Community Association Law

Community Association Law

Cases and Materials on
Common Interest Communities

Second Edition

Wayne S. Hyatt
HYATT & STUBBLEFIELD, P.C.
ADJUNCT PROFESSOR OF LAW
EMORY UNIVERSITY SCHOOL OF LAW (1983–85; 1988–2002)
VANDERBILT UNIVERSITY LAW SCHOOL (1998–2001)

Susan F. French
PROFESSOR OF LAW
UNIVERSITY OF CALIFORNIA AT LOS ANGELES

CAROLINA ACADEMIC PRESS
Durham, North Carolina

ISBN: 978-1-59460-246-7
LCCN: 2008929632

Carolina Academic Press
700 Kent Street
Durham, North Carolina 27701
Telephone (919) 489-7486
Fax (919) 493-5668
www.cap-press.com

Printed in the United States of America

Summary of Contents

Contents

Table of Cases

Preface to the First Edition

Common interest communities, their associations, and community association law as such did not exist at the time the authors went to law school. Today the community association is the most popular form of residential, and increasingly nonresidential, development. Tens of millions of Americans live in community association developments. The law has experienced a similar evolution.

This book is structured to provide a thorough introduction to the substantive law of common interest communities and community associations. Moreover, and to some perhaps more importantly, it seeks to assist the student to grasp the obvious and the subtle qualities of both the theory and the practice of community association law.

The Notes and Problems throughout the book are taken from reported cases and from the contributed experiences of practitioners throughout the United States as well as the experiences of the authors and of men and women who deal with these issues daily. These questions and issues seek to probe the emerging questions and themes arising from the practice.

As noted earlier, the field of community association law is quite young, and it is a composite of both old and new. The basic principles undergirding community association law rest in property and servitude law, but they encompass much more. The threads of corporate law, municipal law, contract law, and other disciplines weave throughout. The relationship to, yet the departure from, these various legal fields and how the resulting principles apply and grow are all much a part of the subject.

It is important to consider where community association law has come from, and it is also important to consider where it is going and how that evolution is proceeding. The evolution, however, has not been linear, and one must note the variations and twists as different state courts address the issues and reflect changes in developmental experience. The number and complexity of judicial decisions dealing with community associations as well as the number and variety of statutes dealing with the subject are significantly on the increase.

The authors' experiences have framed a perspective which believes in the community association concept and in the capacity of the community association. It is a perspective which appreciates the great flexibility inherent in the concepts, legal forms, and developmental options. Experience is valuable only if one realistically learns from the entire experience and not just those portions which are "good" or which fit a preconceived pattern or desired result. This book will, therefore, reflect these experiences and perspectives and will attempt honestly and fully to raise and, in most cases, address the positives and the negatives.

These include concerns over the juxtaposition of the group and the individual, the various methods of individual and group ownership, and the relationship between residential and nonresidential development, among others. These and other questions raise questions of law and of policy. They involve property law as well as social, political, and economic questions. Finally, they involve both scholarly theoretical and mundanely practical considerations.

The authors wish to express thanks for invaluable assistance in the preparation of this book. First, clients and students have contributed and supported the effort in so many ways. Ideas, questions, challenges to advanced "realities" have all made concepts sharper, more realistic, and useful to teacher as well as student.

Second, several Hyatt & Stubblefield staff members have, once again, shown their willingness to exceed even unreasonable expectations in supporting this project and, indeed, making it possible. Vivian Smith and Kara Silverstein have patiently and thoroughly processed the words, over and over.

Christine Barsody fulfills so many functions and does so well and cheerfully. She has been "managing editor," reviewer, interviewer for the retrospectives and observations, and in so many additional ways a most significant contributor. We appreciate more than can be expressed the tangible and intangible support she provides so generously and selflessly.

Finally, it is fair to say that this book would have been neither complete nor completed without Michael S. Rodgers. As a student in the community associations law class, a research assistant, and now a Hyatt & Stubblefield associate, Michael has been actively and creatively engaged in this project since its inception. He has served effectively in many ways as an editor and author; he has brought insight, dedication, and patience to the process. It has been a pleasure working with him, and the authors are confident that, in the future, he will write respected books of his own and that he will use them successfully in his own classroom.

1998

Preface to the Second Edition

Much has taken place in the common interest communities field since the first edition of this book. First, there are thousands of new common interest communities and millions of new owner-residents in those communities. New approaches, new challenges, experience in operation and management all flow from this increased utility of the form of ownership and governance known as "community association law."

Second, professors and students have examined the concepts and questions contained in this book and have provided quite valuable feedback. "Teaching a book" is a real test of and for a book; teaching this one has been a helpful experience. Students as well as teachers have provided very helpful suggestions. The authors appreciate their doing so.

Third, the development industry, broadly defined, has employed new applications of community association law and the design and nature of common interest communities. These innovations have been both in response to and as means to move the real estate market. "Creating community," community stewardship, innovative funding, involvement in cultural and educational activities were all in the future at the time of the first edition. They are all part of the tool box of common interest community developers today.

Fourth, the most significant event in community association law since the first edition is the publication of the Restatement (Third) of Property, Servitudes (2000). This monumental work contains an entire chapter dealing with common interest communities as well as numerous other sections applicable to issues of creation and application of servitudes. This second edition brings the Restatement directly into this book with both "black letter" and Reporter's notes enriching the discussion. Both student and teacher would do well to spend some time with, at least, Chapter 6 of the Restatement.

Another appropriate tool for teacher and student would be Hyatt, Condominium and Homeowners Association Practice: Community Association Law (Third Edition). That work serves as a companion to this casebook.

Once again there are special people to thank for invaluable assistance. In addition to clients, ALI-ABA course attendees, students, and fellow teachers, these include Hyatt & Stubblefield attorneys and staff members who have assisted in so many ways. We particularly thank Lauren Hester and Christine Barsody. Once again and throughout the time between edition one and edition two, Chris has selflessly and generously provided tangible and intangible support.

Finally the authors' heartfelt appreciation goes to those of you who use this book, whether professor, student or practitioner. Of course we are glad that you do so, but more importantly we hope that the book enhances your knowledge of and appreciation for common interest communities and community association law.

2008

Pueblo Bonito at Chaco Canyon, New Mexico. Master Planned Community, Circa 1000 A.D. Photo by Amanda Hyatt.

Community Association Law

Chapter 1

Introduction to Common Interest Communities and Community Associations

A. The Phenomenal Rise of Common Interest Communities

One of the most important stories about housing development in the United States in the last half century has been the rise of common interest communities and their governing bodies, community associations. Of the 126 million housing units in the United States in 2006, approximately 23 million were located in common interest communities, and of the total resident population of 298 million people, approximately 57 million lived in those communities. That is 18% of the housing units and 19% of the population. This is up from just 701,000 housing units out of 63 million (1%) and 2 million out of a population of 203 million (.9%) in 1970.[A] The number of community associations rose from 10,000 to 286,000 over that same period of time.

What accounts for this tremendous increase? Some of the most important factors were increasing land prices, environmental concerns, increasing demand for amenities, and the decreasing ability of municipal governments to provide services and community amenities. Increasing land prices and environmental concerns led to a major shift in zoning laws from Euclidian zoning, which controlled density by requiring open space on each lot, to planned unit development zoning, which allowed clustering of units and aggregating open space into more usable spaces. Increased land prices also led to adoption of the condominium form of ownership, which allowed people who could not afford, or did not want, detached single family homes to become owners rather than renters.

Increased demand for amenities led developers to provide swimming pools, tennis courts, club houses, and the like in residential developments. These amenities could be brought within reach of middle class buyers by spreading the costs across numerous owners. This trend was heightened by the property tax revolts that rolled across the country beginning with California's adoption of Proposition 13 in 1978. Limiting the ability of local

---

A. These figures are taken from statistics provided by the Community Associations Institute, http://www.caionline.org/about/facts.cfm visited Jan. 12, 2008, and the U.S. Census Bureau, http://www.census.gov/.

governments to raise property taxes severely reduced their ability to provide publicly-owned, taxpayer-supported recreational amenities.

These changes in the way residential housing was developed led to a tremendous change in the ownership of property. Open spaces that would have been parceled out among individual lot owners under Euclidian zoning became common property in planned unit developments, and recreational facilities that previously would have been provided by municipal governments and owned by the public became private property provided by the developer. All this privately owned common property required maintenance and management. Although some developers wanted to hold on to some of this common property, for the most part, neither they nor the local government wanted the responsibility. The almost universally adopted solution was to vest title to the common areas and facilities in the home owners, as tenants in common, or in an association controlled by the home owners. Developers imposed covenants on individual lots or units, requiring the homeowners to pay assessments to the community association to maintain these common properties and providing for management by an association of the property owners. Mandatory contribution to the support of common properties coupled with a governance scheme that provides a form of representative government nicely solves the collective action problems that would otherwise result from shared ownership of the common properties.

As the ability of local governments to raise taxes became more constrained after 1978, they increasingly turned to community associations as a way to shift the costs of new development to the home owners. Developers had long been required to assume the costs of providing infrastructure like streets, sewers, drainage, new schools and parks through exactions, but once the development was completed, these facilities were traditionally dedicated to the public and local government provided the services needed to maintain them. However, local governments discovered that the planned unit zoning approval process gave them the power to insist that these facilities remain in private hands and be supported by the homeowners, allowing local governments to reap the benefits of an increased tax base without the costs of servicing the new development. Today, many local governments resist projects that involve public ownership and maintenance of infrastructure and recreation facilities and insist that a community association be established to provide and pay for the services that municipalities formerly provided.[B] In some parts of the country, almost all new housing is located in common interest communities governed by community associations.

Two other factors that have contributed to the rise in common interest communities governed by community associations are fear of crime and the desire for exclusivity. These factors have been particularly important in the rising number of gated communities. In FORTRESS AMERICA: GATED COMMUNITIES IN THE UNITED STATES (1997),[C] Edward J. Blakely and Mary Gail Snyder found three basic types of gated communities, which they labeled lifestyle communities, prestige communities, and security zones. Lifestyle communities include retirement communities and golf and leisure communities, which would not necessarily need gates to accomplish their purposes but often do include them. Prestige communities depend on the gates to project a sense of exclusivity and privilege. Security zone communities provide a psychological sense of safety from crime and traffic

---

B. Steven Siegel, *The Public Role in Establishing Private Residential Communities: Towards a New Formulation of Local Government Land Use Policies that Eliminates the Legal Requirements to Privatize New Communities in the United States*, 38 Urb. Law. 859 (2006).

C. Reviewed at http://www.h-net.org/reviews/showrev.cgi?path=10356889206864.

through gates and security guards. Private ownership of streets and other shared facilities makes it possible to exclude the public from these developments.

The increased privatization of municipal services through common interest communities and the rise of gated communities throughout the world has generated considerable debate about the likely effects of this change in living patterns. Much concern has been expressed that common interest communities allow the "secession of the successful" from public life and lead to withdrawal of support for public schools, public parks, and public services.[D]

Balancing this concern, however, are the many benefits that common interest communities can bring to the people who live there. Increased amenities and security features available through sharing resources via common interest communities are used in lower income housing as well as in housing for the well to do. Because property owners control the association that provides the amenities and services, they have more control than they would have if the amenities and services were provided by local government. In addition, the level of amenities and services selected by the developer initially, and then maintained by the property owners, is likely to be more varied and better tailored to the desires of the owners than facilities provided by public authorities. A study of house sales in Northern Virginia, published in 2005, found that houses in common interest communities sold for 5.4% more than comparable houses that were not in common interest communities.[E]

There is a substantial and growing body of scholarship on common interest communities and community associations, which you may want to read as you pursue your study of this very interesting type of shared ownership and this most local form of governance. Here is a small sample of recent books and articles to get you going.

Michael Lassel, CELEBRATION: THE STORY OF A TOWN (2004); Evan McKenzie, PRIVATOPIA (1996); Valerie Jaffee, Note, *Private Law or Social Norms? The Use of Restrictive Covenants in Beaver Hills*, 116 Yale L.J. 1302 (2007); Lior Jacob Strahilevitz, *Exclusionary Amenities in Residential Communities*, 92 Va. L. Rev. 437 (2006); David L. Callies & Adrienne I. Suarez, *Privatization and the Providing of Public Facilities Through Private Means*, 21 J.L. & Pol. 477 (2006); Paula A. Franzese, *Privatization & Its Discontents: Common Interest Communities & the Rise of Government for "The Nice,"* 37 Urb. Law. 335 (2005); Susan F. French, *Making Common Interest Communities Work: The Next Step*, 37 Urb. Law. 359 (2005); Lee Anne Fennell, *Contracting Communities*, 2004 U. Ill. L. Rev. 829; Mark A. Rogers, *Community Association Law: Administrative Law as a Solution by Analogy*, 53 Emory L. J. 1457 (2004); Wayne S. Hyatt, *Reinvention Redux: Continuing the Evolution of Master-Planned Communities*, 38 Real. Prop. Prob. & Tr. J. 45 (2003); Paula A. Franzese, *Building Community in Common Interest Communities: The Promise of the Restatement (Third) of Servitudes*, 38 Real Prop. Prob. & Tr. J. 17 (2003); Paula A. Franzese, *Does It Take A Village? Privatization, Patterns of Restrictiveness & the Demise of Community*, 47 Vill. L. Rev. 553 (2002); Gerald Korngold, *The Emergence of Private Land Use Controls in Large-Scale Subdivisions: The Companion Story to Village of Euclid v. Ambler Realty Co.*, 51 Case W. L. Rev. 617 (2001). The Research Network on Private Urban Governance (http://www.gated-communities.de/) includes lists of publications from some international conferences on gated communities around the world.

D. Robert B. Reich coined the phrase in the title to an article published in the New York Times Magazine on Jan. 20, 1991. A copy of the article is posted at http://www-personal.umich.edu/~gmarkus/secession.html.

E. Amanda Agan & Alexander Tabarrok, *What Are Private Governments Worth?* Regulation, Fall 2005, http://www.cato.org/pubs/regulation/regv28n3/v28n3-2.pdf.

B. Defining a Common Interest Community

Restatement (Third)[F] § 1.8 Common-Interest Community Defined

A "common-interest community" is a real-estate development or neighborhood in which individually owned lots or units are burdened by a servitude that imposes an obligation that cannot be avoided by nonuse or withdrawal

(1) to pay for the use of, or contribute to the maintenance of, property held or enjoyed in common by the individual owners, or

(2) to pay dues or assessments to an association that provides services or facilities to the common property or to the individually owned property, or that enforces other servitudes burdening the property in the development or neighborhood.

Common interest communities range widely in size and function, from two-unit condominiums to entire towns. Their functions may be as simple as maintaining an entrance sign or as complex as providing all the facilities and services that are ordinarily provided by a municipality. What they have in common are the three defining characteristics listed in the Restatement:

- Individually owned property
- Burdened by a servitude that imposes an obligation to pay for
  ○ Use or maintenance of common property or
  ○ Services or facilities provided by an association, and
- The obligation cannot be avoided by nonuse of the facilities or withdrawal from the association.

Although this definition captures the universe of common interest communities, it is important to realize that not all common interest communities are governed by the same laws. In many states statutes apply only to one or more subsets of common interest communities, like condominiums for example. Even in states that have adopted a "comprehensive" statute like California's Davis-Stirling Act or the Uniform Common Interest Ownership Act (UCIOA), the statute may not reach all common interest communities. Where there is no governing statute, common law and other statutes, like the non-profit corporations act, govern. Chapter 6 of the Restatement (Third) is a valuable resource for determining the common law of common interest communities and community associations.

Committee to Save the Beverly Highlands Homes Association v. Beverly Highlands Homes Association

California Court of Appeal
112 Cal. Rptr. 2d 732, rev. den. (Cal. Ct. App. 2001)

... Defendant The Beverly Highlands Homes Association (Association) is a nonprofit mutual benefit corporation.... Its members are the owners of buildable lots in the Beverly Highlands, which is located in an area of Los Angeles north of Sunset Boulevard near

---

F. Restatement (Third) as used throughout this book means the RESTATEMENT (THIRD) OF PROPERTY, SERVITUDES (2000).

West Hollywood. The Association itself does not own any of the lots in the Beverly High-lands. A description of the property included within the Beverly Highlands, a statement as to the powers of the Association, and restrictions as to use of the property within the Beverly Highlands are set forth in the Beverly Highlands Declaration of Restrictions (Declaration). This document was recorded on June 27, 1952....

Four of the lots in the Beverly Highlands are called open area non-buildable lots. Owners of these lots are not members of the Association.... [These lots, 53, 62, 65, and 66 are restricted by the Declaration to use only as open areas for planting, natural growth, and vegetation. The Declaration states that] "the Association may, by its written authorization, permit the location of television antennas to serve any or all of the building sites" [on Lots 53 and 62. The Declaration also states] ... The Association is responsible for any planting and maintenance of these lots until such time as they may be dedicated to the public for park use."[2] ...

The Association is governed by a Board of Directors (Board) pursuant to its by-laws.... The Association was suspended as a corporation on April 2, 1972. It was revived on April 19, 1989.... In August, [1996] the Board discussed purchasing Lot 66, one of the open area non-buildable lots, in order for the Association to fall within the purview of the Davis-Stirling Common Interest Development Act ... (Civ.Code, § 1350 et seq.). At the September 9 Board meeting, the Board decided not to purchase Lot 66....

In February 1997, the Board sent a letter to Association members regarding amendment of the Declaration to ensure preservation of the views from the members' properties. The Board expressed the opinion that in order to be able to amend the Declaration at that time, the Association would have to own real property within the Beverly High-lands.[G] The Board enclosed a ballot asking members whether they "support[ed] going forward with purchase by the Association of real property making the Beverly Highlands Homes Association subject to the provisions of the Davis-Stirling Act, in order to amend the [Declaration] at this time." The response to the letter was 16 yes votes and 40 no votes.

... On December 1, [1997] the Board sent a letter and a ballot asking Association members to vote on dissolution [of the association].... The votes were counted on January 15, 1998. There were 129 votes out of 205 eligible voters. Of those 129, 94 voted in favor of dissolving the Association and 35 voted against dissolution. The Board then voted unanimously to approve dissolution of the Association....

[Plaintiffs, dissenting members of the Association, sued] the Association, the Board, and Board members.... In five causes of action, plaintiffs sought (1) to enjoin wrongful dissolution of a nonprofit corporation, (2) removal of the Board, (3) an order permitting inspection of the minutes of the Board meetings, (4) an order that an annual meeting of the Association and an election be held, and (5) declaratory relief. Plaintiffs also sought injunctive relief during the pendency of the litigation....

The Davis-Stirling Act, enacted in 1985..., regulates common interest developments. A common interest development is a community apartment project, condominium pro-

---

2. Lot 53 was the subject of a previous lawsuit. (*Simon v. Clavin* (Jun. 8, 1978), 2 Civ. No. 51491.) The lot was deeded to the state for nonpayment of taxes, then purchased at a public auction.... The purchaser sought to free the property from the restrictions contained in the Declaration.... The court held that the restrictions were enforceable as equitable servitudes unless their enforcement would be inequitable....

G. Davis-Stirling, § 1355(b) provides that "a declaration which fails to include provisions permitting its amendment at all times ... may be amended at any time." Apparently the Beverly High-lands declaration did not include an amendment power. — Eds.

ject, planned development or stock cooperative. (§ 1351 (c).) The Act "applies and a common interest development is created whenever a separate interest coupled with an interest in the common area or membership in the association is, or has been, conveyed, provided, all of the following are recorded: (a) A declaration. (b) A condominium plan, if any exists. (c) A final map or parcel map...." ... The Act also provides that "[a] common interest development shall be managed by an association which may be incorporated or unincorporated." (§ 1363 (a).)

A planned development is one "having either or both of the following features: (1) The common area is owned either by ... the association or in common by the owners of the separate interests who possess appurtenant rights to the beneficial use and enjoyment of the common area. (2) A power exists in the association to enforce an obligation of an owner of a separate interest with respect to the beneficial use and enjoyment of the common area by means of an assessment which may become a lien upon the separate interests in accordance with Section 1367." (§ 1351 (k).) A "'separate interest'" is "a separately owned lot, parcel, area, or space." (*Id.*, (*l*)(3).) A "'[c]ommon area'" is "the entire common interest development except the separate interests therein. The estate in the common area may be a fee, a life estate, an estate for years, or any combination of the foregoing. However, the common area for a planned development specified in paragraph (2) of subdivision (k) may consist of mutual or reciprocal easement rights appurtenant to the separate interests." (§ 1351 (b).) ...

The trial court ruled that the Beverly Highlands was a common interest development within the meaning of the Davis-Stirling Act. Under Corporations Code section 8724,[6] therefore, the approval of 100 percent of the members was required for dissolution of the Association and a transfer of the Association's assets. Additionally, Civil Code section 1363, subdivision (a), requires that a common interest development have an association to manage it. Hence, the court concluded, the Association "was not properly dissolved by any proper vote as required by law."[7]

...

The gravamen of defendants' contention is that the Beverly Highlands is not a common interest development within the meaning of the Davis-Stirling Act. The decision to dissolve the Association, therefore, was governed by Corporations Code section 8610, not section 8724. The vote on the dissolution issue was sufficient to meet the requirements of section 8610, so the Association properly was dissolved....

Returning to defendants' contention that the Beverly Highlands is not a common interest development within the meaning of the Davis-Stirling Act, defendants first look to

---

6. Corporations Code section 8724 provides: "Without the approval of 100 percent of the members, ... so long as there is any lot, parcel, area, apartment or unit for which an owners association (as defined in ... [the Davis-Stirling Act]) is obligated to provide management, maintenance, preservation or control: (a) The owners association or any person acting on its behalf shall not: (1) Transfer all or substantially all of its assets; or (2) File a certificate of dissolution; and (b) No court shall enter an order declaring the owners association duly wound up and dissolved."....

In contrast to Corporations Code section 8724, section 8610 of the Corporations Code permits a corporation to "elect voluntarily to wind up and dissolve (1) by approval of a majority of all members..., or (2) by approval of the board and approval of the members...." ... Section 5034 of the Corporations Code defines approval of the members as approval of the majority of the members.

7. Only 94 out of 205 eligible voters, or approximately 46 percent of the members, voted in favor of dissolution. The 94 voters were a majority of the 129 votes received on the question of dissolution, however.

section 1374 of the Civil Code. This provides: "Nothing in this title may be construed to apply to a development wherein there does not exist a common area as defined in subdivision (b) of Section 1351...."

Civil Code section 1351, subdivision (b), defines a "[c]ommon area" as "the entire common interest development except the separate interests therein. The estate in the common area may be a fee, a life estate, an estate for years, or any combination of the foregoing. However, the common area for a planned development specified in paragraph (2) of subdivision (k) may consist of mutual or reciprocal easement rights appurtenant to the separate interests." It is undisputed that the only portions of the Beverly Highlands which might meet the definition of "common area" are the four non-buildable lots, Lots 53, 62, 65 and 66.

The Association has no estate in Lots 53, 62, 65 and 66. Plaintiffs, in essence, admit that the separate interests in the Beverly Highlands do not include mutual or reciprocal easement rights to use of these lots. They argue that the restrictions on the use of these lots "share the fundamental characteristics of an easement. Not all restrictions create property interests amounting to easement rights, but those that limit ownership rights for the common benefit and enjoyment do." They cite no authority in support of this argument.

"An easement is an interest in the land of another, which entitles the owner of the easement to a limited use or enjoyment of the other's land." (4 Witkin, Summary of Cal. Law (9th ed. 1987) Real Property, §434, p. 614....) An easement appurtenant to the land is "attached to the land of the owner of the easement, and benefits him as the owner or possessor of that land." (*Id.*, §435, p. 615.)

"An easement differs from a covenant running with the land and from an equitable servitude, in that these are created by promises concerning the land, which may be enforceable by or binding upon successors to the estate of either party, while an easement is an interest in the land, created by grant or prescription." (4 Witkin, *supra*....) A covenant running with the land is created by language in a deed or other document showing an agreement to do or refrain from doing something with respect to use of the land.... An equitable servitude may be created when a covenant does not run with the land but equity requires that it be enforced....

... [T]he Declaration does not create any easement rights to the use of Lots 53, 62, 65 and 66. Article X of the Declaration addresses easement rights, setting forth the easement rights to which the properties in Beverly Highlands are subject. Section 10.04 restricts use of Lots 65 and 66 to "open areas for planting purposes," with no structures or roads to be constructed over them. This restriction "shall not be deemed or construed as a present dedication of said lots to the public or to the owners of building sites in said property for park or other purposes." The Declaration reserved the right, however, to make such a dedication in the future.

Similarly, section 10.05 restricts use of Lots 53 and 62 to "open areas for natural growth and vegetation, areas for planting purposes and areas within which the Association may, by its written authorization, permit the location of television antennas to serve any or all of the building sites," with no other structure, road or way to be constructed over them. Again, this restriction "shall not be deemed or construed as a present dedication of said lots to the public or to the owners of building sites in said property for planting or other purposes." The Declaration again reserved the "right to dedicate said lots to the public as open areas for the nurture of natural growth and vegetation or for planting purposes." ...

Generally, planned developments are governed by CC&Rs (covenants, conditions and restrictions) or declarations. These are enforceable as covenants running with the land or equitable servitudes. (See, *e.g.*, *Citizens for Covenant Compliance v. Anderson* (1995) 12 Cal.4th 345, 352–355, 47 Cal.Rptr.2d 898, 906 P.2d 1314; *Nahrstedt v. Lakeside Village Condominium Assn.* (1994) 8 Cal.4th 361, 379, 33 Cal.Rptr.2d 63, 878 P.2d 1275.)

The language in the Declaration at issue here clearly creates covenants running with the land or equitable servitudes as to Lots 53, 62, 65 and 66. It creates restrictions as to the use of that land.[9] It does not give the owners of the other lots in the Beverly Highlands any interest in those lots or any right to use those lots for their own enjoyment. Hence, it does not create any "mutual or reciprocal easement rights appurtenant to the separate interests." ...

Nothing in the legislative history of the Davis-Stirling Act cited by plaintiffs leads to any different conclusion. Rather, everything they cite points to the conclusion that in order for a planned development to fall within the Act, there must be, at a minimum, appurtenant easement rights to a portion of the development. And, as previously stated, they cite no authority for the proposition that restrictions on the use of a property are the equivalent of an easement.

Southern Cal. Edison Co. v. Bourgerie (1973) 9 Cal.3d 169, 107 Cal.Rptr. 76, 507 P.2d 964, cited by plaintiffs, holds only "that building restrictions constitute property rights for purposes of eminent domain proceedings." ... *Nahrstedt v. Lakeside Village Condominium Assn., supra*, ... also cited by plaintiffs, notes that "[u]nder the law of equitable servitudes, courts may enforce a promise about the use of land even though the person who made the promise has transferred the land to another. [Citation.] The underlying idea is that a landowner's promise to refrain from particular conduct pertaining to land creates in the beneficiary of that promise 'an equitable interest in the land of the promisor.' [Citations.]" ... *Nahrstedt* does not hold that this enforceable "'equitable interest in the land'" is an actual interest in the land, such as an easement, which entitles the promisee to use the promisor's land. Rather, it holds that the equitable servitudes may be enforced to restrict the promisor's use of his or her own property....

Accordingly, we must conclude that the Beverly Highlands has no common area within the meaning of Civil Code section 1351, subdivision (b). Therefore, the Davis-Stirling Act does not apply to it.... The trial court erred in finding that Beverly Highlands was a common interest development within the meaning of the Davis-Stirling Act....

Defendants assert that even if the Association is dissolved, the Beverly Highlands property owners still can enforce the Declaration. While this assertion is of no relevance to this appeal, it is correct. Article XVI of the Declaration gives the individual Beverly Highlands property owners the right to enforce the Declaration.

...

Under Corporations Code section 8613, once voluntary dissolution of the Association was approved, the Board could continue acting to wind up and settle the Association's affairs. No corporate activities unnecessary to the winding up could take place. An annual meeting and election of new Board members were unnecessary to the winding up....

The judgment is reversed. Defendants are to recover their costs on appeal.

---

9. In *Simon v. Clavin*, the court found the restrictions imposed on Lot 53 by the Declaration may be enforceable as equitable servitudes....

Notes & Questions

1. Did the court reach the right result in the *Beverly Highlands* case? Is there any reason to require approval of 100% of the property owners to dissolve an association that owns no common property? Should the interests of the plaintiffs in continuing the association have been subordinated to the decision of the majority? Note that only a majority of those voting was required to dissolve the association, not a majority of the lots.

2. UCIOA § 1-103(7) defines a common interest community as "real estate with respect to which a person, by virtue of his ownership of a unit, is obligated to pay for real estate taxes, insurance premiums, maintenance, or improvement of other real estate described in a declaration." Would the Beverly Highlands Homes Association qualify as a common interest community under this definition? Would it be relevant that (4) of that same statute defines "common elements" as "(i) in the case of ... (B) a planned community, any real estate within a planned community which is owned or leased by the association, other than a unit, and (ii) in all common interest communities, any other interests in real estate for the benefit of unit owners which are subject to the declaration?"

3. In Hawaii's Planned Community Associations Act, Hawaii Rev. Stats. Ch. 421J, adopted in 1997, a "planned community association" is defined as an organization "to which authority is granted by a declaration which governs a planned community." A declaration is defined as "any recorded instrument ... that imposes on an association maintenance or operational responsibilities for the common area and creates the authority in the association to impose on units ... any mandatory payment of ... a regular annual assessment...." Under the Act, H.R.S. § 421J-10, the association is entitled to attorneys fees and costs in actions to collect delinquent assessments.

In *Kaanapali Hillside Homeowners' Ass'n v. Doran*, 162 P.3d 1277 (HI, 2007), the Hawai'i Supreme Court held that an association created by a charter of incorporation to manage common property and collect assessments from lot owners was not a planned community association entitled to attorney fees and costs under the Planned Community Associations Act because its authority to collect assessments was granted by the corporate charter, rather than by a recorded declaration. However, the association was nonetheless entitled under another statute, H.R.S. § 607-14, to its fees and costs in a successful action to collect assessments from a lot owner. That statute, which provides for an award of attorneys fees and costs to the prevailing party in an action for assumpsit, generally limits the award to 25% of the judgment, but exempts planned community associations from the 25% limit. The Kaanapali Hillside Homeowners' Association qualified for the exemption because "planned community association" was defined as "a nonprofit homeowners or community association existing pursuant to covenants running with the land."

The court speculated that in using two different definitions of planned community association, the legislature may have contemplated that some groups would not qualify under the Planned Community Associations Act but should nevertheless be allowed a full recovery of attorney fees. Subsequent to the decision, legislation has been proposed that would broaden the definition of association in Chapter 421J to eliminate the recording requirement and apply the same definition in § 607-14.

C. Types of Housing Developments and the Need for Community Associations

Americans live in several different types of housing structures: detached single-family, attached single-family, which are often called townhouses, and multi-unit structures. Multi-unit structures range from two-unit duplexes to large high-rises. Under Euclidian zoning, most housing was developed on single parcels which had required setbacks and height limits imposed on a structure-by-structure basis. Although individual ownership of single-family detached houses and townhouses was common, individual ownership of units in multi-unit structures was rare. Multi-unit structures were generally occupied by renters rather than by owners. Although the cooperative form of ownership enabled apartment dwellers to achieve something close to ownership, cooperatives are rarely used outside of New York.

Two important developments of the 1960s significantly changed the housing picture: development of the condominium and planned unit development zoning. Condominium statutes enabled developers to create and sell fee simple interests in units in multi-unit structures. When mortgage and title insurance became available, condominium development took off both in new construction and in conversion of existing apartment buildings. Planned unit development (PUD) zoning freed developers from the strictures of Euclidian zoning, allowing them much greater flexibility in siting structures and in combining housing types. With PUD zoning, it became possible to create developments that included detached houses, townhouses, and multi-unit structures. Using the condominium, it also became possible for the developer to offer fee simple ownership to all of the units in a project. PUD zoning also made it possible for developers to combine commercial uses with residential uses (mixed-use projects). It also became possible to create much larger scale projects, now known as master planned communities, which include multiple types of neighborhoods and sometimes create whole new towns.

Condominiums are required by statute to have governing associations to manage the common property, which in a multi-unit structure, at a minimum, will include the roof and will often include hallways, elevators, parking spaces and other property. Although the association may often be either incorporated or unincorporated, it is required to have a governing board elected by the unit owners. Cooperatives are structured as corporations in which ownership of shares includes a proprietary lease of a unit. As corporations, they, too, are required to have a governing board elected by the shareholders. Thus, development of either a condominium or cooperative always requires creation of a community association which has the responsibility of managing the common property with funds provided by the unit owners or proprietary lessees.

Detached housing and attached townhouse developments do not necessarily require the creation of community associations. A so-called standard subdivision created under Euclidian type zoning may have no common property and no need for an association. Even if all the lots are subject to building and use restrictions, enforcement may be left to the individual lot owners. Even with attached townhouses, simple party-wall agreements between adjoining property owners may be sufficient to handle the problems that are likely to arise. However, in any development where there is shared common property, the developer should create a community association with the power to manage the common property and to assess the individual lot owners to pay for it. Even if there is no common property, it is often a good idea to create a community association in a development where the lots are subject to restrictive covenants. The association can spread the costs of covenant enforcement over the entire development, solving the free rider problem that arises where covenant enforcement is left to individual lot owners.

Modern statutes like UCIOA and California's Davis-Stirling Act require the creation of associations with assessment powers in developments that are not condominiums but include common property.[H] That has not always been the case, however, and is still not the case in a number of states. What happens when the developer does not make provisions for managing and maintaining common property? Cases in the next Chapter address the problem.

Before going on to the next Chapter, you may want a quick recap of the salient features of common interest communities and a brush-up on basic servitudes law—the law that underlies the creation of common interest communities.

D. Legal Underpinnings of Common Interest Communities

Common interest communities offer individually owned lots or units combined with community financed facilities and services. They differ from rental projects in that the lots or units are individually owned, and they differ from standard subdivision development in that the community facilities are private rather than public. Common interest developments are attractive to purchasers because they combine the advantages of property ownership with the savings available from spreading the costs of common facilities and services across the community.

They also provide protection against changes in the use and physical character of land and buildings in the community (a feature common to standard subdivisions with deed restrictions, too), but they also provide an institutional structure for collective enforcement of restrictions and management of common facilities and services. Because the community facilities are private, rather than public, the common interest community is able to limit access to its facilities, internalizing the benefits for members and excluding the general public. This feature, too, may be attractive in the eyes of many purchasers.

The legal device developers use to create common interest communities is the servitude, a generic term that includes both easements and covenants.[I] Servitudes serve the purpose because they allow the developer to create burdens and benefits that run with the land for an indefinite and potentially unlimited period of time, giving permanence to the arrangements. By a declaration, or other appropriate instrument, the developer imposes servitudes on the land that (1) give all lot or unit owners rights to use the common facilities, (2) require owners to pay assessments to maintain those facilities, and (3) restrict use of the land in the community. Usually, the declaration also provides for creation of a

---

H. UCIOA §§ 1-202 and 1-203 exempt cooperatives and planned community developments of 12 units or less or planned communities with limited common expense liability.

I. Statutes have supplemented and simplified, and in some cases supplanted, the common law of servitudes that applies to common interest communities. The statutes, however, may apply only to certain types of common interest communities, like condominiums, and may leave many questions unanswered. Wherever specific statutory rules are not available, the common law of servitudes provides the default rules.

property owners association to manage the community's affairs. As part of the consideration for the developer's conveyance of the land, the original buyers in the common interest community agree to creation of the servitudes, binding themselves and their successors.

The critical feature of a servitude is that the burdens and benefits run with the land. Subsequent purchasers of property in the community have the same rights and responsibilities as the original purchasers, whether or not the rights are assigned to them and whether or not they assume the burdens. Simply by acquiring title to the property, subsequent purchasers become part of the common interest community. This feature is essential to the success of the common interest community. Continuance of the plan does not depend on having each new owner expressly agree to assume the obligations. Owners cannot free-ride on the contributions of others to the common facilities or services, and disaffected owners cannot opt out of the plan by foregoing use of the common facilities or services.

Although servitudes create the basic structure of the common interest community, the bodies of law relevant to the study of community associations include more than what is usually thought of as servitudes law. The servitudes that constitute the common interest community generally provide for creation of an association and give the association powers similar to those of a local government. Most associations are incorporated and corporate law governs, or at least provides the default rules that govern questions relating to powers of the association, its organization, voting rights, elections, and powers and duties of officers and directors.

Normally, the servitudes also give the association powers to assess the members to provide for community facilities and services, to make rules and regulations governing activities within the community, and to enforce the covenants, rules, and regulations. These powers resemble the powers of a local governmental body much more closely than they resemble the powers of a corporation, and analogies drawn from municipal law may be appropriate in determining their interpretation and application.

The servitudes used in common interest communities are easements, which give the individual property owners the right to use the common areas and facilities (roads, recreation facilities, and the like), restrictive covenants, which limit the uses that can be made of the individual properties (*i.e.*, residential uses only, no nuisances, etc.), and affirmative covenants, which require all owners to pay assessments to support the common facilities and may require other affirmative actions as well (submission of plans for improvements to an architectural control committee, keeping yards free of weeds, etc.) Before proceeding further, a brief background note on servitudes law may be useful to you.

1. Background of Servitudes Law[J]

As you probably remember from your basic property course, servitudes have a long and complicated history. Roman law developed an elaborate system of servitudes for rights of way, aqueducts, agricultural uses, and urban encroachments and building restrictions. It apparently did not, however, recognize benefits in gross, or permit the attachment of

---

J. What we present here is a very brief background note. If you need (or want) to know more, we suggest you begin with Susan F. French, *Toward A Modern Law of Servitudes: Reweaving the Ancient Strands*, 55 So. Calif. L. Rev. 1261 (1982), and Uriel Reichman, *Toward a Unified Concept of Servitudes*, 55 So. Calif. L. Rev. 1179 (1982).

affirmative burdens to land. Although not admitted directly, the Roman law probably influenced the development of easement law in England, and Louisiana law, of course, retains substantial traces of Roman law.

Medieval English law recognized a variety of "rights of commons" and other "incorporeal hereditaments,"[K] some of which resembled servitudes. Although an early case suggests that the benefit of a covenant might run with land,[L] running covenants law did not really take shape until the 16th century. Even then, the law only clearly applied to lease covenants.[M] It was not until the 19th century, when the industrial revolution created significant new demands for land and conflicting uses that the modern law of servitudes as a tool for land use development began to emerge. During the 19th century, easements, real covenants, and equitable servitudes became distinct, albeit overlapping, legal devices, each with its own set of requirements and characteristics.

In the latter half of the 20th century, the law moved toward unifying the law of servitudes, eliminating overlapping categories, and arriving at a single body of law governing those that remain. The American Law Institute assumed a leading role in this movement with its Restatement of the Law Third Property, (Servitudes) project, which was completed in 2000.

Prior to the Restatement project, the study of servitudes law tended to focus on the different requirements and limitations on creating and transferring easements, real covenants, and equitable servitudes which were developed in the 19th and early 20th centuries. A thumbnail sketch of the principal doctrines covered would include the following:

A. Easements

1. At one time, a single deed could not be used to transfer the fee simple to one grantee and create an easement in a third person. This rule, which is still followed in a few states (notably New York), requires that separate deeds be used, the first to create the easement, the second to transfer the fee simple subject to the easement. Third party beneficiary doctrine did not operate in this area of the law.

2. Benefits in gross were not permitted in English law, but are permitted in American law. However, the benefits of an easement in gross that is not "commercial" in character (like a pipeline easement) may not be assignable.

B. Real Covenants (enforceable in actions at law by judgments for damages)

1. *Horizontal Privity.* English law did not permit enforcement of affirmative covenant burdens (like covenants to pay assessments) against successors, except in leases. The technical device used to impose this constraint was the horizontal privity requirement. Ab-

---

K. Incorporeal hereditaments included such diverse rights as advowsons, tithes, offices, commons, ways, dignities, franchies, corodies or pensions, annuities and rents according to Blackstone, 2 W. Blackstone, *Commentaries on English Law* at 21.

L. Packenham's Case, a 14th century case, dealt with a covenant requiring performance of services in the manor chapel. Arnold, *Fourteenth-Century Promises*, 35 Cambridge L.J. 321, 323 (1976) notes that the 14th century precedents on covenants are "paltry" and such discussions as are reported are "amateurish and tentative."

M. Henry VIII procured passage of the Grantees of Reversions Act, 1540, 32 Hen. 8, ch. 34, which established that the benefit of a lessee's covenants runs with the reversion. He had a direct interest in the subject because on dissolution of the monasteries, the crown became the successor to church lands, many of which were leased out to others. The statute permitted the crown to enforce the lessees' covenants. Spencer's Case, 77 Eng. Rep. 72 (Q.B. 1583), established that the burden of a lessee's covenants runs with the term to an assignee of the lessee. Spencer's Case is the origin of several rules that later proved troublesome, at least if there is privity.

sent privity, defined as a "tenurial relationship" between covenantor and covenantee, the covenant could not be enforced against an assignee of the covenantor. In the United States, privity was redefined to include a grantor-grantee relationship, which permitted enforcement of affirmative covenants created when a fee simple was transferred. Affirmative covenants imposed by subdivision developers could thus be enforced against successors to the original purchasers in actions at law.

Horizontal privity in its attenuated American version served little purpose other than to prevent enforcement of covenants entered into between land owners in actions at law.

2. *Vertical Privity*. This doctrine, which is much more fully developed in landlord-tenant law than in servitudes law, permits burdens to run only against successors to the same estate as that held by the original covenantor. It thus permits enforcement at law against assignees, but prevents enforcement against sublessees. If applied to common interest community covenants, it would prevent enforcement of assessment covenants against lessees and life tenants of lot or unit owners. In fact, there is almost no vertical privity case law outside the landlord tenant area.

3. *Touch or Concern*. This doctrine, which was always very fuzzy in content, limited the kinds of arrangements that could be implemented with servitudes. Variously applied to require that the burden of the covenant relate to use of the land, or that both burden and benefit, relate to use of the land in some way, it gave courts a tool for refusing to enforce covenants that for some reason or another appeared undesirable. In the landlord tenant area, it was sometimes applied to prevent enforcement at law against assignees of covenants to maintain insurance on the leased premises and to pay taxes on other land of the landlord. In the common interest development context, it has occasionally been used to justify decisions refusing enforcement of covenants to pay for utilities and recreational or social facilities.

C. Equitable Servitudes (covenants enforceable in equity, primarily by injunction)

1. *Horizontal Privity*. The English chancery court invented the equitable servitude to permit the enforcement of covenants made by and between fee owners in *Tulk v. Moxhay*.[N] Dispensing with the privity requirement, the court declared that a covenant (an equity) would be enforced against anyone who purchased the property with notice of the covenant. Later decisions limited the doctrine to negative covenants (or covenants that could be enforced by ordinary injunction) and refused to permit benefits in gross (adopting the English rule on easements). American courts broadened the doctrine, permitting enforcement of affirmative covenants,[O] and sometimes permitting enforcement by persons who held benefits in gross.

2. *Vertical Privity*. Courts generally dispensed with vertical privity in enforcing covenants in equity. An injunction would be issued against any possessor or user of the land who violated a covenant. American commentators suggested that succession to some interest held by the original covenantor (relaxed vertical privity) was required, but there are no cases refusing enforcement against an adverse possessor or other trespasser.

3. *Touch or Concern*. Although there are some cases which appear to hold that touch or concern does not apply to enforcement in equity, most cases appear to apply the same requirement as that applied to enforcement at law.

N. 41 Eng. Rep. 1143 (Ch. 1848).

O. Covenants to pay money were enforced by imposition of an equitable lien on the burdened property, rather than by entry of a judgment for money damages.

4. *Notice.* Prior to 1925 there was not an effective recording system in England. The possibility that a purchaser would be bound to a servitude of which he or she had no notice led to the refusal to enforce covenants at law against successors (through the horizontal privity requirement), and the emphasis on notice in *Tulk v. Moxhay* as a requirement for enforcement in equity. American recording systems render all covenants, whether legal or equitable interests, unenforceable against purchasers without notice. Thus, the notice requirement had little independent force in American law.

5. *No Benefits in Gross.* American law generally followed the English law in refusing to recognize that equitable servitudes could have benefits in gross, even though American courts had long recognized easements in gross. The principal applications of the rule were to prevent enforcement of covenants against competition (on the ground the benefit was to the business interests of the covenantee not the land) and to prevent enforcement by original covenantees who had sold their land and were no longer part of the neighborhood. Potentially it could have applied to prevent enforcement of covenants by property owners associations, by municipalities that required covenants in order to approve a project, or by conservation organizations or other state agencies.

2. Restatement (Third) of Property, Servitudes (2000)

The Restatement takes the position that most of these traditional doctrinal requirements are obsolete and should be discarded. Instead of the old formulations, modern law only requires intent and compliance with the Statute of Frauds for creation of a servitude. Horizontal privity is irrelevant. There is no limit on the persons or entities that can be made beneficiaries of servitudes, whether they own land to be benefited by enforcement of the servitude or not. The third party beneficiary doctrine applies to servitudes. If adopted by the courts, this rule permits developers to retain enforcement rights that remain effective even after a project is sold out, allows governmental agencies to enforce servitudes imposed as a condition of granting approval for a project, and permits creation of conservation, preservation, and other servitudes without resort to statute, or without acquisition of a parcel of land to which the benefits may be made appurtenant.

Substantively, the Restatement takes the position that servitudes are valid unless illegal or against public policy. The touch or concern doctrine has been superseded by a more explicit focus on public policy. Servitudes that impose unreasonable restraints on alienation or competition, or that are unconscionable are expressly declared to be invalid because they are against public policy. Instead of asking whether a servitude relates to use of the land in some way (touches or concerns), courts are invited to ask whether there is a reason to prohibit land owners from creating the kind of arrangement embodied in the servitude, and if there is, whether the reason is sufficiently compelling that the court should refuse to give effect to the agreement reached by the original parties.

The Restatement resolves most of the conundrums that bedeviled students in the traditional basic property course, making way for us to focus on servitude questions that have more relevance to the study of community association law: interpretation, enforcement, modification, and termination of servitudes.

> *You can dream, create, design, and build the most wonderful place in the world, but it requires people to make the dream a reality.*
>
> — *Walt Disney*

Chapter 2

Creating Common Interest Communities

Real estate developments that include both individually owned lots and shared recreational facilities, or roads or other infrastructure, usually provide for management and support of the common facilities by a community association in which all lot owners are members and are required to pay assessments. There are some developments, however, in which the developer did not create any mechanism for management and support of the common property. Voluntary efforts may suffice to maintain the common property, but often break down over time. What happens then?

A. Common Interest Communities Based on Implication

A developer can only impose servitudes on the property while the developer still owns it. Once the property has been conveyed to purchasers, the developer no longer has power to impose a servitude requiring payment of assessments to maintain common property. If the developer has not created the servitude before beginning to sell lots, it can only be created later with consent of the lot owner. Lot owners who find themselves with common property but no enforceable obligation to contribute to its maintenance could agree to create an association with assessment powers to bind themselves and their successors, but it would bind only those who consented. There are very likely to be free riders and hold outs, which will increase the costs for the others. Developers who fail to provide a structure for support and management of common property create substantial problems for the future.

The Restatement (Third) provides a common law solution:

§ 6.3 Power To Create A Common-Interest Community Association

(1) If creation of an association has not otherwise been provided for in a common-interest community, and has not been expressly excluded by the declaration, the developer, or the owners of a majority of the lots or units not owned by the developer, may create an association to manage the common property and enforce the servitudes contained in the declaration. All members of the common-interest community are automatically members of the association, which is governed by the provisions of this Chapter.

(2) If necessary for the management of common property, a court, on petition of owners of less than a majority of the lots or units, may authorize creation of an association....

a. Rationale. Except in the smallest of common-interest communities, an association is usually desirable, if not absolutely necessary, to provide a collective vehicle for the management of commonly held property. Virtually all newer common-interest communities provide for an association, and modern statutes require them for communities above a minimum size. Unless creation of an association has been expressly precluded, failure to create an association is more likely the result of the developer's oversight or desire to save expenses than a choice to require either direct democracy or unanimous approval of the lot owners for decisions regarding management of the common property.

… Even if creation of an association has been expressly excluded by the declaration, or owners of less than a majority of the lots or units in the community petition for creation of an association, a court may authorize creation of an association where necessary for management of the common property, or to protect the public from having to maintain the property, or provide the services required by the declaration. The judicial power to authorize creation of an association is that of a court of equity with its attendant flexibility and discretion to fashion remedies to correct mistakes and oversights and to protect the public interest. Unless the decree provides otherwise, an association so created enjoys the powers and is subject to the duties and limitations that apply to associations under this Chapter.

b. Creation by developer, owners, or court. This section permits the creation of an association either by the developer or by owners, other than the developer, of a majority of lots. The association, once created, enjoys the powers and is subject to the same constraints as other associations covered by this Chapter, including the provisions of Part E governing the developer's relationship with the community. The provision permitting the developer to create the association is designed to permit the developer to cure what was probably an oversight in setting up the project, or to respond to a need for collective management that was not apparent when the project was designed. The underlying theory is that the developer may be in the best position to accomplish creation of the association at the least cost to the owners. However, if it appears that the lot owners relied on the absence of an association in purchasing their interests, or that the developer is seeking an unfair advantage by setting up the association, the lot owners, other than the developer, should be able, either to prevent creation of an association, or to take control of the process.

The basis for creation of an association is the need for management of common property the lot owners are obligated to maintain. That obligation is normally expressly created in the declaration or other governing documents, but is sometimes implied from the circumstances surrounding creation of the development. Once the obligation to support the common property is established, owners of a majority of the lots have the power to create an association with the powers set forth in this Chapter.

Illustration:

1. Lake Shore Estates is a subdivision of 20 lots. Lot 5, restricted for use as a community park and beach, is owned in common, subject to reciprocal easements for park and beach use. The owners of 15 of the lots bring an action to establish the duty of all lot owners to contribute equally to the costs of maintaining the park and beach. On the basis that the parties must have intended

that all lots contribute to maintenance of the park and beach, a judicial decree is entered requiring all lots in the subdivision to contribute equally to the costs of operating and maintaining Lot 5. A majority of the owners is entitled to create an association for the purpose of managing the common areas and levying assessments to maintain them.

If necessary for the management of the common property, a court may authorize creation of an association even though owners of less than a majority of the lots have joined in the petition. This would be appropriate where the size of the community and difficulty of securing participation by owners of a majority of the lots is considerable and there is strong need for collective management of the common property. Unless failure to grant the petition would be unfair to the minority, however, a court should seldom authorize formation of an association over the objection of the majority.

. . .

Several courts have faced a situation in which the developer has provided for creation of an association but has not imposed an express obligation on the lot owners to pay assessments.

Evergreen Highlands Association v. West

Supreme Court of Colorado, En Banc
73 P.3d 1 (Colo. 2003)

I. INTRODUCTION

We granted certiorari in this case to determine whether, pursuant to the modification clause of the Evergreen Highlands Subdivision covenants, the requisite majority of lot owners may "change or modify" the existing covenants by the addition of a new covenant which: (1) requires all lot owners to be members of the homeowners association, (2) assesses mandatory dues on all lot owners in the subdivision to pay for the maintenance of common areas, and (3) imposes liens on those lots whose owners fail to pay the mandatory dues....

We also granted certiorari on the related question of whether, in the absence of a covenant imposing mandatory dues, the homeowners association has the implied power to collect assessments from all lot owners to pay for the maintenance of common areas of the subdivision....

II. FACTS AND PROCEDURAL HISTORY

Petitioner Evergreen Highlands Association, a Colorado non-profit corporation ("Association"), is the homeowner association for Evergreen Highlands Subdivision-Unit 4 ("Evergreen Highlands") in Jefferson County. The subdivision consists of sixty-three lots, associated roads, and a 22.3 acre park area which is open to use by all residents of the subdivision. The Association holds title to and maintains the park area, which contains hiking and equestrian trails, a barn and stables, a ball field, a fishing pond, and tennis courts. The park area is almost completely surrounded by private homeowners' lots, with no fence or other boundary separating the park area from the homes. Respondent Robert A. West owns one of the lots bordering directly on the park area, and has used the facilities there to play tennis, fish, and walk his dog.

Evergreen Highlands Subdivision was created and its plat filed in 1972. The plat indicated that the park area was to be conveyed to the homeowners association. Protective covenants for Evergreen Highlands were also filed in 1972, but did not require lot owners to be members of or pay dues to the Association. The Association, however, was incorporated in 1973 for the purposes of maintaining the common area and facilities, enforcing the covenants, paying taxes on the common area, and determining annual fees. The developer conveyed the park area to the Association in 1976. Between the years of 1976 and 1995, when the modification of the covenants at issue in this case occurred, the Association relied on voluntary assessments from lot owners to pay for maintenance of and improvements to the park area. Such expenses included property taxes, insurance for the park area and its structures, weed spraying, tennis court resurfacing, and barn and stable maintenance.

Article 13 of the original Evergreen Highlands covenants provides that a majority of lot owners may agree to modify the covenants, stating in relevant part as follows:

[T]he owners of seventy-five percent of the lots which are subject to these covenants may release all or part of the land so restricted from any one or more of said restrictions, *or may change or modify any one or more of said restrictions,* by executing and acknowledging an appropriate agreement or agreements in writing for such purposes and filing the same in the Office of the County Clerk and Recorder of Jefferson County, Colorado.

Protective Covenants for Evergreen Highlands-Unit 4, art. 13 (Nov. 6, 1972) (emphasis added) (hereinafter "modification clause"). In 1995, pursuant to the modification clause, at least seventy-five percent of Evergreen Highlands' lot owners voted to add a new Article 16 to the covenants. This article required all lot owners to be members of and pay assessments to the Association, and permitted the Association to impose liens on the property of any owners who failed to pay their assessment. Assessments were set at fifty dollars per year per lot.

Respondent purchased his lot in 1986 when membership in the Association and payment of assessments was voluntary, a fact that Respondent contends positively influenced his decision to purchase in Evergreen Highlands. Respondent was not among the majority of homeowners who approved the 1995 amendment to the covenants, and he subsequently refused to pay his lot assessment. When the Association threatened to record a lien against his property, Respondent filed this lawsuit challenging the validity of the 1995 amendment. The Association counterclaimed for a declaratory judgment that it had the implied power to collect assessments from all lot owners in the subdivision, and accordingly sought damages from West for breach of the implied contract.[1] The district court ruled in favor of the Association on the ground that the amendment was valid and binding; therefore, it never reached the merits of the Association's counterclaims.

The court of appeals reversed, finding that the terms "change or modify" as set forth in the modification clause of the covenants did not allow for the addition of a wholly new covenant, but only for modifications to the existing covenants.... The court of appeals did not address the issue of whether the Association had the implied power to collect assessments from lot owners, and therefore whether Respondent was in breach of an implied contract. We granted certiorari[2] and now reverse and remand.

---

1. The Association also counterclaimed that West was unjustly enriched; this issue was not appealed to us.

2. We granted certiorari on the following issues:

1. Where a planned community's covenants empower a certain percentage of the owners to "change or modify any one or more" of the covenants, may the specified percentage of owners adopt a covenant requiring all owners to pay assessments to the homeowner associa-

III. ANALYSIS

[NOTE: Only the portion of the court's opinion addressing the question whether the association has an implied power to collect assessments is included here. The question whether the amendment power included the power to convert the association to a mandatory membership association with assessment powers is included in Chapter 9 on Amendments. — Eds.]

...

We next examine the question of whether the Association has an implied right to levy assessments against lot owners in order to maintain common areas of the subdivision. Although many subdivisions have covenants which mandate the payment of assessments for this purpose, others, such as Evergreen Highlands, do not.[3] Without the implied authority to levy assessments, these latter communities are placed in the untenable position of being obligated to maintain facilities and infrastructure without any viable economic means by which to do so. In order to avoid the grave public policy concerns this outcome would create, we today adopt the approach taken by many other states as well as the Restatement of Property, which provides that "the power to raise funds reasonably necessary to carry out the functions of a common interest community will be implied if not expressly granted by the declaration." Restatement (Third) of Property: Servitudes § 6.5 cmt. *b* (2000). We therefore hold that, even in the absence of an express covenant mandating the payment of assessments, the Association has the implied power to levy assessments against lot owners in order to raise the necessary funds to maintain the common areas of the subdivision.

B. The Implied Power of Homeowners Associations to Impose Mandatory Dues on Lot Owners for the Maintenance of Common Areas

The Association additionally argues that, even in the absence of an express covenant imposing mandatory assessments, it has the implied power to collect assessments from its members. To this end, the Association brought a counterclaim against West for breach of an implied contract obligating him to pay a proportionate share for repair, upkeep, and maintenance of the common area. The Association now argues that, based on West's breach of the implied contract, it is entitled as a matter of law to collect the unpaid assessments from Respondent.

We agree. Our review of case law from other states, the Restatement of Property (Servitudes), and the declarations for Evergreen Highlands in effect when West purchased his property, as supported by our understanding of the purpose of the Colorado Common Interest Ownership Act ("CCIOA"),[6] convinces us that such an implied power exists in these circumstances. We therefore hold that Evergreen Highlands is a common interest community by implication, and that the Association has the implied power to levy assessments against lot owners to provide for maintenance of and improvements to common areas of the subdivision.

---

tion?
2. Does a planned community's homeowner association have the implied power to collect assessments from all owners to defray the cost of maintaining common areas?
3. Amicus Curiae Community Associations Institute, a national nonprofit research and education organization, estimates that approximately 2,000 Colorado communities, housing an estimated 450,000 people, fall into the latter category.
6. CCIOA is located at sections 38-33.3-101 through 38-33.3-304, 10 C.R.S. (2002).

This being a question of first impression in Colorado, we first examine case law from other jurisdictions and find it largely in concurrence with our holding. When faced with this issue, a substantial number of states have arrived at the conclusion that homeowner associations have the implied power to levy dues or assessments even in the absence of express authority. *See, e.g., Spinnler Point Colony Ass'n, Inc. v. Nash,* 689 A.2d 1026, 1028–29 (Pa.Commw.Ct.1997) (holding that where ownership in a residential community allows owners to utilize common areas, "there is an implied agreement to accept the proportionate costs for maintaining and repairing these facilities."); *Meadow Run & Mountain Lake Park Ass'n v. Berkel,* 409 Pa.Super. 637, 598 A.2d 1024, 1026 (1991) (same); *Seaview Ass'n of Fire Island, N.Y., Inc. v. Williams,* 69 N.Y.2d 987, 517 N.Y.S.2d 709, 510 N.E.2d 793, 794 (1987) (holding that when lot purchaser has knowledge that homeowners association provides facilities and services to community residents, purchase creates an implied-in-fact contract to pay a proportionate share of those facilities and services); *Perry v. Bridgetown Cmty. Ass'n, Inc.,* 486 So. 2d 1230, 1234 (Miss.1986) ("A landowner who willfully purchases property subject to control of the association and derives benefits from membership in the association implies his consent to be charged assessments and dues common to all other members."). *But see Popponesset Beach Ass'n, Inc. v. Marchillo,* 39 Mass.App.Ct. 586, 658 N.E.2d 983, 987–88 (1996) (holding that where lot owner had no notice in his chain of title of assessments and had not used the common areas, there existed no implied-in-fact contract to pay past and future assessments).[7]

Reflecting this considerable body of law, the newest version of the Restatement of Property (Servitudes) provides that "a common-interest community has the power to raise the funds reasonably necessary to carry out its functions by levying assessments against the individually owned property in the community...."Restatement (Third) of Property: Servitudes § 6.5(1)(a) (2000). In addition, as explained in a comment to that section, the power to levy assessments "will be implied if not expressly granted by the declaration or by statute." *Id.* at § 6.5 cmt. b; *see also* Wayne S. Hyatt, *Condominium and Homeowner Association Practice: Community Association Law* 36 (1981) ("The assessment is not equivalent to membership dues or some other discretionary charge.... As long as legitimate expenses are incurred, the individual member must bear his or her share.").

We find the Restatement and case law from other states persuasive in analyzing the issue before us today. In addition, these authorities are in harmony with the legislative purpose motivating the enactment of CCIOA. *See, e.g.,* § 38-33.3-102(1)(b), 10 C.R.S. (2002) ("That the continuation of the economic prosperity of Colorado is dependent upon the strengthening of homeowner associations ... through enhancing the financial stability of associations by increasing the association's powers to collect delinquent assessments"); § 38-33.3-102(1)(d) ("That it is the policy of this state to promote effective and efficient property management through defined operational requirements that preserve flexibility for such homeowner associations").

Respondent, however, argues that the implied power to mandate assessments can only be imputed to "common interest communities," which both CCIOA and the Restatement define as residential communities in which there exists a mandatory obligation or servi-

---

7. We note that in contrast to *Marchillo,* testimony in this case showed that West had, in fact, availed himself of the benefits of the park area.

tude imposed on individual owners to pay for common elements of the community.[8] Respondent therefore contends that because the original covenants did not impose such a servitude, Evergreen Highlands is not a common interest community, and accordingly cannot have the implied power to levy assessments against its members pursuant to these authorities.

Respondent's argument, however, relies on the assumption that the servitude or obligation to pay which would have defined Evergreen Highlands as a common interest community was required to have been made express in the covenants or in his deed. This assumption is incorrect. CCIOA provides only that the obligation must arise from the "declarations," which are defined as "any recorded instruments however denominated, that create a common interest community, including any amendments to those instruments and also including, but not limited to, plats and maps." § 38-33.3-103(13), 10 C.R.S. (2002); *see also* Restatement (Third) of Property: Servitudes § 6.2(5)(2000) ("'Declaration' means the recorded document or documents containing the servitudes that create and govern the common-interest community.").

The declarations in effect for Evergreen Highlands in 1986 incorporated all documents recorded up to that date, and included not only: (1) the covenants, but also; (2) the 1972 plat, which noted that the park area would be conveyed to the homeowners association; (3) the 1973 Articles of Incorporation for the Association stating that the Association's purposes were to "own, acquire, build, operate, and maintain" the common area and facilities, to pay taxes on same, and to "determine annual membership or use fees"; and (4) the 1976 deed whereby the developer quit-claimed his ownership in the park area to the Association.

At the time Respondent purchased his lot in 1986, the Evergreen Highlands' declarations made clear that a homeowners association existed, it owned and maintained the park area, and it had the power to impose annual membership or use fees on lot owners. These declarations were sufficient to create a common interest community by implication. As explained by the Restatement:

> An implied obligation may ... be found where the declaration expressly creates an association for the purpose of managing common property or enforcing use restrictions and design controls, but fails to include a mechanism for providing the funds necessary to carry out its functions. When such an implied obligation is established, the lots are a common-interest community within the meaning of this Chapter.

---

8. CCIOA defines a "common interest community" as:
> real estate described in a declaration with respect to which a person, by virtue of such person's ownership of a unit, is obligated to pay for real estate taxes, insurance premiums, maintenance, or improvement of other real estate described in a declaration.... § 38-33.3-103(8), 10 C.R.S. (2002).

The Restatement defines a "common interest community" as:
> a real estate development or neighborhood in which individually owned lots or units are burdened by a servitude that imposes an obligation that cannot be avoided by nonuse or withdrawal
>   (a) to pay for the use of, or contribute to the maintenance of, property held or enjoyed in common by the individual owners, or
>   (b) to pay dues or assessments to an association that provides services or facilities to the common property or to the individually owned property, or that enforces other servitudes burdening the property in the development or neighborhood.

Restatement (Third) of Property: Servitudes § 6.2 cmt. a (2000); *see also id.* at illus. 2 (citing an example virtually identical to that of Evergreen Highlands and finding it a common interest community by judicial decree).

We accordingly adopt the position taken by the Restatement and many other states, and hold that the declarations for Evergreen Highlands were sufficient to create a common interest community by implication. The Association therefore has the implicit power to levy assessments against lot owners for the purpose of maintaining the common area of the subdivision. Respondent, as a lot owner, has an implied duty to pay his proportionate share of the cost of maintaining and operating the common area. We therefore remand the case to the court of appeals with orders to return it to the trial court to calculate Petitioner's damages in a manner consistent with this opinion....

Justice COATS, concurring only in the judgment of the court and Part III. A. of the majority opinion.

I agree with the majority's determination that the Evergreen Highlands covenants permitted the adoption of the 1995 amendment by 75 percent of the lot owners and that the trial court was justified in finding the amendment binding on all lot owners, whether they voted for it or not. Because the amendment is an express covenant providing for the imposition of mandatory assessments, I would not address the hypothetical question whether the Association would have the implied power to collect assessments in the absence of such an express provision. I would especially not, under these circumstances, legislate a new category of common-interest community and impute powers to that entity, as I believe the majority does.

Whether or not it was adequately preserved for appeal, the Association's alternate argument concerning implied powers was addressed by neither the district nor the appellate court below. In light of this court's finding of a valid, express covenant providing for the imposition of mandatory assessments, resolution of the implied powers question is not only unnecessary but actually premised upon a condition held by the court not to exist in this case. Perhaps most importantly, however, in its attempt to formulate and announce a new rule of general applicability (unanchored by its effect on the outcome of any existing case or controversy), the majority needlessly construes Colorado's Common Interest Ownership Act and the American Law Institute's restatement of the law concerning common-interest communities, and does so in a way that, in my opinion, is at least questionable.

Unsurprisingly, other jurisdictions have found on occasion, in the particular circumstances of individual cases, an implied power of a community to levy mandatory assessments on individual lot owners, flowing from an implied-in-fact contract.... Without restricting those fact-specific holdings in any way, the Restatement suggests the more general concept of a "common-interest community," defined by certain common characteristics, from which its powers, including the implied power to levy assessments, necessarily flow. While its definition is perhaps broader than that of Colorado's Common Interest Ownership Act, even the Restatement would categorize as a "common-interest community" only a development or neighborhood in which individually owned lots are burdened by a servitude that imposes an obligation to support common property or pay assessments to an association with the responsibility of maintaining it or enforcing servitudes on the property in the development. *See* Restatement (Third) of Property: Servitudes § 6.2 (2000).

The Restatement specifically emphasizes that "[i]t does not purport to authorize the imposition of assessments by property-owner groups that are not common-interest communities." *Id.* at § 6.5 cmt. a. Although it makes no attempt to describe all of the circumstances under which a qualifying servitude might be found, the Restatement imputes the power of assessment as a general matter only to communities in which membership in the association is mandatory or the individual lots are so burdened. Rather than suggesting that all residential developments or neighborhood organizations necessarily have the power of assessment, the Restatement merely finds that a power of assessment is implied from the need to enforce existing servitudes on individual lots.

In relying on the Restatement as authority for its broad notion of a "common interest community by implication," the majority, in my view, needlessly dilutes the necessary characteristics of a common-interest community from which its inherent powers derive and injects a kind of circularity into its reasoning. If the declarations in this case actually "made clear that a homeowners association ... had the power to impose annual membership or use fees on lot owners," ... without their voluntary participation, injecting the general concept of a common-interest community would seem to be superfluous. The power to levy assessments on lot owners would already be express, or at least be clearly implied by the particular provisions of the declarations. And to the extent that the majority's expansive definition of "declarations," as including the Association's Articles of Incorporation, is dependent upon their character as "governing documents" of a common-interest community, the servitude necessary to create the common-interest community in the first place certainly could not be inferred from the articles themselves.

Even if I considered guidance from this court to be both important and appropriate in some situations, I would nevertheless be reluctant to give it were I to find no greater clarity or consensus concerning the applicable legal principles than I find here. I fear that the majority's discussion of implied powers of assessment is likely to raise more questions than it resolves. Because I consider this dictum to be both gratuitous and highly questionable, I would omit it altogether. I therefore concur only in the judgment of the court and Part III. A. of the majority opinion.

Notes & Questions

1. Is the concurring opinion correct in asserting that the Restatement does not recognize an implied obligation to pay assessments as sufficient to characterize a development as a common interest community?

2. If the association could not acquire the power to assess lot owners for maintenance of the park and roads, what other options would it have? The law of easements might provide a solution. Assuming that the lot owners had easements to use the park and roads, they could be required to contribute to maintenance of the easements. However, required contributions are usually based on use of the easements, not ownership of lots. Restatement (Third) § 4.13. Lot owners like West could avoid any responsibility for sharing in the costs by avoiding use of the park and roads.

If the lot owners owned the park as tenants in common instead of having easements in land owned by the association, the law of concurrent estates would apply. Co-tenants each have the right to use the whole of the property but their only duty with respect to maintenance would ordinarily be just to avoid waste, which probably would not provide a very satisfactory level of maintenance. It certainly would not allow for improvement of the park.

Other alternatives the association could explore would be opening the park up to outsiders and charging user fees or trying to get a public body to accept dedication of the park and roads and take over their maintenance. Both of these options would involve a loss of exclusivity for the Evergreen Highlands owners and if the park became public, a loss of control over the level of maintenance that would be provided.

Lake Tishomingo, courtesy of John M. Folluo.

Lake Tishomingo Property Owners Ass'n v. Cronin
Supreme Court of Missouri, 1984,
679 S.W.2d 852

WELLIVER, J. Lake Tishomingo Property Owners Association, respondent, brought this action seeking to enforce liens on real property owned by appellants resulting from their failure to pay a special assessment levied by respondent for the purpose of maintaining certain common property. It is undisputed that the special assessment was not authorized by the covenant restrictions contained in the original indenture and no provision in the original covenants permitted their subsequent modification. The question before us is whether a consent decree, entered as final judgment in an earlier suit, which amended the original covenants so as to permit special assessments can now be enforced against these property owners. The Circuit Court of Jefferson County ordered enforcement of the liens.... We affirm the judgment of the trial court....

I

Lake Tishomingo Subdivision is a lake community located in Jefferson County consisting of a 120 acre man-made lake surrounded by approximately 930 lots. Its developer, Lake Development Enterprises, Inc. (LDE), platted the property and constructed the lake in the late 1940's. It is clear from the record that the subdivision was designed to be, and remains, a high quality residential community. The present dispute grew out of the need to dredge the lake due to an accumulation of sediments. There is no substantial dispute as to the seriousness of the problem or the necessity of the operation. Water depth had decreased as much as six feet in areas making boating impossible in parts of the lake, fishing was deteriorating, the water was polluted, and the lake suffered from an over-abundance of aquatic weeds. Dredging the lake emerged as the only solution after numerous individual attempts to remediate the problem failed. An engineering firm, hired by respondent to study the problem, made specific recommendations and estimated the cost of the dredging operation at approximately $170,000.

The cost estimate far exceeded the revenues that could be generated by the annual assessment prescribed by the subdivision's covenant restrictions, set at fifty-five cents per front foot. A group of residents, including appellant Albert Beyer, unsuccessfully sought to obtain financial assistance from the federal government. When that effort failed, respondent's Board of Directors proposed and adopted a resolution calling for a special election to amend the existing covenants to allow a one-time special assessment of $2.60 per front foot to finance the cost of the dredging. Respondent's directors proposed this course of action in reliance of a provision in a consent decree previously rendered final which authorized:

> [c]hanges in, or additions, to, the said subdivision restrictions ... [upon approval] by a simple majority of the votes cast at an election wherein each lot owner in the subdivision shall be entitled to cast one vote for each ten (10) front feet of lot owned by him, but not less than five (5) nor more than ten (10) votes per platted lot. (Said changes or additions may be for the purpose of assessments, extension of the restrictions, and other matters consistent with the purposes of the subdivision and the trust ...)

The proposition was adopted by a majority of the votes cast. Out of 4,913 possible votes 2,904 were cast; 1,976 voted for the proposition, 928 voted against it. Two hundred forty-six property owners voted in the election; 163 voted for the special assessment, 83 voted against it. Respondent recorded the amendment and levied the assessment.

Respondent filed this suit in 1978 against seventy-six property owners who had failed to pay the special assessment....

The [consent] decree as finally approved [in 1972] purported to work three significant changes in the original covenants. First, all the rights, powers and obligations of LDE as the original grantor were transferred to the Lake Tishomingo Property Owners Association (LTPOA), respondent herein, as trustee for the benefit of the lot owners in the subdivision; second, LDE's legal title to the subdivision's common areas was ordered conveyed to LTPOA to hold in trust for the benefit of the lot owners; and finally, the court approved the method, described earlier, for amending the subdivision restrictions.

None of the parties ... sought appellate review of the [1972] consent decree and its provisions have otherwise gone unchallenged until respondent filed this suit. Appellants agree that residents of the subdivision have viewed and dealt with respondent as the legitimate successor-in-interest to LDE. Property owners have participated in periodic elections to elect the members of respondent's Board of Directors, public meetings are regularly held, and committees have been established to study specific issues in the community. Respondent has annually levied the regular assessment and property owners, including all of the appellants, have paid it without challenge. Although the record is not clear on the question, it does not appear that an attempt had been made to change or add to the original covenants prior to the attempt giving rise to the present suit.

Appellants are correct in contending that the courts in both of the prior actions were powerless to amend or reform the original covenants. The records are less than clear that all successors in title were parties to those actions and, in any event, reformation or amendment of the covenants was permissible only upon proof of fraud or mistake, ... neither of which was alleged or proven in those proceedings. The Courts' exercise of power in excess of their jurisdiction renders that part of the consent decree which amended the original covenants void and subject to collateral attack in this proceeding.... That which remains of the consent decree is the designation of respondent as successor trustee and holder of title to the common properties of the subdivision and the extension of the existing covenants for a period of twenty-five years,[7] matters accepted by all parties.

It is clear to us that all the property owners in the subdivision, except appellants, have recognized at least a contractual obligation to bear their fair share of the cost of preserving the common properties for the benefit of all owners in the subdivision. On the record before us the equitable obligation of these appellants cannot be disputed. While the Court is powerless to reform or amend the original covenants, we cannot close our eyes to the fact that, when compared to the cost of the dredging operation, the assessment permitted by the original covenants was tantamount to no assessment at all. The assessment voluntarily made by the large majority of lot owners appears fair and equitable. The evidence regarding the dredging operation reflects that it was both reasonable and necessary for the preservation of the property value of the more than 900 lots in the subdivision. Under the unique circumstances attending this case, our sense of fairness and justice compels us to enforce the clear equitable obligation of appellants to bear their share of the costs necessary for preserving the common property essential for continuation of the subdivision. See *Weatherby Lake Improvement Co. v. Sherman*, 611 S.W.2d 326 (Mo.App.1980). Thus understood, the voluntary assessment made and honored by the great majority of property owners was enforceable by the trial court under the court's power to render equity....

For these reasons, the judgment of the trial court is Affirmed.

Retrospective and Observations

A lawyer named Albert George Byer and his wife, a St. Louis realtor, moved from downtown to the Lake Tishomingo area. Lake Tishomingo began in 1946 and was initially a second home project. Dan Reardon, a St. Louis attorney, was successful in attaining a judgment in which the court allowed the initial restrictions for Lake Tishomingo to be amended. The initial term of the restriction was up for renewal, and the court agreed to extend the term for another 25 years. Mr. Reardon's suit also asked that the court allow owners to vote to increase assessments. Albert Byer opposed the suit and filed an objection, but he was unsuccessful.

After Jack C. Stewart became involved in the case in 1970, Missouri's intermediate appeals court said that the court did not have jurisdiction. The court declared the amendment void and said that the judge in the appeals court had no jurisdiction. Mr. Stewart filed for transfer to the Supreme Court of Missouri. The Missouri Supreme Court is reluctant to take cases from lower courts unless there was a mistake in the judgment of the court or there is an unusual question. Mr. Stewart convinced the Supreme Court to look at the case from the prospective that covenants are not a restraint on alienation but that the owners

----

7. The original indenture authorized the extension of the covenants for a period not exceeding twenty-five years upon agreement of the owners of a majority of the front feet in the subdivision. Clearly a majority have so agreed.

were relying on the restrictions and covenants in place at Lake Tishomingo in order to retain their property value.

Initially the Supreme Court "bombed" the association on the assessments issue but allowed renewal of the covenants. Mr. Stewart filed a motion for rehearing, and somehow the Supreme Court reversed itself, conceding to Mr. Stewart's argument that since the roads in the project were created by a plat, and Missouri law required that everyone that uses roads has an obligation to maintain them, the owners at Lake Tishomingo were required to pay the special assessment for road maintenance.

Albert Byer ended up in court two more times when the association attempted to collect the special assessment against him. A final judgment in one of the cases allowed the association to collect $24,000, which included the special assessment plus attorneys fees. The association executed the judgment on his home in order to collect. Mr. Byer died while appealing another assessment collection attempt by the association, and his wife settled the case.

Mr. Stewart noted that in response to this case, and in response to a second case where he represented a property owners association, Missouri courts have dumped the old law which said that covenants must be construed in favor of the free use of property and have adopted the rule that *sometimes* covenants must be *liberally* construed.

Currently, homes at Lake Tishomingo are in better shape than they were in the 70's when the suits were active. At that time, most of the homes were second homes, and now they are principal residences. The covenants at Lake Tishomingo will be up for renewal again soon.

Problem

The developer of a resort community excluded the hotel site from the land described in the declaration of covenants, conditions, and restrictions (CC&Rs) for the rest of the community at the request of the hotel site owner. The hotel site owner agreed that the hotel site could be subjected to the CC&Rs when the hotel business became stronger and could afford to pay assessments. The hotel has now become successful, due largely to the success of the resort community, but the new owner refuses to submit the hotel property to the CC&Rs or to pay assessments to the association. Does the developer or the association have any recourse against the hotel's current owner?

B. Creating Community Associations

As we have seen, developers who create common interest communities should also create community associations with assessment powers to provide for support and management of the common property. Ideally, this should be accomplished by recording a declaration for the development that includes covenants running with the land that provide for creation of an association, make all lot or unit owners members of the association, and require all lot or unit owners to pay assessments to the association to enable it to carry out its functions.

The developer should also create the association. Usually, a not-for-profit, mutual benefit corporation is used to structure the association, but other organizational forms are sometimes used. The corporate form provides some protection against liability as well as back-up rules for governance of the association. Unincorporated associations may be used where these advantages are not thought to be necessary. In Virginia, for example condominium associations practitioners generally believe that the condominium statute provides adequate protection and guidelines for operation so that it is not necessary to incur the expenses involved in incorporation. Historically, community associations were organized as trusts in Massachusetts. The common areas were held in trust for the benefit of the homeowners, who elected the trustees.

1. The Governing Documents

The basic document for a common interest community is the Declaration, which describes the land included in the community, spells out any restrictive covenants on use of the land, identifies common property, obligates lot or unit owners to belong to and pay assessments to the association, describes the functions and powers of the association, and provides for governance of the association. In providing for governance, the declaration should identify the number of votes allocated to each lot or unit and the basis on which assessments may be made. Very often one vote is allocated to each lot or unit and assessments are equal. However, that is not always the case. Votes and assessments may vary depending on the size or value of a lot or unit or the nature of the activity allowed. Commercial units, for example, may be treated differently from residential units. The declaration should also include provisions for amendment. Although it was common at an earlier time to limit the duration of the covenants, terminating covenants can cause severe problems to a community that owns common property. Better practice is to provide that the lot owners have an option to terminate after a set period and at regular intervals thereafter by a specified percentage of affirmative votes or simply to give the declaration indefinite duration.

"rule against perpetuities" issue?

If the association is incorporated, articles of incorporation will be necessary. Whether or not the association is incorporated, a set of bylaws should be prepared. The bylaws will contain the details of governance of the association. One way to think about the relationship between the declaration and the bylaws is to regard the declaration as the constitution of the community and the bylaws as the statutes. Fundamental provisions dealing with property rights and voting rights belong in the declaration; operational provisions belong in the bylaws. The declaration must always be recorded. Practice varies as to recording of the bylaws. Bylaws may be recorded either because required by local law or because the attorney believes it is the better practice. Recording ensures that all purchasers will have record notice of the contents of the bylaws but may also make them more difficult to amend.

In every state, it is important to be familiar with local laws which may specify what the declaration must contain and what documents must be recorded for various purposes. In Hawaii, for example, the obligation to pay assessments must be in a recorded document, rather than in the association's articles of incorporation, in order to bring an association within the provisions of the state's Planned Community Act. See *Kaanapali Hillside Homeowners' Ass'n v. Doran*, 162 P.3d 1277 (Haw. 2007), discussed in Chapter 1.

In addition to the documents needed to create the association, documents will be needed to identify the lots or units and to convey them to purchasers. A plat map shows the boundaries of the development and locates the building sites, the lot lines, and the common areas. The plat provides a visual representation of the property described in the declaration and furnishes the basis for legal descriptions needed to convey title to the lots and units. The plat map also usually shows the location of roads and easements. Condominium developments also require floor plans that show the boundaries of the units—both horizontal and vertical. You may also find floor plans used where there is attached housing, even if it is not structured as a condominium. Finally, there are the contracts for sale and the deeds to the lots or units. A deed to a condominium unit conveys both the unit and the undivided interests in the common areas that pass with title to the unit.

The deeds to the initial purchasers should specify that the conveyance is made subject to the recorded declaration. When the first lot or unit is sold subject to the declaration, all the property described in the declaration becomes bound by the terms of the declaration, which become servitudes that run with the land. Until the first lot is sold, the developer can withdraw the declaration, but afterwards, the servitudes can be changed only as permitted in the declaration or by statute. Although the initial deeds should provide that the property is conveyed subject to the terms of the declaration, once the servitudes have become effective, failure to include a reference to the declaration in a deed to a purchaser does not exempt that purchaser's property from the servitude regime created by the declaration.

In *Citizens for Covenant Compliance v. Anderson*, 906 P.2d 1314 (Cal. 1995), the Andersons planned to operate a winery and raise llamas on their property. When the neighbors objected on the ground that these activities would violate the restrictive covenants, the Andersons claimed their lots were not covered by the restrictions because the original deeds from the subdivider did not refer to the restrictions. The Supreme Court of California held that the restrictions did bind their lots. Because the declaration of restrictions stated that all lots in the subdivision were bound and benefited and was recorded before lots in the subdivision were sold, purchasers of lots had constructive notice of the restrictions and were bound by them. The Court said: "subsequent purchasers who have constructive notice of the recorded declaration are deemed to intend and agree to be bound by, and to accept the benefits of, the common plan...."

---

2. Control of the Association

One of the attractive features of creating a community association is that it provides a practical vehicle to the developer for an exit strategy. The developer can turn over responsibility for architectural control, providing services, managing common areas, and complying with governmental mandates to the association and move on to other projects. Until the developer is ready to turn over control, or is required to by law or the declaration, the developer retains control of the association by controlling elections to the board of directors. This can be accomplished either by creating a special class of voting membership for the lots or units owned by the developer or simply by giving the developer the right to appoint board members until certain percentages of lots or units have been sold or certain time periods have elapsed. At some point the developer will convey the common property to the association and relinquish any special powers over election of the board of directors. If the developer still has unsold lots or units, the developer will have the same voting rights as any other owner in the association, but no more. If the units have not yet been built, questions often arise as to whether assessments are due for those units and whether the developer is entitled to votes for them. We take up those questions in the chapters on financing the association and voting rights. We take up issues surrounding the transition period and the developer's obligations to the property owners in Chapter 11.

3. Creating Community

Housing developments today are often marketed as places that will provide buyers with a sense of community. Whether a common interest community can become a real community, rather than just a place to live, or worse, a group of warring neighbors who wield restrictive covenants and association rules as cudgels against each other, may depend on the extent and nature of the restrictive covenants and the structure of the association. In a project that develops over time, the developer can play a significant role in developing a sense of community by setting a tone of cooperation and providing opportunities for residents to engage in constructive, community-building ways.

Seven Oaks Governance Documents

Declaration of CCRs (recorded in land records)	By-Laws (recorded as exhibit to CCRs)	Articles of Incorporation (filed with Secretary of State)
Supplemental Declarations Recorded at time of annexation of each Village; may contain additional covenants, easements applicable only to that Village.	Sets out administrative procedures for governance of association: • meetings, voting, quorums • selection of Board of Directors • purposes and powers • due process procedures • officers and roles • committees • rights of Class "B" member	• Incorporates association as nonprofit corporation • Sets out general purposes and powers of association • May be amended by Voting Members representing 2/3 of total Class "A" votes and consists of Class "B" member.
Design Guidelines (unrecorded) Adopted by NCC; amended by NCC, but only with Declarant's written consent as long as Declarant owns property subject to CCRs.	May be amended: By Declarant • to bring into compliance with applicable law, etc. • to enable issuance of title insurance on Units • if required by secondary mortgage market (e.g., FNMA, HLCMC, VA/FHA) By Members • upon approval of Voting Members representing 75% of total Class "A" votes not held by developer, and consent of developer for 30 years.	
Use Guidelines & Restrictions (unrecorded) Initial guidelines set forth in CCRs; supplemented and amended by the Board and Voting Members.		

Newspaper stories often portray association-governed communities as highly regimented places that fine grandmothers for kissing friends, insist that dogs go on a diet, and persecute people who park unapproved vehicles in their driveways or paint their doors the wrong color. Scholars, too, have claimed that associations destroy community rather than building it. There is some truth to these claims—but there are many associations that function well. A survey done for the Community Association Institute in 2005 and again in 2007 reports that 72% of respondents rated their experience living in a community association positive while only 9% responded that it was negative. http://www.cairf.org/research/zogby.pdf.

In "*A New Look: Community Governance Structures that Work in the Market and in Practice*," (Conservation and Façade Easements and Community Stewardship Organizations course of study Materials, ALI-ABA, 2006) Wayne Hyatt wrote:

> This paper sets forth some suggestions as a blueprint for change. The objective is not only to make suggestions but to begin constructive, creative dialogue seeking an array of theories and techniques that meet the needs of the common interest community of the future and that truly represent "community."

I. Introduction

Nothing will ever be attempted if all possible objections must first be overcome.

—Samuel Johnson

Much has been written and spoken about the need for a restoration of community in the United States. There have been excellent articles discussing community theory, the dynamics of the group and the individual, the effects of individualism, and many other related topics. There continues to be excellent literature on traditional neighborhood design and its consequences upon the development of community. However, there is little focus upon one of the key components of the process: residential development utilizing a mandatory membership association. These associations are called *community* associations; but are they really creating and fostering community or are they impeding the very concept they stand for?

This paper discusses concepts of community association structure and governance and proposes new approaches for the creation of *community* in master planned communities. The concepts discussed are designed in large part to "build community" among residents by encouraging interaction and participation rather than simply imposing restrictions and providing amenities.

These concepts represent change and growth in community association structure. That change has occurred in response to changing markets and expectations and negative perceptions of common interest communities. Certain basic guiding principles help frame the discussion. One principle is that the discussion and the resulting proposed course of action be theoretically sound and complete, yet non-legalistic. The course of action must be well-premised in case and statutory law with regard to both problems and solutions. It is meaningless to hypothesize about ideas that clearly are not legally enforceable.

Another principle is that the discussion must have a foundation in reality. The discussion must reflect the fact that evolution in community association formation and operation must not be so daring as to make developments unmarketable, nor should it be so complex as to make projects unmanageable. Moreover, after evolution, "ordinary people" must understand the end product. Evolution must produce a synergy between governance needs and governance capacity.

The final, related principle is that any structure proposed and any technique for implementing such a structure must be balanced against the obvious, fundamental, and primary interest of developers in protecting its real estate assets and its reputation as a community developer.

Project creation, if there is to be community, requires several approaches that are different from the norm. First, community documentation and indeed the entire development plan must seek to destroy the command and control mentality and methodology so dominant in existing community associations. There must be a movement from an emphasis upon people and property management to building and sustaining community. There must be the creation of systems, documents, and design approaches that *empower*, not *impose*. The governance structure must be as concerned with relationships of individuals as with ownership of property. And finally, there must be a recognition that the developer, in fact all of those involved in a master planned community, can do good and do well at the same time. The reality is that community, just like "green," sells. People would rather live in dynamic "communities" that are great places to live rather than sterile environments that are just great places to look at.

To accomplish these objectives requires a tailored governance strategy. Such a strategy would deal with everything from ownership of facilities, the provision of services, and the integration of components and uses with flexibility tied to sufficient assurances so that the buyer knows what she is entitled to expect. The development team must be cognizant of the risks, perhaps of the impossibility, of accomplishing the creation of community within a framework of an organization whose purpose, function, funding and mindset are all founded on maintenance and regulation.

Governance that seeks to create community will involve two major components or approaches. First is the softening of the corporate edges of the traditional approach to community association structure. This helps to lessen the emphasis on command and control. One accomplishes this by restructuring the governance mechanisms and permitting the use of judgments rather than reliance solely upon lists of rules or prohibitions. It is more a matter of regulation than prohibition, standards more than rules. It gives the board of directors the power to deal with needs in a realistic way and not a formulaic, one-size-fits-all approach. It provides for periodic review and accountability of that board to the members of the association, and it makes clear that the board is not under an obligation to sue every time an issue arises but rather is empowered to use its judgment to seek the most appropriate resolution.

Such a governance structure also implements some leveling mechanisms. These can include the statement of Bill of Rights as discussed in Chapter 4 B., *infra* in the notes quoting Professor French's article on the "bill of rights." Professor Hyatt has long used this bill of rights in his community documentation to great effect.

Governance designed to create and to sustain community frequently takes advantage of organizational structures set forth in the Internal Revenue Code in Sections 501(c)(3) and 501(c)(4), which may be called community councils, or community assemblies. Through these devices common interest communities may partner with exempt organizations for environmental, educational, health, arts, and other appropriate activities that create not only for the common interest community but for the public and the surrounding "community" a heightened quality of life and preserved environment. The governing documents frequently provide for creative and flexible funding mechanisms emanating from the common interest community and provide for designated staff within the exempt organization and approaches not normally seen. These could include involving the youth of the community, encouraging and rewarding volunteering, the creation of alliances with other nonprofits or community groups, and a host of innovative strategic partnerships.

4. Community Stewardship Entities

One application of these more creative community building structures is to involve the common interest community in strategic partnerships for the preservation of the environment. If one defines a sustainable development as "a development that preserves and protects the environment (the land, air, water and the critters therein as well as unique and special resources)," one can add that a sustainable development is also one in which there is a livable environment, one that provides a meaningful quality of life, opportunities for harmonious interaction, sharing and participation. There is an opportunity to combine true stewardship functions and community functions thus integrating conservation and community into development.

A major player in such an approach is a community stewardship entity (CSE). This is an organization whose mission is to foster and sustain a harmonious relationship among people and privately protected land. It is a formal partnership among developer, conservationists, and others with an interest in the process whose purpose is to address local land development and conservation issues cooperatively and to create and maintain a "sustainable development."

The CSE helps to create both a sense of place and a sense of preservation, and it includes funding and other mechanisms tied to the development to ensure both its successful operation and its continuity over long periods of time.

The community stewardship entity becomes a part of the conservation toolbox addressing such issues as land acquisition, relationships with land trusts, as well as protecting public lands. The CSE can manage buffers, corridors, and other related portions of protected lands in conjunction with private lands, and it can provide education concerning appropriate activities on such protected lands. It provides a mechanism for the protection of open space for scenic values, environmental and habitat protection, and public enjoyment. It also provides innovative approaches for ownership, management, and funding.

For more information about the structure and operation of CSEs as well as examples of successful operation see "Best Practice: Sustainability Through Community Governance," prepared by Wayne S. Hyatt for the 2007 Sustainable Development Council meeting (Urban Land Institute Fall Meeting, Las Vegas, Nevada); ALI-ABA printed course materials, "Conservation and Preservation Easements and Community Stewardship Entities"; The Sonoran Institute's brochure, "Building Conservation Within Communities"; and W. Hyatt, *Reinvention Redux: Continuing the Evolution of Master-Planned Communities*, 38 *Real Prop. Prob. T. Journal* 45 (2003).

5. Cohousing

Cohousing is a type of common interest community that is sometimes called an "intentional community" because it creates an environment where people are deliberately brought together for many activities. Cohousing communities are like other common interest communities in that they combine individual ownership of lots or units with common spaces and facilities. They are different, however, in that they are <u>relatively small, the common</u> <u>spaces usually include a communal kitchen or common house, often include a community</u> <u>garden, are usually developed by a group of people who come together to form the community,</u> <u>and often are designed to appeal across generations and income groups.</u> They are usually designed to be eco-friendly and members are actively encouraged to develop close bonds.

The Cohousing Association of the United States' website states:

Cohousing communities combine the advantages of private homes with the benefits of more sustainable living, including shared common facilities and ongoing connections with neighbors. These intentional neighborhoods, created and managed by residents, offer an innovative solution to today's environmental and social challenges. http://www.cohousing.org/default.aspx.

Cohousing communities use the same legal structures as other common interest communities—condominium or servitude regimes that impose obligations to support common property and provide governance structures, restrictive covenants, and architectural controls. They are different, however, in that they ordinarily operate on the basis of consensus rather than majority vote. There are usually provisions that in cases of necessity a decision can be taken by majority vote if consensus cannot be reached, but striving for consensus is the ideal.

6. Condominium Conversions

Condominiums are not always built from the ground up. Often apartments or cooperatives are converted into condominiums. Although conversion benefits people who wish to share ownership and responsibility for their property, conversion often burdens tenants in possession at the time the structure is converted. For example, such tenants are often forced out of their residence with little notice and few housing alternatives. In 1988, Congress passed the Condominium and Cooperative Relief Act (CCARA), 15 U.S.C. §§ 3601–3616, which encourages state and local governments to implement legislation requiring developers to provide current tenants with adequate notice and a first right to purchase units in the project. Congress also encouraged tenant-sponsored conversions by requiring the <u>secretary of HUD</u> to expedite the processing and decision making on finance applications so that tenant organizations can convert their residences more easily. This Act is one of the few instances of federal involvement in the field of common interest development. For general information on CCARA see Paul Barron, Federal Regulation of Real Estate and Mortgage Lending, §§ 4.01–4.06 (3d ed. 1992); and see *Bay Colony Condo. Owners Ass'n v. Origer,* 586 F. Supp. 30 (N.D. Ill. 1984) (upholding constitutionality of CCARA).

7. The Attorney's Role

The attorney representing a developer in the creation of a common interest community plays a far greater role than merely filling in the obvious variables in a form set of "CCR's."[P]

P. Although this section addresses the role of the attorney who represents a developer, every attorney, and the law schools who teach them, should strive for four essentials: professionalism and integrity, the ability to read and understand people, the ability to solve problems, and an understanding

She has a complex task of insuring that the various real estate law principles are properly utilized and for selectively creating the governance structure from the applicable principles of other areas of law that, together, comprise "community association law." She best accomplishes this by seeing a common interest community as consisting of both "product" and "process."

The attorney should keep in mind that three strategies must be developed and embodied in the legal documentation and development plan:

- a governance strategy

- an amenity strategy

- an exit strategy.

While doing this work, the attorney will do well to keep in mind three objectives:

- minimize liability

- maximize marketability

- maximize flexibility.

In addition, the governing instruments and the development plan must meet certain specific, legal objectives in order for the project itself to be workable. In studying them, ask how these might change with variations in the size of the development, the nature of common property, and the uses of property in the development. These objectives include:

- *specifying who owns what.* This includes defining what is owned as well as by whom. It requires delineating the common area, limited common area, and privately owned property

- *establishing a system of interlocking relationships* among and between owners. This includes the mandatory nature of the association as well as its structure

- *creating an array of protective standards and restrictions* which institutionalize the land and development plan prepared by other professionals. This is the delicate balancing act of creating provisions that are both flexible yet specific, reasonable, and enforceable. These matters are subjects for Chapters 3, 7, and 8.

- *determining the scope of and creating the necessary administrative vehicle* to maintain and preserve the project. All of the discussions in Chapters 3 and 5 fall into this category.

- *implementing an association financing plan* which is adequate, enforceable, and changeable. This involves both the powers to assess and the procedures and protections for collection. This is the subject of Chapter 6.

- *anticipating the need for and creating a plan to transfer control of the association* at some point in the future from the developer or developers to the various owners. Chapter 11 discusses this topic.

- *creating and preserving developer/declarant rights* with respect to the community. This includes those provisions necessary for the ongoing development of the project. Both Chapters 7 and 11 deal with these issues.

The interdependence of various players within a community the last point illustrates gives rise to one other essential consideration in approaching a discussion of project cre-

---

of the multidisciplinary nature of most transactions. Wayne S. Hyatt, *A Lawyer's Lament: Law Schools and the Profession of Law*, 60 Vand. L. Rev. 385 (2007).

ation: within every successful common interest community, without regard to its type, there is a balancing of the interests of the disparate parties involved. The attorney has direct responsibility to insure that balance is not lost.

As most attorneys are aware, they are responsible for providing their client with competent representation. Although this responsibility generally does not extend to non-clients, under certain circumstances an attorney may owe a duty of care to third parties. For example, an attorney who prepares a public offering statement will likely owe a duty of care to homebuyers who rely on this document when making their purchase. See *Atlantic Paradise Ass'n, Inc. v. Perskie, Nehmad, & Zeltner*, 284 N.J. Super. 678, 666 A.2d 211 (1995) (*cert. denied*, 143 N.J. 518 (1996) (finding that an attorney in preparing a public offering statement owes a duty to non-clients when the attorney knows or should know that a third party will rely on his services).

An attorney also may be liable for fraud if the representations contained in the public offering statement are untrue. See UCIOA § 4-102(c) (1982) (providing that "the person who prepared all or a part of the public offering statement is liable under sections 4-108 ... and 5-106 for any false or misleading statement set forth therein or for any omissions of a material fact therefrom with respect to that portion of the public offering statement which he prepared ..."); see also *Gustafson v. Sentinel of Landmark*, No. 13654 (Va. Cir. Ct. May 10, 1985) (holding that an attorney's failure to provide purchasers with proper offering statements and his failure to register the condominium constitutes fraud).

Some commentators have argued that UCIOA imposes a duty of due diligence on the attorney to ensure that the information contained in a public offering statement is true. Gurdon H. Buck, *Drafting Documents for Condominiums, PUDs, and Golf Course Communities* 643–53 (ALI-ABA 1994). The attorney may not solely rely upon the representations of his or her client but must provide some assurances that the statements are true. *Id.* at 653. Accordingly, an attorney may wish to verify the accuracy of the client's representations by individually investigating the facts. In the related context of federal securities registration, see *Escott v. Barchris Constr. Corp.*, 283 F. Supp. 463 (S.D.N.Y. 1968) (holding that an attorney is liable for not checking matters "easily verifiable"); *Seiffer v. Topsy's Int'l Inc.*, 487 F. Supp. 653 (D. Kan. 1980) (holding that an attorney is liable because he knew or should have known of misleading financial information in the prospectus through careful investigation); and, see also *Feit v. Leasco Data Processing Equip. Corp.*, 332 F. Supp. 544 (E.D.N.Y. 1971) (holding that a lawyer has an obligation reasonably to verify the truth of statements contained in documents that he signed).

Problem

You are driving from the airport in a distant city with a new client who has retained you to act as counsel in preparing the necessary documents for a new thousand-acre, mixed-use master-planned community the client is developing. The project will include retail, office, residential, golf and other recreational properties, and a nice size lake. Prior to leaving your office, you reviewed preliminary plats and project descriptions.

As you drive, the client asks what your initial thoughts, questions, and suggestions are concerning the documents and the association's governance structure, the amenities, and her potential exposure. Tell her.

As you study each successive chapter, revisit this problem, and consider how your answer changes and how the materials you study frame your evolving answer.

8. Layered Associations & Master Planned Communities

Large community associations and master planned communities almost always contain enough quantity and different types of housing (known as "product" in the trade) that it will make sense to organize subassociations. Any condominiums in the development will be required by statute to have their own associations, but it may often make sense to create suborganizations for other parts of the community as well although this approach is no longer the preferred approach. There are some services that should be provided and paid for at the community level, but there are others that can be better handled at a smaller scale. Different organizational structures can be used to implement layered associations. One approach creates separate associations—one master, or umbrella, association with subassociations. The other more prevalent approach uses just one association but creates groupings within the larger association that are often called neighborhoods, villages, or some other market-friendly term, which serve as cost-service centers serving local needs. We will look at the options for organizing large-scale projects when we consider association governance in Chapter 5. By way of introduction, however, we take up two cases that raise basic questions about creation of layered associations.

Bellevue Pacific Center Condominium Owners Association v. Bellevue Pacific Tower Condominium Association

Court of Appeals of Washington
100 P.3d 832 (Wash. Ct. App. 2004)

GROSSE, J....

FACTS

Bellevue Pacific Center (Center) is a condominium. It was created by the Bellevue Pacific Center Limited Partnership (partnership) which recorded declaration and covenants, conditions, restrictions and reservations (declaration) for the Center. The Center's Condominium Association (Center Association) conducts the Center's affairs. The Center is a high-rise, mixed-use complex in downtown Bellevue. The declaration for the Center created three separate units including one comprised of a tower of 171 residential units of various sizes and worth, a unit of commercial office and retail spaces, and a parking garage unit. The separate residential condominium known as the Bellevue Pacific Tower Condominium (Tower) is contained within the Center. The partnership created the Tower by recording a separate declaration. The Tower Condominium Association (Tower Association) controls the residential tower's affairs. Thus, there is a condominium within a condominium. The partnership has owned the commercial and garage units since declarations were filed for the Center and the Tower.

The Center's declaration twice states that votes in its association are allocated equally among the three units comprising the Center: one unit, one vote, or a total of three votes. The declaration indicates that "[c]ommon [e]xpense[s]" are to be allocated based on square footage. The partnership admits the major decisions concerning the operation of the Center requires two of the three unit votes, and that it initially owns two of the three units. But the partnership points out that eventually this may not be so.

The Tower's declaration establishes the Tower Association. The declaration assigns voting rights in the Tower Association based on the declared value of each unit; however, common expenses are allocated among the Tower units based on square footage. The declaration for the Tower includes a provision establishing a period of declarant control and indicates a time when the declarant necessarily had to give up control of the Tower. The relationship between the Center and the Tower was fully disclosed to each person who purchased a residence in the Tower.

By a typical vote of 2 to 1, the Center Association's board divided expenses and assessed the three units. Members of the Tower Association believed they were being overcharged and refused to pay the Association's assessment. The Center Association filed suit to collect the Tower Association's share of the overdue assessment. In response, the Tower Association filed an answer and counterclaim against the partnership and its affiliate, the management company. The pleadings alleged the partnership and the management company mismanaged the Center and assessed improper charges against the Tower Association. These claims were resolved by settlement.

But also included in the Tower Association's pleadings was a claim for declaratory judgment seeking a declaration that the voting rights allocation set forth in the Center's declaration violated the Washington Condominium Act (WCA or Act), RCW 64.34.010-.920. The partnership moved for partial summary judgment dismissing the claim. The trial court granted the motion. The Tower Association briefed an additional issue not directly addressed in the pleadings, claiming the Center Association was a master association under RCW 64.34.276, thus providing only members of the Tower Association with the right to vote for directors of the Center. If the Center Association is deemed a master association, the residential homeowners gain control of the Center's board. The partnership moved for partial summary judgment on this claim and the trial court granted it as well.

The Tower Association moved for reconsideration of the first order on summary judgment, which dismissed its claim that the voting rights allocation was illegal. The motion was denied.

The Tower Association appeals the orders on summary judgment.

ANALYSIS

… The overarching argument of the Tower Association is that the WCA is to be interpreted with consumer protection in mind, … and that the voting scheme set forth in the Center's declaration is contrary to the WCA and constitutes discrimination or is unconscionable. The Tower Association argues that the Act provides that a declarant must transfer control of the condominium to the owners and that the Center Association's voting scheme prevents the transfer of control because the declarant owns two of the three units of the Center Association.

Initially, the Tower Association claims the voting scheme of the Center Association board (each of the three units gets one vote) violates RCW 64.34.224(1). That section provides:

The declaration shall allocate a fraction or percentage of undivided interests in the common elements and in the common expenses of the association, and a portion of the votes in the association, to each unit and state the formulas or methods used to establish those allocations. Those allocations may not discriminate in favor of units owned by the declarant or an affiliate of the declarant.

The Tower Association claims the allocation of votes discriminates in favor of the declarant partnership because it owns two of the three units. But assigning one vote to each unit does not in itself discriminate as each unit retains the same voting power regardless of ownership. There is nothing in the WCA that prevents a declarant from owning a majority of the condominium units. Nothing in the WCA or public policy requires that the residential unit owners must have control of a mixed-use building. The sunset of declarant control is not provided for in the Center condominium declaration because it is not required under the declaration and further is not required by RCW 64.34.308.

The Tower Association argues its point differently, claiming the voting scheme violates RCW 64.34.308 and .312, requiring a declarant to relinquish control to the condominium owners. Under RCW 64.34.308(4)(a), a declarant may have a period of control during which time the declarant has the power to appoint and remove board members and officers, and veto proposed action of the board or association. RCW 64.34.312 provides that *if* a period of declarant control is provided under RCW 64.34.308, then the declarant must transfer the property within a specified time following termination of declarant control.

Here, the declarant partnership did not provide for a period of declarant control for the Center Association, but provided control to the three units with equal votes. Therefore, RCW 64.34.308 and .312 do not apply to the instant facts. While true that the partnership has control, this is due to its ownership of two of the three units not due to its being the declarant. The Tower Association seemingly argues that the statutes prevent a declarant from owning majority control through voting. We disagree.

Even had there been a sunset of declarant control provided in the Center's declaration, nowhere in the WCA is there a prohibition of a declarant owning a majority of the units. The scheme here, while certainly favoring the declarant/partnership is not in violation of the statute. The definition contained in RCW 64.34.020(32) defines a unit owner to include a declarant who owns a unit. Under RCW 64.34.308(6), within 30 days after any declarant control is terminated, the unit owners shall elect a board of directors, at least of a majority of those directors must be unit owners. That is what happened here.

The control disapproved of by statute is the unilateral ability of the declarant to appoint and remove officers as well as veto association actions. Here, the Center's declaration did not provide for such control, and the control exercised was due to its majority control of the Center Association units through ownership, not unilateral control granted by the declaration.

Second, the Tower Association claims the partnership discriminated against the residential owners through misallocation of the developer's ownership interest. RCW 64.34.224(1) provides:

The declaration shall allocate a fraction or percentage of undivided interests in the common elements and in the common expenses of the association, and a portion of the votes in the association, to each unit and state the formulas or methods used to establish those allocations. Those allocations may not discriminate in favor of units owned by the declarant or an affiliate of the declarant.

No case in Washington has described what it means to "discriminate" in favor of units owned by the developer.[3] The Tower Association claims that by looking to the totality of the management arrangements for the Center, the developer established a voting scheme for the Center Association that is biased in favor of the developer's ownership interests, thus the residential homeowners are necessarily discriminated against.

3. See Parents Involved in Cmty. Sch. v. Seattle Sch. Dist. No. 1, 149 Wash.2d 660, 686, 72 P.3d 151 (2003) (quoting Webster's Third New International Dictionary 648) (1993) (two definitions provided for "discriminate" or "discriminate against," here, "'to make a difference in treatment or favor on a class or categorical basis in disregard of individual merit.'").

However, the Center's declaration allocates one vote to each unit. It provides that common expenses are to be shared in proportion to the square footage of the units. Nothing in the allocation is illegal or improper. The statute permits the declarant to allocate votes by size, value, and number of units or other appropriate basis.

The comment to the WCA as well as the Uniform Act approves of an allocation scheme similar to the one here; votes assigned equally to each unit and expenses divided proportionately according to size.

> 1. RCW 64.32 [the former Condominium Act] requires a single common basis related to the "value" of the units to be used in the allocation of common element interests, votes in the association, and common expense liabilities. This Act departs radically from such requirements by permitting each of these allocations to be made on different bases, and by permitting allocations which are unrelated to value.

Thus, all three allocations might be made equally among all units, or in proportion to the relative size of each unit, or on the basis of any other formula the declarant may select, regardless of the values of those units. Moreover, "size" might be used, for example, in allocating common expenses and common element interests, while equality is used in allocating votes in the association. This section does not require that the formulas used by the declarant be justified, but it does require that the formulas be explained. The sole restriction on the formulas to be used in these allocations is that they not discriminate in favor of the units owned by the declarant or an affiliate of the declarant. Otherwise, each of the separate allocations may be made on any basis which the declarant chooses, and none of the allocations need be tied to any other allocation.[4]

But it is the last sentence of RCW 64.34.224(1) that the Tower Association raises, that there can be no discrimination in favor of units owned by the declarant. But as long as all units have the same voting rights and bear the same share of common expenses regardless of who owns them, there is no discrimination in favor of units owned by the declarant.

Implicit in the Tower Association's argument under RCW 64.34.224 is the assumption that there never should have been separate condominiums for the Tower and the Center. But the WCA does not require this and there is no violation of the statute through discriminatory voting other than the usual "majority wins" which is necessarily a type of discrimination, but it is not illegal.

Next, the Tower Association claims the Center Association's voting scheme is unconscionable under RCW 64.34.080 because it allows a declarant to retain control of an association in contravention of the WCA's clear intent to transfer control to the condominium owners. Again, the Center's declaration did not authorize a period of declarant control. The Center has always been subject to a one unit, one vote form of board governance. Control has always been vested in the three unit owners, even though initially the partnership/declarant controlled the Tower units that later was turned over to the homeowners association.

Under RCW 64.34.080(2), a party raising the claim of unconscionability may present evidence as to the commercial setting of the negotiations, whether a party took advantage of another party by reason of mental or physical infirmity, inability to understand the language of the agreement, or illiteracy, as well as evidence relating to the effect of the contract or clause challenged. The Tower Association does not raise or argue any of these points, but instead argues that the contract is one of adhesion that allows the partnership

---

4. 2 Senate Journal, 51st Leg., Reg. Sess., at 2061 cmt. (Wash.1990).

to illegally retain control over the Tower unit. The Tower Association argues that because the residential unit constitutes 53 percent of the Center's square footage, and 88 percent of the Center's declared value, the voting scheme allocating one vote to each of the Center units is unconscionable because it allows the Center Association to use resources provided by the residents and their association to the benefit of the declarant/partnership owned commercial and garage units.

But the declaration itself is not a contract under RCW 64.34.080. It is a document that unilaterally creates a type of real property. The declaration is not a contract that can be called unconscionable. As long as the declaration complies with the Act, neither the declarant/partnership nor the Tower unit owners may change the voting scheme except by approval of all unit owners affected by an amendment....

[handwritten margin note: Declaration is not a contract; Ok, then what principles of interpretation apply?]

The trial court also dismissed the Tower Association's argument that the Center Association is a "master association" under RCW 64.34.276, necessarily rejecting the Tower Association's argument that only the Tower Association members are allowed to elect the Center's board of directors under the alternatives found in RCW 64.34.276(5)(a)-(d). The Tower Association claims the trial court erred in this determination.

RCW 64.34.020(23) defines "[m]aster association" to mean "an organization described in RCW 64.34.276, whether or not it is also an association described in RCW 64.34.300." RCW 64.34.276(1) describes a master association as:

> (1) If the declaration provides that any of the powers described in RCW 64.34.304 [powers of a homeowners' association] are to be exercised by or may be delegated to a profit or nonprofit corporation which exercises those or other powers on behalf of a development consisting of one or more condominiums or for the benefit of the unit owners of one or more condominiums, all provisions of this chapter applicable to unit owners' associations apply to any such corporation, except as modified by this section.

The comment to this section indicates that the use of master associations was common in large or multi-phased condominiums under prior acts.... Therefore, a declarant would set up a master or umbrella organization to provide management services for a series of condominiums. Master associations thus are entities to which other condominium associations delegate a portion of their power.

For RCW 64.34.276(1) to apply, three elements must be present: (1) the declaration of the owners' associations must provide that powers granted to them by the WCA are to be exercised or delegated to another corporation; (2) that corporation exercises those powers on behalf of the development; and (3) there is one or more condominiums. There is no doubt that the first two of these elements are not present in this case.

Because the declaration did not create a master association, the Tower Association's argument necessarily has to be that the Center Association is a *de facto* master association. However, RCW 64.34.276(1), the master association statute, requires that the delegation of powers to a master association appear in a declaration....

The trial court is affirmed.

Notes & Questions

1. Are the owners of units in the Tower condominium being unfairly treated? If you were a member of the Washington Supreme Court, would you grant review of the decision? If so, how do you think you would decide it?

2. Should the residential unit owners have anticipated that they could be at the mercy of the owners of the owners of the garage and commercial segments of the project? Would you have foreseen the difficulties if you had been called on to advise a prospective buyer?

Brandon Farms Property Owners Association, Inc. v. Brandon Farms Condominium Association, Inc.

Supreme Court of New Jersey
852 A.2d 132 (N.J. 2004)

Justice WALLACE delivered the opinion of the court.

In this case, the primary issue is whether the Condominium Act (Act), *N.J.S.A.* 46:8B-1 to -38, permits a developer to require a condominium association to be responsible for assessments owed by individuals of the association to an "umbrella" organization. The trial court invalidated the scheme. In an unpublished opinion, the Appellate Division reversed. We granted certification, ... and we also granted *amicus curiae* status to the Community Association Institute. We now reverse the judgment of the Appellate Division and hold that under the Act, a builder or developer may not make a condominium association responsible for an association member's failure to pay assessments owed to an umbrella organization.

I.

The essential facts are not disputed. Brandon Farms is a 556-acre development of single-family detached homes, townhouses, and condominiums located in the townships of Lawrence and Hopewell. The Declaration of Covenants and Restrictions (Declaration), filed by the developer, created the Brandon Farms Property Owners Association (Property Owners Association) to serve as the umbrella organization charged with maintaining and managing the common property intended for the beneficial use of all homeowners in the community. Although the Property Owners Association is not responsible for the common elements of the condominiums, which are the responsibility of the respective condominium associations, the Declaration governs both the Property Owners Association and the Brandon Farms Condominium Association (Condominium Association). Section 7.02 of the Declaration authorizes the Property Owners Association to collect and disburse assessments and charges necessary to fulfill its mandate.

Each owner of the 1,293 total units in Brandon Farms, whether single-family house or condominium unit, is a member of the Property Owners Association. Membership is divided into three classes: Class A consists of owners of single-family, detached homes on certain designated parcels; Class B consists of owners of single-family homes and some condominium unit owners who are members of the Twin Pines Condominium Association; and Class C consists of 469 owners of condominium units in the Condominium Association. Thus, the owners of condominium units in Class C are members of both the Property Owners Association and the Condominium Association.

All Class A and C members pay a recreational limited common expense assessment to the Property Owners Association in return for access to the community's swimming pool and clubhouse. Class B members, however, are not assessed that charge, but must pay an optional recreational facilities fee to use the pool and clubhouse. In addition to the recreational limited common expense assessment paid by members of Class A and Class C, every homeowner in Brandon Farms is responsible for paying a general common expense assessment levied by the Property Owners Association.

The Brandon Farms community also includes affordable housing units pursuant to an Affordable Housing Plan filed with the Mercer County Clerk's office. All affordable housing units are Class C condominiums and the owners are members of the Condominium Association. Those units comprise approximately 28% of the Condominium Association membership and 10.3% of the Property Owners Association membership.

Consistent with the Declaration, owners of affordable housing units pay reduced assessments. The general common expense assessment is apportioned so that affordable housing owners pay 70% of the normal charge. The resulting shortfall is covered through a second tier assessment placed on all non-affordable housing homeowners. Affordable housing owners also pay 50% of the normal recreational limited common expense assessment, with the shortfall apportioned equally among Class A homeowners and non-affordable homeowners in Class C.

The Condominium Association was established pursuant to the Master Deed to manage the common affairs of the Class C members and to maintain the common elements of the condominiums. The Condominium Association assesses its members for costs and expenses separate and apart from the assessments by the Property Owners Association.

Section 7.02 of the Declaration provides, "Each such [Property Owners Association], assessment … shall be a continuing lien in favor of the [Property Owners Association] upon the Home against which each such assessment is made and shall also be the personal obligation of the Owner of such Home at the time when the assessment fell due." Section 7.06 of the Declaration provides that all recreational limited common expense assessments "shall be allocated among all Class A and C Members of the [Property Owners Association]." Although Class A and B members are required to pay their assessments directly to the Property Owners Association, the Condominium Association is responsible for the payment of the assessments of Class C members.

Section 7.21 of the Declaration, which is the critical key area of contention in this case, provides:

> Despite anything to the contrary herein, the primary responsibility for the payment to [the Property Owners Association] of all Assessments, other than Miscellaneous Assessments, assessed against Class C Members, shall be that of the Condominium Association rather than that of the individual Class C Members. Therefore, the [Property Owners Association] shall levy an aggregate assessment against the Condominium Association to cover all of the individual Assessments for Class C Members, which Condominium Association shall be responsible for payment of the entire aggregate Assessment when due, together with all appropriate late fees, fines, penalties and charges and [sic] regardless of whether all of the individual Class C Members pay the Condominium Association or not.

Initially, the Property Owners Association directly billed and collected assessments from all members, including Class C members. When the developer no longer controlled the Property Owners Association, the homeowners in control sought to enforce the provision of section 7.21 that required the Condominium Association to be responsible for the collection and payment of assessments owed by Class C members. The Condominium Association refused to undertake those responsibilities.

On September 11, 2001, the Property Owners Association filed a complaint in the Chancery Division alleging that the Condominium Association breached section 7.21 of the Declaration and demanding immediate payment of all outstanding assessments, late fees, fines, penalties and charges. The Condominium Association answered generally denying the allegations. Subsequently, parties agreed to a stipulated statement of facts and filed cross-motions for summary judgment.

The stipulation provided that (1) as of November 13, 2001, there were 138 delinquent units of which 59 units or 43% were Class C units; (2) the total delinquent amount for all Property Owner Association members was $23,528.90 of which the Condominium Association members accounted for $14,266.65, and (3) Class A and B members were insulated from having to compensate for the default as to Property Owners Association assessments to Class C members, but Class C members nevertheless had to contribute for the defaults of Class A and B members.

The trial court found that section 7.21 of the Declaration was void and unenforceable because it violated the Act by requiring Class C members to be solely responsible for Class C deficiencies while requiring all classes to make up for the delinquencies of Class A and B members. The court held that "[w]hile [section] 7.21 is not expressly in violation of the Act, the letter and spirit of the Act are undermined by this provision." The court ordered the Property Owners Association to "collect its assessment from each individual unit owner and spread any deficiencies thereafter evenly among all the classes and members of the [Property Owners Association]."

The Property Owners Association appealed. The Appellate Division reversed. The court noted, "[T]he regulatory framework created by the Declaration is not unlike many governance schemes used to oversee the common properties and recreational facilities in other planned unit developments." The panel held that section 7.21 did not violate the Act because that section rendered the assessments "common expenses" of the condominium units. Further, the panel concluded that the developer had a reasonable basis for implementing section 7.21 and that that provision was enforceable. Condominium Association's motion for reconsideration or clarification was denied.

II.

The Condominium Association contends that section 7.21 is void and unenforceable because it violates the letter and spirit of the Act by treating the Condominium Association members as a unit rather than individually. The Condominium Association claims it is inequitable to hold it responsible for the full assessment, regardless of whether the unit owner pays, when the Condominium Association is not a member of the Property Owners Association. Further, the Condominium Association contends that the developer designed section 7.21 to insulate Class A and B members from the risk of non-payment of assessments by affordable home owners in Class C to make sales of Class A and B units more attractive. It asserts that this governance scheme is contrary to public policy because of the disproportionate and negative impact on affordable homeowners.

The Property Owners Association maintains that the trial court erred in applying the Act to an umbrella Property Owners Association and in declaring section 7.21 void. It asserts that section 7.21 must be given full effect because the Declaration is a lawfully recorded instrument under which thousands of homeowners have purchased their homes. With respect to the affordable housing units, it asserts that the additional expenses generated by affordable housing units are borne by all members of the Property Owners Association and that, in any event, affordable unit owners who pay their assessments do not create a problem. It maintains that the class distinctions within the community simply reflect a different status with regard to recreational facility access, and that without section 7.21, Class C members who fail to pay the assessment would unfairly impose financial burdens on Class A and B members. It argues that section 7.21 does not violate the Act or any other law because the assessments clearly constitute a common expense as defined in *N.J.S.A.* 46:8B-3e and thus the Condominium Association is obligated to pay the assessments on behalf of its members.

III.

The Act, adopted in 1970,[Q] establishes a comprehensive scheme for regulating condominiums and their associations. *Fox v. Kings Grant Maint. Ass'n,* 167 *N.J.* 208, 218, 770 A.2d 707 (2001). A condominium is defined as "the form of ownership of real property under a master deed providing for ownership by one or more owners of units of improvements together with an undivided interest in common elements appurtenant to each such unit." The developer must "execute and file a master deed describing the land, identifying the units, defining the common elements, and providing for an association of unit owners." The condominium property consists of all the land and property covered by the master deed and all improvements. The individual owner of a condominium unit owns the unit, … along with a "proportionate undivided interest in the common elements." Each unit owner is responsible for a proportionate share of the common expenses, which includes "(i) all expenses of administration, maintenance, repair and replacement of the common elements; (ii) expenses agreed upon as common by all unit owners; and (iii) expenses declared common by [the Act] or by the master deed or the bylaws." *N.J.S.A.* 46:8B-3e. If the unit owner fails to pay the common expenses charged to the unit, that amount shall be a lien against such unit. A unit owner is presumed to have agreed to pay his proportionate share of common expenses and may not avoid liability for those expenses by waiver of the right to use the common elements.… Accordingly, a unit owner having a fee simple title "enjoys exclusive ownership of his or her individual unit, [retains] an undivided interest as a tenant in common in the [common] facilities [and grounds,]" *Fox, supra,* … and is required to pay a proportionate share of the common expenses,.…

The Act provides that a condominium association "shall be responsible for the administration and management of the condominium and condominium property, including but not limited to the conduct of all activities of common interest to the unit owners." The association is charged with the maintenance of the common elements and the "assessment and collection of funds for common expenses and the payment thereof," along with various other duties. The association is authorized to record a lien against any unit owner for any unpaid assessment duly made by the association.…

Once the unit owners elect a majority of the members of the association's governing board, the developer has sixty days to turn over various documents to the association, including all contracts to which the association is a party. The Act declares that:

> Any management, employment, service or maintenance contract or contract for the supply of equipment or material which is directly or indirectly made by or on behalf of the association, prior to the unit owners having elected at least 75% of the members of the governing board … shall not be entered into for a period in excess of two years. Any such contract or lease may not be renewed or extended for periods in excess of two years and at the end of any two-year period, the association may terminate any further renewals or extensions thereof.
>
> Notwithstanding the above, any management contract or agreement entered into after the effective date of this amendatory act shall terminate 90 days after

---

Q. The Act referred to is New Jersey's Condominium Act, N.J.S.A. Chapter 46:8B. Many of the court's citations to individual sections of the Act have been omitted for easier reading of the opinion. — Eds.

the first meeting of a governing board ... in which the unit owners constitute a majority of the members, unless the board ratifies the contract or agreement. [N.J.S.A. 46:8B-12.2 (emphasis added).]

Any agreement contrary to the Act is void. *N.J.S.A.* 46:8B-7. The Act neither provides for nor prohibits the creation of an umbrella association. The Act states only that the legal structure of a condominium association may take the form of "any entity recognized by the laws of New Jersey, including but not limited to a business corporation or a nonprofit corporation." ... Nevertheless, our courts have recognized and approved the use of umbrella associations in a planned unit development. (... *State v. Panther Valley Prop. Owners Ass'n*, 307 *N.J.Super.* 319, 327, 704 *A.2d* 1010 (App.Div.1998), and *Holbert v. Great Gorge Vill. Condo. Council, Inc.*, 281 *N.J.Super.* 222, 225–228, 656 *A.2d* 1315 (Ch.Div.1994)); Wendell A. Smith & Dennis A. Estis, *New Jersey Condominium & Community Association Law* § 4.1c (2003).

In *Fox,* we addressed the powers and responsibilities of an umbrella property owners association in connection with a condominium association. There, pursuant to the direction of the municipal planning board, the Kings Grant Planned Unit Development (Kings Grant) included sectionalized communities of single-family homes, townhouses, and condominiums, along with the development of community facilities for all Kings Grant unit owners such as recreational facilities, commercial centers, and open spaces.... Kings Grant established an umbrella association to be "fully responsible for 'the maintenance, management, preservation, administration, upkeep and care of *all common property*.'" The declaration filed by Kings Grant provided, "Common property shall also mean and refer to all lands, buildings, improvements and facilities *including, without limitation, common elements as that term is defined in N.J.S.A. 46:8B-1.*" The declaration also provided "that every sub association within Kings Grant ...'irrevocably delegated'... all of its powers and duties for the maintenance, preservation, administration and operation of common property" to the umbrella organization. Each unit owner was a member of the umbrella organization but could not participate directly in its management.... Instead, each community in Kings Grant elected one delegate for every fifty units to represent its interests. The chosen delegate cast votes equal to the number of units within the delegate's representative community.

The last Kings Grant community to be developed was Waters Edge Condominium Community (Waters Edge). Waters Edge's master deed established a condominium association and also declared that "certain powers and duties" of the association were irrevocably delegated to the umbrella organization's board of trustees. A number of Waters Edge unit owners objected to the umbrella organization's interference with the condominium association's affairs. They filed a complaint against the umbrella organization, its project manager, and its board of trustees. The trial court granted partial summary judgment in favor of the umbrella organization upholding its authority to maintain and manage all of the common property within Kings Grant. The court also granted partial summary judgment in favor of the plaintiffs, finding the umbrella organization had no right to interfere with Waters Edge condominium association's membership meetings and elections. The Appellate Division affirmed.

Justice Stein, writing for a unanimous Court, reversed, concluding that "a delegation of power to the umbrella association that [goes beyond regulation of] roads, facilities and services shared by all or several of the communities within the Kings Grant project is [not] reconcilable with the Act." In reaching that conclusion, Justice Stein reviewed various provisions of the Condominium Act and explained:

> N.J.S.A. 46:8B-12.1 and N.J.S.A. 46:8B-12.2 reflect more than the orderly transition of power between the developer and unit owners. They demonstrate the

Legislature's understanding that in a condominium community, the unit owners' interests take precedence over any outside interest, whether that interest is a developer, an umbrella association, or any other outside party. Furthermore, those provisions demonstrate that condominium ownership differs significantly from traditional forms of property ownership, and that because unit owners have an undivided interest in their community's common elements any governance scheme that conflicts with the recognition of that interest is inconsistent with and in violation of the Act.

... The [Act] contains no provision giving the developer the right to use the property interests of ... unit owners as a bargaining chip for the developer's own interests. To the contrary, the Legislature included specific language in the [Act] to prevent a developer's lingering control over a condominium association.

Although the Court recognized that an umbrella organization could serve a useful purpose in controlling common elements shared by several associations, it found no intent by the Legislature to diminish the statutory power of condominium unit owners to control their common elements. The Court concluded that the Kings Grant governance scheme that granted irrevocable control over all common elements to the umbrella organization "plainly violate[d] both the letter and spirit of the [Act]."

IV.

We now address the essential issue in this case, whether section 7.21 of the Declaration complies with the Act. The short answer is that it does not.

Condominium Association members are proportionately liable for the payment of all expenses declared common by their master deed.... Section 15.00 of the Master Deed provides: "Owners of Units in the Condominium, in addition to taking title subject to this Master Deed, also take title subject to the [Declaration].... Owners of units in the Condominium are members of the [Condominium Association] and the [Property Owners Association]." However, section 7.21 of the Declaration, requires the Condominium Association, not the unit owners, to be responsible for collection and payment of all Property Owners Association assessments.

The Property Owners Association and *amicus* argue that the relevant assessments are a "common expense" ... and that section 7.21 constitutes an "agreement" under which the Condominium Association acquired an interest in the Property Owners Association. The Appellate Division agreed and concluded that because the Property Owners Association assessments are common expenses under the Act, they should be treated similarly to other common expenses incurred by the Condominium Association in its day-to-day operation. We find several weaknesses in the "agreement" approach.

Initially, we note that the Condominium Association is a corporation and can act only through its officers or governing board, ... which never agreed to be responsible for collection and payment of the Property Owners Association assessments owed by Class C members. The "agreement" approach is predicated on the fact that the individual unit owners took title subject to the Master Deed, which incorporates the Declaration that contained section 7.21. Yet, that approach fails to recognize that the unit owners have no authority to bind the Condominium Association; thus, the unit owners could not enter into this agreement. *Berman v. Gurwicz*, 189 *N.J.Super.* 89, 106–07, 458 A.2d 1311 (Ch.Div.1981), *aff'd*, 189 *N.J.Super.* 49, 458 A.2d 1289 (App.Div.), *certif. denied*, 94 *N.J.* 549, 468 A.2d 197 (1983) (ruling that recreation lease executed by unit owners before incorporation of Condominium Association, and not adopted subsequently, was unenforceable against association). Section 7:21 neglects to account for the Legislature's intent in the Act "to ensure that the *unit owners*—not the developer—exercise control over their condominium boards" and for the condominium board to make decisions on behalf of its members....

Further, the Act expressly prohibits the developer from entering into a long-term management contract or agreement on behalf of a condominium association. *N.J.S.A.* 46:4B-12.2. If the developer does enter into such an agreement, once the association sheds the developer's control, the board may ratify or reject it. Here, the developer created the so-called agreement before the Condominium Association came into existence, and once the Condominium Association existed, it never adopted or ratified, but instead refused to enforce the agreement.

Clearly, the Condominium Association has the authority to enter into an agreement to collect common expenses owed by the individual unit owners. *See N.J.S.A.* 46:8B-13 (requiring bylaws to provide for administration of association and "the manner of collecting from unit owners their respective shares of common expenses"). Absent such an express agreement however, neither the developer nor the umbrella association may bind the Condominium Association to collect and be responsible for the payment of assessments when an individual unit owner fails to pay.

We conclude that the Property Owners Association's attempt to enforce section 7.21 as an agreement violates the Act, and pursuant to *N.J.S.A.* 46:8B-7, any agreement contrary to the Act is void. Consequently, section 7.21 is void and unenforceable.

The Appellate Division also disagreed with the trial court's conclusion that section 7.21 was inequitable because it required "Class C members to solely bear the burden of Class C deficiencies even though all classes were required to compensate for the default of a Class A or Class B member." The Appellate Division was concerned that declaring section 7.21 void would constitute an invalid abrogation of a restrictive covenant agreed to by all the members of the Property Owners Association.

We are satisfied that the trial court properly analyzed that issue in concluding that section 7.21 violates the Act. Because we are in accord with the trial court's analysis, we quote and adopt it as our own.

[T]his court is persuaded that § 7.21 of the Declaration, requiring Class C members to solely bear the burden of Class C deficiencies even though when a Class A or Class B member defaults all classes are required to compensate, is inequitable. While § 7.21 is not expressly in violation of the Act, the letter and spirit of the Act are undermined by this provision.

For example, in discussing responsibility for common expenses of a condominium association under the Act, the New Jersey [L]egislature indicated that unit owners should be charged the "percentage of their respective undivided interests in the common elements," or an amount described in the master deed or bylaws. *N.J.S.A.* 46:8B-17. Similarly, *N.J.S.A.* 46:8B-3(e) defines common expenses in part as "expenses for which the unit owners are proportionately liable." When measuring the proportionality of interests called for by the [Act] against the potentially disproportionate allocation of [Property Owners Association] common expenses forced upon Class C members by § 7.21, this court is satisfied the letter and spirit of the Act is being violated.

We recognize that a court's power to declare provisions in a master deed and related documents void as against public policy "'must be exercised with caution and only in cases that are free from doubt.'" ... We have declared void contracts that "violate statutes, promote crime, interfere with the administration of justice, encourage divorce, violate public morality, or restrain trade." ...."The sources of public policy include federal and state legislation and judicial decisions."

Section 7.21 puts the developer's interests ahead of unit owners' interests. By insulating single family homeowners in Class A and Class B from the perceived risk of default by affordable housing unit owners and other Class C members, the developer made the single family dwellings in Class A and Class B more attractive. Thus, section 7.21 violates the public policy set forth in the Act by putting the developer's interest in selling Class A and Class B homes ahead of the Condominium Association's interests....

Moreover, if section 7.21 were enforced, the affordable housing unit owners, who are solely in Class C, would bear a disproportionate burden of their neighbor's delinquencies. Sections 7.05 and 7.06 set forth reduced assessments for affordable housing units. If the assessments are treated as common expenses and collected proportionately from all Class C unit owners, once delinquencies are addressed, the reductions established in the Declaration for affordable housing units would be significantly altered. In that event, an affordable housing unit owner who paid the assessment would be required to pay assessment rates significantly higher than the discounted rates set forth in the Declaration and in amounts substantially higher than that paid by Class A and B members. Thus, a prospective affordable unit buyer relying on the reduced assessment for affordable units would not have realized that section 7.21 might convert the assessment into a common expense and thereby substantially reduce or eliminate the discount for affordable units.

We recognized in *Fox, supra,* that a delegation of power to the umbrella association limited to roads, facilities, and services shared by all or several of the communities within the planned unit development was reconcilable with the Act. We now add to that declaration that assessments imposed under such authority should be proportionate to similarly situated unit members of a development to ensure it is consistent with the purposes of the Act. Here, where the assessments by the Property Owners Association result in a disproportionate assessment for affordable housing unit owners and other Class C members who receive the same benefits as Class A members, such assessments violate the letter and spirit of the Act.

V.

We reverse the judgment of the Appellate Division and reinstate the judgment of the trial court.

Notes & Questions

1. Would the Washington court that decided the *Bellevue Pacific Center* case have come out the same way as the New Jersey Court did in *Brandon Farms*? The New Jersey court concluded that even though § 7.21 of the Declaration was not expressly prohibited, it was void because it undermined and thus violated the letter and spirit of the Act. If the Washington court had adopted a less literal or formal approach to interpretation of the Washington Condominium Act, would or should it have come out differently?

2. Why do you suppose the developer billed property owner association assessments directly to unit owners rather than using § 7.21 during the period that the developer retained control of the association?

3. Note that the Community Associations Institute (CAI) participated in the case as an amicus arguing in favor of the position taken by the property owners association that all purchasers in Brandon Farms had agreed to the terms of the Declaration, and therefore, apparently, the court should hold them to it. The argument that the terms of the recorded declaration form the basis of a contract among the developer and all property owners is made frequently by those seeking to uphold the terms and enforce them against the association, other owners, or the developer.

4. Including "affordable" housing units in a project that is otherwise not "affordable" poses significant organizational challenges: affordable unit owners may not be able to pay the same level of assessments as others; owners of other units may resent subsidizing services and facilities for the affordable unit owners; owners of affordable units will resist increasing assessments to pay for improving services and facilities and maybe even to cover rising operating and maintenance costs. How well do you think the Brandon Farms developer handled those challenges?

5. When individual owners default in payment of their assessments, other owners are left holding the bag. Someone has to pay for the association's expenses, and the other owners are it. If including affordable units in a development increases the risk of defaults, how can the developer protect other affordable unit owners and, at the same time, make the non-affordable units attractive to wealthier buyers? Did the New Jersey Supreme Court accurately assess the public policy issues at stake in *Brandon Farms*? Is the situation any different from that which results when property owners default on payment of their real property taxes?

Chapter 3

Functions & Powers of a Common Interest Community

As the size and scope of common interest communities have expanded over the years, particularly since the 1960s, their functions and powers have also expanded. Today, of course, there is still a wide range of common interest communities, from those with only a small bit of property and very simple maintenance functions to those with significant amounts of common property and a variety of functions that may encompass some or all of the functions usually performed by municipal governments. Whatever their size and intended functions, however, common interest communities need some powers to act.

The two primary sources of association powers are statutes (common interest community statutes — condominium acts, planned community acts, and the like — and corporation statutes) and the declaration and other governing documents. As common interest communities have proliferated and courts have become persuaded that they play an important role in the American real estate market, courts have gradually adopted broader views about the sources and interpretation of community powers. The older view insisted on a fairly narrow reading of powers, limiting them to those expressly granted by statute or the governing documents. The newer view reads powers broadly to allow common interest communities to carry out their intended functions and may even find that they have inherent powers to do so. The Restatement (Third) and the Uniform Common Interest Ownership Act (UCIOA) both take the view that common interest communities have inherent powers.

> Restatement (Third) § 6.4 Powers of a Common-Interest Community: In General
>
> In addition to the powers granted by statute and the governing documents, a common-interest community has the powers reasonably necessary to manage the common property, administer the servitude regime, and carry out other functions set forth in the declaration.... The community's powers may be exercised through an association or directly by the members acting collectively if there is no association....
>
> UCIOA § 3-102 Powers of Unit Owners' Association
>
> (a) Except as provided in subsection (b), and subject to the provisions of the declaration, the association may
>
> (1) adopt and amend bylaws and rules and regulations;
>
> (2) adopt and amend budgets for revenues, expenditures, and reserves and collect assessments for common expenses from unit owners;
>
> (3) hire and discharge managing agents and other employees, agents, and independent contractors;

(4) institute, defend, or intervene in litigation or administrative proceedings in its own name on behalf of itself or two or more unit owners on matters affecting the common interest community;

(5) make contracts and incur liabilities;

(6) regulate the use, maintenance, repair, replacement, and modification of common elements;

(7) cause additional improvements to be made as a part of the common elements;

(8) acquire, hold, encumber, and convey in its own name any right, title, or interest to real estate or personal property [subject to limits on common elements and cooperative properties]

(9) grant easements, leases, licenses, and concessions through or over the common elements;

(10) impose and receive any payments, fees, or charges for the use, rental, or operation of the common elements, other than limited common elements..., and for services provided to unit owners;

(11) impose charges for late payment of assessments, and, after notice and an opportunity to be heard, levy reasonable fines for violations of the declaration, bylaws, rules, and regulations of the association;

(12) impose reasonable charges for the preparation and recordation of amendments to the declaration, resale certificates..., or statements of unpaid assessments;

(13) provide for the indemnification of its officers and executive board and maintain directors' and officers' liability insurance;

(14) assign its right to future income, including the right to receive common expense assessments, but only to the extent the declaration expressly so provides;

(15) exercise any other powers conferred by the declaration or bylaws;

(16) exercise all other powers that may be exercised in this State by legal entities of the same type ...;

(17) exercise any other powers necessary and proper for the governance and operation of the association; and

(18) by regulation, require that disputes between the executive board and unit owners or between two or more unit owners regarding the common interest community must be submitted to nonbinding alternative dispute resolution in the manner described in the regulation as a prerequisite to commencement of a judicial proceeding.

(b) The declaration may not impose limitations on the power of the association to deal with the declarant which are more restrictive than the limitations imposed on the power of the association to deal with other persons.

In the balance of this chapter, we look at a number of cases that address questions about the nature, extent, and source of the powers of community associations. In Chapter 4, we take up the question whether these powers are or should be limited by the constitutional constraints that apply to similar powers held by governmental bodies, and in Chapter 5, we look at the statutory and common law constraints that apply to the exercise of common interest community powers.

A. Managing the Common Property

Restatement (Third) § 6.6 Power To Manage, Acquire, and Improve Common Property

Except as limited by statute or the governing documents, a common-interest community has the power reasonably necessary to manage and protect the common property, including the power to make substantial alterations, improvements, and additions to the common property in order to carry out functions authorized by the governing documents.

Schaefer v. Eastman Community Association

Supreme Court of New Hampshire
836 A.2d 752 (N.H. 2003)

DUGGAN, J. This case involves a dispute between the plaintiffs, certain homeowners in the planned, private community of Eastman, and the defendant, Eastman Community Association (ECA or association), a non-profit corporation that governs Eastman. ECA appeals a decision by the Superior Court ... finding that ECA did not have authority under its Declaration of Covenants and Restrictions ... to close Snow Hill ski area. We reverse.

Eastman is a planned, private, four seasons, recreational community located primarily within the town of Grantham. The community is organized into groupings of residences, known as "Special Places," some of which contain the recreational activities or amenities offered at Eastman. The amenities include a golf course, tennis courts, an indoor pool, cross country skiing, hiking, and a lake with beaches and facilities for boating and swimming. Until September 1999, Eastman also offered downhill skiing at its own ski area known as Snow Hill. While the association owns and maintains the recreational amenities, the residents of Eastman own their homes and also own indivisible, equal interests in the common property.

The Articles of Agreement establish ECA as a non-profit corporation organized under RSA chapter 292. The articles provide that ECA's affairs shall be managed by a board of directors, subject to the powers and limitations set forth in the declaration. The declaration is the governing document for the Eastman community and sets forth the residents' rights and privileges and the terms of the association's operation. All property within Eastman is subject to the declaration. Pursuant to the declaration, the association operates by means of a three-tiered representative form of government: Special Place Associations, the Association Council, and the ECA Board of Directors.

Each Special Place has its own Special Place Association, which consists of all property owners within the Special Place. Each member of the Special Place Association is entitled to vote on: (1) the election of representatives to the Association Council; (2) the matters affecting the conduct of the affairs of their Special Place; and (3) all matters affecting the conduct of the affairs of ECA by making recommendations to the appropriate bodies.

The Association Council consists of representatives from each Special Place. Representation on the council is proportional to the size of the various Special Places and currently totals eighty-seven members. The council has the power to: (1) remove members of the ECA Board of Directors; (2) propose amendments to the declaration; (3) propose special assessments; (4) make recommendations to the ECA Board of Directors; and (5) appoint a Finance and Budget Committee to prepare and present to the ECA Board of Directors the annual operating and capital expenditure budgets for the association.

The ECA Board of Directors (board) is comprised of nine directors who are elected by the property owners for three-year terms. The board has numerous powers enumerated in the declaration and has the ultimate responsibility for making decisions regarding policies, finances and administration at Eastman.

As early as 1984, the residents and the governing bodies debated whether the Snow Hill ski area should remain open. In 1994, the results of the Eastman Long Range Planning Committee's survey of Eastman residents indicated that Snow Hill ski area was of little importance to the families and the community. In 1998, Cilley & Associates conducted a survey that found that of 695 respondents, sixty-eight percent had never used Snow Hill. ECA also commissioned other studies performed by area college business students to assist their analysis of whether Snow Hill should remain open.

On August 27, 1999, the Eastman Recreation Committee, a subcommittee of the council, voted eight to zero, with two members abstaining, to recommend closing Snow Hill ski area to the board and accept Ski Whaleback, Ltd.'s offer to purchase Snow Hill's chairlift. On September 4, 1999, the council held a meeting and voted forty-three to nineteen to recommend to the board closing Snow Hill and selling the chair lift to Whaleback. On September 17, 1999, the board voted eight to one to close Snow Hill and sell the chairlift to Whaleback.

The plaintiffs subsequently filed an action in superior court seeking: (1) to enjoin ECA from closing Snow Hill and selling the chairlift; ... At the first part of a bifurcated trial, the plaintiffs argued, and the superior court agreed, that ECA acted *ultra vires* in closing the Snow Hill ski area because the declaration did not provide for the closing of an amenity. The court enjoined the closure of Snow Hill until and unless:

> (a) there is a future amendment of the Declaration of Covenants providing a lawful process for the closure of a major amenity or

> (b) a determination is made to do so by the Board of Directors based on financial conditions, or other substantial conditions establishing that continuation of alpine ski operations would be inequitable, unreasonable or oppressive, within the context of an overall, four-season, recreational and residential community.

In accordance with the superior court's order, ECA amended the declaration to specifically provide for the closing of an amenity.... The amendments became effective on January 20, 2001.

...

At the second part of the bifurcated trial, the plaintiffs argued, and the superior court agreed, that the amendment to the declaration did not provide a lawful procedure for closing an amenity and thus the second vote to close Snow Hill ski area was invalid. Specifically, the superior court ruled that the amenity closing procedure was unlawful because it did not "reflect the disparate impact that the closing of a major amenity would cause," nor did it "reflect an appropriate vote in accordance therewith[,]" namely, the unanimous consent of the Snow Hill Special Place representatives to the council.... This appeal followed.

ECA first argues that the trial court erred in finding that the board's September 17, 1999 vote to close Snow Hill ski area was *ultra vires*. Because we hold that the board acted within its authority under the declaration when it voted to close Snow Hill ski area on September 17, 1999, we need not address the other issues raised by ECA.

"When a court is called upon to assess the validity of [an action taken] by a board of directors, it first determines whether the board acted within its scope of authority and, second, whether the [action] reflects reasoned or arbitrary and capricious decision making." *Beachwood Villas Condo. v. Poor*, 448 So. 2d 1143, 1144 (Fla.Dist.Ct.App.1984); *accord Lamden v. La Jolla Shores Clubdominium Homeowners Ass'n.*, 21 Cal.4th 249, 87 Cal.Rptr.2d 237, 980 P.2d 940, 944 (1999). Because the reasonableness of the board's decision to close Snow Hill ski area was not questioned below or on appeal, we are only concerned with the scope of the board's authority.

Inquiry into this area begins with a review of the association's legal documents. The association's legal documents are "a contract that governs the legal rights between the [a]ssociation and [property] owners." *Lacy v. Sutton Place Condo. Ass'n. Inc.*, 684 A.2d 390, 393 (D.C.1996). Because the association is a corporation, it may not act in any way not authorized by the articles or the declaration. "[A]cts beyond the scope of the powers so [authorized] are *ultra vires*." *Seabrook Island Prop. Owners Ass'n. v. Pelzer*, 292 S.C. 343, 356 S.E.2d 411, 414 (App.1987). Accordingly, whether the association's action was within its authority requires us to interpret the articles and declaration. This is a question of law that we review *de novo*.

In determining whether the declaration provides the board with the authority to close Snow Hill ski area, we should be mindful that the declaration is the association's "constitution." *See Beachwood Villas Condo.*.... Generally, declarations and other governing documents contain "broad statements of general policy with due notice that the board of directors is empowered to implement these policies and address day-to-day problems in the [association's] operation." Thus, the declaration should not be so narrowly construed so as to eviscerate the association's intended role as the governing body of the community. Rather, a broad view of the powers delegated to the association "is justified by the important role these communities play in maintaining property values and providing municipal-like services.... If unable to act, the common property may fall into disrepair...." *Restatement (Third) of Property* § 6.4 comment *a* at 90 (2000); *cf. Joslin v. Pine River Dev. Corp.*, 116 N.H. 814, 817, 367 A.2d 599 (1976) ("[P]rivate land use restrictions 'have been particularly important in the twentieth century when the value of property often depends in large measure upon maintaining the character of the neighborhood in which it is situated.'").

Because an association's power should be interpreted broadly, the association, through its appropriate governing body, is "entitled to exercise all powers of the community except those reserved to the members." *Restatement (Third) of Property* § 6.16. Accordingly, "provided that a [board's action] does not contravene either an express provision of the declaration or a right reasonably inferable therefrom, it will be found valid, within the scope of the board's authority." *Beachwood Villas Condo.*.... This rule preserves the concept of delegated management and carries out the expectations of property owners who purchased property subject to, and with notice of, the association's governing instruments. Moreover, the rights of property owners are safeguarded by the terms of the governing instruments and through their power to remove or replace the board members through the election process. *See Restatement (Third) of Property* § 6.16 comment *b* at 289....

In the present case, the decision to close Snow Hill ski area does not contravene an express provision of the declaration, nor is it a decision reserved to the members. Rather, the defendant relies upon three provisions of Article 7.6 of the declaration that affirmatively provide the association with authority to close the Snow Hill ski area. These provisions provide that:

The Board shall take all such measures as may be necessary to: ...

(h) take steps necessary to protect the Association's assets and insure its financial stability[;] ...

(j) buy and sell property when deemed in the best interests of the Association; ...

(n) take such other action as it may deem necessary to further the purposes of this Declaration or to be in the best interests of this Association.

Because the decision to close the ski area or any other amenity may be necessary to insure financial stability or be in the best interests of the association, it is a decision that is reserved in Article 7.6 for the association to make, through the board, and thus within the board's authority.

The plaintiffs argue that ... ECA lacked authority to close the ski area because it was neither "necessary to insure ECA's financial stability," nor "in the best interests of Eastman." This argument is misplaced. Whether the association's decision was in fact either necessary to ECA's financial stability or in the best interests of Eastman is a question of the reasonableness of the association's action. So long as ECA's action "does not contravene either an express provision of the declaration or a right reasonably inferable therefrom, it will be found valid, within the scope of the board's authority." *Beachwood Villas Condo.* The plaintiffs, both in their brief and at oral argument, argued that the "reasonableness of ECA's decision is not relevant here because the Board did not act within its authority, and thus, there was no need for the trial court to address ECA's reasonableness argument." Because the plaintiffs only claimed, both here and at the trial court, that the association lacked authority to act as it did, and did not allege that the action was unreasonable, these arguments are not relevant to the question presented to us for review.

The plaintiffs also argue that, because the declaration does not expressly authorize ECA to close an amenity, such authority cannot "reasonably be inferred from the [d]eclaration in light of ECA's express purpose to preserve and maintain the recreational amenities, as set forth in the preamble, and in light of the fact that ECA from its inception has promoted the availability of downhill skiing at Eastman." Essentially, the plaintiffs are asking that we narrowly construe the board's powers enumerated in the declaration because of the general purposes of the ECA and Eastman's promotional materials.

The plaintiffs argue that the board's powers must be narrowly construed to deny the board the authority to close the ski area because such an interpretation is consistent with the general purposes of the community. The plaintiffs assert that the general purposes of the community are found in the preamble of the declaration and ECA's statement of purpose. The preamble states that Eastman is to be "a planned residential and recreational community with permanent parks, open spaces and other common facilities for the benefit of such community and the health, safety, and social welfare of the Owners ... within such community." In addition, the preamble further states that ECA is to "provide for the preservation, maintenance and improvement of said parks, open spaces and common facilities." ECA's statement of purpose states that ECA "was established in order to hold, maintain, and administer the Community's facilities and Open Spaces within Eastman."

In addition, the plaintiffs argue that a narrow interpretation of the board's powers would be consistent with promotional materials distributed by Eastman. The plaintiffs point to a number of materials that specifically promote the Snow Hill ski area, which they relied upon in deciding to purchase a home at Eastman. For example, a Community Services Guide that was published shortly before ECA closed the ski area promoted Eastman as:

> [A] recreational community for all seasons offering residents the best of all worlds in its 3500 acres of protected natural environment ... a 325-acre lake for swimming, boating, fishing and other water sports ... a championship 18-hole golf course, tennis courts, and indoor pool ... miles of nature trails, 30 kilometers of cross-country ski trails ... its own downhill ski run, softball diamond, volleyball and basketball courts....

Another brochure stated: "Each neighborhood within the community focuses on a lake, golf course, ski slopes or other 'special places' and is designed to bring together families with common interests." Many brochures directly promoted the ski area by describing Snow Hill as "skiing past evergreens glistening with snow" and as "the perfect 'Special Place' for active, young families who will enjoy skiing from their front doors, down the slope to the lift facilities in winter." Finally, the "Prospective Buyer's Guide to Eastman," which was prepared and distributed by ECA, emphasized Eastman's recreational amenities, including its own downhill ski area and double chairlift.

Accordingly, the plaintiffs argue, that "[w]hen considered in the overall scheme of Eastman and the purposes of ECA set forth in the [d]eclaration, discontinuance of downhill skiing at Snow Hill is not authorized by the [d]eclaration." We disagree. While the plaintiffs may have relied upon the assertions contained in Eastman's promotional materials and the overall general purposes of the ECA, neither limit the broad authority granted to ECA and its governing bodies in the declaration. Because the decision to close Snow Hill ski area does not contravene an express provision of the declaration and there are several provisions of the declaration that reserve such decision-making to the board, the board had the authority, under the declaration, to close the ski area despite the promotional materials or the stated general purposes. Moreover, the plaintiffs purchased their properties subject to, and on notice of, the terms of the declaration, not the promotional materials provided by Eastman.

We should note that, while the board had the authority to act as it did, the plaintiffs or other similarly situated homeowners are not without recourse. The plaintiffs and other homeowners have the power under the declaration to remove or replace their community representatives at the different levels of the governing bodies through the election process. Moreover, our decision today does not give the board *carte blanche*. As a constraint on the board's broad authority under the declaration and in order to protect the rights of property owners, the board's actions must still be reasonable.... *Lamden*.... As previously noted, the plaintiffs did not allege here or below that the board's action was unreasonable. Thus, we need not address the reasonableness of the decision.

[handwritten margin note: Note: board's action still must be "reasonable".]

1. Power to Make Repairs

Telluride Lodge Ass'n v. Zoline

Court of Appeals of Colorado
707 P.2d 998 (Colo. Ct. App. 1985)

TURSI, J. Defendants ... appeal from a judgment of the trial court ordering them to pay certain assessments levied against their condominium units and authorizing plaintiff, The Telluride Lodge Association..., to foreclose on liens against the units. The association cross-appeals the trial court's denial of its request for attorney fees. We affirm the judgment against the defendants, reverse the denial of attorney fees, and remand for further proceedings.

Defendants owned several units in the condominium complex governed by the association pursuant to the declaration creating the condominium. In 1977, the town of Telluride determined that the flat roofs on the buildings in the complex were unsafe because they were leaking severely and were unable to support heavy snow. The complex was ordered to be condemned unless repairs were effected.

At a meeting of the board of directors of the association, three different repair plans were reviewed. The defendants favored a plan which involved little alteration of the exterior of the roofs, but involved extensive visual and structural changes to the interior of each unit. The association elected a different plan calling for the construction and installation of pitched roofs over the flat roofs. This plan, however, eliminated certain clerestory windows in the unit.

The association assessed each unit owner an annual per unit fee to cover the cost of the repair and reconstruction. When defendants refused to pay this assessment, the association filed a notice of lien against defendants' units.

Defendants contend that the association had no authority to undertake the remodeling of the roofs over the objection of several unit owners. They argue that there is no common law authority for this action, citing *Rico Reduction & Mining Co. v. Musgrave*, 14 Colo. 79, 23 P. 458 (1890) for the rule that a co-tenant may not make improvements on jointly owned property without the consent of the other co-tenants. That rule is inapposite.

Here, the authority for the association to make repairs and improvements is vested in it by the declaration and the necessary consent of the condominium unit owners thereto is found in the declaration and the owners' acceptance of their deeds.

Section 9.1 of the declaration reads:

> The Common Elements. The Association shall.... be responsible for the exclusive management, control, operation, maintenance, repair, payment of ... and improvement of the Common Elements and all improvements thereon ... and shall keep the same in good, clean, attractive and sanitary condition, order and repair.

Section 10.1 reads:

> Agreement to Pay Assessment. Each Owner of any Condominium Unit by the acceptance of a deed therefor, whether or not it be so expressed in the deed, shall be deemed to covenant and agree with each other and with the Association to pay to the Association monthly assessments made by the Association for the purposes provided in this Declaration, and special assessments for capital improvements and other matters as provided in this Declaration.

... Defendants argue that even if the association had authority under the declaration to construct the pitched roofs, the association's actions were nonetheless unreasonable. The court found that the association had consulted three qualified architects and made its decision to adopt the pitched roof plan in good faith. There being evidence to sustain these findings, we may not set them aside....

Accordingly, the judgment of the trial court as set forth in its findings, conclusions, and order, is affirmed; its denial of plaintiff's motion for attorney fees is reversed, and the cause is remanded for further proceedings on that motion.

Cedar Cove Efficiency Condo. Ass'n, Inc. v. Cedar Cove Properties

District Court of Appeal of Florida
558 So. 2d 475 (Fla. Dist. Ct. App. 1990)

Appellant, a condominium association, challenges the trial court's final judgments denying those parts of claims for special assessments relating to repair costs of balcony and exterior closet doors.[1] It contends that under chapter 718, Florida Statutes, and the condominium documents it is well within its authority to specially assess the members of the association, including appellee,[2] for the cost of these repairs. We agree and reverse.

The association argues that the balconies are "limited common elements" and that the expense of repair and maintenance of all common elements are "common expenses" for which it may assess its members pro rata. Appellee contends that the balconies are included within the vertical boundaries of the condominium documents' definition of a "unit" and that under the Condominium Act, common elements are those portions of condominium property which are not included in the units. It points out that the condominium documents require the unit owner to maintain and repair all portions of a unit except those maintained by the association.

The pertinent portions of the Condominium Act and the condominium documents provide (emphasis added):

Chapter 718, Florida Statutes (1987) §718.103:

(6) "Common elements" means the portions of the condominium property which are not included in the units.

(7) "Common expenses" means all expenses and assessments which are properly incurred by the association for the condominium

(16) "Limited common elements" means those common elements which are reserved for the use of a certain condominium unit or units to the exclusion of other units, as specified in the declaration of condominium.

(23) "Unit" means a part of the condominium property which is subject to exclusive ownership. A unit may be in improvements land, or land and improvements together, as specified in the declaration.

§718.113:

(1) Maintenance of the common elements is the responsibility of the association. The declaration may provide that limited common elements shall be maintained by those entitled to use the limited common elements.

Declaration Of Condominium

[Definitions] ...

6.1 *Common Expense Fund*: ... the Association shall estimate ... charges ... assessed to the owners (by) percentage attributable to each unit. If the estimated sum proves inadequate for any reason, ... the Board may, at any time, levy a further assessment.... The common expense fund shall be assessed to cover the fol-

---

1. Case no. 89-392 involved expenses for initial balcony repairs at $1,000/voting unit and case no. 89-1472 involved further repairs to the balconies and the exterior closet doors at $1,200/voting unit, with a total $2,500/voting unit assessment.

2. Appellee challenges assessments to its units located on the ground floor of the condominium.

lowing:.... (c) The expense of maintenance, operation, repair or replacement of the common elements including, *but not limited to*, preservation of landscaping, employment of personnel needed, preservation or repair of walls, drives, streets, and building exteriors as the board may, from time to time deem appropriate.

7.3 *Units; Association Responsibility*: the Association shall maintain and replace

(1) All portions of a unit, *except interior surfaces*, contributing to the support of the building, which portions shall include but not be limited to the outside walls of the buildings.

7.4 *Units; Owner Responsibility*: The responsibility of the unit owner shall be

(1) To maintain, repair and replace at his expense all portions of his unit *except* the portions to be maintained, repaired and replaced by the Association.

7.7 *Responsibility*. If the damage is only to those parts of one condominium unit for which the responsibility of maintenance and repair is that of the condominium unit owner, then the said owner shall be responsible for reconstruction and repair after casualty. *In all other instances, the responsibility of reconstruction and repair after casualty shall be that of the association.*

7.9 *Assessments*. If the proceeds of insurance are not sufficient to defray the costs of reconstruction and repair by the Association, or if at any time during reconstruction and repair, or upon completion of reconstruction or repair, the funds for the payment of the costs of reconstruction or repair are insufficient, assessments shall be made against the condominium unit owners who owned the damaged condominium units, and against all condominium unit owners in the case of damage to the common elements, in sufficient amounts to provide funds for the payment of such costs. Such assessments against condominium unit owners for damage to condominium units shall be in proportion to the cost of reconstruction and repair of their respective units. Such assessments on account of damage in common elements shall be in proportion to the owners obligation of common expense.

III. *Vertical Boundaries of Units*: The vertical boundaries of each unit *shall be the exterior of the outside walls* of the units. Where there may be attached to such outside walls *a balcony*, loggia, terrace, patio, a stairway, a stoop, landing steps, projecting cornices and copings, or other portion of the building, serving only the unit being bounded, *such boundary shall be deemed to include all of such structures and fixtures thereon.* However, as respects an interior wall, or walls between such units, including walls between balconies, the vertical boundaries of each unit shall be fixed at the center line of such walls between units, provided that such walls are not to be deemed party walls, but instead are part of the limited common elements as defined elsewhere in this Declaration, serving the only units affected. Every portion of a dwelling contributing to the support of an abutting unit shall be burdened with an easement of support for the benefit of such abutting unit.

Articles of Incorporation

ARTICLE III

2. The Association shall have all the powers of a Condominium Association under and pursuant to Chapter 718, Florida Statutes, the Condominium Act, and shall have all of the powers necessary to implement the purposes of the Association, including, but not limited to the following: ...

c. To maintain, repair, replace and operate condominium property; specifically including all portions of the condominium property to which the Association has the right and power to maintain, repair, replace and operate in accordance with the Declaration of Condominium, the by-laws, and Chapter 718 of the Florida Statutes, the Condominium Act....

e. To reconstruct improvements on the condominium property after casualty or other loss, and the further improvement of the property.

By-laws

6.5 *Special Assessments.* Special assessments, if required, shall be levied and paid in the same manner as heretofore provided for regular assessments. Special assessments can be of two kinds: (1) those chargeable to all members in the same proportions as regular assessments to meet shortages or emergencies, to construct, *reconstruct, repair,* or replace all or any part of the common elements (including fixtures and personal property related thereto) *and for other purposes as shall have been approved by the members at a duly convened meeting;....*

... [T]he trial court found that the association had failed to establish its foreclosure claim.... [I]t found that the balconies were "limited common elements". The court construed the condominium documents, which contained no specific provision for "limited common element" maintenance responsibility, to provide that individual unit owners should maintain their own balconies. It based its conclusion upon the finding that "... balconies are included within the definition of what a unit is ...", upon the variation in balcony sizes between units, and upon the absence of ground floor unit balconies.

Competent substantial evidence supports the court's construction of "limited common elements" to include balconies and exterior closet doors, the simple maintenance of which may be the responsibility of individual unit owners. However, the court also found that the balconies and doors were included within the condominium documents' definition of a "unit." These two findings present an inherent conflict.

Our review of the condominium documents discloses no definition of a "unit." We assume that the trial court was referring to the schedule "B," part II description of the vertical boundaries of a "unit" as a "definition" of "unit." In our opinion, this description is not a definition, but rather a characterization of the area a unit purchaser is entitled to use.

Construing the statute and condominium documents as a whole, and considering the evidence presented, we find that the association is obligated to provide repair and maintenance as the board may deem appropriate. Section 4.4 of the declaration of condominium specifically provides that the association is liable for the maintenance or repair of damage caused by the elements or by other owners. The record indicates that repairs to balconies and exterior closet doors were in fact necessitated by the elements. Under Florida law, the association is authorized to do what is necessary to protect the structural integrity of the building, its aesthetics and its members from liability for unsafe, or decrepit building exterior conditions including balconies and exterior closet doors.

Appellee concedes the association's authorization to regulate and maintain the condominium's aesthetics, including the building exteriors, so long as it exercises good business judgment. The "business judgment rule" will protect a board of directors as long as the board has acted in a reasonable manner...."If, in the good business judgment of the association, such alteration or improvement is necessary or beneficial in the maintenance, repair, or replacement of the common elements, all unit owners should equally bear the cost as provided in the declaration, by-laws and statutes." *Tiffany Plaza Condo. v. Spencer*, 416 So. 2d 823, 826 (Fla. 2d DCA 1982).

Where the repairs have been found to be reasonable, courts have held that consent of the members is not required. Ground floor units derive several benefits from the association's exercise of its business judgment in repairing and maintaining the balconies and doors, including the promotion of market value and sales through pleasant and uniform aesthetics, and the avoidance of damages liability. The association's exercise of authority in this case is reasonable to accomplish such purposes and carries greater weight since it operated pursuant to almost unanimous consent not obtained from members in the cases cited above.

The Act's definition of "limited common elements" implies they are a subset of "common elements" and therefore a "common expense" properly within the scope of the association's authority. Sections 6.1 and 6.2 of the declaration of condominium authorize the association to levy an assessment to maintain and repair all unit exteriors and common elements. Even if the balconies and closet doors are not considered "common elements", it is difficult to refute their classification as part of the unit exterior. The balconies and doors fall within the scope of the association's broad authority to maintain condominium exteriors.

Section 7.3 authorizes the association to maintain and replace all portions of a unit including outside boundary walls of units. This authorization specifically includes the trial court's "description" of balconies and doors as included within the vertical boundaries of a "unit." Section 7.7 requires, as a prerequisite, a clear line of distinction between maintenance that is the responsibility of the unit owner and maintenance that is the responsibility of the association. Since it is not clear from the condominium documents whether or not a limited common element is the responsibility of the unit owner, we hold that maintenance and repair of the balconies and doors falls within the scope of "all other instances" and can only be construed as the association/board's responsibility.

Section 7.9 provides authority for the subject assessments only if the balconies and doors are considered common expenses. We find the "unit" interpretations fashioned below too restrictive of the condominium association's authority in the circumstances. Operation of incorporated condominium associations are commonly compared to the discretionary management function of a municipal corporation which also derives its powers, duties and existence from the state acting through its legislative body. Our interpretation reasonably extracts authorization of this discretionary management function from the Act and condominium documents construed as a whole.

The articles and the by-laws provide broad authority for the association to conduct reconstruction and repair operations for casualty or other loss and for other purposes approved by the members at a meeting. The weather damage, the repair of which was overwhelmingly approved by its members, falls within the meaning of "other purposes." Therefore, it is well within the broad scope of authority granted the association to assess all unit owners for the subject repairs and improvements.

The express terms of the Condominium Act and the condominium documents grant broad authority to the association to regulate the use of the common elements and building exterior. *See Juno By the Sea North Condo v. Manfredonia*, 397 So. 2d 297, 304 (Fla. 4th DCA 1981). The judgments below strictly construe the statutes and documents in a manner which does not provide buyers with the legislative interpretation polestar, "what the buyer sees is what the buyer gets." If a particular unit owner were to damage his own balcony or all balconies, it might be patently unfair, arbitrary and capricious for the association to assess all owners for the repair. But where, as here, the damage is due to the elements, it is prudent and reasonable for all association members to pay a proportionate share of the expenses of repair. It is clear that the intent of the condominium documents places repair and maintenance responsibility for all building exteriors upon the association and that the subject balconies and doors are included within this responsibility. The expenses incurred by the association, in reliance upon the near unanimous consent of its members to repair balconies and closet doors located on the condominium exteriors are valid and reasonable. We cannot say then, construing the statutes and condominium documents as a whole, that the association was without the authority to levy the subject assessments, nor that it acted unreasonably, arbitrarily or capriciously in protecting the condominium aesthetics and in protecting all members from possible damages liability. Reversed and Remanded.

Notes & Questions

1. Why are balconies designated as limited common areas rather than simply as common areas (or elements) if the association has the responsibility to repair them?

2. In multi-unit structures, how should maintenance responsibilities be allocated as between unit owners and the association? If ownership is the determining criteria, how should ownership lines—both horizontal and vertical—between attached units be drawn in setting the project?

3. What is the rationale for treating maintenance expenses for limited common elements as common expenses payable ratably by all unit owners?

2. Power to Make Improvements, Alterations & Restorations

Ordinary maintenance can generally be carried out by the association's board without securing the approval of the members, but capital improvements may require additional authorization, particularly if a special assessment will be needed to fund the work. Rebuilding or restoring structures or facilities after a disaster is usually treated differently from replacements necessitated by wear and tear and obsolescence. Even if a project is approved by the required percentage of owners, it may be challenged on the ground that the community lacks the power to engage in such a project—that it is *ultra vires*. Even if a project is *ultra vires*, meaning not authorized by statute, the governing documents, or common law, the owners could still undertake the project and assess themselves to pay for it, but the assessments would bind all of the lots or units only if 100% of the owners gave their consent.

Parker v. Figure "8" Beach Homeowners' Association, Inc.

Court of Appeals of North Carolina
611 S.E.2d 874 (N.C. Ct. App. 2005)

HUDSON, Judge. This case concerns a dispute between a coastal homeowner's association and one of its members about the association's authority to levy a special assessment for dredging and maintenance of a waterway. On 21 February 2002, plaintiff Raymond Clifton Parker sued for judgment declaring that a vote on the assessment, the assessment itself, and a contract between defendant New Hanover County . . . and defendant Figure "8" Beach Homeowners' Association, Inc. ("HOA") were *ultra vires,* inappropriately obtained, and null and void. . . . [The trial court granted defendant's motion for summary judgment.] We affirm.

Plaintiff owns property on Figure 8 Island ("Figure 8"), a privately owned island of 563 lots in New Hanover County. Mason Inlet runs along the south end of the island, separating it from the Town of Wrightsville Beach. Figure 8 is governed pursuant to the HOA bylaws and applicable restrictive covenants. Figure 8 property owners, including plaintiff, are members of the HOA. On 29 January 1993, the covenants were amended to add "channel dredging; beach renourishment" as purposes for which annual assessments could be used. . . . [A] covenant obligates property owners to pay an annual assessment in an amount fixed by the HOA board, which can also levy additional assessments as it deems necessary. Any assessment for new capital improvements costing more than $60,000 requires approval by a majority of HOA members eligible to vote.

In 1999, the county, the HOA, and several other homeowner associations in the Wrightsville Beach area had been considering measures to deal with erosion, channel dredging and other beach-related maintenance matters. The homeowner associations formed a coalition called the Mason Inlet Preservation Group ("MIPG"), which undertook a project to relocate Mason Inlet. The sand dredged from the project would be used to renourish Figure 8's beaches. The county commissioners voted to sponsor the project and pay for it through a special assessment on the property owners of Wrightsville Beach and Figure 8. Over the next two years, the project moved through the permitting and planning process, and in November 2001, the county obtained from the U.S. Army Corps of Engineers a permit to relocate Mason Inlet. The permit required that the county maintain the relocated inlet for thirty years through regular dredging. On 5 November 2001, the county commission voted 3–2 against the project based on concerns about the cost of maintaining the relocated inlet.

The Figure 8 HOA board quickly developed a plan to seek reversal of the commissioners' vote. Having determined that the costly maintenance was a capital improvement, the board approved immediate solicitation of a vote by HOA members to approve a special assessment covering the maintenance costs of the relocated inlet. On 14 November 2001, the board mailed letters and ballots to all eligible HOA voters. A majority of the ballots returned voted in favor of the special assessment associated with the project.

. . .

This Court has set forth the following standard for interpreting covenants imposing affirmative obligations:

> Covenants that impose affirmative obligations on property owners are strictly construed and unenforceable unless the obligations are imposed in clear and unambiguous language that is sufficiently definite to assist courts in its application. To be enforceable, such covenants must contain some ascertainable standard by which a court can objectively determine both that the amount of the assessment and the purpose for which it is levied fall within the contemplation of the covenant. Assessment provisions in restrictive covenants (1) must contain a sufficient standard by which to measure . . . liability for assessments, . . . (2) must identify with particularity the property to be maintained, and (3) must provide guidance to a reviewing court as to which facilities and properties the . . . association . . . chooses to maintain.

Allen v. Sea Gate Assn., 119 N.C.App. 761, 764, 460 S.E.2d 197, 199 (1995) (internal quotation marks omitted) (citing *Figure Eight Beach Homeowners Ass'n, Inc. v. Parker and Laing*, 62 N.C.App. 367, 376, 303 S.E.2d 336, 341 (1983) and *Beech Mountain Property Owners' Assoc. v. Seifart*, 48 N.C.App. 286, 295–96, 269 S.E.2d 178, 183–84 (1980), *disc. review denied*,309 N.C. 320, 307 S.E.2d 170 (1983)).

We first consider whether the covenants "contain a sufficient standard by which to measure" the HOA's liability for assessments, and whether the covenants "identify with particularity the property to be maintained," and provide us guidance as to which facilities and properties are to be maintained. Regarding annual assessments, the covenant provides:

> 8(c). The funds arising from such assessment or charges or additional assessment may be used for any or all of the following purposes: Maintaining, operating, improving or replacing the bridges; protection of the property from erosion; collecting and disposing of garbage, ashes, rubbish and the like; *maintenance, improvement* and lighting *of* the streets, roads, drives, rights of way, community land and facilities, tennis courts, *marsh and waterways;* employing watchmen; enforcing these restrictions; paying taxes, indebtedness to the Association, insurance premiums, *governmental charges of all kinds and descriptions* and, in addition, doing any other things necessary or desirable in the opinion of the Association to keep the property in neat and good order and to provide for the health, welfare and safety of owners and residents of Figure Eight Island. (Emphasis supplied).

The 29 January 1993 amendment added the language "channel dredging; beach renourishment" to paragraph 8(c). Taken together, the language of this paragraph provides for assessments to be used for channel dredging and maintenance of marshes and waterways and for payment of governmental charges of all kinds and descriptions. Maps included in the covenants depict and refer to several of the areas which the assessment would be used to dredge and maintain.

One area covered by the assessment which is not immediately adjacent to Figure 8, and thus not depicted in the maps, is that where the to-be-opened Mason Creek would flow into the Atlantic Intracoastal Waterway ("AIW"). This area was of concern to the Army Corp of Engineers and the HOA because the planned relocation of Mason Inlet and the reopening of Mason Creek could create problems with sand build up at this juncture with the AIW. Plaintiff contends that because this area is neither named nor depicted in the covenants, it is not specifically identified and could not have been intended for inclusion in the covenants' maintenance provisions. Our courts have stated that "[r]estrictive covenants are strictly construed, but they should not be construed 'in an unreasonable manner or a manner that defeats the plain and obvious purpose of the covenant.'" ... (quoting *Cumberland Homes, Inc. v. Carolina Lakes Prop. Owners' Ass'n*, 158 N.C.App. 518, 521, 581 S.E.2d 94, 97 (2003)).

[handwritten margin note: Part of the area impacted not specified.]

Concerning this location the trial court noted in finding 14:

> 14. Figure Eight Island has a boating community, with a marina near its main clubhouse and with several private docks on the back, or "sound side," of the island. Boating access to the AIW has been enhanced for residents on the southern back side of the island with the dredging and reopening of Mason's Creek, and the entire island's boating community is benefitted by once again having a navigable inlet on the southern end to the Atlantic Ocean. Periodic dredging of shoaling sands within the intersection of Mason's Creek and the AIW, occurring at a location some 4,500 feet from the southern end of the island proper, nev-

ertheless directly benefits the navigability of channels for the Figure Eight Island boating community and the boaters' access to Mason Inlet, Wrightsville Beach and points both south and north on the AIW.

This finding is supported by the exhibits before the trial court, such as the aerial photo of the island and the environmental assessment report created by the U.S. Army Corp. of Engineers. As several aspects of the overall Mason Inlet relocation plan would have an impact on the confluence of AIW and Mason Creek, we believe that the court's construction of the covenants was reasonable and that the evidence adequately supports this finding, which in turn supports the legal conclusion that the "authority of the Figure 8 HOA to assess its property owners/members upon a vote of the membership is lawfully authorized."

In addition, the HOA ballot clearly specified the possible cost involved and the period of time dredging maintenance could be required....

HOA members who voted were informed of the location of the area to be maintained as well as the cost involved and the duration of the commitment upon which they were voting....

Affirmed.

Notes & Questions

1. North Carolina traditionally has required much more specificity than most states in covenants giving an association power to levy assessments. That may change for communities that can take advantage of the broad assessment power conferred by Uniform Planned Community Act, which became effective in North Carolina on January 1, 1999.

2. A Star News article of Oct. 5, 2007 reports that Mason Inlet maintenance dredging in the winter of 2007–2008 is a $1 million project which will be paid for by homeowners from the north end of Wrightsville Beach and Figure Eight Island, "who are on the hook to pay all bills associated with the inlet's monitoring and maintenance through 2030." Prior to the current dredging project, the cost of relocating the inlet had reached $8 million. So far, the county has resisted pleas from the homeowners to help fund the project, which they claim has benefited all county residents by renourishing the beaches. The county commissioners say "a contract is a contract." http://www.starnewsonline.com/article/20071005/NEWS/710050374/1004/news01. For pictures of the relocation project, see http://cirp.wes.army.mil/cirp/news/masoninlet/index.html and http://www.appliedtm.com/projects/coastal/mason-inlet.htm.

A Note on Environmental Risks: Can Developers Bind Future Owners on Agreements to Assume Them?

The developers of the Shell Island Resort on Wrightsville Beach, near Mason Inlet, signed development permits in the 1980s that stated: "In signing this permit, the permittee acknowledges the risks of erosion associated with developing on the site and recognizes that current state regulations do not allow shoreline erosion control structures such as seawalls to be erected for developments initiated after June 1, 1979." It appears that the maps on which granting of the permits was based were not accurate. By the mid 1990s, the inlet was moving south at the rate of 1 foot per day and after Hurricane Fran in 1996, the resort buildings were "imminently threatened" by the inlet waters. The condominium owners association and individual owners unsuccessfully challenged North Carolina's refusal to grant them a permit to build erosion control structures to protect their property in *Shell Island Homeowners Ass'n, Inc. v. Tomlinson*, 517 S.E.2d 406 (N.C.App.,1999). The Shell Island Homeowners Association now pays part of the Mason Inlet maintenance and dredging costs. See *North Carolina Seawall Ban Stands Up to Legal Challenge*, Coastal Services, March/April 2000, http://www.csc.noaa.gov/magazine/2000/02/nc.html.

Should developers be allowed to sign away rights of future buyers to claim that permits for development should not have been issued? In *1515–1519 Lakeview Boulevard Condo. Ass'n v. Apartment Sales Corp.*,43 P.3d 1233 (Wash. 2002), the Supreme Court of Washington held that a covenant exculpating the City of Seattle from liability for damages arising out of soil movements ran with the land. The covenant was agreed to by the developer to secure a permit to build condominium units in an area that was at risk for landslides. Thus, when the condominium was destroyed in a landslide, the unit owners had no remedy against the city for having issued the building permit. The court held that the covenant touched and concerned the land and met other requirements for a running covenant.

Tiffany Plaza Condo. Ass'n, Inc. v. Spencer
Court of Appeals of Florida
416 So. 2d 823 (Fla. Dist. Ct. App. 1982)

CAMPBELL, J.... Tiffany Plaza Condominium [created in 1975] is a forty-two unit residential condominium located at Longboat Key, Florida. Appellees, plaintiffs below, are the individual owners of six of the residential units in the condominium. Their action in the trial court was to prevent the collection of an assessment imposed upon them by the association for construction of a rock revetment on the sand and beach between the condominium and the mean high-water line of the Gulf of Mexico. The beach between the condominium and the mean high-water line is a "common element" of the condominium....

At an annual meeting on February 7, 1981, a vote regarding construction of the rock revetment was taken by members of the association. Thirty-two voted for and eight voted against. Two members were absent. The board of directors of the association then voted to assess all members for their pro rata share of the cost of constructing the rock revetment. Appellees objected and filed their action seeking an exemption from payment by reason of article 5.2(b) of the declaration of condominium. The association defended on the basis that the rock revetment was not an alteration or improvement of a common element as contemplated by article 5.2(b), but was part of the maintenance, repair and replacement of a common element which the association had responsibility for under several provisions of the declaration, by-laws and statutes.... *[margin note: "alteration" or "maintenance"]*

The relevant parts of the declaration, by-laws and statutes are as follows:

Declaration of Condominium

2.6 *Common expenses include*

(a) Expenses of administration; expenses of maintenance, operation, repair or replacement of the common elements, and of the portions of apartments to be maintained by the Association.

4.5 *Liability for Common Expenses or Limited Common Expenses*: Each apartment owner shall be liable for a proportional share of the common expenses or limited common expenses, such share being the same as the undivided share in the common elements which is appurtenant to his apartment.

5. *Maintenance, Alteration and Improvements*: Responsibility for the maintenance of the condominium property and restrictions upon the alteration and improvement thereof, shall be as follows: ...

5.2 *Limited Common Elements and Common Elements:*

(a) *By the Association:* The maintenance and operation of the limited common elements and the common elements shall be the responsibility and expense of the Association.

(b) *Alteration and Improvement*: After the completion of the improvements included in the limited common elements and the common elements which are contemplated by this Declaration, there shall be no alteration nor further improvement of the limited common elements and common elements, without prior approval in writing of the record owners of the apartments; provided, however, that any alteration or improvement of the limited common elements or the common elements bearing the approval in writing of the record owners of not less than 75% of the common elements, and which does not interfere with the rights of any owners without their consent, may be done if the owners who do not approve are relieved from the initial cost thereof. The share of any cost not so assessed shall be assessed to the other apartment owners in the shares which their shares in the common elements bear to each other. There shall be no change in the shares and rights of an apartment owner in the common elements which are altered or further improved, whether or not the apartment owner contributes to the cost thereof....

Chapter 718, Florida Statutes (1981)

718.113 Maintenance: limitation upon improvement.—

(1) Maintenance of the common elements is the responsibility of the association. The declaration may provide that limited common elements shall be maintained by those entitled to use the limited common elements.

(2) There shall be no material alteration or substantial additions to the common elements except in a manner provided in the declaration.

Construing the declaration, by-laws and statutes as a whole, we conclude that article 5.2(b) of the declaration is not intended to relieve an objecting unit owner of the pro rata assessment for the cost of an alteration or improvement when it is reasonably necessary for the maintenance, repair or replacement of a common element. If, in the good business judgment of the association, such alteration or improvement is necessary or beneficial in the maintenance, repair or replacement of the common elements, all unit owners should equally bear the cost.... The trial court erred when it concluded that objecting owners should be relieved from the initial costs thereof even when the alteration or improvement was for the purpose of maintenance of the common elements.

[I]t is clear to us that the association could properly assess all unit owners for the replacement or repair of the beachfront common element if it was damaged by erosion or otherwise. Likewise, it seems to us that if, in the good business judgment of association, alteration or improvement of the beachfront by the addition of a rock revetment would protect the beach from damage and the necessity of subsequent repair or replacement, then that cost also should be borne equally by all unit owners....

In *Trafalgar Towers Ass'n # 2, Inc. v. Zimet*, 314 So. 2d 595 (Fla. Dist. Ct. App. 1975), the court found that the hiring of a resident manager and the purchase of a condominium unit to house the resident manager was in furtherance of the association's duty to maintain the common elements of the condominium. This case is analogous to *Trafalgar*, and we approve the reasoning of our colleagues in the fourth district as applied to this case.

Sterling Village Condominium, Inc. v. Breitenbach, 251 So. 2d 685 (Fla. Dist. Ct. App. 1971), is also helpful. There the court disapproved of the substitution by two unit owners of glass jalousies for wire screening around the porches or screen enclosures that constituted common elements without the consent of the management representing the other unit owners of the condominium. In doing so, the court held that the substitution was a material alteration prohibited without the consent of the management since it was a change, not merely for maintenance, but one which affected and influenced the function, use and appearance of the common elements.

Reversed and Remanded.

Montgomery v. Columbia Knoll Condo. Council

Supreme Court of Virginia
344 S.E. 2d 912 (Va. 1986)

STEPHENSON, J.... The parties have stipulated the facts. [Plaintiffs own] one unit in the Columbia Knoll Condominium.... The Columbia Knoll Condominium Council of Co-owners (the Council), an association of all unit owners, is responsible for the administration of the Condominium.

The Condominium units do not have individual meters for electrical and gas consumption. Therefore, the utility expenses are apportioned among the unit owners according to the size of their units. Based upon professional advice, the Council's board of directors recommended the replacement of all windows in the Condominium with insulated windows as the most effective means of reducing the common utility expenses.

At a meeting of the Council, a majority of the unit owners present voted to replace all the windows at a cost of $125,399.06. The Montgomerys were among the 29% present who opposed the expenditure.

Consequently, the Montgomerys instituted a declaratory judgment proceeding to challenge the Council's authority to replace the windows in their unit and to assess them the cost thereof without their consent. The trial court ruled that the Council acted within its authority, reasoning that "there exists a direct, tangible, demonstrable connection between the [Council's proposed action] and the common good." The Montgomery's appeal. The Condominium Act, Code § 55-79.39, *et seq.*, provides in part:

> [A]ll powers and responsibilities with regard to maintenance, repair, renovation, restoration, and replacement of the condominium shall belong (1) to the [Council] in the case of the *common elements*, and (2) to the individual unit owner in the case of any *unit or any part thereof*. Code § 55-79.79. (Emphasis added.)

The Council does not dispute that the windows in the Montgomery's unit are "part" of their unit. Indeed, the Condominium's master deed expressly defines a "unit" as including the windows. Thus, the Montgomerys contend that, because the windows are part of their unit and not "common elements," the Council has no authority to replace them.

"unit" is defined to include windows.

The Council, on the other hand, contends that it had authority to install the insulated windows because its action was a "reasonable [restriction] on the use of units" and "serve[s] the best interest of all of the [unit] owners."* In support of this contention, the Council cites the following provision of the Condominium's by-laws:

VI/SECTION 2. Maintenance and Repair.

(a) Every co-owner must perform promptly all maintenance and repair work within his own [unit] which, if omitted, would affect the Project and its entirety or in a part belonging to other co-owners, and is expressly responsible for the damages and liabilities which may result from his failure to do so.

The Council's reliance upon this provision is misplaced. This provision clearly is limited to "maintenance and repair," terms which, by definition, do not include improvements. "Maintenance" means to preserve or to keep "in a state of repair," *Webster's Third New International Dictionary*, 1362 (1981), and "repair" means to fix or "restore . . . what is torn or broken." . . .

The installation of insulated windows clearly is an improvement—an enhancement in quality—to the individual units; it cannot be characterized as maintenance or repair. Nothing in the statute or the Condominium instruments authorizes the Council to improve the Montgomery's unit against their will and at their expense. We conclude, therefore, that the Council exceeded its authority. . . . Reversed.

Notes & Questions

1. Do you see any relevant distinctions between putting in a rock revetment to protect against erosion (not an alteration or improvement) and putting in new windows to protect against energy loss (an improvement)? Are the cases (*Tiffany Plaza* and *Montgomery*) distinguishable on some other basis?

2. Should unit owners be protected against decisions to make material alterations, substantial additions, and improvements by the board or a majority of the owners? Does it make sense to allow the project to go ahead without unanimous consent so long as the dissenting owners are not required to pay their share? Does it make sense to provide, as the declaration in *Tiffany Plaza* does, that there shall be no change in the shares or rights of the non-paying owners?

3. Power to Enter Individual Units

River Terrace Condo. Ass'n v. Lewis
Court of Appeals of Ohio
514 N.E.2d 732 (Ohio Ct. App. 1986)

BLACK, J. . . . River Terrace Condominium Association . . . obtained an order permanently enjoining . . . Dora Stewart Lewis from refusing to give access to Unit 2-B in the River

---

* The Council relies in part on Article VI, Section 6 of the Condominium's by-laws to support its assertion of authority. We find no merit to this argument. Section 6, entitled "Rules of Conduct," governs the conduct of the unit owners, assuring the aesthetics of the common elements and the safety and peaceful enjoyment of all owners. Section 6 has no application whatsoever to the Council's authority over the unit owners' fee simple interest in their individual units.

Terrace Condominium ... so that the Association could spray to exterminate cockroaches. The injunction was issued after the trial court sustained the Association's motion for summary judgment. Dora Stewart Lewis appeals....

The facts pertinent to this appeal are not complicated. Beginning in the first floor lobby of the Condominium, cockroaches were discovered in the common areas and certain "units" on the first, second and third floors. On the second floor, they were found in the hallway outside appellant's Unit 2-B and in an adjoining unit that shares a common wall with Unit 2-B. An exterminating company was engaged to spray insecticide to eliminate the infestation on a planned basis, treating half the infested areas and units on one visit and the other half on the next visit two weeks later.

Lewis refused to allow the exterminator to enter her unit, stating in her letter of January 26, 1985 that: "I cannot tolerate spray, also the residuals left. I lost one of my dogs because of an overloading to her system of 'phenols' years ago."[3] She testified at the hearing on a preliminary injunction that she had never seen any cockroaches in Unit 2-B (the Association had no proof to the contrary), and that if the spraying were allowed, she would leave the Condominium.[4]

On February 10, 1985, the board of trustees (the statutory board of managers) of the Association adopted the following resolution at a special meeting:

> Resolved that the Board of the River Terrace Association take any measures necessary for the extermination of roaches in all apartments and common areas in the River Terrace and further take any necessary action to accomplish same.

A copy of the resolution was delivered to Lewis that day, but she continued to deny entry for spraying. At the regular meeting of the board of trustees held on February 19, 1985, the board appointed a committee that was empowered to file suit for the Association, but decided "to approach the growing problem" by three steps; give two Association members a chance to see if they could obtain cooperation from Lewis; consult the board of health; and finally proceed to "[g]o forward at once with a lawyer." The instant action for injunctive relief followed.

A full evidentiary hearing was held on the Association's motion for a preliminary injunction, during the course of which the Association's expert testified that cockroaches "carry bacteria and other things that would lead to disease-producing organisms"; that they nest in clusters and leave droppings that contaminate wherever they live, migrate along conduits, electrical wiring, plumbing lines, and air conditioning ducts; and that they move away from areas that have been sprayed with insecticides. The expert was of the opinion that if cockroaches were found on two sides of a unit, there is "a very good likelihood" that the insects will be found in that unit, especially if it is untreated. Other than general statements about the effect of insecticides on humans, Lewis presented no

---

3. Lewis concluded her letter as follows: "I am having this copied. A copy will go to the executor of my estate. I want West Shell to sign a statement accepting responsibility, knowingly involving in my health [sic] in adverse ways. That statement is not signed and the apartment is sprayed and due to my work I die — West Shell can be sued by my heirs as a contributor to my demise by using unnatural unhealthy means of pest controlling on 'their' deciding in conjunction with other products employed in the building under 'their' management, my resting place."

4. The extent of appellant's testimony about her reason for refusing entry for spraying was as follows: "Q. Have you ever seen any roaches in Unit 2-B? A. No. "Q. Now, have you denied access to the building association to Units 1-D and 2-B for spraying insecticide? "A. Yes. "Q. And if that spraying is allowed, could you tell us how that would affect your view as to living at River Terrace?" A. I'd leave." Q. You would?" A. I'd leave." On cross-examination, appellant conceded that she was not living in Unit 2-B at that time and entered that unit only from time to time.

evidence of any nature upon which a trier of fact could conclude that the insecticides being used in the Condominium would, with reasonable certainty, adversely affect her health.

The Association had sought a preliminary injunction allowing entry into appellant's unit for two purposes: to spray insecticides and to replace valves in the heating, ventilating and air conditioning ("HVAC") system. While the court issued a preliminary injunction allowing entry for the replacement of HVAC valves, it declined to do so for the roach problem, stating that "The evidence does not indicate that the failure to grant a preliminary injunction *prior to the final hearing* would cause irreparable injury to the plaintiff." (Emphasis added.) However, the court found that there was evidence of cockroaches in Unit 2-B and the board "was not arbitrary in fulfilling the authority placed in it by statute and the Declaration and by-laws of the condominium association." The court concluded that the Association had a right of access to deal with the roach problem.

No further evidentiary hearings were held. About a month after the order on the preliminary injunction, the Association filed a motion for summary judgment and later filed an affidavit in substantiation of its position that the decision to enter Unit 2-B was reasonable. Lewis countered with a memorandum and two affidavits, hers and that of her expert, Dr. Susan W. Fisher, both of which will be discussed in detail below. After reviewing the several affidavits, the appellant's answers to interrogatories and the transcripts of the evidence taken at the hearing on the preliminary injunction, the trial court found that reasonable minds could only come to the conclusion that the Association was acting reasonably within its authority, that the Association's means of "spraying for roaches" was reasonable, and that there was no evidence that the use of insecticides in this instance was excessive or any way injurious to the health of the occupants of the Condominium. The court found that the Association had no adequate remedy at law and was entitled to an order permanently enjoining Lewis from refusing access to Unit 2-B for spraying to exterminate cockroaches. An injunction was issued, and this appeal followed.

In her first assignment of error appellant contends that the Association "failed to establish any legal right to enter Unit 2-B to spray insecticide." We disagree because we find the right of entry is patent.

Under R.C. Chapter 5311 and the Declaration and by-laws for this Condominium, while the owner of a unit has exclusive ownership of and responsibility for his unit, R.C. 5311.03(B), the owner's freedom of action is of necessity limited by the fact that the unit is one of many units (in this instance one of fifty-seven) that are physically and legally supported by, and supportive of, all other units and the common areas. It is not an independent, separate entity in the nature of a castle. Under Section 2, Article V of the Declaration and the by-laws, unit ownership extends only to "the undecorated interior surfaces of the perimeter walls" and does not include the conduits, wires, pipes and ducts within those boundaries that serve any other unit. All the rest of the Condominium constitutes "common areas." ... Thus, all of the conduits, wires, pipes and ducts that carry utility and other services throughout the Condominium are "common areas," and these are the highways through which the insects and other pests including cockroaches travel and migrate. They enter and leave individual units along these highways. In the nature of things, an infestation of cockroaches in the Condominium is a common problem, not an individual problem.

Under R.C. 5311.03(F), each unit is "subject to the right of access for the purpose of maintenance, repair, or service of [1] any common area and facility located within its boundaries or [2] of any portion of the unit itself." The entry must be authorized by the board of managers..., and no maintenance of a portion of the unit may be authorized unless it is necessary in the board's opinion for "public safety" or to prevent damage to any other part of the condominium. We construe "public safety" to mean "common safety of the occupants of the condominium," because we believe it is not intended that the board of managers can act only when the perceived danger is to the general public.

This right of entry is also set forth in Section 2, Article XIV of the Declaration and by-laws as follows:

> Section 2. Right of Entry for Repair, Maintenance and Restoration. The Association shall have a right of entry and access to, over, upon and through all the Condominium Property, including each Unit, to enable the Association to perform its obligations, rights and duties pursuant hereto with regard to maintenance, repair, restoration and/or servicing of any items, things or areas of or in the Condominium Property.

There is no question in our minds that the extermination of cockroaches from a condominium falls within the meaning of "maintenance." The Association established that it had a legal right of entry to spray the insecticides, and under R.C. 5311.19 and 5311.23, the Association was fully entitled to enforce its right of access.

. . .

The core issue before the court was whether the decision by the board of trustees to enter Unit 2-B in the interest of common (public) safety was valid and enforceable. In reviewing such a decision, as in reviewing the validity of any rule adopted by a board of managers of a condominium association, the trial court does not substitute its judgment for that of the board of managers or weigh the various elements and considerations to be taken into account as though the court were acting *de novo*. Instead, the court applies the test of reasonableness; that is, the court determines whether under all the facts and circumstances disclosed by the evidence, the action taken (or the rule adopted) by the board of managers was reasonable. We believe there are three major questions subsumed in the test of reasonableness: (1) whether the decision was arbitrary or capricious; (2) whether it was nondiscriminatory and even-handed; and (3) whether it was made in good faith for the common welfare of the owners and occupants of the condominium.[8]

We hold the evidence was sufficient to support ... [the trial court's conclusion that the decision was reasonable]. The infestation of cockroaches could not be tolerated and demanded action; the means of extermination was a customary means reasonably related to eliminating the threat to the safety and enjoyment of the condominium; the plan was to spray insecticides only where cockroaches were found; all residential units in the condominium were subject to spraying in a nondiscriminatory fashion; and the decision to enter Unit 2-B and all other infested units was made in good faith for the common welfare of River Terrace's owners and occupants.

The evidence offered by appellant Lewis to prove that the extermination plan was unreasonable was sketchy: appellant had seen no cockroaches in Unit 2-B; she could not tolerate the spray or "residuals"; her dog had died years ago of "overloading" of "phenols"; and the pest control used was an "unnatural, unhealthy means." This makes it obvious that the proposed spraying was distasteful to Lewis, but we note the absence of any claim or evidence that the specific chemical substances used by the exterminator, the concentration proposed, the durability and toxicity of the "residuals" or the harmful effects

---

8. The test of reasonableness has been used in Ohio in reviewing condominium rules, *Prestwick Landowners' Assn. v. Underhill* (1980), 69 Ohio App.2d 45, 23 O.O.3d 36, 429 N.E.2d 1191, as it has been applied in other states. . . .

on appellant's own health would make the spraying of her unit an unreasonable procedure....

The judgment of the trial court is Affirmed.

Bruce E. Cohan, M.D., P.C. v.
Riverside Park Place Condo. Ass'n, Inc.

Court of Appeals of Michigan
365 N.W.2d 201 (Mich. Ct. App. 1985)

... [Plaintiff appeals from order ... denying plaintiff's motion ... for relief from an October 3, 1980, judgment ordering plaintiff to submit to an inspection of unit 26 of Riverside Condominiums in Ann Arbor. The October 3, 1980, judgment was affirmed by this Court in *Bruce E. Cohan, MD, PC v. Riverside Park Place Condominium Ass'n, Inc.,* ... [in 1983]. The basis of the present appeal is the trial court's failure to consider the constitutionality of the court ordered inspection without a search warrant. We decline to disturb the trial court's refusal to set aside the October 3, 1980, judgment on two grounds.

[The 1980 order required Cohan to submit to an inspection for covenant compliance after the association had denied him permission to enclose the balcony of his unit. At the time of this appeal, the inspection had already occurred and the issue was moot.—Eds.]

...

Nevertheless, we decline to base our opinion on the technical ground of mootness alone. The excellence of plaintiff's counsel's brief and the persistence with which plaintiff has pursued appellate relief justify a decision on the merits. Does plaintiff have a Fourth Amendment claim? Plaintiff asserts that under Fourth Amendment principles a search warrant must be obtained before entry can be made into unit 26.

The flaw in plaintiff's argument is that the purpose of the Fourth Amendment "is to safeguard the privacy and security of individuals against arbitrary invasions by governmental officials." *Camera v. Municipal Court of the City and County of San Francisco,* 387 U.S. 523, 528 (1967) ... In the present case, the right to inspect was not asserted by any governmental entity. Instead, it was asserted by a private association with whom plaintiff contracted when the condominium was purchased. The association's right to inspect is a question of contract between two private parties, as both the lower court and this Court have found. The inspection of the common elements and limited common elements within unit 26 by defendants thus does not reach constitutional magnitude for Fourth Amendment purposes.

Even if governmental action were involved in the present case, the inspection ordered by the lower court and affirmed by this Court in *Cohan, supra,* does not rise to the level of an "unreasonable search and seizure." Plaintiff contends that, for Fourth Amendment purposes, an inspection of a home is the equivalent of a search and that searches and seizures inside a home without a warrant are presumptively unreasonable ... [citations omitted]. These propositions are clearly correct. However, even assuming arguendo that the present case involved a search by a governmental unit, as in the cases cited by plaintiff, the cases are not on point with the present case.

The Michigan Condominium Act, M.C.L. §559.101 *et seq.;* M.S.A. §26.50(101) *et seq.,* makes it clear that the owner of a condominium unit, while he may have a fee simple interest, does not have an exclusive interest in the condominium property. Throughout the act, the titleholder of a condominium unit is referred to as a "co-owner." M.C.L. § 559.106; M.S.A. § 26.50(106) defines a co-owner as a person who owns a condominium unit within the condominium project. This language employed by the Legislature makes it apparent that the titleholder of a condominium unit has fundamental property rights, but he nevertheless enjoys them coextensively with other members of the condominium project.

…

Given this balance of interests, it cannot be said that the association's inspection of the common elements and limited common elements within plaintiff's condominium unit amounts to a constitutional violation as an unreasonable search and seizure. The common limited elements are co-owned by the association. Plaintiff, as a co-owner of those elements of his condominium unit has relinquished some aspects of his right of privacy in his home. Therefore, the exercise of the right to inspection when balanced against plaintiff's interest in his co-owned property meets the test of reasonableness, making a warrant unnecessary.

We do not intend by this opinion to hold that condominium owners are not without Fourth Amendment rights in some particulars. It may well be that in certain instances entry into a condominium unit will require a warrant. However, this is not necessary under the instant factual situation. Affirmed.

4. Power to Allocate Interests in Common Areas

There is a substantial amount of litigation over efforts by the board, or a majority of unit owners, to acquire exclusive use rights to parts of the common areas. Most cases involve condominiums where common areas, or common "elements" as they are called, are owned by the unit owners as tenants in common. When changes are attempted in rights to use common areas, disadvantaged owners claim that they have been illegally deprived of part of their property. Similar questions can arise in non-condominium developments, but because the association, rather than the lot owners, is the owner of the common areas, the claim is framed in terms of interference with the owners' easements in the common areas.

The many citations in the following case illustrate the prevalence of the problem.

The Ridgely Condo. v. Smyrnioudis
Court of Appeals of Maryland
681 A.2d 494 (Md. 1996)

MURPHY, J. This case involves a judgment enjoining the Ridgely Condominium Association, Inc. (Association) from enforcing a bylaw amendment which prohibited clients of the condominium's seven first-floor commercial unit owners from entering and leaving the commercial units via the condominium lobby.

I

A condominium is a "communal form of estate in property consisting of individually owned units which are supported by collectively held facilities and areas." *Andrews v. City of Greenbelt,* 293 Md. 69, 71, 441 A.2d 1064 (1982).

The term condominium may be defined generally as a system for providing separate ownership of individual units in multiple-unit developments. In addition to the interest acquired in a particular apartment, each unit owner also is a tenant in common in the underlying fee and in the spaces and building parts used in common by all the unit owners.

Condo =
exclusive and
) "unit"
and t-i-c.
for "common
elements"

... A condominium owner, therefore, holds a hybrid property interest consisting of an exclusive ownership of a particular unit or apartment and a tenancy in common with the other co-owners in the common elements....

In exchange for the benefits of owning property in common, condominium owners agree to be bound by rules[2] governing the administration, maintenance, and use of the property.... *Dulaney Towers v. O'Brey,* 46 Md.App. 464, 466, 418 A.2d 1233 (1980) ("The courts stress that communal living requires that fair consideration must be given to the rights and privileges of all owners and occupants of the condominium so as to provide a harmonious residential atmosphere.").

The Maryland Condominium Act (the Act), Maryland Code (1996 Repl.Vol.) §§ 11-101 et seq. of the Real Property Article, regulates the formation, management, and termination of condominiums in Maryland. The Act was originally enacted ... [in] 1963, as the Horizontal Property Act[3] in response to § 104 of the Federal Housing Act of 1961, ... which made federal mortgage insurance available to condominiums in states where title and ownership were established for such units. The Act was based on the Federal Housing Administration's Model Horizontal Property Act of 1961....

Under the Act, property becomes a condominium upon the recording of a declaration, bylaws, and a condominium plat. § 11-102. The declaration must include the name of the condominium; a description of the entire project, the units, and the common elements; and the percentage interests in the common elements and votes appurtenant to each unit.... The declaration may be amended with the written consent of at least 80% of the unit owners, except that unanimous consent of the owners is required for some amendments, such as altering percentage interests in common elements, changing the use of units from residential to nonresidential and vice versa, and redesignating general common elements as limited common elements. §§ 11-103(b); 11-107(c).

The bylaws govern the administration of the condominium and must include the form of the condominium administration and its powers, meeting procedures, and fee collection procedures. § 11-104(a), (b). The former § 11-111(f) also required the bylaws to include restrictions on the use of units and common elements.... The 1974 amendments made inclusion of such use restrictions in the bylaws optional. Section 11-104(c) now provides: "The bylaws may also contain any other provision regarding the management and operation of the condominium including any restriction on or requirement respecting the use and maintenance of the units and the common elements." The bylaws may be amended by at least a 2/3 vote of the unit owners. § 11-104(e)(2).

The Council of Unit Owners, which may delegate its powers to a Board of Directors, governs the affairs of the condominium and may adopt rules for the condominium. §§ 11-109(a), (b), 111(a). If there is any conflict between the provisions of the various documents governing the condominium, the statute controls, then the declaration, plat, bylaws, and rules in that order. § 11-124(e).

---

2. The term "rule" is used in this opinion in its generic sense to encompass any regulation in any form enacted by a condominium board of directors or council of unit owners, or contained in the condominium's original documents.

3. "The concept of 'horizontal property' or 'strata' ownership simply means that the area above land can be divided into a series of strata or planes capable of severed ownership, making the ownership of things affixed to land separable from the ownership of the land itself."

II

The Ridgely, located at 205 East Joppa Road in Towson, Maryland, was established in June, 1975. According to Article XV, § 1 of the Association's by-laws, all of the 239 units in the building are residential, except for the seven units on the first floor which "may be used as professional offices." Each of the seven commercial units is accessible both through the lobby and directly through a door located outside of the building. There are no porches or canopies protecting the exterior entrances to the commercial units.

The accounting firm of Smyrnioudis & Wilhelm occupies unit 102. Nicholas Smyrnioudis, Jr. and his father ... have owned the unit since 1977. Clients entered the office through both the lobby and outside exterior doors until the office was remodeled in 1987 at a cost of approximately $40,000. The exterior door now opens into a conference room. Nicholas Smyrnioudis, Jr. testified that switching the reception area and conference room would involve removing an eleven foot reception counter, non-bearing walls, and carpeting.

Mary Granger operated a mail list brokerage and management company in unit 104, which she purchased in 1985. The three or four clients who visited each month used both the lobby and exterior doors. During the pendency of this litigation, Granger sold her unit to Philip R. Grillo, who also operates a business in the unit. Visitors to all of the other commercial units use the exterior doors exclusively.

In 1990, the Association remodeled the lobby of the Ridgely at a cost of approximately $125,000. The lobby, which is among the condominium's common elements, is elaborately decorated with marble floors, dark wood-paneled walls and decorative furniture. The cost of the remodeling was paid out of condominium fees to which both the commercial and residential tenants contribute. Nicholas Smyrnioudis, Jr. testified that use of the lobby is important for his business because of its appearance and because it allows clients to avoid wet grass, ice, rain, and snow. Mary Granger also testified that the lobby "lends to our credibility as a professional business" and "makes a nice impression." In addition, she testified that using the exterior door in the winter makes it difficult to keep the office warm.

The president of the Association, Calvin Coblentz, testified that members of the Association had become concerned about security around the time the lobby was renovated. A card system was installed for the garage doors and elevators in the garage, fire exits were made inaccessible from outside the building, and lighting was added in the parking areas.[6]

In May of 1990, the Board of Directors, in response to members' security concerns, sought to have the commercial unit owners voluntarily agree to have visitors use the exterior entrances to their units exclusively. When this effort failed to achieve full compliance, the Board of Directors, in the spring of 1991, adopted a resolution which provided that: "Effective September 1, 1991, clients of commercial units owners and tenants shall not utilize the Condominium's lobbies."

On August 27, 1991, ... [commercial unit owners] (appellees) filed suit in the Circuit Court for Baltimore County against the Association seeking to enjoin the enactment or enforcement of rules restricting the use of the lobby by the appellees' clients.

---

6. Officer John S. Reginaldi, Crime Prevention Coordinator for the Towson precinct of the Baltimore County Police Department testified at the trial that the Ridgely "is relatively safe other than the fact of the commercial businesses using the main entrances." To improve security, he recommended that the commercial units use the exterior entrances.

On or about October 1, 1991, the members of the Association voted to amend the by-laws. Originally, Article XV, § 1 of the by-laws provided: "All units shall be used as a single family residence, except that up to a maximum of seven (7) units on the first floor may be used as professional offices." The amendment added:

> provided however, that all clients of, or visitors to, professional office owners or their tenants shall be required to use the exterior entrances of each such professional office for ingress and egress.
>
> No visitor or clients of any owner of a professional office or tenant thereof, shall be permitted in any other area of the building, unless accompanied by the owner of the office unit or the tenant of such office unit. For the purpose of this section, the terms "clients" or "visitor" of professional office owner or tenant, shall include the clients or visitor and all person(s) who may accompany such client or visitor to such professional office.

. . .

The appellees filed an amended complaint on September 27, 1991. Pending trial, the parties reached an agreement which allowed commercial visitors to use the lobby, but required them to sign in and wait at the front desk for an escort.

After a trial, Judge John F. Fader, II, enjoined the Association from enforcing the bylaw.... Judge Fader determined that "the proper standard of review is whether the Condominium's rule is reasonable." The restriction, he said, "is unenforceable for failure to reasonably relate to the health, happiness and enjoyment of unit owners." Safety concerns, he noted, had prompted the adoption of the restriction, but there was no evidence that any commercial visitors had threatened the building's security. Judge Fader added:

> There was no indication that the prohibition of all access by commercial tenants and their clients/patients was the only method, the least intrusive method, or the best means available to lessen the possibility of unauthorized persons entering the building, or of authorized individuals causing trouble. In prohibiting commercial access via the main lobby, the Board reacted to a situation, which objectively was not dire, and which did not require the stringent regulation initiated by the Board.

Judge Fader also held that the restriction "fails the reasonableness test since it has a discriminatory impact on commercial unit owners."

On appeal, the Court of Special Appeals affirmed.... At the outset, it said that "our review of the record convinces us that this case actually concerns an access restriction that has diluted appellees' respective percentage interests in the Condominium lobby." In a footnote, the court said that, "To deny the use of the lobby to clients of the commercial unit owners constitutes an *ultra vires* taking of a portion of their percentage interest in the common areas in derogation of the Ridgely Condominium declaration as well as certain provisions of the Maryland Condominium Act." Nonetheless, the court declined to base its decision on that issue since it was not argued by the parties in the circuit court.

The court held that the reasonableness test is the proper standard of review for evaluating restrictions contained in a bylaw amendment. Courts apply a more deferential standard of review to recorded use restrictions, the court said, because unit owners have notice of the restrictions when they purchase their units. In contrast, the court concluded that the more restrictive reasonableness standard is appropriate in this case, because owners did not have notice of the restriction when they purchased their units.

The court emphasized the disparate impact of the restriction on the commercial unit owners, and indicated that § 11-108 may require any use restriction that does not apply equally to all unit owners to be stated in the declaration. Thus, the court held that application of a deferential standard of review is particularly inappropriate where the use restriction has a discriminatory impact.

III

The Association filed a petition for a *writ* of certiorari, which we granted, and which presented this question: "Did the trial court and the Court of Special Appeals apply the appropriate standard of review for evaluating the propriety of a condominium by-law amendment?" In their brief and before the lower courts, the appellees argued that courts should apply a reasonableness test in reviewing the validity of condominium bylaw amendments. At oral argument before us, however, they argued in addition that the bylaw amendment at issue violated both the declaration and the Act by "taking" a property right. Such changes in property interests, they maintained, may only be accomplished by amending the declaration with the unanimous consent of the unit owners. Although this point was not briefed by the parties and was only briefly alluded to in the opinion of the Court of Special Appeals, the appellees urge this Court to reach the issue.

Under Rule 8-131(b), we "ordinarily will consider only an issue that has been raised in the petition for certiorari or any cross-petition and that has been preserved for review by the Court of Appeals." Appellees' argument is directly responsive to the question in the petition for certiorari. They assert that the test for evaluating the propriety of the by-law amendment is whether it deprives a unit owner of a property right. Consequently, in our view, the argument is encompassed within the question presented in the certiorari petition.

IV

In reviewing the validity of a rule, a court must determine whether the Board of Directors or Council of Unit Owners had the authority to promulgate the rule at issue under the Act, declaration, and by-laws. *Dulaney Towers, supra,* 46 Md. App. at 466; *Johnson v. Hobson,* 505 A.2d 1313, 1317 (D.C.App. 1986); *Juno by the Sea North Condo. v. Manfredonia,* 397 So. 2d 297 (Fla.Dist.Ct.App. 1981); 68 Op.Atty.Gen. 112, 119 (1983). Since we find that the Association did not have the authority to enact the rule at issue here by amending the by-laws, we do not reach the question briefed by the parties.

The Association contends that the rule is merely a use restriction which the Council of Unit Owners may enact by amending the by-laws with a 2/3 vote of the unit owners.[8] Cases addressing the propriety of use restrictions fall generally into two categories. In the first class of cases, which we will refer to as "exclusive use" cases, some courts rule that granting exclusive use of common elements to one or few unit owners changes the percentage interest of the excluded unit owners in the common elements. E.g., *Kaplan v. Boudreaux,* 410 Mass. 435, 573 N.E.2d 495 (1991). In the second class of cases, which we will refer to as "equality" cases, some courts rule that if a restriction applies equally to all the unit owners, it does not change their respective percentage interests in the common elements. E.g., *Jarvis v. Stage Neck Owners Ass'n,* 464 A.2d 952 (Me. 1983).

The Supreme Judicial Court of Massachusetts, in *Kaplan,* ... reviewed a bylaw amendment granting exclusive use of a path, which was part of the condominium's common el-

---

8. The Ridgely by-laws, Article XXI, § 1, require a vote of 75% of the unit owners to amend the by-laws.

ements, to one unit. <u>The statute required consent of all the unit owners to alter the percentage interests in the common elements.</u> The court found that it was not necessary to "transfer ... the sum total of a unit owner's interests in a portion of the common area" in order to "affect [the] percentage interest in the common area." Rather, "transfer of an interest that is smaller than an 'ownership' interest would suffice to alter the percentage interest held by each [owner]." <u>The court</u> held that the amendment affected an interest in land because it resembled an easement and <u>concluded that the amendment changed the relative percentage interests of the unit owners in the common elements.</u> Therefore, <u>consent of all the unit owners was required to enact the amendment.</u> see also *Makeever v. Lyle*, 125 Ariz. 384, 609 P.2d 1084, 1089 (Ariz.Ct.App. 1980) (<u>converting general common elements to exclusive use of one owner constitutes taking of other owners' property without authority</u>); *Preston v. Bass*, 13 Ark. App. 94, 680 S.W.2d 115, 116 (1984) (Board approval of carport in common area created limited common element requiring <u>100% vote</u> of unit owners); *Penney v. Association of Apt. Owners*, 70 Haw. 469, 776 P.2d 393, 395 (1989) (change from general to limited common element altered unit owners' percentage interests); *Carney v. Donley*, 261 Ill. App. 3d 1002, 633 N.E.2d 1015, 1020, 199 Ill. Dec. 219 (1994) (board did not have authority to approve balcony extensions into common area); *Sawko v. Dominion Plaza One Condo. Ass'n*, 218 Ill. App. 3d 521, 578 N.E.2d 621, 627, 161 Ill. Dec. 263 (Ill.App.Ct. 1991) (<u>assigning parking spaces to some units diminished other owners' interests in common elements</u>); *Stuewe v. Lauletta*, 93 Ill. App. 3d 1029, 418 N.E.2d 138, 140, 49 Ill. Dec. 494 (Ill.App.Ct. 1981) (developer's grant of parking space to one unit gave exclusive easement and <u>diminished other owners' interests in common elements</u>); *Strauss v. Oyster River Condo. Trust*, 417 Mass. 442, 631 N.E.2d 979, 981 (1994) (additions built in common area changed percentage interests of unit owners); *Grimes v. Moreland*, 41 Ohio Misc. 69, 322 N.E.2d 699, 702 (1974) ("placing fences and [air conditioner] compressors on condominium common areas constitutes a taking of property and an ouster of co-tenants from common areas"); cf. *Alpert v. Le'Lisa Condo.*, 107 Md. App. 239, 247, 667 A.2d 947 (1995) (parking spaces assigned to 20 of 32 unit owners did not become limited common elements because they would not be conveyed with the unit); *Juno by the Sea, supra*, 397 So. 2d 297, 303 (assigning parking spaces to 50 of 70 unit owners did not convert general into limited common elements because spaces would not be conveyed with the unit). Compare *Parrillo v. 1300 Lake Shore Drive Condo.*, 103 Ill. App. 3d 810, 431 N.E.2d 1221, 1223, 59 Ill. Dec. 464 (1981) (enclosing limited common element would not change unit owners' percentage interests in common elements because use was already exclusive) with *Gaffny v. Reid*, 628 A.2d 155, 157 (Me. 1993) (cottage encroaching on limited common area violated other owners' property rights despite prior exclusivity of use).

In contrast, the Supreme Judicial Court of Maine, in *Jarvis, supra*, 464 A.2d at 954, reviewed an agreement approved by 80% of the unit owners which granted an adjacent resort hotel use of the condominium's pool, tennis courts, and parking area. The court discussed *Stuewe, supra*, 418 N.E.2d 138, and *Makeever, supra*, 609 P.2d 1084, and said:

> There is a <u>distinct difference between</u> these cases, in <u>which exclusive use, control and/or ownership of the common areas is taken from some or all of the unit owners</u> and cases in which some reasonable <u>restrictions or regulation of the common areas is imposed on all owners.</u> In the first instance, each owner's percentage interest in the common area is altered. In the second instance, the percentage ownership interest is unaffected.
>
> ... Since the agreement did not increase or decrease the common elements and did not grant any owner exclusive use, it did not alter the percentage interests of the unit

owners.... [S]ee also *Schaumburg State Bank v. Bank of Wheaton*, 197 Ill. App. 3d 713, 555 N.E.2d 48, 52–53, 144 Ill. Dec. 151, *cert. denied*, 133 Ill. 2d 573, 561 N.E.2d 707, 149 Ill. Dec. 337 (1990) (declaration amendment granting nonexclusive easement over driveway to neighbor did not change unit owners' percentage interests in common element); *Bd. of Dir. of By the Sea Council v. Sondock*, 644 S.W.2d 774, 781 (Tx.App. 1982) (declaration amendment allowing removal of carports did not change unit owners' percentage interests in common element because applied equally to all unit owners); cf. *Coventry Square Condo. Ass'n v. Halpern*, 181 N.J. Super. 93, 436 A.2d 580, 582 (1981) (bylaw amendment requiring security deposit from rented units only created "a special class of owners" and was unreasonable, arbitrary, and unnecessary).

Here, the rule at issue affected an "interest" in property. The bylaw amendment revoked the commercial unit owners' right to have their clients use the lobby. That right resembles an easement, which is an interest in property. In *Condry v. Laurie*, 184 Md. 317, 320, 41 A.2d 66 (1945), we discussed the difference between a license and an easement:

> While an easement implies an interest in land, a license is merely a personal privilege to do some particular act or series of acts on land without possessing any estate or interest therein. In *De Haro v. United States*, 72 U.S. 599, ... Justice Davis spoke of the incidents of a license as follows: "It is an authority to do a lawful act, which, without it, would be unlawful, and while it remains unrevoked is a justification for the acts which it authorizes to be done. It ceases with the death of either party, and cannot be transferred or alienated by the licensee, because it is a personal matter, and is limited to the original parties to it."

The right which the bylaw amendment revoked was not "a mere personal privilege," ... but was appurtenant to the condominium unit and would be conveyed with the unit. Since the right resembles an easement, we hold that the bylaw amendment affected an interest in the appellees' property....

Here, however, and unlike the exclusive use cases, such as *Kaplan*, ... the bylaw amendment did not grant one or few unit owners exclusive use of a common area. Nonetheless, unlike the equality cases, such as *Jarvis*, ... the bylaw amendment disparately affected a portion of the unit owners by revoking a property interest they acquired when they purchased their units, without affecting the rights of the other unit owners.

In terms of the Maryland Condominium Act the lobby was a general common element, the use of which all of the tenants enjoyed equally.... By by-law amendment, the Association has attempted to deny that mutuality of use of a general common element. Further, under § 11-106(a), "each unit in a condominium has all of the incidents of real property." By by-law amendment, the Association has attempted to reduce the "easement" that the professional office units enjoyed in the lobby, and that "easement" is one of the incidents of the ownership of a professional office unit.

For these reasons, we hold that it was beyond the power of the Association by by-law amendment to purport to deprive the owners of the professional office units of their rights under the declaration and under the Maryland Condominium Act to the enjoyment of the lobby for the ingress and egress of their business invitees.

Judgment Affirmed with costs.

Notes & Questions

1. Where a development will include mixed uses, should some special consideration be given to protecting the interests of the numerically smaller group? Should that protection

be structural in form (*i.e.*, separate associations for each use), should that protection simply be provisions in the declaration that give the smaller group veto power over certain actions, or should that protection be in some other form?

2. Did the court give sufficient weight to the security concerns of the residential owners? How could their interests best be balanced with those of the commercial owners?

White v. Boundary Association, Inc.

Supreme Court of Virginia
624 S.E.2d 5 (Va. 2006)

KEENAN, Justice. In this appeal, we consider whether a board of directors of a property owners' association was authorized by the Property Owners' Association Act, Code §§ 55-508 through -516.2 (POAA), and the terms of a declaration of covenants, conditions and restrictions, to assign parking spaces for the exclusive use of individual unit owners.

Ralph J. and Mary R. White ... are owners in fee simple of unit number nine in the Boundary, Inc. subdivision ... in the City of Williamsburg. The subdivision occupies 0.66 acres and is comprised of nine townhouses, which are each owned in fee simple, and a common area. The common area includes sidewalks, plantings, a private one-way street through the subdivision, and parking spaces for 18 cars.

The individual properties and the common area of the subdivision are subject to a Declaration of Covenants, Conditions and Restrictions.... A board of directors..., consisting of four officers elected by the owners, manages the business affairs of the Association. Article III, section 1 of the Association's bylaws authorizes the Board to "adopt such rules and regulations for the conduct of [its] meetings and the management of the corporation, as [it] may deem proper, not inconsistent with these by-laws and the laws of this State."

The Declaration directly addresses the subdivision's common area. Article I, section 4 of the Declaration defines "[c]ommon area" as "all real property owned by Boundary Association Inc. for the common use and enjoyment of the owners." Article II, section 1, titled "Owner's Easements of Enjoyment," states that

[e]very owner shall have a right and easement of enjoyment in and to the Common Area which shall be appurtenant to and shall pass with the title to every lot, subject to the following provisions:

(a) The right of Boundary Association Inc. to charge reasonable admission and other fees for the use of any recreational facility situated in the Common Area;

(b) The right of Boundary Association Inc. to suspend the voting rights and right to use of the recreational facilities by an owner for any period during which any assessment against his lot remains unpaid; and for a period not to exceed 60 days for any infraction of its published rules and regulations;

(c) The right of Boundary Association Inc. to dedicate or transfer all or any part of the Common Area to any public agency, authority, or utility for such purposes and subject to such conditions as may be agreed to by the members.

The Board issued two relevant sets of parking regulations concerning the subdivision's common area. One set of regulations, adopted in July 2003..., designated two parking spaces for each unit, thereby assigning all the parking spaces in the subdivision.... [A]nother set of regulations ... (the October regulations), ... permitted the assigned unit owners to have vehicles towed from their designated spaces.

Immediately following the Board's adoption of the October regulations, the Whites ... [sued]. The Whites alleged that the Association exceeded its authority under the POAA and violated the explicit terms of the Declaration by adopting regulations that designated portions of the common area for the exclusive use of the various unit owners. The Whites sought a judgment declaring the parking regulations void and unenforceable, and that any allocation of portions of the common area for the exclusive use of particular unit owners violated both the Declaration and the POAA.... The Whites also sought reimbursement of their attorneys' fees.

The Association asserted various grounds of defense and affirmative defenses, including that the Whites had failed to state a claim upon which relief could be granted, and that the action was barred by the doctrines of waiver, estoppel, and laches. The Association also requested payment of its attorneys' fees.

The Whites and the Association filed cross motions for summary judgment. The ... circuit court granted the Association's cross motion for summary judgment, denied the Whites' motion, and granted the Association's request for attorneys' fees. The Whites appeal....

The Whites argue that the Association exceeded its authority under the POAA, which permits the adoption of common area regulations under valid bylaws "except where expressly reserved by the declaration to the members." Code § 55-513(A). The Whites contend that Article II, section 1 of the Declaration contains such an express reservation by giving every owner "a right and easement of enjoyment in and to the [c]ommon [a]rea," and that the Association may restrict this right only under the three circumstances enumerated in the Declaration. The Whites further maintain that the Association's assignment of exclusive use and towing rights in designated parking spaces is effectively a licensing of the common area, a power not granted to the Association by the Declaration.

In response, the Association contends that neither the Declaration nor the terms of the bylaws limits the Board's authority with regard to "the management of the corporation." Therefore, the Association argues, the parking regulations were a proper exercise of the Board's authority under the bylaws to establish rules regarding the common area. We disagree with the Association's arguments.

We observe that the POAA contains certain provisions applicable to the use of common areas managed by a property owners' association. Code § 55-513(A) states that a board of directors "shall have the power to establish, adopt, and enforce rules and regulations with respect to use of the common areas and with respect to such other areas of responsibility assigned to the association by the declaration, except where expressly reserved by the declaration to the members." Because the statute is unambiguous, we apply its terms in accordance with the plain meaning expressed....

We also consider the terms of the Declaration, which constitutes the contract collectively entered into by all the unit owners in the subdivision. *See Sully Station II Cmty. Ass'n, Inc. v. Dye*, 259 Va. 282, 284, 525 S.E.2d 555, 556 (2000); *Unit Owners Ass'n v. Gillman*, 223 Va. 752, 766, 292 S.E.2d 378, 385 (1982)....

The Declaration expressly granted each unit owner an easement of enjoyment in the common area. Each unit owner, as a dominant tenant, acquired an indefeasible right to enjoyment of the common area that, under the plain terms of the Declaration, was subject to change only under the three stated circumstances or by a vote of 65 percent of the unit owners.[2]

---

2. The Declaration states that it could be amended by a vote of 80 percent of the unit owners through May 21 2000, and, thereafter, by a vote of 65 percent of the unit owners.

These provisions in the Declaration render invalid any rule or regulation adopted under the bylaws that has the effect of divesting the unit owners of property rights granted in their easements. Thus, we must determine whether the present parking policy effectively divests the unit owners of such property rights.

We previously considered a mandatory parking policy of a property owners' association in *Sully Station II*. There, an association was authorized by its declaration to "license portions of the [c]ommon [a]rea to [m]embers on a uniform, non-preferential basis." ... The association's board of trustees adopted a parking policy that assigned two reserved spaces in the common area to each unit that did not have a garage. Those units with garages did not receive any assigned parking spaces. As a result, 78 of the 94 parking spaces that earlier were available to all unit owners were then reserved for the exclusive use of owners of units that did not have garages. ...

The property owners' association in *Sully Station II* argued that its action was valid and enforceable because the community's supplementary declaration authorized the board of trustees to issue rules and regulations for the assignment of parking spaces. ... We explained that the challenged parking policy effected a licensing of the common area by entitling certain unit owners to exclude other owners from using portions of the common area. ... We held that the parking policy constituted a preferential licensing, which was prohibited under the terms of the declaration, because that policy conferred a special privilege on the owners of the units without garages.

In the present case, we likewise conclude that the Board's parking policy confers a license on the individual unit owners, granting a special privilege permitting them to exclude others from using assigned portions of the common area. Because the Declaration does not authorize the Board to license portions of the common area, the Board was not permitted to obtain the same result by a rule or regulation that effectively divested the unit owners of access to certain portions of the common area included in their easement of enjoyment. Therefore, we hold that the parking policy is invalid because it effectively, and without authority, divested the unit owners of a property right granted in the Declaration that "run[s] with and bind[s] the land."[3]

In reaching this conclusion, we recognize that the POAA permits a property owners' association to adopt and enforce "rules and regulations with respect to use of the common areas." Code § 55-513(A). However, this statutory authority is subject to a significant limitation, namely, a declaration's express reservations of rights and privileges to the association members. Here, as we have stated, the Declaration expressly reserved to each individual unit owner an "easement of enjoyment in and to the [c]ommon [a]rea" that was limited by only three conditions, none of which are applicable here. Thus, these easements could not effectively be changed under a bylaw giving the Board authority for "management of the corporation." Accordingly, we conclude that the Board's action imposing the parking policy exceeded its authority under the POAA. ...

Based on our conclusion that the Board exceeded its authority in adopting the parking policy, the circuit court's award of attorneys' fees and costs to the Board as the "prevailing party" under Code § 55-515(A) also was erroneous. The Whites are the prevailing

---

Here's how to do it.

3. We further note that the Declaration provides a mechanism for validly implementing parking regulations such as those adopted by the Board in this case. Licensing of the common area may be accomplished by Board action upon amendment of the Declaration by 65 percent of the unit owners expressly authorizing such licensing of that area.

parties under that statute and, as such, are "entitled to recover [the] reasonable attorneys' fees and costs expended" in prosecuting their claims. . . .

For these reasons, we will reverse the circuit court's judgment and enter final judgment in favor of the Whites declaring the parking policy void and unenforceable. We also will remand the case to the circuit court, pursuant to the Whites' request, for determination of an award of attorneys' fees allowed under Code § 55-515(A).

Notes & Questions

1. Did the court in *White* reach a sensible result? Who are the winners and losers when parking spaces are assigned to individual units? Are the owners' rights to use any parking space in the common areas worthy of as much protection as the rights of the owners in *Ridgely* to use the lobby entrance?

2. Courts do not always reach the same result with respect to the association's power to assign parking spaces. Although some differences may be explainable by the terms of the particular governing documents and some by different attitudes about the balance between individual property rights and the collective rights of the owners as a whole, some may also be due to differences in the physical situation of the development.

In *Juno by the Sea North Condo. Ass'n, Inc. v. Manfredonia*, 397 So. 2d 297 (Fla. Dist. Ct. App. 1981), the court upheld a board's power to assign common element parking spaces for the exclusive use of individual units. The 70-unit complex had 97 parking spaces: 20 covered spaces that were sold as exclusive use, limited common elements on a first-come-first-served basis to purchasers, 50 more spaces adjacent to the building, and 27 spaces in a lot across the street. The two open lots were common elements but were not designated as limited common elements. The court upheld the board's action in assigning exclusive use of the 50 spaces adjacent to the building to the units that did not have one of the covered spaces over a claim that it improperly converted common elements into limited common elements. Because all parking spaces were maintained by the association, the allocation alleviated the unfairness that would otherwise result to the 50 owners who lacked exclusive covered spaces and avoided the chaotic parking situation that prevailed before adoption of the rule.

3. *Alterations in unit's share of common elements.* By declaration or statute, it is common to forbid alterations in a unit's boundaries or share of the common elements without the unit's owner's express consent. Do you see why? Does it make sense to use these provisions to prevent the board, or even a majority of the owners, from assigning parking spaces? Would these provisions also prevent assigning time-slots to various groups for use of the community's pool or other recreation facilities? Should it be necessary to handle these questions in the governing documents?

4. *Discrimination against nonresident owners.* In *Thanasoulis v. Winston Tower 200 Ass'n*, 542 A.2d 900 (N.J. 1988), owners were guaranteed the right to lease one parking space per unit in the garage, which was a common element of the condominium. The board adopted a policy of charging higher rates to owners who rented out their units than to resident owners. The New Jersey Supreme court invalidated the policy on the ground that it, in effect, changed the proportionate interests of the unit owners in the common elements and shares of common expenses, which exceeded the powers of the board.

5. If the development lacks adequate parking, does the association have the power to buy additional land or parking spaces (and assess the owners to pay for it) absent express authorization in the governing documents? We take up this question next.

5. Power to Acquire Additional Property

Whether a community has the power to acquire additional property for use of by its members is a different question from the question whether the developer may increase the size of the community by adding additional land or units.

Candlelight Hills Civic Ass'n, Inc. v. Goodwin
Court of Appeals of Texas
763 S.W.2d 474 (Tx. Ct. App. 1988)

DRAUGHN, J. Appellant Candlelight Hills Civic Association, Inc., a subdivision homeowners association, appeals the trial court's declaratory judgment which narrowly construed the subdivision's restrictive covenants....

We find that the restrictive covenants are unambiguous and, when liberally construed pursuant to § 202.003, Tex. Prop. Code Ann..., manifest the intent to allow acquisition of real property with the maintenance fund. We affirm the lower court's decision regarding the nonpooling of the subsection's votes and the inadmissibility of parol evidence, but reverse its decision disallowing the use of maintenance funds to acquire real property.

... Appellant raises these issues in ... points of error: (1) whether parol evidence was admissible to show the grantor's intent concerning the deed restrictions; (2) whether the restrictive covenants allow maintenance funds to be expended to acquire real property; [and] (3) whether the homeowners' votes could be pooled....

Appellant, the subdivision homeowner's association..., was organized as a Texas non-profit corporation.... Appellant's membership is composed of all lot owners and residents of the Candlelight Hills subdivision. Candlelight Hills is itself divided into six subsections with identical restrictive covenants between the subsections, save for a differing percentage vote required to alter the maintenance fees assessed. The restrictive covenants allow the assessment of maintenance fees which are collected from each homeowner and pooled to create a maintenance fund. The maintenance fund is administered by appellant pursuant to the Restrictions, Covenants, Conditions and Maintenance Charges found in each deed and pursuant to appellant's articles of incorporation, its by-laws, and the Texas Non-Profit Corporation Act. The purposes and intent of the maintenance fund are at the center of the present controversy.

Appellant sought to employ the maintenance fund to acquire a recreational facility for use by the Candlelight Hills subdivision by assuming the indebtedness of the owner. The appellant sought to acquire and maintain this recreational facility through an increase in the annual assessment of maintenance fees, provided a sufficient number of lot owners and residents voted for the proposed acquisition. Appellee ... Goodwin, a Candlelight Hills resident, filed suit to prevent appellant's acquisition of the recreational facility....

In response to appellee's suit, the trial court ruled that the restrictive covenants were unambiguous and did not intend the use of maintenance fees to acquire real property. It excluded deposition testimony of the developer of Candlelight Hills regarding his alleged intent as expressed in the restrictive covenants. It also ruled that the restrictive covenants did not permit the pooling of votes between the different subsections. From that judgment, appellant brings this appeal....

Our determination ... [is] contingent upon a ... fundamental finding as to whether the restrictive covenants are ambiguous. We have long held that the issue of whether an instrument is ambiguous is a question of law.... We find that the lower court correctly ruled that the restrictive covenants are unambiguous.

Appellant asserts that the deposition of T.D. Gardner, the developer of Candlelight Hills, was admissible to show the alleged intent of the restrictive covenants. The admissibility of parol evidence hinges upon the ambiguity of the restrictive covenants. The court is not looking for the subjective intent of the developer; instead, it is the objective intent, the intent expressed or apparent in the writing which is sought.... We find the trial court properly excluded the developer's deposition, as this was parol evidence regarding his subjective intent. Since the deed is not ambiguous on its face, extrinsic evidence is not admissible....

[not ambiguous → no extrinsic evidence,]

[T]he entire instrument in which the restrictive covenants are found is construed as a matter of law.... We note that rules of construction require that: 1) a deed will be enforced as written, even if it does not express original intent; 2) where there is no ambiguity, the entire instrument is reviewed to discern the intent of the party; 3) deeds are construed to confer the greatest estate to the grantee; 4) all promises and agreements are presumed to have been merged fully into and expressed by the written document; and 5) an unambiguous written document will be enforced as written and cannot be varied or contradicted by parol testimony, unless clearly alleged and proven that it was procured by fraud, mistake, or accident....

[Canons of interpretation]

Additional rules of construction have been added to the Property Code by the Texas Legislature, effective June 1987, which apply to "all restrictive covenants regardless of the date on which they were created." § 202.002, Tex. Prop. Code Ann.... A restrictive covenant must now be liberally construed to give effect to its purposes and intent. § 202.003.... The covenant should not be hedged about with strict construction, but given a liberal construction to carry out its evident purpose. With the preceding rules of construction in mind, we must look to the entire document and the necessary references within the document's language to discern its purposes and intent.

[Texas Code requires "liberally construed"]

The Restrictions, Covenants, Conditions and Maintenance Charges, that is, the restrictive covenants, contain a paragraph [4.6] which establishes the general purposes for which the maintenance fund may be employed ...:

> The total fund accumulated from this annual maintenance charge, in so far as the same may be sufficient, may be applied towards the payment of maintenance expenses incurred for any or all of the following purposes: Lighting, improving and maintaining streets, parks, parkways, bridle paths and esplanades; subsidizing bus service; collecting and disposing of garbage, ashes, rubbish and the like; caring for vacant lots; payment of legal and all other expenses incurred in connection with the collection, enforcement and administration of the "MAINTENANCE FUND" and the enforcement of all covenants and restrictions for the Subdivision; employing private policemen and watchmen; *doing any other thing necessary or desirable in the opinion of the Trustees of the Association* to keep the property in the Subdivision neat and in good order, *or which they consider of general benefit to the owners or occupants of the Subdivision*. It is understood that the judgment of the Trustees of the Association in the expenditure of said funds shall be final and conclusive so long as such judgment is exercised in good faith. (emphasis added)

... Construed liberally, this language permits the use of the maintenance fund to purchase real property if such purchase will be of general benefit to the owners and occupants of the subdivision. The term "maintenance expenses" does not, standing alone, fatally

[Holding]

limit the use of the maintenance fund; first, because the term is modified by the enumerated purposes of Paragraph 4:6, which include doing any thing of general benefit to the owners or occupants of the subdivision; and second, because it is modified by any express provisions and any necessary references found in other provisions of the restrictive covenants.

Appellee asserts that the list of purposes under paragraph 4:6 is inclusive, as well as illustrative of the type of permissible purposes for the fund. However, appellee's construction is too narrow. For example, the maintenance fund can be employed for "improvements" to parks and esplanades. The term "improvements" is construed in a property context and is commonly understood to contemplate the purchase of additional land, buildings, and construction of facilities.... The maintenance fund, therefore, need not solely be expended to maintain the status quo of the subdivision; but may be expended to acquire real property for improvements to its parks, streets, bridle paths, parkways, and esplanades, as well as any other thing necessary or desirable of general benefit to the owners or occupants of the subdivision.

... Paragraph 4:2 mandates the payment of the maintenance fund to a "Texas nonprofit corporation," that is, the appellant. This necessarily implicates the appellant's articles of incorporation and by-laws as well as the Texas Non-Profit Corporation Act. Thus, in addition to the express provisions in the restrictive covenants, the appellant is inhered with the powers and purposes enumerated in its articles of incorporation and by-laws. These powers and purposes necessarily modify the express provisions of the restrictive covenants via explicit reference in Paragraph 4:2, which is found in the maintenance fund section of the restrictive covenants.

One of appellant's overriding purposes as stated in its articles and by-laws is to maintain a residential character within Candlelight Hills. Additional, supportive purposes are directed specifically at safeguarding individual and collective property owners, encouraging improvements in the appearance of the homes, promoting wholesome social and recreational activities, and taking concerted actions on matters affecting the welfare of the community. The purchase of real property is consistent with the promotion of social and recreational activities and with taking concerted action on matters affecting the welfare of the community.

Appellant's by-laws define "properties" as any real property owned by appellant or later "brought within the jurisdiction of the Association...." Thus, the by-laws reasonably recognize appellant's power to purchase real property. Importantly, the only money which appellant controls is the maintenance fund, thus any purchase necessarily derives from this fund. The by-laws further define "common area" as "any real property *owned by the Association ... for the common use and enjoyment of owners*" in Candlelight Hills (emphasis added). This provision recognizes that appellant can own property in its own name for the benefit of the subdivision. One of the enumerated duties in appellant's by-laws is to cause any common area to be maintained including *improving* the streets, parks, parkways, and any other thing necessary or desirable for the general benefit of the owners of Candlelight Hills. Consistently, the intents and purposes of appellant, explicitly found in appellant's articles and by-laws and referenced in the restrictive covenants, must necessarily allow the expenditure of the maintenance fund to acquire real property, so long as the subdivision is benefitted.

The interaction of the Non-Profit Corporation Act is seen in its authorization of the purchase of real property without the need for an express enumeration of this power. Art. 1396-2.03, Tex. Bus. Corp. Act (Vernon 1980). The authority to purchase real property without express enumeration is implicitly integrated into the intent of the restrictive covenants via paragraph 4:2's recognition of a "Texas non-profit corporation." Also implicitly integrated into the restrictive covenants from the Texas Non-Profit Corporation Act is the right of the appellant to purchase real property that it might require under its purposes. Article 1396-2.02 Tex. Bus. Corp. Act. (Vernon 1980). The purposes of the present association include maintaining the social, recreational and well-being of the subdivision and the performing of such things permitted by the restrictions, all of which is mirrored in Paragraph 4:6's authority to take action of general benefit to the subdivision.

Appellee asserts that the power of appellant to purchase real property is not in question; rather, it is whether "maintenance" fees may be expended for such an acquisition. He asserts that a broad construction of the term "maintenance fees" allows the indiscriminate purchase of property which will be secured by a vendors lien upon recalcitrant homeowners. However, we find that no indiscriminant authority to purchase property is possible under the restrictive covenants nor through the limitations placed upon the trustees in their articles of incorporation, their by-laws, or the Non-profit Corporation Act,

First, limitations on the indiscriminant authority to purchase real property is found first in Paragraph 4:2, which places the maintenance fund under the fiduciary umbrella of a non-profit organization pursuant to the Texas Non-Profit Corporation Act, Art. 1396-1.01 *et seq.* The second limitation is found in Paragraph 4:3 which dictates a necessary consensus for approval of an assessment increase. The third limitation is found in Paragraph 4:6 which anchors any expenditure to the subdivision's benefit. The fourth limitation is again found in Paragraph 4:6 which imposes upon the Trustees a duty of good faith. The fifth limitation upon indiscriminant purchase power is found in Paragraph 4:7 which authorizes a revocation of the maintenance assessment upon the agreement of the homeowners. The sixth limitation is found in Paragraph 4:8 which requires the membership of the homeowners association to be composed of all homeowners in Candlelight Hills. Paragraph 4:8 also contains the seventh limitation on purchase power which entitles each homeowner to one vote, regardless of whether the homeowner is current in his payment of any maintenance fee assessed. The eighth limitation is found in Paragraph 4:8 which requires the Board of Trustees to be selected from the homeowners association. The ninth limitation is found in § 202.001 of the Texas Property Code which establishes the standard for the exercise of discretionary authority. The exercise of discretionary authority must not be arbitrary, capricious, or discriminatory.

… We must give full and consistent effect to every provision within the restrictive covenants. Thus, the presence of so many safeguards evidences an intent to allow full discretionary authority to rest in the Board of Trustees. The exercise of this authority to acquire real property is consistent with this intent. It is from the body of the maintenance fund, as confined by these express safeguards, that the appellant can exercise its power to purchase real property.

Further evidence of the intent to allow the acquisition of real property with the maintenance fund is found in Paragraph 4:8. Paragraph 4:8 authorizes the appellant's trustees to borrow money for the purposes of the maintenance fund, giving as security present or future funds. The power to borrow money, make contracts, and incur liabilities is also found in Article 1396-2.02, Tex. Bus. Corp. Act. (Vernon 1980). Appellant's articles of incorporation establishes one of appellant's purposes as the performance of all functions and any and all things that may be permitted or required by the restrictive covenants. The coupling of explicit authority in appellant's by-laws with the express authorization of Paragraph 4:8, and reinforced by Article 1396-2.02, evidences the intent to allow the Trustees to enter into any contracts which they deem necessary to carry out the expressed purposes.

[handwritten margin note: Limits on ability to acquire.]

… The purposes and intent of the restrictive covenants are to benefit the subdivision. This benefit is realized through the use of the trustees' powers to contract and to administer a maintenance fund in furtherance of these covenants according to the purposes established in the restrictive covenants, the articles of incorporation, the by-laws, and the Non-Profit Corporation Act.

… We recognize that the framers realized that other beneficial purposes might arise which would be too numerous to enumerate in a written document to be filed of record. Therefore, the document creates an interrelated framework which allows the subdivision to benefit and grow, while its interests are protected.

Having purchased his lot subject to a deed which included a good faith discretionary power to use the maintenance fund for the benefit of the subdivision, appellee had no guarantee that the fund would never be used to purchase real property beneficial to the subdivision.… Accordingly, we sustain the appellant's first point of error and reverse the lower court's judgment. We hold that the restrictive covenants allow the expenditure of maintenance funds for the purchase of real property.

Appellant asserts in its third point of error that the trial court erred in declaring that votes of each subsection could not be pooled. Paragraph 4:3 of the restrictive covenants … specifically ascribes voting rights on a subsection basis. The votes of the separate subsections had been pooled by appellant to determine whether the proposed expenditure of the maintenance fund had gathered the requisite percentage of votes to pass the proposal. Appellant asserts that the votes can be pooled to determine the individual subsection's percentage required by the restrictive covenants. The authority cited by appellant in support of its contention, however, is inapposite to its position. The court in *Zent v. Murrow*, 476 S.W.2d 875 (Tex.Civ.App.-Austin 1972, no writ), found that under the deeds of various subsections of a subdivision, the developer created different areas with provisions for amendment which varied according to the area. Because the different provisions for amendment applied to different sections, the evident intent of the developer was to restrict the power of one area to affect lot owners in other sections. The court in *Zent* held that the lot owners in one section were not authorized to amend the restrictions of another section. Likewise, the developer in the case before us has created several sections within Candlelight Hills subdivision by virtue of the definition located in the Preamble. Each section contains its unique requisite percentage of votes necessary to authorize an increase in maintenance fees. Though some of the requisite percentages are identical between subsections, the subsections' votes were intended to be tabulated separately to avoid "uncertainties and possible discrimination." *Zent*.…

In further support of the non-pooling of votes, it is evident that an express pooling clause exists for the pooling of the maintenance fees collected from each subsection to create a maintenance fund, as reflected in Paragraph 4:9. However, there is no equivalent pooling clause in the voting segment of the restrictive covenants. The nonexistence of a pooled vote provision, when juxtaposed with an express provision to pool maintenance funds, evidences the intent to forbid the pooling of votes. The lower court correctly construed the restrictive covenants to not intend any pooling of votes between subsections which might force a subsection to be carried against its express wishes. Therefore, we overrule appellant's third point of error.

Notes & Questions

1. Is it likely that purchasers in the Candlelight Hills Subdivision understand that their maintenance fund might be used to purchase additional property that might in turn re-

quire more maintenance funds? Do you agree with the court that the governing documents and the non-profit corporations act provide adequate safeguards for the homeowners? What are the risks for individual homeowners?

2. The court held that the association could not aggregate votes across the six sections of Candlelight Hills to obtain the percentage of favorable votes required to authorize the increase in maintenance fees for the purchase. What is the purpose of requiring that the increase be approved in each section?

3. Expanding the size of the community to include additional lots or units ordinarily dilutes the existing owners' interests in the common property. The benefit of being able to spread the maintenance costs across a larger base may be outweighed by increased use of the common property. In a condominium, where unit owners own the common elements as tenants in common, increasing the number of units changes the property rights by reducing the size of the proportionate shares. UCIOA § 2-105(a)(4) requires that the declaration state the maximum number of units the declarant (developer) can create; § 2-122 prohibits amendments to increase the number "to foreclose the possibility of an increase in the density of the project beyond that which was originally contemplated." This means that the maximum number of units can be increased only with the consent of 100% of the owners.

UCIOA § 2-121 allows the merger or consolidation of two or more common interest communities with the same type of ownership on approval in each community by the number of votes that would be required to terminate the community (80% or more under UCIOA § 2-118).

B. Making Rules to Govern the Community

Hidden Harbour Estates v. Norman

District Court of Appeals of Florida
309 So. 2d 180 (Fla. Dist. Ct. App. 1975)

DOWNEY, J. The question presented on this appeal is whether the board of directors of a condominium association may adopt a rule or regulation prohibiting the use of alcoholic beverages in certain areas of the common elements of the condominium.

Appellant is the condominium association formed ... to operate a 202 unit condominium known as Hidden Harbour. Article 3.3(f) of appellant's articles of incorporation provides, *inter alia*, that the association shall have the power "to make and amend reasonable rules and regulations respecting the use of the condominium property." A similar provision is contained in the Declaration of Condominium.

Among the common elements of the condominium is a club house used for social occasions. Pursuant to the association's rule making power the directors of the association adopted a rule prohibiting the use of alcoholic beverages in the club house and adjacent areas. Appellees, as the owners of one condominium unit, objected to the rule, which incidentally had been approved by the condominium owners voting by a margin of 2 to 1 (126 to 63). Being dissatisfied with the association's action, appellees brought this injunction suit to prohibit the enforcement of the rule. After a trial on the merits at which appellees showed there had been no untoward incidents occurring in the club house during social events when alcoholic beverages were consumed, the trial court granted a permanent injunction against enforcement of said rule. The trial court was of the view that rules and regulations adopted in pursuance of the management and operation of the condominium "must have some reasonable relationship to the protection of life, property or the general welfare of the residents of the condominium in order for it to be valid and enforceable." In its final judgment the trial court further held that any resident of the condominium might engage in any lawful action in the club house or on any common condominium property unless such action was engaged in or carried on in such a manner as to constitute a nuisance.

With all due respect to the veteran trial judge, we disagree. It appears to us that inherent in the condominium concept is the principle that to promote the health, happiness, and peace of mind of the majority of the unit owners, since they are living in such close proximity and using facilities in common, each unit owner must give up a certain degree of freedom of choice which he might otherwise enjoy in separate, privately owned property. Condominium unit owners comprise a little democratic sub society of necessity more restrictive as it pertains to use of condominium property than may be existent outside the condominium organization. The Declaration of Condominium involved herein is replete with examples of the curtailment of individual rights usually associated with the private ownership of property. It provides, for example, that no sale may be effectuated without approval; no minors may be permanent residents; no pets are allowed.

Certainly, the association is not at liberty to adopt arbitrary or capricious rules bearing no relationship to the health, happiness and enjoyment of life of the various unit owners. On the contrary, we believe the test is reasonableness. If a rule is reasonable the association can adopt it; if not, it cannot. It is not necessary that conduct be so offensive as to constitute a nuisance in order to justify regulation thereof. Of course, this means that each case must be considered upon the peculiar facts and circumstances thereto appertaining.

Finally, restrictions on the use of alcoholic beverages are widespread throughout both governmental and private sectors; there is nothing unreasonable or unusual about a group of people electing to prohibit their use in commonly owned areas.

. . .

Reversed and Remanded.

———————

Retrospective and Observations

Hidden Harbour Estates began as a development of mobile homes that the owner rented to individuals. He later converted to condominium ownership. The only common area was the clubhouse. At one point, the board surveyed the owners of units in Hidden Harbour Estates asking them whether they would prefer to have alcoholic drinks available at the clubhouse or whether alcohol should be prohibited. The results of the poll were submitted to an accounting firm which tabulated them and found that over 70% of the unit owners did not want alcohol to be served at the clubhouse. The board then decided to prohibit alcohol. Norman challenged the rule.

The president of the association at the time was Layton Mosay. Mr. Mosay was a retired Presbyterian minister of a large congregation in St. Louis. Bo Smith, the circuit court judge, said that it was unconstitutional to prohibit drinking in the clubhouse. Layton Mosay asked Walter Meginniss to appeal the case.

Mr. Meginniss told an interesting story about this case. On the Sunday before he was to do the oral argument in the appeals case, he and his son went golfing at their club. After they golfed, they went into the clubhouse to enjoy a couple of beers, and another club member said that he had heard that Mr. Meginniss was going to be arguing that "alcohol" case. Mr. Meginniss acknowledged that indeed he was going to be arguing it, and the gentlemen said, "Imagine that, Meginniss defending prohibition."

———————

Recall the discussion at the outset of this section. What difference does it make where the power rests or who makes the decision? The board has a great deal of power, but it is only the representative of the membership, while the governing documents contain the rules all owners agreed to when they purchased. Did they really agree, or is that a legal fiction that serves a policy purpose, and does that matter? From the perspective of the ability to compel compliance, it may well not matter; however, from the point of view of community understanding and acceptance, it can matter a great deal.

Restatement (Third) § 6.7 Power To Adopt Rules Governing Use Of Property

(1) Except as limited by statute or the governing documents, a common-interest community has an implied power to adopt reasonable rules to

(a) govern the use of the common property, and

(b) govern the use of individually owned property to protect the common property.

(2) If the declaration grants a general power to adopt rules, the common-interest community also has the power to adopt reasonable rules designed to

(a) protect community members from unreasonable interference in the enjoyment of their individual lots or units and the common property caused by use of other individually owned lots or units; and

(b) restrict the leasing of units to meet valid underwriting requirements of institutional lenders.

(3) Absent specific authorization in the declaration, the common-interest community does not have the power to adopt rules, other than those authorized under subsections (1) and (2), that restrict the use or occupancy of, or behavior within, individually owned lots or units.

UCIOA § 3-102 (c)

Unless otherwise permitted by the declaration or this Act, an association may adopt rules and regulations that affect the use of or behavior in units that may be used for residential purposes only to:

(1) prevent any use of a unit which violates the declaration;

(2) regulate any behavior in or occupancy of a unit which violates the declaration or adversely affects the use and enjoyment of other units or the common elements by other unit owners; or

(3) restrict the leasing of residential units to the extent those rules are reasonably designed to meet underwriting requirements of institutional lenders who regularly lend money secured by first mortgages or units in common interest communities or regularly purchase those mortgages. Otherwise, the association may not regulate any use of or behavior in units.

Weldy v. Northbrook Condominium Association, Inc.
Supreme Court of Connecticut
904 A.2d 188 (Conn. 2006)

ZARELLA, J. The sole issue in this certified appeal is whether a resolution adopted by the board of directors of a condominium association providing that leashes or restraints for household pets shall not exceed twenty feet in length constitutes an illegal amendment of the condominium declaration.... The plaintiffs [unit owners] ... brought an action to enjoin the defendants, Northbrook Condominium Association, Inc.... and the association's five member board of directors ... from enforcing the resolution. The trial court granted the defendants' motion for summary judgment.... [p]laintiffs appealed to the Appellate Court, which reversed] ... On appeal to this court, the defendants claim that the board did not act beyond the scope of its authority in adopting the resolution because it constituted a clarification of, rather than an amendment to, the pet restraint provision in the declaration and thus did not require approval by a two-thirds vote of the unit owners and mortgagees. We agree and, accordingly, reverse the judgment of the Appellate Court.

The opinion of the Appellate Court sets forth the following relevant facts....

...

"Article nine of the condominium's declaration governs 'use, purposes and restrictions' of the condominium property. [Article] 9(e) addresses pet ownership and provides in relevant part that all 'dogs, cats or household pets shall be restrained by leash or other comparable means and shall be accompanied by an owner at all times....' [Article] 9 (l) confers on the board 'the power to make such regulations as may be necessary to carry out the intent of [the] use restrictions....'

Pursuant to § 4(b)(5) of the condominium's bylaws, the board possesses the power to adopt and amend 'rules and regulations covering the details of the operation and use of the property, provided, however, that those rules and regulations contained in the [d]eclaration shall be amended in the manner provided for amending the [d]eclaration.'

Article eighteen of the declaration provides that the declaration may be amended only on the vote of two thirds of the unit owners and mortgagees of the condominium.

"On June 27, 2003, the board, by letter, informed the condominium's owners and residents of 'new regulations to the pet rules.' The board cited the previously quoted language from [article] 9(e) of the declaration and stated that the word 'leash' was not defined. It further noted 'instances where pets have caused injury to other pets' and the board's 'opinion [that] leashes that exceed twenty feet in length do not permit owners to control their dogs sufficiently to ensure the safety of other pets and/or unit owners.' According to the letter, the board, therefore, had adopted an 'additional clarification pertaining to pets.' The 'clarification' provided in relevant part that '[l]eashes or comparable restraints for dogs, cats or household pets shall not exceed [twenty] feet in length.'

"The plaintiffs own a nine and one-half year old black Labrador retriever. Prior to June 27, 2003, the plaintiffs played ball and Frisbee with and otherwise exercised their dog in a common area behind their unit. To do so, they used a leash that was seventy-five feet in length.

...

The Appellate Court ... conclud[ed] that the twenty foot limitation constituted an improper amendment to the condominium declaration in violation of General Statutes § 47-245(b) of the Common Interest Ownership Act; ... and in violation of the provision in the condominium declaration ... because it added "more particular restrictions" to the leash provision in the declaration defining the rights of condominium owners to have their pets in a common area.... We granted the defendants' petition for certification to appeal.[1] ...

On appeal, the defendants ... contend that the intent of the policy in article 9(e) of the declaration is to promote a safe and nonintimidating environment for unit owners and their guests,[2] and that a dog on an excessively long leash cannot be restrained properly in the physically restricted context of a condominium development. Accordingly, the leash restriction gives meaning to, and acts in concert with, the declaration provision. The plaintiffs respond that, because leashes are commonly sold in lengths of thirty to fifty feet, the board in effect illegally amended the declaration by prohibiting leashes more than twenty feet in length. The plaintiffs argue, therefore, that the leash restriction cannot be enforced. We agree with the defendants that the board acted within the scope of its authority in adopting the restriction.

...

"When a court is called upon to assess the validity of [an action taken] by a board of directors, it first determines whether the board acted within its scope of authority and, second, whether the [action] reflects reasoned or arbitrary and capricious decision making." *Beachwood Villas Condominium v. Poor*, 448 So. 2d 1143, 1144 (Fla.App.1984); cf. *Lamden v. La Jolla Shores Clubdominium Homeowners Assn.*, 21 Cal.4th 249, 256, 87 Cal.Rptr.2d 237, 980 P.2d 940 (1999). Because the plaintiffs do not contend that the leash restriction itself is unreasonable, the only issue before the court is whether the board exceeded the scope of its authority in adopting the restriction. We therefore turn to an examination of the relevant statutory provisions.

Condominium developments are of relatively recent origin and provide a unique type of shelter that affords some of the benefits of property ownership without the corresponding burdens.... The statutory scheme in Connecticut governing condominium developments is the Common Interest Ownership Act (act).[3] ... The act "is a comprehensive legislative scheme regulating all forms of common interest ownership that is largely modeled on the Uniform Common Interest Ownership Act."... See generally Unif. Common Interest Ownership Act of 1994, 7 U.L.A. 835 (2005). The act [General Statutes Ch. § 47-200 et seq.] addresses "the creation, organization and management of common interest communities and contemplates the voluntary participation of the owners. It entails the drafting and filing of a declaration describing the location and configuration of the real property, development rights, and restrictions on its use, occupancy and alienation; ... the enactment of bylaws; ... the establishment of a unit owners' association [to manage

---

1. The following issue was certified for review: "Did the Appellate Court properly limit the extent to which a condominium's board of directors is empowered to adopt rules and regulations?" ...

2. In an affidavit dated November 25, 2003, Steve Robifker, president of the board, stated that the intent of the pet policy in article 9(e) of the declaration "is to promote a safe and non-intimidating environment for unit owners and their guests," and that the board had voted unanimously on June 27, 2003, to adopt the leash restriction to clarify the declaration's pet policy after "multiple dog related incidents...."

3. The act was passed in 1983 "to remedy problems arising from unconscionable lease agreements in condominiums and other residential common interest communities created prior to 1984." *Celantano v. Oaks Condominium Assn.*, 265 Conn. 579, 597, 830 A.2d 164 (2003).

the condominium community]; ... and an executive board to act on ... behalf [of the association].... It anticipates group decision-making relating to the development of a budget, the maintenance and repair of the common elements, the placement of insurance, and the provision for common expenses and common liabilities.

Several provisions of the act are of particular significance in the present case. Except in certain designated situations, a declaration may be amended "only by vote or agreement of unit owners of units to which at least sixty-seven per cent of the votes in the association are allocated...." ... A condominium association also is empowered, subject to the declaration provisions, to "[a]dopt and amend bylaws and rules and regulations"; ... and to "[r]egulate the use ... of common elements...."... The condominium's board of directors is not permitted, however, to amend the declaration on behalf of the association....

With the foregoing statutory framework as a backdrop, we turn to an examination of the relevant condominium documents in order to determine whether the board was empowered to adopt the leash restriction for the purpose of clarifying the declaration. This issue presents a question of law that we review *de novo*....

. . .

The leash restriction that the board adopted on June 27, 2003,[4] specifically provides: "Leashes or comparable restraints for dogs, cats or household pets shall not exceed [twenty] feet in length. Pets must be materially attached to the owner in order to be restrained. It is the responsibility of every owner of a cat, dog, or other household pet to restrain that pet while in the [c]ommon [a]rea. Further, it is the specific responsibility of the owner of any pet with an anti-social personality to avoid a conflict with other residents or pets in the community."

Because the issue on appeal is one of first impression, we look for guidance to other jurisdictions that have considered the limits of a board's delegated authority to enact regulations governing a condominium community. With respect to the interpretation of declaration provisions, several jurisdictions have recognized that the declaration is the condominium association's "constitution." *Beachwood Villas Condominium v. Poor*, supra, 448 So. 2d at 1145; accord *Schaefer v. Eastman Community Assn.*, 150 N.H. 187, 191, 836 A.2d 752 (2003). "Generally, declarations and other governing documents contain broad statements of general policy with due notice that the board of directors is empowered to implement these policies and address day-to-day problems in the [association's] operation.... Thus, the declaration should not be so narrowly construed so as to eviscerate the association's intended role as the governing body of the community. Rather, a broad view of the powers delegated to the association is justified by the important role these communities play in maintaining property values and providing municipal-like services.... If unable to act, the common property may fall into disrepair. [2 Restatement (Third), Property, Servitudes §6.4, p. 90, comment (a) (2000)]....

"Because an association's power should be interpreted broadly, the association, through its appropriate governing body, is entitled to exercise all powers of the community except those reserved to the members. [Id., §6.16, p. 289]." ...

---

4. In a letter to unit owners and residents, the board announced that it had adopted the leash restriction for the following reasons: (1) the word "leash" was undefined in the declaration; (2) the board had the responsibility to protect the entire community, including people and pets, from other pets that might have antisocial personalities; (3) there had been several instances in which pets had caused injury to other pets; and (4) in the opinion of the board, leashes that exceeded twenty feet in length did not permit owners to control their dogs sufficiently to ensure the safety of other pets and unit owners.

This broad view of the powers delegated to the condominium's board of directors is consistent with the principle "inherent in the condominium concept ... that to promote the health, happiness, and peace of mind of the majority of the unit owners since they are living in such close proximity and using facilities in common, each unit owner must give up a certain degree of freedom of choice which he might otherwise enjoy in separate, privately owned property. Condominium unit owners comprise a little democratic sub society of necessity more restrictive as it pertains to [the] use of condominium property than may be existent outside the condominium organization." *Hidden Harbour Estates, Inc. v. Norman*, 309 So. 2d 180, 181–82 (Fla.App.1975).

Accordingly, the standard of review most commonly employed in reviewing a board's authority to adopt rules or regulations is that, "provided ... a board-enacted rule does not contravene either an express provision of the declaration or a right reasonably inferable therefrom, it will be found valid, within the scope of the board's authority. This test ... is fair and functional; it safeguards the rights of unit owners and preserves unfettered the concept of delegated board management." *Beachwood Villas Condominium v. Poor*, supra; cf. *Meadow Bridge Condominium Assn. v. Bosca*, 187 Mich.App. 280, 282, 466 N.W.2d 303 (1990) ("a rule or regulation is a tool to implement or manage existing structural law, while an amendment presumptively changes existing structural law" [internal quotation marks omitted]).

Applying these principles in the present case, we conclude that the twenty foot leash limitation is not more restrictive than the declaration but simply implements the declaration's expressed intent that household pets brought to the common areas of the property be restrained properly and controlled by their owners at all times. An excessively long leash would not achieve this objective within the limited confines of the walkways, parking lots, landscaped and recreational areas that typically comprise the common elements of a condominium development because a pet attached to a seventy-five foot leash would have the ability to stray far from its owner, especially if the owner's attention was diverted from the pet. This could endanger persons walking between the owner and the pet as well as persons and vehicles moving in a parking lot or accessway that must take evasive action to avoid a darting animal. Consequently, the leash restriction does not contravene an express provision of the declaration but is a means of implementing the policy embodied therein by increasing the likelihood that a pet will remain under its owner's control, thereby contributing to "a safe and non-intimidating environment for unit owners and their guests."

This conclusion finds support in other cases in which courts have determined that the board of directors acted within the scope of its authority in regulating an activity specifically addressed in the declaration or bylaws. See, e.g., *O'Buck v. Cottonwood Village Condominium Assn., Inc.*, 750 P.2d 813, 815–17 (Alaska 1988) (board acted within scope of authority in banning television antennas on buildings because declaration authorized board to adopt rules and regulations governing use of common areas, including roofs and walls of buildings, and to require action by owners to preserve uniform exterior building appearance); *Meadow Bridge Condominium Assn. v. Bosca*, supra (board empowered to adopt regulation prospectively prohibiting new dogs because bylaws provided that no animals could be maintained by owner without specific approval by association, and bylaws authorized association "to adopt such additional rules and regulations with respect to animals as it may deem proper" [internal quotation marks omitted]).

Correspondingly, the present case is distinguishable from cases in which courts have concluded that the board was not empowered to act because the regulation in question conflicted with an express provision in the declaration. See, e.g., *In re 560 Ocean Club, L.P.*,

133 B.R. 310, 317–18 (Bankr.D.N.J.1991) (board not authorized to adopt regulation requiring minimum of ninety days during summer months and thirty days at other times for short-term leases because declaration merely granted board power to approve or disapprove leases, not to restrict their duration); *Westbridge Condominium Assn., Inc. v. Lawrence,* 554 A.2d 1163, 1164, 1167 (D.C.1989) (board exceeded scope of authority in imposing move-in fee on unit owner because declaration provided only one method for assessing common elements expenses, consisting of pro rata allocation of costs among all unit owners, thereby limiting board's power to impose move-in fee under alternative method of assessment); *Mohnani v. La Cancha Condominium Assn., Inc.,* 590 So. 2d 36, 38 (Fla.App.1991) (board not empowered to adopt regulation that owner could not lease unit for two years following acquisition because regulation contravened declaration provision and rights reasonably inferable therefrom that owners could lease units upon board approval within thirty days following board's receipt of written notice from owner of intent to lease); *Thanasoulis v. Winston Towers 200 Assn., Inc.,* 110 N.J. 650, 659–60, 542 A.2d 900 (1988) (board acted beyond scope of authority in adopting rule charging nonresident owners higher monthly parking fees than resident owners because master deed provided that right of unit owner to use common elements, including parking spaces, was indivisible from owner's interest in condominium itself, and rule thus constituted "change [in] a unit" within meaning of relevant statute by severing owner's property right to parking space [internal quotation marks omitted]); *Ronaldson v. Countryside Manor Condominium Board of Managers,* 189 App.Div.2d 808, 808–809, 592 N.Y.S.2d 459 (board acted outside scope of authority in adopting regulation permitting unit owners to build six foot fences to enclose property at rear of respective units because declaration provided that common elements included entire property, including enclosed areas), appeal dismissed, 82 N.Y.2d 706, 619 N.E.2d 663, 601 N.Y.S.2d 585 (1993); *Sully Station II Community Assn., Inc. v. Dye,* 259 Va. 282, 285, 289, 525 S.E.2d 555 (2000) (board exceeded authority in adopting parking policy under which two reserved parking spaces in common area were assigned to owners of nongaraged units because policy constituted licensing of portion of common area, and declaration granted association right to license those parking spaces to members only on uniform, nonpreferential basis).

The plaintiffs nonetheless argue that the leash restriction is inconsistent with the relevant declaration provision because the twenty foot limitation redefines and changes the everyday meaning of the word "leash," a term applied to restraints sold commercially in lengths of thirty, fifty and even seventy-five feet. We disagree.

Webster's Third New International Dictionary defines the word "leash" as "a thong, cord or chain attached to an animal's collar ... and held in the hand for the purpose of leading, checking, or controlling the ... animal or fastened to an object to secure or tether it...." The twenty foot leash restriction does not add to or change the general provision of the declaration that pets must be controlled in the common areas of the property, nor does it redefine the everyday meaning of the word "leash." It merely ensures that a leash will be more likely to achieve its purpose in a high density residential setting because it will prevent a pet from straying more than twenty feet from its owner. See *Meadow Bridge Condominium Assn. v. Bosca,* supra (regulation prospectively prohibiting new dogs on condominium property did not constitute amendment because it was "not inconsistent with the original bylaw and [did] nothing to change the general rule"). The twenty foot leash restriction is therefore consistent with the declaration.

The plaintiffs also argue that the leash restriction deprives unit owners of a right reasonably inferred from the language of the declaration to restrain their pets on a longer leash. See, e.g., *Beachwood Villas Condominium v. Poor,* supra (board rule invalid if in contravention of right reasonably inferable from provision of declaration). The plaintiffs argue that the principle that communal living requires individuals to give "fair consideration … to the rights and privileges of all owners and occupants" of the community; *Dulaney Towers Maintenance Corp. v. O'Brey*, 46 Md.App. 464, 466, 418 A.2d 1233 (1980); does not apply in this case because they exercise their dog in a secluded area of the property and thus do not interfere with other persons or animals, even though the leash they use is seventy-five feet in length. This claim has no merit.

We first note the obvious fact that the declaration provision is restrictive in nature because it seeks to protect unit owners from unnecessary inconvenience and annoyance by unrestrained pets through the imposition of a physical restraint *and* by requiring that pets be accompanied by their owners at all times. We also recognize that leashes are sold in varying lengths. The fact that the plaintiffs' dog does not interfere with others has no bearing, however, on whether a reasonable inference may be drawn from the declaration that unit owners have a right to use a leash of virtually any length when permitting their pets to walk, run or otherwise traverse across and exercise within the common areas of the property. At some point, depending on the circumstances, a leash beyond a certain length ceases to function as an effective restraint. Similarly, to the extent that the declaration mandates that a pet be "accompanied" by its owner, a pet that has wandered seventy-five feet from its owner, even if attached to a very long leash, can hardly be said, in most situations, to be "accompanied by" and under the control of the owner. In the present case, the board determined that, in light of the physical limitations of the condominium setting in question, a leash of more than twenty feet could not perform as intended. Accordingly, the plaintiffs' claim must fail because the condominium declaration, which seeks to impose a measure of control over pets on the property, does not support an inference that a leash of any length can fulfill its anticipated purpose merely because one end of the leash is attached to the collar of a pet and the other is held by the owner.

Two cases on which the plaintiffs rely, namely, *In re 560 Ocean Club, L.P.,* and *Mohnani,* are inapposite. In the former case, the court determined that the board of directors acted beyond the scope of its authority when it imposed a requirement that all short-term leases be at least ninety days during the summer months and thirty days during other times because the declaration did not address restrictions on the duration of leases but merely granted the board authority to approve or disapprove the leases. *In re 560 Ocean Club, L.P.* In the latter case, the court concluded that the board exceeded its authority in adopting a regulation that owners could not lease their units for a period of two years from the date on which ownership was acquired because the regulation was inconsistent with the declaration and rights reasonably inferable therefrom.… The declaration specified that owners could lease their units following written notice to the board of their intent to do so, and that the board was required within thirty days to approve the transaction or to furnish a lessee approved by the association, thus conceivably allowing an owner to lease the unit within thirty days of acquiring ownership. These cases are distinguishable because the regulations adopted by the respective boards clearly conflicted with the governing declaration provisions. That is not the situation in the present case for all of the reasons that we previously have discussed. We therefore conclude that the board acted within the scope of its authority in adopting the resolution restricting the length of leashes to no more than twenty feet pursuant to article 9 (*l*) of the condominium declaration.

The judgment of the Appellate Court is reversed and the case is remanded to that court with direction to affirm the judgment of the trial court.

Notes & Questions

1. The court in *Weldy*, like the court in *Hidden Harbour*, emphasizes the special nature of condominium developments, particularly that the residents live in close proximity and use facilities in common. Does this suggest that a board in a different kind of development, one with single-family homes on large lots, for example, would not have the power to require that dogs be kept on short leashes while in the common areas? Or that the board could not ban alcohol use in a club house that was located at some distance from the residences?

2. Pet restrictions generate a substantial amount of controversy in common interest communities. This case involved a rule tightening a restriction contained in the declaration. Other cases you will encounter later in this book involve the validity of restrictions, including outright bans, contained in the original declaration or adopted as an amendment by the owners. Rules adopted by the board may be subjected to more judicial scrutiny for "reasonableness" than provisions in the original declaration, which are valid unless they are illegal, unconstitutional, or violate public policy according to Restatement (Third) § 3.01, or unless they are "unreasonable" under California's Davis-Stirling Act. Do you see why different standards of validity are applied? What standard would be appropriate for amendments adopted by more than half, but fewer than all, of the owners?

3. Both Restatement (Third) § 6.7 and UCIOA 3-102 place strict limitations on the ability of the association to adopt rules that restrict the use or occupancy of individual units. How do those provisions limit the ability of the association to adopt rules (as opposed to amendments to the declaration) that ban or limit pet ownership?

Problems

1. The Board of a 20-unit condominium in a 4-story structure adopts a rule banning smoking in all parts of the building including individual units. The new rule is supported by 80% of the unit owners. Is the rule valid? Would it make any difference if the rule was adopted in a townhouse development? In a single-family detached development with 15-foot minimum side yard setbacks?

2. The Board adopts a rule banning occupancy of any unit by a registered sex offender. Is the rule valid?

C. Representing the Community

1. Advocating for the Community

Homeowner associations often take an active role in local government planning processes by appearing at public hearings on zoning and planning matters, lobbying city council members and legislators, and the like, whenever they think their property values or quality of life will be affected by decisions to permit new development, create public parks or other facilities, etc. Although some may be troubled by this activity, it is seldom challenged in legal proceedings. What does get challenged is the expenditure of community funds for these purposes.

Spitser v. Kentwood Home Guardians

Court of Appeals of California
100 Cal.Rptr. 798 (Cal. Ct. App. 1972)

DUNN, A.J. On 28 October 70 plaintiffs, husband and wife, filed an action for declaratory and injunctive relief against defendant, a non-profit corporation.... [Both parties filed motions for summary judgment].... Defendant's motion was denied and plaintiffs' motion was granted.... Defendant has appealed from that judgment.

The parties are agreed on all facts. The declarations supporting the motions show that in September 1940 an oil company became the owner of real property in the Westchester area of the City of Los Angeles. It subdivided the property, thereafter known as "Kentwood," and developed various tracts in it for residential purposes. Each tract was made subject to a recorded Declaration of Protective Restrictions. In March 1943 the oil company formed defendant, Kentwood Home Guardians, as a non-profit corporation, its articles of incorporation reciting that its primary purpose was to enforce the Declarations. On 4 March 70 plaintiffs became owners of a residence in one tract. On 7 April 70 defendant filed a complaint against the City of Los Angeles seeking an injunction to abate noise originating from the city's operation of the nearby Los Angeles International Airport. To finance this lawsuit defendant assessed Kentwood property owners, assessing plaintiffs a total of $8.40. The propriety of that assessment is here the point of contention.

Defendant/appellant takes the position that the Declaration of Protective Restrictions authorized its action and the assessment. Plaintiffs/respondents concede that defendant may make assessments, but not to finance such a lawsuit. Respondents do not dispute that the restrictions on the subdivided land contained in the recorded Declarations are binding upon them.... It is the extent of those restrictions which they questioned.

The Declarations state that the restrictions are imposed as part of a general plan of improvement, development, building, occupation and maintenance; the Declarations endow Kentwood Home Guardians with "the power to enforce the conditions, restrictions, reservations and charges hereinafter set forth." Article III, paragraph 5, states: "No noxious or offensive trade or activity shall be carried on upon said property or any part thereof, nor shall anything be done or maintained thereon which may be or become an annoyance or nuisance to the neighborhood." Article IX authorizes defendant to make an annual assessment, not to exceed 20 cents per front foot upon each lot, and to spend the money collected "for the purposes hereinafter specified or purposes incidental thereto," any unpaid and delinquent assessment becoming an enforceable lien on such lot.

Paragraph 8 of Article IX requires defendant to apply sums collected "toward the payment of the cost of any or all of the following.... (E) Expenses, if any, incident to the enforcement of the restrictions, conditions, charges and agreements contained in this Declaration.... Defendant/appellant contends the expense of litigation was properly incurred under the authorization of Article III, paragraph 5. To the contrary, plaintiffs/respondents argue the language of the article demonstrates that legal action is authorized to abate only a nuisance generated upon Kentwood, itself, and that no authority is given defendant to levy an assessment whose purpose is to defray the expense of enjoining nuisance originating off the premises. Respondents emphasize the language of Article III, paragraph 5, as follows: "No noxious or offensive trade or activity shall be carried on upon said property, or any part thereof, nor shall anything be done or maintained *thereon* which may be or become an annoyance or nuisance to the neighborhood." (Emphasis respondents'.)

In its briefs, appellant asserts that the "obvious purposes of the declaration were to protect ... Kentwood for the welfare of all residents ... and, to safeguard the community from nuisance, trespass, or other activity constituting a source of annoyance to the residents," also contending that: "Appellant ... may abate a nuisance to residents of Kentwood *whether the source* of the nuisance or the perpetrator of same *is within or without* Kentwood." (Emphasis added.) The trial court held otherwise. Its judgment declared, in part: "The Declaration of Protective Restrictions permits legal action to be taken by defendant only against noise sources which are located within the boundaries of Kentwood."

We agree with the trial court. Article III of the Declaration, entitled "Uses of Property," bans the use of Kentwood lots in a manner annoying to, or so as to be a nuisance to, the neighborhood. Article IX, entitled "Provisions for Upkeep," allows use of assessment funds to enforce these and other restrictions upon the use of the property. Appellant is not thereby authorized or required to protect Kentwood from annoyances or nuisance emanating from outside areas; appellant is not made an aegis to shield Kentwood from the outside world. It may assist a lot owner to protect the value of his investment if it is endangered by the conduct of other lot occupiers or owners on their own lots. The Declaration unambiguously reflects this intent.

. . .

Appellant next argues that airplanes flying overhead create noise within the boundaries of Kentwood, itself, which noise therefore constitutes an abatable nuisance.... This argument may be valid but it does not answer the question: is this an activity "upon said property" by a person against whom appellant is authorized to proceed under the Declaration of Protective Restrictions? The fact Kentwood lot owners, individually or collectively, may have their rights invaded, with a corresponding right of access to the courts, does not endow appellant with the right to sue airport authorities or airlines on their behalf, and to charge lot owners for the costs of suit. The language of the Declaration specifies that "No noxious or offensive trade or activity shall be carried on upon the property...." From this and the other language we believe it clear that appellant may not assess lot owners with the costs of suit brought against third parties merely because noises arise from overhead. It would be incongruous to believe the parties intended that airplane noises originating next door could not be abated by appellant on their behalf but that it could file a suit against third parties, seeking to abate noises of airplanes because they were overhead and not next door.

Affirmed.

Owens v. Tiber Island Condo. Ass'n

District of Columbia Court of Appeals
373 A.2d 890 (D.C. Ct. App. 1977)

KELLY, J. Appellee Tiber Island Condominium, which is located between 4th and 6th and M and N Streets, S.W., is organized under the District of Columbia's Horizontal Property Act. D.C. Code 1973, §5-901 *et seq.* Appellants James and Kathleen Owens own a condominium unit in Tiber Island.... In a suit between the parties, the trial court granted summary judgment for Tiber Island on the Owens' original claim and on its own counterclaim. In determining whether these rulings were proper, the key issue is whether Tiber Island's Board of Directors was authorized to file a suit against the Washington Metropolitan Area Transit Authority (WMATA) protesting construction of a subway in the area where the condominium is located.

The dispute began on September 10, 1971, when WMATA circulated a notice of public hearing on the construction of a subway tunnel and a Waterfront Metro Station to be located under M Street, S.W., between 3rd and 6th Streets. Feeling that their lives and property values might be adversely affected by the subway construction, residents of Tiber Island sought specific information about construction sites, noise levels, hours and length of construction, possible acquisition of property, ground vibration, location of vent shafts, effects on utilities and the like. The Board did not obtain the desired information and after an unsatisfactory meeting with WMATA representatives on March 19, 1973, requested its counsel, Mr. Thomas Truitt, to assess its legal options. At the next Board meeting on March 26, 1974, Mr. Truitt reported that in his opinion WMATA was unlikely to cooperate or negotiate with Tiber Island unless it was clear that the condominium would, if necessary, resort to court action. It was decided that the Board had the authority to bring a suit against WMATA and a resolution authorizing retention of legal counsel to institute legal proceedings if a voluntary settlement could not be reached was adopted.

Subsequent negotiations were unsuccessful and on June 24, 1974, Tiber Island filed suit in the District Court for the District of Columbia seeking an injunction against construction, scheduled to begin June 28, until WMATA had complied with the requirements of D.C. Code 1973, § 1-1431 *et seq.* On June 29, the Owens and two other co-owners threatened to intervene in the law suit if Tiber Island did not withdraw as a named plaintiff. Before a motion to intervene could be filed, however, WMATA and Tiber Island reached a settlement agreement.

On July 5, 1974, the Board notified the condominium owners of a special meeting to be held July 23, 1974, for the purpose of voting on a revised budget for 1974, including an assessment for legal fees incurred in reaching the agreement with WMATA. At the meeting thirty-six owners were there in person and twenty-one by proxy. The Owens were present and registered their protest of the Board's actions in bringing the suit as being unlawful *per se.* Nevertheless, the owners approved a resolution revising the budget and authorizing the Board to assess the members a total of $7,300 to fund the revision. The additional assessment was to be paid in five monthly installments. The Owens' pro rata share was $163.70.

The Owens refused to pay the subsequent assessment and filed the present action, alleging that the Board had unlawfully instituted the civil action against WMATA, had illegally assessed the Owens for its maintenance, and had breached its fiduciary duty to the condominium owners. Tiber Island counterclaimed for the amount of the assessment. Tiber Island's subsequent motions for summary judgment on both claims were granted and the Owens appeal....

II.

The trial court granted summary judgment in favor of Tiber Island on the Owens' claim and on its counterclaim.[2] ... There are no factual issues in dispute here....

It is undisputed that (1) that the Board on March 26, 1974, unanimously adopted a resolution authorizing a suit against WMATA; (2) that on July 23, the council of co-owners, with appellants present, and in accordance with the by-laws, approved a revised budget which included the assessment to pay for the legal expenses incurred in the suit against WMATA; and (3) that the appellants were assessed their pro rata share and have refused

---

2. The motion for summary judgment on the counterclaim was granted on January 10, 1975. The Owens appealed this ruling and the appeal was dismissed by this court as an interlocutory, and therefore, non-appealable order under D.C. Code 1973, § 11-721.

to pay it. The question is, therefore, whether Tiber Island's Board had the authority, either *ab initio* under the Horizontal Property Act and its by-laws or by subsequent ratification by the council of co-owners, to sue WMATA on behalf of the condominium.

The applicable section of the Horizontal Property Act is D.C. Code 1973, § 5-924(a), which provides:

> Without limiting the right of any co-owner, actions may be brought on behalf of two or more of the unit owners, as their respective interests may appear, by the manager, or board of directors, or of administration with respect to any cause of action relating to the common elements or more than one unit.

The issue then is whether the law suit relates to the common elements or more than one unit of the condominium. In our opinion it does both.

D.C. Code 1973, § 5-902(f) defines "general common elements" and the aspects of the subway construction which concerned the members of Tiber Island fit into at least one category of the definition, *i.e.*, D.C. Code 1973, § 5-902(f)(7), which reads:

> all other elements of the building rationally of common use or necessary to its existence, upkeep, and safety.

The settlement agreement with WMATA included regulation of construction hours and sites, noise levels, protective barricades, location of dome relief vents and mucking holes, general cleanliness of the area, noise and vibration from the trains once the subway was in operation. All of these matters are rationally necessary to the condominium's existence, upkeep, and safety. Furthermore, the subway construction affected more than one of Tiber Island's units in terms of the environment, property values, and general aesthetic considerations.

The Board was also authorized by the by-laws to

> enforce by legal means the provisions of the Declaration of Condominium, these by-laws and the regulations for the use of the Condominium adopted by it, and to bring any proceeding authorized to be instituted on behalf of the Council of Co-Owners in the Horizontal Property Act.

> ...

It is clear, therefore, that the Board was authorized both under D.C. Code 1973, § 5-924(a) and its own by-laws to bring the suit against WMATA on behalf of the condominium.

III.

The Owens also contend that in the absence of any agreement to the contrary, legal fees of the WMATA suit should be borne by the co-owners named in the suit as plaintiffs and by Tiber Island, thereby reducing Tiber Island's share to one-ninth of the total fee. During the meeting of July 23, the Owens raised this same point and it was explained to them that counsel was retained only by the condominium. The other eight were invited to become named plaintiffs solely to make a better presentation of the case. In any event, the co-owners agreed by the required vote to pay the legal fees incurred and in our opinion this effectively disposes of the matter.

The Owens argue that their due process rights were violated by the assessment schedule basing each co-owner's share on his percentage of ownership. We fail to see any state action in the establishment of the assessment schedule by the condominium and since the Owens voluntarily agreed to the schedule when they bought a unit, any attempt to change it now should be by an attempt to alter the declaration and by-laws by the processes provided for in the by-laws.

No state action

Accordingly, the judgments on appeal are Affirmed.

Notes & Questions

1. Do the different results in *Spitser* and *Owens* stem from a difference in the functions and powers of the two communities identified in the governing documents and statutes? In the absence of specific provisions in the governing documents or statutes authorizing or prohibiting an association from using community funds to pay for lawsuits like those in *Spitser* and *Owens*, what should the default rules be? Should they differentiate between issues that affect property values and others?

2. Although not posed as an advocacy question, a similar question arose in *Parker v. Figure "8" Beach Homeowners' Ass'n, Inc.*, discussed earlier in this chapter. Would the court's rationale there for upholding the association's power to spend money to dredge the channel at a point removed from the development have supported a different result in *Spitser*?

3. Does an association open itself up to liability by opposing zoning changes needed by other projects? *Anchorage Joint Venture v. Anchorage Condo. Ass'n*, 670 P.2d 1249 (Colo. Ct. App. 1983), held that the association had a constitutionally protected right to seek to overturn the grant of variances in a judicial proceeding and so was not liable to the developer for damages caused by delay in the project.

2. Standing to Sue on Behalf of the Community Members

Rest. (3d) § 6.11 Association's Standing To Sue And Defend

Except as limited by statute or the governing documents, the association has the power to institute, defend, or intervene in litigation or administrative proceedings in its own name, on behalf of itself, or on behalf of member property owners in a common-interest community on matters affecting the community.

a. Historical note and rationale. In early cases involving construction-defect litigation in condominiums, developers were able to persuade courts in Florida that associations lacked standing to pursue the litigation because the common elements were owned by the members as tenants in common, rather than by the association. Some other states followed. When the association lacks standing, the owners are forced to sue individually or in a class action, losing the benefits that would otherwise be available from collective action through their association. The Florida legislature and courts subsequently changed course, and most recent legislation and decisions have recognized the association's standing to sue on its own behalf and on behalf of its members if either meets the normal standing requirement.

If either the members on behalf of whom the association sues or the association meets normal standing requirements, the question whether the association has the right to bring a suit on behalf of the members is an internal question, which can be raised only by a member of the association. The question is whether the association has breached a duty owed to members under § 6.13 by exceeding the authority granted to it by the governing documents, by violating the duty to treat members fairly, or otherwise.

The rule stated in this section is modeled on § 3-102(a)(4) of the Uniform Common Interest Ownership Act. It makes clear that an association may sue or defend suits even though the suit involves only property in which the association has no ownership interest. In suits where no common property is involved, the association functions much like the plaintiff in class-action litigation, and questions about the rights and duties between the association and the members with respect to the suit will normally be determined by the principles used in class-action litigation.

As this excerpt from the Restatement indicates, standing questions are frequently raised when the association sues the developer for construction defects. As those suits frequently arise just after the transition from developer control of the association, we take them up in Chapter 11.

Notes & Questions

1. "NIMBY" (*not in my backyard*) *suits.* Often, homeowners will fight the placement of undesirable but necessary facilities such as landfills, sanitariums, prisons, and the like in their neighborhoods because of their adverse effects on property values and aesthetics. Often, community associations in close proximity to the proposed facilities will cooperate on litigation and lobbying strategies to oppose construction. See, *e.g., Gedney Ass'n v. State of New York Dept. of Mental Hygiene*, 112 Misc. 2d 209, 446 N.Y.S.2d 876 (1982) (action filed to challenge the decision to construct residential facilities for mentally disabled persons; association standing upheld); *Connor v. Cuomo*, 161 Misc. 2d 889, 614 N.Y.S.2d 1011 (1994) (community associations brought action seeking to enjoin construction of community residence for homeless mentally ill individuals).

2. *Limitations on community association standing.* Can a homeowner's association sue local and state authorities for alleged violations of state and federal environmental statutes? See, *Ringbolt Farms Homeowners Ass'n v. Town of Hull*, 714 F. Supp. 1246 (D. Mass. 1989). Should there be a limit on the type of claims a community association can bring? Should the proximity of the alleged harm and its relationship to property values in the community be relevant?

3. *Combating Racial Discrimination.* Common interest communities may have standing to bring claims alleging that real estate companies engage in discrimination in the sale and rental of real estate through "racial steering." *See Sherman Park Com'ty Ass'n v. Wauwatosa Realty Co.*, 486 F. Supp. 838 (E.D. Wis. 1980) (community association and individuals who acted as "testers" posing as home seekers for the purpose of comparing the treatment afforded to persons of different races had standing to sue); and *see generally, Gladstone Realtors v. Village of Bellwood*, 441 U.S. 91 (1979) (municipal corporation had standing to sue on "racial steering" case).

4. *Tax assessments and "common interest."* The court in *In Re Objections & Defenses to Real Property Taxes*, 410 N.W.2d 321 (Minn. 1987), held that a condominium association had standing to bring an action challenging tax assessments of all units which comprised the condominium because the Minnesota condominium statute provides standing to an association which asserts a claim on behalf of two or more unit owners. Moreover, the court looked to the tax statute, which authorized actions to determine the validity of a tax on real property by any person having an estate, right, title, or interest in or lien upon such property. Since the association had a statutorily created lien on every unit for payment of future assessments, the court concluded that the association had the authority to challenge the tax assessments as a lienor. In contrast, the court in *Bonavista Condo. Ass'n v. Bystrom*, 520 So. 2d 84 (Fla. Dist. Ct. App. 1988), denied a condominium asso-

ciation standing to challenge *ad valorem* assessments on individual units and held that unit owner dissatisfaction with their taxes was not a "common interest" which is a necessary element under the state's statutes regarding association standing.

5. *Necessity of joinder.* Where a state statute expressly provides for community association standing to sue as the real party in interest, joinder of the unit owners is not typically needed. See, *e.g., Orange Grove Terrace Owner's Ass'n v. Bryant Properties, Inc.,* 176 Cal. App. 3d 1217, 222 Cal. Rptr. 523 (1986), where the court refused to distinguish between the community association and the unit owners since the association was a real party in interest on behalf of everyone. When might joinder of unit owners be required?

6. *Capacity to sue versus real party in interest.* In *Equitable Life Assur. Soc. v. Tinsley Mill Village,* 249 Ga. 769, 294 S.E.2d 495 (1982), the Georgia Supreme Court distinguished between the association's capacity to sue as provided by statute and the necessity of being the real party in interest for certain actions. Only the persons who own, lease, or have a legal interest in the affected property are the real parties in interest. In this case, the court found that only the real parties in interest could maintain an action for damages and an injunction in a nuisance action concerning upstream development activities. When would an association be a real party in interest? Can an association, like condominium association, that owns no real property be a real party in interest?

7. *Standing and zoning board decisions.* Just as standing is required to bring a civil action, it is also required to seek judicial review of zoning board decisions.

In *Douglaston Civic Ass'n. v. Galvin,* 36 N.Y.2d 1, 362 N.Y.S.2d 830 (1974), a property owner's association had standing to assert the rights of its members where their units may be affected by rezoning, variance, exception, or other determinations of the zoning board. The court emphasized that the relationship between zoning board decisions and public health and welfare justified the association's standing in the matter. The court also examined practical factors which favored an association's representative capacity, including: its capacity to assume an adversary position; the size and composition of the community it seeks to protect; the potential adverse effect of the zoning decision to the entire group; and the availability of full participating membership by the property owners in the affected neighborhood. In *Tuxedo Conservation & Taxpayers Ass'n. v. Town Board of Tuxedo,* 408 N.Y.S.2d 668, *aff'd* 418 N.Y.S.2d 638 (1979), a property owner's association was granted standing to challenge a special permit for a 3,900-unit development under the same criteria set forth in *Douglaston.* The *Tuxedo* court also held that there was no need to prove actual harm as a prerequisite to challenge the zoning decision. It was sufficient that the challenged permit might adversely affect the members of the association.

In contrast, the court in *Chabau v. Dade County,* 385 So. 2d 129 (Fla. Dist. Ct. App. 1980), declined to follow *Douglaston* and *Tuxedo,* and it held that a community association must suffer some injury itself to have standing in a suit challenging zoning board decisions. Other jurisdictions may limit the standing of community associations to instances in which the association actually owns real property which is adversely affected by the zoning board decision. See, *e.g.,* 8 A.L.R. 4th 1087; *Lindenwood Improv. Ass'n v. Lawrence,* 278 S.W.2d 30 (Mo. App. 1995) (plaintiff association is not an "aggrieved person" within the meaning of the local statute).

Problems

1. Dr. Joe B. Ray filed an application to rezone land from residential to business so he can open medical offices on the premises. After investigating, the zoning administrator

recommended that the application be denied and sent it on to the planning commission. The planning commission, after hearing evidence and arguments, voted to disapprove the application. The commission then advised Ray of his right to appeal.

One month later the commission reconsidered the petition and granted Ray's rezoning request. The reconsideration violated the commission's bylaws, which state that "an application that has been denied will not be reconsidered for a period of six months and then only if the applicant has furnished proof that there has been substantial change in circumstances surrounding the application to warrant reconsideration."

The Lynnwood Property Owners Association, located nearby is unhappy about the zoning change. Does it have standing to challenge the validity of the commission's actions? See *Lynnwood Property Owners Ass'n v. Lands Described in Complaint*, 359 So. 2d 357 (Ala. 1978) (yes, Association was deprived of procedural due process when the commission failed to follow its own rules).

2. The Greenwood Association's board of directors is concerned because ABC Co. proposes to build a landfill on property next to the community. The board determines to appear before the zoning authorities in opposition and budgets association funds for a zoning attorney. Mr. Jones, an association member, objects because he is a stockholder in ABC Co. and claims the association should not use "his" funds to oppose him. May the board properly become involved?

D. Other Functions & Powers of Common Interest Communities

Raising funds to finance community functions, administering design controls, and enforcing the community's covenants and rules are important common interest community functions and entail many community powers, but they are covered in separate chapters. So, too, is the very important power to amend the governing documents of the community.

Chapter 4

Constitutional & Public Policy Constraints on Common Interest Communities

Most common interest communities are created on privately owned land, by private actors, using private law devices: servitudes and associations (which may be incorporated, unincorporated, or trusts). Even though they are often created at the insistence of local governmental bodies interested in shifting the cost of providing municipal services to the homeowners, common interest communities are almost never treated as state actors subject to the constitutional constraints placed on public governments. One significant consequence is that enforcement of association restrictions and rules does not subject members to § 1983 liability[R] for depriving anyone of "rights, privileges, or immunities secured by the Constitution or laws." Another is that arguments that voting rights within the association should be based on one person one vote, or that tenants should be allowed to vote, are almost never raised and, if they were, would be unlikely to gain traction.[S]

Shelley v. Kraemer, 334 U.S. 1 (1948), held that state courts could not enforce privately created racially restrictive covenants on the ground that to do so would constitute state action that denied the targeted group equal protection of the law. *Shelley* could have been extended to subject court enforcement of all servitudes, and other contracts, to equal protection constraints, but it has had little application outside the context of racial and religious restrictive covenants, where, of course, it is still good law.

Free speech claims have given rise to much of the litigation over the question whether common interest communities are bound by constitutional norms. In the two cases that follow, we look first at a claim that the First Amendment to the U.S. Constitution applies and then, second, at a claim that New Jersey's Constitution's free speech provision applies.

R. "§ 1983 liability" refers to liability under 42 U.S.C. § 1983, which provides in relevant part: "Every person who, under color of any statute, ordinance, regulation, custom, or usage of any State or Territory or the District of Columbia, subjects or causes to be subjected, any citizen of the United States or other person within the jurisdiction thereof to the deprivation of any rights, privileges, or immunities secured by the Constitution and laws, shall be liable to the party injured in an action at law, suit in equity, or other proper proceeding for redress."

S. Even if common interest communities were state actors, they would not necessarily be subject to the one person one-vote rule. See *Salyer Land* Co. v. *Tulare Lake Basin Water Storage*, 410 U.S. 719 (1973) (limiting voters to land owners and allocating number of votes based on assessed valuation of land in water storage district elections did not violate Equal Protection Clause).

A. Constitutional Constraints

1. Rights of Members within the Community

City of Ladue v. Gilleo

Supreme Court of the United States

512 U.S. 43 (1994)

STEVENS, J. An ordinance of the City of Ladue prohibits homeowners from displaying any signs on their property except "residence identification" signs, "for sale" signs, and signs warning of safety hazards. The ordinance permits commercial establishments, churches, and nonprofit organizations to erect certain signs that are not allowed at residences. The question presented is whether the ordinance violates a Ladue resident's right to free speech.[1]

I

Respondent Margaret P. Gilleo owns one of the 57 single-family homes in the Willow Hill subdivision of Ladue.[2] On December 8, 1990, she placed on her front lawn a 24- by 36-inch sign printed with the words "Say No to War in the Persian Gulf, Call Congress Now." After that sign disappeared, Gilleo put up another but it was knocked to the ground. When Gilleo reported these incidents to the police, they advised her that such signs were prohibited in Ladue. The City Council denied her petition for a variance.[3] Gilleo then filed this action under 42 U.S.C. § 1983 against the City, the Mayor, and members of the City Council, alleging that Ladue's sign ordinance violated her First Amendment right of free speech.

The District Court issued a preliminary injunction against enforcement of the ordinance.... Gilleo then placed an 8.5- by 11-inch sign in the second story window of her home stating, "For Peace in the Gulf." The Ladue City Council responded to the injunction by repealing its ordinance and enacting a replacement.[4] Like its predecessor, the new ordinance contains a general prohibition of "signs" and defines that term broadly.[5] The

---

1. The First Amendment provides: "Congress shall make no law ... abridging the freedom of speech, or of the press ..." The Fourteenth Amendment makes this limitation applicable to the States, see *Gitlow v. New York*, 268 U.S. 652 (1925), and to their political subdivisions, see Lovell v. Griffin, 303 U.S. 444 (1938).

2. Ladue is a suburb of St. Louis, Missouri. It has a population of almost 9,000, and an area of about 8.5 square miles, of which only 3% is zoned for commercial or industrial use.

3. The ordinance then in effect gave the Council the authority to "permit a variation in the strict application of the provisions and requirements of this chapter ... where the public interest will be best served by permitting such variation." ...

4. The new ordinance eliminates the provision allowing for variances and contains a grandfather clause exempting signs already lawfully in place.

5. Section 35-2 of the ordinance declares that "No sign shall be erected [or] maintained" in the City except in conformity with the ordinance; § 35-3 authorizes the City to remove nonconforming signs.... Section 35-1 defines "sign" as:

> A name, word, letter, writing, identification, description, or illustration which is erected, placed upon, affixed to, painted or represented upon a building or structure, or any part thereof, or any manner upon a parcel of land or lot, and which publicizes an object, product, place, activity, opinion, person, institution, organization or place of business, or which is used to advertise or promote the interests of any person. The word 'sign' shall also include 'banners', 'pennants', 'insignia', 'bulletins boards', 'ground signs', 'billboard', 'poster billboards', 'illuminated signs', 'projecting signs', 'temporary signs', 'marquees', 'roof signs', 'yard signs', 'electric signs', 'wall signs', and 'window signs', wherever placed out of doors in view of the general public or wherever placed indoors as a window sign....

ordinance prohibits all signs except those that fall within one of ten exemptions. Thus, "residential identification signs" no larger than one square foot are allowed, as are signs advertising "that the property is for sale, lease or exchange" and identifying the owner or agent.... Also exempted are signs "for churches, religious institutions, and schools," "commercial signs in commercially or industrial zoned districts," and on-site signs advertising "gasoline filling stations."[6] Unlike its predecessor, the new ordinance contains a lengthy "Declaration of Findings, Policies, Interests, and Purposes," part of which recites that the

> proliferation of an unlimited number of signs in private, residential, commercial, industrial, and public areas of the City of Ladue would create ugliness, visual blight and clutter, tarnish the natural beauty of the landscape as well as the residential and commercial architecture, impair property values, substantially impinge upon the privacy and special ambience of the community, and may cause safety and traffic hazards to motorists, pedestrians, and children[.]

Gilleo amended her complaint to challenge the new ordinance, which explicitly prohibits window signs like hers. The District Court held the ordinance unconstitutional, and the Court of Appeals affirmed....

We granted the City of Ladue's petition for certiorari ... and now affirm.

II

While signs are a form of expression protected by the Free Speech Clause, they pose distinctive problems that are subject to municipalities' police powers. Unlike oral speech, signs take up space and may obstruct views, distract motorists, displace alternative uses for land, and pose other problems that legitimately call for regulation. It is common ground that governments may regulate the physical characteristics of signs—just as they can, within reasonable bounds and absent censorial purpose, regulate audible expression in its capacity as noise.... However, because regulation of a medium inevitably affects communication itself, it is not surprising that we have had occasion to review the constitutionality of municipal ordinances prohibiting the display of certain outdoor signs.

In *Linmark Associates, Inc. v. Willingboro,* 431 U.S. 85 (1977), we addressed an ordinance that sought to maintain stable, integrated neighborhoods by prohibiting homeowners from placing "For Sale" or "Sold" signs on their property. Although we recognized the importance of Willingboro's objective, we held that the First Amendment prevented the township from "achieving its goal by restricting the free flow of truthful information." In some respects *Linmark* is the mirror image of this case. For instead of prohibiting "For Sale" signs without banning any other signs, Ladue has exempted such signs from an otherwise virtually complete ban. Moreover, whereas in *Linmark* we noted that the ordinance was not concerned with the promotion of esthetic values unrelated to the content of the prohibited speech, ... here Ladue relies squarely on that content-neutral justification for its ordinance.

---

6. The full catalog of exceptions, each subject to special size limitations, is as follows: "municipal signs"; "subdivision and residence identification" signs; "road signs and driveway signs for danger, direction, or identification"; "health inspection signs"; "signs for churches, religious institutions, and schools" (subject to regulations set forth in § 35-5); "identification signs" for other not-for-profit organizations; signs "identifying the location of public transportation stops"; "ground signs advertising the sale or rental of real property," subject to the conditions, set forth in § 35-10, that such signs may "not be attached to any tree, fence or utility pole" and may contain only the fact of proposed sale or rental and the seller or agent's name and address or telephone number; "commercial signs in commercially zoned or industrial zoned districts," subject to restrictions set out elsewhere in the ordinance; and signs that "identify safety hazards." § 35-4....

III

...

Gilleo ... asserts a constitutional right to display an antiwar sign at her own home. Therefore, we first ask whether Ladue may properly prohibit Gilleo from displaying her sign, and then, only if necessary, consider the separate question whether it was improper for the City simultaneously to permit certain other signs. In examining the propriety of Ladue's near-total prohibition of residential signs, we will assume, arguendo, the validity of the City's submission that the various exemptions are free of impermissible content or viewpoint discrimination.[11]

IV

In *Linmark* we held that the City's interest in maintaining a stable, racially integrated neighborhood was not sufficient to support a prohibition of residential "For Sale" signs. We recognized that even such a narrow sign prohibition would have a deleterious effect on residents' ability to convey important information because alternatives were "far from satisfactory." Ladue's sign ordinance is supported principally by the City's interest in minimizing the visual clutter associated with signs, an interest that is concededly valid but certainly no more compelling than the interests at stake in *Linmark*. Moreover, whereas the ordinance in Linmark applied only to a form of commercial speech, Ladue's ordinance covers even such absolutely pivotal speech as a sign protesting an imminent governmental decision to go to war.

The impact on free communication of Ladue's broad sign prohibition, moreover, is manifestly greater than in *Linmark*. Gilleo and other residents of Ladue are forbidden to display virtually any "sign" on their property. The ordinance defines that term sweepingly. A prohibition is not always invalid merely because it applies to a sizeable category of speech; the sign ban we upheld in *Vincent*, for example, was quite broad. But in *Vincent*[T] we specifically noted that the category of speech in question—signs placed on public property—was not a "uniquely valuable or important mode of communication," and that there was no evidence that "appellees' ability to communicate effectively is threatened by ever-increasing restrictions on expression." ...

Here, in contrast, Ladue has almost completely foreclosed a venerable means of communication that is both unique and important. It has totally foreclosed that medium to political, religious, or personal messages. Signs that react to a local happening or express a view on a controversial issue both reflect and animate change in the life of a community. Often placed on lawns or in windows, residential signs play an important part in political campaigns, during which they are displayed to signal the resident's support for particular candidates, parties, or causes.[12] They may not afford the same opportunities for conveying complex ideas as do other media, but residential signs have long been an important and distinct medium of expression.

---

11. Because we set to one side the content discrimination question, we need not address the City's argument that the ordinance, although speaking in subject-matter terms, merely targets the "undesirable secondary effects" associated with certain kinds of signs. See *Renton v. Playtime Theatres, Inc.*, 475 U.S. 41, 49 (1986). The inquiry we undertake below into the adequacy of alternative channels of communication would also apply to a provision justified on those grounds. ...

T. Widmar v. Vincent, 454 U.S. 263 (1981) — Eds.

12. "Small [political campaign] posters have maximum effect when they go up in the windows of homes, for this demonstrates that citizens of the district are supporting your candidate—an impact that money can't buy." D. Simpson, *Winning Elections: A Handbook in Participatory Politics*, 87 (rev. ed. 1981).

Our prior decisions have voiced particular concern with laws that foreclose an entire medium of expression. Thus, we have held invalid ordinances that completely banned the distribution of pamphlets within the municipality, *Lovell v. Griffin*, 303 U.S. 444 (1938); handbills on the public streets, *Jamison v. Texas*, 318 U.S. 413 (1943); the door-to-door distribution of literature, *Martin v. Struthers*, 319 U.S. 141 (1943); *Schneider v. State*, 308 U.S. 147 (1939), and live entertainment, *Schad v. Mount Ephraim*, 452 U.S. 61 (1981). See also *Frisby v. Schultz*, 487 U.S. 474 (1988) (picketing focused upon individual residence is "fundamentally different from more generally directed means of communication that may not be completely banned in residential areas"). Although prohibitions foreclosing entire media may be completely free of content or viewpoint discrimination, the danger they pose to the freedom of speech is readily apparent—by eliminating a common means of speaking, such measures can suppress too much speech.[13]

Ladue contends, however, that its ordinance is a mere regulation of the "time, place, or manner" of speech because residents remain free to convey their desired messages by other means, such as hand-held signs, "letters, handbills, flyers, telephone calls, newspaper advertisements, bumper stickers, speeches, and neighborhood or community meetings."... However, even regulations that do not foreclose an entire medium of expression, but merely shift the time, place, or manner of its use, must "leave open ample alternative channels for communication." *Clark v. Community for Creative Non-Violence*, 468 U.S. 288, 293 (1984). In this case, we are not persuaded that adequate substitutes exist for the important medium of speech that Ladue has closed off.

Displaying a sign from one's own residence often carries a message quite distinct from placing the same sign someplace else, or conveying the same text or picture by other means. Precisely because of their location, such signs provide information about the identity of the "speaker." As an early and eminent student of rhetoric observed, the identity of the speaker is an important component of many attempts to persuade. A sign advocating "Peace in the Gulf" in the front lawn of a retired general or decorated war veteran may provoke a different reaction than the same sign in a 10-year-old child's bedroom window or the same message on a bumper sticker of a passing automobile. An espousal of socialism may carry different implications when displayed on the grounds of a stately mansion than when pasted on a factory wall or an ambulatory sandwich board.

Residential signs are an unusually cheap and convenient form of communication. Especially for persons of modest means or limited mobility, a yard or window sign may have no practical substitute.... Even for the affluent, the added costs in money or time of taking out a newspaper advertisement, handing out leaflets on the street, or standing in front of one's house with a hand-held sign may make the difference between participating and not participating in some public debate. Furthermore, a person who puts up a sign at her residence often intends to reach neighbors, an audience that could not be reached nearly as well by other means.[16]

---

13. See Stone, *Content-Neutral Restrictions*, 54 U. Chi. L. Rev. 46, 57–58 (1987):
    The Court long has recognized that by limiting the availability of particular means of communication, content-neutral restrictions can significantly impair the ability of individuals to communicate their views to others.... To ensure 'the widest possible dissemination of information' [*Associated Press v. United States*, 326 U.S. 1, 20 (1945),] and the 'unfettered interchange of ideas,' [*Roth v. United States*, 354 U.S. 476 (1957),] the first amendment prohibits not only content-based restrictions that censor particular points of view, but also content-neutral restrictions that unduly constrict the opportunities for free expression.

16. Counsel for Ladue has also cited flags as a viable alternative to signs. Counsel observed that the ordinance does not restrict flags of any stripe, including flags bearing written messages.... Even

A special respect for individual liberty in the home has long been part of our culture and our law, see, e.g., *Payton v. New York*, 445 U.S. 573, 596–597 (1980); that principle has special resonance when the government seeks to constrain a person's ability to speak there.... Most Americans would be understandably dismayed, given that tradition, to learn that it was illegal to display from their window an 8- by 11-inch sign expressing their political views. Whereas the government's need to mediate among various competing uses, including expressive ones, for public streets and facilities is constant and unavoidable, ... its need to regulate temperate speech from the home is surely much less pressing....

Our decision that Ladue's ban on almost all residential signs violates the First Amendment by no means leaves the City powerless to address the ills that may be associated with residential signs.[17] It bears mentioning that individual residents themselves have strong incentives to keep their own property values up and to prevent "visual clutter" in their own yards and neighborhoods—incentives markedly different from those of persons who erect signs on others' land, in others' neighborhoods, or on public property. Residents' self-interest diminishes the danger of the "unlimited" proliferation of residential signs that concerns the City of Ladue. We are confident that more temperate measures could in large part satisfy Ladue's stated regulatory needs without harm to the First Amendment rights of its citizens. As currently framed, however, the ordinance abridges those rights....

Midlake on Big Boulder Lake, Condo. Ass'n v. Cappuccio

Superior Court of Pennsylvania
673 A.2d 340 (Pa. Super. Ct. 1996)

CIRILLO, J. Plaintiff/appellant Midlake on Big Boulder Lake, Condominium Association ... appeals from the order enjoining and prohibiting Midlake from enforcing a section of the association's Declaration, which prohibits owner/members from posting signs on their respective properties. We reverse.

Midlake is a condominium association located in Kidder Township, Carbon County, Pennsylvania with the condominium units located along Big Boulder Lake. The association was established, under Pennsylvania's Uniform Condominium Act,[2] by the community developer, Northeast Land Company. A Declaration was filed with the Carbon County Recorder and Deeds Office at the time of the formation of Midlake.

Ronald and Sondra Cappuccio ... acquired a unit by deed in January 1989, which was duly recorded. The declaration was incorporated in the deed. By October, 1989, the property values in the area had plummeted, and the Cappuccios placed two computer-gener-

----

assuming that flags are nearly as affordable and legible as signs, we do not think the mere possibility that another medium could be used in an unconventional manner to carry the same messages alters the fact that Ladue has banned a distinct and traditionally important medium of expression....

17. Nor do we hold that every kind of sign must be permitted in residential areas. Different considerations might well apply, for example, in the case of signs (whether political or otherwise) displayed by residents for a fee, or in the case of off-site commercial advertisements on residential property. We also are not confronted here with mere regulations short of a ban.

2. 68 P.S. §3101. The Act provides that a declaration for a condominium must contain any restrictions created by the declarant on use, occupancy, and alienation of the unit. Midlake has complied with the law, and it is not disputed that the Cappuccios were aware of the restriction at the time of purchase. Mr. Cappuccio is an attorney, licensed to practice in New Jersey.

ated signs in the windows of their condominium which read: "For Sale by Owner. Call xxx-xxx-xxxx." The posting of these signs was in violation of Section 7.1.5 of the Declaration, which states:

> No unit owner (except declarant in connection with its leasing and marketing and sale of units) may erect any sign on or in a unit or in a common element or limited common element which is visible from the outdoors without, in each instance, having obtained the prior written permission of the Executive Board.

Midlake contacted the Cappuccios to enforce the Declaration. When the Cappuccios refused to comply, Midlake brought an action in equity to compel the Cappuccios to take down the signs. The signs were removed, however, around March 1993, when the Cappuccios leased their unit. Midlake offered to withdraw its complaint if the Cappuccios would sign a stipulation stating that they would refrain from posting signs in the future. The Cappuccios refused.

A non-jury trial was held.... The trial court noted that the matter was undeniably moot, but decided the matter after determining that the freedom of speech issue affected the interest of all the owners at Midlake, and could otherwise repeatedly escape review. The trial court then dismissed Midlake's complaint, and granted the Cappuccios' counterclaim, prohibiting Midlake from enforcing Section 7.1.5 of the declaration. In its opinion, the trial court reasoned that despite the fact that "it is beyond cavil that the first section of the Fourteenth Amendment applies only to the states, and erects no shield against purely private conduct, however discriminatory or wrongful," to enforce the restrictive covenant would be "state action" under *Shelley v. Kraemer....* We find that the application of *Shelley* by the trial court in this case was an error of law.

...

Initially, we note that the Cappuccios admit that "if the Plaintiff, instead of being a private organization established under the laws of the Commonwealth of Pennsylvania, were instead a municipal governmental organization, the restrictions would clearly be unconstitutional." Midlake, however, is a private organization, and as such, cannot abridge the rights of the First Amendment of the Constitution. *Flagg Bros., Inc. v. Brooks*, 436 U.S. 149 (1978). Accordingly, the condominium restriction against placing signs in the unit without prior approval by the board of directors is not an impermissible infringement of free speech in violation of the United States Constitution.

Next, the "state action" test, as directed by our supreme court, "is applied by the courts in determining whether, in a given case, a state's involvement in private activity is sufficient to justify the application of a federal constitutional prohibition of state action to that conduct." *Hartford Accident & Indemnity Co. v. Insurance Commissioner of Commonwealth*, 505 Pa. 571, 482 A.2d 542, 549 (1984). This court subsequently determined, after a thorough review of the relevant federal law, that *Shelley v. Kramer*, is not applicable to the enforcement of a restrictive covenant in a contract between private parties, by stating:

> Where a state court enforces the right of private persons to take actions which are permitted but not compelled by law, there is no state action for constitutional purposes in the absence of a finding that racial discrimination is involved as existed in the *Shelley* case....

The Cappuccios alternatively argue that since Midlake was organized under the laws of the Commonwealth, the establishment of the organization was therefore state action. This argument is meritless, and we summarily reject it. See *Jackson v. Metropolitan Edi-*

son Co., 419 U.S. 345, 350 (1974) ("The mere fact that a business is subject to state regulation does not itself convert its action into that of the state")....

The Cappuccios also weakly assert that Midlake is comparable to a company town, such as that described in *Marsh v. Alabama*, 326 U.S. 501 (1946), since it has many of the same types of facilities. Despite the trial court's statement regarding a "mini municipality," there is no correlation between Midlake and a company town or municipality. Midlake's facilities are entirely privately run. While there is sewer service, private streets, and private maintenance, Midlake provides no facilities for community public use that are typically found in a municipality, such as schools, libraries, and other public functions. We need not discuss this issue further.

In conclusion, Midlake is a private organization and there is no racial discrimination or bias, such as that exhibited by *Shelley*, pertinent to the restrictive covenant, which the parties entered into without any compulsion of law. There is, therefore, no state action in the court's judicial enforcement of the condominium association's Declaration....

The courts of this Commonwealth have vigorously defended the rights which are guaranteed to our citizens by both the federal and our Commonwealth's constitutions. One of the fundamental precepts which we recognize, however, is the individual's freedom to contractually restrict, or even give up, those rights. The Cappuccios contractually agreed to abide by the provisions in the Declaration at the time of purchase, thereby relinquishing their freedom of speech concerns regarding placing signs on this property. Accordingly, we reverse.

Margin note left: Priv. org, no rac. discrim. so no "state action"

Margin note left: Indivs have freedom to contractually restrict or even give up, those rpts

Notes & Questions

1. In the last paragraph of the opinion, the court says that the Cappuccios contractually relinquished their freedom of speech with respect to placing signs on their property. Is this accurate? Isn't the court really saying that the Cappuccios have no constitutional right to be protected against speech restrictions imposed by the common interest community because it is a private, rather than a state actor? If that is the case, the Cappuccios have contractually given up a property right — the right to use their property as they please for anything allowed by zoning that is not a nuisance — rather than a constitutional right (the right that government not restrict their ability to speak freely).

2. Should developers be able to require that property purchasers give up the right to place signs on their property? Should there be any difference between "for sale" signs and political signs? Are there legitimate reasons for banning all signs?

3. The Midlake declaration banned all signs except signs the developer used in marketing units. Should the developer be allowed to prohibit unit owners from posting "for sale" signs on their properties while the developer has signs advertising the remaining unsold units?

Gerber v. Longboat Harbour North Condo., Inc.

United States District Court for the Middle District of Florida
724 F.Supp. 884 (U.S.D.C., M.D. Fla. 1989)

KOVACHEVICH, J....

I.

This case raises important constitutional issues involving freedom of speech, secured by the First Amendment to the United States Constitution and made applicable to the

States through the Fourteenth Amendment. At the center of the dispute stands one American who seeks to display the flag of our nation in defiance of condominium documents which forbid such display except on designated occasions. Plaintiff, an Air Force Veteran, will not have the Defendant determine the occasions on which he expresses his deep love and respect for America.

Defendant's motion to dismiss is predicated upon its assertion that, since it is not a governmental entity and has not assumed substantially all of the functions of a governmental entity,[2] the provisions of the First Amendment as incorporated in the Fourteenth Amendment simply do not apply.

Before launching into an examination of the merits of defendant's argument, this Court *sua sponte* points out that the Florida Legislature's recent enactment of § 718.113(4) clearly eviscerates Defendant's chances of prevailing on its motion. Florida Statutes § 718.113(4) states in its entirety

> Any [condominium] unit owner may display one portable, removable United States flag in a respectful way regardless of any declaration rules or requirements dealing with flags or decorations.

Signed by Governor Martinez on June 27, 1989, this provision renders any consideration of Defendant's motion unnecessary at least with respect to facts occurring after the law's effective date. This Court will not strain to reach Constitutional issues in advance of the necessity of doing so. *Ashwander v. Tennessee Valley Authority*, 297 U.S. 288, 346–48, (1936) (Brandeis, J. concurring).

While this Court does not challenge the wisdom of Mr. Justice Brandeis' teaching, the issue of whether a Constitutional question must be resolved in a particular case must first be passed upon by the trial judge. Since the Plaintiff in the instant litigation seeks damages for the inability to exercise fundamental Constitutional rights prior to the passage of the statutory provision, and the statute is prospective only, it is necessary that this Court examine carefully the question of application *vel non* of the First and Fourteenth Amendments to this particular situation.

II.

In 1947, the United States Supreme Court sounded the death knell for those among our number who would deny minorities the housing of their choice simply because of the color of their skin through racially restrictive covenants. In *Shelley v. Kraemer*, 334 U.S. 1 (1948), the six participating justices held that, while the Fourteenth Amendment does not reach purely private conduct, judicial enforcement of restrictive covenants constitutes state action, triggering the protections of the Fourteenth Amendment's Due Process and Equal Protection Clauses.

Applying the principles of *Shelley* to the situation sub judice, this Court finds that judicial enforcement of private agreements contained in a declaration of condominium constitute state action and bring the heretofore private conduct within the ken of the Fourteenth Amendment, through which the First Amendment guarantee of free speech is made applicable to the states.

It cannot be gainsaid that judicial enforcement of a racially restrictive covenant constitutes state action. It offends logic to suppose that equal protection of the law could be

---

2. The landmark case finding a private entity to be the functional equivalent of a state actor is of course *Marsh v. Alabama*, 326 U.S. 501 (1945)....

guaranteed by the very government whose judicial arm seeks to deny it. To suggest that judicial enforcement of private covenants abridging protected speech is not state action is, *mutatis mutandis*, equally repugnant to reason. Defendant's actions in denying Plaintiff his Constitutionally guaranteed right to display the American Flag were illegal *ab initio*, and this Court so holds.

Defendant deems it important that the association's proscription of flag display applied to all residents. Apparently it believes this renders their conduct benign, since its effects were distributed among all occupants. But the racially restrictive covenants in *Shelley* applied to all homeowners who were signators of the covenant. This Court cannot see how or why prohibiting all residents from displaying the symbol of our nation ceases to become a Constitutional violation. It is to suggest that a wrongful act loses its wrongful character merely by being performed on a large enough scale.

This Court has read and weighed the opinion of the Florida Second District Court of Appeal in *Quail Creek Property Owners Association, Inc. v. Hunter, ...* 538 So. 2d 1288 (FL. 1989). This Court cannot agree with its conclusion that judicial enforcement of racially restrictive covenants is state action and judicial enforcement of covenants which restrict one's right to patriotic speech is not state action. Enforcement of private agreements by the judicial branch of government is state action for purposes of the Fourteenth Amendment, as the Highest Court in the land declared it to be in *Shelley*; it cannot be said that the terms of the agreement either increase or decrease the extent to which government is involved. It is an exercise in sophistry to posit that courts act as the state when enforcing racially restrictive covenants but not when giving effect to other provisions of the same covenant.

This Court is well aware that it is not infallible. That decisions are appealed and trial courts reversed is a fact of life to which this jurist is quite accustomed. But the *ratio decidendi* of this case is indistinguishable from that of the *Shelley* court. Judicial enforcement of private agreements which are violative of the Fourteenth Amendment cannot be both state action and not state action at the same time. To conclude otherwise violates a syntactically analytic truth.

III.

It is a curious ordering of values, and a questionable jurisprudence, which would forbid a man from displaying the symbol of his country while staunchly defending the rights of others to deface, desecrate, and destroy that same symbol. Had Mr. Gerber chosen to burn his flag rather than display it in a dignified manner, public spirited lawyers would have appeared to help him protect his constitutional right to burn old glory. But to proudly display the United States Flag Mr. Gerber was forced to commence a federal lawsuit at his own expense.

The legislature of the state of Florida has, through the enactment of Florida Statutes §718.113(4), recognized that the right of each condominium owner to display the United States Flag is fundamental. The flag is a unique national symbol: thirteen stripes, alternating red and white; fifty white stars in a blue field, representing the union of the fifty states into one nation. It is, like the flags of other nations, the physical embodiment of sovereignty. But as America is unique among nations, so is our flag unique among flags. The first three words of our Constitution, "We the People", represent the profound difference between our government structure and the traditional view of governmental power. The government of the United States derives its powers from the people, in whom such power is inherent. It is the people of the United States who are the true sovereigns, and it is the sovereignty of the people that is represented by the white stars in a blue field on our nation's flag.

This Court will not countenance such treading upon the rights of those who would respectfully display the flag in front of their own home.

IV.

Defendant in its brief addressing the impact of § 718.113 raises several points. Most noteworthy is its assertion that the statute impairs existing contracts in violation of both the Federal and Florida Constitutions. This Court disagrees.

Section 718.113 merely recognizes by state statute a right that this Court determines to have already existed to display the American flag. Since the statute did not create rights, but merely recognized them, it does not impair existing contract rights.

V.

In summary, this Court finds that the Condominium Association's conduct was sufficiently attributable to the state to constitute action by the state. This action acted to deprive the Plaintiff of his rights, privileges and immunities secured by the First and Fourteenth Amendments to the United States Constitution within the meaning of 42 U.S.C. § 1983.[3] Defendant also violated § 718.113, Florida Statutes, for the time period subsequent to its effective date. This Court has jurisdiction to adjudicate claims for violation of this state statute under its pendent jurisdiction.

Accordingly, it is now Ordered

(1) That Plaintiff's motion for Summary Judgment be, and the same is, GRANTED.

(2) That Defendant be Enjoined from interfering with Plaintiff's display of the Flag in compliance with the terms of § 718.113, Florida Statutes.

(3) That Plaintiff be awarded costs and reasonable attorneys' fees in accordance with the provisions of 42 U.S.C. § 1988.

Notes & Questions

1. Enforcement of flag restrictions against people flying American flags on their own property drew such public outrage that Congress passed the Freedom to Display the American Flag Act of 2005, 4 U.S.C.A. § 5:

> Sec. 3. Right to Display the Flag of the United States.
>
> A condominium association, cooperative association, or residential real estate management[U] association may not adopt or enforce any policy, or enter into any

[handwritten: 2005 Fed. law allowing display of flag!]

---

3. "Every person who, under color of any statute, ordinance, regulation, custom, or usage, of any State or Territory or the District of Columbia, subjects, or causes to be subjected, any citizen of the United States or other persons within the jurisdiction thereof to the deprivation of any rights, privileges, or immunities secured by the Constitution and laws, shall be liable to the party injured in an action at law, suit in equity, or other proper proceeding for redress. For purposes of this section, any act of Congress applicable to the District of Columbia shall be considered to be a statute of the District of Columbia."

U. "Residential real estate management associations" includes most community associations that are not condominium or cooperative associations. The term is defined in 26 U.S.C.A. § 528, the section that exempts most homeowner associations from paying income tax on the assessments they collect — Eds.

agreement, that would restrict or prevent a member of the association from displaying the flag of the United States on residential property within the association with respect to which such member has a separate ownership interest or a right to exclusive possession or use.

Sec. 4. Limitations. "Nothing in this Act [this note] shall be considered to permit any display or use that is inconsistent with—

(1) any provision of chapter 1 of title 4, United States Code [4 U.S.C.A. § 1 et seq.], or any rule or custom pertaining to the proper display or use of the flag of the United States (as established pursuant to such chapter or any otherwise applicable provision of law); or

(2) any reasonable restriction pertaining to the time, place, or manner of displaying the flag of the United States necessary to protect a substantial interest of the condominium association, cooperative association, or residential real estate management association.

2. The logic of Judge Kovachevich seems impeccable—or does it? Why haven't other courts followed it?

Goldberg v. 400 East Ohio Condominium Ass'n

United States District Court For The Northern District Of Illinois, Eastern Division
12 F. Supp. 2d 820 (N.D. Ill. 1998)

MEMORANDUM OPINION AND ORDER

MARVIN E. ASPEN, Chief Judge: A less creative plaintiff, after observing that Illinois's Condominium Property Act forbids condominium boards of managers from adopting any rule which ""impair[s] any rights guaranteed by the *First Amendment to the Constitution*" and provides that any such rule is "void as against public policy and [is] ineffective," *765 ILCS 605/18.4*, 18.4(h) (West), would have brought suit under that law in state court after her condominium's board enacted a rule which barred all "canvassing or distributing of materials to individual units" other than those materials related to political campaigning.... She would have prevailed if she showed that the regulation impaired a *First Amendment* right or even that the regulation was simply unreasonable—and to that end it would have been the board's burden to prove that the canvassing or distribution was "'antagonistic to the legitimate objectives of the condominium association.'" *Apple II Condominium Ass'n v. Worth Bank & Trust Co., 277 Ill. App. 3d 345, 659 N.E.2d 93, 98, ... (Ill. App. Ct. 1995)* (quoting *Hidden Harbour Estates, Inc. v. Basso, 393 So. 2d 637, 640 (Fla. Dist. Ct. App. 1981)); see also RESTATEMENT (THIRD) OF PROPERTY (SERVITUDES) §6.13 (1998)*. Alternatively she could have used that law to defend against any attempt to collect on the lien which the condominium association placed on her unit as a penalty for her leafletting activities. *See Hinojosa, 679 N.E.2d at 409; 765 ILCS 605/9(g)(1) (West)*....

Unfortunately for her, Marcy Goldberg (or maybe her attorney) has a more active imagination; she sued her condominium association and its board of directors under *42 U.S.C. § 1983* for a violation of the *First Amendment* itself. This leveraged her into federal court (and brought with it the tantalizing possibility of attorneys fees, *see 42 U.S.C. § 1988(b)*;..., but she now faces a motion to dismiss on the ground that the board did not act "under color of" state law, as *§ 1983* requires.

Goldberg takes two stabs at the problem. She first asks for an extension of *Shelley v. Kraemer, 334 U.S. 1 (1948)*, where the Supreme Court held that a state court's enforcement of a racially restrictive covenant constituted sufficient action by the state to satisfy the *Fourteenth Amendment's* state action requirement. Since *§ 1983*'s "under color of" law requirement is "'just as broad as'" the *Fourteenth Amendment's* state action requirement, *Hafer v. Melo, 502 U.S. 21, 28, 116 L. Ed. 2d 301, 112 S. Ct. 358 (1991)* (quoting *Lugar v. Edmondson Oil Co., 457 U.S. 922, 929, 73 L. Ed. 2d 482, 102 S. Ct. 2744 (1982)*), Goldberg reasons that her *First Amendment* rights were violated when her condominium association enacted its rule....

Her principal support for this argument is the decision in *Gerber v. Longboat Harbour N. Condominium, Inc., 724 F. Supp. 884 (M.D. Fla. 1989), vacated in part on other grounds by 757 F. Supp. 1339 (M.D. Fla. 1991)* (motion to reconsider), where the court held unconstitutional a condominium rule prohibiting residents from flying the American flag except on specified holidays.[1] We are not persuaded by this opinion, which, after citing *Shelley*, reasoned as follows:

> Applying the principles of *Shelley* to the situation sub judice, this Court finds that judicial enforcement of private agreements contained in a declaration of private agreements contained in a declaration of condominium constitute[s] state action and bring[s] the heretofore private conduct within the ken of the *Fourteenth Amendment*....
>
> It cannot be gainsaid that judicial enforcement of a racially restrictive covenant constitutes state action. It offends logic to suppose that equal protection of the law could be guaranteed by the very government whose judicial arm seeks to deny it. To suggest that judicial enforcement of private covenants abridging protected speech is not state action is, *mutatis mutandis*, equally repugnant to reason. Defendant's actions in denying Plaintiff his Constitutionally protected right to display the American Flag were illegal *ab initio*, and this Court so holds.

724 F. Supp. at 886. The court concluded that "the *ratio decidendi* in this case is indistinguishable from that of the *Shelley* Court" and that "to conclude otherwise violates a syntactically analytic truth."

The problem is that there is no indication (in either of the two opinions in the case) that the condominium association *actually* secured any sort of judgment or order from a state court. *See generally Leon Friedman, New Developments in Civil Rights Litigation*

---

1. The citation to a decision by a federal district court in Florida is not as random as it might appear. The 1998 version of the Historical and Practice Notes to 765 ILCS 605/18.4(h) state that the First Amendment part of that subsection "is modeled on provisions in the Florida Condominium Act," and *Gerber* relies in part on a Florida condominium statute. Gerber, 724 F. Supp. at 886 (citing FLA. STAT. ch. 718.113(4)). We should point out that one of Goldberg's attorneys, who as a state legislator sponsored amendments to the Condominium Act, is the author of the Historical and Practice Notes to section 18.4; actually he is the author of every signed Note to the Condominium Act (at least one of which even quotes statements he made as a legislator). In that capacity he changed the 1997 version of the Notes, which stated that "Thus, for example, a board of managers could not prohibit unit owners or their tenants from knocking on their neighbors' doors for purposes of political campaigning," to read "Thus, for example, a board of managers could not prohibit unit owners or their tenants from knocking on their neighbors' doors for purposes of condominium or political campaigning." The underlined portion is new and is not supported by any citation or reference to any change to the statute, but we note that it purports to make a state law claim by Goldberg all the more viable, as her leafletting activities concerned condominium governance.... It is difficult, of course, to imagine how subsection 18.4(h) was concerned with condominium campaigning in 1998 but not in 1997 or when it was enacted, as the Florida statute on which 18.4(h) is presumably based, FLA. STAT. ch. 718.123, refers only to campaigning for "public office." It is even more difficult to imagine how it is not at all concerned with commercial speech, as the Notes have consistently claimed. We discuss the commercial speech point further, *infra*, but we observe here that these Notes may be ripe for another revision.

and Trends in Section 1983 Actions, 554 PLI/LIT 7, 25 (1996) (citing *Gerber*). In *Shelley* itself, of course, the petitioners were subject to state court orders divesting them of title in the properties at issue.... This was crucial, as the Court's holding was premised on the idea that the "participation of the State consists in the *enforcement* of the restrictions...." *Id. at 13* (emphasis added). Reinforcing the point, the Supreme Court stated that "but for the *active intervention* of the state courts.... petitioners would have been free to occupy the properties...." *Id. at 19* (emphasis added). It is difficult to understand, then, how the court in *Gerber* found state *action* before the state *acted*.

In fact, old-fashioned patriotism, rather than old-fashioned legal reasoning, is the source of the *Gerber* opinion's persuasive force. The plaintiff we are told, was an Air Force veteran who wished to "express[] his deep love and respect for America."... The court did not hide its sympathy for his predicament: [most of quotation from Gerber about values omitted—Eds.].

> This Court will not countenance such treading upon the rights of those who would respectfully display the flag in front of their own home.

Id. at 887.

We think the better view is that there is no state action inherent in the possible future state court enforcement of a private property agreement. *See Quail Creek Property Owners Ass'n, Inc. v. Hunter*, 538 So. 2d 1288, 1289 (Fla. Dist. Ct. App. 1989) (per curiam). Put another way, *Gerber* is not good law. Since we know from Goldberg's complaint that her condominium association has not secured a state judgment against her, ... we hold that she cannot establish state action under *Shelley*. We express no opinion on whether it would be proper to extend *Shelley* to condominium rules actually enforced by state courts. *See, e.g.*, Note, *Judicial Review of Condominium Rulemaking*, 94 HARV. L. REV. 647, 656–58 (1981) (describing some problems in the use of *Shelley* as the vehicle to review rules promulgated by condominium associations).

Goldberg's second argument that the condominium association acted "under color of" law relies on the idea that condominium associations have powers "traditionally associated with the state." ... She points to the association's power to make rules, conduct hearings, issue decisions, and impose fines and liens. There are two problems with this line of reasoning. First, it "confuse[s] an entity and its attributes." RICHARD A. POSNER, OVERCOMING LAW 211 (1995). Dogs breathe, eat, sleep, run, and play, but they are not humans, who also do all of those things. And it is not as though the attributes that Goldberg cites are those which have been described by the Supreme Court as possibly *exclusive* state functions. *See Flagg Brothers, Inc. v. Brooks*, 436 U.S. 149, 158, 163, 56 L. Ed. 2d 185, 98 S. Ct. 1729 (1978) (government elections, the comprehensive ownership and operation of a town, education, fire and police protection, and tax collection); *see also Edmonson v. Leesville Concrete Co., Inc.*, 500 U.S. 614 (1991) (jury system). Demonstrating that condominiums do certain things that state governments also do doesn't show that condominiums are acting as the state or in the state's place.

Second, it proves too much. The National Basketball Association makes rules, conducts hearings, issues decisions, and imposes fines, but it seems unlikely that the privately run sports league is a government actor. (This example misses the lien power of condominiums, but the private actor in *Flagg Brothers* had the power to impose and enforce its own lien, *436 U.S. at 151 n.1, 155*.) The same holds true for unions and corporations to varying degrees—in fact the Condominium Property Act provides that condominium associations have the powers of a not for profit corporation, *765 ILCS*

605/18.3 (West). We also observe that if Goldberg were correct we would have to consider whether the *Eleventh Amendment* would bar any part of this suit....

One aspect of Goldberg's argument bears further discussion. She posits that the Illinois General Assembly itself recognized that condominium associations would act as the state by enacting the statute which states that "no [condominium] rule or regulation may impair any rights guaranteed by the *First Amendment....*" *765 ILCS 605/18.4(h)* (West). Given that only a state actor can "violate" the *First Amendment*, she argues that this provision amounts to an acknowledgment that condominium associations are state actors.

We disagree. The statute forbids a board from "impairing any rights guaranteed by the *First Amendment*," not from violating the Amendment itself. It is also strange that Goldberg's evidence of an exercise of state power is an action by a putatively private entity which allegedly *violates* state law. In any event, Goldberg fails to elucidate why, if the General Assembly wanted to acknowledge that condominium associations are state actors, it singled out the *First Amendment*. Ordinary state actors are bound by most of the rest of the Constitution, too. The statute's 1998 Historical and Practice Notes provide this explanation: "This provision was adopted in response to boards who were attempting to severely restrict *First Amendment* activity of owners and occupants, especially political activity." In keeping with its "political activity" comment, the Notes even attempt to exclude "commercial signs" from the provision's coverage, despite the fact that commercial speech falls within the *First Amendment's* purview.... In light of the Notes and of the Florida statute, ... we think that the "*First Amendment*" limitation in the Condominium Property Act simply prohibits condominium boards from unduly restricting ordinary political speech or activities, and we see no good reason to construe that limitation as a recognition that the board exercises government power.

The motion to dismiss is granted. It is so ordered.

Committee For a Better Twin Rivers (CBTR) v. Twin Rivers Homeowners' Association (TRHA)

Supreme Court of New Jersey
929 A.2d 1060 (N.J. 2007)

Justice WALLACE, JR. delivered the opinion of the Court.

In this appeal, we determine whether the rules and regulations enacted by a homeowners' association governing the posting of signs, the use of the community room, and access to its newsletter violated our state constitutional guarantees of free expression....

We start from the proposition that all citizens of this State, including the residents of Twin Rivers, possess the constitutional right to free speech and assembly. We acknowledge, however, that those rights are not absolute, as citizens may waive or otherwise curtail their rights. This case presents us with a hybrid setting to apply the standards set forth in *State v. Schmid*, 423 A.2d 615 (N.J. 1980), *appeal dismissed sub nom. Princeton University v. Schmid*, 455 U.S. 100, 102 and *New Jersey Coalition Against War in the Middle East v. J.M.B. Realty Corp.*, 650 A.2d 757 (N.J. 1994), *cert. denied*, 516 U.S. 812, (1995). In applying the *Schmid/Coalition* multi-faceted standard, we conclude that the Association's policies, as set forth in its rules and regulations, do not violate our constitution.

I.

... Twin Rivers is a planned unit development consisting of privately owned condominium duplexes, townhouses, single-family homes, apartments, and commercial buildings located in East Windsor, New Jersey. The community covers approximately one square mile and has a population of approximately 10,000 residents. The Twin Rivers Community Trust (Trust) is a private corporation that owns Twin Rivers's common property and facilities. The Trust was created by indenture on November 13, 1969, for the stated purpose of owning, managing, operating, and maintaining the residential common property of Twin Rivers. The administrator of the Trust certified that "Trust-owned property and facilities are for the exclusive use of Twin Rivers residents and their invited guests," and that the "general public is not invited" to use them.

The Twin Rivers Homeowners' Association (Association) is a private corporation that serves as trustee of the Trust. The Trust authorizes the Association to make rules and regulations for the conduct of its members while occupying the land owned or controlled by the Trust, to provide services to its members, and to maintain the common lands and facilities in Twin Rivers. The Association maintains the Trust's private residential roads, provides street lighting and snow removal, assigns parking spaces in its parking lots, and collects rubbish in portions of Twin Rivers. By acquiring property in Twin Rivers, the owner automatically becomes a member of the Association and subject to its Articles of Incorporation (Articles) and Bylaws.

The Articles authorize the Association to exercise all of the powers, rights, and privileges provided to corporations organized under the New Jersey Nonprofit Corporation Act.... The Bylaws additionally authorize the Association to adopt, publish, and enforce rules governing the use of common areas and facilities. The Bylaws may be amended by a majority of a quorum of members present in person or by proxy at a regular or special meeting of the members.

The Association is governed by a Board of Directors (Board), whose members are elected by all eligible voting members of the Association. The Board is responsible for making and enforcing the rules, and for providing services to its members that are financed through mandatory assessments levied against residents pursuant to an annual budget adopted by the Board.

Prior to the commencement of this litigation, various residents of Twin Rivers formed a committee, known as the Committee for a Better Twin Rivers (Committee), for the purpose of affecting the manner in which Twin Rivers was governed. Eventually, the Committee and three individual residents of Twin Rivers (collectively, plaintiffs) filed a nine-count complaint against the Association and Scott Pohl, the president of the Association, seeking to invalidate various rules and regulations. Plaintiffs subsequently amended their complaint to include the Trust as a defendant. The thrust of the complaint was that the Association had effectively replaced the role of the municipality in the lives of its residents, and therefore, the Association's internal rules and regulations should be subject to the free speech and free association clauses of the New Jersey Constitution. Although plaintiffs' complaint consisted of nine counts, only the first three counts are relevant to this appeal.

In count one of the complaint, plaintiffs sought to invalidate the Association's policy relating to the posting of signs. The Association's sign policy provided that residents may post a sign in any window of their residence and outside in the flower beds so long as the sign was no more than three feet from the residence. In essence, the policy limits signs to one per lawn and one per window. The policy also forbids the posting of signs on utility poles and natural features within the community. The stated purpose for the sign policy is to avoid the clutter of signs and to preserve the aesthetic value of the common areas, as well as to allow for lawn maintenance and leaf collection. Plaintiffs sought injunctive relief to permit the posting of political signs on the property of community residents "and on common elements under reasonable regulation," on the basis that the current policy was unconstitutional.

In count two, plaintiffs complained of the Association's policy in respect of the use of its community room. In general, the community room is available to residents of Twin Rivers, as well as clubs, organizations, and committees approved by the Trust who want to rent the room for parties or other events. When the complaint was filed, the community room policy involved a two-tiered rental charge system that differentiated between the uses of the room. However, during the pendency of this action, the Association amended the community room policy to eliminate the tier system in favor of a uniform rental fee of $165 and a refundable security deposit of $250. Additionally, a certificate of insurance naming the Association as an insured was required. The rental fees were intended to cover the costs associated with the maintenance of the room.

Plaintiffs asserted that the community room policy denied them equal protection of the laws and unreasonably and unconstitutionally violated their right to access the community room on a fair and equitable basis. They sought temporary and permanent injunctions "to allow [p]laintiffs to utilize the community room in the same manner as other similarly situated entities." Plaintiffs also urged that the rental fees were excessive because they were not related to the actual rental costs incurred by the Association.

In count three, plaintiffs alleged they were denied equal access to the Association's monthly newspaper, Twin Rivers Today (Today). The purpose of the newspaper is to provide residents with news and information that concerns the community. The editorial committee of Today selects the content of the newspaper. The paper is delivered to all Twin Rivers residents, but not to the general public. Plaintiffs sought a declaration that all Twin Rivers residents should have "equal access" to the pages of Today. Also, plaintiffs sought a permanent injunction enjoining the president of the Board from using Today "as his own personal political trumpet."

The Association filed a motion for summary judgment, and plaintiffs filed a cross-motion for summary judgment. The material facts were not disputed. The trial court issued a comprehensive opinion, granting defendants' motion for summary judgment on the sign claims in count one and on the newspaper claims in count three. The court, however, granted plaintiffs partial relief in respect of the community room claims in count two.

Central to the trial court's decision was the determination that Twin Rivers was not a "quasi-municipality," and thus was not subject to the New Jersey Constitution's free speech and association clauses. The court noted that while the Association asserted considerable influence on the lives of Twin Rivers residents, that impact was a function of the contractual relationship that residents entered into when they elected to purchase property in Twin Rivers. The court applied the traditional test for evaluating the reasonableness of restrictive covenants and found that the covenant relating to the posting of signs was reasonable and enforceable. Although the trial court upheld the amended policy of a unified rate for the community room, it found that the regulations for use of the community room were impermissibly vague. The court directed the Association to modify the regulations to provide clear standards for the granting or withholding of permission for the room's use. Further, the court concluded that plaintiffs were not denied access to the Association's newspaper and that it would be improper under constitutional principles of free press for the court to exert control over its contents.

Plaintiffs appealed. In a published opinion, the Appellate Division reversed the trial court, holding that the Association was subject to state constitutional standards with respect to its internal rules and regulations. *Comm. for a Better Twin Rivers v. Twin Rivers Homeowners' Ass'n*, 890 A.2d 947 (App.Div.2006). "[I]n balancing the interests of the parties," the panel found that "plaintiffs' rights to engage in expressive exercises ... must take precedence over the [Association's] private property interests." ... The panel thus remanded counts one, two, and three for reconsideration in light of that determination....

The Association petitioned this Court for certification on whether the New Jersey Constitution applies to its internal rules and regulations. Plaintiffs cross-petitioned for certification on an issue unrelated to this appeal. We granted the Association's petition and denied plaintiffs' cross-petition....

II.

The Association argues that the test in *State v. Schmid, supra,* controls the disposition of this appeal, and contends that under that test, it was error to impose constitutional obligations on its private property. The Association urges this Court to follow the vast majority of other jurisdictions that have refused to impose constitutional obligations on the internal membership rules of private homeowners' associations. In support of that view, the Association emphasizes that it does not invite public use of its property, and its members participate in the decision-making process of the Association. Additionally, its members are afforded extensive statutory protections, and the business judgment rule protects members from arbitrary decision-making. Further, the Association contends that the relationship with its members is a contractual one, set forth in reasonable and lawful restrictive covenants that appear in all property deeds.

Defendant Pohl argues that the First Amendment bars a court from asserting control over the content and editorial policies of the Association's newspaper, maintaining that the First Amendment gives the Association discretion to determine the content of its newspaper. He urges this Court to reinstate the trial court's grant of summary judgment in favor of the Association dismissing count three.

In contrast, plaintiffs ask this Court to affirm the judgment of the Appellate Division to find that the New Jersey Constitution limits the manner in which the Association interacts with its members. They urge that political speech is entitled to heightened protection and that they should have the right to post political signs beyond the Association's restricted sign policy. Plaintiffs further contend that the excessive fees charged for the use of the community room are not reasonably related to the actual costs incurred by the Association. Finally, plaintiffs claim that the State Constitution requires that the Association publish plaintiffs' views on an equal basis with which the Association's views are published in its newspaper.

We granted amicus curiae status to the Community Association Institute, the Public Advocate of New Jersey, and the AARP Foundation. The latter two entities favor plaintiffs' position, while the Community Association Institute supports the Association's position.

III.

Our constitution affirmatively grants to individuals the rights of speech and assembly.

Every person may freely speak, write and publish his sentiments on all subjects, being responsible for the abuse of that right. No law shall be passed to restrain or abridge the liberty of speech or of the press. [N.J. Const. art. I, ¶ 6.]....

The people have the right freely to assemble together, to consult for the common good, to make known their opinions to their representatives, and to petition for redress of grievances. [N.J. Const. art. I, ¶ 18].

This Court has long held that the rights of speech and assembly cannot be curtailed by the government.... Moreover, under limited circumstances, we have determined that those constitutional rights may be enforced against private entities. *Schmid*,.... In fact, our constitutional guarantee of free expression "is an affirmative right, broader than practically all others in the nation." *Green Party v. Hartz Mountain Indus., Inc.*, 752 A.2d 315 (N.J. 2000). Here, we must determine whether this case presents one of those limited circumstances where, in the setting of a private community, the Association's rules and regulations are limited by the constitutional rights of plaintiffs.

A.

Federal case law has evolved to require that there must be "state action" to enforce constitutional rights against private entities. *Marsh v. Alabama*, 326 U.S. 501, (1946), is recognized as the leading case in this area of law. In *Marsh,* a private company owned and controlled all aspects of the town.... The company refused to allow solicitation and the distribution of religious literature.... Marsh was arrested for trespassing while distributing religious literature on company-owned land that was otherwise open to the public. The Court explained that "[t]he more an owner, for his advantage, opens up his property for use by the public in general, the more do his rights become circumscribed by the statutory and constitutional rights of those who use it." The Court then balanced the constitutional rights of the property owners against the First Amendment rights of Marsh to find that "the latter occupy a preferred position." The Court concluded that, in those limited circumstances, the property owner's action constituted "state action" and violated the First Amendment....

The United States Supreme Court later considered the application of *Marsh* to shopping centers. In the first case to address the issue, the Court held that the reasoning of *Marsh* applied to a shopping mall.... However, the Court subsequently retreated from that position and, in a later case, concluded that the First Amendment affords no general right of free speech in privately owned shopping centers. See *PruneYard Shopping Ctr. v. Robins,* 447 U.S. 74, 80–81, (1980) (noting that although First Amendment did not grant right of free expression in shopping centers, states may adopt greater free speech rights); *Hudgens v. NLRB*, 424 U.S. 507, 520–21 (1976).

B.

Our jurisprudence has not been as confining. We briefly outline the development of our law expanding the application of free speech or similar constitutional rights against non-governmental entities.

In *State v. Shack*, 277 A.2d 369 (N.J. 1971), this Court was asked to apply the principles of *Marsh* to a private farm operation.... However, the Court declined to rule on the constitutional challenge, noting only that *Marsh* was inapplicable because the land in question was not open to the public....

Almost ten years passed before this Court decided the landmark *Schmid* case. In *Schmid, supra,* Princeton University, a private, non-profit institution, prohibited persons not affiliated with the university from soliciting and distributing political literature on campus. The defendant, a non-student, was arrested and convicted for trespassing while distributing Labor Party materials on the Princeton campus. Princeton's regulations required off-campus organizations to obtain permission before distributing materials. The defendant claimed that his arrest was unconstitutional because distribution of political material was protected by both the First Amendment and Article I of the New Jersey Constitution. Princeton argued that as a private institution, it was not subject to the strictures of the federal or State Constitutions.

Analyzing Princeton's claim, the Court recognized that the

> constitutional equipoise between expressional rights and property rights must be similarly gauged on a scale measuring the nature and extent of the public's use of such property. Thus, even as against the exercise of important rights of speech, assembly, petition and the like, private property itself remains protected under due process standards from untoward interference with or confiscatory restrictions upon its reasonable use. [423 A.2d 615.]

The Court crafted "the test to be applied to ascertain the parameters of the rights of speech and assembly upon privately owned property and the extent to which such property reasonably can be restricted to accommodate these rights." That test requires courts to consider

(1) the nature, purposes, and primary use of such private property, generally, its "normal" use,

(2) the extent and nature of the public's invitation to use that property, and (3) the purpose of the expressional activity undertaken upon such property in relation to both the private and public use of the property.

The Court explained that such a test would allow the court "to ascertain whether in a given case owners of private property may be required to permit, subject to suitable restrictions, the reasonable exercise by individuals of the constitutional freedoms of speech and assembly." In assessing the reasonableness of any restrictions, the court shall consider "whether there exist convenient and feasible alternative means to individuals to engage in substantially the same expressional activity." The Court applied the test to Princeton and found that the university had invited the public to use its facilities, the defendant's expressional activities were consonant with both the private and public uses of Princeton's campus, and Princeton's regulations contained no standards for governing the exercise of free speech. Therefore, the Court concluded that Princeton violated the defendant's constitutional rights of speech and assembly.

In *Bluvias v. Winfield Mutual Housing Corp.*, 540 A.2d 1324 (N.J. Super.App.Div.), *certif. granted*, 546 A.2d 538 (1988), the Appellate Division considered a constitutional challenge brought against a mutual housing corporation under circumstances similar to the present case. In *Bluvias*, with the exception of the streets, the Winfield Mutual Housing Corporation (Corporation) owned the entire Township of Winfield (Township), including the municipal building, school, shopping area, and the dwelling units. The Corporation had acquired the property in late 1950 from the federal government. Pursuant to the terms of its mortgage, each member of the Corporation was required to execute a mutual ownership contract to establish the right to "'perpetual use in a dwelling unit' in the project and imposed restrictions on becoming a 'member' of the Corporation." If a member ceased to occupy the dwelling unit, the Corporation had the right to acquire the unit for a set price. Even after the Corporation paid off the mortgage and the restriction on transfer lapsed, a majority of the members voted to continue the restrictions.

... The plaintiffs brought suit against the Corporation, asserting that the bylaws and rules of the Corporation violated their constitutional right to sell their property. The Appellate Division found that the nature of the Corporation, although it owned all the land, was not a company town under the definitions of *Marsh* and *Schmid*. Because the Township had its own government and included citizens who were not members of the Corporation, and because all powers usually held by a municipality were exercised by the Township, the panel concluded that the actions of the Corporation were private, not public.

We granted certification to consider "whether the membership by-laws promulgated by [the Corporation] constitute[d] governmental action and a denial of equal protection under the Federal and New Jersey Constitutions." *Bluvias v. Winfield Mut. Hous. Corp.*, 556 A.2d 321 (N.J. 1989).... Later, however, we dismissed the appeal as improvidently granted because we found "no issue of constitutional dimension." We noted that the Corporation, although it owned all of the property and dwelling units within the Township, was not a state actor under *Marsh*, and thus, it was not subject to constitutional standards. Further, we noted that "[a] duly-elected governing body and a board of education established under law administer[s] any necessary governmental services" within the Township.

The Court expanded the *Schmid* test in *New Jersey Coalition Against War in the Middle East v. J.M.B. Realty Corp.*, 650 A.2d 757 (N.J. 1994), *cert. denied*, 516 U.S. 812 (1995). In *Coalition*, the plaintiffs sought judicial approval to permit their members to distribute leaflets in shopping centers to support opposition to any military action in the Middle East. The Court concluded that "each of the elements of the [*Schmid*] standard and their ultimate balance support the conclusion that leafletting is constitutionally required to be permitted." Thus, the Court not only relied on the three-pronged test in *Schmid*, but also on the general balancing of expressional rights and private interests. Nevertheless, the Court recognized that regional shopping centers have broad powers to adopt reasonable conditions "concerning the time, place, and manner of such leafletting." The Court limited its holding to "leafletting and associated speech in support of, or in opposition to, causes, candidates, and parties-political and societal free speech." To avoid future questions, the Court addressed the "horribles" the defendants asserted would be the inevitable consequence of its decision. The Court emphasized that "[n]o highway strip mall, no football stadium, no theatre, no single high suburban store, no stand-alone use, and no small to medium shopping center sufficiently satisfies the standard of *Schmid* to warrant the constitutional extension of free speech to those premises, and we so hold."

This Court has also addressed the proper standard for determining the reasonableness of restrictions that shopping mall owners may impose on leafletting and other political and societal speech. *Green Party, supra*,.... In *Green Party*, the plaintiffs sought to invalidate three regulations the shopping mall adopted to limit leafletting and other similar activities. The mall required the plaintiffs to obtain a $1,000,000 insurance policy, "to limit their access to the mall to one day, or a few days a year," and to execute a "hold harmless" agreement in favor of the mall.

The Court applied the principles of *Schmid* and *Coalition*, explaining that in balancing the rights of citizens to speak and assemble against the private property rights of mall owners, the court must consider the nature and importance of the affected right, the extent to which the restriction impedes that right, and the mall's need for retaining the restriction. The Court emphasized that "[t]he more important the constitutional right sought to be exercised, the greater the mall's need must be to justify interference with the exercise of that right." The Court concluded that the proofs in favor of the mall's restrictions did not establish that they were intended "to achieve legitimate business objectives while preserving the leafleteers['] expressive rights." Consequently, the Court invalidated the conditions imposed for insurance and the hold harmless agreement, noting that a "hold harmless agreement related to the actual activities of the leafleteers that cause liability to be created would not be objectionable." Although the Court recognized that the parties may have reached an agreement concerning the number of days when leafletting may be sought, the Court found that "more than one day per year is reasonably required to exercise the expressive rights requested."

C.

Our review of the case law in other jurisdictions reveals that only a handful of states recognize a constitutional right to engage in free speech, assembly, or electoral activity on privately owned property held open to the public, such as a shopping mall or a college campus. *[citations omitted]* Those ... [states] based their determinations, in part, on the open and public nature of the shopping mall. Further, the Supreme Court of Oregon, which originally found a constitutional right to engage in free speech and related activities, appears to have retreated from that position....

Many other states have declined to recognize a constitutional right to free speech in privately owned malls, largely on the ground that malls are not "state actors." [citations omitted]

We note also that, in the context of an apartment complex, the California Supreme Court modified its position ... and now requires state action before free speech rights will be recognized. *Golden Gateway Ctr. v. Golden Gateway Tenants Ass'n,* 29 P.3d 797, 803 (Cal. 2001). In *Golden Gateway Center* ... [t]he regulations for the complex [a residential apartment complex] banned all solicitation inside the building. The tenants association claimed a right to distribute a newsletter and leaflets under the California Constitution's free speech clause. The California Supreme Court noted that "state action" on the part of the apartment complex was a prerequisite to the tenants' free speech claim. The court found that the apartment complex was privately owned and that access was restricted to tenants and their invitees. Thus, the court held that the apartment complex was not the "functional equivalent of a traditional public forum" and was not a state actor for purposes of the application of California's free speech clause.

... [T]he vast majority of other jurisdictions that have interpreted a state constitutional provision with language similar to our constitution's free speech provision require "state action" as a precondition to imposing constitutional obligations on private property owners.... [citations omitted] Those courts recognize either explicitly or implicitly the principle that "the fundamental nature of a constitution is to govern the relationship between the people and their government, not to control the rights of the people vis-à-vis each other." *Southcenter Joint Venture,* 780 P.2d [1282] at 1286 [Wash. 1989]....

IV.

We concluded in *Schmid,* that the rights of free speech and assembly under our constitution are not only secure from interference by governmental or public bodies, but under certain circumstances from the interference by the owner of private property as well. Simply stated, we have not followed the approach of other jurisdictions to require some state action before the free speech and assembly clauses under our constitution may be invoked.

With those general principles as a backdrop, we turn now to apply the *Schmid/Coalition* test to the present matter.... [W]e have not followed the approach of other jurisdictions to require some state action before the free speech and assembly clauses under our constitution may be invoked. Even in the absence of state action, we must determine whether the acts of a homeowners' association violated its members' free speech and association rights in the setting of this private housing association.

This case presents an additional complication: it involves restrictions on conduct both on the private housing association's property and on the homeowners' properties. However, "[i]t is the extent of the restriction, and the circumstances of the restriction that are critical, not the identity of the party restricting free speech." *Coalition, supra.* We conclude that the three-pronged test in *Schmid* and the general balancing of expressional rights and private property interests in *Coalition* are the appropriate standards to decide this case.

Holding:

... [T]he *Schmid* test takes into account ... [three factors].

The first *Schmid* factor requires that we consider the nature, purposes, and primary use of the property. Twin Rivers is a common interest community "in which the property is burdened by servitudes requiring property owners to contribute to maintenance of commonly held property or to pay dues or assessments to an owners association that provides services or facilities to the community." *Restatement (Third) of Property: Servitudes* § 6[.2] (2000). We have recognized that "[a] common-interest community is distinguishable from any other form of real property ownership because 'there is a commonality of interest, an interdependence directly tied to the use, enjoyment, and ownership of property.'" *Fox v. Kings Grant Maint. Ass'n*, 770 A.2d 707 (N.J. 2001) (quoting Wayne S. Hyatt, *Condominium and Homeowner Association Practice: Community Association Law* § 2.01 at 25 (2d ed.1988)).

The primary use of the property in Twin Rivers is residential. There are privately owned businesses within the borders of Twin Rivers, but the Association derives no revenue from them. East Windsor Township, not Twin Rivers, provides for the school system, the police and fire departments, the municipal court system, and the first aid services. Twin Rivers offers its residents services in the form of landscape maintenance, upkeep of trust-owned roads, removal of trash from certain sections of the community, and cleaning of snow. Thus, we find the nature, purposes, and primary use of Twin Rivers's property is for private purposes and does not favor a finding that the Association's rules and regulations violated plaintiffs' constitutional rights.

primary use = residential

nature is for private purposes

The second *Schmid* factor requires that we examine the extent and nature of the public's invitation to use the property. A public invitation to use the premises may be express or implied. As we explained in *Coalition, supra,* an implied invitation can be inferred where the property owner permits and encourages public use of the property. Here, the Association has not invited the public to use its property. Although Twin Rivers is not a gated community and its roads are accessible to public traffic, we agree with the Association's position that "Trust-owned property and facilities are for the exclusive use of Twin Rivers residents and their invited guests." Moreover, the mere fact that owners may sell or rent property to members of the public who are invited to come into Twin Rivers and inspect such property hardly implicates a public invitation. We conclude that the limited nature of the public's invitation to use the property does not favor a finding that the Association's rules and regulations violated plaintiffs' constitutional rights.

limited inv. to public.

The third *Schmid* factor concerns the purpose of the expressional activity in relation to both the private and public use of the property. This part of the test requires that we examine "the compatibility of the free speech sought to be exercised with the uses of the property." Essentially, we must look to the fairness of the restrictions imposed by the Association in relation to plaintiffs' free speech rights. In this case, plaintiffs' expressional activities—posting political signs, free use of the community room, and access to the community newspaper—involve political-like speech aimed at affecting the manner in which Twin Rivers is managed.

Not unreasonably restricted. (handwritten)

We find that plaintiffs' expressional activities are not <u>unreasonably restricted</u>. As the Association points out, the relationship between it and the homeowners is a contractual one, formalized in reasonable covenants that appear in all deeds. Moreover, unlike the university in *Schmid,* and the shopping center in *Coalition,* Twin Rivers is not a private forum that invites the public on its property to either facilitate academic discourse or to encourage public commerce. Rather, Twin Rivers is a private, residential community whose residents have contractually agreed to abide by the common rules and regulations of the Association. The mutual benefit and reciprocal nature of those rules and regulations, and their enforcement, is essential to the fundamental nature of the communal living arrangement that Twin Rivers residents enjoy. We further conclude that this factor does not weigh in favor of finding that the Association's rules and regulations violated plaintiffs' constitutional rights.

We are mindful that at least in regard to the signs on the property of the homeowners, it is the private homeowner's property and not that of the Association that is impacted. The private property owner not only is "protected under due process standards from untoward interference with or confiscatory restrictions upon its reasonable use," *Schmid,* but also our constitution affirmatively grants the homeowner free speech and assembly rights that may be exercised on that property. Notably, the Association permits expressional activities to take place on plaintiffs' property but with some minor restrictions. Homeowners are permitted to place a single sign in each window and signs may be placed in the flower beds adjacent to the homes. Those limitations are clearly not an "untoward interference with" or a "confiscatory restriction" on the reasonable use by plaintiffs' on their property to implicate due process standards.

Holding: (handwritten)
— not a municip (handwritten)

The outcome of the balancing of the expressional rights and the privacy interests is obvious. "We do not interfere lightly with private property rights." *Coalition, supra.* We find that the minor restrictions on plaintiffs' expressional activities are not unreasonable or oppressive, and the Association is not acting as a municipality. The Association's restrictions concerning the placement of the signs, the use of the community room, and access to its newspaper are reasonable "concerning the time, place, and manner of" such restrictions. Neither singularly nor in combination is the *Schmid/Coalition* test satisfied in favor of concluding that a constitutional right was infringed here. Consequently, we conclude that in balancing plaintiffs' expressional rights against the Association's private property interest, the Association's policies do not violate the free speech and right of assembly clauses of the New Jersey Constitution.

Additionally, plaintiffs have other means of expression beyond the Association's newspaper. Plaintiffs can walk through the neighborhood, ring the doorbells of their neighbors, and advance their views. As found by the trial court, plaintiffs can distribute their own newsletter to residents, and have done so. As members of the Association, plaintiffs can vote, run for office, and participate through the elective process in the decision-making of the Association. Thus, plaintiffs may seek to garner a majority to change the rules and regulations to reduce or eliminate the restrictions they now challenge.

V.

We recognize the concerns of plaintiffs that bear on the extent and exercise of their constitutional rights in this and other similar common interest communities. At a minimum, any restrictions on the exercise of those rights must be reasonable as to time, place, and manner. Our holding does not suggest, however, that residents of a homeowners' association may never successfully seek constitutional redress against a governing association that unreasonably infringes their free speech rights.

Moreover, common interest residents have other protections. First, the business judgment rule protects common interest community residents from arbitrary decision-making. *See Thanasoulis v. Winston Towers 200 Ass'n, Inc.*, 542 A.2d 900 (N.J. 1988) (Garibaldi, J., dissenting in part and concurring in part). That is, a homeowners' association's governing body has "a fiduciary relationship to the unit owners, comparable to the obligation that a board of directors of a corporation owes to its stockholders." *Siller v. Hartz Mountain Assocs.*, 461 A.2d 568 (N.J.), *cert. denied*, 464 U.S. 961 (1983). Pursuant to the business judgment rule, a homeowners' association's rules and regulations will be invalidated (1) if they are not authorized by statute or by the bylaws or master deed, or (2) if the association's actions are "fraudulent, self-dealing or unconscionable." *Owners of the Manor Homes of Whittingham v. Whittingham Homeowners Ass'n*, 842 A.2d 853 (N.J. Super. App.Div.2004); *see, e.g., Siller.* Our Appellate Division has uniformly invoked the business judgment rule in cases involving homeowners' associations. *See, e.g., Whittingham; Walker v. Briarwood Condo Ass'n*, 644 A.2d 634 (App.Div.1994); *see also Mulligan v. Panther Valley Prop. Owners Ass'n*, 766 A.2d 1186 (N.J. Super. App.Div.2001).

Second, residents are protected by *N.J.S.A.* 45:22A-44 of the PREDFDA [Planned Real Estate Development Full Disclosure Act], which provides:

Powers and duties of associations

a. Subject to the master deed, declaration of covenants and restrictions or other instruments of creation, the association may do all that it is legally entitled to do under the laws applicable to its form of organization.

b. The association shall exercise its powers and discharge its functions in a manner that protects and furthers the health, safety and general welfare of the residents of the community. [emphasis added]

c. The association shall provide a fair and efficient procedure for the resolution of disputes between individual unit owners and the association, and between unit owners, which shall be readily available as an alternative to litigation.

Although we have not yet had the opportunity to interpret *N.J.S.A.* 45:22A-44, restrictive covenants established by homeowners' associations that unreasonably limit speech and association rights could be challenged under subsection (b) of the statute.

Finally, residents are protected under traditional principles of property law — principles that specifically account for the rights afforded under our constitution's free speech and association clauses. Our courts have recognized that restrictive covenants on real property that violate public policy are void as unenforceable. *See, e.g., Clarke v. Kurtz*, 196 A. 727 (N.J. Eq. & A.1938) ("The equitable grounds on which restrictions of this nature may be enforced at the instance of a subsequent grantee of the common grantor are well defined. One owning a tract of land may convey a portion of it, and by appropriate covenant or agreement may lawfully restrict the use of the part conveyed for the benefit of the unsold portion, *providing that the nature of the restricted use is not contrary to principles of public policy.*" (emphasis added)); *Courts at Beachgate v. Bird*, 545 A.2d 243 (N.J. Super. Ch.Div.1988) (noting that "[r]estrictions in a master deed" should be enforced "unless those provisions 'are wholly arbitrary in their application, in violation of public policy, or that they abrogate some fundamental constitutional right'").

In *Davidson Bros. v. D. Katz & Sons, Inc.*, we enumerated the factors that courts should consider in determining whether restrictive covenants are "reasonable," and thus enforceable:

[handwritten margin note: Traditional property law affords free speech protection]

[handwritten margin note: Courts the following regardly enforceability:]

1. The intention of the parties when the covenant was executed, and whether the parties had a viable purpose which did not at the time interfere with existing commercial laws, such as antitrust laws, or public policy.

2. Whether the covenant had an impact on the considerations exchanged when the covenant was originally executed....

3. Whether the covenant clearly and expressly sets forth the restrictions.

4. Whether the covenant was in writing, recorded, and if so, whether the subsequent grantee had actual notice of the covenant.

5. Whether the covenant is reasonable concerning area, time or duration....

6. Whether the covenant imposes an unreasonable restraint on trade or secures a monopoly for the covenantor....

7. Whether the covenant interferes with the public interest.

8. Whether, even if the covenant was reasonable at the time it was executed, "changed circumstances" now make the covenant unreasonable.

[579 *A.2d* 288 (1990)]....

Our constitution and the fundamental rights it protects play a pivotal role in evidencing public policy.... [citations omitted]. Indeed, in *Hennessey v. Coastal Eagle Point Oil Co.,* 609 *A.2d* 11 (N.J. 1992), we found that in New Jersey, the "highest source of public policy" is our constitution. Thus, restrictive covenants that unreasonably restrict speech — a right most substantial in our constitutional scheme — may be declared unenforceable as a matter of public policy.

VI.

The judgment of the Appellate Division is reversed and we reinstate the judgment of the trial court.

For reversal and reinstatement—Chief Justice ZAZZALI and Justices LONG, LaVECCHIA, ALBIN, WALLACE, RIVERA-SOTO and HOENS.

Opposed-None.

Notes & Questions

1. Prof. Frank Askin of Rutgers-Newark University Law School represented the plaintiffs in *Twin Rivers*. Prof. Askin, who founded the Constitutional Litigation Clinic at Rutgers in 1970, has written several articles expressing concerns over the impact that increased privatization of public spaces and residential communities is having on free speech rights. See Frank Askin, *Community Associations and the New Jersey Constitution*, New Jersey Lawyer, the Magazine, April, 2005; *Twin Rivers: Why the Appellate Division Got It Right*, New Jersey Lawyer, the Magazine, Oct. 2006.

In *Free Speech, Private Space, and The Constitution*, 29 Rutgers L.J. 947, at 960–61 (1998), he wrote:

Once upon a time, the United States Supreme Court held that the First Amendment offered special solicitude for "the poorly financed causes of little people."[67] It was that notion that gave rise to decisions which protected the right of grassroots proselytizers to disseminate their messages in privately owned company

---

67. Martin v. Struthers, 319 U.S. 141, 146 (1943).

towns, at private shopping centers, as well as by going door to door along the public streets. But the United States Supreme Court backed away from doctrines which extended constitutional protections to privately owned forums that had replaced public spaces; more and more of the nation's residential streets are now off-limits in private gated communities. As a consequence, the public forum for the "poorly financed causes of little people" is shrinking away. If grass roots organizers cannot go to the new town squares or go door to door in gated communities to disseminate their messages, their opportunity to be heard is greatly reduced in the modern age.

2. The New Jersey Supreme Court's decision in *Twin Rivers* is criticized in a casenote in the Harvard Law Review for having used its *Schmid* and *Coalition* precedents as if the interests at stake were those of the public instead of focusing on the fact that it was the community residents' rights that were being curtailed. Part of the critique of the court's application *Schmid-Coalition* test is stated at 121 Harv. L. Rev. 644, 648:

> By focusing on the general public when the aggrieved parties were Twin Rivers residents, the court essentially created a test that invariably favors private property rights. Since CICs are by definition private communities, consideration of the property's nature and purposes will always weigh in favor of the rights of homeowners' associations. Similarly, since CICs by their nature exclude the public, the second prong, examining the public's invitation to use the property, will always favor the homeowners' associations.... Like the state action requirement used in other jurisdictions, the court's misguided application of the Schmid-Coalition test accords no import to the value of the restricted practice or the nature of the complainant's asserted right, frustrating the test' core purpose.

3. A number of commentators have called for protecting First Amendment rights of common interest community residents by treating the community as if it were a public governmental unit. See, *e.g*, Adrienne Iwamoto Suarez, *Covenants, Conditions, and Restrictions ... on Free Speech? First Amendment Rights in Common Interest Communities*, 40 Real Prop. Prob. & Tr. J. 739 (2006); Steven Siegel, *The Constitution and Private Government: Toward the Recognition of Constitutional Rights in Private Residential Communities Fifty Years After* Marsh v. Alabama, 6 Wm. & Mary Bill Rts.J. 461 (1997).

4. Do members need constitutional protection against their common interest communities? The court in *Twin Rivers* suggests that there are ample protections available through state statutes, the common law of servitudes, and exercise of political power within the community. We take up these alternate means of protection for fundamental rights in Section B of this Chapter.

2. Rights of Outsiders to Gain Access to a Common Interest Community

The Guttenberg Taxpayers and Rentpayers Ass'n v. Galaxy Towers Condo. Ass'n

Superior Court of New Jersey, Appellate Division
686 A.2d 344 (N.J. Super. App. Div. 1995)

PER CURIAM. On April 4, 1994, plaintiffs filed a complaint in the Chancery Division and obtained an order for defendants to show cause why they should not be preliminarily and permanently enjoined from preventing plaintiffs from distributing pamphlets or flyers on defendants' property in anticipation of a school board election on April 19, 1994. A hearing on the order to show cause took place on April 15, 1994, at the conclusion of which the Chancery judge denied plaintiffs' application for a preliminary injunction and also dismissed the matter for failure to state a cause of action. On April 26, 1994, an order was entered in accordance with the judge's ruling. On June 7, 1994, plaintiffs filed a notice of appeal.

Defendant Galaxy Towers Condominium Association is a nonprofit corporation that manages condominium property known as Galaxy Towers in Guttenberg. The association is governed by a nine member board of directors, elected by the owners of the condominium units. All of the owners and directors are members of the association. Defendant, Bernard Furman, is the president of the board of directors.

Plaintiff Guttenberg Taxpayers and Rentpayers Association is a nonprofit, unincorporated association involved in political activities in Guttenberg. Plaintiff Thomas G. Rizzi is an association trustee, and plaintiff Bill Scoullos is a candidate for the Guttenberg School Board.

Galaxy Towers is a private, residential property made up of 1075 condominium units located in three high-rise buildings, with related common elements, such as hallways, elevators, lobbies and a parking garage. Security personnel are employed by the condominium association to guard the lobby and garage. There is a shopping center located within the Galaxy Towers complex, known as the Galaxy Mall, owned by a third party. The mall is entirely open to the public and contains entrances to Galaxy Towers. There is a bus stop on the Galaxy Towers property for approximately 100 commuters who utilize a private bus service.

According to the certification of Sanford Simon, vice-president of the condominium association, the public is never invited into or permitted to enter Galaxy Towers without permission. Regulations applicable to all residents prohibit anyone from door-to-door canvassing or solicitation. These regulations also apply to outsiders, thereby preventing anyone from visiting or soliciting at any apartment unannounced or without the permission of an owner or resident. Simon certified that at no time has any political candidate, party or group been granted permission to distribute materials within Galaxy Towers.

The Town of Guttenberg is divided into six voting districts. Residents of Galaxy Towers constitute approximately thirty percent of the total number of registered voters in Guttenberg, and approximately eighty-seven percent of the registered voters in District Six. The polling place for this district is located in the Galaxy Mall.

The condominium association from time to time, in its regular newsletter and special notices and bulletins, endorses candidates for local elective office. The record is unclear as to whether the association distributes these materials by mail, door-to-door, or by leaving the material in a central location in the complex.[1]

In April 1993, plaintiff Rizzi sought the association's consent to distribute political literature door-to-door in Galaxy Towers by leaving materials under the doors of the units without disturbing the residents and also to leave such materials at the concierge desk in each lobby of the towers. The association denied this request. Rizzi made a similar request in December 1993, and was denied. After the taxpayers' association fielded a slate of candidates for the April 1994 school board election, it sought permission to place its

---

1. We were advised at oral argument by the attorney for the defendants that he understands distribution is by door-to-door delivery.

material on tables in the lobbies and to go door-to-door. It appears that before the hearing on the order to show cause, the condominium association distributed a flyer to unit owners endorsing several candidates in the school board election.

Condo assoc. distributed flyer supporting certain candidates.

The Chancery judge rejected plaintiffs' request for a preliminary injunction based on his application of the tripartite test enunciated by our Supreme Court in *State v. Schmid*, 84 N.J. 535, 423 A.2d 615 (1980), appeal dismissed *sub. nom Princeton University v. Schmid*, 455 U.S. 100 … (1982). The judge found that the normal or primary use of the property was for residential purposes and that there was no indication that there had been any public invitation to use the property. He also found that this was not a case where plaintiffs had a "right of reply" because the distribution of election material by the condominium association was, in effect, a distribution by the unit owners themselves. He added that plaintiffs had a "reasonable alternative" — namely, distributing their literature by mail to the unit owners of the condominium.

Trial judge says cld. mail to honowrs.

Although the school board election in question has already been held, the issues raised in this appeal will not be considered moot as they present matters of great public importance. …

Plaintiffs claim that under the test enunciated by our Supreme Court to ascertain the parameters of the right of free speech upon private property in New Jersey and under the common law, they should be given the opportunity to respond to electioneering by a residential association that represents approximately thirty percent of the municipal electorate. Plaintiffs maintain that the public interest in allowing citizens to be exposed to both sides of a political controversy is sufficient to allow them to go onto private property for the limited purpose of exercising their "right of reply," once that property is used by others for the same purpose. Plaintiffs ask that we reverse and instruct the trial court to enter a permanent injunction allowing them to enter defendants' property to respond to any election-related materials distributed on behalf of the condominium association.

Is there a right to respond?

Plaintiffs see their proposed activity as sanctioned by the common law principle of protecting important public activities from unreasonable restraints by private property owners, pointing to the holding in *State v. Kolcz*, 114 N.J. Super. 408, 276 A.2d 595 (County Ct. 1971). In that case, defendants were convicted of trespassing when they attempted to circulate a petition to change the form of the municipal government at a planned retirement community. Under the rules and regulations governing the community, solicitors and unauthorized persons were not to be admitted. Defendants sought to ask the residents of the development to sign the petition by going door-to-door to the dwelling units. Between twenty and twenty-five percent of the municipality's registered voters resided in the development. Evidence was offered that a district committeeman of one of the major political parties, who was a resident of the development, engaged in door-to-door campaigning, and that other residents of the community who were political candidates were introduced at the community's social affairs.

The court equated the retirement community to a municipality because "it is in many essential regards a self-sufficient community." In the court's view, while the corporate officers of the community could speak for its residents on certain matters, they could not bar what they knew to be a bona fide political endeavor. To hold otherwise, according to the court, would, in effect, create a political "isolation booth."

Plaintiffs further assert that Galaxy Towers is the functional equivalent of a "company-owned town," as illustrated in *Marsh v. Alabama*, 326 U.S. 501 (1946). See also *State v. Shack*, 58 N.J. 297, 277 A.2d 369 (1971) (the ownership of real property does not include the right to bar access to governmental services available to migrant workers); *Laguna Publishing*

Co. v. Golden Rain Found., 131 Cal. App. 3d 816, 182 Cal. Rptr. 813 (1982), appeal dismissed, 459 U.S. 1192, 103 S. Ct. 1170, 75 L. Ed. 2d 422 (1983) (give-away newspaper excluded from a private, residential, walled community demonstrated unequal treatment as competitor allowed entry).

The issues presented are not capable of satisfactory review because of the absence of a proper factual record. Our Supreme Court in *Schmid, supra,* promulgated the following test:

> Under the State Constitution, the test to be applied to ascertain the parameters of the rights of speech and assembly upon privately owned property and the extent to which such property reasonably can be restricted to accommodate these rights involves several elements. This standard must take into account (1) the nature, purposes, and primary use of such private property, generally, its "normal" use, (2) the extent and nature of the public's invitation to use that property, and (3) the purpose of the expressional activity undertaken upon such property in relation to both the private and public use of the property. This is a multi-faceted test which must be applied to ascertain whether in a given case owners of private property may be required to permit, subject to suitable restrictions, the reasonable exercise by individuals of the constitutional freedoms of speech and assembly....

Following the Chancery judge's ruling, our Supreme Court handed down its opinion in *New Jersey Coalition Against War v. J.M.B. Realty Corp.*, 138 N.J. 326, 650 A.2d 757 (1994). The Court held that the first two factors of the *Schmid* test—the normal use of the property and the nature and extent of the public invitation—are best considered together where "they are most closely interrelated." These two factors, according to the Court, are primarily factual. Similarly, with respect to the second factor, the Court stated:

> The factual issue is the overall nature and extent of the invitation to the public, not somehow restricted to the subjective "purpose" of defendants' uses, and certainly not limited to whether defendants extended an explicit invitation to plaintiff to speak. The issue is whether defendants' actual conduct, the multitude of uses they permitted and encouraged, including expressive uses, amounted to an implied invitation and, if so, the nature and extent of that invitation.

The Court described the third factor as examining the "compatibility" of the free speech sought to be exercised with the uses of the property. The Court pointed out that:

> the test to determine the existence of the constitutional obligation is multifaceted; the outcome depends on a consideration of all three factors of the standard and ultimately on a balancing between the protections to be accorded the rights of private property owners and the free speech rights of individuals to leaflet on their property.

Thus, the applicable tests as announced by our Supreme Court are vitally dependent on the factual circumstances presented in each case. Consequently, we are satisfied that the important constitutional issues presented here may not be decided without a full factual record being developed. The required balancing of property rights and free speech rights depends on a discreet consideration of the facts concerning the use of the property, as well as the practices of the condominium association with regard to its endorsement of political candidates and issues, and other activities deemed pertinent under the present case law.

We reverse the dismissal of plaintiffs' complaint and remand for a plenary hearing. We do not retain jurisdiction.

———————

The Guttenberg Taxpayers and Rentpayers Ass'n v. Galaxy Towers Condo. Ass'n

Superior Court of New Jersey, Chancery Division
688 A.2d 156 (N.J. Super. Ch. Div. 1996)

GREENBERG, J. In this action, the court is required to determine whether a condominium association that actively endorses candidates for political office by distributing campaign flyers to its residents, can deny access to its privately-owned property, to plaintiffs, a citizen group that wishes to engage in the same type of activity. Plaintiffs seek a declaratory judgment finding that defendants' actions prohibiting such access violate the New Jersey Constitution's guarantee of freedom of speech, N.J.S.A. Const. Art. 1, Par. 6 (1971), and permanently enjoining defendants from engaging in this type of activity.

[This decision was entered after a bench trial held on remand from the Appellate Division. — Eds.]

. . .

The courts of this State that have applied the *Schmid* standard in favor of public access have required an initial determination that there is some type of public dedication of the property.... This court finds that in this case, this factual predicate is met.

Galaxy is routinely used for political campaigning. During election time in Guttenberg, distributing political leaflets and handbills is part of the normal, everyday activities that occur on the property. The residents of Galaxy have come to expect as a matter of course, that during election time there will be a flurry of election materials placed under their doors, and available in the common areas of their residential development.

The activities engaged in by the Association are similar in nature to what would be expected from a political organization, from its endorsement of candidates to its get-out-the-vote drives during election time. This court finds that there consistently has been at election time, significant dedication of this property from private to political and thus public use.

Political speech "occupies a preferred position in our system of constitutionally-protected interests." ... *Murdock v. Pennsylvania*, 319 U.S. 105 (1943). Since the Association has made distribution of political flyers a normal use of its property, any invasion of privacy by allowing similar distribution of plaintiffs' literature, subject to reasonable regulations imposed by defendants (conceivably including requiring such distribution by defendant's agents), would be minimal and would not grant more access than necessary to serve a significant constitutional purpose.

The conclusion reached in this matter is extremely fact sensitive. Because the nature of the private property at issue here is quite different from the type of property at issue in *Schmid* or *Coalition*, this court draws guidance from *State v. Kolcz*, 114 N.J. Super. 408, 276 A.2d 595 (1971). *Kolcz* involved Rossmoor community, a "planned retirement village," that in many ways resembles the self-enclosed environment that exists at Galaxy. The corporate officers of the Rossmoor community prohibited people from soliciting door-to-door.... The defendants in *Kolcz* were members of a citizen group that were seeking signatures on a political petition, but who were denied admittance into Rossmoor. Noting that "there is no substitute for door-to-door communication," the court determined that the corporate officers could not "bar what it knows to be a bona fide political endeavor." The court went on to hold that

> although the guaranties of free speech and free press will not be used to force a community to admit peddlers or solicitors of publications to the homes of its

residents ... such guaranties should be used to insure that each individual alone decides what political and religious information he wishes to receive.... This court does not wish to open wide the gates of Rossmoor and thereby allow anyone to come in at anytime, for any purpose. Nevertheless, this court feels compelled to hold ajar the gates of Rossmoor under the present circumstances. To hold otherwise would in effect, create a political 'isolation booth'.

This court finds that in this case, plaintiffs have no adequate meaningful substitute for "door-to-door" communication with the residents of Galaxy. Defendant's contention that plaintiff is able to carry a campaign to the residents by mail and leafletting on public property and at the public voting place (to which plaintiff replies it is not financially able effectively to mail in time to respond to defendant's last minute campaign tactics and is unable to obtain access to a meaningful number of residents on "the street"), misses the point. A level playing field requires equal access to this condominium because it has become in essence a political "company town" (a more constitutionally impaired status than the Rossmoor political "isolation booth") in which political access controlled by the Association is the only "game in town." Distribution of plaintiffs' literature in essentially the same manner in which the Association's literature is distributed is the only effective way plaintiffs can be guaranteed equal access to the registered voters in Galaxy, who represent a substantial percent of the registered voters of Guttenberg.

In light of the above conclusion, it is unnecessary to consider whether defendants' activities have resulted as a matter of law in an "implied invitation" to plaintiffs to respond.

In view of the foregoing, judgment shall be entered against defendants and in favor of plaintiffs.

Retrospective and Observations

Frank Askin, the Rutgers Law School professor and a member of the board of The American Civil Liberties Union of New Jersey, who represented plaintiffs in the *Twin Rivers* case, represented The Guttenberg Taxpayers and Rentpayers Association in this case. According to Prof. Askin, Guttenberg, New Jersey, is an old, working-class community into which was dropped a very large, wealthy enclave. Almost a quarter of Guttenberg's registered voters live in The Galaxy.

In Prof. Askin's opinion, Bernard Furman, who served as president of the Galaxy Condominium Association for 10 years had successfully built a formidable political machine. He persuaded residents to register to vote; he mobilized Association members to attend City Council meetings; he even assembled parades to the mayor's office in order to win political concessions. Under his leadership, the Association was able to gain tax abatements from the City.

The first election which followed the decision in favor of The Guttenberg Taxpayers and Rentpayers Association was the first election in some time where the Galaxy Towers-backed candidate lost. The Association appealed the appellate division's decision to the New Jersey Supreme Court, but *certiorari* was denied.

Notes & Questions

1. As the *Guttenberg* cases illustrate, getting involved in local politics may obtain benefits for the community. In *Guttenberg*, it was favorable tax treatment. In other cases, it might be to obtain influence in zoning and planning decisions that could have an impact on the community. Does a community open itself up to having to provide access for political canvassers if it engages in political activity? If so, is that a bad thing? Are there good reasons to allow common interest communities to insulate themselves from uninvited contact by outsiders? Compare Laura T. Rahe, *The Right To Exclude: Preserving the Autonomy of the Homeowners' Association*, 34 Urb. Law. 521 (2002) with David J. Kennedy, Note, *Residential Associations as State Actors: Regulating the Impact of Gated Communities on Nonmembers*, 105 Yale L.J. 761 (1995).

2. Are the *Guttenberg* cases still good law after *Twin Rivers*?

3. Margaret Farrand Saxton, *Protecting the Marketplace of Ideas: Access for Solicitors in Common Interest Communities*, 51 UCLA L. Rev. 1437 (2004) suggests that to protect residents' rights to receive and distribute information, courts should uphold no-access rules only when a community association "can demonstrate that all residents have affirmatively and specifically consented to such rules, or to the CIC association board's authority to pass them at a later date."

Are Community Associations Really Mini-Governments?

Aside from *Shelley v. Kraemer*, the primary argument for treating community associations as state actors subject to the Fourteenth Amendment to the United States Constitution is that these associations perform governmental functions—that they are "mini-governments."[v] The extent to which this is true, of course, depends on the size and functions of the community, but at the larger end of the scale, there is no doubt that community associations do function as mini-governments. But, should they be treated like public governments? In a 2005 article, *Making Common Interest Communities Work: The Next Step*, 37 Urban Lawyer 359, Prof. Susan French analyzed the nature of community associations:

Community associations (CAs) are similar to public governments in that:

- CAs manage communal property they own, which may include the streets, parks, and other types of "public" property within the community.

- CAs enforce land use restrictions included in the CC&Rs. These restrictions may be very similar to those in zoning and design control ordinances adopted by local governments.

- CAs adopt rules and regulations governing use of property within the CA. Rules governing use of common property within the CA may be very similar to ordinances adopted by local government.

- CAs levy assessments on property in the community to support their operations. Like local property taxes, CA assessments are generally secured by a lien that may be foreclosed in the event of default.

V. Uriel Reichman, Residential Private Governments: An Introductory Survey, 43 U. Chi. L. Rev. 253 (1976), was one of the first to write about the governmental character of community associations.

- CAs may provide services such as utilities, street maintenance, snow removal, recreational activities, and security patrols that either substitute for, or supplement, services that would otherwise be provided by local government.
- Majority rule in some form generally governs much of the decision making in CAs as it does in local government.

CAs are similar to private businesses or private associations in that:

- CAs are based on explicit private contracts. Most CAs are created when a developer sells lots or units subject to the CC&Rs, which spell out the obligations of owners and the association. Purchasers agree to the terms by entering the sales contract or accepting the deed.
- CA governance is based on a corporate model. Voting rights are based on property ownership, not residency, as in cities. Most CAs are organized as incorporated or unincorporated associations governed by a board of directors elected by owners of individual lots or units. The number of votes allocated to each lot or unit is determined by the governing documents. To the extent not overridden by the CC&Rs or a statute governing CAs, the state's corporation code, or law of unincorporated associations, governs operations of the association.
- Size and function of CAs are primarily determined by the governing documents and vary much more widely than those found in local governments. A CA may do as little as managing a two-unit condominium—or maintaining a sign and bit of landscaping at the entrance to a community consisting of a few single-family detached houses—or as much as running a master-planned community with many thousands of residents.[14]
- CA officers and directors are not government officials subject to § 1983 liability or entitled to sovereign immunity.

CAs are different from local governments or private businesses, but may be similar to private associations in that:

- Elected officials (officers and directors) of CAs are not paid and ordinarily do not treat their service as part of their careers. Many CA officers and directors lack training.
- CAs are not ordinarily conducted for profit.
- CA members are required to pay assessments that are not subject to the constraints imposed on property taxes or entitled to the federal income tax deduction allowed for local property taxes.

CAs are different from private businesses, or other private associations, in that:

- CAs govern communities of homes and generally have much more power to affect the quality of residents' lives. CAs typically restrict land use and regulate behavior within the community.

---

14. Rancho Bernardo, California, for example, is a master-planned community of 7,000 acres with a mix of commercial, industrial, and residential uses and about 45,000 inhabitants. Although part of the City of San Diego, it is governed by its CC&Rs that provide for a community council, a planning board, and a recreation council, which represent the community at city functions. For more information, visit the Rancho Bernardo Chamber of Commerce's website at http://www.ranchobernardo chamber.com (last visited May 11, 2005).

- CA management may affect the value of the owners' homes, which for many are their largest single investment.

- Exit is often more difficult for unhappy residents than for unhappy investors in business enterprises or other private associations.

Finally, CAs are different from cities and corporations in that their restrictions, rules, and regulations are often much more invasive.[15] The design controls administered by a CA may be either highly detailed or quite vague allowing, for example, the architectural control committee to disapprove designs that are not "in harmony" with the rest of the development.[16] The controls often extend to color schemes and landscaping as well as design and location of structures, going well beyond the controls typically imposed by cities.... Other restrictions and rules are often more detailed and leave less room for individual autonomy than most city ordinances.[18]

In addition, enforcement is more likely. Unlike local ordinances, which must be enforced by some local official, CC&Rs can be enforced by any property owner in the common interest community as well as by the association. Also, unlike many local governments, which lack sufficient inspectors to spot violations, CAs often hire management companies that either conduct inspections or respond to complaints by residents. CAs thus may have much more power than cities to affect the lives of their residents.

If, as French suggests, community associations are really different from cities, business corporations, and other private associations, what protections should the law afford their members? In addition to the many statutes that govern various aspects of association powers and governance, which we encounter throughout this book, the common law of servitudes imposes substantial limitations on the burdens that can be imposed on common interest community members.

B. Public Policy Constraints

The law of servitudes has long imposed substantive constraints on the kinds of covenants that can be made to run with the land. Many of these constraints were traditionally imposed under the rubric of the touch or concern doctrine, but others have been stated in more direct language. The Restatement (Third) gives a contemporary statement of the rules governing validity of servitudes (rights and obligations that can be made to run with the land).

Restatement (Third) § 3.1 Validity of Servitudes: General Rule

A servitude created as provided in Chapter 2 is valid unless it is illegal or unconstitutional or violates public policy. Servitudes that are invalid because they violate public policy include, but are not limited to:

(1) a servitude that is arbitrary, spiteful, or capricious;

---

15. RESTATEMENT (THIRD) OF PROPERTY: SERVITUDES § 6.9 cmt. *c.*
16. See id. § 6.9, reporter's note.
18. Id. §§ 6.7, 3.1.

(2) a servitude that unreasonably burdens a fundamental constitutional right;

(3) a servitude that imposes an unreasonable restraint on alienation under § 3.4 or § 3.5;

(4) a servitude that imposes an unreasonable restraint on trade or competition under § 3.6; and

(5) a servitude that is unconscionable under § 3.7.

h. Servitudes that unreasonably burden fundamental constitutional rights are invalid. The term "constitutional rights" is used in this context to identify certain important rights that raise public-policy concerns when adversely affected by servitudes. The importance accorded by the federal constitution to protection of these rights against governmental action suggests that there is also a public interest in protecting them against private action. When a servitude inhibits the exercise of rights that are important to the public good, like participation in political debate, for example, public harm results that may justify invalidation of the servitude. Similarly, when a servitude deprives citizens of rights that are fundamental to personal security or well being, public harm may result that justifies invalidation. In assessing the extent of public harm, the possibility that validation will result in more widespread use of similar servitudes should be taken into account. A servitude that "unreasonably burdens" such a right, in this context, is one that creates risks of societal harm that outweigh the benefits of validating the servitude. This standard is similar to that used for determining whether a restraint on alienation is unreasonable under § 3.4. It is also similar to that applied to determine when a contract term is unenforceable on grounds of public policy under § 178 of the Restatement Second of Contracts.

Fundamental constitutional rights include freedom of speech, press, religion, privacy, and association. They include rights to be free from unreasonable searches, excessive penalties, and expropriation of property. They also include rights to procedural fairness in the administration and enforcement of servitudes. Servitudes that burden other rights ordinarily enjoyed by property owners may also create risks of public harm that justify invalidation of the servitude on grounds of public policy. The emphasis on constitutional rights in this Comment is not intended to limit the general principle that a servitude that creates risks of societal harm outweighing the benefits of validating the servitude violates public policy.

The question whether a servitude unreasonably burdens a fundamental constitutional right is determined as a matter of property law, not of constitutional law. Constitutional-law decisions may be useful, but are not controlling, in determining when a servitude goes too far. When private parties create and enforce servitudes they are not governmental actors, and, except where state action is found under *Shelley v. Kraemer*, see Comment *d*, they are not subject to the limits placed on government by the Fourteenth Amendment. One factor to consider in determining whether private parties should be permitted to create servitudes that would be forbidden to governmental bodies is the geographical scope of the private party's power to impose servitudes on an unwilling purchaser compared to that of the government. A person who is unwilling to accept a particular servitude may be able to find other property in the same vicinity that is not subject to the offensive servitude, but would have to leave the jurisdiction to be free of a state law or city ordinance. Another factor is that the coercive power of the government includes criminal sanctions while servitude beneficiaries are limited to civil proceedings. In addition, the moral and political force of the statement made by a governmental body may be considerably different from a similar statement made by a privately created servitude.

In determining whether a servitude imposes an unreasonable burden, the purpose of the servitude, its importance to the beneficiaries, the strength of the challenger's consent to acquire the property despite the burden of the servitude, and the extent to which it interferes with the fundamental right are relevant considerations. Purposes have varying degrees of legitimacy and importance. Through the touch-or-concern doctrine, courts traditionally limited servitudes to those that had an effect on the use or value of land; servitudes that controlled individual or business behavior in ways that did not affect the land were invalid. Although such servitudes are no longer categorically invalid, strong justification is required for a servitude that burdens fundamental rights of successive landowners for a purpose unrelated to the use or value of the beneficiary's land.

In assessing the strength of the beneficiaries' interests in validation of the servitude and of the burdened party's consent, notice is relevant. If the servitude and its application to the situation in question should have been readily apparent, the beneficiary's claims to reliance on the servitude are entitled to greater weight than if the servitude was buried in a mass of boilerplate or obscure verbiage, or an ordinary purchaser would not necessarily understand that it would apply to the situation in question. In assessing the degree to which the servitude burdens the right, the availability of reasonable alternatives for exercise of the right, or for amendment of the servitude are relevant considerations. In an appropriate case, the ease with which the burdened party could avoid the problem by disposing of the burdened property might be relevant.

In subdivisions and common-interest residential communities with reciprocal servitudes, the legitimate interests of the landowners in controlling activities of other landowners are generally limited to controlling use of common areas and controlling activities that create external effects in the neighborhood. Use of servitudes to control activity involving the exercise of fundamental rights on individually owned property is generally not legitimate unless the activity produces spill-over effects that have an adverse impact on other property in the subdivision or community.

What kinds of common interest community restrictions might be invalid as unreasonable burdens on fundamental constitutional rights? The Restatement offers several illustrations:

Restatement (Third) § 3.1 Illustrations:

5. The declaration of servitudes for Harmony Village includes a provision prohibiting owners and residents from criticizing actions taken by the board of directors or the architectural-control committee except at regularly scheduled meetings of the board. A resident unhappy about a board decision to construct a new tennis court distributed a flyer to residents criticizing the board decision. Exercising its power to enforce the servitudes by fines, the board imposed a $1,000 fine on the resident. In the absence of other facts or circumstances, the conclusion would be justified that the prohibition on criticism of board actions is invalid because it unreasonably burdens freedom of speech.

6. Able purchased a lot in Green Acres, a 200-lot single-family residential subdivision subject to a Declaration of Covenants. The covenants restrict lots to single-family residential use, and among many other provisions, define "single family" as "a group of people related by blood or marriage operating as a single housekeeping unit." Able lived alone at the time of the purchase, but subsequently became romantically involved with a person who eventually moved into the house. The two live together as a single housekeeping unit but do not marry. In the absence of other facts or circumstances showing strong justification for the servitude, the conclusion would be justified that application of the covenant to prohibit occupancy by an unmarried couple is invalid. The covenant substantially burdens the privacy and association interests of the landowner, attempts to control activity that produces little or no external effect on other property in the subdivision, and provides little benefit to the other property in the subdivision. It may also be relevant that an ordinary purchaser might not understand that the covenants prohibited living in the house with a partner to whom one was not married.

7. Same facts as Illustration 6. The Green Acres covenants also include a provision that prohibits all signs and banners visible from the street abutting any lot other than small identification signs with the name and address of the owners or occupants of the property. The covenant is challenged by a resident who displays a political yard sign of normal size. In the absence of other facts or circumstances, the conclusion would be justified that application of the covenant to prohibit political yard signs is invalid because the harm to the public interest in citizen participation in political debate outweighs the value of validating the servitude. This application of the covenant substantially burdens free speech because political yard signs have a unique value; reasonable alternative means of exercising the right are not available.

11. The Declaration of Covenants for Bayview Condominiums provides that the common property and the affairs of the condominium association shall be managed by a Board of Directors elected by the unit owners. The Declaration provides that the Directors may conduct business in closed sessions except at the annual meeting and are required to provide owners with access to association records only during a one-month period prior to the annual meeting. In the absence of other facts or circumstances, the conclusion would be justified that these provisions unreasonably burden the rights of unit owners to procedural fairness. The interest of the association and other owners in efficiency and saving costs by preventing owners from appearing at board meetings and by limiting their access to association records are not strong and are outweighed by the public interest in maintaining common-interest communities as desirable residential communities. Ordinary purchasers, particularly first-time buyers in common-interest communities, may not appreciate the importance of these kinds of covenant provisions. It should be noted that in some states these provisions would also be illegal under corporation or common-interest-community statutes.

12. Same facts as Illustration 11. The Declaration also gives the Board of Directors the power to enter individually owned units at any time, without notice, to inspect for violation of the covenants or rules or regulations of the condominium association. In the absence of other facts or circumstances, the conclusion would be justified that this covenant unreasonably burdens fundamental rights to freedom from unreasonable searches and rights to privacy.

What kinds of restrictions would not be invalid as unreasonable burdens on fundamental constitutional rights?

10. Covenants for Green Acres also prohibit construction or alteration of the exterior of any structure on any lot without submission of plans to the Green Acres architectural review committee for approval. The committee is expressly authorized to reject plans for structures or alterations that would not be in harmony with existing construction in Green Acres. The owner of Lot 5 submitted plans for a new house drawn by an innovative architect. There were no other similar houses in Green Acres. The committee rejected the plans. The owner challenges the covenant on the ground that it unreasonably burdens freedom of expression. In the absence of other facts or circumstances, the conclusion would be justified that the covenant is valid. The meaning of the covenant should have been apparent to an ordinary purchaser, and the public interest in allowing free expression through architecture does not outweigh the public interest in permitting developers and other lot owners in a development from determining the esthetic character of the development.

13. Same facts as Illustration 12, except that at least three working days' notice must be given unless there is an emergency requiring immediate access to locate or repair conditions damaging, or threatening to damage, common elements or other units. In cases of emergency, an attempt to notify the occupant before entry must be made unless unreasonable under the circumstances. In the absence of other facts or circumstances the conclusion would be justified that this covenant is valid. The interests of the association and other owners in securing compliance with covenants, rules, and regulations, and in preventing damage to common elements and other units, outweigh the limited burdens on privacy and freedom from unreasonable searches.

The Constitution of a Private Residential Government Should Include a Bill of Rights

Susan F. French, 27 Wake Forest Law Review 345 (1992)

. . .

By definition, owners of property in common interest communities are required to give up the freedom to choose to abandon their interests in commonly owned facilities.... To this extent, the loss of freedom is inherent in the concept of a common interest community. Beyond required contributions to support the common facilities, however, people who buy into common interest developments are often asked to give up significantly greater degrees of freedom to obtain the advantages offered by ownership of property in the community.... The degree of freedom prospective purchasers are asked to give up is determined by the developer, who creates the constitution for the new community in its recorded declaration of servitudes.

Developers probably conceive of the documents they use to create common interest communities as instruments for enhancing the quality of life and promoting property values, rather than as instruments for oppression. Since their primary interest is usually in making money, they draft common interest community constitutions with an eye on what will sell, rather than on the extent to which the law will permit them to deprive community members of their liberty.... [O]ther factors being equal, rational consumers should select a community on the basis of the degree of freedom of choice they wish to give up.

. . .

Although there are obvious advantages to be gained by purchasing housing in a common interest community, there are also severe risks. If the developer has created a community with rigid restrictions, the association may not be able to adapt to changing conditions, thus property values may fall. If the developer has created a community with flexible restrictions, the community association may adopt changes that substantially reduce the value of units to their owners or force them to move. Dreams of homeownership can turn sour for people whose building or landscaping plans are not approved and for people who learn too late that they will not be permitted to put up political signs, for sale signs, or holiday decorations. Dreams can turn to nightmares for homeowners who are forced to a choice of moving or giving up beloved pets, lovers, or even children.

As our collective experience with life in common interest communities increases, more of us will become aware of the risks involved in buying a home in a common interest community. As public awareness changes, we can expect developers to adapt new communities to our changing views of the advantages and risks involved....

I think one promising line of thought is to pursue the analogy that has been drawn between community associations and governments. Community associations are forms of democratic local government. The broader their powers, the more they resemble other local governments. As the resemblance to government grows stronger, the more people will fear the lack of controls that limit the powers of public governments. People will feel comfortable with this most local form of government only if it is subjected to the same kinds of restrictions we, as a people, have imposed on our other levels of government. In drafting the constitutions of private residential governments, developers should include a bill of rights to ensure future citizens of the community that the majority cannot unite to deprive them of the liberties they are not willing to sacrifice for the advantages of ownership in the community. Inclusion of a bill of rights should substantially reduce the concerns of people who worry that their neighbors will turn their dreams of homeownership into nightmares.

Since different common interest communities are designed to appeal to various segments of the larger community, the contents of the constitution and bill of rights for any particular development should be tailored to the interests and fears of the group the developer intends to target. People who are interested in living in communities designed for special activates or interest groups will obviously be willing to give up more or different liberties than those who simply want good housing in a good neighborhood that will retain its value. Even within the group of those who are simply looking for housing, the degrees of liberty people are willing to give up to acquire various amenities will vary. However, certain fears are likely to appear with sufficient frequency that developers should consider addressing them in the constitutions for any community they create.

The fear of interference with personal freedom to live as one wishes and financial fears of being treated unequally or being prevented from selling or renting the property are likely to surface in many potential purchasers.[21] So, too, is the fear that restraints on alienation will prevent the owner from leasing or selling the property when necessary or con-

21. Robert Ellickson suggests that prospective members of common interest communities should fear subsequently adopted redistributive policies if their exit costs from the community would be high because of transaction costs, loss of irreplaceable surplus value, or capitalization of the redistributive tax into a lower value for the member's share of the community. To reassure prospective members, he suggests that a form of takings clause should be included in the association documents or implied by the courts. Robert C. Ellickson, *Cities and Homeowner Associations*, 130 U. Pa. L. Rev. 1519, 1525, 1535 (1982).

venient. Although there are countervailing reasons why owners might want the community association to have the power to determine life styles and activities within the community and to control resales or prevent rentals, limiting the association's ability to do so will probably result in reassuring more potential buyers than it will frighten. The following Proposed Provisions for a Homeowner's Bill of Rights is intended to give developers and their lawyers a starting point for thinking about the kinds of provisions that might have wide appeal to potential purchasers of homes in common interest developments.

Proposed Provisions for a Homeowner's Bill of Rights

In exercising the powers to make rules and regulations for the governance of the community, and the use and occupancy of both common and individually owned property within it, the community association shall observe the following principles and limitations:

1. *Equal Treatment*: Similarly situated owners and residents shall be treated similarly.

2. *Speech*: The rights of residents to display political signs and symbols of the kinds normally displayed in or outside of residences located in single-family residential neighborhoods in their individually owned property shall not be abridged, except that the association may adopt reasonable time, place, and manner restrictions for the purpose of minimizing damage and disturbance to other owners and residents.

3. *Religious and Holiday Displays*: The rights of residents to display religious and holiday signs, symbols, and decorations of the kinds normally displayed in or outside of residences located in single-family residential neighborhoods in their individually owned property shall not be abridged, except that the association may adopt reasonable time, place, and manner restrictions for the purpose of minimizing damage and disturbance to other owners and residents.

4. *Household Composition*: The association shall make no rule that interferes with the freedom of residents to determine the composition of their households, except that the association shall have the power to require that all occupants be members of a single housekeeping unit, and to limit the total number of occupants permitted in each lot or unit on the basis of the size and facilities of the unit and its fair share use of the common facilities, including parking.

5. *Activities Within Individually Owned Property*: The association shall make no rule that interferes with the activities of the residents carried on within the confines of their individually owned properties, except that the association may prohibit activities not normally associated with property restricted to residential use, and it may restrict or prohibit any activities that impose monetary costs on the association or other owners, that create a danger to the health or safety of other residents, that generate excessive noise or traffic, that create unsightly conditions visible outside the unit, that block the views from other units, or that create a nuisance.

5. *Pets*: Unless the keeping of pets is prohibited at the time of the sale of the first lot or unit, no rule prohibiting the keeping of ordinary household pets shall be adopted thereafter over the objection of any owner expressed in writing to the association. The association may adopt reasonable regulations designed to minimize damage and disturbance to other owners and residents, including regula-

tions requiring damage deposits, waste removal, leash controls, noise controls, occupancy limits based on size and facilities of the unit and fair share use of the common areas. Nothing in this provision shall prevent the association from requiring removal of any animal that presents an actual threat to the health or safety of residents or from requiring abatement of any nuisance.

6. *Allocation of Burdens and Benefits*: The initial allocation of financial burdens and rights to use common facilities among the various lots or units shall not be changed to the detriment of any unit owner over that owner's objection expressed in writing to the association. Nothing in this provision shall prevent the association from changing the common facilities available, from adopting generally applicable rules for use of common facilities, or from denying use privileges to those who abuse the facilities, violate rules for use of common facilities or fail to pay assessments.

7. *Alienation*: The association shall not adopt rules that prohibit transfer of any lot or unit, or require consent of the association for transfer of any lot or unit, for any period greater than [two] months. The association shall not impose any fee on transfer of any unit greater than an amount reasonably based on the costs of the transfer to the association.

The idea that members of common interest communities need enumerated protections has taken hold with others who now advocate legislative enactment of a Bill of Rights. The AARP, which appeared as an *amicus* in the *Twin Rivers* case on the side of the plaintiffs, is promoting a Bill of Rights for Homeowners in Associations which includes the following rights:

- the right to security against foreclosure
- the right to resolve disputes without litigation
- the right to fairness in litigation (if the homeowner prevails, the association shall pay attorney fees)
- the right to be told of all rules and charges
- the right to stability in rules and charges
- the right to individual autonomy
- the right to oversight of associations and directors
- the right to vote and run for office
- the right to reasonable associations and directors
- the right to an ombudsperson for homeowners

The proposed Right to Individual Autonomy provides:

Homeowners shall not surrender any essential rights of individual autonomy because they live in a common-interest community. Homeowners shall have the right to peaceful advocacy during elections and other votes as well as use of common areas.

The AARP proposal is summarized at www.aarp.org/research/legal/legalrights/ing 128_homeowner.html.

The National Conference of Commissioners on Uniform State Laws has also considered a draft of a homeowner's bill of rights as part of its larger project of revising UCIOA that is currently underway. See http://www.nccusl.org/Update/CommitteeSearchResults.aspx?committee=244 for copies of drafts under consideration.

B. Public Policy Constraints.

Nahrstedt v. Lakeside Village Condo. Ass'n, Inc

Supreme Court of California
878 P.2d 1275 (1994)

KENNARD, J. A homeowner in a 530-unit condominium complex sued to prevent the homeowners association from enforcing a restriction against keeping cats, dogs, and other animals in the condominium development. The owner asserted that the restriction, which was contained in the project's declaration recorded by the condominium project's developer, was "unreasonable" as applied to her because she kept her three cats[W] indoors and because her cats were "noiseless" and "created no nuisance." Agreeing with the premise underlying the owner's complaint, the Court of Appeal concluded that the homeowners association could enforce the restriction only upon proof that plaintiff's cats would be likely to interfere with the right of other homeowners "to the peaceful and quiet enjoyment of their property." ...

Those of us who have cats or dogs can attest to their wonderful companionship and affection. Not surprisingly, studies have confirmed this effect. (See, *e.g.*, Waltham Symposium 20, *Pets, Benefits and Practice* (BVA Publications 1990); Melson, *The Benefits of Animals to Our Lives* (Fall 1990) People, Animals, Environment, at pp. 15–17). But the issue before us is not whether in the abstract pets can have a beneficial effect on humans. Rather, the narrow issue here is whether a pet restriction that is contained in the recorded declaration of a condominium complex is enforceable against the challenge of a homeowner.... [T]he Legislature, in Civil Code section 1354, has required that courts enforce the covenants, conditions and restrictions contained in the recorded declaration of a common interest development "unless unreasonable."

Because a stable and predictable living environment is crucial to the success of condominiums and other common interest residential developments, and because recorded use restrictions are a primary means of ensuring this stability and predictability, the Legislature in section 1354 has afforded such restrictions a presumption of validity and has required of challengers that they demonstrate the restriction's "unreasonableness" by the deferential standard applicable to equitable servitudes. Under this standard established by the Legislature, enforcement of a restriction does not depend upon the conduct of a particular condominium owner. Rather, the restriction must be uniformly enforced in the condominium development to which it was intended to apply unless the plaintiff owner can show that the burdens it imposes on affected properties so substantially outweigh the benefits of the restriction that it should not be enforced against any owner....

I

Lakeside Village is a large condominium development in Culver City, Los Angeles County. It consists of 530 units spread throughout 12 separate 3-story buildings. The residents share common lobbies and hallways, in addition to laundry and trash facilities.

The Lakeside Village project is subject to certain covenants, conditions and restrictions (hereafter CC & R's) ... included in the developer's declaration recorded ... April

---

W. The appellate court in Nahrstedt personified Ms. Nahrstedt's cats by giving them fictional names: Fluffin, Muffin, and Ruffin. 25 Cal.App. 4th 1473, 1490 (1992).—Eds.

17, 1978, at the inception of the development project. Ownership of a unit includes membership in the ... the Lakeside Village Condominium Association..., the body that enforces the project's CC & R's, including the pet restriction, which provides in relevant part: "No animals (which shall mean dogs and cats), livestock, reptiles or poultry shall be kept in any unit."

In January 1988, plaintiff Natore Nahrstedt purchased a Lakeside Village condominium and moved in with her three cats. When the Association learned of the cats' presence, it demanded their removal and assessed fines against Nahrstedt for each successive month that she remained in violation of the condominium project's pet restriction.

Nahrstedt then brought this lawsuit against the Association, its officers, and two of its employees, asking the trial court to invalidate the assessments, to enjoin future assessments, to award damages for violation of her privacy when the Association "peered" into her condominium unit, to award damages for infliction of emotional distress, and to declare the pet restriction "unreasonable" as applied to indoor cats (such as hers) that are not allowed free run of the project's common areas. Nahrstedt also alleged she did not know of the pet restriction when she bought her condominium....

The Association demurred to the complaint. The Association argued that the pet restriction furthers the collective "health, happiness and peace of mind" of persons living in close proximity within the Lakeside Village condominium development, and therefore is reasonable as a matter of law. The trial court sustained the demurrer as to each cause of action and dismissed Nahrstedt's complaint. Nahrstedt appealed.

A divided Court of Appeal reversed the trial court's judgment of dismissal. In the majority's view, the complaint stated a claim for declaratory relief based on its allegations that Nahrstedt's three cats are kept inside her condominium unit and do not bother her neighbors. According to the majority, whether a condominium use restriction is "unreasonable," as that term is used in section 1354, hinges on the facts of a particular homeowner's case. Thus, the majority reasoned, Nahrstedt would be entitled to declaratory relief if application of the pet restriction in her case would not be reasonable. The Court of Appeal also revived Nahrstedt's causes of action for invasion of privacy, invalidation of the assessments, and injunctive relief, as well as her action for emotional distress based on a theory of negligence.

... [W]e granted review to decide when a condominium owner can prevent enforcement of a use restriction that the project's developer has included in the recorded declaration of CC& R's.

II

...

Use restrictions are an inherent part of any common interest development and are crucial to the stable, planned environment of any shared ownership arrangement. (Note, Community Association Use Restrictions: Applying the Business Judgment Doctrine (1988) 64 Chi. Kent L. Rev. 653, 673 ...; see also Natelson, *Consent, Coercion and "Reasonableness," supra,* 51 Ohio State L.J. at p. 47.) The viability of shared ownership of improved real property rests on the existence of extensive reciprocal servitudes, together with the ability of each co-owner to prevent the property's partition....

The restrictions on the use of property in any common interest development may limit activities conducted in the common areas as well as in the confines of the home itself. (Reichman, *Residential Private Governments* (1976) 43 U.Chi.L.Rev. 253, 270....) Commonly, use restrictions preclude alteration of building exteriors, limit the number of persons that can occupy each unit, and place limitations on — or prohibit altogether — the keeping of pets....[5]

Restrictions on property use are not the only characteristic of common interest ownership. Ordinarily, such ownership also entails mandatory membership in an owners association, which, through an elected board of directors, is empowered to enforce any use restrictions contained in the project's declaration or master deed and to enact new rules governing the use and occupancy of property within the project.... Because of its considerable power in managing and regulating a common interest development, the governing board of an owners association must guard against the potential for the abuse of that power.[6] As Professor Natelson observes, owners associations "can be a powerful force for good or for ill" in their members' lives.... Therefore, anyone who buys a unit in a common interest development with knowledge of its owners association's discretionary power accepts "the risk that the power may be used in a way that benefits the commonality but harms the individual." ... Generally, courts will uphold decisions made by the governing board of an owners association so long as they represent good faith efforts to further the purposes of the common interest development, are consistent with the development's governing documents, and comply with public policy....

Thus, subordination of individual property rights to the collective judgment of the owners association together with restrictions on the use of real property comprise the chief attributes of owning property in a common interest development. As the Florida District Court of Appeal observed in *Hidden Harbour Estates, Inc. v. Norman* (Fla.Dist.Ct.App.1975) 309 So. 2d 180, a decision frequently cited in condominium cases: "[I]nherent in the condominium concept is the principle that to promote the health, happiness, and peace of mind of the majority of the unit owners since they are living in such close proximity and using facilities in common, each unit owner must give up a certain degree of freedom of choice which he [or she] might otherwise enjoy in separate, privately owned property. Condominium unit owners comprise a little democratic sub-society of necessity more restrictive as it pertains to use of condominium property than may be existent outside the condominium organization." (... see also Leyser, *The Ownership of Flats — A Comparative Study, supra,* 7 Int'l & Comp.L.Q. at p. 38 [explaining the French system's recognition that "flat ownership" has limitations that considerably exceed those of "normal" real property ownership, "limitations arising out of the rights of the other flat owners."].)

Notwithstanding the limitations on personal autonomy that are inherent in the concept of shared ownership of residential property, common interest developments have increased in popularity in recent years, in part because they generally provide a more affordable alternative to ownership of a single-family home. (See *Frances T. v. Village Green Owners Ass'n* (1986) 42 Cal.3d 490, 500, fn. 9, 229 Cal.Rptr. 456, 723 P.2d 573 [noting that common interest developments at that time accounted for as much as 70 percent of the new housing market in Los Angeles and San Diego Counties]; ...; see also McKenzie, *Welcome Home*[.] *Do as We Say.*, N.Y. Times (Aug. 18, 1994) p. 23A, col. 1 [stating that 32 million Americans are members of some 150,000 homeowners associations and predicting that between 25 to 30 percent of Americans will live in community association housing by the year 2000.])

---

5. Even the dissent recognizes that pet restrictions have a long pedigree. (See dis. opn., post, p.82, fn. 5 of 33 Cal. Rptr. 2d, p. 1294, fn. 5 of 878 P.2d, citing Crimmins, The Quotable Cat (1992) p. 58 [English nuns living in a nunnery prohibited in 1205 from keeping any pet except a cat].)

6. The power to regulate pertains to a "wide spectrum of activities," such as the volume of playing music, hours of social gatherings, use of patio furniture and barbecues, and rental of units. (Note, Business Judgment, *supra* 64 Chi. Kent L. Rev. at p. 669.)

One significant factor in the continued popularity of the common interest form of property ownership is the ability of homeowners to enforce restrictive CC & R's against other owners (including future purchasers) of project units....

III

In California, common interest developments are subject to the provisions of the Davis-Stirling Common Interest Development Act ... (§ 1350 *et seq.*) ...

Subdivision (a) of section 1354, states in relevant part:

> The covenants and restrictions in the declaration shall be enforceable equitable servitudes, *unless unreasonable,* and shall inure to the benefit of and bind all owners of separate interests in the development. (Italics added.)

... [A]lthough under general rules governing equitable servitudes a subsequent purchaser of land subject to restrictions must have actual notice[3] of the restrictions, actual notice is not required to enforce recorded use restrictions covered by section 1354 against a subsequent purchaser. Rather, the inclusion of covenants and restrictions in the declaration recorded with the county recorder provides sufficient notice to permit the enforcement of such recorded covenants and restrictions as equitable servitudes....

In choosing equitable servitude law as the standard for enforcing CC & R's in common interest developments, the Legislature has manifested a preference in favor of their enforcement. This preference is underscored by the use of the word "shall" in the first phrase of section 1354.

... The Legislature's use of the phrase "unless unreasonable" in section 1354 was a marked change from the prior version of that statutory provision, which stated that "restrictions shall be enforceable equitable servitudes *where reasonable.*" Under settled principles of statutory construction, such a material alteration of a statute's phrasing signals the Legislature's intent to give an enactment a new meaning.... Here, the change in statutory language, from "where reasonable" to "unless unreasonable," cloaked use restrictions contained in a condominium development's recorded declaration with a presumption of reasonableness by shifting the burden of proving otherwise to the party challenging the use restriction.

How is that burden satisfied? To answer this question, we must examine the principles governing enforcement of equitable servitudes.

... Like any promise given in exchange for consideration, an agreement to refrain from a particular use of land is subject to contract principles, under which courts try "to effectuate the legitimate desires of the covenanting parties." (*Hannula v. Hacienda Homes* (1949) 34 Cal.2d 442, 444–445, 211 P.2d 302.) When landowners express the intention to limit land use, "that intention should be carried out." (*Id.*...; Epstein, *Notice and Freedom of Contract in the Law of Servitudes* (1982) 55 So. Cal. L. Rev. 1353, 1359 ["We may not understand why property owners want certain obligations to run with the land, but as it is *their* land ... some very strong reason should be advanced" before courts should override those obligations....].)

Thus, when enforcing equitable servitudes, courts are generally disinclined to question the wisdom of agreed-to restrictions. (Note, *Covenants and Equitable Servitudes in Cal-*

---

3. The statement that actual notice is necessary to enforce a covenant in equity against a subsequent purchaser may have been true in English law, but is not an accurate statement of American law. In the United States, constructive notice imparted by the recording act is sufficient. See Restatement of Property Third, (Servitudes) § 7.13, Tent. Draft No. 6 (1997). Eds.

ifornia, ... 29 Hastings L.J. at p. 577 ...) This rule does not apply, however, when the restriction does not comport with public policy. (*Ibid.*) Equity will not enforce any restrictive covenant that violates public policy. (See *Shelley v. Kraemer* (1948) 334 U.S. 1 ...; Cal. Civ. Code § 53, subd. (b) [voiding property use restrictions based on "sex, race, color, religion, ancestry, national origin, or disability"].) Nor will courts enforce as equitable servitudes those restrictions that are arbitrary, that is, bearing no rational relationship to the protection, preservation, operation or purpose of the affected land. (See *Laguna Royale Owners Ass'n. v. Darger, supra,* 119 Cal.App.3d 670, 684, 174 Cal.Rptr. 136.)

These limitations on the equitable enforcement of restrictive servitudes that are either arbitrary or violate fundamental public policy are specific applications of the general rule that courts will not enforce a restrictive covenant when "the harm caused by the restriction is so disproportionate to the benefit produced" by its enforcement that the restriction "ought not to be enforced." (Rest., Property, § 539, com. *f....*) When a use restriction bears no relationship to the land it burdens, or violates a fundamental policy inuring to the public at large, the resulting harm will always be disproportionate to any benefit.

Sometimes lesser burdens too can be so disproportionate to any benefit flowing from the restriction that the restriction "ought not to be enforced." ... For instance, courts will not enforce a land use restriction when a change in surrounding properties effectively defeats the intended purpose of the restriction, rendering it of little benefit to the remaining property owners.... In such cases, enforcing the restriction would be oppressive or inequitable.... Note, *Restrictive Covenants: Injunctions: Changed Conditions in the Neighborhood as a Bar to Enforcement of Equitable Servitudes* (1927) 16 Cal.L.Rev. 58.)

As the first Restatement of Property points out, the test for determining when the harmful effects of a land-use restriction are so disproportionate to its benefit "is necessarily vague." ... Application of the test requires the accommodation of two policies that sometimes conflict: "One of these is that [persons] should be required to live up to their promises; the other that land should be developed to its normal capacity." Reconciliation of these policies in determining whether the burdens of a recorded use restriction are so disproportionate to its benefits depends on the effect of the challenged restriction on "promoting or limiting the use of land in the locality...."

From the authorities discussed above, we distill these principles: An equitable servitude will be enforced unless it violates public policy; it bears no rational relationship to the protection, preservation, operation or purpose of the affected land; or it otherwise imposes burdens on the affected land that are so disproportionate to the restriction's beneficial effects that the restriction should not be enforced.

... [U]nder subdivision (a) of section 1354 the use restrictions for a common interest development that are set forth in the recorded declaration are "enforceable equitable servitudes, unless unreasonable." In other words, such restrictions should be enforced unless they are wholly arbitrary, violate a fundamental public policy, or impose a burden on the use of affected land that far outweighs any benefit.

This interpretation of section 1354 ... is consistent with the views of legal commentators as well as judicial decisions in other jurisdictions that have applied a presumption of validity to the recorded land use restrictions of a common interest development. (*Noble v. Murphy, supra,* 612 N.E.2d 266, 270; *Hidden Harbour Estates v. Basso, supra,* 393 So. 2d 637, 639–640; Note, *Judicial Review of Condominium Rulemaking, supra,* 94 Harv.L.Rev. 647, 653.) As these authorities point out, and as we discussed previously, recorded CC & R's are the primary means of achieving the stability and predictability so essential to the success of a shared ownership housing development. In general, then, enforcement of a common interest development's recorded CC & R's will both encourage the development of land and ensure that promises are kept, thereby fulfilling both of the policies identified by the Restatement. (See Rest., Property, § 539, com. f, p. 3230.)

When courts accord a presumption of validity to all such recorded use restrictions and measure them against deferential standards of equitable servitude law, it discourages lawsuits by owners of individual units seeking personal exemptions from the restrictions. This also promotes stability and predictability in two ways. It provides substantial assurance to prospective condominium purchasers that they may rely with confidence on the promises embodied in the project's recorded CC & R's. And it protects all owners in the planned development from unanticipated increases in association fees to fund the defense of legal challenges to recorded restrictions.

How courts enforce recorded use restrictions affects not only those who have made their homes in planned developments, but also the owners associations charged with the fiduciary obligation to enforce those restrictions.... When courts treat recorded use restrictions as presumptively valid, and place on the challenger the burden of proving the restriction "unreasonable" under the deferential standards applicable to equitable servitudes, associations can proceed to enforce reasonable restrictive covenants without fear that their actions will embroil them in costly and prolonged legal proceedings. Of course, when an association determines that a unit owner has violated a use restriction, the association must do so in good faith, not in an arbitrary or capricious manner, and its enforcement procedures must be fair and applied uniformly....

There is an additional beneficiary of legal rules that are protective of recorded use restrictions: the judicial system. Fewer lawsuits challenging such restrictions will be brought, and those that are filed may be disposed of more expeditiously, if the rules courts use in evaluating such restrictions are clear, simple, and not subject to exceptions based on the peculiar circumstances or hardships of individual residents in condominiums and other shared-ownership developments.

Contrary to the dissent's accusations that the majority's decision "fray[s]" the "social fabric", we are of the view that our social fabric is best preserved if courts uphold and enforce solemn written instruments that embody the expectations of the parties rather than treat them as "worthless paper" as the dissent would. Our social fabric is founded on the stability of expectation and obligation that arises from the consistent enforcement of the terms of deeds, contracts, wills, statutes, and other writings. To allow one person to escape obligations under a written instrument upsets the expectations of all the other parties governed by that instrument (here, the owners of the other 529 units) that the instrument will be uniformly and predictably enforced.

The salutary effect of enforcing written instruments and the statutes that apply to them is particularly true in the case of the declaration of a common interest development.... [C]ommon interest developments are a more intensive and efficient form of land use that greatly benefits society and expands opportunities for home ownership. In turn, however, a common interest development creates a community of property owners living in close proximity to each other, typically much closer than if each owned his or her separate plot of land. This proximity is feasible, and units in a common interest development are marketable, largely because the recorded declaration of CC & R's assures owners of a stable and predictable environment.

Refusing to enforce the CC & R's contained in a recorded declaration, or enforcing them only after protracted litigation that would require justification of their application on a case-by-case basis, would impose great strain on the social fabric of the common interest development. It would frustrate owners who had purchased their units in reliance on the CC & R's. It would put the owners and the homeowners association in the difficult and divisive position of deciding whether particular CC & R's should be applied to a particular owner. Here, for example, deciding whether a particular animal is "confined to an owner's unit and create[s] no noise, odor, or nuisance" is a fact-intensive determination that can only be made by examining in detail the behavior of the particular animal and the behavior of the particular owner. Homeowners associations are ill-equipped to make such investigations, and any decision they might make in a particular case could be divisive or subject to claims of partiality.

Enforcing the CC & R's contained in a recorded declaration only after protracted case-by-case litigation would impose substantial litigation costs on the owners through their homeowners association, which would have to defend not only against owners contesting the application of the CC & R's to them, but also against owners contesting any case-by-case exceptions the homeowners association might make. In short, it is difficult to imagine what could more disrupt the harmony of a common interest development than the course proposed by the dissent....

IV

... Nahrstedt could prevent enforcement of the Lakeside Village pet restriction by proving that the restriction is arbitrary, that it is substantially more burdensome than beneficial to the affected properties, or that it violates a fundamental public policy.... Nahrstedt's complaint fails to adequately allege any of these three grounds of unreasonableness.

We conclude, as a matter of law, that the recorded pet restriction of the Lakeside Village condominium development prohibiting cats or dogs but allowing some other pets [fish and birds other than poultry] is not arbitrary, but is rationally related to health, sanitation and noise concerns legitimately held by residents of a high-density condominium project such as Lakeside Village, which includes 530 units in 12 separate 3-story buildings.

Nahrstedt's complaint alleges no facts that could possibly support a finding that the burden of the restriction on the affected property is so disproportionate to its benefit that the restriction is unreasonable and should not be enforced. Also, the complaint's allegations center on Nahrstedt and her cats (that she keeps them inside her condominium unit and that they do not bother her neighbors), without any reference to the effect on the condominium development as a whole, thus rendering the allegations legally insufficient to overcome section 1354's presumption of the restriction's validity.

Nahrstedt's complaint does contend that the restriction violates her right to privacy under the California Constitution, article I, section 1.[11] According to Nahrstedt, this state constitutional provision (enacted by voters initiative in 1972) guarantees her the right to keep cats in her Lakeside Village condominium notwithstanding the existence of [the] restriction.... Because a land-use restriction in violation of a state constitutional provision presumably would conflict with public policy ... we construe Nahrstedt's contention as a claim that the Lakeside Village pet restriction violates a fundamental public policy and for that reason cannot be enforced.... The pertinent question, therefore, is whether the privacy provision in our state Constitution implicitly guarantees condominium owners

---

11. That provision states: "All people are by nature free and independent and have inalienable rights. Among these are enjoying and defending life and liberty, acquiring, possessing, and protecting property, and pursuing and obtaining safety, happiness, and *privacy*." (Italics added.)

or residents the right to keep cats or dogs as household pets. We conclude that California's Constitution confers no such right.

We recently held, in *Hill v. National Collegiate Athletic Assn.* (1994) 7 Cal.4th 1, 26 Cal.Rptr.2d 834, 865 P.2d 633, that the privacy provision in our state Constitution does not "encompass all conceivable assertions of individual rights" or create "an unbridled right" of personal freedom.... The legally recognized privacy interests that fall within the protection of the state Constitution are generally of two classes: (1) interests in precluding dissemination of confidential information ("'informational privacy'"); and (2) interests in making personal decisions or in conducting personal activities free of interference, observation, or intrusion ("'autonomy privacy'"). The threshold question in deciding whether "established social norms safeguard a particular type of information or protect a personal decision from public or private intervention," we explained in *Hill,* must be determined from "the usual sources of positive law governing the right to privacy—common law development, constitutional development, statutory enactment, and the ballots arguments accompanying the Privacy Initiative." ...

From these sources we discern no fundamental public policy that would favor the keeping of pets in a condominium project. There is no federal or state constitutional provision or any California statute that confers a general right to keep household pets in condominiums or other common interest developments.[12] There is nothing in the ballot arguments relating to the privacy provision in our state Constitution that would be of help to plaintiff's argument in this case. The ballot arguments focused on the conduct of government and business in "'collecting and stockpiling unnecessary information ... and misusing information gathered for one purpose in order to serve other purposes or to embarrass ...'" ... Nor does case law offer any support for the position that the recognized scope of autonomy privacy encompasses the right to keep pets: courts that have considered condominium pet restrictions have uniformly upheld them. (*Noble v. Murphy, supra,* 612 N.E.2d 266 [upholding total ban on pets]; *Wilshire Condominium Ass'n, Inc. v. Kohlbrand, supra,* 368 So. 2d 629 [upholding pet restriction]; *Dulaney Towers Maintenance v. O'Brey, supra,* 418 A.2d 1233 [same].)

Because this case does not involve a disabled person needing guide dog assistance or an elderly person living in public housing, we do not address the public policy implications of recorded CC & R's that are in conflict with these statutes.

Our conclusion that Nahrstedt's complaint states no claim entitling her to declaratory relief disposes of her primary cause of action challenging enforcement of the Lakeside Village condominium project's pet restriction, but does not address other causes of action (for invasion of privacy, invalidation of assessments, injunctive relief, and seeking damages for emotional distress) revived by the Court of Appeal. Because the Court of Appeal's decision regarding those other causes of action may have been influenced by its conclusion that Nahrstedt had stated a claim for declaratory relief, we remand this case to the Court of Appeal so it can reconsider whether Nahrstedt's complaint is sufficient to state those other causes of action.

---

12. With respect to either disabled individuals living in rented housing or elderly persons living in publicly funded housing, the situation is otherwise. The Legislature has declared its intent that, in specified circumstances, these two classes of Californians be allowed to keep pets. Thus, section 54.1, which guarantees equal access to housing accommodations to individuals with disabilities, permits landlords to refuse to rent to tenants who have dogs, *except* when the prospective tenant is a disabled person needing the services of a guide, service, or signal dog. (*Id.* at subd. (b)(5).) And, under Health and Safety Code section 19901, elderly residents in publicly funded housing are entitled to have up to two household pets.

...

We reverse the judgment of the Court of Appeal, and remand for further proceedings consistent with the views expressed in this opinion.

LUCAS, C.J., and MOSK, BAXTER, GEORGE and WERDEGAR, JJ., concur.

ARABIAN, Justice, dissenting.

"There are two means of refuge from the misery of life: music and cats."[1]

I respectfully dissent. While technical merit may commend the majority's analysis,[2] its application to the facts presented reflects a narrow, indeed chary, view of the law that eschews the human spirit in favor of arbitrary efficiency. In my view, the resolution of this case well illustrates the conventional wisdom, and fundamental truth, of the Spanish proverb, "It is better to be a mouse in a cat's mouth than a man in a lawyer's hands."

As explained below, I find the provision known as the "pet restriction" contained in the covenants, conditions, and restrictions (CC & R's) governing the Lakeside Village project patently arbitrary and unreasonable within the meaning of Civil Code section 1354. Beyond dispute, human beings have long enjoyed an abiding and cherished association with their household animals. Given the substantial benefits derived from pet ownership, the undue burden on the use of property imposed on condominium owners who can maintain pets within the confines of their units without creating a nuisance or disturbing the quiet enjoyment of others substantially outweighs whatever meager utility the restriction may serve in the abstract. It certainly does not promote "health, happiness [or] peace of mind" commensurate with its tariff on the quality of life for those who value the companionship of animals. Worse, it contributes to the fraying of our social fabric.[3]

1. The pleadings.

...

In relevant part, plaintiff has alleged that she is the owner of a condominium unit located in Lakeside Village; that she has three cats which she brought with her when she moved there; that she maintains her cats entirely within the confines of her unit and has "never released [them] in any common area"; that they are "noiseless, create no nuisance, [and] have not destroyed any portion of [her] unit, or the common area"; and that they provide her companionship. She further alleges the homeowners association is seeking to enforce a recorded restriction that prohibits keeping any pets except domestic fish and birds.

The majority acknowledge that under their interpretation of Civil Code section 1354 "the test for determining when the harmful effects of a land-use restriction are disproportionate to benefit 'is necessarily vague.'" ... Nevertheless, in their view the foregoing

---

1. Albert Schweitzer.

2. The majority invest substantial interpretive significance regarding the enforceability of condominium restrictions in the replacement of "where reasonable" in former Civil Code section 1355 with "unless unreasonable" in Civil Code section 1354.... Other than the statutory language itself, however, they cite no evidence the Legislature considered this a "material alteration" or intended a "marked change" in the statute's interpretation. Although I fail to see other than a semantical distinction carrying little import as to legislative intent, I find the pet restriction at issue here unenforceable under either standard.

3. The majority imply that if enough owners find the restriction too oppressive, they can act collectively to alter or rescind it.... However, realistically speaking, implementing this alternative would only serve to exacerbate the divisiveness rampant in our society and to which the majority decision itself contributes.

allegations are deficient because they do not specifically state facts to "support a finding that the burden on the affected property is so disproportionate to its benefit that the restriction is unreasonable and should not be enforced." ... They also fail to make "any reference to the effect on the condominium development as a whole...." This narrow assessment of plaintiff's complaint does not comport with the rule of liberal construction that should prevail on demurrer.... When considered less grudgingly, the pleadings are sufficient to allege that the pet restriction is unreasonable as a matter of law.

Generically stated, plaintiff challenges this restriction to the extent it precludes not only her but anyone else living in Lakeside Village from enjoying the substantial pleasures of pet ownership while affording no discernible benefit to other unit owners if the animals are maintained without any detriment to the latter's quiet enjoyment of their own space and the common areas. In essence, she avers that when pets are kept out of sight, do not make noise, do not generate odors, and do not otherwise create a nuisance, reasonable expectations as to the quality of life within the condominium project are not impaired. At the same time, taking into consideration the well-established and long-standing historical and cultural relationship between human beings and their pets and the value they impart ... enforcement of the restriction significantly and unduly burdens the use of land for those deprived of their companionship. Considered from this perspective, I find plaintiff's complaint states a cause of action for declaratory relief....

2. The burden.

Under the majority's construction of Civil Code section 1354, the pet restriction is unreasonable, and hence unenforceable, if the "burdens [imposed] on the affected land ... are so disproportionate to the restriction's beneficial effects that the restriction should not be enforced." ... What, then, is the burden at issue here?

Both recorded and unrecorded history bear witness to the domestication of animals as household pets.[5] Throughout the ages, dogs and cats have provided human beings with a variety of services in addition to their companionship — shepherding flocks, guarding life and property, hunting game, ridding the house and barn of vermin. Of course, the modern classic example is the assist dog, which facilitates a sense of independence and security for disabled persons by enabling them to navigate their environment, alerting them to important sounds, and bringing the world within their reach.[6] Emotionally, they allow a connection full of sensation and delicacy of feeling.

---

5. Archeologists in Israel found some of the earliest evidence of a domesticated animal when they unearthed the 12,000-year-old skeleton of a woman who was buried with her hand resting on the body of her dog. (Clutton-Brock, Dog (1991) p. 35.) Romans warned intruders "*Cave canem*" to alert them to the presence of canine protectors. (*Id.*, p. 34.) Cats were known to be household pets in Egypt 5,000 years ago and often mummified and entombed with their owners. (Clutton-Brock, Cat (1991) p. 46.) According to the English Nuns Rule in 1205, "Ye shall not possess any beast, my dear sisters, except only a cat." (Crimmins, The Quotable Cat (1992) p. 58.)

6. Although it is possible only to estimate the total, well in excess of 10,000 individuals avail themselves of the benefits of guide, alert, and service dogs in California alone.... State law guarantees them the right to live with their animals free from discrimination on that basis. (See Gov.Code, § 12955, subd. (*l*) [impermissible discrimination under the Fair Employment and Housing Act (FEHA) "includes ... *restrictive covenants,* zoning laws, denial of use permits, and other actions ... that make housing opportunities unavailable." (Italics added.)]; see also Civ.Code, § 53; cf. 42 U.S.C. §§ 3601, 3604(f)(3)(B) [federal fair housing act].) Thus, to the extent the pet restriction contains no exception for assist dogs, it clearly violates public policy. At oral argument, counsel for the association allowed that an individual who required assistance of this kind could seek a waiver of the pet restriction, although he in no manner assured that the association's board would necessarily accede to such an effort to enforce the mandate of FEHA. In any event, this "concession" only serves to prove the point of discriminatory impact: disabled persons who have dogs to assist them in normalizing their daily lives do not

Throughout the ages, art and literature, as well as mythology, depict humans in all walks of life and social strata with cats and dogs, illustrating their widespread acceptance in everyday life.[7] Some religions have even incorporated them into their worship.... Dogs and cats are also admired for the purity of their character traits.[9] Closer to home, our own culture is populated with examples of the well-established place pets have found in our hearts and homes.[10]

In addition to these historical and cultural references, the value of pets in daily life is a matter of common knowledge and understanding as well as extensive documentation. People of all ages, but particularly the elderly and the young, enjoy their companionship. Those who suffer from serious disease or injury and are confined to their home or bed experience a therapeutic, even spiritual, benefit from their presence.[11] Animals provide comfort at the death of a family member or dear friend, and for the lonely can offer a reason for living when life seems to have lost its meaning.... In recognition of these benefits, both Congress and the state Legislature have expressly guaranteed that elderly and handicapped persons living in public-assistance housing cannot be deprived of their pets. (12 U.S.C. § 1701r-1; Health & Saf.Code, § 19901.) Not only have children and animals always been natural companions, children learn responsibility and discipline from pet ownership while developing an important sense of kindness and protection for animals.[13] Single adults may find certain pets can afford a feeling of security. Families benefit from the experience of sharing that having a pet encourages. While pet ownership may not be a fundamental right as such, unquestionably it is an integral aspect of our daily existence, which cannot be lightly dismissed and should not suffer unwarranted intrusion into its circle of privacy.

3. The benefit.

What is gained from an uncompromising prohibition against pets that are confined to an owner's unit and create no noise, odor, or nuisance?

To the extent such animals are not seen, heard, or smelled any more than if they were not kept in the first place, there is no corresponding or concomitant benefit. Pets that remain within the four corners of their owners' condominium space can have no deleterious or offensive effect on the project's common areas or any neighboring unit. Certainly, if other owners and residents are totally *unaware* of their presence, prohibiting pets does not in any respect foster the "health, happiness [or] peace of mind" of anyone except the homeowners association's board of directors, who are thereby able to promote a form of

---

have the equal access to housing guaranteed under state law if they must go, hat in hand as an Oliver Twist supplicant, to request an association board's "permission" to live as normal a life as they are capable of with canine assistance.

7. For example, poetry runs the gamut from the doggerel of Ogden Nash to T.S. Eliot's "Old Possum's Book of Practical Cats."

9. For example, the Odyssey chronicles the faithfulness of Odysseus's dog. The legendary terrier "Greyfriars' Bobby" is synonymous with loyalty. In 1601, when the Earl of Southampton was being held in the Tower of London, his cat is reputed to have located his master's cell and climbed down the chimney to join him during his imprisonment. (Clutton-Brock, Cat, *supra*, p. 16.) And military annals document the wartime bravery and courage of dogs in the K-9 Corps.

10. The President and his family often set a national example in this regard. Chelsea Clinton's cat "Socks" is only the latest in a long line of White House pets, including Franklin Roosevelt's "Fala" and the Bushes' "Millie."

11. See, e.g., Siegel, *Companion Animals: In Sickness and in Health* (1993) 49 Journal of Social Issues 157.

13. See, e.g., Melson, *The Benefits of Animals to Our Lives* (Fall 1990), People, Animals, Environment at pages 15–17.

sophisticated bigotry. In light of the substantial and disproportionate burden imposed for those who must forego virtually any and all association with pets, this lack of benefit renders a categorical ban unreasonable....

The proffered justification is all the more spurious when measured against the terms of the pet restriction itself, which contains an exception for domestic fish and birds. A squawking bird can readily create the very kind of disturbance supposedly prevented by banning other types of pets. At the same time, many animals prohibited by the restriction, such as hamsters and the like, turtles, and small reptiles, make no sound whatsoever. Disposal of bird droppings in common trash areas poses as much of a health concern as cat litter or rabbit pellets, which likewise can be handled in a manner that avoids potential problems. Birds are also known to carry disease and provoke allergies. Neither is maintaining fish without possible risk of interfering with the quiet enjoyment of condominium neighbors. Aquarium water must be changed and disposed of in the common drainage system. Leakage from a fish tank could cause serious water damage to the owner's unit, those below, and common areas. Defendants and the majority purport such solicitude for the "health, sanitation and noise concerns" of other unit owners, but fail to explain how the possession of pets, such as plaintiff's cats, under the circumstances alleged in her complaint, jeopardizes that goal any more than the fish and birds expressly allowed by the pet restriction. This inconsistency underscores its unreasonableness and discriminatory impact.[14]

4. The majority's burden/benefit analysis.

From the statement of the facts through the conclusion, the majority's analysis gives scant acknowledgment to any of the foregoing considerations but simply takes refuge behind the "presumption of validity" now accorded *all* CC & R's irrespective of subject matter. They never objectively scrutinize defendants' blandishments of protecting "health and happiness" or realistically assess the substantial impact on affected unit owners and *their* use of *their* property. As this court has often recognized, "deference is not abdication." ... Regardless of how limited an inquiry is permitted under applicable law, it must nevertheless be made.

Here, such inquiry should start with an evaluation of the interest that will suffer upon enforcement of the pet restriction. In determining the "burden on the use of land," due recognition must be given to the fact that this particular "use" transcends the impersonal and mundane matters typically regulated by condominium CC & R's, such as whether someone can place a doormat in the hallway or hang a towel on the patio rail or have food in the pool area, and reaches the very quality of life of hundreds of owners and residents. Nonetheless, the majority accept uncritically the proffered justification of preserving "health and happiness" and essentially consider only one criterion to determine enforceability: was the restriction recorded in the original declaration?[15] If so, it is "pre-

---

14. On a related point, the association rules and regulations already contain a procedure for dealing with problems arising from bird and fish ownership. There appears no reason it could not be utilized to deal with similar concerns about other types of pets such as plaintiff's cats.

15. The majority purport to rely on several out-of-state cases to support their conclusions as to the validity of the pet restriction. These decisions are either distinguishable or reflect the same lack of objective analysis. *Hidden Harbour Estates, Inc. v. Norman*..., involved a prohibition against the consumption of alcoholic beverages in the condominium project club house, one of the *common areas* used by all the owners. *Hidden Harbour Estates v. Basso* (Fla.Dist.Ct.App.1981) 393 So. 2d 637 likewise did not concern a restriction on pets but a ban on the construction of private wells, which had the potential for creating serious salination problems in the *common* drinking water. Of those cases involving pet restrictions, only *Noble v. Murphy* (1993) 34 Mass.App.Ct. 452, 612 N.E.2d 266, dealt with a categorical prohibition (See *Dulaney Towers Maintenance v. O'Brey* (1980), 46 Md.App. 464, 418 A.2d 1233; *Wilshire Condominium Ass'n, Inc. v. Kohlbrand* (Fla.Dist.Ct.App.1979) 368 So. 2d 629.) The court there also failed to give any consideration to the qualitative nature of the restriction or the

sumptively valid," unless in violation of public policy. Given the application of the law to the facts alleged and by an inversion of relative interests, it is difficult to hypothesize any CC & R's that would not pass muster.[16] Such sanctity has not been afforded any writing save the commandments delivered to Moses on Mount Sinai, and they were set in stone, not upon worthless paper.

Moreover, unlike most conduct controlled by CC & R's, the activity at issue here is strictly confined to the owner's interior space; it does not in any manner invade other units or the common areas. Owning a home of one's own has always epitomized the American dream. More than simply embodying the notion of having "one's castle," it represents the sense of freedom and self-determination emblematic of our national character. Granted, those who live in multi-unit developments cannot exercise this freedom to the same extent possible on a large estate. But owning pets that do not disturb the quiet enjoyment of others does not reasonably come within this compromise. Nevertheless, with no demonstrated or discernible benefit, the majority arbitrarily sacrifice the dream to the tyranny of the "commonality."

5. Conclusion.

Our true task in this turmoil is to strike a balance between the governing rights accorded a condominium association and the individual freedom of its members. To fulfill that function, a reviewing court must view with a skeptic's eye restrictions driven by fear, anxiety, or intolerance. In any community, we do not exist *in vacuo*. There are many annoyances which we tolerate because not to do so would be repressive and place the freedom of others at risk.

In contravention, the majority's failure to consider the real burden imposed by the pet restriction unfortunately belittles and trivializes the interest at stake here. Pet ownership substantially enhances the quality of life for those who desire it. When others are not only undisturbed by, but *completely unaware of,* the presence of pets being enjoyed by their neighbors, the balance of benefit and burden is rendered disproportionate and unreasonable, rebutting any presumption of validity. Their view, shorn of grace and guiding philosophy, is devoid of the humanity that must temper the interpretation and application of all laws, for in a civilized society that is the source of their authority. As judicial architects of the rules of life, we better serve when we construct halls of harmony rather than walls of wrath.

I would affirm the judgment of the Court of Appeal.

Notes & Questions

1. *Due process and restrictive covenants.* After his exposure to the community association in *Nahrstedt*, Justice Arabian "became convinced that the authority [of associations]—unrestrained by basic principles of due process or even rationality—threatens fundamental interests heretofore assumed as sacrosanct incidents of home ownership. Given the growing popularity of multi-unit developments and the presumption of reasonableness the law accords recorded restrictions, vast numbers of people are vulnerable

---

burden it imposed on those arbitrarily deprived of the opportunity to own pets that could be confined to their units and kept without disturbing the quiet enjoyment of other unit owners.

16. Under the facts of this case, the majority do more than simply accord the restriction a presumption of reasonableness. They encourage and endorse the enforcing body to disregard the privacy interests of law-abiding property owners. If pets are maintained in the manner alleged in plaintiff's complaint, then only snoopers are in a position to claim a violation of the restriction.

to significant limitations on their conduct enforced by their neighbors without account-ability or independent review." See Armand Arabian, *Condos, Cats, & CC&Rs: Invasion of the Castle Common*, 23 Pepp. L. Rev. 1, 2 (1995). Inspired in part by Susan F. French, *The Constitution of a Private Residential Government Should Include a Bill of Rights*, 27 Wake Forest L. Rev. 345, 350 (1992) he proposed legislation to prohibit covenants or rules restricting the use of a unit or the common areas "(1) without reasonable justification based on economic, aesthetic, health, or safety considerations; or (2) in a manner that de-nies a civil right granted or guaranteed under the United States Constitution, the California Constitution, or a federal, state, county, or local statute, ordinance or regulation." How does his proposed legislation differ from the rule adopted by the majority?

2. *Costs of litigation.* In contrast to Justice Arabian, most commentators believe the decision reached by the majority is necessary to protect community associations from the costs that would be involved if individual owners were entitled to exemptions on the ground that their particular use did not cause the harm the restriction was designed to protect against. Inviting courts to second-guess association decisions may be costly both because of the additional litigation likely to ensue and because courts may not under-stand the situation that led to association action. For an interesting and thorough analy-sis of the *Nahrstedt* decision, see Carl B. Kress, *Beyond Nahrstedt: Reviewing Restrictions Governing Life in a Property Owner Association*, 42 UCLA L. Rev. 837 (1995).

3. *Aftermath.* The California legislature came to the aid of pet-loving homeowners in 2000 when it enacted

Civil Code § 1360.5. Pets within common interest developments:

(a) No governing documents shall prohibit the owner of a separate interest within a common interest development from keeping at least one pet within the com-mon interest development, subject to reasonable rules and regulations of the as-sociation. This section may not be construed to affect any other rights provided by law to an owner of a separate interest to keep a pet within the development.

(b) For purposes of this section, "pet" means any domesticated bird, cat, dog, aquatic animal kept within an aquarium, or other animal as agreed to between the association and the homeowner.

(c) If the association implements a rule or regulation restricting the number of pets an owner may keep, the new rule or regulation shall not apply to prohibit an owner from continuing to keep any pet that the owner currently keeps in his or her separate interest if the pet otherwise conforms with the previous rules or regulations relating to pets.

(d) For the purposes of this section, "governing documents" shall include, but are not limited to, the conditions, covenants, and restrictions of the common interest development, and the bylaws, rules, and regulations of the association.

(e) This section shall become operative on January 1, 2001, and shall only apply to governing documents entered into, amended, or otherwise modified on or after that date.

4. *Other cases. Coventry Square Condo. Ass'n. v. Halpern*, 436 A.2d 580 (N.J. Super. 1981) invalidated a by-law provision which required a limited class of residents to pay a security deposit on the ground that it was arbitrary. *Davidson Bros., Inc. v. D. Katz & Sons, Inc.*, 274 N.J. Super. 159, 643 A.2d 642 (1994) refused to enforce a covenant not to use a site for a grocery store that would compete with the covenantee's grocery store on the ground that it violated public policy by unduly restricting the shopping opportuni-

ties of low income residents. These and other bases for invalidating enforcement of use restrictions and other governing document provisions are considered throughout this book, and particularly in Chapters 7 and 8.

Chapter 5

Association Governance

Chapter 3 addressed the powers of the community association. In this chapter we consider how those powers are exercised, how the community "governance" works. Corporate law provides a legal framework for the many community associations that are incorporated, and the law of unincorporated associations provides a framework for many others. However, community associations are different from other corporations and associations and principles from municipal law and even trust law sometimes come into play. In many states, special statutes, like those based on UCIOA, provide the primary law governing some or all community associations. For questions not covered by those statutes, nonprofit corporation statutes and the evolving common law of community associations must provide the answers.

Restatement (Third) § 6.16 Representative Government

Except as otherwise provided by statute or the governing documents, an association in a common-interest community is governed by a board elected by its members. The board is entitled to exercise all powers of the community except those reserved to the members.

Governance issues revolve around four basic questions: Who may act? How may they act? What rules apply? And what do the rules mean? Who may act addresses the concern whether actions may be taken by the board of directors or whether a vote of the membership is required. If the latter, what percentage of affirmative votes is necessary? How they may act raises questions of the standard or standards applicable to governance actions. Two primary approaches have been taken to judicial review of association actions: the rule of reasonableness and the business judgment rule. The Restatement (Third) takes a middle ground, requiring that the association act reasonably in exercising its discretionary powers but placing the burden of proof on the member challenging the association's action. In thinking about which standard should be applied, consider the extent to which results will be predictable, the autonomy of the governing body will be respected, and the interests of community members will be protected.

Restatement (Third) § 6.13 Duties Of A Common-Interest Community To Its Members

(1) In addition to duties imposed by statute and the governing documents, the association has the following duties to the members of the common-interest community:

(a) to use ordinary care and prudence in managing the property and financial affairs of the community that are subject to its control;

(b) to treat members fairly;

(c) to act reasonably in the exercise of its discretionary powers including rulemaking, enforcement, and design-control powers;

(d) to provide members reasonable access to information about the association, the common property, and the financial affairs of the association.

(2) A member challenging an action of the association under this section has the burden of proving a breach of duty by the association. Except when the breach alleged is ultra vires action by the association, the member has the additional burden of proving that the breach has caused, or threatens to cause, injury to the member individually or to the interests of the common-interest community.

A. Rights of Members

1. Membership and Voting Rights

I do not believe that democracy can survive except as a formality if the ordinary citizen's role is limited to voting, and if he is incapable of initiative or all possibility of influencing the political, social, and economic structures that surround him.

—Saul Alinsky

Membership and voting rights in a common interest community are established by the governing documents. Typically the membership provisions are included in the declaration, but some provisions may be found in the bylaws, or occasionally in the articles of incorporation.

Restatement (Third) § 6.17 Voting Rights

Except as otherwise provided by statute or the declaration, votes are allocated to members on the basis of the number of lots or units owned that are currently subject to an obligation to pay assessments or dues. One vote is allocated to each such lot or unit. Unless a contrary interpretation is required by statute or by the governing documents, a requirement for approval by a certain percentage of "owners" means approval by that percentage of votes.

In the vast majority of communities, membership is tied to ownership. In examining governance issues, consider when and whether some basis other than ownership might be appropriate.

In many communities there are a large number of tenants who have resided there for years, have made substantial investments in improvements, and consider the community their "home" as much as the owner residents do. Traditionally, however, tenants have not been given the right to vote, serve on committees or boards, or otherwise participate in community governance. The justification often given for their exclusion is that their economic interests are different from those of the owners, but that is generally true of renters and does not justify denying them voting rights in public elections. Nor do the different interests of resident and nonresident owners lead to different voting rights in common interest communities. If tenants should be given participation rights, how extensive should they be?

Unlike prospective tenants, and subject to some statutory and regulatory limits, developers can control the extent of their participation rights in community associations. Faulty drafting or inadequate foresight, however, can lead to litigation over their rights, as the next case demonstrates.

Investors Ltd. v. Sun Mountain Condo.

Court of Appeals of Idaho
683 P.2d 891 (Id. Ct. App. 1984)

SWANSTROM, J. Investors Limited of Sun Valley (Investors), as the present developer of the Sun Mountain Condominium project, filed suit against Sun Mountain Condominiums Homeowners Association seeking a declaratory judgment holding that it has voting rights in the Association....

The issue in this case is whether Investors is the "owner" of platted but unbuilt condominium units and is thereby entitled to voting rights in the Association, the "management body" of the condominium project. We hold that Investors is not an owner, but limit our holding to the facts in this case and base it upon the particular language in the condominium documents.

The facts in this case are not disputed. In 1972, a condominium declaration and plats for the Sun Mountain Condominiums, Phase I, were filed with the Blaine County Recorder. The project, to be built in Ketchum, Idaho, was to consist of three buildings, each containing four units, on a parcel of approximately one acre. The original developer built one of the buildings shown on the plats and sold the first four units to individual purchasers. The remaining two buildings are yet to be built.

In September of 1979, Investors purchased the Sun Mountain project from the original developer. Later, Investors submitted to the City of Ketchum amended plans for the project, showing that three additional buildings would be built on the remaining land, rather than two as shown on the original plats. The Association, consisting of the owners of the four units in the building that had been completed, objected to Investors' new plans which would significantly reduce each owner's share of the common area.

Under Idaho law, prior to the first sale of a condominium, the declaration and the plat or plats may be amended or revoked by a subsequently recorded instrument executed and acknowledged by the record owner and the holder of any recorded security interest in all of the property comprising the condominium project.... However, after the first sale of a condominium, the declaration and plats can be amended only if the proposed amendment is consented to by the requisite percentage of "the voting power of the owners of the project," always more than fifty percent, as specified in the declaration. I.C. § 55-1505(2)(k). Here the declaration recorded by the declarant in 1972 stated:

> This Declaration shall not be revoked nor shall any of the provisions herein be amended unless the Owners representing an aggregate ownership interest of 85% or more of the Condominiums, as reflected on the real estate records of Blaine County, Idaho ... consent and agree to such revocation or amendment by instruments duly recorded.

It is undisputed that the four owners of the completed condominiums represent an aggregate ownership of thirty-three percent of the total condominiums originally planned and platted for Sun Mountain Condominiums, Phase I. The original developer had never voted in, attempted to control or to manage the Association, nor had it ever been assessed or paid any of the assessments of the Association. The owners of the four com-

Completed condos rep. 4/12 orig. contemplated units. (33%)

pleted units comprised the Association and paid one hundred percent of all of its assessments. All four owners opposed Investors' plans to add an additional building to the project. However, to overcome the Association's resistance to its plans, Investors tried to gain control of the Association by asserting its voting rights as the "owner" of eight unbuilt condominium units.[1] The Association rejected Investors' claim of voting rights and refused to allow it to participate in Association affairs. Investors then filed this suit.

...

A key provision of the [Sun Mountain Condominium] declaration is section 7.1 which states: "Every Owner shall be entitled and required to be a member of the Association.... No person or entity other than an Owner may be a member of the Association." Investors contends that, as the record owner of the entire unimproved and unsold portion of the project, it is an "owner" and is entitled to membership in the Association. The Association contends, on the other hand, that the term "owner" refers only to the owners of condominium units which have been built and are physically extant.

Investors, at oral argument, contended this project was to be developed in stages, indicating an intent that the term "owner" should apply to all platted condominiums, whether built or unbuilt. Arguably, the use of the term "Phase I" implies that other phases could follow, but that argument invites us to speculate on things outside the record. This we will not do. The record before us indicates that all three buildings platted in Phase I of the project were to be built and offered for sale at the same time. This is reflected in several parts of the recorded declaration.

As explained below, we think the term "owner," as used in the declaration, is unambiguous. A plain reading of the declaration supports the Association's position that "owner" is defined by reference to physically existing units. However, we note at the outset that even if the definition were susceptible of differing interpretations, in this instance we would reach the same result. Investors' predecessor was the "declarant" who prepared and filed the condominium declaration in 1972. The predecessor chose the language used in the declaration to define membership rights and voting rights in the Association. The declarant could easily have made clear, specific provisions in the declaration for retaining some control in the Association until all or part of the units were completed and sold, if this was the intent. Because the declaration was drafted by Investor's predecessor in interest, the basic tenets of contract law require that we construe the provisions of the document in favor of the nondrafting party....

Moreover, the condominium statutes do not require any deviation from a plain reading of the declaration. The Condominium Property Act (1965 Idaho Sess.Laws, chapter 225, p. 515) is a "first generation" act that is yet to be amended. Unlike many modern statutes governing development and sales of condominiums, the Idaho law does not prohibit or restrict the developer from retaining control over the managing body of condominium owners by reason of the developer's ownership of built but unsold units. The Idaho act is simply silent on the subject. Compare, e.g., Fla.Stat. §§ 718.301, 302 (1981). See also P.J. Rohan, "The Model Condominium Code" —A Blueprint For Modernizing Condominium Legislation, 78 Colum.L.Rev. 587–608 (1978). On the other hand, there is nothing in the Idaho act that suggests the term "owner" as defined in the declaration here should be construed to include ownership of unbuilt units.

---

1. The actual number of votes which can be cast by a member of the Association is determined by that member's percentage interest in the common area, as shown by an exhibit filed with the condominium declaration. This percentage interest can vary from unit to unit.

We now focus upon the declaration itself. Section 2.7 defines "<u>owner</u>" as "any person or entity, including Declarant, at any time owning a condominium." Condominium is defined by the declaration as follows:

> "Condominium" means a separate interest in a <u>Unit</u> together with an undivided interest in common in the Common Area (expressed as a percentage of the entire ownership interest in the Common Area) as set forth in Exhibit B attached hereto and by this reference made a part hereof.

A unit is defined more specifically in section 2.2 of the declaration as follows, in part:

> "Unit" means the separate interest in a condominium as bounded by the interior surface of the perimeter walls, floors, ceilings, windows and doors thereof and the interior surfaces of the built-in fireplaces as shown and numbered on the condominium map to be filed for record, together with all fixtures and improvements therein contained.

Section 1.4 of the declaration recites:

> This condominium project will provide a means for ownership in fee simple of separate interests in Units and for co-ownership with others, <u>as tenants in common, of Common Area</u>, as those terms are herein defined.

Section 4.1 recites:

> The project is hereby divided into Condominiums, each consisting of a separate interest in a Unit and an undivided interest in common in the Common Area in accordance with the attached Exhibits A & B setting forth the Common Area appurtenant to each Unit. The percentage of ownership interest in the Common Area which is to be allocated to each Unit for purposes of tax assessment under Section 55-1514 of the Idaho Code and for purposes of liability as provided by Section 55-1515 of such Code shall be the same as set forth in Exhibit B. Exhibit B also contains a legal description of each Unit in Building [blank] consisting of the identifying number of such Unit as shown on the Condominium Map. Such undivided interests in the Common Area are hereby declared to be appurtenant to the respective Units.

According to section 2.4, "<u>Building means one of the buildings constructed on the Real Property pursuant to this Declaration</u>, excepting all automobile parking structures."

Sections 4.4 and 4.5 state:

> Title to a Condominium may be held or owned by any entity and in any manner in which title to any other real property may be held or owned in the State of Idaho.

> No part of a Condominium or of the legal rights comprising ownership of a Condominium may be separated from any other part thereof during the period of Condominium Ownership prescribed herein, so that each Unit and the undivided interest in the Common Area appurtenant to such Unit shall always be conveyed, devised, encumbered, and otherwise affected only as a complete Condominium. Every gift, devise, bequest, transfer, encumbrance, conveyance or other disposition of a Condominium or any part thereof shall be presumed to be a gift, devise, bequest, transfer, encumbrance, or conveyance, respectively, of the entire Condominium; together with all appurtenant rights created by law or by this Declaration.

It is clear from the foregoing provisions that to be an "owner" — and thus a member of the Association — one must own a condominium. A condominium does not exist under this declaration unless there is both ownership of a separate interest in real property (a unit) and an undivided interest in real property (the common area of the project). A developer, like anyone else, must have both interests before he is an "owner" within the meaning of the declaration. The declaration treats a "unit" as part of a "building" and refers to "building," in section 2.4, as one of the buildings constructed on the property.

We do not question that Investors is a "record owner" of the property committed to the Sun Mountain Condominiums, Phase I project who has a "real property" interest in that project. I.C. § 55-1505. Likewise, in construing the term "owner" as used in this declaration, we are not suggesting that either a developer or a purchaser of an unbuilt condominium has no recognizable real property interest in a unit. That question is not before us. It may well be that, in spite of historic and long-standing prohibitions to the contrary, a developer can enter into valid contracts to sell "future interests" in unbuilt condominiums once statutory requirements for filing declarations, plats and other documents have been met. See, *e.g., State Savings & Loan Association v. Kauaian Development Company, Inc.*, 50 Hawaii 540, 445 P.2d 109 (1968), modified in appeal taken after remand, 62 Hawaii 188, 613 P.2d 1315 (1980). Recognition of this concept implies that contract purchasers of planned but unbuilt condominiums can acquire equitable ownerships of a real property interest in the "property" as defined by I.C. § 55-1503(c). The district judge here indicated his awareness of the public policy stated in the Condominium Property Act "to permit and facilitate the construction and development of condominiums and condominium projects, together with the financing of the same." I.C. § 55-1502. He expressed the view that practical considerations in condominium development, financing and sales require courts to willingly accept and clearly define this "new" form of property ownership. He stated that "common practice in the selling of condominiums necessitates a finding that parties do own condominiums before they are built." We are not challenging that statement here. We are not called upon to determine the broad range of ownership rights. We are simply construing the language employed in this particular declaration, which defines membership rights in the Association.

We conclude that because Investors is not an "owner" of a condominium it is not entitled to membership in the Association. Accordingly, we reverse the summary judgment order and remand for further proceedings. Costs to appellant. No attorney fees awarded on appeal.

Reversed and Remanded.

Notes & Questions

1. *Association membership.* The primary dispute in *Investors* was the developer's membership status and voting rights and his interest in unbuilt condominium units. Why is the dispute over membership important? What rights may be affected or implicated by membership status? See UCIOA Sections: 1-103 (32) ("Unit Owner"), 2-105 (Contents of Declaration), 2-107 (Allocation of Allocated Interest), 2-112 (Relocation of Unit Boundaries), 2-117 (Amendment of Declaration), 2-118 (Termination of Common Interest Community), 3-103 (Executive Board Members and Officers), 3-106 (Bylaws), 3-109 (Quorums), and 3-115 (Assessments for Common Expense).

2. *Mandatory membership.* The association, as the community's managing body, has, among other powers, the authority to collect assessments on each member's unit and to

require that homeowners obtain approval prior to making any changes to the exterior of the unit. See, *e.g.,* UCIOA § 3-102. The association's power often invites disputes over the mandatory nature of association membership. See *Duffy v. Sunburst Farms E. Mut. Water and Agric. Co.,* 604 P.2d 1124 (Az. 1980) (unit owner challenging the mandatory membership requirements of the association). In *Duffy,* a majority of the homeowners voted to amend the declaration and make membership in the association voluntary. The court upheld this amendment even though many of the owners voting for it were not "members in good standing" (*i.e.,* they were delinquent on assessments) and, hence, were not eligible to vote under the by-laws. Nevertheless, read literally, the declaration provision only required a majority vote of "owners" not "Members." Do you agree with the outcome? Why would homeowners want to withdraw as members? See also *Anthony v. Brea Glenbrook Club,* 58 Cal. App. 3d 506, 130 Cal. Rptr. 32 (1976) (holding that mandatory membership requirements can be enforced as equitable servitudes or as covenants running with the land). Which aspects of the common interest community scheme imply that mandatory membership requirements can be enforced as covenants running with the land or as an equitable servitude? If homeowners are permitted to withdraw from association membership, what are possible consequences?

3. *Membership and unbuilt units.* In *Investors,* the court ruled that the developer was not a "unit owner" as described and defined in the CCRs. The court interpreted the term "unit" to denote an actual physical structure. Compare the *Investors* decision with the holding in *Mountain View Condo. Homeowners Ass'n, Inc. v. Scott,* 180 Ariz. 216, 883 P.2d 453 (1994). In *Mountain View,* the court held that the ownership interests of completed condominium units were indistinguishable from uncompleted units for the purpose of paying assessments to the association. In reaching its decision, the court noted that the declaration of covenants said nothing about a requirement of an actual physical structure before becoming "unit" owner and, hence, a member. How do you explain the seemingly opposite outcomes? Which approach do you agree with and why? See also UCIOA §§ 2-107 and 3-115.

4. *The declaration and membership.* The declaration is the key document that controls membership and other essential aspects of the common interest community. Under corporate law, the articles of incorporation and by-laws are also instrumental in defining the rights and privileges of membership. Could the developer in *Investors* have avoided the dispute regarding his membership status by drafting the governing documents differently? How would you draft such terms? See UCIOA §§ 1-103 and 2-105.

5. *The Uniform Act and membership.* UCIOA § 1-103 (32) defines "unit owner" as an owner of a *physical portion* of the common interest community designated for separate use or occupancy. Imagine that you are the developer's attorney in *Investors.* What arguments can you make that the definition in UCIOA § 1-103 (32) includes owners of unbuilt units?

Problem

A community has a large number of renters. Many of the tenants have been there for years and consider the community their home. T, leader of a small group of civic-minded tenants, has attended many board meetings. Tonight during "citizens time," she requested the board to permit tenants to serve on committees and the board itself. As board chair, how do you respond? As association counsel? The following day you discuss the question with Developer as the two of you discuss the documents for a new project. What would you suggest??

2. Meetings, Elections, Quorum, Voting and Proxies

Restatement (Third) § 6.18 Meetings And Elections

Except to the extent the association is properly controlled by the developer under § 6.19, and subject to reasonable procedures set forth in the governing documents or adopted by the association, members of a common-interest community have the right to vote in elections for the board of directors and on other matters properly presented to the members, to attend and participate in meetings of the members, and to stand for election to the board of directors. Except when the board properly meets in executive session, members of the association are entitled to attend meetings of the board of directors and to a reasonable opportunity to present their views to the board.

Lake Forest Property Owners' Ass'n v. Smith

Supreme Court of Alabama
571 So. 2d 1047 (Ala. 1990)

MADDOX, J. Lake Forest Property Owners' Association, Inc. ("the Association"), appeals from a declaratory judgment in favor of James C. Smith, Diane Millar, James Childs, and Susan D. Bedford, all members of the Association, holding that the Association's board of directors was without authority to cast certain "residual" votes at its annual meeting.

The stipulated facts pertinent to this appeal are as follows: From 1971 until 1979, Lake Forest, Inc., developed and operated a "planned unit development" in Baldwin County, Alabama, that consisted of approximately 4,200 lots as well as a sewer system, water system, roads, and recreational facilities, including a country club, a golf course, a yacht club, and other amenities. On July 1, 1971, Lake Forest, Inc., granted the Association an option to purchase all of the common facilities in the development. Those common facilities consisted of the country club, the yacht club, the marina, the golf course, the lake, any facilities or area for the common use of Lake Forest members, and the guard and security service. The Association was incorporated on July 29, 1971, at which time it adopted its by-laws.

On October 19, 1978, at a special meeting of the Association, the membership voted to exercise the option. At that time, the Association also elected its board of directors. On February 2, 1979, Lake Forest, Inc., sold the common facilities to the Association. In November 1988, Lake Forest, Inc., merged with its parent corporation, Purcell Company, Inc. ("Purcell").

On October 16, 1989, the Association held its annual meeting, for the primary purpose of electing four members to the board of directors. The by-laws required that at least two people be nominated for each vacancy; consequently, the nominating committee recommended eight persons for the four available positions in the proxy it sent with the notice of the meeting. Prior to the meeting, several members, referred to as the "reform group," circulated a proxy proposing its own slate of directors.

The applicable section of the Association's by-laws dealing with voting states, in part:

3.7. Voting. Each full Voting Member shall be entitled to one vote for each lot owned for which dues, charges, initiation fee and assessment are current, for the election of each member of the Board of Directors and one vote for each and every action which may require a vote of the membership of the Corporation; provided however, Lake Forest, Inc., or its *successor*, shall be entitled to cast the number of votes equal to <u>one vote for each quarter (1/4) acre of property which it owns</u> in Lake Forest Development, for the election of each Director of the Board and for each and every other matter which may require a vote of the membership of the Corporation.

(Emphasis added.)

Two weeks prior to the annual meeting, the Association's board of directors adopted a resolution that <u>instructed the president to cast a total of 1,227 votes for its nominees.</u> Of those votes, <u>1,184,</u> the "residual" votes, represented each 1/4 acre of real property referred to in section 3.7 of the by-laws (<u>the common areas</u>), while 43 of the votes <u>represented lots the Association owned.</u> Pursuant to the resolution, the president also cast the same number of votes, 1,227, in favor of two amendments to the by-laws and in favor of a dues increase from $27.50 to $35.00 a month.[2] The results of the board of directors election were as follows:

Board's Nominees	Total Votes Received	Votes Received Without "Residual" Votes & Votes Representing Lots Owned
Coxwell	1,905	678
Sadler	1,691	464
Yoder	1,665	438
Agostinelli	1,635	408
Coats	431	431
Debrule	349	349
Deloney	317	317
		3,085 (45%)

Reform Group Nominees	Total Votes Received	
Smith	851	
Millar	804	
Childs	793	
Bedford	702	
Stoddard	402	
Maye	264	
	3,816 (55%)	

The trial court entered an order based on the stipulated facts and made the following conclusions of Law:

1. That Defendant, <u>Lake Forest Property Owners' Association, Inc., is not a 'Successor' of Lake Forest, Inc., as that term is intended in Section 3.7 of the by-laws of Lake Forest Property Owners' Association, Inc.</u>

2. That Defendant, Lake Forest Property Owners' Association, Inc., was <u>without authority to cast 1,184 votes representing one vote per quarter acre of real property owned by Defendant,</u> for the election of Directors or for an increase in the dues.

---

2. The two amendments were defeated and are not a subject of this appeal.

3. That Defendant, Lake Forest Property Owners' Association, Inc., did have authority to cast 43 votes representing lots owned by Defendant for the election of Directors and for an increase in the dues.... [T]he increase in dues is adjudged to have been defeated and the vote for Directors is adjudged to have been as follows:

dissidents

Smith	851
Millar	804
Childs	793
Coxwell	721
Bedford	702
Sadler	507
Yoder	481
Agostinelli	451
Coats	431
Studdard	402
Debrule	349
Deloney	317
Maye	264

The Association argues that, by virtue of its purchase of the common amenities and its assumption of the obligations of Lake Forest, Inc., it is the "successor" to Lake Forest, Inc., as that term is used in section 3.7 of the by-laws. The reform group nominees argue that Purcell, rather than the Association, is the successor to Lake Forest, Inc.

We recognize initially that because the facts below were undisputed, the *ore tenus* rule is inapplicable in this case. Instead, "the appellate court shall sit in judgment on the evidence *de novo*, indulging no presumption in favor of the trial court's application of the law to the facts." *Justice v. Arab Lumber & Supply, Inc.*, 533 So. 2d 538, 542 (Ala.1988) (citations omitted).

It is generally acknowledged that there is no precise legal definition of "successor" that would be applicable in all contexts. *Safer v. Perper*, 569 F.2d 87, 95 (D.C.Cir.1977). Rather, the determination of whether an entity is a "successor" is made on a case-by-case basis according to the facts. *Howard Johnson Co. v. Detroit Local Joint Executive Board*, 417 U.S. 249, 256, 94 S.Ct. 2236, 2240, 41 L.Ed.2d 46 (1974).

Although there are no Alabama cases dealing with the definition of "successor" in the precise factual context presented here, first *National Bank of Birmingham v. Adams*, 281 Ala. 404, 410, 203 So. 2d 124, 129 (1967), supports the reform group's argument that Purcell, by virtue of the merger with Lake Forest, Inc., is, in fact, the successor to Lake Forest, Inc.:

> We think that it is clear under the Alabama decisions and indeed the decisions of most if not all jurisdictions, that the surviving corporation in a merger situation is the successor to the constituent corporation. If it is not the successor to the constituent corporation, what is it with regard thereto?

Look to the purchase agreement.

In this case, the purchase agreement between Lake Forest, Inc., and the Association refers several times to Lake Forest, Inc., and "its successors," without mentioning the Association as its "successor." Indeed, that agreement makes it clear that the Association was the purchaser of the common facilities rather than the successor to Lake Forest, Inc. "In the non-labor contractual cases, 'successor' has often been defined as 'one who takes the place that another has left, and sustains the like part or character.'" *Safer*, 569 F.2d at 95, quoting *Wawak Co. v. Kaiser*, 90 F.2d 694, 697 (7th Cir.1937) (citations omitted). After the merger, Purcell took the place that Lake Forest, Inc., left, and Purcell now stands in its place as the owner of the 800 unsold lots that Lake Forest, Inc., retained when it sold the common facilities to the Association. Therefore, the trial judge's holding that the Association is not the successor to Lake Forest, Inc., as well as his determination that the Association did not have the authority to cast the 1,184 residual votes, is affirmed.

[handwritten margin note: Purcell still owns 800 unsold lots.]

The reform group also argues that the trial judge erred in ruling that the president of the Association's board of directors properly cast 43 votes for the dues increase and for the board's nominees. Section 2.4 of the Association's by-laws, entitled "Dues, Charges and Assessments," specifically states that "[t]he Board of Directors [has] no authority to increase dues." We agree with the reform group that the board of directors may not do indirectly (by casting 43 votes for the number of lots the Association owns) what it is prohibited from doing directly.

With regard to the 43 votes cast for the board's nominees, the reform group argues that the Association never qualified itself as a "full voting member" pursuant to section 2.1 of the by-laws and, thus, was not entitled to vote based on the number of lots it owned. Section 2.1 of the by-laws reads, in part, as follows:

> Section 2.1 Persons Who Shall be Members: The membership of the Corporation shall consist of two classes of members: the first class of which shall be called Full Voting Members; the second class of which shall be called Associate Members.

> The Full Voting Membership shall be limited to those persons who purchase lots in the Lake Forest development from Lake Forest, Inc., or its successors, on or after July 1, 1971....

> In the event a lot is purchased by a corporation, the corporation must immediately designate an individual who will be the club member. This individual must go through the process of applying through the membership committee. When approved this member must then sign a notarized statement that he will be responsible for dues, charges, assessments, including interest on such charges, assessments, collection costs and attorney's fees.

There is no evidence in the record that the Association ever designated any individual to represent the 43 lots it owns. Moreover, there is no evidence that any dues have been paid on those 43 lots. The beginning of section 3.7 reads: "Each Full Voting Member shall be entitled to one vote for each lot owned for which dues, charges, initiation fee and assessment are current...." Thus, the Association did not have the authority to cast 43 votes for either the nominees or the dues increase, and the trial judge's holding to the contrary is reversed.

The judgment of the trial court is affirmed in part and reversed in part and the cause is remanded for proceedings consistent with this opinion.

Affirmed in part; Reversed in part and Remanded.

Islander Beach Club Condo. Ass'n v. Johnston

Florida District Court of Appeal
623 So. 2d 628 (Fla. Dist. Ct. App. 1993)

HARRIS, C.J. The issue on appeal is whether sealed voting proxies sent to a time-share condominium association prior to the election of board members (but not to be opened until the election) become "official records" of the association upon their receipt and subject to examination by association members prior to the election. We hold that they do not become official records subject to opening and inspecting until after the election and reverse.

Islander Beach Club Condominium Association of Volusia County, Inc. ("Islander") is a not-for-profit corporation charged with the operation of the Islander Beach Club condominium. Islander scheduled a meeting to be held December 5, 1992 to elect three directors to the board of administration of the condominium. Islander asserts in its brief that its Board of Directors adopted a procedure whereby all voting proxies received from time-share unit week owners are, upon receipt, retained in a secure area and left unopened until an independent CPA firm opens the proxies shortly before the election in order to verify the proxies against Islander's list of unit week owners.[3]

Appellee Richard P. Johnston is an individual owner of three condominium unit weeks at Islander Beach Club. Johnston was in the process of waging a proxy fight to obtain votes so that he could be elected to one of the board member positions. Toward that end, Johnston demanded to see the voting proxies as they were received by the association. Because it considered the proxies "non-public" until they were opened three days before the election, Islander refused Johnston's request.

Johnston sued, requesting that the court issue an injunction prohibiting Islander from denying Johnston immediate access to the proxies. After an evidentiary hearing on the matter, the trial court issued the injunction which directed Islander to permit Johnston to open and inspect the voting proxies as they were received.

Section 718.111(12) provides in pertinent part:

(12) OFFICIAL RECORDS. —

(a) From the inception of the association, the association shall maintain each of the following items, when applicable, which shall constitute the official records of the association:

12. Ballots, sign-in sheets, voting proxies, and all other papers relating to elections, which shall be maintained for a period of 1 year from the date of the meeting to which the document relates. [Emphasis added] ...

(c) The official records of the association are open to inspection by any association member or the authorized representative of such member at all reasonable times.

The most logical interpretation of this provision is that voting proxies do not become "official records" subject to inspection by any association member until after the election for which they were given. The statute groups voting proxies together with ballots and sign-in sheets, neither of which even exist prior to an election. In addition, subsection (a)12 seems to focus on post election preservation of the records, as evidenced by the provision that these records must be maintained for a period of one year "from the date of" the election. Further the proxies received do not become "voting proxies" until they have been verified as legitimate and submitted for counting. This does not mean that the existence

---

3. This procedure is not required by the Florida Condominium Statutes, the declaration of condominium or the association's by-laws. While it is an efficient procedure to eliminate delay at a meeting to collect and account for proxies, it should not be the exclusive procedure by which a member may exercise a proxy. A member's right to name a proxy to present the written authorization at a meeting prior to an election should not be eliminated by action of a board of directors.

of the sealed proxies may be kept secret or that the proxies in their sealed condition should not be available for inspection as they come in. Whatever information management has should be available to the membership.

The statutory provision pertaining to the use of proxies in condominium association elections further supports the conclusion that the contents of the proxy envelope do not become official records until after an election. Pursuant to Section 718.112(2)(b)3, Florida Statutes, any proxy given is effective "only for the specific meeting for which originally given." This section also provides that all proxies are revocable at any time prior to their actual exercise at the election. Therefore, the sealed proxies in the instant case technically had no legal effect until the votes were cast at the election. Because the proxies in question were exerciseable only at the election which had not yet occurred and were revocable at any time, until the association officers had access to the contents of the proxy envelope, they were not "official records" of Islander.

[handwritten margin note: proxies may be reversed at any time.]

Reversed and Remanded.

Creative applications of organizational forms used in municipal and state government may provide models for developers of common interest communities. The following graphic illustrates a Voting Member (or voting delegate) system that works very well in larger communities because it permits greater participation which assures that the various interests within the community are represented in the governance structure.

Voting Members

- Voting representatives (or delegates) of Class "A" Members (i.e., homeowner members)
- Each Neighborhood elects equal number or proportional number of Voting Members
- Voting members vote on specific issues on behalf of Class "A" Members, such as:
  - Board elections
  - Rule-making issues
  - Expansion of the community
  - Common expense and assessment issues

Under this scheme, the community is divided into areas of like product of approximately the same numerical strength. These may be called parcels, villages, neighborhoods, or many other terms (in a more traditional development, these would be treated as "sub-associations"). The project size, configuration, housing type, and other such factors will influence the structure of the Neighborhoods. These are set either at the outset, or as the project develops, and they may subsequently be realigned at the Neighborhoods' request.

Neighborhoods are grouped into electoral districts, or voting groups, for the purpose of voting and electing directors. These may be based on geographic area, one or more housing types, or other bases. Each represents a political unit within the community association. The goal is to insure that the governing structure is composed of representatives of all constituent groups rather than to allow one highly dense area to control all decision-making.

Often, Neighborhoods are represented by a Voting Member or representative who casts all of the votes from the area he or she represents. The governing documents may require or permit the Voting Members to poll their members before casting votes, a practice that differs markedly from that of most city councils and other local governments. Allocation of seats on the board of directors should be set up to ensure a balanced and proportionate number of directors for each voting group or Neighborhood. Many community associations also have one or more at-large directors, which can reduce the parochial effect of district elections.

Notes & Questions

1. *Allocating votes.* How many votes should each unit owner receive? One vote per unit? Or should votes be weighted proportionally to the value of each unit? Or the square footage of each unit? Should the votes be proportional to the assessment burden of each unit? What factors might be relevant in drafting a voting scheme for different types of developments (*i.e.*, single-family homes, "stacked" apartment style units, etc.)? See UCIOA § 2-107; Model Nonprofit Corporation Act (MNCA) § 7.21.

2. *Multiple membership classes.* The Lake Forest Property Owners' Association used a two-tier voting system, full voting members and associate voting members. Only the full voting members (those whose dues, charges, initiation fees and assessments were current) could vote at the annual meeting. Is such a two-tier system permissible? Is it constitutional? Compare the voting scheme in the *Lake Forest Property Owners'* decision with the voting scheme in *Roberts v. United States Jaycees*, 468 U.S. 609 (1984) (holding that the Jaycees had to give full member voting rights to women in a two-tier scheme).

The Jaycees are a non-profit, national membership organization whose objective is to pursue educational and charitable purposes that promote development of young men's civic organizations. The Jaycees by-laws provided for multiple classes of members. Regular membership was limited to young men between the ages of 18 and 35, while associate membership was available to persons ineligible for regular membership, principally women and older men. An associate member could not vote or hold local or national office. The Minnesota Supreme Court held that the scheme violated the Minnesota Human Rights Act which prohibits discrimination in places of public accommodation on account of an individual's race, color, sex, creed or national origin. The United States Supreme Court upheld that decision. Can you think of reasons why the voting scheme at issue in *Lake Forest Property Owners'* could be challenged under equal protection laws? Could it be challenged under other constitutional or public policy reasons? Why might *Roberts* not apply in the community association context?

3. *Voting and Uniform Act requirements.* The court in *Islander Beach Club* applied the voting proxy requirements of the Florida condominium statute but never mentioned what effect, if any, the community's by-law provisions would have on proxy issues. Can the by-laws vary or supplement the voting and quorum requirements of the local condominium act? See UCIOA §§ 1-104, 3-109 and 3-110; Texas Prop. Code §§ 82.709; 82.110 (1997); and O.C.G.A. § 44-3-79 (1997). How would you draft a proxy provision for *Islander Beach Club Condominium Association*?

4. *Voting and corporate laws.* The Islander Beach Club Condominium Association was organized as a Florida not-for profit corporation. Consequently, the association's voting scheme may have implicated the state's corporation law. Courts often apply well settled principles of corporate law to resolve disputes that are not adequately addressed in the association's governing documents. For example, see *Greenback Townhomes Homeowners Ass'n v. Rizan*, 166 Cal. App. 3d 843, 212 Cal. Rptr. 678 (1985). The Greenback Townhomes Homeowners Association, a non-profit organization, sought to amend its by-laws to conform to changes in California's non-profit corporations code.

The proposed amendment required approval by 75% of all members; however, the association was unable to obtain this requisite percentage to approve the amendment. Nevertheless, the court applied principles of corporate law to permit a corporation, upon court approval, to make by-law amendments or to take other actions where the nonprofit corporation failed to obtain the requisite number of votes because of poor record keeping, voter apathy, etc. Are there reasons why such judicial interference should be limited? In what other ways would court-approved amendments be needed or desirable? How would you draft a voting provision to avoid the problem in *Greenback*?

Note that some states require associations to organize as corporations, either for profit or not-for-profit. See Alabama Uniform Condominium Act § 35-8a-301. Can you think of reasons why an association might wish to be incorporated? Why might a nonprofit corporate status be desirable? How relevant are corporate legal principles to unincorporated associations? What rule of law applies?

5. *Voting and the rights of the minority.* The questions: who may act? and how many votes are required? are implicit in any discussion of actions requiring membership approval. Even if the threshold question whether membership approval is required has been resolved, how many votes remains an issue. Documents frequently provide that some decisions may be taken by a majority vote, while others require a super majority vote. Some governance structures call for delegate voting rather than giving all members a right to vote on certain issues. In all situations where a majority may make a decision, questions concerning the rights of the minority arise, particularly when the decision affects an economic interest of the minority.

6. *Homeowner access to association records.* A unit owner demanded access to association financial records in order to examine employee compensation. The association's board refused. Result? See *Grillo v. Montebello Condo. Unit Owners Ass'n*, 243 Va. 475, 416 S.E.2d 444 (1992).

7. *Meetings and requisite notice.* An important, but sometimes overlooked, aspect of community association governance is the need to follow the required notice and meeting provisions of the by-laws and/or state law. Typically advance notice of at least 30 days is required before the annual or regular meeting of the members. Often notice is required to be sent by U.S. Mail or delivered in person. See generally Model Nonprofit Corporations Act (MNCA) §§ 7.01–7.24, UCIOA § 3-108-3-110. How might the type of development affect your drafting of by-law provisions governing meetings, notice, and quorum requirements (for example, second-home vacation properties vs. primary residences)? What alternate forms of notice may be acceptable or desirable in the computer and electronic age? Why might you wish to draft a quorum requirement lower than 50% of all members/votes entitled to be cast? Consider these same drafting issues with respect to similar board meeting provisions. See MNCA §§ 8.20–8.24.

Problems

1. Your best association client just called. The members are scheduled to vote on a much needed assessment increase. The CCRs require an absolute majority, and there is a problem. One investor-owner who had title to 20% of the units, has gone into bankruptcy. The trustee has taken title to the units and refuses to vote. The investor has written a letter in opposition to the assessment and contends that the letter is his "proxy." What advice do you give?

2. The association's president is also concerned about gathering proxies. Apparently, a small group of owners opposed to the assessment increase has sent letters to all own-

ers requesting proxies. In response, <u>the board has adopted a rule that only the association officers may cast more than three proxies</u>. In addition, the rule prohibits anyone delinquent in at least one month's assessment from voting someone's proxy. The association president is very pleased with this tactic and explains it proudly. He asks for your opinion, expecting the best. What do you think? Who is your client in this situation? What difference does that make? The <u>association is not incorporated</u>. Does that make any difference?

3. You and the president are also concerned over the fact that there are a number of absentee owners who do not attend meetings or respond to mailings. What if you send a ballot with instructions that if the ballot is not returned, it will be interpreted as a yes vote. <u>Does silence equal consent?</u> Does it affect your answer if the absentee owner is an institution rather than a private individual? Why?

4. You and your developer client are discussing the voting group/voting member approach shown in the graphic in Section A.2. She is very interested but also wants some further explanation. How, in the future, can the structure be changed, and what circumstances would require or justify change? Are there state law concerns and, if so, how are they addressed? Should the "representatives" have an obligation to poll their constituents before voting? If so, on all or some issues? If some, which?

5. The delegate system is in place and has been quite successful with one exception. That exception is that in the last several elections for delegates, no one has turned out from several delegate districts. The result is that no one represents those districts and, consequently, the delegates are having difficulty mustering the necessary votes to make decisions. The association's president proposes to you that she simply act on behalf of any district that is unrepresented. What is your reaction?

Assume that the president is a developer appointee on a board still under developer control. Does that make a difference in your response? Assume further that the president proposes that the notice for the next delegate election will contain a bold-face statement that should any delegate district be unrepresented, the president of the association would act as that delegate. How would this affect your response?

3. Actions Requiring Membership Approval

Gier's Liquor & Sporting Goods v. Ass'n of Unit Owners of Driftwood Shores Surfside Inn Condo.

Oregon Court of Appeals
862 P.2d 560 (Or. Ct. App. 1993)

DE MUNIZ, J. <u>Plaintiff</u>, a California corporation, owns a condominium unit at <u>Driftwood Shores Surfside Inn Condominium</u> (Driftwood). Defendant is an association of the owners of <u>88 units of Driftwood</u>. Defendant was formed under the Oregon Condominium Act and its predecessor statutes pursuant to a Declaration of Unit Ownership. ORS ch 100. Defendant is governed by its declaration and by-laws, ORS 100.100; ORS 100.415, and it operates through its board of directors. <u>In May, 1985, Driftwood's restaurant and conference facility was destroyed by fire</u>. That facility was located on property subject to defendant's declaration. In September, 1985, at a duly constituted meeting, 52 percent of the owners selected real property adjacent to Driftwood as the site for a new facility. <u>That property was not owned by defendant</u>. The owners also approved financing of $1,200,000 to fund the

prop. for new dvo. not owned by Driftwood.

project. At two later meetings, the owners approved an additional 10 percent financing and an assessment on each unit to pay for the financing of the facility.

Plaintiff notified defendant that it objected to the facility and demanded that it not be assessed. The facility was constructed and has been operating since October, 1986. Plaintiff has not paid the assessments. In June, 1988, defendant filed a lien against plaintiff's condominium unit. Plaintiff then brought this action alleging a cloud on its title. Defendant filed a counterclaim against plaintiff to foreclose its lien and joined cross-defendants, who are the beneficiaries of a trust deed granted by plaintiff. Plaintiff and defendant filed cross-motions for summary judgment, based on stipulated facts. The trial court found for defendant and held that cross-defendants' interest was subrogated to that of defendant for purposes of foreclosure. We affirm.

Plaintiff's argument focuses on defendant's purchase of the additional real property, on which the facility was built. It argues that, under ORS 100.125,[4] defendant may annex real property only if its declaration complies with ORS 100.105(2)[5] and a supplemental declaration and plat are recorded. Plaintiff argues that neither condition was met here.

Defendant argues that the statutes on which plaintiff relies apply only when real property is annexed to the condominium and that it acquired, but did not annex, the property in dispute here. Plaintiff counters, citing dictionary definitions to show that "acquire" and "annex" mean the same thing. It argues that to accept defendant's distinction would render the Condominium Act meaningless by allowing an association to circumvent the act's requirements.

Dictionary definitions are not required in order to determine that the legislature authorized a condominium association to own real property that is not subject to the annexation requirements of chapter 100. ORS 100.405(4) provides, in part:

> Subject to the provisions of the condominium's declaration and by-laws ... the association may:
>
> (h) Acquire by purchase, lease, devise, gift or voluntary grant real property or any interest therein and take, hold, possess and dispose of real property or any interest therein[.]

That provision is not limited to acquiring real property that may only be submitted to condominium form of ownership. See ORS 100.020. Rather, the legislature has provided that an association may acquire real property, if its declaration and by-laws so permit. *Towerhill Condo. Assoc. v. American Condo. Homes*, 66 Or.App. 342, 347, 675 P.2d 1051 (1984).

Plaintiff argues that defendant's declaration and by-laws do not provide the authority to purchase real property. It contends that, to make the purchase, defendant would have to amend its declaration, which requires a vote of 75 percent of the owners, and that such a vote did not take place.

---

4. ORS 100.125 provides:
    If the declaration complies with ORS 100.105(2), until the termination date, additional property may be annexed to the condominium by the recording of a supplemental declaration and plat in accordance with ORS 100.115 and 100.120.
5. ORS 100.105(2) provides, in part:
    In the event the declarant proposes to annex additional property to the condominium under ORS 100.125, the declaration shall also contain a general description of the plan of development[.]

However, an amendment is not required if the board already has the authority to purchase real property. Article III of defendant's by-laws deals with the board of directors. Section 2 provides, as relevant:

> POWERS. The Board of Directors shall be vested with the management of all the affairs of [defendant], including, but without being limited to, the power to direct the purchase by [defendant] of such property as the purposes thereof shall require, to provide for the incurring of debts on behalf of [defendant] and the issuance of note and other evidences of such debts, and to provide for the mortgage pledge or hypothecation of all, or any part of the assets of [defendant] to accomplish the purposes of [defendant]; provided that the purchase by the Board of Directors of capital assets or improvements, may not exceed the sum of TWO THOUSAND DOLLARS ($2,000) without the enactment of resolution authorizing additional purchases of capital assets or improvements to the common elements by more than fifty percent (50%) of the voting qualified unit owners.

Plaintiff argues that section 2 only authorizes the Board to purchase such things as are necessary for the "day-to-day operation" of defendant. Defendant argues that plaintiff's reading is "very narrow and excruciatingly limited."

We agree with defendant that the language of section 2 shows that "property" is to be broadly construed. The board is authorized to incur debts that may exceed $2,000 if more than 50 percent of the voting owners concur. The board may mortgage the assets of defendant in doing so. We agree with defendant that the board's unlimited power to mortgage defendant's assets demonstrates that the board has authority to make substantial purchases of property—real or personal. That conclusion is further reflected in the board's authority to acquire capital assets in excess of $2,000.

Defendant relies on Article VI, section 1, of its by-laws as authority for the assessment to pay for the facility. That section provides, in part:

> EXPENSES AND ASSESSMENT. Each unit owner shall contribute pro rata based on his percentage of ownership in the general common elements, towards the common condominium expenses, including, but not limited to, the cost of operation, maintenance, repair and replacement.... The Board of Directors shall fix a monthly assessment for each unit in an amount sufficient to provide for all current expenses. (Emphasis supplied.)

Plaintiff argues that "repair and replacement" as a "common condominium expense" has no relationship to the purchase of real property. Although that might be true in some instances, we do not agree that the relationship does not exist here.

ORS 100.005(8)(a) and (c) define as common expenses "administration, maintenance, repair or replacement of the common elements," and expenses "agreed upon as common ... by the declaration or the by-laws of the particular condominium." Under exhibit C of the declaration here, the common elements consist of

> the underlying land, sewage treatment plant, sewage effluent line and easement for effluent line, swimming pool and recreation building, elevators, walkways, stairs, V shaped area between the north and south wings of building "D," reception lobby, manager's office, telephone service room, cover over entry, asphalt, curbing, sea barrier, underground utility lines, project lighting and all other improvements not located within a living unit. (Emphasis supplied.)

The restaurant and conference facility was part of the common elements before it was destroyed by fire. As noted above, the by-laws authorize assessment for the repair and replacement of common elements. The replacement of the restaurant and conference facility here included the cost of the real property. Plaintiff is liable for the assessment.

…

Affirmed on appeal and on cross-appeal.

Notes & Questions

1. *Assessment and homeowner approval.* The *Gier's Liquor* case illustrates both the scope of the board's power to act unilaterally and limitations upon its actions. Review UCIOA § 3-102 which enumerates powers of community associations. Should membership approval be necessary to approve the annual budget and assessment? To enact a rule affecting the common elements or regulation? A use restriction affecting individual units? Amendments to the declaration that conform the declaration with changes in state law? Review UCIOA and MNCA generally for provisions that require member approval. In drafting the governing documents, when would you require membership approval? Explain.

2. *Member challenges to board actions.* The board often has broad authority to make decisions which substantially impact the community, often without the members' consent. What standards might courts impose before addressing member challenges to unilateral board actions? See, *e.g., Beechwood Villas Condo. v. Poor,* 448 So. 2d 1143 (Fla. Dist. Ct. App. 1984) (holding that, in assessing the validity of actions taken by the board, the court should first determine whether the Directors had the authority to take the action, and second whether the action was arbitrary and capricious); and *Hidden Harbour Estates v. Norman,* 309 So. 2d 180, 182 (Fla. Dist. Ct. App. 1975) (" … the test of reasonableness. If a rule is reasonable, the association can adopt it; if not, it cannot)." See also, *Condominium Rulemaking — Presumptions, Burdens and Abuses: A Call for Substantive Judicial Review in Florida,* 34 U. Fla. L. Rev. 219 (1982); *Judicial Review of Condominium Rulemaking,* 94 Harv. L. Rev. 647 (1981). This topic will be more fully addressed in Section 5.02(B).

3. *Ultra vires doctrine.* Challenges to board actions as being *ultra vires* often arise in the corporations context, including actions taken by the board of directors of homeowner associations. As you may recall from your corporation law class, an act is *ultra vires* when the corporation is without authority to perform it under any circumstances or for any purpose. The *ultra vires* doctrine states that any contract made by a corporation beyond the scope of its corporate power is unlawful. See *Community Fed. Sav. & Loan Ass'n of Independence, Mo. v. Fields,* 128 F.2d 705, 708 (8th Cir. 1942); and *Buddin v. Golden Bay Manor, Inc.,* 585 So. 2d 435 (Fla. Dist. Ct. App. 1991). What documents can a homeowner rely on to challenge board actions as *ultra vires*? What is the effect if there are ambiguities or inconsistent treatment of board powers in the different documents? Do the association's by-laws prevail over the terms of the declaration? See UCIOA § 2-103.

The Real World: A Developer's Insight

My goal is to eliminate all associations. So far, the only way to do that is to eliminate commonly owned property, which I am not yet willing to do.

The real issue is not necessarily what is in the documents (some reasonableness applies), but the fact that associations cannot manage themselves. With very few exceptions, operation of an association is a pain in the rear! It is a thankless, time-consuming job that, for the most part, is petty, combative, and just plain silly.

I would like to see associations run much like a city or county. Everyone elects council persons and a chairman, whose term is two years. Instead of sending a request, such as fencing, doghouses, etc., you must present your issues for the council's approval. The meeting is open, and anyone can attend. The request is voted on after some discussion, and they move on to the next case. It would be quicker and cut down on the need to shuffle paperwork.

—Bruce E. Smith

B. Board of Directors

Restatement (Third) § 6.14 Duties Of Directors And Officers Of An Association

The directors and officers of an association have a duty to act in good faith, to act in compliance with the law and the governing documents, to deal fairly with the association and its members, and to use ordinary care and prudence in performing their functions.

Generally speaking, the board of directors is responsible for establishing policy and supervising the implementation of that policy. In the common interest community setting, board members frequently confuse the distinction between making and executing policy. This confusion is compounded by the fact that often directors are also officers who have a genuine sense of responsibility to ensure that "things get done." Understanding the roles and responsibilities of the directors, officers, and agents or employees is important. It is just as important for the association's members to appreciate the distinctions among these parties and their roles. All concerned must have a clear picture of how the members' expectations concerning association operation and what services it is to perform coincide with the directors' powers and responsibilities. Frequently, directors' expectations will not be in sync with those of the members.

Governing documents and state law dictate the composition of the board, frequency of meetings, notice requirements and other procedural matters relating to actual operation of the board of directors. Differences in the community's size and nature can result in different approaches to the board's structure and function. The larger the community, the greater the likelihood of a large board. In a resort or second home community, boards meet less frequently, and it is common for them to meet by telephone conference call in addition to meeting in person.

Board members are generally elected by and from the membership. They are thus responsible to that membership, and successful boards are comprised of individuals who have learned how to be responsive as well. What differences exist in the community association board's context from that experienced in traditional corporate boards? How do these differences affect, first, the board's operation and, second, the legal principles applicable to that operation?

We should note that in different states (or perhaps by personal choice), the board may not be "of directors," but "of managers," or "of trustees," or some other term. The duties and applicable principles are the same, and for the present purposes, we shall use the term board of directors.

Beginning an analysis of the board of directors, one should keep in mind the questions posed in the introduction to this chapter about roles and sources of power, about the nature of the community association as an incorporated entity or one that has the "nature" of a corporation. Most of the controversy concerning governance of community associations deals with actions taken or not taken by the board. We have also discussed questions concerning the sources of the board's power. In this section, you will revisit some of those issues; as you do so, consider what the scope of that power is.

The question of the scope of the board's power is an important one, for it requires an analysis not only of expressed and implied powers but also of the ways and means for exercising those powers and whether there are limits on those powers. Courts do not directly discuss the subject of limits when considering cases involving community association actions. They speak of reasonableness or free use of property or other maxims. What is really at issue is: how far can and should a board go? How much power does and should it have? Since the board is the entity charged with the responsibility of acting and given the powers to act on the association's behalf, the association's purposes are important to that analysis as well.

1. Powers

The board of directors of a condominium association is charged with specific responsibilities and owes a duty to the membership to carry out these responsibilities in a manner that serves the best interest of the membership. A typical document provision might contain the following language:

> Powers and Duties. The Board of Directors shall manage the affairs of the Association and shall have all the powers and duties necessary for the administration of the Condominium and may do all such acts and things as are not by the Declaration, Article of Incorporation, or these by-laws directed to be done and exercised exclusively by the members. The Board shall have the power to adopt such rules and regulations as it deems necessary and appropriate and to impose sanctions for violations thereof, including, without limitation, monetary fines. In addition to the duties imposed by these by-laws or by any resolution of the Association that may hereafter be adopted, the Board of Directors shall have the power to and be responsible for, the following, in way of explanation, but not limitation:
>
> (a) preparing and adopting an annual budget in which there shall be established the contribution of each Owner to the common expenses;
>
> (b) making assessments to defray the common expenses, establishing the means and methods of collecting such assessments, and establishing the period of the installment payments of the annual assessment (unless otherwise determined by the Board of Directors, the annual assessment against the appropriate share of the common expenses shall be payable in equal monthly installments, each such installment to be due and payable in advance on the first day of each month for said month.);
>
> (c) providing for the operation, care, upkeep, and maintenance of all of the Common Elements;

(d) designating, hiring, and dismissing the personnel necessary for the main-tenance, operation, repair, and replacement of the Association, its prop-erty, and the Common Elements and, when appropriate, providing for the compensation of such personnel and for the purchase in the performance of their duties.

(e) collecting the assessments, depositing the proceeds thereof in a bank de-pository that it shall approve, and using the proceeds to administer the Association;

(f) making and amending rules and regulations;

(g) opening bank accounts on behalf of the Association and designating the signatories required;

(h) making and contracting for the making of repairs, additions and im-provements to, or alterations of the Common Elements and the Limited Common Elements in accordance with the other provisions of the Dec-laration and these by-laws, after damage or destruction by fire or other casualty;

(i) enforcing by legal means the provisions of the Declaration, these by-laws, and the rules and regulations adopted by it, and bringing any proceedings that may be instituted on behalf of or against the Owners concerning the Association;

(j) obtaining and carrying insurance against casualties and liabilities, as pro-vided in the Declaration, and paying the premium cost thereof;

(k) paying the costs of all services rendered to the Association or its members and not chargeable to Owners;

(l) keeping books with detailed accounts of the receipts and expenditures af-fecting the Association and its administration, specifying the maintenance and repair expenses and any other expenses incurred; and

(m) contracting with any person for the performance of various duties and func-tions. The Board shall have the power to enter into common management agreements with (by way of illustration, but not limitation) trusts, condo-miniums, or property owners' associations. Any and all functions of the Association shall be fully transferable by the Board, in whole or in part, to any other entity.

———————

Consider the breadth of the enumerated powers as you examine the cases and questions.

There are some basic considerations in guiding the board in the exercise of these pow-ers. First, there is an obligation to act. This means that the board must make a decision when confronted with a germane issue. That is not to say how it must decide the issue but that it may not refuse to consider it and thus refuse to meet its duty. Remember that not taking action is just as much an affirmative decision as deciding to act.

In addition to the obligation to act when action is required, there is the question of how the board is to act. In the sections dealing with board liability and standards of judicial review, we will address these issues in some detail. You should see now the threads com-prising that discussion: reasonableness, business judgment, and the possible applicabil-ity of the Constitution. The questions remain: Which rules apply? When? Why?

a. Express Powers

At least one court has held that a board has all power not expressly reserved for the membership in the governing documents. This traditional statement of an extremely broad power illustrates that, in many cases, community association boards will be faced with tasks not anticipated or even capable of being anticipated at the time the documents were drafted. The fact remains that there is, by necessity, a balancing act as attorneys, courts, and board members examine the scope of a board's authority as they face various operational issues over the life of the community association. That balancing involves striving to find the ability to meet immediate needs while, at the same time, being consistent with reasonable expectations of the members, protecting the members' interest, and allowing a degree of independence and autonomy.

Certainly, boards have powers granted in their governing documents; however, it is not always clear exactly what the scope of those powers might be. In addition, there are instances in which boards, and their counsel, are faced with the necessity of interpreting existing law or documentation.

What is the board of directors' obligation to act? Does the board have the ability to make a decision that it will refrain from taking an action, or does it have an obligation in all cases to take some affirmative action? Clearly, there is a difference between making a conscious decision not to take an affirmative step and merely doing so through inactivity. What might the legal consequences be from each?

As you consider the standards applicable to testing board decisions, also consider whether and to what extent a standard or rule is or is not met based upon the method by which the board acts. Consider also the importance of the board's discretion not to be compelled, in all instances, to follow a predetermined course. What is the role of the association's counsel in these matters? How does one advise the board, particularly when the board's preferred outcome is not to take an action?

In addition to resolving the question of its obligation to act, the board is also faced with the question of how to act. In answering this question, the board and its counsel are concerned not only with the board's powers and the standards interpreting and applying those powers, but they are also concerned about internal procedures, intraboard relationships, and other factors that are inherent in successfully discharging the board's roles and responsibilities. The fact that in almost every case the board is comprised of uncompensated volunteers, many of whom are inexperienced in board governance, further exacerbates the challenge.

Ryan v. Baptiste
Court of Appeals of Missouri
565 S.W.2d 196 (Mo. Ct. App. 1978)

REINHARD, J. Defendants, Members of the Board of Managers of the Burtonwood Manor Condominium, have appealed from a judgment of the Circuit Court granting a mandatory injunction against them and denying their counterclaim for damages. The defendants were ordered to remove locks from the doors of the exterior entrance-ways of the building in which plaintiff's condominium unit was located. Following several occurrences of vandalism and theft, defendants installed locks on the entrance-ways. Keys were provided to unit owners. Plaintiff objects to installation of the locks arguing that the presence of the locks infringed on the easement rights granted in the condominium by-laws.

In addition to granting injunctive relief to plaintiff, the court ruled against defendants on their counterclaim for damages to the locks and doors allegedly caused by plaintiff.

Burtonwood Manor Condominium was created by filing a "Declaration of Condominium by-laws and Indenture" with the Office of the Recorder of Deeds of St. Louis County, pursuant to § 448.010, RSMo.1969. Plaintiff is one of the original purchasers and owned one of eight units in building 29 of the Burtonwood complex. The by-laws provide for administration of the condominium by a nine-member Board of Managers. Article 7.1(n) states that among the powers and duties of the Board of Managers are "Promulgation of administrative rules and regulations and such reasonable rules and regulations as it may deem advisable for the use, operation, maintenance, conservation and beautification of the 'Common Elements' and for the health, comfort, safety, and general welfare of the unit owners and occupants of said property."

Easements in and to all common elements are granted to unit owners in § 4.2 of the By-laws. Maintenance and repair of the common elements is a duty reserved of the by-laws. Any structural alterations deemed "necessary or proper for the maintenance and operation of the property" may be undertaken by the Board "for the benefit of all unit owners" under § 7.1(f) of the by-laws.

. . .

This case requires a consideration and balancing of rights of the individual unit owner and of the entire residential community. Members of the Board of Managers are elected by the condominium owners to oversee and protect the rights and interests of the community at large. Accordingly, the Board is vested with considerable discretion with which to execute its managerial and administrative responsibilities. The individual unit owner, though extended certain rights and responsibilities, does not possess absolute control over his own property common to all owners. The condominium by-laws represent a form of private law making, and individual owners come together and agree to subordinate some of their traditional individual ownership rights and privileges when they choose this type of ownership experience.

. . .

The Board of Managers of Burtonwood is the designated decision-making body of the condominium association and exercises broad discretion in the maintenance and operation of the development. Nevertheless, the Board is not at liberty to promulgate arbitrary and capricious rules which bear no relationship to the health, happiness and enjoyment of life of the unit owners. Thus, in reviewing the action of the Board in this case, we believe the standard to be applied is reasonableness. *Hidden Harbour Estates, Inc. v. Norman, supra.* See also *Forest Park Cooperative, Inc. v. Hellman,* 2Misc.2d 183, 152 N.Y.S.2d 685 (1956); *Amoruso v. Board of Mgrs. of Westchester Hills Con.,* 38 A.D.2d 845, 330 N.Y.S.2d 107 (1972). Applying this standard, we conclude the installation of the locks on doors providing entry to common passageways of the condominium building was a reasonable exercise of the Board's authority. The need for locked entranceways was indicated by several reports of vandalism and theft. While the locks could be expected to create a minor inconvenience, it cannot be concluded they in any way interfered with residents' easement rights or constituted an unreasonable infringement upon their use and enjoyment of the premises. Rather, the decision to install the locks was a reasonable attempt to increase the security and thereby protect the rights and interests of the residential community.

The injunction must be dissolved, and in view of our determination that the action of the Board was reasonable, the trial court's judgment in favor of plaintiff on defendants' counterclaim must be reversed. The cause is remanded with instructions to dissolve the injunction and enter a judgment for defendants on plaintiff's petition. Defendants' counterclaim is remanded for a new trial.

Reversed and Remanded.

Salvatore v. Gelburd

Appellate Court of Illinois
565 N.E.2d 204 (Ill. Ct. App. 1990)

JIGANTI, J. This case involves a dispute over the proper interpretation of a declaration of condominium ownership. The plaintiff, Kenneth Salvatore, and the defendants, Michael and Marilyn Gelburd, filed cross motions for summary judgment, arguing contrary interpretations of the same clause of the condominium declaration. The trial court granted the defendants' motion and the plaintiff appeals.

The plaintiff, Kenneth Salvatore, and the defendants, Michael and Marilyn Gelburd, are owners of adjoining units in a three-unit condominium complex, 1950 North Howe, Chicago, Illinois. During the summer of 1988, the Gelburds built a storage shed on the roof of their unit. By definition of the condominium declaration, a roof is considered a common element of ownership. The Gelburds installed a wooden railing around the roof of the shed and a stairway enabling them to use the shed's roof as a sun deck. In the fall of 1988 Salvatore complained that chairs and a table on the roof of the shed were being blown about by the wind, causing loud noises to emanate from the roof. On November 1, 1988, the condominium association held a meeting attended by the plaintiff and the defendants. At the meeting, it was agreed that the Gelburds would remove the railing and the stairway and cease using the roof of the shed as a deck. The Gelburds also agreed to inform any subsequent purchasers of their unit that the shed roof was not to be used as a deck.

In November the Gelburds removed the railing and the table and chairs from the shed roof. On January 17, 1989, another association meeting was held. At the meeting, the association voted to ratify the construction of the Gelburds' rooftop storage shed if they complied with the conditions agreed to at the November 1 meeting. In March of 1989, the Gelburds removed the stairway to the storage shed. In April, the condominium association acknowledged through a letter to the Gelburds that they had complied with the requirements for ratification of their rooftop storage shed.

The plaintiff alleges that under section 4.09(b) of the Declaration of Condominium Ownership for the 1950 North Howe Condominium, the shed constructed by the defendants on their roof is a prohibited alteration which the Board is without authority to ratify. The parties filed cross motions for summary judgment. The trial court granted the defendants' motion and the plaintiff appeals.

The facts of this case are not disputed. At issue is whether the trial court erred in construing as it did section 4.09(b) of the condominium declaration. Section 4.09(b) reads in pertinent part as follows:

4.09 Additions, Alterations or Improvements

(b) Except as otherwise provided in Section 7.01(a) hereof, no additions, alterations or improvements shall be made by a Unit Owner to any part of the Common Elements and no additions, alterations or improvements shall be made by a Unit Owner to his Unit ... without the prior written consent of the Board. ...

If an addition, alteration or improvement is made by a Unit Owner without the prior written consent of the Board, then the Board <u>may</u>, in its discretion, take any of the following actions:

...

(3) <u>Ratify the action taken by the Unit Owner</u>, and the Board may (but shall not be required to) condition such ratification upon the same conditions which it may impose upon the giving of its prior consent under this Section. (Emphasis added.)

The plaintiff insists that under a proper reading of section 4.09(b), the condominium association did not have the authority to ratify the construction of the Gelburds' rooftop shed. Salvatore refers to the "<u>Doctrine of the Last Antecedent Clause</u>" in <u>arguing that</u> the phrase in the condominium declaration, "<u>without the prior written consent of the Board,</u>" <u>applies only to the immediate preceding clause "no additions, alterations or improvements shall be made by a Unit Owner to his Unit</u>." (See *Tondre v. Pontiac School District No. 105* (1975), 33 Ill.App.3d 838, 342 N.E.2d 290.) Therefore, Salvatore maintains, the <u>Board may consent only to alterations by a unit owner to the owner's unit, and not to any alterations to the common elements</u>. Salvatore also argues that a contrary holding renders section 7.01(a) of the declaration redundant and superfluous. Section 7.01(a) is noted in section 4.09(b) as an exception to 4.09(b). Section 7.01(a) specifies that a common wall between two units owned by the same unit owner may be removed or altered with Board approval. Salvatore argues that the situation described in section 7.01(a) is the one and only instance in which the Board may approve an alteration to a common element.

The Gelburds contend, and the trial court agreed, that under the terms of the condominium declaration the Board had the authority to ratify the construction of the Gelburds' rooftop storage shed. Viewing the instrument as a whole, <u>we do not believe that the trial court erred in its interpretation of the condominium declaration.</u> (*Shelton v. Andres* (1985), 106 Ill.2d 153, 87 Ill. Dec. 954, 478 N.E.2d 311.) Throughout the declaration, numerous references are made to the Board's authority and responsibility to administer the property. For example, the Board is vested with the authority to adopt and amend such reasonable rules and regulations as it may deem advisable. With respect to the common elements, the Board has among other powers the authority to lease or grant licenses, concessions or contracts to any part of the common elements. The Board may also consent to obstructions or storage otherwise prohibited in the common elements. In consideration of all its language and provisions, we believe that <u>one of the purposes of the condominium declaration was to give the Board broad powers to administer the cooperative aspect of the condominium ownership.</u>

A strict application of the plaintiff's rules of grammar and construction effect a technically literal construction of section 4.09(b) of the condominium declaration. We are concerned, however, with the <u>natural and obvious import of the language, and not a forced interpretation</u>. (*The Pennsylvania Railroad Co. v. Chicago, Rock Island and Pacific Railroad Co.* (1958), 12 Ill.2d 574, 147 N.E.2d 363.) In the present case, we believe that the phrases in section 4.09(b), "without the prior written consent of the Board," and "the Board may ... [r]atify the action taken," naturally refer to additions, alterations or improvements to common elements as well as unit elements. The language of section 4.09(b) comports with the tenor of the language throughout the condominium declaration which in effect <u>gives</u> overriding powers of administration to the Board. <u>Viewing the instrument as a whole, the</u> trial court's interpretation of section 4.09(b) was fair and reasonable.

(*Shelton v. Andres* (1985), 106 Ill.2d 153, 87 Ill. Dec. 954, 478 N.E.2d 311.) For these reasons, the ruling of the trial court is affirmed.

Affirmed.

Ochs v. L'Enfant Trust and W. End Condo. Ass'n

District of Columbia Court of Appeals
504 A.2d 1110 (D.C. Ct. App. 1986)

PAIR, J. Appellant Laurance J. Ochs is an owner in fee simple of a unit in the West End Condominium on 21st Street, Northwest, and a member of its owner association, appellee West End Condominium Association (hereinafter the "Association"). Brought into question in this appeal are separate orders of the Superior Court which together validated the Association's grant of a conservation easement to appellee L'Enfant Trust (hereinafter the "Trust"), upheld the Association's special assessment to appellant for use in financing the easement, and awarded the Association attorney fees in connection with the litigation in the amount of $10,000.

As grounds for reversal, appellant principally maintains that (1) the grant of the conservation easement was not in accordance with law and the condominium documents; (2) the Association's allocation of the easement assessment to less than all of its members was improper; and (3) the trial court erroneously included in its award of attorney fees the costs and legal expenses incurred by the Association in defending his suit to have the easement grant declared void. We agree only with appellant's last contention and, accordingly, remand this case to the trial court for further proceedings on this issue.

I

The Association is comprised of the owners of 34 units in the West End Condominium, a "horizontal property regime" recognized as such under the District of Columbia Condominium Act of 1976, D.C. Code § 45-1801 *et seq.* (1981). In late 1981, the Association was approached by the Trust, a non-profit foundation, regarding the possibility of the Association donating to it a "conservation easement" in the facade of the condominium building. The proposed easement was designed primarily to help preserve the historic nature of the neighborhood, which is known to some as the DuPont Circle Historic District. The easement would constitute an encumbrance on the property and would grant to the Trust the right to review and approve any Association decision affecting the exterior of the building, whether structural or cosmetic in nature. The condominium owners would be directly affected by the conveyance of the easement, particularly insofar as it encumbered their individual, undivided percentage interests in the building's facade, which is designated a "common element" in the condominium instruments.

[The events which precipitated the granting of the conservation easement to the Trust were as follows. In May 1982, the Association's president sent notice to all members notifying them of the upcoming special meeting to discuss granting the conservation easement. Members were told that a special assessment would be necessary to effectuate the easement but that they would in turn realize a charitable deduction in their income taxes. The members were also informed that an amendment to the condominium declaration and by-laws would be necessary to grant this conservation easement.

At the special meeting, a motion was passed for the Board to pursue the matter with the Trust, commission an appraiser to determine the value of the charitable contribution, and obtain a letter ruling from the IRS regarding the validity of such a deduction.

Subsequently, the owners were notified that the easement was worth approximately $265,000 (or 8% of the buildings' value), that the Trust would accept the easement, and that the IRS would allow the charitable deduction. On October 1, 1982, the Board circulated a voting package necessary to grant the easement, amend the governing documents, and impose a special assessment of $17,263 to pay for the costs of the transaction. The owners were also informed that one unit owner would not be assessed his share of the expenses, since, as a foreign resident and tax payer, he was not entitled to take the charitable deduction on the transaction and, in the Board's judgment, it would not be fair to assess him for an expense for which he received no benefit.

By November 2nd, the Board had received more than 2/3 of the necessary votes to approve the easement "package." The owners were notified that their share of the special assessment was due by December 7th, and thereafter a late fee would be imposed for each week the assessment was not paid.

On November 10, the appellant, Laurance Ochs, informed the Board that he objected to the granting of the easement and related assessment on the ground that it was impermissible under the governing documents. Specifically, he claimed that every unit owner must consent to the easement as each owner has an individual interest in the common elements of the building, including the facade. He also objected to the mail-ballot procedure. Nevertheless, the Board (after meeting with Mr. Ochs and others) granted the conservation easement to the Trust on December 16, 1982, thereby restricting the association's control over the building's facade. — Eds.]

II

On January 13, 1983, appellant filed in the Superior Court a "Complaint to Quiet Title and Damages for Trespass" on the basis of the Association's conveyance of the conservation easement to the Trust. Appellant prayed for, *inter alia*, a declaration that the Trust had "no estate, right, title, lien or interest in or to said real property or any part thereof," an order enjoining the Trust and the Association from interfering with his possession, use and enjoyment of the property, compensatory damages of $10,000, and punitive damages in the sum of $30,000. The Trust and the Association filed a timely answer in which they denied appellant's allegations, and which they amended to include a counterclaim against appellant for the special assessment that had been levied against him ($707.27), late fees ($725 through February 16 and $75 per week thereafter in which the assessment remained unpaid), interest on the judgment, costs, and reasonable attorney fees. Shortly thereafter, appellant filed an answer to the counterclaim alleging that the counterclaim was predicated "on illegal acts undertaken by [the Association] contrary to the West End Condominium's Declaration and by-laws." More specifically, the answer alleged that the Association was without authority to levy the special assessment and, in any event, did not do so according to his percentage interest in the condominium, for he was being required to pay partially for a non-assessed unit owner's contribution.

...

On January 26, 1984, a non-jury trial was held on the Association's counterclaim which resulted in a judgment for the Association.

...

Appellant then appealed this judgment, as well as the trial court's earlier judgments which summarily disposed of his claim against the Association and the Trust, and which held him liable for the Association's special assessment and attendant late fees.

III

A. Appellant's first four contentions pertain to the trial court's grant of summary judgment to appellees on his initial claim which, as we have noted, sought a declaration that the conservation easement grant was invalid, as well as related compensatory and punitive damages. Specifically, appellant contends that (1) D.C. Code § 45-1848(b) (1981), *infra*, upon which the trial court based its decision, is subordinate to, or should be read together with the common law rules of tenancies in common which preclude the type of encumbrance here conveyed; (2) the Condominium Declaration and by-laws, and *id.* §§ 45-1821(f) and 45-1838(e), prohibited the Association from encumbering his undivided percentage interest in the building's facade, a common element; (3) the execution of the conservation easement deed deprived him of a vested property interest in violation of the due process clause of the Fifth Amendment; and (4) the Board of Directors obtained the necessary unit owner votes by procedures violative of the condominium instruments and *id.* § 45-1845(d).

. . .

In our view, the trial court here correctly determined that on appellant's claim there was no genuine issue as to any material fact and that appellees were entitled to judgment as a matter of law.

In so holding, the court properly applied D.C. Code § 45-1848(b), which reads:

> Except to the extent prohibited by the condominium instruments, and subject to any restrictions and limitations specified therein, the executive organ of the unit owners' association, if any, and if not, then the unit owners' association itself, shall have the irrevocable power as attorney-in-fact on behalf of all unit owners and their successors in title to grant easements through the common elements and accept easements benefiting the condominium or any part thereof. [Emphasis added.]

Because there was no factual dispute regarding the nature of the easement, the trial court was entitled to decide, as a matter of law, whether it was properly granted by the Board to the Trust pursuant to § 45-1848(b).

Unmistakably, in the planning stages the Board was working under the assumption that two-thirds of the unit owners would have to assent to the conveyance of the conservation easement to the Trust. Indeed, if the Board had thought otherwise, it would not have circulated the initial ballot respecting the proposed easement to all unit owners. But in our view, this assumption was erroneous. Section 45-1848(b) vested authority in the Board to grant the conservation easement in question without approval by the unit owners. As the "executive organ" of the Association,[1] the Board was empowered "to grant easements through the common elements," as it did here by conveying the "Conservation Easement Deed of Gift" in the building's facade to the Trust.

Given this statutory authority, the only question is whether such authority was prohibited by, or subject to any restrictions and limitations specified in the Association's con-

---

1. In Paragraph 4.1 of the Condominium Declaration (as amended), and in By-laws Article IV, 4.1, the Board of Directors is defined as the "Executive Organ" of the Association within the meaning of the Condominium Act.

dominium instruments. *Id.* § 45-1848(b). We have closely examined these instruments (the Condominium Declaration and by-laws) and have found nothing which would in any way prohibit or restrict the Board's power to act as attorney-in-fact on behalf of the unit owners to grant an easement in the facade of the condominium building. Consequently, on the basis of the unambiguous import of § 45-1848(b), we hold that the Superior Court did not err in rejecting appellant's challenge to the conveyance of the conservation easement to the Trust.

Appellant's related claims concerning the validity of the easement conveyance are without merit.[2] Appellant maintains that execution of the easement deed deprived him of a vested property interest in violation of the due process clause of the Fifth Amendment. This argument must fail as it takes "'significant government involvement' in order for the challenged action to fall within the ambit of the constitutional protection." *Bryant v. Jefferson Federal Savings and Loan Association*, 166 U.S.App.D.C. 178, 180, 509 F.2d 511, 513 (1974) (citing *Moose Lodge No. 107 v. Irvis*, 407 U.S. 163, 173, 92 S.Ct. 1965, 32 L.Ed.2d 627 (1972); *Reitman v. Mulkey*, 387 U.S. 369, 380, 87 S.Ct. 1627, 1633, 18 L.Ed.2d 830 (1967)). Since the only government action complained of here is the City Council's promulgation of s 45-1848(b), we hold that appellant's constitutional claim is insufficient as a matter of law.[3] *Cf. Bryant, supra*, 166 U.S.App.D.C. at 180–81, 509 F.2d at 513–15; *Bichel Optical Laboratories, Inc. v. Marquette National Bank of Minneapolis*, 487 F.2d 906, 907 (8th Cir.1973); *Adams v. Southern California First National Bank*, 492 F.2d 324, 330–31 (9th Cir.1973), cert. denied, 419 U.S. 1006, 95 S.Ct. 325, 42 L.Ed.2d 282 (1974).

And finally, as we have already intimated, since the Board of Directors had statutory authority under § 45-1848(b) to grant the conservation easement without unit owner approval, it is of no significance that an insufficient number of owners' votes may have been properly cast.[4] Consequently, for the aforesaid reasons, the trial court properly granted the Association and the Trust summary judgment on appellant's claim.

B. Appellant next challenges the trial court's ruling that he was liable for the Board's special assessment levied against him for use in financing the conveyance of the conservation easement. Appellant contends that "[t]he special assessment levied by the Board of Directors was not levied against each unit owner in proportion to the share interest of

---

2. Two of these claims may be dismissed with little discussion. First, we need not decide whether the common law rules of tenancies in common would preclude the action taken by the Board of Directors in the case at bar, for the District of Columbia City Council has passed specific legislation, *i.e.*, § 45-1848(b), permitting the action here challenged—the Board's granting of an easement through a common element. Secondly, nothing in the Condominium Declaration or By-laws, or for that matter the statutory authority cited by appellant, D.C. Code §§ 45-1821(f) and 45-1838(e) (1981), would divest the Board of such authority. Sections 45-1821(f) and 45-1838(e) of the Condominium Act preclude certain action which would affect unit owners' interests in condominium common elements. However, even if read to proscribe the easement grant to the Trust, those sections, by their terms, are subordinate to conflicting provisions of the Condominium Act. And § 45-1848(b) necessarily permits the infringement of unit owners' interests in common elements, as it empowers the executive organs of unit owner associations to grant easements through condominium common elements.

3. Indeed, § 45-1848(b) is subject to the restrictions and limitations specified in condominium instruments. Thus, its application can be avoided altogether if a condominium association so decides.

4. By this statement, we are not suggesting that this may have been the case, only that this issue need not be reached. And, for this reason, appellant's reliance on § 45-1845(d) does not help him. In any event, appellant's position draws little sympathy for, as the records bears out, two-thirds of the unit owners did eventually approve the easement conveyance.

each unit owner as required by the by-laws and D.C. Code § 45-1852 (1981), and was not an assessment authorized under the by-laws or the D.C. Condominium Act."[5]

We have no doubt that the Board could lawfully assess appellant for his share of the cost of financing the conveyance of the conservation easement. Article VI, 6.1(C) of the by-laws provides that "[a] Unit Owner shall be personally liable for all lawful assessments, or installments thereof, levied against his Condominium Unit...."[6] A unit owner may be *specially assessed* under by-laws Article VI, 6.1(E), which provides in pertinent part as follows:

> Special Assessments. In addition to the assessments authorized above, the Board of Directors may levy a special assessment for the purpose of defraying the cost of any unexpected repair or other nonrecurring contingency, or to meet any deficiencies occurring from time to time.... Any such special assessments shall be assessed in the manner set forth in Paragraph D of this Section 6.1 ... with respect to additional assessments payable to the reserve fund for capital improvement, replacements and major repairs. [Emphasis added.]

It is fair to say that the assessment for the conservation easement was for the purpose of defraying the cost of a "nonrecurring contingency," *i.e.*, the easement in perpetuity to the Trust.

Appellant nevertheless complains that he has been wrongfully burdened with a portion of another's share of the special assessment. We cannot agree. It is true that the Board of Directors did not assess the owner of two units in the building because, as a non-United States federal income taxpayer, he could not reap the charitable deduction benefits of the easement. But the authority for assessing around this individual is contained in D.C. Code § 45-1852(b), applied by the trial court, which reads:

> To the extent that the condominium instruments expressly so provide, any other common expenses benefiting less than all of the condominium units ... shall be specially assessed against the condominium unit or units involved, in accordance with such reasonable provisions as the condominium instruments may make for such cases.

Appellant suggests that the condominium instruments do not "expressly so provide," and points to by-laws Article VI, 6.1(E), which provides that special assessments "shall be assessed in the manner set forth in Paragraph D of this Section 6.1." The applicable portion of Section 6.1(D) states that an assessment shall be levied against the unit owners "in proportion to the respective Par Value of their Units."

By-laws Article VI, 6.6, however, would appear to satisfy § 45-1852(b)'s requirement that the condominium instruments expressly allow for disproportionate assessment since it provides in part that:

---

5. The special assessment was worded in part as follows:
  For the sole complete purpose of executing a conservation easement as defined in ... the Internal Revenue Code ... the West End Condominium Unit Owners Association authorizes a special assessment of $17,263 for defraying and meeting all costs incurred for such act.... All unit owners will be assessed in proportion to their ownership percentage in the Condominium, except that the unit owner of units 102 and 106 will not be assessed any amount for such assessment and such assessment is waived for that unit owner, with the increment that would otherwise be due from units 102 and 106 being apportioned among the remaining unit owners in proportion to their percentage interest in the building.
6. Paragraph 21 of the Condominium Declaration also contains such a provision.

> Whenever in the judgment of the Board of Directors the Common Elements shall require additions, alterations or improvements costing in excess of $5,000 during any period of 12 consecutive months, and the making of such additions, alterations or improvements shall have been approved by the Unit Owners of apartment units to which a majority of the votes in the Association appertain, the Board of Directors shall proceed with such additions, alterations and improvements and shall assess all Unit Owners for the cost thereof as a Common Expense.... Notwithstanding the foregoing, if, in the opinion of not less than 80% of the members of the Board of Directors, such additions, alterations or improvements are exclusively or substantially exclusively for the benefit of the Unit Owner or Unit Owners requesting the same, such requesting Unit Owner or Unit Owners shall be assessed therefor, in such proportion as they jointly approve, if more than one Unit Owner, or, if they are unable to agree thereon, in such proportions as may be determined by the Board of Directors.

In our opinion, this by-law, though admittedly ambiguous, vested discretion in the Association's Board of Directors to assess around the non-United States taxpayer-unit owner, who would be unable to take advantage of the charitable deduction concomitant with conveyance of the conservation easement.

Affirmed in part, Reversed in part and Remanded.

b. Implied Powers

When and how does the need for implied powers arise? What truly is the distinction between an implied power and express power, or is one merely the extension of the other? In some contexts, courts will treat the board as having all power not expressly taken from it, while in others the approach is more ad hoc, focusing on whether the action taken and the power exercised are directly inferable from the express powers. It is important to keep these distinctions in mind as you read this section.

There are, of course, conflicting policy issues. On the one hand, there is the importance of the board's ability to meet the needs and demands which the community association must address and which, as time and circumstances change, will also change. This is complicated by the growing trend toward privatization and "load shedding" from municipal government to the private sector, particularly to the community association. At the same time, there is a need for a degree of certainty on the part of purchasers, particularly as to the extent of their economic responsibilities for actions taken by the association.

In large measure, the analysis centers on whether the proposed action is within a range of potential actions that the association might take in the future that could have been anticipated at the time of purchase. If so, it is not so much the power that is being implied as the outcome. The board would thus have whatever powers are necessary to effectuate the expressed or implied expectations of the parties.

There are serious, conflicting policies involved as you move from express powers to implied powers. The purchaser knows or has the opportunity to know of the express power. There is at least constructive notice, but candor compels the observation that for too many purchasers, that is all the notice there is. When the action taken, or the method of making the decision, or executing the decision is not within the scope of the express powers, but rather rests entirely upon a concept of implied powers, there is a much more serious concern over the parties' expectations and the justification for the community association to be involved in the particular activity at all.

There is, on the other hand, an equally compelling argument that the association must be able to discharge the responsibilities imposed upon it. When those responsibilities come from the result of "privatization" imposing responsibilities on the private sector instead of the public, or when they arise from unanticipated circumstances or needs, should the community association be deemed to have the ability to meet the need? What if the unanticipated situation was something that could have been anticipated? Is there a presumption that the power or situation was purposefully omitted?

Conversely, is there not an assumption that the owner-members have the expectation that their community association will be able to meet any legitimate need, or is the use of the modifier "legitimate" a step in a circle of reasoning? The point is that there will be needs that have not been anticipated but must be met nonetheless. Deciding when and why is the difficult task. Not all owner-members will see the situation in the same light, have the same financial capacity to respond, or necessarily agree to allow the group, rather than the individual, to address the problem.

In giving effect to the parties' expectations, you must also extrapolate to a degree. Expectations, as you will see more clearly in Chapter 10, can change and as times and circumstances change there will be modifications in what people honestly believe they originally expected, intended, and relied upon in the purchase. The word *community* has meaning as well, and you must confront the dilemma that there will be many different individual interests involved in the community setting. To say that *the* individual must be afforded *his* right in a given situation may well result in the compromise of another individual's view of *her* right. This is particularly true in situations in which the owners generally bought in expectations of a systematic approach to the community-wide set of procedures, rules, etc. All of this becomes important in attempting to balance the interests of the group and of the individuals comprising the group. It is a part of the discussion of implied powers because that is how many of the cases arise.

There are standards that guide the analysis of implied powers. The cases reflect an evolution in judicial thinking regarding this power and a guarded acceptance. There are, and need to be, limits. What should they be? How should the standard be drawn, or should there not be *a* standard but rather be consideration on a case by case basis? If the latter, how does that mesh with a test of predictability, autonomy, and fairness?

In all of these cases and circumstances, remember that the issue is whether there is an implied power not an implied purpose. The association has the purposes contained within its charter. That is what makes an action *intra vires*. Such a finding is assumed to be a condition precedent to any finding of an approved implied power.

Beachwood Villas Condo. v. Poor

Florida District Court of Appeal
448 So. 2d 1143 (Fla. Dist. Ct. App. 1984)

HURLEY, J. At issue is the validity of two rules enacted by a condominium board of directors. The trial court invalidated both rules because it determined that the board exceeded the scope of its authority. We reverse.

The board of directors of the Beachwood Villas Condominium Association enacted Rules 31 and 33 to regulate unit rentals and the occupancy of units by guests during the owner's absence. Rule 31, the rental rule, requires that: (1) the minimum rental period be not less than one month, (2) the number of rentals not exceed six per year, (3) the occupancy rate not exceed a specified number which is calculated to the size of the unit,

(4) tenants not have pets without the approval of the board, and (5) a processing fee of $25.00 be paid. Rule 33, the guest rule, requires: (1) board approval for the "transfer" of a unit to guests when the guests are to occupy the unit during the owner's absence, (2) that the number of transfers (either by rental or guest occupancy) not exceed six per year, and (3) that the occupancy rate not exceed a specified number which is calculated to the size of the unit. The trial court found that the board lacked authority to enact either rule. We respectfully disagree.

Hidden Harbour Estates, Inc. v. Basso, 393 So. 2d 637 (Fla. 4th DCA 1981), suggested that condominium rules falling under the generic heading of use restrictions emanate from one of two sources: the declaration of condominium or the board of directors. Those contained in the declaration "are clothed with a very strong presumption of validity....," *id.* at 639, because the law requires their full disclosure prior to the time of purchase and, thus, the purchaser has adequate notice. *See* Section 718.503(2)(a), Florida Statutes (1983). Board rules, on the other hand, are treated differently. When a court is called upon to assess the validity of a rule enacted by a board of directors, it first determines whether the board acted within its scope of authority and, second, whether the rule reflects reasoned or arbitrary and capricious decision making. *See, e.g., Hidden Harbour Estates, Inc. v. Norman*, 309 So. 2d 180 (Fla. 4th DCA 1975); *Sterling Village Condo., Inc. v. Breitenbach*, 251 So. 2d 685 (Fla. 4th DCA 1971); *see generally* Note, *Condominium Rulemaking—Presumptions, Burdens and Abuses: A Call for Substantive Judicial Review in Florida*, 34 U.Fla.L.Rev. 219 (1982); Note, *Judicial Review of Condominium Rulemaking*, 94 Harv.L.Rev. 647 (1981).

The reasonableness of rules 31 and 33 was not questioned below and, therefore, we are concerned only with the scope of the board's authority. Inquiries into this area, as we indicated in *Juno by the Sea North Condo., Inc. v. Manfredonia*, 397 So. 2d 297 (Fla. 4th DCA 1980) (on rehearing), begin with a review of the applicable statutes and the condominium's legal documents, *i.e.*, the declaration and by-laws.

> By express terms in the statute and in the declaration the association has been granted broad authority to regulate the use of both the common element and limited common element property.
>
> In general, that power may be exercised as long as the exercise is reasonable, is not violative of any constitutional restrictions, and does not exceed any specific limitations set out in the statutes or condominium documents.

Id. at 302.

Since there has not been any suggestion that either rule violates the Condominium Act, Section 718, Florida Statutes (1983), we begin by viewing the Beachwood Villas declaration of condominium. Article X provides that "[t]he operation of the condominium property shall be governed by the by-laws of the Association which are ... made a part hereof." In turn, Article IV of the by-laws states that "[a]ll of the powers and duties of the Association shall be exercised by the board of directors...." More specific is Article VII, Section 2, which states that "[t]he Board of Directors may, from time to time, adopt or amend previously adopted rules and regulations governing and restricting the use and maintenance of the condominium units...."

It is obvious from the foregoing that the board of directors is empowered to pass rules and regulations for the governance of the condominium. The question remains, however, whether the topics encompassed in rules 31 and 33 are legitimate subjects for board rulemaking. Put another way, must regulations governing rental of units and occupancy of units by guests during an owner's absence be included in the declaration of condominium. At least one court has held that "[u]se restrictions to be valid, must be clearly inferable [sic] from the Declaration." *Mavrakis v. Playa Del Sol Association*, No. 77-6049, slip op. at 4 (S.D. Fla. May 11, 1978). This test is rooted in the concept that declarations of condominium are somewhat like covenants running with the land. *See Pepe v. Whispering Sands Condo. Association*, 351 So. 2d 755 (Fla. 2d DCA 1977). Even so, we believe that this test is too stringent. A declaration of condominium is "the condominium's 'constitution.'" *Schmidt v. Sherrill*, 442 So. 2d 963, 965 (Fla. 4th DCA 1984). Often, it contains broad statements of general policy with due notice that the board of directors is empowered to implement these policies and address day-to-day problems in the condominium's operation through the rulemaking process. It would be impossible to list all restrictive uses in a declaration of condominium. Parking regulations, limitations on the use of the swimming pool, tennis court and card room—the list is endless and subject to constant modification. Therefore, we have formulated the appropriate test in this fashion: provided that a board-enacted rule does not contravene either an express provision of the declaration or a right reasonably inferable therefrom, it will be found valid, within the scope of the board's authority.[1] This test, in our view, is fair and functional; it safeguards the rights of unit owners and preserves unfettered the concept of delegated board management.

Inasmuch as rules 31 and 33 do not contravene either an express provision of the declaration or any right reasonably inferable therefrom, we hold that the board's enactments are valid and plainly within the scope of its authority. Accordingly, we reverse the order on appeal and remand the cause for further proceedings consistent with this opinion.

Reversed and Remanded.

Lovering v. Seabrook Island Property Owners Ass'n
Supreme Court of South Carolina
352 S.E.2d 707 (S.C. 1987)

Respondents, who are both Seabrook Island property owners, commenced these actions to challenge the validity of an assessment imposed by Petitioner Seabrook Island Property Owners Association (Association) to pay for bridge repairs and a beach renourishment project. The circuit court granted summary judgment for the Association and Petitioner Seabrook Island Company (Company), and respondents appealed.

The Court of Appeals reversed, holding that the actions of the Association were *ultra vires*. *Lovering v. Seabrook Island Property Owners Ass'n*, 289 S.C. 77, 344 S.E.2d 862 (Ct.App.1986). The Association and the Company now seek a writ of certiorari. We grant certiorari, dispense with further briefing, and affirm as modified.

It is undisputed that the Association had no express power to impose the assessment at issue. The Association and the Company argue, however, that the power to levy this

---

1. In *Tower House Condo., Inc. v. Millman*, 410 So. 2d 926 (Fla.3d DCA 1981), the court invalidated a condominium bylaw because it was inconsistent with the declaration. Likewise, *Scarfone v. Culverhouse*, 443 So. 2d 122 (Fla. 2d DCA 1983), invalidated board action which was authorized by and inconsistent with the declaration. In the same vein, a facially neutral rule or board decision may be attacked on the ground that it places an unreasonable or arbitrary limitation on a use permitted by the declaration. *See Lyons v. King*, 397 So. 2d 964 (Fla. 4th DCA 1981). As indicated, however, this allegation has not been raised in the case at bar.

"Implied or incidental"

↓

"reas. necs. to execut'n of the corp's express powers"

special assessment was an <u>implied or incidental power</u> of the Association's authority under its by-laws to maintain and preserve the amenities and values of the development.

Implied or incidental powers are those which are reasonably necessary to the execution of the corporation's express powers, not those which are merely convenient or useful. *South Carolina Elec. & Gas Co. v. South Carolina Public Service Auth.*, 215 S.C. 193, 54 S.E.2d 777 (1949); *Creech v. South Carolina Public Service Auth.*, 200 S.C. 127, 20 S.E.2d 645 (1942).

Assuming, without deciding, that the Association had the responsibility of maintaining the streets and the beach, the by-laws provided the mechanism of an annual maintenance charge to finance the necessary repairs. Furthermore, the Association could have financed the repairs by use of its statutory authority to borrow funds under S.C.Code Ann. § 33-31-100(2)(1976), a course of action the Association apparently considered and rejected. <u>Since the power to levy a special assessment was not necessary for the Association to carry out its express powers,</u> even if more convenient than the available fund raising methods, <u>it could not be an implied or incidental power.</u>

Alternate means to carry out express powers

The Association and the Company also argue that the assessment was an allowable adjustment to the annual maintenance charge. The assessment in question was based on the Association's calculation of the "value received" by each property owner from the repairs. The by-laws, however, specifically provide that adjustments to the annual maintenance charge are to be based on the assessed value of the property as fixed by the county tax assessor. Thus, an adjustment based on the "value received" by the individual property owners was invalid.

Spec. assess. was "ultra vires"

Based on the foregoing, <u>the Court of Appeals correctly held that the imposition of the special assessment was *ultra vires*.</u> The court then, however, further held that the Company owned the bridges and the beach and was responsible for their maintenance. The issue of property ownership was not raised before the circuit court or by exception on appeal and should not have been decided by the Court of Appeals. Accordingly, the portion of the Court of Appeals' opinion relating to this issue is vacated and the case is

Affirmed as modified.

Notes & Questions

1. *Board.* Typically, the board of directors of community associations is elected and serves in the same manner as any board of directors of a for-profit corporation. Can you think of possible differences between incorporated and unincorporated association boards? See Model Business Corporations Act, §§ 8.03 and 8.04.

2. *By-laws and director authority.* Typically, the by-laws grant <u>broad authority</u> to the board of directors and the officers of the association to carry out their respective duties, much like any corporation. For example:

> *Board of Directors.* The Board of Directors shall be responsible for the affairs of the Association and shall <u>have all the powers and duties necessary for the administration of the Association's affairs and, as provided by law, may do all acts and things as are not by the Declaration, Articles, or these By-laws directed to be done and exercised exclusively by the members....</u>

Broad "catch all"

What are some examples of board actions that are "necessary for the administration of the association's affairs?" Looking at the sample language above, what are some possible restrictions on board actions? If you were a developer/declarant, what issues might concern you regarding board powers and the rights of members and declarant? In what areas might you wish expressly to limit the authority of the board of directors?

3. *Delegation of board powers.* Traditionally, one envisions the operations of a corporation being guided by policy decisions made exclusively by its board of directors. In reality, however, this "traditional method" of corporate governance is varied, most often by necessity or practicality. For example, certain policy decisions may be delegated to committees who have more expertise in or commit more time to particular issues (*i.e.*, finance, administration, marketing, etc.). Accordingly, a question arises as to the extent to which a board may delegate its express powers to other board members, officers, committees, and other third parties. See generally, Brandon, *Corporate Governance* §§ 4.01–4.40 (Michie Co. 1993); and *Fletcher Cyclopedia of the Law of Private Corporations*, Vol. 19 §§ 3.01–3.21 (Perm Ed). In the community association context, what policy decisions do you believe should remain with the board of directors? What decisions may be delegated to others and by what process?

4. *Board actions and meetings.* As in corporations, formalities are imposed on community association board actions by the respective state's corporate code. Additional requirements may also be imposed by a condominium or common interest community association statute. For example, an association's board of directors is usually required to give notice to homeowners of upcoming meetings, and there are usually quorum requirements. Similarly, there are likely to be requirements associated with conducting board meetings. What requirements may be imposed upon the board before they may take action on association affairs? Compare UCIOA §§ 3-108 and 3-109 with Model Business Corporations Act §§ 8.22 and 8.24.

5. *Member access to board meetings and board meeting minutes.* Should members be permitted to attend all board meetings? Or obtain the minutes from all such meetings? How might such openness to the board of directors decision-making process be disadvantageous? Advantageous? Should a homeowner who is in alleged violation of the restrictive covenants be entitled to review board meeting minutes in which his violation was discussed? See generally Nevada Common Interest Ownership Act Article III, Nev. Rev. Stat. Ann. § 116.31085 (Michie 1997) (Provisions regarding executive board meetings).

6. *Board composition during declarant control period.* Disputes sometimes arise between the developer/declarant and the association members regarding selection of members for the association's board of directors. The Uniform Condominium Act and the Uniform Common Interest Ownership Act impose board membership requirements in an attempt to balance the interests of association members and the developer/declarant.

UCA, UCIOA § 3-103 (d) permits the declarant to control the operation of the association for a specified period of time. Section 3-103(d) reads:

> Subject to subsection (e), the declaration may provide for a period of declarant control of the association, during which a declarant, or persons designated by him, may appoint and remove the officers and members of the executive board....

UCA, UCIOA § 3-103 (e) promotes input from association members by requiring that a certain percentage of the board of directors be elected by the unit owners. Section 3-103(e) reads:

> Not later than 60 days after conveyance of 25 percent of the units that may be created to unit owners other than a declarant, at least one member and not less than 25 percent of the members of the executive board must be elected by unit owners other than the declarant. Not later than 60 days after conveyance 50 per-

cent of the units which may be created to unit owners other than a declarant, not less than 33 1/3 percent of the members of the executive board must be elected by unit owners other than the declarant.

Can you think of reasons why the declarant would want to maintain control over the association on specific matters for a longer period? What association issues or what matters are likely to be important to the developer/declarant until the development is completed? Absent board member appointments, how else may a declarant retain control over specific, important issues? Issues surrounding the period of declarant control will be considered in more detail in Chapter 11.

7. *Limitations on implied powers*. In *Beachwood Villas*, the court enunciated the following standard: "Provided that a board-enacted rule does not contravene either an express provision of the declaration or a right reasonably inferable therefrom, it will be found valid, within the scope of the board's authority." Do you agree that this test is "fair and functional?" What standards should apply to other, non-rulemaking actions of the board arising from its implied powers (such as the assessment at issue in *Lovering*)? In challenging a board of directors' action which is not expressly provided for, where could you look for limitations on the board's authority in the community association context? See generally *Tower House Condo., Inc. v. Millman*, 410 So. 2d 926 (Fla. Dist. Ct. App. 1981); and *Scarfone v. Culverhouse*, 443 So. 2d 122 (Fla. Dist. Ct. App. 1983).

Note: *Community Association Management*

Community association management encompasses much more than simply ensuring that lawns in the common area are mowed regularly. Managing an association is similar to running a small business. It requires sound financial planning, establishing and implementing policies and procedures, supervising employees and subcontractors, and coordinating committee and volunteer activities.

During a community's creation and the initial sales period, it is common for the developer to manage the association through the developer-appointed board of directors and officers and employees of the development company. This arrangement provides the developer with extensive control over the community's direction during initial stages of development. Moreover, many developer responsibilities at this stage overlap with what will ultimately become association management responsibilities. Note that the burden to the developer of managing the nascent association is not as significant as it may later become when the homeowners control the association.

At some point during the development process, the association may need to evaluate whether to self-manage or whether to retain a professional management company. Factors which may influence such decisions include the community's size, complexity, needs and resources. It should also be noted that an association can usually choose from a "menu" of professional management services to fit its needs and budget.

The self-management system requires the association's members to coordinate all operational activities of the association and the community. Directors, officers and appointees of the board oversee various tasks, including hiring sub-contractors for maintenance work, acquiring insurance, filing association tax forms, and invoicing and collecting assessments. In other words, the members provide the services that a management company might otherwise provide.

Self management has the advantage of keeping direct management costs to the association and its members low and fosters a sense of community pride among the homeowner volunteers. However, this method has serious disadvantages as well. Self-management requires an active, intelligent, and large pool of volunteers from which to chose its leaders. In many communities, there are often too few talented residents who wish to contribute such large amounts of time to their association. Also, the savings thought to accompany self-management may not always be as large as generally assumed. For example, management firms do not have the same "learning costs" as a frequently changing volunteer base, and such firms can often negotiate better prices for certain resources based upon their representation of multiple clients.

Contract management has many forms. Most commonly, the association can contract with either the developer (or a subsidiary of the developer) or an independent, professional management company that can provide management services from a distance or with on-site staff.

The developer-managed community may have some limited advantages, particularly in the time period immediately following transition (see Chapter 11). For example, it is likely that the same staff that has a working relationship with the members and is familiar with the needs of the particular community will be retained. Disadvantages include the perceived need of the community to break away from developer control and the lack of competitive bidding for services.

Often, the benefit of the professional management company lies in its ability to distribute certain costs among several different community association clients. For example, management company staff can specialize in certain areas (*i.e.*, newsletter production, assessment collection, etc.) and some costs can be shared (*i.e.*, computer systems and software, other office equipment, etc.). Typically, the professional management company will provide a single account representative to attend board meetings and coordinate the association's operational activities. For larger communities, the management company may hire on-site personnel to handle all or a few of its operational matters.

Of course, it is important to note that contracting for management of the association's day-to-day affairs is not a complete divestiture of the board's responsibilities. For example, although a management company (and an accountant) may assist the board in preparing the annual budget, the ultimate decision rests with the board itself, and not the management company. Also, state law and the community's own governing documents may require that certain actions be taken by the association's directors and officers, such as adopting new rules or approving sanctions against members.

For a review of relevant case law concerning community association management companies, see generally *Raintree Corp. v. Rowe*, 248 S.E.2d 904 (N.C. Ct. App. 1978) (only homeowners association, not management company, may enforce collection of delinquent assessments); *Mitchell v. Stetson Management Co.*, No. 79M31493 (Dist. Ct. Cook Co., Ill. 1980) (individual homeowner may not sue management company over the level of its service as only the association has standing to enforce its contractual rights); *Nichols v. Kirkpatrick Management, Inc.*, 536 N.E.2d 565 (Ind. Ct. App. 1989) (duty to repair condominium roof was upon the condominium association, not its management company); *Planned Community Services, Inc. v. Spielman*, 371 S.E.2d 193 (Ga. Ct. App. 1988) (management company not liable for slip and fall injury on condominium property); *Gentry v. Northeast Management Co.*, 472 F. Supp. 1248 (N.D. Tex. 1979) (management company for condominium not liable for racial discrimination due to lack of evidence);

Johnson v. Nationwide Indus., Inc., 450 F. Supp. 948 (N.D. Ill. 1978) (no illegal tying agreement between condominium developer and management company since the only "product" involved was the sale of a condominium unit).

Problem

A developer built a community with the intent of selling a specific number of affordable units. To preserve the affordable nature of these units, the resale price is limited (via a cap on the amount of appreciation over time). The board is concerned that some owners are circumventing the CCRs and the intent to maintain affordable units by leasing the affordable units at market rates rather than selling. The president calls you for advice. What do you tell her?

2. Propriety of Board Actions: Standards of Judicial Review

> … in a society that has come to value the individual's freedom above the individual's commitments, we too often lack the integrity to transform our talk into action.
>
> — *Stephen L. Carter*

Courts have usually applied either what they call the "business judgment rule" or the "reasonableness" standard in determining the propriety of actions or nonactions taken by community association boards. Considerable confusion can arise in this area because boards make several different kinds of decisions and the appropriate standard of judicial review depends on the nature of the decision. Business decisions about management of the common property may call for substantial deference by the judiciary, while legislative decisions about allocation of assessment burdens or imposition of restrictions on occupancy or use of individual units may call for substantial judicial scrutiny. Decisions to grant variances from architectural standards, or to deny approval for building plans may call for different levels of scrutiny, as may adjudicatory decisions imposing fines and other penalties.

In reading the cases that follow, consider the extent to which community associations should be left to govern themselves — leaving unhappy residents to their political remedies — and when it is appropriate for the courts to step in. When courts do become involved, when should they limit their review to the processes followed by the association, and when should they review the merits of the actions taken or not taken? You might also think about whether the size of the association and the scope of its functions, and whether it is self-managed or run by a management company, should matter.

Another issue that arises is whether a different standard should be applied to decisions made by developer-appointed boards. Is it appropriate to hold them to a higher "fiduciary" standard because of the potential conflicts of interest between the developer and the homeowners?

Directors' actions take different forms and arise in different settings. For example, the board may act on its own, may apply a provision from the declaration, or may deal with a by-law provision. The document provision may have been adopted by amendment, or it might be in the original declaration. Consider the extent to which courts should become involved in reviewing each of these kinds of actions. Finally, think about whether any of these disputes could have been avoided by better drafted documents. Would you draft the documents to give greater or less protection to dissenting homeowners? How would you balance their interests against the interests of the larger community?

a. The Business Judgment Rule

Levandusky v. One Fifth Ave. Apartment Corp.

Court of Appeals of New York
553 N.E. 2d 1317 (N.Y. 1990)

KAYE, J. This appeal by a residential cooperative corporation concerning apartment renovations by one of its proprietary lessees, factually centers on a two-inch steam riser and three air conditioners, but fundamentally presents the legal question of what standard of review should apply when a board of directors of a cooperative corporation seeks to enforce a matter of building policy against a tenant-shareholder. We conclude that the business judgment rule furnishes the correct standard of review.

In the main, the parties agree that the operative events transpired as follows. In 1987, respondent (Ronald Levandusky) decided to enlarge the kitchen area of his apartment at One Fifth Avenue in New York City. According to Levandusky, some time after reaching that decision, and while he was president of the cooperative's board of directors, he told Elliot Glass, the architect retained by the corporation, that he intended to realign or "jog" a steam riser in the kitchen area, and Glass orally approved the alteration. According to Glass, however, the conversation was a general one; Levandusky never specifically told him that he intended to move any particular pipe, and Glass never gave him approval to do so. In any event, Levandusky's proprietary lease provided that no "alteration of or addition to the water, gas or steam risers or pipes" could be made without appellant's prior written consent.

Levandusky had his architect prepare plans for the renovation, which were approved by Glass and submitted for approval to the board of directors. Although the plans show details of a number of other proposed structural modifications, including changes in plumbing risers, no change in the steam riser is shown or discussed anywhere in the plans.

The board approved Levandusky's plans at a meeting held March 14, 1988, and the next day he executed an "Alteration Agreement" with appellant, which incorporated "Renovation Guidelines" that had originally been drafted, in large part, by Levandusky himself. These guidelines, like the proprietary lease, specified that advance written approval was required for any renovation affecting the building's heating system. Board consideration of the plans appropriately detailed to indicate all structural changes—was to follow their submission to the corporation's architect, and the board reserved the power to disapprove any plans, even those that had received the architect's approval.

In late spring 1988, the building's managing agent learned from Levandusky that he intended to move the steam riser in his apartment, and so informed the board. Both Levandusky and the board contacted John Flynn, an engineer who had served as consulting agent for the board. In a letter and in a subsequent presentation at a June 13 board meeting, Flynn opined that relocating steam risers was technically feasible and, if carefully done, would not necessarily cause any problem. However, he also advised that any change in an established old piping system risked causing difficulties ("gremlins"). In Flynn's view, such alterations were to be avoided whenever possible.

At the June 13 meeting, which Levandusky attended, the board enacted a resolution to "reaffirm the policy—no relocation of risers." At a June 23 meeting, the board voted to deny

[handwritten margin note: "mon'ry riser denied."]

[handwritten margin note: "Levandsky does it any way!"]

Levandusky a variance to move his riser, and to modify its previous approval of his renovation plans, conditioning approval upon an acceptable redesign of the kitchen area.

Levandusky nonetheless hired a contractor, who severed and jogged the kitchen steam riser. In August 1988, when the board learned of this, it issued a "stop work" order, pursuant to the "Renovation Guidelines." Levandusky then commenced this article 78 proceeding, seeking to have the stop work order set aside. The corporation cross-petitioned for an order compelling Levandusky to return the riser to its original position. The board also sought an order compelling him to remove certain air-conditioning units he had installed, which allegedly were not in conformity with the requirements of the Landmarks Preservation Commission.

Supreme Court initially granted Levandusky's petition, and annulled the stop work order, on the ground that there was no evidence that the jogged pipe had caused any damage, but on the contrary, the building engineer had inspected it and believed it would likely not have any adverse effect. Therefore, balancing the hardship to Levandusky in redoing the already completed renovations against the harm to the building, the court determined that the board's decision to stop the renovations was arbitrary and capricious, and should be annulled. Both counterclaims were dismissed, the court ruling that the corporation had no standing to complain of violations of the Landmarks Preservation Law, particularly as the building had not been cited for any violation.

On reargument, however, Supreme Court withdrew its decision, dismissed Levandusky's petition, and ordered him to restore the riser to its original position and submit redrawn plans to the board, on the ground that the court was precluded by the business judgment rule from reviewing the board's determination. The court adhered to its original ruling with respect to the branch of the cross motion concerning the air conditioners, notwithstanding that the Landmarks Preservation Commission had in the interim cited them as violations.

On Levandusky's appeal, the Appellate Division, 150 A.D.2d 167, 540N.Y.S.2d 440 modified the judgment. The court was unanimous in affirming the Supreme Court's disposition of the air conditioner claim, but divided concerning the stop work order. A majority of the court agreed with Supreme Court's original decision, while two Justices dissented on the ground that the board's action was within the scope of its business judgment and hence not subject to judicial review. Concluding that the business judgment rule applies to the decisions of cooperative governing associations enforcing building policy, and that the action taken by the board in this case falls within the purview of the rule, we now modify the order of the Appellate Division.

At the outset, we agree with the Appellate Division that the corporation's cross claim concerning Levandusky's three air conditioning units was properly dismissed, as the appropriate forum for resolution of the complaint at this stage is an administrative review proceeding. That brings us to the issue that divided the Appellate Division: the standard to be applied in judicial review of this challenge to a decision of the board of directors of a residential cooperative corporation.

[handwritten margin note: "Issue:"]

As cooperative and condominium home ownership has grown increasingly popular, courts confronting disputes between tenant-owners and governing boards have fashioned a variety of rules for adjudicating such claims (*see generally*, Goldberg, *Community Association Use Restrictions: Applying the Business Judgment Doctrine*, 64 Chi-Kent L.Rev. 653 [1988] [hereinafter Goldberg, *Community Association Use Restrictions*]; Note, *Judicial Review of Condominium Rulemaking*, 94 Harv.L.Rev. 647 [1981]). In the process, several salient characteristics of the governing board homeowner relationship have been identified as relevant to the judicial inquiry.

As courts and commentators have noted, the cooperative or condominium association is a quasi-government—a "little democratic sub society of necessity" (*Hidden Harbour Estates v. Norman*, 309 So. 2d 180, 182 [Fla.Dist.Ct.App.]). The proprietary lessees or condominium owners consent to be governed, in certain respects, by the decisions of a board. Like a municipal government, such governing boards are responsible for running the day-to-day affairs of the cooperative and to that end, often have broad powers in areas that range from financial decisionmaking to promulgating regulations regarding pets and parking spaces (*see generally*, Note, *Promulgation and Enforcement of House Rules*, 48 St John's L.Rev. 1132 [1974]). Authority to approve or disapprove structural alterations, as in this case, is commonly given to the governing board. (*See*, Siegler, *Apartment Alterations*, N.Y.L.J., May 4, 1988, at 1, col.1.)

Through the exercise of this authority, to which would-be apartment owners must generally acquiesce, a governing board may significantly restrict the bundle of rights a property owner normally enjoys. Moreover, as with any authority to govern, the broad powers of a cooperative board hold potential for abuse through arbitrary and malicious decisionmaking, favoritism, discrimination and the like.

On the other hand, agreement to submit to the decisionmaking authority of a cooperative board is voluntary in a sense that submission to government authority is not; there is always the freedom not to purchase the apartment. The stability offered by community control, through a board, has its own economic and social benefits, and purchase of a cooperative apartment represents a voluntary choice to cede certain of the privileges of single ownership to a governing body, often made up of fellow tenants who volunteer their time, without compensation. The board, in return, takes on the burden of managing the property for the benefit of the proprietary lessees. As one court observed: "Every man may justly consider his home his castle and himself as the king thereof; nonetheless his sovereign fiat to use his property as he pleases must yield, at least in degree, where ownership is in common or cooperation with others. The benefits of condominium living and ownership demand no less." (*Sterling Vil. Condo. v. Breitenbach*, 251 So. 2d 685, 688, n. 6 [Fla.Dist.Ct.App.].)

It is apparent, then, that a standard for judicial review of the actions of a cooperative or condominium governing board must be sensitive to a variety of concerns—sometimes competing concerns. Even when the governing board acts within the scope of its authority, some check on its potential powers to regulate residents' conduct, life-style and property rights is necessary to protect individual residents from abusive exercise, notwithstanding that the residents have, to an extent, consented to be regulated and even selected their representatives (*see*, Note, *The Rule of Law in Residential Associations*, 99 Harv.L.Rev. 472 [1985]). At the same time, the chosen standard of review should not undermine the purposes for which the residential community and its governing structure were formed: protection of the interest of the entire community of residents in an environment managed by the board for the common benefit.

We conclude that these goals are best served by a standard of review that is analogous to the business judgment rule applied by courts to determine challenges to decisions made by corporate directors (*see*, *Auerbach v. Bennett*, 47 N.Y.2d 619, 629, 419 N.Y.S.2d 920, 393 N.E.2d 994). A number of courts in this and other states have applied such a standard in reviewing the decisions of cooperative and condominium boards (*see, e.g., Kirsch v. Holiday Summer Homes*, 143 A.D.2d 811, 533 N.Y.S.2d 144; *Schoninger v. Yardarm Beach Homeowners' Assn.*, 134 A.D.2d 1, 523 N.Y.S.2d 523; *Van Camp v. Sherman*, 132 A.D.2d 453, 517 N.Y.S.2d 152; *Papalexiou v. Tower W. Condo.*, 167 N.J.Super. 516, 401 A.2d 280; *Schwarzmann v. Association of Apt. Owners*, 33 Wash.App.

397, 655 P.2d 1177; *Rywalt v. Writer Corp.*, 34 Colo.App. 334, 526 P.2d 316). We agree with those courts that such a test best balances the individual and collective interests at stake.

Developed in the context of commercial enterprises, the business judgment rule prohibits judicial inquiry into actions of corporate directors "taken in good faith and in the exercise of honest judgment in the lawful and legitimate furtherance of corporate purposes." (*Auerbach v. Bennett*, 47 N.Y.2d 619, 629, 419 N.Y.S.2d 920, 393 N.E.2d 994, *supra*.) So long as the corporation's directors have not breached their fiduciary obligation to the corporation, "the exercise of [their powers] for the common and general interests of the corporation may not be questioned, although the results show that what they did was unwise or inexpedient." (*Pollitz v. Wabash R.R. Co.*, 207 N.Y. 113, 124, 100 N.E. 721.)

Application of a similar doctrine is appropriate because a cooperative corporation is— in fact and function—a corporation, acting through the management of its board of directors, and subject to the Business Corporation Law. There is no cause to create a special new category in law for corporate actions by coop boards.

We emphasize that reference to the business judgment rule is for the purpose of analogy only. Clearly, in light of the doctrine's origins in the quite different world of commerce, the fiduciary principles identified in the existing case law—primarily emphasizing avoidance of self-dealing and financial self-aggrandizement—will of necessity be adapted over time in order to apply to directors of not-for-profit homeowners' cooperative corporations (see, *Goldberg, Community Association Use Restrictions, op. cit.*, at 677–683). For present purposes, we need not, nor should we determine the entire range of the fiduciary obligations of a cooperative board, other than to note that the board owes its duty of loyalty to the cooperative—that is, it must act for the benefit of the residents collectively. So long as the board acts for the purposes of the cooperative, within the scope of its authority and in good faith, courts will not substitute their judgment for the board's. Stated somewhat differently, unless a resident challenging the board's action is able to demonstrate a breach of this duty, judicial review is not available.

In reaching this conclusion, we reject the test seemingly applied by the Appellate Division majority and explicitly applied by Supreme Court in its initial decision. That inquiry was directed at the *reasonableness* of the board's decision; having itself found that relocation of the riser posed no "dangerous aspect" to the building, the Appellate Division concluded that the renovation should remain. Like the business judgment rule, this reasonableness standard—originating in the quite different world of governmental agency decisionmaking has found favor with courts reviewing board decisions (see, e.g., *Amoruso v. Board of Managers*, 38 A.D.2d 845, 330 N.Y.S.2d 107; *Lenox Manor v. Gianni*, 120 Misc.2d 202, 465 N.Y.S.2d 809; see, Note, *Judicial Review of Condominium Rulemaking, op. cit.*, at 659–661 [discussing cases from other jurisdictions]).

As applied in condominium and cooperative cases, review of a board's decision under a reasonableness standard has much in common with the rule we adopt today. A primary focus of the inquiry is whether board action is in furtherance of a legitimate purpose of the cooperative or condominium, in which case it will generally be upheld. The difference between the reasonableness test and the rule we adopt is twofold. First—unlike the business judgment rule, which places on the owner seeking review the burden to demonstrate a breach of the board's fiduciary duty—reasonableness review requires the board to demonstrate that its decision was reasonable. Second, although in practice a certain amount of deference appears to be accorded to board decisions, reasonableness review permits— indeed, in theory requires—the court itself to evaluate the merits or wisdom of the board's decision (*see, e.g., Hidden Harbour Estates v. Basso*, 393 So. 2d 637, 640 [Fla.Dist.Ct.App.]), just as the Appellate Division did in the present case.

The more limited judicial review embodied in the business judgment rule is preferable. In the context of the decisions of a for-profit corporation, "courts are ill equipped and infrequently called on to evaluate what are and must be essentially business judgments ... by definition the responsibility for business judgments must rest with the corporate directors; their individual capabilities and experience peculiarly qualify them for the discharge of that responsibility." (*Auerbach v. Bennett*, 47 N.Y.2d, *supra*, at 630–631, 419 N.Y.S.2d 920, 393 N.E.2d 994). Even if decisions of a cooperative board do not generally involve expertise beyond the usual ken of the judiciary, at the least board members will possess experience of the peculiar needs of their building and its residents not shared by the court.

Several related concerns persuade us that such a rule should apply here. As this case exemplifies, board decisions concerning what residents may or may not do with their living space may be highly charged and emotional. A cooperative or condominium is by nature a myriad of often competing views regarding personal living space, and decisions taken to benefit the collective interest may be unpalatable to one resident or another, creating the prospect that board decisions will be subjected to undue court involvement and judicial second-guessing. Allowing an owner who is simply dissatisfied with particular board action a second opportunity to reopen the matter completely before a court, which—generally without knowing the property—may or may not agree with the reasonableness of the board's determination, threatens the stability of the common living arrangement.

Moreover, the prospect that each board decision may be subjected to full judicial review hampers the effectiveness of the board's managing authority. The business judgment rule protects the board's business decisions and managerial authority from indiscriminate attack. At the same time, it permits review of improper decisions, as when the challenger demonstrates that the board's action has no legitimate relationship to the welfare of the cooperative, deliberately singles out individuals for harmful treatment, is taken without notice or consideration of the relevant facts, or is beyond the scope of the board's authority.

Levandusky failed to meet this burden, and Supreme Court properly dismissed his petition. His argument that having once granted its approval, the board was powerless to rescind its decision after he had spent considerable sums on the renovations is without merit. There is no dispute that Levandusky failed to comply with the provisions of the "Alteration Agreement" or "Renovation Guidelines" designed to give the board explicit written notice before it approved a change in the building's heating system. Once made aware of Levandusky's intent, the board promptly consulted its engineer, and notified Levandusky that it would not depart from a policy of refusing to permit the movement of pipes. That he then went ahead and moved the pipe hardly allows him to claim reliance on the board's initial approval of his plans. Indeed, recognition of such an argument would frustrate any systematic effort to enforce uniform policies.

Levandusky's additional allegations that the board's decision was motivated by the personal animosity of another board member toward him, and that the board had in fact permitted other residents to jog their steam risers, are wholly conclusory. The board submitted evidence—unrefuted by Levandusky—that it was acting pursuant to the advice of its engineer, and that it had not previously approved such jogging. Finally, the fact that allowing Levandusky an exception to the policy might not have resulted in harm to the building does not require that the exception be allowed. Under the rule we articulate today, we decline to review the merits of the board's determination that it was preferable to adhere to a uniform policy regarding the building's piping system.

Turning to the concurrence, it is apparent that in many respects we are in agreement concerning the appropriate standard of judicial review of cooperative board decisions; it is more a matter of label that divides us. For these additional reasons, we believe our choice is the better one.

For the guidance of the courts and all other interested parties, obviously a single standard for judicial review of the propriety of board action is desirable, irrespective of the happenstance of the form of the lawsuit challenging that action.* Unlike challenges to administrative agency decisions, which take the form of article 78 proceedings, challenges to the propriety of corporate board action have been lodged as derivative suits, injunction actions, and all manner of civil suits, including article 78 proceedings. While the nomenclature will vary with the form of suit, we see no purpose in allowing the form of the action to dictate the substance of the standard by which the legitimacy of corporate action is to be measured.

By the same token, unnecessary confusion is generated by prescribing different standards for different categories of issues that come before cooperative boards—for example, a standard of business judgment for choices between competing economic options, but rationality for the administration of corporate by-laws and rules governing shareholder-tenant rights (*see*, concurring opn., at 545, at 816 of 554 N.Y.S.2d, at 1326 of 553 N.E.2d). There is no need for two rules when one will do, particularly since corporate action often partakes of each category of issues. Indeed, even the decision here might be portrayed as the administration of corporate by-laws and rules governing shareholder-tenant rights, or more broadly as a policy choice based on the economic consequences of tampering with the building's piping system.

Finally, we reiterate that "business judgment" appears to strike the best balance. It establishes that board action undertaken in furtherance of a legitimate corporate purpose will generally not be pronounced "arbitrary and capricious or an abuse of discretion" (CPLR 7803[3]) in article 78 proceedings, or otherwise unlawful in other types of litigation. It is preferable to a standard that requires Judges, rather than directors, to decide what action is "reasonable" for the cooperative. It avoids drawing sometimes elusive semantic distinctions between what is "reasonable" and what is "rational" (the concurrence rejects the former but embraces the latter as the appropriate test). And it better protects tenant-shareholders against bad faith and self-dealing than a test that insulates board decisions "if there is a rational basis to explain them" or if "an articulable and rational basis for the board's decision exists." (Concurring opn., at 548, at 817 of 554 N.Y.S.2d, at 1327 of 553 N.E.2d.) The mere presence of an engineer's report, for example—"certainly a rational explanation for the board's decision" (concurring opn., at 548, at 817 of 554 N.Y.S.2d, at 1327 of 553 N.E.2d)—should not end all inquiry, foreclosing review of nonconclusory assertions of malevolent conduct; under the business judgment test, it would not.

---

* We of course do not disregard the form of action. In determining whether appellant's decision was "arbitrary and capricious or an abuse of discretion" (CPLR 7803[3]), we would use "business judgment," the concurrence some form of "rationality" or "reasonableness." By analogy, we hold today in *Akpan v. Koch*, 75 N.Y.2d 561, 574, 555 N.Y.S.2d 16, 22,554 N.E.2d 53, 59 ([decided today]) that because a governmental agency took the required "hard look" under the State's environmental protection laws, its action cannot be characterized as arbitrary and capricious or an abuse of discretion under CPLR 7803(3). So too here, board action that comes within the business judgment rule cannot be characterized as arbitrary and capricious, or an abuse of discretion.

Accordingly, the order of the Appellate Division should be modified, with costs to appellant, by reinstating Supreme Court's judgment to the extent it granted appellant's cross motions regarding the steam riser and severed and set down for assessment the issue of damages and, as so modified, affirmed.

...

Affirmed as modified.

Retrospective and Observations

Joel Sharrow, who represented the cooperative in this case, relayed the interesting note that after the outcome of this suit, members of the existing board were voted out, and Levandusky became a member of the board of directors.

Note: The Business Judgment Rule Compared with the Rule of Reasonableness

The business judgment rule is most traditionally seen in cases arising from the board's exercise of its business responsibilities. Conversely, the rule of reasonableness is most frequently seen in cases generally characterized as part of the "governmental" powers of the community association. However, there are no bright lines, and one must always watch for the components of one rule being used under the title of another.

In the preceding section, we questioned the differences that might apply in the business judgment rule when the board is developer appointed as opposed to being homeowner elected. It is appropriate to visit these questions again in the context of the rule of reasonableness; however, the underlying principles which may support a distinction in the application of business judgment, fiduciary, and combined standards may well not exist when looking at the rule of reasonableness.

The Pennsylvania Supreme Court, relying in part on the American Law Institute's Principles of Corporate Governance, well stated the business judgment rule and what it means:

> The business judgment rule insulates an officer or director of a corporation from liability for a business decision made in good faith if he is not interested in the subject of the business judgment, is informed with respect to the subject of the business judgment to the extent he reasonably believes to be appropriate under the circumstances, and rationally believes that the business judgment is in the best interests of the corporation. *Cuker v. Mikalauskas*, 692 A.2d 1042, 1045 (1997).

The business judgment rule is used both to defend a board[X] when it and its members are subject to suit and, as the business judgment doctrine or principle, to defend the board's decisions.[Y] Most cases present the latter situation in which some association member contests the board's decision, and the board relies upon business judgment to defend.

X. The business judgment rule has been used as a type of "shield" by some boards when faced with suit. In *Seafirst Corp. v. Jenkins*, corporate officers and directors used it as a means of showing they exercised due care in fulfillment of their responsibilities when charged with negligent mismanagement. 644 F. Supp. 1152 (W.D. Wash. 1986).

Y. "As the name implies, a necessary predicate for the application of the business judgment rule is that the directors' decision is that of a *business* judgment and not a decision ... which construes

Technically, it is the business judgment doctrine or principle which is invoked to defend the decision, but in most community association cases the distinction in nomenclature between doctrine and rule is not observed. There may, however, be a difference in the underlying rationale. For example, the business judgment rule rather than doctrine may be used to support the business or entrepreneurial decisions of the board. Both the rule and the doctrine rest upon notions of judicial restraint and the relative competence of directors and judges in making decisions. The doctrine weighs in on the side of third parties who deal with the corporation and need certainty. The rule serves as an incentive to induce individuals to become directors.

Actually, what is being done in these cases is the assertion of a rule that defends the *procedure* under which the board has acted and the right of the board to be the sole arbiter of the issue involved. The result is that if the procedure is valid, the court will not second guess the substance of the board's action. Consequently, the court upholds the decision without subjecting the wisdom of the board's action to judicial scrutiny. As the Delaware Supreme Court explained, the business judgment rule is "a *presumption* that in making a business decision the directors of a corporation acted on an informed basis, in good faith and in the honest belief that the action taken was in the best interests of the company." (*Aronson v. Lewis*, 473 A.2d 805, 812 (Del. 1984).) (Emphasis supplied.) A complaining party, of course, may challenge and require a court to examine each component.

A serious question arises whether, in the community association context, *all* board decisions should be protected by the business judgment doctrine. Some courts have held that the business judgment rule does not apply because of the "governmental" nature of the board's action. The gravamen of such decisions is the fundamental nature of the action and its effect upon some right of the property owner. Such decisions articulate the premise that this corporate standard is irrelevant in a case testing the validity of a non business action.

The practitioner and the board member are both concerned about the enforceability of the decision itself and are far more concerned about that than a damage award in most cases. Resolution of litigation through settlement or court order that leaves the board's decision altered or set aside has potentially far greater impact than might result in some other commercial setting and certainly more so than in typical civil litigation. The issue in common interest community litigation is not only the immediate issue at trial but the larger issue of board governance and the very structure of the common interest community.

Conversely there is the need to separate the presumption that works well in the business setting from political-social-regulator decisions. A presumption of validity may not be as appropriate in those circumstances. This gives rise to a need for a more structured process and one that affords protection to association and member alike giving due regard to the rights of the other members of the association as well.

Courts do not apply the business judgment doctrine in some corporate cases. One is analogous: internal corporate matters and shareholder voice. This departure illustrates the appropriateness for departures in other "internal governance" areas as, for example, voting, voice, rule making, and enforcing. In applying this heightened scrutiny, however, courts do not substitute their own judgment but do afford closer scrutiny.

There are additional justifications for a departure from or a modification of the business judgment doctrine in some internal matters. These certainly include the nature of

---

and applies a statute and a corporate bylaw." *Lake Monticello Owners' Ass'n v. Lake,* 463 S.E.2d 652, 656 (Va. 1995).

the business, the significance of the investment, the liquidity factor, and most importantly the power the association has over the members.

A troublesome issue in applying the business judgment rule is self interest. Directors are members thus are affected by each decision. But directors frequently act in their own interest without breaching the duty of loyalty. The key issue is whether the directors are taking advantage of their position to improve their situation above and at the expense of non director members.

Finally, consider the basic justifications for the business judgment rule and test them against the common interest community context. First, the rule encourages competent people to serve by providing a degree of "safe harbor." Second, it acknowledges that making decisions involves a degree of risk and thus protects discretion without "second guessing" the decision. Third, it provides for judicial efficiency in that it keeps courts from becoming involved in decisions that are better made by those closer to the situation or with greater skill or understanding.

Lamden v. La Jolla Shores Clubdominium Homeowners Association

Supreme Court of California
980 P.2d 940 (1999)

OPINION BY: WERDEGAR, J., expressing the unanimous view of the court.

A building in a condominium development suffered from termite infestation. The board of directors of the development's community association ... decided to treat the infestation locally ("spot-treat"), rather than fumigate. Alleging the board's decision diminished the value of her unit, the owner of a condominium in the development sued the community association. In adjudicating her claims, under what standard should a court evaluate the board's decision?

As will appear, we conclude as follows: Where a duly constituted community association board, upon reasonable investigation, in good faith and with regard for the best interests of the community association and its members, exercises discretion within the scope of its authority under relevant statutes, covenants and restrictions to select among means for discharging an obligation to maintain and repair a development's common areas, courts should defer to the board's authority and presumed expertise. Thus, we adopt today for California courts a rule of judicial deference to community association board decisionmaking that applies, regardless of an association's corporate status, when owners in common interest developments seek to litigate ordinary maintenance decisions entrusted to the discretion of their associations' boards of directors....

BACKGROUND

Plaintiff Gertrude M. Lamden owns a condominium unit in one of three buildings comprising the La Jolla Shores Clubdominium condominium development....[2] ...

2. The Development was built, and its governing declaration of restrictions recorded, in 1971. In 1973 Lamden and her husband bought unit 375, one of 42 units in the complex's largest building. Until 1977 the Lamdens used their unit only as a rental. From 1977 until 1988 they lived in the unit; since 1988 the unit has again been used only as a rental.

In the late 1980's, attempting to remedy water intrusion and mildew damage, the Association hired a contractor to renovate exterior siding on all three buildings in the Development. The contractor replaced the siding on the southern exposure of Building Three and removed damaged drywall and framing. Where the contractor encountered termites, a termite extermination company provided spot-treatment and replaced damaged material.

Lamden remodeled the interior of her condominium in 1990. At that time, the Association's manager arranged for a termite extermination company to spot-treat areas where Lamden had encountered termites.

The following year, both Lamden and the Association obtained termite inspection reports recommending fumigation, but the Association's Board decided against that approach. As the Court of Appeal explained, the Board based its decision not to fumigate on concerns about the cost of fumigation, logistical problems with temporarily relocating residents, concern that fumigation residue could affect residents' health and safety, awareness that upcoming walkway renovations would include replacement of damaged areas, pet moving expenses, anticipated breakage by the termite company, lost rental income and the likelihood that termite infestation would recur even if primary treatment were utilized. The Board decided to continue to rely on secondary treatment until a more widespread problem was demonstrated.

In 1991 and 1992, the Association engaged a company to repair water intrusion damage to four units in Building Three. The company removed siding in the balcony area, repaired and waterproofed the decks, and repaired joints between the decks and the walls of the units. The siding of the unit below Lamden's and one of its walls were repaired. Where termite infestation or damage became apparent during this project, spot-treatment was applied and damaged material removed.

In 1993 and 1994, the Association commissioned major renovation of the Development's walkway system, the underpinnings of which had suffered water and termite damage. The $1.6 million walkway project was monitored by a structural engineer and an on-site architect.

In 1994, Lamden brought this action for damages, an injunction and declaratory relief. She purported to state numerous causes of action based on the Association's refusal to fumigate for termites, naming as defendants certain individual members of the Board as well as the Association. Her amended complaint included claims sounding in breach of contract (viz., the governing declaration of restrictions …), breach of fiduciary duty, and negligence. She alleged that the Association, in opting for secondary over primary treatment, had breached *Civil Code section 1364* … and the Declaration … in failing adequately to repair, replace and maintain the common areas of the Development.

Lamden further alleged that, as a proximate result of the Association's breaching its responsibilities, she had suffered diminution in the value of her condominium unit, repair expenses, and fees and costs in connection with this litigation. She also alleged that the Association's continued breach had caused and would continue to cause her irreparable harm by damaging the structural integrity and soundness of her unit, and that she has no adequate remedy at law. At trial, Lamden waived any damages claims and dismissed with prejudice the individual defendants. Presently, she seeks only an injunction and declaratory relief.

… As to the Association's actions, the trial court stated, "the Board did take appropriate action." The court noted the Board "did come up with a plan," viz., to engage a pest control service to "come out and [spot] treat [termite infestation] when it was found."

The trial judge opined he might, "from a personal relations standpoint," have acted sooner or differently under the circumstances than did the Association, but nevertheless concluded "the Board did have a rational basis for their decision to reject fumigation, and do ... what they did." Ultimately, the court gave judgment for the Association, applying what it called a "business judgment test." Lamden appealed.

Citing *Frances T. v. Village Green Owners Assn.* (1986) 42 Cal. 3d 490, ... 723 P.2d 573 ... (*Frances T.*), the Court of Appeal agreed with Lamden that the trial court had applied the wrong standard of care in assessing the Association's actions. In the Court of Appeal's view, relevant statutes, the governing Declaration and principles of common law imposed on the Association an objective duty of reasonable care in repairing and maintaining the Development's common areas near Lamden's unit as occasioned by the presence of termites. The court also concluded that, had the trial court analyzed the Association's actions under an objective standard of reasonableness, an outcome more favorable to Lamden likely would have resulted. Accordingly, the Court of Appeal reversed the judgment of the trial court.

We granted the Association's petition for review.

DISCUSSION

"In a community apartment project, condominium project, or stock cooperative ... unless otherwise provided in the declaration, the association is responsible for the repair and maintenance of the common area occasioned by the presence of wood-destroying pests or organisms." (*Civ. Code, § 1364, subd. (b)(1)*.) The Declaration in this case charges the Association with "management, maintenance and preservation" of the Development's common areas....

... [T]he parties ... differ only as to the standard against which the Association's performance in discharging this obligation properly should be assessed: a deferential "business judgment" standard or a more intrusive one of "objective reasonableness." ... The Association would have us decide this case through application of "the business judgment rule." ...

"The common law business judgment rule has two components—one which immunizes [corporate] directors from personal liability if they act in accordance with its requirements, and another which insulates from court intervention those management decisions which are made by directors in good faith in what the directors believe is the organization's best interest." (*Lee v. Interinsurance Exchange (1996) 50 Cal. App. 4th 694, 714* ...) A hallmark of the business judgment rule is that, when the rule's requirements are met, a court will not substitute its judgment for that of the corporation's board of directors.... [I]n California the component of the common law rule relating to directors' personal liability is defined by statute....

According to the Association, uniformly applying a business judgment standard in judicial review of community association board decisions would promote certainty, stability and predictability in common interest development governance. Plaintiff, on the other hand, contends general application of a business judgment standard to board decisions would undermine individual owners' ability ... to enforce, as equitable servitudes, the CC&R's in a common interest development's declaration.[5] Stressing residents' interest in a

---

5. *Civil Code section 1354, subdivision (a)* provides: "The covenants and restrictions in the declaration shall be enforceable equitable servitudes, unless unreasonable, and shall inure to the benefit of and bind all owners of separate interests in the development. Unless the declaration states otherwise, these servitudes may be enforced by any owner of a separate interest or by the association, or by both."

stable and predictable living environment, as embodied in a given development's particular CC&R's, plaintiff encourages us to impose on community associations an objective standard of reasonableness in carrying out their duties under governing CC&R's or public policy.

Two reasons why "bus. judg. rule" does not apply.

For at least two reasons, ... the "business judgment rule" ... does not directly apply to this case. First, the statutory protections for individual directors (*Corp. Code, § 309, subd. (c), 7231, subd. (c)*) do not apply, as no individual directors are defendants here....

... [B]y its terms, *section 7231* protects only "[a] *person* who performs the duties of a director" ...; it contains no reference to the component of the common law business judgment rule that somewhat insulates ordinary corporate business *decisions*, per se, from judicial review.... Moreover, plaintiff here is seeking only injunctive and declaratory relief, and it is not clear that such a prayer implicates *section 7231*. The statute speaks only of protection against "*liability* based upon any alleged failure to discharge the person's obligations...." ...

Assoc. is not incorp.

Second, neither the California statute nor the common law business judgment rule, strictly speaking, protects *noncorporate* entities, and the defendant in this case, the Association, is not incorporated.[6]

"judicial deference" rule.

... For the foregoing reasons, the "business judgment rule" ... has no direct application to the instant controversy. The precise question presented, then, is whether we should in this case adopt for California courts a rule—analogous perhaps to the business judgment rule—of judicial deference to community association board decisionmaking that would apply, regardless of an association's corporate status, when owners in common interest developments seek to litigate ordinary maintenance decisions entrusted to the discretion of their associations' boards of directors. (Cf. *Levandusky v. One Fifth Ave. Apt. Corp.*, ... [(1990) 75 N.Y.2d 530, 538, 557 N.E.2d 1317] [referring "for the purpose of analogy only" to the business judgment rule in adopting a rule of deference].)

Our existing jurisprudence specifically addressing the governance of common interest developments is not voluminous. While we have not previously examined the question of what standard or test generally governs judicial review of decisions made by the board of directors of a community association, we have examined related questions.

Fifty years ago, in *Hannula v. Hacienda Homes (1949) 34 Cal. 2d 442*..., we held that the decision by the board of directors of a real estate development company to deny, under a restrictive covenant in a deed, the owner of a fractional part of a lot permission to build a dwelling thereon "must be a reasonable determination made in good faith." ... Sixteen years ago, we held that a condominium owners association is a "business establishment" within the meaning of the Unruh Civil Rights Act.... (*O'Connor v. Village Green Owners Assn. (1983) 33 Cal. 3d 790, 796* ...; but see *Harris v. Capital Growth Investors XIV (1991) 52 Cal. 3d 1142*, ... [declining to extend *O'Connor*]; *Curran v. Mount Diablo Council of the Boy Scouts (1998) 17 Cal. 4th 670, 697* ... [same].) And 10 years ago, in *Frances T.*..., we considered "whether a condominium owners association and the individual members of its board of directors may be held liable for injuries to a unit owner caused by third-party criminal conduct." ...

In *Frances T.*, ... [we concluded that a] community association ... may be held to a landlord's standard of care as to residents' safety in the common areas ... and [that] the plaintiff had alleged particularized facts stating a cause of action against both the association and the individual members of the board.... The plaintiff failed, however, to state a cause

---

6. The parties do not dispute that the component of the common law business judgment rule calling for deference to corporate decisions survives the Legislature's codification, in *section 7231*, of the component shielding individual directors from liability....

of action for breach of contract, as neither the development's governing CC&R's nor the association's bylaws obligated the defendants to install additional lighting. The plaintiff failed likewise to state a cause of action for breach of fiduciary duties, as the defendants had fulfilled their duty to the plaintiff as a shareholder, and the plaintiff had alleged no facts to show that the association's board members had a fiduciary duty to serve as the condominium project's landlord....

More recently, in *Nahrstedt v. Lakeside Village Condominium Assn. (1994) 8 Cal. 4th 361 ... (Nahrstedt)*, we confronted the question, "When restrictions limiting the use of property within a common interest development satisfy the requirements of covenants running with the land or of equitable servitudes, what standard or test governs their enforceability?"...

In *Nahrstedt*, ... we distilled from numerous authorities the principle that "[a]n equitable servitude will be enforced unless it violates public policy; it bears no rational relationship to the protection, preservation, operation or purpose of the affected land; or it otherwise imposes burdens on the affected land that are so disproportionate to the restriction's beneficial effects that the restriction should not be enforced." ... Applying this principle, and noting that a common interest development's recorded use restrictions are "enforceable equitable servitudes, unless unreasonable" (*Civ. Code, § 1354, subd. (a)*), we held that "such restrictions should be enforced unless they are wholly arbitrary, violate a fundamental public policy, or impose a burden on the use of affected land that far outweighs any benefit"....

In deciding *Nahrstedt*, ... [we observed:] "Because of its considerable power in managing and regulating a common interest development," ..."the governing board of an owners association must guard against the potential for the abuse of that power." ... We also noted that a community association's governing board's power to regulate "pertains to a 'wide spectrum of activities,' such as the volume of playing music, hours of social gatherings, use of patio furniture and barbecues, and rental of units." ...

We declared in *Nahrstedt* that, "when an association determines that a unit owner has violated a use restriction, the association must do so in good faith, not in an arbitrary or capricious manner, and its enforcement procedures must be fair and applied uniformly." (... citing *Ironwood Owners Assn. IX v. Solomon (1986) 178 Cal. App. 3d 766, 772* ...; *Cohen v. Kite Hill Community Assn. (1983) 142 Cal. App. 3d 642, 650*....) Nevertheless, we stated, "Generally, courts will uphold decisions made by the governing board of an owners association so long as they represent good faith efforts to further the purposes of the common interest development, are consistent with the development's governing documents, and comply with public policy." (*Nahrstedt*, ... citing Natelson, *Consent, Coercion, and "Reasonableness" in Private Law: The Special Case of the Property Owners Association* (1990) *51 Ohio State L.J. 41, 43*.)

The plaintiff in this case, like the plaintiff in *Nahrstedt*, ... disagrees with a particular aspect of the development's overall governance as it has impacted her. Whereas the restriction at issue in *Nahrstedt* (a ban on pets), however, was promulgated at the development's inception and enshrined in its founding CC&R's, the decision plaintiff challenges in this case (the choice of secondary over primary termite treatment) was promulgated by the Association's Board long after the Development's inception and after plaintiff had acquired her unit. Our holding in *Nahrstedt*, which established the standard for judicial review of recorded use restrictions that satisfy the requirements of covenants running with the land or equitable servitudes ... therefore, does not directly govern this case, which concerns the standard for judicial review of discretionary economic decisions made by the governing boards of community associations.

In *Nahrstedt*, moreover, some of our reasoning arguably suggested a distinction between originating CC&R's and subsequently promulgated use restrictions. Specifically, we reasoned in *Nahrstedt* that giving deference to a development's originating CC&R's "protects the general expectations of condominium owners 'that restrictions in place at the time they purchase their units will be enforceable.'" (... quoting Note, *Judicial Review of Condominium Rulemaking* (1981) 94 Harv. L.Rev. 647, 653.) Thus, our conclusion that judicial review of a common interest development's founding CC&R's should proceed under a deferential standard was, as plaintiff points out, at least partly derived from our understanding (invoked there by way of contrast) that the factors justifying such deference will not *necessarily* be present when a court considers subsequent, unrecorded community association board decisions. (... discussing *Hidden Harbour Estates v. Basso (Fla.Dist.Ct.App. 1981) 393 So. 2d 637, 639–640.*)

Nevertheless, having reviewed the record in this case, and in light of the foregoing authorities, we conclude that the Board's decision here to use secondary, rather than primary, treatment in addressing the Development's termite problem, a matter entrusted to its discretion under the Declaration and *Civil Code section 1364*, falls within *Nahrstedt*'s pronouncement that "Generally, courts will uphold decisions made by the governing board of an owners association so long as they represent good faith efforts to further the purposes of the common interest development, are consistent with the development's governing documents, and comply with public policy." ... Moreover, our deferring to the Board's discretion in this matter, which ... is broadly conferred in the Development's CC&R's, is consistent with *Nahrstedt*'s holding that CC&R's "should be enforced unless they are wholly arbitrary, violate a fundamental public policy, or impose a burden on the use of affected land that far outweighs any benefit." ...

Here, the ... trial court found that the Board acted upon reasonable investigation, in good faith, and in a manner the Board believed was in the best interests of the Association and its members.... Contrary to the Court of Appeal, we conclude the trial court was correct to defer to the Board's decision. We hold that, where a duly constituted community association board, upon reasonable investigation, in good faith and with regard for the best interests of the community association and its members, exercises discretion within the scope of its authority under relevant statutes, covenants and restrictions to select among means for discharging an obligation to maintain and repair a development's common areas, courts should defer to the board's authority and presumed expertise.

The foregoing conclusion is consistent with our previous pronouncements, as reviewed above, and also with those of California courts, generally, respecting various aspects of association decisionmaking. [Discussion of additional California cases omitted.—Eds.]

Our conclusion also accords with our recognition in *Frances T.* that the relationship between the individual owners and the managing association of a common interest development is complex.... On the one hand, each individual owner has an economic interest in the proper business management of the development as a whole for the sake of maximizing the value of his or her investment. In this aspect, the relationship between homeowner and association is somewhat analogous to that between shareholder and corporation. On the other hand, each individual owner, at least while residing in the development, has a personal, not strictly economic, interest in the appropriate management of the development for the sake of maintaining its security against criminal conduct and other foreseeable risks of physical injury. In this aspect, the relationship between owner and association is somewhat analogous to that between tenant and landlord. (See generally, *Frances T.,* ... [business judgment rule "applies to parties ... to whom the directors owe a fiduciary obligation," but "does not abrogate the common law duty which every person owes to others—that is, a duty to refrain from conduct that imposes an unreasonable risk of injury on third parties"].)

Relying on *Frances T.*, the Court of Appeal held that a landlord-like common law duty required the Association ... to exercise reasonable care in order to protect plaintiff's unit from undue damage.... Contrary to the Court of Appeal, however, we do not believe this case implicates such duties. *Frances T.* involved a common interest development resident who suffered "'physical injury, not pecuniary harm.... '" ... Plaintiff here, by contrast, has not resided in the Development since the time that significant termite infestation was discovered, and she alleges neither a failure by the Association to maintain the common areas in a reasonably safe condition, nor knowledge on the Board's part of any unreasonable risk of physical injury stemming from its failure to do so.... Accordingly, *Frances T.* is inapplicable.

Plaintiff warns that judicial deference to the Board's decision in this case would not be appropriate, lest every community association be free to do as little or as much as it pleases in satisfying its obligations to its members. We do not agree. Our respecting the Association's discretion, under this Declaration, to choose among modes of termite treatment does not foreclose the possibility that more restrictive provisions relating to the same or other topics might be "otherwise provided in the declaration[s]" (*Civ. Code, § 1364, subd. (b)(1)*) of other common interest developments.... [W]e have before us ... a declaration constituting a general scheme for maintenance, protection and enhancement of value of the Development, one that entrusts to the Association the management, maintenance and preservation of the Development's common areas and confers on the Board the power and authority to maintain and repair those areas.

Thus, the Association's obligation at issue in this case is broadly cast, plainly conferring on the Association the discretion to select, as it did, among available means for addressing the Development's termite infestation. Under the circumstances, our respecting that discretion obviously does not foreclose community association governance provisions that, within the bounds of the law, might more narrowly circumscribe association or board discretion.

Citing Restatement Third of Property, Servitudes, Tentative Draft No. 7,[9] plaintiff suggests that deference to community association discretion will undermine individual owners' previously discussed right ... to enforce recorded CC&R's as equitable servitudes, but we think not. "Under well-accepted principles of condominium law, a homeowner can sue the association for damages and an injunction to compel the association to enforce

---

9. The Restatement tentative draft proposes that "In addition to duties imposed by statute and the governing documents, the association has the following duties to the members of the common interest community: [P] (a) to use ordinary care and prudence in managing the property and financial affairs of the community that are subject to its control." (Rest.3d Property, Servitudes (Tent. Draft No. 7, Apr. 15, 1998) ch. 6, § 6.13, p. 325.) "The business judgment rule is not adopted, because the fit between community associations and other types of corporations is not very close, and it provides too little protection against careless or risky management of community property and financial affairs." ... It is not clear to what extent the Restatement tentative draft supports plaintiff's position. As the Association points out, a "member challenging an action of the association under this section has the burden of proving a breach of duty by the association" and, when the action is one within association discretion, "the additional burden of proving that the breach has caused, or threatens to cause, injury to the member individually or to the interests of the common interest community." ... Depending upon how it is interpreted, such a standard might be inconsistent with the standard we announced in Nahrstedt, viz., that a use restriction is enforceable "not by reference to facts that are specific to the objecting homeowner, but by reference to the common interest development as a whole." ...

the provisions of the declaration.... More importantly here, the homeowner can sue directly to enforce the declaration." (*Posey v. Leavitt (1991) 229 Cal. App. 3d 1236, 1246–1247*, citing *Cohen v. Kite Hill Community Assn., supra.*) Nothing we say here departs from those principles.

Finally, plaintiff contends a rule of judicial deference will insulate community association boards' decisions from judicial review. We disagree. As illustrated by *Fountain Valley Chateau Blanc Homeowner's Assn. v. Department of Veterans Affairs (1998) 67 Cal. App. 4th 743, 754–755 ...* (*Fountain Valley*), judicial oversight affords significant protection against overreaching by such boards.

In *Fountain Valley*, a homeowners association, threatening litigation against an elderly homeowner with Hodgkin's disease, gained access to the interior of his residence and demanded he remove a number of personal items, including books and papers not constituting "standard reading material," claiming the items posed a fire hazard.... The homeowner settled the original complaint..., but cross-complained for violation of privacy, trespass, negligence and breach of contract. The jury returned a verdict in his favor, finding specifically that the association had acted <u>unreasonably.</u>

Putting aside the question whether the jury, rather than the court, should have determined the ultimate question of the reasonableness *vel non* of the association's actions, the Court of Appeal held that, in light of the operative facts found by the jury, it was "virtually impossible" to say the association had acted reasonably.... The city fire department had found no fire hazard, and the association "did not have a good faith, albeit mistaken, belief in that danger." In the absence of such good faith belief, the court determined the jury's verdict must stand, thus impliedly finding no basis for judicial deference to the association's decision.

Plaintiff suggests that our previous pronouncements establish that when, as here, a community association is charged generally with maintaining the common areas, any member of the association may obtain judicial review of the reasonableness of its choice of means for doing so. To the contrary, in *Nahrstedt* we emphasized that "anyone who buys a unit in a common interest development with knowledge of its owners association's discretionary power accepts the risk that the power may be used in a way that benefits the commonality but harms the individual.'" (... quoting Natelson, *Consent, Coercion, and "Reasonableness" in Private Law: The Special Case of the Property Owners Association, supra,* 51 Ohio State L.J. at p. 67.)[10]

Nor did we in *Nahrstedt* impose on community associations strict liability for the consequences of their ordinary discretionary economic decisions. As the Association points out, unlike the categorical ban on pets at issue in *Nahrstedt*—which arguably is either valid or not—the Declaration here, in assigning the Association a duty to maintain and repair the common areas, does not specify *how* the Association is to act, just that it should. Neither the Declaration nor *Civil Code section 1364* reasonably can be construed to mandate any particular mode of termite treatment.

Still less do the governing provisions require that the Association render the Development constantly or absolutely termite-free. Plainly, we must reject any per se rule "requiring a condominium association and its individual members to indemnify any individual

---

10. In this connection we note that, insofar as the record discloses, plaintiff is the only condominium owner who has challenged the Association's decision not to fumigate her building. To permit one owner to impose her will on all others and in contravention of the governing board's good faith decision would turn the principle of benefit to "'the commonality but harm [to] the individual'" (*Nahrstedt ...*) on its head.

homeowner for any reduction in value to an individual unit caused by damage.... Under this theory the association and individual members would not only have the duty to repair as required by the CC&Rs, but the responsibility to reimburse an individual homeowner for the diminution in value of such unit regardless if the repairs had been made or the success of such repairs." (*Kaye v. Mount La Jolla Homeowners Assn. (1988) 204 Cal. App. 3d 1476, 1487* ... [disapproving cause of action for lateral and subjacent support based on association's failure, despite efforts, to remedy subsidence problem].)

The formulation we have articulated affords homeowners, community associations, courts and advocates a clear standard for judicial review of discretionary economic decisions by community association boards, mandating a degree of deference to the latter's business judgments sufficient to discourage meritless litigation, yet at the same time without either eviscerating the long-established duty to guard against unreasonable risks to residents' personal safety owed by associations that "function as a landlord in maintaining the common areas" (*Frances T.*) or modifying the enforceability of a common interest development's CC&R's....

Common sense suggests that judicial deference in such cases as this is appropriate, in view of the relative competence, over that of courts, possessed by owners and directors of common interest developments to make the detailed and peculiar economic decisions necessary in the maintenance of those developments. A deferential standard will, by minimizing the likelihood of unproductive litigation over their governing associations' discretionary economic decisions, foster stability, certainty and predictability in the governance and management of common interest developments. Beneficial corollaries include enhancement of the incentives for essential voluntary owner participation in common interest development governance and conservation of scarce judicial resources.

DISPOSITION

... [T]he judgment of the Court of Appeal is reversed.

Notes & Questions

1. In what types of cases will the California Court apply its deferential standard? Is it willing to give substantive review to a wider range of cases than the New York Court?

2. Note how both parties in *Lamden* argued that their positions furthered stability and predictability in the life of community residents, arguments based on *Nahrstedt*. Which one was right? How important are stability and predictability and what are their costs?

3. The court in *Lamden* said that its decision is compatible with the decisions in *Cohen v. Kite Hill Community Ass'n* and *Laguna Royale Owners Ass'n v. Darger*, which are both reproduced in the next section. After you have read those cases, consider the range of situations in which the Lamden rule will properly be applied.

Schwarzmann v. Ass'n of Apartment Owners of Bridgehaven

Court of Appeals of Washington
655 P.2d 1177 (Wash. Ct. App. 1982)

DURHAM J. Robert and Eleonore Schwarzmann appeal an order granting defendants' motion for partial summary judgment and dismissal of claims, and denying the Schwarzmanns' motion for reconsideration. This case addresses the individual liability of members of the condominium board of directors for damages to the condominium unit of the Schwarzmanns, as well as for medical and emotional injuries allegedly incurred by them. Plaintiffs' claims against the condominium association remain unaffected by this decision.

In 1971, the Schwarzmanns purchased a unit in the Bridgehaven condominium in Seattle and have resided there since December of that year. Bridgehaven Association is an unincorporated association with a 7-member Board of Directors (Board). The Association and the Board are responsible for the maintenance and repair of common areas of the condominium. These common areas include portions of the building outside the interior surfaces of the perimeter walls, floors, ceilings, windows and doors of the individual apartment units. Roof and attic areas above the individual units are part of the common areas.

In November 1978, spots appeared in the Schwarzmanns' ceiling. They reported this at the December 6, 1978 board meeting. Several days later, the Board sent building chairman Nick Buono to look at the spots. At that time, the Schwarzmanns noticed additional spots on their ceiling.

On December 31, 1978, water leaked from the Schwarzmanns' ceiling onto their furniture and carpet. In response to this, the Board had a representative of Evergreen Roofing Company inspect the problem on January 2 and January 5, 1979. Evergreen, which had re-roofed all the Bridgehaven buildings the previous fall, determined that the Schwarzmanns' problem was caused by condensation occurring in the attic area over the Schwarzmanns' unit.

The Schwarzmanns presented their problem at the annual meeting of the Association on January 8, 1979. The condominium owners instructed the Board to hold an emergency meeting to consider the situation. Three days later, Buono arrived at the Schwarzmanns' unit with a representative from the Cooper Mechanical Company. He concluded that the water problem was not caused by the heating system, the air cleaner, or any condensation from inside the unit.

The Schwarzmanns then hired Northwest Inspection Engineers. An inspector traced the source of the water problem to generally improper ventilation in the attic space over the Schwarzmanns' unit. A copy of his report was sent to the Board on January 17, 1979.

Unsatisfied with lack of action by the Board, the Schwarzmanns had their attorney send a demand letter to the Association on January 31, 1979. On February 14, 1979, Board president McKinstry sent a letter to the Schwarzmanns stating that the Board would not accept responsibility for the water problem, for the following reasons:

> The roof does not leak.
>
> There is ample ventilation in the "attic" areas above the bedrooms, utility room and kitchen.
>
> The venting has functioned well for over seven years.
>
> All cathedral ceilinged units at Bridgehaven have the same type of insulation.
>
> No other similar unit at Bridgehaven has suffered any appreciable damage.
>
> No other owner has the type of heat you have installed.

Furthermore, the Board believed that the Schwarzmanns' problem was caused by the condensation of moist air compounded by unusually cold weather.

On March 5, 1979, the Schwarzmanns distributed a letter to Bridgehaven residents seeking their aid in obtaining corrective action by the Board. Pursuant to a special meeting, on March 19, 1979 the Board sent a ventilation installer and three residents to further inspect and evaluate the water problem. The installer reported that the toilet and exhaust systems had been installed correctly and that "[i]f there is a problem of sweating or moisture it must be caused by something other than the existing exhaust systems".

The Schwarzmanns' attorney sent a second demand letter to the Board on March 30, 1979, requesting corrective action within 30 days. The Schwarzmanns apparently did not receive a satisfactory response, and brought this action in June 1979. They sought damages for the diminished use of their unit, the interference caused to their daily lives, and the pain, suffering, medical fees, and costs which were exacerbated by the above. The Schwarzmanns also sought a variety of equitable relief.

The trial court dismissed the Schwarzmanns' claims as to all individual defendants and granted summary judgment of dismissal against the Schwarzmanns' claims for emotional and medical damages.

The Schwarzmanns first claim that the trial court erred by granting summary judgment of dismissal to all the individually named defendants. The issue of personal liability of a member of a condominium board of directors is one of first impression in this state.

Although there is no case law directly on point, RCW 64.32.240 and the corporate "business judgment rule" are closely related. RCW 64.32.240 is part of the Horizontal Property Regimes Act, RCW 64.32, and states, in pertinent part:

> Actions relating to the common areas and facilities for damages arising out of tortious conduct shall be maintained only against the association of apartment owners and any judgment lien or other charge resulting therefrom shall be deemed a common expense, which judgment lien or other charge shall be removed from any apartment and its percentage of undivided interest in the common areas and facilities upon payment by the respective owner of his proportionate share thereof based on the percentage of undivided interest owned by such apartment owner.

The Schwarzmanns assert that this provision was enacted to alleviate difficulties faced by plaintiffs who might want to sue unincorporated associations of condominium owners. They argue that such potential plaintiffs would face procedural problems initiating a suit; *i.e.*, they would have to sue every member of a condominium development individually. Therefore, the Schwarzmanns contend, the Legislature included RCW 64.32.240 simply to facilitate lawsuits against condominium associations, rather than to bar actions by individual condominium owners against individual board members.

No legislative history or case was suggested or independently found which supports this statutory interpretation. Absent a showing that a literal reading of a statute is obviously contrary to legislative intent, the language of a statute should be followed. *Hatfield v. Greco*, 87 Wn.2d 780, 557 P.2d 340 (1976). Additionally, words in common usage should be given their plain and ordinary meaning. *Washington ex rel. Edwards v. Heimann*, 633 F.2d 886, 891 (9th Cir. 1980). RCW 64.32.240 mandates that "[a]ctions relating to the common areas and facilities for damages arising out of tortious conduct shall be maintained *only* against the association of apartment owners". (Italics ours.) Nothing in this statute suggests that tort actions may also be brought against individual association members.

Irrespective of our reading of RCW 64.32.240, the Board members' actions nonetheless fell within the parameters of the "business judgment rule." In *Nursing Home Bldg. Corp. v. DeHart*, 13 Wn. App. 489, 498–99, 535 P.2d 137 (1975), we explained that:

> Courts are reluctant to interfere with the internal management of corporations and generally refuse to substitute their judgment for that of the directors. *See Sanders v. E-Z*

Park, Inc., 57 Wn.2d 474, 358 P.2d 138 (1960). The "business judgment rule" immunizes management from liability in a corporate transaction undertaken within both the power of the corporation and the authority of management where there is a reasonable basis to indicate that the transaction was made in good faith. An excellent statement of the "business judgment rule" is found in W. Fletcher § 1039 at pages 621–25:

> It is too well settled to admit of controversy that ordinarily neither the directors nor the other officers of a corporation are liable for mere mistake or errors of judgment, either of law or fact. In other words, directors of a commercial corporation may take chances, the same kind of chances that a man would take in his own business. Because they are given this wide latitude, the law will not hold directors liable for honest errors, for mistakes of judgment, when they act without corrupt motive and in good faith, that is, for mistakes which may properly be classified under the head of honest mistakes. And that is true even though the errors may be so gross that they may demonstrate the unfitness of the directors to manage the corporate affairs. This rule is commonly referred to as the "business judgment rule." (Footnotes omitted.) See also H. Henn, Law of Corporations § 242 (1970).

While *DeHart* did not involve a condominium board of directors, these same principles have been applied to the governing bodies of condominiums elsewhere. *See Rywalt v. Writer Corp.*, 34 Colo. App. 334, 526 P.2d 316 (1974); *Papalexiou v. Tower W. Condo.*, 167 N.J. Super. 516, 401 A.2d 280 (1979); *see also* Comment, *Judicial Review of Condominium Rulemaking*, 94 Harv. L. Rev. 647, 663–66 (1981).

Like their corporate counterparts, condominium directors have a fiduciary responsibility to exercise ordinary care in performing their duties and are required to act reasonably and in good faith. *Papalexiou*, 401 A.2d at 286. The trial court found no evidence of bad faith or improper motive which would demonstrate that the board members breached a duty owed to the plaintiffs. Nor do we find any such evidence. Absent a showing of fraud, dishonesty, or incompetence, it is not the court's job to second-guess the actions of directors. *Papalexiou v. Tower West Condo., supra.*

Plaintiffs also urge this court to "pierce the corporate veil" of the condominium association, in order to find the board members individually liable. This is only appropriate where an officer or director commits or condones a wrongful act in the course of carrying out his duties, *see Johnson v. Harrigan-Peach Land Dev. Co.*, 79 Wn.2d 745, 489 P.2d 923 (1971); *see also State v. Ralph Williams' N.W. Chrysler Plymouth, Inc.*, 87 Wn.2d 298, 322, 553 P.2d 423 (1976), dismissed, 430 U.S. 952, 51 L. Ed. 2d 801, 97 S. Ct. 1594 (1977), and a lack of good faith can be shown. *See Olympic Fish Prods., Inc. v. Lloyd*, 93 Wn.2d 596, 599, 611 P.2d 737 (1980); *see generally* Harris, *Washington's Doctrine of Corporate Disregard*, 56 Wash. L. Rev. 253 (1981). Once again, there is a lack of substantial evidence that any of the individually named defendants acted in bad faith, or somehow knowingly participated in or condoned wrongful or negligent conduct.

The Schwarzmanns next assign error to the dismissal of their claim for emotional distress damages.

...

Our review of the record on appeal reveals no evidence of ill motive or recklessness on the part of the Board. The Board merely exercised its discretion, as duly elected administrators of the condominium. A party is not liable for damages for emotional distress when it had a legal right to act as it did. *Bowe v. Eaton*, 17 Wn. App. 840, 843–44, 565 P.2d 826 (1977).

As for plaintiffs' claim of negligent infliction of emotional distress, this case is clearly not within the guidelines of the leading Washington cases.

…

A summary judgment should be upheld only if there are no genuine issues of material fact and if the prevailing parties are entitled to judgment as a matter of law. *Teagle v. Fischer & Porter Co.*, 89 Wn.2d 149, 152, 570 P.2d 438 (1977). The trial court's oral decision indicates that it gave thorough consideration to all facts which might favor plaintiffs' position and found there to be no genuine issues of material fact. We agree. The trial court's use of summary judgment was appropriate in this case.

We Affirm.

———————

Retrospective and Observations

The Schwarzmanns' Perspective

Carolyn Hayek represented the Schwarzmanns in this case which had a "really bad outcome." According to Ms. Hayek, the Schwarzmanns were conscientious unit owners who followed all the rules promulgated by the board. They only sued the board when leaks in their unit became a threat to their furniture and their lifestyle.

The Schwarzmanns had a "water problem" in their condominium unit, and they did not know the source of that water. In Ms. Hayek's view, the association was very amateurish and seemed to be dominated by certain personalities, one of which was "an old codger who thinks he knows everything." The rest of the board relied on this man's opinion regarding the cause of the problem and its solution. That particular board member seemed to have a personality conflict with the Schwarzmanns and tried everything he could to deny their right to a solution to the water problem. The association claimed that the Schwarzmanns were to blame for the problem because they used their dryer too much.

At the point when Ms. Hayek became involved, she tried to educate the board, but that seemed to make them more combative. The board's insurance company then got involved. The insurance company's attorney did understand that the association was responsible for fixing problems to the common elements. The association hired an expert who cut a hole in the ceiling of the Schwarzmanns' unit to analyze the problem. The report indicated that the cause of the leak was poor building design along with a ventilation problem. All the dryers in that building in the condominium (which Ms. Hayek thinks housed six units) were vented to the attic above the Schwarzmanns' unit on the third floor. On cold days, condensation ran through the ceiling of the Schwarzmanns' unit.

Prior to the trial, the association did solve the ventilation problem, but the Schwarzmanns felt that they were entitled to compensation for the damages to their unit as well as to emotional and medical distress. For several months, they had been unable to entertain or have family gatherings in their unit, they had a hole in their ceiling, and Ms. Schwarzmann had to obtain medical attention because she was being ostracized by other tenant owners. At trial, the judge was "cozy" with the insurance company's attorney and treated the Schwarzmanns and their counsel as if they were silly. Although Ms. Hayek was prepared to try the case on the facts, once the trial began, the judge immediately granted summary judg-

Croton River Club, courtesy of David Cohen.

ment to the association. Ms. Hayek said the motion for summary judgment came out of nowhere. The trial court never heard the facts in the case and never allowed testimony by any of Hayek's witnesses.

Interestingly, Ms. Hayek became a judge herself although she has now resigned from the bench. During the time she was a judge, many people advised her to make each side feel that it had been heard and that the judgment was fair no matter what the outcome.

In Re Croton River Club, Inc.

U.S. Court of Appeals, Second Circuit
52 F.3d 41 (2d Cir. 1995)

WINTER, C.J. Defendants appeal from Judge Goettel's affirmance of two decisions by Bankruptcy Judge Schwartzberg. The first decision granted partial summary judgment to plaintiff-appellee on the ground that the allocation of a portion of the budget of a homeowners' association to a marina was not protected by the business judgment rule. The second decision was entered after an evidentiary hearing and concluded that the allocation was unreasonable. The bankruptcy court then substituted a different allocation. We affirm, although we hold that the decision barring any change in the new allocation is no longer in force because the marina has been sold.

BACKGROUND

Croton River Club, Inc. ("Croton") sponsored and developed a planned community named Half Moon Bay on the banks of the Hudson River. Croton planned to build 326 residential units within 13 buildings. The development's amenities were to include tennis courts, a restaurant, a public park, automobile parking, a swimming pool, a community building, a lagoon, and a marina with 300 boat slips. Croton intended to construct an infrastructure including an access road with a bridge across the nearby Metro North railroad tracks, street lighting, a sewage pumping station, landscaping, a garbage processing center, a riverfront promenade, and a sound barrier along the Metro North tracks. The Half Moon Bay Homeowners Association, Inc. (the "Homeowners Association") is a New York non-profit corporation that oversees the common elements of the Half Moon Bay development.

On February 14, 1991, Croton filed for bankruptcy under Chapter 11 of the Bankruptcy Code, 11 U.S.C. §§ 1101 *et seq.*, when construction of Half Moon Bay was still incomplete. Most of the infrastructure was in place, but only 120 residential units and 162 marina slips had been constructed. Croton had sold 71 of the residential units and the remaining 49 were still not entirely complete.

At issue in the present matter is the allocation of the project's budget to the marina. At various stages of the development of Half Moon Bay, the sponsor—Croton—set an allocation for the marina of 14.25% of designated line items that reflected services used by both the marina and the residential units.

In December 1990, a group of residential unit owners from the Half Moon Bay development (hereafter "homeowners") initiated a derivative action against Croton and others seeking declaratory and injunctive relief and $6 million in damages. The derivative action alleged a failure by Croton to fulfill the offering plan and a breach of fiduciary duty by the Board of Directors of the Homeowners Association.

In July 1991, Croton entered into a stipulation and settlement agreement (the "Settlement") with HMB Acquisition Corp. and the homeowners. The HMB Acquisition Corp. wanted to purchase several of the assets connected to the Half Moon Bay site, but the settlement of all disputes between Croton and the homeowners was a condition for closing the sale.

The Settlement thus provided that:

> the budgets set by the [Half Moon Bay Homeowners Association, Inc.], and the allocations under the control of the [Half Moon Bay Homeowners Association, Inc.] (including the allocation of expenses to the Marina parcel), shall be finally decided by a vote of the homeowner-in-residence members of the [Half Moon Bay Homeowners Association, Inc.] Board.

The Settlement also restricted use of the Half Moon Bay site by owners of marina slips. Subsequent to the Settlement, Croton sold the residential units and the partially developed land to HMB Acquisition Corp. This sale included neither the marina nor the parcel of land intended for the restaurant.

In December 1991, the Homeowners Association Board of Directors set allocations for the 1992 budget. As indicated in the portion of the Settlement quoted above, only the Board members who owned residential units were entitled to vote on the budget. The allocation to be paid by the owners of marina slips (the "Marina Allocation") was set at approximately $160,000, or 53% of an expanded list of line items. The Marina Allocation was a three-fold percentage increase in the amount of the allocation from previous years and over an eight-fold increase in the dollar amount of the allocation initially recommended by the managing agent for the Homeowners Association.

On May 21, 1992, Croton commenced an adversary proceeding on behalf of itself and all others similarly situated to invalidate the Marina Allocation. The bankruptcy judge held that the business judgment rule did not protect the Marina Allocation and ruled, after two days of evidentiary hearings, that the marina slip owners should pay an allocation based on a 14.25% multiplier (as they had in previous years) applied to an independently arrived at list of line items that, in the court's view, represented shared expenses. Appellants appealed to the district court claiming that the bankruptcy court: (i) should have applied the business judgment rule to the allocation and (ii) erred in creating and enforcing its own allocation of expenses common to the marina slip owners and the residential unit owners. The district court upheld the bankruptcy court, although the district court held that the bankruptcy court had not created its own allocation but had "simply struck down the 53% allocation which automatically reinstated the 14.25% figure." Therefore, the district court believed that it "need not reach whether or not Judge Schwartzberg would have had the power to set a new allocation had there been sufficient evidence on the record."

Appellants brought the present appeal. At oral argument, it was disclosed that the marina has been sold.

DISCUSSION

The first issue is whether the business judgment rule protects the Marina Allocation determined by the Board of the Homeowners Association. In *Levandusky v. One Fifth Avenue Apartment Corp.*, 75 N.Y.2d 530, 554 N.Y.S.2d 807, 553 N.E.2d 1317 (1990), the New York Court of Appeals held that the business judgment rule informs the standard of review for the actions of cooperative and condominium governing boards. The business judgment rule, as developed in the commercial context, precludes judicial inquiry into the actions of corporate directors so long as those actions were taken in good faith and after a reasonable investigation. *See id.* 554 N.Y.S.2d at 811, 553 N.E.2d at 1321–22.

It is black-letter, settled law that when a corporate director or officer has an interest in a decision, the business judgment rule does not apply. *See, e.g., Alpert v. 28 Williams St. Corp.*, 63 N.Y.2d 557, 483 N.Y.S.2d 667, 674–75, 473 N.E.2d 19, 26 (1984) (when merger creates inherent conflict of interest, burden to prove good faith and fairness of merger shifts to interested directors); *Lewis v. S.L.&E., Inc.*, 629 F.2d 764, 769 (2d Cir. 1980). In commercial matters, moreover, if the business judgment rule does not protect a board's decision, then the burden falls upon the board to demonstrate that its actions were reasonable and/or fair. *See, e.g., Alpert v. 28 Williams St. Corp.*, 483 N.Y.S.2d at 674–75, 473 N.E.2d at 26.

The bankruptcy court apparently relied upon this body of law in determining that the business judgment rule did not apply and in applying a reasonableness test. See *Ludwig v. 25 Plaza Tenants Corp.*, 184 A.D.2d 623, 584 N.Y.S.2d 907, 908 (1992). We are less certain that *Levandusky* adopts in wholesale fashion the rule that the protection of the business judgment rule is not available for decisions rendered by condominium board members who are not disinterested. *Levandusky* emphasized that the business judgment rule was to be looked to for purposes of analogy only and that the rule would have to be adapted in light of the somewhat different context of boards of not-for-profit cooperative condominiums. *Levandusky,* 554 N.Y.S.2d at 811–12, 553 N.E.2d at 1321–22. It is the case with regard to such boards that members will be condominium owners and will rarely be wholly disinterested. Arguably, therefore, one possible adaptation of the business judgment rule under *Levandusky* would be to discard the aspect of the rule that calls for independent judicial scrutiny of decisions by interested boards for reasonableness.

It can also be argued, however, that while the typical conflicts of interest that inhere in such boards will not be sufficient to deprive decisions of the business judgment rule's protection, some conflicts of interest may be so blatant and of such a magnitude that judicial scrutiny for reasonableness under *Levandusky* is called for. The conflict of interest in the instant matter is obvious and of great magnitude. The members of the board who voted for the Marina Allocation were all residential owners and were selected to represent the residential owners as a whole. Simple arithmetic demonstrates that the higher the

Marina Allocation, the smaller the contribution by residential owners. If 71 residential units have been sold, the approximately $140,000 added to the Marina Allocation would thus save each residential owner up to $2,000 dollars annually.[1] Moreover, vesting the residential owners with complete power over the budget allocation left them without any incentive for self-restraint based on the need to have the cooperation of marina owners in resolving future budgetary matters where there was no conflict. However, we need not resolve the issue of the extent to which board decisions must be disinterested because the Marina Allocation fails both the reasonableness and good faith tests.

The Homeowners Association failed to carry the burden of showing reasonableness. First, the Marina Allocation included a number of line items representing expenses that either did not benefit or only tangentially benefited the marina slipowners. For example, the salary of the manager of the residences was a line item included in the Marina Allocation. Marina slipowners were thus to pay over half of that salary even though the manager has no duties relating to the marina. In addition, expenses relating to the pool were also a line item even though marina slipowners cannot use the pool. Second, a 53% allocation for the marina is facially unreasonable because the different wear and tear on property resulting from year-long residential use is significantly greater than seasonal riverbank use.

As noted, moreover, the business judgment rule does not protect actions taken in bad faith, *see, e.g., Alpert v. 28 Williams St. Corp.*, 483 N.Y.S.2d at 674–75, 473 N.E.2d at 26, and we believe that the Marina Allocation is so unreasonable that bad faith must be inferred. The inclusion of line items that neither concern nor substantially benefit the marina and the failure to take the seasonal nature of marina use into account cannot be reconciled with a good faith requirement. The record strongly indicates that the dominating consideration in fashioning the Marina Allocation was the residential owners' desire to lessen their own costs and that the incantations of the business judgment rule are driven by the lack of a legitimate rationale for the Allocation.

. . .

Affirmed in part, Modified in part.

Retrospective and Observations

The Association's Perspective

This case is the evolution of one of 14 separate cases involving the Croton River Club which began on the trial court level. Steven Kershenbaum, the association's attorney, said that this was a very interesting decision and that the final results were different from what was indicated in the reported opinion.

Mr. Kershenbaum began working with community association developers in the '60s and has done so ever since. It was only at the persuasion of David Cohen that he agreed to represent "the people." Mr. Cohen is the owner of a prestigious, private publishing house named Oceana Publishing Company. His company publishes professional books and has several authors who are lawyers.

Mr. Cohen was sincerely devoted to saving the land in the project at Croton River Club, and he spent 20–30 hours each week for over four years trying to pre-

---

1. There may have been some overlap between residential and marina owners. However, in the case of overlap, the allocation would be irrelevant because the total payment of the individual owner would not be affected.

serve the site along the Hudson River. According to Mr. Kershenbaum, this case is the antithesis of what normally happens. Mr. Cohen was able to catalyze the owners into a cohesive group. When the developer realized it was facing a formidable group, it distributed information to the other homeowners that David Cohen was a bad guy and that he was selling them down the river.

Eventually, the developer filed a RICO suit against Mr. Cohen, 10 John Does, and Mr. Kershenbaum. The suit basically claimed that the defendants had conspired against the developer. After pleadings had been submitted to the court, the developer duplicated the entire set of pleadings and distributed copies to the residents. Although the federal judge warned the developer never to do that again, the experience severely eroded homeowner support. Mr. Kershenbaum was successful in getting the court to remove the RICO case.

After four years, Mr. Cohen grew tired of fighting, sold his unit, and moved. Today, there are some homeowners still trying to fight the current developer (there have been four). At one point, the homeowners successfully convinced the town not to renew the site plan on which the initial developer spent millions of dollars and much time. Originally, the site plan featured five separate condominium buildings. Only one has been built.

According to Mr. Kershenbaum, the homeowners' organization is losing its steam, and its successes are eroding.

The business judgment rule obviously permits, indeed requires, the exercise of judgment. Does it allow directors to decide not to do something? Would it not be an advantage if they had an express power to refrain from taking action? Much of the concern over some community association activities rests upon the fact that suits are brought to enforce rules, for example, that in particular circumstances perhaps should not be brought, as for example, when there is a technical violation that will have no real negative impact on the community. Or the utility of enforcement will be outweighed by the cost. Time, cost, utility, divisiveness, and other factors can make a strong case for there to be no action even though there is a technical violation. Does the business judgment rule protect the board when it decides to refrain from acting?

In his major work on corporations, Fletcher states that the "control of litigation and the decision to litigate or not is in the directors, and until they improperly fail or refuse to sue or defend in the corporate name, the stockholder cannot do so." The critical word is "improperly." The directors may properly refuse. What are some of the reasons that might make such a decision proper?

Acknowledging these principles, however, does not diminish the justification for the board to have a more flexible approach to governance nor for the initial governing documents to create and to institutionalize rule making as a dynamic process rather than a static recitation of scores of prohibitions, many of which will never have relevance in a particular community.

What is needed is a legal framework within which a board and the association membership may operate to implement or manage existing covenants to permit the governance process to evolve with the needs and desires and changes within that community. Recognizing the difference between regulation and prohibition, an alternative approach involves creation of a more legitimate governance structure and contemplates that the governing documents will initially contain only the limited number of prohibitions and significant restrictions the developer believes to be vital to the overall development plan for the community. Coupled with these initial provisions would be a method to permit changes and modifications in restrictions and the adoption, modification, or abrogation of regulations to be made in the "legislative process" of the community as time passes and circumstances change.

Notes & Questions

1. *Judicial review.* The business judgment rule does not establish a standard of conduct. Rather, it provides a threshold for judicial review.

> [T]he court will examine the decision only to the extent necessary to verify the presence of a business decision, disinterestedness and independence, due care, good faith, and the absence of an abuse of discretion. If these elements are present — and they are presumed to be present — and the case does not involve fraud, illegality, ultra vires conduct or waste, then the court will not second guess the merits of the decision.

Denis J. Block *et al., The Business Judgment Rule: Fiduciary Duties of Corporate Directors,* Ch. 2 sec. A 2. (4th ed. 1993 & Supp. 1995). See, *Aronson v. Lewis,* 473 A.2d 805 (Del. 1984); 1 ALI, Prin. Of Corp. Gov.: Analysis and Recommendation, §4.01(c) (1994); *Cuker v. Mikalauskas,* 692 A.2d 1042 (Penn. 1997). The court's inquiry is limited to whether the board acted within the scope of its authority under the by-laws and whether the action was taken in good faith to further a legitimate interest of the community association. Absent a showing of fraud, self-dealing or unconscionability, a court will not call into question the wisdom of the business decision. See *Schoninger v. Yardarm Beach Homeowners' Ass'n,* 134 A.D.2d 1, 523 N.Y.S.2d 523 (1987); *Rywalt v. Writer Corp.,* 34 Colo. App. 334, 526 P.2d 316 (1974). As one court put it:

> [A]s agents for the owners, they [the Board of Managers] cannot be held responsible to them [owners] except for willful conduct or bad faith. Only under such circumstances would unit owners be willing to assume responsibility without compensation in an effort to improve the lot of all unit owners. This type of gratuitous quasi-public service should be encouraged by exoneration from personal liability rather than be discouraged by imposition of personal and individual liability.

Kleinman v. High Point of Hartsdale I Condo., 438 N.Y.S. 2d 47 (1979).

2. *The fifth element.* Confusion with the reasonableness test stems from the fifth element of the business judgment rule — that the challenged activity not demonstrate an abuse of discretion. While superficially recognizing the discretion accorded to director's decisions, this element potentially opens the door to judicial scrutiny of the underlying merits of the challenged action. It also opens the door for confusion as courts weave the business judgment rule and the reasonableness test in many ways. See *Dulaney Towers Maintenance Corp. v. O'Brey,* 418 A.2d 1233 (Spec. App. Md. 1980), *Holleman v. Mission Trace Homeowner's Ass'n,* 556 S.W.2d 632 (Tex. Civ. App. 1977), and *Papalexiou v. Tower West Condo.,* 401 A.2d 280 (Sup. Ct. N.J. Ch. Div. 1979). Block *et al., supra,* at 38 n. 174, ("where a shareholder contends that the directors' judgment is so unwise or unreasonable as to fall outside the permissible bounds of the director's sound discretion, a court should ... be able to conduct its own analysis of the reasonableness of that business judgment.") See also *Cramer v General Tel. & Elecs. Corp.,* 582 F.2d 259, 275 (3d Cir. 1978), *cert. denied,* 439 U.S. 1129 (1979). This inquiry has been described as the "off-

the-wall" test, rejecting "egregious" decisions which "cannot be attributed to any rational business purpose." Block *et al.*, at 39 n. 174 (citing Arsht, *The Business Judgment Rule Revisited*, 8 Hofstra L. Rev. 93, 122 (1979). See also E. Veasey, *Duty of Loyalty: Criticality of the Counselor's Role*, 45 Bus. Law. 2065, 2071 (1990).

The Delaware Court of Chancery's 1989 decision in *In re RJR Nabisco Shareholders Litigation*, closed the door on the residual power of courts to review the merits of the underlying decision. The Chancery Court found that shareholders were protected by the good faith requirement of the business judgment rule from 'egregious' decisions. This court determined that it was inappropriate to open the door to search for bad faith where the elements of the business judgment rule have not been rebutted. Block *et al.*, at 39, [1988–89 Transfer Binder] Fed. Sec. L. Rep. (CCH) ¶94,194 (Del. Ch. Jan. 31, 1989), *appeal refused*, 556 A.2d 1070 (unpublished opinion, text available at 1989 Del. Lexis 42 and 1989 WL 16907) (Del. Feb. 2, 1989).

3. *Conflicts of interest.* Since the board members/directors are also home or condominium unit owners, there is added difficulty over just what will constitute a conflict that will trigger judicial review.

4. *Tyranny of the minority.* Seemingly, broad judicial review provides for a "checks and balances" approach to association governance. However, limiting judicial review preserves the value of centralized decision-making and protects unit owners against unwarranted interference from one of their number. The business judgment rule not only protects directors from unit owners, but also serves the more important function of protecting the unit owners from each other. Block *et al.*, at 11 (citing Dooley & Veasey, *The Role of the Board in Derivative Litigation: Delaware Law and the Current ALI Proposals Compared*, 44 Bus. Law. 503, 522 (1989), quoted in *Waltuch v. Conticommodity Servs., Inc.*, 833 F. Supp. 302, 306 (S.D.N.Y. 1993), and *Granada Invs., Inc. v. DWG Corp.*, 823 F. Supp. 448, 455–6 (N.D. Ohio 1993)).

5. *Presumption or defense.* The business judgment rule is a presumption and not merely a defense to a breach of fiduciary duty claim against a director. Michael Bradley and Cindy A. Schipani, *The Relevance of the Duty of Care Std. In Corporate Governance*, 75 Iowa L. Rev. 1, 23 (1989). At least 21 states follow the presumption rationale. See Block *et al.*, at 12. Flowing from the presumption, the burden of demonstrating a board's lack of good faith, by a preponderance of the evidence, falls upon the challenger of the board action. The shareholder bears a heavy burden to overcome the presumption. Block *et al.*, at 14 n. 74. In fact, shareholders must make allegations and proffers of fact giving rise to the possibility that the business judgment rule will not apply in order to obtain discovery. A shareholder challenge may not amount to a fishing expedition in the absence of tenable proffers. *Id.* at 15 n. 76, (citing *Washington Bancorp. v. Said*, 812 F. Supp. 1256, 127 n. 51 (D.D.C. 1993)).

6. *Fairness test.* If facts sufficient to overcome the presumption of the business judgment rule are established, the business judgment rule has no application. Instead, the court will scrutinize the challenged activity under the fairness doctrine. Block *et al* at 15 n. 77. Application of the fairness doctrine is not necessarily outcome determinative. Block *et al.* at 16. The burden of proof is shifted to the board to establish that the challenged transaction was entirely fair to the association. See Craig W. Palm & Mark A. Kearney, *A Primer on the Basics of Director's Duties in Delaware: The Rules of the Game (Part I)*, 40 Vill. L. Rev., 1297, 1317 (1995).

7. *Duty of care.* The duty of care in the corporations context should not be confused with the duty of care in the tort situations. In tort, the duty establishes an objective stan-

dard measuring the reasonableness of a decision or course of action. In contrast, the duty of care for corporations focuses on whether a director took the proper steps to render an informed decision. Whether the decision, in and of itself, is ultimately reasonable is not the focus of this inquiry. *Fletcher* at § 1032. The most common standard imposed by statute or through common law is the ordinary prudent person standard. States that follow the Model Business Corporations Act typically require the director to act in good faith and in the best interests of the corporation by exercising the care of an ordinarily prudent person under like circumstances. Other states impose a similar duty, in the absence of parallel statutory language, through case law. *Fletcher* at 1032, Model Bus. Corp. Act, § 35, Model Bus. Corp. Act (1984) § 8.30(A) and *Daniels v. Berry,* 148 S.C. 446, 146 S.E. 420 (1929).

8. *Duty of loyalty.* What does the duty of loyalty mean in a community association? Could a director claim that she is protected by the business judgment rule when she has acted in self-interest yet still acted as she honestly believed to be in the best interest of the community association? Is there a situation in which the common interest community director does not have an interest in the outcome of the decision? Expectations of members of the association are, of course, very important in evaluating actions. Do not these expectations include—indeed mandate—that the directors will have a degree of "self interest" in every board decision? Possible conflicts of interest are equally, and possibly more, likely for directors appointed by the developer. When should such conflicts provide the basis for judicial review of board decisions?

9. *Limited liability.* Liability stemming from a breach of the duty of care has been limited by statutes. Some statutes eliminate director liability for breaches of the duty of care altogether, while preserving liability for breaches of the duty of loyalty. Some extend the protection to breaches of the duty of loyalty. Some provide protection to officers as well as directors. Still others approach director liability from the opposite extreme, prohibiting the elimination of liability for recklessness or abdication of the director's responsibilities. Virginia has dropped the "ordinarily prudent person" language altogether, requiring only the exercise of good faith judgment in the best interests of the corporation. *Fletcher Cyclopedia of Corporations,* Vol. 3A Ch.11 § 1034 (Perm. Ed.) (citing state statutes); Va. Code Ann. 12.1-690(A). Even though individual directors are exculpated by statute, however, the action taken by the board may be overturned by a court.

b. The Reasonableness Standard

The business judgment rule is most traditionally seen in cases arising from the board's exercise of its <u>business responsibilities</u>. The rule of <u>reasonableness</u> conversely is most frequently seen in cases generally characterized as part of the "<u>governmental</u>" powers of the community association. In this section, we examine the rule of reasonableness, and as we do so, we further explore the association's governmental powers and how those powers are exercised within the context of association governance.

Courts generally follow one of three approaches in testing the propriety of board actions: the <u>business judgment rule</u>, <u>equitable reasonableness</u>, and what some have called "<u>constitutional reasonableness</u>." The discussion of the rule or rules for evaluating board action, therefore, is not one just concerning <u>business judgment</u> versus <u>reasonableness</u> but one also of how to define and to apply the reasonableness rule.

The debate over the rule turns in large part on how one views the common interest community itself. To satisfy constitutional requirements, <u>municipalities must only show that</u>

their actions bear a rational relationship to a legitimate state interest. A private common interest community, under the reasonableness rule, must do more. Some scholars and practitioners ask why, insisting that the common interest community is a private organization comprised of property owners who have voluntarily bought into the community and its association. They argue that courts should not second-guess the community's board's decisions.

Others question the basic premise that the purchase in a common interest community is voluntary. These scholars insist that there is an element of coercion inherent in the purchase because the common interest community is the best available housing choice and the buyer must take the governance in order to obtain the housing product and all of the attributes that come with it. Therefore, they insist, the individual should be freed from the restrictions, or the courts should exercise review at a level equivalent to substantive due process, and put the burden on the community association to justify its actions. This is "constitutional reasonableness." Note that "constitutional reasonableness" is a higher standard than a city must meet.

Do the facts support these assertions? Is there not a "coercive" element in every home purchase, whether it is location or school district, or something that leads the purchaser to select the house despite a higher price or other features the buyer does not necessarily want? More importantly, consider the effects of the more extreme interpretation of the reasonableness rule and how it should be applied. First, it shifts the burden of proof from the person attacking the action to the board. This requires that the board prove to the court that its actions were reasonable. Second, the result is that in many cases the court makes the decision, substituting its judgment for that of the common interest community's governing board.

Are there situations in which the more stringent "constitutional reasonableness" is appropriate and those in which it is not? What if the community association seeks to regulate actions on the common property or the exterior of units in one situation and seeks to proscribe conduct in the unit itself in another? Might there be justification for a more rigorous review in one case than the other?

Purchasers' expectations are very important in evaluating actions. How does that consideration fit into this discussion? For example, if the CCRs or a properly adopted board resolution says no pets are allowed, is it appropriate for one owner's desire to have a pet be placed above the interests of the other owners? Is a standard of review fair if it allows the court to substitute its judgment for that of the community's board as to the appropriateness of an action? ?

Many of these cases questioning the validity of restrictions or board actions involve very emotional issues: pets, the American flag, artistic expression, etc. Others involve interpersonal disputes among or between neighbors in which there may be no "right" answer, just one that reflects one point of view or another. In these cases, is court intervention wise or should the community be left to resolve the disputes through its governance processes?

The rule of reasonableness can be seen as the analog of due process in the private setting with both substantive and procedural aspects. Substantively, the question is whether the action is within the board's authority and whether it bears a rational relationship to the association's purposes.

Procedural reasonableness looks to notice and whether or not the board followed the prescribed procedures in making its decisions. Keep in mind that there are differences between due process as you have studied it in constitutional, municipal, or other areas of the law applicable to municipal corporations and that applicable in the private setting. It is the internal "constitution" of the common interest community which sets the standards, unless the standards set by the governing documents themselves violate procedural fairness norms.

Reasonableness and the role of the court may vary depending on context. For example, a board's decision interpreting a provision in declaration might be treated differently from <u>a decision to enforce that provision</u>. The deference given to the board's interpretation of a provision in the governing documents might well differ from the deference given to a decision as to whether or how to implement that decision.

As you study the cases in this section, consider how they might have been decided <u>under the business judgment rule</u>. Reflect upon the role of the concept of reasonableness in the application of the business judgment rule itself. If properly applied does that rule accomplish the same objectives and protect the same interests as the rule of reasonableness or does reasonableness provide needed protection to homeowners? Also, be sure to note the context in which the question arises — the business judgment rule may be better suited to resolve some cases, the reasonableness rule may be better suited to others. Finally, consider whether Restatement § 6.13 provides a better solution.

Cohen v. Kite Hill Community Ass'n

Court of Appeals of California
191 Cal. Rptr. 209 (Cal. Ct. App. 1983)

McDANIEL, J. This is an appeal from a judgment of dismissal entered after an order sustaining the demurrer of defendant, Kite Hill Community Association (the Association), to the plaintiffs' fourth amended complaint. Because we conclude that the plaintiffs finally succeeded in pleading a cause of action, we shall reverse the judgment.

FACTS[1]

As reflected by the allegations of plaintiffs' complaint, Kite Hill is a residential community located in the rolling hills of Southern Orange County.

Plaintiffs, Mr. and Mrs. Cohen, purchased a lot in Kite Hill which afforded a panoramic view of the surrounding countryside. They paid a premium for this view.

The Association, a nonprofit corporation duly organized and existing under the laws of California, is composed of all of the homeowners in Kite Hill. It was organized by the developer, S & S Construction Company, for the purpose of administering and enforcing the Declaration of Covenants, Conditions and Restrictions (the Declaration) which was recorded as to the entire tract and incorporated by reference into the respective deeds by which all Kite Hill residents acquired their homes in this tract. The Declaration was also attached as an exhibit to the complaint.

Every owner of a lot in Kite Hill is automatically a member of the Association and subject to payment of regular and special assessments to the Association for the purpose of carrying out its community functions.

Shortly after the Cohens purchased their home, they submitted to the Association's Architectural Committee (the Committee) plans for certain improvements and land-

---

1. On appeal, we deem the Association's demurrer to have admitted all well-pleaded material facts. (Thompson v. County of Alameda, 27 Cal.3d 741, 746, 167 Cal.Rptr. 70, 614 P.2d 728).

scaping in their front and rear yards. The Declaration requires that such plans be submitted to the Committee in writing and be approved before any construction can begin.

One part of the plan approved by the Committee was a slump stone and wrought iron fence (a two foot slump stone base topped by a three foot iron fence). This is the type of fence designated by the Declaration for use in a lot such as the Cohens'; *i.e.*, a side yard with a view.

Shortly thereafter, plaintiffs' neighbors, the Ehles, received approval from the Committee to construct a solid slump stone fence immediately adjacent to the Cohens' slump stone and wrought iron fence. The Ehles' is the type of fence designated in the Declaration for a side yard *without* a view.

Plaintiffs objected to the installation of the nonconforming fence because they believed that it would materially obstruct their view. However, their efforts to persuade the Ehles and the Association to modify or prevent the construction were unsuccessful.

The Cohens then initiated this lawsuit against the Ehles and the Association, and contemporaneously sought a temporary restraining order to prevent the Ehles from completing construction of the fence. Although the attorneys for plaintiffs and the Ehles stipulated to the issuance of a temporary restraining order pending a hearing, the fence was substantially completed by the time the hearing occurred. The trial court denied the temporary restraining order, and the plaintiffs withdrew their application for a preliminary injunction.[2]

Plaintiffs' complaint[3] alleged that the Association and its Architectural Committee, in approving the Ehles' construction plans, had: (1) breached the covenants contained in the Declaration; (2) breached their fiduciary duty owed to plaintiffs; (3) breached their duty of good faith and fair dealing; (4) been negligent; and (5) committed "willful misconduct or other intentional conduct."

In the key charging allegations, the complaint alleged that the "solid wall of slump block as approved by the Association and installed by Defendants Ehle is not a permitted fence under Exhibit 'C' of the Kite Hill Restrictions ..."; that the "approval by the Architectural Committee of the Architectural [sic] plans of Defendants Ehle ... is in violation of the mandates of the Kite Hill Restrictions and a clear abuse of their discretion"; that the Association acted "with full knowledge of their breach of the recorded Kite Hill Restrictions ... [and] ... in willful, conscious and reckless disregard for Plaintiffs' rights"; and, that "as a direct and proximate result of the Defendant's [sic] violation of the Kite Hill Restrictions the Plaintiffs have been damaged for the loss of use and enjoyment of their property and for diminution in the value of their property...."

Plaintiffs sought damages and a mandatory injunction to compel the Association to take certain steps to force the Ehles to comply with the architectural standards set forth in the Declaration.

The Association demurred to the plaintiffs' complaint on the ground that it failed to state a cause of action and that it was "uncertain and unintelligible." The trial court sustained the Association's demurrer to the complaint. After the judgment of dismissal, plaintiffs filed this appeal.

---

2. Plaintiffs also named as defendants their other neighbors, the Lees, for construction of certain improvements without the approval of the Committee, as well as S & S Construction Company.

3. Plaintiffs amended their complaint several times. The trial court sustained the Association's demurrer to their Fourth Amended Complaint.

DISCUSSION

A. The Association's Duties Under the Declaration

The fundamental question presented here is whether plaintiffs' complaint alleged facts sufficient to state a cause of action against the Association. More precisely, did the complaint allege facts sufficient to establish that the Association owed a duty to plaintiffs and that the former breached that duty, thereby entitling plaintiffs to some or all of the remedies sought? Such a determination must be based on the terms and conditions of the Declaration. We shall proceed, therefore, to an examination of the relevant provisions of this document before turning to the central question of duty.

...

Another important function of the Association is to preserve the aesthetic quality and property values within the community. To this end, the Declaration contains an elaborate and detailed list of restrictions on the types of construction, improvements, landscaping and general activities which individual homeowners may install and engage in on their individual properties.

Article VII of the Declaration is concerned specifically with "Architectural and Landscaping Control" and contains 11 sections. Section 1 in pertinent part provides:

> Architectural Approval. No fence, wall, building, sign or other structure (including basketball standards), or exterior addition to or change or alteration thereof (including painting) or landscaping, shall be commenced, constructed, erected, placed, altered, maintained or permitted to remain on the Project or any portion thereof, until plans and specifications shall have been submitted to and approved in writing by an architectural committee, initially to be appointed by the Declarant (the 'Architectural Committee') ... plans and specifications shall be submitted in writing over the signature of the Owner of the property or all such Owner's authorized agent. Approval shall be based, among other things, on adequacy of site dimensions; adequacy of structural design and material; conformity and harmony of external design with neighboring structures; effect of location and use of improvements and landscaping on neighboring property, improvements, landscaping, operations and uses; relation of topography, grade and finished ground elevation of the property being improved to that of neighboring property; proper facing of main elevations with respect to nearby streets; preservation of view and aesthetic beauty with respect to fences, walls and landscaping; ... and conformity of the plans and specifications to the purpose and general plan and intent of this Declaration. In any event, the Architectural Committee shall have the right, but not the obligation, to require any Member to remove, trim, top, or prune any shrub, tree, bush, plant or hedge which such Committee reasonably believes materially obstructs the view of any Lot.... (Emphasis added.)

With regard specifically to fences, Article VII, section 11 provides:

> In the event that any Owner of a Lot within the Project wishes to install a fence ('fence ') on his Lot in addition to complying with the other provisions of this Article, any such Owner shall also comply with the requirements of Exhibit 'C' attached hereto and incorporated herein by this reference, which Exhibit sets forth the specifications for any Fence. The location of any Fence shall be as determined by the Architectural Committee in its sole and absolute discretion; provided, however, that any Fence shall be located in such a fashion as to assure

adequate access to adjacent real property in order that said real property may be maintained. (Emphasis added.)

"Exhibit C" is a series of diagrams which both illustrate the type and dimensions of the fences which are approved for use in the Project, and indicate where each fence may properly be located. Thus, "Sheet 1" of Exhibit C (as amended) shows a solid slump block fence. The diagram specifies what type of block may be used, the dimensions of the blocks, and the maximum allowable height of the fence. This diagram is labeled "Slump Block Wall @ Sideyard Without View." "Sheet 2" illustrates a second fence, this one consisting of a two-foot slump block foundation topped by a three-foot wrought iron bar section, for a total maximum height of five feet. Sheet 2 is labeled, "Slump Block & Wrought Iron Wall @ Rear & Sideyard W/View."

As noted, the Declaration provides that all plans for any improvements must be submitted to the Architectural Committee. According to the Declaration, the Committee must consist of "not less than three nor more than five members." The Committee is empowered, "in its sole discretion," to amend the restrictions, or, "[w]here circumstances such as topography, location of property lines, location of trees, configuration of Lots, or other matters require, may ... [allow] reasonable variances ... provided ... that all such variances [are] in keeping with the general plan for the improvement and development of the Project."

The Association is charged, in the Declaration, with the broad affirmative duty of "administering and enforcing these covenants, conditions and restrictions." The Declaration vests the Association with the equivalent means of enforcing its obligations, as well. Thus, Article XVI, section 4, entitled "Enforcement," provides that the Association "shall have the right to enforce by proceedings at law or in equity all covenants, conditions, restrictions, easements, reservations, liens and charges now or hereafter imposed by the Declaration ... including, without limitation, the right to prosecute a proceeding at law or in equity against the person or persons who have violated or are attempting to violate any of these covenants, conditions, restrictions ... to enjoin or prevent them from doing so, to cause said violation to be remedied and/or to recover damages for said violation."

In addition to the affirmative duties recited above, the Declaration also contains several so-called "exculpatory" clauses. These clauses purport to absolve the Association from any affirmative duty to enforce any of the covenants, conditions and restrictions in the Declaration, and to immunize the Association from liability for any of its acts of malfeasance or nonfeasance. Thus, the concluding sentence of Article VII, Section 1 states: "The [Association] shall not be required to comply with any of the provisions of this Section 1." Section 4 of the same Article provides that the Association "shall (not) be liable in damages to anyone submitting plans or specifications to them for approval, or to any Owner of property affected by this Declaration by reason of mistake in judgment, negligence or nonfeasance arising out of or in connection with the approval or disapproval or failure to approve or disapprove any such plans or specifications, ..." Moreover, just in case any doubt remained as to the intent to establish the Association's immunity to suit, Article XVI, Section 12 provides: "To the fullest extent permitted by law, neither the Board, any committees of the Association nor any member shall be liable to any Member or Owner or the Association for any damage, loss or prejudice suffered or claimed on account of any decision, approval or disapproval of plans or specifications (whether or not defective), course of action, act, omission, error, negligence or the like made in good faith within which such Board, committee, or persons reasonably believed to be the scope of their duties."

Having set forth the relevant provisions in the Declaration, we now turn to the central legal issue, the nature and extent of the Association's duty to plaintiffs with reference to the codefendants' fence.

It is a settled rule of law that homeowners' associations must exercise their authority to approve or disapprove an individual homeowner's construction or improvement plans in conformity with the declaration of covenants and restrictions, and in good faith. (*Hannula v. Hacienda Homes,* 34 Cal.2d 442, 447, 211 P.2d 302; *Bramwell v. Kuhle,* 183 Cal.App.2d 767, 779, 6 Cal.Rptr. 839.) As the court in *Hannula* stated: "Each of the decisions enforcing like restrictions has held that the refusal to approve plans must be a reasonable determination made in good faith." (*Hannula v. Hacienda Homes, supra,* 34 Cal.2d 442, 447, 211 P.2d 302.) The same requirement of good faith applies equally to the approval of plans. "The converse should likewise be true, ...' [T]he power to approve plans ... must not be exercised capriciously or arbitrarily.'" (*Bramwell v. Kuhle, supra,* 183 Cal.App.2d 767, 779, 6 Cal.Rptr. 839; *see also Norris v. Phillips* (Colo.App.1981) 626 P.2d 717, 719.)

Furthermore, in recognition of the increasingly important role played by private homeowners' associations in such public-service functions as maintenance and repair of public areas and utilities, street and common area lighting, sanitation and the regulation and enforcement of zoning ordinances, the courts have recognized that such associations owe a fiduciary duty to their members. (*See Raven's Cove Townhomes, Inc. v. Knuppe Development Co.,* 114 Cal.App.3d 783, 799, 171 Cal.Rptr. 334.)

In a thoughtful article on *Concepts of Liability in the Development and Administration of Condominium and Home Owners Associations,* 12 Wake Forest Law Review at page 915, the authors note the increasingly "quasi-governmental" nature of the responsibilities of such associations:

> The other essential role directly relates to the association's regulatory powers; and upon analysis of the association's functions, one clearly sees the association as a quasi-government entity paralleling in almost every case the powers, duties, and responsibilities of a municipal government. As a 'mini-government,' the association provides to its members, in almost every case, utility services, road maintenance, street and common area lighting, and refuse removal. In many cases, it also provides security services and various forms of communication within the community. There is, moreover, a clear analogy to the municipal police and public safety functions. All of these functions are financed through assessments or taxes levied upon the members of the community, with powers vested in the board of directors, council of co-owners, board of managers, or other similar body clearly analogous to the governing body of a municipality. Terminology varies from region to region; however, the duties and responsibilities remain the same. (Id. at p. 918, fns. omitted.)

As reflected by the law review article noted, membership in an association is usually mandatory. Such is true here. And the powers of such associations are extensive.

> By his acceptance, the purchaser automatically becomes a member of the association created by the declaration and submits to the authority of the association and to the restrictions upon the use and enjoyment of the property contained in the declaration. Because each owner automatically becomes a member of the association upon taking title and because the association is empowered to levy and to collect assessments, to make and to enforce rules, and to permit or to deny certain uses of the property, the association has the power, and in many

cases the obligation, to exert tremendous influence on the bundle of rights normally enjoyed as a concomitant part of fee simple ownership of property. (Id. at p. 917.)

With power, of course, comes the potential for abuse. Therefore, the Association must be held to a high standard of responsibility: "The business and governmental aspects of the association and the association's relationship to its members clearly give rise to a special sense of responsibility upon the officers and directors.... This special responsibility is manifested in the requirements of fiduciary duties and the requirements of due process, equal protection, and fair dealing." (*Id.* at p. 921.) (*See Raven's Cove Townhomes, Inc. v. Knuppe Development Co., supra,* 114 Cal.App.3d 783, 792–799, 171 Cal.Rptr. 334.)

The Kite Hill Community Association's approval of a fence not in conformity with the Declaration is analogous to the administrative award of a zoning variance. In the zoning context as well as here, a departure from the master plan in the Declaration stands to affect most adversely those who hold rights in neighboring property. Hence, what the California Supreme Court has stated with regard to judicial review of grants of variances applies equally well to the Association's actions herein:

> [C]ourts must meaningfully review grants of variances in order to protect the interests of those who hold rights in property nearby the parcel for which a variance is sought. A zoning scheme, after all, is similar in some respects to a contract; each party foregoes rights to use its land as it wishes in return for the assurance that the use of neighboring property will be similarly restricted, the rationale being that such mutual restriction can enhance total community welfare. [Citations.] If the interest of these parties in preventing unjustified variance awards for neighboring land is not sufficiently protected, the consequence will be subversion of the critical reciprocity upon which zoning regulation rests. (*Topanga Ass'n. for a Scenic Community v. County of Los Angeles*, 11 Cal.3d 506, 517–518, 113 Cal.Rptr. 836, 522 P.2d 12.)

For nearly identical reasons, we conclude that the courts must be available to protect neighboring property interests from arbitrary actions by homeowner associations.

Thus, it follows that the trial court must review the Association's decision approving the Ehles' fence to insure that it was neither arbitrary nor in violation of the restrictions contained in the Declaration. (See cases cited in 40 A.L.R.3d 86.) Moreover, where the matter is up for review on appeal from a judgment of dismissal upon the sustaining of a demurrer, the standard of review is the same, *i.e.*, to test as a matter of law whether the action of the Association could have been arbitrary. In our view, the complaint has succeeded in pleading this possibility, and a trial is necessary to determine if the Association action was in fact arbitrary.

Turning to the next point, there is no merit in the Association's argument that its duty of good faith extended only to its members as a group and not to its members individually. The Declaration expressly provides that the Committee's approval of improvements "shall be based, among other things, on ... [the] effect of location and use of improvements and landscaping on *neighboring* property, improvements, landscaping, operations and uses;...." (Emphasis added.)

The Association advanced the proposition (during oral argument) that the Committee's approval of improvement plans could be "arbitrary" as to an individual homeowner, yet reasonable in light of the overriding interests of the community. Nonsense. Like any community, Kite Hill consists of individual members who form in the aggregate an organic whole. Thus, like any government, the Association must balance individual interests against the general welfare. No decision of the Committee could possibly be deemed "arbitrary" as to an individual homeowner if it were based upon a superseding duty to the community at large. The Association's duty of good faith subsumes an obligation to reconcile in a fair and equitable way the interests of the community with the interests of the individuals residing therein.

Nor is there merit in the argument that a homeowner aggrieved by a decision of the Association with regard to a neighbor's improvement should be limited to suit against that neighbor. As earlier noted, the covenants and restrictions create an affirmative duty on the part of the Association to protect individual homeowners affected by the improvement. More importantly, the Declaration clothes the Association with full authority to undertake all necessary legal actions to fulfill its protective duties.

Furthermore, it is apparent that but for the allegedly arbitrary approval by the Committee of the codefendants' fence, plaintiffs might never have been forced to pursue a legal remedy in the first place.

Moreover, in any action by plaintiffs against their neighbors, the sole question for determination will be whether the actions of the Architectural Committee have been arbitrary. In an action to determine whether the Committee's ruling was arbitrary or sound, the Association would obviously be a proper, if not an indispensable, party.

A nearly identical situation confronted the court in *Norris v. Phillips, supra*, 626 P.2d 717. Plaintiffs owned property adjacent to defendants' in a residential community. Despite plaintiffs' objections the Architectural Control Committee approved defendants' plan to construct a barn on their property. Plaintiffs filed suit against their neighbors as well as against the committee seeking to enjoin construction, but the committee was dismissed from the suit and the dismissal was not appealed. Plaintiffs prevailed at trial. The Court of Appeal reversed, holding that the trial court had failed to apply the correct standard in measuring the committee's actions. "[T]he trial court's determination of a breach of covenant, without a determination that the Architectural Control Committee acted unreasonably or in bad faith, was in error." (*Id.* at p. 719.) Rather than remand for a determination using the proper standard of review, however, the *Norris* court reversed. They did so because the committee had earlier been dismissed. "In such a challenge, the Architectural Control Committee is an indispensable party. In that the architectural control committee was dismissed out of this suit and that dismissal has not been appealed, a remand for a determination that the committee acted unreasonably or in bad faith is not possible." (*Id.* at p. 719, fn. 1.)

Similarly, plaintiffs' suit here turns on the good faith and lack of arbitrariness of the Committee's approval, assessed in the light of all of the provisions of the Declaration. It appears from the record that the fence in question was not in conformity with the provisions of the Declaration, particularly the provisions contained in Exhibit C, inasmuch as the codefendants placed a solid stone fence on a sideyard with a view, whereas Exhibit C clearly requires a wrought iron open fence. Although the Declaration vests "sole discretion" in the Committee and allows for reasonable variances, their decisions must be "in keeping with the general plan for the improvement and development of the Project," and of course, must be made in good faith and not be arbitrary. These are clearly questions of fact for a jury. Accordingly, the Association was a proper defendant in the action below, and dismissing it from the action was error.

. . .

In sum, we hold that the Association in reviewing the codefendants' improvement plan owed a fiduciary duty to plaintiffs to act in good faith and to avoid arbitrary action, and that there is an issue of fact raised by the pleadings as to whether the Association did so. As a consequence, the demurrer was improperly sustained.

The judgment is Reversed.

Retrospective and Observations

The Cohen's Perspective

The Cohens were a couple who had been married several years and had no children. She was a research chemist with Union Oil, and he was a mid-level marketing executive with a major computer company. This was their dream home.

The lot which the Cohens purchased overlooked a regional park which included a lake, greenbelts, and picnic areas. The lot was at the top of a hill and had a 180° view of surrounding communities. When the Cohens moved in, the developer had already erected rear yard fences at the end of the yard but had not built side yard fences.

The Cohens were the first in their neighborhood to submit plans for a side yard fence and to receive approval from the architectural review committee ("ARC"). The neighbors on the right, the Ehles, then submitted their plans for a side yard fence and improvements to their backyard, and notification was sent to the Cohens. The Cohens objected. They did not want the fence to march 40 feet down the property line between their home and the Ehles'. As things turned out, the Ehles built a fence which was 4 inches away from the Cohens' fence.

Following the Cohens' objection to the Ehles' plans, the Cohens began negotiations with their neighbors and with the association. At the point where Mr. Cohen wanted clarification about the trees and the location of the trees which the Ehles planned, negotiations broke down, and the Cohens sued the association.

As often happens, the litigation went on for years. After four years, the Cohens moved. Ms. Cohen quit her job, and Mr. Cohen took an assignment with his company in the San Diego area. The case eventually settled, and the Cohens received several hundred thousand dollars.

Richard Neuland, their first attorney, noted several things about the case. After litigation began, the Cohens' neighbor on the other side did not submit plans for their fence and landscaping before installing them, and the ARC did nothing. They installed a patio, a large gazebo, and extensive landscaping. This precluded the view on that side of the Cohens. At the time, the board was controlled by the developer which introduced a policy for the ARC in which "view" was defined as the view between prolongation of the rear lot line into space. The policy did not address side yard views, but the CCRs spoke of views across property lines.

Mr. Neuland stressed that the Cohens were very quiet, reserved people who spent close to $25,000 implementing landscaping and improvements to their front and back yards. The Ehles were very outgoing, likable people who turned all of the other neighbors against the Cohens because of the problems the Cohens created with the association.

The Association's Perspective

The association's attorney, Martin Lee, argued that it was nonsense that the association arbitrarily decided what was good for one owner in order to maintain the common good for all other owners. He maintains that the court would not listen to him but that the same argument was used in *Nahrstedt*.

The case was finally settled between developer and the plaintiff.

Judge Walland was the Superior Court Judge. Between the time that this case was decided and when it went up on appeal, Judge Walland became a member of the Appellate Court and recused himself when the case went before the appeals court.

Laguna Royale Owners Ass'n v. Darger
Court of Appeals of California
174 Cal. Rptr. 136 (Cal. Ct. App. 1981)

KAUFMAN, J. Defendants Stanford P. Darger and Darlene B. Darger (the Dargers) were the owners of a leasehold condominium[1] in Laguna Royale, a 78-unit community apartment complex on the ocean front in South Laguna Beach. The Dargers purported to assign three one-quarter undivided interests in the property to three other couples: Wendell P. Paxton and Daila D. Paxton, Keith I. Gustaveson and Elsie Gustaveson, and Keith C. Brown and Geneva B. Brown (collectively the other defendants) without the approval of Laguna Royale Owners Association (Association). Association instituted this action to obtain a declaration that the assignments from the Dargers to defendants were invalid because they were made in violation of a provision of the instrument by which the Dargers acquired the property, prohibiting assignment or transfer of interests in the property without the consent and approval of Association's predecessor in interest. Following trial to the court judgment was rendered in favor of Association invalidating the assignments from the Dargers to the other defendants. Defendants appeal.

FACTS

The Laguna Royale development is built on land leased by the developer from the landowner in a 99-year ground lease executed in 1961. As the units were completed, the developer sold each one by executing a Subassignment and Occupancy Agreement with the purchaser. This document conveyed an undivided 1/78 interest in the leasehold estate for a term of 99 years, a right to exclusive use of a designated unit and one or more garage spaces and a right to joint use of common areas and facilities; it also contained certain restrictions. The restriction pertinent to this action is paragraph 7, which provides in relevant part:

> 7. Subassignee (the purchaser) shall not assign or otherwise transfer this agreement, ... nor shall subassignee sublet ... without the consent of and approval of Lessee....[2]

---

1. A "condominium" is defined in Civil Code section 783, which reads in part as follows:
    A condominium is an estate in real property consisting of an undivided interest in common in a portion of a parcel of real property together with a separate interest in space in a residential, industrial or commercial building on such real property, such as an apartment, office or store ... (P) Such estate may, with respect to the duration of its enjoyment, be either (1) an estate of inheritance or perpetual estate, (2) an estate for life, or (3) an estate for years, such as a leasehold or a subleasehold.
(For a general discussion of condominiums, *see* Hanna, California Condominium Handbook (1975); Comment, Community Apartments: *Condominiums or Stock Cooperatives?* (1962) 50 Cal.L.Rev. 299; Comment, *Fee in Condominium* (1964) 37 So.Cal.L.Rev. 82.)
2. In full, paragraph 7 reads:
    Subassignee shall not assign or otherwise transfer this agreement, or any right or inter-

Upon the sale of all units and completion of the project, the developer entered into an "Assignment Agreement" with the Association, transferring and assigning to the Association all the developer's rights, powers and duties under the Subassignment and Occupancy Agreements, including inter alia the "right to approve or disapprove assignments or transfers of interests in Laguna Royale pursuant to Paragraph 7 of the Subassignment and Occupancy Agreements.

In 1965, Ramona G. Sutton acquired unit 41, consisting of some 3,000 square feet, by a Subassignment and Occupancy Agreement with the developer. In 1973 the Dargers purchased unit 41 from the executrix of Mrs. Sutton's estate.[3] As owner of a unit in the project, the Dargers automatically became members of the Association and were bound by the Association's by-laws.[4]

The Dargers reside in Salt Lake City, Utah, where Mr. Darger became a vice president of a large banking chain not long after the Dargers acquired their unit at Laguna Royale. The responsibilities of Mr. Darger's new position made it difficult for them to get away, and they attempted unsuccessfully to lease their unit through real estate agents in Laguna Beach. On October 30, 1973, Mr. Darger wrote to Mr. Yount, then chairman of the board of governors of the Association, in which he stated in part:

> It has been suggested that we might sell shares in our apartment to two or three other couples here. These associates would be aware of the restrictions regarding children under 16 living there, as well as the restrictions regarding pets, and would submit themselves to the regular investigation of the Board given prospective purchasers and lessees. I would expect that the apartment will remain vacant most of the time, as now, and not more than one of the families will occupy the apartment at one time.

By letter dated November 12, 1973, Mr. Yount responded in relevant part:

---

est herein, or in or to any of the buildings and improvements on the leased premises nor shall subassignee sublet said premises or any part thereof without the consent and approval of Lessee, and no assignment or transfer, whether voluntary or involuntary, by operation of law, under legal process or proceedings, by assignment for benefit of creditors, by receivership, in bankruptcy, or otherwise, and no such subletting shall be valid or effective without such consent and approval. Should Lessee consent to any such assignment, transfer or subletting, none of the restrictions of this article shall be thereby waived and the same shall apply to each successive encumbrance, assignment, transfer or subletting hereunder and shall be severally binding upon each and every assignee, transferee, subtenant and other successor in interest of subassignee. (P) The death of subassignee shall not be deemed to effect a transfer of this agreement within the meaning of this paragraph, but the right of the successors in interest of subassignee to use and occupy the subject premises shall be subject to approval of lessee as in the case of a voluntary assignment by subassignee.

3. The transfer was accomplished through an assignment and assumption agreement, not disputed by the parties or in issue on appeal.

4. Article II, section 2 of the bylaws provides:

Section 2. Ownership. (P) A person shall be considered to become an owner of a unit for purposes of membership in the Association upon recordation of a Subassignment and Occupancy Agreement that has been approved by the Board of Governors, by which the person acquires an undivided 1/78 interest in the leasehold covering Laguna Royale, plus the exclusive right to use and occupy an apartment to be used as a residence.

Article VII of the bylaws provides:

Section 1. By-Laws a contract. (P) These By-Laws shall constitute a binding contract among the owners of units in Laguna Royale.... Section 2. Assigns. (P) These By-Laws shall inure to the benefit of and be binding upon the heirs, grantees, successors, assigns, ... who agree to be bound by these By-Laws.

Following receipt of your letter of October 30, 1973 regarding the possibility of selling shares in your apartment #41, we discussed the matter at the regular meeting of the Board of Governors held on November 10, 1973.

Prior to the meeting we had referred the letter to our attorney, Mr. James Ralston Smith, for Laguna Royale Owner's Association for his opinion. We received his opinion prior to the meeting and this is quoted as follows: 'As to the request of Mr. Darger, as owner of apartment # 41, to sell undivided interests in that apartment to other parties, it is my opinion that if such other parties otherwise qualified and indicate no intended use of the apartment other than single family owner's use, there would be no legal basis to refuse such transfers. However, State law restricts more than four (4) transfers of undivided interests, without qualifying as a subdivision.

The letter then indicated that a number of members of the board of governors had voiced some objections to multiple ownership of a unit and then stated:

The Board of Governors is quite sympathetic with your problem of being unable to lease your apartment; however, because of the reasons given above, it is our opinion that the multiple ownership would not be beneficial to the other unit owners. We believe that our opinion is shared by the majority of the unit owners of Laguna Royale. Even in view of the Boards' (sic) opinion, we would have no alternative except to approve the transfer which you suggested, providing you would comply with the legal opinion of Mr. Smith.

Thereafter Mr. Darger discussed the possibility of joint ownership with some of his associates in Salt Lake City and in late 1974 or early 1975 he reached a point where he believed he was ready to proceed. He made an appointment with John Russell Henry, then chairman of the board of governors of the Association, and met with him for the purpose of going over the agreement that Mr. Darger's Salt Lake City attorney had prepared, to make sure that everything that the board might want to be in the agreement was included from the beginning. Mr. Darger agreed in writing to pay the fees incurred by the board in having the board's attorney review the instrument.

The document prepared by Mr. Darger's attorney contemplated five owners,[5] and the board's attorney indicated both to the board and Mr. Darger personally that, in his opinion, ownership of undivided interests in the unit by more than four persons would violate California subdivision laws. Thereafter, in a letter dated November 25, 1975, to Mr. Henry, Mr. Darger stated that because of a possible violation of the subdivision laws and for other reasons, we plan for a total of four shares, including my own."

Subsequently Mr. Darger received from Mr. Henry a letter dated January 12, 1976, which read in part:

The matter of multiple ownership of Apt. 41 has been studied in depth and detail with our own attorney, and the ultimate decision being that to do so would be contrary to recorded Lease, Subassignment and Occupancy agreement. In this connection you are respectfully requested to refer to Paragraphs 4[6] and 7 of

---

5. Apparently title to the unit would have been transferred to a trustee for the benefit of the five beneficial owners.

6. Paragraph 4 of the Subassignment and Occupancy Agreement reads: "The premises covered hereby shall be used solely for residential purposes, and no sign of any kind shall be displayed in or upon any portions of said building. Subassignee shall use or suffer or permit any person to use said premises, or any portion thereof, for any purpose tending to injure the reputation thereof, or to dis-

such Agreement which limit use of units solely to residential purposes, without exception, and require written consent by your Board of Governors for any assignment thereof.

A few days later Mr. Darger received from Mr. Henry another letter dated January 16, 1976, that read in part:

> The Board has determined that the transfer as you requested would create and impose an undue, unreasonable burden and disadvantage on the other owners' and residents' enjoyment of their apartments and the common facilities. Further, your requested transfer would be contrary to and in conflict with the close community living nature of Laguna Royale and would be contrary to the single family character of the private residential purpose to which all apartments are restricted under the recorded Master Lease and the Subassignment and Occupancy Agreement, as well as the By-Laws and House Rules, by which all owners are bound.

On February 23, 1976, Mr. Darger sent a formal letter request for approval to transfer unit 41 from the Dargers to themselves and the other defendants on condition that "the three new couples subsequently receiv(e) individual approvals after a 'Request For Approval Of Sale Or Lease' form has been filed with the Board for each, and each has submitted to a personal interview by the Board for its consideration." The letter further requested that if approval was not given, "the Board specify its reasons for denial and indicate how the request made herein differs from the situation of the owners of at least two other units where there is multiple ownership between more than one party who have no family or corporate relationship, (and) in light of the written and verbal approvals for such a transfer of apartment # 41 that have been extended by the Board to us over the past two and one half years."

By a letter from its attorney to the Dargers dated March 16, 1976, Association advised the Dargers that it would not consent to the requested transfer. It was denied that written and verbal approvals had been given the Dargers in the past, and it was stated in relevant part:

> The reason the Association will not consent to your requested transfer is that the Board feels it is obligated to protect and preserve the private single family residential character of Laguna Royale, together with the use and quiet enjoyment of all apartment owners of their respective apartments and the common facilities, taking into consideration the close community living circumstances of Laguna Royale.
>
> The Board feels strongly about its power of consent to assignments and other transfers of leasehold interests and considers the protection and preservation of that power to be critical in maintaining the character of Laguna Royale for the benefit of all owners as a whole. A four family ownership of a single apartment, with the guests of each owner potentially involved, would compound the use of the apartment and common facilities well beyond the normal and usual private single family residential character to the detriment of other owners and would frustrate effective controls over general security, guest occupants and rule compliance, as has been the case in the past.
>
> Provision 7 of the Subassignment and Occupancy Agreement, under which all apartment leasehold interests are held, requires the unqualified consent to any transfer. Provision 10 of said agreement provides for the termination of the leasehold interest in the event of a violation of Provision 7, or other breach....

turb the neighborhood or occupants of adjoining property, or to constitute a nuisance, or in violation of any public law, ordinance or regulation."

No apartments in Laguna Royale are held by multiple families in the manner that you have requested. In any event, any consents given by the Association to transfers in the past cannot be regarded as setting any precedent or in any way limiting or impairing the power of the Association to refuse its consent to any present or future transfer. In this regard, the language of Provision 7 of the Sub-assignment and Occupancy Agreement provides that consent given to any particular transfer shall not operate as a waiver for any other transfer.

[handwritten margin note: Reply that no units are held by "multi party" arrangement.]

After consultation with legal counsel the Dargers proceeded nevertheless, and on June 11 they executed instruments purporting to assign undivided one-fourth interests in the property to themselves and the other three couples. The instruments were recorded on June 30, and on July 3, 1976, the Dargers informed Association by letter of the transfers enclosing on Association's forms a separate "Request For Approval Of Sale Or Lease" and financial statement prepared and executed by each of the other couples. These papers show that the other defendants all reside in Salt Lake City, Utah. Each executed request form contains a warranty by the purchaser that if the application is approved no child under 16 years of age "will make residency at this property" and an agreement that the purchaser "will abide by and conform to the terms and conditions of the master lease, ... all amendments described in the Subassignment and Occupancy Agreement ... and the by-laws of the Laguna Royale Owners ... Association."

After unsuccessfully demanding that the other defendants retransfer their purported interests to the Dargers, the Association filed this action.

At trial the testimony confirmed that no more than one family of defendants used the property at a time and, although the matter was not examined in detail, answers to questions by one or more defendants indicated that 13-week periods had been agreed upon for exclusive use by each of the four families. It was also indicated that for substantial periods during the year, no use at all was being made of the unit. The evidence also showed that a number of Laguna Royale units were owned by several unrelated persons, but that in each case the owners used the unit "as a family."

No formal findings were made. However, in its notice of intended decision the court stated in relevant part:

> The Court concludes that the Subassignment and Occupancy Agreement, ... is in law a sublease.... Therefore, Civil Code Section 711 does not apply to void the requirement that consent be given to the transfer of defendant Darger's interest. The provisions of Title 10 of the Administrative Code, Section 2792.25, as cited in Ritchey v. Villa Nueva Condo. [1978] 81 Cal.App.3d 688, 146 Cal.Rptr. 716, only govern the restrictions of condominiums by laws, and not restrictions that may exist because of leasehold interests. The plaintiff association had the right to approve any transfer of defendant Darger's interest. The Court finds that the plaintiff association acted reasonably in refusing to grant consent to the proposed transfer by Darger to the other defendants. Plaintiff is entitled to a declaration that the assignments by Darger to the other defendants are invalid. Plaintiff is awarded attorney fees in the amount of $2500.

[handwritten margin note: Trial Ct. finds did have ability to transfer.]

Judgment was entered accordingly.

CONTENTIONS, ISSUES AND DISCUSSION

Defendants contend paragraph 7 of the Subassignment and Occupancy Agreement prohibiting assignments or transfers without the consent of Association is invalid because it is in violation of their constitutional rights to associate with persons of their choosing

[handwritten margin note: OK. Defs. argue invalid as infringes "constitutional right to associate."]

unlawful restraint on alienation

(U.S.Const., 1st amend.; Cal.Const., art. I, § 1), because it constitutes an unlawful restraint on alienation (Civ.Code, § 711), and because it does not comply with a regulation of the Real Estate Commissioner (Cal.Admin.Code, tit. 10, § 2792.25). Failing those, defendants contend finally that if by its finding that Association acted reasonably in refusing to approve the transfers, the court meant to indicate that Association had the duty to act reasonably in withholding consent and did so, that determination is not supported by substantial evidence and is contrary to law.

Association contends that the prohibition against transfer or assignment without its consent is not invalid on any of the bases urged by defendants. It argues primarily that its right to withhold approval or consent is absolute, that in exercising its power it is not required to adhere to a standard of reasonableness but may withhold approval or consent for any reason or for no reason at all. Secondarily, it argues that the evidence supports the finding it acted reasonably in disapproving the transfers to the other defendants.

Holding: May grant consent but must be "reas-"

We reject Association's contention that its right to give or withhold approval or consent is absolute. We likewise reject defendants' contention that the claimed right to approve or disapprove transfers is an invalid restraint on alienation because it is repugnant to the conveyance of a fee. We hold that in exercising its power to approve or disapprove transfers or assignments Association must act reasonably, exercising its power in a fair and nondiscriminatory manner and withholding approval only for a reason or reasons rationally related to the protection, preservation and proper operation of the property and the purposes of Association as set forth in its governing instruments. We hold that the restriction on transfer contained in paragraph 7 of the Subassignment and Occupancy Agreement (hereafter simply paragraph 7), thus limited, does not violate defendants' constitutional rights of association and is not invalid as an unreasonable restraint on alienation. However, we conclude that in view of the present provisions of Association's by-laws, its refusal to consent to the transfers to defendants was unreasonable as a matter of law. Accordingly, we reverse the judgment with directions to enter judgment for defendants.

Decision: the Board was not reasonable.

Having so concluded and disposed of the appeal it is unnecessary for us to decide whether the Real Estate Commissioner's regulation, which was not in effect when the Subassignment and Occupancy Agreement here involved was executed, could validly be applied to paragraph 7 or whether, if applied, it would invalidate the provisions of paragraph 7.

As indicated, the initial positions of the parties are at opposite extremes. Association contends that the Subassignment and Occupancy Agreement constitutes a sublease and that under the law applicable to leasehold interests, when a lease contains a provision permitting subletting only upon consent of the lessor, the lessor is under no obligation to give consent and, in fact, may withhold consent arbitrarily. (*See, e. g., Richard v. Degen & Brody, Inc.* (1960) 181 Cal.App.2d 289, 298–299, 5 Cal.Rptr. 263; 4 Miller & Starr, Current Law of California Real Estate, § 27:92, pp. 415–416; *see also* cases cited in Anno. 31 A.L.R.2d 831 (1953).) Defendants on the other hand contend that the Subassignment and Occupancy Agreement conveys, in essence, a fee,[7] and that under California law when a fee simple interest is granted, any restriction on the subsequent conveyance of the grantee's interest contained in the original grant is repugnant to the interest conveyed

---

7. It is unclear to us how the Subassignment and Occupancy Agreement could convey a fee interest when the entire interest in the land underlying the development is only a 99-year ground lease. It would appear that defendants' argument more appropriately ought to be that once consent was given pursuant to the Subassignment and Occupancy Agreement to the transfer from the estate of Ramona Sutton to the Dargers, the rule in *Dumpor's Case* (1578) 76 Eng.Rep. 1110, became applicable and that thereafter no consent to any further assignment was required. (See 3 Witkin, *Summary of Cal. Law* (8th ed. 1973) Real Property, § 491, p. 2170.)

and is therefore void. (*See, e. g., Murray v. Green* (1883) 64 Cal. 363, 367, 28 P. 118; *Title Guarantee & Trust Co. v. Garrott* (1919) 42 Cal.App. 152, 155, 183 P. 470; *see also* 3 Witkin, Summary of Cal. Law (8th ed. 1973) Real Property, § 314, p. 2023.)

We reject the extreme contentions of both parties; the rules of law they propose, borrowed from the law of landlord and tenant developed during the feudal period in English history (*see Green v. Superior Court* (1974) 10 Cal.3d 616, 622, 111 Cal.Rptr. 704, 517 P.2d 1168), are entirely inappropriate tools for use in affecting an accommodation of the competing interests involved in the use and transfer of a condominium. Even assuming the continued vitality of the rule that a lessor may arbitrarily withhold consent to a sublease (*but see* Note, *Effect of Leasehold Provision Requiring the Lessor's Consent to Assignment* (1970) 21 Hast.L.J. 516), there is little or no similarity in the relationship between a condominium owner and his fellow owners and that between lessor and lessee or sublessor and sublessee. Even when the right to the underlying land is no more than an undivided interest in a ground lease or sublease, ownership of a condominium constitutes a statutorily recognized estate in real property (*see* Civ.Code, § 783 (see fn. 1, *ante*)), and in our society the right freely to use and dispose of one's property is a valued and protected right. (U.S.Const., amends. 5 and 14; Cal.Const., art. I, § 7, subd. (a); *see* 5 Witkin, Summary of Cal. Law (8th ed. 1974) Constitutional Law, § 273, p. 3563.) Ownership and use of condominiums is an increasingly significant form of "home ownership" which has evolved in recent years to meet the desire of our people to own their own dwelling place, in the face of heavy concentrations of population in urban areas, the limited availability of housing, and, thus, the impossibly inflated cost of individual homes in such areas.

On the other hand condominium living involves a certain closeness to and with one's neighbors, and, as stated in *Hidden Harbour Estates, Inc. v. Norman* (Fla.App.1975) 309 So. 2d 180, 181–182: "(I)nherent in the condominium concept is the principle that to promote the health, happiness, and peace of mind of the majority of the unit owners since they are living in such close proximity and using facilities in common, each unit owner must give up a certain degree of freedom of choice which he might otherwise enjoy in separate, privately owned property." (*See also White Egret Condo. v. Franklin* (Fla.1979) 379 So. 2d 346, 350; *Seagate Condo. Association, Inc. v. Duffy* (Fla.App.1976) 330 So. 2d 484, 486.) Thus, it is essential to successful condominium living and the maintenance of the value of these increasingly significant property interests that the owners as a group have the authority to regulate reasonably the use and alienation of the condominiums.

Happily, there is no impediment to our adoption of such a rule; indeed, the existing law suggests such a rule. In the only California appellate decision of which we are aware dealing with the problem of restraints on alienation of a condominium, *Ritchey v. Villa Nueva Condo. Assn., supra*, 81 Cal.App.3d 688, 695, 146 Cal.Rptr. 716, the court upheld as a reasonable restriction on an owner's right to sell his unit to families with children, a duly adopted amendment to the condominium by-laws restricting occupancy to persons 18 years and over. And, of course, Civil Code section 1355 pertaining to condominiums expressly authorizes the recordation of a declaration of project restrictions and subsequent amendments thereto, "which restrictions shall be enforceable equitable servitudes where reasonable, and shall inure to and bind all owners of condominiums in the project."

Reasonable restrictions on the alienation of condominiums are entirely consistent with Civil Code section 711 in which the California law on unlawful restraints on alienation has its origins.[8] The day has long since passed when the rule in California was that all re-

---

8. Civil Code section 711 reads: "Conditions restraining alienation, when repugnant to the interest created, are void."

straints on alienation were unlawful under the statute; it is now the settled law in this jurisdiction that only unreasonable restraints on alienation are invalid.

. . .

Nor does the right of Association reasonably to approve or disapprove the assignment or transfer of the Dargers' ownership interest violate defendants' constitutional right to associate freely with persons of their choosing. Preliminarily, there is considerable doubt of whether the actions of Association constitute state action so as to bring into play the constitutional guarantees. (*Cf. Moose Lodge No. 107 v. Irvis* (1972) 407 U.S. 163, 173, 92 S.Ct. 1965, 1971, 32 L.Ed.2d 627, 637; *Newby v. Alto Riviera Apartments* (1976) 60 Cal.App.3d 288, 293–295, 131 Cal.Rptr. 547; *see generally* 5 Witkin, Summary of Cal. Law (8th ed. 1974) Constitutional Law, § 338, pp. 3631–3632.) In any event, however, the constitutionally guaranteed freedom of association, like most other constitutionally protected rights, is not absolute but is subject to reasonable restriction in the interests of the general welfare. (*Village of Belle Terre v. Boraas* (1974) 416 U.S. 1, 9, 94 S.Ct. 1536, 1541, 39 L.Ed.2d 797, 804; *White Egret Condo. v. Franklin, supra,* 379 So. 2d at pp. 349–351.) Moreover, it may be persuasively argued that if any constitutional right is at issue it is the due process right of an owner of property to use and dispose of it as he chooses. (*See generally* 5 Witkin, Summary of Cal. Law (8th ed. 1974) Constitutional Law, § 273, p. 3563.) And, of course, property rights are subject to reasonable regulation to promote the general welfare. (*Home Building & Loan Assoc. v. Blaisdell* (1934) 290 U.S. 398, 428, 434–436, 54 S.Ct. 231, 236, 238–239, 78 L.Ed. 413, 423, 426–428; *Sonoma County Organization of Public Employees v. County of Sonoma* (1979) 23 Cal.3d 296, 305, 152 Cal.Rptr. 903, 591 P.2d 1; *In re Marriage of Bouquet* (1976) 16 Cal.3d 583, 592, 128 Cal.Rptr. 427, 546 P.2d 1371.) Finally, any determination of the validity or invalidity of Association's right to approve or disapprove assignments or transfers of the Dargers' interest will of necessity impinge upon someone's constitutional freedom of association. A determination that the power granted the Association is invalid would adversely affect the constitutional right of association of the remaining owners at least as much as a contrary determination would affect the same right of the Dargers. (*Cf. Presbytery of Riverside v. Community Church of Palm Springs* (1979) 89 Cal.App.3d 910, 925, 152 Cal.Rptr. 854.)

Having concluded that a reasonable restriction on the right of alienation of a condominium is lawful, we must now determine whether Association's refusal to approve the transfer of the Dargers' interest to the other defendants was reasonable in the circumstances of the case at bench. The criteria for testing the reasonableness of an exercise of such a power by an owners' association are (1) whether the reason for withholding approval is rationally related to the protection, preservation or proper operation of the property and the purposes of the Association as set forth in its governing instruments and (2) whether the power was exercised in a fair and nondiscriminatory manner. (*Cf. Pinsker v. Pacific Coast Society of Orthodontists* (1974) 12 Cal.3d 541, 550, 116 Cal.Rptr. 245, 526 P.2d 253; *Lewin v. St. Joseph Hospital of Orange* (1978) 82 Cal.App.3d 368, 388, 146 Cal.Rptr. 892; *Ascherman v. Saint Francis Memorial Hosp.* (1975) 45 Cal.App.3d 507, 511–512, 119 Cal.Rptr. 507.) Another consideration might be the nature and severity of the consequences of application of the restriction (*e.g.,* transfer declared void, estate forfeited, action for damages). (*See* 3 Witkin, Summary of Cal. Law (8th ed. 1974) Real Property, § 315, p. 2025; Rest. Property, §§ 404–406.)

As to the last observation, a potential problem in the case at bench was avoided by the nature of the relief granted in the court below. Although in its complaint Association asserted a right to terminate the Dargers' ownership interest because of their assignments without Board approval and although there is some reference in the briefs to a "forfeiture," the judgment of the trial court simply invalidated the transfers to the other defendants, leaving the Dargers as the owners of the unit as they were at the outset. If Association's disapproval of the transfers was otherwise reasonable, we would find nothing unreasonable in the invalidation of the transfers.

To determine whether or not Association's disapproval of the transfers to the other defendants was reasonable it is necessary to isolate the reason or reasons approval was withheld. Aside from the assertion that it had the power to withhold approval arbitrarily, essentially three reasons were given by the Association for its refusal to approve the transfers: (1) the multiple ownership of undivided interests; (2) the use the defendants proposed to make of the unit would violate a bylaw restricting use of all apartments to "single family residential use"; and (3) the use proposed would be inconsistent with "the private single family residential character of Laguna Royale, together with the use and quiet enjoyment of all apartment owners of their respective apartments and the common facilities, taking into consideration the close community living circumstances of Laguna Royale." As to (3) Association asserted: "A four family ownership of a single apartment, with the guests of each owner potentially involved, would compound the use of the apartment and common facilities well beyond the normal and usual private single family residential character to the detriment of other owners and would frustrate effective controls over general security, guest occupants and rule compliance, ..." We examine each of these reasons in light of the indicia of reasonableness referred to above.

Insofar as approval was withheld based on multiple ownership alone, Association's action was clearly unreasonable. In the first place, multiple ownership has no necessary connection to intensive use. Twenty, yea a hundred, persons could own undivided interests in a condominium for investment purposes and lease the condominium on a long-term basis to a single occupant whose use of the premises would probably be less intense in every respect than that considered "normal and usual." Secondly, the Association by-laws specifically contemplate multiple ownership; in Section 7 of Article III, dealing with voting at meetings, it is stated: "Where there is more than one record owner of a unit, any or all of the record owners may attend (the meeting) but only one vote will be permitted for said unit. In the event of disagreement among the record owners of a unit, the vote for that unit shall be cast by a majority of the record owners." Finally, the evidence is uncontroverted that a number of units are owned by several unrelated persons. Although those owners at the time of trial used their units "as a family," there is nothing in the governing instruments as they presently exist that would prevent them from changing the character of their use.

We turn to the assertion that the use of the premises proposed by defendants would be in violation of section 1 of article VIII of the by-laws which provides: "All apartment unit uses are restricted and limited to single family residential use and shall not be used or occupied for any other purpose" and paragraph 4 of the Subassignment and Occupation Agreement which provides: "The premises covered hereby shall be used solely for residential purposes, ..." The term "single family residential use" is not otherwise defined, and if there is any ambiguity or uncertainty in the meaning of the term it must be resolved most favorably to free alienation. (*Randol v. Scott* (1895) 110 Cal. 590, 595–596, 42 P. 976; *Burns v. McGraw* (1946) 75 Cal.App.2d 481, 485–486, 171 P.2d 148; *Riley v. Stoves* (1974) 22 Ariz.App. 223, 526 P.2d 747, 749.) Actually, there is no evidence that defendants proposed to use the property other than for single family residential purposes. It is uncontroverted that they planned to and did use the property one family at a time for residential purposes. Thus, the proposed use was not in violation of the restriction to single family residential use.[9] (*White Egret Condo. v. Franklin, supra,* 379 So. 2d at p. 352).

---

9. In the trial court counsel for Association argued that "single family residential use" meant the same thing as "single family residential" customarily found in zoning ordinances, typically in con-

The reasonableness of Association's disapproval of the transfers from the Dargers to the other defendants must stand or fall in the final analysis on the third reason offered by the Association for its action: the prospect that defendants' proposed use of the apartment and common facilities would be so greatly in excess of that considered "usual and normal" as to be inconsistent with the quiet enjoyment of the premises by the other occupants and the maintenance of security.[10]

There can be no doubt that the reason given is <u>rationally related</u> to the proper operation of the property and the purposes of the Association as set forth in its governing instruments. The by-laws provide that "(t)he purpose of the Association is to manage and maintain the community apartment project ... on a non-profit basis for the benefit of all owners of Laguna Royale." By subdivision (M)(6) of section 2 of Article V of the by-laws the Board is empowered to "prescribe reasonable regulations pertaining to ... (r)egulating the purchase and/or lease of an apartment to a buyer or sublessee who has no children under 16 years of age that will occupy the apartment temporarily or full time as a resident." This power is said by the by-laws to be given the Board in recognition of "the prime importance of both security and quiet enjoyment of the Apartments owned by each member, and of the common recreational areas.

We reject defendants' contention that the Association had established a practice of approving or disapproving transfers solely on the basis of factors relating to the character, reputation and financial responsibility of the proposed transferee. There was testimony that during personal interviews with proposed transferees, the Board always inquired into the use proposed to be made of the premises.

The difficulty with upholding the Association's disapproval of the transfers by the Dargers to the other defendants is twofold. First, no evidence was introduced to establish that the intensity or nature of the use proposed by defendants would in fact be inconsistent with the peaceful enjoyment of the premises by the other occupants or impair security. We may take judicial notice as a matter of common knowledge that the use of a single apartment by four families for 13 weeks each during the year would create some problems not presented by the use of a single, permanent resident family. The moving in and out would, of course, be more frequent, and it might be that some temporary residents would not be as considerate of their fellow occupants as more permanent residents. However, we are not prepared to take judicial notice that the consecutive use of unit 41 by these four families, one at a time, would be so intense or disruptive as to interfere substantially with the peaceful enjoyment of the premises by the other occupants or the maintenance of building security.

Secondly, and most persuasive, a provision of the by-laws, subdivision (A) of section 1 of article VIII, provides:

> Residential use and purpose, as used herein and as referred to in the lease, subassignment and occupancy agreement pertaining to and affecting each apartment unit in LAGUNA ROYALE shall be and is hereby deemed to exclude and prohibit the rental of any apartment unit for a period of time of less than ninety

---

nection with the zoning designation R-1. We cannot conceive a decision that the ownership of a private dwelling in an R-1 zone by four families to be used by each family 13 weeks each with no use being made by more than one family at any time would be a use in violation of the R-1 zoning. We note also that our conclusion is in accord with the opinion originally expressed by the attorney for the Association that under the existing governing instruments there was nothing the Board could do legally to prevent multiple ownership if the interests were no smaller than quarter interests.

10. It is probable that this was the principal reason Association refused to approve the transfers. Defendants' proposed use of the unit has been characterized from time to time during these proceedings as "time sharing."

(90) days, as it is deemed and agreed that rentals of apartment units for less than ninety (90) day periods of time are contrary to the close community apartment character of LAGUNA ROYALE; interfere with and complicate the orderly administration and process of the security system and program and maintenance program of LAGUNA ROYALE, and interfere with the orderly management and administration of the common areas and facilities of LAGUNA ROYALE. Accordingly, no owner shall rent an apartment unit for a period of time of less than ninety (90) days.

The point is self-evident: under the present by-laws the Dargers could effect the same use of the property as is proposed by defendants by simply leasing to each couple for a period of 90 days each year.[11]

Under these circumstances we are constrained to hold that Board's refusal to approve the transfers to the other defendants on the basis of the prospect of intensified use was unreasonable as a matter of law.

The judgment is Reversed.

GARDNER, J., dissenting. I dissent.

Stripped to its essentials, this is a case in which the other owners of a condominium are attempting to stop the owner of one unit from embarking on a time sharing enterprise. The majority properly conclude that the owners as a group have the authority to regulate reasonably the use and alienation of the units. The majority then conclude that the Board's refusal to approve this transfer was unreasonable as a matter of law. To the contrary, I would find it to be entirely reasonable and would affirm the judgment of the trial court.

The use of a unit on a time sharing basis is inconsistent with the quiet enjoyment of the premises by the other occupants. Time sharing is a remarkable gimmick. P. T. Barnum would have loved it. It ordinarily brings enormous profits to the seller and in this case would bring chaos to the other residents. Here we have only four occupants but if this transfer is permitted there is nothing to stop a more greedy occupant of a unit from conveying to 52 or 365 other occupants.

If as an occupant of a condominium I must anticipate that my neighbors are going to change with clock like regularity I might just as well move into a hotel and get room service.

A Note on the Meaning of Reasonableness

Excerpt From Wayne S. Hyatt, *Common Interest Communities: Evolution And Reinvention*
31 J. Marshall L. Rev. 303, 348–355 (1998)

Scholarly commentary on reasonableness is extensive. Although some commentary reflects an inherent predilection that common interest communities are seriously flawed,

---

11. We note that on the form supplied by the Board to be filled in and executed by proposed purchasers or lessees, it is indicated that no lease less than six months in duration will be approved. While the Board is authorized by the bylaws to promulgate regulations concerning sales and leases of the units, its regulations must be consistent with the bylaws and cannot supersede or, in effect, amend a provision of the bylaws. The bylaws provide that they may be amended only by majority vote of the owners.

and some shows an inadequate understanding of the common interest community it-self, much commentary has raised legitimate questions and proposed theoretical solu-tions. Regrettably, many of those suggested solutions call for a blanket response to highly particularized situations or are impractical to implement. These solutions, how-ever, served to help frame responses from both the courts and practitioners. Without becoming too detailed and thus losing sight of the scope and purpose of this article, it is appropriate to examine some of the commentary, the problems identified, and the proposed solutions.[207]

The discussion among scholars essentially concerns the nature and extent of the reg-ulation appropriate for community associations. There is a general consensus that the association has a restrictive aspect and an ability to control its members to some extent.[208] There is less agreement upon the consequence or the approach courts should take in test-ing association action. This disagreement however, is less sharply drawn when the asso-ciation's actions affect third parties.[209]

When a court tests a municipality's actions, in the absence of the strict scrutiny re-quired to protect a "fundamental" right, courts apply the rationality standard, which re-quires that in order for a government action to be valid it must only be rationally related to a legitimate governmental interest. Some commentators reject application of this same standard to the "private government." They argue for a higher standard and de-

---

207. Much of the discussion is a debate between two views of social structure. Communitarian-ism and liberalism appear to be the two most pervasive theories of the notion of community. Com-munitarians advocate the attentiveness to group needs and group norms. G. Robinson, *Communities*, 83 Va. L. Rev. 269, 270 (1997). Conversely, liberals promote individual autonomy and diversity within the community. *Id.* However, Robinson notes that the two movements must resolve similar internal contradictions of ideology. *Id.* at 272. Specifically, both movements must resolve the social reality that both beliefs condone community by isolationism; that neither are readily assimilated into the larger society. *Id.* at 272–3. Robinson concluded by observing that the two seemingly opposed theo-ries are at times difficult to distinguish. *Id.* at 346.

Professor Alexander also sees little opposition between communitarianism and liberalism when he notes that the communitarian theory "understands group activity and individuality as simultaneously present aspects of the human personality, or self." Alexander, *Dilemmas of Group Autonomy: Resi-dential Associations and Community*, 75 Cornell L. Rev. 1, 2 (1989). Alexander attempts to converge the divergent gaps between communitarianism and liberalism by including liberal ideals within com-munitarian dogma. *Id.* He then applies his "communitarian" theory to residential associations by not-ing that residential associations are communitarian in character because of their desire as a group to isolate themselves. *Id.* at 50. His argument is theory, not fact, based. Alexander then contends that com-munities, by their very nature, exclude, thereby limiting their ability to develop sympathy for others and contradicting the communitarian teachings. *Id.* at 52. One questions the applicability of his the-ory to common interest community reality.

Conversely, Robinson, in attempting to define the concept of "community" and how this concept fits within the larger framework of society, sees very little overlap in the philosophies of two opposed concepts, communitarianism and liberalism. He states that communitarians emphasize group needs and group norms. *Id.* at 270. Likewise, liberals insist on individual autonomy and diversity. *Id.* More-over, Robinson addresses the notion of exclusion of gated communities by asking: what is the differ-ence between "privatized" and "traditional" communities; who set the terms and conditions of "community living;" given a conflict between communal and social norms, how do we decide which comes first? *Id.* at 306.

208. "The typical controversy is not one that arises from terms in the original covenants; it arises from the subsequent exercise of regulatory power delegated to a representative of the homeowners (ini-tially to the developer of the common interest property and thence to the homeowners' association) by the original covenants." *Id.* at 289.

209. *See, e.g.,* Evan McKenzie 31 J. Marshall L. Rev. 395 (1998).

fine "reasonableness" to include both procedural and substantive components. Such a reasonable standard is, therefore, higher than that applicable to local government. Is this appropriate?

Several commentators[211] argue that this higher standard is appropriate. They base their contentions upon the argument that common interest communities are not voluntary, at least under their definition of voluntary. These commentators[212] find "coercion" in the market place from the popularity of the common interest community and the lack of alternative housing.[213] These scholars are also concerned because they find further coercion once the buyer becomes a member subject to the governance process of the community association itself. They expect to find and thus assume a universal finding of exclusiveness,[214] regimentation,[215] and loss of personal freedom to act as an individual,[216] among other concerns about the individual member's relationship to the group.[217]

Other scholars disagree and assert that the reasonableness standard is too severe,[218]

---

211. See G. Alexander, *Dilemmas of Group Autonomy: Residential Associations and Community*, 75 Cornell L. Rev. 1 (1989); *see also* note *Freedom, Coercion and the Law of Servitudes*, 73 Cornell L. Rev. 883 (1988).

212. See Alexander *supra*:

Several commentators have criticized reasonableness review on the basis of familiar notions of private ordering. In effect, they seek to secure a strong form of autonomy for these residential groups, requiring only that groups govern themselves consistently with their own internal scheme of values and preferences. Their arguments for strong autonomy reflect the pluralist/public choice approach to the nature and status of groups. With respect to the specific debate over residential associations, I argue that communitarian theory justifies substantive judicial review under the reasonableness standard as a dialogic form of legal intervention. The experience with residential associations indicates why we should reject strong group autonomy for social groups in general as a social condition that would pervert, rather than advance, the ideal of a community. *Id.* at 7.

213. *Id.*

214. *E.g.*, Brower *supra* at 205, 207 Note 99 Harv 472, 475; Kennedy *supra*.

215. *E.g.*, Arabian *supra* at 17; Brower *supra* at 205.

216. Note 99 Harv at 474; McKenzie *supra* at 26.

217. Alexander argues for judicial activism in communities, where courts "serve as a bridge between communities and society" to keep the majoritarian forces within the community from denying a community's ability to formulate the conception of the "good." Alexander, *supra* at 55–56. He apparently sees the judiciary as a cure-all for the struggle between the individual and the group. *Id.*

A recognized communitarian leader disagrees with this argument:

Any form of social encouragement or pressure is quickly branded "coercion." [A]s I see it, suasion is not coercion, because coercion entails the use of force. Moral suasion carries no threat of imprisonment, deportation, physical harm to one's loved ones, or even destruction of property. As a result, the ultimate decision of how to conduct oneself when one is subject to suasion, as distinct from coercion, rests with the individual. Etzioni, *supra* at 38.

218. In fact, the view has been met with considerable skepticism. Professor Stewart Sterk, in refuting Alexander's notion of judicial activism in community association affairs, argues that the self-interest of association members provides an "institutional protection" against enactment of harsh restrictions, hence the association's rules should be enforceable, without court intervention. S. Sterk, Minority Protection in Residential Private Governments, 77 B.U.L. Rev. 273, 333 (1997). Sterk also notes that due to the interdependence of association members, community associations should enjoy a greater latitude and freedom to choose its associates than the courts afford individual sellers or landlords. *Id.* at 337. Sterk generally argues that as long as the rules have a similar impact on all units, the legal system should let the association decision stand. *Id.*

Professor Gillette also refutes Alexander's view on judicial activism by contending that community association residents should implement *their* vision of *their* community [emphasis added]. C. Gillette, *Courts, Covenants, and Communities*, 61 U. Chi. L. Rev. 1375, 1379 (1994). Gillette argues that the more privatized this vision, the more the law should defer to the association because the political

especially in light of the voluntary nature of the purchase[219] and the doctrines applicable to consensual undertakings and private ordering.[220] These commentators would have the courts refrain from involvement in most cases. However, perhaps the leading scholar on this side of the argument has appropriately defined reasonableness[221] and would look to a private "takings clause" in order to compensate member owners who are aggrieved by regulations that economically disadvantage their property rights.[222]

Still other scholars have sought a middle ground or variations on these central themes.[223] More recently, others have advanced what may be more pragmatic yet the-

---

processes in municipal decision making helps to accommodate the diverse and competing interests that exist in a municipality. *Id.* at 1379–80 and 1410. Moreover, Gillette shows that judicial intervention is not always adept at distinguishing process failures from situations in which the minority was simply outvoted. *Id.* at 1411.

Robinson is also hesitant to allow the judiciary to solve community problems. Robinson notes that Alexander "conflates communitarian norms with the social policy of the state. This is a dangerous confusion when one assumes that "the state is the embodiment of community norms." Robinson, *supra* note 130, at 295. Professor Robinson comments on the debate in community by viewing judicial activism not as a question of community versus individual but a question of choosing one concept of community over another. *Id.*

219. R. Epstein, *Covenants and Constitutions*, 73 Cornell L. Rev. 906 (1988); U. Reichman, *Residential Private Governments: An Introductory Survey*, 43 U. Chi. L. Rev. 253 (1976); *See also* note *The Rule of Law in Residential Associations*, 99 Harv. L. Rev. 472 (1985).

220. *Id.*

221. See Ellickson, *supra*:

'Reasonable,' the most ubiquitous legal adjective, is not self-defining. In reviewing an association's legislative or administrative decisions, many judges have viewed the "reasonableness" standard as entitling them to undertake an independent cost-benefit analysis of the decision under review and to invalidate association decisions that are not cost-justified by general societal standards. This variant of reasonableness review ignores the contractarian underpinnings of the private association. As some courts have recognized, respect for private ordering requires a court applying the reasonableness standard to comb the association's original documents to find the association's collective purposes, and then to determine whether the association's actions have been consonant with those purposes. To illustrate, the reasonableness of a board rule banning alcoholic beverages from the swimming pool area cannot be determined in the abstract for all associations. So long as the rule at issue does not violate fundamental external norms that constrain the contracting process, the rule's validity should not be tested according to external values, for example, the precise package of values that would constrain a comparable action by a public organization. Rather, the validity of the rule should be judged according to the enacting association's own original purposes. *Id.* at 1530.

222. The practicality of this proposal is questionable.

223. See, Gillette *supra*:

Judicial intervention, however, is not always beneficial. Courts are not necessarily adept at distinguishing process failures from situations in which the minority was simply outvoted by a sympathetic but unpersuaded majority.... As in those cases, however judicial intervention is not an unqualified benefit. Courts that err when construing ambiguities, or that restrict associations from enforcing covenants, impose on associations the very activities that a majority of the association had agreed to avoid. Indeed, the desire to avoid the externalities from such activity may have been the primary motivating factor for joining the association to begin with. Judicial misconstruction thus distorts the signals sent by covenants about the nature of the association. Judicial scrutiny of the meaning or reasonableness of covenants, therefore, is desirable only if the risk of judicial error is outweighed by the possibility that the association will enforce covenants in a manner inconsistent with the common vision of association members. *Id.* at 1411–12.

oretically sound arguments that reflect realities of the common interest community experience.[224]

During this scholarly debate on the reasonableness standard, courts and practitioners have been applying and developing a substantial body of "community association law."[225] Reasonableness has been a major component in that body of law. In many cases courts have simply required that the action be reasonable without defining what that means.[226] They have then applied the facts and found for[227] or against[228] the association again without articulation of a jurisprudential definition.[229]

The case law is moving with community association evolution and is more reflective of the practical realities than scholarly disputation. Two leading cases illustrate the point: *Nahrstedt v. Lakeside Village Condo. Ass'n, Inc.*[230] and *Hidden Harbor Estates, Inc. v. Basso.*[231]

---

224. The need for flexibility in servitudes brings forth an argument that a community association must be governed by "standards" instead of "rules." J. Winokur, *Ancient Strands Rewoven, or Fashioned Out of Whole Cloth: First Impressions of the Emerging Restatement of Servitudes*, 27 Conn. L. Rev. 131, 149 (1994). Implicit in the concept of "standards" according to Winokur, is the ability of the board to use discretion in applying standards. *Id.* at 150. Winokur does see advantages to stead-fast rule governance, namely the elimination of arbitrary or bias decision making, and increased predictability. *Id.* at 149. The difficulty in governance by standards to Professor Winokur is that if Ms. Nahrstedt were allowed her cats, the association would have risked (1) the waiver of the "no pet" rule and (2) liability for nonenforcement to a stricter neighbor. *Id.* at 149 (note 94). Both concerns can be resolved and have been discussed as part of the "precedent problem." Winokur argues that if true discretionary standard governance is to take place, boards must be protected from these legal risks. *Id.* at 149 (note 94). As discussed above and as provided in the Restatement, they are if they act properly.

225. *See generally, Perry v. Bridgetown Community Ass'n, Inc.*, 486 So. 2d 1230 (Miss. 1986).

226. See, *e.g., Hidden Harbor Estates v. Norman*, 309 So. 2d 179 (Fla. Dist. Ct. App. 1975). This case is perhaps the prime example of this approach, and courts often cite it.

227. *Id.* (holding that the rule prohibiting alcoholic beverages in common areas was reasonable); *Gillman v. Pebble Cove Home Owners Ass'n, Inc.*, 546 N.Y.S. 2d 134 (A.D. 2 Dept. 1989).

228. *See Hidden Harbor Estates, Inc. v. Basso*, 393 So. 2d 637 (Fla. Dist. Ct. App. 1981) (holding that the rule prohibiting an owner from drilling a water well was reasonable); *Bear Creek Village Condo. Ass'n v. Clark*, No. 10401 (Mich. App. March 23, 1989) (finding that the rule prohibiting dogs that exceed a certain height or weight requirement was unreasonable.).

229. One interesting application is *Papalexiou v. Tower W. Condo.*, 401 A.2d 280 (N.J. Super. Ch. 1979) (court stated that reasonableness was the rule but applied the business judgment rule).

230. 878 P.2d 1275 (1994). This California case, much misrepresented as to the severity of its facts, *see, e.g.,* Carl B. Kress, Comment, *Beyond Nahrstedt: Reviewing Restrictions Governing Life in Property Owner Associations*, 42 UCLA L. Rev. 837, 857–58 (1995) for a clarification and "emotion reducer," well illustrates the correct result. Even though the court was applying a statute, its articulation of reasonableness is relevant and appropriate as the standard. The court stated that the servitude would be enforced unless it violated public policy, bore "no rational relationship to the protection, preservation, operation, or purposes of the affected land; or it otherwise imposes burdens on the affected land that are so disproportionate to the ... beneficial effects ... that it should not be enforced." *Nahrstedt* at 1287. The court specifically rejected a case by case analysis of a restriction looking instead to the community effect. *Id.*

The courts' test of reasonableness was applied against a covenant provision. It is, however, a valid definition of "reasonableness" for any community association purpose.

231. 393 So. 2d 637 (Fla. 1981). This case drew a sharp distinction between board created restrictions and those contained in the covenant. The latter did not require reasonableness because they were agreed to upon purchase. The former, however, were subject to a test of reasonableness as a "fetter" on the board's discretion. *Id.* at 639–40. See *Korandovich v. Vista Plantation Condominium Ass'n*, 634 So. 2d 273, 275 (Fla. Dist. Ct. App. 1994) (holding that association's decision to prohibit supplemental address numbers adjacent to storm doors is subject to rule of reasonableness where declaration is silent on the issue); *Worthinglen Condominium Unit Owners' Ass'n v. Brown*, 566 N.E.2d 1275, 1279 (Ohio Ct. App. 1989) (using a reasonableness test to determine that amendments to a

The cases basically apply somewhat the approach of the business judgment doctrine, by exhibiting a respect for the elected decision maker and displaying a reluctance to substitute the court's judgment just because the judge might see the preferred outcome differently.[232] The courts, generally, look at procedure not outcome.

The appropriate standard is one which fairly responds to owner expectations and to association purposes. It is one that acknowledges that courts have no greater, and perhaps less, capacity to govern associations than those elected to do so;[233] that admits to the fallacies of the arguments favoring of a substantive reasonableness review;[234] that elevates private actors to the standard applicable to public actors,[235] but no higher; that gives an appropriate degree of autonomy,[236] certainty, and predictability to community governance, and it accords with community association law and the emerging Restatement. The appropriate standard is reasonableness, premised upon an examination of the association's purposes and the rational relationship of the action to those purposes.

Notes & Questions

1. What approach do you believe appropriate? How would you resolve the policy disagreements? Is it possible that the "debate" is really about something other than common interest communities?

2. *Reasonableness test.* In *River Terrace Condo. Ass'n v. Lewis* (case printed in Chapter 3 A.3.), the court reviewed the reasonableness of the board's decision to spray insecticide within a resident's unit. The court asked whether, under all the facts and circumstances, the decision was: (1) arbitrary or capricious, (2) nondiscriminatory and even-handed, and (3) made in good faith for the common welfare of the owners and occupants of the condominium. 33 Ohio App. 3d 52, 514 N.E.2d 732 (1986). In *Hidden Harbour Estates v. Norman,* also in Chapter 3), a rule prohibiting alcoholic beverages in the clubhouse was upheld as a reasonable measure "to promote the health, happiness and peace of mind of a majority of the unit owners." 309 So. 2d 180 (Fla. Dist. Ct. App. 1975). *Ryan v. Baptiste, supra* in this chapter, modified the reasonableness test by investing the board with substantial discretion to determine what is reasonable in a given context. 565 S.W.2d 196 (Mo. Ct. App. 1976). Note, however, that in

---

condominium declaration were enforceable against owners who acquired units prior to adoption of the amendment).

232. *See, e.g.,* Valenti v. Hopkins, 926 P.2d 813, 817–18 (Or. 1996) (holding that an association's decision is entitled to the court's deference, regardless of whether the members were "skilled" or "neutral").

233. Clayton P. Gillette, *Mediating Institutions: Beyond the Public/Private Distinction: Courts, Covenants, and Communities,* 61 U. Chi. L. Rev. 1375, 1378–79 (1994).

234. *Id.* at 1379. ("It is through resolution of these disputes that the legal system reveals the value we ultimately place on autonomous associations.")

235. See Ellickson *supra* at 1520. ("The first puzzle is that courts are more vigorous in reviewing the substantive validity of regulations adopted by established homeowners associations than regulations adopted by established cities. Considering the "private" nature of the association, one might have expected exactly the opposite judicial treatment.")

236. Robinson, *supra:*

> Power and discretion may provide opportunity for arbitrariness, but they may also indicate a desire for communal autonomy and to that extent may be an argument against outside interference.... But one can also see the case in a somewhat broader light as a recognition that individual autonomy and community self-governance are two sides of the same coin. *Id.* at 290–91.

Papalexiou v. Tower W. Condo., the court stated that the directors' actions must satisfy the reasonableness test, but then proceeded to apply the business judgment rule, 401 A.2d 280, 284 (1979). See also *Holleman v. Mission Trace Homeowner's Ass'n*, 556 S.W.2d 632 (Tex. Civ. App. 1977); *Dulaney Towers Maintenance Corp. v. O'Brey*, 418 A.2d 1233 (Md. Ct. Spec. App. 1980).

3. *Rule making: substantive reasonableness.* Courts have assessed both the substantive and procedural aspects of rulemaking to determine reasonableness. The governing documents and applicable statutes determine the boundaries of the board's rule-making power. See, e.g., *Makeever v. Lyle*, 125 Ariz. 384, 388–89, 609 P.2d 1084, 1088–89 (1980) (association may not deprive owner of interest in the common elements without authorization from the declaration, by-laws, or applicable statutes); *Juno by the Sea North Condo. Ass'n, Inc., v. Manfredonia*, 397 So. 2d 297, 303 n. 5 (Fla. Dist Ct. App. 1980) (association may not enact "eminently reasonable" regulation requiring each unit to be cleaned by an "association paid cleaning service since association authority within individual units is limited), *rev. denied*, 402 So. 2d 611 (Fla. 1981); *LeFebvre v. Osterndorf*, 87 Wis. 2d 525, 533, 275 N.W.2d 154, 159" (1979) (restriction on unit owner's ability to rent the unit is reasonable absent any record of discrimination or malice); *Cf. Drabinsky v. Sea Gate Ass'n*, 239 N.Y. 321, 146 N.E. 614 (1925) (even in the absence of a recorded declaration, an association can adopt reasonable rules to regulate the community in accord with the founders' intent).

4. *Rule making: procedural reasonableness.* Courts have measured the reasonableness of a rule by determining whether a unit owner had notice of the board's authority to promulgate a particular rule. See *Juno by the Sea North Condo. Ass'n, Inc.*, 397 So. 2d 297, (Fla. Dist. Ct. App. 1980) (parking regulations were reasonable since, in part, prospective purchasers had notice of parking assignment policy). And association actions have been struck for failure to follow the enactment procedures established in the condominium documents. See, e.g., *Pepe v. Whispering Sands Condo. Ass'n, Inc.*, 351 So. 2d 755, 757–58 (Fla. Dist. Ct. App. 1977) (association cannot consolidate budgets absent authority in the declaration); *Garrison Apartments, Inc. v. Sabourin*, 449 N.Y.S.2d 629, 633–34 (Civ. Ct. 1982) (assessment invalidated where board failed to follow proper procedures).

5. *Overcoming director protection statutes.* In light of the director protection statutes, such as Delaware's section 102(b)(7), how might a potential plaintiff frame a complaint to have a better chance of prevailing against homeowner association directors? See Comment, *Limiting Corporate Director's Liability: Delaware's Section 102(b)(7) and the Erosion of the Duty of Care*, 136 U. Pa. L. Rev. 239, 273 (1987); and Richards, *Delaware Shareholders May Limit Director's Liability Under New Law*, N.Y.L.J., Aug 11, 1986, at 35.

6. *Board guidance in decision-making.* Does the reasonableness test or the business judgment rule provide the board with better guidance for future rulemaking? See Lewis A. Schiller, *Limitations on the Enforceability of Condominium Rules*, 22 Stetson L. Rev. 1133 (1993).

7. *Burden of proof.* Who has the burden of proof in a suit challenging the reasonableness of restrictions found in the declaration or regulations adopted by the Board? See, e.g. *Hidden Harbour Estates v. Norman*, 309 So. 2d 179 (Fla. 1975); *Hidden Harbour Estates v. Basso*, 309 So. 2d 180; 393 So. 2d 637 (Fla. Dist. Ct. App. 1981); see also *Nahrstedt v. Lakeside Village Condo. Ass'n, Inc.*, 878 P.2d 1275 (Cal. 1994) (*en banc*); and Armand Arabian, *Condo's, Cats, and CC&R's: Invasion of the Castle Common*, 23 Pepperdine L. Rev.

1, 11–15 (1995). What policies might justify placing the burden of proof on the home-owners or on the association?

Problems

1. Happy Homes Condominium is not totally happy. Mr. and Ms. Sensitive complain strongly that multiple mold spores in their unit cause allergic reactions for them and for their dog. The Sensitives' attorney has made demands that the association cure the problem and is threatening litigation. The association's manager reported that the cause of the problem was the Sensitive's dog and that she was sure there was really no problem. On this basis, the board voted to take no action.

Sometime later, another unit owner, next door to the Sensitives, reported the same problem. The president did not place the issue on the next board meeting agenda but included it in his oral report to the board (no questions were asked and only a few comments made). The problem continues.

Tonight, a board member is suffering allergies and suggests that the board authorize repairs. He does not have a dog. To make matters worse, the Sensitives have sued. The president demands that you have the suit dismissed since the board's business decisions are protected. As association attorney, you are in attendance and are asked your views on the matter. What do you say? Would it make any difference to your answer if a majority of the board members were declarant appointees? What arguments should the Sensitive's attorney make? In the absence of a litigation issue, how would you advise the board knowing the facts as presented? What if the mold allegedly resulted from irrigation of the common areas?

2. Tony is a developer-appointed director on the condominium association board. Three directors are developer appointees, and two are owner-elected. The board is considering the question of potential construction defects within several key components of the condominium. Transition of control is approaching but because the statute of limitations is also nearing its expiration, the board feels that it must address these issues.

Tony is concerned about personal liability and wonders whether he should withdraw from deliberations. If he does so, at least one other appointee is likely to do so as well. He asks you for advice and a recommendation. You are counsel for the association. How do you respond? As counsel for the developer, would your response be different?

C. Governance Structures for Large Communities

> *The perpetual obstacle to human advancement is custom.*
>
> —*John Stuart Mill*

There are some unique aspects of governance in larger communities. By "larger," we mean projects in excess of 500 acres or 500 units, although most truly large projects are 1,000 units and up. Project size is important but not as important as the number of units and the mix of product within the community. That mix may include single-family attached and single-family detached product of various lot sizes and configurations, rental, and nonresidential components. In the larger project, there is a much greater likelihood that there will be discrete areas of substantially dissimilar product. Generally, there will be more "governmental" activities assumed by the private association. For example, an association might provide fire services, security services and more of the indicia of a local government than would be seen in the much smaller common interest community. These unique aspects of large projects call for unique applications of governance methods and principles.

In larger communities, there are problems that stem purely from size. High density of one product type can result in a dominance by that product's residents in the governance process. For example, an extremely dense area may have sufficient voting capability to elect the board. This would be to the detriment of broad-based representation generally, and specifically to other areas that, while smaller, have an important economic interest in the operation of the association. Challenges of homogeneity arise from differences in product type, needs, demographics, economic capabilities and desires of owners, the presence of tenants, and a variety of other factors.

There are also cost and time "people" demands. The larger and more complex the governance structures, the greater the demand on volunteer time, as well as the greater the cost from duplication of services. There may be parallels between consolidation of city and county governments and the large-scale community association. Just as a metropolitan area with multiple small and large city governments and several county governments may well benefit from a consolidation of all into one, so can the common interest community find genuine advantages from reducing and more finely tuning its governance structure.

While time and cost economies are one primary need of a large scale governance structure, there are others. The local components, that is the groupings of different product type, have their own localized needs, and the governance structure must be empowered to satisfy them. Although a single-family detached dwelling may need no exterior building or ground maintenance, a single-family attached dwelling will probably desire such services. The governance structure and the service delivery systems implicit therein must, therefore, be able to meet both needs.

In a monolithic structure, there is a greater likelihood that everyone will be assessed the same. In a structure with many different associations, there may be different assessments, but there will be duplication of services resulting in unnecessary expenditures and, consequently, unnecessary charges to owners. Thus, a large scale governance structure will seek ways to deliver different services while doing so in a cost-effective manner with charges being differentiated within the community either on an assessment or user fee basis. This provides greater flexibility to accommodate needs within a community of different economic levels—affordable housing, age restricted housing, and other groupings—which might need or desire a level of services and assessments more consistent with the economic situation of the different groups. Ultimately, the successful large-scale governance structure will be one which serves as a vehicle for sharing, yet maintaining the maximum appropriate degree of autonomy.

The traditional approach involves the so-called "umbrella and subassociation." The umbrella is the "master" association that provides governance for the entire community. It is empowered to deal with community-wide matters and has design review, assessment, and rule making powers over all components of the community. The "sub" associations are those established for individual neighborhoods or products. They are most typically created by builders as they develop individual subdivisions. The results can be 5, 10, 20, or even more associations within the overall jurisdiction of the single umbrella or master. Each association has its own board of directors, management structure, insurance policy, and all of the other indicia of association governance and operation. The result is a dramatic demand on time, volunteers, and cost. The accompanying graphic shows how this might be structured in a typical project.

Typical Umbrella Community Association Structure

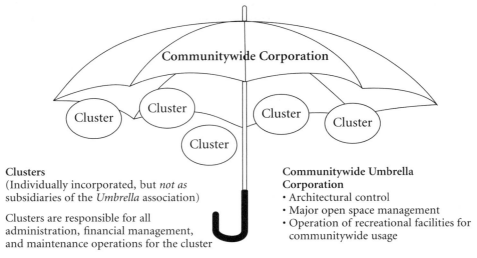

Clusters
(Individually incorporated, but *not as* subsidiaries of the *Umbrella* association)

Clusters are responsible for all administration, financial management, and maintenance operations for the cluster

Communitywide Umbrella Corporation
• Architectural control
• Major open space management
• Operation of recreational facilities for communitywide usage

In comparison with the unified community association, the *umbrella* association structure lacks
• The better controls of centralized administration and financial management
• Centralized communications
• The economics of scale of centralized maintenance operations
• Uniform quality control of community appearances
• Effective centralized community code adoption and enforcement

There is an alternative.

The consolidated government model works well in the large scale setting resulting in one community-wide association with no subordinate associations except as may be required by law. The obvious circumstance under which a subordinate association would be necessary is when there is a condominium (due to state law requirements and ownership issues). In all other circumstances, individual developments can be treated as semi-autonomous, localized units for both cost accounting and decision making. These local units, frequently called neighborhoods, villages, or some other user- and market-friendly term which connotes both a pleasant place to live as well as a governmental unit, can direct the association to provide particularized services and can be charged therefor. The challenge to the drafting attorney is to recognize the advantages of a creative application of lessons learned in high school civics.

Generally, the single association structure is considered a positive approach because it provides efficiency, economy, and it is market wise yet risk averse. It provides a unified system for assessments, architectural control, meetings, regulations, insurance, and other factors that result in a unified community. It provides a centralized organization with one board, one management contract, and far fewer meetings, resulting in cost reductions and a more systematic maintenance standard. It can enhance developer control and reduce the problems that come from diverse groups. Accordingly, drafters need to be careful that they protect the interests of these diverse groups and build in methods for meaningful participation during the control period.

The unified system allows neighborhood services and market segmentation. This permits various groups of attached and detached product and the nonresidential product to receive what they need and that for which they can and will pay. It provides an excellent vehicle for owner input through a centralized communication structure, yet has localized, semi-autonomous governmental units. It enhances leadership development because it provides opportunities to participate without the necessity of multiple corporate structures. It is a great plus for cost control because it avoids duplication and allows a balance of representatives on the ultimate governing structure.

In addition to unifying the product from a business and economic perspective, it is important that the single association structure for large communities have a well-considered representative mechanism as well. This is normally done by grouping the neighborhoods into voting groups or electoral districts, permitting representative voting, and insuring that different groups are brought together for the purpose of selecting directors. On the one hand, this insures proportionate representation while avoiding the probability of one very dense area having the capacity to select all or most of the directors. The accompanying graphic (see next page) illustrates this structure.

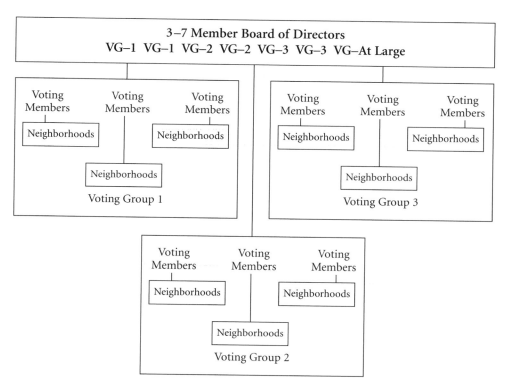

- Class "A" Members within each Neighborhood elect one Voting Member to represent them on any matters requiring a membership vote.
- Voting Groups are established at the option of Declarant. If established, the Voting Members within each Voting Group will vote on a separate slate for election of directors, with each Voting Group electing an equal number of directors and any additional director elected at large by all Voting Members (without regard to Voting Groups).

As you can see, the neighborhood, which in the more traditional approach would be the subassociation, may be the same as or different from an electoral district depending upon project size, configuration, housing type, neighborhood size, and other such factors. It is important that both the developer-declarant and, subsequently the association, be able to change or subsequently to create neighborhoods as the project changes and grows. Generally, neighborhoods are composed of the same product type in the same general range of price point or economic expectations.

These neighborhoods are brought together to form voting groups or electoral districts. This formation might reflect geographical area, similar housing type, approximate unit density, desired maintenance or service level, and other such matters. There is not a requirement that they be equal in population, although that is certainly a desirable characteristic. Initially the developer, and subsequently the board, may establish or reestablish voting groups. However, after being established, owners of residences within a district have a say in any subsequent change.

The process is further simplified by each neighborhood selecting a voting representative or a voting member. This person, frequently the head of the neighborhood committee which is responsible for notifying the association's board of directors of desired levels of service unique for that neighborhood, acts as that neighborhood's representative and casts the number of votes equal to the number of units within the neighborhood when all voting members come together to cast votes on association business.

Frequently, voting representatives meet with their constituents prior to voting and in some cases, the documents require that this be done on some or all issues. More commonly, the voting representative has the capacity to vote as he or she deems appropriate but also has the power to poll the constituents. The result is a simplified, more cost effective system resulting in time and cost economies while affording a significant degree of autonomy, participation, and simplicity in governance.

Problems

1. As a legislative intern, you are assigned to draft legislation affecting the operation of common interest communities. Your state has a well developed body of corporate law. Most of it deals with for-profit corporations; there is a rudimentary not-for-profit code, but there are few cases. There is even less law dealing with unincorporated organizations. Your research indicates, however, that most condominium associations are unincorporated, HOAs are incorporated as not-for-profit, yet both appear to function as for-profit corporations. Your senator asks whether this is appropriate. What are the justifications and counter arguments for such an approach? If the approach is justified, what might call for special treatment?

2. You also discover that there are those who argue that, because of the nature of these communities, their governance structures should be held to a reasonableness standard or even required to meet constitutional tests. Local governmental actions are only required to meet a rational relationship test. What arguments support these positions? Are they justified? Does it depend upon the circumstances and, if so, what circumstances? Once again, your senator raises questions. She asks whether communities and their boards have different responsibilities in different situations and whether, therefore, the applicable rules might vary. What do you think? How would you state the rule or rules and the guidelines as to when each applies?

Chapter 6

Financing the Community

"Follow the money." Although many developers and residents of common interest communities hope to provide a structure that will encourage development of a strong sense of "community," the signature characteristic of common interest communities is that they allow owners to share common property and resources without the free rider problems that otherwise might plague common ownership arrangements. Money to pay for the expenses of the common property and services is the lifeblood of the common interest community. In this chapter we follow the money to learn how communities raise the money they need, the choices developers face, and the kinds of problems and issues that may arise around community fund raising.

One important issue arising out of community financing is that, unlike property taxes, funds paid to support common property and services in common interest communities are not deductible from state or federal income taxes. Particularly when they are required to shoulder what would otherwise be public expenses for roads, parks, or other types of services usually provided by local government, residents of common interest communities may feel that they are unfairly subjected to double taxation. They pay the same local taxes as people who live in other parts of the larger community but have to pay extra to provide their own municipal services. Opponents of allowing tax deductions or credits for common interest community assessments argue that the benefits of private control over the services and facilities justify denying the deductions.

Other important issues arise out of the way common expense burdens are allocated to lots or units in the community, a choice that is usually made by the developer. Most commonly, the developer provides for assessments against each lot or unit and the assessments are for equal shares of the expenses. However, some condominium developments allocate shares on the basis of square footage or market value of the units. Another choice, very occasionally used, is to allocate expense shares among the lots on the basis of their appraised value for tax purposes. As you can imagine, interesting questions arise when a state, like California, caps the rate of tax assessment increases for current owners but raises assessments to market value on each sale of the property.

The developer's choice of method for allocating common expenses is critical because it is usually extremely difficult, if not impossible, to change it later. Like voting rights, a lot's or unit's allocated share of the expense burden is viewed as part of the "property" acquired by the first purchaser. Even if the initial allocation turns out to be unfair, it probably cannot be changed without agreement by 100% of the owners. A question worth considering is whether by statute or the declaration changes should be allowed by something less than a unanimous vote, and if so, what safeguards should be included.

In deciding how common expenses should be allocated, a developer (and the developer's lawyer) should select a method that most accurately reflects the costs that will be generated by each lot or unit and the value of the benefits the payor will receive from the common expenditures. The inclusion of "affordable" units in the development significantly complicates the expense allocation question and requires creative thinking by both developer and lawyer.

Another important issue arises in developments where the governing documents placed a cap on the amount of common expenses that owners are required to pay, either in absolute dollar terms or in terms of the annual percentage increase that is allowed. When compliance with the cap prevents the community from raising sufficient funds to cover its expenses, what should be done? Some homeowners may claim they have vested rights in the specified caps while others may claim their expectations of continuing maintenance of common property and services should be met. Although caps may help with initial marketing of a project, they are usually a very bad idea because of the significant problems they will create when inflation or other changes make the amounts that can be raised inadequate.

We begin our study of community financing by examining the community's power to raise the money needed to finance community operations using the Restatement (Third) as a starting point.

A. The Power to Assess

Restatement (Third) § 6.5 Power To Raise Funds: Assessments, Fees, And Borrowing

(1) Except as limited by statute or the declaration:

(a) a common-interest community has the power to raise the funds reasonably necessary to carry out its functions by levying assessments against the individually owned property in the community and by charging fees for services or for the use of common property;

(b) assessments may be allocated among the individually owned properties on any reasonable basis, and are secured by a lien against the individually owned properties.

(2) Unless expressly authorized by the declaration, fees for services rendered, or for the use of common property, must be reasonably related to the costs of providing the service, or providing and maintaining the common property, or the value of the use or service.

(3) An association may borrow money, but in the absence of authority granted by the declaration, it may not assign future revenues or create a security interest in common property to secure a loan without the approval of at least a majority of the voting power in the community, or greater percentage if required by the governing documents.

The most common method of financing common interest community operations is to levy assessments against individual lots or units for their shares of common expenses. Assessments may be levied on an annual, quarterly, monthly, or some other basis, but an annual assessment, payable monthly, is the most common. Common techniques and problems are discussed in the Note on Collection Practices and Issues, *infra*.

The governing documents usually provide for both regular and special assessments. Regular assessments should be based on an annual budget that covers reserves as well as anticipated regular expenses. Special assessments are used to deal with unanticipated expenses and major repairs or replacements not covered by reserves. Although owners sometimes question regular assessments on the ground that particular expenditures are *ultra vires*, they are more likely to contest special assessments either because they have been caught by surprise, due to the differences in budgeting procedures, or because they do not believe the purpose of the assessment is legitimate.

In addition to assessments, community associations may have other, sometimes creative, funding mechanisms. User fees—charges for use of some facility or service imposed on a per-use basis or an annual or other time basis—allow an association to allocate the costs to those who value a facility or service rather than imposing the burden on all owners.

Transfer fees imposed on the transfer of individual lots or units at the time of resale or, in some instances, at the time of the original sale by the developer or builder, are a relatively new addition to the funding tools in master planned communities but have long been used in cooperatives. To be understood and accepted by owners outside the cooperative context, transfer fees must be used for purposes perceived to have value in the community. Environmental programs, community activities, or educational activities, for example, may be funded with transfer fees. For planning purposes, however, it is important to remember that the amount of fees generated will depend on the number of sales. When the housing market is slow, the programs they support may run short of funds if care has not been taken to create reserves to compensate for uneven cash flow. Finally, a few community associations receive income from business activities they conduct in addition to maintenance and operation of the common property. Associations that operate businesses, of course, have additional tax and business issues to contend with.

Assessments usually create personal liability on the part of the lot or unit owner and a lien against the property for unpaid assessments. However, even with these protections, assessments are not always paid. In that case, the other owners have to pick up the slack through increases in their assessments. As you read through the cases in this chapter, think about the best ways to protect the financial interests of owners in common interest communities.

Rodruck v. Sand Point

Washington Supreme Court
295 P.2d 714 (Wash. 1956)   *Note old date.*

SCHWELLENBACH, J. This is an appeal from judgments entered in two cases consolidated for trial. Plaintiffs and interveners are owners of tracts in the plat of the residential district known as the Sand Point Country Club, located in Seattle. The district contains two hundred thirteen residential lots and is elliptical in shape. One may enter the residential area [only] at three points at the southern boundary from East 75th Street (a city thoroughfare ...).

...

[In March of 1928, Samuel Hayes incorporated the Sand Point Country Club and conveyed all of the property in the residential district to it. On December 28, 1928, Hayes incorporated the Sand Point Maintenance Commission. December 31, 1928, the Sand Point Country Club conveyed to the maintenance commission, in trust, "easement of access," and also certain easements for water, sewage, and telephone utilities. In 1942, different owners sold lot 22 to plaintiff Burke, lot 198 to plaintiff Rodruck, and lot 202 to intervener Tippery. By virtue of the purchase, each plaintiff became a member of the maintenance commission. The maintenance commission reorganized and amended its by-laws in May, 1951, and in January of 1953, the district was annexed to the city of Seattle. Subsequent to the annexation, the city of Seattle levied against the property of the commission for the area's share of the cost of improving East 75th Street, and the commission, in turn, levied against the property of the members. — Eds.]

Plaintiff Rodruck in his complaint sought (1) an order declaring the corporate reorganization of 1951 void; and (2) an order declaring the corporation to have no power to levy assessments for the improvement of East 75th Street. Tippery, as intervener in the Rodruck suit, sought (1) to have his title quieted as against the filed covenants and restrictions; (2) an adjudication that the streets in the district are public; and (3) an order declaring the amended articles of incorporation of 1951 to be of no effect. Plaintiff Burke sought (1) an order declaring his right to withdraw from membership in the commission; (2) an adjudication declaring that the streets in the area are public; (3) an adjudication that the purported covenants in the Declaration of Protective Restrictions, as amended, are void; and (4) an injunction enjoining the city of Seattle from taking further steps with regard to the levy of assessments against the area....

...

[Defendant commission cross-complained seeking judgment for unpaid assessments. The trial court granted a motion for dismissal on the issue of the character of the streets and stated that the streets within the district were private streets. The court entered judgment dismissing the complaints of plaintiffs and intervener and ordered recovery by defendant commission on its cross-complaint in the amounts prayed for. Plaintiffs appealed. — Eds.]

It is contended that the trial court erred in finding that the streets within the area are private streets; in finding that no evidence was produced which permits the court to relieve appellants or their tracts from the obligations of membership in the maintenance commission; in entering decrees dismissing appellants' actions and in granting judgments against them with interest and costs, including attorneys' fees; in finding that the maintenance commission is duly organized under the laws of the state; in finding that appellants Rodruck are barred by *res judicata* from questioning the rights of the commission to levy assessments and foreclose against them and their property; in finding that certain causes of action are barred by the statute of limitations; and in refusing to find that the commission has no power to levy assessments for the improvement of East 75th Street.

...

[Appellants failed to prove that the use of the streets by the public was adverse. The court acknowledged that future adverse use might render the streets public, but stated that "a member of the public must enter from 75th Street, and, to get out, must go back to 75th Street" and therefore it is difficult "to believe that any outsider had any idea that he was using these streets as a matter of right." — Eds.]

We will now consider the contention that the corporate reorganization of 1951 was invalid and the consequent amended articles of incorporation and by-laws void. The maintenance commission was originally incorporated as a social club under chapter CLVIII of the Laws of 1895, p. 400. Its by-laws were amended in 1939, and on May 15, 1951, the commission was reorganized under RCW 24.04 as a nonprofit corporation. May 28, 1951, the secretary of state issued his certificate acknowledging the filing of the amended articles of incorporation.

Appellants assert that the meeting to reorganize was irregular in several respects, and further that under RCW 24.04.120 the commission was incapable of reorganizing as a nonprofit corporation. These assertions question the authority of the commission to act as a nonprofit corporation.

The commission, through its compliance with statutory procedure, the issuance of the certificate of reorganization, and its subsequent activity as a reorganized corporation, is at the least a de facto nonprofit corporation. Its authority to act as such cannot be questioned in this action

. . .

The commission under its articles of incorporation and by-laws had the right to assess its members for maintenance work and improvements to the streets, and the deeds from the Hayes Investment Company to appellants' predecessors in interest embodied a covenant running with the land in that respect, which is binding upon the appellants as subsequent grantees. Each of the certificates of title held by the appellants recites that it is subject to restrictions and reservations contained in the deed from the Hayes Investment Company to their predecessors in interest. Each of those deeds contain[s] this statement:

> The said property is hereby conveyed subject to the provisions of the by-laws of said Sand Point Maintenance Commission, which is, as aforestated, a Washington corporation, with its principal place of business at Seattle, Washington, organized for the purpose, among others, of taking title, in trust, to and improving and maintaining certain properties constituting easements of access (including parking strips, parking areas and bridle path) the cost thereof, including installation and maintenance of water, sewerage, gas, electric light and power and telephone, and such other service and service lines as may be deemed useful by said commission, to be assessed by it to and paid by the owners of tracts in said residential district, in the manner provided in the by-laws of said corporation. Said properties and areas are particularly described in certain deeds of conveyance from Sand Point Country Club and others to said Commission heretofore recorded and filed, respectively, in the offices of the Auditor and of the Registrar of Titles for said County, copies of which the Grantee acknowledges he has received and read; and there has been issued to the Grantee one share of stock in said corporation, which said share shall be inseparably appurtenant to the tract hereby conveyed, and said tract and each portion thereof and undivided interest therein (if at any time so comprised), shall be subject to the lien of such assessments, and the owner thereof liable therefor, as shall be levied from time to time by said Commission under and in accordance with its by-laws and any amendments thereof, which assessments shall be superior to any and all other liens created and permitted by the Grantee, his heirs, personal representatives and assigns, except as otherwise may be provided by said Commission; and the Grantee, for himself, his heirs, personal representatives and assigns, by the acceptance of this deed, binds himself and his heirs, personal representatives and assigns, to all of the provisions, restrictions, conditions and regulations now or hereafter imposed by the by-laws of said Commission, and any amendments thereof, all of which shall constitute covenants running with the land.

In order that a covenant might be said to run with the land, it is essential that the promise "touch" or "concern" the land. Clark, *Covenants and Interests Running With Land* (2d ed.) 94.

In *Seattle v. Fender*, 42 Wn. (2d) 213, 254 P. (2d) 470, we quoted with approval from *Pelser v. Gingold*, 214 Minn. 281, 8 N. W. (2d) 36:

> A covenant is said to run with the land when it touches or concerns the land granted or demised. Generally speaking, a covenant touches or concerns the land if it is such as to benefit the grantor or the lessor, or the grantee or lessee, as the case may be. As the term implies, the covenant must concern the occupation or enjoyment of the land granted or demised and the liability to perform it, and the right to take advantage of it must pass to the assignee. Conversely, if the covenant does not touch or concern the occupation or enjoyment of the land, it is the collateral and personal obligation of the grantor or lessor and does not run with the land.

The main consideration in deciding whether covenants run with the land appears to be whether the covenant in question is so related to the land as to enhance its value and confer a benefit upon it.

Specifically, a covenant creating a lien against the land for the expense of repairs, or for dividing the expense of repairs, may run with the land and follow it into the hands of subsequent purchasers....

In *Neponsit Property Owners' Ass'n v. Emigrant Industrial Sav. Bank*, 278 N. Y. 248, 15 N. E. (2d) 793, 118 A. L. R. 973, the association sought to foreclose a lien upon land owned by the defendant. The lien claim was based upon a covenant in the deed from the association's assignor to defendant's predecessor in interest. Defendant's deed conveyed the property to him subject to the covenant contained in the original deed. That covenant was intended to create a charge or obligation to pay a fixed sum of money to be "devoted to the maintenance of the roads, paths, parks, beach, sewers, and such other public purposes as shall from time to time be determined by the party of the first part (the grantor), its successors, or assigns." The court determined that the covenant to pay money for use in connection with but not upon the land subject to the burden of the covenant "touched" or "concerned" the land. The court said:

> Thus, unless we exalt technical form over substance, the distinction between covenants which run with land and covenants which are personal, must depend upon the effect of the covenant on the legal rights which otherwise would flow from ownership of land and which are connected with the land. The problem then is: Does the covenant in purpose and effect substantially alter these rights? ...

> Looking at the problem presented in this case from the same point of view and stressing the intent and substantial effect of the covenant rather than its form, it seems clear that the covenant may properly be said to touch and concern the land of the defendant and its burden should run with the land. True, it calls for payment of a sum of money to be expended for 'public purposes' upon land other than the land conveyed by Neponsit Realty Company to plaintiff's predecessor in title. By that conveyance the grantee, however, obtained not only title to particular lots, but an easement or right of common enjoyment with other property owners in roads, beaches, public parks or spaces and improvements in the same tract. For full enjoyment in common by the defendant and other property owners of these easements or rights, the roads and public places must be maintained. In order that the burden of maintaining public improvements should rest upon the land benefited by the improvements, the grantor exacted from the grantee of the land with its appurtenant easement or right of enjoyment a covenant that the burden of paying the cost should be inseparably attached to the land which enjoys the benefit. It is plain that any distinction or definition which would

exclude such a covenant from the classification of covenants which 'touch' or 'concern' the land would be based on form and not on substance.

The covenant in question in substance concerns the enjoyment and value of the land demised to appellants, and the reasoning of the *Neponsit* case is applicable. The appellants, by taking ownership of the land, obtained a right of common enjoyment with the other property owners in the streets. The covenant attached the burden of paying a share of the cost of maintaining the streets to the land enjoying the benefit. In purpose and effect, it substantially altered the rights connected with the land conveyed.

Under the covenant, the maintenance commission is obliged to maintain and repair the streets. Performance on the part of the commission has and will inure to the benefit of appellants' property. Appellants, as property owners, enjoy the roads as maintained by the commission. The assessments for maintenance and repair "touch" or "concern" the land....

It is asserted that the Hayes Investment Company deeds and the by-laws of the commission are too indefinite to fulfill the requirements of a covenant or promise; that there is no fixed limit to the amount that may be charged and no standard to guide the board of trustees in making the assessments.

The articles of incorporation, by-laws, and deeds are correlated documents.... Both the original articles and by-laws and the amended articles and by-laws included, among the corporate purposes and powers, the maintenance and improvement of the streets, alleys, sidewalks, etc. It was for the commission as trustee, through its board of trustees, to determine what work was to be done in maintaining and improving the streets and what charge would be made against the members for such work. The right to demand payment of the charges levied carried with it an obligation on the part of the commission to exercise the discretion vested in it fairly and within the scope of the corporate functions outlined in its charter and by-laws. Appellants, as members of the commission and subsequent grantees under the Hayes Investment Company deeds, are bound by a sound exercise of that discretion. Members may attack assessments deemed to be unreasonable and the result of an abuse of discretion, but the plan of operation does not fail in its entirety merely because such discretion has been vested in the commission. The scope of the work to be done is discretionary; the amounts of the individual assessments are governed by a set standard,

> ... according as the area of such tract bears to the entire area of the tracts assessed, that is, on the square footage basis, and without reference to the value of the front footage thereof; ...

Nassau County v. Kensington Ass'n, 21 N. Y. S. (2d) 208, relied upon by appellants, is not in point. In that case, certain property was laid out as a residential area. An association was formed, made up of the property owners in the district, for the common welfare of its members. Deeds taken by parties buying property in the district contained this covenant: "And the said parties of the second part agree to pay to the Kensington Association five dollars per year for each lot in the property hereby conveyed; said payments to be binding on any subsequent owners of the said lots." The court ruled that the covenant did not run with the land and emphasized that the association was not committed by the terms of the covenant to use the funds collected for any particular purpose or in fact to spend the money at all.

We are not faced with the same situation. The covenant in the Hayes deed clearly states the purposes for which the funds realized through assessments are to be collected and spent, and the commission is obliged thereby to spend such funds for those designated purposes.

In this instance, as has been noted, the maintenance and repair of the enumerated facilities is designated in the commission's charter as a purpose of the formation of the commission. Appellants, as members of the commission, were bound by provisions therein commensurate with promotion of the corporate objects. The by-laws, in effect, constitute a contract between the commission and its members....

Appellants assert further that to recognize the power of assessment, as recited in the deeds to their grantors and incorporated by reference in their deeds, would result in allowing a change or modification of the filed restrictions without complying with the procedure set forth for that purpose.

Reliance is had upon *Van Deusen v. Ruth*, 343 Mo. 1096, 125 S. W. (2d) 1. In that case, restrictions were filed applicable to a certain real-estate subdivision. It was provided therein that the restrictions could be modified or amended by following a definite procedure set out in the instrument. Thereafter, in compliance with that procedure, an instrument was filed purporting to prohibit the erection of commercial buildings which had been permitted under the original restrictions. The court canceled the second instrument.

There, the attempted modification and amendment destroyed in part the subject matter of the restrictions then in effect. New and additional burdens resulted from the deletion enforced in the instrument of modification. The restrictions of record in this case make no mention of the power of assessment. The power to assess is in no way connected with the filed restrictions. The latter are not denominated as exclusive, and we do not consider them as being so. Each of the restrictions remained in full force and effect as within the contemplation of the instrument as filed.

The assessments now due and owing to the commission were levied in accordance with authority vested in that body. They are binding obligations as against appellants and the property to which they hold title in the Sand Point district. The amounts due have been established by the evidence in the sums found by the trial court.

The judgments are Affirmed.

Fogarty v. Hemlock Farms Community Ass'n

Commonwealth Court of Pennsylvania
685 A.2d 241 (Pa. Commw. Ct. 1996)

SMITH, D. Dennis Fogarty and Mary M. Fogarty (the Fogartys) appeal from an order of the Court of Common Pleas of Pike County that granted a motion for summary judgment on behalf of Hemlock Farms Community Association, Inc. (HFCA), holding that HFCA has the power to levy special assessments for the construction of three capital improvements—a community mail office, an administration building and a community clubhouse—and that the Fogartys are obligated to pay their assessment. The questions presented are whether HFCA exceeded its authority under the Fogartys' deed covenant by imposing the special assessments and whether HFCA violated the debt ceiling limitations set forth in Section 6.8(b) of its by-laws when it incurred debt for the construction.

In 1969 the Fogartys purchased a property in the Hemlock Farms Community in Blooming Grove Township, Pike County. Under a protective covenant contained in their

Hemlock Farms Community Clubhouse, courtesy of Michael J. Sibio, PCAM, of Hemlock Farms Management Co.

deed, the Fogartys are required to become members of HFCA, which is an association comprised of all the homeowners in the Hemlock Farms Community. The deed covenant also requires the Fogartys to pay annual dues and fees, as well as assessments for control, maintenance and repair of streets, roads and recreational facilities.

On July 14, 1990, the membership of HFCA passed a resolution that imposed special assessments upon all members to offset construction costs for the three improvements. HFCA's Board of Directors estimated that the costs of the project would be $2,675,000. HFCA imposed a $151 assessment on the Fogartys in September 1990 and a $119 assessment in June 1991. The Fogartys refused to pay the assessments and filed an action in the trial court seeking a declaration that the assessments were invalid in that they were not authorized by the covenants in the Fogarty's deed or by HFCA's by-laws. Following the close of discovery, both parties filed motions for summary judgment. The trial court granted summary judgment on behalf of HFCA and upheld the special assessments. The Fogartys appeal.

The Fogartys contend that the trial court erred in determining that HFCA was authorized by the deed covenant and its by-laws to impose these special assessments. In part, Paragraph 10 of the deed covenant provides:

> The Purchaser agrees to join the Hemlock Farms Community Association, the only qualification for election to membership being ownership or prospective ownership of a Lot or Lots or acreage within the development, and to maintain such membership, and pay (i) such annual fees or dues as the Association may by its by-laws prescribe, (ii) such assessments as the Association may charge for the repair and maintenance of the streets and roads and (iii) such assessments

as the association may charge for control, maintenance and administration of beach and other recreational facilities, and (iv) fire service fee of $18.00 per year in respect of each and every Lot owned by the Purchaser on which a house has not been erected.

The Fogartys contend that the deed covenant is nonrestrictive. They cite *Birchwood Lakes Community Ass'n, Inc. v. Comis*, 296 Pa. Super. 77, 442 A.2d 304 (1982), for the proposition that if an agreement in a non-restrictive covenant is not clearly expressed or is susceptible to more than one interpretation, the words of the deed must be construed most strongly against the grantor and most favorably toward the grantee, unless the grantee drafted the deed.

Although the Fogartys do not challenge HFCA's decision to construct the new improvements, they argue that HFCA must pay for these improvements through annual fees and borrowing as specified in the deed covenant. The Fogartys claim that Paragraph 10 does not authorize special assessments for these types of capital improvements but only authorizes special assessments for the maintenance and repair of streets and roads and for the control, maintenance and administration of the beach and other recreational facilities.

The trial court, however, determined that the deed covenant did not prohibit the levying of special assessments and that HFCA is authorized by its by-laws to levy special assessments. The trial court further determined that HFCA may, by the implied intent of the parties, levy authorized special assessments for the building of improvements that benefit all association members, in the absence of an express agreement prohibiting such assessments. To support its decision, the trial court relied on *Meadow Run and Mountain Lake Park Ass'n v. Berkel*, 409 Pa. Super. 637, 642, 598 A.2d 1024, 1027 (1991), *appeal denied*, 530 Pa. 666, 610 A.2d 46 (1992), where the Court held that:

> Absent an express agreement prohibiting assessments, when an association of property owners in a private development is referred to in the chain of title and has the authority to regulate each property owner's use of common facilities, inherent in that authority is the ability to impose reasonable assessments on the property owners to fund the maintenance of those facilities.

The Fogartys argue that *Meadow Run & Mountain Lake Park Ass'n* is distinguishable from the present case. In that case, the homeowners' association passed a resolution assessing each homeowner $300 for the repair of dams and roads. The appellants argued that there was no specifically expressed deed covenant authorizing such an assessment. Nevertheless, the Superior Court reasoned that because all property owners' deeds notified them that they had the right to use the facilities and that they were bound by certain rules regarding that right, there existed implied rules and regulations regarding the maintenance of those facilities. The Fogartys claim that the deed in the present case, in contrast, expressly limits the imposition of special assessments only to the maintenance and repair of roads and recreational facilities.

The Fogartys also rely on the basic principle of contract law that the intent of the parties to a contract is to be determined solely from its express language and that any ambiguities or doubtful language must be construed most strongly against the drafter.... They refer also to the maxim *expressio unius est exclusio alterius* to support their position that because the deed covenant specifically lists all obligations that the HFCA may require them to meet, special assessments for items not contained in the covenant are thereby excluded.

On the other hand, HFCA contends that because it is a nonprofit corporation operating in the Commonwealth, it is governed by provisions of the Nonprofit Corporation Law of 1988 (NCL), 15 Pa. C.S. §§5101–6162. Specifically, HFCA relies on Section 5544(a) of the NCL, 15 Pa. C.S. §5544(a), relating to fees, dues and assessments, which provides:

(a) General rule.—A nonprofit corporation may levy dues or assessments, or both, on its members, if authority to do so is conferred by the by-laws, subject to any limitations therein contained. Such dues or assessments, or both, may be imposed upon all members of the same class either alike or in different amounts or proportions, and upon a different basis upon different classes of members. Members of one or more classes may be made exempt from either dues or assessments, or both, in the manner or to the extent provided in the by-laws.

Noting that the Fogartys are required by the deed covenant to become HFCA members, HFCA refers to the following pertinent by-law provisions by which the Fogartys are governed:

Section 2.4. Obligations of membership.

The obligations of membership shall be: ...

(b) To pay all dues, assessments and user fees, including those relating to receipt of water or other utility service, levied pursuant to the authority granted by these by-laws.

Section 3.1 Powers.

Subject to the restrictions of these by-laws, the Board of Directors shall: ...

(b) Promulgate rules and regulations and levy dues, fees and special assessments in respect thereof and take any other lawful action in respect thereto.

Section 6.3. Dues, fees and assessments.

(a) Membership dues, fees, utility charges and assessments shall be fixed by the Board and vary reasonably as between improved, unimproved and adjacent lots.

HFCA contends that, pursuant to these provisions, its Board of Directors has the power to promulgate and levy special assessments for various purposes and that the deed covenants refer strictly to the obligations of the buyers and do not impose any restrictions on corporate authority to make capital improvements. HFCA further argues that *Meadow Run & Mountain Lake Park Ass'n* supports the position that where no express agreement prohibiting special assessments exists in the deed covenant and where property owners are required to join the association, the property owners are thereby bound by the by-laws. This Court agrees with HFCA.

In *Meadow Run & Mountain Lake Park Ass'n*, the Superior Court further stated:

Residential communities such as Meadow Run and Mountain Lake Park, are "analogous to mini-governments" and as such are dependent on the collection of assessments to maintain and provide essential and recreational facilities. *Holiday Pocono Civic Association, Inc. v. Benick*, 7 D. & C. 3d 378 (1978). When ownership of property within a residential community allows the owners to utilize roads and other common areas of the development, there is an implied [sic] agreement to accept the proportionate costs for maintaining and repairing these facilities....

In the present case, all members of HFCA will benefit from the new mail office, administration building and clubhouse. Although the Fogartys' deed does not mention an assessment for these improvements, it does not impose restrictions on the authority granted to HFCA under its by-laws to construct such facilities. Therefore, absent lan-

Holding

guage in the deed covenant prohibiting HFCA from levying special assessments for capital improvements, the Fogartys may be assessed their proportionate costs to construct the new improvements.

The Fogartys further argue that the capital improvements made by HFCA were unauthorized because the debt created by HFCA violated the debt ceiling restrictions of the bylaws. Section 6.8(b) of the by-laws provides:

> Debt ceiling. No debts to finance capital expenses or capital projects shall be incurred which shall have the effect of increasing the annual debt service of the Association for interest and amortization above ten percentum (10%) of the annual operating expense budget for any one (1) year; provided, however, that where the Board determines that additional debt service is necessary in order to provide adequate water service to the membership, the Board may, by a two-thirds vote of its members, exceed the ten percent (10%) limitations set forth above, but the total debt service shall not exceed twenty percent (20%).

The Fogartys assert that ten percent of the 1990 operating budget amounted to $281,024.70. On April 27, 1991, after raising nearly $800,000 through the special assessments, HFCA obtained a construction and term loan in the maximum amount of $1,875,000 from the First National Bank of Pike County. The loan required an annual payment of ten percent of the outstanding principal and interest at the rate of prime plus one percent. The prime rate on that date was nine percent.

The Fogartys claim that the potential annual principal payment of $187,500 and accompanying interest payment of $187,500 amounted to $375,000, an amount that exceeds ten percent of the previous operating budget. To the contrary, HFCA contends that the Fogartys' argument is premature in that HFCA's borrowing did not exceed the debt limitation. This Court's review of the record indicates that HFCA did not borrow the full $1,875,000 but, in fact, borrowed much less. The parties do not dispute that the annual debt never exceeded the debt ceiling in Section 6.8(b) of HFCA's by-laws.

Annual debt never exceeded debt ceiling.

Declaratory judgment is available only where an actual controversy exists; it is not appropriate to determine rights in anticipation of events that may never occur. *Pennsylvania Protection & Advocacy, Inc. v. Department of Education*, 148 Pa. Commw. 153, 609 A.2d 909 (Pa. Cmwlth. 1992). Such is the case here. HFCA never violated the debt ceiling, and, as a consequence, the Fogartys' action for declaratory judgment on this issue was properly dismissed. In view of the foregoing, the order of the trial court is affirmed.

Retrospective and Observations

The association's perspective.

Hemlock Farms is a well-established, 4000+ acre community in Pike County, Pennsylvania. As with many communities in that area of Pennsylvania, it was built originally as a second home community and has now transitioned to a primary home community. Original plans for the community included recreational facilities that would accommodate a 50% build-out. As build-out continued beyond 50%, the association realized that it would have to expand recreational facilities. Dennis and Mary Fogarty objected to those plans and sued the association claiming that the association was not authorized to impose a special assessment against association members in order to build the capital improvements.

The Fogartys continue to live at Hemlock Farm, and the association continues its strategic planning. The case was appealed to the Pennsylvania Supreme Court, but the court denied certiorari.

Alan Young, the association's attorney, observed that in every community it seems that 5% of the owners cause 85% of the problems.

Notes & Questions

1. *Authority to assess. Rodruck* involved a dispute over the authority of a maintenance commission to levy assessments against members of a residential community for maintenance of streets, alleys, sidewalks, etc. Typically, community associations are explicitly provided with broad authority to maintain common property and to assess for such maintenance. For example, a typical provision granting authority to the association may provide:

> The assessments provided for herein shall be used for the general purposes of promoting the recreation, health, safety, welfare, common benefit, and enjoyment of the Owners and occupants of Units, including the maintenance of real and personal property as may be more specifically authorized from time to time by the Board of Directors.

See WAYNE S. HYATT, CONDOMINIUMS AND HOME OWNER ASSOCIATIONS: A GUIDE TO THE DEVELOPMENT PROCESS, 200–205 (1985). What association actions may fall within the authority granted by the above provision?

2. *Vagueness as to assessment authority.* An assessment must be imposed for legitimate association matters; otherwise, it may be subject to successful challenge by association members. In addition to the intended purpose and use of assessments, the governing documents should provide a procedure by which assessments are levied and collected. See generally WAYNE S. HYATT & PHILIP S. DOWNER, CONDOMINIUM AND HOMEOWNER ASSOCIATION LITIGATION: COMMUNITY ASSOCIATION LAW (1987).

What happens when the covenant providing the assessment authority is vague as to the purpose, method, or procedure for collection?

In *Beech Mountain Property Owners Ass'n v. Seifart*, 48 N.C. App. 286, 269 S.E.2d 178 (1980), the court refused to enforce an assessment where the covenants were unclear and ambiguous. The declaration in question provided that the association could make "reasonable assessment charges for road maintenance and maintenance of the trails and recreational areas." The court noted two policy arguments supporting its decision not to enforce the covenant for assessments. First, the court held that a purchaser would not be adequately informed about which roads and trails would be maintained (there were 58 miles of gravel roads in the resort). Second, the covenant provisions did not provide any specific standards by which the association's authority to levy such an assessment could be objectively determined. Compare the language at issue in *Beech Mountain Property Owners Ass'n* with the language of the governing documents in *Rodruck*. Are there differences? Would the "typical provision" described in note 1 above create an enforceable assessment power under *Beech Mountain*? How would you draft the governing documents to ensure that assessment powers meet the *Beech Mountain* standard? Do you think that degree of specificity is desirable as a policy matter?

An assessing power may be struck when:

3. *Implied power to assess.* Generally, covenants in the declaration provide authority for the association to collect assessments from each owner. Where the declaration does not specifically provide for assessment for a particular purpose, the association may be challenged by homeowners who refuse to pay. See, *e.g., Wendover Road Property Owners Ass'n v. Kornicks*, 28 Ohio App. 3d 101, 502 N.E. 2d 226 (1985) (declining to apply quasi-contract or unjust enrichment theories to require a property owner to pay assessments when the deed conveying the property did not provide for such an assessment); *Board of Directors of Carriage Way Property Owners Ass'n v. Western National Bank of Cicero*, 139 Ill. App. 3d 542, 487 N.E.2d 974 (1985). The declaration at issue in *Carriage Way* authorized assessments *only* for maintenance of sewers. The association, however, attempted to collect assessments for other common area maintenance and was challenged. The association argued that when a declaration was deficient, as in this case, the owners should nonetheless be required to pay a proportionate share of common expenses based on a theory of unjust enrichment or implied or quasi-contract. The court rejected this argument and held that the owners were not required to pay these other expenses. Note that the common property in these cases was limited to easements and that absence of assessment authority may not have seriously compromised the ability to maintain the easements in usable condition. Easement law provides that all users of the easement can be required to contribute to maintenance based on their degree of use. See Restatement (Third) § 4.10, Duties of Repair and Maintenance. Why isn't easement law generally sufficient to handle the problems of maintaining common property in common interest communities?

Some courts have held that an association has the authority to collect assessments despite the absence of express language in the declaration. For example, in *Meadow Run and Mountain Lake Park Ass'n v. Berkel*, 409 Pa. Super. 637, 598 A.2d 1024 (1991), the court held that there was an implied agreement to accept proportionate costs for maintaining and repairing common facilities when the property owner availed himself of the use of the common areas. Consider the policy reasons supporting such a result. Does the common benefit received support common responsibility? See also Robert G. Natelson, Law of Property Owners Associations § 6.1 (1989).

4. *Withholding payment of assessments.* Generally, unit owners may not withhold payment for valid assessments even when the association has failed to provide the intended service or provided deficient service. See, *e.g., Rivers Edge Condo. Ass'n v. Rere, Inc.*, 390 Pa. Super. 196; 568 A.2d 261 (1990); *Forest Villas Condo. Ass'n, Inc. v. Camerio*, 205 Ga. App. 617, 422 S.E.2d 884 (1994). Homeowner defenses to assessment payment will be considered more thoroughly later in this chapter and in Chapter 8. See also Freedman and Alter, Law of Condominium and Property Owners' Associations, § 5.3 (1992).

Problem

The Broken Bush HOA board is looking for new revenue sources. Because design review is time consuming and staff intensive, they decide to charge a $250 fee for processing applications and an additional $750 deposit to ensure that construction does not result in damage to the common area. Six months after the board began this charge, a builder objected, saying that the CCRs do not authorize it.

The board calls association counsel, you. What do you advise? Where do you look for authority? How should such a charge be set? What are other ways the board can raise revenue? If you were drafting CCRs for a new project, how would you deal with this issue?

B. Governing Documents Provide Assessment Method

Seabrook Island Property Owners Ass'n v. Pelzer
Court of Appeals of South Carolina
356 S.E.2d 411 (S.C. Ct. App. 1987)

BELL, J. Seabrook Island Property Owners Association instituted this action against J. Randolph Pelzer to collect an unpaid annual assessment for 1984 on two lots owned by Pelzer at Seabrook Island. Pelzer counterclaimed, alleging the assessment was invalid. He also sought a refund of assessments he had previously paid for the years 1976 through 1983, alleging that they, too, were invalid. The Association replied to the counterclaim, raising the defense of estoppel as to past assessments. The circuit court entered judgment for the Association in the sum of $992.25, representing the unpaid 1984 assessment, and dismissed Pelzer's counterclaim with prejudice. Pelzer appeals. We affirm in part and reverse in part.

The Association is a non-profit corporation organized under the laws of South Carolina. Its purpose is to preserve the amenities of Seabrook Island and to maintain roads, open spaces, and landscaping for all property owners of the Seabrook Island development. Its membership is composed of all property owners on Seabrook Island.

The Association is governed by protective covenants and by-laws. These authorize it to collect from each property owner an annual maintenance charge. The authority to assess and the method of assessment are prescribed in Paragraph 7 of the protective covenants and in Article VIII, Section 1, of the by-laws. Paragraph 7 of the protective covenants provides, in pertinent part:

> Each lot and lot owner in the subdivision shall be subject to an annual maintenance charge based upon the assessed valuation of the premises and any improvements thereon as fixed each year by the Tax Assessor of Charleston County, South Carolina, for County taxation purposes.

Article VIII, Section 1, of the by-laws states:

> The Board of Directors ... shall have the right and power to subject the property situated on Seabrook Island ... to an annual maintenance charge....

> The annual charge may be increased, adjusted or reduced from year to year by the Board of Directors ... and such maintenance charge may be set at a fixed rate for unimproved property and a fixed rate for improved property. After reassessment of all the property on Seabrook Island by the Tax Assessor of Charleston County, the annual charge may be increased, adjusted or reduced from year to year by the Board of Directors ... based on the dollar [sic] of the assessed valuation of the premises and any improvements constructed thereon ... as fixed each year by the Tax Assessor of Charleston County, South Carolina, for County taxation purposes.

In 1984, Pelzer received two bills for maintenance charges on his improved and unimproved lots, respectively. Although he had paid previous assessments from 1976 through 1983 without protest, he investigated the manner in which the assessments were fixed in connection with litigation for clients challenging special assessments for beach renourishment and bridge repair.[1] As a result of his investigation, Pelzer concluded the Association had been improp-

---

1. Pelzer was the plaintiffs' attorney in Lovering v. Seabrook Island Property Owners Association, 289 S.C. 77, 344 S.E.2d 862 (Ct.App. 1986) *aff'd as modified*, 291 S.C. 201, 352 S.E.2d 707 (1987).

erly assessing his properties, because the annual maintenance charge was not based upon assessed valuation for taxation purposes as required by the restrictive covenants and by-laws.
He, therefore, requested the Association in writing to reassess the property on a valid basis
and refused to pay the annual maintenance charges for which he had been billed.

[handwritten margin note: Invalid as not based upon criteria set forth in the cov. / by-laws]

I

The Association admits it has been assessing all property owners on a fixed fee basis
without regard to the value of their property. Owners of improved lots are assessed at
one uniform fee, regardless of the value of their lots; owners of unimproved lots are assessed at another uniform fee, regardless of the value of their lots. The flat fee for improved property for 1984 was $610.00; the fee for unimproved property was $315.00.

[handwritten margin note: Assoc. admits assessed on "fixed fee" basis.]

The Association defends this flat fee system of assessment as a "business judgment" of
the Board of Directors. It contends a flat fee is authorized under the clause in Article VIII,
Section 1, which says "such maintenance charge may be set at a fixed rate for unimproved
property and a fixed rate for improved property." We reject this argument.

In *Lovering v. Seabrook Island Property Owners Association*, 291 S.C. 201, 352 S.E.2d
707 (1987), our Supreme Court construed the Association's by-laws to provide that "adjustments to the annual maintenance charge are to be based on the assessed value of the
property as fixed by the county tax assessor."…. This is the plain import of both the restrictive covenants and the by-laws.

The authorization to set the maintenance charge at a "fixed rate" does not permit a
"flat fee" system of charges. A "rate" is a proportional charge based on value, not a flat fee.
A "fixed rate" is a fixed amount of assessment per stated amount of valuation. The "rate"
of assessment is the proportion or ratio the maintenance charge bears to the assessed
value of the property. Typically, it is expressed as a percentage or millage of the property's assessed value: *i.e.*, so many cents or mills per dollar of value.

Under the by-laws, the Board of Directors may set one rate for improved property and
another rate for unimproved property. For example, improved property might be assessed at 1.5% of value while unimproved property is assessed at 1% of value. This does
not, however, authorize the Board to fix the annual maintenance charge on some basis
other than assessed value for county tax purposes.

The Association argues that its flat fee system of charges is reasonable and was adopted
in good faith in the exercise of business judgment. This argument misses the point. Restrictive covenants are contractual in nature and bind the parties thereto in the same
manner as any other contract. *Palmetto Dunes Resort v. Brown*, 287 S.C. 1, 336 S.E.2d 15
(Ct.App.1985). Moreover, a corporation may exercise only those powers which are granted
to it by law, by its charter or articles of incorporation, and by any by-laws made pursuant
thereto; acts beyond the scope of the powers so granted are *ultra vires*. *Lovering v. Seabrook
Island Property Owners Association*, 289 S.C. 77, 344 S.E.2d 862 (Ct.App.1986), *aff'd as
modified*, 291 S.C. 201, 352 S.E.2d 707 (1987). The "business judgment" rule applies to
intra vires action of the corporation, not to *ultra vires* acts.…

[handwritten margin note: Assoc. must follow its own covenants and by-laws.]

The restrictive covenants and the by-laws require annual maintenance charges to be based
on property values. A system of charges that violates this requirement cannot be defended
on the ground that it is a reasonable alternative. The Association is bound to follow the
covenants and its own by-laws.

Since the flat fee annual maintenance charge violates the restrictive covenants and the
by-laws, we reverse the judgment against Pelzer for the 1984 charges on his two lots.

II

In his first counterclaim, Pelzer also sought a <u>refund</u> of all assessments paid in excess of what was due under a proper method of assessment for the years 1976 through 1983. The circuit court held <u>Pelzer was estopped</u> to assert his claim for a refund and dismissed the counterclaim with prejudice. <u>We affirm</u>.

As regards refund of payments from 1976 through 1983, <u>the equities clearly favor the Association</u>. The annual charges for those years were assessed in good faith. Pelzer had <u>constructive knowledge</u> that the maintenance charges were not being assessed in accordance with the restrictive covenants and by-laws. Nevertheless, he acquiesced in the method of assessment and paid the charges. The Association expended the moneys for purposes authorized by the by-laws. Pelzer received the benefit of those expenditures. <u>He cannot now return the benefits or restore the Association to its former position</u>.

For these reasons, the circuit court correctly held Pelzer is estopped to claim a refund. If a party stands by and sees another dealing with his property in a manner inconsistent with his rights and makes no objection while the other changes his position, his silence is acquiescence and it estops him from later seeking relief....

Holding re: No refund.

Affirmed in part, Reversed in part.

Retrospective and Observations

Randy Pelzer was an attorney who lived at Seabrook Island. In the process of representing the Loverings and the Wallers in other cases against Seabrook Island Property Owners Association, Mr. Pelzer decided that the Association's method of determining assessments on property at Seabrook Island was not in accordance with the declaration and by-laws.

The case was appealed to the South Carolina Supreme Court, but certiorari was denied. David Wheeler, the Association's attorney, notes that the case is often cited in other South Carolina cases because of the court's decision that <u>Mr. Pelzer was estopped from claiming a refund on assessments he paid between 1976 and 1983</u>.

Notes & Questions

1. *Methods of assessment.* The *Seabrook* case mentioned several methods of assessment, including flat fee and fixed rate assessment methods. Here are some proposed methods of assessing owners for common element or common area expenses:

Value assessment. The value of the unit is assessed based on either par value or market value in relation to the value of the project as a whole. In other words, if an owner's property value represented 1/25 of the entire value of the community, then that owner would pay 1/25 of the common expenses.

Square footage assessment. The ratio of the square footage of the unit to the total square footage determines the assigned percentage of interest. Owners with larger lots or units pay a higher percentage of the assessment costs.

Equality principle. All units have an equal ownership, vote, and assessment liability regardless of factors such as value and square footage.

See Wayne S. Hyatt, Condominium and Homeowner Association Practice: Community Association Law, p. 109 (3d Ed. 2000).

What do you think the rationale is behind each assessment method mentioned above? What are the pros and cons of each assessment method? Are some of the assessment methods more viable in the condominium context than in other types of homeowner associations or cooperatives and vice versa? Which method of assessment is best to assess owners for "limited" common areas or elements which are used by less than all of the owners in the community?

2. *Modifying the assessment method.* Common elements are areas subject to community use. The condominium form of ownership grants to each unit owner the title to his unit plus an undivided interest in common elements (everything outside a unit). In other homeowner associations, title to the common area is held by the association. In all instances, unit owners typically pay for a percentage of the common area expenses. See UCIOA § 2-107 and commentary. Given the ownership differences between these different forms of communities, do you think that it would be harder to change the method of assessment in a condominium community than in other forms of common interest communities? Consider the following case:

In *Thiess v. Island House Ass'n, Inc.*, 311 So. 2d 142 (Fla. Dist. Ct. App. 1976), a condominium association sought to change the method of assessing units for common element expenses by amending the declaration. Prior to the amendment, the declaration provided that each unit owner would own 1/73 of the common elements and would be responsible for 1/73 of the common expenses. The amendment proposed a change to the declaration whereby each owner would be assessed based on the value of his or her unit. Since the apartment units were valued higher than the villas in the condominium community, under the new assessment method, apartment unit owners would pay more of the common area expenses.

Although the amendment was approved by a majority of the unit owners, a group of apartment unit owners voted against the new assessment method and challenged the amendment. The court held that the amendment was ineffective without 100 percent approval of all owners. The court reasoned that the association's surplus generated by common element assessments was a property interest owned by each unit owner. In short, the court considered the assessment method to be part of "a bundle of rights and responsibilities" that was intricately intertwined with the owners' property interests, and as such, it could not be modified without the consent of each owner.

Contrast the *Thiess* decision with the *Seabrook Island* case (which involved a noncondominium property owners association). In *Seabrook Island*, the court found the change in assessment method invalid because (1) it violated restrictive covenants which required the proportionate value method of assessment, and (2) amendment of the assessment method by the association exceeded the powers granted to it in the declaration and by-laws. Accordingly, the association's action was *ultra vires*. In both cases, the change in assessment method was held invalid. Had the board in *Seabrook Island* amended the declaration with a homeowner vote to provide for per lot assessments, would result be the same? If the *Thiess* case had not involved a condominium association, would the court have reached the same result?

In *Cebular v. Cooper Arms Homeowners Ass'n*, 47 Cal. Rptr.3 d 666 (Cal. Ct. App. 2006), a condominium unit owner unsuccessfully challenged the unequal allocation of assessments in the declaration. When the Cooper Arms was converted from a stock cooperative to a condominium in 1995, undivided interests in the common area were allocated on the same basis as cooperative stock had previously been allocated among apartment owners, which did not necessarily reflect size or location of the units. Unit 215 thus had 19 interests and plaintiff's unit 1101 had 85 interests. Although the declaration stated that the association should have only one class of voting membership, votes were allocated on the same basis as interests in the common area, and assessments were similarly unequal. The court rejected claims that the assessment formula was arbitrary and inequitable or otherwise illegal. It found that because the assessments were tied to voting rights, they were not "wholly arbitrary," and that equal assessments were not legally required.

3. *Assessments for common area expenses where member access is restricted.* An association has the authority to collect payments from owners to cover common area or common element expenses. An association's authority to require that members contribute for maintenance of common areas is premised upon the rationale that those who have access to these areas must pay a share of the maintenance expenses. What happens when common area resources are appropriated in a way that restricts access of a group of unit owners who contribute to those expenses?

Consider *Lyman v. Boonin*, 397 Pa. Super. 543, 580 A.2d 765 (1990); *vacated and remanded*, 635 A.2d 1029 (Pa. 1993) in which a condominium association enacted a policy that gave on-site parking priority to resident unit owners over nonresident unit owners. The policy addressed the shortage of parking spaces and the practice of some unit owners who sublet unneeded parking spaces to others without regard to a waiting list. The parking regulation was problematic given the ownership interests held by all unit owners. Effectively, the policy deprived nonresident unit owners of their property interests in the common elements. The court held that the association had the authority to establish a system of priority; however, the association's policy must provide a method by which all unit owners are compensated for use of the commonly owned parking spaces. How could non-parking unit owners be "compensated?"

4. *Assessments for limited common areas.* Disputes sometimes arise over the proper amount or method of assessment for maintenance of limited common areas or elements. In *Tosney v. Chelmsford*, 397 Mass. 683 (1986), garden apartment owners challenged the limited common area assessment imposed on them and not on other townhouse owners. The limited common elements in question were elevators, parking areas, and air conditioning and heating units for the garden apartments. Even though the declaration did not create these as limited common areas, the townhouse unit owners did not derive any benefit from them. The court held that it was neither ethical nor logical to require the townhouse owners to pay for maintenance of what were in effect limited common elements of the garden apartment owners.

The court also noted that most, if not all, states require that limited common elements be designated as such in the declaration or master deed, or an amendment of such documents. See, *e.g.*, UCIOA Section 2-108. Nonetheless, the court in *Tosney* held that an agreement entered into between the developer and the association which provided for limited common element assessments on garden apartments was valid and enforceable against those owners. Do you believe it is proper to hold owners to terms of an agreement between the association and the developer? Why or why not? Is there a benefit received? What would have been a preferable way for the developer subsequently to designate limited common areas?

5. *Annual assessments vs. special assessments.* As *Seabrook Island* illustrates, the declaration and by-laws authorize the association to assess and collect from each owner his or her proportionate share of common expenses. The governing documents also

usually authorize the collection procedure for assessments, permissible uses of assessments, and, occasionally, the maximum amount of annual increases. Typically, the governing documents distinguish between annual assessments and special assessments. An annual assessment covers charges the association has determined are necessary for ongoing maintenance of the community plus reserves necessary for future major repairs (such as roof replacement). A special assessment, on the other hand, covers unanticipated contingencies. Consider the following sample special assessment provision:

> Special Assessments. In addition to the other assessments authorized herein, the Association may levy special assessments in any year. So long as the total amount of special assessments allocable to each Unit does not exceed $500.00 in any one fiscal year, the Board may impose the special assessment. Any special assessment which would cause the amount of special assessments allocable to any Unit to exceed this limitation shall be effective only if approved by a Majority of the Members. Special assessments shall be paid as determined by the Board, and the Board may permit special assessments to be paid in installments extending beyond the fiscal year in which the special assessment is imposed.

Should the special assessment provision contain specific references as to the type of expenses it may fund, or should it be purposefully vague? If the purpose is to cover unanticipated needs, is it not counter intuitive to limit special assessments to a specified lists of purposes? Requiring a vote of the members is a better approach. What if a declaration did not provide for any assessments other than annual assessments? How would a community address unexpected maintenance expenses? The above sample provision provides for a homeowner vote before special assessments over $500 can be imposed. What are the benefits and disadvantages of this policy?

6. *Specific assessments.* Specific assessments are generally imposed to pay for common expenses which benefit one or a few units within a community. Such common expenses "must be assessed exclusively against the units benefited." UCIOA § 3-115(c)(2). Thus, specific assessments are assessments against a particular unit or units for expenses which the association incurs or expects to incur as a result of providing benefits, items, or services to the unit owner at the owner's request or as a result of bringing the unit into compliance with the governing documents. For example, the Board may specifically assess an owner for the cost of providing a lawn mowing service or other maintenance services which the association is not obligated to provide but does so as a convenience. Another example is when a homeowner refuses to comply with the governing documents and the association must pay someone to correct the violation (for example, towing junk cars from the owner's driveway). Sometimes specific assessments are referred to as default assessments or benefited assessments.

7. *Transfer fees.* An increasingly common practice is to draft governing documents to include the payment of "transfer fees" to the association on the sale of homes in the community. These fees may be imposed on the initial unit sale from the developer/builder to the homeowner as well as upon all subsequent sales from homeowner to homeowner. The purpose of the transfer fee is twofold. First, it compensates the community association for administrative expenses associated with such events (*i.e.*, updating membership lists and mailing lists). Second, it provides a convenient means to raise additional revenue for operation and common element reserve funds and for special community programs (*e.g.*, charitable foundation programs targeting neighborhood schools or providing other worthwhile neighborhood services). One perceived problem with transfer fees is

the appearance that the assessment burden is placed unfairly upon units which are more frequently sold (versus the unit owner who lives in the same house for 20 or 30 years). What factors may support the "fairness" of such transfer fees?

In thinking about whether and how to use transfer fees, remember that the amount of money they will generate will fluctuate depending on the state of the economy and other factors affecting sales within the community. Note, also, that their use is highly limited in California by Civil Code § 1366.1, which provides:

> An association shall not impose or collect an assessment or fee <u>that exceeds the amount necessary to defray the costs for which it is levied</u>.

Problems

1. Your developer client is planning a mixed income housing development. There will be both market rate and affordable housing. Developer is concerned that the association's budget and required assessment will make the monthly housing cost too high for the affordable housing units. She asks you for advice on how to address this issue in the documents and in the association's operation. What do you suggest? What policy concerns complicate the resolution?

Developer is considering efforts to preserve the affordable nature of the housing thus insuring that all units remain within an affordable price range upon resale. Can this be done? How might this be done through document drafting? What policy considerations support doing so? Not doing so? What do you advise?

2. Meeting with your developer client, you are considering various issues in preparation for the drafting of the CCRs for your client's new project. She has asked you a number of questions, and you are currently discussing assessment issues. One of the questions she asks is when assessments should begin. How do you advise her?

3. Seven Oaks Community Association has several churches located in its community, but they are not subject to the CCRs. By agreement with the declarant, each church is subject to design review and pays an assessment to the association. This payment has become a point of contention; the churches feel it is too high, that they should not have to pay at all. The board asks you if they can waive the assessment. Can they? The declarant proposes that it and each church modify the agreements to remove the assessment obligation. One board member objects arguing that the modification cannot be done without board consent. Do you agree? What are the association's rights and powers, and, if any, who may exercise them?

If you had originally represented the developer, how would you suggest churches be treated? Is there a potential problem in determining what qualifies as a church? How could you address the problem?

C. Assessing Unbuilt Units

What else can an unbuilt unit be? If land has been submitted to a condominium declaration or to a set of CCRs, by definition there are only certain types of property within that regime. As you know, in a condominium, submitted property is either a unit or common element. Thus, if land has been submitted to a condominium declaration and is not a unit, it is part of the common property. Therefore it is not subject to future development in the absence of extraordinary powers and reserved rights. Conversely, if the developer designated the property as a unit or a unit to be built, is it not a unit subject to assessment?

There are, of course, differences in this regard between condominium and homeowners associations. Property in the latter can be subject to further subdivision, and submitting property to CCRs does not necessarily mean that the property has to be either common area or units. Always ask what else it can be and what the property is. Statutory provisions applicable to the particular regime are also important. The policy questions of owners' expectations, the owners' capability, and uniform treatment of all owners are also important considerations. Each of these affect the basis of your analysis of the cases.

Developers and builders may sometimes assert that an unbuilt unit does not yet exist and, thus, cannot be assessed because there is nothing against which to levy an assessment. When does the unit come into existence? What controls? The documents themselves define these terms and are capable of postponing the creation of units in some contexts. Therefore, against whom should any ambiguity be construed? Are these questions answered differently in the condominium and non-condominium common interest community?

Pilgrim Place Condo. Ass'n v. KRE Properties, Inc.

Supreme Judicial Court of Maine
666 A.2d 500 (Me. 1995)

ROBERTS, J. KRE Properties, Inc., appeals from a judgment entered in the Superior Court (York County, Fritzsche, J.) affirming a summary judgment entered in the District Court (Biddeford, Gaulin, J.) that awarded unpaid condominium assessments to Pilgrim Place Condominium Association. KRE's principal contention is that the court erred in holding that KRE was liable for assessments on units owned by it that were not built at the time of the assessments. We affirm the judgment.

In 1988 Pilgrim Place, Inc., created a condominium by recording a condominium declaration on real estate in Old Orchard Beach. Although Pilgrim Place created 48 units, it was required by the terms of the declaration to build only 24. It had the option of building the remaining 24 units within the declarant control period. According to the Pilgrim Place condominium declaration, all present and future owners were entitled to one vote per unit in the management of the condominium. Each unit owner, including the declarant, owned an undivided 1/48th (2.083%) interest in the common elements of the condominium and was, in return, responsible for 2.083% of the common expenses. Until the condominium association made a common expense assessment, the declarant was responsible for all common expenses. After the first common expense assessment, all unit owners were liable for their pro rata share of the common expenses. The declaration required the association to adjust the pro rata share to reflect the actual number of units built at the end of the declarant control period in the event that fewer than 48 units were ultimately constructed. The declarant control period was to expire five years after the conveyance of the first unit, or sixty days after the conveyance of 75% of the units, whichever came sooner. During Pilgrim Place's period of control of the condominium association, annual budgets were calculated and assessments were made pursuant to the declaration based on 48 total units.

In 1990 Maine Savings Bank foreclosed on Pilgrim Place's interest in the condominium. KRE acquired title at a foreclosure sale to units 25–48, which were unbuilt, along with all the special declarant rights. The premises were conveyed "subject to any unpaid condominium assessments, other condominium charges or lien[s] therefor[], now or hereafter due." During KRE's period of control from 1990 until the expiration of its development rights in December 1992, it built 16 units. KRE paid no assessments on any of its unbuilt units. Moreover, the management company hired by KRE to run the condominium assessed the annual expenses for maintenance of the common areas based only on units actually built.

In 1993 the association filed this action seeking condominium fees on the units owned by KRE from the time it acquired them at the foreclosure sale. The District Court entered a summary judgment in favor of the association for approximately $36,000 plus interest and attorney fees. The judgment reflected unpaid fees accrued on existing units from the time of KRE's acquisition of development rights to the time of KRE's sale of those units and fees on unbuilt units from the time of KRE's acquisition of development rights to the expiration of the declarant control period, at which time the development rights expired. On appeal by KRE, the Superior Court affirmed the judgment and this appeal followed.

KRE's basic contention is that pursuant to the Maine Condominium Act, 33 M.R.S.A. §§ 1601-101 to 1604-118 (1988 & Supp. 1994), and the Pilgrim Place condominium declaration, an assessment cannot be levied against units that are declared but not built. We disagree. The Act neither compels nor prohibits an assessment against such units. A condominium is created by the act of recording a declaration, not by the erection of a physical structure. *See id.* § 1602-101(a). The Pilgrim Place declaration explicitly creates 48 condominium interests in real estate or units. Each of those units must be owned either by the declarant or a purchaser of a completed unit. *See id.* § 1601-103(27). KRE is the declarant of the Pilgrim Place condominium because it is the successor to the original declarant's special rights to construct additional units. *See id.* § 1601-103(9).

According to the Pilgrim Place condominium declaration, the declarant has the same obligation as any other unit owner, and the declaration provides that the owner of each unit pay 1/48th of the common expenses. Moreover, section 1602-107 prohibits discrimination in favor of the declarant in the allocation of liability for common expenses. KRE's reliance on the definition of "unit" in section 1601-103(26) as "a *physical* portion of a condominium" is unpersuasive. The definition is of a physical portion "designated," *i.e.*, intended in the future, "for separate ownership or occupancy."

No provision of the Act requires any distinction between built and unbuilt units in the assessment for common expenses. In fact, the only distinction in the Act is the prohibition in section 1602-101 against conveyance of a unit to a purchaser until the unit is substantially complete. The Act implicitly recognizes that the creation of units owned by the declarant and the concomitant obligation to pay assessments may occur prior to the actual construction of the physical units. In addition, the provision in the declaration allowing the association to modify the pro rata share assessed against each unit only after the declarant control period expires also implies that the assessments must be against every declared unit prior to that time.

Other courts have applied their states' statutes in accord with our interpretation. In *Mountain View Condo. Homeowners Ass'n v. Scott,* 180 Ariz. 216, 883 P.2d 453, 457 (Ariz. App. Div. 2 1994), the court was faced with a question identical to the one presented in this case. Interpreting Arizona's version of the Uniform Condominium Act, the court held that the obligation to pay assessments rests with the successor declarant regardless whether the units are built. In so doing, the Arizona court cited *Bradley v. Mullenix,* 763

S.W.2d 272 (Mo. App. 1988). In *Bradley*, as in this case, neither the statute nor the declaration drew any distinction between built and unbuilt units for purposes of assessing common expenses.

Finally, we conclude that KRE did not generate any issue of fact material to any of those defenses that it preserved in the District Court.

Judgment Affirmed.

Notes & Questions

1. *Developer liability for assessments on unbuilt units. Bear Creek Master Ass'n v. Edwards*, 31 Cal. Rptr. 3d 337 (Cal. Ct. App. 2005) also held a successor owner of unbuilt units liable to pay assessments. Under the CC&Rs and the Davis-Stirling Act, all units in a phase become liable for assessments after the first unit is sold. The statutory definition of a condominium as a "separate interest in space," rather than a structure, applies to condominium projects begun before the 1985 adoption of the Davis-Stirling Act.

The declarant/developer in *Pilgrim Place* was held liable for assessments on units that were provided for in the declaration but not yet built. How can a declarant avoid assessments for unbuilt units? See UCIOA §§ 2-105, 2-107, 3-115. Phasing also serves other developmental objectives. What might those objectives be?

2. *Phasing in unbuilt units.* The developer in *Pilgrim Place* was required to pay assessments because the units were already subject to the declaration and because Maine's Condominium Act prohibits a declarant from allocating common expenses in a way that decreases or eliminates the declarant's obligation to contribute to such expenses. One way to avoid this problem is to pre-sell the units prior to subjecting them to the declaration. Another more common option is slowly to subject new units in "phases" to minimize the assessment burden. What rights would the declarant reserve in the declaration to ensure that new units can be annexed without express approval of existing unit owners. Consider the following language:

> Unilateral Annexation by Declarant. The Declarant, as the owner of unbuilt units, shall have the unilateral privilege at any time to subject all or any portions of real property owned by declarant to this Declaration.

Why is such language necessary? What problems could arise if the declarant failed to provide this unilateral power? See *Dunes South Homeowners Ass'n, infra*. See also, *Fairway Villas Venture v. Fairway Villas Condo. Ass'n*, 815 S.W.2d 912 (Tex. App. 1991) (developer liable for assessments on unbuilt units).

3. *Unbuilt units: benefits and burdens.* The *Mountain View* and *Pilgrim Place* cases illustrate that unit owners include owners of both built and unbuilt units for the purpose of common assessments. Recall the situation in *Investors Ltd. of Sun Valley v. Sun Mountain Condo.*, 683 P.2d 891 (Idaho Ct. App. 1984), in Chapter 5. There the developer who owned unbuilt units in a condominium community asserted that he was entitled to vote on an amendment to the declaration because he was a unit owner and, hence, a member entitled to vote. The court held that ownership of unbuilt units was not the same as built units for purposes of voting on the amendments. The court interpreted several provisions of the governing documents to determine that only owners of built units were entitled to vote. The case does not expressly state whether the developer was required to pay for assessments on the unbuilt units. If the developer in *Investors Ltd. of Sun Valley* was required to pay assessments on its unbuilt units, should he have had voting privi-

leges, too? Are there any salient differences between voting rights and the obligation to pay assessments in this context?

Problem

The declarant submitted all 50 acres of soybeans he owns to a condominium declaration. The declaration stated that the condominium contained 100 units, parking, and a pool. Declarant built the pool, parking, and one building containing 10 units. He then ran out of financing. The balance of the land remains a soybean field. It produces a good crop each season. Several months after all 10 units are sold and occupied, one of the 10 unit owners calls you and asks about collecting assessments from the other 90 units. How do you advise the owner?

D. Declarant Exemption from Paying Assessments

Why treat the declarant's units differently? Economic and marketing issues may support a developer's argument that it should be exempt from assessments. In the early years, operating costs rarely are as high as projected in the budget. The developer subsidizes much of what would otherwise be common expenses either as a part of developing and marketing the project or with indirect subsidies. In part, this is done to keep the early buyers from having to carry the full cost of operating the community.

In addition, unbuilt units do not contribute to all costs or receive benefits from all line items in the community's budget. For example, an unbuilt unit does not contribute to the costs of management services, insurance, water, social activities, etc. Thus, there are arguments in support of treating unbuilt units or the developer's units differently from sold units. There are, however, arguments of expectations and fairness that contradict these assertions. What is the lawyer's role in resolving them? How should the document be drafted to balance these competing interests?

Traditionally, the issue is addressed most commonly and successfully by phasing the project. This means that land is submitted to the common interest community regime in stages so that unbuilt units are not made subject to the regime and built units that are as yet unsold are subjected to it as close to the actual time of closing as possible.

As alternatives to assessing units whether or not they have been subjected to the governance regime, developers frequently fund either the deficit between that which the owners have paid in assessments and what it actually cost to operate the association, or they provide a direct operating subsidy. What are the pros and cons of each?

The deficit funding mechanism may have greater appeal when one considers potential tax consequences to the association. In each association's budget, there is or should be consideration of amounts, if any, to be placed in an operating or in a long-term capital reserve. Reserves are discussed later in this chapter. Here, however, it is appropriate to address the question whether the subsidy or deficit funding should include funding for the reserve or whether that is an item which can be deferred. What are the policy and economic interests involved?

Finally, developers often make in-kind contributions to the association's operation. This might be direct and intentional with a request being made for a credit against assessments, or it might be indirect and incidental. For example, repairing and replacing roads at the conclusion of construction might be in lieu of putting funds in reserves each year for future road repair. If the developer is permitted to make such contributions, how should they be valued? Should this opportunity be open to all owners? Certainly, there are circumstances in which such contributions may genuinely benefit the association. Consider what guidelines might be appropriate to deal with such payments.

Dunes South Homeowners Ass'n Inc. v. First Flight Builders, Inc.

Supreme Court of North Carolina
459 S.E.2d 477 (N.C. 1995)

FRYE, J. Plaintiff presents two issues on this appeal: (1) whether defendant, the developer of a condominium project subject to the provisions of Chapter 47A of the North Carolina General Statutes as it existed in 1980, may exempt itself from the payment of its pro rata share of maintenance assessments for units it owns; and (2) whether all or a portion of plaintiff's claim for assessments for the years 1986 through 1993 is barred by the statute of limitations. We conclude that the provisions of Chapter 47A of the General Statutes prohibit defendant from unilaterally exempting itself from the payment of its pro rata share of maintenance assessments. Furthermore, we conclude that no portion of plaintiff's claim is barred by the statute of limitations. Accordingly, we reverse the decision of the Court of Appeals and remand this case to that court for further remand to Superior Court, Dare County, for reinstatement of the order granting plaintiff's motion for summary judgment.

Dunes South is a condominium development in which units are sold by time-share weeks. Defendant is the original developer of the Dunes South project and at the time of the institution of this action owned a number of units within the development, some of which had been previously conveyed by defendant and later reacquired, as well as some which had not previously been conveyed by defendant. On 7 August 1980, in accordance with Chapter 47A of the North Carolina General Statutes, defendant filed the original "Declaration of Covenants and Restrictions" (Declaration). This Declaration provided that defendant, as well as other unit owners in the development, would pay annual, per-unit maintenance assessments to plaintiff homeowners association. The Declaration further provided that it could be amended at any time with approval of two-thirds of the membership in plaintiff homeowners association. Subsequently, on 21 January 1983, defendant, as holder of two-thirds of the votes in the association, filed a "Dunes South Supplemental Declaration of Covenants and Restrictions" (Supplemental Declaration). This Supplemental Declaration purported to exempt defendant from the obligation to pay annual per-unit maintenance assessments on units "remaining unsold" and instead provided that defendant would pay for any operating expenses in excess of the per-unit assessments collected from other unit owners.

On 17 February 1993, plaintiff homeowners association filed this action for money judgment and to foreclose upon a lien for unpaid maintenance assessments on Dunes South units owned by defendant. In its answer, defendant did "not admit the validity of the liens claimed against such units for unpaid assessments nor the validity of the assessment amount." Plaintiff then filed a motion for summary judgment supported by an affidavit listing seventy-six units previously conveyed and then reacquired by defendant and setting out the amount of maintenance assessments allegedly owed by defendant on these units for the years 1986 through 1993. On 24 November 1993, defendant filed a motion for leave to amend its answer to allege that at least a portion of plaintiff's claim was barred by N.C.G.S. § 1-52(1), the three-year statute of limitations for filing an action based on contract. On that same day, Mr. Gerald Friedman, president of defendant corporation, filed an affidavit stating, in pertinent part:

> 5. Pursuant to the terms of the Supplemental Declaration of Covenants and Restrictions, First Flight Builders, Inc. was only responsible for the actual operating expenses incurred by plaintiff in excess of the collections of assessments on units within Dunes South and was not responsible for paying per unit annual assessments on unit[s] owned by First Flight Builders, Inc.

On 29 November 1993, the trial court entered an order allowing defendant to amend its answer. However, on 30 November 1993, Judge Watts entered an order allowing plaintiff's motion for summary judgment, from which defendant appealed.

The Court of Appeals vacated the trial court's order, concluding that summary judgment for plaintiff was improper since the term "remaining unsold" in the Supplemental Declaration was ambiguous and therefore created a question for the jury as to whether defendant was liable to plaintiff for the maintenance assessments on units previously conveyed and then reacquired by defendant. *Dunes South Homeowners Assn. v. First Flight Builders*, 117 N.C. App. 360, 368, 451 S.E.2d 636, 640–41 (1994). In addition, the Court of Appeals held that plaintiff's claim for assessments for the years 1986 through 1990 was barred by the statute of limitations for actions based on contract, N.C.G.S. § 1-52(1) (1983). *Dunes South*, 117 N.C. App. at 366, 451 S.E.2d at 640. Judge Eagles dissented, concluding that the terms of the Supplemental Declaration were not ambiguous and that the trial court properly granted plaintiff's motion for summary judgment as to those assessments not barred by the statute of limitations. *Id.* at 369, 451 S.E.2d at 641. Plaintiff appeals to this Court based on Judge Eagles' dissent. Additionally, plaintiff's petition for discretionary review as to an additional issue was allowed by this Court on 9 February 1995.

Plaintiff first contends that the Court of Appeals erred in ignoring the provisions of Chapter 47A of the North Carolina General Statutes when it reversed the trial court's grant of summary judgment in plaintiff's favor. Plaintiff argues that under the provisions of Chapter 47A, more specifically N.C.G.S. § 47A-12, defendant developer was bound to contribute its pro rata share of the maintenance expenses for the common areas of the condominium project and was prohibited from unilaterally exempting itself from the payment of the maintenance assessments at issue in this case. Accordingly, plaintiff argues that, regardless of the language of the Supplemental Declaration, defendant is obligated to pay the maintenance assessments at issue here. We agree.

By executing and recording a declaration of unit ownership, defendant submitted its condominium project to the provisions of Chapter 47A of the General Statutes.... N.C.G.S. § 47A-12 provides, in pertinent part:

> The unit owners are bound to contribute pro rata, in the percentages computed according to G.S. 47A-6 of this Chapter, toward the expenses of administration and of maintenance and repair of the general common areas and facilities and, in proper cases of the limited common areas and facilities, of the building and toward any other expense lawfully agreed upon. No unit owner may exempt himself from contributing toward such expense by waiver of the use or enjoyment of the common areas and facilities or by abandonment of the unit belonging to him....

A "unit owner" is defined as "a person, corporation, partnership, association, trust or other legal entity, or any combination thereof, who owns a unit within the building."... Neither the definition of "unit owner" nor the provisions of N.C.G.S. § 47A-12 makes any distinction between a developer and any other unit owner. Defendant developer, as a corporation owning several units within the condominium project, qualified as a "unit owner" under section 47A-3(14). Thus, defendant was "bound to contribute pro rata ... toward the expenses of administration and of maintenance and repair of the general common areas and facilities."...*. Consistent with this statutory requirement, defendant covenanted, in its original Declaration, to pay annual, per-unit maintenance assessments for each unit it owned.

The crucial issue then becomes whether defendant may, through provisions in the Supplemental Declaration, exempt itself from its statutory obligation as a unit owner to pay its pro rata share of the maintenance expenses for common areas. Having submitted the project to the provisions of Chapter 47A, defendant's obligation, as a unit owner, to contribute its pro rata share of maintenance expenses derived not only from its Declaration, but also from the provisions of N.C.G.S. §47A-12. Section 47A-12 is but one of several sections within Chapter 47A which evidence the legislature's intent to ensure the orderly, reliable and fair government of condominium projects and to protect each owner's interest in his or her own unit as well as the common areas and facilities. For example, N.C.G.S. §47A-6(b) protects the unit owners' interests in the common areas, providing that the ratio of the undivided interest of each unit owner in the common areas shall have a permanent character and shall not be altered except with the unanimous consent of all unit owners expressed in an amended declaration.... Likewise, we believe that the provisions of section 47A-12 are designed to protect unit owners from shouldering a disproportionate share of the maintenance expenses for common areas when other unit owners, including the developer, attempt to unilaterally exempt themselves from contributing their pro rata share of maintenance expenses.

Section 47A-12 explicitly states that each unit owner is "*bound to contribute*" pro rata toward maintenance expenses for the common areas.... In addition, this section also addresses two methods by which an individual unit owner might attempt to unilaterally exempt itself from paying its share of maintenance expenses, providing that "[n]o unit owner may exempt himself from contributing toward such expense by waiver of the use or enjoyment of the common areas and facilities or by abandonment of the unit belonging to him." In light of the purposes behind Chapter 47A and the language of N.C.G.S. §47A-12, we do not believe that the legislature intended to allow a developer, as a unit owner, to unilaterally exempt itself from the payment of its pro rata share of the maintenance expenses for the common areas. This is exactly what defendant attempted to do. Accordingly, we conclude that the Supplemental Declaration filed by defendant in this case was ineffective to exempt it from paying the maintenance assessments at issue here.

Having determined that defendant is obligated to pay its pro rata share of the common expenses, we must now determine what, if any, portion of defendant's obligation to plaintiff is barred by the statute of limitations.

...

[The court concluded that no portion of plaintiff's claim was barred by the statute of limitations.—Eds.]

[W]e reverse the decision of the Court of Appeals and remand this case to that court for further remand to Superior Court, Dare County, for reinstatement of the court's order granting plaintiff's motion for summary judgment.

Notes & Questions

1. *Developer responsibility for assessments.* Statutory provisions typically prohibit a declarant from unilaterally exempting itself from assessments which are applicable to all

owners, as the court held in *Dunes South*. UCIOA § 2-107 (a) provides that a declarant may not allocate assessments in a manner that discriminates in favor of the declarant or an affiliate. What are possible reasons for exempting developers/declarants from paying assessments on unbuilt or unsold units? Given that assessments are partly premised on the notion that those who use the common area should contribute to its maintenance, what is the rationale for assessing unsold units?

2. *Developer/declarant payment of in-kind contribution in lieu of assessments.* A developer that owns a large number of units may become financially burdened with the responsibility of paying assessments on all of its units. One way that a developer can pay for assessments without making substantial cash outlays is to pay the assessed amounts through in-kind contributions. For instance, a developer might agree to contribute maintenance services to the association on the development site with the employees it has in return for a decrease in the dollar amount the developer may owe for assessments. How would one value in-kind contributions for the purpose of reducing the developer's assessment amount? Should such an arrangement be provided for in the declaration?

3. *Subsidy.* In addition to declarant assessments, some declarants/developers provide a subsidy to the new association. A subsidy differs from a declarant assessment in that assessments must be paid by the declarant, whereas subsidies are most often voluntary contributions. There are many ways that a declarant can subsidize the community. For instance, the developer may agree to subsidize landscaping costs with in-kind contributions. The developer may also make a loan to the association to be paid back over a period of time, or the developer/declarant might agree to pay a fixed dollar amount to the association each year. Why would a developer wish to subsidize association operations? What effect would a subsidy have on the annual assessments? What effect would it have on marketability of the development?

4. *Developer subsidies and "lowballing."* At first blush, it may seem as though the burden to a developer of assuming the financial responsibility for common area maintenance would outweigh the benefits. However, a developer may be more successful at attracting new buyers if the community's assessments are inexpensive, or at least, reflect the eventual per unit assessment level when all units have been sold. As more units are sold, there will be less need for a developer subsidy.

Sometimes, a developer will be accused of "lowballing" assessments. Lowballing is a term used to describe a developer practice of setting assessments unrealistically low to enhance initial unit sales. Later, the assessment is increased dramatically. If an owner purchases a unit in reliance on the low assessment amount, what are possible causes of action against the developer?

Problem

Your developer client is considering the draft CCRs you have prepared. She intends to sell off lots in the development to different builders, who will then sell the newly built homes to the public. She has questions about the assessment process.

"When do the builders start paying assessments?" she asks. You have explained how, in this noncondominium HOA, her property can be exempt and why she will fund deficits. How do you respond to her question about the builders? How do the builders' obligations affect hers? What are the practical and the policy considerations? Would your answers be different if your client were building a condominium? Why?

E. Special Assessments

Special assessments are imposed when the normal budget is insufficient and operating funds cannot cover expenditures. They are most commonly needed when there are unanticipated expenditures resulting from extraordinary circumstances or substantial increases in basic services, such as landscaping services.

The governing documents often limit the uses to which special assessments may be put. Is there wisdom in this approach? Experience has shown that language such as "unexpected repair, replacement, or maintenance" of property as the basis for special assessments does not serve well when there is a substantial increase in *service* charges. Consider, therefore, what is needed in the authorizing language: whether there should be limits imposed, whether the appropriate limit should be vested in the discretion and judgment of the board, or whether a vote of the membership should be required. If the latter, consider whether a majority or something higher than a majority vote should be required.

Washington Courte Condo. Ass'n v. Cosmopolitan Nat'l Bank

Appellate Court of Illinois
523 N. E. 2d 1245 (Ill. App. Ct. 1988)

BILANDIC, J. Defendants are the owners of six of the 44 units, which are part of plaintiff, Washington Courte Condominium Association-Four (hereinafter plaintiff or Association). A special assessment was adopted by a two-thirds vote of the members of the Association. Defendants paid the special assessment installments for about six months. Thereafter, they refused to pay any further installments. Pursuant to Ill.Rev.Stat.1985, ch. 110, par. 9-102(a)7, the plaintiff Association sued for possession of the units, delinquent installments and attorney fees. After a jury trial, judgment was entered in favor of plaintiff and against the six defendant unit owners for possession, delinquent installments and attorney fees. Defendants filed this timely appeal. Defendants contend that the subject matter of the special assessment should have been included in the annual budget of the Association and not in a special assessment. Therefore, the special assessment is invalid and the judgment for plaintiff must be reversed. We disagree.

The Association was created pursuant to the provisions of the Condominium Property Act for the purpose of facilitating the administration and operation of the property involved in this litigation. (Ill.Rev.Stat.1985, ch. 30, par 301 *et seq.*) Serious construction defects affecting the common elements were discovered. In 1983, the Association retained counsel to institute legal proceedings seeking $1.5 million in damages against the developers (who retained ownership of two of the 44 units). This action was authorized by the unit owners and 30 of the 44 unit owners signed the agreement retaining counsel.

As the developer litigation progressed, legal fees and costs were incurred. The board of directors of the Association determined that a special assessment would be necessary to pay the accrued fees and costs and to provide for future fees and costs relating to this developer litigation. The Condominium Property Act provides that "[any] non-recurring common expense, ... shall be separately assessed against all unit owners.... subject to approval by the affirmative vote of at least two-thirds of the unit owners voting at a meeting called for the purpose of approving the assessment." (Ill.Rev.Stat.1985, ch. 30, par. 309(d).) A notice of special meeting of the unit owners to consider the proposed special assessment to support the developer litigation was properly served on all of the unit owners in accordance with the Condominium Property Act and the by-laws of the Association.

A special meeting was held on June 17, 1985, and the special assessment was adopted with the approval of more than two-thirds of the unit owners. One of the defendants voted "No" and the others abstained. Following the meeting, all of the unit owners, including the defendants, paid their respective portions of the approved special assessment. In November 1985, defendants ceased paying their respective portions of the special assessment because they contended that the fees were too high or that they did not like the lawyer. None of them objected to the notice of the special meeting of June 17, 1985, nor the manner in which the meeting was conducted and the assessment adopted. When defendants persisted in their refusal to pay their share of the special assessment, plaintiff Association commenced this action.

I

It is undisputed that any defenses going to the validity and enforceability of the special assessment is germane to the issues. However, defendants failed to establish any such defenses. The maintenance of litigation to recover damages from the developers for alleged serious construction defects is the type of "non-recurring common expense" which is properly the subject matter of a special assessment. (Ill.Rev.Stat.1985, ch. 30, par. 309(d).) Defendants received proper notice, attended the special meeting where the assessment was adopted, and even paid the assessment for approximately six months.

Defendants' argument that the costs of maintaining the developer litigation should be the subject of the budget adopted each year by the board to cover "anticipated common expenses" is without merit. (Ill.Rev.Stat.1985, ch. 30, par. 309(c).) Litigation, by its very nature, is unpredictable in duration and cost. A special committee was set up to review all bills before they were submitted for payment. The record does not reveal that defendants ever sought to rescind or repeal the special assessment at any duly constituted meeting, or even attempted to call a meeting for that purpose. Merely because six unit owners suddenly do not like a lawyer or think costs are too high is not a basis for overruling the will of their fellow unit owners who adopted the special assessment by an extraordinary vote of over two-thirds of the unit owners.

Defendants failed to establish that the special assessment was not valid.

. . .

For the foregoing reasons, the judgment of the circuit court of Cook County is Affirmed.

Notes & Questions

1. *Drafting special assessment provisions.* How specific should the special assessment provisions of the declaration be? Compare the pros and cons of a special assessment provision which specifies each possible use of the funds versus a vague and expansive provision. Which approach to drafting special assessment provisions do you believe "works" better? Recall *Lovering v. Seabrook Island Property Owners Ass'n, supra.*

2. *Separate assessments for "nonrecurring expenses."* Some governing documents provide for assessments for "nonrecurring" expenses. For example, in *Azar v. Old Willow Falls Condo. Ass'n,* 593 N.E.2d 583, (Ill. App. Ct.1992), the court held that legal fees and engineering and roofing costs are properly characterized as nonrecurring expenses and were valid as such under the association's by-laws. What other expenses could be characterized

as "nonrecurring?" Do you see any potential problems with using the "nonrecurring" expense standard to determine when an association may properly levy special assessments?

3. *Member approval of special assessments.* A number of lawsuits have arisen over procedural requirements for levying special assessments. Often, special assessments require homeowner approval and greater homeowner involvement than annual assessments. For instance, an applicable statute or the governing documents may require a special meeting to consider special assessments and a super-majority vote of homeowners to approve. See *Azar v. Old Willow Falls Condo. Ass'n*, 593 N.E.2d 583 (Ill. App. Ct. 1992) (2/3 vote of members needed to pass special assessment under Illinois Condominium Act). Despite these formalities, some courts have permitted the association to levy special assessments to cover "emergency" repairs without homeowner approval. See *Farrington v. Casa Solana Condo. Ass'n, Inc.* 5175 So. 2d 70 (Fla. Dist. Ct. App. 1987) (holding that levy of special assessment is valid without approval of owners for emergency waterproofing repairs). Should "emergency" special assessments be authorized in the declaration? Do you see potential problems with permitting the association board to determine when and what circumstances constitute an "emergency?" What advantages do you see in also permitting the board unilaterally to levy special assessments?

4. *Lump sum payment of special assessment.* In situations where the association incurs substantial costs to cover unexpected expenses (*e.g.*, roof repairs or structural repairs), should the association be permitted to require a one-time, lump sum payment from each unit owner? In *Braeshire Condo. Board of Managers v. Brinkmeyer*, 841 S.W.2d 217 (Mo. Ct. App. 1992), a group of owners challenged the association's authority to require payment of the special assessments in two installments, as opposed to the ordinary twelve month installments used for annual assessments. The court upheld the association's payment plan as it was not contrary to the by-laws. What benefits or burdens may result from having such assessments paid over several months versus a one-payment plan? Should an association be required to maintain a cash reserve for such emergencies and to use the reserve fund before assessing the owners? Are there any drawbacks to "draining" reserve funds in this manner?

5. *Limit on special assessment amounts.* Is it desirable to limit the annual special assessment amount? See *Azar v. Old Wilow Falls Condo. Ass'n*, 593 N.E.2d 583 (Ill. App. Ct. 1992) (holding that association could not impose an assessment in excess of the maximum assessment amount authorized by the association's by-laws). Compare with municipal taxation units and the rationale for such. See, *e.g.*, S. D. Codified Laws § 9-47-1 (Michie 1997) (limiting special assessments levied by local governments to $10 per thousand of taxable valuation of all property within the municipality). Other than special assessments, how else might an association raise funds for needed repairs?

6. *Special assessments to cover judgments against the association.* In *Washington Courte*, the court upheld a special assessment to recover legal fees arising from a suit against the developer for defective construction. Do you think special assessments are appropriate to cover litigation expenses in defense of *ultra vires* acts of the board? Is there a difference between association defense actions versus association-initiated actions for the purpose of levying special assessments? Should the developer in the *Washington Courte* case who still owned two units be required to pay special assessments to fund litigation against it? See *Ocean Trail Unit Owners Ass'n v. Mead*, 650 So. 2d 4. (Fla. 1994) (holding that condominium association could impose a special assessment on unit owners to cover attorneys fees and other legal costs incurred as a result of the unit owners suit against the association). These issues will be addressed subsequently in Chapter 10.

Problems

1. Seven Oaks Condominium continues to be beset by leak problems in the garden apartment units. The roofs of the townhouses and highrise units, which are of concrete, do not leak. The leaking garden units were built with a board and tar roof structure. Now in a third consecutive rainy season, the association board is concerned. Last night it rained, and already the calls have begun. There are leaks in many units; in a few, plaster ceilings have given way, and now homeowners are complaining because of the interior damage.

The townhouse and highrise directors are considering a special assessment against the leaking units. The manager is urging suit be filed against the developer immediately in order to get some money. Various owners are threatening suit against the board and the manager.

As the association's attorney, you are preparing your response to the board's request for an analysis of their situation, the legal issues involved, and the strengths and weaknesses of the association's position.

Please respond.

2. A new client is sitting in your office seeking your advice. She and her husband own a unit in Seven Oaks, which has a homeowners association. She explained that Seven Oaks is to be built in phases, and she resides in a unit in the 60-unit first phase, all the units of which are built and sold. Although her deed and the deeds of most Phase I owners required membership in the HOA, the CCRs were not recorded until all Phase I units were sold and Phase II was underway.

There are now four sets of CCRs recorded, one on each phase. All have the same substantive provisions. Phase I has a large open space in its common area which DevCo, the developer/declarant, now wishes to use for the site of a 5,000 square foot clubhouse to serve all owners in the 350-unit development. DevCo controls the association and asserts it has the right to build the facility as it will benefit all units. In addition, DevCo, through the management company, is seeking each owner's signature to a single set of CCRs "in order to avoid title problems."

The CCRs, mirroring the other three, state that control passes to owners when 70% of the units are sold. The board of directors DevCo appointed has imposed a special assessment to fund clubhouse construction. To deal with delinquents, the board adopted a procedure stating that owners who do not pay their assessments are not "in good standing" and thus may not vote. In addition, the board has just adopted a rule which permits the owners in Phases II–IV to use the existing pool and tennis facilities adjacent to the clubhouse site.

Your client has questions. In addition, she has not yet paid the clubhouse assessments. Your new client asks for your analysis of her situation. Please provide a concise, thorough response.

F. Collecting Assessments

1. Assessment Collection

Case law is generally well settled that, if properly drafted, the affirmative covenant to pay assessments to the association runs with the land and is binding on all successors-in-title. The covenant must run with the land to assure continued compliance with the scheme of development for the community and to assure the continued viability of the association and, consequently, preservation and enhancement of property values. Early decisions in some jurisdictions held that certain covenants to pay assessments did not comply with traditional legal requirements for running with the land. However, more recent decisions essentially have narrowed those rulings to the specific language of the covenants in question and have been more generous in interpreting covenant language to be sufficient to run with the land.

In many homeowners association covenants and in condominium statutes, the independent obligation to pay assessments is expressly established and stated. For example, the statute may provide that no owner is exempted from the obligation to pay assessments for any reason whatsoever, including nonuse or abandonment of the unit or nonuse of the amenities. A number of courts have upheld this concept of independent covenants, holding that an owner's dissatisfaction or displeasure with some aspect of the association or the association's conduct of its operations and duties (most commonly, maintenance duties) cannot justify unilaterally withholding or refusing to pay assessments. Instead, the owner is legally obligated to continue to pay the assessment and may resolve his maintenance or other complaints only through association procedures or, if necessary, through a separate, independent claim (or counterclaim) against the association.

Often, assessments are not paid because an owner is angry at the board of directors. The owner may be dissatisfied with the physical maintenance of the community or with the board's handling of an association matter or may be involved in a personal dispute with a board member or manager. Sometimes an owner refuses to pay assessments as an attempt to get the board's attention on another issue.

In contrast to the owner's perspective, however, is the directors' perspective. The board generally has a duty set out in the governing documents to collect assessments and to do so in a uniform and consistent manner. Many board members feel an obligation to collect assessments and all related charges out of a sense of fairness to the many owners who regularly pay their respective shares of the assessments. Additionally, the perspective of many directors is that people are obligated to pay their bills.

Perhaps the most common defense of nonpayment of assessments is the argument that the owner did not know about it, that she was not told of it when she purchased. The obvious, but not always dispositive, response is that the assessment obligation arises from a recorded instrument and that all owners take with constructive notice. Is that enough?

Another argument is "lack of power." Variations are arguments that the board made the wrong decision that something should be done or how it should be done; that the action to be taken will cost too much; or because of its cost, there should be a different vote. Frequently, owners object because they assert that they do not use the facility or service for which the assessment is levied. What should be the result? The issue, of course, is whether there is a power and whether that power to assess has been properly exercised. The benefit may be direct for some and indirect for others. Should the distinction matter?

Occasionally, a developer receives assessment payments directly or excuses payment of an assessment for a period of time in order to induce a purchaser to buy. Is this appropriate and valid? Consider to whom the assessment is owed, and whether there are circumstances under which a third party can excuse the payment. Obviously, there is a difference in a developer's telling a purchaser that she is excused from paying the assessment if the developer timely makes payment in lieu thereof. What, if any, other circumstances might be appropriate?

There is also an issue of multiple lot purchases. In the event a buyer purchases two lots and builds his house in the middle of the resulting tract, frequently he argues he is responsible for one not two assessments. Does he have one or two votes? How and under what circumstances might it be appropriate and possible to treat this ownership differently from each lot carrying a separate obligation?

If assessments are a share of common expenses, does an individual owner have the ability to withhold assessments because he is dissatisfied with something that the association has done or not done? What if the dissatisfaction relates not to the association's actions but to the developer's failure to comply with its responsibilities or to meet the representations made in order to induce purchases?

Certainly there are legitimate objections that owners might have to actions of the association or developer, but those normally have little to do with the obligation of each and every owner, as individuals and as a group of owners comprising the association, to meet the common obligations. Consider, therefore, the question of fairness and the expectations of the parties as you look at arguments that basically say that a "rent strike" or an "assessment strike" is appropriate. There is an interesting question of the responsibility, and perhaps liability, of an attorney who suggests that her client put her assessment "in escrow" because she is unhappy with the way the association is operating. Consider these issues as you review the cases and notes in this section.

a. Collection

While the purpose of this book is not to outline the technical procedures for managing an association, it is worthwhile to understand how provisions and powers in the association's governing documents are implemented in the day-to-day management of the development. The community association board is put in a unique and often uncomfortable position when enforcing collection procedures against a fellow homeowner-neighbor. Boards may be reluctant to file liens against a neighbor or to instigate foreclosure proceedings. Therefore, a wide range of enforcement alternatives should be outlined in the documents in addition to the more formal approaches. These various approaches taken by the association in collecting assessments can create different legal issues. It is vitally important that once procedures for enforcement of assessment collections are established, the board adopt them in a resolution and follow them strictly.

Annually, the association drafts and approves its budget for the coming year. From that budget, annual assessments are determined and levied against each unit. The governing documents or board resolution may allow payments of the assessments on a monthly or quarterly basis. Statutes may outline, to some extent, procedures and timelines for notice and filing liens. Generally, though, enforcement procedures available to the association for collection of delinquent accounts are provided in the community's governing documents, specifically in the association's by-laws, and can be further detailed by board resolution. The vast majority of owners pay their assessments in a timely manner, and most of those who are late will pay once they are reminded of the due date and amount. However, in every community, a small number of owners do not pay assessments for a variety of reasons ranging from financial difficulty to retaliation against the board of directors. The association has a variety of techniques from which to choose in creating a collection policy to be applied consistently in every case to avoid allegations that the policy is applied arbitrarily.

A typical collection process begins with reminder notices 10 to 15 days after the assessment was due. Generally, after the assessment is 30 days overdue, the association begins its duly authorized enforcement procedures. A common, but proper, practice is for the association to suspend the delinquent owner's amenity use privileges or voting rights.

The association also may be empowered to charge late fees or accelerate the delinquent owner's assessments. Once an account is 30 days overdue, the association assesses a late fee and accelerates and notifies the owner that the entire remaining annual assessment is due and payable. This acceleration allows the association, should the owner remain delinquent, to file a lien on the owner's unit or file suit against the owner for the entire year's assessment. If the power to accelerate is not specifically granted in the community's governing documents, is a duly adopted board resolution valid? What general language would support an implied power to do so?

The association's next step may be to file a lien against the delinquent owner's unit. Statutes may prescribe the timing and filing procedures of the lien. The association can also file a suit at law against the owner personally. From these steps, the association may foreclose on its lien or file suit and obtain a judgment. Once a judgment is obtained, the association may levy on personal property for public auction or begin garnishment procedures. Although collection procedures up to this point should be applied consistently, steps the association takes from here may be based on a case-by-case basis. What factors should the association take into account when deciding on a course of action to recover the assessments, late fees, and attorneys fees the owner has now amassed?

b. Collecting from Delinquent Members

i. Late Fees and Sanctions

Villas at Hidden Lakes Condo. Ass'n v. Geupel Constr. Co.

Court of Appeals of Arizona

847 P.2d 117 (Ariz. Ct. App. 1992)

TOCI, J. In this appeal, defendants Geupel Construction Company and R.G.W. Investment Co., Inc. ("Developer") challenge the trial court's grant of summary judgment in favor of plaintiff, The Villas at Hidden Lakes Condominium Association ("Association"). The Association, a group of condominium owners organized under a declaration of horizontal property regime ("Declaration"), claimed the Developer owed the Association for delinquent monthly assessments on units formerly owned by Developer. The Association had enacted a late payment charge on past due assessments and had applied the late payment charge retroactively to the Developer's alleged delinquent assessments. Developer disagreed, asserting that it owed no assessments because it had exercised the right to temporarily withdraw twenty-three units from the project. When Developer did not pay, the Association filed suit.

We reverse the granting of summary judgment and remand for proceedings consistent with this opinion. We hold that: (1) because the Developer lawfully withdrew twenty-three units from the original fifty-three unit development, the twenty-three lots in Phase Two were not subject to the monthly assessments and late charges; (2) although the Association possessed the necessary contractual and statutory authority to impose late fees, it exercised its power unreasonably by making the late fees retroactive; and (3) because the affidavit in support of summary judgment did not contain admissible evidence of the Developer's liability for assessments, interest, and late charges, the Association did not establish a *prima facie* case against the Developer entitling it to summary judgment.

FACTUAL AND PROCEDURAL HISTORY

…

[Paradise Isle Associates ("Developer") built a condominium project in northeast Phoenix called The Villas at Hidden Lakes and recorded its declaration of horizontal property regime ("Declaration One") on August 30, 1985. The Developer later recorded an amended Declaration on October 11, 1985 ("Declaration Two"). The Developer formed The Villas at Hidden Lakes Homeowner's [sic] Association under Declaration Two in October of 1985. According to Declaration Two the Developer would pay to the Association monthly assessments on each of the condominium units it owned, beginning on May 1, 1986. On July 24, 1986, after four units had been sold, Developer withdrew twenty-three of the original fifty-three units from the project and stopped paying assessments on these twenty-three units. The Association sued to recover the unpaid unit assessments, late fees, and interest. It also sought to foreclose a lien on a lot then owned by Developer. By the time the trial court entered judgment, the late fees totaled $47,160. Developer counterclaimed, alleging that the lien was invalid and that it did not owe the assessments and late payment fees because it had withdrawn the twenty-three lots from the project. Alternatively, the Developer asserted that the late fees exceeded the twelve percent interest specified in the Association by-laws for delinquent assessments and were therefore unenforceable. — Eds.]

THE SEQUENCING OF THE PROJECT

…

[The Association first argued that because the Developer had already sold five units, it did not have authority to "unilaterally" amend the Declaration. The court found that the Developer had satisfied the amendment provisions found in the governing Declaration itself. The Association also contended that even if the developer had authority to amend the Declaration, the entire recorded Amendment was invalid because it referred to the revoked Declaration One. The court disagreed: the Amendment was valid because it clearly identified the property and precisely stated its purpose, and the Developer re-recorded the Amendment to correct the erroneous reference to the revoked declaration. The Association then argued that the Amendment was invalid because it exempted the twenty-three withdrawn units from monthly assessment payments, and that such unequal treatment of individual units was unlawful without approval by one hundred percent of the owners. The court disagreed because, even though the twenty-three units were temporarily withdrawn from the project, once the units were rededicated they would again be subject to the covenants and restrictions. The Association further contended that the Declaration required "approval of all the Owners of the units" in order to terminate the horizontal property regime. The court stated that while termination of the regime required one hundred percent owner approval, withdrawal of property required only sixty-seven percent of the votes of the owners and the termination vote was therefore valid. Lastly, the Association argued that the Developer was estopped from claiming that no assessments were due on the twenty-three withdrawn lots in Phase Two. The court held that the Association did not establish a prima facie case of equitable estoppel, and the trial court erred in granting summary judgment for two reasons: 1) the original Declaration gave constructive notice that the owners holding "sixty-seven (67%) of the votes in the association" could consent to withdrawal of units from the development, and 2) neither the Association or the five unit owners presented admissible evidence that they suffered any injury from the withdrawal of the twenty-three lots in Phase Two. The court remanded this issue to the trial court. — Eds.]

THE LATE FEE PENALTY

1. Did the Association Have the Authority to Impose Late Fees?

Both Declaration Two and A.R.S. section 33-1242 of the Uniform Condominium Act (UCA) support the Association's right to charge late payment penalties on overdue assessments.

Article Five, section one is the only authority in Declaration Two for assessment of late fees.[4] That section states that the assessments, "late payment penalties, if any, together with interest, costs, and reasonable attorney's fees," shall be a lien upon the unit. In addition, Arizona's UCA, A.R.S. section 33-1242, provides:

> Subject to the provisions of the declaration, the association may:
>
> . . .
>
> 11. Impose charges for late payment of assessments and, after notice and an opportunity to be heard, impose reasonable monetary penalties upon unit owners for violations of the declaration, by-laws and rules of the association.

The Developer argues that this section does not give the Association authority to impose late fees in excess of the contractual twelve percent interest rate because the UCA only applies to condominiums created after January 1, 1986. See A.R.S. § 33-1201(A) (establishing effective date of UCA). The Developer points out that the Association filed its governing declaration (Declaration Two) before the effective date of the UCA.

The UCA, however, "applies to condominiums created within this state before the effective date of this chapter to the extent the provisions of this chapter are not in conflict with chapter 4.1 of this title. . . ." A.R.S. § 33-1201(B). Chapter 4.1 (which is former A.R.S. sections 33-551 through 33-561, repealed by the current UCA) contains no language that prevents the assessment of late charges by a condominium homeowner's association. Therefore, the Association had authority under section 33-1242 to impose late fees.

The Developer argues, nevertheless, that even if the UCA applies, the Association may not exercise rights authorized by section 33-1242(11) because this section is expressly "[s]ubject to the provisions of the declaration." The Developer never tells us where the Declaration expressly prohibits the imposition of late charges. We have carefully reviewed Declaration Two and find no such prohibition. Thus, we conclude the Association may exercise the powers granted to it in the Declaration and in A.R.S. section 33-1242(11).

---

4. Section 1. PERSONAL OBLIGATION OF ASSESSMENTS. The Declarant, for each Dwelling owned within the Property, hereby covenants, and each Owner, by acceptance of a deed, except as provided for in this Article, whether or not it shall be so expressed in such deed, is deemed to covenant and agree to pay to the Association: (1) annual assessments (paid as provided herein) for commonly metered utilities, insurance, maintenance, management, utilities for common areas, and other general expenses including reserves for contingencies, maintenance, repair and replacement, hereafter referred to as "annual assessments;" (2) special assessments for capital improvements; and (3) supplemental assessments. Such assessments are to be established and collected as provided in this Declaration, Articles and by-laws. The annual, special and supplemental assessments, *late payment penalties*, if any, together with interest, costs, and reasonable attorney's fees, shall be a lien upon the Unit as created by the Articles or by-laws. Each such assessment, together with interest, costs, and reasonable attorney's fees, shall also be the personal obligation of the person who was the Owner of such Unit at the time the assessment was levied. The personal obligation for delinquent assessments shall not pass to successors in title unless expressly assumed by them, or unless prior to the transfer of title as evidence by the records of the County Recorder or other appropriate governmental agency, a lien for such assessment shall have been filed or recorded. (Emphasis added.)

2. Was the Developer Personally Liable for Late Fees?

Count One of the Association's complaint claimed that Developer was personally liable for late charges on delinquent assessments. The Developer argues Declaration Two excludes late payment penalties from the list of items that may become a personal liability of an owner. The Developer also argues the Association's exclusive remedy is a lien against each lot for the amount of the late charges. Based on our interpretation of Declaration Two, we hold that the Declaration creates a personal obligation for late fees and that a former owner may be personally liable for such charges. Article Five, section one, of Declaration Two, provides in part:

Section 1. PERSONAL OBLIGATION OF ASSESSMENTS

...

The annual, special and supplemental assessments, late payment penalties, if any, together with interest, costs, and reasonable attorney's fees, shall be a lien upon the Unit as created by the Articles or by-laws. Each such assessment, together with interest, costs, and reasonable attorney's fees, shall also be the personal obligation of the person who was the Owner of such Unit at the time the assessment was levied.

(Emphasis added.) Developer argues the exclusion of late payment penalties from the list of items in the second sentence clearly signifies that such payments may not become a personal liability of an owner. We reject this argument.

First, the title of this section, "Personal Obligation of Assessments," says that the assessments specified in section one are meant to be the personal obligation of the lot owner. Second, the four kinds of assessments specifically listed in the first sentence are collectively referred to in the second sentence as "each such assessment." Both sentences merely describe the same four assessments in different ways. We hold, therefore, that the words "each such assessment" in the second sentence refer to and include the assessment for late fees listed in the first sentence and personally bind the lot owners.

3. Were the Late Fees Reasonable?

Although the Association by Declaration and statute has the power to impose charges for late fees, it cannot abuse its discretion or exercise its power unreasonably. We hold that because the Association had not adopted a schedule of penalties for late payments at the time the Developer's assessments became delinquent, the retroactive imposition of monetary penalties on such assessments was unreasonable.

The Association adopted the late charge in October 1987, and applied it to monthly assessments already delinquent. The Association calculated the late charge by multiplying the number of units owned by Developer by the number of months Developer owned each unit. It then multiplied the product of this calculation by the $10 late fee. According to the Association, at the moment it adopted the late charge penalty, Developer was automatically liable for $2,170 in late charges for past delinquencies. Thus, in November, the month following adoption of the late charge, instead of charging a late fee of $520 for fifty-two delinquent assessments,[5] the Association assessed the Developer a late payment penalty of $3,070. The Association claimed a similar sum for each following month in which the pre-October 1986 assessments were unpaid. Fifteen months later, according to the Association, the Developer owed $47,160 in late charges.

---

5. The Association made no claim for assessments on Unit 33, the first unit sold.

The Developer contends the Association had no statutory or contractual power to impose late fees in excess of the twelve percent interest specified in the governing by-laws. We disagree. Article Five, section one of the Declaration and A.R.S. section 33-1242(11) clearly give the Association the power to impose charges for late fees and interest. Nevertheless, we find that neither the language of the Declaration authorizing the imposition of "late payment" fees nor the provisions of A.R.S. section 33-1242 empower the Association to assess unreasonable late payment fees.

Courts have regularly imposed a reasonableness standard on rules and regulations adopted by condominium homeowners' associations. *See, e.g., Makeever v. Lyle*, 125 Ariz. 384, 388, 609 P.2d 1084, 1088 (App.1980) (condominium associations may exercise broad powers "if they are not arbitrary and capricious, bearing no reasonable relationship to the fundamental condominium concept"); *Ryan v. Baptiste*, 565 S.W.2d 196, 198 (Mo.App.1978); *Rhue v. Cheyenne Homes, Inc.*, 449 P.2d 361, 363 (Colo.1969) (refusal of committee to approve house plans must be reasonable and not arbitrary and capricious); see also *Chateau Village North Condo. v. Jordan*, 643 P.2d 791, 792 (Colo.App.1982); *Unit Owners Ass'n of Buildamerica-1 v. Gillman*, 223 Va. 752, 292 S.E.2d 378, 386 (1982) ("[A]mendments to condominium restrictions, rules and regulations should be measured by a standard of reasonableness, and ... courts should refuse to enforce regulations that are found to be unreasonable."); *Worthinglen Condo. Owners' Ass'n v. Brown*, 57 Ohio App.3d 73, 76, 566 N.E.2d 1275, 1277 (1989) (If, in the context of surrounding circumstances, the amendment is unreasonable, arbitrary or capricious, it is invalid.).

We note that late charges are ordinarily imposed in connection with an installment debt. There, the late payment penalty, usually a flat fee or percentage of the installment due, is set forth in the loan documents. The obligor knows, in advance of the due date, that a late charge in a sum certain will be assessed for each late payment. In an installment debt, the obligor can choose between paying on time or paying late and incurring a specific late charge.

Here, however, although the Association always had the power to enact a late payment penalty, it did not do so until October, 1987. Before that date, the Association did not require an owner to make a choice between making a timely monthly assessment payment and incurring a late penalty for failing to make a timely payment. We conclude that an owner who may have acted on the premise that the Association's only penalty for late payment of a monthly assessment was an interest charge of 12%, and who might have timely paid the monthly assessment rather than a late payment penalty, should not be subject to a late payment charge enacted many months after the date of delinquency. For that reason, we hold that, as a matter of law, the Association's imposition of a retroactive late fee was unreasonable, arbitrary, and an abuse of discretion.

Thus, the Association cannot use assessments delinquent before October 1987, as the base for post-October late payment calculations. We strike all late fees imposed on assessments delinquent before October 1987, and remand to the trial court for a recalculation of the late fees.

. . .

CONCLUSION

Based on the foregoing, we reverse the trial court's grant of summary judgment on all counts and remand for proceedings consistent with this opinion.

Reversed and Remanded.

ii. Self-Help Remedies

San Antonio Villa Del Sol Homeowners Ass'n v. Miller

Court of Appeals of Texas
761 S.W.2d 460 (Tex. Ct. App. 1988)

DIAL, J. This is an appeal arising from a suit filed by appellee, William B. Miller, against San Antonio Villa Del Sol Homeowners Association, appellant in this matter ("Association"), the Association's Board of Directors, Marie Gates, Hilda Hewitt, and David Acosta ("The Board"), and Dorothy Wearmouth, Property Manager of the Association. In his suit, Miller claimed that the defendants harassed him by turning off a portion of his utilities. The Association counterclaimed to collect unpaid monthly assessments and a special assessment made in 1984.

Following a non-jury trial, the court held that the 1984 assessment was not valid and that the defendants lacked the authority to terminate Miller's utilities. The court further held that Miller owed $3,604.51 in monthly maintenance fees, to be offset by $600.00, incurred as a result of moving into another apartment. Finally, the trial court denied the Association its request for $313.00 of accrued interest on Miller's overdue payments. Appellant comes before this Court to challenge the trial court's findings that the 1984 special assessment was illegal and that the Association is not entitled to prejudgment interest.

Pursuant to the Condominium Declaration, the Association exists to maintain, repair, and replace the common elements of the San Antonio Villa Del Sol and acts through its Board of Directors. Prior to 1984 and in compliance with the Declaration, Miller purchased a condominium and acquired a .0076 interest in its common elements.

On November 26, 1984, following the discovery of a gas leak, the property manager contacted E.L. Smith Plumbing to inspect the premises. The inspection revealed that the gas pipelines needed replacement, because the required major repairs would not last long.

The Board solicited bids for the pipeline project and accepted E.L. Smith's bid of $61,500.00. In addition, the Board also voted to specially assess the owners for the plumbing services and goods related to the gas lines.

Miller claimed the Board's action was illegal and refused to pay his share of the assessment, $454.86. In December, 1984, Miller stopped paying his monthly maintenance fee of $117.37, which goes toward such common expenses as garbage collection, grounds upkeep, gas, water and security. In November, 1985, after filing a lien on Miller's unit and bringing suit against him, the Association notified him that if his assessments were not paid, his gas and water would be disconnected. Miller did not respond, and the Association partially disconnected his gas and water. As of the date of trial, Miller owed $3,604.51 in monthly assessments and $313.81 in accrued interest.

The trial court ruled that the 1984 special assessment was illegal and, therefore, appellant was not entitled to the $454.86 from appellee. The Association was, however, entitled to $3,604.51 in back payments from Miller less $600.00 moving expenses incurred by Miller. Finally, the trial court denied appellant's request for prejudgment interest. Appellant advances ten points of error challenging the trial court's findings concerning prejudgment interest, the special assessment and the $600.00 offset in favor of Miller. Appellee has failed to file a brief.

. . .

In its first point of error, appellant contends that the trial court erred by failing to award prejudgment interest on the monthly maintenance fees. At trial, Miller admitted that he had not paid his monthly maintenance fees since December, 1984. The trial court found that Miller was liable to appellant for these fees totaling $6,304.51 but denied appellant his request for prejudgment interest. It appears from the record that the trial court, in denying the award for prejudgment interest, factored into consideration that Miller acted in good faith when he failed to make his monthly payments.

Prejudgment interest is recoverable as a matter of right when an ascertainable sum of money is determined to have been due and payable at a definite time prior to judgment. *Miner-Dederick Constr. Corp. v. Mid-County Rental Serv.*, 603 S.W.2d 193, 200 (Tex.1980); *Howze v. Surety Corp.*, 584 S.W.2d 263, 268 (Tex.1979); *Ceco Corp. v. Steves Sash & Door Co.*, 714 S.W.2d 322, 328 (Tex.App.—San Antonio 1986), rev'd in part on other grounds, 751 S.W.2d 473 (Tex.1988). The trial court does not have discretion to increase or reduce prejudgment interest. *Matthews v. DeSoto*, 721 S.W.2d 286, 287 (Tex.1986).

In this case, the trial court determined that Miller owed the Association $3,604.51 less $600 offset. The contract specifies a rate of interest of 10% per annum. We reverse the trial court and remand the case with instructions that the trial court calculate the pre-judgment interest. Tex.Rev.Civ.Stat.Ann. art. 5069-1.05, § 1(1) (Vernon Supp.1988).

In points two through six, appellant challenges the trial court's finding that the 1984 special assessment was illegal. In points two and three, appellant claims alternatively that there is no evidence or insufficient evidence to show that section 21.2 of the Condominium Declaration applies to this special assessment. Section 21.2 reads as follows:

> The Association, acting solely through the Board, may include in the regular assessments amounts to be used for the replacement of or addition to capital items or improvements in the Property. Such assessment for capital improvement or replacement shall in no event exceed 30% of the common assessment for the operation and maintenance of the Property without the assessment having been first voted on and approved by two-thirds (2/3) or more vote in percentage ownership interest of those present in person or by proxy at a meeting of the Association duly called for that purpose.

The gist of appellant's argument in points two and three is that there is no evidence or insufficient evidence to show that the replacement of the gas pipeline is a capital item or capital improvement. In addressing a no evidence point, we must consider only the evidence and inferences tending to support the finding. *Garza v. Alviar*, 395 S.W.2d 821, 823 (Tex.1965). On the other hand, when we are deciding an insufficient evidence point, we consider all the evidence and affirm the point only if the evidence supporting the finding is so weak or the evidence to the contrary is so overwhelming. *Id.*

At trial, Mr. Michaud, the plumber who performed the work in question, testified that the condition of the gas pipes was very bad, very dangerous and not feasible to repair. The pipes had to be replaced. This testimony provides us with sufficient evidence that the work performed could reasonably be classified as a capital improvement. Points two and three are overruled.

In points of error four and five, appellant alternatively contends that there is no evidence or insufficient evidence to support the finding that appellant did not reasonably judge the plumbing services and goods to be necessary to preserve and maintain the integrity of the common elements of the property. The thrust of appellant's argument concerns the applicability of section 21.3 of the Declaration, which sets forth two exceptions to section

21.2. Although appellant, pursuant to Rule 298, requested an additional finding pertaining to reasonableness, the trial court declined to make such a finding. We infer from the brief that appellant's real complaint is the trial court's failure to make the requested finding.

The trial court's failure to comply with Tex.R.Civ.P. 298 concerning additional findings is not reversible if the requested finding is covered by and directly contrary to the original findings filed by the trial court. *Shelby Int'l., Inc. v. Wiener*, 563 S.W.2d 324, 328 (Tex.Civ.App.—Houston [1st Dist.] 1978, no *writ*); *Wentz v. Hancock*, 236 S.W.2d 175, 176 (Tex.Civ.App.—Austin 1951, *writ ref'd*). The trial court found that appellant violated section 21.2 of the Declaration. By making this finding, the trial court has impliedly rejected the application of the exceptions in section 21.3. Such a finding is in direct opposition to appellant's requested finding. Therefore, the trial court's failure to comply with appellant's request is not reversible error if the finding made is supported by the evidence. To determine the necessary evidentiary support, we must consider the concomitant arguments under point of error six.

In its sixth point of error, appellant contends that the trial court erred in concluding as a matter of law that the 1984 special assessment was invalid and thus of no force and effect. The trial court based its conclusion on its finding that the assessment by the Association violated section 21.2 of the Declaration. Appellant points out that section 21.3 of the Declaration sets forth the following exception to rule 21.2:

> The 30% of the common assessment limitation provided at paragraph 21.2, above, shall not apply in connection with damage or destruction referred to in section 12 hereof or to such structural alteration or capital additions to or capital improvements of the common elements as are necessary in the Board's reasonable judgment to preserve or maintain the integrity of the common elements of the property. (emphasis added).

Therefore, if the Board reasonably believed its actions were necessary to preserve or maintain the integrity of the common elements, membership approval was not required. Because the trial court did not apply the 21.3 exception, it apparently concluded that the Association's actions were unreasonable.

The evidence was not disputed that after a gas leak was discovered, the property manager arranged for an inspection of the premises. The plumber who conducted the inspection advised that the most feasible way to handle the problem was to replace the gas pipes. The Board solicited bids for the job and accepted E.L. Smith's bid of $61,500.00. The reserve funds were insufficient to pay for the cost of the work; therefore, the Board voted to specially assess the homeowners for the services pertaining to the gas lines which were owned by the Association as common elements.

We find no evidence to suggest that the Association acted unreasonably when it levied the special assessment. In fact, the Association's actions comport in every way with reasonable behavior as set out in prior case law.

The reasonableness standard in this case must be measured in the context of the uniqueness of condominium living. *Pooser v. Lovett Square Townhomes Owners' Ass'n*, 702 S.W.2d 226, 231 (Tex.App.—Houston [1st Dist.] 1985, *writ ref'd n.r.e.*); *Raymond v. Aquarius Condo. Owners Ass'n*, 662 S.W.2d 82, 89 (Tex.App.—Corpus Christi 1983, no *writ*). Each condominium owner relinquishes some degree of freedom of choice and agrees to subordinate some of his traditional ownership rights when he elects this type of ownership experience. The Association is vested with considerable discretion to determine the necessary expenses for the operation of the condominium project and to assess the owners' pro rata share of such common expenses. *Pooser*, 702 S.W.2d at 231; *Raymond*, 662 S.W.2d at 89.

Clearly, the Association complied with the reasonableness standard set out in *Pooser* and *Raymond*. Furthermore, there is no evidence that the Association acted unreasonably. Therefore, points of error four, five, and six are sustained.

In points of error seven through ten, appellant challenges the trial court's finding that the Association acted illegally and outside the scope of its authority when it disconnected Miller's utilities. In so doing, appellant also challenges the $600.00 offset awarded to Miller.

In *Raymond, supra*, a condominium owner also challenged the legality of an assessment by the owners' association. The court referred to two sections of the Texas Condominium Act: § 15, which states that no owner is exempt from contributing towards expenses for the common elements; and § 9, which states that by accepting an individual unit, a condominium owner accepts the terms, conditions and restrictions of the Condominium Declaration. *Raymond*, 662 S.W.2d at 87. In addition, the court cited paragraph 9 of the Condominium Declaration, which says that each unit owner "shall" pay his proportionate share of the common expenses. *Id.* The court concluded that the Board of Directors acted within the scope of its authority granted in the by-laws. *Id.*

Similarly, in the case at bar, Miller has challenged the action of the Association. The record indicates that for eleven months, Miller had not paid his monthly maintenance fees but enjoyed the benefit of the maintenance services. At trial, Miller admitted that because he was not paying his maintenance fees, his neighbors in effect were paying his fees.

Section 5.2 of the by-laws authorizes the Board to make assessments for common expenses, and section 5.6 gives the Association the rights and remedies contained in the Condominium Act and the Declaration to enforce the collection of these assessments. Section 6.2 states that the remedies available in the by-laws are in addition to any other available remedies.

By failing to pay his monthly maintenance fees, Miller was in violation of section 21.1.1 of the Declaration. Section 6.1.1 of the by-laws permits the Association to take action that will abate a condition that is clearly contrary to the intent and meaning of the by-laws. The record shows that the Association sent notice to Miller that if his assessments were not paid, the gas and water in his condominium would be disconnected. After Miller failed to respond, the Association partially disconnected his utilities.

Clearly, a condominium dweller who does not pay his share of the maintenance fee, admits that the other owners are in essence paying his way, and fails to respond to notice of disconnection is in violation of the meaning and intent of the by-laws. The Association took appropriate action to abate this condition. Its actions were neither arbitrary nor capricious and fit squarely within the reasonableness standard set out in *Pooser* and *Raymond*. Therefore, we sustain points of error seven through ten, and in so doing we reverse the $600.00 offset in favor of Miller.

We reverse those portions of the judgment (1) that deny pre-judgment interest, (2) that hold that William B. Miller did not have to pay the special assessment in the amount of $454.86, and (3) that award William B. Miller an offset in the amount of $600.

We remand the case to the trial court with instructions to enter a judgment in conformity with this opinion.

Reversed and Remanded.

iii. Liens

Most association covenants establish a right of lien against the unit or home for delinquent assessments. State law controls the steps necessary to perfect the lien against third parties and the rights of collection against any successors-in-interest to the title of the unit. The practical value of an association's lien rights varies in accordance with the authority for the lien, the procedures for perfection and enforcement, and lien priority.

Inwood North Homeowners' Ass'n v. Harris

Supreme Court of Texas
736 S.W.2d 632 (Tex. 1987)

ROBERTSON, J. This case involves a suit between a homeowners' association and homeowners who are delinquent in their payment of neighborhood assessments. The issue before this court is whether the homestead laws of Texas protect the homeowners against foreclosure for their failure to pay the assessments.

The trial court granted a default judgment against the several homeowners in the amounts they were in arrears, but refused to allow the homeowners' association to foreclose on the homes to collect the sums due. The court of appeals affirmed, 707 S.W.2d 127. We reverse the judgment of the court of appeals.

In December 1980, Inwood North Associates filed a declaration of covenants and restrictions for the Inwood North subdivision in the Harris County real property records. The declaration provided that all the lots within the subdivision were impressed with certain covenants and restrictions and that such would run with the land and be binding upon all parties acquiring rights to any of the property therein. The declaration thereafter created Inwood North Homeowners' Association, a nonprofit corporation, to enforce the various restrictive covenants and to ensure the preservation of the uniform development plan. Under Article IV of the declaration, each person receiving a deed for a lot in the subdivision "is deemed to covenant and agree to pay the Association the following: (a) annual assessment or charges; and (b) special assessments for capital improvements. These assessments, plus interest and costs of collection, were designated to be "a charge on the land and shall be secured by a continuing Vendor's Lien upon the Lot against which such assessments or charges are made."

Many lots in the subdivision were bought between 1981–83, and the respondents here were among the purchasers. The deeds given to the various homeowners contained specific references to the maintenance charges, or in some cases to the property records where the declaration was filed. When some of the homeowners became lax in the payment of their assessment charges, the Association brought suit to recover the amounts due and sought to foreclose on the "Vendor's Lien" contained in the declaration. While many of the delinquent sums were subsequently received, several homeowners failed to settle their accounts. When these homeowners failed to appear at trial after being properly served, the trial court rendered a default judgment against them.

In upholding the trial court's refusal to order foreclosure, the court of appeals held that no proper vendor's lien was formed by the declarations, thus holding the homestead laws of this State precluded foreclosure. While we recognize that no vendor's lien was present, we disagree with the result reached by the court of appeals.

It is unquestioned that an owner of land may contract with respect to their property as they see fit, provided the contracts do not contravene public policy. *Goodstein v. Huff-*

man, 222 S.W.2d 259, 260 (Tex.Civ.App.—Dallas 1949, *writ ref'd*). Therefore, the developer of the subdivision, as owner of all land subject to the declaration, is entitled to create liens on his land to secure the payment of assessments. *Cf. Hodges v. Roberts*, 74 Tex. 517, 519–20, 12 S.W. 222, 223 (1889). The declarations in question provided that the assessments "shall be secured by a continuing vendor's lien." It does not seem likely that a true vendor's lien exists in the present case because the assessment charges were not part of the purchase price of the property. Furthermore, there is no deed of trust which would have acknowledged the prior lien. *Lifemark Corp. v. Merritt*, 655 S.W.2d 310, 313 (Tex.App.—Houston [14th Dist.] 1983, *writ ref'd n.r.e.*). Much more probable is its existence as a contractual lien, as several older decisions hold that a contractual lien will be enforced regardless of the fact that it was improperly designated as a "vendor's lien." *E.g. Maryland Casualty Co. v. Willig*, 10 S.W.2d 415, 419 (Tex.Civ.App.—Waco 1928, *writ ref'd*).

Creation of a contractual lien depends only on evidence apparent from the language of the agreement that the parties intended to create a lien. *Dabney v. Schutze*, 228 S.W. 176, 177 (Tex. Comm'n App.1921, judgmt adopted). Furthermore, under *Moore v. Smith*, 443 S.W.2d 552 (Tex. 1969), this court must consider the assessment provisions and lien as a whole and must not overthrow the clear and explicit intentions of the parties. See *Cartwright v. Trueblood*, 90 Tex. 535, 39 S.W. 930, 932 (1897). It seems clear from the language used in the agreement that the owner intended to provide for such liens, and we would be remiss in not conforming this decision to such an intent. With this decision made we turn to the crux of this case; the effect of Texas homestead law on the lien in question.

As a general rule, a homestead is protected against all debts of those who live in that homestead. The only debts which may be collected by foreclosure on the homestead are delineated in Article XVI, §50 of the Texas Constitution. That section provides:

> The homestead of a family, or of a single adult person, shall be, and is hereby protected from forced sale for the payment of all debts except for the purchase money, the taxes due thereon, or for work and material used in constructing improvements thereon, and in this last case, only when the work and material are contracted for in writing.... No mortgage, trust deed or other lien on the homestead shall ever be valid, except for the purchase money therefor, or improvements made thereon, as hereinbefore provided, whether such mortgage, or trust deed, or other lien, shall have been created by the owner alone, or together with his or her spouse....

Tex. Const. Art. XVI, §50 (1845, amended 1973).

Since the early days of Texas jurisprudence, it has been expressed that the

> homestead exemption was founded on principles of soundest policy.... Its design was not only to protect citizens and their families from destitution, but also to cherish and support in bosoms of individuals, those feelings of sublime independence which are so essential to maintenance of free institutions.

Franklin v. Coffee, 18 Tex. 413, 416 (1857). This court has often said that interpretation of the homestead laws are to be made liberally. *E.g., Cocke v. Conquest*, 120 Tex. 43, 35 S.W.2d 673, 678 (1931). Homestead rights, however, may not be construed so as to avoid or destroy pre-existing rights. *Minnehoma Financial Co. v. Ditto*, 566 S.W.2d 354, 357 (Tex.Civ.App.—Fort Worth 1978, *writ ref'd n.r.e.*). It has long been held that an encumbrance existing against property cannot be affected by the subsequent impression of the homestead exception on the land. *Farmer v. Simpson*, 6 Tex. 303, 310 (1851). As said by this court many years ago, "[A] previously acquired lien, whether general or special, voluntary or involuntary, cannot be subsequently defeated by the voluntary act of a debtor in attempting to make property his homestead." *Gage v. Neblett*, 57 Tex. 374, 378 (1882). Thus, we reaffirm that when the property has not become a homestead at the execution of the mortgage, deed of trust or other lien, the homestead protections have no application even if the property later becomes a homestead.

Thus, this case revolves around when the lien attached on the property. If it occurred simultaneously to or after the homeowners took title, there is authority which would deem the homestead right superior. *See Freiberg v. Walzem*, 85 Tex. 264, 20 S.W. 60, 61 (1892). On the other hand, if the lien attached prior to the claimed homestead right and the lien is an obligation that would run with the land, there would be a right to foreclose.

In Texas, a covenant runs with the land when it touches and concerns the land; relates to a thing in existence or specifically binds the parties and their assigns; is intended by the original parties to run with the land; and when the successor to the burden has notice. *Westland Oil Devel. Corp. v. Gulf Oil Corp.*, 637 S.W.2d 903, 910–11 (Tex.1982); Williams, *Restrictions on the Use of Land; Covenants Running with the Land at Law*, 27 Tex.L.Rev. 419, 423 (1949). The covenant to pay maintenance assessments for the purpose of repairing and improving the common areas and recreational facilities of Inwood North touches and concerns the land. *See* 5 R. Powell, *The Law Of Real Property* § 673[2] at 60–46 (15th ed. 1986) (a covenant to pay for the maintenance of subdivision facilities both benefits and burdens the property of each individual landowner, thus, it runs with the land); *see also Restatement Of Property* § 537 at 3224 (1944). The Declaration of Covenants evidences the intent of the original parties that the covenant run with the land, and the covenant specifically binds the parties, their successors and assigns. Because the property in question was conveyed in a succession of fee simple estates, the requirement of privity is satisfied. *Westland Oil*, 637 S.W.2d at 910–11. Consequently, the covenant in question satisfies the requirements of a covenant running with the land. Furthermore, the deeds signed by each of the homeowners made reference to the assessments that would be due, thus each of the homeowners had notice of what their obligations were, and a purchaser with constructive notice of restrictive covenants becomes bound by them. *Selected Lands Corp. v. Speich*, 702 S.W.2d 197, 199–200 (Tex.App.—Houston [1st Dist.] 1985, *writ* ref'd n.r.e.). Moreover, a purchaser is bound by the terms of instruments in his chain of title. *Cooksey v. Sinder*, 682 S.W.2d 252, 253 (Tex.1984). Therefore, as the homeowners had constructive notice of the lien and foreclosure provisions in the declarations, they are bound by them.

The record discloses that the liens were contracted for several years before the homeowners took possession of their houses. Because the restrictions were placed on the land before it became the homestead of the parties, and because the restrictions contain valid contractual liens which run with the land, the homeowners were subject to the liens in question and an order of foreclosure would have been proper.[1]

---

1. In reaching this decision we are mindful of the decisions of several other states which have chosen to uphold homeowners' associations' rights to foreclose for delinquent assessments. While we recognize that the decisions of these other jurisdictions are arguably distinguishable for one reason or another, we note that no reported case in any jurisdiction has reached anything other than the result we announce today. See *Boyle v. Lake Forest Property Owners Ass'n, Inc.*, 538 F.Supp. 765, 769 (S.D.Ala.1982); *Bessemer v. Gersten*, 381 So. 2d 1344, 1348 (Fla.1980); *Kell v. Bella Vista Village Property Owners Ass'n*, 258 Ark. 757, 528 S.W.2d 651, 653 (1975); *William H. Bond, Jr. & Assoc., Inc. v. Lake O'The Hills Maintenance Ass'n*, 381 So. 2d 1043, 1044 (Miss.1980). Of particular importance is *Bessemer*, as it involved very similar facts to the present case. In *Bessemer*, the Florida Supreme Court held that the homeowners "in accepting the deed with actual or constructive notice of the lien provisions of the declaration of restrictions, manifests the intent to let the real property stand as security for the debt." *Bessemer* at 1348. The court thereafter allowed foreclosure, saying

Furthermore, a second and equally important theory supports our holding today. A homestead right in real property cannot rise any higher than the right, title or interest acquired by the homestead claimant. *Sayers v. Pyland*, 139 Tex. 57, 161 S.W.2d 769, 773 (1942). A homestead may attach to an interest less than an unqualified fee simple title. A homestead may attach to any possessory interest, subject to the inherent characteristics and limitations of the right, title or interest in the property. *Gann v. Montgomery*, 210 S.W.2d 255, 258 (Tex.Civ.App. — Ft. Worth 1948, *writ ref'd n.r.e.*). The homestead, however, will not operate to circumvent an inherent characteristic of the property acquired. *Sayers*, 161 S.W.2d at 773. The concept of community association and mandatory membership is an inherent property interest. The declaration defines the rights and obligations of property ownership. The mutual and reciprocal obligation undertaken by all purchasers in Inwood Homes creates an inherent property interest possessed by each purchaser. The obligation to pay association dues and the corresponding right to demand that maximum services be provided within the association's budget are characteristics of that property interest. Moreover, the right to require that all property owners pay assessment fees is an inherent property right. That no owner has to pay more than a pro rata share is an essential characteristic of the property interest.

We see no distinction in pro rata fee simple ownership of common elements and in pro rata common ownership in an association, mandated by the declaration, which owns the common elements. The function of the association, with its attendant responsibilities, is the same in *Inwood North* as in *Johnson v. First Southern Properties, Inc.*, 687 S.W.2d 399 (Tex.App. — Houston [14th Dist.] 1985, *writ ref'd n.r.e.*).[2]

The purchase of a lot in Inwood Homes carries with the purchase, as an inherent part of the property interest, the obligation to pay association fees for maintenance and ownership of common facilities and services. The remedy of foreclosure is an inherent characteristic of the property right. It is generally the only method by which other owners will not be forced to pay more than their fair share or be forced to accept reduced services. If we were not dealing with a homestead, no one would have a problem declaring that a lien exists to secure the payment of the Homeowners' Association assessments. Our focus in this case has been on whether the lien is enforceable against a homestead claim. In making that determination, we have considered the debt, the lien, the homestead claim, and the property interest to which the homestead attached. In so doing, we have found the lien in the present case to be superior, and worthy of protection against the homestead claim.

In conclusion, we hold that under the facts in the present case, the Homeowners' Association is entitled to the foreclosure of the contractual lien it has on the houses of delinquent owners. We recognize the harshness of the remedy of foreclosure, particularly when such a small sum is compared with the immeasurable value of homestead. Under the laws of this state, however, we are bound to enforce the agreements into which the homeowners entered concerning the payment of assessments. Thus, the judgments of the trial court so that it may issue an order of foreclosure consistent with this opinion.

[T]he creation of the lien by acceptance of the deed relates back to the time of the filing of the declaration of restrictions. Thus, with regard to the time of attachment of the lien, this case is to be treated as if the respondents (homeowners) had taken title subject to a valid pre-existing lien. Since the acquisition of homestead status does not defeat prior liens ... the lienor's right prevails over the respondent's homestead right. *Bessemer* at 1348.

2. For an analysis of *Johnson* and applicable homestead principles, see Note, *The Texas Homestead and Condominium Assessments*, 38 Baylor L.Rev. 987 (1986).

Reversed and Remanded.

c. Consequences of Failing to Collect Assessments

The relationship between a community association board and its members is a unique one. Often board members may be reluctant to be aggressive in collecting assessments against their neighbors. However, failure to do so could lead to the community's gradual decline.

Even aggressive procedures, such as foreclosing on a lien, repossessing personal property, or garnishing a delinquent owner's income, will not guarantee that the association will recover assessments, late charges, attorneys fees and other administrative costs. Assessment debts in some situations can be discharged in bankruptcy. Foreclosing on a lien and collecting on a judgment take a great deal of time, and public auctions and sheriff's sales do not often bring a good price on repossessed or foreclosed property. First priority mortgagees and any other higher priority creditors must be paid before the association receives any payments. Garnishment of wages and other assets assumes the delinquent owner has income, and this is often not the case.

In many cases, unless the owner is hiding assets, there is little the association can do but wait to see if the owner gets back on his or her feet which may take years, and in the meantime, unpaid assessments keep mounting.

However, the community's common expenses need to be met. Unpaid assessments and the costs incurred by the association in trying to collect, in turn, become expenses of the association. In order for these and all other expenses to be paid, they are included as a common expense and paid by assessments to all other unit owners in the community. In other words, if the association incurs $10,000 in unpaid assessments and other expenses, that $10,000 will be allocated to each of the other unit owners in their annual assessment. Not only is the association hurt by increased debt, all members are burdened with their pro rata share of that expense.

Continuing a trend of uncollected assessments can be detrimental to the amount and quality of amenities and services the association is able to provide community residents. In order to keep assessments reasonable within its market, the association may have to cut back on services it provides to its members, close costly amenities such as the neighborhood pool, or begin charging use fees for the amenities it maintains. Common and recreational facilities may fall into disrepair and landscaping may be ignored because of a lack of funds. The end result could be a decline in property values within the community.

Assessments are generally the community's primary funding source. When one member of the community chooses not to pay his or her assessments, everyone in the community pays the price in the increase of assessments, decrease of association services and decline of the community's appearance and quality of living.

Notes & Questions

1. *Late fee calculations.* Essentially, there are two methods of imposing late fees on community association assessments. The most popular method is charging interest for each month the payment is delinquent under the concept that such interest is the "cost" to the association for not timely receiving payment. Also, depending upon the imposed interest rate, the interest method deters homeowners from delaying payment of assessments because it is "cheaper" than deferring other debt payments (for example, credit cards).

The other popular late fee method is imposing flat rate penalties for late payments (or, conversely providing "discounts" for those who pay early). For example, an association may make a special assessment for $100.00 if paid within 30 days, and thereafter the amount due becomes $150.00. Sometimes, the community association's documents may stipulate a flat-rate late fee of "x" dollars for each month the assessment is delinquent (regardless of the amount of the overdue assessment). Finally, the governing documents may attempt to impose both flat-rate penalties and interest.

Discuss what factors may influence the desirability of each late fee payment method. Which options (or under what circumstances) may run the risk of being excessive and unenforceable by a court? See UCIOA § 3-115.

For additional review of the late fee and interest legal issues, see the following cases: *400 Condo. Ass'n v. Wright*, 608 N.E.2d 446 (Ill. App. Ct. 1992); *Broad Street School Condo. Corp. v. Minneman*, No. 0111179 (Conn. Super. Ct., April 23, 1997); *First Fed. Savings Bank of Georgia v. Eaglewood Court Condo. Ass'n, Inc.*, 367 S.E.2d 876 (Ga. App. 1988); *First Fed. Savings Bank v. WSB Investments, Inc.*, 586 N.E.2d 1159 (Ohio App. 1990); *Hershiser v. Yorkshire Condo. Ass'n, Inc.*, 410 S.E.2d 455 (Ga. App. 1991); *King James Landing Ass'n, Inc. v. Della Rata, Inc.*, No. 1844 (Md. Ct. Sp. App. June 24, 1994); *Lee v. Braeburn Valley West Civic Ass'n*, 794 S.W.2d 44 (Tex. App. 1990); and *Tygrett v. University Gardens Homeowners Ass'n*, 687 S.W.2d 481 (Tex. App. 1985). See also Feldman, *Drafting Effective Contracts: A Practitioner's Guide* (1989 and 1996 Supp.) (concerning interest, usury, and consumer protections); *Modern Business Law and the Regulatory Environment*, Ch. 55 (3d Ed. 1996) (concerning consumer protection laws and debt collection practices). See *Pine Island Ridge Condo. "F" Ass'n v. Waters*, printed *infra* (denying delinquent owner the right to lease unit; applying reasonableness test).

2. *Limits on self-help measures?* How far can or should community associations go in trying to compel delinquent assessment payments? Suppose the homeowner in *San Antonio Villa del Sol* had infant children and was located in the frigid winter conditions of the mid-west (versus sunny Texas). Would cutting off the gas and heat be viewed as a reasonable means to compel payment? As counsel for a community association, what factors would you advise the board of directors to consider before proceeding with self-help measures? What limits may be placed on a board's decision to deny rights to a development owner? Recall that the nonpaying member is still receiving benefits that the other owners must pay for and that there is a need to have all pay or services decline.

3. *Denying voting privileges.* In *Mountain Home Properties*, the court held that the association could not deny the new owner's voting privileges since California Civil Code Section 1466 prevented holding the new owner liable for the prior owner's violation. However, typically an association may prevent the current delinquent owner from exercising such voting rights. For example, in *How v. Mars*, 513 N.W.2d 511 (Neb. 1994), the court held that both the by-laws and the state's non-profit corporations code expressly permitted such action.

Most non-profit organizations provide that only "members in good standing" may vote. However, some association governance documents have failed similarly to provide for such treatment. Is it fair to prohibit voting for failure to pay assessments? What reasons support or reject denial of such voting privileges? Is this a fundamental difference between community associations and public governments?

4. *Timing of community association liens.* Review footnote 1 of *Inwood North Homeowner's Association* and the cases cited therein. Why is it so important for the assessment lien to arise at or before the time of closing of each new home sale? Why do most community

association documents subordinate their lien to the first mortgage? See WAYNE S. HYATT, CONDOMINIUMS AND HOME OWNER ASSOCIATIONS: A GUIDE TO THE DEVELOPMENT PROCESS, § 6.20 (1985 and 1995 supp.) (concerning subordination of assessment liens and secondary mortgage market requirements); and see generally, *Powell on Real Property*, 632 (Perm Ed.) (concerning liens, mortgages, and foreclosure issues).

For additional cases reviewing the legal issues of the association assessment lien, see generally *American Holidays, Inc. v. Foxtail Owners Ass'n*, 821 P.2d 577 (Wyo. 1991) (concerning timing of declaration-provided lien); *Carroll v. Oak Hall Assoc., L.P.*, 898 S.W.2d 603 (Mo. App. 1994) (interpretation of Missouri's condominium statute and its lien provision); *First Fed. Savings and Loan of Charleston v. Bailey*, 450 S.E.2d 77 (S.C. App. 1994) (concerning mortgage priority over assessment lien); *Hudson House Condo. Ass'n, Inc. v. Brooks*, 223 Conn. 610 (1992) (applying Connecticut's Common Interest Ownership Act lien provisions); *In re Beckley*, 210 Bankr. 391 (M.D. Fla. 1997) (concerning effect of bankruptcy on assessment lien); and *Rittenhouse Park Community Ass'n v. Katznelson*, 539 A.2d 334 (N.J. Super. Ch. Div. 1987) (issues regarding notice of lien provision in declaration).

5. *Assessment obligations on subsequent purchasers.* The facts of the *Mountain Home Properties* case concerned the subsequent conveyance of lots after nonjudicial foreclosure by the original lender. Irrespective of the application of California Civil Code § 1466, the new owner essentially argued that the association's assessment lien could not attach to the mortgage company's property title upon foreclosure since its deed and lien were superior to the association's. This court passed on determining whether the association's lien survived foreclosure. What do you think? Review footnote 4 of *Mountain Home Properties*. See *Board of Directors of Olde Salem Homeowners' Ass'n v. Secretary of Veteran Affairs*, 589 N.E.2d 761 (Ill. App. Ct. 1992) (concerning subsequent purchases for past due assessments after foreclosure sale); and *Long Island Savings Bank, F.S.B. v. Gomez*, 568 N.Y.S.2d 536 (N.Y. Sup. Ct. 1991) (effect of mortgage foreclosure on association assessment lien). See also Nelson and Whitman, *Real Estate Finance Law* Ch. 7 (2ed. 1985 and 1989 Supp.) (concerning foreclosure); *Powell on Real Property* 37.28 (Perm. Ed.) (concerning mortgage priority rules).

In the last paragraph of the *Mountain Home Properties* opinion, the court states: "There does not appear to be anything reasonable about compelling respondent to pay the debts of another as a condition precedent to obtaining membership in the association." Do you agree with this statement? From the association's perspective, why might this requirement be reasonable? What other methods may the association (or document drafter) take to compel payment of past due assessments in such resale solutions? For additional consideration of California Civil Code Section 1466, see *Cerro de Alcala Homeowner's Ass'n v. Burns*, 216 Cal. Rptr. 84 (Cal. App. Dep't Super. Ct. 1985) (vacating condominium unit does not release owner of assessment obligation under § 1466; must take affirmative steps to abandon unit to apply).

6. *Fair Debt Collection Practices Act.* Case law is split on whether community association assessments are debts for the purposes of the Fair Debt Collection Practices Act. See *Bryan v. Clayton*, 698 So. 2d 472 (Fla. Dist. Ct. App. 1997) (holding that assessments are not covered by this statute); *Vasatka v. Wolin-Levin, Inc.*, No. 94-C-4129 (N.D. Ill. 1995) (letter notifying owner of past due assessments need not comply with the act). But see *Newnan v. Boehm, Pearlstein & Bright, Ltd.*, 119 F.2d 477 (7th Cir. 1997) (past due assessment is "debt" under the act); *Thies v. Law Office of William A. Wyman*, 969 F. Supp. 604 (S. D. Cal. 1997) (past due assessments subject to the act). Do you agree that community association assessments are charges which arise out of a transaction "primarily for personal, family, or household purposes"? See Fair Debt Collection Practices Act, 15 U.S.C

§ 1692 (1997). Consider the association attorney's potential exposure. Is an assessment in a condominium a "debt" as that term is used in the Fair Debt Collection Practices Act? May an attorney who writes an assessment collection letter violate that Act? *Newman v. Boehm, Pearlstein & Bright*, 119 F.3d 477 (7th Cir. 1997). Does a debt require the offer or extension of credit not found in the typical assessment setting? *Zimmerman v. HBO Affiliate Group*, 834 F.2d 1168, 69 (3rd Cir 1987).

2. Payment to Developer Is Not Payment to Association

What happens when there is a payment to the developer or builder rather than to the association or when the builder-seller, as part of the sale, tells the buyer that there will be an exemption for the buyer? The declarant may attempt to provide an exemption; however, the amount due is a "share of common expense." The assessment is an obligation all owners are mutually bound to honor. Thus, can anyone excuse it?

There are also circumstances in which the seller makes arrangements with the buyer to satisfy the assessment for her. This operates as a substitution of primary responsibility for the payment. The owner is still liable but if the seller makes the payment, all is well. If he does not, the association has an action against the owner, and the owner has an action against the seller. The association receives its funds.

Pine Island Ridge Condo. "F" Ass'n v. Waters
Court of Appeals of Florida
374 So. 2d 1033 (Fla. Ct. App. 1979)

MOORE, J. By its complaint in the trial court appellant sought to foreclose a lien on appellees' condominium unit by reason of appellees failure to pay their monthly maintenance assessments. The appellees responded to the complaint with a general denial that any amounts whatsoever were due to appellant and alleged, as an affirmative defense, prepayment of all maintenance fees, recreation fees and country club dues for a period of five years. In a three count counterclaim appellees sought a declaratory judgment, damages for slander of title, and compensatory and punitive damages for interference by appellant with appellees' use and enjoyment of their property.

The case was tried before the judge, sitting without a jury, on stipulated facts, the pertinent ones of which are: (1) the appellees are the fee simple owners of the condominium unit, (2) the condominium unit is subject to the Declaration of Condominium, Articles of Incorporation, and by-laws of the appellant association which is empowered to make and collect maintenance assessments, (3) assessments in specified amounts were made against appellees' unit, (4) appellees refused to pay any and all of said assessments, and (5) the appellant filed an appropriate claim of lien against appellees' unit.

It was further stipulated that: (6) the appellant, Pine Island Ridge Condominium "F" Association, Inc., is not the successor in right, title and interest to the developer, Pine Island Ridge, Inc., the seller from whom appellees purchased their unit, (7) that appellees paid the seller a $2,000.00 premium as pre-payment of all maintenance fees, recreation fees, and country club dues for a period of five years, (8) that appellant refused to allow appellees to lease their unit while fees were in default, and (9) that appellant is a separate corporation distinct from Pine Island Ridge, Inc., the developer and seller of the subject condominium.

Final judgment was entered by the court against the appellant on its foreclosure action and for the appellees on their counterclaim, finding that the appellees had pre-paid all maintenance fees, recreation fees and country club dues for a period of five years. The final judgment also provided for the appellees to recover from the appellant all damages for loss of rental income plus costs and attorney's fees. We reverse.

Appellees' pre-payment agreement clearly specifies that it was entered into with the developer, Pine Island Ridge, Inc., not the condominium association. The developer agreed to pay to the association, on behalf of appellees, all maintenance, recreation fees and country club dues for a period of five years commencing October 1, 1974.[1] At no time did the association approve or ratify this agreement, nor did it release the appellees from their obligation for maintenance fees assessed pursuant to the Declaration of Condominium. As this court stated in *Hidden Harbour Estates, Inc. v. Norman*, 309 So. 2d 180 (Fla. 4th DCA 1975), "condominium unit owners comprise a little democratic subsociety. . . ." As such each purchaser justifiably relies on the terms and conditions contained in the recorded Declaration of Condominium, Articles of Incorporation and by-laws in purchasing individual units. The sub-society operates through its association which cannot be bound by separate agreements between one buyer and the seller, which agreements have never been recorded or approved or ratified by the association. It is unfortunate that in the instant case the developer failed to abide by the agreement; however, this does not excuse the appellees (who may well have an action against the developer) from paying all properly assessed maintenance fees. Although the appellees obviously acted in good faith so also did the remaining condominium unit owners. ". . . (W)here one of two innocent parties must suffer a loss, the one who made possible the loss must bear it." *Griffin v. Gulf Life Insurance Co.*, 146 So. 2d 901 (Fla. 1st DCA 1962). We therefore hold that the association acted properly in commencing an action to foreclose its lien.

Turning now to the final judgment in favor of the appellees for loss of rental income we hold that the refusal to allow appellees to lease their unit was reasonable. In another context we held in *Seagate Condo. Association, Inc. v. Duffy*, 330 So. 2d 484 (Fla. 4th DCA 1976) that the test with respect to restraints on alienation and use is reasonableness. Since the Declaration of Condominium herein specifies that a unit owner must obtain the approval of the association prior to leasing his unit we feel it is reasonable to withhold such approval from an owner who is in default of monthly assessments, thereby placing an added burden upon other owners. The appellees are not entitled therefore to damages for such refusal.

The final judgment is reversed and this cause remanded for further proceedings consistent with this opinion.

Remanded and Reversed.

3. Offsets Against Association Assessments

Offsets can arise in several situations. One type is a form of owner self-help. Another is the case of an owner who objects to paying because of some grievance against the association or against the developer or builder. Analogous to a "rent strike," these argu-

---

1. It is interesting to note the form used by the developer in agreeing to make such payments is captioned: "Advance Payments Made Pursuant To This Contract May Be Used For Construction Purposes By The Developer."

ments are predicated upon the premise that there is a right of offset solely as determined by the delinquent owner.

Another offset situation is one in which there is an "in-kind" contribution. In other words, there is some service performed in lieu of the payment of money. Is this a valid approach? What problems do you see in using it? Is it available to all owners, and if not, should it be available to some? Why?

Windham Creek Owners Ass'n v. Lacey

State Court of Fulton County
C.A. No. 596388 (Fulton Co. St. Ct. 1977)

FINDING OF FACTS, CONCLUSIONS OF LAW AND ORDER

This case having come on for trial before this court on September 28, 1977 and this court having received evidence and heard testimony from the parties and having otherwise been fully advised in the premises hereby makes its Findings of Facts, Conclusions of Law and Order as follows:

FINDING OF FACTS

Defendant is an owner of a condominium unit at Windham Creek, a condominium which at the time of the filing of this suit was duly submitted to the Apartment Ownership Act, Ga. L. 1963, at 561 *et seq.*, Ga. Code Ann. Chapter 85-16(b) *et seq.*, hereinafter referred to as the "Act."

Plaintiff is a Condominium Association formed for the purpose of exercising the powers of the association as duly authorized by the Act.

The Declaration of Covenants, Conditions and Restrictions for Windham Creek (hereinafter referred to as the "Declaration") as amended in compliance with the Act was filed for record in the Office of the Clerk of Fulton County Superior Court and governs the rights and obligations of the parties herein.

Said Declaration provides that each owner by acceptance of a deed conveying a unit hereby is deemed to covenant to pay the association assessments as fixed from time to time as therein provided.

Said Declaration provides that such assessment shall become a charge and a continuing lien upon the property against which such assessment is made.

Said Declaration provides that if the assessment is not paid within 30 days after the date due the association may bring an action of law against the owner personally obligated to pay the same or foreclose its lien against such owner's residence.

The Declaration provides that the Association may file suit in the collection of unpaid assessments in which case attorney's fees of 15% of the principal amount of the suit may be collected upon proper notice, under Ga. Code Ann. Section 20-506, to the Defendant.

Plaintiff filed a lien on Defendant's property.

Defendant has failed to pay the Association assessments in the amount of $26.00 per month for a period of 24 months for a total of $624.00.

Whatever work Defendant performed on the common area of the Association was performed as a volunteer and in no way obligated the Association to Defendant.

The Association substantially complied with this responsibility to provide certain services to its members including Defendant.

CONCLUSIONS OF LAW

Defendant owes Plaintiff $624.00, principal, plus attorney's fees of 15% of the principal and interest at the legal rate of 7 per-cent per annum for the period beginning October 23, 1976 and ending September 28, 1977.

The Third-party Complaint against Third-party Defendant William C. Cato, is hereby dismissed.

The Fact that the developer, Third-party Defendant Cato, may or may not have properly or fully performed his obligations as builder is no defense to Defendant Lacey's obligation to pay the association assessment including payments for the period of time during which the developer controlled the association.

ORDER

Upon the above Findings of Fact and Conclusions of Law, it is hereby ordered, adjudged, and decreed:

1. That Plaintiff have a judgment against Defendant in the principal amount of $624.00 plus attorney's fees in the amount of $93.60, interest in the amount of $21.84 and costs in the amount of $16.00.

2. That the lien filed by Plaintiff is hereby foreclosed pursuant to the Act.

So Ordered.

LaFreniere v. Fitzgerald

Supreme Court of Texas
669 S.W.2d 117 (Tex. 1984)

WALLACE, J. This is a suit by the C-H Council of Co-Owners, Inc. (Council) and four owners of individual condominium units (Fitzgerald) to recover past due maintenance and operation expense assessments from the owner (LaFreniere) of the remaining units within the complex. LaFreniere answered and counterclaimed for amounts already paid by him on behalf of the Council. The trial court rendered judgment on the jury verdict denying recovery to all parties. The court of appeals reversed the judgment of the trial court and remanded the cause for trial. 658 S.W.2d 692. We reverse the judgment of the court of appeals and affirm the judgment of the trial court.

LaFreniere owned a high-rise apartment house, the Cliff-House, which he converted to condominiums. After the apartments were converted LaFreniere attempted to sell the individual condominium units; however, after three years he still owned approximately 60% of the units. LaFreniere was, at all pertinent times, president of the Council and was in complete charge of the operation of the condominium project. The Council was a nonprofit corporation which managed the condominium project. Each owner was assessed twelve cents per month per square foot of individually owned floor space. This money was used for operation and maintenance of the common elements in the project. Fitzgerald and the Council sued LaFreniere alleging that he owed for past due assessments. LaFreniere answered that he had paid expenses on behalf of the Council in excess of the past due assessments and counterclaimed for this excess.

The controlling issue presented in this appeal is whether there was any evidence to support the jury verdict that LaFreniere had expended a sum of money on behalf of the Council equal to his past due assessments. The Council and Fitzgerald contended that

LaFreniere owed past due assessments in the amount of $153,477.26. LaFreniere contended that he had paid Council expenses of $177,285.06. To support his contention, LaFreniere introduced canceled checks into evidence which he claimed represented amounts previously paid by him on behalf of the Council. The court of appeals held that LaFreniere's Exhibits 41 through 45, which included these canceled checks, were hearsay and were not properly admitted into evidence because LaFreniere failed to establish the proper predicate for their admission as required by Tex.Rev.Civ.Stat.Ann. art. 3737e (Vernon Supp.1984). In particular, the court of appeals found that LaFreniere had not proven that he had personal knowledge of the facts reflected in those exhibits, such personal knowledge requirement being a necessary prerequisite to admission of the business records under 3737e. See Tex.Rev.Civ.Stat.Ann. art. 3737e § 1(b) (Vernon Supp.1984). The court further found that these exhibits were the only evidence of LaFreniere's payments and since these exhibits were improperly admitted there was no evidence to support the jury's answers which entitled LaFreniere to an offset.

The exhibits consisted of canceled checks supported by invoices or other memoranda representing payments made by LaFreniere. The checks in question totaled over 550 in number and amounted to payments of $177,285.06. All but six of these checks were signed by LaFreniere. The checks signed by LaFreniere totaled $176,516.09. The remaining six checks were signed by LaFreniere's bookkeeper at his instructions. LaFreniere was the sole stockholder and manager of the corporation. LaFreniere testified that each of the checks was drawn on either his personal account or his corporate account. He further testified that each check was issued in the regular course of his business, at or about the time of the rendition of the services paid for by the checks and that the checks were kept in the regular course of his business. He also testified that to his knowledge each of the checks and the documents on which they were based represented proper expenses of the Council.

We hold that the trial court properly admitted the invoices and checks as business records pursuant to Article 3737e. Section 1 of that article requires that for memoranda or records of an act to be admitted as an exception to the hearsay rule that:

a. It was made in the regular course of business;

b. It was the regular course of that business for an employee or representative of such business with personal knowledge of such act, event or condition to make such memorandum or record or to transmit information thereof to be included in such memorandum or record;

c. It was made at or near the time of the act, event or condition or reasonably soon thereafter.

The court of appeals' holding that the record was inadmissible was based on their conclusion that the requirement of personal knowledge within § (1)(b) had not been met. The trial judge shall determine from all of the evidence offered whether the personal knowledge required by Article 3737e § (1)(b) is present. As recited above, LaFreniere testified that each invoice was submitted for services performed for the Council and that each check was issued by him in payment of that invoice. This meets the personal knowledge requirement of § (1)(b).

The court of appeals held that the Council and Fitzgerald were entitled to attorney's fees. Since we hold that the trial court was correct in denying recovery to the Council and Fitzgerald on their cause of action, they are not entitled to attorney's fees. *Jay-Lor Textiles v. Pacific Compress Warehouse*, 547 S.W.2d 738, 743 (Tex.Civ.App. — Corpus Christi 1977, *writ* ref'd n.r.e.).

The judgment of the court of appeals is Reversed.

Pooser v. Lovett Square Townhomes Owners' Ass'n

Court of Appeals of Texas
702 S.W.2d 226 (Tex. Ct. App. 1985)

BASS, J. This is an appeal from a final judgment in favor of appellees in a suit by appellants to enjoin the collection of condominium maintenance fees. Trial was to the court. We affirm.

Appellants, James E. Pooser, *et ux*, and James E. Ross, *et ux*, d/b/a Ross Ventures, were the owners of two condominium homes at Lovett Square, a condominium project in Houston, Texas. Ross Ventures purchased Unit No. 10 several years prior to trial. Pooser purchased Unit No. 9 about the same time and then sold it to Ross Ventures, who later conveyed it to a third party.

In 1983, appellants brought suit against Lovett Square Townhomes Owners' Association [appellee], to enjoin the collection of past-due maintenance assessments until certain claimed offsets against said assessments had been satisfied. Ross and Pooser claim that the appellee breached its duty to keep their roofs in good condition and repair, resulting in the expenditure of money by appellants to repair leaking roofs and damage resulting from such leakage for which they seek credit.

Appellee filed a counterclaim for past-due assessments, interest and attorney's fees, arguing that the leakage problems were caused by defective design and construction of the roofs by the architect and developers of Lovett Square.

The court entered judgment denying the relief sought by appellants and granting appellee relief on its counterclaim. Upon request, the trial court entered its findings of fact and conclusions of law.

. . .

Appellants essentially raise factual insufficiency points of error. In deciding a factual insufficiency point, we are required to review all the evidence, including that contrary to the finding of the court, and decide whether the judgment was so against the great weight and preponderance of the evidence as to be manifestly unjust. [Citations omitted—Eds.]

In their first point of error, appellants allege that the court erred in making findings of fact numbers 9 and 10, because they are in conflict with finding of fact number 8. These findings are as follows:

8. All condominium units at Lovett Square suffer serious leaking problems. These problems consist primarily of water seepage at the perimeters of the various roofs, through the metal flashing construction joining the walls and roofs. These roofing problems are the result of the defective design and construction of the roofs at Lovett Square. Because of these initial defects left by the builders and developers of Lovett Square, all units continue to suffer serious leakage problems.

9. The Association has not failed and refused to keep in good order, condition and repair the roofs and outside walls of the Plaintiffs' condominium units. The Association has undertaken all reasonable and usual maintenance measures, and has kept the roofs in at least as good order, condition and repair as were the roofs at the time of the construction of Lovett Square was completed and the units sold. Lovett Square's roofing problems are the result of the defective design and construction of the project, not of any failure to maintain the roofs.

10. The Association has taken several steps to deal with the leakage problem at Lovett Square. First, the Association has retained counsel to file suit against the developers and architect of Lovett Square, and that lawsuit is now pending in the 80th District Court of Harris County, Texas. Second, the Association has sought expert advice concerning the roof problem, and in particular has retained Moisture Systems, Inc., a professional roof consulting firm, to evaluate the problem and devise a solution. Third, the Association has retained Moisture Systems, Inc. to draft plans and specifications for the proper repair of the roofs based on the study it had recently completed at the time of trial. Because the Association recognized that some condominium units suffered serious leakage problems that they could not await the completion of a lawsuit against the developers and architect, nor could they await the completion of an expert study and plans and specifications, the Association adopted an intermediate plan: The Association voted to allow those homeowners with such serious problems to repair their own roofs at their own expense, with the understanding that the Association would allow a reasonable setoff (based on the amount, if any, which such repairs later save the Association) against anticipated future special assessments for roof repairs, to compensate the homeowner in part for his initial expenditures. Approximately seven homeowners, including not only Plaintiff Ross but also three members of the Board of Managers, had taken this option and repaired their roofs at their own expense.

Appellants argue that there is a conflict "between the finding that there are serious leaking problems on one hand and the finding that the Association has not failed and refused to keep the roofs in a good state of repair on the other." Appellants ignore the final sentences of findings of fact numbers eight and nine, which state that the leakage problems do not result from the failure of appellee to properly maintain the roofs, but rather from the defective design and construction of the project. Appellants' first point of error is overruled.

Appellants' second point of error alleges that the court erred in making finding of fact number nine (set forth above) because it is "contrary to the evidence." Appellants contend that their condominium units "were leased in good order and condition," and started leaking later. Appellant Ross stated that in his opinion, the roofs had deteriorated following the purchase of the units and as a result of appellee's failure to maintain the roofs.

Ross' testimony is controverted by D.B. Hales, a roof design and construction consultant, who testified that he had substantial experience in the evaluation of roof leakage problems. He had conducted an extensive study of the roofs at Lovett Square. Based on his expertise and the study completed, Hales concluded that the roofing problems were caused primarily by defective design and secondly by poor construction. Hales also found numerous instances where maintenance had been performed, and found no evidence of any failure of the appellee to maintain the roofs as originally designed and constructed.

The testimony of Stephen M. Vaughan also disputes appellants' position. Vaughan testified that he had been a resident of Lovett Square since 1981, and was currently president of the board of managers of the Owners' Association. According to Vaughan, virtually every unit in the complex leaks, and more than half of the units have very serious leakage problems. He stated that the leakage problems in his unit began at the time of purchase, and that since 1982, he has actively participated with the homeowners in pursuing the developers to solve the leakage dilemma.

The record shows that it was always the understanding of the homeowners that the leakage problem did not result from poor maintenance on the part of appellee. This understanding is reflected in the course of action taken by the Association in seeking expert advice to evaluate the problem and devise a solution, and in filing suit against the developers and architects of the project. Ross was aware of such understanding, having been present at the Association meeting in April 1982, wherein the developer tendered control of the corporation to the homeowners. A plan was initiated at that meeting to pursue the developer to correct the leakage problems. It was set forth that the roof repairs were the developer's obligation, and the developer, Joubert, assured the homeowners at said meeting that he would cure the problem. A policy was approved by unanimous vote at subsequent board and membership meetings to implement offsets against anticipated future special assessments for roof repairs, at the time the entire complex was repaired or at the conclusion of the lawsuit against the developer, for those who had already fixed their roofs at their own expense.

Mr. Ross announced at the April 1982, meeting that he would not pay his assessments and would fix his roof and eventually offset the resulting cost against the homeowners' assessment. Subsequently, appellants chose not to participate in the Association's decisions or follow the Association's adopted plan. Appellants were not treated any differently than five to seven homeowners with serious roof leakage problems who followed the Association's policy and continued to pay their assessments. Now, appellants challenge appellee's alleged lack of maintenance and repair subsequent to appellants' actions. Ross admitted that roof repairs were effectuated on Unit No. 9 prior to or close to the April 1982, turnover and that he went ahead with roof repairs on Unit No. 10 about the same time. Appellants cannot seek credit in equity with unclean hands. *Howard v. Richeson*, 13 Tex. 553 (1855); *Regional Properties, Inc. v. Financial & Real Estate Consulting Co.*, 752 F.2d 178, 183 (5th Cir.1985). We overrule point of error two.

In point of error three, appellants claim that the court erred in making conclusion of law number five because the obligation of appellee to maintain the common areas is not independent of the right to collect maintenance funds. Conclusion of law number five reads in pertinent part: "The obligation of homeowners under the Declaration to pay maintenance assessments is independent of the Association's duty to maintain the common areas."

Vaughan admitted that the financial reserve of the project was weak and, therefore, substantially aggravated by appellants' overdue payments. He also testified that the maintenance funds were crucial to the operation of Lovett Square. The amount of assessments averaged $7,500.00 per month, barely covering the cost of operation of $7,500.00 to $9,000.00 per month. Operational costs included management expenses, maintenance costs of the common areas, and insurance coverage on the common elements. Appellants failed to pay their assessments from December 1980, through November 1984, and continued to reap the general benefits from assessments paid by other homeowners. The total amount of assessments owing by appellants was $16,558.36. Mr. Vaughan was of the opinion that if all of the homeowners chose appellants' course of action, Lovett Square would have to close down.

Neither the Lovett Square Declaration nor the Condominium Act mandates that the duty to pay assessments is contingent upon the obligation to repair common elements. Rather, payment in this case makes maintenance and repair more plausible. In fact, the declaration provides for no exemption whatsoever from payment of the assessments, stating in pertinent part: "No Owner is or shall be exempt from such obligation to make such payment by waiver of use of the Common Areas, or any portion thereof, or because of any restriction of such use pursuant to this Declaration, the by-laws or the Rules and Regulations, *or for any other reason*." (Emphasis supplied.) This contractual provision is consistent with the policy that apartment owners in condominiums accept the terms, conditions, and restrictions in their Condominium Declaration by acceptance of deeds to the individual apartment units. *See Raymond v. Aquarius Condo. Owners Association, Inc.*, 662 S.W.2d 82, 87 (Tex.App.—Corpus Christi 1983, no *writ); Board of Directors of By The Sea Council of Co-Owners, Inc. v. Sondock*, 644 S.W.2d 774, 780 (Tex.App.—Corpus Christi 1982, *writ ref'd n.r.e.*); Tex.Prop.Code Ann. sec. 81.001-81.210 (Vernon 1984) (hereinafter Condominium Act). The court determined that the appellants' right to offset against the assessments was not abrogated but would accrue at some later date, and would not entitle appellants to circumvent their continuing obligation to timely pay their fair share of assessments. Appellants' third point of error is overruled.

Appellants' fourth point of error claims that the court erred in making conclusion of law number six because "reasonable action is not a substitute for the unambiguous requirements of the statute, by-laws, and Declarations of the Condominium Association." Conclusion of law number six reads as follows:

> So long as a condominium association or board of managers has acted reasonably in the exercise of its duties under the condominium declaration, a condominium owner is not entitled to recover damages, or to avoid maintenance assessments, because of his disagreement with the actions taken by the association or board.

The court did not hold that the appellee had no duty to properly maintain the common elements of the project. Such duty was clearly provided for in the by-laws of Lovett Square. That the roofs are common elements was also undisputed. What was in dispute was the reasonableness of appellee's course of action. The record reflects that numerous repairs and steps were made to resolve the leakage problem. The majority of homeowners had rejected the proposal of levying special assessments to immediately cure the problem. Homeowners with particularly serious leakage problems, however, were allowed to immediately repair their roofs at their own expense and receive reimbursement later. This step was the result of three factors: appellee's financial reserve was weak; time was needed to discover the causes of leakage and devise proper solutions; and the roofing problem was always understood to be the developer's obligation.

The reasonableness of appellee's course of action must be measured in the context of the uniqueness of condominium living. "Condominium unit owners constitute a democratic subsociety, of necessity more restrictive in the use of condominium property than might be acceptable given traditional forms of property ownership. Therefore, each constituent must relinquish some degree of freedom of choice and agree to subordinate some of his traditional ownership rights when he elects this type of ownership experience." *Raymond*, 662 S.W.2d at 89; see *Board of Directors of By The Sea Council of Co-Owners, Inc.*, 644 S.W.2d at 780–81. The relinquishment of certain ownership rights is consistent with the condominium concept in Texas, which envisions the ownership of two estates merged into one: the fee simple ownership of an apartment or unit in a condominium project and a tenancy in common with other co-owners in the common elements. *Dutcher v. Owens*, 647 S.W.2d 948, 949 (Tex.1983).

The association was vested with considerable discretion in exerting managerial and administrative responsibilities, including the privilege to determine the necessary expenses for the operation of the condominium project, as well as solutions to the leakage problem, and to assess the owners their pro rata share for such "common expenses." There is no evidence that the Association's actions were either arbitrary or capricious. By purchasing a condominium unit, appellants delegated decision making authority concerning the common areas to appellee. Appellants then chose not to participate in their Association or to vote or run for office.

We follow *Raymond* and apply a standard of reasonableness in evaluating appellee's conduct. The delegation of authority to the condominium association is implicit in the condominium scheme, and the record shows reasonable efforts of appellee to solve the leakage problem. Appellants' fourth point of error is overruled.

Appellants' fifth point of error states that the court erred in making conclusion of law number seven, "because such a construction of the statute would abrogate the very purpose of the Condominium Act." Conclusion of law number seven reads as follows:

> The Declaration's requirement that the Association, through its Board of Managers, shall have the duty 'to keep in good order, condition and repair all of the general and limited common elements,' does not require the Association to construct common elements that were never completed by the original developer, or to repair defects in the original design and construction of the project. This requirement states, instead, a duty to maintain the common areas in the condition in which they were originally constructed, reasonable wear and tear excepted.

Again, the standard that we must apply defines the extent of appellee's duties of maintenance and repair to be one of reasonableness. The by-laws of the Association require appellee to keep the common elements "in good order, condition and repair," not to reconstruct such elements. The Condominium Act expressly provides that the by-laws of a condominium regime govern the administration of the buildings that comprise the regime. Further, administrative expenses are referred to in the Act as those covering "maintenance and repair" (*i.e.*, maintenance assessments), which are shared pro rata in the condominium project. The Act does not contemplate that administrative expenses include those necessary for the reconstruction or replacement of common elements, absent agreements to the contrary. Tex.Prop.Code Ann. sec. 81.202, 81.204. Faced with defectively designed and constructed roofing, appellee did all it could, save reconstruct and replace the roofs, to remedy the leakage problem. The court applied the proper standard. We overrule appellants' fifth point of error.

Appellants' final point of error alleges that the court erred in failing to enter judgment for appellants. Based upon the Declaration of the Association, the Condominium Act, and the record in this cause, we conclude that the court entered the proper judgment. Appellants' sixth point of error is overruled.

The judgment is Affirmed.

Notes & Questions

1. *Developer control and in-kind contributions.* Obviously, the developer in *LaFreniere* continued to pay many of the association's expenses "out of his own pocket" for several years. Accordingly, it is not too surprising that the other owners questioned how much he paid in this fashion versus paying outright assessments per unit. In light of the various assessment issues raised in this Chapter, how would you have advised LaFreniere from the beginning concerning this funding practice? What alternatives would be preferable and may have prevented the homeowner litigation?

2. *Permissible offsets.* To address the immediate roof problems, the Lovett Square Townhomes Association devised a plan whereby owners could repair some roofs at their own expense and later receive an offset based upon *possible future savings* to the association for such repairs. Although the court did not address this point directly, why might a homeowner question this offset policy in light of the fact that the roofs are condominium com-

mon property? What other temporary or emergency options might the association have considered to address the most severely leaking roofs? If a homeowner experienced property damage from the leaking roofs and could not get the association to take action timely to repair the problem, what other courses of action should the homeowner consider?

Problem

There are 30 members in the homeowners association, but only 27 pay assessments. Owners of the three homes down the short side road from the other 27 believe that they are exempt. One of the three objected to paying when he purchased because, "I really do not receive any benefits." The developer then caused the board it controlled to adopt a resolution exempting the three homes.

For several years the 27 have paid all costs. Now there is a problem. A new owner has learned that the three do not pay and is refusing to pay a special assessment imposed for needed road repairs.

The association now has an owner-elected board which hires you. They ask for your analysis and recommendations.

4. Effect of Foreclosures

Highland Lakes Country Club & Community Ass'n v. Franzino

Supreme Court of New Jersey
892 A.2d 646 (N.J. 2006)

Justice LaVecchia delivered the opinion of the Court.

In this matter, a homeowners' association in a common-interest community seeks to compel a current homeowner to pay his unpaid membership fees, dues, and common assessments as well as arrears attributable to prior owners of the property....

A.

Highland Lakes Country Club and Community Association (the Association) is a private, single-family, residential community governed by a not-for-profit corporation. Restrictive membership covenants contained in the community's master deed, in subsequent deeds used in the transfer of title to property, and in the Association's Bylaws require all property owners in the community to join the Association.[1] ... At issue is the Association's position that, based on deed language requiring adherence to Bylaw requirements, arrears on membership charges that were accrued by predecessors in title may be enforced both as a contractual obligation undertaken by an acquiring property owner and as an equitable servitude on the property. We thus turn to the relevant language in the Bylaws that, coupled with the deed covenants, is asserted to provide notice that a purchaser in this community acquires the property with a concomitant obligation to pay arrears accrued by prior owners and that the property may be subject to an equitable servitude for such arrears.

---

1. In a Master Deed recorded in 1936, and in the form of deed thereafter used to convey property in the community, there are two membership covenants. In covenants (s) and (t), the purchaser acknowledges that membership in the Association is required of homeowners, affirms that membership has been applied for, and agrees to abide by the Association's requirements, stating specifically that "the buyer further agrees to comply with and conform to the By-Laws of such association."

Article III of the Bylaws includes the following provisions:

SECTION VIII. Membership privileges in the Club will not be granted on resale or other transfer of ownership of property until all Club dues, assessments and initiation fees in arrears are paid in full. (Amended 8/15/93)

SECTION IX. Membership in the Club shall be granted automatically to new owners upon proof of conveyance of title to property in Highland Lakes satisfactory to the Membership Committee. The effective date of the membership of such new owners shall coincide with the effective date of the acquisition of title by such new owners, and such membership shall continue for the entire duration of ownership....

SECTION X. All members shall comply with the By-Laws and Rules and Regulations of Highland Lakes Country Club and Community Association. (Amended 8/16/81)

SECTION XI. (Adopted 8/18/85) The Club shall have a lien on the real property in Highland Lakes of a member for all of such member's unpaid dues, assessments and initiation fees, together with the late payment charges thereon and reasonable attorney's fees for the collection thereof, which lien shall be effective and may be foreclosed in the following manner: ...

B.

The history of this litigation, culminating in the present claim for arrears filed against homeowner, Robert Franzino, may be summarized as follows. On June 22, 1972, Gregory and Marilyn Donchevich purchased the Highland Lakes home that is the subject of this appeal. The Doncheviches gave a purchase money mortgage to Forman Mortgage Company. Through a series of assignments, Oxford Financial Companies (Oxford) came to hold the mortgage on the property. On December 12, 1990, Oxford filed a complaint in foreclosure against the Doncheviches. The Association was joined as a party because it had a docketed judgment for arrears owed by the Doncheviches.... In Oxford's prayers for relief it sought a judgment barring and foreclosing all defendants of all equity or redemption in and to the property.... The Association asserted in a counterclaim that it had a lien on the property by virtue of the docketed judgment against the Doncheviches and because the recorded deed and Bylaws placed all persons owning property in the community on constructive notice that arrears would constitute an equitable servitude on their property. Moreover, the Association asserted that its recorded covenants had priority over the purchase money mortgage.

While Oxford's foreclosure action was pending, the Association was a party to another action before the Appellate Division that also involved whether the Association's assertion of a lien for arrears based on its covenant language would have priority over a purchase money mortgage on a home within the community. *Fortune Sav. Bank v. Von Glahn....* In respect of the issue of priority of payment, Oxford and the Association consented to be bound in their action by the decision in the *Fortune* appeal....

The Appellate Division decided the *Fortune* appeal in October, 1991, in favor of the purchase money mortgage holder, granting it priority in payment over the Association's asserted lien. Thereafter, a final judgment was entered in Oxford's favor in its foreclosure action. In ordering the sale of the Doncheviches' property to pay Oxford, the court also ordered that the defendant Association was "absolutely debarred and foreclosed of and from all equity of redemption of, in, and to said property when sold." In October, 1992, consistent with the court's order, a sheriff's sale was conducted and Oxford purchased the Doncheviches' property for $100.00. The Writ of Execution authorized a sale of the property to pay, in the first place, $54,228.31 to Oxford on its mortgage, together with interest on the principal sum in default on the mortgage.... There is no record of there being a surplus from the foreclosure after payment on the purchase money mortgage or that the Association ever made application for surplus monies....

The property was deeded to Oxford on June 1, 1993. On October 1, 1993, Oxford received a letter from Highland demanding payment in the amount of $851.66 for fees, dues, and assessments that had accrued on the property since the date that Oxford took ownership of the property. In addition, the Association demanded payment for the fees, dues, and assessments still owing from the Doncheviches. The letter advised that neither Oxford nor any subsequent purchaser would be allowed any of the privileges of membership until all arrears were paid. Oxford never paid any assessments on the property....

On March 18, 1994, Franzino purchased the property from Oxford for $64,948.00....

Franzino moved into the property, forwarding to the Association payment for his initiation fee as well as his first year's dues. The Association deposited the monies and informed Franzino that it applied his payment to the amounts owed by Oxford and the Doncheviches from their periods of ownership. The Association also advised Franzino that he would not be permitted any membership privileges until all arrears were paid in full. Franzino refused on the basis that the arrears of past owners were not his responsibility. He has refused to pay his own assessments since then.

This action ensued. The Association's complaint ... alleged that Franzino owed $6,750.14 for past amounts due, plus interest and the costs of suit. Franzino ... filed a counterclaim that ... sought a declaratory judgment on his responsibility for the arrears of prior owners of his property, and he requested compensatory and punitive damages attributable to the Association's denial of membership privileges until those arrears were paid in full.

On cross motions for summary judgment, the trial court granted summary judgment to the Association and dismissed Franzino's counterclaims. Damages totaling $13,555.64 were awarded to the Association. Franzino was held liable for those arrears that were attributable to his period of ownership of the property, and for the arrears attributable to the Doncheviches and Oxford when they held the property. The trial court stated that although the Appellate Division's unpublished decision in *Fortune* established that a purchase money mortgage had priority over the Association's covenant lien in respect of the order of payment from monies available from the foreclosure and sale of the property, the foreclosure action did not extinguish Highland's contractual right to collect the assessments of prior owners from the current owner of the property.

Franzino appealed.... In an unpublished decision, the Appellate Division reversed. The panel explained that

> [b]ecause a homeowner's responsibility to pay Highland's fees is based on restrictive membership covenants included in Highland's deeds and bylaws, because the bylaws specifically state that unpaid assessments are a lien "effective from and after the date of recording," and because no such lien was recorded when Franzino purchased [the property], we reverse....

II.

A.

...

Lacking any statutory origin, homeowners' associations are created in New Jersey by the filing of a declaration of covenants, conditions, and restrictions contained in deeds and association bylaws. E. Richard Kennedy & Mark D. Imbriani, *The Rights of Tenants in Condominium and Homeowner Association Communities,* 174 *N.J. Law.* 18, 18 (1996). The covenants include restrictions and conditions that run with the land and bind all current and future property owners. Gemma Giantomasi, Note, *A Balancing Act: The Foreclosure Power of Homeowners' Associations,* 72 Fordham L. Rev. 2503, 2508 (2004). The bylaws set forth the rules and regulations that govern an association's members.... Because such documents are instruments affecting title to real estate, homeowners' associations may record their governing documents. *See N.J.S.A.* 46:16-1 and -2. Once recorded, the recordation can serve as notice to subsequent judgment creditors and purchasers. *See N.J.S.A.* 46:21-1. It is well established that membership obligations requiring homeowners in a community to join an association and to pay a fair share toward community maintenance are enforceable as contractual obligations. *See Paulinskill Lake Ass'n,* ... 165 *N.J.Super.* [43] at 45, 397 A.2d 698 [App. Div. 1998]. Moreover, such recorded covenants also can create a lien on the property. *See Leisuretowne Ass'n, Inc. v. McCarthy,* 193 *N.J.Super.* 494, 501, 475 A.2d 62 (App.Div.1984) (affirming foreclosure on lien arising from defendants' nonpayment of monthly maintenance fees required by recorded covenants)....

B.

...

III.

A.

In this matter, the Association seeks to hold Franzino liable for arrears for common assessments on the property that arose during the period of the property's ownership by the Doncheviches, the period of ownership by Oxford, and the period during which he owned the property. We begin with the Association's claim that Franzino purchased the property with a preexisting lien created when the Doncheviches went into arrears on their common assessments....

Here, any lien that may have been created when the Doncheviches went into arrears on Association common assessments was extinguished by operation of the foreclosure judgment and subsequent sheriff's sale. We reject the Association's argument that liens created through operation of its covenants and bylaws language are entitled to survive a foreclosure judgment. The Association's position is contrary to foreclosure's essential purpose of transferring a lien claim from the property to the monies generated by the foreclosure sale, thus clearing title to the property.[5] Accordingly, we hold that the Association's asserted lien for the Doncheviches' arrears, arising from the covenant language in the Doncheviches' deed and governing Bylaws, was extinguished by operation of the foreclosure judgment and sale. The property was no longer encumbered by that lien. That said, although that lien became unenforceable, the underlying debt that gave rise to that lien was not affected.

It has long been the law in New Jersey that extinguishment of a lien does not affect the validity of the underlying debt that gave rise to the lien.... [Citations omitted—Eds.] On that basis, the Association urges that the debt underlying the lien filed against the prior owners of the property remained unsatisfied and, by operation of the master deed and Bylaws, was assumed by Franzino when he acquired the property to which that debt

---

5. Of course, the Association may pursue the Doncheviches personally on the debt owed. However, foreclosure is a *quasi in rem* action and, therefore, after the lien is extinguished by operation of the foreclosure judgment, the property no longer secures the debt.

referred. The Association urges that Franzino's purchase of the property, subject to the deed and Bylaw covenants, created new contractual agreements binding him to pay both his common assessments on the property and those arrears that were accrued by his predecessors in title. The covenant language thus created a debt, for present and past arrears, and also created anew a special remedy for that debt in respect of the property—an equitable servitude on the property to secure Franzino's payment of those debts.

As to whether the covenant language is sufficiently specific to impose a new debt obligation for the arrears of past owners, we turn to the language itself to see whether it expresses such intent with sufficient clarity to provide fair notice of the obligation alleged.

B.

Article III, Section VIII of the Bylaws, states that "*[m]embership privileges* in the Club will not be granted on resale or other transfer of ownership of property until all Club dues, assessments and initiation fees in arrears are paid in full."(emphasis added). Although Section VIII does not include specific reference to arrears "accrued by predecessors in title," its import plainly conveys the message that "all arrears" means "all." It informs a new owner that until all arrears are satisfied the privilege of association membership will be withheld. It is, in essence, notice that privilege denial will be used as leverage to compel satisfaction of all arrears.

Section IX, which speaks to actual "membership" in the Association as opposed to addressing the privileges of membership, addresses a new owner's obligation and states that the new owner's duty to pay dues and common assessments commences with the date from which membership is recognized, namely the date of conveyance....

Our obligation when interpreting contractual provisions is clear. [Canons of construction omitted—Eds.]

... Viewed in its proper context, Section VIII applies to a "resale or other transfer of ownership of property" and makes clear that, in those circumstances, membership privileges in the Association will not be available to the purchaser until all "dues, assessments and initiation fees *in arrears* are paid in full."(emphasis added). Common sense tells us that at "resale or other transfer of ownership of property" there are and there can be no "dues, assessments and initiation fees in arrears" other than those already due from prior owners. Thus, Section VIII undoubtedly addresses those "dues, assessments and initiation fees" that are "in arrears" at the time of a "resale or other transfer of ownership of property" and imposes the obligation of their satisfaction on the new owner of the property.

...

Read as written, and in context, ... the Association's Bylaws are not ambiguous. Therefore, nothing here should be read to relieve Franzino of the obligation to which he became bound under the master deed and Bylaws when he acquired the property: the obligation to inquire about and to ensure satisfaction of all "dues, assessments and initiation fees *in arrears*," ...

D.

We conclude that there was a debt owed to the Association by Franzino's predecessors in title relating to the property that preceded Franzino's acquisition. Franzino acquired the obligation to pay for that debt when he acquired the property without requiring satisfaction of the arrears debt prior to closing title. Accordingly, we uphold the continuing validity of the underlying debts owed to the Association and separately incurred by defendant Franzino and his predecessors in title Gregory and Marylyn Donchevich and Oxford Financial Companies, and hold further that any liens in favor of the Association applicable to the property were either extinguished or never perfected.

...

IV.

The judgment of the Appellate Division is reversed and the judgment of the Law Division is reinstated.

Justice WALLACE, dissenting.

I respectfully dissent. I concur with the Appellate Division decision that the Association's Bylaws are ambiguous.

Swan Creek Village Homeowners Association v. Warne
Supreme Court of Utah
134 P.3d 1122 (Utah 2006)

PARRISH, Justice:

...

FACTUAL AND PROCEDURAL BACKGROUND

Swan Creek Village, located in Rich County, Utah, was designed as a 500-plus home development to be completed in multiple phases. In 1979, the developer incorporated the Swan Creek Village Homeowners Association (the "Original Association") and thereafter recorded with Rich County a "Declaration of Reservations, Restrictions and Covenants of Swan Creek Village" (the "Declaration"). The Declaration recognized that the Original Association had been created for the purpose of furthering the community welfare of the property owners in the Swan Creek subdivision, and it bestowed upon the Original Association the power to perform many functions as an agent of the lot owners, including the power to impose, collect, and disburse assessments.

The developer declared bankruptcy and pulled out of Swan Creek midway through its development. Abandoned by the developer, the Original Association failed to file its annual report or pay its filing fee and was involuntarily dissolved on March 31, 1986. Mark Bryner, a lot owner, attempted to have the Original Association reinstated. But his attempt failed because his application to reinstate the Original Association was filed more than one year from the time of its dissolution....

In a continued effort to secure a vehicle for the collective governance of Swan Creek, Bryner incorporated a new homeowners association (the "HOA"), using the identical name and articles of incorporation used by the Original Association. A certificate of incorporation for the HOA was issued on April 28, 1988. Shortly thereafter, Bryner called a meeting of all Swan Creek lot owners. More than 100 people, representing almost half of the lot owners, attended the meeting and elected a board of directors for the HOA....

On May 13, 1989, the board of directors voted to levy a special assessment of $5,900 (the "1989 Assessment") against each lot to cover the cost of certain improvements that had been made to Swan Creek. This 1989 Assessment was levied against all lots in Swan Creek; however, credits were given to those lot owners who had already contributed to the improvements in question.

In the early 1990s, the HOA was party to litigation in the First Judicial District Court for Rich County, State of Utah. One of the issues raised by the litigation was the authority of the HOA to levy assessments pursuant to the terms of the Declaration. The court ruled in favor of the HOA, concluding that the HOA was properly formed and had the authority to impose assessments on the owners of lots in Swan Creek. However, the court limited its holding to the action before it....

When certain lot owners failed to pay the 1989 Assessment, the HOA placed liens on the corresponding lots. Rich County owned four of these lots, having earlier been issued fee simple title by the Rich County Auditor in payment of general taxes, interest, costs, and penalties.... Warne purchased these four lots at a May 24, 1994 tax sale....

Shortly thereafter, the HOA sent ... Warne and other lot owners a letter demanding payment of the 1989 Assessment. After certain lot owners argued that the 1994 tax sale had extinguished any obligation for the 1989 Assessment, the HOA imposed a new assessment (the "1996 Assessment") and issued the following statement:

> The Homeowners association of Swan Creek Village levied an improvement assessment in the amount of $5,900 on May 13, 1989. There have been questions on the legality of this assessment on lots purchased at tax sale after this date. In order to remove any question concerning the validity of this assessment and lien after tax sale, a new assessment is being made at this time.

The 1996 assessment was identical to the 1989 Assessment and, like the 1989 Assessment, was levied against all lots constructed in the first two phases of the development. Like the 1989 Assessment, the 1996 Assessment gave credits to those who had already contributed to the improvements for which the 1996 Assessment was levied. Swan Creek directed notice of the 1996 Assessment to ... Warne, who refused to pay.

The HOA filed suit ... on May 3, 2001, seeking to enforce and collect the 1996 Assessment....

ANALYSIS

...

III. THE STATUTE OF LIMITATIONS DOES NOT BAR THE HOA'S CLAIM

We next turn to ... Warne's contention that the HOA's claim is barred by the applicable statute of limitations. This case is an action on a "contract ... founded upon an instrument in writing" governed by the six-year limitations period of Utah Code section 78-12-23(2) (2002).

... Warne asserts that the statute of limitations began running in 1989 because the 1996 Assessment was merely an attempt to revive the 1989 Assessment. We disagree. Even if the 1996 Assessment represented an effort to collect amounts unpaid from earlier assessments, it was still a new assessment. In so concluding, we do not decide whether the 1996 Assessment was valid, an issue we address below....

IV. THE SWAN CREEK HOMEOWNERS ASSOCIATION HAS ASSESSMENT AUTHORITY OVER LOT OWNERS IN THE SUBDIVISION

We now turn to ... Warne's claim that the HOA lacks authority to impose assessments on property owners in the Swan Creek subdivision. Although ... Warne recognizes that the Original Association would have had authority to levy such assessments ... she claims that the HOA lacked this authority because it is not the association contemplated under the Declaration and because an insufficient number of lot owners voted to ratify its authority. In essence, she urges us to conclude that the assessment power terminated with the defunct Original Association, thereby leaving the HOA without assessment authority.

... [W]e find that the HOA's authority to impose assessments on Swan Creek lot owners pursuant to the terms of the Declaration has been repeatedly ratified by the lot owners over a period of many years. Therefore, using our equitable powers, we declare the HOA to be a valid association authorized to impose assessments pursuant to the terms of the Declaration....

Although we have not previously addressed ratification in the context of homeowners associations, such an exercise of our equitable powers is consistent with over a hundred years of Utah case law in similar contexts.... [Utah history omitted—Eds.]

Other courts have called on such equitable principles in affirming the authority of homeowners associations. [Discussion of *Evergreen Highlands Ass'n v. West, Seaview Ass'n v. Williams,* and *Perry v. Bridgetown Cmty. Ass'n* omitted—Eds.]

...

V. THE VALIDITY OF THE 1996 ASSESSMENT DEPENDS ON THE TERMS OF THE DECLARATION AND THE NATURE OF THE IMPROVEMENTS

Having determined that the HOA has authority to levy assessments on the Swan Creek property owners, we address whether ... Warne was required to pay the 1996 Assessment. Warne argues that the 1996 Assessment was invalid because it was, in reality, an attempt to resuscitate the 1986 Assessment that had been extinguished by the tax sale. We agree.

It is well-settled that liens on real property are extinguished by a tax sale.... A similar rule applies to foreclosure sales. *See* Restatement (Third) of Property §6.5 cmt. 9 (2000).... We therefore conclude that the lien securing the 1989 Assessment was extinguished by the tax sale and that Alicia Warne had no obligation to pay the 1989 Assessment.

Although the tax sale extinguished the 1989 Assessment, it did not extinguish the HOA's authority to levy new assessments on property purchased at the sale. *See* Restatement (Third) of Property §6.5 cmt. 9 (2000). We must therefore confront the thorny issue presented here—whether an association may levy on property purchased at such a sale a new assessment for previously incurred obligations. While this is an issue of first impression in Utah, courts from other jurisdictions have addressed it. *See, e.g., Kingsmill Vill. Condo. Ass'n v. Homebanc Fed. Sav. Bank,* 204 Ga.App. 900, 420 S.E.2d 771 (1992).

In *Kingsmill Village,* a bank acquired a condominium at a foreclosure sale, and the court held that it was not solely responsible for an unpaid assessment levied on the property prior to the bank's assuming title.... The court reasoned that after the foreclosure sale, the unpaid assessment became part of the common expenses. Therefore, the court suggested that the association could require the bank to pay only a pro rata portion of the assessment. Reasoning that the "substance" of the claim was a "recoupment of past assessments," the court refused to allow "[a] party [to] do indirectly what the law does not allow to be done directly." ...; *see also First Fed. Sav. Bank v. Eaglewood Court Condo. Ass'n,* 186 Ga.App. 605, 367 S.E.2d 876, 877 (1988) (holding that mortgagee which foreclosed condominium unit was not liable for an unpaid assessment but rather a pro rata amount of the unpaid share according to statute); *Lakes of the N. Ass'n v. TWIGA Ltd. P'-ship,* 241 Mich.App. 91, 614 N.W.2d 682, 687 (2000) (indicating that "parties agree that a lien for past due assessments ... does not survive a tax sale," but legislative intent was that covenants do subsist); *Micheve, L.L.C. v. Wyndham Place at Freehold Condo. Ass'n,*

370 N.J.Super. 524, 851 A.2d 743, 746–47 (Ct.App.Div.2004) (indicating that a condominium statute did not permit an association to collect back maintenance fees from buyer after sheriff's sale).

Many of these decisions are premised on state statutes that bear on the validity of reassessments following foreclosures. But at the time the HOA filed this action, Utah had no such statute. We therefore decline to follow the rules adopted by these courts. Instead, we conclude that basic principles of contract law govern the validity of the 1996 Assessment. Specifically, we hold that the validity of the assessment against Alicia Warne turns upon the specific provisions of the Declaration establishing the homeowners association and conferring its assessment authority. We choose this approach because both Utah statutes and case law recognize that such associations are controlled by their governing documents, which in fact constitute a contract between the association and the property owners.[3]

...

Had the Declaration authorized selective imposition of assessments under circumstances such as those presented here, we would be constrained to uphold them. Such an approach would be consistent with the principle that the Declaration constitutes a contract between the HOA and its members and with the fact that a recorded Declaration imparts notice of its contractual terms to all who acquire property subject to it. In the absence of such explicit authorization, however, we must agree with Alicia Warne that the HOA lacks authority to revive assessments extinguished by tax sale.

... Paragraph 17(d) of the Declaration, which outlines the powers of the association, states that the association has "the power to assess and collect from *every member* of the association *a uniform monthly charge per single-family residential lot within the sub-division*" (emphasis added). Paragraph 9 of the Declaration states that "[e]ach lot owner shall pay the management committee or association his *allocated portion* of the cash requirement deemed necessary ... to manage and to meet the expenses incident to the running of the association and upkeep of the development" (emphasis added). And paragraph 10 defines the cash requirement as the "aggregate sum" to be paid by "all the owners then in existence."

Nothing in the Declaration suggests that the HOA may impose nonuniform assessments or levy assessments on only selected lot owners or that it may achieve that result by purporting to impose a new assessment on all lot owners and then relieving certain lot owners from responsibility for the assessment by crediting them for payments made toward prior assessments. Indeed, paragraph 17(d)(2) of the Declaration provides that every person acquiring a lot thereby is "held to have agreed to pay the association all charges that the association *shall* make" (emphasis added). It is significant that the Declaration uses the future tense — it does not provide that those acquiring lots are liable for prior assessments. This interpretation is consistent with paragraph 11 of the Declaration, which states that "[e]ach monthly assessment and each special assessment shall be separate, distinct and personal to the owners of the lot against which the same is assessed."

We accordingly vacate the summary judgment entered in favor of the HOA and enter judgment in favor of Alicia Warne. Because this result may initially appear unfair to those lot owners who paid the assessment at issue, we note that the HOA could have prevented this result by foreclosing on its lien prior to the tax sale or by appearing at the tax sale and

---

3. Although not in effect at the time of this action, such an approach is also consistent with the Community Association Act, which provides that the amount and timing of any assessments must be "in accordance with the terms of the ... declaration." Utah Code Ann. § 57-8a-201(2) (Supp.2005).

bidding on the lots. Moreover, Alicia Warne will not be entirely relieved from responsibility for the assessment because the HOA retains the authority to levy assessments for the common expenses of the association. Any revenue shortfall resulting from the unpaid assessments will presumably contribute to the common expenses of the association, and it remains within the authority of the HOA to impose a new assessment on all lots (including those owned by Alicia Warne) requiring lot owners to pay their pro rata share of those expenses.

Notes & Questions

1. How can a common interest community protect itself against defaulting owners? Would it be a good idea to include a provision in the declaration that purchasers of units will not be able to enjoy common property without payment of unpaid assessments imposed on the property during prior ownerships? Even if you think it would be a good idea — which it may well not be — be sure to check to see whether new owners can be made liable for delinquent assessments.

2. *Foreclosure of tax liens.* Statutes often provide that the purchaser at a property tax lien foreclosure sale takes the property free from liens and encumbrances. Does this include common interest community covenants authorizing the association to impose assessments? In *Westwood Homeowners Ass'n v. Lane County*, 864 P.2d 350 (Ore. 1993), the Supreme Court of Oregon, sitting *en banc*, held that the assessment power survives the tax sale. It reasoned that "encumbrances" may have different meanings dependent on context and that, in the context of common interest communities, the legislature could not have meant to include, and thus extinguish, the servitudes. It thus held that "encumbrances" as used in the tax foreclosure statute does not include servitudes.

G. Reserve Funds — When, Why, and How

Some association expenses are incurred yearly and are therefore rather obvious elements of the association's budget of common expenses. However, some types of expenses are expected to arise only once every few years, once in the association's lifetime, or are unforeseeable by even the most conscientious board of directors. Through the creation and maintenance of a reserve fund, the association can prepare itself to handle periodic and unanticipated expenses without disrupting the association's normal operation and services.

For example, a particular community might maintain a clubhouse which is used by owners for social gatherings. The association's budget would normally include annual operational expenses for the clubhouse, such as the cost of providing electricity or phone service to the structure, but probably would not include the cost of a major repair, such as replacing the clubhouse roof. However, if the association's budget includes a reserve fund, the board will have considered the expected lifespan of the roof and will have reserved an adequate amount of money over several years of assessments to pay for the new roof when it becomes necessary. Although including a reserve fund in the common expenses increases the annual assessment slightly for each homeowner, the potential results of failure to fund a reserve are much less attractive and probably more costly in the long run.

If replacement of the aged roof became necessary in the absence of a reserve fund, the association would likely have to choose between the unappealing options of a substantial annual assessment increase for the year in which the roof must be replaced, levy of a costly special assessment to fund the replacement, or neglect of the clubhouse. Furthermore, if the association's governing documents include a provision which sets a maximum assessment increase or places a cap on the dollar amount of the annual assessment, the association may not have the authority to implement an increase sufficient to fund the replacement. If the governing documents require that a special assessment be approved by the membership, the membership may choose to forgo funding the replacement.

Reserve funds are created through the assessment provisions of the association's governing documents and are included in the budget. When budgeting for the reserve fund, the board should take into consideration the number and nature of replaceable assets which comprise the common areas or other areas of the community which are left to the care of the association. The board must also anticipate the expected life of each asset and the expected cost of repair or replacement. Based upon this analysis, the board sets the required reserve contribution in an amount sufficient to meet the projected needs. The reserve contribution is then included in the annual assessment. The association may also choose to budget for an operating reserve in addition to the capital reserve. An operating reserve is used to cover expenses that could not have been anticipated and is generally based upon a percentage of the association's total expenses rather than upon anticipated short-term or long-term expenses, as is the basis for the capital reserve.

Whether the developer or board considers a reserve fund to be necessary to a particular community depends largely upon whether the association is responsible for assets or facilities for which it reasonably anticipates future capital repairs, maintenance, and replacement needs. Failure of a developer-controlled board of directors to establish a reserve fund for an association can result in liability to the developer and its appointees on the board for breach of fiduciary duty. See, *e.g.*, *Ravens Cove Townhomes, Inc. v. Knuppe Dev. Co.*, 115 Cal. App. 3d 787 (1981). The issue, however, is why there is no reserve. There is no independent duty to create a reserve fund. The issue is one of business judgment and the rationale for the decision.

While failure to have an adequate reserve may call into question whether sound business judgment was used in making financial decisions, an association which chooses to employ reserve funds must consider issues beyond the size of the fund. The association must address the tax consequences of creating such reserves, whether the association will be permitted to invest any of the funds held in reserve, and under what circumstances access to the reserve funds will be allowed.

H. Association Taxation Issues

"Double taxation" is a frequent argument made for different reasons and justifications. One argument rests upon the fact that the community association provides services local government normally provides, *e.g.*, trash collection, snow removal, yet the members continue to pay the same rate of tax. See generally *New Jersey State League of Municipalities v. State of New Jersey*, 257 N.J. Super. 509, 608 A.2d 965 (1992). The second argument rests upon the local assessors' computing and imposing property tax on the common property. Those who see double tax do so in the fact that the members' individual property is subject to tax and that the appraised value is increased because of the presence and availability of the common facilities. The theory is that the "value" of the common property is built into the value of the homes. Tax on the homes and the common property thus results in "two bites of the apple."

Under applicable provisions of the Internal Revenue Code, a community association, whether or not it is incorporated, is defined as a "corporation" for income tax purposes and thus is potentially subject to federal income tax. I.R.C. Section 528 defines what is taxable income for a homeowners association and specifies the tax rate applicable to such income. The association may have part of its income exempted from federal income tax if the association meets certain requirements—which almost all do. A qualifying association must (1) be organized and operated to provide for the acquisition, construction, management, maintenance, and care of association property; (2) derive 60 percent or more of its income from membership dues, fees, and assessments levied on its residents; and (3) have expenditures for the acquisition, construction, management, maintenance, and care of association property which total 90 percent or more of the association's expenditures for the taxable year. For such a qualifying association, "exempt function income," which includes membership dues, fees, and owner assessments, is not subject to federal income tax. However, other income sources such as interest on reserve accounts, facilities fees for nonmembers, transportation, and on-site shop sales are subject to federal income tax. Typically, most states follow the federal lead in the area of income taxation and tax under the same or similar scheme.

Other taxation issues may arise depending on the *situs* state, county, or municipality. For example, a municipality may attempt to impose a sales tax on assessments or try to derive some other sort of local tax revenue from the community association.

The Real World: A Developer's Insight

When an association sets its budget, skimping on a management company is not a good place to look to save money. In general, associations end up accepting bids from management companies which are low bidders, making the management fee a small percentage of the association's budget. Also, many associations interview the management company but never meet the person who will manage the association. This usually comes as a surprise, and I have not seen it work out very often.

It is critical to pick the absolutely best person as a manager.

— *Ted Lennon*

* * * *

Reston now has the problem of deciding what pools to close since they cannot support them on the user fee system. Formerly, the whole community subsidized the pools in the community-wide assessments, lending proof that creating a huge community with everyone having access to and paying for the same amenities is a wasteful idea.

— *Jim Todd*

Chapter 7

Design Standards and Control

Restatement (Third) § 6.9 Design-Control Powers

Except to the extent provided by statute or authorized by the declaration, a common-interest community may not impose restrictions on the structures or landscaping that may be placed on individually owned property, or on the design, materials, colors, or plants that may be used.

a. Rationale. Although design controls are a common feature of common-interest communities, they are not necessary to the effective functioning of the community. Unlike powers to manage common property, to raise funds to carry out the purposes of the community, or to enforce the declaration, powers to control the design of individual properties within the community do not necessarily further public interests or fulfill reasonable expectations of the property owners. Design controls may contribute to the maintenance of property values, but they may also interfere with freedom of expression and contribute to the creation of communities lacking in variety or architectural interest. Long tradition supports the individual's right to determine the aesthetic qualities of the home and, within limits imposed by zoning and building codes, to construct structures that suit his or her tastes and needs. Purchasers in communities without design controls may have a reliance interest in the absence of such controls that should be protected.

Some form of design control is typically included in the governing documents of a common interest community. Controls vary widely from highly specific requirements to broad standards like "harmony." The nature of the controls used in a community can make a significant difference in enforceability and, perhaps more importantly, in the image of the community they convey. The normal structure and phraseology of well-drafted documents relating to the design control process strive to strike a balance among permissiveness, requesting compliance, and mandating choice.

One should also ask who sets the standards and how may standards change. What factors mitigate in support of change and against change? Another area of inquiry concerns differences, if any, between design standards and use restrictions. If there be any differences, one must consider the nature of such differences and whether the differences impact enforcement.

Design standards and design control are truly flash points in the structure and operation of common interest communities. One might ask why homeowners care so much about the way their homes look and their unfettered right to make the decisions on these subjects. However, for several different reasons, homeowners do have extremely strong feelings. Even when buying into a community marked by interdependence, individuals still see their "homes as their castles." Others feel home design is an aesthetic statement of who they are and what they wish to be. Still others feel that design standards and control are very important as they are applied to their neighbors. It is the neighbor, after all, who might "do something wrong." In such situations, it is, of course, unnecessary to apply the rules to themselves. Cases concerning design standards present opportunities not only for legal analysis but also for development of well-tuned people skills.

When addressing this subject, we see a situation in which there are needs for both certainty and flexibility. The result is that articulation of a standard is a very important yet difficult task. Individuals need to have sufficient guidance so that they know what is expected, but at the same time as styles, materials, and markets change, there is also a need for standards to evolve in order to reflect change. Must everything be written down, or may the reviewing authority have wide discretion? How does the use of discretion and subjective decision making affect enforcement?

A real challenge is the creation of the standard and the method of communicating it. In the early years of common interest development, most guidelines reflected the language in the FHA form which required that a structure be "in harmony" with its surroundings. There was a great deal of subjectivism in determining whether or not something was acceptable. Increasingly, one now sees "pattern books" which are very specific as to what is or is not permitted on a particular lot. Times and circumstances change, and the method of determining and applying the standards changes with it.

It is also instructive to consider the relationship between the design review process in the private setting and the zoning and building approval process in the public setting. Note the distinction between public law and private law and consider how one affects the other. To what extent does one supplement the other? Interestingly, in some situations, public law will be more restrictive than private standards.

The individual homeowner and her association's design committee are obviously significant parties in this process, but there are others as well. The declarant-developer has an interest in the process and its long-term, uniformly applied application. The merchant builder, the term most frequently applied to the home builder who buys lots or parcels of improved property from the developer for the construction of homes, also has an interest. Not only is he concerned about standards, but most importantly, he will be interested in having maximum flexibility to do what is necessary to satisfy the potential buyer of the home. Thus, a potential conflict between two major players is created from the outset.

The interest of the individual owner is apparent, both as it pertains to her home and to the homes surrounding her. The association representing the group of owners has an interest more parallel to the developer's in the desires for long-term, wide-spread uniformity and quality. At the same time, the association becomes the enforcement agent tasked with resolving any potential disputes. It, therefore, also has an interest in insuring a procedurally appropriate and judicially understood system.

Often overlooked is local government which has a considerable stake in the process. Local government can very frequently shift responsibility to the association's design process, but most frequently, a developer passes on to the association, through the design process, the responsibilities local government imposed as a part of zoning and permitting. In some cases, the association's design approval becomes a condition precedent for local government's acceptance of applications for building permits. In this way, city officials do not become embroiled in granting approvals and then having work begin without association approval.

Initial considerations in addressing design cases include the economic interests and expectations of the various parties and a balance between conformity and individualism.

These vary from party to party, and the lawyer's job in drafting will include developing a system reflecting each. How might this be done? What provisions would be necessary and which desirable? How might this process change depending upon the size and complexity of the project? Some have argued that there are constitutional ramifications which arise as the public and private permitting processes become more intertwined. The attorney for the developer and the attorney for the association might look at these issues differently. What might their perspectives be?

A. Validity of Architectural Standards

If there is anything the nonconformist hates worse than a conformist it's another nonconformist who doesn't conform to the prevailing standards of nonconformity.

—Bill Vaughn

Rhue v. Cheyenne Homes, Inc.
Supreme Court of Colorado
449 P.2d 361 (Colo. 1969)

PRINGLE, J. In the trial court, Cheyenne Homes, Inc., obtained an injunction prohibiting Leonard Rhue and Family Homes, Inc., hereinafter referred to as plaintiffs in error, from moving a thirty year old Spanish style house into a new subdivision which was about 80% improved and which contained only modern ranch style or split level homes.

At the time that the subdivision in which the plaintiffs in error seek to locate this house was platted, the owner placed upon the entire area certain restrictive covenants contained in a "Declaration of Protective Covenants," which was duly recorded. As recited in the document, these protective covenants were for the purpose of "protecting the present and future values of the properties located" in the subdivision. Admittedly, the house which the plaintiffs in error wish to put in the subdivision does not violate any of the few specific restrictions contained in the protective covenants. However, paragraph C-2 of the recorded protective covenants contains the following declaration:

> C-2 No building shall be erected, placed or altered on any lot until the construction plans and specifications and a plan showing the location of the structure shall have been approved by the architectural control committee . . .

Plaintiffs in error failed to submit their plans to the architectural control committee, and the trial court, in entering its injunction, held (1) that such failure constituted a breach of the restrictive covenants, and (2) that the placing of the house would not be in harmony with the existing neighborhood and would depreciate property values in the area.

Plaintiffs in error contend that restriction C-2 is not enforceable because no specific standards are contained therein to guide the committee in determining the approval or disapproval of plans when submitted. We disagree.

It is no secret that housing today is developed by subdividers who, through the use of restrictive covenants, guarantee to the purchaser that his house will be protected against adjacent construction which will impair its value, and that a general plan of construction will be followed. Modern legal authority recognizes this reality and recognizes also that the approval of plans by an architectural control committee is one method by which guarantees of value and general plan of construction can be accomplished and maintained.

Holding

So long as the intention of the covenant is clear and, in the present case it is clearly to protect present and future property values in the subdivision, covenants such as the one before us have been upheld against the contention that they lacked specific restrictions providing a framework within which the architectural committee must act. *Winslette v. Keeler,* 220 Ga. 100, 137 S.E.2d 288; *Kirkley v. Seipelt,* 212 Md. 127, 128 A.2d 430; *Fairfax Community Assoc. v. Boughton,* 127 N.E.2d 641 (Ohio Ct. C.P.); *Hannula v. Hacienda Homes,* 34 Cal.2d 442, 211 P.2d 302, 19 A.L.R.2d 1268. In *Kirkley v. Seipelt, supra,* the plaintiff in error argued unsuccessfully that a covenant requiring approval of plans failed in the test of reasonableness because there were no standards to guide the approving party.

Nelson v. Farr, 143 Colo. 423, 354 P.2d 163, upon which plaintiffs in error solely rely, is not dispositive of the instant case. We were concerned there with the propriety of an injunction which imposed certain restrictions on land, even though there were no recorded instruments restricting the use of the affected land.

We have recognized in Colorado that restrictive covenants placed on land for the benefit of purchasers within a subdivision are valid and not against public policy, and are enforceable in equity against all purchasers. *Pagel v. Gisi,* 132 Colo. 181, 286 P.2d 636; *Seeger v. Puckett,* 115 Colo. 185, 171 P.2d 415. While we have here enunciated the proposition that the covenant requiring approval of the architectural committee before erection of a house in the subdivision is enforceable, we point out that there is a corollary to that proposition which affords protection and due process of law to a purchaser of a lot in the subdivision, namely, that a refusal to approve plans must be reasonable and made in good faith and must not be arbitrary or capricious. *Kirkley v. Seipelt, supra; Winslette v. Keeler, supra; Hannula v. Hacienda Homes, supra.*

Note: A refusal must be reasonable and made in good faith and must not be arbitrary or capricious.

Since two of the three committee members testified that they would disapprove the plans if they were presented to them, we examine the evidence to determine if such refusal is warranted under the rules we have laid down. There was testimony that the house was about thirty years old, and that the other houses were no older than two years. The house of plaintiffs in error has a stucco exterior and a red tile roof. The other houses are commonly known as ranch style or split level, and are predominantly of brick construction with asphalt shingle roofs. There was further testimony that the style of the house would devalue the surrounding properties because it was "not compatible" with the houses already in place.

One member of the committee expressed concern that the house of plaintiffs in error would devalue surrounding property. The other added that he thought the covenant gave the architectural committee the authority to refuse approval to plans for property which would seriously affect the market value of other homes in the area. Clearly, a judgment of disapproval of the plans by the committee is reasonable and in good faith and in harmony with the purposes declared in the covenant.

The judgment is Affirmed.

Notes & Questions

1. *Vague standards are not per se invalid.* At issue in *Rhue v. Cheyenne Homes, Inc.,* 168 Colo. 6, 449 P.2d 361 (1969) was the validity of a covenant to protect present and future values of the properties. The court held that such language was not fatally vague, so long as the covenant's intention and purpose was clear. Other courts have upheld the validity

of covenant restrictions that were arguably less clear and certain than the covenants in *Rhue*. For instance, in *Normandy Square Assoc. v. Ells,* 213 Neb. 60, 327 N.W.2d 101 (1982), the Nebraska Supreme Court held that a protective covenant which provided that structures must conform to the harmony of external design and location in relation to surrounding structures was not *per se* ambiguous, and in the proper circumstances, is enforceable provided that authority is exercised reasonably within the framework of the covenant's purpose. The court reasoned that the validity of that standard must be applied on a case-by-case basis. Do you find the courts' holdings in *Rhue* and *Normandy Square* problematic in that they do not provide potential purchasers with clear standards relating to construction and modification of their property? If not, consider the rationale and holding of the cases in Note 2. Can there be absolute standards while still meeting the need for flexibility as styles, codes, materials, etc., change?

2. *Clear and concise guidelines may be required to enforce covenants.* Unlike the general covenants upheld in *Rhue* and *Normandy*, some courts find covenants invalid where the covenant lacks sufficient guidelines to enable an owner to determine which structures are acceptable under the covenants. In *Prestwick Landowners Ass'n v. Underhill,* 69 Ohio App. 2d 45, 429 N.E.2d 1191 (1980), the court invalidated a covenant which required the architectural design committee's consent before erecting fences and other structures. The homeowner in that case challenged the committee's decision to disapprove a fence he proposed to erect. The court held that the covenant was invalid because of the lack of *de facto* guidelines to give notice to a lot owner as to the kind of fence that would qualify for architectural committee consent. Minutes from a board meeting showed that the committee would make a case-by-case determination. The court found that such a system increased the possibility that the committee would exercise its authority in an unreasonable, arbitrary and capricious manner. Which rule do you think is best, general standards or *de facto* guidelines? Why?

3. *Drafting Considerations.* In *Ross v. Newman,* 291 N.W.2d 228 (Neb. 1980), the Nebraska Supreme Court held that a covenant was invalid and unenforceable where the provision lacked clarity. The provision in question restricted clustered residences from being altered without express written approval by a majority of the owners of townhome lots. The documents provided that the owners look at general appearance, exterior color, harmony of external design and location in relation to surrounding topography and other relevant architecture factors (location within lot boundary lines, quality of construction, size, and suitability for clustered residential purposes). The court noted that the provision was unclear as to what alterations were subject to the committee's approval. The court further noted that the owner/appellant, as well as other owners, had installed exterior front doors, beveled glass windows, door knockers, different colored front doors, and patios, all without vote under the covenant.

The language in this provision gives much more guidance than language in the covenants in *Rhue* and *Normandy Square*, yet the court found the language unclear. Based upon the facts of the case, do you think that the court's decision could have been better grounded in the arbitrary application of the covenant with respect to prior changes? Do you think the court would have reached the same result if the committee had required approval of all alterations in the past? How might the documents have been better drafted in *Ross* to avoid the above outcome?

4. *Arbitrary and capricious.* Courts have consistently enforced covenants where the committee's enforcement is not arbitrary and capricious. See, e.g., *Sprunk v. Creekwood Condo. Unit Owners' Ass'n,* 60 Ohio App. 3d 52, 573 N.E.2d 197 (1989); *Normandy Square Ass'n v. Ells,* 213 Neb. 60, 327 N.W.2d 101 (1982).

5. *Equal application of restriction to all owners.* A finding of arbitrary and capricious application of a restrictive covenant can sometimes turn on the fact that the committee did not apply the covenant restriction to all lot owners equally. For instance, a court found an amendment to a covenant null and void where the amendment excepted one lot owner from application of building restrictions placed on the use of land in the subdivision. *Riley v. Boyle*, 6 Ariz. App. 523, 434 P.2d 525 (1967); see also *Cowherd Dev. Co. v. Littick*, 361 Mo. 1001, 238 S.W. 2d 346 (1951).

6. *Equal application of covenant to all types of construction that may fall within a provision.* Consider the following hypothetical. A covenant provides that there shall be no changes to the exterior of any structures. The architectural review committee failed to require approval of certain changes to the exterior (*e.g.,* changes in door color, door style and installation of windows that vary from the style used in the development). However, when a property owner sought to add a skylight to his unit, the committee protested. Do you believe that the previous facts give rise to a claim of arbitrary enforcement of covenants? See *Normandy Square, supra.* If an association enforces the covenant in an arbitrary manner, should the committee be deemed to waive the right to challenge future acts by owners? What policy arguments support a negative response to that question? See Chapter 8 D regarding defenses to covenant enforcement.

7. *Blanket prohibitions vs. reasonable restrictions on use.* Some courts have approached blanket prohibitions on certain structures by balancing the equities of the case. That is, courts look at the overall scheme of development and how the proposed modification or addition would affect the overall quality of the development. In balancing the equities, the court can look at the burden imposed on the owner's free use of his property and the association's purpose for the blanket restriction and how any changes would be contrary to the restriction's purpose. See, *e.g., Westfield Homes v. Herrick*, 229 Ill. App. 3d 455, 593 N.E.2d 97 (1992). How else might a court approach blanket prohibitions?

8. *Prohibitions in line with the overall aesthetic appearance of the development.* Courts are more likely to uphold the reasonableness of a covenant where it bears a relation to the overall development. For instance, in one case a homeowner challenged the prohibition of clothes lines in open areas of the development. Although the restriction did not expressly prohibit clothes lines, the court found that the prohibition was reasonable in light of the fact that the overall development plan emphasized the community's aesthetic quality by maintaining open common areas. *Beckett Ridge Ass'n.-I v. Agne*, 26 Ohio App. 3d 74, 498 N.E.2d 223 (1985); see also *Leblanc v. Webster*, 483 S.W.2d 647 (Mo. Ct. App. 1972). Do you think bans on clothes lines are less likely to be upheld today given increased concerns about energy costs and global warming?

B. Scope of Architectural Committee's Authority

Davis v. Huey

Supreme Court of Texas
620 S.W.2d 561 (Tex. 1981)

WALLACE, J. Petitioners Tom H. Davis and Hattie Davis, husband and wife, appealed from a permanent injunction entered by the District Court ordering them to remove a portion of their residence built in a residential subdivision without approval of the developer pursuant to restrictive covenants of record. The Court of Civil Appeals affirmed the trial court judgment. 608 S.W.2d 944. We reverse the judgment of the Court of Civil Appeals and render judgment that Respondents, Robert M. and Mary Paige Huey, take nothing.

This is the second time this controversy has appeared before this Court. In 1977, the Hueys filed suit against the Davises alleging violation of restrictive covenants and seeking a temporary injunction to halt construction of their house and ordering the removal of the structure. The trial court denied the application for injunctive relief. The court of civil appeals reversed the judgment of the trial court on the grounds that there was no evidence that the developer had acted in an unreasonable and arbitrary manner in refusing to approve the construction plans for the Davises' house. *Huey v. Davis*, 556 S.W.2d 860 (Tex. Civ. App.—Austin 1977), *reversed*, 571 S.W.2d 859 (Tex. 1978). This Court reversed the judgment of the court of civil appeals on the grounds that the lower court exceeded the scope of appellate review of a temporary injunction and improperly granted premature review of the merits of the case. *Davis v. Huey*, 571 S.W.2d 859 (Tex. 1978).

Northwest Hills, Section 7, a residential subdivision in Austin, Texas, was developed by the Austin Corporation. In 1965, prior to the sale of any lots in the subdivision, the Austin Corporation filed in the Deed Records of Travis County certain restrictive covenants applicable to the subdivision. These covenants are contained in ten paragraphs, numbers 7 and 8 being the ones primarily at issue in this cause. Paragraph 7 establishes the setback, front-line, side-line and rear-line limits of the lot in question. Paragraph 7 provides:

7. <u>Set-Back, Front Line, Side Line and Rear Line</u>

No structure shall be located or erected on any lot nearer to the front plot line than <u>twenty-five (25) feet</u>, nor nearer than five (5) feet to any side plot line except that the total combined setback from both sides shall in no event be less than fifteen (15) feet, <u>nor nearer than fifteen (15) feet to the rear plot line</u>.

Paragraph 8 provides that prior to the commencement of construction on a lot, the lot owner is required to submit the construction plans to the developer or an architectural committee for approval. Paragraph 8 provides:

8. Architectural Control and Building Plans

For the purpose of insuring the development of the subdivision as a residential area of high standards, the Developers, or in the alternative an Architectural committee <u>appointed at intervals of not more than five years</u> by the then owners of a majority of the lots in Northwest Hills <u>Section Seven</u> Addition, reserve <u>the right to regulate and control the buildings or structures or other improvements placed on each lot</u>. No building, wall or other structure shall be placed upon such lot until the plan therefor and the plot plan have been approved in writing by the Developers. Refusal of approval of plans and specifications by the Developers, or by the said Architectural Committee, may be based on any ground, including purely aesthetic grounds, which in the sole and uncontrolled discretion of the Developers or Architectural Committee shall seem sufficient. No alterations in the exterior appearance of any building of [sic] structure shall be made without like approval. No house or other structure shall remain unfinished for more than two years after the same has been commenced.

The <u>Davises' lot adjoins the Huey lot</u> on the canyon rim in an area located within Section 7 of Northwest Hills. The Davises purchased their lot in May, 1976. The record is not precise on this point, but the Hueys apparently purchased their lot in late 1973 or early 1974. The Davises originally proposed to build a house on their lot to be situated twenty-

complied w/
setback

five feet from the rear plot line. It is underlined that the proposed placement of the house complied with the set-back restrictions in Paragraph 7. However, the developer, Austin Corporation, acting through David B. Barrow, Jr., refused to approve the Davises' plans on the basis that the proposed placement of the house on the lot was inconsistent with

denied "on
any ground"
involved.

the general plan of the subdivision. In refusing approval, Barrow relied on the general authority of Paragraph 8 to refuse approval of a plan "on any ground, including purely aesthetic grounds, which in the sole and uncontrolled discretion" of the developer shall seem sufficient. After negotiations between the parties regarding placement of the house proved fruitless, the Davises began construction despite the lack of approval of their plans. Thereafter, the Hueys instituted proceedings, in which Barrow and Austin Corporation, intervened seeking to halt construction on the grounds that the disapproval of the plans was a reasonable, good faith exercise of the authority granted by Paragraph 8; that the completion of the house would reduce the value of the surrounding property because of its size and placement; and, the proposed construction would block the views of the Hueys and other neighbors.

The trial court rendered judgment[2] permanently enjoining the Davises from further construction on their lot until the plans had been approved by the Austin Corporation and ordering them to remove a part of the house already constructed. The court of civil appeals affirmed holding *inter alia* that a covenant requiring written approval of building plans by the developer prior to any placement of any structure on a lot in a subdivision was valid and enforceable when exercised reasonably and pursuant to a general plan or scheme; that evidence supported the findings that there was a general plan or scheme created by the developer; and, that the developer acted reasonably in disapproving Davises' plans. 608 S.W.2d 944.

On appeal to this Court, the Davises primarily attack the validity of the developer's exercise of approval authority pursuant to Paragraph 8, contending that the lower courts failed to properly construe the restrictive covenants. The Davises bring additional points complaining of the lower courts' rulings on evidentiary questions, equity matters, the reshuffling of the jury panel, motions for mistrial, a motion for continuance, the taxing of costs, and the application of the doctrine of the "law of the case." However, in light of

---

2. The case was submitted to the jury on two special issues. In answer to Special Issue One, the jury found that the developer, in refusing to approve the Davises' plans, "acted reasonably and in pursuance of a general plan or scheme to insure the development of the subdivision as a residential area of high standards." In answer to Special Issue Two, the jury failed to find that the only reason considered by the developer in refusing to approve the Davises' plans was the effect of the Davises' house upon the view from the Huey's house. In connection with Special Issue One, the jury was instructed as follows:

> Under the provisions of Paragraph 8 of the restrictive covenants, the developer had the right to refuse to approve plans or plot plan provided that he acted reasonably and provided that his refusal was in pursuance of a general plan or scheme to insure the development of the subdivision as a residential area of high standards.
> You are further instructed that the term "general plan or scheme" means that the restrictions employed by the developer are substantially uniform and are imposed upon substantially all of the lots in the restricted area and that such plan or scheme was intended, understood, and relied upon by the developer and substantially all of the purchasers of lots in the subdivision, and has been maintained from the beginning without material departure therefrom.
> You are further instructed that by the recordation of the restrictions upon Section 7 of Northwest Hills, subsequent purchasers of lots within the subdivision were charged with knowledge of the content of such restrictions.

In addition, the trial court, upon request, filed extensive findings of fact and conclusions of law. See *Davis v. Huey*, 608 S.W.2d 944, 949–50 (Tex. Civ. App—Austin 1980).

our holding that the Davises' lot was not burdened by the restriction sought to be imposed, it is unnecessary to consider these points.

It has been stated that housing today is ordinarily developed by subdividers, who, through the use of restrictive covenants, guarantee to the homeowner that his house will be protected against adjacent construction which will impair its value, and that a general plan of construction will be followed. *Rhue v. Cheyenne Homes, Inc.*, 168 Colo. 6, 449 P.2d 361, 362 (Colo. 1969). Restrictions enhance the value of the subdivision property and form an inducement for purchasers to buy lots within the subdivision. *Finley v. Carr*, 273 S.W.2d 439, 443 (Tex. Civ. App.—Waco 1954, *writ ref'd*). A covenant requiring submission of plans and prior approval before construction is one method by which guarantees of value and of adherence to a general scheme of development can be accomplished and maintained. *Rhue v. Cheyenne Homes, Inc., supra.*

In *Baker v. Henderson*, 137 Tex. 266, 153 S.W.2d 465 (1941), the court set out fundamental rules regarding the application of restrictive covenants in conveyances:

> Restrictive clauses in instruments concerning real estate must be construed strictly, favoring the grantee and against the grantor, and all doubt should be resolved in favor of the free and unrestrictive use of the premises.

> Being in derogation of the fee conveyed by the deed, if there be any ambiguity in the terms of the restrictions, or substantial doubt of its meaning, the ambiguity and doubt should be resolved in favor of the free use of the land. *Settegast v. Foley Bros. Dry Goods Co.*, 114 Tex. 452, 270 S.W. 1014; *Regland v. Overton*, Tex. Civ. App., 44 S.W.2d 768, 771; *Holliday v. Sphar*, 262 Ky. 45, 89 S.W.2d 327; Thompson on Real Property, sec. 3361; 18 C.J., p. 387, and authorities under notes 19 and 20; 26 C.J.S., Deeds, § 163. In Regland v. Overton, supra [44 S.W.2d 771], the court quotes from Thompson on Real Property as follows: "In this country real estate is an article of commerce. The uses to which it should be devoted are constantly changing as the business of the country increases, and as its new wants are developed. Hence, it is contrary to the well-recognized business policy of the country to tie up real estate where the fee is conveyed with restrictions and prohibitions as to its use; and, hence, in the construction of deeds containing restrictions and prohibitions as to the use of the property by a grantee, all doubts should, as a general rule, be resolved in favor of a free use of property and against restrictions."

Id. at 471; accord, *McDonald v. Painter*, 441 S.W.2d 179, 183 (Tex. 1969); *Southampton Civic Club v. Couch*, 159 Tex. 464, 322 S.W.2d 516, 518 (1958); *Settegast v. Foley Bros. Dry Goods Co.*, 114 Tex. 452, 270 S.W. 1014, 1016 (1925).

Although covenants restricting the free use of property are not favored, when restrictions are confined to a lawful purpose and are within reasonable bounds and the language employed is clear, such covenants will be enforced. *Wald v. West MacGregor Protective Assoc.*, 332 S.W.2d 338, 343 (Tex. Civ. App.—Houston 1960, *writ ref'd n.r.e.*). However, a purchaser is bound by only those restrictive covenants attaching to the property of which he has actual or constructive notice. One who purchases for value and without notice takes the land free from the restriction. See, *e.g., Hill v. Trigg*, 286 S.W. 182, 184 (Tex. Comm'n App. 1926); *Fleming v. Adams*, 392 S.W.2d 491, 496 (Tex. Civ. App.—Houston 1965, *writ ref'd n.r.e.*); *Keith v. Seymour*, 335 S.W.2d 862, 871 (Tex. Civ. App.—Houston 1960, *writ ref'd n.r.e.*). See *generally*, 20 Am. Jur. 2d *Covenants, Conditions and Restrictions* §§ 304–11 (1965).

The majority view with respect to covenants requiring submission of plans and prior consent to construction is that such clauses, even if vesting the approving authority with broad discretionary powers, are valid and enforceable so long as the authority to consent is exercised reasonably and in good faith. Other cases have apparently taken the position that a discretionary approval covenant will not permit the approving authority to impose limitations more restrictive than those specific restrictions affecting the lot owner's use of the property. Under this view, a restriction requiring approval of plans will not justify the imposition of building design or site requirements which are more onerous than those specifically stipulated by other restrictions of record.

We find that the better reasoned view is that covenants requiring submission of plans and prior consent before construction are valid insofar as they furnish adequate notice to the property owner of the specific restriction sought to be enforced. Therefore, the question before this Court is whether the approval clause set out in Paragraph 8 of the restrictions placed the Davises on notice that their lot was subject to more stringent building site restrictions than those set out in the specific restriction governing set-back and side-lines, Paragraph 7. We hold that as a matter of law Paragraph 8 failed to provide the Davises with notice of the placement restrictions sought to be enforced and therefore the developer's refusal to approve the plans exceeded the authority granted by the restrictive covenants and was void.

In *Curlee v. Walker*, 112 Tex. 40, 244 S.W. 497, 498 (1922), quoting with approval from *Hooper v. Lottman*, 171 S.W. 270, 272 (Tex. Civ. App.—El Paso 1914, no writ), the court stated rules pertaining to covenants in a subdivision:

> So the general rule may be safely stated to be that where there is a general plan or scheme adopted by the owner of a tract, for the development and improvement of the property by which it is divided into streets and lots, and which contemplates a restriction as to the uses to which lots may be put, or the character and location of improvements thereon, to be secured by a covenant embodying the restriction to be inserted in the deed to purchasers; and it appears from the language of the deed itself, construed in the light of the surrounding circumstances, that such covenants are intended for the benefit of all the lands, and that each purchaser is to be subject thereto, and to have the benefit thereof, and such covenants are inserted in all the deeds for lots sold in pursuance of the plan, a purchaser and his assigns may enforce the covenant against any other purchaser, and his assigns, if he has bought with actual or constructive knowledge of the scheme, and the covenant was part of the subject matter of his purchase.

In addition, in order to enforce restrictions based on a general plan or scheme, it is essential that the party seeking to enforce the restrictions on the use of land establish that the purchaser had notice of the limitations on his title. *E.g., McCart v. Cain*, 416 S.W.2d 463, 465 (Tex. Civ. App.—Fort Worth 1967, *writ ref'd n.r.e.*); *Fleming v. Adams*, 392 S.W.2d 491, 496 (Tex. Civ. App.—Houston 1965, *writ ref'd n.r.e.*); *Alexander Schroeder Lumber Co. v. Corona*, 288 S.W.2d 829, 832 (Tex. Civ. App.—Galveston 1956, *writ ref'd n.r.e.*. Thus, the Hueys have the burden of showing that under the scheme or plan adopted in Section 7, Northwest Hills, it was intended that Paragraph 8, in addition to the specific set-back requirements of Paragraph 7, was intended to regulate placement of buildings on all lots within the subdivision, and that the Davises had notice of such scheme, purpose and intention when they purchased the lot in question, for, unless they had such knowledge or notice, it cannot be said that they entered into the scheme or assumed the mutual obligation. See *Monk v. Danna*, 110 S.W.2d 84, 87 (Tex. Civ. App.—Dallas 1937, *writ dism'd*). Moreover, the meaning of Paragraph 8 and accordingly the nature of the notice thereby furnished to the Davises, is determined at the date of the inception of the general plan or scheme, *i.e.,* in 1965, the date of filing of the restrictions in the Deed

Records of Travis County. See *Curb v. Benson*, 564 S.W.2d 432, 433 (Tex. Civ. App.—Austin 1978, *writ ref'd n.r.e.*); *Green Avenue Apartments v. Chambers*, 239 S.W.2d 675, 686 (Tex. Civ. App.—Beaumont 1951, no *writ*).

It is undisputed that Austin Corporation, by impressing upon all lots in Section 7 a uniform set of restrictive covenants, intended to establish a scheme or plan to insure the development of a "residential area of high standards." There is also little dispute that the developer has implemented in the subdivision a general scheme or plan which has resulted in a residential area of high standards. David B. Barrow, Jr., who, acting on behalf of Austin Corporation, refused to approve the Davises' plans testified that his disapproval was in furtherance of an intention to maintain Section 7 as a residential area of high standards. Barrow testified that his refusal to approve the Davises' plans was essentially based on the placement of the house on the lot because, in his view, the proposed construction was incompatible with the houses in the surrounding area. He stated that in the area of the Davises' lot all the houses are located roughly equidistant from the street, have a rear area of back yard, have only minor variations in size, and are located on their lots so as to avoid interference with neighbors' views. Barrow stated that the Davises' house was incompatible with the surrounding houses because of its larger dimensions, its placement near the rear of the lot, and its obstruction of the views from neighboring houses. However, it is to be emphasized that Barrow also acknowledged that "in the abstract," the Davises' house would not detract from and was not inconsistent with a residential area of high standards. Thus, it is apparent that in the view of Barrow, the Davises' plans were consistent with a residential area of high standards but were incompatible with a general plan or scheme involving the placement of houses on lots in Section 7.

However, there is nothing in the record which will support a holding that a general plan or scheme had been adopted by the developer with respect to placement so as to place the Davises on notice of such restrictions. Barrow testified that at the time the restrictions were filed, the developers had no definite intentions concerning the regulation of placement under Paragraph 8. In addition, other than the specific restrictions on building site and size, there is no language in any of the covenants, particularly in Paragraph 8, which would place a purchaser on notice that his lot was subject to the placement limitation sought to be enforced.[5] *See Brown v. Wehner*, 610 S.W.2d 168, 170 (Tex. Civ. App.—Houston [1st Dist.] 1980, *writ ref'd n.r.e.*). Even more significant is the following testimony of Barrow:

> Q All right. Now, it is true, as I recall it, sir, that you made your decision on where you were going to allow someone to build on Lot 22 at a later date after some other people chose to build their houses up near the fronts of their lots?
>
> A Yes, sir.
>
> Q So the Hueys' choice, you are letting influence what the Davises do, rather than the restrictive covenants, isn't that true?
>
> A The—yes, sir, all the homes along the street in that area influenced the decision.

Based on the language of the restrictive covenants and Barrow's testimony, it is clear that a general scheme regarding the placement of houses on lots in Section 7 did not exist at the time the restrictions were filed but that the placement restrictions sought to be im-

---

5. In comparison, the Austin Corporation inserted the following clause in the restrictive covenants for Section 12 of Northwest Hills: "The Developer reserves the right to determine the location and height of all houses located in block W."

posed were in response to developing conditions in the subdivision. Thus, the limitations on the Davises' free use of their property were not based on the restrictive covenants but rather on the voluntary decisions of neighboring lot owners who had the good fortune to construct their houses prior to the Davises. The personal decisions of adjoining lot owners do not appear in the Davises' chain of title or in any other instrument of record. Therefore, the Davises did not purchase with notice of the limitation sought to be imposed and their lot is not burdened by the placement restriction. See *Golf View Improvement Ass'n v. Uznis*, 342 Mich. 128, 68 N.W.2d 785, 787 (Mich. 1955); *Carranor Woods Property Owners' Ass'n v. Driscoll*, 106 Ohio App. 95, 153 N.E.2d 681, 686 (Ohio Ct. App. 1957); see also *Wiley v. Schorr*, 594 S.W.2d 484, 487 (Tex. Civ. App.—San Antonio 1979, writ ref'd n.r.e.).

·A contrary holding would be inconsistent with the basic concept underlying the use of restrictive covenants that each purchaser in a restricted subdivision is subjected to the burden and entitled to the benefit of the covenant. In the instant case, under the theory advanced by the developer, lot owners who built their houses early in the development of the subdivision had a relatively free hand in deciding on placement of their houses on their lots, limited only by the specific restrictions. However, once these houses were constructed the surrounding undeveloped lots were burdened to the extent that placement of houses on these lots could not be inconsistent with the developed lots as determined by the approving authority in the subdivision. Thus, lot owners who built their houses early in the development of the subdivision received the benefits of the covenants but not the burdens. In contrast, the Davises were burdened by the restrictions but essentially will receive no benefits because their house was constructed after other lot owners had decided on placement of their houses. See *Curlee v. Walker, supra*. Thus, the placement restriction sought to be enforced in this cause clearly lacks the mutuality of obligation central to the purpose of restrictive covenants. See Thompson On Real Property § 3164 (1962).

Accordingly, we hold that the refusal of the developer to approve the Davises' plans exceeded his authority under the restrictive covenants and was void.

Accordingly, we reverse the judgments of the courts below and render judgment that the Hueys take nothing.

Notes & Questions

1. *Notice as a prerequisite to enforcing a restrictive covenant.* Generally, an association's authority to enforce a covenant against an owner requires either actual notice or constructive notice of violation of a restriction. See, *e.g., Coffman v. James*, 177 So. 2d 25 (Fla. Dist. Ct. App. 1965).

2. *Approval ineffective where the architectural committee was not properly elected.* What happens when a architectural design committee gives approval where it has no authority to do so? Consider the following case. The association held a meeting at which it elected a committee (Committee I) to oversee and control the architecture of the development. A homeowner requested that Committee I approve his specifications for building a home. Committee I took no action. The developer then appointed a new committee (Committee II), which purportedly had the authority to approve architectural changes, etc. Committee II approved the homeowner's plans, and the owner began construction. The association sought to enjoin the owner's construction. The court issued an injunction against the owner, finding that the approval to go ahead with the construction was invalid

because Committee II had no authority to approve or disapprove such plans. *Trieweiler v. Spicher*, 254 Mont. 321, 838 P.2d 382 (1992).

3. *Delegation to committee of the developer's/landlord's rights.* The First Union National Bank leased property from the plaintiff. The lease provided that any improvement or modification to the leasehold had to comply with rules and regulations of the architectural committee of the landlord/developer. First Union National Bank obtained approval of the modification from the architectural committee and began construction. The landlord objected to the changes and sought to enjoin First National Bank's construction. The landlord also sought contractual damages for making changes to the leasehold without proper authorization. The court held that the lease did not expressly designate the architectural committee as the developer/landlord's agent for approval of alterations to the leasehold and that consent by committee did not waive the landlord's right to reject alterations to the property. *Winslow v. First Union Nat'l Bank of Florida*, 639 So. 2d 86 (Fla. Dist. Ct. App. 1994).

4. "*Harmony*" *covenant.* A number of restrictive covenants provide that the architectural committee has the authority to approve or disapprove modifications to units in a development in order to protect conformity and harmony of external design. See, *e.g.*, *Winslette v. Keeler*, 220 Ga. 100, 137 S.E.2d 288 (1964). In *Winslette*, the court held that the following harmony covenant was not so vague as to render it unenforceable. The provision stated, "No building shall be erected, placed or altered ... until the building plans, specifications and plat plan showing the location of such building have been approved in writing by the developer, his agents, successors or assigns as to conformity and harmony of external design and general quality with existing standards of the neighborhood...." Do you think that the court was correct in holding that the covenant was not so vague as to render it unenforceable? How much discretion should a committee be given with regard to rejecting modifications or additions that are not in harmony with the existing development? How important are internal operating procedures to guide the committee and to ensure consistency?

5. *Benefits and burdens.* Do you agree with the *Davis* opinion that those who build their homes early received the benefits but not the burdens of the covenants, and those who built subsequently received the burdens but not the benefits? Must the general scheme of development be decided at the inception of the development? Or can it be defined or established by the developer as homes are approved and constructed? On the surface, the *Davis* court appears to take the former position, but is that really the proposition they are advancing? What factors are most significant in explaining the *Davis* outcome?

C. Construing Document Terminology

The old adage that one picture is worth a thousand words is certainly true in the design standards process. The most effective design standards contain considerable illustrative material. In fact, there is more illustration and less text with the text primarily intended to explain and elaborate the illustration. One sees pictures side by side with a line struck through one or subheadings of "this" and "not this." This approach allows all concerned to have a greater sense of what is intended.

The design documentation is normally found in two separate instruments. The design standards, design guidelines, pattern books, or other similarly named documents provide the renderings and architectural and design texts. The CCRs provide the teeth and the obligation to comply. The latter document empowers while the former sets forth and explains.

The more forward-looking documents provide for limited exceptions. Evolution and technology, design excellence, and the unique characteristics of a lot might be examples where the review process would permit a waiver. Generally, however, the empowering documents make very clear that the final decision rests with the reviewing body, which is granted considerable discretion to decide what is or is not appropriate under the particular circumstances.

Lakes at Mercer Island Homeowners' Ass'n v. Witrak

Court of Appeals of Washington
810 P.2d 27 (Wash. Ct. App. 1991)

FORREST, J. The Lakes at Mercer Island Homeowners Association (Homeowners) appeal the trial court's grant of summary judgment, arguing that issues of fact were presented relating to Bonnie Witrak's compliance with provisions of the Homeowners Declaration of Covenants, Conditions and Restrictions (CCR). We reverse.

Bonnie Witrak and Tom Gumprecht live in a residential subdivision located on Mercer Island, known as "The Lakes at Mercer Island" (The Lakes). In spring of 1987, John and Maryann Deming began construction on the lot adjacent to Witrak. In May 1987, Witrak planted 55 pyramidalis trees on her property to screen her property from the Demings. She did not seek the approval of the Homeowners Architectural Control Committee (ACC), nor was it required. She then built a six-foot fence on the lot line between the two properties. Prior to construction, Witrak had sought and obtained ACC approval to build the fence pursuant to Article II section 8 of the CCR.

In January 1988, Witrak hired an architect to design an addition to her home. In July 1988, she submitted the architect's plans to the ACC. It denied approval of the addition by letter dated August 15, 1988. Witrak requested that the ACC reconsider. It refused. A meeting between Witrak, the ACC and the Homeowners Board of Directors on September 19, 1988 did not change the ACC's decision.

On September 23, 1988, workers began excavation on Witrak's property. By September 25, 1988, they had planted a row of 30 Douglas Fir trees, each between 25–30 feet in height immediately adjacent to the Witrak/Deming boundary line. On September 26, Witrak renewed her request for approval of the proposed addition. The ACC again refused to allow the remodel, they also claimed the trees were planted in violation of the CCR and referred the matter to the Board. Witrak refused to remove the trees. The Board filed suit on October 18, 1988, seeking an order that the trees be removed. Both parties moved for summary judgment. On December 22, 1989, the trial court held that there were no material facts in dispute and concluded, as a matter of law, that the language of the CCR did not prohibit the trees. The Homeowners' motion for reconsideration was denied. This appeal followed.

After reading the relevant provisions of the CCR the trial court concluded as a matter of law that the trees did not constitute a wall or fence. The material portion of Article II, section 8 of the CCR states:

Landscaping and Fencing....

> Fences, walls or shrubs are permitted to delineate the lot lines of each lot, subject to Architectural Control Committee approval. In any event, no fence

erected within the subdivision shall be over six feet (6') in height. No barbed wire, chain link or corrugated fiberglass fences shall be erected on any lot. All fences, open and solid, are to meet the standards set by the Architectural Control Committee and must be approved by the Committee prior to construction.

While restrictive covenants were once disfavored by the courts, upholding the common law right of free use of privately owned land, modern courts have recognized the necessity of enforcing such restrictions to protect the public and private property owners from the increased pressures of urbanization.[1] The primary objective in interpreting restrictive covenants is to determine the intent of the parties to the agreement.[2]

We agree with the reasoning expressed by the Missouri Court of Appeals in *Thomas v. Depaoli*[3] that the clear intent of a restrictive covenant is determined by the purposes sought to be accomplished by the covenant. The *Thomas* court determined that a fence which obstructed the view of neighbors was a "building" as contemplated in a set-back restriction.[4] This reasoning is consistent with prior Washington law. In *Foster v. Nehls*[5] the court declined to specifically define "one and one-half stories in height," opting instead to determine the purpose of the restriction and enjoin the building of a structure that obstructed a neighbor's view.

Witrak suggests the courts must adopt literal definitions for the words of a covenant, claiming restrictive covenants should be "strictly" construed. While it is true that the courts should not give a covenant a broader than intended application, it is well settled that a covenant should not be read in such a way that defeats the plain and obvious meaning of the restriction.[6] Witrak also contends that any doubts regarding the interpretation of the covenants should be resolved in her favor.[7] While such a rule may have some validity when the conflict is between a homeowner and the maker of the covenants, it has limited value when the conflict is between homeowners.[8] In such a case the court should place special emphasis on arriving at an interpretation that protects the homeowners' collective interests.

The trial court appears to apply a "plain meaning" interpretation of the covenants. However, this decision was made prior to the Supreme Court holding in *Berg v. Hudesman*[9] rejecting such analysis in favor of the "context rule." In *Berg* the Supreme Court recognized that even the most ordinary words are only understood in the context of the surrounding document, the subject matter and objective of the contract, the surrounding circumstances, the subsequent acts and conduct of the parties, and the reasonable-

---

1. *Thayer v. Thompson*, 36 Wash.App. 794, 796–97, 677 P.2d 787, review denied, 101 Wash.2d 1016 (1984).

2. *Burton v. Douglas Cy.*, 65 Wash.2d 619, 621–22, 399 P.2d 68 (1965); *Hagemann v. Worth*, 56 Wash.App. 85, 782 P.2d 1072 (1989); *Thayer v. Thompson*, 36 Wash.App. at 796, 677 P.2d 787; *Fairwood Greens Homeowners Assoc. v. Young*, 26 Wash.App. 758, 614 P.2d 219 (1980); *Foster v. Nehls*, 15 Wash.App. 749, 551 P.2d 768 (1976), review denied, 88 Wash.2d 1001 (1977).

3. 778 S.W.2d 745, 748 (Mo.App.1989).

4. The *Thomas* court cited the following: "The marked tendency of the courts is to give effect to the intention of the parties, and, in so doing, to extend the meaning of the term to cover structures that ordinarily would not fall within the strict definition of the word." *Thomas*, at 748, quoting 26 C.J.S. Deeds § 164(1), p. 1108 (1956).

5. 15 Wash.App. 749, 750, 551 P.2d 768 (1976).

6. *Fairwood Greens*, 26 Wash.App. at 762, 614 P.2d 219.

7. See *Fairwood Greens*, at 761–762, 614 P.2d 219.

8. The Homeowners Association in this case is made up of other homeowners and clearly reflects objections by Witrak's neighbors.

9. 115 Wash.2d 657, 801 P.2d 222 (1990).

ness of the respective interpretations of the contract.[10] The wooden fence previously built by Witrak was approved because it did not block the Demings' light or view. Witrak's proposed remodel was denied because it would adversely affect the neighbors' "outlook." It is only after such considerations that the language can be interpreted to arrive at the intent of the parties. Of particular interest to this case is the *Berg* court's emphasis on rejecting interpretations that are unreasonable and imprudent and accepting those which make the contract reasonable and just.[11]

The overall purpose of the CCR seems clear: protect the aesthetic harmony of the community, preserve an open natural appearance, and maintain the view and light of each property owner. Adopting a definition of "fence" as excluding trees and being limited only to a structure frustrates the purpose of the covenants. Article II, section 8, specifically cites height, placement and appearance as primary factors to ACC approval of fences. In view of the overall purposes and the specific control of "fences, walls and shrubs" delineating a boundary, it is almost inconceivable that the developer had any actual intent to allow a row of trees immediately adjacent to a property line without any control. If such is the meaning, it surely was not deliberate.

Contrary to Witrak's contention, even the literal meaning of "fences" does not exclude a row of trees along a property line. A common and ordinary meaning of "fence" is "a barrier," *Webster's Third New International Dictionary* 837 (1969), or "a hedge, structure, or partition, erected for the purpose of inclosing a piece of land, or to divide a piece of land ... or to separate two contiguous estates." *Black's Law Dictionary* 745 (4th ed. 1968). These definitions preclude a summary judgment that trees may under no circumstances constitute a fence.

Witrak urges the court to reject as a matter of law the notion that fences may be naturally grown because it is not expressly provided for in the covenant. We are not persuaded. Normally, a property owner can plant a row of trees or other foliage to create a barrier between two contiguous pieces of property. Such "fencing" occurs on a regular basis. Prior courts have recognized that planting large bushy trees close together along a property line is indeed a "fence."[12] Shrubs performing the role of a fence in delineating property lines are expressly subject to ACC control. The difference between a "shrub" and a "tree" seems to be primarily botanical rather than functional.[13] What is the difference for these purposes between a line of 15' cedar trees and line of 15' laurel shrubs? Given the covenant's clear concern with height and obstruction of neighbors' light and view, it would be a strange reading indeed that would require prior approval of relatively low shrubbery delineating a lot line but allow a property owner to plant large trees along the same lot line without ACC approval. Clearly the language cannot be interpreted as a matter of law to require such a result.

---

10. *Berg*, 115 Wash.2d at 666–67, 801 P.2d 222. This reasoning is consistent with rules of statutory interpretation that words which are capable of various meanings are best understood in a given case from the context in which it is used. See *Moran v. Washington Fruit & Produce*, 60 Wash.App. 548, 555, 804 P.2d 1287 (1991).

11. *Berg*, 115 Wash.2d at 672, 801 P.2d 222.

12. *Clyde Hill v. Roisen*, 111 Wash.2d 912, 767 P.2d 1375 (1989). (While the Court was discussing a city fence ordinance that specifically defined "naturally grown fences", the Court recognized that absent the legal definition, the trees were "factually" a fence. This discussion clearly indicates that it is not a strained interpretation of the covenant to include naturally grown barriers as a "fence".)

13. *Webster's New World Dictionary*, 1351 (college edition, 1968) defines "shrub" as "a bushy, woody plant with several permanent stems instead of a single trunk", while a "tree" is "a woody perennial plant with one main stem or trunk which develops many branches ... 2. a treelike bush or shrub...." *Webster's*, at 1552.

Witrak contends that since trees are expressly referred to in other sections of the CCR limiting their placement they may not be considered a fence. This argument is unpersuasive. The sections specifically dealing with trees address other concerns and do not limit the interpretation that should be given to Article II, section 8. Also unpersuasive is Witrak's argument that the trees do not delineate the lot line. The fact that the trees are slightly inside the legal boundary and there is a wooden fence on the boundary is immaterial. The trees are planted in such a manner that visually they mark the property line which makes it impossible to say as a matter of law that they do not delineate the lot line.[14]

The Homeowners also argue that the trees should be considered part of Witrak's remodel plans and require prior ACC approval pursuant to Article VII, section 5.[15] Witrak asserts that the trees were planted in response to her long-standing concern for privacy and were totally independent of the remodeling plan. This claim seems disingenuous considering the timing of planting the trees promptly following rejection of her remodel plans and their resubmission the following day. The claim is even less credible given Witrak's letter to the Homeowners suggesting the trees "improved" the planned remodeling and eliminated the basis for objection. Apparently Witrak assumed that since the trees obstructed the Demings' view and light just as the proposed remodel would have, the remodel should be allowed. Whether the trees are a part of the remodeling plan presents an issue of fact.[16]

While treating the trees as a "fence" or "shrubs" subject to ACC approval seems more harmonious with the overall purposes of the covenants, it remains an issue of fact to be determined after consideration of all relevant evidence. In addition, Witrak's claim that the pertinent covenants have been waived is a possible defense to this action that is yet to be litigated.[17] Therefore this matter is returned for a trial on the merits. The award of attorney fees will abide the outcome of the trial.

Reversed and Remanded.

Retrospective and Observations

Michael Fields was involved in this case literally from the beginning. He was the first chairperson of Lakes at Mercer Island Architectural Control Committee ("ACC"), and he later represented the association, although his specialty is family law.

Mr. Fields commented that in some sense, this case involved balancing the characteristics of community association life: the individual doing what he wants

---

14. The weakness of Witrak's position became clear during oral argument when counsel was given the hypothetical removal of the 6-foot wooden fence. Under Witrak's theory the trees would then unquestionably delineate the lot line.

15. Article VII, section 5 reads in pertinent part: "All plans and specifications required to be submitted to the Committee shall ... set forth the following with respect to the proposed structure: the elevation of the structure with reference to the existing and finished lot grade; the general design, the interior layout; the exterior finish materials and color including roof materials; the landscape plan; and such other information...." (Emphasis added.)

16. Given our decisions regarding Article II, section 8 and Article VII, section 5, it is unnecessary to determine if the trees also amount to "improvements" under Article VII, section 6. Although a broad definition of "improvements" may include trees, in this case it more likely refers to structures.

17. Witrak extensively argues that there are many such trees planted at The Lakes and the ACC has never disapproved of these trees. While this does not defeat the Homeowners' claim that trees may be "fences" it could possibly defeat the cause of action.

to do with his property versus the quasi-community preserving a standard. The risk comes when people such as members of an ACC use their power inappropriately. According to Mr. Fields, such committees, in an effort to be accommodating, often are not as attentive to the rules set up by the association and to the CCRs. The three people who initially wanted to be part of the ACC at Lakes at Mercer Island all came to the committee from the same approach, that of "not wanting to have a dictatorial mentality." They tried to approach each request fairly, seeking input from the applicant's neighbors and trying to make suggestions to the plan if it was not approved.

This incident arose from the first application to the ACC. Unfortunately, it involved a "Hatfield and McCoy" situation. Bonnie Witrak decided to build a 2,000 square foot addition to her home. The plans that she submitted clearly would have taken away her neighbor's view of Seattle, and the ACC disapproved the plans. Witrak asked for reconsideration, and the ACC responded with a letter that basically said, "Let's get together and talk about this."

The ACC met with two members of the board of directors; Ms. Witrak; her husband, Tom Gumprecht; his attorney; and their neighbor, Mr. Deming, whose view was affected. At the outset of the meeting, Mr. Gumprecht said, "He'll never agree to anything," referring to Mr. Deming. Mr. Fields then turned to Mr. Deming and said, "If we can work out a plan where your view of Seattle is only partially obstructed, would you agree to that?" Mr. Deming agreed that he would try to compromise, whereupon Mr. Gumprecht walked out of the meeting.

Later that week, Mr. Fields ran into Mr. Gumprecht on the street, and Mr. Gumprecht said that he had the perfect compromise and asked to meet again with the ACC for a re-reconsideration.

The following Friday evening, between 11 p.m. and midnight, eight semis loaded with 30 mature Douglas Furs arrived at the subdivision. The trees were planted along the property line between Witrak and the Demings. The trees completely obliterated the Demings' view from their property.

Ms. Witrak and Gumprecht then approached the ACC and said that there was no problem with their addition obstructing the view of the Demings because they had planted beautiful trees and obstruction of the view was not an issue any longer. At this point, Witrak sued the association for summary judgment, and the association counter sued for summary judgment. The trial court entered summary judgment in favor of Ms. Witrak, and the association appealed. Mr. Fields took the case on appeal without any fee to the association. The appeals court reversed the decision of the trial court and remanded the case. It then settled, with each side paying its own attorneys fees and Witrak paying for removal of the trees.

Interestingly, while the case was pending appeal, Witrak sold the house, and someone actually bought it.

Mr. Fields stated that the same thing happened when Ms. Witrak purchased another house. She brought in trees, the association sued her, the case went to trial, and the court decided that Ms. Witrak must remove the trees and pay the association's legal costs. Ms. Witrak spent over six figures on that case.

Sterling Village Condominium, Inc. v. Breitenbach

District Court of Appeal of Florida
251 So. 2d 685 (Fla. Dist. Ct. App. 1971)

DRIVER, J. Appellant, Sterling Village Condominium, Inc., plaintiff below, is the managing corporation for Sterling Village Condominiums. The officers and directors of appellant corporation are drawn from unit owners in the condominium. Appellees, Edward V. Breitenbach and Anna Mae Breitenbach, his wife, were the defendants below. Hereinafter the parties will be referred to as plaintiff and defendants, in accordance with their respective positions before the trial court.

Defendants, Breitenbachs, own two units in Sterling Village Condominiums. Defendants' units, in common with other units in the condominium complex, had as a part thereof screen enclosures, or porches. Mr. and Mrs. Breitenbach attempted to obtain consent from the plaintiff to replace the screen with glass jalousies. Consent was denied, notwithstanding which defendants proceeded to remove the screen from the enclosures and substitute glass jalousies in its stead.

Plaintiff filed suit against defendants, seeking a mandatory injunction to require defendants to remove the glass jalousies and return the enclosures to their original screened condition. Defendants answered, and the case was tried to the court without jury. The court denied the mandatory injunction on the grounds that the substitution of glass jalousies for screen did not amount to a "substantial" alteration or addition and that, consequently, no consent was required to make the change. This appeal followed.

The use, management, and control of the units in Sterling Village Condominiums are controlled by Florida Statute 711, the Florida Condominium Act, and by the Declaration of Condominiums of Sterling Village Condominium, Inc. Defendants bound themselves by the Declaration of Condominiums when they purchased the two units owned by them in the complex. Florida Statutes, Chapter 711.13, F.S.A. provides *inter alia*:

> 2. There shall be no material alteration or substantial addition to the common elements except in a manner provided in the declaration.

The pertinent provisions of the Declaration of Condominiums of Sterling Village declare:

ARTICLE XIV, Paragraph C.

Each unit owner agrees as follows:

2. Not to make or cause to be made any structural addition or alteration to his unit, or to the common elements, without prior consent of the Association....

3. To make no alteration, decoration, repair, replacement, or change of the common elements, or to any outside or exterior portion of the building whether within a unit or part of the common elements; ...

ARTICLE XIV, Paragraph E.

The Association shall determine the exterior color scheme of the building and all exteriors, and shall be responsible for the maintenance thereof, and no owner shall paint an exterior wall, door, window, or balcony, or any exterior surface or replace anything thereon or affixed thereto, without the written consent of the Association.

ARTICLE XV.

Where the limited common elements consist of screened porches, the condominium unit owner or owners who have the right to exclusive use of said screened porch shall be responsible for the maintenance, care, preservation and replacement of the screening on said screened porch at his own cost and expense....

ARTICLE XV, LIMITED COMMON ELEMENTS.

... Those areas reserved for the use of a certain unit owner or certain unit owners to the exclusion of other unit owners are designated limited common elements....

An alteration, as applied to buildings, is:

To vary; change; or make different; to change from one form or state to another without destroying identity; a change within the superficial elements of an existing structure. (*Black's Law Dictionary*, Fourth Edition, 1951)

An addition, by contrast, is:

To add to the depth or height, or to the interior accommodations of a building. (*Black's Law Dictionary, supra.*)

The use of screens and glass jalousies is so widespread in Florida that their respective characteristics and properties are common knowledge of which we take judicial notice.

The screen enclosures are defined by the Declaration of Condominiums as being "limited common elements". We hold under the above definitions of alteration and addition that removal of wire screening and substituting glass jalousies in its stead is an addition or alteration to the common elements. The pivotal issue to be resolved, then, is: Were the additions or alterations "Substantial" or "Material"?

"Substantial" is:

Belonging to substance; actually existing; real; not seeming or imaginary; not illusive; solid; true; veritable; (*Black's Law Dictionary*, Fourth Edition 1951)

... Something worthwhile as distinguished from something without value or merely nominal." (*Black's Law Dictionary*, Fourth Edition 1951)

"Material" is:

That which is important; that which has influence or effect. (*Black's Law Dictionary*, Fourth Edition 1951)

The just quoted definition of "material" is taken from cases dealing with legal instruments but no definition of the term as applied to buildings was cited in the Briefs, and independent research has failed to find a definition of the term as applicable to buildings.

It is to be assumed that the term "material" was used in the Declaration of Condominiums as having the meaning attached to it in everyday parlance by men and women of ordinary learning and knowledge. We hold that as applied to buildings the term "material alteration or addition" means to palpably or perceptively vary or change the form, shape, elements or specifications of a building from its original design or plan, or existing condition, in such a manner as to appreciably affect or influence its function, use, or appearance.

Patently, the substitution of glass jalousies for wire screening is a change in the elements and specifications of the enclosures as they were originally designed or existing at the time of the change. It is equally apparent that this change affects and influences the function, use, and appearance of the building. Screen keeps out neither rain, dust, nor wind; jalousies, on the other hand, convert an area otherwise subject to the vagaries of the elements to an all-weather enclosure, making the interior appreciably resistant to wind, rain, dust, and cold or heat as the case may be. Such change amounts to a material alteration.

Defendant called the only expert witness to testify, Mr. Ames Bennett, an architect. Mr. Bennett, upon cross examination, testified:

Question: All right. With reference to that one or two apartments that had those jalousies installed, would you define that as a material alteration?

Witness: Yes.

In view of the foregoing we are impelled to the holding that the substitution of glass jalousies for screen was a material and substantial alteration within the meaning of those terms, and that consent was required to be given by the Association to such changes, and no consent having been obtained we must necessarily reverse.

...

Daily in this state thousands of citizens are investing millions of dollars in condominium property. Chapter 711, F.S.A., 1967, the Florida Condominium Act, and the Articles or Declarations of Condominiums provided for thereunder ought to be construed strictly to assure these investors that what the buyer sees the buyer gets. Every man may justly consider his home his castle and himself as the king thereof; nonetheless his sovereign fiat to use his property as he pleases must yield, at least in degree, where ownership is in common or cooperation with others. The benefits of condominium living and ownership demand no less. The individual ought not be permitted to disrupt the integrity of the common scheme through his desire for change, however laudable that change might be.

The other points, arguments, and theories covered in the briefs and record have not been overlooked; however, discussion of them being unnecessary to our decision, we will not unduly lengthen this opinion by reviewing them.

The Judgment appealed from is reversed and this cause remanded for entry of a judgment directing appellees to remove the glass jalousies and restore the screen enclosures in keeping with the comprehensive plans and specifications of Sterling Village Condominiums, Inc.; or, in the alternative, obtain consent of appellant to said change.

Reversed and Remanded.

Palmetto Dunes Resort v. Brown

Court of Appeals of South Carolina
336 S.E.2d 15 (S.C. Ct. App. 1985)

SANDERS, C. J. Respondent Palmetto Dunes Resort sued appellant George F. Brown seeking an injunction prohibiting him from constructing a house on a lot which he owned in a subdivision it had developed. The trial court granted the injunction. We affirm.

Palmetto Dunes developed a residential and resort subdivision on Hilton Head Island. It recorded an instrument containing covenants that restricted certain tracts designated as "Limited Residential" areas. The covenant central to this appeal provides that no building may be constructed upon any lot without Palmetto Dunes' written approval of the building plans and the building location plans, and accords Palmetto Dunes the discretion to disapprove plans for "purely aesthetic considerations."

Palmetto Dunes also created a nine person committee known as the Architectural Review Board to evaluate the exterior positioning and aesthetics of proposed homes, and to approve or disapprove plans pursuant to the covenant. In addition, Palmetto Dunes published a document entitled *Policy, Procedures and Building Guidelines to Follow When Building in Palmetto Dunes Resort*, which describes the approval process and the operation of the Board. The preamble of this document explains that the restrictive covenants were established to "assure and preserve certain high standards of aesthetics and materials ... and to create certain procedures to enable the community to permanently control the quality of its neighborhoods."

The document goes on to provide that the Board is concerned with "all elements of aesthetics," and specifies the "major considerations" to be: "(1) how the house will look to the neighbors (2) color of stain (3) roof line (4) window treatments and exposure (5) general harmony with area and natural surroundings (6) landscaping plans."

The procedures described in the document require an owner to submit an "Application for Residential Construction" along with a "site plan" and "elevation drawing" to the Board. The document admonishes that the Board "often withholds final approval and makes suggestions for improvements that [its] experience [has] shown to be wise."

In December 1980, Brown purchased an unimproved lot subject to the restrictive covenants discussed above on which he intended to build his personal residence. He was familiar with the "policy, procedures and building guidelines" as published by Palmetto Dunes. In February 1981, he filed an application for approval of construction along with proposed building and site plans. The Board reviewed the application and refused to approve the plans. The minutes of the Board's meeting state: "[Brown's] house is rejected due to aesthetics and the uniform opinion of the Board is that the finished product does not represent the quality we are striving for." The chairman of the Board informed Brown by letter that, although other matters concerning the plans were discussed, the general reason for the rejection "was on the basis of aesthetics." The chairman suggested that Brown work on the plans to make them more "pleasing and acceptable."

At the next meeting of the Board, in March 1981, Brown appeared personally to present proposed "cosmetic" changes to make the plans acceptable, such as landscaping alternatives and the installation of dormer windows in the roof over the garage entrance. The Board continued to find the plans unacceptable. The minutes from the meeting state: "It was the unanimous decision of those present that the house is still unapprovable. The garage front and roofline overpower the house entirely too much."

By a second letter, the chairman of the Board informed Brown of its decision that: "The house is still unacceptable to the Board—basically because the garage simply overpowers the house, both the front elevation and the roof line."

Shortly thereafter, Brown's lot was discovered with trees marked for cutting and with stakes placed as if construction was imminent. On March 16, 1981, Palmetto Dunes sought and obtained a temporary order restraining Brown from commencing construction on the lot. Brown then agreed not to attempt construction until there was a final adjudication of the dispute, and the trial judge issued a temporary injunction *pendente lite*.

The hearing on Palmetto Dunes' suit for a permanent injunction was held in February 1983. Brown defended on the primary grounds: (1) that the language in the covenant allowing Palmetto Dunes to refuse approval for aesthetic reasons was unenforceable as a matter of law; and (2) that even if the provision was otherwise enforceable, it should not be enforced in his case because Palmetto Dunes exercised its authority to disapprove plans in an unreasonable manner. The trial judge granted Palmetto Dunes its requested relief, and this appeal followed.

I

Although Brown accepts the concept of requiring approval of plans before construction, he challenges the validity of the covenant here on the ground that it lacks objective standards to guide the Board in its approval or disapproval of plans.[1] Specifically, he argues that the provision allowing disapproval for "purely aesthetic considerations" is vague and ambiguous, thereby enabling Palmetto Dunes to be arbitrary in its decisions.

Rejecting similar arguments, courts have upheld covenants that provide no criteria to guide the approving authority in deciding upon the suitability of proposed construction. See *Rhue v. Cheyenne Homes, Inc.*, 168 Colo. 6, 449 P.2d 361 (1969); *Hannula v. Hacienda Homes, Inc.*, 34 Cal.2d 442, 211 P.2d 302, 19 A.L.R.2d 1268 (1949); *Kirkley v. Seipelt*, 212 Md. 127, 128 A.2d 430 (1957). Other courts confronted with similar arguments have upheld covenants whose criteria for approval can hardly be said to be more specific than the "aesthetic considerations" criterion involved here. See *Snowmass American Corp. v. Schoenheit*, 524 P.2d 645 (Colo.App.1974) (stated purpose of all covenants was to establish and maintain mountain residential area "of the highest possible quality" and protect its "value, desirability and attractiveness"); *Winslette v. Keeler*, 220 Ga. 100, 137 S.E.2d 288 (1964) (covenant required building to be in "conformity and harmony of external design and general quality with the existing standards of the neighborhood"); *Normandy Square Association, Inc. v. Ells*, 213 Neb. 60, 327 N.W.2d 101 (1982) (covenant required plans to be approved "as to the harmony of external design and location in relation to the surrounding structures and topography"); *Syrian Antiochian Orthodox Archdiocese v. Palisades Associates*, 110 N.J.Super. 34, 264 A.2d 257 (1970) (covenant allowed disapproval of plans "which are not suitable or desirable in [grantor's] opinion").

Our Supreme Court has held that to be valid and enforceable a restrictive covenant must, among other things, "not be too indefinite." *Vickery v. Powell*, 267 S.C. 23, 28, 225 S.E.2d 856, 858 (1976). "Restrictive covenants are contractual in nature," so that the paramount rule of construction is to ascertain and give effect to the intent of the parties as determined from the whole document. *Hoffman v. Cohen*, 262 S.C. 71, 75, 202 S.E.2d 363, 365 (1974); *Easterby v. Heilbron*, 26 S.C.L. (1 McMul.) 462 (1840).

Applying these principles, we find the "aesthetic considerations" clause is not indefinite. Its settled intent, viewed in relation to the entire document, is to vest in Palmetto

---

1. Brown does not contest that aspect of the covenant which requires the approval of plans before construction. He acknowledges that such covenants encumbering residential subdivisions as part of a uniform plan of development have been generally sustained. See Annot., 40 A.L.R.3d 864 (1971). Moreover, he indicated at trial that he wanted the Board to continue functioning. He acknowledged that Palmetto Dunes is a high quality, well-planned development and that the Board is "essential." While not necessary to our decision, we note the holdings of other courts that such covenants are a proper means to assure conformance of proposed structures with the design and development of a subdivision so as to not detract from its appearance and thereby enhance and maintain property values. See *Rhue v. Cheyenne Homes, Inc.*, 168 Colo. 6, 449 P.2d 361 (1969); *Kirkley v. Seipelt*, 212 Md. 127, 128 A.2d 430 (1957); *Jones v. Northwest Real Estate Co.*, 149 Md. 271, 131 A. 446 (1925). Covenants requiring consent to construction have been involved in cases before our Supreme Court. See *Baron v. Knohl*, 282 S.C. 21, 316 S.E.2d 674 (1984); *Circle Square Co. v. Atlantis Development Co.*, 267 S.C. 618, 230 S.E.2d 704 (1976). Although the validity of the covenants requiring consent to build was not questioned in those appeals, in *Circle Square* the court remarked on the effect of restrictive covenants generally on the development of Hilton Head Island:

Hilton Head Island has been developed as a pleasing and appealing resort and retirement community, and the success of the Island's development is due in no small part to careful planning of development and enforcement of that planning through restrictive covenants. 267 S.C. at 630, 230 S.E.2d at 709.

Dunes the authority to disapprove plans based upon its judgment of their aesthetic suitability within Palmetto Dunes Resort. Brown displayed his understanding of this by proposing to make cosmetic changes to the house following the initial rejection. The parties voluntarily bound themselves to this arrangement, which they had the right to do. See *Winslette v. Keeler*, 220 Ga. 100, 137 S.E.2d 288; *Kirkley v. Seipelt*, 212 Md. 127, 128 A.2d 430.

Brown urges that the phrase "aesthetic considerations" is ambiguous so that we must apply the rule of construction that requires ambiguities in a restrictive covenant to be strictly construed against the party seeking to enforce it. See *Donald E. Baltz, Inc. v. R.V. Chandler and Co.*, 248 S.C. 484, 151 S.E.2d 441 (1966). We conclude, however, that this rule is not applicable here. "[T]his rule of strict construction should not be applied so as to defeat the plain and obvious purpose of the instrument." *Davey v. Artistic Builders, Inc.*, 263 S.C. 431, 436, 211 S.E.2d 235, 237 (1975).

The covenant, by making no attempt to set forth objective "aesthetic considerations," implicitly recognizes, as do we, that it is impossible to establish absolute standards to guide a judgment of taste.[2] But this does not compel the conclusion that the covenant is ambiguous. We agree with the trial judge that although people may reasonably differ as to whether a house is aesthetically appropriate, the covenant is unambiguous in leaving this solitary judgment to Palmetto Dunes. The plain and obvious purpose of the covenant is to vest this discretion in Palmetto Dunes, which is constrained only to exercise its judgment reasonably and in good faith. See *Kirkley v. Seipelt*, 212 Md. 127, 128 A.2d 430.

II

We next consider whether the trial judge correctly ruled that Palmetto Dunes reasonably and in good faith disapproved Brown's plans. This being an action in equity tried by a single judge, we may decide whether the evidence supports this factual finding based upon our own view of the preponderance of the evidence. See *Mims v. Edgefield County Water and Sewer Authority*, 278 S.C. 554, 299 S.E.2d 484 (1983); *Townes Associates, Ltd. v. City of Greenville*, 266 S.C. 81, 221 S.E.2d 773 (1976) (dictum).

The Board's formally stated reason for disapproval was that the garage "overpowers" the house. The members of the Board who testified at trial expressed their dissatisfaction with the house in consistent terms. These witnesses, who were sequestered, testified variously that: the garage was proportionately too big for the house; the proposed construction "looked like ... a house with a garage and a little piece of it was residential area;" the house "just looked like too much garage;" the "garage looked larger than the house [and]

---

2. Great minds have struggled for centuries to define "aesthetic considerations." In the tradition of Western thought, three writers have provided guidance in the language of common speech. One is the theologian, St. Thomas Aquinas. The second is Immanuel Kant, the most significant philosopher since Aristotle and Plato. The third is Mortimer J. Adler, chairman of the Board of Editors for the *Encyclopedia Britannica*. In the thirteenth century, Aquinas made a stab at defining beauty: "Beauty relates to the knowing power, for beautiful things are those which please when seen." St. Thomas Aquinas, *Summa Theologica*, I-I, q. 5, art. 4, *reprinted in* 19 *Great Books of the Western World* 26 (R. Hutchins ed. 1952). Five hundred years later, Kant explained more precisely: "The judgment of taste, therefore, is not a cognitive judgment, and so not logical, but is aesthetic—which means that it is one whose determining ground *cannot be other than subjective*." I. Kant, *The Critique of Judgment* 41 (Judge J.C. Meredith trans. 1952). More recently, Adler agreed: "In the presence of the most eloquent statements about beauty, we are left speechless—speechless in the sense that we cannot find other words for expressing what we think or hope we understand." M. Adler, *Six Great Ideas* 103–04 (1981). The law, in all its majesty, cannot compel the definition of the indefinable. We reject the alternative of holding that aesthetic considerations have no place in restrictive covenants.

gave ... the feeling that the house was tacked onto the garage;" the plans looked "like there's a garage with a house added to it rather than a house with a garage added to it;" the garage was "predominant" over the house; the "house looked like a large, two-story garage with a small house appended to it."

These comments aptly describe the frontal appearance of the house. From the front, the house appears to be apportioned neatly into halves. The two-car garage appears to comprise one of the halves, and a residential area the other. The roof above the garage extends very noticeably higher than the roof over the other half of the house. These features give the garage, as articulated by the Board, its overpowering effect.

The Board's reason for disapproval for "aesthetic considerations" must bear a reasonable relation to the other buildings or general plan of development. See *Jones v. Northwest Real Estate Co.*, 149 Md. 271, 131 A. 446 (1925). Under the covenant, the Board had the right to disapprove proposed construction that would tend to mar the general appearance of Palmetto Dunes subdivision and thus diminish the overall quality of the development. Upon a thorough review of the testimony and documentary evidence, we find that the Board's reasons for disapproval bear a sufficient relation to the general plan of development to be sustainable.

...

[The court found that the evidence did not justify a finding that the Board acted unreasonably when it disapproved Brown's plans, even through it had previously approved similar plans. The Board was qualified to make the decision, it followed the required procedures, and the circumstantial evidence presented was not sufficient. The court also found: the trial judge's factual findings were correct; the trial judge did not abuse his discretion regarding the reception of evidence; and the fact that one of the decisions cited by the trial court was later reversed was not significant enough to require reversal.—Eds.]

Affirmed.

Retrospective and Observations

George Brown's Perspective

James Herring had practiced law for 15 or 16 years when he tried this case, and he was stunned at its outcome. He described it as David v. Goliath.

The irony in this case is that the same plan that Mr. Brown submitted had twice before been approved by the architectural review board. Just prior to the architectural review board's review of Mr. Brown's plans, minutes from a board meeting indicated that the architectural review board must become cautious about approving any plan which contained prefabricated elements. After that board meeting, the next plans to come before the architectural review board were Mr. Brown's. Because of the directive from the board of directors, the architectural review board felt compelled to disapprove his plans.

Mr. Herring called the results of the trial and appeals courts amazing. Mr. Herring found the approval process a necessary part of a planned community; however, the application in this set of facts was oppressive.

Interestingly, Mr. Herring noted that he and opposing counsel both used a Texas case, *Davis v. Huey*, in their briefs. Opposing counsel used the appellate decision, and Mr. Herring used the Supreme court decision which overturned the appeals case. However, opposing counsel drafted the order, and the court signed it without noticing anything. When the case was appealed, Mr. Herring said that the court was bored and did not understand why he was there. Mr. Herring noted that this case was an exercise in sophistry. He also noted that over the years (he has practiced law for 33 years) there is an adage that comes from the bench that really bothers him. He has been told by several judges that no one is guaranteed a perfect trial.

The Association's Perspective

Joseph Barker, the association's attorney, noted that George Brown was a small-time developer who developed projects near the Spanish Wells area. Mr. Barker pointed out that it was interesting that for his own projects, Mr. Brown copied the Palmetto Dunes Resort Covenants, Conditions and Restrictions.

Mr. Barker found it ironic that Mr. Brown questioned the Palmetto Dunes covenants when he used the identical set for his projects. According to Mr. Barker, Mr. Brown's house was a "horror."

This case added strength to local architectural review boards.

Notes & Questions

1. *Plain meaning vs. contextual interpretation of covenant*. In *Lakes at Mercer Island Homeowners Ass'n v. Witrak*, 810 P.2d 27 (Wash. Ct. App. 1991), the court rejected the plain meaning construction of restrictive covenants in favor of a contextual rule that looks to the covenant's intent and purpose. The court recognized that the plain meaning standard might be appropriate when there is a dispute between the covenant's drafter and an owner, but that the contextual interpretation standard should be applied when there is a conflict between owners. Do you think the court was merely exalting form over substance in holding that the two standards may be used depending on who the disagreeing parties are, or do you think that there is a legitimate reason to use the two standards in different situations? Which rule of construction do you think is better? Why?

2. *Provision requiring approval by committee within a set time period*. Covenants generally require the architectural committee to approve or disapprove proposed changes within a certain period of time. Some courts have held that a committee's failure to respond within the specified time period is tantamount to approval. See, *e.g.*, *Mendenhall Village Single Homes Ass'n v. Dolan*, 655 A.2d 308 (Del. 1995), *Aurora Shores Homeowners Ass'n v. Hardy*, 37 Ohio App. 3d 169, 525 N.E.2d 26 (1987). As a practical matter, do you think that courts should refuse to enforce restrictions where the committee failed to approve or disapprove the submitted plans within the specified time period and the owner began changes or modifications? In effect, if the court refuses to enforce the restrictive covenant and does not enjoin the owner's activities, the owner will be free to carry on changes or modifications that may disrupt the overall appearance and uniformity of the development. Would a better remedy be to require the association to pay any reasonable costs incurred by the property owner as a result of the committee's delay or failure to approve or disapprove the owner's proposal? Should an owner who violates the covenant be able to pay damages in lieu of compliance? How would you compute such damages? What about the rights of the neighbors to enforce the covenants? Have they been completely delegated to the architectural review in such instances?

3. *Restrictions on use of property for residential purposes only*. Courts have reached different conclusions as to whether the language in a covenant bars certain business activi-

ties on premises. The scope of such a restriction depends largely on the language in the restrictive covenant. See, *e.g., Waller v. Thomas*, 545 S.W.2d 745 (Tenn. Ct. App. 1976).

In *Monigle v. Darlington*, 32 Del. Ch. 137, 81 A.2d 129 (1951), the court held that operation of a beauty salon did not violate architectural design restrictions where the covenants provided that the property must be used for residential purposes only and that the erection and maintenance of any noxious, or offensive thing, trade or business whatsoever on the property was prohibited.

In contrast, the court in *Laux v. Phillips*, 37 Del. Ch. 435, 144 A.2d 409 (1958), found that operation of a beauty salon was barred by a restrictive covenant that stated no structures should be used for "carrying on any business or trade." The language of the two provisions is similar. Based on the language of the covenants, what argument can you make in support of the contrary conclusions reached by those courts? If you were the beauty salon owner, what factors would you examine to support your business use?

In *Knudtson v. Trainor*, 345 N.W.2d 4 (Neb. 1984) the court held that use of a house as a group home for five mentally retarded women was a residential use within the meaning of the covenant.

4. *Restriction on use of residence to one or two families*. Does the language, "single family residence," indicate that only one family (mother, father, children) can live in any one residence? See Gerald Korngold, *Single Family Use Covenants: For Achieving a Balance Between Traditional Family Life and Individual Autonomy*, 22 U.C. Davis L. Rev. 951 (1989) for an excellent discussion of the policy issues such covenants may raise if interpreted to allow only traditional families. Group homes for disabled persons may be allowed in single family developments either by regarding such groups as a "family" or by finding that interpreting the covenant to exclude them would violate the federal Fair Housing Act. See *Hill v. Community of Damien of Molokai*, 911 P.2d 861 (N.M. 1996).

Groups of college students—and even law students—can usually be excluded as not constituting a single family. See, *e.g., Sterling Village Condo. v. Breitenbach*, 251 So. 2d 685 (Fla. Dist. Ct. App. 1971). Do you see why?

5. "*Aesthetics considerations*." Is it possible to explain the different outcomes in *Davis v. Huey*, printed in Chapter 7 and the *Palmetto Dunes* case? How broadly should the term "aesthetic consideration" be defined?

Problem

What activities trigger the necessity for architectural review committee approval? What constitutes a "structure" or an "addition or alteration?" If there is damage within the common interest community, and the owner undertakes restoration, how does one differentiate among the concepts of repair, restore, and improve? Which, if any, would necessitate design review?

D. Judicial Review of Architectural Committee Actions

What is the scope of judicial review? If the property owner is aggrieved by a decision of the design review body, the matter often winds up in court. At that point, there is a genuine issue as to which rules the court should apply in testing the design committee's decision. May the court substitute its own judgment for the committee's? Does the court have sufficient information or are there intangible factors that support traditional deference to the association's committee?

The design review process is normally administered by an entity which may be called the new construction committee, the design review board, the architectural control committee, or a variety of other names. As it pertains to new construction, the developer normally retains control over the approval process or appoints the members of the association's committee. As time passes and more homes are sold, the process gradually shifts to the association.

The association's committee, frequently known as the modifications committee, takes over responsibility for changes in existing products, usually well before the declarant-developer has completed the development. For example, modifications of existing homes, additions to exteriors, etc., become subject to the jurisdiction of the association's committee. At this point, who has a greater breadth of knowledge, committee members who are a part of the community, or a judge? Should this matter?

Generally, all homeowners have purchased in reliance upon some expectations of the existence and enforcement of standards. They have an economic expectation that these standards will, in the main, be upheld. What impact does this have upon judicial review? Does this generally-held expectation affect the individual's desire for free expression in the exterior of her home. These and other policy issues are implicit in questions of judicial review and, in fact, in the action of the design committee itself.

Ironwood Owners Ass'n IX v. Solomon

Court of Appeals of California
224 Cal.Rptr. 18 (Cal. Ct. App. 1986)

KAUFMAN, J. Defendants Bernard and Perlee Solomon (Solomons) appeal from a summary judgment in favor of plaintiff Ironwood Owners Association IX (Association). The judgment granted the Association a mandatory injunction compelling the removal of eight date palm trees from the Solomons' property. The Association was also granted declaratory relief, the court finding the Solomons in violation of the Association's Declaration of Covenants, Conditions and Restrictions (CCRs) for having planted the date palm trees without previously filing a plan with and obtaining the written approval of the Association's Architectural Control Committee.

Facts

The Solomons purchased a residential lot in the Ironwood Country Club, a planned unit development, in March 1979. They do not dispute that they bought the property with full notice of the CCRs, which were duly recorded in Riverside County in December 1978.

The date palm trees in question were planted sometime during July 1983 and have remained there since. The Solomons have admitted and it is therefore undisputed that they did not file a plan regarding the palm trees with the Association's Architectural Control Committee and accordingly never received a permit or approval for the landscaping addition.

The Association is, pursuant to section 1.02 of the CCRs, "a non-profit California corporation, the members of which [are] all of the several Owners of the Real Property." The Association's members elect a board of directors to conduct the Association's business affairs. Under section 2.04[2] the board has the power to "enforce all of the applicable provisions" of the Association's bylaws, its articles of incorporation, and the CCRs (subd. (a)), to "delegate any of the powers or duties imposed upon it herein to such committees, officers or employees as the Board shall deem appropriate" (subd. (e)), and to "take such other action and incur such other obligations ... as shall be reasonably necessary to perform the Association's obligations hereunder or to comply with the provisions or objections [sic] of [the CCRs]" (subd. (i)).

The Architectural Control Committee is a body of three persons first appointed by Silver Spur Associates, the original owner and conveyor of the property; committee vacancies are now filled by the board of directors. The following provisions from the CCRs describe the powers and duties of and procedures to be followed by the Architectural Control Committee:

> 4.02 *Duties of Architectural Control Committee.* All plans and specifications for any structure or improvement whatsoever to be erected on or moved upon or to any Residential Lot, and the proposed location thereof on any such Residential Lot, and construction material, the roofs and exterior color schemes, any later changes or additions after initial approval thereof, and any remodeling, reconstruction, alterations or additions thereto on any such Residential Lot shall be subject to and shall require the approval in writing, before any such work is commenced, of the Architectural Control Committee.

> 4.03 *Submission of Plans.* There shall be submitted to the Architectural Control Committee two complete sets of plans and specifications for any and all proposed Improvements to be constructed on any Residential Lot, and no structures or improvements of any kind shall be erected, altered, placed or maintained upon any Residential Lot unless and until the final plans, elevations and specifications therefor have received such written approval as herein provided. Such plans shall include plot plans showing the location on the Residential Lot of the building, wall, fence or other structure proposed to be constructed, altered, placed or maintained thereon, together with the proposed construction material, color schemes for roofs, and exteriors thereof, and proposed landscape planting.

> 4.04 *Approval of Plans.* The Architectural Control Committee shall approve or disapprove plans, specifications and details within thirty days from the receipt thereof or shall notify the Owner submitting them that an additional period of time, not to exceed thirty days, is required for such approval or disapproval. Plans, specifications and details not approved or disapproved, or for which time is not extended within the time limits provided herein, shall be deemed approved as submitted. One set of said plans and specifications and details with the approval or disapproval of the Architectural Control Committee endorsed thereon shall be returned to the Owner submitting them and the other copy thereof shall be retained by the Architectural Control Committee for its permanent files. Applicants for Architectural Control Committee action may, but need not, be given the opportunity to be heard in support of their application.

> ...

> 4.05 *Standards for Disapproval.* The Architectural Control Committee shall have the right to disapprove any plans, specifications or details submitted to it if:

---

2. All further citations will be to the CCRs unless otherwise noted.

(i)   said plans do not comply with all of the provisions of [the CCRs];

(ii) the design or color scheme of the proposed building or other structure is not in harmony with the general surroundings of the Real Property or with the adjacent buildings or structures;

(iii) the plans and specifications submitted are incomplete; or

(iv) the Architectural Control Committee deems the plans, specifications or details, or any part thereof, to be contrary to the best interest, welfare or rights of all or any of the other Owners.

DISCUSSION

1. CCRs Require Submission of Landscaping Plan

We have concluded the court ruled correctly that the CCRs require the submission of a plan to the Architectural Control Committee for substantial landscaping changes such as the planting of eight tall date palm trees. Section 4.02 gives the Committee power and duty to review "additions" to residential lots, and we interpret this term broadly to include any substantial change in the structure and appearance of buildings and landscapes. We note that in drafting the CCRs, the original conveyor of the subdivision property included section 8.02(b) which provides for liberal construction of its provisions.[3] (See also Civ.Code, § 1370 [formerly Civ.Code, § 1359].) Furthermore, "proposed landscape planting" is specifically enumerated in section 4.03 as an item to be described in plans for such additions filed with the Committee, which clearly shows the Committee was to take landscaping into account when it weighed the esthetic aspects of plans it received.

Because no extrinsic evidence bearing on the interpretation of these provisions of the CCRs was shown to exist,[4] this question was solely one of law (*Estate of Dodge* (1971) 6 Cal.3d 311, 318, 98 Cal.Rptr. 801, 491 P.2d 385) and was therefore properly determined by the court on summary judgment. (See *Milton v. Hudson Sales Corp.* (1957) 152 Cal.App.2d 418, 433, 313 P.2d 936.) The court's declaratory conclusion that the Solomons were and are required under the CCRs to submit a plan to the Architectural Control Committee proposing the addition of the eight date palm trees will be affirmed.

2. Association's Request for Injunction Does Pose Questions of Material Fact

The Association's request for a mandatory injunction compelling the removal of the Solomons' palm trees was in effect a request to enforce an administrative decision on its part disapproving the palm trees as not meeting the standards set forth in section 4.05 of the CCRs. That this is so is demonstrated by the final letter sent by the Association's counsel to the Solomons demanding removal of the palm trees: "Despite the provisions [of the CCRs] referenced above, you unilaterally installed the date palm trees on your property, substantially changing the *uniform development, harmony and balance* of the improvements within the Association. The fact that you did not obtain

---

3. Section 8.02(b) provides: "The provisions of [the CCRs] shall be liberally construed to accomplish [their] purpose of creating a uniform plan for the operation of the project for the mutual benefit of all Owners."

4. At oral argument counsel for the Solomons indicated that in Mr. Solomon's deposition he stated it was not his understanding that landscaping restrictions of this sort applied to the Solomons' property or that the Solomons were required to submit plans for approval of the date palms. But evidence of Mr. Solomon's subjective belief would have been irrelevant; the test is an objective one. (See 1 Witkin, Summary of Cal.Law (1973) Contracts, § 522, p. 445, and authorities there cited.)

approval from the Architectural Control Committee is not even at issue." (Emphasis added.)

Despite the Association's being correct in its contention the Solomons violated the CCRs by failing to submit a plan, more was required to establish its right to enforce the CCRs by mandatory injunction.[5] When a homeowners' association seeks to enforce the provisions of its CCRs to compel an act by one of its member owners, it is incumbent upon it to show that it has followed its own standards and procedures prior to pursuing such a remedy, that those procedures were fair and reasonable and that its substantive decision was made in good faith, and is reasonable, not arbitrary or capricious. (*Cohen v. Kite Hill Community Assn.* (1983) 142 Cal.App.3d 642, 650–651, 191 Cal.Rptr. 209, and cases there cited; *Laguna Royale Owners Assn. v. Darger* (1981) 119 Cal.App.3d 670, 683–684, 174 Cal.Rptr. 136; *cf. Pinsker v. Pacific Coast Society of Orthodontists* (1974) 12 Cal.3d 541, 550, 116 Cal.Rptr. 245, 526 P.2d 253; *Lewin v. St. Joseph Hospital of Orange* (1978) 82 Cal.App.3d 368, 388, 146 Cal.Rptr. 892; also cf. Code Civ.Proc., § 1094.5.)

"The criteria for testing the reasonableness of an exercise of such a power by an owners' association are (1) whether the reason for withholding approval is rationally related to the protection, preservation or proper operation of the property and the purposes of the Association as set forth in its governing instruments and (2) whether the power was exercised in a fair and nondiscriminatory manner." (*Laguna Royale Owners Assn. v. Darger, supra*, 119 Cal.App.3d 670, 683–684, 174 Cal.Rptr. 136.)

Several questions of material fact therefore remained before the trial court when it granted summary judgment in this case. First is the question whether the Association followed its own procedures as set forth in the CCRs. According to the CCRs the Association is governed by a board of directors, but there is nothing in the record showing any decision in respect to this matter by the Association's board of directors. Secondly, the record does not document and the parties do not indicate that the Architectural Control Committee ever met to consider whether or not the Solomons' palm trees violated the standards set forth in section 4.05 of the CCRs. The record contains no indication that either the board or the Architectural Control Committee made any findings, formal or informal, as to whether the palm trees met the standard in section 4.05 upon which the disapproval of the palm trees was apparently based.

There is some indication in the record that the Association attempted to assess the esthetic impact of the palm trees on the community. The matter was discussed at several meetings, members of the board communicated in writing and over the phone with Bernard Solomon, and at least two "polls" were conducted to elicit community opinion. As a matter of law, however, these acts on the part of the Association without appropriate decisions by the governing board or the proper committee did not constitute a reasonable application of the CCRs to the palm trees dispute. The CCRs carefully and thoroughly provide for the establishment of an Architectural Control Committee and impose upon it specifically defined duties, procedures and standards in the consideration of such matters. The record as it stands discloses a manifest disregard for these provisions: whatever decision was made does not appear to be that of the governing body or the committee designated to make the decision; no findings of any sort bridge the analytic gap between facts and the conclusions of the decision maker, whoever that was; and

---

5. Even had the basis for the injunction been solely the failure to submit plans for approval, the record would still be deficient. There is nothing showing final board action on that basis either. Moreover, had that been the sole basis, the injunction should properly have been in the alternative, *e.g.*, either to remove the trees or submit a plan. Here the order was unconditional and absolute.

the record provides no means for ascertaining what standard was employed in the decision making process.[6]

To be successful on a motion for summary judgment, the moving party must show it is entitled to judgment as a matter of law. (*Baldwin v. State of California* (1972) 6 Cal.3d 424, 439, 99 Cal.Rptr. 145, 491 P.2d 1121; *Stationers Corp. v. Dun & Bradstreet, Inc.* (1965) 62 Cal.2d 412, 417, 42 Cal.Rptr. 449, 398 P.2d 785.) Having failed to establish that its actions were regular, fair and reasonable as a matter of law, the Association was not entitled to a mandatory injunction on summary judgment and the trial court erred in granting that relief.

DISPOSITION

That portion of the trial court's judgment granting the Association declaratory relief and affirming its interpretation of the Declaration of Covenants, Conditions and Restrictions (PP 1 and 2) is affirmed. Otherwise, the judgment is reversed. Each party shall bear its own costs on appeal.

Affirmed in part and Reversed in part.

Souza v. Columbia Park and Recreation Ass'n, Inc.

Court of Special Appeals of Maryland
522 A.2d 1376 (Md. Ct. Spec. App. 1987)

WENNER, J. Appellants, Anthony R. Souza and Roseanne S. Souza, purchased Lot 243, Section 1, Area 2, in the Village of Hickory Ridge, Columbia, Maryland, in 1979. The lot was shown on a recorded plat[1] of the Hickory Ridge Subdivision, and was purchased with the knowledge that the property was subject to the "Hickory Ridge Village Covenants," recorded at *Liber* 559, *folio* 437 of the land records of Howard County.

Section 8.01 of Article VIII of the Hickory Ridge Village Covenants provides in pertinent part:

Without the prior written approval of the Architectural Committee:

(a) No lot shall be split, divided, or subdivided for sale, resale, gift, transfer or otherwise;....

The Souzas wanted to divide their lot into four smaller parcels and in accordance with the covenants sought the approval of the Architectural Committee. The Committee denied the Souzas' request to subdivide the lot, and its decision was appealed to the Hickory Ridge Appeals Board. The Board upheld the decision of the Committee. Nonetheless, the Souzas obtained subdivision approval from Howard County[2] and recorded a plat subdividing the property.[3] The Columbia Park and Recreation Association, Inc., *et al.*, appellees, filed suit in the Circuit Court for Howard County to enforce the restrictive covenants and sought an injunction directing the Souzas to re-join the parcels to recre-

---

6. From comments made at oral argument it may appear that these things were in fact done and are simply not reflected in the record. That of course may be properly shown in subsequent proceedings.

1. Howard County Land Records Plat Book 25, folio 34.

2. The Howard County Zoning Regulations apparently permitted the subdivision of Lot 243. This appeal is limited to the effects of the Hickory Ridge Village Covenants.

3. Plat No. 5807, among the Land Records of Howard County.

ate the original Lot 243. The Circuit Court (Nissel, J.) granted the relief sought by appellees and this appeal followed. We shall affirm.

The Souzas argue, as they did below, that the covenant prohibiting subdivision of their lot unless approval is obtained from the Committee is unenforceable since it contains no criteria explaining how an application to subdivide will be evaluated. Moreover, they contend that the denial by the Committee and the Board of their request for subdivision approval was arbitrary and unreasonable, and as such it was error for the trial court to affirm those decisions.

We think it important to note at the outset that appellants purchased a platted lot in an already subdivided area of a well-known planned community, a community in which they had lived for several years prior to purchasing Lot 243. The Deed, Agreement and Declaration of Hickory Ridge Village Covenants clearly state that the covenants "shall run with, bind and burden the Property..." and "shall be binding upon (i) the Grantee, her heirs, executors, administrators and assigns...." In addition, appellants agree that the covenants apply to and govern their use of their lot; they only question the enforceability of the covenants and the propriety of the actions of the Committee and the Board.

I.

As we have observed, appellants argue that the covenant in question contains no criteria for the evaluation of applications to subdivide and should, therefore, be declared unenforceable. We agree with the trial court that in accordance with *Kirkley v. Seipelt*, 212 Md. 127, 128 A.2d 430 (1957) such covenants are enforceable provided that "any refusal to approve ... would have to be based upon a reason that bears some relation to the other buildings or the general plan of development; and this refusal would have to be a reasonable determination made in good faith, and not high-handed, whimsical or captious in manner." *Id.* at 133, 128 A.2d 430. See, also, *Thompson v. Gue*, 256 Md. 32, 34 n. 1, 259 A.2d 272 (1969); *Carroll County v. Buckworth*, 234 Md. 547, 200 A.2d 145 (1964). Appellants' reliance on *Harbor View Improvement Assn., Inc. v. Downey, et al.*, 270 Md. 365, 311 A.2d 422 (1973) is misplaced, inasmuch as Downey is distinguishable on its facts from the case *sub judice*. Although the covenant at issue in *Kirkley* required approval to build or alter a building, we see no reason why we should not apply its rationale to the case *sub judice* because, as the Court said in *Kirkley*, "the parties had a right voluntarily to make this kind of a contract between themselves..." 212 Md. at 133, 128 A.2d 430.

We hold that the covenant in question is enforceable within the standards enumerated in *Kirkley*.

II.

In denying appellants' request for approval to subdivide Lot 243, the Architectural Appeals Board gave the following reasons:

> It is the opinion of this Appeals Board that any subdivision of Lot 243 would be contrary to the best interest of the community.

> We think it is important to uphold the original design concept of Clemens Crossing. The interspersion of estate lots among smaller lots has been a viable, successful arrangement. Lots were purchased, homes were built and major decisions were made based on the Final Development Plan for this area. Such planning and adherence to plan is a fundamental part of the Columbia concept.

Furthermore, the environmental factors which were considered in the original design concept are still present and continue to be valid reasons for limiting development on Lot 243 to one residential unit.

The Board's language clearly indicates that the decision to disapprove the application to subdivide was based upon a desire to adhere to the development plan and to protect the interests of those who had bought lots in the neighborhood and built upon them in reliance upon the plan for the area. The Committee also considered the environmental factors which were considered by the developer when he made the original subdivision of the property.

We agree with the trial court's determination that "[t]he refusals of Defendants' [appellants'] application appear ... to have been based upon reasons bearing a relation to the general plan of development of the Hickory Ridge Community." Inasmuch as we have no basis on which to find that the action denying the application was in bad faith, highhanded or in any way improper,[4] we hold that the trial judge's determination is not clearly erroneous. Rule 1086.

Judgment Affirmed.

Europco Management Co. of America v. Smith

District Court of Appeal of Florida
572 So. 2d 963 (Fla. Dist. Ct. App. 1990)

ZEHMER, J. Europco Management Company of America appeals a final order, entered at the end of the plaintiff's case in a nonjury trial, dismissing its action for a mandatory injunction to enforce certain protective covenants of the Southwind II housing development against homeowners Stephen and Ruth Smith. We reverse, holding that the evidence presented by Europco was sufficient to establish a *prima facie* case.

Europco is the owner and developer of Southwind II, a 200-acre golf course subdivision containing single-family, high-priced homes.[1] Protective covenants, which have been recorded in the official records of Okaloosa County and run with the title to the land in Southwind II, contain various restrictions on the use of the land in the subdivision and the construction and alteration of the structures built thereon. The covenants principally involved in this case recite that:

(4) MINIMUM SQUARE FOOTAGE FOR ANY PRINCIPAL RESIDENCE....
(c) *No lot clearing or construction of any kind, including but not limited to construction of main structure, garages, fences or ancillary structures, shall be permitted to commence or allowed to remain on any lot until the plans, design, colors and location of said improvements on the lot have been approved by Developer acting through the Bluewater Bay Architectural Review Committee or such other representative as Developer may designate from time to time.*

. . .

(5) OTHER STRUCTURES. *Construction of structures other than the main residence and a garage shall not be permitted on any lot of the Subdivision except for*

---

4. Appellants raise as improper conduct the alleged *ex parte* contact of Howard Research & Development Corporation, the developer of Columbia, with members of the Board; however, they point us to no case law which prohibits *ex parte* contact with members of non-public boards or committees.
   1. Southwind II is part of Bluewater Bay Resort Community in Okaloosa County.

the following ancillary structures which may be permitted subject to approval by Developer of location, architectural design and exterior finishes: pet house (up to 25 square feet and not more than 5 feet high), hothouse or greenhouse (up to 100 square feet and not more than 15 feet high), poolhouse, outdoor fireplace or barbecue pit (up to 9 square feet and not more than 10 feet high), and swimming pools and mechanical installation in connection therewith. *Any such ancillary structures permitted hereunder shall be attractively landscaped, constructed in a harmonious design with the main structure* and located only in the lot area to the rear of the main residence and not visible from the street. *No ancillary structure shall be built or placed on a lot until the quality, style, color and design have been approved by the Developer in the manner provided for herein.*

(9) DESIGN AND LOCATION OF IMPROVEMENTS AND TREE REMOVAL TO BE APPROVED BY DEVELOPER. For the purpose of further insuring the development to be a residential area of highest quality and standards, *and in order that all improvements on each lot shall present an attractive and pleasing appearance from all sides of view, the Developer reserves the exclusive power and discretion to control and approve the* landscaping plan and the location on the lot and *design of all building, structures and other improvements to be built on each lot. Included in the power and discretion to approve such design is the right to approve the architectural design, appearance, color, finish and materials of all exterior building surfaces.* A lot owner shall be required to submit such information as Developer may request in order to facilitate Developer's approval process. One set of the plans required to be submitted for approval will be retained by Developer. *If the finished building or other structure does not comply with the approved plans, Developer retains the right to cause the necessary changes to be made at owner's expense, the cost of which shall be a lien upon the property involved.* Any changes in plans must first be reapproved by the Developer in accordance with the procedures specified from time to time by Developer.... (Emphasis added.)

The Smiths purchased a home in Southwind II and required, as a condition of the sale, that the builder add a screen porch to the rear of the house. The builder, however, did not obtain the developer's approval before completing the addition and consummating the sale transaction. Subsequent to the purchase transaction, Europco sought an injunction against the Smiths on the ground that they had caused an addition to their house to be built without first seeking approval as required by the protective covenants. Europco further alleged that when approval was eventually requested, it was denied because the addition violated the developer's established policy prohibiting additions constructed of a design and material different from that of the primary structure. The complaint requested an injunction requiring the Smiths to either remove the addition or make it comply with the protective covenants and the builder's policy. The Smiths' answer denied the essential allegations of the complaint and raised the affirmative defenses of estoppel and laches.[2]

At trial, Jerry Zivan, the chief executive officer of Europco, testified that he had created an advisory committee for the architectural review of projects in Southwind II, and that the committee consisted of 3 representatives of the developer, 5 representatives of

---

2. The Smiths also filed a third-party complaint against the builder, Barber Construction Company, Inc., wherein they alleged that Barber added the porch and sold them the home without obtaining the developer's permission and thus should indemnify the Smiths if they are required to make the addition conform.

the homeowners, and 2 other representatives. Zivan testified that on July 16, 1987, the architectural review committee was making a routine inspection for an application involving property in Southwind II when a member noticed Mr. Barber, a contractor, constructing an addition on the back of a house. Zivan talked to Barber, confirmed that no request for approval of the addition had been submitted, and requested that Barber immediately cease construction. Barber agreed to stop work on the addition, and submitted an application for approval of the addition to the committee that day. One week later, as part of their review of the application, the committee visited the house and found the addition had been completed. Zivan instructed the committee that they were not to consider the fact that the addition was completed without committee approval; rather, they were to apply the same standards in reviewing the application that would otherwise be applied. Zivan testified that the committee rejected the application because the materials used on the exterior of the addition were not harmonious with those used on the exterior of the primary residence (horizontal cedar lap siding on the addition, brick and stucco on the original structure), and because the primary residence had 16" to 24" roof overhangs whereas the addition had none. Zivan testified that he subsequently met with Barber and John Recher, a real estate broker representing the Smiths, who then had made a contract to purchase the home. Zivan informed Barber and Recher of the committee's rejection of the application and asked that the house be made to conform to the restrictions. Barber and Recher requested permission to complete the painting of the addition so that the Smiths could close on a permanent loan, and promised to thereafter make whatever changes were necessary. After the addition was painted and the loan closed, the Smiths refused to have the conforming changes made.

Linda Morgan testified that she is the administrative assistant for the architectural review committee and is responsible for keeping records of all its transactions and business. She fills out an application form for each homeowner or builder who intends to build or make an addition and personally presents the application to the committee; all comments are recorded on the application and a copy is returned to the applicant. She stated that the applicant is invited to communicate with the committee through her or by letter, and that every applicant receives the same treatment.

Douglas Kirby, chairperson of the homeowner group on the architectural review committee, stated that the committee found the addition to the Smiths' house unacceptable due to the lack of a roof overhang and the inconsistency in building materials.

Nancy Beaukenkamp, one of the homeowner representatives on the committee, is a graduate architect from Cornell University. She cited the same reasons for rejecting the application. The court questioned Beaukenkamp about the committee's procedure of not allowing a homeowner to present an application in person. Beaukenkamp stated that the purpose of this procedure is to ensure that the members of the committee are able to be objective in making their decisions; she stated that she did not feel they could do so if their neighbors were appearing before them in person.

After Europco rested its case, the Smiths filed a motion for "directed verdict," alleging that they had been denied due process of law since they had been precluded from appearing personally before the committee. The court treated the Smiths' motion as one for involuntary dismissal pursuant to Rule 1.420(b), Florida Rules of Civil Procedure (1990),[3] and granted it. The court ruled that the Smiths had been denied due process in

---

3. Fla.R.Civ.P. 1.420(b) states, in pertinent part, After a party seeking affirmative relief in an action tried by the court without a jury has completed the presentation of his evidence, any other party may move for a dismissal on the ground that on the facts and the law the party seeking affirmative

that they were denied an opportunity to appear in person before the architectural review committee. The court further ruled that Europco had failed to prove by a preponderance of the evidence that the addition "diminished the value of the surrounding property in the subdivision, that the [Smiths'] addition changed the consistent pattern of development of the subdivision or that the [Smiths'] addition was noticeably different as to quality or appearance than other homes in the subdivision." Last, the court ruled that Europco's attempted application of the restrictive covenants to the Smiths was arbitrary and unreasonable.

Appealing, Europco first asserts that the trial court erred in ruling that the Smiths were denied due process because they were not afforded an opportunity to appear in person before the architectural review committee. No authority is cited by the trial court in support of this proposition and we know of none. The undisputed facts of this case show that Europco complied with all necessary due process requirements for enforcement of a protective covenant such as involved in this case. See *Majestic View Condominium Association, Inc. v. Bolotin*, 429 So. 2d 438 (Fla. 4th DCA 1983) (Due process requirements for enforcement of a protective covenant are (1) constructive or actual notice of the existence of the restriction prior to enforcement; (2) a reasonable demand for compliance with the restriction after the breach has occurred; and (3) compliance with any applicable procedural due process considerations that require notice of the commencement of the litigation and an opportunity to be heard in court.)

The developer is not required to provide a forum at which the applicant can personally appear and be heard. Notice and opportunity to personally appear and be heard in court is all that is necessary. The Smiths have not defended this ruling in their answer brief, and when questioned about it at oral argument conceded the issue, stating that they had "abandoned" it. We therefore reverse this ruling.

Europco next argues that the remaining rulings on which the trial court based its dismissal constitute reversible error because they not only conflict with applicable legal principles but also manifest the court's complete disregard for the evidence presented and amount to the substitution of the trial court's judgment for that of the witnesses to whom the discretion of approval was delegated. We find ourselves in agreement with these contentions.

An involuntary dismissal is only proper when the evidence considered in the light most favorable to the non-moving party fails to establish a *prima facie* case in favor of that party. *Alpha Electric Supply, Inc. v. Jewel Builders, Inc.*, 349 So. 2d 699 (Fla. 4th DCA 1977). Where, as here, one party seeks an injunction to prevent the violation of a restrictive covenant, a *prima facie* case is established by evidence showing the alleged violation. See *Stephl v. Moore*, 94 Fla. 313, 114 So. 455 (Fla. 1927). In this case, the testimony of Zivan, Kirby, and Beaukenkamp was sufficient to establish that the addition to the Smiths' house was constructed in clear violation of the covenants quoted above. Reading all the covenants in *pari materia* demonstrates rather clearly the intent that the developer reserve control over the architectural design and aesthetics of the structures and landscapes in the project, and that such control, although amounting to plenary discretion in such matters, is to be fairly exercised in a reasonable manner by the developer directly or through delegation to a committee. The covenants make specific provisions for enforcement of the restrictions by resort to liens and court proceedings, but do not predicate

---

relief has shown no right to relief, without waiving the right to offer evidence if the motion is not granted. The court as trier of the facts may then determine them and render judgment against the party seeking affirmative relief or may decline to render judgment until the close of all the evidence.

enforcement solely on a showing of diminished value to the surrounding property.[5] They simply vest in the developer or a delegated committee reasonable authority and discretion to control exterior architectural design and construction so as to maintain the consistency and compatibility of the design and appearance with the entire project pursuant to reasonable policies and standards uniformly and fairly, not arbitrarily, applied. There is no requirement that such policies and standards be in writing, as contended by the Smiths.

All three witnesses established without contradiction (1) that the addition was built without the approval of the architectural review committee, and (2) that the application was rejected because the materials used on the exterior of the addition were not harmonious with the materials used on the exterior of the primary residence and the design of the addition's roof overhangs was not compatible with the design of the existing structure.

This record demonstrates nothing arbitrary or unreasonable about either the requirement for prior approval of home additions or the policy requiring use of consistent materials and roof lines for additions to existing structures. There is no evidence that these requirements were unfairly and inconsistently applied. The evidence thus established a *prima facie* case that the builder's construction of the porch addition without approval violated the clear intent of the protective covenants, and it was reversible error for the trial court to rule otherwise.

[The appeals court decided the trial court erred regarding the defendant's burden of proof. Contrary to the trial court's ruling, the burden is on the party challenging enforcement of a restrictive covenant to show there has been a breach of authority and discretion. To enforce a restrictive covenant, there must be a breach of the covenant, but the complainant does not need to show irreparable injury or nuisance. The trial court also erred in ruling that, "[T]he attempted application of the restrictive covenants by [Europco] was arbitrary and unreasonable as to [the Smiths]." The Smith's raised this issue in their motion for involuntary dismissal at the close of Europco's case, but, as an affirmative defense (with the burden resting upon the attacking party) it should have been raised in their answer. — Eds.]

The appealed order is Reversed and this cause is Remanded.

Valenti v. Hopkins

Supreme Court of Oregon
926 P.2d 813 (Or. 1996)

VAN HOOMISSEN, J. This is an action to enforce restrictive covenants in a residential subdivision. After the subdivision's architectural control committee (ACC) approved defendants' house plans, plaintiffs brought this action, asserting that defendants' construction would obstruct plaintiffs' view in violation of the subdivision's restrictive covenants. The trial court denied injunctive relief. The Court of Appeals gave no deference to the ACC's determination and, on *de novo* review, held that defendants had vio-

---

5. The recitation in paragraph 38 of the covenants ("All parties agree that these Covenants and Restrictions shall instead be construed to accomplish their purpose consistent with continued support of the value of lots") means only that the general restrictions on aesthetic changes are intended to preserve value, not that enforcement of the restrictions is limited to instances of diminished value to surrounding lots, as is made clear in the next sentence of that paragraph ("These Covenants are to be construed reasonably to accomplish their purpose").

lated the restrictive covenants. The Court of Appeals, therefore, reversed and remanded the case to the trial court to fashion a remedy. *Valenti v. Hopkins*, 131 Ore. App. 100, 883 P.2d 882 (1994). The issue is whether the decision of a contractually created private architectural control committee is reviewable *de novo* by the courts, with no deference being given to the committee's interpretation of the enabling restrictive covenants or to its conclusions on the merits. For the reasons that follow, we reverse the decision of the Court of Appeals.

In 1988, plaintiffs purchased their two-story home in the West Ridge Subdivision in Deschutes County. At that time, plaintiffs had an unobstructed view of the Cascade mountains to the west and of the Paulina and Ochoco mountains to the east. At the time plaintiffs purchased their home, the subdivision's restrictive covenants provided that "the height of improvements ... on a lot shall not materially restrict the view of other lot owners" and that the ACC "shall be the sole judge of the suitability of such heights."

Plaintiffs' lot and house are on the east side of West Ridge Avenue. In 1990, defendants purchased a lot across West Ridge Avenue to the west of plaintiffs' home. In March 1990, defendants submitted their house plans to the ACC. Plaintiffs objected on the ground that defendants' proposed house would obstruct their view of the mountains to the west. Plaintiffs understood that the view from their first floor would be obstructed by any house built on defendants' lot; however, they expected the ACC to protect the view from their second floor. The ACC rejected defendants' plans for reasons unrelated to plaintiffs' objection. Defendants then submitted alternate plans for a two-story house, which the ACC approved. Defendants later withdrew those plans and, instead, proposed to build another type of house of the same basic design. With some alterations unrelated to height, the ACC approved those plans. Most importantly, the ACC interpreted the subdivision's amended covenants to mean that, because plaintiffs' home was located on the east side of West Ridge Avenue, plaintiffs' lot was not "adjacent" to defendants' lot within the meaning of Article III, section 4, and, therefore, that plaintiffs did not have a protected western view.[5] After the ACC approved defendants' plans, they began construction. As expected, their house obstructed plaintiffs' second-floor view of the mountains to the west.

Plaintiffs then filed this action in circuit court, seeking injunctive relief and specific performance of the covenants or monetary damages. The trial court concluded that the ACC had not acted "arbitrarily or unreasonably" in approving defendants' plans, dismissed plaintiffs' complaint, and awarded defendants attorney fees. The court relied primarily on *Lincoln Const. v. Thomas J. Parker & Assoc.*, 289 Ore. 687, 617 P.2d 606 (1980) (recognizing a "fraud, bad faith, or failure to exercise honest judgment" stan-

---

5. In a letter to plaintiffs, in the context of an unrelated dispute with another neighbor, the ACC explained its position as follows:

> Previous committees have established ground rules concerning a homeowner's view that are essentially as follows:
>
> 1. Persons with homes on the West side of the street shall have views to the West out the back of their homes.
>
> 2. Persons with homes on the East side of the street shall have views out the back of their homes to the East.
>
> ...
>
> Western views, of the Cascade Mountains, are considered the prime views and this is reflected in the fact that lots on the West side of Westridge sell for considerably more than lots on the East side. No one on the East side of the street is guaranteed a Westerly view."

Although plaintiffs argue that the ACC's specific decision in their case was "arbitrary, capricious, unfair and unreasonable," they do not argue that the ACC lacked authority to interpret the covenants.

dard of review for decisions of private entities like the ACC). Plaintiffs appealed, contending that the trial court erred in failing to find that defendants had breached the amended covenants, in failing to conclude that the ACC's decision was "arbitrary and unreasonable," and in failing to grant appropriate relief from defendants' alleged breach. Defendants cross-appealed, arguing that plaintiffs' complaint did not state sufficient facts to constitute a claim, because they did not challenge the reasonableness of the ACC's decision. Defendants also argued that the trial court's award of attorney fees was inadequate.

The Court of Appeals rejected defendants' first cross-assignment of error and then concluded that it was not required to defer to the ACC's interpretation of the enabling covenant or to its findings on the merits, relying on *Hanson v. Salishan Properties, Inc.*, 267 Ore. 199, 515 P.2d 1325 (1973). The court proceeded to review the trial court's decision *de novo* and concluded that, within the meaning of the covenants, plaintiffs' and defendants' lots were "adjacent" and that plaintiffs were entitled to protection of their view to the west over defendants' lot. The court found that defendants' house materially obstructed plaintiffs' view and concluded that defendants had breached the covenants. Accordingly, the court remanded the case to the trial court to fashion a remedy. *Valenti*, 131 Ore. App. at 109. We allowed defendants' petition for review to determine the proper role of the courts in reviewing decisions of a contractually created private design committee charged with enforcing a subdivision's restrictive covenants.

This court has referred to restrictive covenants, such as those at issue here, as "contractual obligations imposed upon all lot owners." *Ludgate v. Somerville*, 121 Ore. 643, 648, 256 P. 1043 (1927). Generally, restrictive covenants such as those found here are enforceable. See *Alloway v. Moyer*, 275 Ore. 397, 400–01, 550 P.2d 1379 (1976) (the defendant must comply with a reasonable construction of the restriction); *Donaldson v. White*, 261 Ore. 314, 493 P.2d 1380 (1972) (restrictive covenant enforced); *Snashall v. Jewell*, 228 Ore. 130, 363 P.2d 566 (1961) (same). As a general rule, the construction of a contract is a question of law. Unambiguous contracts must be enforced according to their terms; whether the terms of a contract are ambiguous is, in the first instance, a question of law. *Pacific First Bank v. New Morgan Park Corp.*, 319 Ore. 342, 347, 876 P.2d 761 (1994).

In *Hanson*, the plaintiffs sought a permanent injunction prohibiting the defendant, a neighboring leaseholder, from building a specific kind of house on his leased beachfront lot that, the plaintiffs alleged, would interfere with their views of the beach and the ocean. Lease covenants provided that lessees "shall restrict the height of improvements ... to the end that the view of other ... tenants shall be preserved to the greatest extent reasonably possible." *Hanson*, 267 Ore. at 202.

Pursuant to "Architectural Considerations" incorporated into the lease, the defendant submitted construction plans to an architectural committee, which approved them. After the plaintiffs obtained a favorable judgment from the trial court, this court reversed, stating:

> The more serious restriction is that height will be limited to the end that views 'shall be preserved to the greatest extent reasonably possible.' *The sort of a structure which will so preserve the view is, of course, a matter of opinion* [emphasis added]. The documents in question leave such a decision to the Architectural Committee. The committee was of the opinion that a few feet of additional height to the [defendants'] house would obstruct less view of consequence than would be the case if the usable square footage in the second story were added to the first floor, thereby creating additional width.... Unless this court can find that

the decision of the Architectural Committee *did not* [original emphasis] preserve the view of upland owners to the greatest extent reasonably possible, that committee's decision should not be disturbed. From the evidence in this case we cannot say with any conviction that its decision did not so preserve plaintiffs' view." *Id.* at 204.

Hanson did not purport to establish, even in *dictum,* a nondeferential standard of review for decisions of architectural committees charged with applying and enforcing restrictive covenants of a subdivision.

Friberg v. Elrod, 136 Ore. 186, 296 P. 1061 (1931), was a suit to foreclose a mechanic's lien for labor performed under a construction contract. The contract provided that "the engineer shall be the sole judge of the ... quality of the work done by the contractor" and that "all disputes or disagreements between the parties hereto shall be submitted to and decided by the engineer and his decision shall be binding upon both parties." 136 Ore. at 189. The defendant argued that the plaintiff's lien claim already had been decided by the engineer and that the engineer's final estimate of the amount to be paid to the plaintiff under the contract should be accepted. This court agreed, holding:

> Where a contract stipulates that a certain engineer is expressly clothed with the broad authority to determine all questions arising in relation to the work, ... and provides that after the completion of the work the engineer shall make a final estimate of the amount of work done, and the value thereof to be paid by the builder, ... the contract does not create a mere naked agreement to submit differences to arbitration, such stipulations are of the very essence of the contract, and such agreement is not subject to revocation by either party, and *an award...,* *in the absence of fraud or of such gross mistake as would imply bad faith or a failure to exercise honest judgment, is binding on both parties to the contract....*" *Id.* at 194–95 (emphasis added).

Friberg applied a deferential standard of review to carry out the expressed intention of the parties to avoid costly and time-consuming litigation and to promote finality by upholding the decision of a contractually designated third party. The consistent policy of the law is to encourage the private resolution of disputes.

Lincoln was an action for breach of contract between a road builder and a supplier of gravel. In that case, this court recognized:

> Parties to contracts often provide for resolution of disputes by a skilled, neutral third person. The rationale is that a quick resolution of their differences is commercially more practicable than a potentially expensive lawsuit. When a contract clearly expresses that a third person is to make final decisions respecting specified matters, such agreement is enforceable. Such third person's determination is final, absent a showing of fraud, bad faith, or a failure to exercise honest judgment." 289 Ore. at 692–93 (citing *Friberg,* 136 Ore. at 195).[6]

The *Lincoln* court explained the rationale for deferring to a designated third party's decision:

> Normally, when contracting parties agree to abide by determinations made by a third person, they do so in the belief that the third person will make such de-

---

6. Strictly speaking, the court's restatement of the *Friberg* principle was not essential to the decision in *Lincoln* because, in *Lincoln,* this court determined that neither of the alleged contractually designated "third parties" had made a binding determination. 289 Ore. at 693. But the dictum was a strong one, and we find it to be instructive.

terminations in good faith, and in a fair, impartial manner. To a substantial degree, the honesty, integrity and objectivity of such third person is a factor in the decision of one to agree that a third person make such determinations. *Id.* at 693.

In this case, plaintiffs argue that the ACC's members are neither "skilled" nor "neutral" and, therefore, that their decision is not entitled to deference under the *Friberg* standard. We reject that argument. Plaintiffs approved the covenants including the provisions for the creation and authority of the ACC — knowing that the ACC's members would be owners of lots in the subdivision who, like themselves, would not necessarily have any expertise in the matters they might be asked to resolve. We proceed to examine the restrictive covenants here to determine whether the *Friberg* standard of review is applicable in these circumstances.

The subdivision's covenants expressly provide that "the [ACC] will be responsible for approval of plans and specifications of private areas and for promulgation and enforcement of its rules and regulations governing the use and maintenance of private areas and improvements thereon." They further provide that "consent of the [ACC] is required for all new construction" and that "the [ACC] may at its discretion withhold consent with respect to any proposal which the [ACC] finds would be inappropriate for the particular lot or would be incompatible with the neighboring homes and terrain within [the subdivision]." The ACC is given broad authority to consider "height, ... view, effect on other lots ... and any other factor it reasonably believes to be relevant" in determining whether or not to consent to any proposal. The covenants provide that "the height of improvements ... on a lot shall not materially obstruct the view of adjacent lot owners," but they further provide that "the [ACC] *shall judge* the suitability of such heights and may impose restrictions." (Emphasis added.) We take the use of the words "shall judge" to mean that in the context of the broad range of authority granted, the ACC is intended to be the final arbiter both as to the applicable law and the facts, with respect to height restrictions.

In summary, the collective wording of the restrictive covenants set out above clearly expresses that the ACC is to make final decisions respecting the relevant issues. We therefore hold that the standard of review articulated in *Friberg* and discussed in *Lincoln* — review for fraud, bad faith, or failure to exercise honest judgment — is the appropriate standard of review of the ACC's interpretation of the language in the covenants here and of its decision on the merits. Plaintiffs neither have alleged nor proved that the ACC's interpretation of the language in the covenants or its decision on the merits in this case was the result of fraud, bad faith, or a failure to exercise honest judgment.

We hold that the Court of Appeals erred in deciding *de novo* that defendants had breached the covenants. We reverse the decision of the Court of Appeals and remand the case to that court for consideration of defendants' assignment of error concerning attorney fees.

The decision of the Court of Appeals is reversed. The case is remanded to the Court of Appeals for further consideration.

The Real World: A Developer's Insight

In the Wyndham community, our architectural review committee allowed construction of a free-standing, two-car garage in the rear yard of a custom lot. An argument ensued with the neighbor, who based his objection on the forward-facing garage doors which were prohibited by the design guidelines but approved by the committee. After stirring substantial controversy with other homeowners, they threatened to "call the press." Our committee (a member of which was a registered architect) represented that (1) it had the right to approve, (2) the building was compatible in style to the main house and the neighborhood and was, in fact, a part of the architectural vernacular of the city, and (3) the front-facing doors were so far set back from the street that the intent of the "no front-loading garages" guideline had not been compromised. The homeowners did not accept the argument.

We debated reversing our approval, which would at minimum have caused us to "buy" the garage from its owner (who was one of our builders) and expose us to a suit from him, along with our guidelines becoming suspect. We decided to take our chances. I invited the media into my office, explained the whole situation honestly with the result that we got favorable coverage for our responsible planning, while the wealthy homeowners made no headway with the public, who thought the whole thing was silly. In the end, the garage stayed.

There is a moral to this story: Stand your ground when it makes sense to do so, involve professionals in the design review process for credibility, and don't be afraid of the press. Always deal openly with them.

—Daniel C. Van Epp

Notes & Questions

1. *Standard of validity.* For a regulation to be valid, it must (1) have been adopted in a good faith effort to further a community purpose, as evidenced by the documents and applicable statutes, (2) represent a reasonable means of advancing the purpose, (3) not run counter to superior documents, and (4) be consistent with public policy. See ROBERT G. NATELSON, LAW OF PROPERTY OWNERS ASSOCIATIONS, § 4.2, p.123–25 (1989); and RESTATEMENT (THIRD) §6.7.

2. *Document language.* Courts have repeatedly upheld the validity of architectural controls. See generally, Grasser, *The Legal Aspect of Architectural Control in Community Associations,* Community Ass'n L. Rep. 1 (June & July 1982). Although document language requiring "conformity and harmony in external *design* and general quality with existing standards" has been upheld, precise standards can further restrict a reviewing court's discretion. But see *Prestwick Landowners' Ass'n v. Underhill,* 69 Ohio App. 2d 45, 429 N.E.2d 1191 (1980) ("harmony" is an insufficient standard). From a drafting standpoint, precision in architectural standards may often be preferred. See *Winslette v. Keeler,* 220 Ga. 100, 137 S.E.2d 288 (1964); *Pinewood Greens Homeowner's Ass'n v. Murtha,* C.A. No. 48301 (19th Jud. Cir. Ct. Va. 1976); see also ROBERT G. NATELSON, LAW OF PROPERTY OWNERS ASSOCIATIONS, §4.7, p.153 (1989) (VA Form 26-8201 describes "harmony of external design" as a standard of review).

3. *Timely objection.* Of the potential defenses raised by a violating unit owner, estoppel, laches and the statute of limitations are the most frequently seen. The Board may be estopped from enforcing architectural rules when an objection is made over a year after the exterior change. *Plaza Del Prado Condo. Ass'n, Inc. v. Richman,* 345 So. 2d 851 (Fla. Dist Ct. App. 1977). If a unit owner spends a considerable sum of money completing a project before an objection is raised, a court may find it inequitable to order removal of the violation under the laches defense. See W. Hyatt & P. Downer, COMMUNITY AND

Homeowner Association Litigation, § 2.25 (1987). Unless there is a continuing violation, the statute of limitations may also limit the board's right to enforce an architectural standard. *Id.* at § 2.24. These defenses are addressed in more detail in Chapter 8. Also note that failure to enforce an architectural violation may trigger a claim against the board for breach of a fiduciary duty. *Id.* at § 2.20; and see *Cohen v. Kite Hill Community Ass'n*, 142 Cal. App. 3d 642, 191 Cal. Rptr. 209 (1983).

4. *Consistency.* Architectural standards which are enforced "reasonably, uniformly, consistently, and in good faith" are more apt to survive judicial scrutiny. See *Friedberg v. Riverpoint Bldg. Comm'n*, 218 Va. 659, 239 S.E.2d 106 (1977). Consistency problems often arise when there is significant turnover among the enforcement body members in a short period of time. However, transition of association control from developer to homeowners does not usually prevent the association from enforcing restrictions that the developer failed to assert. *Estates of Fort Lauderdale Property Owner's Ass'n, Inc. v. Kalet*, 492 So. 2d 1340 (Fla. Dist. Ct. App. 1986). Similarly, dormant restrictions may be enforced by a newly elected board against new or continuing violations (depending on the specific facts and circumstances of cause). *Id.*

Should the documents provide a detailed laundry list of architectural standards? Will such a list likely minimize a reviewing court's discretion? What are the potential downsides to this technique? *Bush Terrace Homeowners Ass'n v. Ridgeway*, 437 N.W.2d 765 (Minn. App. 1989).

5. *Improper Procedure.* In *The Fountains of Palm Beach Condo., Inc. v. Farkas*, 355 So. 2d 163 (Fla. Dist. Ct. App. 1978), the defendant/owner's husband attempted to obtain permission to construct a patio on the common elements. The management firm indicated that it had no objection but informed the owner that transition to the unit owner association was underway. The association informed the owner that it did not yet possess the power to grant or deny the request until transition was complete. The owner proceeded with construction, and the association filed suit, seeking a mandatory injunction requiring the removal of the patio slab at the owner's expense. Because the declaration required prior written consent before undertaking structural changes the owner failed to follow the proper procedures and was ordered to remove the improvements.

Courts may scrutinize the board's adherence to established procedure during the regulation-making process to gauge the validity of a regulation. See, *e.g., Coventry Square Condo. Ass'n. v. Halpern*, 181 N.J. Super. 93, 436 A.2d 580 (1981) (board did not provide notice to unit owners of new regulation nor were specific records kept to support the board's decision to promulgate the regulation). See also Robert G. Natelson, Law of Property Owners Associations, §4.4.3, p.133 (noting "judicial trend" of considering the procedures followed by a board of directors and committees to evaluate regulation validity).

6. *Injunctive relief.* Why might the association prefer an injunction or court order requiring an offending structure to be removed rather than damages? See, *e.g., Ass'n of Owners of Regency Park v. Thomassen*, 878 S.W.2d 560 (Tenn. Ct. App. 1994) (condominium association sought injunction to require unit owner to remove partially complete deck and stairs constructed from her unit).

7. *Selective Enforcement.* In addition to developer transition and board/committee turnover, what other factors may trigger inconsistent or selective enforcement of restrictions? See, *e.g., Chattel Shipping and Inv., Inc., v. Brickell Place Condo. Ass'n, Inc.*, 481 So. 2d 29 (Fla. Dist. Ct. App. 1986). See also Chapter 8 D.2.

8. *Effect of Architectural Violation on Subsequent Owner.* If a unit owner installs new windows without obtaining board approval and sells the unit, can the purchaser be required to remove and replace the windows at his or her own expense? See, *e.g., Courts at Beachgate v. Bird*, 226 N.J. Super. 631, 545 A.2d 243 (1988). What remedies might the purchaser have in such situations?

9. *Case comparison.* How do you explain the different outcomes in *Ironwood Owners Ass'n IX* and *Souza*?

10. *Due process.* In the *Europco* case, the court held that there was no requirement for the homeowner to have the opportunity to appear in person before the architectural control committee. Rather, the opportunity to be heard in court is the only requirement of due process in that case. Do you agree? Why might it be advantageous to deny homeowners the opportunity to appear before the architectural control committee?

Chapter 8

Enforcement in the Community

If Chapters 3 and 5 are the "pure science" of governance, this chapter represents "applied science." Here we address the real world issues of enforcing the regulations contained either in governing documents or board resolutions. We look at enforcement techniques, potential remedies, and the effects that these have upon the community and its governance structure.

There is an ongoing tension between community and governance in the operation of common interest communities. The very name, "common interest community," denotes a development of shared "common interests." But, as you have seen, not all members share the same view as to what the common interest is. Sharing resources can raise conflicts, too, and communities sometimes find it necessary to enforce cooperation and compliance with community rules and norms of acceptable behavior. The rights of individuals and, sometimes, the positive aspects of individualism are circumscribed. A question to ask as you read these materials is whether the restrictions put in place by the developer and the rules and enforcement policies adopted by the association have struck the right balance between securing the common good and recognizing the rights of individual members of the community. You should also consider the appropriate role of the judiciary in reviewing community enforcement decisions. When is judicial deference to community decision making appropriate, and when should judges take a more active role to protect individual members of the community?

A. Enforcing the Community's CCRs, Rules and Regulations

There will always be a tension between the needs of the individual and the needs of the group. Both must be honored.

—John W. Gardner

Restatement (Third) § 6.8 Enforcement Powers

Except to the extent limited by statute or the governing documents, a common-interest community has the power to enforce the governing documents, the rules and regulations adopted pursuant to § 6.7, and the obligation to pay assessments and other charges imposed pursuant to § 6.5. In addition to seeking court enforcement, the association may adopt reasonable rules and procedures to encourage compliance and deter violations, including the imposition of fines, penalties, late fees, and the withdrawal of privileges to use common recreational and social facilities.

1. Introduction

The word "community" evokes a group of people living and working in the same locale, sharing values and aspirations, and existing under a system of laws and regulations. Certainly the use and ownership of facilities and the sharing of rights and responsibilities as they pertain to those responsibilities define the concept of community. However, the term means more.

The successful community has a balance, a purpose, order, and group rights and responsibilities and still respects individual rights and the right to be an individual. Successful communities have diversity in uses, population, demographics, and, indeed, in their very character. They are both inclusive and exclusive, and they have well-developed systems for both interdependence and independence.

The dynamic tension between independence and interdependence establishes the true challenge in creating both community and governance. That challenge is most vividly seen when attorney and client, in the common interest community setting, address the subject of enforcement. This challenge arises from the conflict between individual rights and common, community rights. It is made more difficult by a significant trend in American society toward a "language of rights" in which an individual's desire or predilection is transformed into a justiciable right.

In *Rights Talk*, Professor Mary Ann Glendon points out that in American society there is a "tendency to frame nearly every social controversy in terms of a clash of rights [which] impedes compromise, mutual understanding, and the discovery of common ground." *Rights Talk* (1991), Preface at xi. Quoting the United States Supreme Court in the *Charles River Bridge* case, she further points out that "'we must not forget that the community also have rights, and that the happiness and well being of every citizen depends on their faithful preservation.'" *Id.* at 26 (quoting *Charles River Bridge v. Warren Bridge*, 36 U.S. 420, 548 (1837)).

Finally, she points out that "American political discourse generally seems poorly equipped to take into account social 'environments' — the criss-crossing networks of associations and relationships that constitute the fine grain of society.... Our legal and political vocabulary deal handily with rights-bearing individuals, market actors, and the state, but they do not afford us a ready way of bringing into focus smaller groups and systems where the values and practices that sustain our republic are shaped, practiced, transformed, and transmitted from one generation to the next...." *Id.* at 115,120.

The discussion of the group versus the individual thus frames the issue and sets the tone for the entire discussion of enforcement. Enforcement becomes the measure of how well the drafter and the implementer of a community association plan balance community and governance. The language used in the governing documents, board resolutions, and the internal association debate all must reflect both individual rights and the common, community rights. It is not an easy task.

Language that seeks to empower and not to impose, that seeks reasonable regulation rather than absolute prohibition, stands the greatest chance of success. What is involved? Certainly the initial drafting approaches are very important. Here the governing documents both set a tone and have the opportunity to provide processes for reconciling conflict and for determining when enforcement should be undertaken, relaxed, or forgone. Appropriate provisions can allow for the exercise of independent judgment, and they can make clear that the board has and should accept the discretion to fashion remedies to resolve the conflict.

The specter of "bad precedent" must be dispelled. Enforcement often results from the fear of setting a bad precedent if there is a decision not to enforce. Subsequently, enforcement results because there is a precedent calling for it. In neither case perhaps do the facts require or justify enforcement. Combining flexible procedures, a true understanding of and commitment to shared values and goals, and the exercise of judgment would permit creative, alternative remedies in some cases and acknowledgment of the inappropriateness of enforcement in others. Such an approach gives rise to a system which is dynamic and supportive of the rights both of the individual and the community.

Just as the community structure must be able to respond differently to different situations, so must the individual's expectation. This may require a greater change than can be effected by the drafter of community association documentation; however, that drafter can, by well chosen, focused phraseology, move toward defining expectations, thus lowering the clamor of the rhetoric of rights. As we shall subsequently see, the attorney also plays a significant role.

Finally, it is worth considering why restrictions exist in the first place and how they should be established. Consider what people expect when they buy into a community. If a community is a place of shared values and subject to a set of laws and regulations, these restrictions in the common interest are the ribs that give structure to the body politic. Restrictions can be both positive and negative, and each should be chosen wisely to fit the particular needs and character of the individual community.

2. Who May Enforce

Enforcement rights are determined initially by the governing documents or by statute. In addition, the common law of servitudes recognizes implied enforcement rights in all lots subject to a common plan of development. See Restatement (Third) § 2.14. When the governing documents grant enforcement rights to the community association, the normal implication is that the power is to be exercised by the board of directors. However, questions may arise whether some actions may be taken only with approval of the membership.

When the association chooses not to pursue an enforcement action, individual lot owners generally have the right to do so. That right may be curtailed by the governing documents, however, and interesting questions sometimes arise as to the association's ability to foreclose individual action, particularly when the association settles an action. If a case concerns common property rather than individual units, may individual members require the board to go forward? In the event that the board settles a case over the objection of homeowners, is that settlement *res judicata*?

Third parties and local government may also be interested parties in many enforcement activities. Local government may be looking to and relying on the association to perform certain functions or to insure that certain activities are prohibited. In many cases, the zoning and permitting process will have imposed upon the developer contingent responsibilities, which are then passed to the association. Accordingly, local government expects the association to insure compliance. Whether third parties, like neighboring land owners or conservation organizations, may enforce community restrictions depends on whether they are third party beneficiaries of the covenants. Although some older case law denied third party beneficiary rights to persons who did not own land in the vicinity, modern law recognizes that such rights can be expressly created in the governing documents. See Restatement (Third) § 2.6.

In the absence of statutory authority, the right to enforce covenants is determined by the common law of servitudes. We begin with two cases that illuminate the boundaries of rights to enforce covenants and the recognition of enforcement rights in community associations.

Stegall v. Housing Auth. of the City of Charlotte, N.C.

Supreme Court of North Carolina
178 S.E.2d 824 (N.C. 1971)

Action for a declaratory judgment and injunction. Plaintiffs, who own lots fronting on Wyanoke Avenue in the City of Charlotte, brought this action ... in behalf of themselves and 20 other such lot owners. They seek to have the adjacent property of defendant Williams, an 8.38-acre tract, which he purchased from Garrison, declared subject to the restriction "that only one single-family residence may be erected on any one lot."

In brief summary the complaint alleges: (1) The deed from Garrison to Williams imposed the foregoing restriction. (2) Williams has granted to defendant Summers Development Company an option to purchase the 8.38 acres for the construction thereon of 50 or more multi-family units. (3) Defendants City of Charlotte and Housing Authority of the City of Charlotte have jointly announced the proposed construction of a 54 unit multi-family duplex development on the tract. Plaintiffs pray that each defendant be enjoined from using "the restricted property" for any purpose other than single-family residences.

Plaintiffs did not make Williams a party to the action. However, upon his motion the court allowed him to intervene as a party-defendant. Answering, each defendant alleged that the covenants in the deed from Garrison to Williams were personal to Garrison; that they were not inserted pursuant to any general plan of development; and that plaintiffs were not entitled to enforce the covenants. Defendants City of Charlotte and Housing Authority denied that either had any present or contingent interest in "the subject land."

The case was tried by Judge Fountain without a jury. The record evidence and testimony disclosed the following:

By deed recorded 8 January 1945, F. B. Garrison and wife acquired a tract of land in Charlotte Township, Mecklenburg County, containing 59.77 acres, more or less. This deed subjected the land conveyed to no restrictive covenants. Thereafter, the Garrisons made three conveyances from this tract: (1) In February 1946, by a deed which imposed no restrictions, they conveyed four acres, more or less, to Queen City Lumber and Supply Company, which has since used the property as a lumber yard and commercial sales area. (2) In June 1949 they conveyed to J. E. Jones, Russell Cannaday, and defendant Williams, a partnership, 37 acres, more or less. This deed likewise contained no restrictive covenants. (3) In July 1958, 18 acres, more or less, were conveyed to defendant Williams. It is 8.38 acres of this tract which is the subject of this action.

In the deed from Garrison to Williams, between the description of the 18 acres conveyed and the habendum clause, appears the following:

The above land is conveyed subject to the following restrictions:

1. That is shall be used for residential purposes only.
2. That only one single-family residence may be erected on any one lot.

By the three conveyances referred to above, F. B. Garrison and wife disposed of the entire 59.77-acre tract except for a lot with a frontage of about 210 feet on the north side of Bascon Street, a depth of approximately 532 feet, and a rear boundary of about 100 feet. This lot is subject to no restrictive covenants. It is, however, traversed by 100 feet of the 200-foot right-of-way of the Seaboard Airline Railroad, and is unsuitable for building. Wyanoke Avenue dead-ends in Bascon Street opposite this lot. Garrison owns no rental property within the 59.77-acre tract which he formerly owned. He does, however, own rental property "somewhere in the area."

By a map recorded 19 October 1959, defendant Williams subdivided the northern portion of the 18-acre tract into lots fronting on each side of Wyanoke Avenue. Those lots on the east side of Wyanoke were plotted as lots 37–40 in Block 6 of Walnut Hills; those on the west side, as lots 1–6 in Block 8. On the same day, Williams and his partner, Russell Cannaday, recorded an agreement whereby these lots were subjected to restrictive covenants "running with the land" and "binding on all parties and all persons claiming under them for a period of twenty-five (25) years...." After that time the covenants would be automatically extended for successive periods of ten (10) years unless a majority of those then owning lots agreed by recorded instrument to change the covenants in whole or in part. These covenants, *inter alia*, restricted each lot to residential purposes, and forbade the construction of any dwelling containing less than 864 square feet of living area and costing less than $8,000.00 based on cost levels prevailing as of 19 October 1959.

By map registered 11 August 1960, Williams and Cannaday subdivided and added to Walnut Hills lots 7–11 of Block 8 and lots 32–36 of Block 6. Restrictions substantially the same as those imposed upon the first subdivision were imposed upon the second.

That portion of the 18-acre tract not covered by the subdivision maps of 19 October 1959 and 11 August 1960—the 8.38 acres in suit—is still owned by defendant Williams. It has never been subdivided. On 2 April 1970 Williams granted to defendant Summers Development Company an option to purchase this remaining land for the sum of $70,000.00. The option was expressly made subject to "existing zoning of R-6MF" (multi-family zoning), "water and sewerage available at the site," and to "Charlotte Housing Authority approval of the site for the construction of fifty (50) or more multi-family units."

The transcript contains no evidence that either the City of Charlotte or the Housing Authority of the City of Charlotte has any legal or equitable interest in the 8-acre tract, which is the subject of this action.

Without objection, Mr. Garrison testified that at the time he conveyed the 18.38-acre tract to Williams "what he had in mind was protecting his rental property that he had somewhere in the area." Also without objection, plaintiff Stegall testified that at the time he purchased his lot No. 7 he asked Mr. Williams what he was going to do with the 8.38-acre tract of land at the foot of Wyanoke Avenue, and Williams told him that he was going to build single-family dwellings.

Judge Fountain found facts in accordance with the foregoing evidence and concluded as a matter of law that restriction No. 2 in the deed from Garrison to Williams "is vague and creates at most a personal covenant enforceable only by defendant Williams' immediate grantors, F. B. Garrison and his wife, upon a suit by them and upon a proper showing of benefit to them to be derived from the enforcement of the said clause." Accordingly, Judge Fountain decreed that clause No. 2 is invalid and unenforceable by plaintiffs and that they are not entitled to injunctive relief. Plaintiffs excepted and appealed.

SHARP, J. The question presented is whether plaintiffs, who own lots in the northern half of the 18-acre tract conveyed by Garrison to Williams, may enjoin the erection of multi-family units on the southern half of the tract by virtue of the restriction in Williams' deed "that only one single-family residence may be erected on any one lot." Plaintiffs, as grantees of Williams, contend that the restriction is a covenant running with the land which is enforceable by any subsequent grantee of Williams. Defendants contend (1) that it is a personal covenant between Williams and Garrison, not intended for plaintiffs' benefit, and (2) that the restriction is void for vagueness.

A grantee of land cannot benefit from covenants contained in the deed to his vendor "except such as attach to, and run with, the land." 20 Am. Jur. 2d Covenants, Conditions, Etc. §§ 20, 292 (1965). A restriction which is merely a personal covenant with the grantor does not run with the land and can be enforced by him only.... Whether restrictions imposed upon land by a grantor create a personal obligation or impose a servitude upon the land enforceable by subsequent purchasers from his grantee is determined by the intention of the parties at the time the deed containing the restriction was delivered. Ordinarily this intention must be ascertained from the deed itself, but when the language used is ambiguous it is proper to consider the situation of the parties and the circumstances surrounding their transaction. However, this intention may not be established by parol. Neither the testimony nor the declarations of a party is competent to prove intent. The instrument must be construed most favorably to the grantee, and all doubts and ambiguities are resolved in favor of the unrestricted use of the property....

In July 1958, at the time Garrison conveyed the 18 acres by metes and bounds to Williams, no part of the 18 acres had been subdivided into building lots, and there was in existence no map or general plan of development for that tract. The first map of Walnut Hills, Williams' subdivision of the northern portion of the tract, was dated, approved by the Charlotte-Mecklenburg Planning Commission, and recorded on 19 October 1959. From 8 January 1945, the date the Garrisons acquired the 59.77-acre tract from which they sold the 18 acres to Williams, they never subdivided the property into lots or made any plans for developing it themselves. It was divided into three separate tracts by the three sales above noted.

Restrictions in a deed will be regarded as for the personal benefit of the grantor unless a contrary intention appears, and the burden of showing that they constitute covenants running with the land is upon the party claiming the benefit of the restriction. 26 C.J.S. Deeds § 167(3) (1956); 7 Thompson, *Real Property* § 3152 (1962 Replacement). "These principles apply with especial force to persons who (as here) are not parties to the instrument containing the restriction." *Stevenson v. Spivey*, 132 Va. 115, 120, 110 S.E. 367, 368, 21 A.L.R. 1276, 1278. In the absence of a general plan of subdivision, development and sales subject to uniform restrictions, restrictions limiting the use of a portion of the property sold are deemed to be personal to the grantor and for the benefit of land retained. *Sheets v. Dillon*, 221 N.C. 426, 20 S.E. 2d 344. Furthermore, "where ... a deed containing a covenant restricting the use of land embraces and conveys all the land affected thereby, such covenant stands only as a personal covenant between the parties." *Craven County v. Trust Co.*, 237 N.C. 502, 516–517, 75 S.E. 2d 620, 631.

For all practical purposes, after the Garrisons conveyed the 18 acres to Williams, they had disposed of the entire 59.77-acre tract. The lot retained, which is less than an acre, is useless because encumbered by the railroad right-of-way. Indeed, Garrison testified that he would be glad to give it to the City. Thus, the restriction which the Garrisons inserted in their deed to Williams could not have been for the benefit of any part of the

59.77-acre tract. Having parted with all their interest in the 18 acres the Garrisons had no right to limit its free use by imposing upon it a covenant running with the land except for the benefit of other lands then owned by them.... "[T]he existence of the dominant estate is ordinarily essential to the validity of the servitude granted, and the destruction of the dominant estate releases the servitude." *Welitoff v. Kohl*, 105 N.J. Eq. 181, 188, 147 Atl. 390, 393, 66 A.L.R. 1317, 1323. "A restrictive covenant can be enforced only by the owner of some part of the dominant land for the benefit of which the covenant was made. It cannot be enforced by the grantor who created the covenant, nor by his heirs, after he or they have parted with all interest in any land benefited by the covenant." 7 Thompson, *Real Property* § 3172 (1962 Replacement). Accord, 26 C.J.S. Deeds § 162(3) at 1094 (1956); *Kent v. Koch*, 333 P. 2d 411 (Dist. Ct. App. Cal.)....

One who seeks to enforce a restrictive covenant "must show that he is the owner of or has an interest in the premises in favor of which the benefit or privilege has been created; otherwise, he has no interest in the covenant and is a mere intruder." *Los Angeles University v. Swarth*, 107 F. 798, 804 (C.C.S.D. Cal.). Garrison testified that at the time the restriction in question was inserted in Williams' deed he owned property "in the area." The record, however, does not disclose its location or distance from the 18-acre tract. Unless it was close enough to the 18-acre tract to be adversely affected by Williams' disregard of the covenant restricting the use of "any one lot" to "one single-family residence," the Garrisons themselves could not enforce the covenant.

The meager and imprecise language by which the Garrisons attempted to impose restrictions upon Williams' 18 acres makes it impossible to ascertain their real purpose. If the "one-family lot" restriction was inserted for the benefit of other lands retained by the Garrisons it would have been very easy for them to have specified the land. Furthermore, "[T]he word *lot* has no definite significance with reference to dimensions, and, as an indication of quantity, the term is of the vaguest import and contains no legal or other meaning in this respect. How much and what it includes must be determined by the facts and circumstances of each particular case. A lot may be large or it may be small but the term is most frequently used to describe a small parcel than a large parcel." 54 C.J.S. at 840 (1948). Had Williams extended Wyanoke Avenue through the 8.38-acre tract and divided it into 30-X-50-foot lots on which he had erected a series of one-family townhouses with party walls, could Garrison have successfully contended that he had violated the restriction against multiple-unit dwellings?

Be that as it may, on this record the Garrisons own "no ascertainable property capable of being benefited" by the restrictions in suit. *See Re Union of London & Smith's Bank Limited's Conveyance*, 1 Ch. 611, 89 A.L.R. 797. If the Garrisons, as Williams' grantors, could not enforce the restriction against Williams, *a fortiorari*, plaintiffs, as the grantee of Williams, could not enforce it against Williams.

Plaintiffs Stegall and Hogan own two of the 21 lots comprising the Walnut Hills subdivision. All of these lots are subject to identical restrictions which Williams, pursuant to a general plan of development, specifically imposed upon them individually by number. The owner of any one of these 21 lots may enforce these restrictions against any other owner, for they are covenants running with the land.... The adjoining 8.38-acre tract in suit, however, was not made a part of Walnut Hills, and Williams has not subjected it to these restrictions. The ruling of the court below that "the purported restriction contained in clause numbered 2" in the deed from Garrison to Williams was not a covenant running with the 18-acre tract therein conveyed and that plaintiffs have no right to enforce it is correct. The judgment of Fountain, J., is Affirmed.

Notes & Questions

1. Did the buyers of lots in the Walnut Hills subdivision have reasonable expectations that they could prevent use of the remaining part of the Williams tract for other than single family residences? Who was the intended beneficiary of the covenant between Garrison and Williams?

2. If Garrison had intended to retain enforcement rights against subsequent purchasers from Williams, should he have been allowed to do so? If he had no property to benefit from enforcement of the covenant, what other interest might he have had in enforcement that would be sufficient to give him standing to sue for its enforcement?

3. Should a developer of a subdivision subject to restrictions be able to retain enforcement rights after selling the last lot?

Merrionette Manor Homes Improvement Ass'n v. Heda

Appellate Court of Illinois
136 N.E.2d 556 (Ill. App. Ct. 1956)

SCHWARTZ, J. The question before this court is whether or not the plaintiff, an association of home owners organized as a nonprofit corporation, whose membership consists of the owners of real property within an area subjected to planned and uniform restrictive covenants, has sufficient interest to bring suit to enjoin alleged violations. The association has no legal title to any property in the area, but the prospect of the formation of such an association for the purpose of requiring conformance was set forth in the declaration establishing the restrictive covenants. On motion of defendants the trial court dismissed the suit, and plaintiff appealed. Defendants filed no brief in this court and we must therefore decide the case on the brief of appellant and our own research.

The original subdivider of the property was the Merrionette Manor Corporation which on December 29, 1948, recorded its declaration of covenants designed to preserve the plan of the subdivision, the character of the homes and the arrangement for land usage. The covenant involved in the instant case reads as follows:

> A vestibule, no more than one story in height, may be erected by any owner of any residential unit which shall not extend beyond the confines of the present front stoop, and may only be erected when the owner of the attached adjacent dwelling unit shall simultaneously erect a similar vestibule of the same design and construction to conform to the entire residential unit.

Other covenants prohibited the construction of trailers, tents, shacks, barns, noxious or offensive trades or activities, signs, advertisements, billboards, and other uses considered objectionable. It was further stated that in the event of the formation of a property owners association whose purpose "shall specifically include the control of all properties in the area with respect to conformance," the declarant could at its option assign the control therein set up to the property owners association.

Following this declaration of covenants, the declarant caused to be incorporated the Merrionette Manor Homes Improvement Association, plaintiff in this case, including in the purposes of the corporation the encouraging of enforcement, preservation and maintenance of protective covenants; safeguarding the owners of residences against improper use of surrounding building sites and generally to promote and encourage pride of ownership and harmonious maintenance of properties among the various owners resident in the subdivision. The plaintiff association is the assignee of the declarant as to the right to bring an action to enforce the covenants.

Defendants purchased the property in question, which was half of a duplex house, in June 1952. The deed to the property provided that title was taken subject to the restrictive covenants referred to. Despite the covenants and the warning that such action would result in plaintiff's seeking legal and equitable relief, defendants constructed a vestibule without the joint and simultaneous construction of a like vestibule by the owner of the adjacent dwelling unit and without having plans therefor approved by the declarant or the plaintiff or any agent of the declarant or the plaintiff. Thereupon this suit was instituted.

[handwritten margin note: Deed sold restrictions.]

The question is one of first impression in Illinois. Home owners associations such as the plaintiff appear to be a relatively modern device, a natural outgrowth of the development of housing projects on a large scale, particularly in urban communities where the general good of all within the community requires adherence to some common standards. Everybody's business is no one's business. Hence, the enforcement of such standards had to be centralized and home owners associations came into being. While the general question of who may enforce restrictive covenants has been discussed in many cases, the particular question here presented has been considered in but one case, that of *Neponsit Property Owners' Ass'n v. Emigrant Industrial Sav. Bank*, 278 N.Y. 248, 15 N.E.2d 793. The case is squarely in point. There, as in the instant case, the plaintiff had not succeeded to the ownership of any property in the area nor did the plaintiff own any other property in the residential tract to which any easement or right of enjoyment was appurtenant. The plaintiff association was created solely to act as the assignee of the benefit of the covenant. The court considered the argument that such covenants cannot be enforced when there is no privity of estate between the parties, and pointed out that the enforcement of such covenants rests upon equitable principles, citing *Tulk v. Moxhay*, 2 Phillips 774; *Trustees of Columbia College v. Lynch*, 70 N. Y. 440, 26 Am. Rep. 615; *Korn v. Campbell*, 192 N. Y. 490, 85 N. E. 687, 37 L. R. A. (N. S.) 1, 127 Am. St. Rep. 925. The court said that no right to enforce a restrictive covenant where the plaintiff did not own property which would benefit by such enforcement had been sustained in New York, but as illustrating that this is not true in some jurisdictions, cited *Van Sant v. Rose*, 260 Ill. 401, 103 N.E. 194, which we will later discuss. The court concluded that it is not necessary to lay down any definite rule as to "when, or even whether, covenants in a deed will be enforced, upon equitable principles, against subsequent purchasers with notice, at the suit of a party without privity of contract or estate." The court there considered that the solution was to look at the real character of the association, not to ignore the corporate form nor to draw aside the veil, but to recognize that the association was acting as the agent or representative of the property owners, and that the property owners were expected to and did look to that organization as the medium through which enjoyment of their common rights might be preserved equally for all. The court concluded its opinion with the following:

[handwritten margin note: Plaintiff HOA did not appear to own any property.]

> Only blind adherence to an ancient formula devised to meet entirely different conditions could constrain the court to hold that a corporation formed as a medium for the enjoyment of common rights of property owners owns no property which would benefit by enforcement of common rights and has no cause of action in equity to enforce the covenant upon which such common rights depends.... In substance, if not in form ... there is privity of estate between the plaintiff and the defendant.

This is a strong and well-reasoned precedent of the highest court in the largest state of the union. Unless Illinois decisions are to the contrary, it is one which we should follow. To that end we will examine the pertinent Illinois cases.

In *Van Sant v. Rose*, 260 Ill. 401, 103 N.E. 194, cited in the *Neponsit* case, the defendants contended that in order to entitle a complainant to relief against the violation of a restrictive covenant prohibiting the erection of a flat building, such complainant must show some right or beneficial interest in the land affected by the covenant or in adjoining lands which would be injured as a result of failure to keep the covenant. The court held that while a bill to enjoin a breach of restrictive covenants cannot be maintained by one having no connection with or interest in their enforcement, the fact that the plaintiffs owned no property in the vicinity that would be affected by a breach of the covenants or that they would in any other manner sustain damages did not deprive them of their interest and right to sue. The plaintiffs in that case were the original grantors and covenantees, but the opinion makes it clear that the law of Illinois with respect to covenants is not so strictly defined as to require in all cases that the one seeking enforcement must show some right or beneficial interest in the land affected by the covenant or in the adjoining lands.

In *Hays v. St. Paul Methodist Episcopal Church*, 196 Ill. 633, 63 N.E. 1040, the court refused to enforce the restriction on the ground that it was not intended for the benefit of the complainant, but in its discussion of the general principles applicable to such cases said that in the case of building line restrictions imposed upon land sold in lots or parcels by agreements made with each purchaser, the inference is that the agreements are intended for the common benefit of all and *each may enforce the restriction against the others.*

In *Brandenburg v. Country Club Bldg. Corp.*, 332 Ill. 136, at page 145, 163 N.E. 440, at page 444, the court said:

> The owner of real estate has the right to convey it subject to any restriction he may see fit to impose, and the only restriction upon such right is that it must be exercised with proper regard to public policy and that the conveyance must not be in restraint of trade. The purchasers from the grantee in a conveyance which imposes upon the grantee restrictions in the use of the land not opposed to public policy will be bound by the restrictions, and equity will enforce them upon equitable principles by injunction against their violation at the suit of any person in whom the right to enforce them is vested.

> ...

Nothing in the Illinois cases we have examined indicates a policy or trend opposed to what we think are the sound conclusions of the *Neponsit* case. The primary purpose of the plaintiff association is to enforce the covenants on behalf of and for the good of all 541 property owners who constitute its membership. The enforcement of such covenants as those here involved is based on sound equitable principles. It will, in a proper case, extend to requiring a defendant to repair an injury already done or to remove a structure already erected, but it is not every case which will call for such relief. Each case must be decided on its own circumstances....

The trial court should overrule the motion to dismiss and require the defendants to answer.

The order is reversed and the cause remanded, with directions to take such further proceedings as are not inconsistent with the views herein expressed....

Notes & Questions

1. *Parties to the declaration have standing to enforce restrictive covenants.* A fundamental question in the enforcement of a community association's CCRs is who may enforce and how? In general, parties to a common declaration (including unit owners and the community association, if any) have standing to enforce restrictive covenants against one another. Enforcement through the judicial process is usually sought by seeking an injunction, specific performance, or damages. For a thorough review of the law in this area, see 51 A.L.R.3d 556; see also *Inwood North Homeowners Ass'n, Inc. v. Meir*, 625 S.W.2d 742 (Tx. Ct. Civ. App. 1981) (holding that the association is entitled to an injunction requiring removal of an air conditioning unit placed in a window); *Greenspan v. Rehberg*, 56 Mich. App. 310 (1984) (holding that a covenant requiring purchaser to expand and improve right-of-way will be specifically enforced even thought the construction required by the court was not within the contemplation of the parties); *Woodlands Golf Ass'n, Inc. v. Feld*, 429 So. 2d 846 (Fla. Dist. Ct. App. 1983) (holding that an owner is entitled to damages for breach of a covenant providing lot owners with the right to apply for membership in a golf club, where the club advised owner that membership was not available). See also *Roehrs v. Lees*, 429 A.2d 388 (N.J. Super. App. Div. 1981) (reviewing law of who may sue to enforce restrictive covenants).

2. *Standing of non-parties.* With respect to non-parties (*i.e.*, those who were not an original party to the covenant), the question of who has standing is often determined by the intent of the original parties to the covenant. If the original parties intended their agreement to benefit the land of the person seeking to enforce the restriction, then that person typically has standing to seek enforcement of the restriction. ROBERT G. NATELSON, LAW OF PROPERTY OWNERS ASSOCIATIONS, § 5.1 (1989); *Restrictive Covenants— Who May Enforce*, 51 A.L.R.3d 556. See also *Westgate Terrace Community Ass'n, Inc. v. Burger King Corp.*, 383 N.E.2d 1355 (Ill. App. Ct. 1978) (claimant who is not an intended beneficiary lacks standing to enforce a servitude); *Ludwig v. Spoklie*, 930 P.2d 56 (Mont. 1996) (holding that an owner of a servient estate lacked standing to enforce a restrictive covenant because the owner was not the intended beneficiary of the agreement).

3. *Standing of community associations.* As *Merrionette Manor Homes* illustrates, community associations typically have authority and standing to seek enforcement of their own restrictive covenants. Most often, this enforcement authority is provided in the express language of the CC&Rs. See, *Conestoga Pines Homeowners Ass'n v. Black*, 689 P.2d 1176 (Colo. Ct. App. 1984) (holding that an association can sue to enforce restrictive covenants in the CC&Rs). Regardless of whether a community association holds title to real property, in developments where reciprocal servitudes give property owners enforcement rights against each other, homeowners may form such an association to provide a mechanism for collective enforcement. See *Restatement (Third)*, § 6.3.

4. *No injury is needed to enjoin a CC&Rs violation.* A breach of a restrictive covenant is sufficient grounds to enjoin its violation, as each homeowner is entitled to the benefit of the covenants. See *Turner Advertising Co. v. Garcia*, 311 S.E.2d 466 (Ga. 1984) (holding that the beneficiary of a restrictive covenant need not show injury for an injunction to be issued, only that a breach of the covenants has occurred).

5. *Standing of municipalities.* Absent statutory authority, municipalities cannot enforce privately created covenants. See, *e.g.*, *Maplewood Tp. v. Margolis*, 141 A. 564 (N.J. 1928) (holding that town had no right to seek enforcement of restrictive covenants between private parties). Older cases sometimes held that municipalities could not even enforce covenants to which they were a party on the ground that they did not own adjacent land

that would be benefited by the covenant, following the English case, *London County Council v. Allen*, [1914] 3 K.B. 642. That case was based on reasoning that treated restrictive covenants like easements, which in England were valid only if there was a dominant estate. Easements in gross were not recognized. In the United States, of course, easements in gross are valid, and there is no reason that municipalities should not be able to enforce covenants to which they are parties so long as they have some legitimate interest in the enforcement. When a developer is required to impose particular covenants on purchasers in a common interest community in order to secure approval for a project, should the agency that insisted on the covenant be treated as a third party beneficiary with enforcement rights?

Problem

Amanda, Bob, and Cathy are neighbors. Amanda owns Lot 2, and Bob and Cathy own Lot 1 and Lot 3, respectively. Amanda conveys Lot 2 to Dave. The deed to Lot 2 includes a restriction that Dave not operate a business on Lot 2. The restriction was for Bob's benefit as owner of Lot 1. Dave is now operating his veterinary practice out of Lot 2. Cathy comes to you for legal advice on whether she can sue Dave for his business use of Lot 2 and under what legal theory and/or remedy.

> Restatement (Third) § 8.1 Right To Enforce A Servitude
>
> **A person who holds the benefit of a servitude under any provision of this Restatement has a legal right to enforce the servitude. Ownership of land intended to benefit from enforcement of the servitude is not a prerequisite to enforcement, but a person who holds the benefit of a covenant in gross must establish a legitimate interest in enforcing the covenant.**
>
> Restatement (Third) § 8.2 Absence Of Privity Does Not Determine Availability Of Remedy
>
> **Lack of privity between the parties who created the servitude or between the originally burdened party and the person against whom enforcement is sought does not prevent enforcement by a remedy traditionally classified as a legal remedy. The fact that a covenant imposes an affirmative burden does not prevent enforcement by a remedy traditionally classified as an equitable remedy.**

B. Duty to Enforce

The duty to enforce should not be confused with a mandate to pursue enforcement in all cases. Examine whether or not enforcement is obligatory. Consider circumstances under which it might be appropriate not to enforce or to find alternatives to the traditional enforcement procedures and remedies.

Well-drafted documents clearly state that the board has the ability to exercise judgment. If the board is guided by the business judgment rule, it has the ability to exercise its discretion in accordance with its "judgment." It has the ability to decide what is appropriate under each set of circumstances.

The board must address certain considerations. Good faith and fair dealing among the membership as a whole, as well as consistent application of the community's core values, require adherence to the regulatory scheme. Principles prohibiting discrimination call for rational justifications when different persons are treated differently.

A board may well make the determination that the cost of prosecuting the enforcement far outweighs any community benefit to be received. Under such circumstances, it may decide not to pursue enforcement. Alternatively, the board and its counsel might recognize that the facts may lead to a bad judicial decision at best or one that runs a substantial risk of making "bad law" for the association. Under these circumstances, good judgment might justify adopting an alternative to enforcement.

The duty to enforce is a part of the duty to govern, and governing involves judgment and selectivity.

Morris v. Kadrmas

Supreme Court of Wyoming
812 P.2d 549 (Wy. 1991)

ROONEY, J. Appellant [Morris] brought this action against appellees [Kadrmas] requesting relief in the form of injunction and monetary damages for violations of the protective covenants on the Valley West Subdivision near Sheridan. The action was also against the Valley West Subdivision Land Owners Committee in the form of mandamus and declaratory judgment for failure to enforce the covenants. The district court dismissed the action against the Committee. Appellant appeals from a subsequent grant of appellees' motion for summary judgment and denial of appellant's similar motion. Appellant owns lot 23 in the subdivision. Appellees own lot 24 therein. We reverse and remand.

The issues presented by appellant in this appeal are whether or not appellees violated the protective covenants by placing a 60' x 40' garage and shop building on lot 24 without (1) an accompanying residential structure, (2) with only a 12-foot set back from the lot line, and (3) with a metal roof. There is no issue of fact in this case. Appellees acknowledge the erection of the 60' x 40' metal-roofed garage and shop building without accompanying residential structure, and with only a 12-foot set back from the lot line, but they contend that such was proper since it had Committee approval. They word the issues on appeal:

> A. Did the District Court properly grant summary judgment to Appellees in view of the uncontroverted evidence that the Control Committee charged with the duty to approve construction and enforce the protective covenants of the subdivision did, in fact, review and approve the building plans and specifications submitted by Appellees in accordance with what the Committee perceived to be its delegated authority?

> B. If not, does the failure of the Appellant to appeal from the 'Order of Dismissal' granted to the Control Committee nevertheless prevent him from perfecting this appeal?

The Declaration of Protective Covenants, executed and recorded by the original owners of the land and developers of the subdivision, provided in pertinent part:

> Said conditions, restrictions, covenants and reservations are imposed upon said above described realty as an obligation or charge against the same for the benefit of each and every lot, tract and parcel therein contained and the owner or

owners thereof, and with the right of enforcement vested in the owner or owners of any one or more of the other lots above described, and said conditions, restrictions, covenants and reservations will be imposed upon each and every lot in said above described real estate, and are as follows:

(1) That said lots shall be used for residence purposes exclusively and only one residence shall be permitted on each lot and that no buildings or structures, other than one-family residences with the customary out buildings, including a private garage and one barn, shall be erected, maintained or permitted on any such lot.... No residence building thereon shall exceed one and one-half stories in height, except with prior approval of ... the Control Committee.... At the time 75% of the lots in the Subdivision shall have been sold and conveyed by the undersigned owners, the purchasers (owners) of said lots shall elect a Control Committee consisting of three (3) members who shall then replace the undersigned owners or their successors in interest as the approval authority for the provisions of these covenants.

...

(2) That no residence or other allowable structure erected upon any of said lots shall be erected, maintained or located nearer than 25 feet to the front lot line, nor nearer than 25 feet to any side lot line, except with the prior approval of the approval authority.

...

(4) ... All pitched roofs shall have cedar shingles or shakes, except flat and low-pitched roofs may have natural gravel or shale roofs; exceptions: Sierra Forest Tone by Flintkote or as approved by the approval authority....

...

(12) The approval authority shall have the right to vary the limitations provided by these restrictions and covenants to the extent of 10% of the requirements, and shall have the right to enforce these covenants.

...

(21) These covenants are to run with the land and shall be binding on all parties and all persons claiming under them for a period of twenty-five (25) years from the date these covenants are recorded, after which time said covenants shall be automatically extended for successive periods of ten (10) years unless an instrument signed by 75% of the then owners of the lots has been recorded, agreeing to change said covenants in whole or in part.

(22) The approval authority shall have the sole and exclusive right and authority to determine compliance with the covenants contained herein and allocate and assess the costs for the improvements, maintenance and repair of all utilities and roadways. Upon the violation of any covenants or upon the failure to pay any assessments, written notice of such violation or failure shall be directed to the violator who shall have ten (10) days after receipt of said notice or after said notice should have been received in the ordinary course of mail, to correct the violation or pay the assessment due. If said violation is not corrected or payment is not made, owner or the approval authority may re-enter and take possession of the violator's premises and correct the violation at the violator's sole expense. In addition, damage may be assessed at the option of the owner or approval authority against the violator at the rate of $25.00 per

day for each day the violation continues after the said 10-day notice. In the event suit is required to collect any sums due or enjoin the violation of any of the covenants contained herein, the violator, in addition to any of the other penalties provided herein or which may be assessed by the Court shall be liable for all attorney fees and costs incurred by the owner or approval authority in bringing such action.

We review a summary judgment in the same light as the district court, using the same materials and following the same standards. *Baros v. Wells*, 780 P.2d 341 (Wyo. 1989).

COMMITTEE APPROVAL

Appellees' contention that approval of the building plans and specifications by the Committee was sufficient authorization to disregard the covenants running with the land to the extent that the violations thereof were contained in such plans and specifications is incorrect. The Committee has no authority to vary the terms of the covenants other than as provided in the Declaration of Protective Covenants themselves.

[handwritten margin note: Committee has no authority to vary wvel in accordau w/ terms of CC Rs.]

Covenant No. 1 requires the existence of a residence for accompanying "customary out buildings." Authority is not given to the Committee to make an exception to this requirement. The only authority given to the Committee in the covenant to approve a variance is with reference to the requirement that no residence building shall exceed one and one-half stories in height. An effort by the Committee to approve a variance in the requirement that an outbuilding must have an accompanying residence is without legal force or effect. Appellees are in violation of this covenant. We held in *Sutherland v. Bock*, 688 P.2d 157 (Wyo. 1984) that, under a covenant such as this one, an outbuilding cannot be justified without the existence of a residential structure on the lot. The covenant is specific in providing that the only building or structure shall be a "one-family residence *with* customary out buildings." (Emphasis added.)

Covenant No. 2 provides that no structure "shall be erected, maintained or located ... nearer than 25 feet to any side lot line" except "with the prior approval" of the Committee. However, the extent to which the Committee can exercise this approval is limited by Covenant No. 12 which allows a variance of the covenants "to the extent of 10% of the requirements." Accordingly, the Committee cannot authorize a set back of less than 22.5 feet. An effort by the Committee to approve a set back of 12 feet is without legal force or effect. Appellees are in violation of this covenant.

Covenant No. 4 requires all pitched roofs to have cedar shingles or shakes "or as approved" by the Committee. Again, it may be said that Covenant No. 12 limits the extent to which the committee could exercise the approval. However, the application of Covenant No. 12 is obviously only to the limitations capable of being restricted in degree or in percentage. The limitation relating to the type of roof lacks this capability. The Committee did not exceed its authority in approving a metal roof on the building. Appellees suggest that Covenant No. 12 creates an ambiguity in the Declaration. There is no ambiguity under our holding that the obvious intent of the declarants was that the covenant applies only to the limitations capable of being restricted in degree or in percentage. If covenants number 12 creates a conflict or ambiguity in the covenants as suggested by appellees, the following reasoning used by us with reference to contract interpretation is applicable. We have held that a construction leading to a conclusion that a contract encompasses inconsistent provisions is to be avoided if that is reasonably possible, and provisions which apparently conflict must be reconciled, if such can be done by any reasonable interpretation, before a construction is adopted nullifying any provisions of that instrument. *See, e.g., Shepard v. Top Hat Land & Cattle Co.*, 560 P.2d 730 (Wyo. 1977).

PROPRIETY OF APPEAL

Appellees argue that "Appellant's quarrel, if any, is with the Control Committee for the action it took in approving the building plans and authorizing" the construction of the building in accordance therewith—although in violation of the covenants—and that appellant's failure to appeal the order dismissing his complaint against the Committee is "fatal" to this appeal. In effect, appellees contend that any error by the district court was in dismissing the complaint against the Committee and not with granting appellees' motion for summary judgment.

Such argument and contention is faulty for more than one reason. It is premised on the false assumption that appellant's injury could result only from the action of the Committee and not from the action of appellees or from the actions of both. Appellees recognized the correct potential by filing, as an alternative to the motion to dismiss, a third party complaint[1] for the purpose of making the Committee liable for any judgment against them in favor of appellant; but the summary judgment made it unnecessary to consider the issues resulting therefrom. The lack of authority in the Commission to approve the erection of the outbuilding without the previous, concurrent, or imminent erection of a residence, and the lack of its authority to vary the set back from the lot line to the extent it did makes pertinent consideration by the trial court of appellees' third party complaint, but it does not prevent appellant from pursuing a legal claim against appellees.

The introductory paragraph to the covenants recites that they are for the "benefit of each and every lot ... and the owner or owners thereof, and with the right of enforcement vested in the owner or owners." Although Covenant No. 22 gives the Committee "sole and exclusive right and authority to determine compliance with the covenants," it also recognizes the legal right, among others, of the *owner* to "correct the violation at the violator's sole expense," and to hold the violator "liable for all attorney fees and costs incurred" in bringing an action to enjoin the violation of any of the covenants.

The motion of the Committee to dismiss appellees' claim recited as the basis for dismissal that "[p]ursuant to the Covenants, the right of enforcement is vested in the owner or owners of any one or more of the lots." The district court granted the Committee's motion to dismiss. In granting appellees' motion for summary judgment against appellant, the court did so upon the finding that "the Control Committee approved the building of the lot and that the land owners are stuck with what the Control Committee did." If the right of enforcement is vested in appellant, it is difficult to understand why he cannot use the right rather than being "stuck with" whatever action the Committee decides to take. The two holdings are inconsistent.

Additionally, an appeal can be taken only from a final order. W.R.C.P. 41(a)(2) states that a dismissal is without prejudice "unless otherwise specified in the order." There was no such specification in the order dismissing the Committee from the action. W.R.C.P. 54 provides in pertinent part:

(a) A judgment is the final determination of the rights of the parties in action....

(b) ... [W]hen multiple parties are involved, the court may direct the entry of a final judgment as to one (1) or more but fewer than all of the ... parties only

---

1. A third party complaint was filed rather than a cross-claim inasmuch as the trial court had previously granted the Committee's motion to dismiss.

upon an express determination that there is no just reason for delay and upon an express direction for the entry of judgment."

See *Wheatland Irrigation District v. Two-Bar Muleshoe Water Co.*, 431 P.2d 257 (Wyo. 1967).

Appellees note that they spent money in erecting the building and indicate that estoppel may prevent action against them. However, they did not plead such as an affirmative defense. W.R.C.P. 8(c) provides: "In pleading to a preceding pleading, a party shall set forth affirmatively ... estoppel, ... waiver." Estoppel must be pleaded. *Prazma v. Kaehne*, 768 P.2d 586 (Wyo. 1989).[2]

Injunctive relief is available to appellant. A covenant can be enforced without regard to the amount of damages which would result from a breach and even if there is no substantial monetary damage. It is proper even in the absence of a showing of irreparable harm or uncompensable injury. *Dice v. Central Natrona County Improvement & Service District*, 684 P.2d 815 (Wyo. 1989). The propriety of the injunctive relief here requested is also provided in the covenants. Covenant No. 1 states that no structure, other than a one-family residence with customary outbuildings, shall be "erected, *maintained*, or permitted on any such lot." (Emphasis added.) Covenant No. 2 states that no structure "erected on any of said lots shall be erected, *maintained*, or located nearer than 25 feet to any side lot line." (Emphasis added.) The introductory paragraph to the covenants provides that the right of enforcement of the covenants is vested in "the owner or owners of any one or more of the" lots, and that covenant number 22 provides for corrective action for violation of the covenants to be available to "the owner or approval authority."

REMAND

Accordingly, we reverse the summary judgment entered in favor of appellees and direct a grant of appellant's motion for summary judgment and the issuance of an injunction directing appellees to cause the barn to be razed (1) unless construction of a residence is commenced within 30 days of the mandate herein, with completion within a reasonable time, and (2) unless the barn is moved within 30 days of the mandate herein to comply with the ten percent requirement of Covenant No. 2. Since our reversal makes pertinent the issues presented in appellees' proposed third party complaint, we direct the grant of (1) appellees' motion for leave to file the same, and (2) the conduct of the usual resulting proceedings.

Reversed and Remanded.

---

2. The elements of estoppel may not here exist even if properly pleaded by appellees. In estoppel, the court can presume assent to an adverse right by one who has knowledge of relevant facts and acquiesces for an unreasonable length of time in asserting the right. *Marken v. Goodall*, 357 F.Supp. 317 (1972) aff'd 478 F.2d 1052 (D.Wyo. 1973). Appellant lives in Ranchester. His lot in this subdivision is vacant. In his deposition, he testified that he purchased the lot on January 14, 1976 for $12,600, that he considered the transaction an investment which could be hurt by the covenant violations of appellees, that he might want to trade the lot and that he might decide to build on it. He further testified that he gets "out there a couple of times a summer" and first saw the barn on one of these trips in May of 1989, at which time the building was "almost completed," and that, within a week thereafter, he telephonically told appellee Wayne Kadrmas that he objected to the covenant violations. Appellant's attorney sent a notice letter to appellees on October 24, 1989, and this action was filed on February 12, 1990. Of interest is the deposition testimony of Gary Laughton, a member of the Committee, in which he said to appellee Wayne Kadrmas at the time Kadrmas was staking out the barn location that the set back "had to be twenty-five feet. I said that is what the covenants said it had to be." Kadrmas responded, "I have equipment coming in and I have staked it out and this is about where it has to be built."

If in your own judgment you cannot be an honest lawyer, resolve to be honest without being a lawyer.

—*Abraham Lincoln*

C. Enforcement Methods

Often associations look for alternative enforcement techniques that are less costly than litigation. One device is to record a "notice of violation" in the public records. What is the efficacy of such technique? What are the risks? Some states have strict statutory limits on what may be recorded. What if the notice is not specifically on the list? See *Ward v. The Superior Court of Los Angeles*, 63 Cal.Rptr.2d 731 (Cal. Ct. App. 1997) (notice of non-compliance not a recordable document; homeowners entitled to expungement as cloud on title).

Alternative dispute resolution should be considered in all enforcement circumstances, even when not required by statute. Negotiation, mediation, and, perhaps, arbitration are possibilities depending upon the circumstances and the documents. There are substantial benefits to be realized through ADR, including saving time, money, and the social capital so important to maintaining the sense of community.

There are other enforcement methods as well. Consider why a board might look to a variety of enforcement techniques. A minor violation might well not justify litigation under any circumstances. The more extreme the enforcement method, the greater the damage to the social fabric of the community. Devices employed by the board without the need for professional help or the intervention of third party tribunals lower cost, save time, and often have a more immediate positive impact. Imposition of fines, denial of privileges, and use of various self-help measures all fall into these categories.

Fines, late fees, withdrawal of privileges to use common recreational and social facilities, notices of violations, and other enforcement techniques may be used unless prohibited by statute or the governing documents. Late fees are routinely used to encourage prompt payment of assessments and other fees or charges due the association and are included in the association's lien for unpaid assessments. So long as the amount is reasonable and property owners have the opportunity to correct errors in the association's records, late fees generally present little difficulty.

1. Fines

Fines and other monetary penalties are commonly used to deter violations of use restrictions and rules governing use of common property or individual units. They may also be useful to encourage compliance with prior approval requirements. They are particularly potent enforcement tools if the amount is secured by the association's lien for unpaid assessments and charges against the property, so potent that California law (Ca. Civ. Code § 1367(c)) prohibits inclusion of most fines in the association's lien.

Occasionally, the power to impose fines or penalties has been denied community associations on the ground that only the government may exercise such powers, but the weight of authority makes it clear that fines and penalties are legitimate tools of the common interest community. The amounts must be reasonable, and the procedures adopted must provide property owners with notice of their potential liabilities and a reasonable opportunity to present the facts and any defenses they may have. Consider and apply these standards as you read the *BuildAmerica-1* case.

Unit Owners Ass'n of BuildAmerica-1 v. Gillman

Supreme Court of Virginia
292 S.E.2d 378 (Va. 1982)

HARRISON, Jr., J. The Unit Owners Association of BuildAmerica-1, a condominium, filed its bill to enforce liens recorded against condominium units owned by Harry F. Gillman and Saundra K. Gillman based upon fines it had levied for alleged violations by them of its rules and regulations. It also sought to enjoin the Gillmans from bringing their garbage trucks onto the common elements of the condominium. The Gillmans filed their bill against the Board of Managers of the Association, seeking a declaratory judgment of their rights under the bylaws of the Association, injunctive relief, and the recovery of damages. The causes were consolidated, and upon trial, the lower court found the provision in the bylaws of the Association providing for the collection of fines to be unlawful, unconstitutional, and therefore unenforceable. The court did grant the Association certain injunctive relief and a judgment for $1250, representing counsel fees incurred by it. The Association and the Gillmans noted appeals.

The Association contends here that Article III, paragraph 2(m) of its bylaws, providing for the levying of fines, is not unlawful or unconstitutional as violative of the due process guarantees of either the federal or state constitutions, and that the award made by the trial court of counsel fees is unreasonably low. The Gillmans contend on appeal that the trial court failed to construe properly the bylaws, rules, and regulations of the Association as applied to them; erred in not applying the equitable defense of laches and estoppel against the Association; and erred in granting an injunction order which lacked standards for compliance or ascertainable scope and which, because of its vagueness, will give rise to further litigation.

The condominium involved is located in the southern part of Fairfax County and is described as a single, large industrial structure comprised of twenty-six small warehouse or garage-type units, surrounded by a parking area. The paved, blacktop parking area, which is a common element of the condominium, is designed to allow vehicles to drive around the entire length of the structure and to facilitate on-site parking in spaces which were lined off but undesignated.

The condominium was established under the Condominium Act, Code § 55-79.39, *et seq.*, by master deed of John R. Pflug, Jr., dated August 16, 1974, and recorded in Fairfax County along with the bylaws of the Association. Article 6 of the deed provides that "[a]ll present and future owners, tenants, visitors and occupants of units shall be subject to, and shall comply with the provisions of this deed, the By-Laws and Rules and Regulations … [of the condominium] as they may be amended from time to time." The deed stipulates that the condominium shall be administered by an Association whose membership is comprised of unit owners.

Article III, Section 2 of the bylaws of the Association prescribes the powers and duties of its Board of Managers to include the operation, care, upkeep, and maintenance of the common elements, controlling the general use of all common elements, and taking all other necessary action for the sound management of the condominium. Article V, Section 11(c) enumerates certain restrictions on the use of units, and provides that "[n]o nuisances shall be allowed on the Condominium nor shall any use or practice be allowed which is a source of reasonable annoyance or which unreasonably interferes with the peaceful possession or proper use of the Condominium by its owners and occupants." Regulation 15 for the Condominium provides that "[n]o noxious or offensive activity shall be carried on in any Unit or in the common elements, nor shall anything be done therein, either willfully or negligently, which may be or become an annoyance or nuisance to the other Unit Owners or occupants."

By deed dated July 12, 1976, the Gillmans purchased Unit 17, and one year later, on July 13, 1977, purchased Unit 21 of the condominium. In each deed are the following provisions:

> SUBJECT TO the reservations, restrictions on use, and all covenants and obligations set forth in the Master Deed, dated August 16, 1974 and recorded in Deed Book 4088 at page 266 and as set forth in the By-laws of the Unit Owners Association attached thereto and as it may be amended from time to time, all of which restrictions, payments of charges and all other covenants, agreements, obligations, conditions and provisions are incorporated in this Deed by reference and shall constitute covenants running with the land, to the extent set forth in said documents and as provided by law and all of which are accepted by the Grantees as binding and to be binding on the Grantees and their successors, heirs and administrators, executors and assigns or the heirs and assigns of the survivor of them, as the same may be.

> AND the Grantors do hereby covenant and agree that the purpose for which the Unit may be used is for such uses as may be permitted under the zoning ordinances subject to such limitations as may be contained in the Master Deed and the By-laws of the Unit Owners Association.

The Gillmans, trading as Gillmans Five Star Trash Service, owned and operated a fleet of trash-collecting-trucks. From the date of their purchase of the units, and in the course of operating their business, they have been using these units and the common elements of the condominium as a location on which to repair, clean, and park overnight several of their vehicles. The Gillmans testified that they purchased the condominiums for this express purpose and that this purpose was clearly stated to Pflug, the grantor and declarant in the master deed, as well as to his employee, Roger Thornton. While this testimony was contradicted, it does appear that when the Gillmans purchased the last unit from the Association, Thornton wrote a letter for the Gillmans to sign, requesting a loan from a local bank to finance their purchase, and setting forth in the letter that the intended use of the condominium was for a storage facility for the Gillmans' commercial vehicles and trash receptacles used in their business. Further, to encourage the Gillmans' purchase of the second unit, Pflug accepted a second deed of trust on the unit.

The Gillmans apparently conducted their operations out of their units without incident or complaint until the spring of 1978. Between May 2 and August 10, 1978, they received a series of four letters from the Association complaining about the manner in which they were parking vehicles, of oil and gas leakage from their trucks, and of offensive odors which emanated from the vehicles. They were finally ordered to remove their trucks from the condominium on or before June 12, 1978, or have the trucks physically removed by the Association and be subjected to a special assessment for the cost of removal.

On August 10, 1978, the Association, by its attorney, notified the Gillmans that it had imposed a fine on their units based upon their continuing violation of the bylaws, rules, and regulations of the Association. The fines were imposed pursuant to Article III, Section 2(m) of the bylaws, which gives the Board of Managers the power to:

> [Levy] fines against Unit owners for violation of the Rules and Regulations established by it to govern the conduct of the Unit owners, provided, however, that no fine may be levied in an amount in excess of $25 for any one violation. But for each day a violation continues after notice, it shall be considered a separate violation.... Where a Unit owner is fined for an infraction of the Rules and Regulations and fails to pay the fine within 10 days after notification thereof, the Board may levy an additional fine or fines to enforce payment of the initial fine.

The Board of Managers imposed a fine of $25 against each truck for each day that such truck had allegedly "produced noxious odors on the Common Elements of the Condominium." The fine imposed for five trucks was $125 a day, a total of $8000 for the period June 7 through August 10, 1978. The Gillmans were also advised that if they did not pay the $8000 within ten days, an additional fine of $8000 would be imposed; and further, that the Managers would impose a similar $25 fine for each day that any truck continued to generate an intolerable odor while parked on the common elements.

This action by its counsel was formally ratified at a special meeting of the Board of Managers held August 31, 1978. At that meeting, counsel explained Virginia's Condominium Act to the Managers, with particular reference to "the right of assessment and the right to lien for failure to pay assessments based on the unit owners pro rata portion of condominium expenses." It was his opinion that the Association had "a sound foundation for assessing against Gillmans' and [recovering] the cost of attorneys' fees if we do prevail." However, he advised the Board that "it's a matter of Gillmans' attorney's theory versus our theory of the condominium act." At this meeting, the Board also amended the Association's rules and regulations to provide that no unit owner be allowed to maintain on the condominium property more than three trucks per unit with an empty weight of 10,000 pounds or over.

The Gillmans did not pay the $8000 fine within ten days, and the Board levied an additional fine of $8000. Ultimately it levied fines totaling $20,500 on the Gillmans for their alleged violations and filed memoranda of liens in that amount in the Clerk's Office of Fairfax County, pursuant to Code § 55-79.84(a) (1979 Cum.Supp.), which provides, in part:

> The unit owners' association shall have a lien on every condominium unit for unpaid assessments levied against that condominium unit in accordance with the provisions of this chapter and all lawful provisions of the condominium instruments....

On November 2, 1978, the Association filed its suit to enforce the liens and enjoin the Gillmans from parking their trucks on the common elements. The next day the Gillmans filed suit for a declaratory judgment.

The condominium is built in a zone that permits the operation of a trash-and-garbage-collection-business such as that conducted by the Gillmans. There is nothing in the master deed, or in the bylaws, which prohibited a sale by Pflug of one or more units for use by a purchaser in conducting such a business, and in using, repairing, and storing vehicles in connection therewith. Purchasers of other units from Pflug were charged with knowledge of the permitted uses.

Although it may have been planned originally that each unit owner would be allocated four parking spaces per unit, this understanding admittedly was not observed by the various unit owners. Prior to August 31, 1978, there were no restrictions or limits on the number of vehicles that each unit owner could own, use, store, or park in the units or on the common elements. The Association fined the Gillmans because their trucks caused an "odoriferous nuisance" in that they "produced noxious odors on the common element of the condominium," which were "offensive and intolerable to the other unit owners."

The Gillmans deny that they operated their business or trucks in the manner alleged by the Association; admit that they have parked their trucks on the common elements of the condominium; and claim that they have a vested property right to do so. They testified that the Association had made no objection for more than two years to the manner in which they had operated their business, and emphasize the conveyance to them of a second unit after they had been conducting a garbage-and-trash-collecting-business from their first unit for a full year. They further say their business was being operated in compliance with the zoning laws of Fairfax County and consistent with uses of other unit owners and owners of surrounding properties. At trial, the Gillmans introduced copies of numerous inspection reports made by representatives of Prince William and Fairfax Counties reflecting the cleanliness of the trucks and full compliance with all health regulations.

John T. Summers, an inspector for the Fairfax Health Department, was accepted as an expert witness. He had inspected the Gillmans' operation some twenty-five times. He said the Gillmans had cooperated fully with the Health Department, and he found no violations and observed no significant health hazards. When asked to evaluate the cleanliness of the Gillmans' trucks in comparison to those of other such companies, Summers stated they "were no better nor no worse" than other trash trucks. He testified that on warm humid days he had noted some odor from the trucks, but this was only when one was close to a truck, and even then he found the odor slight.

Four unit owners, members of the Board of Managers, testified that they detected offensive odors emanating from the Gillman trucks. Carl Moorefield said that he could smell "rotten garbage" from the front of his unit even when the Gillman trucks were not on the premises. He also said that the trucks leaked oil and hydraulic fluid and caused damage to the surface of the driveway area. Moorefield admitted that he had seen heavy vehicles, other than those of the Gillmans', on the common elements of the condominium, and that he routinely had ten or eleven employee automobiles associated with his operation parked on the common elements during the day.

Board member William Crawford testified that to his knowledge "at least five trucks were parked [by the Gillmans] on the premises every day." Crawford said the trucks were leaking oil and hydraulic fluid on the parking area and they were often parked and repaired in the driveway area, thereby interfering with other vehicles. He complained of an odor emitted by the trucks and said that he had seen maggots on the pavement which he attributed to the Gillman trucks.

William Rydell, unit owner, operated a retail automobile glass shop. He said that the odor of the Gillman trucks bothered his customers more than it bothered him. He admitted that while the Gillman trucks sometimes leaked oil and hydraulic fluid, his own trucks "leaked some of the same," the difference apparently being one of degree. He said that while the Gillman trucks caused congestion, everyone at the condominium caused congestion to others at some time or another. Rydell regularly used seven or eight trucks in his business.

Pflug testified that he then owned only one unit of the condominium and that it was rented. He said that when the Gillmans' problem was brought to his attention, he visited the condominium and found the odor nauseating. In characterizing the Gillman trucks, he said "they stink."

No condominium shall come into existence in Virginia except on the recordation of condominium instruments pursuant to the provisions of Chapter 4.2 of the Code of Virginia, cited as the Condominium Act. Code § 55-79.39, *et seq.* The entire condominium concept, and all pertaining to it, is therefore a statutory creation. For a review of the historical background and nature of this method of real estate ownership, Virginia's present Condominium Act, and its predecessor, the Horizontal Property Act, Acts 1962, c. 627, reference is made to Mr. Justice Compton's opinion in *United Masonry v. Jefferson Mews,* 218 Va. 360, 237 S.E.2d 171 (1977).

We consider first the Association's assignment which questions the action of the trial court in setting aside as unlawful the fines levied against the Gillmans. The Association argues that the requirement of the Condominium Act (Code § 55-79.73(a)) that "a set of bylaws providing for the self-government of the condominium by an association of all the unit owners" is designed to foster the evolution of a condominium into "a self-governing community" and a "fully self-governing democracy." It argues that there is no limitation inherent in the Condominium Act on the powers that may be created by the condominium documents, relying upon Code § 55-79.80(c), which provides: "This section shall not be construed to prohibit the grant, by the condominium instruments, of other powers and responsibilities to the unit owners' association or its executive organ."

The Association further contends that consistent with "the deference to the condominium documents" that appears throughout the Condominium Act, Virginia Code § 55-79.84 does not limit the lien it permits to assessments levied "in accordance with the provisions of this chapter," but extends the lien also to assessments levied "in accordance with the provisions ... of the condominium instruments." It maintains that since the bylaws of the Association give its Board of Managers the power to levy a fine against a unit owner, and to collect such fine as if it were a common charge, every unit owner purchased subject to this power.

We do not agree that it was ever the intent of the General Assembly of Virginia that the owners of units in a condominium be a completely autonomous body, or that such would be permitted under the federal and state constitutions. Admittedly, the Act is designed to and does permit the exercise of wide powers by an association of unit owners. However, these powers are limited by general law and by the Condominium Act itself. Code § 1-13.17 provides that "[w]hen ... any ... number of persons, are authorized to make ... bylaws, rules, regulations ... it shall be understood that the same must not be inconsistent with the Constitution and laws of the United States or of this State." The Condominium Act also sets limits on the powers that may be created by the condominium documents. All unlawful provisions therein are void. Code § 55-79.52(a). "Common expenses" mean expenditures lawfully made or incurred. Code § 55-79.41(b).

We find no language in the Condominium Act which authorizes the executive or governing body of a condominium to levy fines, impose penalties, or exact forfeitures for violation of bylaws and regulations by unit owners. Code § 55-79.83 provides in detail the various circumstances under which common expenses associated with the maintenance, repair, renovation, restoration, or replacement of any common element shall be assessed. Code § 55-79.84 provides that a unit owners' association shall have a lien on every condominium unit for unpaid assessments levied against that condominium unit in accordance with the provisions of the Condominium Act and all lawful provisions of the condominium instrument.

The Condominium Act provides the manner in which an association shall compel compliance with condominium instruments. Code § 55-79.53 reads as follows:

> The declarant, every unit owner, and all those entitled to occupy a unit shall comply with all lawful provisions of this chapter and all provisions of the con-

dominium instruments. Any lack of such compliance shall be grounds for an action or suit to recover sums due, for damages or injunctive relief, or for any other remedy available at law or in equity, maintainable by the unit owners' association, or by its executive organ or any managing agent on behalf of such association, or, in any proper case, by one or more aggrieved unit owners on their own behalf or as a class action.

The statute does not purport to grant an association the power to secure compliance with its bylaws, rules, and regulations by the imposition of a fine or the exaction of a penalty. The accepted definition of "fine" is found in *Black's Law Dictionary* 569 (5th ed. 1979), and is as follows:

> To impose a pecuniary punishment or mulct. To sentence a person convicted of an offense to pay a penalty in money. A pecuniary punishment imposed by lawful tribunal upon person convicted of crime or misdemeanor. A pecuniary penalty. It may include a forfeiture or penalty recoverable in a civil action, and, in criminal convictions, may be in addition to imprisonment.

The Condominium Act authorizes assessments, not fines. The term "assessment" is in no way synonymous with the word "fine" or the word "penalty." Assessment is defined in *Black's, supra,* at p. 106, as follows:

> In a general sense, the process of ascertaining and adjusting the shares respectively to be contributed by several persons towards a common beneficial object according to the benefit received. A valuation or a determination as to the value of property....

The imposition of a fine is a governmental power. The sovereign cannot be preempted of this power, and the power cannot be delegated or exercised other than in accordance with the provisions of the Constitutions of the United States and of Virginia. Neither can a fine be imposed disguised as an assessment.

The controversy here arose over the alleged objectionable manner in which the Gillmans were conducting their business from their privately owned units and on the common elements in which they jointly had an interest with other unit owners. The trucks emitted an offensive odor, as would be expected of trucks that haul garbage and are periodically disinfected. However, the Gillmans were operating a lawful business in a permitted zone and apparently to the satisfaction of the health authorities of two counties. They maintained that they were complying with the law and with the bylaws, rules, and regulations of the Association. Assuming that the Gillman trucks, and their mode of operation, created noxious and offensive odors and amounted to a nuisance, Code § 55-79.53 provided the Association with a remedy to correct the condition and obtain compliance with its bylaws and regulations. Instead of proceeding in that manner and having the rights of the respective parties determined as provided by law, the Board of Managers called a special meeting, the four members who attended decided what they objected to was a "nuisance," fined the Gillmans $20,500, and encumbered their property. The mischief that could be wrought if it were constitutionally permissible for a condominium association to levy fines on and exact penalties of unit owners is dramatically illustrated by this case. Pflug frankly admitted that he regretted selling any units to the Gillmans, and said the sale was "... a bad deal ... the worst one I've ever made" and that the only way to solve the pavement problem was "to get rid of all Gillmans' trucks." Moorefield, another member of the Board "fining" the Gillmans, testified that the imposition of fines better served the purpose of getting the Gillmans out of the condominium since the only way this could be accomplished was to "ruin them." We think it clear that the

Gillmans were being punished, not assessed, and hold the action of the Association to have been impermissible.

We now turn our attention to the Gillmans' assignments of error in which they question the action of the Association in amending its rules and regulations. They allege that their purchases of units were made after full disclosure of their intended use to the declarant Pflug, that their use of the property was in accordance with the zoning ordinance and with the understanding they had of permitted uses, and that their continued and alleged reasonable use of the common elements for the repair and parking of their trash collection vehicles was ratified by the Association.... They object to the amendment to the rules and regulations attempting to reduce the number of trucks the Gillmans are allowed on the parking area....

The narrow issue is the right of a condominium association to amend its rules, regulations, and bylaws from time to time. As we have heretofore pointed out, the bylaws of the Association recorded with the master deed expressly provide for such amendments. And the master deed conveyed the units to the Gillmans with the express understanding that the rules, regulations, and bylaws of the Association were subject to amendment. The power exercised by the Association is contractual in nature and is the creature of the condominium documents to which all unit owners subjected themselves in purchasing their units. It is a power exercised in accordance with the private consensus of the unit owners. While the unit owners are vested with an undivided interest in the common elements, the authority to control the use of the common elements is vested in the Association by the condominium documents and such amendments thereof as may thereafter be adopted.

A regulation which restricts the use of parking spaces and the weight of vehicles permitted to occupy such spaces is in no sense a zoning regulation adopted under the police power....

. . .

It is our conclusion that amendments to condominium restrictions, rules, and regulations should be measured by a standard of reasonableness, and that courts should refuse to enforce regulations that are found to be unreasonable. In doing so, inquiry must be made whether an association has acted within the scope of its authority as defined under the Condominium Act and by its own master deed and bylaws, and whether it has abused its discretion by promulgating arbitrary and capricious rules and regulations bearing no relation to the purposes of the condominium.

[handwritten margin note: Amendmts to bylaws are governd by Standard of "reasonablness" Test!]

. . .

We are unable to determine from the record before us the reasonableness of the regulation adopted by the Board of Managers of the Association restricting the number and weight of vehicles that may be parked on the common elements....

. . .

We find no merit in the Gillmans' assignment which raises the equitable defense of laches and estoppel against the Association. We do not address the question of the adequacy of attorneys' fees, the Gillmans having substantially prevailed. Accordingly, we affirm the decree of the court below directing that fines levied on the Gillmans by the Association be set aside and vacated, and the assessment liens released of record. The action of the court below granting the injunctions is reversed, and the injunctions are dissolved. The trial court's allowance of a fee to counsel for the Association is reversed. The case is remanded for further proceedings not inconsistent with the views expressed in this opinion.

Judgment Affirmed in part, Reversed in part and case Remanded.

Notes & Questions

1. *Fine or assessment?* The court in *Unit Owners Ass'n of BuildAmerica-1* engaged in some discussion about the difference between a fine and an assessment. According to the court, a fine is a "pecuniary punishment" or "penalty." The court noted that a fine is different than an assessment. Unlike a fine, an assessment is a fee levied against each owner for his or her proportional share of upkeep and repair expenses for common areas. For a discussion on fines and other community association charges, see WAYNE S. HYATT, CONDOMINIUM AND HOMEOWNER ASSOCIATION PRACTICE: COMMUNITY ASSOCIATION LAW, §§6.03–6.07; UCIOA §3-1.2.

2. *Late charge or impermissible fine?* The amount assessed in *Unit Owners Ass'n of Build-America-1* was characterized as a "fine" by the association. The court held that the fines were clearly impermissible under the state's condominium statute. A more difficult question is, at what point does a late fee or other charge become an impermissible fine? See *Vernon Manor Cooperative Apartments, Section I v. Salatino*, 178 N.Y.S.2d 895 (N.Y. Co. Ct.1958) (court concluded that a late charge equal to 100% of the payment in default did not bear any relation to the cost incurred or loss suffered by the owner's default).

UCIOA and UCA authorize charges for late payment of assessments and fines for violating association rules. See, UCIOA §3-102(11) (providing that an association can "impose charges for late payment of assessments and, after notice and opportunity to be heard, levy reasonable fines for violations of the declaration, bylaws, and rules and regulations of the association...."). Under UCIOA, an association must provide for notice and an opportunity to be heard before levying a fine for noncompliance with regulations. UCIOA does not impose a similar requirement for the imposition of late payment charge. Why do you think UCIOA requires notice and opportunity to be heard before fining a party? How are fines and penalties different so as to warrant different treatment?

3. *Authority to impose a fine.* In determining whether the association in *Unit Owners Ass'n of BuildAmerica-1* had authority to levy the fine, the court noted two reasons why the association could not levy the proposed fine. First, the state's Condominium Act did not grant the association authority to secure compliance with by-laws, rules, and regulations with such fines. Second, the Condominium Act authorized assessments for maintenance of common areas but not fines as a penalty for failing to adhere to association rules and regulations.

Other states have upheld the authority to impose a fine for violation of the community's covenants or rules. See *Michaels v. Galaxy Towers Condo. Ass'n*, No. C19283 (N.J. Super. Ct. Aug. 3, 1983) (fine for refusing to provide association an extra door key upheld); *Kittel-Glass v. Oceans Four Condo. Ass'n, Inc.*, 604 So. 2d 827 (Fla. Dist. Ct. App. 1995) (authority to impose fine upheld, however, association must provide the violating party an opportunity for a hearing before imposing fine); *Parnell Woods Condo. Ass'n, Inc. v. Schneider*, No. 159-639 (Wisc. Cir. Ct. Milwaukee Co. Oct. 7, 1982) (parking fine upheld as reasonable and uniformly applied to all violators); *Stewart v. Kopp*, 456 S.E.2d 838 (N.C. 1995) (North Carolina Condominium Act impliedly authorizes fines for up to $150.00 per day for a continuing violation).

4. *Permissible imposed fines.* *Unit Owners Ass'n of BuildAmerica-1* illustrates that not all states permit an association to levy a fine, especially when the state's condominium statute does not authorize it. Nevertheless, some courts have permitted fines against homeowners who breach association regulations. For example, the Ohio Appeals Court permitted a fine against a homeowner who violated the association's requirement that homeowners receive association approval before constructing new docks. *Lake Buckhorn Prop. Owners Ass'n v. Estill*, 1995 WL 617623 (Ohio Ct. App. unpublished opinion).

5. *Reasonableness of regulation and fine as applied.* Some courts evaluate the reasonableness of the underlying regulation before determining whether an association can recover fines for violations. In *Spratt v. Henderson Mill Condo. Ass'n, Inc.*, 481 S.E.2d 879 (Ga. App. 1997), a condominium unit owner challenged the authority of the Henderson Mill Condominium Association to assess a $25 fine for leasing her unit in violation of the declaration. The court first noted that application of the no-leasing rule to Spratt was reasonable. The rule prohibited leasing of units except in cases to avoid undue hardship on the owner. Undue hardship was defined by the declaration to include the owner's death, temporary relocation of residence, and inability to find a buyer at the prevailing market rate. In her application to lease her unit, Spratt did not provide evidence of undue hardship. Instead, she stated that she wanted to move because of traffic around the development and child safety concerns. The court concluded that Spratt did not meet the undue hardship requirements and was therefore subject to penalties for leasing the unit. The court also held that the fines were reasonable as applied to Spratt for two reasons. First, the Association did not impose the fine until over two months after Spratt entered into the prohibited lease agreement. Second, the association charged the same fine to another owner who impermissibly rented his condominium. See also *Glen Devin Condo. Ass'n v. Makhluf*, 1994 Mass. App. Div. 227 (Mass. Dist. Ct. 1994) (finding that monetary sanctions are more cost effective and expeditious method of halting and deterring violations than petitioning a court for injunctive relief).

Problem

You are stopped in the hall by one of your favorite professors who asks if you have time for a question. His wife has placed decorative pieces on the exterior of their house and on the yard. The homeowner association's board has notified her that this is not permitted and that she must remove them. If she does not, the board will levy a daily fine. "Can they do this?," he asks. What if there is no specific authority to fine in the CC&Rs? The board does have specific authority to make rules and to impose sanctions for their violation. Does that make a difference in how you answer?

The professor then tells you that the board wrote that the fine, if unpaid, would become a lien on the professor's property. Would this be so? What authority, if any, would be required? What should the professor and his wife do?

How would you advise the board?

2. Self-Help Measures

Counsel is judged by results, not by intentions.

—Cicero

Withdrawal of privileges to use common recreational and social facilities is not as commonly used as fines or penalties. However, it may be a particularly appropriate method for deterring violation of rules governing use of common facilities and has the advantage of not increasing the financial burdens of the property owner, who may already be struggling to retain the home.

Self help is also available. This can range from actually removing an offending object to turning off utilities. What policy concerns does this create? What guidelines should apply to the use of self help? Also refer to our discussion on self-help in Chapter 6 with respect to assessment collection.

California Riviera Homeowners Ass'n v.
Superior Court of Los Angeles County
California Court of Appeal
56 Cal. Rptr. 2d 564 (Cal. Ct. App. 1996)

MASTERSON, J. We issued an order to show cause in this matter to address the question of whether recordation of a notice of violation that is authorized by covenants, conditions and restrictions (CC&R's) comes within the litigation privilege of Civil Code section 47, subdivision (b). We hold that it does.

BACKGROUND

Stuart Hackel owns a house in the Pacific Palisades area of Los Angeles which is arguably subject to CC&R's recorded by predecessors of the California Riviera Homeowners Association ("California Riviera") and later modified by California Riviera.[1] Article IV, section 10 of the CC&R's prohibits a structure from being erected or maintained closer than 10 feet from the side property lines of each parcel. It further provides that, in the event of breach, California Riviera may record a notice of violation with the county recorder of Los Angeles County, and that it may not initiate any litigation unless such a notice has been recorded.[2]

OPINION

In 1991, Hackel completed a substantial remodel of his house. He was later informed by a realtor that California Riviera had recorded a "Notice of Violation of Restrictions" with respect to the property. The notice stated that Hackel had failed to comply with the 10-foot set-back requirement of the CC&R's.

On December 10, 1992, Hackel filed an action against California Riviera and two of its officers for slander of title, breach of fiduciary duty, declaratory relief, and injunctive relief. Hackel's complaint alleges, in essence, that the set-back requirement of the CC&R's is unenforceable because the right of enforcement was not transferred to California Riviera from its predecessors in the early 1940's, and that long-standing violations of the CC&R's, as well as inconsistent enforcement by California Riviera, have rendered the set-back requirement a nullity. The complaint further alleges that California Riviera exceeded its authority when it modified the CC&R's in the early 1950's by adding article IV, section 10, thereby creating the notice of violation procedure. Finally, Hackel alleges that, irrespective of whether the set-back requirement may be enforced or whether the notice of violation procedure is beyond California Riviera's authority, a notice of violation is not a recordable document as a matter of law.

In August 1993, Hackel filed a motion in respondent superior court requesting among other things that the notice of violation be expunged on the ground that it is not a record-

---

1. For purposes of this opinion we assume, but do not hold, that Hackel is bound by the CC&R's.
2. Article IV, section 10 provides:

> Notice of any breach or violation of any of the [CC&R's] hereby established, ... shall, within a reasonable time after the occurrence of such breach, violation or failure to comply, be executed by the owner of the reversionary rights herein provided for, or by the Art Jury, ... and recorded in the office of the County Recorder of Los Angeles County; and a copy of such notice, ... shall be mailed by registered mail to the person, firm or corporation responsible for such breach or violation of, or failure to comply with, any of said [CC&R's]. Until such notice has been recorded and mailed by registered mail as in this paragraph provided, neither the owner of the reversionary rights, nor the Art Jury ... shall have the right to commence any action against any person, firm or corporation responsible for any breach or violation of any of said [CC&R's] or for failure to comply therewith.

able document. The motion was granted. California Riviera thereafter petitioned this court for a writ of mandate to compel respondent court to reverse its order. The petition was granted in *California Riviera Homeowners Association v. Superior Court (Hackel)*, 37 Cal. App. 4th 1599, 44 Cal. Rptr. 2d 595, 1995. In that opinion, we held that recordation of a notice of violation was not authorized by statute, but that California Riviera's notice could nonetheless be recorded because recordation was specifically authorized by the CC&R's. (At pp. 8, 12.)

While California Riviera's petition for a writ of mandate was pending in this court, it filed a motion for summary adjudication of issues in respondent court, asserting among other things the validity of its affirmative defense that the notice of violation was a publication within the meaning of the litigation privilege of Civil Code section 47, subdivision (b). The motion was denied on the ground that the issue of whether the notice of violation was recordable had not yet been decided.

Following finality of proceedings on the prior petition for a writ of mandate, California Riviera renewed its motion for summary adjudication of issues. The motion was again denied, this time on the ground that the notice of violation was not privileged because it was not "authorized by law." California Riviera again petitioned for a writ of mandate seeking an order to compel respondent court to change its ruling. We issued an order to show cause on the petition to enable us to address a single issue, *i.e.,* whether recordation of California Riviera's notice of violation comes within the litigation privilege. Following briefing and oral argument, we find respondent court's ruling to be in error.

DISCUSSION

With the exception of a claim for malicious prosecution, an absolute privilege exists as to any publication or communication made in a judicial proceeding or other proceeding authorized by law, even if the publication was made with malice or intent to do harm. (Civ. Code, §47, subd. (b); *Silberg v. Anderson* (1990) 50 Cal. 3d 205, 215–216, 266 Cal. Rptr. 638, 786 P.2d 365.) This "litigation privilege" "applies to any publication required or permitted by law in the course of a judicial proceeding to achieve the objects of the litigation, even though the publication is made outside the courtroom and no function of the court or its officers is involved. [Citations.]" (*Id.* at p. 212; see *Moore v. Conliffe* (1994) 7 Cal. 4th 634, 641, 871 P.2d 204; *Albertson v. Raboff* (1956) 46 Cal. 2d 375, 380–381, 295 P.2d 405.) "The privilege to defame in the course of judicial proceedings is not limited to statements during trial but can extend, notwithstanding the phrasing of the statute, to steps taken prior thereto. [Citations.]" (*Lerette v. Dean Witter Organization, Inc.* (1976) 60 Cal. App. 3d 573, 577, 131 Cal. Rptr. 592.) "The usual formulation is that the privilege applies to any communication (1) made in judicial or quasi-judicial proceedings; (2) by litigants or other participants authorized by law; (3) to achieve the objects of the litigation; and (4) that [has] some connection or logical relation to the action. [Citations.]" (*Silberg v. Anderson, supra,* 50 Cal. 3d at p. 212.)

By analogy to several cases in which prelitigation communications were held to come within the litigation privilege, California Riviera asserts that the privilege is also applicable here. We agree. For example, in *Moore v. Conliffe, supra,* 7 Cal. 4th 634, 643, the Supreme Court held that the litigation privilege applied to statements made in connection with a private contractual arbitration, reasoning that such a proceeding "is designed to serve a function analogous to—and typically to eliminate the need to resort to—the court system." In *Lerette v. Dean Witter Organization, Inc., supra,* 60 Cal. App. 3d at page 578, the litigation privilege was applied to a letter demanding settlement of a financial dispute on the ground that the letter was sent as a matter "preliminary to a judicial proceeding." In *Frank Pisano & Associates v. Taggart* (1972) 29 Cal. App. 3d 1, 25, 105 Cal. Rptr. 414, the privilege was applied to a mechanic's lien, the recordation of which was "clearly authorized by law" in conjunction with an action to enforce the lien.

Finally, in *Wilton v. Mountain Wood Homeowners Assn.* (1993) 18 Cal. App. 4th 565, a condominium homeowners association recorded allegedly fraudulent assessment liens against the owner of one of its condominium owners. The owner sued the association, which raised the litigation privilege as a defense. As explained by the *Wilton* court, "Condominium homeowners associations must assess fees on the individual owners in order to maintain the complexes (Civ. Code, § 1366, subd. (a).) When an owner defaults, the association may file a lien on the owner's interest for the amount of the fees. (Civ. Code, § 1367, subd. (b).) If the default is not corrected, the association may pursue any remedy permitted by law, including judicial foreclosure or foreclosure by private power of sale. (Civ. Code, § 1367, subd. (d).)"[3] (18 Cal. App. 4th at p. 568.)

The *Wilton* court found that the homeowners association was entitled to the protection of the litigation privilege. Referring to the mechanic's lien discussed in *Frank Pisano & Associates v. Taggart, supra*, 29 Cal. App. 3d 1, *Wilton* reasoned that both homeowners association's assessment liens and mechanic's liens are required by statute to be filed as a first step in foreclosure actions to remedy defaults, and therefore meet the traditional litigation privilege test reiterated in *Silberg v. Anderson, supra*, 50 Cal. 3d at page 212, of being "required or permitted by law in the course of a judicial proceeding to achieve the objects of the litigation." (*Wilton v. Mountain Wood Homeowners Assn., supra*, 18 Cal. App. 4th at p. 569.)

Relying on this well-established definition of the privilege, respondent court rejected California Riviera's argument for application of the litigation privilege on the ground that, because no statute authorized recordation of a notice of violation, such recordation was not "permitted by law." This interpretation of what constitutes "law" is too narrow. (Cf. *Hambrecht & Quist Venture Partners v. American Medical Internat., Inc.* (1995) 38 Cal. App. 4th 1532, 1540, 1542.) [46 Cal. Rptr. 2d 33].) The broad range of what "law" encompasses includes "'the rules of action or conduct duly prescribed by controlling authority....' [Citation.]" (Id. at p. 1540.) Here, such authority may be found in article IV, section 10 of the CC&R's, which is enforceable under the law of equitable servitudes.[4] We think that the court in *Wilton v. Mountain Wood Homeowners Assn., supra*, 18 Cal. App. 4th 565, put undue emphasis on the existence of statutory authorization for recordation of a document. Thus, for the purpose of the litigation privilege, we find the CC&R's authorization to record a notice of violation is part of the "law."

Moreover, the privilege may apply even if the publisher ultimately resorts to an extrajudicial remedy. For example, in *Wilton* the homeowner argued that the litigation privilege should not apply inasmuch as the association had the statutory power to foreclose either judicially or by private sale (*i.e.*, without litigation). This argument was rejected

---

3. These statutes are part of the Common Interest Development Act (Civ. Code, § 1350 et seq.) which by definition does not apply to California Riviera.

4. We are aware of Hackel's argument that the notice of violation procedure should not qualify for the privilege because it was designed for the express purpose of inducing the homeowner to remedy the alleged violation in order to remove the cloud that the notice places on title. But the avoidance of litigation is the precise purpose for the type of demand letter that was found to come within the litigation privilege in *Lerette v. Dean Witter Organization, Inc., supra*, 60 Cal. App. 3d 573. And the same missive of "comply-or-suffer-a-cloud-on-title," published in this case via the county recorder, was found to be a privileged publication in *Frank Pisano & Associates v. Taggart, supra*, 29 Cal. App. 3d 1, and *Wilton v. Mountain Wood Homeowners Assn., supra*, 18 Cal. App. 4th 565.

on the ground that it was unacceptable to make the privilege "hinge upon factual inquiries into which remedy associations intended to use [because this] might lead associations to resort to judicial foreclosure in every case simply to avoid the risk of tort liability." (18 Cal. App. 4th at p. 570.)

We endorse the pragmatic view espoused in *Wilton*. As applied here, the litigation privilege does not require either the existence of a judicial proceeding or the likelihood that such a proceeding is imminent. California Riviera is entitled to its protection.

DISPOSITION

Let a peremptory writ of mandate issue commanding respondent superior court to vacate its order denying California Riviera's motion for summary adjudication of issues on the ground the notice of violation recorded by California Riviera does not come within the litigation privilege of Civil Code section 47, subdivision (b), and to reconsider the motion and enter a new and different order which recognizes that recordation of the notice of violation comes within the litigation privilege. In all other respects, California Riviera's petition for writ of mandate is denied. The parties are to bear their own costs on this writ petition.

[Note that the preceding case is not of precedent value because the California Supreme Court ordered it depublished and subsequently ruled that a notice of noncompliance was not an instrument contained in the statutorily permitted list of recordable instruments. The case, however serves an instructive purpose. First, other states are more permissive in what may be recorded. Second, it illustrates a self-help approach and its potential consequences. — Eds.]

Note:
Limited
precedential
power

Retrospective and Observations

The Association's Perspective

When Kevin Kane joined this case as replacement counsel for the association, he recognized that the principal issue was having the courts address the recording of a notice of violation of covenant. He discovered that there was no California case law on either side of that issue.

Previously, the California Supreme Court remanded the case back to the court of appeals, and the appeals court determined that the association had a right to record notice of a homeowners' violation under the law of equitable servitudes. The court certified the case for publication and Stuart Hackel, the real party in interest in the case, appealed again for the Supreme Court to hear the case. The Supreme Court denied rehearing, depublished the appeals court opinion, and remanded the case to the trial court. The trial court has requested that the parties try to settle the case. According to Mr. Kane, at the time of publication, settlement is still going nowhere. Hackel continues to challenge the right of an association to record the violation of the covenants, maintaining that the association indiscriminately attacked him while allowing other violations and that the association is estopped from enforcing against him because it has not enforced every violation.

Mr. Kane explained that California has two types of planned communities. The first, common interest communities, are governed by California civil code and are granted the power to levy assessments and collect them, enforce restrictions, etc. The second group of communities is "all others." California Riviera Homeowners Association falls into that category. These communities have no authority to compel owners within the community to pay assessments. As an aside, Mr. Kane cited the example of the community in which Steven Spielberg and Tom Hanks live. Assessments on lots in that community are $50 per year, and associations have a very hard time collecting that. Therefore, communities such as California Riviera do not have the funds to litigate issues such as in this case.

When Mr. Kane joined the case, he investigated Hackel and found that at the time, he had 17 cases in litigation. Hackel's style of development was to go into communities which were built in the 1920's and which had small California bungalows on large parcels of land. He bought up the houses, demolished them, and built huge houses on the parcels because California's real estate trend recently has been toward large square footage homes on small lots. Hackel made his money by charging millions of dollars for the homes. California Riviera is his sixth project, and Mr. Kane feels that Hackel purchased this particular community at a very bad time in the California real estate market. After Hackel purchased homes in the community, housing prices dropped dramatically. Mr. Kane feels that Hackel is using the litigation in this case as a vehicle to recoup his losses at California Riviera.

Stuart Hackel's Perspective

Stuart Hackel's attorney, Ronald Katzman, is of the opinion that in California, an owner is held ransom by the cloud on the title of his property when an association records such things as the notice of violation recorded in *California Riviera*. The owner is deprived of due process. Such actions pit neighbors against neighbors and open Pandora's box.

Notes & Questions

1. *Bylaws, CC&Rs, statute.* An important concern for an association is its ability to enforce any valid rule or regulation it passes. A number of factors could affect an association's rights of self-enforcement.

The first concern is that the relevant documents authorize self-help remedies. How specific the association documents must be with respect to enforcement actions is debatable. For instance, some courts have recognized an association's authority to enforce regulations where the relevant documents do not expressly authorize certain acts. See, *e.g., Western v. Chardonnay Village Condo. Ass'n, Inc.*, 519 So. 2d 243 (La. Ct. App. 1988). *Cf. Grimes v. Moreland*, 322 N.E.2d 699 (Ohio Ct. Com. Pl.1974) (holding that that an association could not convert common elements into private property where the by-laws, declaration, and applicable statute did not authorize such actions).

A second concern is whether a controlling statute permits an association to take self-help measures to enforce its rules and regulations. UCIOA § 3-1.2 grants an association broad authority to enforce rules and regulations of the common interest community including, subsections 15 and 17 which authorize the "exercise of any powers conferred by the declaration," and "the exercise of any powers necessary and proper for the governance and operation of the association." What factors would you consider in drafting an effective "self-help" provision in a declaration?

2. *Adverse consequences of self-help measures. Paxton v. Oxnard Police Dept.*, 21 F.3d 1115 (9th Cir. 1994) 1994 WL 143951, 1994 U.S. App. Lexis 9516, an unpublished opin-

ion, illustrates some of the risks involved in using self help. After discovering that their homes had been built on a <u>toxic waste dump</u>, several owners posted signs protesting lack of action by the city and state. To enforce its sign restrictions, the association cut down one sign with a chain saw and <u>allegedly knocked down the homeowner with a truck</u>, leading to litigation in both state and federal court. Do you think it is advisable for a community association to risk violent confrontation with any homeowner in its attempt to force compliance with community rules? How might the association have prepared better or acted differently in the *Paxton* case?

3. *Constitutional concerns.* In *Paxton*, the homeowners sued the police department alleging a violation of their Fourteenth Amendment due process rights because their property was taken without notice and hearing. The case also raises the issue of First Amendment violations in that the actions may have <u>deprived the homeowners of the right to express their opinion.</u>

3. Alternative Dispute Resolution

Disputes and disagreements can occur in any situation, but disputes between owners in a community or between the governing association and an owner or owners can be a particularly <u>troubling and expensive burden on the community</u>. In a typical business situation, when there is a dispute that leads to a law suit, the parties involved can terminate their business relationship after the conflict has been resolved. However, in a community, short of selling their units and moving out of the community, owners cannot simply sever ties with their neighbors or their community association. Some type of relationship and interaction must continue during and after the conflict. Litigation, which can be a very lengthy adversarial process, does not foster a spirit of cooperation and good will between the parties and as such, tends permanently to strain the relationship.

Not only can relationships among neighbors be irreparably damaged through the costly and adversarial litigation process, but the costs also adversely impact the entire community. If the association is involved, <u>all the association's costs and attorneys fees of the litigation constitute a common expense and are allocated to all residents through assessments.</u> Even if the association is not directly involved, as governing body for the community, it most likely will be impacted in some manner.

Increasingly, community associations' governing documents include provisions for the <u>mandatory use of alternatives to litigation between and among owners and between owners and the association.</u> These methods are designed to aid the parties in working out the solution in a cooperative rather than adversarial manner, thus avoiding and decreasing the emotional and financial costs of litigation for everyone in the community. Parties are encouraged to work together to create solutions to their problems, and the procedures established in the documents <u>typically require less time and money than litigation.</u>

A dispute resolution provision should be included in the community's governing documents. A well-constructed provision defines or specifies the parties bound by the provision, types of claims exempt from the procedures, the procedures to be followed, how costs are allocated between or among the parties, and how the resolution may be enforced by the prevailing party. Certain disputes, including disputes between the community association and an owner regarding assessments, liens, or violations of the restrictive covenants, generally are exempt from the dispute resolution requirements, as they involve explicit powers of the association and are not necessarily subject to negotiation or compromise.

Typically, the dispute resolution process begins with notice by the aggrieved party to the alleged violator describing the disputed issue and a proposed remedy, and offering a meeting between the parties to discuss the matter. Once notice has been given, a period of negotiation begins. Each party involved is required to make a good faith effort to negotiate a solution to the problem, often with the help of a representative of the community association if the conflict is between owners.

Should negotiations fail to yield a solution, the next step is mediation. Mediation offers a more structured approach and involves the participation of a professional mediator. Mediation gives the parties the opportunity to clear up misunderstandings and discover areas of agreement with the help of a neutral third party.[DDD]

If mediation does not result in a mutually acceptable solution, the dispute often may be submitted to arbitration (although sometimes, mediation is provided as the final step before litigation). Arbitration is managed by an arbitrator or arbitration panel whose decision may be binding or non-binding. Arbitration has similarities to conventional litigation in that discovery is permitted and the same rules of evidence apply. Whereas, in the mediation process, the parties work together with a mediator's help to come to an agreement, in arbitration, each party argues his or her case to an arbitrator or arbitration panel, and the arbitrator or panel issues a decision. As with litigation, the parties to an arbitration proceeding attempt to convince a third party that their position is the correct one. Thus, the adversarial nature of the relationship between the parties is more apparent than in the mediation setting.

Alternative dispute resolution provisions may specify whether the arbitration is binding or non-binding, designate the arbitration agency, and limit discovery. Non-binding arbitration solutions may be rejected by either party unless both parties agree to be bound by the arbitrator's decision. Agreements formed in binding arbitration typically are enforceable under state law.

Community associations should anticipate that disputes will arise in their communities and create procedures for resolving those disputes before they occur. How those disputes are handled can be the difference between a good faith resolution between friends and neighbors and a court battle between opposing sides.

Requiring common interest community members to engage in some form of alternative dispute resolution before resorting to the courts is an increasingly popular idea and may be a prerequisite to filing suit in some states. See *e.g.,* Calif. Civ. Code § 1369.510 *et seq.* Does this mean that a developer may require arbitration of disputes over construction or design of the project? *Villa Milano Homeowners Ass'n v. Il Davorge,* 102 Cal. Rptr.2d 1 (Cal. Ct. App. 2000) held that the arbitration clause in the declaration was an adhesion contract, unconscionable, and unenforceable. California Code of Civil Procedure § 1298.7 gives home buyers the right to bring a judicial action for construction or design defect damages despite a binding arbitration clause in the purchase agreement. However, a more recent case, *Shepard v. MacKay Enterprises, Inc.,* 56 Cal.Rptr.3d 326 (Cal. Ct. App. 2007) has held that the Federal Arbitration Act preempts the California statute.

Notes & Questions

1. *Traditional judicial remedies for breach of a restrictive covenant.* Appropriate judicial remedies for a breach of covenant claim may include: declaratory judgment, compen-

---

DDD. "ADR & Construction Defect—Making It Work," 16th Annual Community Association Law Seminar, E. Richard Kennedy and Karyn A. Kennedy, January 22, 1995.

satory, punitive, and nominal damages; prohibitory and mandatory injunctions; specific performance; imposition of an equitable lien; and, under limited circumstances, extinguishment of the servitude. See *Restatement (Third)* § 8.2. Courts enjoy wide discretion in selecting the appropriate remedy and, generally, may give the plaintiff any remedy or combination thereof as is justified by the facts of the case. *Id.* See, *e.g., Schulz v. Zoeller*, 568 S.W.3d 677 (Tx. Ct. Civ. App. 1978) (upholding an injunction requiring removal of a house brought onto the property which violated a restriction prohibiting moveable structures); *M.H. Siegfried Real Estate v. Renfrow*, 592 S.W.2d 488 (Mo. Ct. App. 1979) (holding that a property owner was entitled to an injunction against obstruction of an easement and damages for the length of time the obstruction was maintained); *Mondelli v. Saline Sewer Co.*, 628 S.W.2d 697 (Mo. Ct. App. 1982) (holding that easement holder was entitled to damages proximately caused by wrongful interference with the easement).

2. *Non-judicial enforcement methods.* As reviewed above, community associations may choose to deny privileges to violating unit owners as a means of enforcing the restrictive covenants. For example, the association could choose to suspend the owner's right to vote or suspend association-provided services (such as trash collection and lawn maintenance). Alternatively, the association may choose to restrict access to the community's common areas such as the pool or the clubhouse. See *Korman Co. v. Palmyra Harbour Condo. Ass'n*, No. A-4177-96T2 (N.J. Super. Ct. App. Div., Aug. 7, 1996) (holding that a regulation restricting access to the clubhouse and recreational facilities for an owner who is in violation of the association's rules and regulations is an appropriate exercise of the association's obligation to other owners, provided that such authority is authorized by the association's by-laws).

In extreme enforcement cases, the association may also have the authority to terminate an owner's property interest for continuing violation of the CCRs. See ROBERT G. NATELSON, LAW OF PROPERTY OWNERS ASSOCIATIONS, § 5.4.6. Termination, however, is generally limited to cooperatives where the relationship of owner to the cooperative is based on a proprietary lease. *Cf. Green v. Greenbelt Homes Inc.*, 194 A.2d 273 (1963) (holding that the objectionable conduct of the member was a sufficient breach of the covenant to warrant the corporation's exercise of its right to terminate her interest in the dwelling unit).

3. *Selecting the appropriate remedy.* How does one select the appropriate enforcement remedy? Contributing factors may include the purpose of the applicable servitude and its utility to the parties, the conduct of the parties, the interest of third persons and the public, and the likely costs incurred to serve judicial enforcement. See *Restatement (Third)* § 8.2. Of course, equity under the circumstances is an important consideration. *Id.* at § 8.3. In determining whether a particular remedy is inequitable, the *Restatement* lists seven factors to consider:

> (1) Delay by the complaining party; (2) Failure of the complaining party to object to similar conduct by the defendant or by holders of other property subject to the same general plan of development; (3) fairness of the transaction that created the servitude and the servitude terms; (4) severity of the breach or violation; (5) utility of specific enforcement to the complaining party and others subject to the same general plan, and the public; (6) costs of specific enforcement to the party in breach or violation of the servitude, to third parties, and to the public: and (7) practicability of the remedy.

See, *e.g., Elmwood, Inc. v. Hassett*, 486 N.Y.S.2d 13 (App. Div. 1985) (holding that plaintiff is estopped from seeking an injunction requiring removal of building from parking lot on which plaintiff had easement, because plaintiff did not object until a substantial portion of the construction had been completed); *Perry-Gething Foundation v. Stinson*, 631 N.Y.S.2d 170 (N.Y. App. Div. 1995) (holding that enforcement of the covenant was barred by laches because plaintiffs failed to bring suit despite ongoing construction).

Problem

You are having a further conversation with your client from Seven Oaks who is still unhappy about the proposed new clubhouse construction (see Problem in Chapter 6). Although she still has not executed the revised Declaration, she has been busy.

Her immediate concern is that the board of directors, through the management company, has filed a lien upon her property to enforce a $1,000 fine that board imposed when she distributed a newsletter attacking the board, DevCo, and the clubhouse idea. In addition, she has not yet paid the clubhouse assessments.

Your client asks for your advice as to what her position is and what actions she might take. She is concerned about her own liability as well as wondering whether she has an action against any other party. How do you advise her?

D. Defenses to Enforcement of CCRs, Rules and Regulations

"Litigation:" A machine you go into as a pig and come out as a sausage.

—*Ambrose Bierce*

Whenever the decision to enforce the CCRs is made, the subject of defenses arises. The most common defensive argument, of course, is that the community association does not have the power to do what it seeks to do. A second defense is change of condition. Questions that arise are: How much and what kind of change is required before a court will set aside a covenant? What about a board-made rule? Are they treated differently?

Selective enforcement is perhaps the next most commonly raised defense in enforcement litigation. It is popular because asserting that there has not been uniform enforcement is often accurate. This does not automatically mean that the current enforcement action is barred, however. Nonuniform enforcement exists in many cases because of a change in board memberships and the fact that different board members may have different perspectives on whether and how to enforce.

Failure to have a rationale for non-enforcement and for not documenting that decision may also give rise to the selective enforcement argument. Selective enforcement is much different from making an informed business decision that enforcement is not appropriate in a particular situation and fully documenting that decision. Selective enforcement generally involves three variables: time, uniformity, and rational bases. It may occur when there is board turnover, a lax board of declarant appointees being replaced by home owners who are more aggressive, or permission or tolerance for one type of violation that is then argued to bar enforcement against violations of another type.

Selective enforcement is important to understand because, as a defense, it is creative, it deters sloppy "government," and it happens. Key factors to look for in examining selective enforcement include, whether there has been a consistent enforcement policy by the body then engaged in the action, whether the tolerated violations have been so extensive as to tend to show that no plan of development exists, whether enforcement will still have substantial value in the overall plan of development, and the reasons for the prior non- or limited enforcement.

In addition to these defenses, of course, all of the "normal" litigation defenses including the statute of limitations and laches are raised.

1. Arbitrary Application

Coventry Square Condo. Ass'n v. Halpern

District Court of New Jersey

436 A.2d 580 (N. J. Sup. Ct.1981)

GEHRICKE, J. This is a suit by the Condominium Association in which it seeks to collect a $225 security deposit per unit from all unit owners who rent their premises to tenants pursuant to a by-law effective as of November 1, 1977.

Defendants resist this demand for a deposit, asserting that there is no statutory sanction for so doing; that the by-law relied on by plaintiff exceeds the authority of the board of directors of the Association to so act and the deposit required is really a special assessment levied against a specially created class of owner.

There are no reported cases in our State on the issues raised in this case. This condominium consists of 633 units, of which 80 are occupied by tenants. Forty-two of these rented units are owned by two landlords.

In 1977 the board of directors of the Association, acting on what they perceived to be increased maintenance expenses caused by inadequate watering, excessive glass breakage, more frequent pest control and garbage placement on the wrong days at such tenant-occupied units, passed a regulation effective November 1, 1977 requiring that owners of rented units deposit $225 per unit with the Association as security for such increased costs. Defendants acknowledge that they have not deposited any money with plaintiff pursuant to this regulation.

The regulation was passed by the board after several meetings and much discussion among themselves, but without any special notice of their intention to act at their October 12, 1977 meeting.

Cross-examination by defendants' counsel elicited testimony that plaintiff did not seek to regulate owner-occupants in like fashion because they were easily available and could be easily collected from, and the Association wanted to have the benefit of a part of an owner's security received from the tenant.

Interrogatories propounded by defendants (# 5) reveal that there were no specific records kept of non-owner resident damage.

P-1 in Evidence—the Rules and Regulations of Coventry Square Condominiums provide for the following:

Garbage pick-up, placement at wrong times will be at additional expense to the UNIT.

Lawn care, replacement due to neglect will be at additional expense to the UNIT.

Home owners are the responsible party even if they are not residing in their unit.
(Emphasis supplied)

The provision of the regulation in question which requires that the Association place deposit money in an interest-bearing escrow account clearly demonstrates that the Association is not acquiring any property right in such funds; the language used shows that the Association is a recipient of the owner's money, which is returnable if no damage occurs to common elements attributable to the tenant of an owner. Assessments are, "In general sense, the process of ascertaining and adjusting the shares respectively to be contributed by several persons toward a common beneficial object according to the benefit received." *Black's Law Dictionary* (4 ed. 1951). They are collected for the purpose of making a common expenditure in the future and are not refundable. The money required under this regulation is a deposit, not a special assessment.

The provision for payment by nonresident owners does establish a special class of owner and the concomitant duty to make a security deposit by such members of that specially created class.

While these defendants acknowledged that they were subject to the regulations of the Association, this does not mean that they cannot resist compliance when they believe the regulation to be improper. Samuel Johnson said it best when he told Boswell that "one does not have to be a cook to criticize the cooking."

The Association provides in its regulations for the imposition of costs on unit owners for lawn replacement and untimely garbage placement, and places responsibility on unit owners even if not residing in the unit. A nonresident owner is presumably as available as a resident owner. The assertion by plaintiff that they wish to have benefit of part of any deposit an owner may require from his tenant is difficult to uphold; it appears to be a glossing over of a deliberate attempt to interject the Association into a private contractual relationship between a nonresident owner (landlord) and his tenant. This court can justify neither the intent nor the implementation of such conduct. The Association is not a third-party beneficiary of nonresident's contract with his tenant.

The regulation in question is unreasonable in that it creates a limited class from whom an extraordinary payment of money into escrow is demanded; it is arbitrary in that it seeks to acquire a convenient fund from this limited class arising out of a contractual arrangement between members of this class and their tenants, and it is unnecessary because the provisions already in place for imposition of charges against owners adequately protect the Association against the anticipated damage by tenants.

The court finds that there is no cause for action against defendants, and the complaint is dismissed without costs.

Dismissed.

Notes & Questions

1. *Creation of a limited class.* A restriction is arbitrarily enforced if the restriction does not burden all members of the association equally but imposes a burden only on a limited class of individuals. It is important to note that a restriction may be reasonably related to a lawful objective, yet be unenforceable because the restriction is arbitrarily applied to only a "certain class of individuals." *White Egret Condo., Inc. v. Franklin*, 379 So. 2d 346 (Fla. 1979) (holding that an age restriction prohibiting children under the age of 12 from residing in the complex was arbitrarily enforced since there were other young children living in the complex).

2. *Importance of association record-keeping.* If the association can prove that it took some action, *e.g.*, a letter of non-compliance, fine, etc., with respect to all other similar

violations, the defense of arbitrary enforcement typically will be ineffective. See *Dunlap v. Bavarian Village Condo.*, 780 P.2d 1012 (Alaska 1989) (holding that a restriction was not arbitrarily enforced since the association took steps to eliminate every violation the appellant could identify). In the absence of good record-keeping by the association, how else may the association rebut the arbitrary application defense?

2. Selective Enforcement

Ladner v. Plaza Del Prado Condo. Ass'n, Inc.

District Court of Appeal of Florida
423 So. 2d 927 (Fla. Dist. Ct. App. 1983)

FERGUSON, J. The owners of a condominium unit bring this appeal from a Final Judgment ordering them to restore their terrace railing to its original condition in compliance with the Declaration of Condominium and by-laws. Appellants make two arguments: (1) the order requiring them to correct a non-conforming condition constitutes an impermissible selective enforcement of the rules, (2) a prior decision of this court holding that the action by the condominium association constitutes selective enforcement is the law of the case and is not open to redetermination by the trial court.

We will first address the second point on appeal. The case was before this court previously, *Ladner v. Plaza Del Prado Condominium Association, Inc.*, 384 So. 2d 50 (Fla. 3d DCA 1980), to review an order granting the Condominium Association's motion for preliminary injunction which required appellants to correct the nonconforming condition of their terrace railing. This court reversed the preliminary injunction for the reason that the Association had failed to show that without the injunction they would suffer irreparable harm, citing to *Department of Health and Rehabilitative Services v. Artis*, 345 So. 2d 1109 (Fla. 4th DCA 1977). The opinion, set out in its entirety below, also purports to decide the underlying merits of the case:

> We reverse the decision of the trial court granting the condominium association a temporary mandatory injunction requiring the Ladners to restore the terrace of their apartment to its original condition. *Ordering the Ladners to remove their nonconforming, differently colored terrace railings constitutes selective enforcement of the rules contained in the declaration of condominium and the bylaws contrary to White Egret Condominium, Inc. v. Franklin*, 379 So. 2d 346 (Fla. 1979). Furthermore, no irreparable harm to appellee has been shown. *Department of Health and Rehabilitative Services v. Artis*, 345 So. 2d 1109 (Fla. 4th DCA 1977).
>
> Reversed and remanded for further proceedings.

Ladner, 384 So. 2d 50 (emphasis supplied).

But the narrow issue before this court in the interlocutory appeal from the order granting temporary injunction was whether the Condominium Association had made a showing, reasonably free from doubt, that a preliminary injunction was necessary to prevent great and irreparable injury. *See, e.g., Sackett v. City of Coral Gables*, 246 So. 2d 162 (Fla. 3d DCA 1971). The expression that the Association was selectively enforcing its rules was beyond that necessary to decide the narrow issue raised so is *obiter dictum* and without force. *State ex rel. Biscayne Kennel Club v. Board of Business Regulation*, 276 So. 2d 823 (Fla. 1973); *Pell v. State*, 97 Fla. 650, 122 So. 110 (1929).

There is a second and even more compelling reason why we must reject appellant's argument that the statement made in the prior opinion as to a material point in the controversy constitutes the law of the case. Acceptance of such a proposition would essentially require us to hold that a final judgment of injunction could enter based on facts developed at the preliminary stage before the parties have had an opportunity for a full hearing. The purpose of a temporary injunction[1] is to preserve the status quo until a final hearing when full relief may be granted....

Appellant's first point on appeal goes to the merits of the case. At the hearing on the merits after remand, the trial court made the following findings:

2. That the defendants, William Ladner and Judith Ladner, his wife, are the owners of [a] condominium unit..., purchased with notice of and are subject to the provisions of the Declaration of Condominium as well as the other involved condominium documents, including the bylaws.

3. That the Declaration of Condominium provides in part that no unit owner shall decorate or change the appearance of any portion of the exterior of the apartment building without the prior approval, in writing, of the owners of record of 51% of the condominium units and the approval of the association.

4. That the defendants, without seeking or obtaining requisite prior approval materially altered the railings of the terrace of their condominium unit.

5. The plaintiff association, acting through its Board of Directors, did notify the defendants of their violation of such provision of the Declaration of Condominium and request compliance therewith.

6. That defendants failed to comply with such requests of the Board of Directors resulting in the filing of the instant case.

7. That based upon the evidence presented to the court, the court finds that as a result of the decision in *Plaza Del Prado v. Richman*, 345 So. 2d 851 (Fla. 3d DCA 1977) a certain group of unit owners who had received permission from the developer of the Plaza Del Prado Condominium were allowed to maintain their terrace railings with the alterations permitted by the developer.

8. That as a result of the *Richman* decision, the plaintiff association was without authority to compel compliance with the Declaration of Condominium as to that certain group of unit owners.

Those findings of the trial court are supported by competent and substantial evidence in the record. A finding of fact by a trial judge in a non-jury case will not be set aside on review unless totally unsupported by competent substantial evidence. *Laufer v. Norma Fashions, Inc.*, 418 So. 2d 437 (Fla. 3d DCA 1982); *Oceanic International Corp. v. Lantana Boatyard*, 402 So. 2d 507 (Fla. 4th DCA 1981). The alterations made by unit owners with permission of the developer, before responsibility for enforcement of the Declarations and bylaws was transferred to the Association, are the only alterations which have continued. The Association, since it inherited the responsibility for enforcement, has consistently precluded any further violations of the agreement not to alter the architectural uniformity of the exterior building. That the Association has consistently performed its duty to en-

---

1. Preliminary injunction and temporary injunction are used interchangeably and have the same meaning. Black's Law Dictionary 923 (rev. 4th ed. 1968). The Florida Rules of Civil Procedure, 1.610(a) uses "Preliminary Injunction," and distinguishes it from "Temporary Restraining Order." Fla.R.Civ.P. 1.610(b).

force the mutual agreement entered into by all the unit owners, and has done so only prospectively, whereas the predecessor developer was lax in enforcing those rules, does not constitute selective and arbitrary conduct by the association in violation of the proscriptions of *White Egret Condominium v. Franklin*, 379 So. 2d 346 (Fla. 1979).

 Holding. —O.

Affirmed.

Notes & Questions

1. *Consistent and uniform application.* As *Ladner* illustrates, a restriction which is consistently and uniformly applied generally does not constitute selective enforcement, even if some violations went "unpunished" in the past. See *Chattel Shipping and Investment, Inc. v. Brickell Place Condo. Ass'n, Inc.*, 481 So. 2d 29 (Fla. Dist. Ct. App. 1985) (holding that implementation of a "uniform policy" to enforce a restriction only prospectively is not selective enforcement); *Sugarland Run Homeowners Ass'n, v. Couzins*, 28 Va. Cir. 334 (Va. Cir. Ct. 1992) (holding that restrictive covenants were not selectively enforced because the association employed a "vigorous and methodical approach" to covenant enforcement); *Manor Forest Condo. Ass'n v. Zuccala*, No. CL-9-9888-AF (Fla. Cir. Ct. Palm Beach County. Mar. 12, 1990) (bringing suit against one of many parking violators is not selective enforcement); and *Mountain Park Homeowners Ass'n v. Tydings*, 864 P. 2d 392 (Wash. Ct. App. 1993) (upholding satellite dish enforcement).

On the other hand, if a restriction is not presently applied in a consistent and uniform manner (*i.e.*, a patchwork approach to enforcement), then selective enforcement is more likely to be found. See *White Egret Condo., Inc. v. Franklin*, 379 So. 2d 346 (Fla. 1979) (holding that a restriction prohibiting children was selectively enforced against respondent because the association permitted several children in the complex). But see *Constellation Condo. Ass'n, Inc. v. Harrington*, 467 So. 2d 378 (Fla. Dist. Ct. App. 1985) (plaintiff failed to prove that age restriction was selectively enforced).

2. *Other violations are not evidence of selective enforcement.* Violation of the same restriction by others in the community does not, by itself, support a selective enforcement defense. See *Sugarland Run Homeowners Ass'n, v. Couzins*, 28 Va. Cir. 334 (Va. Cir. Ct. 1992) (holding that evidence of other violations does not indicate selective enforcement). Moreover, violation of other covenants is irrelevant to a determination of whether a specific covenant was selectively enforced. *Mountain Park Homeowners Ass'n, Inc. v. Tydings*, 864 P.2d 392 (Wash. Ct. App. 1993) (holding that the association uniformly enforced its restriction prohibiting antennas despite the fact that other covenants were not being enforced).

3. Waiver

Sharpstown Civic Ass'n, Inc. v. Pickett

Supreme Court of Texas
679 S.W.2d 956 (Tex. 1984)

WALLACE, J. This is a suit to enjoin the violation of deed restrictions on two lots in a residential subdivision. The trial court, based upon a jury verdict, rendered judgment denying a permanent injunction. The court of appeals affirmed. 667 S.W.2d 840. We reverse the judgments of the courts below and render judgment granting the injunction.

Sharpstown Civic Association, Inc., and six resident lot owners of Sharpstown Country Club Terrace, Section Two, in Houston, Harris County, Texas (Sharpstown) brought suit against Ronald I. Pickett, *et al.*, (Pickett) to enjoin the proposed construction of a commercial car wash on the lots in question. Those lots are Lots One and Two, Block 42, Sharpstown Country Club Terrace, Section Two. The two lots form a triangle, the base of which abuts Triolo Lane, a two-lane residential street. One of the longer sides of the triangle abuts South Gessner Road, a four-lane city street. The third side abuts an 80-foot wide drainage easement which abuts an adjoining 150-foot wide utility easement. There is no discernible boundary line between the two lots.

In 1969, Robert Hill purchased the two lots and moved a 12' X 38' one-story wooden building onto Lot One. He built a circular gravel driveway in front of the building and made water, sewage, electricity and telephone connections. The building was used by Mr. Hill as a real estate office. He also rented space to an insurance salesman and to an attorney. This use was continued until mid-November of 1979, when the property was sold to Pickett. Pickett used the building as an office until April of 1980, at which time he erected a sign that announced the future use of the two lots as a commercial car wash. Sharpstown contacted Pickett and objected to the use of the lots as a car wash. The parties were unable to agree on a use of the lots and this suit was filed. Pickett indicated at trial that he was considering using the property for a strip shopping center rather than a car wash. He is now using Lot One as a used car lot.

The jury found in answer to special issues as follows:

(1) Lot One was used for non-residential purposes but Lot Two was not so used;

(2) The non-residential use of Lot One began in the 1970's;

(3) The non-residential use of Lot One was continuous from 1970 until the filing of this suit;

(4) Lots One and Two were used and maintained as one parcel;

(4a) One or more of the Plaintiffs knew of the non-residential use of Lot One but not of Lot Two;

(5) One or more of the Plaintiffs first knew of the non-residential use of Lot One in 1970;

(5a) A person of reasonable prudence should have known of the non-residential use of Lot One;

(6) A person of reasonable prudence should have known of the non-residential use of Lot One commencing in 1970; and

(7) Plaintiffs waived the right to enforce the restrictions against non-residential use of the property.

The issues to be decided are: (1) whether non-residential use of Lot One, without objection by Sharpstown, will support a waiver by Sharpstown of its right to enforce restrictions on Lot Two; (2) whether the use of the small office building on Lot One, without objection by Sharpstown, was sufficient to waive its right to enjoin the use of the lot for use as a commercial car wash or a strip shopping center; and (3) whether there could be waiver of the non-residential use of Lot One absent a showing that each plaintiff (Sharpstown) actually knew of the non-residential use.

Pickett contends that the use of Lot One as a site for the small office building constitutes a use of both lots for that purpose. Sharpstown contends that there is no evidence to substantiate the jury's finding that both lots were used as one parcel. The only evidence of any use of Lot Two was infrequent mowing of the grass plus occasional parking of one or more vehicles on the lot. We hold this does not constitute evidence of use of Lot Two for non-residential use.

Pickett further contends that the use of Lot One for non-residential purposes was sufficient to support waiver of the restrictions on Lot Two because of the location and shape of the two lots. We reject this contention for two reasons. First, the lots are separate and distinct as evidenced by the plat filed of record. Because they are separate lots, whether one or both were used in violation of the restrictions must be determined based upon the use made of each lot. *See Wade v. Magee*, 641 S.W.2d 321 (Tex. App.—El Paso 1982, *writ ref'd n.r.e.*). Second, the jury failed to find any non-residential use of Lot Two, or that any of the plaintiffs knew, or that a reasonable person should have known, of any non-residential use of Lot Two. Pickett thus failed to carry his burden of proof on the issue of non-residential use of Lot Two. The courts below thus erred in denying injunctive relief to Sharpstown as to Lot Two.

The next question is whether the use of Lot One as a site for the small office building, without objection by Sharpstown, constituted a waiver of the use of that lot for a commercial car wash or a strip shopping center. Pickett contends that any non-residential use was sufficient to support every non-residential use. Sharpstown contends that the use of the small office building was not a substantial violation of the restrictions. Therefore, according to Sharpstown, Pickett's stated purpose of building a commercial car wash constituted a new violation of the restrictions and Sharpstown acted promptly to enjoin that use.

Pickett's argument, followed to its logical conclusion, would require us to hold, as an example, that use of residential property for the purpose of giving piano lessons for hire, if continued for a sufficient time, would give rise to the right of the owner of that property to convert it to a service station or other equally undesirable use. We find a more reasonable interpretation of the applicable law to be that in order to support a waiver of residential restrictions the proposed use must not be substantially different in its effect on the neighborhood from any prior violation. To put it another way, the prior violation which has been carried on without objection, if insignificant or insubstantial when compared to the proposed or new use, will not support a waiver of the new and greater violation. *See Arrington v. Cleveland*, 242 S.W.2d 400 (Tex. Civ. App.—Fort Worth 1951, *writ ref'd*); *Wilson v. Gordon*, 224 S.W. 703 (Tex. Civ. App.—Galveston 1920, *writ dism'd*). We hold that Sharpstown waived the restrictions as to the use of Lot One for the purposes for which it was used from 1970 until purchased by Pickett in November of 1979.

Sharpstown contends that there could be no waiver of the right to enjoin the violation of the deed restrictions absent actual notice to each of them of the violations which occurred between 1970 and 1979. The jury found that a reasonably prudent person should have known of the non-residential use of Lot One from 1970 to 1979. This is equivalent to a finding of constructive notice of the non-residential use. A purchaser is bound by these restrictions of which he has constructive notice. *See Davis v. Huey*, 620 S.W.2d 561, 565 (Tex. 1981). There was evidence to support this finding.

We hold that Pickett be enjoined from conducting non-residential activities on Lot Two, and that he be enjoined from conducting non-residential activities on Lot One which are of a more substantial nature than those conducted by his predecessor in title from 1970 to 1979. Therefore, we reverse the judgments of the courts below and render judgment that Pickett be enjoined from using the property as a commercial car wash, a strip shopping center, or a used car lot.

4. Changed Conditions

Marks v. Wingfield

Supreme Court of Virginia
331 S.E.2d 463 (Va. 1985)

STEPHENSON, J. Appellants, Dudley H. Marks and Thurman H. Upchurch (collectively, Marks), sued to enjoin the appellees, Carlton L. Wingfield and others (defendants), from placing campers[2] upon certain subdivision lots owned by the defendants. All lots in the subdivision are subject to the following restrictive covenants:

> 1. No shacks, tents, house trailers or temporary dwellings of any kind whatsoever shall be erected on the property.

> 2. Lots hereby conveyed shall be used and occupied for residential purposes only, and only one single-family residence shall be constructed on any lot.

In their responsive pleadings, defendants denied that they violated the restrictions, and, alternatively, that, even if they had, they claimed that the restrictions were invalid and unenforceable. The trial court ruled in favor of the defendants on both grounds, and this appeal resulted. Thus, we must determine (1) whether the restrictions are valid and enforceable, and, if so, (2) whether the defendants violated them.

The evidence was taken by depositions, and the material facts are undisputed. The subdivision known as "Riverside" was established in 1958 and consists of 19 residential lots fronting on the James River in Amherst County. Riverside, which always has been primarily a recreational area, contains nine permanent houses.

It was not until the late 1970's that campers were placed in the subdivision. During this period, the defendants brought campers to the subdivision. Previously, all dwellings had been permanent structures which complied with the restrictions. When the present suit was instituted, five campers were located within Riverside. A real estate appraiser opined that placing campers or other temporary structures near a single-family residence adversely affects the value of the residence property.

These campers are mobile and are either towed or driven[3] upon the land. They are titled by the Division of Motor Vehicles. Generally, when in place, the campers are supported by jacks or bricks which are placed under them on the ground. However, such supports, although desirable, are not necessary. The campers are suitable for use as temporary dwellings, and, occasionally, some defendants sleep in them overnight. Electric and natural gas utilities are connected to the campers.

The subdivision was subjected to major flooding by the river in 1969 and 1972. The floods, however, did not cause any substantial damage to the permanent houses. Because of the floods, the County adopted regulations requiring that future structures be placed at designated elevations.

First, we address the defendants' contention that the restrictions are invalid and unenforceable because, due to flooding, the character of the neighborhood has changed from residential to recreational. They argue that the area is unsuitable for permanent dwellings; therefore, because the intended purpose of the restrictions has ceased to exist, the covenants are no longer reasonable.

---

2. A camper is "a portable dwelling (as a specially equipped trailer or automotive vehicle) for use during casual travel and camping." Webster's New Collegiate Dictionary 158 (1980).

3. One of the campers is a self-propelled "motor home."

Ordinarily, residential restrictions are recognized as reasonable and valid, *Ault v. Shipley*, 189 Va. 69, 76, 52 S.E.2d 56, 59 (1949), and will be enforced in equity, *Renn v. Whitehurst*, 181 Va. 360, 366, 25 S.E.2d 276, 278–79 (1943). When a party seeks to defeat their enforcement on the ground of changed conditions in the neighborhood, he must prove that conditions in the whole neighborhood have changed so radically as to virtually destroy the essential purposes and objectives of the agreement. *Hening v. Maynard*, 227 Va. 113, 118, 313 S.E.2d 379, 382 (1984); *Ault*, 189 Va. at 76–77, 52 S.E.2d at 59; *Booker v. Old Dominion Land Co.*, 188 Va. 143, 148, 49 S.E.2d 314, 317 (1948); *Deitrick v. Leadbetter*, 175 Va. 170, 177, 8 S.E.2d 276, 279 (1940).

The record discloses only one change of condition in the subdivision since the restrictions were imposed. That change resulted from the County's adoption of an ordinance, as a protection against flood damage, which regulated elevation of structures to be built in the subdivision. However, this did not radically change the residential character of the neighborhood.

While the defendants correctly assert that the subdivision is primarily a recreational area, it was always recreational in nature. It is important to note, however, that in a subdivision containing only 19 lots, nine permanent houses have been built. Clearly, therefore, the area remains residential, as well as recreational, in character.

Finally, the possibility of flooding is no greater now than when the restrictions were imposed. We conclude that the record does not support a finding that there has been such a radical change of conditions in the neighborhood as would make the restrictions unreasonable. Thus, the court erred in this ruling.

Next, we consider whether the defendants violated the covenants. They contend that they did not because the restrictions do not exclude campers.

Restrictive covenants are not favored and must be construed strictly. Moreover, the party who seeks to enforce a restriction has the burden of proving that it proscribes the acts of which he complains. *Hening*, 227 Va. at 117, 313 S.E.2d at 381. Nevertheless, equity will enforce restrictions when they are reasonable and the intention of the parties is clear. *Id.*

We believe it is clear from a reading of both restrictions that the developer and his immediate grantees intended to exclude all types of temporary residences in the subdivision. Indeed, one restriction expressly prohibits "temporary dwellings of any kind whatsoever." Because campers are used as temporary residences, they fall within the prohibition. The mere fact that they have been used sparingly as living quarters is of little significance. More significantly, the campers are susceptible to residential use and, at times, have been so used.

In finding that the restrictions had not been violated, the trial court focused upon the word "erected" and concluded that the campers "are not erected or constructed on the lots," but are "easily movable." The same argument could be applied with equal force, however, to "house trailers" which are expressly prohibited by restriction Number One. We conclude that when the restrictions are read together, such a construction defeats the obvious purpose and objective contemplated by the parties, *i.e.*, to create a residential subdivision containing permanent, single-family dwellings.

We hold, therefore, that because the restrictions are reasonable and enforceable, and prohibit campers on the subdivision lots, the court erred in denying the injunction. Thus, we will reverse the decree of the trial court and remand the cause with directions that an injunction be entered consistent with the views expressed herein.

Reversed and Remanded.

Notes & Questions

1. *Destruction of essential purpose.* As provided in *Marks*, when a party seeks to defeat enforcement of a restrictive covenant on the ground of changed conditions, that party must prove that conditions in the whole neighborhood have changed "so radically as to virtually destroy the essential purposes and objectives" of the covenant in question. See also *Gladstone v. Gregory*, 596 P.2d 491 (1979) (holding that the underlying purpose of a restriction prohibiting construction of a second story addition was not fundamentally thwarted because appellant's view over respondent's home is of value to him and should be protected). A condition which thwarts the original purpose of a restriction may occur within or outside the subdivision. Generally, the source of the changed condition does not matter so long as the change frustrates the purpose of the restriction. See ROBERT G. NATELSON, LAW OF PROPERTY OWNERS ASSOCIATIONS, § 5.5.3 (1989). What are some examples of changed conditions that may release owners from commonly seen use restrictions? See, *e.g., Meyerland Community Improvement Ass'n v. Temple*, 700 S.W.2d 263 (Tex. App. 1985) (non-residential use permitted in some undeveloped parcels due to changes in surrounding area); *Deak v. Heathcote Ass'n*, 595 N.Y.S.2d 556 (N.Y. App. Div. 1993) (unit owner failed to show changed conditions to permit subdivision of his lot); *Gladstone v. Gregory*, 596 P.2d 491 (Nev. 1979).

2. *Commercial encroachments.* Subdivisions in which each lot is restricted to single family residence are frequently surrounded by commercial developments. When a developer buys lots in a subdivision and seeks to construct a commercial development, an interesting issue arises: can certain lots can be "released" from the restrictive covenants under the claims of changed conditions? However, where the residential character of the entire subdivision remains intact, individual lots will not be considered separate and apart from their relation to the entire development and will not be released from the residential restriction. See *Camelback Del Este Homeowners Ass'n v. Warner*, 749 P.2d 930 (Ariz. Ct. App. 1987) (only when the conditions have substantially changed in the subdivision will the court allow a commercial development to encroach the rights of homeowners living in that neighborhood).

5. Estoppel

Woodmoor Improvement Ass'n, Inc. v. Brenner
Court of Appeals of Colorado
919 P.2d 928 (Colo. Ct. App. 1996)

TAUBMAN, J. In this action by a homeowners' association to enforce a restrictive covenant prohibiting homeowners from having "outside aerials or antennas," plaintiff, Woodmoor Improvement Association (WIA), appeals the judgment of the trial court denying its request for injunctive relief and permitting defendants, Leonard I. and Mary Jane Brenner, to maintain a satellite dish antenna on their property. We affirm.

WIA is a non-profit corporation formed for the purpose of ensuring the value of some 2,500 lots in the Woodmoor subdivision through the enforcement of recorded restrictive covenants. Article V, § 10 of the covenants states that: "Outside aerials or antennas are not permitted."

In 1990, the Brenners sought and received approval from WIA's Architectural Control Committee (the Committee) for the construction of a new home with an adjacent satellite dish. The plan and specifications submitted by the Brenners and considered by the Committee clearly indicated that a satellite dish would be situated next to their new home. The Brenners also presented a three-dimensional model of their new home that included a model of the satellite dish and a surrounding wall intended to screen it from the view of passersby.

As conditions to its approval of the building of the satellite dish, the Committee required that the Brenners obscure it from view by surrounding it with a fence or wall and also required that the satellite dish and fence be painted the same color as the house.

Following this approval, the Brenners began construction of their new home. They spent approximately $26,000 for the satellite dish and a sophisticated home entertainment system and spent approximately $4,000 for the fence to enclose the satellite dish.

A monitor appointed by the Committee oversaw the installation of the satellite dish and its accompanying fence and, early in 1993, certified to the WIA board that the satellite dish and surrounding fence had been installed in conformance with the Committee's criteria for approval.

Although a decision of the Committee approving building plans and specifications may be appealed to the Board of Directors of WIA by a member homeowner, no appeals were filed. In 1992, however, when the members of the Committee that had originally approved the Brenner satellite dish were replaced, a new board sought to enforce the covenant prohibiting outside aerials or antennas and requested that the Brenners remove their satellite dish.

When the Brenners refused to do so, WIA brought suit seeking a permanent injunction to prohibit them from maintaining the satellite dish. Following a trial to the court, the court concluded that the Brenners' satellite dish was an aerial or antenna generally prohibited by the covenants, but nevertheless held that WIA was equitably estopped from enforcing that covenant provision against the Brenners. This appeal followed.

I. Architectural Control Committee Authority to Approve Satellite Dish

WIA contends that the Committee lacked authority to approve the Brenners' plans for a satellite dish and, therefore, the Committee's 1990 approval of the Brenners' plans to install a satellite dish must be set aside. We disagree.

Relying on *Stratford v. Littlehorn*, 635 P.2d 910 (Colo. App. 1981), *rev'd* on other grounds, 653 P.2d 1139 (Colo. 1982), and *Wilson v. Goldman*, 699 P.2d 420 (Colo. App. 1985), WIA argues that the Committee had no authority to grant an exception to the express provisions of the covenants. It maintains that because the covenants plainly prohibit "outside aerials or antennas," a term that in its view included satellite dishes, the Committee acted in excess of its authority in 1990 by approving the Brenners' plans for installation of a satellite dish.

In our view, both *Stratford* and *Wilson* are distinguishable. In *Stratford*, the protective covenants of a subdivision prohibited used structures from being moved onto any lot. The architectural control committee of that subdivision nevertheless granted an exception to the express provisions of the covenants. A division of this court concluded that because the covenants at issue were clear, they should have been enforced as written to prohibit residents from moving an older home onto their property.

Here, by contrast, there was a dispute concerning the interpretation of the restrictive covenant that prohibited outside aerials or antennas. Although WIA contends that the meaning of this restrictive covenant is clear, and that it clearly applies to satellite dishes, the Brenners take the opposite view. They have at all times argued that, inasmuch as satellite dishes were not in existence when this covenant was promulgated in 1971, the restrictive covenant at issue does not apply to such devices.

The Brenners presented testimony at trial that members of the Committee had interpreted the covenant at issue to apply only to rooftop aerials or antennas, and not to satellite dishes. Satellite dishes, they contend, were otherwise permitted, subject to additional covenant provisions that required unsightly additions or structures to be screened from public view.

Accordingly, this is not a case where an architectural control committee granted an exception to an unambiguous provision of a covenant. Rather, the Committee was simply interpreting the covenant in favor of the Brenners based upon conflicting interpretations of it.

Wilson is also distinguishable. There, restrictive covenants prohibited fences from being erected around any homeowner's lot. The defendant in that case nevertheless built a fence around his property based on the verbal assurances of only one member of the architectural control committee. An immediate appeal was brought against the defendant by several homeowners and the committee as a whole.

Here, by contrast, the Brenners gained official approval for the satellite dish from the committee as a whole. Also, the record reveals that no appeal was brought against the Brenners until two years after placement of the satellite dish had been approved. Thus, we disagree with WIA and conclude that both *Stratford* and *Wilson* are distinguishable from the facts of the instant case.

II. Equitable Estoppel

WIA next contends that the trial court erred in concluding that it was equitably estopped from applying the covenant regarding outside aerials and antennas to the Brenners. Specifically, it asserts that equitable estoppel does not apply; that, in the alternative, the reliance element of the equitable estoppel test was not met; and finally, that there can be no governmental estoppel as a matter of law. We are not persuaded by any of these contentions.

A.

WIA first asserts that the principles of equitable estoppel do not apply when there is a clear violation of the covenants. We do not agree.

Generally, protective covenants that are clear on their face must be enforced as written. However, equity may fashion a remedy to effect justice suitable to the circumstances of the case. *Wilson v. Goldman, supra.*

The elements of estoppel as they relate to the right to enforce a covenant are full knowledge of the facts, unreasonable delay in the assertion of an available remedy, and intervening reliance by and prejudice to another. *Barker v. Jeremiasen,* 676 P.2d 1259 (Colo. App. 1984).

Further, the doctrine of equitable estoppel may be applied to preclude enforcement by the architectural control committee of a homeowners' association of a restrictive covenant which inures to the benefit of all lot owners in the subdivision. In such case, application of the doctrine requires that the property owner reasonably rely on the actions or representations of the architectural control committee. *First Hyland Greens Ass'n v. Griffith,* 618 P.2d 745 (Colo. App. 1980).

Although WIA argues that *Stratford v. Littlehorn, supra,* and *Wilson v. Goldman, supra,* must control, we have already determined above that those cases are distinguishable from the instant case. Also, because *Stratford* was not decided on the basis of equitable estoppel, it does not preclude application of that doctrine here.

Moreover, even if the Committee's approval of the satellite dish did violate an express provision of the covenants, the principles of equitable estoppel would still apply to the facts of this case. *See Wilson v. Goldman, supra* (violations of restrictive covenants may give way to equitable considerations); *Hargreaves v. Skrbina*, 662 P.2d 1078 (Colo. 1983) (equitable considerations may excuse zoning violations).

Here, the trial court concluded that the Brenners relied on the representations of the Committee to their detriment, that such reliance was reasonable, and that, therefore, WIA was equitably estopped from asserting a violation of the covenants in regard to the satellite dish. These conclusions are amply supported by the record.

The Brenners testified that they spent some $30,000 to install their satellite dish and home entertainment system in express reliance on the Committee's approval of their plans. Subsequently, the Committee's monitor approved the manner in which the satellite dish had been installed. No appeal was taken to the WIA board from the decision of the Committee. Under these circumstances, reliance by the Brenners was reasonable.

Thus, the trial court properly concluded that WIA could be equitably estopped from enforcing its restrictive covenant.

B.

WIA, however, argues that even if the doctrine of equitable estoppel is applicable here and even if the Brenners detrimentally relied on the Committee's approval by paying for a new satellite dish and home entertainment system, the Brenners still did not satisfy the reliance element of the estoppel doctrine.

More specifically, WIA asserts that sufficient reliance for estoppel exists only when a homeowner's action is taken with full knowledge that it both violates the covenants and will not be enforced. Thus, WIA maintains that inasmuch as the Brenners consistently asserted that satellite dishes did not violate the covenants, they could not have reasonably relied on any actions of the Committee. We are not persuaded by this argument.

Barker v. Jeremiasen, supra, upon which WIA relies, is distinguishable from the instant case. There, the court held that the defendants did not establish detrimental reliance by constructing buildings in connection with a horse breeding operation because they believed that such buildings were consistent with the restrictive covenants at issue there. Here, however, the Brenners relied not simply on their own interpretation of a restrictive covenant, but also on the interpretation that was formally approved by the Committee.

Thus, under the circumstances presented here, we conclude that the Brenners adequately demonstrated detrimental reliance in support of their claim of equitable estoppel.

C.

Next, WIA argues that because homeowner associations have been given much of the governing power of a city and estoppel does not lie against a city based on an *ultra vires* act by it, there can be no finding of estoppel against WIA. We disagree.

WIA bases its assertion that homeowner associations have been given much of the governing power of a city on the Colorado Common Interest Ownership Act, § 38-33.3-101, *et seq.*, C.R.S. (1995 Cum. Supp.). That act establishes a comprehensive and uniform framework for the creation and operation of homeowner associations. Nevertheless, WIA cites no authority, and we are aware of none, that supports the proposition that enactment of a legislative scheme governing the operation of homeowners' associations thereby transforms such homeowners' associations into cities or other governmental entities.

Thus, even if we assume that the doctrine of estoppel does not lie against a city or other governmental entity based on its *ultra vires* act, the doctrine of equitable estoppel may be asserted against a homeowners' association.

III.

Finally, WIA contends that because Leonard Brenner served as a director of the WIA board, he breached his fiduciary duty to WIA, a nonprofit corporation, by seeking approval for the satellite dish. We do not agree.

...

Judgment affirmed.

Notes & Questions

1. *Equitable estoppel requirements.* As *Woodmoor Improvement Ass'n, Inc.* states, "the elements of estoppel as they relate to the right to enforce a covenant are full knowledge of the facts, unreasonable delay in the assertion of an available remedy, and intervening reliance by and prejudice to another." Note, however, that where a community association makes specific complaints about a covenant violation, even without taking substantive actions to enforce further, the defense of equitable estoppel may not likely succeed. See *Barker v. Jeremiasen*, 676 P.2d 1259 (Colo. App. 1984). See also *Englewood Golf, Inc. v. Englewood Golf Condo. Villas Ass'n, Inc.*, 547 So. 2d 1050 (Fla. Dist. Ct. App. 1989) (developer not estopped from enforcing its maintenance rights even though association previously assumed responsibility for it); *Knight v. City of Albuquerque*, 794 P.2d 739 (N.M. 1990) (developer estopped from developing property for any use except as a golf course since it designated such use on a plat); and *Armbrust v. Golden*, 594 So. 2d 64 (Ala. 1992) (residents who operated service business from their home were not estopped from enforcing residential covenant against another homeowner whose business was noticeable to passersby).

2. *Prejudicial delay.* As examined in *Woodmoor Improvement Ass'n*, the doctrine of equitable estoppel involves not merely an unreasonable delay in seeking relief but a delay which is relied upon and prejudices another. A delay is prejudicial if it causes the defendant economic harm or prevents the defendant from taking steps to protect himself from additional economic harm. See *Manor Vail Condo. Ass'n v. Town of Vail*, 604 P.2d 1168 (Colo. 1980); *Fifty-Six Sixty Collins Ave. Condo. Inc. v. Dawson*, 354 So. 2d 432 (Fla. Dist. Ct. App. 1978) (association estopped from denying unit owner the right to install shutters as they had been previously approved); *Plaza Del Prado Condo. Ass'n, Inc. v. Richman*, 345 So. 2d 851 (Fla. Dist. Ct. App. 1977) (association estopped from enforcing covenant after waiting one year from violation to assert claim); *Rabon v. Mali*, 344 S.E. 2d 607 (S.C. 1986) (homeowners estopped from enforcing residential covenant since business had been ongoing for some time); *Reynolds v. Four Seasons Condo. Ass'n, Inc.*, 462 So. 2d 738 (Ala. Civ. App. 1984) (condominium board waited too long to enforce enclosure built over one year earlier). What happens when a violation is initially known to occur but the extent or severity of the violation is not known until after completion of the improvement? In other words, a "minor" violation may have been permissible or acceptable, but a subsequent "major" violation is not?

3. *City-state argument.* It is interesting that *Woodmoor Improvement Ass'n* is one of the few cases in which a community association sought to equate itself with a governmental

unit of the state. In this case, Woodmoor Improvement Association asserted that such a status arose out of the Colorado Common Interest Ownership Act—an argument the court summarily rejected. However, why might such an argument be unwise for a community association (*i.e.,* opening Pandora's Box)? Refer to our earlier discussion in Chapter 4 regarding state action and other constitutional issues.

6. Statute of Limitations

Cutujian v. Benedict Hills Estates Ass'n

Court of Appeal of California
49 Cal. Rptr. 2d 166 (Cal. Ct. App. 1996)

CROSKEY, J. In these consolidated appeals, Eric K. Cutujian appeals from a judgment of dismissal after the sustaining without leave to amend of a demurrer to his third amended complaint for nuisance, and from an order after judgment awarding $30,000 in attorney fees, plus costs, to the defendant, Benedict Hills Estates Association (the Association). The trial court's order was based on the conclusion that Cutujian's complaint had not been filed within the relevant statutory period.

However, we conclude that the gravamen of Cutujian's claim is based on the Association's violation of a covenant running with the land and the statute of limitations did not commence to run until April of 1988 when Cutujian made a demand for performance under the covenant. Since Cutujian filed his complaint less than two years later, his action is timely and was improperly dismissed. We therefore reverse both the judgment and the award of attorney fees and costs.

FACTUAL AND PROCEDURAL BACKGROUND

In 1988, Cutujian and his brother jointly purchased a partially improved residential lot in Benedict Hills Estates (hereafter, BHE), a common interest residential development in the County of Los Angeles, located between the cities of Beverly Hills and Los Angeles. The development was subject to a recorded declaration of conditions, covenants and restrictions (CCRs) and was governed by the Association. Among the Association's duties under the CCRs is the maintenance of natural and manmade slopes and corresponding drainage ditches both in the common areas and within individual lots.

BHE was originated in 1976, when the first developer subdivided and graded 229 building pads on 2 tracts of real property located south of Mulholland Drive and east of Benedict Canyon in the County of Los Angeles. The Association was formed shortly after the development began; the CCRs were recorded on January 21, 1976. At the time this action commenced, residences had been built on approximately 90 percent of the 229 lots.

Sometime between 1976 and 1978, a surface slump occurred on the fill slope in the lot which later was purchased by Cutujian. From that time until Cutujian purchased the lot, the lot remained vacant, and no owner attempted to build on it.

Cutujian purchased his lot, located at 3226 Hutton Drive, in early 1988 from Kathleen McCarthy, who apparently purchased it from one of the developers. On April 4, 1988, while escrow was pending, Cutujian demanded that the Association repair the damage to the slope on his lot, as required by the CCRs. The Association did not positively refuse to repair the slump, but stated it believed the slump could be repaired for approximately $3,000, a cost which Cutujian believed to be unrealistically low. After several discussions of costs and the feasibility of repairing the slump at any particular cost,

Cutujian concluded the Association was not going to do the repair. He therefore proceeded to have the slump repaired at his own expense and thereafter initiated the present action to recover his costs.

Cutujian filed his original complaint on August 8, 1989. After the sustaining of a demurrer, Cutujian filed a first amended complaint, and thereafter, upon stipulation by the parties, he filed a second amended complaint on April 29, 1992.

The second amended complaint sought damages against the Association for (1) breach of the CCRs which govern BHE; and (2) negligence. On November 9, 1993, the Association moved for summary judgment, alleging Cutujian's action was barred by the statute of limitations.

While the motion for summary judgment was pending, Cutujian successfully sought leave of the court to file a third amended complaint. In the third amended complaint, Cutujian recast his action as one for damages for a continuing nuisance arising from violation of an equitable servitude, but he pled essentially the same facts as were pled in previous pleadings. The Association demurred, again raising the statute of limitations.

The trial court found the action was barred by the statute of limitations and sustained the demurrer to the third amended complaint without leave to amend. A judgment of dismissal was entered on March 17, 1994. The trial court thereafter awarded costs and attorney fees to the Association as the prevailing party in the action. These timely appeals followed.

CONTENTIONS ON APPEAL

Cutujian contends that: (1) his third amended complaint was for a continuing nuisance, not for breach of a written instrument; (2) his claim for damages was filed within the time allowed for an action for continuing nuisance; (3) even if his claim is in truth a claim for breach of a written instrument, it is nevertheless timely, because the instrument created covenants running with the land;[1] (4) his claims cannot in fairness be affected by the inaction of his predecessors in interest; (5) the trial court awarded excessive and unauthorized attorney fees to the Association.

DISCUSSION

. . .

2. Commencement of Statute of Limitations for Enforcement of Covenant in Recorded CCRs

Cutujian contends the trial court erred in finding his action time-barred, because the surface slump on his property was a continuing nuisance which the Association had a duty to abate, pursuant to the CCRs. The Association contends that (1) Cutujian was bound by admissions, which Cutujian made in previous pleadings, that the surface slump at 3226 Hutton Drive occurred between 1976 and 1978; (2) the slump was not an abatable nuisance; and (3) consequently, Cutujian's action is barred by the three-year statute of limitations governing an action for permanent nuisance. (*Cf. Spar v. Pacific Bell* (1991) 235 Cal.App.3d 1480, 1485 [1 Cal.Rptr.2d 480].) In the alternative, the Association argues

---

1. This contention was raised for the first time in a supplemental letter brief, filed after arguments at the request of this court. In pre-argument briefing, the parties focused only upon the question of whether Cutujian stated a cause of action for a continuing nuisance. However, at the time of oral argument, the court questioned both parties as to the significance of certain authorities, discovered through the court's independent research, which suggested that the facts alleged in Cutujian's complaint might constitute a valid and timely cause of action for breach of the CCRs. In response to such questioning, both parties requested and were granted leave to address the court's questions by way of supplemental letter briefs. Such supplemental briefing has been received and considered.

that Cutujian's third amended complaint was a sham pleading, filed in order to avoid the effect of his previous admissions, which the Association contends conclusively established that the action was barred by the four-year statute of limitations for actions on a written instrument (Code Civ. Proc., § 337) or the three-year statute of limitations for injury to real property (Code Civ. Proc., § 338, subd. (b)).

As we shall explain, we conclude the statute of limitations to enforce the disputed provision of the CCRs began to run in 1988, when Cutujian demanded that the Association fulfill its obligation to repair the slope damage at 3226 Hutton Drive. Consequently, we do not find Cutujian's action to be time-barred.

Unless they are unreasonable, the CCRs in the declaration governing a common interest development may be enforced as equitable servitudes and as covenants running with the land. (Civ. Code, § 1354, subd. (a), 1460 *et seq.*; *Nahrstedt v. Lakeside Village Condominium Assn.* (1994) 8 Cal.4th 361, 375–376 [33 Cal.Rptr.2d 63, 878 P.2d 1275].) The CCRs benefit and bind the owners of all separate interests in the project. (Civ. Code, § 1354, subd. (a).) Unless the declaration provides otherwise, CCRs may be enforced by any owner of a separate interest, by the association or by both. (Civ. Code, § 1354, 1460 *et seq.*; *Nahrstedt v. Lakeside Village Condominium Assn., supra*, 8 Cal.4th at pp. 375–376; *Franklin v. Marie Antoinette Condominium Owners Assn.* (1993) 19 Cal.App.4th 824, 832, fn.11 [23 Cal.Rptr.2d 744]; *see generally*, Sproul & Rosenberry, Advising Cal. Condominium and Homeowners Associations (Cont.Ed.Bar 1991) § 6.43, p. 297; 4 Witkin, *Summary of Cal. Law* (9th ed. 1987) Real Property, § 328, p. 529.) A party who is damaged by a violation of the CCRs may seek money damages. (*Mackinder v. OSCA Development Co.* (1984) 151 Cal.App.3d 728, 737 [198 Cal.Rptr. 864]; *see generally*, Sproul & Rosenberry, Advising Cal. Condominium and Homeowners Associations, *supra*, § 7.37, p. 347.) The statute of limitations for such an action is that for an action arising from a written instrument and is four years. (Code Civ. Proc., § 337.)

The issue in this case is not what statute of limitations applies to Cutujian's action, but when the statute of limitations commenced to run. No California statute or judicial decision directly addresses either the question of when the statute commences for an action to enforce CCRs, or the more general question of when the statute commences for enforcement of a covenant running with the land which requires the performance of an affirmative act. As we have observed above, CCRs are enforceable as covenants running with the land. (*Nahrstedt v. Lakeside Village Condominium Assn., supra*, 8 Cal.4th at pp. 375–376; *Franklin v. Marie Antoinette Condominium Owners Assn., supra*, 19 Cal.App.4th at p. 832, fn. 11.) Courts in other jurisdictions have addressed the question of when the statute of limitations commences for enforcement of such covenants. These courts have generally concluded that the statute does not commence until there is a demand for performance. (*See, e.g., Scherpenseel v. Bitney* (1993) 263 Mont. 68 [865 P.2d 1145, 1150]; *Louisville & Nashville R. Co. v. Pierce* (1950) 313 Ky. 189, 195 [230 S.W.2d 430, 17 A.L.R.2d 1244]; *Parks v. Hines* (1934, Tex.Civ.App.) 68 S.W.2d 364, 367–368, *affd.* by 128 Tex. 289 [96 S.W.2d 970, 973].) Some courts have required that the demand be made within a reasonable time. (*See, e.g., Hustina v. Grand Trunk Western R. Co.* (1942) 303 Mich. 581 [6 N.W.2d 902, 905]; *Whitney v. Cheshire R. Co.* (1911) 210 Mass. 263 [96 N.E. 676, 679].) Some courts have enforced affirmative covenants without discussion of demand on the theory that there was a continuous breach so that a new cause of action arose from day to day as long as the covenant was not performed. (*See, e.g., Carnegie Realty Co. v. Carolina C&O Ry. Co.* (1916) 136 Tenn. 300 [189 S.W. 371, 373]; *Atlanta K. & N. Ry. Co. v. McKinney* (1906) 124 Ga. 929 [53 S.E. 701, 704].)

In *Scherpenseel v. Bitney, supra*, 865 P.2d 1145, the single recent case of which we are aware which discusses the commencement of the statute of limitations to enforce an affirmative covenant running with the land, the Montana Supreme Court analyzed the few existing cases on the subject. The court observed, as have we, that previous cases have taken three separate approaches: (1) holding that the statute commences upon an actual demand for performance; (2) holding that the statute commences upon a demand for performance, but requiring that the demand be made within a reasonable time; (3) holding that, whether or not there is a demand for performance, there is a continuing breach for as long as the duty is not performed, so that a new cause of action arises from day to day. (865 P.2d at p. 1149.)

The action in *Scherpenseel* was an action by a purchaser of real property to enforce a developer's covenant to dedicate and construct a road on the property, and the county's duty to accept and maintain the road. (865 P.2d at p. 1146–1147.) In that context, the Montana Supreme Court concluded the better rule required that the eight-year statute of limitations to enforce an affirmative covenant running with the land commence when the plaintiffs demanded construction of the road, although the covenant was made more than eight years before the demand. (*Id.* at pp. 1149–1150.)

One California decision, *Strosnider v. Pomin* (1942) 52 Cal.App.2d 745 [126 P.2d 915], impliedly adopted this same rule. In *Strosnider*, the Pomins conveyed certain land to Strosnider's predecessor in interest in 1913. By a separate agreement, the Pomins (1) conveyed an easement for a 40-foot right of way over land which they retained, (2) affirmatively covenanted to open and maintain a road over the burdened property along the right-of-way, and (3) covenanted to deed, upon demand, an additional small triangular parcel. (52 Cal.App.2d at p. 746.) From 1913 until nearly the time of the lawsuit, the road was not built; indeed, from time to time, the Pomins erected buildings which encroached upon the right-of-way. However, in 1923, as promised, the Pomins conveyed the triangular parcel, and included in the deed the promised right-of-way, "'to be used in common by the parties hereto, and their heirs, executors and assigns.'" (*Id.* at pp. 746–747.) In addition, in 1937, a son and heir of the Pomins, Ernest Pomin, made an oral promise to Strosnider, who by then had acquired the property, to perform the covenant to open and improve the promised road if Strosnider would dismiss a quiet title action which he had filed respecting the easement. (*Id.* at p. 747.)

Ernest did, in fact, remove the encroachments from the right-of-way and improve and open the road. However, he later erected a fence across the road and refused to allow Strosnider to pass. When Strosnider sued, Ernest raised, among other defenses, the statute of limitations. (52 Cal.App.2d at pp. 747–748.) The court concluded the easement and right to a road had not been extinguished by the failure of Strosnider and his predecessors to (1) use the easement, (2) object to the construction of encroachments on the easement, or (3) demand construction of the road for many years after the original agreement. The court considered the 1923 deed to be evidence that the Pomins acknowledged the easement holder's right to demand the road when a need for it arose. The court observed that the road had apparently not become necessary until shortly before the dispute arose. Where demand for the road was made at that time, and suit was commenced within the allowed time after the demand, the lawsuit was not barred by the statute of limitations. (*Id.* at pp. 749–750.)

Here, the CCRs governing BHE common interest development stated that they would "run with the Property and Additions" and would be binding "upon all parties having or acquiring any right, title or interest in the Property Additions...." The CCRs imposed upon the Association an affirmative duty to maintain the slope areas in the development in a neat and safe condition, a duty which included "the repair and replacement of landscaping and improvements when necessary or appropriate...." It would seem to go without saying that repair of the building pad on the 3226 Hutton Drive lot was not "necessary or appropriate" until a purchaser of the lot actually was ready to build a residence. The pad was damaged, apparently by rainfall, before any purchaser was ready to build. Indeed, over 10 years passed before any owner seriously commenced construction. During all of that time, the Association had a duty to repair the building pad. However, there was little sense in doing so at times when no construction was planned. Nor was there any demand that the damaged pad be repaired. However, immediately upon purchasing the lot with an intent to build—indeed, while escrow was pending—Cutujian observed the damage to the building pad and demanded that it be repaired in accordance with the CCRs.

We believe that the most reasonable rule of law is the one adopted by the Montana Supreme Court in *Scherpenseel v. Bitney, supra,* 865 P.2d 1145, that the statute of limitations to enforce affirmative covenants running with the land, and, in particular, duties included in a declaration of CCRs, commences when a demand for performance is made. Under this rule, Cutujian's lawsuit was timely.

The purpose of statutes of limitation is to promote justice by preventing surprises through the revival of claims that have been allowed to slumber until evidence has been lost, memories have faded, and witnesses have disappeared. (*Telegraphers v. Ry. Express Agency* (1944) 321 U.S. 342, 348 [88 L.Ed. 788, 792, 64 S.Ct. 582].) The theory is that even if one has a just claim it is unjust not to put the adversary on notice to defend within the period of limitation, and the right to be free of stale claims in time comes to prevail over the right to prosecute them. (*Ibid.*) The sound policies underlying statutes of limitation are not circumvented where, as here: (1) the defendant was at all times under an affirmative duty created by a recorded declaration of CCRs; (2) the duty was expressly defined as arising "when necessary or appropriate"; (3) immediately after performance of the duty became necessary, by reason of a lot owner's intent to begin construction of a residence, the lot owner demanded performance; and (4) the defendant, with knowledge of its duty, failed to perform it.

Indeed, if the statute of limitations did commence between 1976 and 1978, and did run by 1982, as the Association argues, the result would certainly be unjust to Cutujian; during that entire time, the Association's Board was controlled by the developers of BHE, one of whom was Cutujian's predecessor in interest, Jerry Oren, or one of Oren's companies. With knowledge of the slump and the need to repair it, and while he was represented on the Association's board, Oren determined not to repair the slump or demand that the Association repair it. Under these circumstances, Cutujian rightly contends it would be unfair if Oren's inaction could foreclose Cutujian's right to performance of the Association's duties. We thus conclude it was when Cutujian demanded that the slope failure on his property be repaired, and the Association failed to comply with the demand, that the statute of limitations began to run for commencement of action for breach of the covenant to repair.

Cutujian commenced this action in August of 1989, well within four years from the date of his demand for performance. The action was thus commenced within the limitation of time in which to file an action to enforce provisions of a declaration of CCRs.

Although we have reached this conclusion on appeal, Cutujian himself was apparently not confident during the proceedings below that his action was timely. Consequently, before the trial court ruled on the Association's motion for summary judgment, Cutujian recast his cause of action for breach of the CCRs as one for a continuing nuisance.[2] He

---

2. The Association contends that by this modification Cutujian abandoned any claim based on a breach of the CCRs and thus has waived any right to replead that claim. We summarily reject this argument. The gravamen of Cutujian's cause of action, however labeled, is based upon the violation by the Association of the duties imposed upon it by the CCRs. The essential facts underlying that claim have been repeatedly alleged in each of the Cutujian's several pleadings. (See generally, *Bay Cities Paving & Grading, Inc. v. Lawyers' Mutual Ins. Co.* (1993) 5 Cal.4th 854, 860 [21 Cal.Rptr.2d 691, 855 P.2d 1263].) In any event, in light of our conclusion regarding the commencement of the statute of

must be given an opportunity to amend his complaint to reinstate the cause of action for breach of the CCRs. (*Leibert v. Transworld Systems, Inc., supra,* 32 Cal.App.4th at p. 1701.)[3]

3. Action for Continuing Nuisance

It is settled that where conduct which violates a duty owed to another also interferes with that party's free use and enjoyment of his property, nuisance liability arises. (Civ. Code, § 3479; *Lussier v. San Lorenzo Valley Water Dist.* (1988) 206 Cal.App.3d 92, 100 [253 Cal.Rptr. 470].) Under this definition of nuisance, the Association's violation of its duty to Cutujian under the CCRs gave rise to liability for the nuisance caused by the slump, which plainly interfered with Cutujian's use of the land. Moreover, the CCRs governing BHE provide that any violation of a duty created by the CCRs will give rise to an action for nuisance. It also appears that the nuisance was abatable, inasmuch as Cutujian was able to abate it. Consequently, it can reasonably be deemed a continuing nuisance for which a new cause of action arises each day on which the nuisance continues. (*Phillips v. City of Pasadena* (1945) 27 Cal.2d 104, 107–108 [162 P.2d 625]; *Mangini v. Aerojet-General Corp.* (1991) 230 Cal.App.3d 1125, 1142–1145 [281 Cal.Rptr. 827].)

Under the above principles, it would appear Cutujian has stated a timely and viable cause of action for a continuing nuisance. As a practical matter, this cause of action is identical to a cause of action for breach of an affirmative covenant running with the land, brought under the theory that breach of such a covenant is a continuous breach giving rise to a new cause of action from day to day as long as the covenant is not performed. Cutujian's nuisance cause of action is thus essentially redundant in view of our conclusion that his cause of action for breach of the CCRs was timely.[4]

. . .

DISPOSITION

The judgment of dismissal and the postjudgment order awarding attorney fees are reversed. The matter is remanded for further proceedings consistent with the views in this opinion. Costs on appeal are awarded to Cutujian.

---

limitations, the Association is not in any way prejudiced by Cutujian's reassertion of his claim based on a violation of the CCRs.

3. When Cutujian filed his supplemental letter brief on October 27, 1995, he attached a proposed fourth amended complaint which alleges the Association violated the CCRs and failed to correct an ongoing and continuing nuisance, in that: (1) the CCRs governing BHE require the Association to maintain the slopes in the development; (2) sometime prior to 1980, a surface slump occurred on property that was subsequently purchased by Cutujian; (3) in 1988, when Cutujian purchased the lot, he demanded that the slump be repaired; and (4) the Association failed and refused to repair the slump. Cutujian had the burden on appeal of establishing that his complaint can be amended to state a cause of action. (*Careau & Co. v. Security Pacific Business Credit, Inc.* (1990) 222 Cal.App.3d 1371, 1386 [272 Cal.Rptr. 387].) The proposed amended complaint sufficiently meets this burden.

4. In addition to its arguments on the main issues in this appeal, the Association raises the following three contentions: (1) the Association's failure to repair the slump caused Cutujian no damage, as he paid a lower price for his lot than would have been demanded, had it not been for the slump; (2) the Association had no duty to repair the slump, as it resulted from an act of God and was thus subject to an exculpatory clause in the CCRs; (3) Cutujian's complaint was subject to demurrer, because he failed to allege facts establishing his standing to sue. The Association's arguments regarding Cutujian's standing to sue and the application of the exculpatory clause in the CCRs are not properly before us, as neither was addressed by the trial court. Indeed, the Association concedes it did not even raise the issue of the exculpatory clause in the trial court. The Association's argument that Cutujian has been fully compensated for any costs which he incurred in repairing the slump is also not properly before us, because it goes to the issue of damages and cannot be resolved at the pleadings stage of the action. We emphasize that our ruling in this case is limited to resolving the dispute over the statute of limitations. We express no view on the merits of the action.

Notes & Question

In finding that Cutujian's claim for a continuing nuisance was redundant to his other claim for a violation of the declaration, the court stated that a cause of action would arise on every day that the nuisance continued (in this case, every day the damage was not repaired by the association). In lieu of its adoption of the Montana rule (that a cause of action only arises when a demand for performance is made), does the court's finding regarding the continuing nuisance claim leave uncertainty over the ultimate issue of when the California four-year statute begins to run? If a homeowner fails to file a lawsuit within four years of his initial demand to the association for repair, may the homeowner still claim a continuing nuisance at anytime thereafter so long as the association continues to violate its duty to repair under the declaration?

Problem

JoAnn wants to build a fence along her front yard line. She has thick hedges on each side, and this fence will well serve to make the yard "child escape proof." The trouble is that the CCRs say no fences. But there are fences scattered throughout the community. While most fences are on rear yards, the developer had permitted some front fences as well. Now that the homeowners are in control of the association, the board has said no fences.

"Can they do this to me?" JoAnn asks you, her attorney friend. How do you advise her? She then tells you of all of the children in the community. "It was not that way before," she explains. Does that matter?

E. Attorneys Fees

Attorneys fees generally are recoverable in assessment collection efforts only if specific authority exists under state statute or if the association covenants establish such a right. However, a number of state statutes expressly provide for the recovery of attorneys fees in assessment collection efforts and those attorneys fees which sometimes may be the reasonable fees actually incurred, rather than being limited to a fixed percentage of the assessment amount due.

In an appropriate case, judgment may be obtained for all costs of collection, including attorneys fees incurred up to the time of the judgment, even when the attorneys fees exceed the original principal amount owed.

Nottingdale Homeowners' Ass'n v. Darby

Supreme Court of Ohio
514 N.E.2d 702 (Ohio 1987)

DOUGLAS, J. This is a case of first impression requiring us to determine whether two parties, in a non-commercial transaction, may lawfully contract to require, in a suit between them, the payment by the unsuccessful party of the prevailing party's attorney fees. We hold that they may do so and, accordingly, reverse the decision of the court of appeals.

A majority of state supreme courts currently recognize and follow the "American Rule" regarding the recovery of attorney fees by the prevailing party in a civil action. This rule provides "that attorneys' fees are not ordinarily recoverable in the absence of a statute *or enforceable contract providing therefor.*" (Emphasis added.) *Fleischmann Distilling Corp. v. Maier Brewing Co.* (1967), 386 U.S. 714, 717, 87 S.Ct. 1404, 1406, 18 L.Ed.2d 475. *See, also, Alyeska Pipeline Service Co. v. Wilderness Society* (1975), 421 U.S. 240, 257, 95 S.Ct. 1612, 1621, 44 L.Ed.2d 141, and Comment d to Section 356 of the Restatement of the Law 2d, Contracts (1981) 160, which provides in part: "Although attorneys' fees are not generally awarded to the winning party, if the parties provide for the award of such fees the court will award a sum that it considers to be reasonable."

Contrary to this majority position, appellees argue, and the court of appeals found, that in Ohio attorney fees are not to be awarded to a successful litigant absent statutory authorization or bad faith by the unsuccessful litigant. In support of their contention that "fee-shifting" agreements are unenforceable in this state, appellees cite case law which stands for the proposition that attorney fees are not taxable as costs against an unsuccessful litigant in the absence of statute. In so doing, appellees ask us to ignore the facts of this case and stand the law of contracts on its proverbial head. We decline to do so.

Appellees rely upon the following cases for support: *State, ex rel. Kabatek, v. Stackhouse* (1983), 6 Ohio St.3d 55, 6 OBR 73, 451 N.E.2d 248; *State, ex rel. Grosser, v. Boy* (1976), 46 Ohio St.2d 184, 75 O.O.2d 228, 347 N.E.2d 539; and *Sorin v. Bd. of Edn.* (1976), 46 Ohio St.2d 177, 75 O.O.2d 224, 347 N.E.2d 527. None of these cases, however, supports the conclusion that parties may not contract under circumstances like those of this case for the payment of attorney fees.

...

As further support for their position, appellees cite *Coe v. Columbus, Piqua & Indiana Ry. Co.* (1859), 10 Ohio St. 372; *Gates v. Toledo* (1897), 57 Ohio St. 105, 48 N.E. 500; and *Miller v. Kyle* (1911), 85 Ohio St. 186, 97 N.E. 372. We find appellees' reliance upon these cases equally misplaced.

...

Appellees, absent any showing of misunderstanding, deception or duress, ask us to disregard the explicit terms of the condominium declaration and condominium by-laws by which they agreed to be bound. As shown above, the law in Ohio does not compel such a result nor are we prompted by appellees' arguments to institute such a rule.

It has long been recognized that persons have a fundamental right to contract freely with the expectation that the terms of the contract will be enforced. This freedom "is as fundamental to our society as the right to write and to speak without restraint." *Blount v. Smith* (1967), 12 Ohio St.2d 41, 47, 41 O.O.2d 250, 253, 231 N.E.2d 301, 305. Government interference with this right must therefore be restricted to those exceptional cases where intrusion is absolutely necessary, such as contracts promoting illegal acts. No such necessity exists in this case.

Appellees, when they purchased a unit in Nottingdale Condominium, freely agreed to be bound by the terms of the condominium declaration. The declaration provides that in any action for foreclosure or to collect delinquent assessments, reasonable attorney fees incurred by the homeowners' association shall be paid by the defaulting unit owner. The matter which prompted this litigation was appellees' continued refusal to pay the monthly sum required of each unit owner for necessary services. While refusing each month to pay the amount due, appellees continued to accept the benefit of these services, including snow removal, trash collection, lawn care, exterior painting, water service, and payment of liability insurance. These services were enjoyed by appellees at the expense of their neighbors, fellow unit owners who faithfully contributed their monthly pro-rata share to the fund which makes the services possible. Repeated good-faith efforts by appellant to collect appellees' unpaid obligations were ignored, necessitating the instant lawsuit. The expenses to prosecute this lawsuit, once again, must come from the fund supported by appellees' fellow unit owners. No amount of legal wrangling can obscure the fact that appellees knowingly accepted the services and must pay for them. To obtain this inevitable result, appellant has been forced by appellees' intransigence to incur large amounts in attorney fees to collect the relatively small amount of past due assessments.[6]

By refusing to enforce the provision which would require appellees to pay appellant's reasonable attorney fees, this court would make it virtually impossible for condominium unit owners' associations to recoup unpaid assessments from recalcitrant unit owners. The expense of collection would render the effort useless. The result would be that a unit owner, who for any reason does not wish to pay his monthly service assessment, can enjoy the benefits of such services and refuse to pay for them, secure in the knowledge that collection by the association will be prohibitively expensive. Under such circumstances, what incentive would exist for the unscrupulous unit owner to pay his assessments? Obviously, very little.

As can be seen, the fee-shifting agreement in this case protects the fund of the unit owners' association from potential bankruptcy, and the conscientious contributors thereto from the burden of paying for the delinquency of others. Without such fee-shifting agreements, unit owners' associations may have to abandon claims against debtors, such as appellees, as too costly to pursue. With such agreements, the debtor will be encouraged to pay to avoid litigation, and if litigation becomes necessary, the association's resources will be protected if its suit proves meritorious. A more ideal arrangement can scarcely be imagined.

In sum, this court will not interfere with the right of the people of this state to contract freely and without needless limitation. A rule of law which prevents parties from agreeing to pay the other's attorney fees, absent a statute or prior declaration of this court to the contrary,[7] is outmoded, unjustified and paternalistic.

Accordingly, we hold that provisions contained within a declaration of condominium ownership and/or condominium by-laws requiring that a defaulting unit owner be responsible for the payment of attorney fees incurred by the unit owners' association in either a collection action or a foreclosure action against the defaulting unit owner for unpaid common assessments are enforceable and not void as against public policy so long as the

---

6. The trial court determined the unpaid assessments to be $2,464.82, with additional late charges of $145. The attorney fees incurred by appellant in collecting this amount were $12,268.89, as of the date of the trial court's decision. The trial court, noting the large amount of these fees, was reluctant to award such an amount "in what should have been a routine and simple case." However, the court recognized that

> the fact that the case did not remain routine and simple is due solely to the activities of the defendant in pursuing what he believed to be the proper course in this matter. The Court can sympathize with the defendant in standing for a principal [sic] in which he believes, but the Court finds, as a matter of law and evidence, that the plaintiff is entitled to recover a reasonable amount for their [sic] fees and expenses of suit. Since the only evidence before the Court is evidence presented by the plaintiff, and since there is nothing to indicate that the amount of fees incurred is not reasonable under all the facts of this case, the Court hereby awards judgment in favor of the plaintiff and against the defendants Darby, in the sum of $12,268.89.

7. A contract of adhesion, where the party with little or no bargaining power has no realistic choice as to terms, would likewise not be supportable.

fees awarded are fair, just and reasonable as determined by the trial court upon full consideration of all of the circumstances of the case.

We, therefore, reverse the judgment of the court of appeals and reinstate the judgment of the trial court.

Judgment Reversed.

LOCHER, J., dissenting. I must vigorously dissent to the position taken by the majority in the case *sub judice*. Today's decision has no basis in Ohio law and defies simple logic. Furthermore, the decision perpetuates the modern "American" rule: sue, sue, sue.

Under a black-letter smoke screen of freedom of contract, the majority turns a basic collection case into a virtual "horn of plenty" filled with attorney fees for appellant. The majority fails to cite one Ohio case in which attorney fees were awarded absent a statute permitting the same or evidence that the unsuccessful party had acted in bad faith. The Ohio Revised Code does not contain any language permitting the recovery of attorney fees in actions such as the one at bar. Moreover, the General Assembly has expressly provided for the recovery of attorney fees, as part of litigation costs, with respect to certain statutory actions.[8]

Also, there is no evidence of bad faith present in the instant action. Appellant initiated this action and the Darbys presented an aggressive but realistic defense. Despite the majority's suggestions, the Darbys were not "deadbeats" who neglected to pay their bills. From 1978 until early 1983, the Darbys faithfully paid their monthly common assessments. The Darbys then discovered an extremely apathetic and unprofessional homeowners' association. They revealed how appellant failed to follow its own by-laws and challenged the legality of appellant's actions brought pursuant to those by-laws.[9] The fact "[t]hat appellees interposed a defense which was ultimately overruled does not, in and of itself, demonstrate bad faith." *State, ex rel. Kabatek, v. Stackhouse* (1983), 6 Ohio St.3d 55, 56, 6 OBR 73, 74, 451 N.E.2d 248, 249. Today's decision sends a harsh message to these individuals who believed that they were being wronged. That message is to pay the money and keep quiet now or you will certainly pay later. The majority ignores the observations of the United States Supreme Court that "'one should not be penalized for merely defending or prosecuting a lawsuit, and that the poor might be unjustly discouraged from instituting actions to vindicate their rights if the penalty for losing included the fees of their opponents' counsel.'" *F.D. Rich Co. v. Industrial Lumber Co.* (1974), 417 U.S. 116, 129, 94 S.Ct. 2157, 2165, 40 L.Ed.2d 703.

---

8. See, e.g., R.C. 163.21, 309.13, 733.61 and 1313.51.

9. I agree with the following statement of the court of appeals contained in footnote 7 of its opinion:

> One particular inconsistency in this case strikes this court immediately. On the one hand, appellee freely admits its unit owners have [sic] failed to live up to their agreement with it in that they have failed to gather a quorum of themselves to conduct annual meetings and elect officers as required by the by-laws, they have raised monthly assessments by thirteen percent (13%) in a single year which is arguably improper, and they have authorized a professional manager to sign assessment liens, something we allow here by our view of R.C. 5311.18. These departures from the provisions of the by-laws of the home owners' association have been excused herein for one reason or another; for example, by finding certain unit owners acted as a de facto board of trustees.

On the other hand, appellee now claims that in spite of their [sic] admitted failure to follow their [sic] by-laws or their [sic] 'loose' interpretation of them, appellant[s] should be held to a strict interpretation of them, and compelled to pay appellee's attorney fees for first alleging and then showing, at least in part, that appellee failed to follow such rules. One could legitimately accuse appellee of simultaneously urging strict construction of the by-law's attorney fee provision while demanding liberal or loose construction of the same by-laws concerning the selection and authority of its board of trustees.

The majority cavalierly trots out a broad freedom of contract rule from a comment to the Restatement of Contracts and a litany of cases from other jurisdictions which do not closely resemble the action currently before this court. In fact, one of the cases cited by the majority, *Farmers Union Oil Co. v. Maixner* (N.D.1985), 376 N.W.2d 43, involved an action on an overdue account brought by an oil company against an agricultural products company. The agreement by the debtor company to pay its creditor's attorney fees was thrown out as being against public policy and void. The majority offers no support for the position it takes under the circumstances presented by this action. Under the instant facts, there is no support under Ohio case law or the case law of any other jurisdiction. Rather, the majority finds the attorney fees provisions to be a "neat idea," as a method of collecting debts.

The majority further finds a homeowners' association to be helpless without such attorney fees provisions. Has R.C. 5311.23 been repealed by the legislature? That section (still in effect) provides that a "unit owner is liable in a civil action for damages caused to any person by his failure to comply with any lawful provision of the condominium instruments." Certainly, a provision requiring payment of common assessments is a lawful provision contained in condominium instruments.

There is no doubt that the principle of freedom of contract is a sound one. However, its use is misplaced under the present circumstances. This action does not involve parties of equal bargaining power. Appellant makes no argument, and there is nothing in the record to indicate, that the Darbys had any opportunity to "bargain away" the attorney fees provisions before entering into this "contract." Purchasing a home is an experience fraught with emotion. When the "right place" is found, the decision to purchase is not only one of cold economics but is emotional as well. Clearly the buyer is at a distinct disadvantage. This case does not present parties in equal bargaining positions. Thus, this court should adhere to Ohio's well-established view that "contracts for the payment of counsel fees upon default in payment of a debt will not be enforced." *Miller v. Kyle* (1911), 85 Ohio St. 186, 192, 97 N.E. 372. *See, also, American Nursing Care of Toledo v. Leisure* (N.D. Ohio 1984), 609 F.Supp. 419, 433; *Federal Deposit Ins. Corp. v. Timbalier Towing Co., Inc.* (N.D.Ohio 1980), 497 F.Supp. 912, 929.

Finally, today's decision does nothing but reinforce the views of many that we have become an overly litigious society. The majority grants carte blanche to those who can insert attorney fees provisions into contracts to sue at will. Why not? The party having difficulty paying his debt because he just lost his job can pick up the tab. It's in the contract. Sue them, it's paid for. Moreover, the majority casually allows this small collection case of approximately $2,600 to become a financial bonanza for the attorneys in an amount nearly five times the amount owed. Former Chief Justice Burger mentioned in his annual report to the midyear meeting of the American Bar Association that he had organized a task force to study the state of justice in this country. In his address, he stated that one of the members of the task force "provided an apt summary of the whole problem: 'some basic institutional reform in the legal profession is what is needed—lawyers have got to stop using the court system as a means of enriching themselves at the expense of their clients. *And the courts have got to stop allowing the lawyers to do it.*'"[10] (Emphasis added.) Unfortunately, today's decision will be viewed by many observers as perpetuating the problem the former Chief Justice speaks of. I cannot join in such a decision.

Therefore, I would hold that in the absence of a statute permitting the same, the attorney fees provisions embodied in the instant condominium instruments should be de-

---

10. Burger, The State of Justice (April 1984), 70 A.B.A.J. 65.

clared to be against public policy and void. Accordingly, I would affirm the decision of the court of appeals.

Problems

The statute of limitations is an important defense in enforcement actions and in actions against the builder/developer. You should consider it when the statute of limitations arises in both contexts.

1. In building the condominium, Developer improperly poured the foundations. Using an inadequate mixture in the concrete, he saved money but created a potential structural maintenance problem. Three years later, the association underwent transition and control of the association passed from Developer to the unit owners.

At that point, the owners' transition team was offered the opportunity to review all of the developer's books and records, and they did a thorough review of financial and budget matters. However, they choose not to incur the expense of having a review of all other records, deciding instead simply to take custody of them.

Two more years passed, and there was a period of intense rain which saturated the soil. Shortly thereafter, one wall of the condominium tower began settling and cracking. Through its attorney, the association made a demand on Developer who denied all responsibility and asserted that because more than three years had passed since he completed construction, the statute of limitations provided an absolute defense to him and to his company.

As counsel for the association, you have finally reviewed every piece of paper the association received from the developer and have found field notes that conclusively establish the fact that the foundations were improperly poured. It is quite clear that if the foundations were proper, the settling would not have occurred.

The board is meeting in an executive session and asks you to evaluate Developer's position. How do you advise them? How would you advise the board of directors considering the investment of the association's reserve funds? What issues and legal considerations are involved?

2. The date is today, and the Board of Directors of Seven Oaks Condominium Association, Inc. is meeting in the living room of its president, Kim Scoson. Four of the seven directors are present as is the association's manager, Nadyne Gideon, and you, the association's attorney. The manager is making her report, and the tension is running high.

"I've told T.R. Zarabi over and over that this is a quiet, adults-only place, but I might as well be talking to a horse. Does he care that the rule says 21 or over only? I say not! First he buys that dog and now he has a female roommate with a ten-year-old kid. He knows that the amendment restricting units to single-family use has been approved but ignores it. He contends that Ahara and her brat kid are family because they went through the wars together, whatever that means. You should fine him and then foreclose the lien."

"What about the rumor he has let her have an interest in the unit?" asked Ginger, the aloof, female board member. "What about our rule requiring all sales to have our approval? Why don't you do something?" she snorted at no one in particular.

"With a name like that, something just has to be wrong with him," asserted Joe Pistol, the truculent treasurer. "We ought to do something. Can't we at least get rid of that kid?"

"That's not as important as the damage to my rug," interjected Riv O'Lee, the normally mild-mannered secretary. "I want something done. My living room was dry when I went to work and wet when I came home. My Two Grey Hills rug is ruined, and I want action."

"Calm down," said Kim, "we'll take care of you. Any objection to using the reserve? ... Done!"

"What about the kid?" repeated Joe.

"I really think we need to deal with Haney's deck construction," said Nadyne. "It's been six weeks since he finished it, and he never did ask permission; he just built the thing."

"Yeah, we do need to do something to him, too," piped in Joe. "His deck is bigger than mine. It's even four feet longer than his patio area under it."

"The point is that the deck was built in violation of last year's rule prohibiting exterior construction. Without objection, I'll order Nadyne here to tear it down."

"Abstain," groused Ginger.

"Done," said Kim.

"Where are we on the cable TV contract?" inquired Riv.

"Don't worry about that," Kim spoke up. "I told Nadyne to handle it. It's all signed. The assessment increase is only $2.50 per month.

"What about the kid?"

"Collections are in good shape with only a 10% delinquency rate. We've filed liens on those turkeys and written the usual 'nasty nice' letter."

"Good."

"Sue the rascals!"

"We've got ten thousand left over,"said Nadyne. "Should I buy some options?"

"Do what's best," said Joe. "But what about that kid?"

"Bingo night went well," reported Ginger. "Everyone enjoyed the clubhouse. Next time we are going to sell cocktails as a fund raiser for the social fund committee. You must all come."

"Good," said Kim. As he picked up his gavel to adjourn the meeting, Kim looked at you and said, "I guess we should get our money's worth with our lawyer here. What do you think about tonight's business, counselor?"

Tell him.

The question we must ask ourselves is not whether we like or do not like what is going on, but what we are going to do about it.

— Winston Churchill

Chapter 9

Amending the Governing Documents

This chapter deals with change. When dealing with a real estate product and with recorded instruments which create and regulate rights relating to that real estate product, change is not easy; quite frequently, it is or is perceived to be threatening. Consequently, the power to amend and the process of amendment are very important issues in creating and operating common interest communities.

When amending the documents, one is altering the existing structure: either adding or deleting provisions or modifying them to change their effect. However, amendments quite often involve a great deal more. Common interest community documents are also amended to create a portion of the community, to terminate all or a portion, and to renew the governance structure which otherwise will expire by its own terms or by operation of law. It is important to understand which of these objectives is being pursued and how the rules may vary.

It is helpful to consider the circumstances in which the various questions relating to amendment might arise. The declarant initially places the declaration of condominium or CCRs on record to create the project. Normally, that declaration covers only a small portion of the project ultimately intended to be encumbered as part of the common interest community. Consequently, the document will be amended in order to "phase" the development. Phasing is the addition of land which is submitted from time to time as development progresses. As this is done, additional or alternative restrictions might be added to that newly submitted phase.

The declarant might also seek to amend the documents in order to enhance the project's acceptability to the financing community or to include a lender's requirements or those of the secondary mortgage market institutions. Alterations in the development plan may result from changes in circumstances, the market, or other external factors. For example, a project originally conceived as having no pets and no children may become unmarketable. Would the developer have the unilateral right to amend the documents to permit pets? Even though there is a reservation of power to make unilateral amendments, other factors might limit the exercise of that power. Finally, there is the question of when an amendment is not an amendment. Changing the design guidelines may, for example, be done without the necessity of amending the declaration.

The association may have an entirely different set of goals and concerns leading to document amendment. Quite frankly, often an association engages in an extensive amendment process following transition of control from the developer. In addition to removing developer control provisions and other sections, the relevance of which have ceased due to cessation of declarant control and of development, the association may desire to fine tune the documentation based upon its actual experience.

Frequently, changes in the law result in association-sponsored amendments. For example, in the mid 1990s, many states adopted indemnification statutes as part of their corporate codes. Many associations modified their relevant documentation in order to take advantage of these provisions. Targeted, specific changes produce amendments dealing with substantive issues that associations experience. Lease controls, pet regulations or, more particularly, "pet amortization provisions," indemnification, and other examples represent a large body of association-sponsored amendments. Finally, there are still many documents which, by their terms or because of operation of law, expire after specified periods. Twenty years is a typical expiration period.

If the CCRs expire after a specified period, the governance structure and the interlocking ownerships expire as well. Amendments to extend the expiration period or to effect a renewal in accordance with the expiration period terms are common. Obtaining all the necessary signatures in such a process can be quite an onerous task. One asks, therefore, why documents contain an expiration period. More recently drafted documents normally do not contain an expiration period but rather provide for perpetual duration unless there is a termination by a specified vote. This is a better approach than putting the burden on the association to renew in the face of an automatic termination. In many instances throughout this book, you have considered the effect of the buyers' expectations and of their reasonable right to rely upon that which has been represented. How do these considerations fit in this amendment context?

Finally, it is important to consider what is being amended and whether that makes a difference in who may make the amendment, what vote is required, and what limitations might apply. For example, quite frequently the power to amend the by-laws rests with the board of directors, while a vote of the entire membership is required to amend the CCRs. The issues of why the board has authority to amend the by-laws while the CCRs require membership vote, who has the power to amend plats and plans, and under what circumstances such amendments are important become quite relevant in the following section.

A. Power to Amend

Restatement (Third) § 6.10 Power To Amend The Declaration

(1) Except as expressly limited by statute or the declaration, the members of a common-interest community have the power to amend the declaration subject to the following requirements:

(a) Unless the declaration specifies a different number, an amendment adopted by members holding a majority of the voting power is effective

(i) to extend the term of the declaration,

(ii) to make administrative changes reasonably necessary for management of the common property or administration of the servitude regime,

(iii) to prohibit or materially restrict uses of individually owned lots or units that threaten to harm or unreasonably interfere with the reasonable use and enjoyment of other property in the community.

(b) Unless the declaration specifies a different number, an amendment adopted by members holding two-thirds of the voting power is effective for all purposes except as stated in subsections (2) and (3).

(2) Amendments that do not apply uniformly to similar lots or units and amendments that would otherwise violate the community's duties to its members under § 6.13 are not effective without the approval of members whose interests would be adversely affected unless the declaration fairly apprises purchasers that such amendments may be made. This subsection does not apply to nonuniform modifications made under circumstances that would justify judicial modification under § 7.10.

(3) Except as otherwise expressly authorized by the declaration, and except as provided in (1), unanimous approval is required

(a) to prohibit or materially restrict the use or occupancy of, or behavior within, individually owned lots or units, or

(b) to change the basis for allocating voting rights or assessments among community members.

UCIOA § 2-117. Amendment of Declaration

(f) By vote or agreement of unit owners of units to which at least 80 percent of the votes in the association are allocated, or any larger percentage specified in the declaration, an amendment to the declaration may prohibit or materially restrict the permitted uses of or behavior in a unit or the number or other qualifications of persons who may occupy units. The amendment must provide reasonable protection for a use or occupancy permitted at the time the amendment was adopted.

Comment

4. The 1994 revision ... deletes the prohibition on amendments which restrict the uses of units....

5. New subsection (f) ... adopted in 1994, responds to the growing belief that restrictions on use and occupancy which unit owners would like to impose after the declaration is recorded ought to be adopted only by a super majority and only after providing protection for those whose use or occupancy will be affected by the amendment. For example, a community may seek to prohibit pets after a number of owners have purchased and occupied their units in reliance on the absence of such a restriction. Under this amendment, if the community votes to impose the limitation, it can do so only with the vote of a high percentage of owners and only on such conditions as reasonably protect the interests of existing pet owners. Whether the amendment "grandfathers" the right of the existing pet to remain or the right of the current owner to have a pet is not determined by the language ... but will depend on the circumstances of each community and its owners.

The only constant in real estate is change.

—Anonymous

When seeking to ascertain the extent of authority to amend that is contained in the governing documents, one must consider both procedural and substantive challenges. Regrettably, the documents are not always well drafted with the consequence being that the answers are not always clear. From a procedural perspective, one must ascertain what law applies to the amendment process. What vote is required? If the documents state that amendments require a two-thirds vote, is there clarity as to the question, "two-thirds of what?" Is it two-thirds of the owners, the lots, the affected lots, those lots which are in good standing because all assessments are paid, or something else entirely? The issues of who may vote, and how, and what vote is required are significant procedural challenges in any amendment process. These issues are considered throughout this Chapter.

There are also substantive questions. The subject matter of the amendment itself may raise questions concerning its permissibility or whether a more significant vote than that specified in the amendment process might be required. For example, under what circumstances might a 50% majority amend the documents to restrict leasing or to impose some other restraint upon ownership? In circumstances in which there is a right appurtenant to the fee interest being changed, one must give careful scrutiny to the validity of the amendment itself. In the presence of carefully drafted documents, associations generally have broad amendment powers, and the courts have upheld an array of significant alterations of personal rights. Under what circumstances might this be appropriate? Under what circumstances might it be appropriate to impose limits?

Board of Directors of By the Sea Council of Co-Owners, Inc. v. Sondock

Court of Appeals of Texas
644 S.W.2d 774 (Tex. Ct. App. 1982)

GONZALEZ, J. The opinion of this Court announced on August 26, 1982 is hereby withdrawn and this opinion is substituted therefor.

This is an appeal in a suit for a permanent injunction. The Board of Directors of By the Sea Council of Co-Owners, Inc., appellants, sought to remove the carports assigned to the apartment owners at the By the Sea Condominium and promoted and obtained an amendment to the Condominium Declaration that gave them authority to remove them. Melvin Sondock, et ux, et al, appellees, filed suit to enjoin the Board from removing the carports and to order the Board to repair the carports.

After a trial without a jury, the trial court granted a permanent injunction which prohibited the Board from removing the covers over the carports, required the Board to repair the carports and to "allot and derive the funds" for the repairs from the annual maintenance fund; declared that the amendment to the Condominium Declaration was void; and ordered that the business records be kept on the premises of the condominium project.

Extensive findings of fact and conclusions of law were made and are recited in the judgment. They are found in an appendix to this opinion.

The Board appealed....

By cross-points, the appellees contend that the trial court erred in: (1) permitting the Board to pay the attorney's fees and court costs from the funds belonging to the Council of Co-Owners, (2) in finding that the amendment in question received the consent of more than 66 2/3 % of the owners, and (3) in denying appellees attorney's fees. We affirm in part and reverse and render in part.

The main issues in this case are the validity of the amendment to Condominium Declaration and whether all owners in the condominium project must be joined as parties in a suit which affects the interest of the absent owners in the context of these facts.

The Declaration establishing the condominium project was adopted pursuant to the Texas Condominium Act, Tex. Rev. Civ. Stat. Ann. art. 1301a, and was recorded as required by the Act.

...

In accordance with the Act, the Declaration for By the Sea defines these various terms, including: (1) the apartments, which are individually owned, and (2) the common elements, which are owned in undivided shares by all of the owners of the individual apartment units. The term "common elements" is further broken down into "general common elements, which are defined to mean all of the common elements except for the limited common elements, and "limited common elements", which are defined in the By the Sea Declaration to include only the parking spaces and the storage lockers, one of each being assigned for the exclusive use of the apartment to which it is assigned.

The Board contends that the nature and use of the common elements may be modified from time to time, provided the Condominium Declaration is properly amended in accordance with the Declaration. We agree....

Amendment to Condominium Declaration

... The Board, pursuant to paragraph 40 of the By-Laws promoted the following amendment to the By-Laws:

> The parking spaces which are 'Limited Common Elements' as defined in Declaration may be covered or uncovered from time to time as determined by the Board of Directors of the By The Sea Council of Co-Owners, Inc.

66 2/3% of the owners consented in writing to this amendment.[2]

Appellees contend that they bought their apartments in reliance upon the continued existence of covered parking and that covers over the parking facilities were vested property rights that could not be taken away without their consent. Specifically, appellees contend that the removal of the covers from their assigned parking would decrease each unit owner's "percentage of undivided interest" in the common elements and this could not be done without 100% approval of all of the owners. Their authority for this proposition is paragraph 11 of the condominium By-Laws.[3]

It is undisputed that each person who purchased a condominium unit in By the Sea Condominium project purchased the unit subject to the terms of the recorded Condominium Declaration and to all of the restrictions and conditions in the Declaration. Paragraph 40 of the Declaration ... provides that the Declaration may be amended by the written consent of unit owners who own more than 66 2/3% of the common elements.

Similarly, section 9 of the Texas Condominium Act also provides that apartment owners in condominiums accept the terms, conditions and restrictions in the Condominium Declaration by acceptance of deeds to the individual apartment units.

_____

2. 40. AMENDMENTS—The provisions of this Declaration may be changed, altered or amended only with the written consent of Unit Owners ... who in the aggregate own at least 66 2/3% of the common elements, and each such amendment shall be filed for record in the same manner as this Declaration ...

3. 11. PROPORTIONATE OWNERSHIP OF COMMON ELEMENTS, SHARE OF COMMON EXPENSES AND VOTING RIGHTS—The percentage interest which each Apartment bears to the entire condominium regime is set out in the following "SCHEDULE OF PERCENTAGE".... The above percentages fixing the *percentage of undivided ownership interest* of each owner in the common elements and his share of the common expenses and voting representation *cannot be changed* except by the written consent of *each and every owner* and mortgagee of all apartment units in this condominium project, duly executed, acknowledged and filed for record; ... [Emphasis supplied.]

Also, paragraph 33 of the Condominium Declaration provides that each purchaser accepts all of the provisions of the Declaration by accepting a deed to the apartment unit and these restrictions and conditions shall be covenants running with the land.[4]

... The trial court ... found that the amendment to permit the elimination of the covered parking did receive written consent of the unit owners, owning an aggregate of more than 66 2/3% of the common elements. However, the court concluded that because the covered parking is "a property right" the covers over the parking facilities could not be eliminated because any such change would require the unanimous consent of all the owners.

Since appellees acquired their condominium units subject to the Condominium Declaration which contains the right to amendment, we have to look at the amendment and determine whether the amendment is arbitrary and capricious, and/or whether the amendment changed the percentage of undivided interest in the common elements or whether it violates any other rule of law.

There are no Texas cases that we have been able to find that are directly in point. Therefore, we will look to other States to see how they have resolved similar disputes.

In *Mayfair Engineering Co. v. Park*, 318 So. 2d 171 (Fla.App.1975), the Condominium Declaration reserved to the developer the right to assign for consideration 35 parking spaces, which were limited common elements of the condominium. The unit owners later objected, arguing that title to the 35 parking spaces became vested in the unit owners and that therefore the developer was no longer the fee owner, and had nothing to assign. The court held that although fee ownership of the 35 parking spaces was in the unit owners, nevertheless such ownership was subject to the restrictions set out in the recorded Declaration. The court stated:

> The unit owners knew or should have known of this reservation clause in Article VIII of the Declaration when they purchased their condominium units and therefore were on notice then of their limited right and interest in the thirty-five parking spaces. Enforcement of the Declaration's terms thus cannot be said to work a hardship upon them. *Id.* at 173.

In *Seagate Condominium Association, Inc., v. Duffy*, 330 So. 2d 484 (Fla. App. 1976), an amendment to a condominium declaration restricted the right of the condominium unit owners to lease their apartments. The court held that the amendment allowing the lease prohibition was valid. The court stated:

> Our courts have on several occasions pointed out the uniqueness of the problems of condominium living and the resultant necessity for a greater degree of control over and limitation upon the rights of the individual owner than might be tolerated given more traditional forms of property ownership....

Kroop v. Caravelle Condominium, Inc., 323 So. 2d 307 (Fla.App. 1975), involved an amendment to a declaration which restricted a unit owner's rights to lease the apartment. After the plaintiff purchased an apartment, the Declaration was amended to prevent any owner from leasing his apartment more than once. The plaintiff contended, among other things, that the amendment was an infringement upon his basic constitutional right to

---

4. 33. RIGHTS AND OBLIGATIONS. — The rights and obligations of the respective Unit Owners under this Declaration and the By-Laws, including amendments thereto, shall be deemed to be covenants running with the land, so long as the project property remains subject to the provisions of the Act ... Upon acceptance or recordation of any deed or other instrument conveying title to the Apartment Unit.... the Owner thereof shall be to have accepted and agreed to and shall be bound by and subject to each and all of the provisions of the Act and of this Declaration and By-Laws, as now existing or hereafter amended.

own, possess and enjoy property. The trial court held that Kroop acquired the apartment with the knowledge that the Condominium Declaration might thereafter be amended and that the amendment was adopted in a proper manner and for a proper purpose. The appellate court affirmed.

In *Ritchey v. Villa Nueva Condominium Association*, 81 Cal.App.3d 688, 146 Cal.Rptr. 695 (1978), the condominium owners approved, by more than 75%, an amendment to the By-Laws which would limit occupancy in a portion of the condominium to persons eighteen years of age or older, if the occupancy would involve a period of 14 days or more. The plaintiff challenged the validity of the amendment, arguing that such an age restriction is *per se* unreasonable. The court acknowledged that the amendment to the By-Laws operated both as a restraint upon the owner's right of alienation and as a limitation upon his right of occupancy, but the court found that the amendment to the By-Laws was reasonable. The plaintiff also argued that when he purchased his condominium apartment it was referred to as "a family unit" and that he relied upon these representations. However, the court held that appellant purchased the apartment subject to the Enabling Declaration which specifically provided that the By-Laws could be amended.

In our case, the Declaration of By the Sea Condominium expressly states that the Declaration can be amended if the appropriate written consents are obtained. Appellees testified they bought their apartments in the belief that they had the right to a covered parking space, just as Mr. Ritchey believed he had a right to permit children to occupy his apartment. Further, as in the Ritchey case, at the time appellees purchased their apartments, the Declaration expressly stated that each purchaser accepted all the provisions of the Declaration, including the right to amend.

The trial court held that the elimination of the covers over the parking facilities had the effect of changing each owner's percentage of undivided ownership in the common elements, which under Section 11 of the Declaration required the unanimous consent of all owners. Section 11 does so provide, but is inapplicable here. If one or more of the unit owners appropriated a part of the common elements to his or her exclusive use, that appropriation would require the unanimous consent of all owners, and would not be permitted under Section 11.... However, our case does not involve such an appropriation. Instead, by the amendment, the covers over the parking facilities may be removed for all owners. No owner has obtained an advantage over any other owner; and no owner has lost his percentage share in the common elements.

[handwritten margin note: No owner has lost his %. All have lost their covered garages!]

In summary, at the time of purchase of their units, appellees knew (or should have known) that they bought subject to all the provisions of the Condominium Declaration. One of these provisions was the right to amend the Declaration. The Declaration was amended properly and the amendment is not arbitrary or capricious. Therefore, appellants' points of error two through six are sustained....

The portion of the judgment of the trial court ordering that the business records of the condominium be kept on the premises is affirmed. The portion of the judgment of the trial court declaring the amendment to the Condominium Declaration void and granting the injunction is reversed and it is here rendered that the amendment to the Condominium Declaration is valid and the injunction is dissolved.... Affirmed in part, Reversed in part.

Notes & Questions

1. *Power to amend.* In upholding the validity of the association's amendment, the court in *Board of Directors of By the Sea Council*, concludes "at the time of purchase ... appellees

knew that they bought subject to all the provisions of the Condominium Declaration. One of these provisions was the right to amend...." But did not the complaining homeowners also buy their units with the expectation of covered parking? Does the reasonableness test, as used in this case, sufficiently protect the minority owners? See generally UCIOA § 2-117.

2. *Express limits on amendment authority*. In *Caughlin Ranch Homeowner's Ass'n v. Caughlin Club*, 849 P.2d 310 (Nev. 1993), an amendment to the CCRs to assess commercial property within the development was held invalid (the documents in effect at the time the commercial property was annexed to the development only provided for assessments against residential parcels). The provision permitting amendments to the CCRs prohibited the addition of new and different covenants. Why might such express limitations be undesirable? In what other manner may a declarant protect certain provisions from being amended under the "normal" amendment process?

3. *Special declarant rights*. UCIOA § 2-104(8) provides that all special declarant rights must be contained in the declaration (*i.e.*, rights reserved for the declarant's benefit and not shared in common with other unit owners). Examples of special declarant rights include easements to further developmental interests, free use of common elements to advance marketing activities, and certain veto rights with respect to community operational matters. Typically, homeowners are without authority to amend these special declarant rights (at least without the declarant's approval). Why do you suppose such protections are needed? How would you draft these protections?

Problem

The CCRs have no amendment provision. All the homes are sold, and there are serious problems with unrealistic use restrictions. The documents need to be changed. The board retains you and asks for your suggestions as to one or more courses of action and the strengths and weaknesses of each. Please do so. Would your advice be different if there were an amendment provision but it required 90% vote? At a meeting?

Assume that the problem is not a "bullet proof" set of CCRs which require unanimous or near unanimous vote, but rather a problem of participation. Many lots have absentee owners who neither attend meetings nor return proxies. Some are foreclosures which lenders own. What is your advice now?

B. Uniform Application of Amendments

The foregoing and following cases illustrate uniformity as an important aspect to the amendment process.

Montoya v. Barreras

Supreme Court of New Mexico
473 P.2d 363 (N.M. 1970)

SISK, J. Twenty of the defendants in a quiet-title action appeal from that portion of the final decree which relieved and excluded from the burden of residential restrictions and covenants one lot owned by plaintiff in a subdivision in Santa Fe, New Mexico in which these defendants also owned lots.

Defendants rely on three points, but because we hold that the second point is controlling and requires reversal the other points need not be discussed. Point II reads as follows:

> The 'Declaration of Protective Covenants to the Linda Vista Addition of the City of Santa Fe' does not permit the removal of restrictions on only one lot in the subdivision while retaining the restrictions on all other lots in the subdivision, and therefore, the trial court erred in overruling appellants' legal defense 1(E).

Legal defense 1(E), as it appears in the amended answer of defendants, reads:

> The Covenant (X) does not permit the relinquishment of the restrictions on only one lot or one portion of the subdivision while retaining the restrictions on other lots in the subdivision.

In 1940, the owner of a tract of land in Santa Fe, New Mexico, whom we will refer to as the grantor, executed and recorded an instrument title 'Declaration of Protective Covenants for the Linda Vista Addition to the City of Santa Fe, New Mexico,' which declared that all of the described tract was encumbered by and subject to twelve paragraphs of restrictions. Paragraph (X) of the restrictive covenants, which contains the language directly in dispute, provides:

> These covenants are to run with the land and shall be binding on all the parties and all persons claiming under them until January 1, 1966, at which time said covenants shall be automatically extended for successive periods of ten (10) years unless by a vote of the majority of the then owners of the lots it is agreed to change the said covenants in whole or in part.

All of the evidence before the trial court was documentary. No plat of the addition is included in the transcript. The parties executed a Stipulation Agreement in which they agreed that during December, 1967, and January and February, 1968, a majority of the owners of lots within the residential subdivision had signed a 'Consent to Change of Protective Covenants' pertaining to the plaintiff's lot, by which they voted for and consented to the removal of all of the restrictions from that one lot and to its use for commercial purposes.

Plaintiff contends that such removal of the residential restrictions from one lot only was proper because the language of paragraph (X) is ambiguous and must be construed strictly against the grantor and in favor of free use of the land. By such construction they argue that the phrase '... change the said covenants in whole or in part' in paragraph (X) is not limited to changing the residential covenants themselves as they affect all of the lots, but permits the complete removal of the covenants from one lot while retaining them on all other lots.

The plaintiff's authorities recite the long-established rules that, if ambiguous, a restriction on property must be construed against its grantor and in favor of free use. But alleging that a restriction is ambiguous does not necessarily make it so. These general rules can have significance only as applied to the particular facts of the individual case. Restrictive covenants must be considered reasonably, though strictly, and an illogical, unnatural, or strained construction must be avoided. *H. J. Griffith Realty Co. v. Hobbs Houses, Inc.*, 68 N.M. 25, 357 P.2d 677 (1960). In the Griffith case this court noted that in construing restrictive covenants, perhaps more than in any other field of law, each case must depend on its own particular facts, and an attempt to apply general rules is unsatisfactory.

The issue to be determined is therefore whether, considering the declaration of restrictive covenants as a whole, paragraph (X) can be reasonably and logically construed to permit the residential restrictions to be removed on one lot only, or on a lot-by-lot basis, by a majority of the owners in the subdivision. We do not believe that it can.

Before applying the general rule that restrictive covenants should be construed in favor of the free use of property, the court must recognize that …"effect is to be given to the intention of the parties as shown by the language of the whole instrument, considered with the circumstances surrounding the transaction, and the object of the parties in making the restrictions." *Hoover v. Waggoman*, 52 N.M. 371, 199 P.2d 991 (1948). *See also Suttle v. Bailey*, 68 N.M. 283, 361 P.2d 325 (1961); *Rowe v. May*, 44 N.M. 264, 101 P.2d 391 (1940).

Considering the entire document, by clear statement and with plain intent, it constitutes a detailed plan for residential development and restriction as to all of the lots in the subdivision. Under the facts and circumstances of this case, we are not faced with the resolution of an ambiguous restriction.

Examination of the entire declaration reveals that the original restrictions were clearly imposed on all of the described property. The declaration describes the property and is then followed by the granting clause which declares that all of the property shall be encumbered by the restrictions. Following this granting clause, twelve paragraphs of restrictive covenants are listed, including the provision in covenant (X) that they may be changed in whole or in part. The phrase "in whole or in part in covenant (X) clearly modifies the words "to change," and the direct object of "to change" is the word "covenants," not the word "lots." Thus, the covenants may be changed in whole or in part, but we cannot construe this language as permitting any such change or changes to apply to only a portion of the lots on which the restrictions were imposed. Nor is there anything in the covenants themselves which can be construed as either expressly or impliedly modifying or changing the granting clause itself, which expresses the intent and purpose that all of the described property is encumbered by the restrictions, whether they remain as originally stated or are subsequently changed in whole or in part. The original restrictions were clearly imposed on all of the described property, and though the restrictions themselves may be changed in whole or in part, the change or changes which might be made must affect all of the described property.

Historically, restrictive covenants have been used to assure uniformity of development and use of residential area to give the owners of lots within such an area some degree of environmental stability. To permit individual lots within an area to be relieved of the burden of such covenants, in the absence of a clear expression in the instrument so providing, would destroy the right to rely on restrictive covenants which has traditionally been upheld by our law of real property. As in *Gorman v. Boehning*, 55 N.M. 306, 232 P.2d 701, 26 A.L.R.2d 868 (1951), the declaration of the grantor in this case contemplates a plan of development limited to residential purposes. To completely insure a plan of residential development, the grantor must impose reciprocal restrictive covenants on the property for the common benefit of all of his grantees and their assigns. *Margate Park Protective Ass'n v. Abate*, 22 N.J.Super. 550, 92 A.2d 110 (1952). *See also Cree Meadows, Inc. v. Palmer*, 68 N.M. 479, 362 P.2d 1007 (1961); *Benbow v. Boney*, 240 S.W.2d 438 (Tex.Civ.App. 1951).

All of the lots in the subdivision were sold subject to the provisions of the declaration. Restrictions as to the use of land are mutual, reciprocal, equitable easements in the nature of servitudes in favor of owners of other lots within the restricted area, and constitute property rights which run with the land. *McFarland v. Hanley*, 258 S.W.2d 3 (Ky.

1953). Where the covenants manifest a general plan of restriction to residential purposes, such covenants constitute valuable property rights of the owners of all lots in the tract. *Gorman v. Boehning, supra.*

In *Riley v. Boyle*, 6 Ariz.App. 523, 434 P.2d 525 (1967), one landowner in a residential subdivision sued to enjoin another from violating two restrictive covenants pertaining to construction requirements. Another restriction provided that:

> The owner or owners of 51% of the lots in this subdivision shall have the right to amend or change these conditions, reservations and restrictions for the beneficial improvement and interest of WESTRIDGE ESTATES.

At least 51% of the owners had signed an amendment which included a provision that one lot was excluded from the effect of two of the restrictions. It was contended that the removal of those restrictions from one lot only was invalid. The court said:

> Only one case dealing with the precise question herein involved has been cited to the court. That is the case of *Cowherd Development Company v. Littick*, 361 Mo. 1001, 238 S.W.2d 346 (1951). It held that a majority of the owners of the lots could exercise the power of extending the restrictions for an additional period of 25 years either as to all of the lots or as to none of the lots but could not keep the restrictions in force as to some lots but not as to others.

The comment is made in the notes of 4 A.L.R. 3d 582:

> It would appear that any action taken by property owners to alter, extend, or revoke existing restrictions must apply to all of the properties which are subject to them. In one case the court held invalid an attempt to retain restrictions as to part of a subdivision while releasing them as to another part.

> This court is satisfied that this is a sound principle. It is to be noted that in the subdivision in question in this case there was no attempt at zoning or imposing one set of restrictions on a part of the subdivision and another set on another part.

> Paragraph 19 of the restrictions, as stated above, gives the power to 51 per cent of the lot owners to change completely the restrictions applicable to the entire subdivision but it does not give the power to change the restrictions as to one or more but less than all the lots. The restrictions imposed pertain to all lots in the subdivision and a fair construction of the words permitting amendments indicate that the power to amend is only as to restrictions for all lots in the subdivision.

> Taking these words to mean that particular lots could be excepted permits the obviously unintended result that 51 per cent of the owners could exempt their own property and leave the other 49 per cent encumbered or could even impose more strict restrictions upon certain lots. Certainly such an interpretation could easily result in a patchwork quilt of different restrictions according to the views of various groups of 51 per cent and completely upset the orderly plan of the subdivision.

The court then held that each owner had the contractual right to have the restrictions enforced against all of the lots unless the partial change in the restrictions voted by 51 per cent of the owners was made equally applicable to all lots in the subdivision and that the attempted exemption of one lot was null and void. Both our case and the *Riley* case, *supra*, deal directly with the partial changing or amending of restrictive covenants, and we agree with the Arizona court that absolution from the restrictions as to only some, but not all, of the lots is not a valid construction where the language of the instrument manifests the intent for orderly residential neighborhood development. In *Cowherd Development Company v. Littick*, 361 Mo. 1001, 238 S.W.2d 346 (1951), in holding that the extension of the restrictions could not apply to part of the lots and not others, the court noted that one of the primary purposes of residential restrictions in a subdivision is to assure purchasers of lots that they may build homes without fear of commercial expansion or encroachment.

The soundness of the reasoning in *Riley v. Boyle, supra*, is evidenced when the results of the interpretation plaintiff would place on paragraph (X) of the restrictions are considered. Plaintiff's interpretation would permit the majority of owners to remove all restrictions from their lots while leaving the burden on the lots of the minority. It would permit the majority of owners, whose lots might not be adversely affected because of their insulated location in the subdivision, to authorize offensive consequences for the minority by removing or imposing restrictions only on certain lots within the area. Because the grantor encumbered all of the property with restrictions, we cannot infer from the declaration the intention that any subsequent change or changes in the restrictions could be made applicable to only one lot or a portion of the lots in the residential subdivision.

Our holding that the declaration does not permit the majority of owners to exempt one lot only from the residential restrictions, contrary to the vested rights of the minority of owners, does not necessarily mean that the plaintiff was or is without a remedy. This court has long recognized that individual lots in a subdivision may be relieved of restrictive covenants if there has been such a change in the conditions which existed when the covenants were imposed as to defeat the intended objects and purposes of the covenants and their enforcement is no longer necessary to afford the protection originally contemplated. *Williams v. Butler*, 76 N.M. 782, 418 P.2d 856 (1966); *Mershon v. Neff*, 67 N.M. 311, 355 P.2d 128 (1960); *Chuba v. Glasgow*, 61 N.M. 302, 299 P.2d 774 (1956). See also the majority opinion and the dissent in *Mason v. Farmer*, 80 N.M. 354, 456 P.2d 187 (1969). In the present case, however, no allegation of change of conditions was raised by the pleadings nor was any finding concerning change of conditions requested or made. To the extent that it relieves and excludes the plaintiff's lot from the operation and effect of the restrictive covenants, the decree is reversed with directions to enter a new decree consistent with this opinion.

Reversed.

Notes & Questions

1. *Flexibility versus expectations.* Part of the holding in *Montoya* was premised upon reliance interests of homeowners buying into the community. Quoting *Cowherd*, it held that "one of the primary purposes of residential restrictions in a subdivision is to assure purchasers of lots that they may build homes without fear of commercial expansion or encroachment." See also *Walton v. Jaskiewica*, 563 A.2d 382 (Md. 1989) (majority of owners could not amend the declaration to exempt one lot from a resubdivision restriction because of the expectation that covenants will be uniformly enforced); *La Esperanza Townhome Ass'n v. Title Security Agency*, 689 P.2d 178 (Ariz. Ct. App. 1984) (changing use of property restricted to townhomes was held void; the court reasoned that amendments must be applied in a uniform manner to all lots in the subdivision so as to maintain the orderly plan of the development). But see *LaBrayere v. LaBrayere*, 676 S.W.2d 522 (Mo. Ct. App. 1984) (developer amendment to re-subdivide lot upheld).

Essentially, courts frequently seek to protect the original, general scheme of development in these cases. On the other hand, and as examined in *Board of Directors of By the*

Sea Council, supra, are not homeowners also put on notice that things may change or be amended in the future? Where is the line drawn between maintaining maximum flexibility to deal with future clients but also preserving the original development scheme? Would the same outcome occur in *Montoya* if the owners were seeking to buy the lot and change its use to common property (*e.g.*, use the lot and home as a community center or re-sale office)?

2. *Change in conditions.* As addressed in *Montoya* and in Chapter 8, units in a subdivision may be relieved of restrictive covenants if there is such a change in conditions that the intended objective and purpose of the original covenants is defeated. What type of changed condition in *Montoya* might have supported the need to relieve that lot of its residential use restriction? Who has the burden of proving such a change? See generally *Gibbs v. Cass*, 431 S.W.2d 662 (Mo. App. 1968); *Meyerland Community Improvement Ass'n v. Temple*, 700 S.W.2d 263 (Tex. App. 1985) (changed conditions and declaration amendment permitted sale of land for non-residential use); and *Black Horse Run Property Owners Ass'n v. Kaleel*, 362 S.E.2d 619 (N.C. App. 1987) (association's acquiescence to covenant violation did not result in a changed condition).

[handwritten margin note: Note: Change ~ CCRs ~ response to "change i conditions"]

3. *Eliminating special exemptions.* Declaration amendments which eliminate special exemption provisions are more likely to be upheld than amendments which create new exemptions. For example, in *Bay Island Towers, Inc. v. Bay Island-Siesta Ass'n*, 316 So. 2d 574 (Fla. Dist. Ct. App. 1975), an amendment which eliminated special treatment of certain lots which could be developed as apartments was valid and effective against a purchaser who intended to build high-rise apartments. How might one draft safeguards against such subsequent amendments? Does the purchaser now have a claim against the developer/declarant after its special exemption was eliminated?

4. *Withdrawal or de-annexation of property.* Note that the association's intention in the *Montoya* case was to withdraw or "de-annex" the subject lot from the terms of the declaration. Typically, this is a limited right reserved to the declarant during the development period. Why might it be acceptable for the declarant to withdraw property from the community association scheme but not the community association some years later?

C. Amendments May Expand Scope of the Servitude Regime

Evergreen Highlands Association v. West

Supreme Court of Colorado, En Banc
73 P.3d 1 (Colo. 2003)

I. INTRODUCTION

We granted certiorari in this case to determine whether, pursuant to the modification clause of the Evergreen Highlands Subdivision covenants, the requisite majority of lot owners may "change or modify" the existing covenants by the addition of a new covenant which: (1) requires all lot owners to be members of the homeowners association, (2) assesses mandatory dues on all lot owners in the subdivision to pay for the maintenance of common areas, and (3) imposes liens on those lots whose owners fail to pay the mandatory dues.

[handwritten margin note: Change to require all lot owners to be members of the HOA.]

The district court held that such an amendment was valid and binding. The court of appeals reversed, finding that the modification clause of Evergreen Highlands' covenants did not allow for the addition of a wholly new covenant, but only for the modification of existing covenants. We now reverse the court of appeals, holding that the addition of a new covenant falls within the permissible scope of the modification clause of the Evergreen Highlands covenants....

II. FACTS AND PROCEDURAL HISTORY

...

Evergreen Highlands Subdivision was created and its plat filed in 1972. The plat indicated that the park area was to be conveyed to the homeowners association. Protective covenants for Evergreen Highlands were also filed in 1972, but did not require lot owners to be members of or pay dues to the Association. The Association, however, was incorporated in 1973 for the purposes of maintaining the common area and facilities, enforcing the covenants, paying taxes on the common area, and determining annual fees. The developer conveyed the park area to the Association in 1976. Between the years of 1976 and 1995, when the modification of the covenants at issue in this case occurred, the Association relied on voluntary assessments from lot owners to pay for maintenance of and improvements to the park area. Such expenses included property taxes, insurance for the park area and its structures, weed spraying, tennis court resurfacing, and barn and stable maintenance.

Article 13 of the original Evergreen Highlands covenants provides that a majority of lot owners may agree to modify the covenants, stating in relevant part as follows:

> [T]he owners of seventy-five percent of the lots which are subject to these covenants may release all or part of the land so restricted from any one or more of said restrictions, *or may change or modify any one or more of said restrictions*, by executing and acknowledging an appropriate agreement or agreements in writing for such purposes and filing the same in the Office of the County Clerk and Recorder of Jefferson County, Colorado.

...

In 1995, pursuant to the modification clause, at least seventy-five percent of Evergreen Highlands' lot owners voted to add a new Article 16 to the covenants. This article required all lot owners to be members of and pay assessments to the Association, and permitted the Association to impose liens on the property of any owners who failed to pay their assessment. Assessments were set at fifty dollars per year per lot.

Respondent purchased his lot in 1986 when membership in the Association and payment of assessments was voluntary, a fact that Respondent contends positively influenced his decision to purchase in Evergreen Highlands. Respondent was not among the majority of homeowners who approved the 1995 amendment to the covenants, and he subsequently refused to pay his lot assessment. When the Association threatened to record a lien against his property, Respondent filed this lawsuit challenging the validity of the 1995 amendment. The Association counterclaimed for a declaratory judgment that it had the implied power to collect assessments from all lot owners in the subdivision, and accordingly sought damages from West for breach of the implied contract.[1] The district court ruled in favor of the Association on the ground that the amendment was valid and binding; therefore, it never reached the merits of the Association's counterclaims.

New Article 16 required all lot owners to be members, pay assessmnt and he sit. assessment

---

1. The Association also counterclaimed that West was unjustly enriched; this issue was not appealed to us.

The court of appeals reversed, finding that the terms "change or modify" as set forth in the modification clause of the covenants did not allow for the addition of a wholly new covenant, but only for modifications to the existing covenants. The court examined two divergent lines of cases from other states and concluded that the particular language used in Evergreen Highlands' modification clause supported the more restrictive interpretation, based on the principle that courts should resolve any ambiguities in covenant language in favor of the free and unrestricted use of property.... The court of appeals did not address the issue of whether the Association had the implied power to collect assessments from lot owners, and therefore whether Respondent was in breach of an implied contract. We granted certiorari and now reverse and remand.

III. ANALYSIS

Interpretation of a covenant is a question of law requiring de novo review.... Courts must construe covenants as a whole based upon their underlying purpose, but will enforce a covenant as written if clear on its face. Ambiguities will be resolved in favor of the free and unrestricted use of property. *Id.; see also Newman v. Wittmer,* 277 Mont. 1, 917 P.2d 926, 929 (1996) (noting that although ambiguities should be resolved in favor of the unrestricted use of property, "the free use of the property must be balanced against the rights of the other purchasers in the subdivision.").

We begin our analysis by examining the modification clause of the Evergreen Highlands covenants in order to determine if its scope is broad enough to allow for the addition of a wholly new covenant by the requisite majority of property owners. Because this is an issue of first impression in Colorado, we examine cases from other jurisdictions interpreting similar covenant modification language. We conclude that the terms "change" and "modify," as used in the Evergreen Highlands covenants, are expansive enough to allow for the addition of a new covenant. We hold that the 1995 amendment to the Evergreen Highlands covenants, approved by the requisite majority of lot owners, is valid and binding on all lot owners in Evergreen Highlands. We therefore reverse the court of appeals.

We next examine the question of whether the Association has an implied right to levy assessments against lot owners in order to maintain common areas of the subdivision. [This part of the opinion is included in Chapter 2, A—Eds.] ...

A. Modification Clause of the Evergreen Highlands Covenants

The Association argues that the court of appeals erred when it held that the language of the Evergreen Highlands' modification clause only provided for "changes to the existing covenants, not the creation and addition of new covenants that have no relation to the existing covenants." ... Specifically, the Association argues that the word "change" is broad enough to encompass not only the modification of existing covenants, but the addition of new covenants as well. Based on our analysis of the language used in the Evergreen Highlands' modification clause, as well as the prevailing case law from other states, we agree.

1. The *Lakeland* Line of Cases

The court of appeals adopted the line of cases following *Lakeland Property Owners Association v. Larson,* 121 Ill.App.3d 805, ... 459 N.E.2d 1164 (1984). That case involved a situation nearly identical to the present one, in which a majority of lot owners voted to add a new covenant creating mandatory assessments and vesting the homeowner association with the power to impose liens for non-payment. Interpreting very similar covenant modification language (allowing a majority of the property owners to "change the said covenants in whole or in part," the court disallowed the adoption of the new covenant.

It held that "[t]he provision … clearly directs itself to changes of existing covenants, not the adding of new covenants which have no relation to existing ones." The *Lakeland* reasoning has been adopted by other states.

In *Caughlin Ranch Homeowners Association v. Caughlin Club,* 109 Nev. 264, 849 P.2d 310 (1993), a subdivision's original covenants imposed assessments only on residential parcels, although the modification clause provided for amendment of the rates. A year after the covenants were filed, a commercial club was developed and began operations on the property. Some six years later, after control of the homeowners association had passed from the developer to the lot owners, the homeowners association amended the covenants to levy assessments against the commercial parcel. Basing its reasoning on *Lakeland,* the Nevada Supreme Court disallowed the amendment, holding that the covenant modification clause allowing "amendments" referred only to "amendments of existing covenants as opposed to the creation of new covenants unrelated to the original covenants."

In *Boyles v. Hausmann,* 246 Neb. 181, 517 N.W.2d 610, 613 (1994), the modification clause allowed the majority of the homeowners to "change [the covenants] in whole or in part." The plaintiffs' lot was allegedly rendered unbuildable when the requisite majority of the homeowners association amended an existing covenant to increase the setback requirements. The *Boyles* court disallowed the additional covenant because, even though the restriction was appended onto an existing covenant, it was "new and different."

Finally, in *Meresse v. Stelma,* 100 Wash.App. 857, 999 P.2d 1267 (2000), the covenants for a six-lot subdivision allowed a majority of the lot owners "to change or alter them [the covenants] in full or in part." Five of the lot owners voted to alter the covenants to increase the access road easement, thereby stripping the sixth lot owner of a portion of his property. The court disallowed the amendment, holding that the amendatory language of the covenants "does not place a purchaser or owner on notice that he or she might be burdened, without assent, by road relocation at the majority's whim."

2. The *Zito* Line of Cases

Despite the fact that the *Lakeland* reasoning has been followed by other courts as recently as 2000, the same court that decided *Lakeland* issued a contrary opinion in 1992 with little explanation.[4] In *Zito v. Gerken,* 225 Ill.App.3d 79, 167 Ill.Dec. 433, 587 N.E.2d 1048 (1992), existing subdivision covenants granted the homeowners association the authority to modify the covenants, although the exact language of the modification clause is not provided. The homeowners association adopted mandatory assessments and disgruntled homeowners sued. This time, however, the Illinois Appellate Court held in favor of the homeowners association, holding that: "[a] restrictive covenant which has been modified, altered or amended will be enforced if it is clear, unambiguous and reasonable"; "[t]he 1987 amendment does not seek to change the character of [the subdivision] or to impose unreasonable burdens upon any lot owners"; and "the terms and conditions of the 1987 amendment impose a minimal collective burden upon the residents."

---

4. *Zito* was issued by a different division of the Illinois Appellate Court with only a "*but see*" reference to the earlier ruling in *Lakeland,* to wit: "The trial court, therefore, erred when it failed to enforce the 1987 amendment to the restrictive covenants. *But see Lakeland Property Owners Ass'n v. Larson* [citation omitted]."

In *Sunday Canyon Property Owners Association v. Annett,* 978 S.W.2d 654 (Tex.Ct.App.1998), the modification language allowed the covenants, upon a majority vote of the lot owners, to be "waived, abandoned, terminated, modified, altered or changed." Based on this language, the court allowed the requisite majority to adopt an amendment creating a homeowners association levying mandatory lot assessments. The court held that, despite the fact that the creation of the homeowners association

> exceeded the original purpose of the right to amend contemplated by purchasers prior to the amendment, it is of no moment. Recognized long ago was the right of persons ... to contract with relation to their property as they see fit in the absence of contraventions of public policy and positive law. That right is derived from ownership of the property, and embraces the ability to impose on the property restrictive covenants and to abrogate or modify them....

Finally, in *Windemere Homeowners Association, Inc. v. McCue,* 297 Mont. 77, 990 P.2d 769 (1999), a majority of homeowners voted to amend the covenants to create a homeowners association authorized to levy the costs of road maintenance against property owners. Basing his argument on *Lakeland, Caughlin,* and *Boyles,* plaintiff homeowner challenged the amendment as an impermissible new covenant. The court, however, held that the modification clause in these covenants was "markedly different" than those in *Lakeland* and its progeny; specifically, the clause, like that in *Sunday Canyon,* allowed a majority of property owners to "waive, abandon, terminate, modify, alter, or change" the covenants. Consequently, the court held that this amendatory language was "broad enough" to justify the amendment.

3. Application to the Evergreen Highlands Covenants

As this summary of cases from other jurisdictions illustrates, there exists a split in the law with respect to this issue. Respondent contends that these cases can be distinguished by how narrowly or broadly the particular modification clause is written, and argues that the amendatory language in Evergreen Highlands' covenants is much more akin to the narrow language found in the *Lakeland* line of cases than the more expansive language found in the *Zito* line of cases. He therefore argues that the *Lakeland* reasoning should prevail here.

There is little substance to the distinction between the "broad" or "narrow" amendatory language upon which Respondent relies. The covenant modification language in *Lakeland* and *Boyles* allowed a majority of lot owners to "change" the covenants, ... and in *Meresse* to "change or alter" the covenants.... The amendatory language in *Sunday Canyon* and in *Windemere,* however, provided that the covenants could be "waived, abandoned, terminated, modified, altered or changed." ... In the latter cases, the first three words — "waived, abandoned, and terminated" — all deal with *ending* a covenant, not adding a new one, and are therefore inapplicable here. The last three words — "modified, altered, or changed" — are the same as those in the *Lakeland* line of cases, with the addition of "altered," which is simply a synonym for "change" and "modify." Thus, distinguishing these cases from one another based on the breadth of the language used is an artificial, and ultimately unpersuasive, distinction.

Moreover, from a linguistic standpoint, the *Lakeland* conclusion that "change or modify" can only apply to the alteration of existing covenants, and not the addition of new and different ones, is not well-founded. Webster defines "change" as "to make different." *Webster's Third New International Dictionary* 373 (1986); *see also Ticor Title Ins. Co. v. Rancho Santa Fe Ass'n,* 177 Cal.App.3d 726, 223 Cal.Rptr. 175, 179 (1986) ("the words 'changed' and 'modified' include any alteration whether involving an increase or decrease."). Applying this definition to the language at issue, covenants could certainly be changed or made different either by the addition, subtraction, or modification of a term. Confining the meaning of the term "change" only to the modification of existing covenants, then, seems illogically narrow.

For these reasons, we find the court of appeals' reliance on a linguistic analysis to distinguish covenant modification language unsatisfactory. We instead conclude that the different outcomes in the *Lakeland* and *Zito* lines of cases are based on the differing factual scenarios and severity of consequences that the cases present. In those cases where courts disallowed the amendment of covenants, the impact upon the objecting lot owner was generally far more substantial and unforeseeable than the amendment at issue here. *See, e.g., Caughlin Ranch,* ... (covenants previously imposing assessments only on private lots amended to assess the sole commercial parcel in the subdivision at a substantially higher rate); *Boyles,* ... (changed setback requirement rendered plaintiff's lot unbuildable); *Meresse* ... (increased access road easement deprived plaintiff of a portion of his private lot).

In contrast, *Zito, Windemere,* and *Sunday Canyon,* like this case, all specifically considered — and allowed — the amendment of covenants in order to impose mandatory assessments on lot owners for the purpose of maintaining common elements of a subdivision. We accordingly find the *Zito* line of cases more applicable to the situation here. This interpretation also avoids the absurd result that could follow from application of the *Lakeland* reasoning; Evergreen Highlands would be unable to adopt a mandatory-assessment covenant when its original covenants were silent on the subject, yet could adopt such a covenant if its original covenants had expressly prohibited a mandatory-assessment covenant.

Moreover, the amendment at issue in this case was changed according to the modification clause of the original Evergreen Highlands covenants, and it is undisputed that Respondent was on actual notice of that clause when he purchased his lot in 1986. In addition, we note that, at fifty dollars per year, the mandatory assessment imposed on Respondent is neither unreasonable nor burdensome.[5] To the contrary, the existence of a well-maintained park area immediately adjacent to Respondent's lot undoubtedly enhances Respondent's property value.

We conclude that the modification clause of the Evergreen Highlands covenants is expansive enough in its scope to allow for the adoption of a new covenant, and hold that the 1995 amendment to the Evergreen Highlands covenants, passed by the requisite majority of lot owners, is valid and binding on all lot owners in Evergreen Highlands.

Notes & Questions

1. In *Holiday Pines Property Owners Ass'n, Inc. v. Wetherington,* 596 So. 2d 84 (Fla. Dist. Ct. App. 1992), the court held that an amendment by the developer that required

---

5. By way of comparison, the amendment approved in *Zito* provided for lot assessments at $100 per year.... The amendment approved in *Sunday Canyon* imposed an open-ended annual assessment for the maintenance and improvement of the roads, water system, and common areas; for providing architectural control over lot improvements; and for promoting "the health, welfare, and safety of the residents." ... Finally, the amendment approved in *Windemere* created a homeowners association that was responsible for maintenance, repair, reconstruction, and snow removal on the common subdivision road, and allowed the association to assess lot owners for the paving of the road....

homeowners to become association members, pay dues, and be subject to the lien enforcement power was both <u>unreasonable and outside the general scheme of development.</u> Can the different outcomes of *Evergreen Highlands* and *Holiday Pines* be explained by *who* was exercising the unilateral amendment power? Should a developer be able to convert a project into a common interest community after lots have been sold without consent of the homeowners? See Restatement (Third) §6.3 in Chapter 2.

2. *Incremental amendments.* In most cases, a vote of association members is required to amend the declaration. Due to "democratic forces" similarly observed in governmental affairs, most changes in common interest communities only incrementally expand or contract the servitude regime because most people prefer the *status quo* until it becomes absolutely necessary to change. Should community association documents be drafted to allow changes to be more readily adopted? Under what circumstances should super majorities be required to adopt amendments?

Note: Developer's Reserved Amendment Powers

In the *Zito* case discussed in *Evergreen Highlands*, the developer had reserved the right to amend the covenants at any time, a right the developer later transferred to the association. It is not infrequent to find that a community association's governing documents permit the developer to make amendments unilaterally, but the power is not usually transferred to the association. Even if the declaration appears to give the developer an unlimited amendment power, courts have generally imposed limitations on how the power can be exercised. In *Flamingo Ranch Estates, Inc. v. Sunshine Ranches Homeowners, Inc.,* 303 So. 2d 665 (Fla. Dist. Ct. App. 1974), a leading case, the Florida District Court of Appeal held that a declarant may unilaterally amend the declaration only if the amendment is reasonable and does not destroy the general scheme of development. The Restatement (Third) takes a similar position.

> Restatement (Third) §6.21 Developer's Power To Waive Provisions Of The Declaration
>
> A developer may not exercise a power to amend or modify the declaration in a way that would materially change the character of the development or the burdens on the existing community members unless the declaration fairly apprises purchasers that the power could be used for the kind of change proposed.

Problem

During the period of declarant control when developer had both control of the board and the majority vote, he amended the documents to permit a portion of the common property to be declared as the site of a unit, changed the requirement that all units be restricted to residential use to permit that newly-created unit to be used for commercial purposes, and then used that unit as a real estate sales office.

Years later when the owners finally achieved control of the association, declarant and its successor, Real Estate Resale Operator, had continually used the real estate office for commercial purposes. In defending against the association's claim that they are violating the declaration, they argue that the owners acquiesced by their silence and that Real Estate Resale Operator has acquired a right through adverse use to continue to operate the commercial facility in the midst of the residential development. The board invites you to a meeting and requests your advice. How do you respond?

D. Amendments May Not Deprive Members of Certain Existing Rights

Twin Lakes Village Property Ass'n, Inc. v. Aune

Supreme Court of Idaho

857 P.2d 611 (Id. 1993)

BISTLINE, J. The stipulated facts and documentary evidence submitted to the trial court show that the Twin Lakes Village Property Association, Inc., ("the association") is a non-profit corporation. In July of 1973, Pack River Properties, Inc., a Washington corporation, created the Twin Lakes Village Subdivision in Kootenai County, Idaho. The subdivision originally had a nine-hole golf course, a clubhouse, tennis courts, and a swimming pool, as well as other amenities, for the use of the association members. Members paid a separate annual fee in order to use the golf course.

In 1985, Pack River gave notice that it would cease to operate the properties at Twin Lakes Village. After the announcement, the membership of the association explored ways to continue the operation of association's amenities and other necessary services.

In 1986, Twin Lakes Investments ("TLI") purchased the Pack River properties. After the acquisition, meetings were held about the future operation of the amenities and services. By September, the association board of directors had developed, for submission to the membership, a plan which included the acquisition by the membership from TLI of the existing nine-hole golf course, together with additional property for the construction of nine more holes of golf course, and all other of the existing membership amenities. The plan was submitted to the membership. The association's board of directors drafted proposed amendments to the articles of incorporation, the bylaws, and the protective covenants in order to accommodate the purchase of the golf course and to provide for its future development and operation, as well as the other services and amenities. These proposed amendments: 1) changed the voting structure of the membership from a weighted system based upon square footage of property owned within the village to a one lot-one vote system; 2) eliminated provisions which forbid any amendment to the bylaws which would (a) deprive a member of a then existing right or privilege or (b) effect a fundamental change in the policies of the association; and 3) permitted the acquisition and improvement of the golf course.

These proposed amendments were passed by the membership on January 24, 1987. After the approval of the amendments, the issue of the property purchase from TLI was submitted to the membership for vote, and was accepted and passed by the majority. This vote was in accordance with the provisions of the newly adopted amended bylaws. TLI, as owners, did not exercise their rights to act, vote or participate in the voting action to approve the purchase by the association.

The board thereafter levied a new assessment on all memberships for the purposes of acquiring, developing and operating the property and for the further development of the golf course by an additional nine holes. This assessment was in addition to the regular annual assessment previously paid by the members before January 24, 1987. The association and TLI entered into an agreement of purchase on April 3, 1987.

The association instituted a declaratory judgment action against those association lot owners who had failed to pay the assessments. The defendant lot owners counterclaimed, arguing that the actions taken by the association were invalid under the original corporate documents. They also sought a declaratory judgment as to the effect of the assessments.

TLI was allowed to intervene in this matter.

The defendants asserted at trial that they were not required to pay the assessment, in part, because the amendments to the bylaws which permitted the purchase of the golf course and amenities were void because they violated Article 8 of the original bylaws (hereinafter "the protective covenants"), which places limitations on the members' ability to amend the bylaws. The protective covenants provide:

> *These By-Laws may be repealed or amended by a vote representing two-thirds of the assessable lands held by the members* present at any regular meeting of the association, or at any special meeting of the association called for that purpose, *except that the members shall not have the power* to change the purposes of the association so as to decrease its rights and powers under the laws of the State, or to waive the requirement of bond or other provision for the safety and security of the property and funds of the association and its members, or *to deprive any member of rights and privileges then existing, or so to amend the By-Laws as to effect a fundamental change in the policies of the association....*

(Emphasis added.) Further, the members argued that the extraordinary assessment imposed to finance the purchase did not pass by the required super-majority of votes as required by the amended bylaws. The district court, sitting without a jury, ruled for the property association. The court held that:

1. The articles of incorporation, the bylaws, and the original protective covenants were properly and lawfully amended.

2. The amendments to these documents did not effect a fundamental change in the policies of the Association.

3. While the original voting system was changed as a result of the amendments, the defendants did not assert or show that the new "one ownership-one vote" system affected the outcome of the vote or that rights were prejudiced by this change.

4. The assessments were lawfully imposed upon its members.

5. The plaintiff was entitled to judgment and prejudgment interest against the defendants.

Some but not all of the defendants appealed from the district court's ruling. (The appellants are hereinafter referred to as the members.)

DISCUSSION

The members make four arguments on appeal:

1. That the amendment of the bylaws that eliminated the protective covenants violated those same covenants.

2. That the protective covenants were violated when the bylaws were amended to change member voting rights to a one lot-one vote system from the previous system, which allotted voting strength on the basis of the amount of property owned within the village.

3. That the amendments to the bylaws that permitted the purchase of the golf course violated the protective covenant that forbids any amendment that changes the fundamental policies of the association.

4. That the assessments imposed against the members in order to purchase and operate the golf course did not pass by the required number of votes.

In order to resolve these issues, we must construe the bylaws. Because corporate documents are equivalent to contracts among the members of the association, the normal rules governing the interpretation of contracts apply.

We conclude, for the reasons expressed below, that: 1) the amendment which eliminated the protective covenants is invalid; 2) the change in voting structure is invalid; 3) the purchase of the golf course did not effect a fundamental change in the policies of the association; but 4) the members are not required to pay the assessments because of the irregularities in the voting on those measures. Consequently, we affirm the order of the district court in part and reverse it in part.

1. The Amendment of the Bylaws Which Eliminated the Protective Covenants is Void.

When the bylaws were amended, the prohibition against depriving any member of then-existing rights and privileges and the prohibition against effecting a fundamental change in the policies of the association were eliminated. The members challenge these changes as violative of the provisions they eliminated.

We agree with the members. If the elimination of those covenants are allowed to stand, the members, who invested substantial sums of money believing they were joining a homeowner's association in order to protect and preserve their investment, could, by majority vote of the other owners, be subjected to unrestricted changes in the nature, purposes, policies, and rules of the association. This would not be so under the protective covenants. The protective covenants created a right to be free from fundamental change and made inalienable all rights and privileges currently possessed by the members. Because the elimination of the protective covenants eliminated those rights, the amendment is in violation thereof and thus is void.

2. The Amendments to the Voting Rights Bylaws are Invalid Because The Amendment Deprived the Members of An Existing Right.

Prior to the 1987 amendments, votes were allocated according to square foot ownership within the plat. That formula was changed to one of "one lot-one vote." Thus those owners who made a larger investment in the association no longer had a larger say in the running of the association as a result of the amendment. The members argue that the amendments that changed the voting system violated the protective covenants by depriving certain members of their then-existing voting rights.

In order to resolve this issue, we must determine the extent of the members' voting rights in order to determine whether the amendments were a deprivation thereof. Prior to the amendments, Article 3 of the articles of incorporation listed among the "rights of the members" that "the voting rights of each membership in the association shall be in the same proportion as the square footage of the lot owned or being purchased bears to the total square footage of land in the plat, exclusive of the platted common areas and public roadways." Thus, the members' voting rights consisted of two separate and independent rights: 1) the right to the vote itself and 2) the right to the manner by which the vote was weighted.

The association argues that the elimination of the second rights only "diminished" the voting rights because the members still have the first right in its entirety. This argument cannot prevail, however, because even if only one of the members' two voting rights was eliminated, the fact remains that the second right was totally eliminated. Thus we declare the amendment that changed the voting structure to be void as violative of Article 8 of the original bylaws because the members were totally deprived of a right then existing.

3. The Amendments Which Permitted the Purchase of the Golf Course Did Not Effect a Fundamental Change in the Policies of the Association.

Finally, the members argue that the purchase of the golf course effected a fundamental change in the policies of the association and is therefore invalid. They point to Article 3, which states, in relevant part

> Pecuniary gain is not the object of this Corporation. The purposes for which this corporation is organized are generally, but not limited to the holding and maintaining in accordance to the By-Laws as from time to time adopted and amended, the common areas ... and any other property it may subsequently acquire.... within said plat; maintaining and supervising control of the architectural design of improvements placed upon the property in said plat, and through the architectural control committee to be created under the By-Laws of this corporation and its other proper officers, to interpret and enforce the protective and restrictive covenants....

The members argue that a fundamental change occurred when the association became the owner and operator of an entrepreneurial venture, here before the main function of the association was as a caretaker of the common areas. The association is quick to point out that the article goes on to provide that "[i]n addition to these general purposes but without limitation thereof," the association "shall have all the powers of corporations provided for under state law including the power to purchase real property, borrow money," and "[t]o acquire and hold as common areas [real property] pursuant to the protective covenants ... and to maintain and improve the same for benefit of the members and to make assessments therefor subject to these Articles and the By-Laws."

We conclude the purchase, financing, improvement, and maintenance of the golf course falls squarely within the powers expressly granted to the association. It necessarily follows that the exercise of the power expressly granted in Article 3 could not be considered a fundamental change in the policies of the association as contemplated by Article 8. Otherwise, the powers never would have been granted to the association and that portion of the Articles of Incorporation would be rendered a nullity. This interpretation is consonant with our rule that various provisions in a contract must be construed, if possible, so to give force and effect to every part thereof....

Our conclusion, that the amendment authorizing the purchase of the golf course did not effect a fundamental change, does not mean the purchase is otherwise valid because, as we held in part 2 above, the method by which the purchase was approved (the one lot-one vote system) was invalid. The association argues that any error in that regard should be deemed harmless because the members have not shown any prejudice from the change in voting structure, *i.e.*, that the result of the balloting would have been different. We disagree. Idaho Rule of Civil Procedure 61 permits a court to reverse a judgment whenever such action is required to do "substantial justice." Given the difficulties in proving prejudice in this case along with the fundamental character of the right to vote, we conclude it would be fundamentally unfair to allow the results of the ballot to bind the members. Thus, although we do not invalidate the purchase of the golf course, we do hold that the members are not liable for any assessments to fund the purchase, maintenance, or operation of the golf course unless the purchase and assessments are properly approved pursuant to the original voting structure.

4. The Assessments Were Not Properly Approved Under The Amended Bylaws.

The final issue raised by the members is whether, assuming the legitimacy of the change in voting structure, the assessments imposed for the purchase and maintenance of the golf course were properly approved under the terms of the amended bylaws. Even though we held in part 3 above that the members are not liable for the assessments currently imposed, we address this issue to give guidance in case the association decides to attempt to impose assessments in the future.

a. Any extraordinary assessment must be passed by a two-thirds majority.

After the acquisition of the golf course was approved, the membership voted to impose a one-time assessment of $4000 to be applied towards the purchase of the golf course. Sixty-three percent of the membership voted in favor of this assessment. The assessment, according to the members, is invalid because it did not pass by a two-thirds majority of the total voting power of the association as required by Article 6 of the amended bylaws.

Article 6 of the amended bylaws provides that extraordinary assessments may not exceed twenty per cent of the budgeted gross expenses, excluding reserves, for that fiscal year without the assent of two-thirds of the voting power of the Association. It is undisputed that the $4000 assessment exceeded the twenty per cent amount. Thus, the members claim that this assessment is invalid because it was approved by sixty-three per cent of the membership instead of the sixty-six per cent required. The association argues that Article 15 permitted the assessment to be approved by a simple majority. Article 15 specifically deals with the acquisition of the golf course and Article 15.3(a) permits a simple majority to determine whether "to purchase the golf course for cash or other consideration to be raised by Extraordinary Assessment and/or third party borrowing." Article 15.3(d) goes on to state that Article 15.3 is intended to "allow all decisions with respect to the acquisition, operation and maintenance to be made by a majority of a quorum of the voting power."

We first note that the Court will read a contract as a whole and will give meaning to all of its terms to the extent possible.... The above quoted language from Article 15, however, only permits a simple majority of the members to authorize the purchase of the golf course. It does not speak to the approval of the *funding method*. The reference to extraordinary assessments and/or third-party borrowing is a condition on the association's power to purchase the golf course, *i.e.*, the purchasing authority granted by 15.3(a) is conditional upon the approval of an extraordinary assessment and/or third party borrowing. The language does not permit the imposition of an extraordinary assessment with only a simple majority vote. The drafters must have intended Article 15.3(a) to incorporate the supermajority provisions of Article 6 because Article 6.4 states that extraordinary assessments may be used to "acquire additional Common Area (*such as the Golf Course*)." (Emphasis added.) To belabor the obvious, the purchase of the golf course would not have been used as an illustration of a permissible purpose of an Article 6 extraordinary assessment if the drafters did not intend Article 6 to set forth the procedures for the approval of the extraordinary assessment to buy the golf course.

Accordingly, we hold that any extraordinary assessment, including those intended to apply to the purchase of the golf course, must receive a two-third majority vote in favor in order to pass.

...

CONCLUSION

We hold that the amendment to the bylaws regarding the members' voting rights is void. All future votes must be conducted under the original voting scheme. We also hold that the amendments to the bylaws that permitted the purchase of the golf course did not effect a fundamental change in the policies of the association. However, because of the irregularities in the voting, we hold that the members are not liable for those assessments. Any future extraordinary assessments must pass by a two-thirds majority. Any future regular assessments for operation and maintenance need only a majority vote to pass. Finally, the amendments to the protective restraints are void. Costs on appeal to the appellants. The respondent's request for attorney fees is denied.

Affirmed in part, Reversed in part.

Notes & Questions

1. *Unanimous consent requirements.* Courts have traditionally protected property owners in common interest communities from amendments that would unfairly change the allocation of burdens in the community or the community's character. Amendments that prohibit or materially restrict property use and amendments that change the voting rights or common expense liability allocated to the lot or unit, require unanimous consent unless the declaration gave fair notice that such changes could be made over the objection of affected property owners. See Restatement (Third) § 6.10.

2. *Amendment procedure.* The underlying problem in the *Twin Lakes Village* case was the improper voting method utilized. Fortunately for the association in that case, properly re-voting under the original voting scheme would reaffirm their original objectives. As counsel for an association considering a similar suspect voting change, how would you advise the association to minimize the risk of being subsequently challenged?

E. Prospective and Retroactive Application of Amendments

Worthinglen Condo. Unit Owners' Ass'n v. Brown
Court of Appeals of Ohio
566 N.E. 2d 1275 (Oh. Ct. App. 1989)

BRYANT, J. Plaintiff-appellant, Worthinglen Condominium Unit Owners' Association ("Worthinglen"), appeals from a judgment of the Franklin County Court of Common Pleas holding an amendment to the condominium declaration to be unenforceable.

Plaintiff sets forth the following as its sole assignment of error:

> The court erred, as a matter of law, in holding that an amendment to a condominium declaration prohibiting unit owners from leasing their units is unenforceable against owners who acquired condominium units prior to the adoption of that amendment.

Plaintiff is a condominium unit owners' association. On March 10, 1988, plaintiff amended the Worthinglen condominium declaration to include a provision that stated, in part:

> No unit shall be used for any other purpose other than a dwelling place for a single family and for purposes necessarily incidental thereto. Notwithstanding any other provision of this Declaration, Exhibits, or By-Laws, each unit shall be occupied by the owner of that unit, and no leasehold interest or general tenancy in others shall be created by the owner of any unit. The above requirement of owner

occupancy and prohibition against leasehold interests or general tenancies shall become <u>effective within ninety (90) days</u> of the recording of an amendment creating such a requirement and prohibition with the office of the Franklin County Recorder, providing that <u>such amendment shall not affect the existing term of any lease in effect at the time of such recording</u>.

At the time the owners amended the declaration, defendant-appellee, Jacqueline L. Brown, owned one unit at Worthinglen, which she leased to third parties. The "grandfather" clause in the amendment allowed <u>her existing lease to continue</u>. However, when defendant's tenants moved out in October 1988, defendant sought to lease her unit to defendants Mr. and Mrs. Yamada.

On October 28, 1988, plaintiff filed an action in the court of common pleas, apparently pursuant to R.C. 5311.19, seeking a temporary restraining order, a preliminary injunction, and a permanent injunction to prevent defendant from leasing her unit to the Yamadas. On November 30, 1988, a referee recommended that the trial court deny plaintiff injunctive relief. On December 1, the trial court adopted the referee's report and plaintiff appealed to this court.

This case launches the court into largely uncharted waters of Ohio law. While other states have set forth parameters regarding the validity of various condominium rules, Ohio jurisdictions for the most part have not. In such a situation, we are tempted to analogize to existing defined areas of the law and apply the interpretations and limits found therein to the condominium issue before us. However, condominiums are unique. More specifically, unlike neighborhoods consisting of single-family dwellings, condominium associations may make rules governing all unit owners, with the approval of a supermajority of the owners. Moreover, given the need in condominium living for a stable environment with the concomitant relinquishing of some measure of individuality, as well as the central role played by the condominium's restrictive scheme in the lives of the current and future owners, we find that none of the readily available analogies so squarely meshes with the issues presented herein as to allow resolution by any single analogy. Indeed, whether we attempt to derive a solution by comparison to real estate or zoning law, corporate law (the business judgment rule), administrative law (review of administrative rule making), or constitutional review (application of *Shelley v. Kraemer* [1948], 334 U.S. 1, 68 S.Ct. 836, 92 L.Ed. 1161), each of the individual theories is lacking in some respect, and may indeed result in different conclusions. Note, *Judicial Review of Condominium Rulemaking* (1981), 94 Harv.L.Rev. 647 (hereinafter "Note").

Hence, we decline to apply by analogy a single, defined body of law to the issue herein. Instead, we examine condominium rules and regulations in the context of the unique character of condominium living. In so doing, we note that a purchaser of a condominium unit voluntarily submits himself to the condominium form of property ownership....

Potential purchasers of condominium units should thus realize that the regime in existence at the time of purchase <u>may not continue indefinitely</u> and that changes in the declaration may take the form of restrictions on the unit owner's use of his property.

We do not, though, endorse the view that a person who voluntarily enters the ranks of condominium ownership surrenders all individual property rights. Individual property receives some protection in the condominium arrangement, although less than that accorded non-condominium property. An example of the protection is set forth in R.C. 5311.05(B)(9), which requires a supermajority (seventy-five percent) to pass amendments to the declaration.

In addressing nearly the identical issue, the court in *Seagate Condominium Assn., Inc. v. Duffy* (Fla. App. 1976), 330 So. 2d 484, 485, noted that restraints on alienation, including restrictions on leasing, are part of the law; only unlimited or absolute restraints are prohibited. As a result, the court chose to assess the validity of restraints by reference to their reasonableness.

We agree with *Seagate* and cases from Ohio and other jurisdictions which generally require that condominium rules meet a "reasonableness" test. See *River Terrace Condominium Assn. v. Lewis* (1986), 33 Ohio App. 3d 52, 57, 514 N.E.2d 732, 737–738, at fn. 8; *O'Buck v. Cottonwood Village Condominium Assn., Inc.* (Alaska 1988), 750 P.2d 813, 817; *Johnson v. Hobson* (D.C. App. 1986), 505 A.2d 1313, 1317; *Hidden Harbour Estates, Inc. v. Norman, supra,* at 182. Accordingly, we adopt the reasonableness test, pursuant to which the validity of condominium rules is measured by whether the rule is reasonable under the surrounding circumstances. If the rule is unreasonable, arbitrary or capricious in those circumstances, it is invalid.

...

["The first question ... of reasonableness is whether the decision or rule was arbitrary or capricious.... The second question is whether the decision or rule is discriminatory or evenhanded.... The third question is whether the decision or rule was made in good faith for the common welfare of the owners and occupants of the condominium...."—Eds.]

We agree that evaluation of any condominium rule under the reasonableness test requires an examination of the foregoing considerations, including the potential hardship to accrue as a result of the amendment. Included therein, by necessity, is not only a consideration of whether the surrounding circumstances render a restriction on an owner's use of his or her property reasonable, but also a determination of whether the rule has been reasonably implemented. *Cf. Winston Towers 200 Assn., Inc. v. Saverio* (Fla. Dist. Ct. App. 1978), 360 So. 2d 470 (bylaw amendment banning pets void and unenforceable against dog owner as attempt to impose retroactive regulation), and *Wilshire Condominium Assn., Inc. v. Kohlbrand* (Fla. Dist. Ct. App. 1979), 368 So. 2d 629, 631 (regulation, in existence when defendant purchased unit, permitting purchasers to retain dogs but forbidding dogs' replacement enforceable). Similarly, in this case, the issue is not only whether plaintiff reasonably may restrict defendant's right to lease her unit, but also whether plaintiff reasonably may do so retroactively.[2]

Defendant, while not contending that the leasing restriction is invalid in itself, urges that it is invalid insofar as it is retroactively applied against a unit owner who bought her unit before the restriction existed, in violation of the notice provisions of Ohio's condominium statutes. Defendant cites *Breene v. Plaza Tower Assn.* (N.D. 1981), 310 N.W.2d 730, in support of her argument. The referee herein also relied on *Breene*.

The condominium association in *Breene* had amended its "declaration of restrictions" to include a provision restricting the unit owners' ability to lease their units. *Id.* at 732–733. The statute involved in that case stated:

> The owner of a project shall, *prior to the conveyance of any condominiums therein,* record a declaration of restrictions relating to such project which restrictions shall be enforceable equitable servitudes where reasonable, and shall inure to and bind all owners of condominiums in the project.'" (Emphasis sic.) *Id.* at 733.

---

2. While *Seagate Condominium Assn., Inc. v. Duffy, supra,* found a retroactive restriction on alienation reasonable, we do not suggest that *Seagate* dictates the appropriate result herein, as the fact of *Seagate* included a transient tourist population not likely to be a motivating factor in plaintiff's adoption of the rule at issue.

The *Breene* court declared that the lease restriction in question was "not legally binding upon Breene" and that any future amendments "would have only a prospective effect." *Id.* at 731. The court noted that the statute required an owner to record all restrictions on the condominium property before conveyance of the property. Since the restriction in *Breene* had not been recorded at the time the unit owners involved in the case had purchased their unit, the court reasoned that the restriction was not binding on the unit owners because the owners had not received notice of the restriction pursuant to the statute. *Id.* at 733–734.

We find the reasoning in *Breene* unpersuasive. Although we note some similarities in the respective facts and statutes involved,[3] we, nevertheless, do not agree with the North Dakota Supreme Court's conclusion that a lease restriction can never be enforced against owners who purchased their units before the restriction was recorded, nor do we believe that retroactive enforcement of a restriction would render any Ohio statutory notice provision a "nullity." *Breene, supra,* at 735. A condominium declaration could satisfy the statutory right to notice of a restriction prior to the purchase of a condominium unit, *id.* at 734, if it adequately set forth whatever restrictions existed at the time of purchase. Moreover, application of defendant's contentions would create a lack of uniformity in condominium living that undermines one of the purposes of condominium rules and regulations.

Defendant also contends more broadly that R.C. 5311.05(B)(9), which requires a declaration to state "[t]he method by which the declaration may be amended," does not sufficiently inform a potential purchaser of a condominium unit of the restrictions that could be placed on his unit. See *Breene, supra,* at 734 ("knowledge of the provisions for amendment" does not constitute adequate notice). However, if a declaration has provided notice under R.C. 5311.05(B)(9) to a potential purchaser that the condominium association may amend the declaration, then the fact that the purchaser has not foreseen a *particular* amendment is not dispositive.

Given the foregoing, we sustain plaintiff's single assignment of error to the extent set forth above. We reverse the judgment of the trial court and remand this matter for consideration of the reasonableness of plaintiff's amendment to the declaration, including the retroactive application thereof, in light of the facts and circumstances present at the time the amendment to the declaration was adopted. Inasmuch as the foregoing opinion addresses issues perhaps not reasonably anticipated by the parties, the trial court on remand may take such additional evidence as may be necessary to determine this action under the guidelines this opinion sets forth.

Reversed and Remanded.

Notes & Questions

1. *Extent of amendment power.* Courts have upheld amendments in a wide variety of contexts directly affecting previously existing rights. For example, associations have amended documents to prohibit children from residing within the community, to prohibit leasing under all but narrowly defined circumstances, to prohibit leasing entirely,

---

3. Ohio's condominium statutes, like North Dakota's, require condominium owners to record property restrictions. R.C. 5311.05(b)(3) requires the condominium developer to record a declaration, which must set forth "[t]he purpose or purposes of the condominium property and the units and commercial facilities situated therein and the restrictions, if any, upon the use or uses thereof [.]" The condominium association must also record amendments to the declaration. R. C. 5311.08(A).

to prohibit pets, and to adopt amendments in other circumstances which one might reasonably argue directly affect the "bundle of rights" one acquired when taking title to the home in the community. What should the standard be? How far can the amendment power extend? See, *e.g.*, *Noble v. Murphy*, 612 N.E.2d 266 (1992) (amendment of bylaws to incorporate pet restriction held valid; *Kroop v. Caravelle Condo., Inc.*, 323 So. 2d 307 (1975) (amendment prohibiting leasing of unit more than once during period of ownership was reasonable and could be applied to owner who purchased unit before amendment was adopted; owner purchased subject to all terms of declaration including term that declaration could be amended).

2. *Prospective amendments.* The benefit of making amendments only prospectively enforceable is two-fold. First, it assists in acquiring the needed number of votes necessary to amend the governing documents (after all, existing owners are exempted from its requirements). Second, it makes a regulation that may otherwise be unreasonable, become reasonable since the rights of existing owners are not interfered with and prospective owners have notice of its requirements. What type of amendments should be prospectively enforced? See, *e.g.*, *Constellation Condo. Ass'n v. Harrington*, 467 So. 2d 378 (Fla. Dist. Ct. App. 1985) (limitation on number of days children under 12 were permitted to reside); *Winston Towers 200 Ass'n, Inc. v. Saverio*, 360 So. 2d 470 (Fla. Dist. Ct. App. 1978) (pet ban).

3. *The* Breene *notice and recordation rule.* Do you agree with the *Worthington* court that the *Breene* notice and recordation rule with respect to amendments "would create a lack of uniformity in condominium living that undermines one of the purposes of condominium rules and regulations?" Are there situations where the *Breene* test may seem more appropriate than the reasonableness test imposed by the *Worthington* court? Review *Breene v. Plaza Tower Ass'n*, 310 N.W.2d 730 (N.D. 1981).

F. Method of Amending Documents

There are interesting questions involved in a very basic issue inherent in any amendment process: what is the vote required to amend? That may be an obvious question, but simply answering it with a percentage number does not necessarily resolve the question. What do the terms mean?

Earlier we discussed the possibilities in seeking to determine whether a percentage of the total number of owners, a percentage of the owners of a total number of lots, a percentage of those owners who are affected or, perhaps "materially adversely affected," by the amendment, or some other variation was appropriate. The most typical situations deal with percentages of owners with questions arising over the treatment of owners of multiple lots.

If Owner has title to six lots of nine, does she represent two-thirds, or does she, in combination with two of the remaining three owners, represent two-thirds? The voting procedure also presents interesting questions. The documentation may clarify whether the vote must be at a meeting or whether it might be done by mailed-in written ballots. May it be done in part at a meeting and in part by ballot? Consider why a board may wish to have the flexibility to achieve the necessary votes through methods other than simply at a meeting.

In many instances, it is difficult to obtain a quorum, much less to have a super majority attend an actual meeting. Combining a meeting with written votes may make the overall process more democratic and more likely to succeed. What about silence as consent? Might the board send out notice that if one does not respond, the lack of response will be deemed to be concurrence? What are the objections to such an approach? Might it be appropriate under any circumstances? Would your reaction be different if silence is invoked as consent against an institutional lender as opposed to an individual homeowner?

Finally, how long might the period to vote be kept open? In the event that the board uses a meeting combined with a written vote in an effort to achieve a super majority, may that period of voting extend for days, weeks, months?

1. Voting Requirements

Harrison v. Air Park Estates Zoning Comm'n

Court of Appeals of Texas
533 S.W.2d 108 (Tex. Ct. App. 1976)

AKIN, J. This is an appeal from a temporary injunction against defendant Ivan Harrison, obtained by plaintiff Air Park Estate Zoning Committee, restraining defendant's completion of an aircraft hangar on property of which he is equitable owner. Plaintiff's property is a part of a larger tract originally owned by Milton J. Noell, which was subdivided into individual lots to provide "homesites for people who like airplanes." The development contemplated that persons buying lots would build both a hangar and a residence on each lot. In 1969, Harrison purchased one of the lots under a note and a contract for deed containing the following restrictions and provisions:

12b ... *A hangar may be built before the home is built....*

16 These covenants ... shall be binding ... until revoked or *modified in whole or in part by a three-fourths majority vote of the then owners of real property therein,* said vote to be on the basis of one vote per lot therein. (Emphasis added.)

Acting under paragraph 16, 12b was modified by written agreement of 76.4%. Of the equitable owners of lots in the development to read as follows:

... A home may be built with a hangar as a later addition but no hangar may be built before a home.... (Emphasis added.)

The documents changing the restriction were filed of record on March 22, 1971, although the modification had been approved and executed on March 24, 1970. All equitable and legal lot owners were notified by plaintiff of this modification on February 19, 1971. [Noell], the developer, owned equitably 42% of the lots which percentage he voted to change 12b.

On April 26, 1974, defendant Harrison submitted to plaintiffs a plan for the construction of a hangar on his lot without first building a house. This plan was disapproved on May 21st by plaintiffs because it violated restriction 12b as modified. Harrison, nevertheless, began construction of the hangar, and this action precipitated suit by the zoning committee to enjoin construction. The trial court issued its temporary injunction and Harrison appeals. We affirm.

Harrison contends that the trial court erred in granting the temporary injunction because: (1) The modification of paragraph 12b was not valid because it was approved by the various lot owners signing circulated documents rather than at a formal meeting, and (2) equity will not permit a grantor (Noell) to sell property under certain restrictions and to retain rights to impose further restrictions.

Since this is a temporary injunction, the principal question presented is whether the trial court abused its discretion in issuing the *writt*.... This inquiry requires a determination of whether a valid vote was taken and whether the modification of paragraph 12b was reasonable.

Validity of Vote

Harrison argues that the method of voting on amending the deed restrictions lacks specificity and is, therefore, ambiguous. He contends that "the very essence of the word vote denotes *an opportunity* by all persons entitled to vote to express their approval or disapproval." [Emphasis added.] Although paragraph 16, *supra,* specifies no particular method of voting, this lack of specificity does not render the paragraph ambiguous. Moreover, Harrison and other lot owners had this opportunity. Consequently, we hold that this was a valid vote in accordance with the contract for deed. This is true because early in 1970 before execution of the document modifying the restrictions, notice was given of a meeting of equitable and legal owners of lots in the subdivision to discuss the modification of 12b. Although notice of the meeting was given to all owners, an insufficient number to modify the restriction attended. Although Harrison attended this meeting, he neither signed the petition nor voiced objection. After this meeting a petition to modify was hand circulated to other lot owners. By this effort the proponents of the modification were successful in securing sufficient votes to change the restriction. We see nothing unfair in obtaining the necessary vote by personal contact with the owners. We conclude, therefore, that this contention is without merit.

Reasonableness of Modification

Harrison also argues that the modification is void because it is more restrictive than the original covenant. We cannot agree with this contention because, even though the modification was more restrictive, it was consistent with the overall plan of development and was neither unreasonable nor prohibited by law. Furthermore, paragraph 16 of the covenants gave the right to amend the restrictions to three-fourths of the owners of the property. Since the subdivision was designed to provide "homesites for people who like airplanes," the apparent purpose of the modification was to protect the rights of the property owners by insuring that both homes and hangars would be built. Because this modification enhanced, rather than abrogated, the original plan specified in the contracts between the developer and the various lot owners, we hold it to be reasonable. *Couch v. Southern Methodist University,* 10 S.W.2d 973 (Tex.Comm'n App.1928, jdgmt. adopted).

[handwritten margin note: new restrict. neither un-reasonable & prohibited by law.]

Landowners have the right to impose any restrictions they choose so long as the restrictions are not against public policy or illegal. *Parker v. Delcoure,* 455 S.W.2d 339, 343 (Tex.Civ.App. — Fort Worth 1970, *writ ref'd n.r.e.*); *Goodstein v. Huffman,* 222 S.W.2d 259, 260 (Tex.Civ.App. — Dallas 1949, *writ ref'd*). The restrictions imposed by Mr. Noell, the original owner and developer of the subdivision, were reasonable and compatible with the purpose of the development, and, the owners of the lots had a right under paragraph 16 of these restrictions to amend them commensurate with the purpose and intent of the development.... Affirmed.

[handwritten margin note: All restrict. legal unless against pub policy or illegal.]

Penney v. Ass'n of Apartment Owners of Hale Kaanapali

Supreme Court of Hawaii
776 P.2d 393 (Haw. 1989)

WAKATSUKI, J. Robert C. Penney and P. Jean Penney (Plaintiffs-Appellants) are owners of an apartment in Hale Kaanapali, a condominium project which has both residential/hotel apartments and apartments used as commercial spaces. Hale Kaanapali Hotel Associates, a Hawaii Limited Partnership, (Defendant-Appellee) is the owner of an apartment designated in the Declaration of the horizontal property regime as Building F constituting a snack bar containing 625 square feet except for the two bathrooms which are common elements within the Building. When a special meeting was called for the purpose of amending the Declaration, Defendant-Appellee had approximately 72.3% of the common interest of the condominium project and controlled another 4.53% interest by proxies. The amendment proposed to change a common area of approximately 2,664 square feet which was used as the Association clubhouse area including the restrooms from a common element to a limited common element for Defendant-Appellee's exclusive use. The proposed amendment was approved by a vote of 76.83% of the interest of all the apartment owners.

Plaintiffs-Appellants contended in the circuit court that the amendment is invalid because approval of 100 percent of the ownership interest is required to change a common element to a limited common area for the exclusive use by an apartment owner. The circuit court held the amendment to the Declaration to be valid. We disagree.

Hawaii Revised Statutes (HRS) § 514A-13(b) (1985) provides:

> The common interest appurtenant to each apartment as expressed in the declaration shall have a permanent character and shall not be altered without the consent of all the apartment owners affected[.]

In contrast, HRS § 514A-13(d)(1) (1985) permits the board of directors of the association of apartment owners "upon the approval of the owners of seventy-five per cent of the common interests, to change the use of the common elements."

Defendant-Appellee contends that the amendment to the Declaration is merely a change in the use of the common elements, and therefore, § 514-13(d)(1) applies. This would require an approval of only 75 percent of the common interests.

The change of use of a common element (e.g., changing from shuffleboard to tennis court, or erecting a maintenance shed on what was open space), and conversion of a common element to a limited common element are significantly different. In the former, the benefit to all the apartment owners is not diminished. In the latter, however, the benefit to all the apartment owners is significantly diminished by the restricted and exclusive use of the limited common area to one or fewer than all of the apartment owners. "In effect, then, the common elements as to all other tenants have thereby been diminished." *Stuewe v. Lauletta*, 93 Ill.App.3d 1029, 1031, 49 Ill.Dec. 494, 496, 418 N.E.2d 138, 140 (1981).

Defendant-Appellee further contends that although there may an alteration to the common elements, § 514A-13(b) requires unanimous consent only when the common interest is altered.

"Common interest" is defined as the percentage of undivided interest in the common elements appertaining to each apartment. HRS § 514A-3 (1985). Since the percentage of undivided interest in the common elements owned by each apartment owner will remain the same, Defendant-Appellee reasons that § 514-13(b) is inapplicable. We disagree.

We agree with the Florida appellate court which stated: An undivided interest [in the common elements] is an undivided interest in the whole and when that whole changes, that interest, if not the percent, also changes. *Tower House Condominium, Inc. v. Millman*, 410 So. 2d 926, 930 (Fla.Dist.Ct.App., 3d Dist. 1981). See also *Grimes v. Moreland*, 41 Ohio Misc. 69, 74, 322 N.E.2d 699, 703 (1974) ("Fencing-in of one area for almost exclusive use of one unit owner will not alter the percentage interest of the other unit owners (each will still have this approximately 6% interest) but it will mean that each unit owner will have 6% of the smaller remaining common area.")

For all intents and purposes, converting a common element to a limited common element diminishes the common interest appurtenant to each apartment. Under HRS § 514A-13(b), we hold that such conversion requires the consent of all the apartment owners.

Converting "common elmt" to "limited common element" requires 100% consent.

The circuit court's summary judgment is vacated and this case is remanded for entry of a judgment in accordance with this opinion.

Reversed and Remanded.

Sky View Financial, Inc. v. Bellinger

Supreme Court of Iowa
554 N.W.2d 694 (Iowa 1996)

NEUMAN, J. Individual owners of a lakefront property development have appealed summary judgment for the land developers in a dispute over the interpretation of voting rights provisions contained in covenants running with the land. The district court interpreted the covenants to require a "one vote per lot" majority for amendment. We affirm.

Plaintiff Sky View Financial and its only two shareholders, Clinton Anderson and Wendell Sollars, are locked in a feud with defendant Sun Valley Iowa Lake Association, a group representing owners of the lake lots. Background facts concerning the controversy are detailed in *Sun Valley Iowa Lake Ass'n v. Anderson*, 551 N.W.2d 621 (Iowa 1996) [hereinafter *Sun Valley*]. Facts pertinent to the current controversy may be summarized as follows:

Quenton Anderson developed farmland into a lake resort area in the 1970s. Buyers of the lake lots formed what would become the first of three property owners associations—the Sun Valley Lake Property Owners Association. In 1988, Anderson sold a major portion of the project to Patten Corporation. Patten established a second landowners association—the Iowa Lakes Association. The two owners associations merged in 1989 with the formation of the Sun Valley Iowa Lake Association, defendants in the current suit [hereinafter "Association"]. In 1992, Patten sold its interest in the development to Sky View Financial. Sky View then deeded some of the lots to Anderson and Sollars, individually.

The appeal before us centers on differences between the restrictive covenants recorded by Patten in 1988 and revisions to those covenants filed by the Association in 1993. At issue are covenants that pertain to voting for amendments on assessments. The 1988 covenants provide in pertinent part:

VII. ASSESSMENTS.

A. GENERAL. Pursuant to the powers granted to it in its Articles and By-Laws, the Association is hereby expressly authorized and empowered to levy annual assessments against all Lots in the Development. Provided, however, except as may be otherwise indicated, *no assessment shall be levied against Lots owned by the Declarant [Patten] or any successor developer.*

....

XVI. TERM AND AMENDMENT. The provisions of this Declaration shall affect and run with the land and shall exist and be binding upon all parties claiming an interest in the Development until January 1, 2015, after which time the same shall be extended for successive periods of ten (10) years each. *This Decla-*

ration may be amended by the affirmative vote of a majority of the Owners of all *Lots in the Development* and by recording an amendment to this Declaration duly executed by the requisite number of such Owners required to effect such amendment. (Emphasis added.)

Pursuant to these covenants, the Association levied annual assessments against the lots owned by Anderson and Sollars. They refused to pay, considering themselves developers and therefore exempt from payment. In April 1993, the Association initiated an action against them to collect delinquent assessments. See generally *Sun Valley*, 551 N.W.2d at 628–29. We ultimately affirmed the district court's finding that Sky View was a successor developer exempt from assessment, but Anderson and Sollars were individual owners who could be assessed. *Id.* at 640.

Meanwhile, two days after filing the *Sun Valley* action, the Association voted to revise the 1988 bylaws and restate the 1988 covenants. The vote took place at an annual meeting of the owners which Sky View officials chose not to attend. The 1993 restated covenants provide in pertinent part:

ARTICLE VII. ASSESSMENTS

A. GENERAL. Pursuant to the powers granted to it in its Articles and By-laws, the Association is hereby expressly authorized and empowered to levy annual, special, and emergency assessments against *all* Lots in the Development.

ARTICLE XVI. TERM AND AMENDMENT

.... This Declaration may be amended by the affirmative vote of a majority of the owners of lots in the development, *whereby each owner possesses the right to cast one vote irrespective of the number of lots owned*, and by recording an amendment to this Declaration duly executed by the requisite number of owners required to affect such amendment. (Emphasis added.)

In accordance with these restated covenants, which removed the exemption for developers, the Association again levied assessments against lots owned by Sky View.

Sky View then brought the present suit seeking a declaratory judgment that the 1993 restated covenants are null and void. The parties filed cross-motions for summary judgment. The Association contended that Sky View's action was barred as a matter of law because it should have been raised as a compulsory counterclaim in the Sun Valley litigation.

The district court entered summary judgment for Sky View. It rejected the Association's preclusion argument, reasoning that the amended covenants did not even exist at the time the prior suit was commenced. The court also declared the 1993 covenants null and void because they were amended by a simple majority vote of the owners (irrespective of number of lots owned) in violation of Article XVI of the 1988 covenants.

On appeal, the Association urges two grounds for reversal. First, it cites error in the court's failure to find Sky View's present action barred by the prior litigation. Second, the Association insists the court erred in its interpretation of Article XVI of the 1988 covenants regarding voting and, hence, erred in its ruling that the 1993 amendments were null and void.

Our review is for the correction of errors at law. Iowa R. App. P. 4.

I. Compulsory Counterclaim.

It appears doubtful that Sky View could have brought or enforced a counterclaim in the *Sun Valley* action for interpretation of contractual language not yet promulgated. Accordingly, we find no error in the district court's refusal to dismiss Sky View's petition under rule 29.

II. Validity of Amendments.

At the heart of this controversy is the question whether, as the Association claims, Article XVI of the 1988 covenants permits amendment by a simple majority of lot owners without regard to the number of lots owned by each party voting.

Because restrictive covenants are contractual in nature, we apply contract-based rules of construction to interpret them. *Compiano v. Kuntz*, 226 N.W.2d 245, 249 (Iowa 1975). Where the wording of a restriction is ambiguous, its meaning must be strictly construed against the party seeking to enforce it. *Iowa Realty Co. v. Jochims*, 503 N.W.2d 385, 386 (Iowa 1993). However, "mere disagreement over the meaning of a word or phrase does not establish ambiguity for purposes of the rule." *Id.* The crux of the parties' disagreement here turns, not on the meaning of the words, but on their import. In the phrase "this Declaration may be amended by the affirmative vote of a majority of the Owners of all Lots in the Development," the Association stresses the word "Owners," while Sky View places emphasis on the phrase "all Lots."

To support its preferred reading, the Association relies on a line of "one vote per owner" cases which holds that phrases like "a majority of the then owners of the lots affected thereby" or "the majority of the owners of the property" refer to voting strength measured by number of owners, not by area owned. *Cieri v. Gorton*, 587 P.2d 14, 17 (Mont. 1978); *Beck v. Council of the City of St. Paul*, 50 N.W.2d 81, 82 (Minn. 1951). In *Cieri*, the court rejected on equitable grounds the efforts of two nonresident owners of sixty-nine undeveloped lots to remove all restrictive covenants from a 110-lot subdivision over the objection of forty-one resident owners. *Cieri*, 587 P.2d at 17. Citing *Beck*, the court framed the issue as "whether the numerical strength of those who are owners in fact is to be determined on a per capita basis or according to the amount or the number of parcels of land which they own." *Id.* (quoting *Beck*, 50 N.W.2d at 83). In both cases, the covenants revealed an emphasis on individual ownership irrespective of acreage owned, thus yielding a "one vote per owner" interpretation. *Cieri*, 587 P.2d at 17; *Beck*, 50 N.W.2d at 83.

A contrary line of cases adopts the "one vote per lot" position. In the leading "lot" case, *Diamond Bar Development Corp. v. Superior Court*, 131 Cal. Rptr. 458 (App. 1976), the owners of a majority of lots (including the developer) voted to amend protective covenants controlling perimeter fencing. Capturing the essence of the controversy, the court described the question as "whether the draftsman feared a majority tyranny based upon sheer numbers of property owners or a majority tyranny based upon extent of ownership." *Id.* at 460. The court looked to the covenant document as a whole, finding evidence of a voting system that favored number of lots owned over mere ownership status. This scheme, the court believed, was consistent with an evident drafting intent that influence over amendments would be "commensurate with the extent of [the owners'] investment." *Id.* at 461. Similarly, in *Cecala v. Thorley*, 764 P.2d 643, 644 (Utah App. 1988), the court found the phrase "majority of owners of lots" susceptible to two reasonable interpretations and, thus, looked to the entire agreement to discern the drafter's intent. Noting that the covenant language manifested an intent that land area ownership control the subdivision development, it rejected the *Beck* and *Cieri* analysis in favor of the "one vote per lot" interpretation in *Diamond Bar*. *Id.* at 645–46.

Guided by these decisions, we first consider the Association's claim that the language at issue is unambiguous and clearly mandates a "one vote per owner" limitation. The claim appears disingenuous given the nature of subsequent amendments. First, the Association found it necessary to amend Article XVI to state that "each owner possesses the right to cast one vote irrespective of the number of lots owned." Were the original language free from ambiguity, no such clarification would be needed. Second, the Association saw fit to amend the voting provisions of the 1988 bylaws. The 1988 bylaws provided that "there shall be one vote and one voting member for each Lot regardless of the number of persons who may have an ownership interest in such Lot, or the manner in which title is held by them." The Association cut this provision from its 1993 bylaws, inserting in its place a rule that "each owner is allowed one vote." If, as the owners argue, the language in the 1988 covenants plainly gives voting strength to a majority of owners and not lots, these self-serving amendments would be unnecessary.

We believe the district court rightly found the covenant language ambiguous and in need of interpretation. Looking first at the controverted language itself, the court wisely reasoned that the reference to "all Lots" would be meaningless unless all lots were considered for voting purposes. Expanding on that notion, the court found from a review of the entire document that "it doesn't seem remotely logical or probable that the developer intended to abdicate [its powers] to the individual property owners once two lots, a majority of two out of three, had been sold." We entirely agree. Although progress on the common areas of the development is well underway, the great majority of lots remain undeveloped. The district court was sensitive to the considerable investment made by Sky View and the power that investment should command relative to individual ownership. Consistent with the covenants, the balance of control will eventually shift as more lots are sold and the developer no longer enjoys majority status.

We find no error in the court's decision to invalidate the purported amendments to the 1988 covenants. We, therefore, affirm the court's judgment for Sky View, Anderson and Sollars.

Affirmed.

Note: Judicial Power to Excuse Compliance with Voting Requirements

> Restatement (Third) § 6.12 Judicial Power To Excuse Compliance With Requirements Of The Governing Documents
>
> A court may excuse compliance with any of the following provisions in a governing document if it finds that the provision unreasonably interferes with the community's ability to manage the common property, administer the servitude regime, or carry out any other function set forth in the declaration, and that compliance is not necessary to protect the legitimate interests of the members or lenders holding security interests:
>
> (1) a provision limiting the amount of any assessment that can be levied against individually owned property;
>
> (2) a provision requiring that an amendment to the declaration be approved by lenders;
>
> (3) a provision requiring the approval of more than a majority of the voting power to adopt an amendment described in § 6.10(1)(a);
>
> (4) a provision requiring approval of more than two-thirds of the voting power to adopt an amendment described by § 6.10(1)(b) that is not subject to the requirements of § 6.10(2) or (3);

(5) a requirement that an amendment to the declaration be signed by members;

(6) a quorum requirement for meetings of members.

Peak Investments v. South Peak Homeowners Association, Inc.

California Court of Appeal
44 Cal.Rptr.3d 892 (Cal. Ct. App. 2006)

SILLS, P.J. South Peak Homeowners Association ... appeals from the trial court's order granting a homeowner's petition to reduce the percentage of homeowner votes needed to approve an amendment to the declaration of covenants, conditions, and restrictions (CC & Rs). The Association claims the trial court improperly reduced the percentage to less than a simple majority of the homeowner votes. We find the Davis-Stirling Common Interest Development Act (Civ.Code, § 1350 et seq.) requires that a proposed amendment to the CC & Rs be approved by at least a simple majority of the total votes in the homeowners association before the trial court can reduce the percentage of votes set by the CC & Rs. Accordingly, we reverse.

FACTS

Peak Investments and Norman and Rita Lesman ... own lot 43 in South Peak, a planned community of custom homes in Laguna Niguel comprising 63 lots. The Association is governed by CC & Rs recorded in April 1984. In 1986, the Association amended the CC & Rs to change the building heights ... and the setback provisions for each lot.... These changes were reflected on Exhibit 1 to the amendment, entitled "Height and Setback Limitations," which listed on a chart each lot number, its maximum height, its minimum setback from front lot line, its minimum setback from side lot lines, and its minimum setback from rear lot lines. The setback limit for lot 43's side lot lines was listed as "20-7," meaning the limit was 20 feet total minimum setback distance for both sides of the lot and 7 feet minimum setback distance for each side of the lot. The second page of Exhibit 1 started with listing lot 31; all the lots from lot 31 through 55 had sideline setbacks of 25-7 except lot 43.

The CC&Rs were amended again in 1990 to modify the building height limitations by removing the 35 foot cap.... The amended section refers to Attachment 2, which appears to be a retyped version of Exhibit 1 to the 1986 amendment. The only difference in the two is the minimum sideline setback for lot 43; that number was changed from 20-7 to 25-7.

The Lesmans purchased lot 43 in June 2001 and apparently wanted to build a larger structure than the 20-7 setback allowed. They contacted the lawyer who prepared the 1990 amendment, Edward Coss, who wrote to the Association's Board of Directors in May 2002, opining that the change in the sideline setback on lot 43 was "an inadvertent typographical error." Coss explained, "I can find no record or other communication to support the change in the side lot lines; in fact, the purpose of Amendment Number Three was limited to building height alterations." Coss enclosed a proposed amendment to the CC & Rs to correct the error for the Association's approval.

For whatever reason, the Board declined to effect the execution of the amendment. In July 2004, the Lesmans proposed an amendment to change the setback for their lot. In accordance with the bylaws, they caused a special meeting of the homeowners to be called to vote on the proposed amendment. The homeowners received a copy of the proposed amendment, which explained the requested change from 25-7 to 20-7; they also received a ballot allowing them to approve or disapprove the amendment or abstain from voting. The ballot noted, "[A]t least 25 percent (25%) of the voting power of the membership (16/63) must be present in person or by proxy in order to achieve a quorum. The written approval of at least 2/3rds of the Members (42 of 63) must be received for the proposed amendment to be approved."

The meeting was held on July 29, 2004, with seventeen homeowners physically present. Thirty-two ballots were cast: Twenty-one voted in favor of the amendment, and eleven voted against it. Because an amendment to the CC & Rs requires the votes of two-thirds of the lot owners…, the proposed amendment failed.

The Lesmans petitioned the superior court to reduce the percentage necessary to amend the CC & Rs because the CC & Rs required a "supermajority" to amend and not enough members attended the special meeting, and to confirm the amendment as validly approved. (Civ.Code, § 1356.) The trial court granted the petition, finding that more than 50 percent of the voters voted in favor of the amendment, as required by the statute. "[I]t seems to me … that this is what [section] 1356 was meant to apply to, the situation where you can't get enough people interested to be there to provide for super majority. It isn't like enough people came and voted against it. There just isn't [*sic*] that many votes.… [T]he only question here is whether 50 percent of the voters voted in favor of the amendment. It appears to me they did, 21 out of 32 or 33." The court also found the amendment was reasonable, another statutory requirement. The Association appeals from the order granting the petition.

DISCUSSION

[margin note: Petition for reduction in the % of affirm. votes req'd to amend CC&Rs.]

Civil Code section 1356, part of the Davis-Stirling Common Interest Development Act…, provides that a homeowners' association, or any member, may petition the superior court for a reduction in the percentage of affirmative votes required to amend the CC & Rs if they require approval by "owners having more than 50 percent of the votes in the association.…" … The court may, but need not, grant the petition if it finds all of the following: Notice was properly given; the balloting was properly conducted; reasonable efforts were made to permit eligible members to vote; "[o]wners having more than 50 percent of the votes, in a single class voting structure, voted in favor of the amendment"; and "the amendment is reasonable.".…)

On appeal, the Association … argues the statute requires an affirmative vote by more than 50 percent of *all* owners, whether or not they attended the meeting (i.e., 32 out of 63), while the trial court mistakenly construed the requirement to be merely more than 50 percent of the owners who attended the meeting (*i.e.*, 17 out of 32).

[margin note: The crux:] → … The phrase in question here is "owners having more than 50 percent of the votes," appearing in section 1356, subdivision (c)(4). The phrase is unqualified by language indicating "the votes" are those cast at a meeting; in the absence of such qualification, it must mean total votes in the Association.

Our interpretation is buttressed by language in other sections of the Act that carefully define votes cast at a meeting. For example, section 1355.5 allows the board of directors of an association to adopt an amendment to the governing documents deleting "any provision which is unequivocally designed and intended, or which by its nature can only have been designed or intended, to facilitate the developer in completing the construction or marketing of the development." … However, the board may not adopt such an amendment "without the approval of the owners, casting a majority of the votes at a meeting or election of the association constituting a quorum.… For the purposes of this section, 'quorum' means more than 50 percent of the owners who own no more than two separate interests in the development." ... Likewise, a rule change by the board of directors of an association may be reversed "by the affirmative vote of a majority of the votes represented and voting at a duly held meeting at which a quorum is present (which affirmative votes also constitute a majority of the required quorum)...." (§ 1357.140, subd. (c).) And absent statutory notice (§ 1365), the board of directors of an association cannot levy assessment increases without the "approval of owners, constituting a quorum, casting a majority of the votes at a meeting or election of the association...." (§ 1366, subds. (a) & (b).)

If a declaration fails to include provisions permitting its amendment, the Act provides that it may be amended after, *inter alia,* "the approval of owners representing more than 50 percent ... of the separate interests in the common interest development has been given...." (§ 1355, subd. (b).) Thus, it appears the Legislature made a conscious decision to provide that a bare majority of all the members would be the minimum required to amend the declaration. The comments to the Restatement of Property explain, "The declaration for a common-interest community functions like a constitution for the community. Like a constitution, the declaration should not be subject to change upon temporary impulse. Unlike rules, which can be adopted with a simple majority of votes cast, amendments require at least a majority of all votes that could be cast, and many types of amendment require substantially more." (Rest.3d, Property, Servitudes (2000) § 6.10, com. *a.*)

[handwritten margin note: Holding. This needs 32/63 not 17/63.]

The Restatement includes a section entitled "Judicial Power to Excuse Compliance with Requirements of the Governing Documents." The section provides that "[a] court may excuse compliance with any of the following provisions in a governing document if it finds that the provision unreasonably interferes with the community's ability to manage the common property, administer the servitude regime, or carry out any other function set forth in the declaration, and that compliance is not necessary to protect the legitimate interests of the members or lenders holding security interests: ... (4) a provision requiring approval of more than two-thirds of the voting power to adopt an amendment...." (Rest.3d, Property, Servitudes, *supra,* § 6.12.) The section's notes state, "The rule that quorum and supermajority requirements may be waived if necessary to permit adoption of amendments necessary to continued existence and proper functioning of the association is based on California Civil Code §§ 1356 and 1357, although it differs in some particulars." (*Id.,* reporter's notes.) Notably, the Restatement section does not require the court to make threshold findings before it can exercise its discretion, as does section 1356.

There is no case law directly on point. The closest is *Blue Lagoon Community Assoc. v. Mitchell* (1997) 55 Cal.App.4th 472, 64 Cal.Rptr.2d 81, in which this court held that a proceeding pursuant to section 1356 was not "adversarial" so as to entitle the party successfully opposing the petition to attorney fees as the prevailing party in an action to enforce the governing documents of a common interest development. (§ 1354, subd. (c).) In so holding, this court commented: "[T]he purpose of Civil Code section 1356 is to give a property owners' association the ability to amend its governing documents when, because of voter apathy or other reasons, important amendments cannot be approved by the normal procedures authorized by the declaration. [Citation.] In essence, it provides the association with a safety valve for those situations where the need for a supermajority vote would hamstring the association." ...

It appears the legislative intent is to require at least a simple majority of all members of an association to amend the CC & Rs. Accordingly, the trial court erred in finding that the affirmative votes of 21 out of 63 owners met the statutory prerequisite that owners having more than 50 percent of the vote voted in favor of the amendment. Because we reach this conclusion, we need not discuss the Association's contention that the amendment was not reasonable. We observe, however, that it appears the Lesmans may be merely attempting to correct a scrivener's error. Nothing in this opinion shall be construed to hamper their ongoing efforts in that regard.

DISPOSITION

The order granting the petition is reversed. In the interest of justice, each party shall bear its own costs.

Notes & Questions

1. The court seems sympathetic to the Lesmans' efforts if they are "merely attempting to correct a scrivener's error." How should they go about doing that?

2. Should the California legislature and the Restatement (Third) have gone farther and allowed a court to excuse compliance with association voting requirements if a majority of those voting had favored the amendment? What are the justifications for allowing owners to defeat possible actions by simply staying away?

2. Notice

Carroll v. El Dorado Estates Div. No. Two Ass'n, Inc.

Supreme Court of Alaska
680 P.2d 1158 (Alaska 1984)

In this case an incorporated association of condominium owners brought suit to enforce a bylaw of the association which bans residential possession of animals, *i.e.*, pets. The court granted summary judgment in the association's favor.

We find that the bylaw was not validly adopted and we reverse.

I.

The El Dorado Estates Division Number Two Association, Inc. [Association] was established pursuant to a condominium declaration filed in 1976. The Association is a corporation which, through its Board of Directors, manages the business affairs of the condominium property on behalf of the unit owners. Under the declaration, the Association also has responsibility for the enforcement of its bylaws and of the rules and regulations of occupancy.

At the time the condominium declaration was filed, pets were permitted. Article IX of the declaration states in part:

> Section 6. Animals. The Association may by rules and regulations prohibit or limit the raising, breeding or keeping of animals in any unit or on the common areas or any part thereof.

Article VIII of the bylaws of the Association permitted pet ownership, subject to certain restrictions.[2]

---

2. Article VIII states in part:

> Section 1. *Rules and Regulations....* f) If any resident shall keep a dog or other pet in his Unit, he shall take all special care required to insure that such pet shall not disturb other condominium residents in any way. If the Board of Directors shall receive a written complaint signed by any Owners concerning a bothersome animal, the Board shall, in its discretion,

[handwritten margin note: pets banned: 20 ; 23 units in person or by proxy.]

At the Association's annual meeting on June 28, 1979, twenty of twenty-three unit owners were present in person or by proxy. A proposed amendment to Article VIII, Section 1, clause (f) of the bylaws was adopted. The amendment prohibited pet ownership, except for existing pets.[3]

In September, 1982, the Association filed a lawsuit seeking an injunction enforcing the amended bylaw against three unit owners, James A. Carroll, James Adkins, and Guy Whitney (collectively referred to as "Carroll"). Carroll's motion to dismiss the complaint on the ground that injunctive relief was not available was denied.

Carroll was the only one of the three who had been a unit owner at the time of the 1979 annual meeting. All three owners conceded that they now own pets in violation of the amended bylaw. They defended the action on the basis that the amendment was invalid, for the following reasons: (1) timely and adequate notice of the purpose of the annual meeting was not given; (2) the proxy solicitation was materially misleading; and (3) the pet ban restricted their ownership rights as set forth in the declaration.

On cross motions for summary judgment the superior court rejected these contentions and granted summary judgment in the Association's favor. The unit owners appeal.

II.

. . .

B. Sufficiency of Notice.

Carroll argues that because the notice of the meeting did not indicate that a pet ban would be considered, it was insufficient. The Association bylaws require that the notice contain a statement of the purpose of the meeting. A mere statement that amendments to the bylaws will be considered, without any specificity as to which bylaws or the general nature of the proposed amendments, is inadequate to fulfill this requirement. Carroll cites several cases in support of this argument. *See Des Moines Life & Annuity Co. v. Midland Insurance Co.*, 6 F.2d 228, 229 (D.C. Minn. 1925); *Blum v. Latter*, 163 So. 2d 189, 193–94 (La. App. 1964); *Klein v. Scranton Life Insurance Co.*, 139 Pa. Super. 369, 11 A.2d 770, 775 (1940); *Mueller v. Merz*, 23 Wis. 2d 588, 127 N.W. 2d 774, 776 (1964).

---

take action to eliminate the problem and may require the Owner of such pet to dispose of the pet, regardless of when the pet was obtained, or whether other Owners are permitted to retain their pets. Residents shall not have on the premises more than one pet. Such pet shall never be permitted in common areas without a handler. Each pet owner shall promptly remove and properly dispose of all animal waste deposited by his pet in the common area whether inside or outside the building; and each pet owner shall be responsible for the repair of all damaged areas, including damage to shrubbery's and lawns.

3. The amendment repealed the provision quoted in n. 2, *supra*, and replaced it with this language:

No animals or pets will be permitted on the premises, that is in the individual units or in the common areas, effective this date and with this By-Laws change. Any unit owner, tenant or guest who presently has an animal or pet may be permitted to keep his or her pet until such time as their pet is disposed of. At this time they may not replace the animal or pet with another. Any unit owner or tenant who presently has an animal or pet in his unit shall take all special care required to insure that such pet shall not disturb other condominium residents in any way. If the Board of Directors shall receive a written complaint signed by an owner concerning a bothersome pet the Board shall take action to eliminate the problem and may require the owner of such a pet to dispose of the pet. Pets may not be permitted in the common areas without a handler. Each pet owner shall promptly remove and properly dispose of all animal wastes deposited by his pet in the common areas whether inside or outside the building; and each pet owner shall be responsible for the repair of all damaged area including damage to shrubbery's and lawns.

The Association contends that its notice was adequate, since it informed the unit owners that "Proposed Amendments to By-Laws" were on the agenda. The corporate cases cited by Carroll are distinguishable, it contends. Even if the notice was inadequate, Carroll's attendance by proxy waives any objection, the Association argues.[4]

The Alaska statutes and the Model Business Corporation Act, unlike the Association's bylaws, do not specifically require that the notice of a corporation's annual meeting specify the purpose of the meeting. Model Business Corp. Act § 29 (1971); AS 10.05.141; AS 10.20.066.[5] However, there are significant differences between memberships in a condominium association and status as a shareholder in the typical corporation. Members of a condominium association have a heightened interest in the affairs of the association inasmuch as it regulates the conditions of their residence. Shareholders typically have only a financial interest in corporate affairs, and, in addition, their ownership interests are often more readily transferable than realty. A higher standard of notice for condominium associations may therefore be appropriate.

The Uniform Condominium Act promulgated by the Commission on Uniform State Laws in 1977 requires that "the notice of any meeting [of the association] must state the time and place of the meeting and the items on the agenda, including the general nature of any proposed amendment to the declaration or bylaws." Uniform Condominium Act § 3-108, 7 U.L.A. 177 (1978). In 1980, a revised Uniform Condominium Act was promulgated, which broadens the notice requirement to include, in addition to changes in the declaration or bylaws, "any budget changes, and any proposal to remove a director or officer." 7 U.L.A. Supp. at 187 (1983). These provisions indicate the importance of advance notification of changes in the bylaws. They add specific content to the general concept of purpose expressed in the association's bylaws. We think it is appropriate to follow the lead of the uniform act and hold that the term purpose includes notice of the general nature of proposed amendments to bylaws.

The importance of prior notice of amendments to the bylaws is also indicated by the fact that the Association's Board of Directors in this case directed the Association's sec-

---

4. Article II, Section 7 of the bylaws states:

Section 7. *Notice of Meetings.* The Secretary shall at least seven (7) days before the date set for each annual and special meeting give written notice thereof to each Unit Owner according to the Association's record of ownership, stating whether it is an annual or special meeting, the authority for the call thereof, the place, day and hour of such meeting and the purpose therefor, in any of the following ways: (a) by leaving the same with him personally, or (b) by leaving the same at his residence or usual place of business, or (c) by mailing it, postage prepaid, addressed to him at his address as it appears on the record of ownership of the Association. If notice is given pursuant to the provisions of this section, the failure of any Unit Owner to receive actual notice of such meeting shall in no way invalidate the meeting or any proceedings thereat. *The presence of any Unit Owner in person or by proxy at any meeting shall be deemed a waiver of any required notice as to such Unit Owner, unless such Unit Owner shall at the opening thereof object to the holding of such meeting for noncompliance with the provisions of this section.*

(Emphasis added).

5. According to *Fletcher Cyclopedia of Corporations*, it is not ordinarily necessary to give specific notice of the business to be conducted at an annual meeting. The reason is that all subjects are proper at such a meeting, and a requirement of advance notification as to topics for an annual meeting would inappropriately restrict the shareholders from bringing things up that they wanted discussed. However, "[a]n exception is made where unusual or extraordinary business not ordinarily brought up at a general meeting, such as an increase of stock, or an amendment of the bylaws in some fundamental particular ... is to be approved at the meeting." 5 E. Smith, *Fletcher Cyclopedia of Corporations* § 2009, at 55 (Rev. ed. 1976) (footnotes omitted).

retary to provide a copy of the proposed amendments with the notice, and it was only by oversight that the notification failed to include a copy.

For these reasons we conclude that the bylaws' requirement that the notice of the annual meeting must include a statement of the purpose of the meeting means that members must be informed of the general nature of proposed amendments to the bylaws. The notice of annual meeting failed to inform the members of the general nature of proposed amendments, and hence did not constitute notice as to that matter.

III.

We hold that the notice of the annual meeting was inadequate to satisfy the requirements of the Association's bylaws. Attendance by proxy was not a waiver of the defective notice.

Article II, Section 7 of the bylaws states in part:

> The presence of any Unit Owner in person or by proxy at any meeting shall be deemed a waiver of any required notice as to such Unit Owner unless such Unit Owner shall at the opening thereof object to the holding of such meeting for noncompliance with the provisions of this section.

Arguably, the waiver provision applies to any defect in notification, including a failure of notice. Without determining the full scope of the waiver provision, we decline to read it so broadly as to encompass notice of the general nature of proposed amendments.[7]

The judgment is Reversed, and this case is Remanded.

Notes & Questions

1. *Voting procedures.* In *Harrison*, the complaining owner essentially alleged that a meeting of the members to vote formally on the proposed amendment was necessary. Why might having votes on document amendments without a membership meeting be disadvantageous? How does one give proper notice of the vote? Is notice needed here? Who can solicit votes and under what process obtain them in the signature or petition voting method? On the other hand, in what circumstances might mail-in ballots or other non-meeting voting methods be advantageous? See generally UCIOA §§ 2-117 and 3-110, MNCA Chapter 7, and recall our discussion on voting in Chapter 5. See also *Bryant v. Lake Highlands Dev. Co. of Texas, Inc.*, 618 S.W.2d 921 (Tex. Civ. App. 1981) (court interpreted declaration voting as per lot, not per owner); *VNNC, Inc. v. Eghbal*, No. 53497-83 (D.C. Landlord-Tenant Ct., Nov. 7, 1983) (in cooperative context analyzing D.C. statute requiring one-unit, one-vote system versus cooperative shares owned). Revisit these questions after reading *La Jolla Mesa Vista Improvement Ass'n*, printed *infra*.

2. *Voting limits.* As the *Penney* case illustrates, not all amendments may be approved under the "normal" majority voting provisions. Some amendments are so fundamental to the community association regime (such as changing condominium common area into

---

7. Carroll argues that the bylaw prohibiting pet ownership improperly eliminates property rights granted in the condominium declaration. Since the pet ownership right granted in the declaration was specifically made conditional and subject to change, this argument lacks merit. Carroll further contends that banning pets was a material amendment to the bylaws requiring the written approval of 100% of the mortgage holders pursuant to Article X of the bylaws. While a change in pet ownership rights is material from the unit owners' perspective, we do not find it material from the mortgage holders' perspective.

some other use) that they require unanimous consent. What other types of amendments may require unanimous consent? Or require consent of the affected owners? See, *e.g.*, UCIOA §§ 2-107, 2-108, 2-112, 2-113, 2-117, 2-118, and 3-112. What are some of the inherent problems with requiring unanimous consent? See *In re Greenback Townhomes Homeowner Ass'n*, 212 Cal. Rptr. 678 (Cal. Ct. App. 1985) (court modification of voting requirements); *City of Gulfport v. Wilson*, 603 So. 2d 295 (Miss. 1992) (amendment of restrictive covenant required a per block vote rather than vote of entire subdivision); *Lake Arrowhead Chalets Timeshare Owners Ass'n v. Lake Arrowhead Chalets Owners Ass'n*, 59 Cal. Rptr. 2d 875 (Cal. Ct. App. 1996) (master association cannot vote to amend voting rights of sub-association members without their approval).

3. *Per owner or per lot?* The court in *Diamond Bar Development Corp. v. Superior Court*, 131 Cal. Rptr. 458 (Cal. Ct. App. 1976), observed that determining the desired voting method (per owner or per lot) was a question "whether the draftsman feared a majority tyranny based upon sheer numbers of property owners or a majority tyranny based upon extent of ownership." The *Sky View* court proceeded to find that it was illogical to assume that the developer (hence, the drafter) intended to lose control of the association as soon as it sold two lots. Nevertheless other courts favored the one person, one vote standard. See *Cieri v. Gorton*, 587 P.2d 14 (Mont. 1978). Is there any reason that a developer would wish to adopt a one person, one vote standard?

4. *Notice requirements.* Notice of meetings and the agenda items are very important in the governance of a community association. The *Carnall* case notes that condominium association homeowners desire a "higher standard of notice" than their corporate shareholder counterparts since they have a "higher interest in the affairs of the association." Do you agree? What about the counter argument that members should be able to bring up and take action on any issue or matter of business during the course of a membership meeting? In short, must a community association call a meeting and send advance notice for every issue which is appropriate for member action? How do you balance the association's need to perform its business function with the homeowners' need to participate in such decisions? From a drafting perspective, how would you approach drafting a notice provision? See UCIOA § 3-108 and MNCA §§ 7.05 and 7.06.

5. *Amendments changing developer's original plan.* In its declaration of condominium, the developer provided that the documents could be amended. Years later, unit owners amended the documents to remove an obligation to pay annual dues to the developer's sports club, a mandatory obligation contained in the documents at the time they purchased. Developer challenged the amendment. What would be the result? What vote would be required to make the change? See *Stream Club, Ltd. v. Thompson*, 536 N.E. 2nd 459 (1989).

G. Power to Extend and Renew Servitude Regime

La Jolla Mesa Vista Improvement Ass'n v. La Jolla Mesa Vista Homeowners Ass'n

Court of Appeals of California
269 Cal. Rptr. 825 (Cal. Ct. App. 1990)

BENKE, J. The residential development which is the subject of this dispute has been governed by a declaration of conditions and restrictions (CCRs) since 1957. By their terms the CCRs were scheduled to expire on January 1, 1987, unless within the six months preceding January 1, 1987, they were extended by a majority of the homeowners in the development.

Between July 1, 1986, and January 1, 1987, a homeowners association circulated a document which extended the effective date of the CCRs to January 1, 2017. The extension also provided substantial modifications of the existing CCRs. The extension proponents, believing they had enough signatures to make the extension and modification effective, recorded their extension on December 24, 1986.

Thereafter a second homeowners association was formed. It filed the instant action which challenges the validity of the extension. The challenge is based primarily on alleged defects in a number of the signatures obtained in support of the petition.

Following a trial without a jury, the superior court found the extension was supported by a sufficient number of valid signatures and entered judgment in favor of the defendants.

We affirm in large measure because we find homeowners who assented in writing to the extension did not have the power to unilaterally revoke their consent.

SUMMARY

The subject of this dispute is La Jolla Mesa Vista Unit No. 1 (La Jolla Mesa Vista) which consists of 94 residential lots located in La Jolla. The original CCRs, recorded by the grantor on May 20, 1957, provided in paragraph 22: "Each and all of the foregoing conditions and restrictions shall terminate on January First, Nineteen Hundred eighty-seven unless the owners of a majority of said lots have executed and recorded at any time within six months prior to January 1, 1987, in the manner required for conveyance of real property, a writing in which they agree that said Conditions and Restrictions shall continue for a further specified period ...; provided, also that the above and foregoing Conditions and Restrictions may be modified, after said termination date, at the times and in the manner hereinabove provided for the extensions of said Conditions and Restrictions; all of which extensions and modifications shall become effective on the expiration date of the Conditions and Restrictions in force at the time of such extension or modification."

The La Jolla Mesa Vista Homeowners Association (Homeowners) was formed by residents to implement the CCRs and to otherwise promote and manage the common interests of the homeowners. In 1985 Homeowners proposed extending the CCRs and conducted meetings in which the comments of individual homeowners were solicited. Thereafter Homeowners retained counsel, who drafted an extension and modification of the existing CCRs. The extension would have modified the CCRs by replacing the 1957 version with a new set of provisions.

Homeowners and its individual members circulated the extension during the last half of 1986. When the extension was recorded on December 24, 1986, signatures from the owners of 52 of the 94 lots had been obtained.[2] However before the extension was recorded, the owners of three of the fifty-two lots signed rescissions of their consent to the extension petition. Between December 24, 1986, and December 31, 1986, four more rescissions were executed.

On January 30, 1987, the La Jolla Mesa Vista Improvement Association (Improvement), an unincorporated association, filed a complaint against Homeowners and four individuals, Jack Bauman, Brendan O'Sullivan, Louis Besbeck and William Knowles.

---

2. Although each signature was not notarized, the persons who obtained the signatures appeared before notaries and attested to the authenticity of the signatures. (See, Civ. Code § 1195).

Improvement alleged it was composed of individual owners of lots in La Jolla Mesa Vista. Improvement alleged Homeowners' recorded extension was not enforceable against its members because a majority of the development's owners had not consented to the extension in the manner required by paragraph 22 of the original CCRs. Improvement also alleged the modification set forth in the petition was beyond the scope of change contemplated or permitted by paragraph 22. Improvement alleged these facts gave rise to claims for quiet title, declaratory relief, slander of title and cancellation of an instrument.

Trial without a jury commenced on March 28, 1988. Initially the defendants argued Improvement lacked standing to contest the extension because it did not itself own any lots in the development. The trial court took the standing defense under submission and proceeded to hear the merits. Thereafter Improvement presented evidence of defects in a number of the signatures on the extension. Improvement presented no evidence with respect to its allegation the modification set forth in the petition was beyond the scope of change permitted by paragraph 22.

Following presentation of the evidence the trial court found no defects in any of the disputed signatures and thus found the extension was valid. The court also found Improvement had standing to brings its claims.

Judgment was entered on August 15, 1988, and Improvement filed a timely notice of appeal.

ISSUES ON APPEAL

Improvement again argues the extension is not supported by validly executed signatures representing a majority of the development's homeowners.[3]

DISCUSSION

[Parts I and II of the opinion are unpublished. — Eds.]

III THE EXTENSION AND MODIFICATION WERE APPROVED BY A MAJORITY OF THE LOT OWNERS

The parties agree approval from 48 lot owners was needed to make the extension and modification effective. The parties further agree that at the time the extension and modification was recorded, signatures purporting to represent 52 lots were on the petition. On this appeal Improvement challenges the signatures provided for 11 of the 52 lots. We find that Improvement's challenges as to seven of the lots have no merit; thus we find the needed majority and do not consider Improvement's challenges to the signatures provided for the remaining lots.

A. Signatures on the Petition Were Binding and Could Not Be Rescinded

As to six of the lots (Nos. 12, 22, 49, 58, 72, 86S), Improvement's challenge is based solely on the fact that after signing the extension the owners of those lots executed purported "rescissions" of their agreement to the extension and modification. The trial court rejected this challenge because it found that by executing the extension the owners bound themselves under a contract which they could not unilaterally rescind without good cause.

---

3. In unpublished portions of the opinion we discuss Homeowners' objection to Improvement's standing and Improvement's contention paragraph 22 of the original CCRs did not permit their wholesale replacement.

(Civ.Code, § 1689.) The trial court further found Improvement had not shown good cause for any of the rescissions.

Like the trial court we find the owner's signature on the petition was sufficient to create a binding contract which could not be unilaterally rescinded. The only case we have been able to locate which deals directly with this issue is *Russell v. Wallace* (1929) 58 App. D.C. 357, 30 F.2d 981, 982 (*Russell*). In *Russell* the court enforced a racially restrictive covenant which had been created by circulation of a written instrument among property owners. The court rejected a property owner's attempt to withdraw from the covenant before all the property owners had assented to its terms. "The chief consideration for the contract was the mutual promise and covenant of the signers, each with the other. Mutual agreements of this kind, entered into for a valuable consideration, are upheld on the theory that the subscribers are banding together for the accomplishment of an object which is of common interest to all, and which can only be obtained by their combined performance. The consideration for each subscriber is the promise already made by others who have signed or by those who will subscribe. The contract becomes, therefore, of such a nature that a subscriber may only withdraw when an unreasonable time has been consumed in procuring the signatures of all the parties who are required to make up the agreement." (*Ibid.*)

Although *Russell* is no longer valid insofar as it holds racially restrictive covenants are enforceable (see *Shelley v. Kraemer* (1948) 334 U.S. 1, 20, 68 S.Ct. 836, 845, 92 L.Ed. 1161), we believe its explanation of covenants established by mutual subscription is still good law. Our conclusion is based on statutes and regulations which govern "common interest developments" in California and holdings in analogous charitable subscription cases.

Common interest developments are the subject of the Davis-Stirling Common Interest Development Act. (Civ.Code, §§ 1350–1373.) They are also subject to regulations promulgated by the Department of Real Estate. (*See* Cal. Code of Regs., tit. 10, § 2792 *et seq.*) Civil Code section 1357, subdivision (a), provides: The Legislature finds that there are common interest developments that have been created with deed restrictions which do not provide a means for the property owners to extend the term of the declaration. The Legislature further finds that covenants and restrictions, contained in the declaration, are an appropriate method for protecting the common plan of developments and to provide for a mechanism for financial support for the upkeep of common areas including, but not limited to, roofs, roads, heating systems, and recreational facilities. If declarations terminate prematurely, common interest developments may deteriorate and the housing supply of affordable units could be impacted adversely. The Legislature further finds and declares that it is in the public interest to provide a vehicle for extending the term of the declaration if owners having more than 50 percent of the votes in the association choose to do so.

In turn Civil Code section 1357, subdivision (b), provides in part:

> A declaration which specifies a termination date, but which contains no provision for extension of the termination date, may be extended by the approval of owners having more than 50 percent of the votes in the association or any greater percentage specified in the declaration for an amendment thereto.

The procedures by which members of common interest developments exercise their rights, including the right to extend CCRs, are set forth, in part, in section 2792.17 of title 10 of the California Code of Regulations. Under section 2792.17, subdivision (f) of title 10 of the Code of Regulations, CCRs should provide that "[a]ny action which may be taken by the vote of members at a regular or special meeting ... may be taken without a meeting if done in compliance with the provisions of Section 7513 of the Corporations Code." Section 7513, subdivision (a), of the Corporations Code in turn provides in part: "[A]ny action which may be taken at any regular or special meeting of members may be taken without a meeting if the corporation distributes a written ballot to every member entitled to vote on the matter. Such ballot shall set forth the proposed action, provide an opportunity to specify approval or disapproval of any proposal, and provide a reasonable time within which to return the ballot to the corporation." Significantly Corporations Code section 7513, subdivision (d), provides: "Unless otherwise provided in the articles or bylaws, *a written ballot may not be revoked.*" (Italics added.)

Although the record does not disclose the common ownership of realty which would make the La Jolla Mesa Vista development a common interest development and therefore directly subject to the foregoing statutory and administrative provisions (see Civ.Code, §1351), those provisions nonetheless are helpful in interpreting the procedures which in fact were employed by the association. Civil Code section 1357 is helpful in that it is a legislative recognition of the practical importance of efforts to renew CCRs. Here without renewal of the CCRs, owners in the La Jolla Mesa Vista development would be without the protection which may be responsible in large part for establishing the value of their residences.

The Department of Real Estate regulations governing the process by which decisions are made by common interest developments are helpful in that by incorporating the election scheme set forth in the Corporations Code, the department has provided administrative recognition that efficient procedures must exist by which collective decisions can be reached. Of particular importance here is the provision in Corporations Code section 7513, subdivision (d), for irrevocable ballots. Plainly where the provisions of Corporations Code section 7513, subdivision (d), apply, individuals cannot unduly delay or frustrate decision making by repeatedly changing their minds. Thus the statute and the regulation which has incorporated its provisions serve as recognition that certainty, finality and promptness in decision making, which are fostered by irrevocable balloting, are important interests shared by all members of a common interest development or other collective endeavor.

In our view the benefits to be derived from renewal of the CCRs coupled with the benefits gained from a procedure which resolves the renewal issue with certainty and finality are sufficient consideration to support the irrevocability of the consents obtained by Homeowners. This conclusion is consistent with a long line of charitable subscription cases. "If 'a number of subscribers promise to contribute money on the faith of the common engagement, for the accomplishment of an object of interest to all, and which cannot be accomplished save by their common performance, then it would seem that the mutual promises constitute reciprocal obligations.'" (*Christian College v. Hendley* (1874) 49 Cal. 347, 350; *see also University of Southern California v. Bryson* (1929) 103 Cal.App. 39, 49, 283 P. 949; *Board of Home Missions & Church Extension v. Manley* (1933) 129 Cal.App. 541, 544, 19 P.2d 21; *First Trust, etc. Bank v. Coe College* (1935) 8 Cal.App.2d 195, 199, 47 P.2d 481.) Here renewal of the CCRs could not be accomplished without the mutual consent of a majority of the homeowners; by analogy to the charitable contribution cases, a person who has given his assent to the extension is bound for a reasonable period of time by the assents previously obtained and by assents which are later obtained.

In sum then we reject Improvement's argument the homeowners were free to rescind their consents to the extension. Where, as here, the written procedures established for obtaining consent to extensions or modifications to CCRs do not give an assenting member of a development the right to unilaterally withdraw his or her consent, such a right will not be implied.

In addition, contrary to Improvement's argument, we have no trouble finding the language used in the extension and modification was in fact sufficient to express the parties intention to be bound by its terms. The extension provides: "The undersigned desire to extend and amend said Declaration of Conditions and Restrictions, all as herein provided. NOW, THEREFORE, the undersigned hereby extend and amend said Declaration of Conditions and Restrictions as follows."

We also have no difficulty upholding the trial court's finding no good cause for rescission existed. Improvement presented no evidence of fraud, mistake, undue influence, or any other grounds for rescission.

...

Having found no valid rescissions and no defect in the consent provided for Lot 80, we have reached the majority of 48 lots needed to uphold the extension.

Judgment Affirmed.

Notes & Questions

1. *Extension and termination of the regime.* Declarations for common interest communities created in an earlier era frequently included termination dates. Why do you think termination dates were included? Modern documents either provide for indefinite duration, with provisions for amendment and termination under certain circumstances, or provide for automatic extension unless a specified percentage of owners take action to modify or terminate the declaration. See UCIOA §2-118. See generally, *White v. Lewis*, 487 S.W.2d 615 (Ark. 1972) and *Boyles v. Hausman*, 509 N.W.2d 676 (Neb. Ct. App. 1993).

2. *Implied powers to renew servitude regime.* As explained in *La Jolla Mesa*, California has provided by statute a means for extending a common interest community regime when covenants terminate without providing a process for renewal. See California Civil Code §1357. What would have happened in the absence of such a statute? Is there an implied power to renew the covenant based upon a majority vote of the owners? Or is 100% approval necessary to revive the expired covenants? See *Brandwein v. Serrano*, 338 N.Y.S.2d 192 (N.Y. Sup. 1972) (considering extension agreement to continue restrictions); and see Restatement (Third) §6.10(b) (concerning vote necessary to extend the declaration).

Problem

Let's revisit a problem from chapter 6. A new client is sitting in your office seeking your advice. She and her husband own a unit in Seven Oaks, a homeowners association development. She explains that Seven Oaks was built in phases, and she resides in a home in the 60-unit first phase. All of the units in her phase are sold and owner-occupied.

There are now four sets of CCRs recorded, one on each phase. All have the same substantive provisions and state, in numerous instances, that certain rights or responsibilities exist unless modified by a majority vote of the association's voting power. Phase I has a large open space in its common area, which DevCo, the declarant/developer, wishes to use as a site for a new clubhouse to serve all owners. DevCo still owns units in the fourth phase, and it has proposed that all documents be amended to authorize construction of the clubhouse and to impose a capital assessment to fund its construction.

Your client is interested in having the clubhouse because of her interest in aerobics. She is asking your advice and specifically has inquired whether the proposed actions are valid and what steps might be necessary in order to ensure that "she gets her clubhouse."

How do you advise her?

Chapter 10

Liability of Associations, Boards and Members

Note the three parties in the title to this chapter. When one thinks about liability in a common interest community, most commonly it is the developer that is thought to be the defendant; however, there are significant liability issues that affect the association, boards of directors, and members of each. It is always important to reflect upon the fact that if an association is held liable, members of that association, directly or indirectly, must be responsible for that liability. This chapter addresses the very important, real world issues of when and under what circumstances liability might arise and what the exposure is for that liability.

There are a number of initial policy questions inherent in these determinations. When and why the association should be liable are one set. How to allocate monetary responsibility and to whom to allocate it involve another. Keep in mind that the association generally has very limited assets, and that common property is owned either in common in the condominium or by the association on behalf of the individual owners subject to an extensive array of covenants in the non-condominium common interest community. These ownership structures make it quite difficult simply to attach the property as one might do in levying upon a judgment in a more typical civil litigation context.

The declarant as the declarant, and the declarant as the project developer are unique roles, and declarant's liability is considered separately in Chapter 11.

A consideration of liability is not complete if one only focuses upon litigation and its consequences. Liability should be studied in the broader context of risk management and risk prevention as well. Consider what the attorney's role is in developing document provisions and procedures in practice to reduce the risk of liability and to manage disputes more effectively when they do arise.

A lawyer seeing herself only in the role of litigator is not only missing a splendid opportunity to affect positive change but also is not fully serving her client. Many litigation cases illustrate situations in which documents were poorly drafted, procedures were not followed or were not in place, and alternative dispute resolution procedures were ignored. In each case, consider how the dispute could have been avoided by the practice of preventive lawyering.

A. Association Liability

What creates association liability? What is different, if anything, in the context of the common interest community from any other transaction in which contract or tort liability arises? Associations have a variety of contractual relationships which, in the ordinary course of business, can give rise to dispute and potential liability. Perhaps the most common is the agreement between the association and a professional management entity or an employment contract with a full-time management employee. In addition, there are a variety of third parties who deal directly or indirectly in a business context with the association. Consider, moreover, the possibility of third parties who have claims arising from contracts between the association and others or who, because of some relationship between the individual and the association, may have an implied contract.

In a tort situation, the initial question always is whether there is a duty. The next questions are whether the association owes a duty, what the nature and extent of that duty is, and to whom it is owed. The association practitioner is wise never to assume nor to concede the existence of such a duty. In the common interest community context, duty normally arises either from representation or from the relationship between the association and another party.

1. Association Liability to Members and Third Parties

White v. Cox
Court of Appeals of California
95 Cal. Rptr. 259 (Cal. Ct. App. 1971)

FLEMING J. Plaintiff White owns a condominium in the Merrywood condominium project and is a member of Merrywood Apartments, a nonprofit unincorporated association which maintains the common areas of Merrywood. In his complaint against Merrywood Apartments for damages for personal injuries White avers he tripped and fell over a water sprinkler negligently maintained by Merrywood Apartments in the common area of Merrywood. The trial court sustained Merrywood's demurrer without leave to amend and entered judgment of dismissal. White appeals.

The question here is whether a member of an unincorporated association of condominium owners may bring an action against the association for damages caused by negligent maintenance of the common areas in the condominium project. In contesting the propriety of such an action defendant association argues that because it is a joint enterprise each member is both principal and agent for every other member, and consequently the negligence of each member must be imputed to every other member. Hence, its argument goes, a member may not maintain an action for negligence against the association because the member himself shares responsibility as a principal for the negligence of which he complains. (6 Am.Jur.2d, Associations and Clubs, §31.)

We first consider the present status of an unincorporated association's liability in tort to its members. In *Marshal v. International Longshoremen's & Warehousemen's Union*, 57 Cal.2d 781 [22 Cal.Rptr. 211, 371 P.2d 987], the court ruled that a member of a labor union organized as an unincorporated association could sue the union for negligent acts which the member had neither participated in nor authorized. The court said: "Under traditional legal concepts the partnership is regarded as an aggregate of individuals with each partner acting as agent for all other partners in the transaction of partnership business, and the agents of the partnership acting as agents for all of the partners. When these concepts are transferred bodily to other forms of voluntary associations such as fraternal organizations, clubs and labor unions, which act normally through elected officers and in which the individual members have little or no authority in the day-to-day operations of the association's affairs, reality is apt to be sacrificed to theoretical formalism. The courts, in recognition of this fact, have from case to case gradually evolved new theories in approaching the problems of such associations, and there is now a respectable body of judicial decision, especially in the field of labor-union law, with which we are here directly concerned, which recognizes the existence of unincorporated labor unions as separate entities for a variety of purposes, and which recognizes as well that the individual members of such unions are not in any true sense principals of the officers of the union or of its agents and employees so as to be bound personally by their acts under the strict application of the doctrine of respondent superior."

In effect, the court found that the traditional immunization of an unincorporated association from liability in tort to its members rested on two supports: (1) an unincorporated association lacks a legal existence separate from its members; (2) each member exercises control over the operations of the association. But the court observed that these supports no longer carried the persuasiveness they once did, and it quoted from its opinion in *DeMille v. American Fed. of Radio Artists*, 31 Cal.2d 139, 149 [187 P.2d 769]: The member and the association are distinct. The union represents the common or group interests of its members, as distinguished from their personal or private interest. 'Structurally and functionally, a labor union is an institution which involves more than the private or personal interests of its members. It represents organized, institutional activity as contrasted with wholly individual activity. This difference is as well defined as that existing between individual members of the union.' (*United States v. White*, 322 U.S. 694, at page 701 [88 L.Ed. 1542, 64 S.Ct. 1248, 152 A.L.R. 1202].) The court then concluded that a union could be held liable in tort for negligence to a member. But it specifically limited the application of its ruling to labor unions, declaring it would leave "to future development the rules to be applied in the case of other types of unincorporated associations." (57 Cal.2d at 787, fn. 1.)

Since *Marshal* in 1962 the rule of non-liability of an unincorporated association to its members has suffered further erosion from both statutory and case law. Under amendments to the Corporations Code in 1967 an unincorporated association, defined as "any partnership or other unincorporated organization of two or more persons" (§ 24000), has been made liable to third persons to the same extent as if the association were a natural person (§ 24001),[2] its property (but not the property of its members) may be levied upon by writ of execution to enforce a judgment against the association (§ 24002), and a system has been created for the designation of agents for service of process (§§ 24003–24007). An unincorporated association may own property (§§ 21200–21201), protect its name and insignia (§§ 21300–21310), engage in commercial ventures (Com. Code, § 1201, subds. 28, 30), and engage in labor activities (Lab. Code, § 1117). Members of nonprofit unincorporated associations remain free from liability for the association's debts incurred in acquiring real property. (Corp. Code, § 21100.)

Since 1962 the trend of case law has flowed toward full recognition of the unincorporated association as a separate legal entity. A member of an unincorporated association does not incur liability for acts of the association or acts of its members which he did not authorize or perform. (*Orser v. George*, 252 Cal.App.2d 660, 670–671 [60 Cal.Rptr. 708].) A partner in a business partnership has been allowed to maintain an action against the

[handwritten margin note: Trend to recog. unincorp. ass. as sep. legal entity.]

---

2. Section 24001, subdivision (a) declares that an unincorporated association is liable to nonmembers for an act or omission of its agents. Section 24001, subdivision (b) adds: "Nothing in this section in any way affects the rules of law which determine the liability between an association and a member of the association."

partnership for the loss of his truck as a result of partnership negligence. (*Smith v. Hensley* (Ky.) 354 S.W.2d 744 [98 A.L.R.2d 340].) In the latter case the court declared that the doctrine of imputed negligence, which would normally bar a partner's recovery against the partnership, was an artificial rule of law which should yield to reason and practical considerations; since the partnership would have been liable for damages to the property of a stranger, no just reason existed for denying recovery for damages to the property of a partner. In affirming a judgment for plaintiff the court said: "... under a realistic approach, seeking to achieve substantial justice, the plaintiff should be held entitled to maintain the action."

In view of these developments over the past decade we conclude that unincorporated associations are now entitled to general recognition as separate legal entities and that as a consequence a member of an unincorporated association may maintain a tort action against his association.

Does this general rule of tort liability of an unincorporated association to its members apply in the specific instance of a condominium? A brief review of the statutory provisions which sanction and regulate the condominium form of ownership will clarify the nature of what we are dealing with. A condominium is an estate in real property consisting of an undivided interest in common in a portion of a parcel of real property together with a separate interest in another portion of the same parcel. (Civ. Code, §783.) A project is the entire parcel of property, a unit is the separate interest, and the common areas are the entire project except for the units. (Civ. Code, §1350.) Transfer of a unit, unless otherwise provided, is presumed to transfer the entire condominium. (Civ. Code, §1352.) Ownership is usually limited to the interior surfaces of the unit, a cotenancy in the common areas, and nonexclusive easements for ingress, egress, and support. (Civ. Code, §1353.) Typically, a condominium consists of an apartment house in which the units consist of individual apartments and the common areas consist of the remainder of the building and the grounds. Individual owners maintain their own apartments, and an association of apartment owners maintains the common areas. The association obtains funds for the care of the common areas by charging dues and levying assessments on each apartment owner.

The original project owner must record a condominium plan (Civ. Code, §1351), and restrictions in the plan become enforceable as equitable servitudes (Civ. Code, §1355). The plan may provide for management of the project by the condominium owners, by a board of governors elected by the owners, or by an elected or appointed agent. Management may acquire property, enforce restrictions, maintain the common areas, insure the owners, and make reasonable assessments. (Civ. Code, §§1355, 1358.) Only under exceptional circumstances may the condominium project be partitioned. (Civ. Code, §1354; Code Civ. Proc., §752b.) Zoning ordinances must be construed to treat condominiums in like manner as similar structures, lots, or parcels. (Civ. Code, §1370.) Condominium projects with five or more condominiums are subject to rules regulating subdivided lands and subdivisions. (Bus. & Prof. Code, §§11004.5, 11535.1.) Individual condominiums are separately assessed and taxed. (Rev. & Tax. Code, §2188.3.) Savings and loan associations may lend money on the security of condominium real property. (Fin. Code, §7153.1.)

California's condominium legislation parallels that of other jurisdictions (*see* Ferrer & Stecher, *Law of Condominium* (1967)), and a review of this legislation brings out the two different aspects of the typical condominium scheme. (1) Operations. These are normally conducted by a management association created to run the common affairs of the condominium owners. The association functions in a manner comparable to other unincorporated associations in that it is controlled by a governing body, acts through designated agents, and functions under the authority of by-laws, etc. (the plan). In this aspect of the condominium scheme the management association of condominium owners functions as a distinct and separate personality from the owners themselves. (2) Ownership. In its system of tenure for real property the condominium draws elements both from tenancy in common and from separate ownership. Tenancy in common has also been brought into the structure of the management association, for under Civil Code section 1358 the management association holds personal property in common for the benefit of the condominium owners. In a formal sense, therefore, the condominium owners are tenants in common of the common areas and the personal property held by the management association, and they are owners in fee of separate units, which are not separate in fact. It is apparent that in its legal structure the condominium first combines elements from several concepts—unincorporated association, separate property, and tenancy in common—and then seeks to delineate separate privileges and responsibilities on the one hand from common privileges and responsibilities on the other. At this juncture we return to the tests used in *Marshall* to determine the tort liability of an association to its members and pose two questions. Does the condominium association possess a separate existence from its members? Do the members retain direct control over the operations of the association?

Our answer to the first question derives from the nature of the condominium and its employment of the concept of separateness. Were separateness not clearly embodied within the condominium project the unit owners would become tenants in common of an estate in real property and remain exposed to all the consequences which flow from such a status. We think the concept of separateness in the condominium project carries over to any management body or association formed to handle the common affairs of the project, and that both the condominium project and the condominium association must be considered separate legal entities from its unit owners and association members.

For answer to our second question we turn to the statutory scheme, whence it clearly appears that in ordinary course a unit owner does not directly control the activities of the management body set up to handle the common affairs of the condominium project. To illustrate from the facts at bench: White owns his individual unit and a one-sixtieth interest in the common areas of Merrywood. An administrator controls the common affairs of Merrywood and maintains the common area where White tripped over the sprinkler. The administrator is appointed by and responsible to a board of governors. The board of governors is elected by the unit owners in an election in which each owner has one vote, owners vote by proxy, and cumulative voting is allowed. White is not a member of the board of governors. The Merrywood condominium plan succinctly warns, "In case management is not to your satisfaction, you may have no recourse." To use the language of the *Marshall* opinion, we would be sacrificing reality to theoretical formalism to rule that White had any effective control over the operation of the common areas of Merrywood, for in fact he had no more control over operations than he would have had as a stockholder in a corporation which owned and operated the project.

With respect to the elements deemed critical in *Marshall* we find no substantial distinction between a condominium and a labor union. A condominium, like a labor union, has a separate existence from its members. Control of a condominium, like control of a labor union, is normally vested in a management body over which the individual member has no direct control. We conclude, therefore, that a condominium possesses sufficient aspects of an unincorporated association to make it liable in tort to its members. The condominium and the condominium association may be sued in the condominium name under authority of section 388 of the Code of Civil Procedure. The condominium and the condominium association may be served in the statutory manner provided for service on an unincorporated association (Corp. Code, §§ 24003–24007), and individual unit owners need not be named or served as parties in a negligence action against the condominium and the condominium association.[3]

Holding /
Conclus.

We conclude (1) the condominium association may be sued for negligence in its common name, (2) by a member of the association, (3) who may obtain a judgment against the condominium and the condominium association.

The judgment of dismissal is Reversed.

ROTH, J. Concurring. I agree that a member of an unincorporated association of condominium owners may sue the association in tort. (Code Civ. Proc., § 388.) However, the majority opinion fails to define or distinguish the extent to which individual unit owners in a condominium project may become liable to another unit owner or to a third person for tortuous conduct arising in the common areas of the condominium project. In footnote 3, the majority declines to hold on "what property execution may be levied to satisfy a judgment against the condominium and the condominium association."

When as at bench a judgment of dismissal entered after a demurrer without leave to amend has been sustained the question of levy of execution may not be properly before this court. However, the question of the identities of the parties liable is not settled in this case[1] nor is the basis of the liability of parties other than the association, to wit, Merrywood Apartments.

The ownership of the common areas in a condominium project is vested in the individual unit owners as tenants in common. (Civ. Code, § 1353, subd. (b).) Thus, even though, as the majority holds, the association may be sued in its separate name, it is apparent that the legal owners of the common areas are not immunized from liability by virtue of the mere existence of the association.

A comparative study of California condominium legislation with that in other states shows that the question of the individual unit owner's tort liability in cases arising in the

---

3. We express no opinion on what property execution may be levied to satisfy a judgment against the condominium and the condominium association. With reference to liens for labor, services, or materials, the last sentence of Civil Code section 1357 reads: "The owner of any condominium may remove his condominium from a lien against two or more condominiums or any part thereof by payment to the holder of the lien of the fraction of the total sum secured by such lien which is attributable to his condominium."

It could be implied from the sense of the section that a condominium owner may satisfy his portion of any liability arising out of the operation of the condominium project by the payment of his proportionate share of the liability. Such a conclusion would conform to what has been written on the subject by text writers (Rohan and Reskin, Condominium Law and Practice (1970), Ch. 10A, and 4 Powell on Real Property, § 633.25), and parallels what has been achieved by statute in other states. Alaska, Massachusetts, and Washington provide that a cause of action in tort relating to the common areas may be maintained only against the association of apartment owners. A judgment lien becomes a common expense and is removed from an individual condominium upon payment by the individual owner of his proportionate share. (Alaska Stat., tit. 34, § 34.07.260; Annot. Laws of Massachusetts, Ch. 183A, § 13; Rev. Code of Washington Annot., § 64.32.240.) District of Columbia, Idaho, and Maryland provide more generally that any judgment lien against two or more condominium owners may be removed from an individual condominium upon payment by the condominium owner of his proportionate share. (Dist. of Columbia Code Encyclopedia, § 5-924(c); Idaho Code, § 55-1515; Annot. Code of Maryland, art. 21, § 138.) In contrast is Mississippi, whose code declares that individual owners have no personal liability for damages caused by the governing body or connected with use of the common area. (Miss. Code Annot., § 896-15.)

1. In addition to Merrywood Apartments, the complaint named Does I through X as defendants.

common areas has not been regulated by statute. The majority's suggestion that section 1357 of the Civil Code, in providing for the aliquot satisfaction of liens for labor, services, or materials, also provides for the distribution of tort liability among the owners is too great a strain on the expressly limited wording of that code section. This suggestion has been questioned by at least one commentator (*Comment*, 77 Harv. L.Rev. 777, 780, fn. 24) and it does not square with the fact that California has followed the lead of most states and failed to provide adequate regulation or protection of the individual owner's interests in the case of torts arising from the common areas. (*See* Rohan, *Perfecting the Condominium as a Housing Tool: Innovations in Tort Liability and Insurance* (1967), 32 Law & Contemp. Prob. 305, 308; Kerr, *Condominium — Statutory Implementation* (1963), 28 St. John's L.Rev. 1, 42–43; *Comment, supra*, 77 Harv. L.Rev. 777, 780.) The absence of an express statutory scheme for the re-distribution of tort liability, such as those found in the Alaska, Massachusetts and Washington legislation, is ample warning that the problem of protecting the individual unit owner from tort liability which, it should be noted, may exceed the value of his unit[2] (whether it be to another unit owner or to a third person) is yet an open question in California.

One practical answer is, of course, insurance taken out by the association to cover liability in respect of the common areas. (See *Kerr, supra*, at p. 43.) It might then be argued depending on the terms of the written declaration between unit owners that, at least as between suing and defendant unit owners, the maximum amount of liability of defendant unit owners has been contractually limited to the maximum of the insurance taken out by the association.[3]

At bench we have the declaration upon which the project at bench is grounded before us only insofar as its terms are reflected by the permit of the Commissioner of Corporations.

The permit, after setting forth the plan of management and powers of the board of governors, sets forth in pertinent part that the board of governors shall have the power to: "Contract and/or pay for fire, casualty, liability and other insurance and bonding of its members, maintenance, gardening, utilities, materials, supplies, services and personnel necessary for the operation of the project, taxes and assessments which may become a lien on the entire project or the common area, and reconstruction of portions of the project which are to be rebuilt after damage or destruction;"

The above excerpt or summary (in the permit) from the declaration is substantially similar to the powers set forth in section 1355, subdivision (b)(2) of the Civil Code, which empowers the board of governors to obtain "... fire, casualty, liability, workmen's compensation and other insurance insuring condominium owners, and for bonding of the members of any management body;"

It occurs to me, therefore, on the limited record before this court that each unit holder of the project has by contract delegated to the board of governors which operates the project the power and responsibility to obtain adequate liability insurance for the project to cover claims of third persons and also adequate insurance to cover negligence actions

---

2. Thus, in California, the co-owners may have to respond for injuries arising out of the common areas in terms of the personal tort liability of tenants in common, which according to the common law and our statutory law results in joint and several liability. (Code Civ. Proc., § 384; 86 C.J.S. Tenancy in Common, § 143.)

3. In California, the governing body of a condominium project may obtain insurance on behalf of, and for the benefit of condominium owners. (Civ. Code, § 1355, *subd.* (b)(2).)

of unit owners against the association and actions which any unit owner might bring against other unit owners because of the negligence of the association.

It seems to me therefore that any failure by management to obtain adequate insurance *Concurring* or any insurance leaves a unit holder injured by negligence of management, (as distinguished *opinion* from independent negligence of a fellow unit owner) with the right to proceed against the association to the extent of its insurance if any and with no right to proceed against other unit owners. A suit by one other than a unit owner is a question not raised by the litigation at bench, and cannot be similarly circumscribed. Generally, tenants in common may be joined as defendants and their liability is joint and several (Code Civ. Proc., § 384), and the apportionment of liability as between unit owners is, of course, a difficult and vexing question. (*See generally*, 86 C.J.S.2d, Tenancy in Common, § 143.)

Notes & Questions

1. *The Uniform Act.* UCIOA § 3-111 limits the liability of unit owners and the association for injury or damages arising out of the use of common elements or arising out of declarant's action or declarant's property prior to its dedication as common area. See UCIOA § 3-111 and commentary for discussion on association and unit owner liability protections.

2. *Knowledge of dangerous conditions.* If an association was unaware of a dangerous condition in the common elements, can it be liable for injury to its members? To its members' guests? To trespassing third parties? See, *e.g.*, *Casey v. Christie Lodge Owners Ass'n, Inc.*, 923 P.2d 365 (Colo. Ct. App. 1996) (member assaulted in parking lot); *Fryberger v. Lake Cable Recreation Ass'n, Inc.*, 533 N.E.2d 738 (Ohio 1988) (injury in lake); *Hallman v. Pointe Arcadia Horizontal Property Regime, Inc.*, 402 S.E.2d 493 (S.C. Ct. App. 1991); *Moody v. Cawdrey & Assoc., Inc.*, 721 P.2d 707 (Haw. 1986) (guest cruelly attacked).

3. *Environmental liability.* Does liability arise from environmental conditions or problems on the common elements under state and federal environmental statutes which typically apply to business and not individual homeowners? See generally *Cyker v. Four Seasons Hotels Ltd.*, No. 90-11929-7 (D. Mass Jan. 4, 1991) (pool chemical contamination of neighboring properties did not create cause of action under Comprehensive Environmental Response, Compensation and Liability Act); *Ellenheath Condo. Ass'n, Inc. v. Pearlman*, No. A-1413-94T3 (N.J. Super. Ct. App. Div. Oct. 24, 1996) (discussion of liability for leaking underground storage tank replacement).

4. *Releases from liability.* Can an association release itself from liability from personal injuries arising from use of common elements (such as exercise equipment) by obtaining signed release forms? See, *Hiett v. Lake Barcroft Community Ass'n, Inc.*, 418 S.E.2d 894 (Va. 1992) (pre-injury release language in triathlon registration form was void as a violation of public policy and could not release defendant association from negligence liability claim).

5. *Liability arising from covenant or rule violations.* Can an association be held liable for injuries sustained on common elements where member's action was in violation of the community's covenant or rules? See *O'Brien v. Christensen*, 662 N.E.2d 205 (Mass. 1996) (injury caused from violative use of entrance area).

6. *Management company liability.* A management company will often jointly be sued for injuries sustained on common elements. Often, the issue concerns the level of maintenance or oversight provided by the management company. See, *e.g.*, *Planned Community Services, Inc. v. Spielman*, 371 S.E.2d 193 (Ga. Ct. App. 1988).

Problems

1. The homes at Golf Villas are lovely and have great views of the golf course. The problem is that some are effectively part of the course ... at least for the errant shot. Sue and Charlie have come to you with their problem. Shots from the 6th tee continue to land in their yard, strike the house, and break the living room window. This morning one shot barely missed the baby. They ask you whether they can sue the association or the golf course. How do you advise them? What are the questions you would ask them? Does the errant golf ball constitute a trespass? Under what circumstances? Remember, "it is generally known that the average golfer does not always hit the ball straight."

2. You just received a call from the president of your favorite condominium association client. It seems that the board decided to publish the names of homeowners delinquent in payment of common expenses. First they posted the names on the bulletin boards of the lobbies of each of the three condominium buildings. At the management company's suggestion, they then decided to publish the names in the association newsletter. This is the first you hear of this approach to assessment collection, and the president advises you that one delinquent has called in a fury, asserting that she has been defamed. How do you advise your client?

It seems that an owner held a meeting of the Arts Guild Board of Trustees in her unit, and many of the prestigious members read items from the bulletin board as they waited for the elevator in the lobby. Several women noticed the complaining owner's name and have now chided her unmercifully about "not paying her bill." Does this affect your advice?

Finally, what questions might you have about the newsletter? Does the newsletter's nature and extent of circulation make a difference to you in formulating your advice?

3. You are at a HOA board meeting, and the board is in intense discussion over the proposal to add a bar at the swimming pool and to provide bar service from 5:00–8:00 p.m. during summer hours. Several members have proposed this as a "fun thing to do" and a great revenue source. You are asked for your advice. What do you say?

2. Association Liability for Security

Frances T. v. Village Green Owners Ass'n

Supreme Court of California, In Bank
229 Cal. Rptr. 456 (Cal. 1986)

BROUSSARD, J. The question presented is whether a condominium owners association and the individual members of its board of directors may be held liable for injuries to a unit owner caused by third-party criminal conduct. Plaintiff, Frances T., brought suit against the Village Green Owners Association (the Association)[1] and individual members of its board of directors for injuries sustained when she was attacked in her condominium unit, a part of the Village Green Condominium Project (Project). Her complaint stated three causes of action: negligence, breach of contract and breach of fiduciary duty. The trial court sustained defendants' general demurrers to plaintiff's three causes of action without leave to amend and entered a judgment of dismissal. Plaintiff appealed.

---

1. Plaintiff erroneously refers to the named party as the Village Green Condominium Project. The correct name is the Village Green Owners Association. The association is a nonprofit corporation, rather than an unincorporated association.

I.

On the night of October 8, 1980, an unidentified person entered plaintiff's condominium unit under cover of darkness and molested, raped and robbed her. At the time of the incident, plaintiff's unit had no exterior lighting. The manner in which her unit came to be without exterior lighting on this particular evening forms the basis of her lawsuit against the defendants.[2]

The Association, of which plaintiff was a member, is a nonprofit corporation composed of owners of individual condominium units. The Association was formed and exists for the purposes set forth in the Project's declaration of covenants, conditions and restrictions (CC&Rs). The board of directors (board) exercises the powers of the Association and conducts, manages and controls the affairs of the Project and the Association. Among other things the Association, through its board, is authorized to enforce the regulations set forth in the CC&Rs. The Association, through the board, is also responsible for the management of the Project and for the maintenance of the Project's common areas.

At the time of the incident, the Project consisted of 92 buildings, each containing several individual condominium units, situated in grassy golf course and parklike areas known as "courts." Plaintiff's unit faced the largest court. She alleges that "the lighting in [the] park-like area was exceedingly poor, and after sunset, aside from the minuscule park light of plaintiff's, the area was in virtual darkness.... Of all condominium units in [plaintiff's court] ... plaintiff's unit was in the darkest place."

Throughout 1980, the Project was subject to what plaintiff terms an "exceptional crimewave" that included car thefts, purse snatchings, dwelling burglaries and robberies. All of the Project's residents, including the board, were aware of and concerned about this "crimewave." From January through July 1980, articles about the crimewave and possible protective measures were published in the Association's newsletter and distributed to the residents of the Project, including the directors. The newsletters show that residents, including the directors, were aware of some of the residents' complaints regarding lighting.[3] In early 1980 the board began to investigate what could be done to improve the lighting in the Project. The investigation was conducted by the Project's architectural guidelines committee.

Plaintiff's unit was first burglarized in April 1980. Believing the incident would not have occurred if there had been adequate lighting at the end of her court, plaintiff caused the following item to be printed in the Association's newsletter: "With reference to other lighting, Fran [T.] of Ct 4, whose home was entered, feels certain (and asked that this be mentioned) that the break-in would not have occurred if there had been adequate lighting at the end of her Court. This has since been corrected. We hope other areas which need improvement will soon be taken care of...."[4]

---

2. Since this case arises from the sustaining of a demurrer, we must assume that the factual allegations in the complaint are true....

3. Many of the Association's newsletters were attached to the complaint as exhibits. The newsletters included such items as: "LIGHTS! LIGHTS! LIGHTS! You are doing a disservice to your neighbors as well as yourself if you keep your front and back doors in darkness. Many who live upstairs are able to gaze out on the Green at night and see perfectly the presence or absence of a prowler where there is a lighted doorway. But where porches are shrouded in darkness, NOTHING is visible. AS A CIVIC DUTY—WON'T YOU KEEP THOSE LIGHTS ON? If you would like to try out a Sensor Light on a 30-day trial basis to see how efficient and economical it is, we are sure it can be arranged through the Court Council and Court Reps."

4. Plaintiff, of course, alleges that nothing was done to correct the lighting problem.

In May 1980 plaintiff and other residents of her court had a meeting. As court representative plaintiff transmitted a formal request to the Project's manager with a copy to the board that more lighting be installed in their court as soon as possible.[5]

Plaintiff submitted another memorandum in August 1980 because the board had taken no action on the previous requests. The memorandum stated that none of the lighting requests from plaintiff's court had been responded to. Plaintiff also requested that a copy of the memorandum be placed in the board's correspondence file.

By late August, the board had still taken no action. Plaintiff then installed additional exterior lighting at her unit, believing that this would protect her from crime. In a letter dated August 29, 1980, however, the site manager told plaintiff that she would have to remove the lighting because it violated the CC & Rs. Plaintiff refused to comply with this request. After appearing at a board meeting, where she requested permission to maintain her lighting until the board improved the general lighting that she believed to be a hazard, she received a communication from the board stating in part:

> The Board has indicated their appreciation for your appearance on October 1, and for the information you presented to them. After deliberation, however, the Board resolved as follows: [P] You are requested to remove the exterior lighting you added to your front door and in your patio and to restore the Association Property to its original condition on or before October 6. If this is not done on or before that date, the Association will have the work done and bill you for the costs incurred.

The site manager subsequently instructed plaintiff that pending their removal, she could not use the additional exterior lighting. The security lights had been installed using the same circuitry used for the original exterior lighting and were operated by the same switches. In order not to use her additional lighting, plaintiff was required to forego the use of all of her exterior lights. In spite of this, however, plaintiff complied with the board's order and cut off the electric power on the circuitry controlling the exterior lighting during the daylight hours of October 8, 1980. As a result, her unit was in total darkness on October 8, 1980, the night she was raped and robbed.

II.

NEGLIGENCE

In her first cause of action plaintiff alleged that the Association and the board negligently failed to complete the investigation of lighting alternatives within a reasonable time, failed to present proposals regarding lighting alternatives to members of the Association, negligently failed to respond to the requests for additional lighting and wrongfully ordered her to remove the lighting that she had installed. She contends that these negligent acts and omissions were the proximate cause of her injuries.

The fundamental issue here is whether petitioners, the condominium Association and its individual directors, owed plaintiff the same duty of care as would a landlord in the traditional landlord-tenant relationship. We conclude that plaintiff has pleaded facts sufficient to state a cause of action for negligence against both the Association and the individual directors.

_____

5. The letter stated: "June 12, 1980. REPORT FROM YOUR COURT REP.... It was requested that the following items be relayed to the on-site mgr. for consideration and action if possible. 1. Lights be installed on the northeast corner of bldg. 18 promptly.... Item No. 1 above was put into the form of a motion with the request that action be taken on this item particularly by the site manager...."

A. The Association's Duty of Care.

The scope of a condominium association's duty to a unit owner in a situation such as this is a question of first impression. Plaintiff contends, and we agree, that under the circumstances of this case the Association should be held to the same standard of care as a landlord.

Defendants based their demurrer to the negligence cause of action on the theory that the Association owed no duty to plaintiff to improve the lighting outside her unit. The Association argues that it would be unfair to impose upon it a duty to provide "expensive security measures" when it is not a landlord in the traditional sense, but a nonprofit association of homeowners. The Association contends that under its own CC & Rs, it cannot permit residents to improve the security of the common areas without prior written permission, nor can it substantially increase its limited budget for common-area improvements without the approval of a majority of the members.

But regardless of these self-imposed constraints, the Association is, for all practical purposes, the Project's "landlord."[6] And traditional tort principles impose on landlords, no less than on homeowner associations that function as a landlord in maintaining the common areas of a large condominium complex, a duty to exercise due care for the residents' safety in those areas under their control. (*See, e.g., Kwaitkowski v. Superior Trading Co.* (1981) 123 Cal.App.3d 324, 328, 176 Cal.Rptr. 494; *O'Hara v. Western Seven Trees Corp., supra,* 75 Cal.App.3d 798, 802–803, 142 Cal.Rptr. 487; *Kline v. 1500 Massachusetts Avenue Apartment Corp.* (D.C. Cir.1970) 439 F.2d 477, 480–481; *Scott v. Watson* (1976) 278 Md. 160, 359 A.2d 548, 552.)

Two previous California decisions support our conclusion that a condominium association may properly be held to a landlord's standard of care as to the common areas under its control. In *White v. Cox, supra,* 17 Cal.App.3d 824, 95 Cal.Rptr. 259, the court held that a condominium owner could sue the unincorporated association for negligently maintaining a sprinkler in a common area of the complex.

. . .

In *O'Connor v. Village Green Owners Assn., supra,* 33 Cal.3d 790, 191 Cal.Rptr. 320, 662 P.2d 427, this court held that the Association's restriction limiting residency in the project to persons over 18 years of age was a violation of the Unruh Civil Rights Act (Civ.Code, §51).[8] In so doing, we were mindful of the Association's role in the day-to-day functioning of the project: "Contrary to the association's attempt to characterize itself as but an organization that 'mows lawns' for owners, the association in reality has a far broader

---

6. Petitioners also suggest that even if the Association and its ruling board function as would a landlord in a rental complex of similar size, plaintiff's status as a unit owner—rather than defendants' effective control over the common areas—should determine the Association's duty of care. We disagree that an unincorporated association has no existence apart from that of its members. (*See Marshall v. International Longshoremen's & Warehousemen's Union* (1962) 57 Cal.2d 781, 783–784, 22 Cal.Rptr. 211, 371 P.2d 987; *White v. Cox* (1971) 17 Cal.App.3d 824, 830, 95 Cal.Rptr. 259.) Constitutional and common law protections do not lose their potency merely because familiar functions are organized into more complex or privatized arrangements. (*See, e.g., PruneYard Shopping Center v. Robins* (1980) 447 U.S. 74, 100 S.Ct. 2035, 64 L.Ed.2d 741; *Shelley v. Kraemer* (1948) 334 U.S. 1, 68 S.Ct. 836, 92 L.Ed. 1161; *Marsh v. Alabama* (1946) 326 U.S. 501, 66 S.Ct. 276, 90 L.Ed. 265.) Similarly, a homeowner's association and its board may not enforce provisions of the CC & Rs in a way that violates statutory or common law. (*See O'Connor v. Village Green Owners Assn.* (1983) 33 Cal.3d 790, 191 Cal.Rptr. 320, 662 P.2d 427.)

8. Section 51 provides in relevant part: "All persons within the jurisdiction of this state are free and equal, and no matter what their sex, race, color, religion, ancestry, or national origin are entitled to the full and equal accommodations, advantages, facilities, privileges, or services in all business establishments of every kind whatsoever."

and more businesslike purpose. The association, through a board of directors, is charged with employing a professional property management firm, with obtaining insurance for the benefit of all owners and with maintaining and repairing all common areas and facilities of the 629-unit project.... *In brief, the association performs all the customary business functions which in the traditional landlord-tenant relationship rest on the landlord's shoulders.*" (*O'Connor v. Village Green Owners Assn.*, supra, 33 Cal.3d 790, 796, 191 Cal.Rptr. 320, 662 P.2d 427, italics added.)[9]

Since there are no reported California cases dealing with the liability of a condominium association in a situation such as this, the parties have analogized this case to four landlord-tenant cases involving similar facts. The reasoning employed by this line of landlord-tenant cases is equally applicable here. In two of these cases the courts found the landlord liable, while in the other two they declined to do so.

O'Hara v. Western Seven Trees Corp., supra, 75 Cal.App.3d 798, 142 Cal.Rptr. 487 established that in some instances a landlord has a duty to take reasonable steps to protect a tenant from the criminal acts of third parties and may be held liable for failing to do so. In *O'Hara* plaintiff alleged that the defendant landlords were aware that a man had raped several tenants and additionally "were aware of the conditions indicating a likelihood that the rapist would repeat his attacks." (*Id.*, at p. 802, 142 Cal.Rptr. 487.) In addressing the question of the landlords' liability the court observed:

> Traditionally, a landlord had no duty to protect his tenants from the criminal acts of others, but an innkeeper was under a duty to protect his guests. [Citations.] But in recent years, the landlord-tenant relationship, at least in the urban, residential context, has given rise to liability under circumstances where landlords have failed to take reasonable steps to protect tenants from criminal activity. [Citations.] ... [S]ince only the landlord is in the position to secure common areas, he has a duty to protect against types of crimes of which he has notice and which are likely to recur if the common areas are not secure.... [Citations.] "(*Id.*, at pp. 802–803, 142 Cal.Rptr. 487, italics added. See also Peterson v. San Francisco Community College Dist. (1984) 36 Cal.3d 799, 806–807, 205 Cal.Rptr. 842, 685 P.2d 1193.)

The court concluded that, as in the case before us, plaintiff had alleged the most important factor pointing to the landlord's liability: foreseeability. "[The landlords] allegedly knew of the past assaults and of conditions making future attacks likely. By not acting affirmatively to protect [the plaintiff], they increased the likelihood that she would also be a victim." (*Id.*, 75 Cal.App.3d, at p. 804, 142 Cal.Rptr. 487.)[10] Moreover, "evidence of

---

9. We also take judicial notice of the fact that a rapidly growing share of California's population reside in condominiums, cooperatives and other types of common-interest housing projects. Homeowner associations manage the housing for an estimated 15 percent of the American population and, for example, as much as 70 percent of the new housing built in Los Angeles and San Diego Counties. (See Bowler & McKenzie, *Invisible Kingdoms* (Dec. 1985) Cal.Law., at p. 55.) Nationally, "[t]hey are growing at a rate of 5,000 a year and represent more than 50 percent of new construction sales in the urban areas. Projects average about 100 units each, so the associations affect some 10 million owners," according to C. James Dowden, executive vice president of the Community Association Institute in Alexandria, Virginia. (*Ibid.*) According to Bowler & McKenzie, *supra*, housing experts estimate that there already are 15,000 common-interest housing associations in California. While in some projects the maintenance of common areas is truly cooperative, in most of the larger projects control of the common area is delegated or controlled by ruling bodies that do not exercise the members" collective will on a one-person, one-vote basis. (*Ibid.*)

10. The court also concluded that several sections of the Restatement Second of Torts suggest that landlords can be held liable under certain circumstances for injuries inflicted during criminal assaults on tenants. Section 302B provides: "An act or an omission may be negligent if the actor realizes or should

prior similar incidents is not the *sine qua non* of a finding of foreseeability." (*Isaacs v. Huntington Memorial Hospital* (1985) 38 Cal.3d 112, 127, 211 Cal.Rptr. 356, 695 P.2d 653.) "[F]oreseeability is determined in light of all the circumstances and not by a rigid application of a mechanical 'prior similars' rule." (*Id.* at p. 126, 211 Cal.Rptr. 356, 695 P.2d 653.)

. . .

Assoc controlled Maintune of comm areas .

As in *O'Hara* and *Kwaitkowski*, it is beyond dispute here that the Association, rather than the unit owners, controlled the maintenance of the common areas. This is clearly illustrated by the fact that when plaintiff attempted to improve security by installing additional exterior lighting, the board ordered her to remove them because they were placed in an area over which the Association exercised exclusive authority.

Defendants further contend that even if the landlord-tenant standard of care is applicable, under this standard the Association owed no duty to the plaintiff. Defendants rely primarily upon *7735 Hollywood Blvd. Venture v. Superior Court* (1981) 116 Cal.App.3d 901, 172 Cal.Rptr. 528 and *Riley v. Marcus* (1981) 125 Cal.App.3d 103, 177 Cal.Rptr. 827 for this contention. Both cases are factually distinguishable from the case before us primarily because the alleged prior criminal acts were not of a nature that would create a duty to better secure the common areas. Both cases are legally questionable because in *Isaacs v. Huntington Memorial Hospital, supra,* 38 Cal.3d 112, 211 Cal.Rptr. 356, 695 P.2d 653, we explicitly rejected the "rigidified foreseeability concept" applied by the court in *Riley* and adopted the court's conclusion in *Kwaitowski* that "'[f]oreseeability does not require prior identical or even similar events.'" (38 Cal.3d at p. 127, 211 Cal.Rptr. 356, 695 P.2d 653.)

The facts alleged here, if proven, demonstrate defendant's awareness of the need for additional lighting and of the fact that lighting could aid in deterring criminal conduct, especially break-ins. As in *O'Hara* and *Kwaitkowski*, the Association was on notice that crimes were being committed against the Project's residents. Correspondence from plaintiff and other residents of her court, along with the articles in the Project's newsletter, demonstrate affirmatively that defendant was aware of the link between the lack of lighting and crime.

Plaintiff's unit had, in fact, been recently burglarized and defendant knew this. It is not necessary, as defendant appears to imply, that the prior crimes be *identical* to the ones perpetrated against the plaintiff. (*Isaacs v. Huntington Memorial Hospital, supra,* 38 Cal.3d 112, 211 Cal.Rptr. 356, 695 P.2d 653; *Kwaitkowski, supra,* 123 Cal.App.3d at p. 329, 176 Cal.Rptr. 494.) Defendant need not have foreseen the precise injury to plaintiff so long as the possibility of this type of harm was foreseeable. (*Isaacs, supra; Kwaitkowski, supra,* at p. 330, 176 Cal.Rptr. 494.)

Thus, plaintiff has alleged facts sufficient to show the existence of a duty, that defendant may have breached that duty of care by failing to respond in a timely manner to the

---

realize that it involves an unreasonable risk of harm to another through the conduct of the other or a third person which is intended to cause harm, *even though such conduct is criminal.*" (Italics added.)

Section 448 provides: "The act of a third person in committing an intentional tort or crime is a superseding cause of harm to another resulting therefrom, although the actor's negligent conduct created a situation which afforded an opportunity to the third person to commit such a tort or crime, *unless the actor* at the time of his negligent conduct *realized or should have realized the likelihood* that such a situation might be created, and *that a third person might* avail himself of the opportunity to *commit such a tort or crime.*" (Italics added.)

Section 449 provides: "If the likelihood that a third person may act in a particular manner is the hazard or one of the hazards which makes the actor negligent, such an act whether innocent, negligent, intentionally tortious, or criminal does not prevent the actor from being liable for harm caused thereby." (Italics added. [Sic])

need for additional lighting and by ordering her to disconnect her additional lights, and that this negligence—if established—was the legal cause of her injuries.

B. Directors' Duty of Care.

Plaintiff's first cause of action also alleged that the individual directors on the Association's board breached a duty of care they owed to her by ordering her to remove the external lighting she had installed for her protection and by failing to repair the Project's hazardous lighting condition within a reasonable period of time.

Individual dirs duty } care?

It is well settled that corporate directors cannot be held *vicariously* liable for the corporation's torts in which they do not participate. Their liability, if any, stems from their own tortious conduct, not from their status as directors or officers of the enterprise. (*See United States Liab. Ins. Co. v. Haidinger-Hayes, Inc.* (1970) 1 Cal.3d 586, 595, 83 Cal.Rptr. 418, 463 P.2d 770.) "[A]n officer or director will not be liable for torts in which he does not personally participate, of which he has no knowledge, or to which he has not consented.... While the corporation itself may be liable for such acts, the individual officer or director will be immune unless he authorizes, directs, or in some meaningful sense actively participates in the wrongful conduct." (*Teledyne Industries, Inc. v. Eon Corporation* (S.D.N.Y.1975) 401 F.Supp. 729, 736–737 (applying California law), *affd.* (2d Cir.1976) 546 F.2d 495.)

[Directors are jointly liable with the corporation and may be joined as defendants if they personally directed or participated in the tortious conduct.] (*United States Liab. Ins. Co. v. Haidinger-Hayes, Inc., supra,* 1 Cal.3d 586, 595, 83 Cal.Rptr. 418, 463 P.2d 770; *Dwyer v. Lanan & Snow Lumber Co.* (1956) 141 Cal.App.2d 838, 841, 297 P.2d 490;....

Dirs. jointly liable w/ the corp. if they personally directed and participated in the tortious conduct.

Directors are liable to third persons injured by their own tortious conduct regardless of whether they acted on behalf of the corporation and regardless of whether the corporation is also liable. (See, *e.g., Tillman v. Wheaton-Haven Recreation Ass'n, Inc., supra,* 517 F.2d 1141, 1144 ["a director who actually votes for the commission of a tort is personally liable, even though the wrongful act is performed in the name of the corporation"]; and *see* rule and authorities cited in 3A Fletcher, *Cyclopedia of the Law of Private Corporations* (Perm. ed. 1986) §§ 1135–1138, pp. 267–298; 18B Am.Jur.2d (1985) Corporations, §§ 1877–1880, pp. 723–729; Knepper, *Liability of Corporate Officers and Directors* (3d ed. 1978) § 5.08 and (1985 supp.) § 5.08; 1 Ballantine & Sterling, *Cal. Corporations Law* (4th ed. 1986) § 101, at pp. 6-3, 6-4; 19 C.J.S., Corporations, § 845, at pp. 271–273.)[11] This liability does not depend on the same grounds as "piercing the corporate veil," on account of inadequate capitalization for instance, but rather on the officer or director's personal participation or specific authorization of the tortious act. (*See* 18B Am.Jur.2d, *supra,* § 1877, at p. 726.)

This rule has its roots in the law of agency. Directors are said to be agents of their corporate principal. (Corp.Code, § 317, subd. (a).) And "[t]he true rule is, of course, that the agent is liable for his own acts, regardless of whether the principal is liable or amenable to judicial action." (*James v. Marinship Corp.* (1944) 25 Cal.2d 721, 742–743, 155 P.2d 329.) Moreover, directors are not subordinate agents of the corporation; rather, their role is as their title suggests: they are policy-makers who direct and ultimately control corpo-

---

11. The fact that directors receive no compensation for their services does not exonerate them from liability that otherwise attaches for a breach of duty. Corporations Code section 7230, subdivision (a) provides, in the context of directors' fiduciary duty to a nonprofit mutual benefit corporation, that "[a]ny duties and liabilities set forth in this article shall apply without regard to whether a director is compensated by the corporation." (See, *e.g., Virginia-Carolina Chemical Co. v. Ehrich* (D.C.S.C.1916) 230 Fed. 1005, 1015–1016; *Weidner v. Engelhart* (N.D.1970) 176 N.W.2d 509, 518; 19 C.J.S., Corporations, § 863, p. 297.)

rate conduct. Unlike ordinary employees or other subordinate agents under their control, a corporate officer is under no compulsion to take action unreasonably injurious to third parties. But like any other employee, directors individually owe a duty of care, independent of the corporate entity's own duty, to refrain from acting in a manner that creates an unreasonable risk of personal injury to third parties. The reason for this rule is that otherwise, a director could inflict injuries upon others and then escape liability behind the shield of his or her representative character, even though the corporation might be insolvent or irresponsible. (*See O'Connell v. Union Drilling & Petroleum Co., supra*, 121 Cal.App. 302, 8 P.2d 867; 18B Am.Jur.2d, *supra*, at p. 729, fn. 13.) Director status therefore neither immunizes a person from individual liability nor subjects him or her to vicarious liability.

Since this appeal follows a dismissal based on plaintiff's failure to state a cause of action, we must next determine the nature of the duty the individual defendants owed to plaintiff. In *United States Liab. Ins. Co. v. Haidinger-Hayes, Inc., supra*, we discussed the two traditional limitations on a <u>corporate officer's or director's personal liability for negligence</u>. First, we concluded that no special agency relationship imposed personal liability on the defendant corporation's president for failing to prevent economic harm to the plaintiff corporation, a client of his principal. This conclusion reflected the oft-stated disinclination to hold an agent personally liable for economic losses when, in the ordinary course of his duties to his own corporation, the agent incidentally harms the pecuniary interests of a third party. "Liability imposed upon agents for active participation in tortious acts of the principal have been mostly restricted to cases involving physical injury, not pecuniary harm, to third persons [citations]." (1 Cal.3d at p. 595, 83 Cal.Rptr. 418, 463 P.2d 770.) Since the harm in that case was pecuniary in nature and resulted from good faith business transactions, we analyzed liability under principles of agency law and denied recovery against the officer as an individual. (*Ibid.*)

In *Haidinger-Hayes*, we also restated the traditional rule that directors are not personally liable to third persons for negligence amounting merely to a breach of duty the officer owes to the corporation alone. "[T]he act must also constitute a breach of duty owed to the third person. More must be shown than breach of the officer's duty *to his corporation* to impose personal liability *to a third person* upon him." (1 Cal.3d at p. 595, 83 Cal.Rptr. 418, 463 P.2d 770, italics in original.) In other words, a distinction must be made between the <u>director's fiduciary duty to the corporation</u> (and its beneficiaries) and the director's <u>ordinary duty to take care not to injure third parties</u>.[12] The former duty is defined by statute,[13] the latter by common law tort principles.

[handwritten margin note: Dir's fiduciary duty to the corp. v. ordinary duty care not to injure 3rd parties.]

12. Like any other citizen, corporate officers have a societal duty to refrain from acts that are unreasonably risky to third persons even when their shareholders or creditors would agree that such conduct serves the institution's best interests. One court succinctly summarized this distinction between a director's institutional duty to corporate insiders and the duty every person owes to the world. "[A]n officer or director of a corporation owes a duty to the corporation which is separate and independent of any duty which he may owe to an employee or to a third person. If he fails to perform a duty owed to the corporation, he may be answerable to that corporation for the damages which it sustained because of his failure or neglect. [P] The only duty which an executive officer of a corporation owes to a third person, whether he be an employee of the corporation or a complete stranger, is the same duty to exercise due care not to injure him which any person owes to another. If an injury is sustained by a third party as the result of the independent negligence of the corporate officer, or as the result of a breach of the duty which that officer, as an individual, owes to the third party, then the injured third party may have a cause of action for damages against the officer personally." (*Saucier v. U.S. Fidelity and Guaranty Company* (La.App.1973) 280 So. 2d 584, 585–586.)

13. The legislative comments indicate that section 7231, the standard of fiduciary responsibility for nonprofit directors, incorporates the standard of care defined in Corporations Code section 309.

Thus, if plaintiff's complaint had alleged only that the Association's CC & Rs and by-laws delegated to the directors a general duty to conduct the affairs of the organization, including the control and management of its property, then she would not have stated a cause of action. It is true that the residents were forced to rely on the directors to oversee management of the property; however, it would be insufficient to allege that because the directors had a duty as agents of the Association to manage its property and to conduct its affairs, that they also necessarily owed a *personal duty* of care to plaintiff regardless of their specific knowledge of the allegedly dangerous condition that led to her injury. As this court suggested in *Haidinger-Hayes*, such a broad application of agency principles to corporate decision-makers would not adequately distinguish the directors' duty of care to third persons, which is quite limited, from their duty to supervise broad areas of corporate activity. Virtually any aspect of corporate conduct can be alleged to have been explicitly or implicitly ratified by the directors. But their authority to oversee broad areas of corporate activity does not, without more, give rise to a duty of care with regard to third persons who might foreseeably be injured by the corporation's activities. "Directors or officers of a corporation do not incur personal liability for torts of the corporation merely by reason of their official position, unless they participate in the wrong or authorize or direct that it be done." (1 Cal.3d at p. 595, 83 Cal.Rptr. 418, 463 P.2d 770.)

On the other hand, we must reject the defendant directors' assertion that a director's liability *to third persons* is controlled by the statutory duty of care he or she owes to the corporation, a standard defined in Corporations Code section 7231. This statutory standard of care, commonly referred to as the "business judgment rule," applies to parties (particularly shareholders and creditors) to whom the directors owe a fiduciary obligation.[14] It does not abrogate the common law duty which every person owes to others— that is, a duty to refrain from conduct that imposes an unreasonable risk of injury on

---

(See Legis. Committee com., Deering's Ann.Corp.Code (1979) foll. § 7231, p. 205; see also 1B Ballantine & Sterling, Cal.Corporation Laws (4th ed. 1984) § 406.01, p. 19–192.) Section 309 defines the standard for determining the personal liability of a director for breach of his fiduciary duty to a profit corporation.

Sections 7231 and 309 provide, in relevant part: "A director shall perform the duties of a director, including duties as a member of any committee of the board upon which the director may serve, in good faith, in a manner such director believes to be in the best interests of the corporation and with such care, including reasonable inquiry, as an ordinarily prudent person in a like position would use under similar circumstances." In addition, a director is entitled to rely on information, opinions and reports provided by the persons specified in the statute. (§ 7231, subd. (b); § 309, subd. (b).)

14. The "business judgment rule" exists in one form or another in every American jurisdiction. (See 3A Fletcher, Cyclopedia of the Law of Private Corporations, *supra*, § 1039.) Nevertheless, no case or treatise we have unearthed mentions corporate officers or directors as a category of defendants who (like infants or public officials) enjoy some limited immunity, under the common law or by statute, from personal liability for their own tortious conduct. (See, e.g., Prosser & Keeton, The Law of Torts (5th ed. 1984) §§ 131–135, pp. 1032–1075.)

The business judgment rule has been justified primarily on two grounds. First, that directors should be given wide latitude in their handling of corporate affairs because the hindsight of the judicial process is an imperfect device for evaluating business decisions. Second, "[t]he rule recognizes that shareholders to a very real degree voluntarily undertake the risk of bad business judgment; investors need not buy stock, for investment markets offer an array of opportunities less vulnerable to mistakes in judgment by corporate officers." (18B Am.Jur.2d, *supra*, s 1704, at pp. 556–557.) Of course, a tort victim cares little whether the tortfeasor acted in good faith to maximize the interests of the enterprise. Unlike shareholders challenging an unprofitable decision, a tort victim's exposure to the risk of harm is generally involuntary and uncompensated. And unlike the review of business judgments that affect only the pecuniary interests of investors, courts have a long and distinguished record of deciding whether a defendant's personal conduct imposed an unreasonable risk of injury on the plaintiff.

third parties.[15] The legal fiction of the corporation as an independent entity—and the special benefit of limited liability permitted thereby—is intended to insulate stockholders from personal liability for corporate acts and to insulate officers from liability for corporate contracts; the corporate fiction, however, was never intended to insulate officers from liability for their own tortious conduct.[16]

To maintain a tort claim against a director in his or her personal capacity, a plaintiff must first show that the director specifically authorized, directed or participated in the allegedly tortious conduct (*United States Liab. Ins. Co. v. Haidinger-Hayes, Inc., supra*, 1 Cal.3d at p. 595, 83 Cal.Rptr. 418, 463 P.2d 770); or that although they specifically knew or reasonably should have known that some hazardous condition or activity under their control could injure plaintiff, they negligently failed to take or order appropriate action to avoid the harm (*Dwyer v. Lanan & Snow Lumber Co., supra*, 141 Cal.App.2d 838, 297 P.2d 490; see also Fletcher, Cyclopedia of the Law of Private Corporations, *supra*, § 1135, at p. 268; Annot., *Personal Civil Liability of Officer or Director of Corporation for Negligence of Subordinate Corporate Employee Causing Personal Injury or Death of Third Person* (1979) 90 A.L.R.3d 916). The plaintiff must also allege and prove that an ordinarily prudent person, knowing what the director knew at that time, would not have acted similarly under the circumstances.

Although the statutory business judgment rule defined in sections 7231 and 309 concerns only the director's fiduciary duty to the corporation, and not to outsiders, we recognize—as the Legislature did—that "[t]he reference to 'ordinarily prudent person' emphasizes the long tradition of the common law, in contrast to standards that might call for some undefined degree of expertise, like 'ordinarily prudent businessman.'" (Legislative Committee com., Deering's Ann. Corp. Code (1977) foll. § 309, p. 205.) We are mindful that directors sometimes must make difficult cost-benefit choices without the benefit of complete or personally verifiable information. For this reason, even if their conduct leads directly to the tortious injury of a third party, directors are not personally liable in tort unless their action, including any claimed reliance on expert advice, was clearly unreasonable under the circumstances known to them at that time. This defense of reasonable reliance is necessary to avoid holding a director personally liable when he or she reasonably follows expert advice or reasonably delegates a decision to a subordinate or subcommittee in a better position to act.[17]

Under the facts as alleged by plaintiff, the directors named as defendants had specific knowledge of a hazardous condition threatening physical injury to the residents, yet they

---

15. The dissent has not cited a single case from any jurisdiction in which directors' liability in tort to third persons has been governed by the business judgment rule. To the contrary, the cases have uniformly applied common law tort principles....

16. Although a director's fiduciary and common law duties are distinct, as a practical matter we recognize that a director's responsibility to the corporation cannot be completely divorced from the public responsibility of the corporation itself. A corporation is a citizen in society, and as such is expected to conform to societal laws and norms. Typically, the corporation's best interests will be served by complying with those laws and norms, if only because of the sanctions which may result from noncompliance. A director who causes his or her corporation to embark upon a course of unlawful or tortious conduct may, as a consequence, be exposed to liability from both within and without the corporation if the conduct falls below the statutory standard.

17. Sections 7231 and 309 employ identical language to provide that "[i]n performing the duties of a director, a director shall be entitled to rely on information, opinions, reports or statements, including financial statements and other financial data, .prepared" by various employees and experts who "the director believes to be reliable and competent in the matters presented." A director who commits a tort because he reasonably relied on such information cannot be held personally liable for the harm that results.

failed to take any action to avoid the harm; moreover, the action they did take may have
exacerbated the risk by causing plaintiff's unit to be without any lighting on the night
she was attacked. Plaintiff has thus pled facts to support two theories of negligence, both
of which state a cause of action under the standard stated above.

[handwritten margin note: Dirs. had specific know. 1) hazardous conditions on litigns.]

First, plaintiff alleges that the directors took affirmative action that made the break-
in more likely when they ordered her to immediately disconnect the lighting she had installed to protect herself from the foreseeable risk of another criminal break-in.[18] Plaintiff
alleges that she installed the additional exterior lighting only after the board ignored repeated requests from residents of her court to improve the lighting condition. Since the
directors were aware of the crimewave and that plaintiff had installed additional lighting
to protect herself, they assumed a duty to exercise their discretion in a manner that would
not increase her risk of injury from crimes that could foreseeably recur if the common
areas were not secure. Instead, according to the complaint, the board's decision actually
increased the risk of harm and was the legal cause of plaintiff's injuries. Since the additional lights were connected to the building circuits and switches, forcing her to immediately turn off all the exterior lights meant extinguishing all the additional lights. The break-in,
rape and robbery occurred on the same night plaintiff complied with the board's order,
with the result that the area outside her unit was cloaked in near-total darkness.

Second, plaintiff alleges that the individual directors breached a duty of care owed to
her by failing to take action to repair the hazardous lighting condition within a reasonable period of time. Some six months passed between the time the board began to investigate complaints about the lighting and the second burglary of plaintiff's unit. The facts,
as alleged, indicated that the directors had actual knowledge of the level and types of
crime in the area, of complaints by residents that the lights provided inadequate security, and of the recent burglary of plaintiff's unit. Therefore, plaintiff alleged, the directors knew the lack of adequate lighting created a risk of recurring criminal activity, yet
they failed to use reasonable care to alleviate the danger, even though the residents necessarily relied on the board to do so.

Directors and officers have frequently been held liable for negligent nonfeasance
where they knew that a condition or instrumentality under their control posed an un-
reasonable risk of injury to the plaintiff, but then failed to take action to prevent it. (*see
Dwyer v. Lanan & Snow Lumber Co., supra,* 141 Cal.App.2d 838, 297 P.2d 490; Adams
v. Fidelity and Casualty Co. of New York (La.App.1958) 107 So. 2d 496; *Schaefer v. D &
J Produce, Inc., supra,* 62 Ohio App.2d 53, 403 N.E.2d 1015; *Curlee v. Donaldson*
(Mo.App.1950) 233 S.W.2d 746; *Saucier v. U.S. Fidelity & Guaranty Co., supra,* 280
So. 2d 584; *see also Barnette v. Doyle* (Wyo.1981) 622 P.2d 1349, 1355–1356; *Preston-Thomas
Const., Inc. v. Central Leasing Corp.* (Okl.App.1973) 518 P.2d 1125, 1127.) *Dwyer* is
directly on point. In that case, the manager of a sawmill informed its president and
director that a backline was poorly secured and might fall, as it had previously. The of-

---

18. Section 11.2(b) of the CC&Rs provides: "Nothing shall be altered or constructed in or removed from the COMMON AREAS or the ASSOCIATION PROPERTY, except upon the written consent of the BOARD." Plaintiff's complaint alleges that the directors instructed her to remove the
lighting on the ground that she had violated the CC&Rs by not securing the board's prior written
consent and by not using a licensed electrician pursuant to a permit obtained from the city. But even
assuming plaintiff violated the CC&Rs in this manner, nothing in the CC&Rs would have prevented
the board from conditioning their approval on compliance with safety regulations or other standards,
or from taking care not to leave her in a worse position. In any event, whether the directors acted
reasonably under the circumstances is a question of fact, not a proper ground for dismissal for failure to state a claim.

ficial failed to take any precautionary action within a reasonable period of time and was found liable to a person injured when the line subsequently fell. (141 Cal.App.2d at p. 841, 297 P.2d 490.) Although a director's obligation to complete a task is ordinarily a duty owed to the corporation alone, in the instant case, as in *Dwyer*, when the only persons in a position to remedy a hazardous condition are made specifically aware of the danger to third parties, then their unreasonable failure to avoid the harm may result in personal liability.[19]

In this case plaintiff's amended complaint alleges that each of the directors participated in the tortious activity. Under our analysis, this allegation is sufficient to withstand a demurrer. However, since only "a director who actually votes for the commission of a tort is personally liable, even though the wrongful act is performed in the name of the corporation," (*Tillman v. Wheaton-Haven Recreation Ass'n, Inc., supra*, 517 F.2d 1141, 1144; *Tillman v. Wheaton-Haven Recreation Ass'n.* (1973) 410 U.S. 431, 440, fn. 12, 93 S.Ct. 1090, 1095, fn. 12, 35 L.Ed.2d 403), plaintiff will have to prove that each director acted negligently as an individual. Of course, the individual directors may then present evidence showing they opposed or did not participate in the alleged tortious conduct. (*Ibid.*)

Under the circumstances plaintiff has alleged particularized facts that state a cause of action for negligence against the individual directors. Of course, the directors may have acted quite reasonably under the circumstances—or the causal link between the lighting and plaintiff's injuries may be too remote—but those are questions for the trier of fact and not appropriate grounds for sustaining a general demurrer to plaintiff's claim. The trial court therefore erred when it sustained the defendant directors' demurrer to plaintiff's negligence cause of action against them and dismissed without leave to amend.

III.

BREACH OF CONTRACT

. . .

IV.

BREACH OF FIDUCIARY DUTY

Plaintiff's third cause of action, alleging that the CC & Rs and bylaws gave rise to a fiduciary duty defendants breached by their acts and omissions, must fail for a similar reason.

. . .

---

19. Some courts have found an alternative basis for such a result in traditional principles of agency law, particularly sections 352 and 354 of the Restatement Second of Agency. Section 352 states that "[a]n agent is not liable for harm to a person other than his principal because of his failure adequately to perform his duties to his principal, unless physical harm results from reliance upon performance of the duties by the agent, or unless the agent has taken control of land or other tangible things." The comment to section 354 explains that an agent relied on to take some action for the protection of a person "should realize that, because reliance has been placed upon performance by him there is an undue risk that his failure will result in harm to the interests of the third person which are protected against negligent invasions." (Rest.2d Agency, § 354, com. a.) Here, the directors, as agents of the Association, undertook to fulfill the Association's duty to secure the common areas against the foreseeable criminal acts of third parties; having undertaken this duty and having induced the residents' reliance, they were not free to desist if doing so created an unreasonable risk of physical injury to the plaintiff. (*See also Miller v. Muscarelle* (1961) 67 N.J.Super. 305, 170 A.2d 437, 446–451, which explains the historical origins and defects of the traditional misfeasance-nonfeasance distinction in the context of corporate agency.)

V.

CONCLUSION

We conclude that the trial court erred in sustaining the Association's and directors' demurrer to the negligence cause of action. We affirm dismissal of plaintiff's other causes of action. The judgment is therefore reversed and remanded to the trial court for further proceedings consistent with this opinion.

Reversed and Remanded.

Retrospective and Observations

Frances Troy's Perspective

According to Terry Steinhart, who represented Frances Troy, Ms. Troy was approximately 65 years old when the rape occurred. Rose Byrd, Chief Justice of the California Supreme Court at that time, took the case under submission after it was argued. There is a law in California that a judge must render an opinion within three months of the end of the arguments. Justice Byrd sat on this case for years. Approaching the age of 70, Ms. Troy became impatient about the results of the case. She spoke with Mr. Steinhart every month or so to get an update and to see whether a decision had been rendered. Ultimately, Ms. Troy told Mr. Steinhart that she was going to write a letter to the Chief Justice to see what was taking so long, and she did just that. Mr. Steinhart followed up her letter with a letter to either the state controller or the state treasurer citing the statute which required a three-month turn around on decisions and requesting that enforcement of that statute, holding a judge's salary until the decision was reached, be invoked against all of the justices of the California Supreme Court. Mr. Steinhart does not know whether their salaries were held, but eventually the California Supreme Court ruled that there was a cause of action in this case.

The Association's Perspective

Jamoa Moberly, attorney for Village Green Owners Association recalled that Village Green is a unique complex, one of the first of its kind built in the 1950s in an area in south central Los Angeles which became a crime-ridden area after the project's inception. Homes at Village Green are one level, bungalow type units.

The personalities of the parties involved in this case were something that Ms. Moberly remembered. It seemed to her that there was a personality conflict between Frances Troy and the board members. Ms. Troy wanted to install lights on her unit after it was burglarized. The board wanted to do it on its time frame, and a conflict arose. When the California Court of Appeals ruled in favor of Frances Troy, the Association decided not to appeal the case because it did not want the case to be heard by the California Supreme Court.

The plaintiff's name in this case was changed after the appeals court decision because of a movement in California to protect anonymity among rape victims and to encourage them to go to court. Ms. Moberly noted that the long term impact of this case is that state law changed to protect board members in similar situations.

On remand, this case eventually settled for $100,000.00 paid by the association's insurance company.

Security: Association Liable for Art Theft

Reprinted from Community Association Law Reporter
(Community Associations Institute, April 1981)
Issacs v. Trustees of Riverview Condo. Trust
Supr. Ct. Of Mass., Cambridge (1980)

Many, many people have read about the *Issacs'* case because it was discussed in an article in the *Boston Globe* and then was picked up by a wire service syndication. People read the article to say that there was a particularly high duty on behalf of a condominium association and its Board to provide security to its members. However, neither the article itself nor the case upon which the article was based makes that point. Both do, however, raise very interesting questions.

The basic facts are actually quite simple. Professor Issacs and his wife were the owners of a condominium unit at Riverview Condominium. When they purchased their unit, they were particularly concerned about security and discussed their concerns with representatives of the developer and of the management entity. Their concern was motivated in large part by the fact that they owned at least three pieces of major art, all by Jackson Pollock. The three paintings were valued at slightly less than $1 million.

When the Issacs purchased their condominium unit, they had, as noted, discussed the need for security with representatives of the developer. A sales agent made representations to them concerning the nature and the quality of security which would be available if they purchased. She also represented how the security system currently in force at the condominium was to work, including locked entrances and exits, a buzzer system, a manned main control desk in the lobby of the building, and other such devices and procedures.

Following their purchase, the Issacs noted on several occasions breaches of the security system and reported these breaches to the management officials. The latter acknowledged the problems and indeed contracted for and obtained an engineering review, outlining what additional security procedures should be taken. The court specifically found that Issacs had been told that the condominium was totally secure; that there was 24-hour-a-day security at the condominium. The sales management representative had said that no unauthorized people could enter 221 Mount Auburn Street. She said that the only people with keys to the condominium apartments were herself and one Frank Brosnahan, who was the superintendent of the building. The Plaintiffs were told the only way to enter the condominium building was by the front door entrance which was controlled by guards. Any unauthorized person would be intercepted by a guard at the front door, which was locked at all times. They were also told that all outside doors were locked and secured at all times, that the building had around-the-clock security, and that his valuable painting collection would be "safe." The Court also found that Issacs was not told that there had been auto thefts from the grounds and that there were in fact no security guards.

In summary, the court found that Issacs made the developer's representatives aware of his need for security, and they assured him that the necessary high degree of security was present in the building. In reliance upon that assurance, Issacs purchased a unit. The high degree of security represented was not present. The Court found that as a proximate cause of negligence of the developer's management personnel, a burglary took place.

The court found that the Defendants had a duty of reasonable care to the Plaintiff to control access to and from the common areas and to provide security adequate to prevent unauthorized access by third parties to the condominium building. Moreover, the court found that the Defendants, "owed the Plaintiff such duties of care, which duties arose out of the discussions of the parties at the time the Plaintiff's condominium purchase was contemplated, the persistent notice of the Plaintiff of security breaches and inadequacies, the Defendants' knowledge of condominium thefts preceding and following the Plaintiff's purchase of his condominium apartment, and the security reports and advice from various sources prior to November 8, 1973." In other words, the court found that there was a special duty due this particular Plaintiff because of the unusual circumstances surrounding this particular Plaintiff.

The court went on to say that "given the Defendant Trustees of the Riverview-Cambridge Condominium Trust and Defendant First Realty Management Corporation's duties of care to the Plaintiff, if the Defendants knew or should have known that such security failures would or could result in a theft of a condominium apartment owner's property, then those Defendants had a duty to act to correct such security failures, and failure to so act may be found to create liability and negligence for said Defendants because of the Plaintiff's loss."

It is important to note at this juncture that, unlike the question posed in the newspaper article, the court is focusing upon the special knowledge which those in control of the Association had concerning the nature of the individual owner's property and the fact that the Defendants had encouraged that owner to purchase a unit in reliance upon their representations that sufficient security was and would be in place.

The court found a breach of these duties and held the Defendants liable for just less than $1 million in damages.

Notes & Questions

1. *Foreseeability.* Should foreseeability of the crime be relevant to determining an association's liability for security lapses? If so, how does one determine what event is or is not foreseeable? See *Admirals Port Condo., Inc. v. Feldman*, 426 So. 2d 1054 (Fla. Dist. Ct. App. 1983) (condominium association not liable to unit owner who was mugged in parking lot since third party criminal acts are not foreseeable). Compare the *Admirals Port* case with *Francis T.* and *Issacs*. What factor may explain the different outcomes?

2. *Providing security services.* Is a community association required to provide security services and other forms of security protection? Even when there have been repeated instances of crime? See, *e.g.*, *Feld v. Merriam*, 506 Pa. 383 (1984) (landlord not liable for failing to provide security services for benefit of tenants).

Problem

CC&Rs often contain a long list of the association's duties. In one is "the duty of surveillance of the common area." In another community, the marketing representations stressed the security aspects of the building and how one could live with confidence in the "secure community" of Happy Halls Condominiums. In still another, the board and design review committee have total control over all activities on the common property. No owner can make any alterations, including those which might be necessary to enhance safety and security without the board's consent, which was substantially delayed because of internal operating procedures.

In each of these instances, think about what duties might have arisen as a result of the drafting and marketing of the communities. Consider as well what role foreseeability may or should play in the context of association tort liability. Does the applicable rule of law depend upon foreseeability? If so, in this context what facts or circumstances might give rise to a foreseeable risk of harm sufficient to establish potential liability? One might question what reasonable expectations might be within the context of a particular community and whether or not those expectations and the particular circumstances the community might otherwise vary the basic rule.

3. Association Liability for Discrimination

As you consider the cases in this section, do not limit your analysis to the effect of federal law. Always consider state law and particularly the state constitution. Too often, practitioners never read their state constitution after they pass the bar. That can be an extremely costly mistake. Importantly, the state constitution may be broader and more protective than that of the United States.

a. Disability Discrimination

Martin v. Constance
United States District Court
843 F. Supp. 1321 (D.C. Mo. 1994)

GUNN, J. This matter is before the Court for disposition on the merits following a bench trial. Plaintiffs, developmentally disabled adults living in a group home owned and operated by the State of Missouri, brought this action to enjoin enforcement of a restrictive covenant which would preclude the continued operation of the group home. The home is located in the residential and historic neighborhood of Compton Heights in the City of St. Louis, Missouri. Defendants are owners of real estate in Compton Heights, and the Compton Heights Neighborhood Association. Joined as defendants necessary for complete relief are the Governor of the State of Missouri, the Director of the Missouri Department of Mental Health and the Superintendent of the St. Louis Developmental Disabilities Treatment Centers. Plaintiffs seek declaratory and injunctive relief under the Fair Housing Act as amended in 1988, 42 U.S.C. § 3604(f), and under 42 U.S.C. § 1983.

I. Background

Compton Heights, a designated historic neighborhood, is subject to a restrictive covenant duly recorded in 1893 which provides in relevant part as follows:

> But one building shall be ... placed upon each of said lots and such building shall never be used or occupied for any purpose except for that of a private residence exclusively nor shall any part or portion thereof ever be used or occupied except solely as a residence, nor shall such building be arranged or ever used or occupied as flats, nor shall said lots or any part thereof ever be used or occupied for trade or business of any kind.

In December 1989 the State began looking into purchasing a certain dwelling in Compton Heights to use as a group home for six mentally retarded/developmentally handicapped adult males and two resident supervisors. Upon learning of the State's intentions, residents of the neighborhood wrote letters to various state officials to voice opposition to the plan. A public meeting was held and it was decided to file an action in state court to seek enforcement of the restrictive covenant to prevent the State from operating the group home. On January 30, 1990, the private defendants filed such an action in state court.

On April 2, 1990, while the action was pending, the State purchased the property, and on April 10, 1990, plaintiffs moved in. On April 18, 1990, plaintiffs moved to intervene in the state-court action. When the motion was denied, plaintiffs filed this action as well as a request for a preliminary injunction enjoining prosecution of the state-court action. On May 23, 1990, following a hearing, this Court granted the preliminary injunction. Trial on plaintiffs' FHA and Section 1983 claims was held on June 6 and 7, 1990.

At the hearing and trial, plaintiffs presented evidence that the group home operates as a functional family. (Tr. 347-48). The inhabitants are screened to assure their suitability for community living and there is little turnover in the makeup of the group. Plaintiffs also presented evidence that the State was committed to preserving the historical significance of the house and would not change its exterior appearance.

Plaintiffs' expert on community integration of the mentally retarded testified that numerous studies on the effect of a group home for developmentally disabled adults on a residential neighborhood all indicate that there is no adverse impact on real estate values, neighborhood stability or crime rates. (Tr. 349-54).

The private defendants presented evidence that the restrictive covenant was on several occasions enforced against businesses. Several Compton Heights residents testified that they opposed the group home because they did not want a rooming house or business in their neighborhood. In addition they expressed concern that the State, as a property owner, was not subject to the same restrictions as private owners and may not maintain the property.

II. FHA Claim

Title 42 U.S.C.A. § 3604(f) (Supp. 1993) provides in relevant part that it shall be unlawful

(1) To discriminate in the sale or rental, or to otherwise make unavailable or deny, a dwelling to any buyer or renter because of a handicap of—

(B) a person residing in or intending to reside in that dwelling after it is so sold … or made available.

(2) To discriminate against any person in the terms, conditions, or privileges of sale or rental of a dwelling … because of a handicap of—

(B) a person residing in or intending to reside in that dwelling after it is so sold … or made available.

(3) For purposes of this subsection, discrimination includes—

(B) a refusal to make reasonable accommodations in rules, policies, [or] practices … when such accommodations may be necessary to afford such person equal opportunity to use and enjoy a dwelling.

…

Plaintiffs' standing is evident. The FHA itself defines "aggrieved person" a person who "(1) claims to have been injured by a discriminatory housing practice; or (2) believes that such person will be injured by a discriminatory housing practice which is about to occur." 42 U.S.C. § 3602(i).[2]

---

2. The Court rejects the private defendants' argument that the FHA is not applicable to them because they are not sellers or renters.

B. Discriminatory Intent

A plaintiff can show a violation of section 3604(f) by one of two methods. The first method is showing discriminatory intent on the part of the defendants. Plaintiff's evidence of discriminatory intent need not show that the handicapped status of the intended inhabitants was the sole factor of the defendant's decision to seek enforcement of the restrictive covenant, only that it was a motivating factor. *See Village of Arlington Heights v. Metropolitan Housing Dev. Corp.*, 429 U.S. 252, 265–66, 50 L. Ed. 2d 450, 97 S. Ct. 555 (1977). "The Court must conduct a sensitive inquiry into such circumstantial and direct evidence of intent as may be available." *Id.* at 266.

Based upon the evidence, the Court finds that the status of the intended residents of the home was a motivating factor in the private defendants' attempt to enforce the restrictive covenant. It is, at least in part, the presence of developmentally handicapped persons to which these defendants object. The Court accords little credibility to other reasons put forward by the private defendants for seeking to enforce the restrictive covenant. The group home would be more closely akin to a family residence, than a business or boarding house with transient occupants. In fact, under Missouri law, a group home has been held not to violate the terms of a restrictive covenant prohibiting use of lots for a purpose "other than that of an exclusive family residence for one family." *See Maull v. Community Living for the Handicapped*, 813 S.W.2d 90 (Mo. Ct. App. 1991).[3]

The private defendants put forward no evidence to support the asserted fear that the State would not maintain the property. The inference of a discriminatory motive is strongly supported by the fact that although the State has made reasonable assurances to address the stated concerns of the residents, they continue to oppose the group home.

The Court concludes that plaintiffs are entitled to an injunction enjoining the enforcement of the restrictive covenant to preclude the operation of the group home in which they live.

C. Discriminatory Effect

Although the Court concludes that plaintiffs have proved a violation of the FHA by showing discriminatory intent, the Court will consider whether plaintiffs have also succeeded on the merits by proving discriminatory effect. Under this method of establishing a violation of section 3604, plaintiffs "need prove no more than that the conduct of defendants actually or predictably resulted in ... discrimination; in other words, that it has a discriminatory effect.... Effect, and not motivation, is the touchstone." *United States v. City of Black Jack*, 508 F.2d 1179, 1184–85 (8th Cir. 1974), *cert. denied*, 422 U.S. 1042, 45 L. Ed. 2d 694, 95 S. Ct. 2656 (1975).

The Court concludes that this is an appropriate case for application of the discriminatory effect (sometimes called the disparate impact) analysis, and that under this analysis plaintiffs have established a violation of section 3604(f). *See, e.g., Stewart B. McKinney Found., Inc. v. Town Plan & Zoning Comm'n*, 790 F. Supp. 1197, 1216–19 (D. Conn. 1992) (disparate impact analysis applied to claim by nonprofit organization that requirement that it obtain special exception for its intended use of residence as home for HIV-infected persons violated section 3604(f)); *United States v. Scott*, 788 F. Supp. 1555 (D. Kan. 1992) (subdivision residents violated FHA by seeking judicial enforcement of facially neutral restrictive covenant to prevent sale of house to operator of group homes for disabled individuals, though there was no showing of residents' bad faith or malice towards handicapped persons).

---

3. See also Mo. Ann. Stat. § 89.020.2 (Vernon Supp. 1993).

Reference to the legislative history of the 1988 amendments to the FHA confirms this conclusion. House Report No. 100-711, 100th Cong., 2d Sess. 24, reprinted in 1988 U.S.C.A.N. 2173, 2184–85, states:

> [Section 3604(f)(2)] is intended to prohibit the application of ... restrictive covenants ... which have the effect of excluding, for example, congregate living arrangements for persons with handicaps.
>
> Another method of making housing unavailable to people with disabilities has been the application or enforcement of otherwise neutral rules and regulations on ... land use in a manner which discriminates against people with disabilities. Such determination often results from false ... assumptions about the needs of handicapped people, as well as unfounded fears of difficulties about the problems that their tenancies may pose. These and similar practices would be prohibited.[4]

The private defendants' argument that the statute only reaches *special* restrictive covenants that specifically prohibit the sale or rental of a dwelling to handicapped individuals is thus without merit. The Court also rejects these defendants' argument that prohibiting this group home from operating would have no discriminatory effect on plaintiffs or handicapped persons in general, because there are other group homes in Missouri. Defendants' reliance on *Familystyle v. City of St. Paul*, 923 F.2d 91 (8th Cir. 1991) (state and city requirements that group homes for mentally ill not be clustered furthered goal of integrating mentally ill into society and did not have discriminatory effect), is misplaced.

D. Refusal to Make Reasonable Accommodation

The Court concludes that the private defendants discriminated against plaintiffs under the definition of "discrimination" set forth in section 3604(f)(3)(B). Even if there was a consistent policy and practice of enforcing the restrictive covenant against perceived violations, the Court finds that under the facts of this case the attempt to enforce the covenant constituted a refusal to make a "reasonable accommodation" necessary to afford plaintiffs an equal opportunity to use and enjoy a dwelling.

A reasonable accommodation would have been not to seek enforcement of the covenant. Such an accommodation would not impose an undue financial or administrative burden on the private defendants, nor would it undermine the basic purpose behind the practice of enforcement, namely, to maintain the residential nature of the neighborhood. *See, e.g., Oxford House, Inc. v. Township of Cherry Hill*, 799 F. Supp. 450, 461–63 (D. N.J. 1992) (municipality's refusal to grant zoning approval to group home for handicapped persons in single family residential zone violates reasonable accommodation provision of FHA).

III. Section 1983 Claim

The private defendants argue that plaintiffs failed to establish an essential element of their section 1983 claim, namely that the private defendants acted "under color of state law." Plaintiffs, relying on *Shelley v. Kramer*, 344 U.S. 1 (1948), argue that the private defendants' resort to the state court to enforce the restrictive covenant constitutes state action. In *Shelley*, the Supreme Court found state action where private parties resorted to

---

4. HUD's regulations on discriminatory conduct under the FHA prohibit "enforcing covenants ... which preclude the sale or rental of a dwelling to any person because of ... a handicap." 24 C.F.R. 100.80(b)(3) (1993).

the state courts to enforce a *facially discriminatory* restrictive covenant. Plaintiffs argue that *Shelley* encompasses judicial action to enforce a *facially neutral* covenant in a discriminatory manner.

This position was rejected in *Casa Marie, Inc. v. Superior Court*, 988 F.2d 252, 259–60 (1st Cir. 1993). The Court agrees with this holding in *Casa Marie*, at least where, as here, there has been no state court decision on the matter.

Plaintiffs argue in the alternative that state action arises from the fact that the covenant the private defendants seek to enforce is recorded in accordance with state regulations. No case law is cited in support of this position, and this Court concludes that it is without merit.

It Is Hereby Ordered, Adjudged And Decreed that judgment is entered in favor of plaintiffs on their claim under the Fair Housing Act as amended in 1988, 42 U.S.C. §§ 3604(f). The private defendants are enjoined from attempting to enforce the restrictive covenant to prevent the group home in question from operating.

It Is Further Ordered that judgment is entered in favor of the private defendants on plaintiffs' claim under 42 U.S.C. § 1983.

Schroeder v. De Bertolo

United States District Court
879 F. Supp. 173 (D.C. P.R. 1995)

PIERAS, JR., J. The Court has before it co-defendants' motions to dismiss, and plaintiffs' motions in opposition to motion to dismiss (docket Nos. 39, 46, 47 and 48). For the reasons set forth below, co-defendants' motions are hereby Denied.

This is an action for monetary damages pursuant to the Fair Housing Amendments Act ("FHAA"), 42 U.S.C. § 3604(f) and § 3617 (1988). During 1981–82, Rosa Amalia Maeso Schroeder purchased a condominium unit in Concordia Gardens Condominium ("Concordia"). Throughout the time Ms. Schroeder lived in Concordia, she suffered from mental illness, until she committed suicide on June 5, 1993. Plaintiffs are Ms. Maeso Schroeder's brothers and sister, suing in their capacity as legal representatives of the estate of their deceased sister, as well as their personal capacity. Defendants are members of the Board of Directors of Concordia Gardens Condominium Association and the handyman who worked at the Condominium.

Plaintiffs allege that defendants initiated groundless claims against decedent for breach of the peace and misappropriation of common property, threatened to file groundless criminal charges against decedent, and entered decedent's dwelling without her consent to search for common property that decedent had allegedly taken from the common areas. Through these actions, plaintiffs allege that defendants intimidated Ms. Maeso Schroeder and intentionally prohibited her from using the common areas at the Concordia Gardens Condominium because of her mental illness. Since decedent's mental illness was a mental impairment which substantially limits one or more of her major life activities, plaintiffs allege that her illness constituted a "handicap" as defined by the FHAA.

Defendants move to dismiss this action for lack of subject matter jurisdiction and for failure to state a claim upon which relief can be granted. First, defendants assert that the protections of Fair Housing Amendments Act apply only in the initial sale or rental of a dwelling. Since Ms. Maeso Schroeder had already purchased a condominium unit, defendants assert that the cited statutory provisions are inapplicable to the case at bar. Second, defendants allege that plaintiffs do not have standing to sue for decedent's alleged injuries. They allege that rights under Fair Housing Act and Fair Housing Amendments Act are decedent's personal rights which were not inherited by decedent's heirs at the time of her death.

...

III. FAIR HOUSING ACT AND FAIR HOUSING AMENDMENTS ACT

Plaintiffs allege that defendants' actions violate Section 3604(f) of the Fair Housing Amendments Act, which prohibits discriminatory housing practices based on an individual's handicap, and Section 3617 of the FHAA, which prohibits a third party from interfering with an individual's exercise of her right to be free from discriminatory housing practices.

"The starting point in every case involving construction of a statute is the language itself," *Ernst & Ernst v. Hochfelder*, 425 U.S. 185, 47 L. Ed. 2d 668, 96 S. Ct. 1375 (1976) (quoting *Blue Chip Stamps v. Manor Drug Stores*, 421 U.S. 723, 44 L. Ed. 2d 539, 95 S. Ct. 1917 (1975)). First, Section 3604(f)(1) makes it unlawful "to discriminate in the sale or rental, *or to otherwise make unavailable or to deny*, a dwelling to any buyer or renter because of a handicap of ... that buyer or renter; (emphasis added)." Further, Section 3604(f)(2), makes it unlawful, "to discriminate against any person in the terms, conditions, or privileges of sale or rental of a dwelling, *or in the provision of services or facilities in connection with such dwelling*, because of a handicap of ... that person" (emphasis added).

Defendants argue that the cited provisions prevent discrimination only in the sale or rental of housing accommodations. Since Ms. Maeso Schroeder was the owner of her condominium unit, they argue, she had already exercised her right to purchase a dwelling. Thus, any discriminatory action which they may have taken against her is beyond the scope of the protections of the FHAA.

The language of the statute does not lend itself to such a narrow interpretation. The phrase "to otherwise make unavailable or deny" sweeps activities which go beyond the initial sale or rental transaction under the scope of the section. Once Ms. Maeso Schroeder became the owner of the unit, her housing rights did not terminate. She had the continuing right to quiet enjoyment and use of her condominium unit and common areas in the building. Her right to obtain a dwelling free from discriminatory conduct of others encompassed the right to maintain that dwelling.

Defendants further argue that the prohibitions of the FHAA only apply to housing providers. Since plaintiff already owned her condominium unit, the condominium board of directors were not providing her with housing. To support this contention, defendants cite to Section 3603, which provides an exemption from the other provisions of the Fair Housing Act for certain single-family houses sold or rented by an owner which fulfill specific criteria. They assert that this exemption demonstrates Congress's intent the FHAA prohibitions only apply to those who are in the business of providing housing.

Neither the statutory language, legislative history, nor cases in other jurisdictions suggest that Congress intended such a narrow construction of the statute and its amendments. The FHAA "is a clear pronouncement of a national commitment to end the unnecessary exclusion of persons with handicaps from the American mainstream." *Helen L. v. DiDario*, 46 F.3d 325, 1995 U.S. App. LEXIS 2233, n.14 (3d Cir. 1995) (quoting H.Rep. No. 711, 100th Cong., 2d Sess. 18 (1988), reprinted in 1988 U.S.C.C.A.N. 2173, 2179 (footnote omitted)).

[Handwritten margin notes:] FHA only apply to sale or rental of accommdt.? → No. too narrow an intrp. FHAA only apply to housing providers? → No.

When interpreting analogous statutory language prohibiting discrimination based on race or gender, courts have broadly held that the activities of neighbors, management companies, realtors, and financiers which go beyond the initial purchase or rental of a dwelling are prohibited by the Fair Housing Act. For example, allegations against a neighbor who interferes with the initial sale or rental of a property have been held sufficient to make out a claim under the Fair Housing Act. *See Sofarelli v. Pinellas County*, 931 F.2d 718 (11th Cir. 1991) (plaintiff, who purchased land and intended to rent a home to minorities, had a claim against his neighbors for their violent and intimidating actions in preventing him from moving his home onto the property which he had purchased). *See also Hogar Agua y Vida en el Desierto v. Suarez*, 829 F. Supp. 19, 1993 (D.P.R. 1993), *vacated, remanded, sub nom.*, 36 F.3d 177 (1st Cir. 1994) (plaintiff's claims against defendants whose actions intimidated the owner of a neighboring property to refuse to sell to an organization providing housing to individuals suffering from AIDS, were seemingly within the scope of the protections of the FHAA).

In addition, allegations that the management of an apartment complex had intentionally allowed the quality of services to decline after the tenants had already begun renting an apartment were sufficient to state a claim under FHA. *See Concerned Tenants Assn. of Indian Trails Apartments v. Indian Trails Apartments*, 496 F. Supp. 522 (N.D.Ill. 1980) (plaintiffs, black tenants, stated a claim against the management of their apartment complex alleging that the quality of the services provided had deteriorated substantially since the time when the racial composition of the complex was primarily white).

Finally, there is a cause of action against neighbors who interfere with the continuing right to use and enjoy the rented or purchased property. *See Evans v. Tubbe*, 657 F.2d 661 (5th Cir. 1981) (plaintiff, black owner of land, alleged sufficient facts to state a claim against her white neighbor who owned a private road providing access to plaintiff's property. Defendant built a gate blocking plaintiff's access to the private road and provided a key to all of plaintiff's white neighbors, but not to plaintiff). *See also Seaphus v. Lilly*, 691 F. Supp. 127 (N.D. Ill. 1988) (plaintiff had alleged facts sufficient to state a claim against owners of neighboring condominium units for interfering with his continued right to enjoy his dwelling free from discrimination by changing the locks to the garage and common doors without providing plaintiff a key, slashing the tires on his cars, and barricading his access to his apartment).

Members of the condominium board of directors are elected by the owners of units in the building to communally represent the interest of all the owners. They are responsible for collecting condominium dues or maintenance fees, and administering that money to maintain the common areas in the building. Other duties of the board include the enforcement of condominium regulations for the benefit of all the owners in the building. Because of their duties and responsibilities, members of the board have the ability to exert indirect control over individual owners in the use of the common areas. <u>Therefore, although defendants were not decedent's direct housing provider, they were in a position to deny or make unavailable a portion of the building to plaintiff</u>, or to discriminate against plaintiff in the provision of housing services or facilities.

Plaintiffs further allege that defendants violated Section 3617 of the FHAA, which prohibits a third party from interfering with individual's free exercise of his or her housing rights:

> It shall be unlawful to coerce, intimidate, threaten, or interfere with any person in the exercise or enjoyment of, or on account of having exercised or enjoyed,..., any right granted or protected by section 3603, 3604, 3605, or 3606 of this title. 42 U.S.C. § 3617.

[Handwritten margin note: Although Condo. Assoc. not direct housing provider, were in a position to deny porti 7 building to plantiff]

By bringing groundless civil claims against decedent and threatening to bring criminal actions, defendants' actions could arguably have intimidated decedent in such a way that she refrained from exercising her right to use the lobby and other common areas of the Condominium whenever she wished. Although defendants did not force decedent to move out of the Condominium, their actions allegedly forced her out of a portion of the physical space which she was entitled to use. By denying plaintiff the right to use the common areas whenever she wished, defendants allegedly discriminated in the provision of facilities, since other condominium owners were allowed to use the common areas whenever they so desired.

In light of the analysis presented, plaintiffs' allegations that defendants entered decedent's dwelling without her permission, brought groundless civil claims against decedent, and threatened to bring groundless criminal charges against her in an attempt to prevent her from using the communal areas of the condominium complex are sufficient to state a claim under the FHAA.

. . .

Phillips v. Perkiomen Crossing Homeowners Ass'n

United States District Court
Wl 58076 (E.D. Pa.)

BUCKWALTER, J. *Pro se* plaintiff Sandra Phillips, on behalf of her daughter Elizabeth Phillips, has sought jurisdiction in this court based upon the Americans with Disabilities Act ("ADA"). Plaintiff claims that defendant Perkiomen Crossing Homeowners Association ("Perkiomen") and its vice president, Dave Redfield, violated the act by allowing the Phillips' neighbors to "harass the family for having handicapped parking...."

There are three ways in which the ADA may apply to a particular case: through the section addressing equal opportunity in employment for individuals with disabilities, through the prohibition against discrimination by public entities, and through the public accommodations requirements placed upon certain private entities. Review of the plaintiff's *pro se* Complaint reveals that none of these sections of the ADA apply to the plaintiff's case for the following reasons.

(1) There is no employment relationship between the parties which would enable Subchapter I of the Act to Apply. Under 42 U.S.C.A. § 12111, the only entities covered by Subchapter I are employers, employment agencies, labor organizations or joint labor-management committees. 42 U.S.C.A. § 12111 (2) (1995). An "employer" is defined under the Act as "a person engaged in an industry affecting commerce who has 15 or more employees for each working day in each of 20 or more calendar weeks...." 42 U.S.C.A. § 12111 (5)(A) (1995). This does not include tax-exempt "bona fide private membership clubs." 42 U.S.C.A. § 12111 (5)(B) (1995). To bring an action under this section, a plaintiff must be an employee of a qualified employer. The record in this case indicates no such relationship between the parties.

(2) Defendant Perkiomen is not a "public entity." Under Subchapter II, Part A, which prohibits discrimination by public entities, "public entity" is defined as "(A) any State or local government; (B) any department, agency, special purpose district, or other instrumentality of a State of States or local government; and (C) the National Railroad Passenger Corporation, and any commuter authority...." 42 U.S.C.A. § 12131 (1995). There is no evidence that Perkiomen is affiliated with state or local government in such as way as to fall under Section 12131.

(3) The location in which the alleged incidents occurred is not a "commercial facility" and Perkiomen is not a qualified private entity under the public accommodations section of the ADA. Sections 12181 *et seq.* require certain private entities to make their facilities amenable to individuals with disabilities. However, these entities are limited to "commercial facilities," defined as "facilities—(A) that are intended for nonresidential use; and (B) whose operations will affect commerce." 42 U.S.C.A. § 12181 (1995). Plaintiff's complaint indicates that the facility in question is a private parking lot for residents of the Perkiomen Crossing housing development.

Since the Americans with Disabilities Act does not apply to the facts as presented by the plaintiff, the court is left without jurisdiction to hear this matter, and so must dismiss the plaintiff's *pro se* Complaint. However, if plaintiff can state a claim arising out of the facts set forth in her complaint over which the court would have jurisdiction, the plaintiff may file an amended complaint by October 9, 1995. An order to this effect follows.

Notes & Questions

1. *Applicability of acts.* As the above cases illustrate, there are essentially two federal acts which may relate to disability discrimination by community associations. Those are the Fair Housing Act as amended in 1988 (also known as the Fair Housing Amendments Act), 42 U.S.C. § 3604(C), and the Americans with Disabilities Act, 42 U.S.C.A. § 12111 (1998). Under each, one must evaluate whether the alleged disability discrimination is covered by the act, whether one has standing to bring such a claim, and whether the association or some other party may be liable for such a claim even if discrimination of some kind occurred.

2. *Public accommodations.* A facility which is intended for nonresidential use and whose operations will affect commerce may trigger application of the ADA. See 42 U.S.C.A. § 12181 (1995). In *Phillips*, the private parking lot was not found to fall under the public accommodations category. What about community facilities that can be rented out to the general public? Or club memberships offered to the public for use of the community swimming pools, tennis courts, and other such recreational activities? Reexamine these issues upon reading the racial discrimination cases and notes provided below.

b. Familial Status, Marital Status, and "Single Families"

Simovits v. Chanticleer Condominium Association

United States District Court, Northern District of Illinois, Eastern Division
933 F.Supp. 1394 (N.D. Ill. 1996)

KEYS, United States Magistrate J.… The Simovits owned a condominium in the Chanticleer Condominium Complex ("Chanticleer"), an eighty-four unit housing facility located in Hinsdale, Illinois. Since 1985, the Association has had a restrictive covenant ("the Covenant") in its Declaration of Condominium Ownership, stating that "no minor children under the age of eighteen (18) years may reside in any unit purchased after the effective date of this amendment," without the prior written approval of the Board of Managers. Residents of Chanticleer who violate the Covenant are subject to injunctive relief and a $10,000 fine. This provision is construed as barring an owner from selling a unit to anyone with children under the age of eighteen.

A large number of Chanticleer's residents are fifty-five years of age or older. However, there is no requirement that residents must be fifty-five years old or older. According to

[handwritten margin note: No resale to anybody with a child < 18 yrs of age.]

the president of the Association, Jim Londos, Chanticleer is intended for people who are "any age over 18." In fact, the last two sales of Chanticleer units have been to people under the age of fifty-five.

The Simovits purchased their Chanticleer condominium in June of 1993, for $130,000. Prior to the closing, they appeared before the Association's screening committee. The purpose of this meeting was to explain the Association's rules and regulations, including the Covenant. Mr. Simovits informed the board that he believed the Covenant to be illegal. Nonetheless, the Simovits signed a statement acknowledging the rules and agreeing to abide by them.[3]

Shortly after moving into Chanticleer, Mr. Simovits ran for a position on the Association's board. During his campaign, he published a newsletter to introduce himself to the residents of Chanticleer. In that newsletter, Mr. Simovits stated that "I like Chanticleer as an adult community and would like to keep it that way." He testified that these comments were politically motivated: "by that time, I knew that many of the residents were elderly and they liked the place as it was. I needed some votes." Mr. Simovits lost the election.

The Simovits put their Chanticleer condominium on the market in May of 1995, for $187,500.[5] A prospective buyer, represented by real estate agent Karen Jones, expressed an interest in the condominium. However, the Simovits decided not to enter into negotiations with that individual because she had a minor child and they did not wish to cause any problems. After several weeks passed without any interested buyers, the Simovits were forced to lower their asking price. They lowered it to $179,500 in July and again, in August, to $169,900. In early November, another prospective buyer, represented by realtor Bonita Swartz, expressed an interest in the Simovits' condominium. According to Ms. Swartz's testimony, the prospect was interested in making an offer on the condominium. At that time, the condominium was on the market for $169,900. The potential buyer had three children, all under the age of eighteen.

[handwritten margin note: Hard time trying to sell to anybody w/ out kids < 18.]

When Mr. Simovits informed Mr. Londos that he had a potential buyer with minor children, Mr. Londos replied that the Covenant prohibited such a sale. Mr. Londos also told Ms. Swartz about the Covenant. Ms. Swartz testified that, after she told the prospective buyer about the rule, the prospect was no longer interested in making an offer.

On the same day he informed Mr. Simovits that he could not sell to this prospective buyer, Mr. Londos contacted the Association's lawyer, who called the Simovits on November 8, 1995, warning them that the Covenant prohibited a sale to a person with minor children. On November 14, 1995, Mr. Londos received a letter from the Association's lawyer regarding the Simovits and the questionable legality of the Covenant. The letter warned Mr. Londos that discriminating against families with children is illegal. The letter stated that the statutory exemptions to the FHA are "strictly construed" and that "unless Chanticleer can produce hard evidence that the community meets these narrowly construed exemptions, the financial liability to Chanticleer could be substantial." Mr. Londos shared the contents of this letter with the Association's board members on the day he received it. Despite the warnings in the letter, the Association decided to continue to prevent the Simovits from selling to a buyer with minor children.

---

3. Mr. Simovits testified that his lawyer informed him that, despite his belief regarding the illegality of the Covenant, he had to sign this statement in order to finalize the closing on the condominium.

5. Mr. Simovits testified that he "was planning to come down possibly about $10,000 or so" from this initial asking price. (R. at 58.)

Immediately after contacting the Association's lawyer in early November, Mr. Londos began to compile a list of all the Chanticleer residents' ages in order to determine the percentage of residents who were fifty-five years of age or older. This was the first time the Association had conducted a survey of this nature. In compiling the survey, Mr. Londos speculated as to the residents' ages. He testified that he "had a pretty good idea ... in [his] head who was of what age." He did not take any steps to verify these presumptions. Consequently, the list contained inaccuracies.

In preparation for the hearing herein, Mr. Londos conducted another similar survey. In this May 21, 1996 survey, conducted two days prior to the hearing, Mr. Londos used signed affidavits to verify the residents' ages. However, he did not obtain affidavits from all of Chanticleer's residents. He resorted to guessing the ages of those residents who did not submit an affidavit.[7]

On April 15, 1996, the Simovits entered into a contract to sell their condominium ... a couple without children, for $145,000. However, the buyers were young, and thus wanted the Covenant waived. The Association agreed to waive it, and the deal closed on April 30, 1996.

The Simovits allege that, as a result of the Covenant, they lost numerous opportunities to sell their condominium at a higher price. They enlisted HOPE Fair Housing Center ("HOPE"), a not-for-profit agency dedicated to promoting equal opportunity housing, to challenge the legality of the Covenant.

The Simovits brought suit for the economic damages that they suffered as a result of the Covenant. They allege that the Covenant diminished the value of their condominium by $30,000. Real estate appraiser Robert A. Napoli testified on behalf of Plaintiffs, and appraisers Brent Baldwin and Anthony Uzemack testified on behalf of Defendant. All agreed that the Simovits' condominium was worth $145,000 with the Covenant. However, the appraisers disagreed as to the condominium's value without the Covenant. To determine the effect of the Covenant on the value of the condominium, Mr. Napoli looked at recent sales prices of five condominiums, similar in size and location to the Simovits', that were not subject to a restrictive covenant. He opined that the Simovits' condominium, without the Covenant, was worth $175,000. Mr. Uzemack, looking at three of the same properties as Mr. Napoli, opined that the Covenant had no "measurable" effect on the value of the Simovits' condominium—that it was worth $145,000, with or without the Covenant.

In addition to diminishing the value of their condominium, the Simovits allege that the Covenant caused them to incur additional mortgage obligations. Because the Covenant delayed the sale of their condominium, the Simovits allege that they paid an extra $3,560.15 in mortgage payments.

Moreover, the Simovits allege that they were emotionally injured as a result of the enforcement of the Covenant. Mr. Simovits testified to a special sensitivity to discrimination due to events in his past.[11] Mrs. Simovits testified that her husband suffered from chest and stomach pains, as well as sleeplessness, as a result of their inability to sell the condominium. Mrs. Simovits testified that she suffered from extreme anxiety, headaches, and abdominal distress due to their inability to sell. Mr. and Mrs. Simovits seek $10,000 each in emotional injury damages.

---

7. Mr. Londos' testimony regarding how he determined the ages of those residents who did not submit an affidavit illustrates the speculative nature of these surveys. When asked how he knew one resident was over the age of fifty-five, Mr. Londos stated that "I have seen her at the meetings. She is definitely over 55." (R. at 256.)

11. Mr. Simovits testified that he "grew up under Nazi occupied Hungary" and that he was "an anti-Communist in Budapest." (R. at 74.)

HOPE also alleges economic injuries as a result of the Covenant. HOPE is suing for the time and money it devoted to helping the Simovits. HOPE alleges that it diverted its time and resources away from housing counseling in order to help the Simovits pursue this action against the Association. According to ... HOPE's executive director, HOPE spent $2,806 in out-of-pocket expenses and $4,424 in staff time on the Simovits' case. Additionally, HOPE asks for $35,000 in monitoring and compliance expenses.

The Simovits and HOPE both seek punitive damages in the amount of $10,000 from the Association. In addition, the Simovits and HOPE seek a 5 year injunction against the Association, requiring them to permit residency at Chanticleer regardless of family status.

DISCUSSION

The following issues are before the Court: (1) whether the Simovits and/or HOPE have standing to sue under the FHA; (2) whether the Association is liable under the FHA for discrimination based on familial status; (3) whether the Association's defenses to liability are viable; and (4) if the Court finds the Association liable and its defenses untenable, what remedies are available to the Simovits and HOPE.

I. STANDING

A. The Simovits' Standing

The Association argues that the Simovits lack standing in this case because they were not the victims of discrimination. However, in order to have standing to sue under the FHA, the Simovits need not be victims of discrimination. See *Gladstone Realtors v. Village of Bellwood*, 441 U.S. 91, 115 (1979) (holding that Caucasian residents have standing under FHA to challenge racial discrimination directed against African-Americans in their neighborhood).

The Simovits' pleadings satisfy the FHA's permissive standing requirements. The Simovits allege that they lost opportunities to sell their condominium at a price higher than the $145,000 obtained.... Also, the Simovits allege that they suffered financial strain due to the additional mortgage payments they incurred.

FHA has permissive standing rights that the Ps meet.

B. HOPE's Standing

The Association alleges that the Simovits are not in the class of people covered by HOPE's mission statement because the Simovits endorsed the Covenant. The Association alleges, therefore, that HOPE lacks standing to sue in this case. However, "the only injury that need be shown to confer standing on a fair-housing agency is deflection of the agency's time and money from counseling to legal efforts directed against discrimination." *City of Chicago*, 982 F.2d at 1095 (quoting *Village of Bellwood v. Dwivedi*, 895 F.2d 1521, 1526 (7th Cir. 1990)).

II. LIABILITY

... [T]he Association's liability under the FHA for discrimination based on familial status turns on whether or not Chanticleer meets the exemption for "housing for older persons" in §3607(b)(2) of the FHA. One category of "housing for older persons" is "housing intended and operated for occupancy by persons 55 years and older." 42 U.S.C. §3607(b)(2)(C).

Exempt from FHA for >55 yrs. old.

Prior to December 28, 1995, the FHA required the following to meet the "55 years and older" exemption: (1) the facility has significant facilities and services specifically designed to meet the physical and social needs of older persons; (2) at least eighty percent of the units are occupied by one person age fifty-five or over; and (3) the complex publishes and adheres to policies which demonstrate an intent to provide housing for persons age fifty-five and older....

However, on December 28, 1995, Congress eliminated this "significant facilities and services" requirement.... Under the Housing for Older Persons Act of 1995, the following are the requirements to qualify as "age 55 years and older" housing: (1) at least eighty percent of the occupied units are occupied by at least one person who is fifty-five years of age or older; (2) the housing facility publishes and adheres to policies and procedures that demonstrate the intent to provide housing for persons age fifty-five or older; and (3) the housing facility complies with HUD rules and regulations for verification of occupancy. 42 U.S.C. § 3607(b)(2)(C)(i)–(iii). The statute requires that the defendant meet all of the above requirements to qualify for the exemption. In addition, the defendant has the burden of proving that it meets the above requirements. See *Massaro v. Mainlands Section 1 & 2 Civic Ass'n*, 3 F.3d 1472, 1475 (11th Cir. 1993), cert. denied, 115 S. Ct. 56 (1994).

A. Eighty Percent Test

The Association has failed to provide reliable evidence that, since 1985, eighty percent of the occupied dwellings at Chanticleer have had at least one person fifty-five years of age or older in residence. The Association relies on the results of the two surveys conducted by Mr. Londos to qualify for the exemption. Such reliance, however, is misplaced. Most significant, in the first survey, is the absence of corroborating source documentation. Mr. Londos merely estimated the ages of the Chanticleer residents, neglecting to verify them by using affidavits or other signed statements. A survey compiled in such an unscientific manner does not provide reliable evidence that eighty percent of the occupied dwellings had at least one person age fifty-five or older in residence. Moreover, the circumstances surrounding the taking of this survey — upon the advice of counsel in response to Mr. Simovits' threat to file a lawsuit — makes it clear that, even if the eighty percent requirement were met, it was merely fortuitous and is not indicative of any intent to provide housing for persons age fifty-five or older.

As to the second survey, the corroborating source documentation is incomplete. Mr. Londos did not obtain affidavits from every resident at Chanticleer, and he speculated as to the ages of those residents from whom he did not obtain an affidavit. Consequently, the survey's results are totally unreliable. Accordingly, the Court finds that the Association has failed to meet the eighty percent test.

B. Policies and Procedures Test

The Association freely admits that it does not publish and adhere to policies and procedures that demonstrate an intent to provide housing for persons aged fifty-five years or older.[18] ... Thus, the Association has, in fact, conceded its liability under the FHA, since qualification for the exemption requires that all three of its requirements be met. HUD provides a list of six nonexclusive factors for determining whether a facility is in compliance with this test. These factors are: (1) the housing facility's written rules and regulations; (2) the manner which the housing is described to prospective residents; (3) the nature of advertising; (4) age verification procedures; (5) lease provisions; and (6) the

---

18. The Association argues that it is in "effective compliance" with this prong of the statute because Chanticleer has a "longstanding reputation" in the community as a facility for older persons. (R. at 39, 350.) However, the "exemptions from the Fair Housing Act are to be construed narrowly, in recognition of the important goal of preventing housing discrimination." See *Massaro*, 3 F.3d at 1475. The Association's argument for "effective compliance" directly conflicts with this principle of narrow construction.

actual practices of the management in enforcing the relevant rules and regulations. 24 C.F.R. § 100.316(b)(1)–(6) (1995).

The Association argues, unpersuasively, that these six factors are no longer applicable, in determining whether on not the policies and procedures prong is met, because HUD eliminated § 100.316 on April 25, 1996. The Federal Register, on which the Association's argument is based, states that "the provisions describing the 'significant facilities and services' requirement for '55 or over' housing in §§ 100.306, 100.307, 100.310, and 100.316 were deleted to conform to the new requirements of '55 or over' housing established by the Housing for Older Persons Act." Regulatory Reinvention; Streamlining of HUD's Regulations Implementing the Fair Housing Act, 61 Fed. Reg. 18,248 (1996). Clearly, only the provisions relating to the "significant facilities and services requirement" were deleted. The provisions in § 100.316 relating to the policies and procedures requirement remain intact.

. . .

III. DEFENSES

The Association makes the argument that the Simovits should be barred from enforcing their rights under the FHA by the equitable defenses of estoppel, laches, unclean hands, and waiver. [The court rejected all four arguments. — Eds.]

IV. REMEDIES

The FHA provides that, where a defendant has engaged in a discriminatory housing practice, "the court may award to the plaintiff actual and punitive damages ... and as the court deems appropriate ... any permanent or temporary injunction." 42 U.S.C. § 3613(c)(1)....

A. Economic Damages

While all three experts are professional real estate appraisers, and all valued the Simovits' condominium the same, with the Covenant, their differences of opinion as to whether and to what extent the Covenant has an impact on the value of the property is inexplicable and irreconcilable and can be attributable only to their alignments with the respective parties. The Defendants' experts' opinion that the Covenant has no impact on the value of the units simply defies logic. On the other hand, Plaintiffs' expert's opinion that the Covenant decreases the value of the property by $30,000 appears excessive. The Court discredits Defendant's experts in this regard and credits plaintiff's expert only to the extent that the Covenant had some adverse impact on the value of the property. The Court, then, is left with the necessity of determining a non-arbitrary figure regarding the diminution in value of the property as a result of the Covenant. [Valuation discussion omitted. — Eds.]

The Simovits are entitled to the difference between the amount at which they sold their property, $145,000, and what they reasonably could have realized but for the Covenant, $157,500. Accordingly, they are awarded $12,500 in damages as compensation for the reduction in value of their condominium.

The Covenant created a delay in selling the condominium (by deterring prospective buyers), causing the Simovits to incur $3,560.15 in additional mortgage obligations. This Court finds that, but for the Covenant, the Simovits would not have incurred these costs. Thus, the Simovits are entitled to the $3,560.15 they paid in unnecessary mortgage payments.

HOPE seeks recovery of $7,230 in economic losses stemming from the time and resources it devoted to helping the Simovits. The Court awards these damages. The Court, however, declines to award the $35,000 in monitoring and compliance costs sought by HOPE.

The goals of monitoring the Association can be achieved through more equitable means, as set forth in the Court's Order below.

B. Emotional Distress Damages

Mr. and Mrs. Simovits seek $10,000 each in emotional injury damages. In order for the Simovits to recover for emotional injuries, a causal connection must exist between their alleged injuries and the Association's discriminatory conduct.... The Court finds that the Association's enforcement of the Covenant did not cause Mr. Simovits any compensable indignity or emotional harm, especially in light of his "feigned" approval of it. Hence, the Simovits suffered, at most, only indirect effects of the "no children" policy; they were not denied housing on the basis of their familial status.

Mrs. Simovits, like her husband, was not the direct victim of the Association's discrimination. She testified that the inability to sell their condominium caused her emotional distress. Although Mrs. Simovits testified to suffering anxiety and headaches, there is no indication that these injuries were atypical of the normal stresses associated with the sale of one's home.... [T]he Record does not support an award for emotional damages for either Mr. or Mrs. Simovits.

No emot'l damgs.

C. Punitive Damages

The Simovits and HOPE seek $10,000 each (for a total of $20,000) in punitive damages from the Association. Under § 3613(c)(1) of the FHA, the court may award punitive damages to a prevailing party in a housing discrimination case. Generally, punitive damages are awarded in cases where the defendant shows a reckless or callous disregard for the plaintiff's rights. The Record in this case contains overwhelming evidence of the Association's reckless disregard for the Simovits' and HOPE's rights. Most significant is the Association's failure to heed the warnings of its lawyer. Despite these warnings, the Association persisted in enforcing the Covenant against the Simovits, and prevented them from selling to buyers with children under the age of eighteen. The Minutes of the Association's November 14, 1995 Board of Managers' meeting show that this was a calculated gamble. Moreover, the Association republished its resident directory containing the rules and regulations, including the Covenant, to all residents in March, 1996. This callous and reckless disregard for the Simovits' rights entitles them to punitive damages.

Likewise, the Association showed a reckless disregard for HOPE's rights. The Association's continued publication and enforcement of the Covenant, despite warnings of the Covenant's illegality, directly conflicted with HOPE's mission of providing equal housing opportunities to the people of DuPage County. This reckless disregard for HOPE's rights entitles them to punitive damages.

There is no formula for determining the amount of punitive damages; however, the size of the award should be sufficient to "'punish [the defendant] for his outrageous conduct and to deter him and others like him from similar conduct in the future.'" Smith, 461 U.S. at 54 (quoting RESTATEMENT 2d of Torts, § 908(1) (1979)). At the end of 1995, the Association had a cash balance of $44,000.[25] A punitive award of $20,000, approximately one-half of its cash reserves, certainly serves the goals of punishment and deterrence.

---

25. According to the Association's audited balance sheet as of December 31, 1995, it had $44,180 in its Replacement Fund. The audit report states that this fund is used to accumulate resources for future repairs and replacements. (R. at Ex. 38.)

Moreover, a $20,000 punitive award is not excessive; the Seventh Circuit has affirmed even larger punitive awards in past housing discrimination cases.[26] Thus, a $10,000 award to the Simovits and another $10,000 award to HOPE constitute reasonable punitive awards.

D. Injunctive Relief

Section 3613(c)(1) also authorizes the Court to order injunctive relief. The testimony herein shows that the Association has no intention of discontinuing the enforcement of the Covenant unless enjoined and that an injunction is necessary to redress its "long-standing reputation ... within the community as a community for older persons." The Court is unaware of the pervasiveness of this reputation; however, it is certain that, since the enactment of the Covenant in 1985, families with children have been wrongfully denied the opportunity to live at Chanticleer. Although this type of harm can not be cured by monetary awards alone, the Court has adequate flexibility in fashioning equitable relief to remedy the effects of the Association's discrimination.

CONCLUSION

The Court finds that the Association is liable for discrimination based on familial status under the FHA. Therefore, the Association shall comply with the following:

ORDER: IT IS HEREBY ORDERED THAT:

1. By the close of business on September 6, 1996, the Association shall pay the Simovits $26,060.15 in damages....

3. From August 1, 1996 through August 1, 1999, the Association is hereby enjoined from attempting to qualify for any of the "housing for older persons" exemptions provided for in § 3607(b)(2) of the FHA.

4. The Association shall, no later than August 15, 1996, remove from its by-laws, rules, regulations and/or Declaration of Condominium Ownership any policies that discriminate against families with children. Written notification of such action shall be sent to all owners and tenants of units at Chanticleer and to HOPE.

5. By the close of business on the first Friday of January, beginning January 3, 1997, and continuing through January 7, 2000, the Association shall submit annual reports to HOPE containing the following information:

a. A copy of every person's application for the Association's approval to purchase at Chanticleer during the prior year, and a statement indicating the person's name and familial status, whether that person was rejected or accepted, the date on which the person was notified of acceptance or rejection, and, if rejected, the reason for such rejection; and

b. Current occupancy statistics of Chanticleer, indicating the ages of all residents occupying each of the units at Chanticleer.

6. By the close of business on August 26, 1996, the Association shall send written notice, to all real estate brokerage firms listed in the Hinsdale Yellow Pages, consisting of a statement explaining that the Association's discriminatory policies are no longer in effect and that families with children are welcome to reside at Chanticleer. A copy of each letter shall also be sent to HOPE.

---

26. In *Phillips v. Hunter Trails Comm. Ass'n*, 685 F.2d 184, 191 (7th Cir. 1982), the Seventh Circuit affirmed a punitive award of $100,000 to a married couple.

Notes & Questions

1. *Martin v. Palm Beach Atlantic Ass'n, Inc.*, 696 So. 2d 919 (Fla. Dist. Ct. App., 1997) held that publication of a rule prohibiting occupancy of units by children, even if rule was not enforced, itself violates the Federal Fair Housing Act (FFHA). Even before the 1988 amendment that prohibited family status discrimination, some courts applied state statutes to protect families with children from discrimination in housing. See *Marina Point Ltd. v. Wolfson*, 640 P.2d 1084 (Cal. 1982) (Unruh Act protects children against discrimination in housing); *Village Green Owners Ass'n v. O'Connor*, 177 Cal. Rptr. 159 (Cal. Ct. App. 1981) (California housing and civil rights laws applied to age restrictions in condominium).

2. *Wilson v. Playa de Serrano*, 123 P.3d 1148 (Ariz. Ct. App. 2006), held that despite the description of Playa de Serrano as "an adult townhouse development" in its 1969 declaration, the association lacked the power to adopt a rule restricting occupancy to persons fifty-five and older to comply with FFHA requirements to qualify as housing for seniors. "Absent a specific authorization in the Declaration, neither the Board nor a majority of the owners in Playa de Serrano has authority to restrict occupancy in the subdivision to persons fifty-five years of age or older." The court cited Restatement (Third) § 6.7(3) (specific authority needed to adopt rules that restrict use or occupancy of individually owned lots or units).

Maryland Commission on Human Relations v. Greenbelt Homes, Inc.

Court of Appeals of Maryland
475 A.2d 1192 (Md. 1984)

COLE, J. In this case we must determine whether enforcing a housing cooperative regulation that operates to prohibit a female resident from having an unrelated adult male reside with her constitutes discrimination on the basis of "marital status" proscribed by Maryland Code (1957, 1979 Repl.Vol.), Art. 49B, § 20. The relevant facts are not disputed.

Greenbelt Homes, Inc. (Greenbelt) is a Maryland corporation operating a housing cooperative in Greenbelt, Maryland. In 1976, Raymond and Marguerite Burgess (Burgess) applied for a Greenbelt membership. Their daughter, C. Lynn Kuhr (Kuhr), and her son were to be the residents of the unit; therefore, Kuhr also was required to file an application with Greenbelt. On this application, Kuhr indicated that only she and her son would be living in the unit. The Greenbelt board of directors granted Burgess permission to have their daughter and her son dwell in their unit and on November 15, 1976, Burgess entered into a mutual ownership contract with Greenbelt purchasing the equity and perpetual use of a housing unit in the Greenbelt Housing Project. This contract provided that the corporation could impose reasonable rules and regulations in managing the project and specifically noted that occupancy of the unit was only for the cooperative member and "his immediate family." If the member violated any provisions of the agreement, the corporation could terminate the contract. Furthermore, a Greenbelt occupancy regulation specifically defined "family members." See *infra* p. 80.

Kuhr and her son moved into the unit shortly after her parents executed the contract. Sometime thereafter Richard Searight, an unrelated adult male, also moved into the unit. Neither Kuhr nor her parents ever sought a waiver of the contractual provision limiting occupancy to immediate family members. In May of 1978, Greenbelt became aware of Mr. Searight's presence in the unit after receiving complaints from other cooperative members about parking and other problems relating to the occupancy of the Kuhr unit. Greenbelt advised Kuhr and her parents that having this unrelated adult occupy the unit violated the mutual ownership contract and urged them to "straighten out" the situation. When the matter had not been resolved by September of 1978, Greenbelt notified Burgess of a board of directors meeting at which they could explain why their contract should not be terminated. Before this meeting, Kuhr notified Greenbelt that Mr. Searight would be vacating the unit (which he in fact did "against his will and against the will of [Kuhr]").

Prior to Searight's exodus, Kuhr filed a housing discrimination complaint with the Maryland Commission on Human Relations (Commission) pursuant to Maryland Code (1957, 1979 Repl.Vol.), Art. 49B, §9(a), alleging that Greenbelt's conduct constituted discrimination on the basis of her "marital status, single." After concluding that there was probable cause to proceed against Greenbelt for discriminatory conduct, the Commission issued its Statement of Charges. *See* Maryland Code (1957, 1979 Repl.Vol.), Art. 49B, §11(a). A hearing examiner reviewed the case on stipulated facts. On August 28, 1980, he dismissed the action with prejudice, concluding that there had been a breach of the ownership contract. The Commission's counsel appealed to a three-member appeal board of the Commission, which reversed the dismissal of the Kuhr complaint and ordered Greenbelt to "cease and desist from discriminating against [Kuhr] in the terms, conditions or privileges of sale or rental of a dwelling...."

The Commission subsequently denied a request to vacate its decision and Greenbelt filed a petition in the Circuit Court for Prince George's County to review and reverse the Commission's decision. Each party moved for summary judgment. The circuit court granted Greenbelt's motion, concluding that *Prince George's County v. Greenbelt Homes*, 49 Md.App. 314, 431 A.2d 745 (1981), controlled and thus sections 19 and 20 of Article 49B had not been violated.

The Commission timely noted an appeal to the Court of Special Appeals and Greenbelt noted a cross-appeal. The Commission filed a petition for writ of certiorari in this Court presenting the following issue:

> Whether the prohibition of unmarried persons of the opposite sex who choose to share a dwelling space in the Greenbelt Housing Project is discrimination on the basis of marital status within the meaning of Section 20 of Article 49B of the Annotated Code of Maryland.

We granted certiorari prior to consideration by the intermediate court to resolve this important issue.

Greenbelt argues that Kuhr breached the mutual ownership contract and, thus, it has the right to terminate her occupancy. The mutual ownership contract provides, in pertinent part, as follows:

> 7(a). Occupancy: The Member shall occupy the dwelling unit covered by this contract as a private dwelling from the date of occupancy ... for himself and his immediate family....

> 7(b). Rules and Regulations Relating to Occupancy and Care of the Dwelling: This Corporation reserves the right to impose any reasonable rules and regulations not inconsistent with the provisions of this contract ... as in its judgment may be necessary or desirable for the management and control of Greenbelt and the Member's dwelling unit and surrounding premises, and for the preservation of good order and comfort therein, and the Member agrees faithfully to observe and comply with such rules and regulations and further agrees that all persons living in the dwelling unit also will observe and comply with such rules and regulation....

13. Termination of Contract by Corporation for Default or for Cause: In the event of default by the Member ... or violation of any of the provisions hereof, the Corporation may terminate this contract.... The Corporation may terminate this Contract ... if its board of directors ... shall determine that the Member for sufficient cause is undesirable as a resident in Greenbelt because of objectionable conduct on the part of the Member or of a person living in his dwelling unit. To violate or disregard the rules and regulations provided for in paragraph 7(b) hereof, after due warning, shall be deemed to be objectionable conduct.

The occupancy regulation amplifying section 7(a) of the contract stated:

That the definition of "family members" as used in GHI Mutual Ownership Contracts be clarified as follows: the following are considered as family members who may live in a GHI unit without getting GHI approval for such occupancy as long as the number of persons does not exceed GHI occupancy standards:

1. Wife, Mother, Stepmother, Mother-in-Law

2. Husband, Father, Stepfather, Father-in-Law

3. Daughter, Stepdaughter, Legally Adopted Daughter, Daughter-in-Law

4. Son, Stepson, Legally Adopted Son, Son-in-Law

5. Sister, Sister-in-Law

6. Brother, Brother-in-Law

7. Grandchildren, Grandparents

8. Foster Children — The number of foster children which a member may care for is determined by the existing family unit to insure that total occupancy standards established by Prince George's County for foster children placement are not exceeded.

The housing of any other person in a GHI unit in excess of 30 days, whether with or without compensation, without approval of the board of directors will be considered a violation of the mutual ownership contract and may result in the termination of such member's contract.

We had occasion to review these contractual provisions in *Green v. Greenbelt Homes*, 232 Md. 496, 194 A.2d 273 (1963). In that case Greenbelt sought to terminate its contract with a woman who, among other violations, was living with an unrelated adult man. The Court addressed the question "whether the provisions of the contract relating to termination were valid." *Id.* at 501, 194 A.2d 273. The Court held that the member had breached her contract with Greenbelt sufficiently to "warrant the corporation exercising its right to terminate the interests of the member in the dwelling unit." *Id.* at 504, 194 A.2d 273. In examining the issue presented in that case, the Court focused on the nature of the cooperative and its relationship to members:

An important factor in the maintenance of a cooperative housing project is the control of the activities of the cooperative members living within the project. In a recent article, Restrictions on the Use of Cooperative Apartment Property, by Arthur E. Wallace, 13 Hastings Law Journal, 357, 363, it is said:

The economic and social interdependence of the tenant-owners demands cooperation on all levels of cooperative life if a tolerable living situation is to be maintained. Each tenant-owner is required to give up some of the freedoms he would otherwise enjoy if he were living in a private dwelling and likewise is privileged to demand the same sacrifices of his cotenant-owners with respect to his rights.

By analogy, the cooperative agreement is really a community within a community governed, like our municipalities, by rules and regulations for the benefit of the whole. Whereas the use of lands within a city is controlled by zoning ordinances, the use of apartments within the cooperative project is controlled by restrictive covenants. The use of the common facilities in the project is controlled on the same theory that the use of city streets and parks is regulated. In both situations compliance with the regulations is the price to be paid to live in and enjoy the benefits of the particular organization." [Id. at 503–04, 194 A.2d 273.]

For these reasons, the Court recognized that the activities of cooperative members may be contractually regulated and that these regulations should be enforced.

The case *sub judice* is strikingly similar. Here, the undisputed facts demonstrate that Kuhr violated a provision of the mutual ownership contract executed by her parents, yet also governing the conduct of all those living in the project.[2] She knew from the date the contract was signed that only her immediate family members were authorized to occupy the dwelling unit. Despite such knowledge, she allowed Mr. Searight, unrelated by blood or marriage, to live with her and at no time sought a waiver from the board of directors so as to justify his presence in the dwelling unit. Greenbelt maintains this breach should be dispositive of the issue before us.

However, as we see it, even this conduct cannot determine the issue if, indeed, the contractual covenant prohibiting persons from residing with unrelated adults violates the State anti-discrimination law. The real issue is whether Greenbelt was precluded from seeking to enforce its membership regulation because such conduct constituted an unlawful discriminatory practice under Maryland Code (1957, 1979 Repl.Vol.), Art. 49B, § 20. Section 20 provides in pertinent part:

It shall be an unlawful discriminatory housing practice, because of race, color, religion, sex, national origin, marital status, or physical or mental handicap, for any person having the right to sell, rent, lease, control, construct, or manage any dwelling constructed or to be constructed, or any agent or employee of such person:

. . .

(2) To discriminate against any person in the terms, conditions, or privileges of sale or rental of a dwelling, or in the provision of services or facilities in connection therewith.

. . .

(6) To include in any transfer, sale, rental or lease of housing any restrictive covenant that discriminates; or for any person to honor or exercise, or attempt to honor or exercise any discriminatory covenant pertaining to housing.

Our cases make clear that when interpreting a statute, if the language is plain, unambiguous and has a definite and sensible meaning, that meaning is presumed to be that intended by the legislature. *See Gietka v. County Executive*, 283 Md. 24, 387 A.2d 291

---

2. Section 7(b) of the mutual ownership contract indicates that all residents are bound by the conditions of occupancy. Furthermore, by signing the membership application Kuhr explicitly agreed "to abide by all the laws, rules and regulations of the corporation."

(1978*); Hunt v. Montgomery County*, 248 Md. 403, 237 A.2d 35 (1968); *Secretary of State v. Bryson*, 244 Md. 418, 224 A.2d 277 (1966); *Central Credit v. Comptroller*, 243 Md. 175, 220 A.2d 568 (1966); *Taylor v. Ogle*, 202 Md. 273, 96 A.2d 24 (1953). Section 20 is couched in language that is clear and unambiguous. This provision of Maryland's anti-discrimination law means precisely what it says: no person shall be discriminated against in regard to housing because of that person's marital status. As we see it, "marital status" connotes whether one is married or not married.

Here, the fact that Kuhr was not married to Mr. Searight was irrelevant. It would have made no difference under the circumstances of this case if Searight had been Kuhr's best girlfriend, her favorite aunt, her destitute cousin, or her infant nephew. The point is that no one of these people, including Mr. Searight, falls within the defined class of family members in the regulation.

Nevertheless, the Commission contends that the regulation allows unmarried couples to be treated differently from married couples and this circumstance offends the statute. We see no merit in this contention. We believe Judge Lowe's opinion in *Prince George's County v. Greenbelt Homes*, 49 Md.App. 314, 319–20, 431 A.2d 745 (1981), states a clear response to the Commission.

> Only marriage as prescribed by law can change the marital status of an individual to a new legal entity of husband and wife. The law of Maryland does not recognize common law marriages (Henderson v. Henderson, 199 Md. 449, 454, 87 A.2d 403 (1952)) or other unions of two or more persons—such as concubinage, syneisaktism, relationships of homosexuals or lesbians—as legally bestowing upon two people a legally cognizable marital status. Such relationships are simply illegitimate unions unrecognized, or in some instances condemned, by the law.

Moreover, in our view, the legislature has intended to promote rather than denigrate the institution of marriage. Subsection 7 of § 20 illustrates the point by making it an unlawful practice "[t]o refuse to consider both applicants' income when both parties to a *marriage* seek to buy or lease any dwelling." [Emphasis supplied.] We find nothing in this statute which tends to elevate an individual's relationship with other persons to the level achieved by marriage. In our view, the directors of a cooperative project may reasonably expect to maintain a more stable community by restricting occupancy to those who enjoy a close and definite familial relationship.

Our conclusion that Kuhr was not discriminated against because of her marital status is buttressed by an analysis of similar cases from other jurisdictions. For instance, the New York courts have addressed a similar issue in *Hudson View Properties v. Weiss*, 106 Misc.2d 251, 431 N.Y.S.2d 632 (1980), *rev'd*, 109 Misc.2d 589, 442 N.Y.S.2d 367 (1981), *rev'd*, 86 A.D.2d 803, 448 N.Y.S.2d 649 (1982), *rev'd*, 59 N.Y.2d 733, 463 N.Y.S.2d 428, 450 N.E.2d 234 (1983). In that case, the landlord served a notice to cure upon Ms. Weiss for "allowing a person who is not a tenant to reside in and occupy the premises." The landlord subsequently served upon the tenant a notice purporting to terminate the tenancy because the violation had not been cured. Ms. Weiss did not surrender the premises and the landlord instituted a holdover proceeding. Ms. Weiss moved to dismiss because:

> the landlord through his attorney has stated that if I marry Mr. Wertheimer, he will withdraw his claim that I have violated the lease and will not seek to evict me. If I remain single, this action will continue. I am moving to dismiss on the grounds that these actions violate the State Human Rights Law [Executive Law] § 296(5)(a) and the City Human Rights Law § B1-7.0(5a) which prohibit discrimination in housing on the basis of marital status." [442 N.Y.S.2d at 369.]

The relevant provision of the New York Human Rights Law (§ 296(5)(a)) stated:

> It shall be an unlawful discriminatory practice for the owner ... or managing agent of, or other person having the right to sell, rent, or lease a housing accommodation ... or any agent or employee thereof: (1) To refuse to sell, rent, lease or otherwise deny to or withhold from any person or group of persons such a housing accommodation because of the ... marital status of such person or persons [L.1975 ch. 803, eff. on the 60th day after August 9, 1975]. [442 N.Y.S.2d at 369.]

The Appellate Term of the Supreme Court, First Department, reversed the lower court's decision to grant the tenant's motion to dismiss, 106 Misc.2d 251, 431 N.Y.S.2d 632 (1980), noting that the landlord's pleading was not defective on its face. *See* 109 Misc.2d 589, 442 N.Y.S.2d 367, 370 (1981). That court was reversed on appeal, 86 A.D.2d 803, 448 N.Y.S.2d 649 (1982); however, the New York Court of Appeals again reversed, agreeing with the intermediate appellate court. *See* 59 N.Y.2d 733, 463 N.Y.S.2d 428, 450 N.E.2d 234 (1983). That court stated:

> In this case, the issue arises not because the tenant is unmarried, but because the lease restricts occupancy of her apartment, as are all apartments in the building, to the tenant and the tenant's immediate family. Tenant admits that an individual not part of her immediate family currently occupies the apartment as his primary residence. Whether or not he could by marriage or otherwise become a part of her immediate family is not an issue. The landlord reserved the right by virtue of the covenant in the lease to restrict the occupants and the tenant agreed to this restriction. Were the additional tenant a female unrelated to the tenant, the lease would be violated without reference to marriage. The fact that the additional tenant here involved is a man with whom the tenant has a loving relationship is simply irrelevant. The applicability of that restriction does not depend on her marital status. [463 N.Y.S.2d at 429.]

The case upon which the New York court in *Hudson View Properties*, relied, *Manhattan Pizza Hut v. New York State, Etc.*, 51 N.Y.2d 506, 434 N.Y.S.2d 961, 415 N.E.2d 950 (1980), held that an employer's anti-nepotism rule, precluding an employee from working under the supervision of a relative (including a spouse) did not violate the human rights law prohibition against discrimination attributable to an individual's "marital status." In construing the meaning of that term the court noted:

> [T]he plain and ordinary meaning of "marital status" is the social condition enjoyed by an individual by reason of his or her having participated or failed to participate in a marriage. Illuminated another way, when one is queried about one's "marital status", the usual and complete answer would be expected to be a choice among "married", "single", etc., but would not be expected to include an identification of one's present or former spouse and certainly not the spouse's occupation. [434 N.Y.S.2d at 964 (emphasis supplied).]

See also Thomson v. Sanborn's Motor Express, Inc., 154 N.J.Super. 555, 382 A.2d 53 (1977); *McFadden v. Elma Country Club*, 26 Wash.App. 195, 613 P.2d 146 (1980). *But cf. Miller v. C.A. Muer Corp.*, 124 Mich.App. 780, 336 N.W.2d 215 (1983).

Accordingly, we hold that § 20's prohibition against marital status discrimination does not preclude a housing cooperative from enforcing a contractual obligation restricting occupancy to persons in the member's immediate family. Thus, Greenbelt did not discriminate against Kuhr based on her "marital status."

Judgment of the circuit court for Prince George's County Affirmed. Appellant to pay the costs.

DAVIDSON, J., dissenting. I agree with the majority that the language of Maryland Code (1957, 1979 Repl.Vol.), Art. 49B, §20 is "clear and unambiguous" and "means precisely what it says: no person shall be discriminated against in regard to housing because of that person's marital status." I further agree with the majority that the term "marital status" "connotes whether one is married or not married."

Here the record shows that under the applicable contractual covenant, C. Lynn Kuhr (Kuhr), a female, was entitled, without Greenbelt approval, to reside in a Greenbelt housing unit with Richard "Searight (Searight), a male, if she was married to him. Kuhr, however, was not entitled, without Greenbelt approval, to reside in a Greenbelt housing unit with Searight if she was not married to him. Manifestly, under the applicable contractual covenant, Kuhr's right to reside in a Greenbelt housing unit with Searight depended upon whether she was "married or not married" and, therefore, depended upon her "marital status."

In sum, Kuhr was prohibited by the applicable contractual covenant from residing in a Greenbelt housing unit with Searight because she was "not married" or, in other words, "single." In my view, she was "discriminated against with regard to housing because of her marital status." *See, e.g., Hess v. Fair Employment & Housing Commission*, 138 Cal.App.3d 232, 234, 187 Cal.Rptr. 712, 714 (1st Dist.1982); *Atkisson v. Kern County Housing Authority*, 59 Cal.App.3d 89, 99, 130 Cal.Rptr. 375, 381 (5th Dist.1976); *Zahorian v. Russell Fitt Real Estate Agency*, 62 N.J. 399, 405, 301 A.2d 754, 757 (1973); *Loveland v. Leslie*, 21 Wash.App. 84, 87, 583 P.2d 664, 666 (Div. 1, 1978). Accordingly, I respectfully dissent.

Notes & Questions

1. *Single family defined*. What is a "single family?" If you were drafting documents, how would you define the term "family?" See generally, *Deep East Texas Regional Mental Health Retardation Services v. Kinnear*, No. 9-93-316-CV (Tex. App. June 6, 1994) (covenant term "single family residence" held to refer to the type of structure built not its use).

2. Gerald Korngold, in *Single Family Use Covenants: For Achieving A Balance Between Traditional Family Life and Individual Autonomy*, 22 U.C. Davis L. Rev. 951 (1989), takes the position that:

> single family use covenants should not be applied to limit personal choices taking place within the home. Rather, they should be enforced only to the extent that they limit fallout projected from a household on the rest of the neighborhood. 'Family' would thus have a flexible meaning in the context of single family use restrictions. This proposal is necessary not only in light of general policy considerations but also because it strikes a proper balance between freedom of contract values and the policy against restrictions on land which are inherent in real covenants law. The approach will protect traditional family life to a great, albeit not the fullest, extent while respecting individual autonomy.

3. Although more than 20 jurisdictions have statutes that bar discrimination in housing based on marital status, most statutes do not define the term. Court decisions are split on the issue whether discrimination against unmarried couples is covered by the statute. See Comment, *The Wages of Living in Sin: Discrimination in Housing Against Unmarried Couples*, 25 U.C. Davis L. Rev. 1055 (1992).

Problem

The association has a provision in its governing documents that limits occupancy of a unit to a "single family." In addition, there is a regulation that prohibits more than two persons per bedroom from residing in any unit. A new owner moves into a three-bedroom unit with six persons in addition to the husband and wife owners. These additional persons include several cousins, a grandparent, and a brother-in-law. You receive a call from the condominium association's manager asking for your advice on whether and how to enforce the rule. What do you advise? Assume, instead, that you receive a call from the new owner asking for advice as to how he should respond to the manager's alarming statement that his occupancy with his "family" violates the governing documents. How do you respond?

c. Racial Discrimination and Civil Rights Statutes

Law schools frequently teach entire courses on the subject of racial discrimination and the application of civil rights statutes. Our goal here is merely to introduce you to the topic and to raise questions about the application of civil rights statutes to community associations.

Tillman v. Wheaton-Haven Recreation Ass'n, Inc.

United States Supreme Court
410 U.S. 431 (1973)

BLACKMUN, J. Wheaton-Haven Recreation Association, Inc., a nonprofit Maryland corporation, was organized in 1958 for the purpose of operating a swimming pool. After a membership drive to raise funds, the Association obtained zoning as a "community pool" and constructed its facility near Silver Spring, Maryland. The Association is essentially a single-function recreational club, furnishing only swimming and related amenities.[1]

Membership is by family units, rather than individuals, and is limited to 325 families.[2] This limit has been reached on at least one occasion. Membership is largely keyed to the geographical area within a three-quarter-mile radius of the pool.[3] A resident (whether or not a homeowner) of that area requires no recommendation before he may apply for membership; the resident receives a preferential place on the waiting list if he applies when the membership is full; and the resident-member who is a homeowner and who sells his home and turns in his membership, confers on the purchaser of his property a first option on the vacancy created by his removal and resignation. A person residing outside the three-quarter-mile area may apply for membership only upon the recommendation of a member; he receives no preferential place on the waiting list if the membership is full; and if he becomes a member, he has no way of conferring an option upon the purchaser of his property. Beyond-the-area members may not exceed 30% of the total. Majority

---

1. Candy, ice cream, and soft drinks have been sold on the premises, but these were merely incidentals for the convenience of swimmers during the season. Aside from meetings of the board of directors and of the general membership, the premises apparently have been utilized only for pool-related activities.

2. Wheaton-Haven presently charges an initiation fee of $375 and annual dues ranging from $50 to $60, depending on the number of persons in the family unit.

3. The Association's bylaws provide that "membership shall be open to bona fide residents (whether or not home owners) of the area within a three-quarter mile radius of the pool," and "may be extended" to others "who shall have been recommended ... by a member."

approval of those present at a meeting of the board of directors or of the general membership is required before an applicant is admitted as a member.

Only members and their guests are admitted to the pool. No one else may gain admission merely by payment of an entrance fee.

In the spring of 1968 petitioner, Harry C. Press, a Negro who had purchased from a nonmember a home within the geographical preference area, inquired about membership in Wheaton-Haven. At that time the Association had no Negro member. In November 1968 the general membership rejected a resolution that would have opened the way for Negro members. Dr. Press was never given an application form, and respondents concede that he was discouraged from applying because of his race.

In July 1968 petitioners Murray and Rosalind N. Tillman, who were husband and wife and members in good standing, brought petitioner Grace Rosner, a Negro, to the pool as their guest. Although Mrs. Rosner was admitted on that occasion, the guest policy was changed by the board of directors, at a special meeting the following day, to limit guests to relatives of members. Respondents concede that one reason for the adoption of this policy was to prevent members from having Negroes as guests at the pool. Under this new policy Mrs. Rosner thereafter was refused admission when the Tillmans sought to have her as their guest. In the fall of 1968 the membership, by resolution, reaffirmed the policy.

In October 1969 petitioners (Mr. and Mrs. Tillman, Dr. and Mrs. Press, and Mrs. Rosner) instituted this civil action against the Association and individuals who were its officers or directors, seeking damages and declaratory and injunctive relief, particularly under the Civil Rights Act of 1866, now 42 U. S. C. §1982,[4] the Civil Rights Act of 1870, now 42 U. S. C. §1981, and Title II of the Civil Rights Act of 1964, 78 Stat. 243, 42 U. S. C. §2000a, *et seq.* The District Court, in an unreported opinion, held that Wheaton-Haven was a private club and exempt from the nondiscrimination provisions of the statutes. It granted summary judgment for defendants. The Court of Appeals affirmed, one judge dissenting. 451 F.2d 1211 (CA4 1971). It later denied rehearing *en banc* over two dissents, *id.*, at 1225. We granted *certiorari*, 406 U.S. 916 (1972), to review the case in the light of *Sullivan v. Little Hunting Park*, 396 U.S. 229 (1969).

I

In *Jones v. Alfred H. Mayer Co.*, 392 U.S. 409 (1968), this Court, after a detailed review of the legislative history of 42 U. S. C. §1982, *id.*, at 422–437, held that the statute reaches beyond state action and is not confined to officially sanctioned segregation. The Court subsequently applied §1982 in Sullivan to private racial discrimination practiced by a nonstock corporation organized to operate a community park and playground facilities, including a swimming pool, for residents of a designated area. The Presses contend that their §1982 claim is controlled by *Sullivan*. We agree.

A. The Court of Appeals held that §1982 would not apply to the Presses because membership rights in Wheaton-Haven could neither be leased nor transferred incident to the acquisition of property. 451 F.2d, at 1216–1217. In *Sullivan*, the Court concluded that the right to enjoy a membership share in the corporation, assigned by a property owner as part of a leasehold he was granting, constituted a right "to ... lease ... property" protected by §1982. 396 U.S., at 236–237. The Court of Appeals distinguished property-

---

4. "All citizens of the United States shall have the same right, in every State and Territory, as is enjoyed by white citizens thereof to inherit, purchase, lease, sell, hold, and convey real and personal property." 42 U. S. C. §1982.

linked membership shares in *Sullivan* from property-linked membership preferences in Wheaton-Haven by emphasizing the speculative nature of the benefits available to residents of the area around Wheaton-Haven. We conclude that the Court of Appeals erroneously characterized the property-linked preferences conferred by Wheaton-Haven's bylaws.

Under the bylaws, a resident of the area within three-quarters of a mile from the pool receives the three preferences noted above: he is allowed to apply for membership without seeking a recommendation from a current member; he receives preference over others, except those with first options, when applying for a membership vacancy; and, if he is an owner-member, he is able to pass to his successor-in-title a first option to acquire the membership Wheaton-Haven purchases from him.[5] If the membership is full, the preference-area resident is placed on the waiting list; other applicants, however, are required to reapply after those on the waiting list obtain memberships.

The Court of Appeals concluded, incorrectly it later appeared, that the membership had never been full,[6] and that the option possibility, therefore, was "far too tenuous a thread to support a conclusion that there is a transfer of membership incident to the purchase of property." 451 F.2d, at 1217. Since the Presses had not purchased their area home from a member, the court found no transaction by which the Presses could have acquired a membership preference. 451 F.2d, at 1217–1218, n. 14.

We differ from the Court of Appeals in our evaluation of the three rights obtained. The record indicates that the membership was full in the spring of 1968 but dropped, perhaps not unexpectedly in view of the season, in the fall of that year. We cannot be certain, either, that the membership would not have remained full in the absence of racial discrimination,[7] or that the membership will never be full in the future. As was observed in dissent in the Court of Appeals:

> Several years from now it may well be that a white neighbor can sell his home at a considerably higher price than Dr. and Mrs. Press because the white owner will be able to assure his purchaser of an option for membership in Wheaton-Haven. Dr. and Mrs. Press, however, are denied this advantage. 451 F.2d, at 1223.

Similarly, the automatic waiting-list preference given to residents of the favored area may have affected the price paid by the Presses when they bought their home. Thus, the purchase price to them, like the rental paid by Freeman in *Sullivan*, may well reflect benefits dependent on residency in the preference area. For them, however, the right to acquire a home in the area is abridged and diluted.

When an organization links membership benefits to residency in a narrow geographical area, that decision infuses those benefits into the bundle of rights for which an individual pays when buying or leasing within the area. The mandate of 42 U. S. C. § 1982

---

5. Under the Wheaton-Haven system, a within-the-area member selling his home may either retain his membership or seek to sell it back to the Association. If Wheaton-Haven is willing to purchase, it pays 80% of the initial cost if the membership is not full, and 90% if the membership is full. The purchaser of the member's home then has a first option on the membership so released by the seller. The practical effect of this system is to prefer applicants who purchase from members over other applicants, particularly at a time when the membership is full.

6. In the court's *per curiam* statement responsive to the petition for rehearing, it described its earlier observation that the membership list had never been full as an "inadvertent misstatement ... now corrected to reflect a full membership list in the spring of 1968." 451 F.2d 1211, 1225.

7. The record reveals that a number of members withdrew when the present suit was filed. Tr. of Oral Arg. in District Court 15.

then operates to guarantee a nonwhite resident, who purchases, leases, or holds this property, the same rights as are enjoyed by a white resident.

B. Respondents contend that even if 42 U. S. C. § 1982 applies, Wheaton-Haven nevertheless is exempt as a private club under § 201 (e) of the Civil Rights Act of 1964, 42 U. S. C. § 2000a (e),[8] with a consequent implied narrowing effect upon the range and application of the older § 1982. In *Sullivan* we found it unnecessary to consider limits on § 1982 as applied to a truly private association because we found "no plan or purpose of exclusiveness" in Little Hunting Park. 396 U.S., at 236. But here, as there, membership "is open to every white person within the geographic area, there being no selective element other than race." *Ibid.* The only restrictions are the stated maximum number of memberships and, as in *Sullivan, id.*, at 234, the requirement of formal board or membership approval. The structure and practices of Wheaton-Haven thus are indistinguishable from those of Little Hunting Park.[9] We hold, as a consequence, that Wheaton-Haven is not a private club and that it is not necessary in this case to consider the issue of any implied limitation on the sweep of § 1982 when its application to a truly private club, within the meaning of § 2000a (e), is under consideration. Cf. *Moose Lodge No. 107 v. Irvis*, 407 U.S. 163 (1972); *Daniel v. Paul*, 395 U.S. 298 (1969).

II

Mrs. Rosner and the Tillmans, relying on 42 U. S. C. §§ 1981,[10] 1982, and 2000a *et seq.*, contend that Wheaton-Haven could not adopt a racially discriminatory policy toward guests. The District Court granted summary judgment for the respondents on these claims also, holding that Wheaton-Haven was a private club and exempt from all three statutes.

The operative language of both § 1981 and § 1982 is traceable to the Act of April 9, 1866, c. 31, § 1, 14 Stat. 27. *Hurd v. Hodge*, 334 U.S. 24, 30–31 n. 7 (1948).[11] In light

---

8. The provisions of this subchapter shall not apply to a private club or other establishment not in fact open to the public, except to the extent that the facilities of such establishment are made available to the customers or patrons of an establishment within the scope of subsection (b) of this section. 42 U. S. C. § 2000a (e).

9. Apparently one applicant was formally rejected during the preceding 12 years of Little Hunting Park's operation. App. 127 and Brief for Petitioner 7, *Sullivan v. Little Hunting Park*, 396 U.S. 229 (1969). At Wheaton-Haven one applicant was formally rejected in the preceding 11 years.

The Court of Appeals found it "inferable from Little Hunting Park's organization and membership provisions that it was built by the same real estate developers who built the four subdivisions from which members were drawn, as an aid to the sale of homes." 451 F.2d, at 1215 n. 8. This inference may be erroneous. App. 24-36 and Tr. of Oral Arg. 24, 31–34, *Sullivan v. Little Hunting Park, supra*. In any event, *Sullivan* did not rest on any relationship between the club and real estate developers.

10. "All persons within the jurisdiction of the United States shall have the same right in every State and Territory to make and enforce contracts, to sue, be parties, give evidence, and to the full and equal benefit of all laws and proceedings for the security of persons and property as is enjoyed by white citizens, and shall be subject to like punishment, pains, penalties, taxes, licenses, and exactions of every kind, and to no other."

11. The Act of Apr. 9, 1866, § 1, read in part:

That all persons born in the United States ... of every race and color ... shall have the same right, in every State and Territory in the United States, to make and enforce contracts, to sue, be parties, and give evidence, to inherit, purchase, lease, sell, hold, and convey real and personal property, and to full and equal benefit of all laws and proceedings for the security of person and property, as is enjoyed by white citizens, and shall be subject to like punishment, pains, and penalties, and to none other, any law, statute, ordinance, regulation, or custom, to the contrary notwithstanding. 14 Stat. 27.

The present codification of § 1981 is derived from Revised Statutes § 1977 (1874), which codified the Act of May 31, 1870, § 16, 16 Stat. 144. Although the 1866 Act rested only on the Thirteenth Amendment, *United States v. Harris*, 106 U.S. 629, 640 (1883); Civil Rights Cases, 109 U.S. 3, 22

of the historical interrelationship between § 1981 and § 1982, we see no reason to construe these sections differently when applied, on these facts, to the claim of Wheaton-Haven that it is a private club. Consequently, our discussion and rejection of Wheaton-Haven's claim that it is exempt from § 1982 disposes of the argument that Wheaton-Haven is exempt from § 1981. On remand the District Court will develop any necessary facts concerning the adoption of the guest policy and will evaluate the claims of the parties[12] free of the misconception that Wheaton-Haven is exempt from §§ 1981, 1982, and 2000a.

The judgment of the Court of Appeals is reversed, and the case is remanded for further proceedings.

It is so ordered.

Notes & Questions

1. *Review of application of civil rights statutes to private communities and club.* For a thorough review of the application of federal civil rights laws to private community association developments and private clubs, see *U.S. v. Landsdowne Swim Club*, 894 F.2d 83 (3rd Cir. 1990) (applying 42 U.S.C. § 2000(E) to private club exemption of Title II of the Civil Rights Act of 1964); *Brown v. Loudaun Golf and Country Club*, 573 F. Supp. 399 (E.D. Va. 1983); *EEOC v. Chicago Club*, No. 92C-6910 (N.D. Ill. Feb. 3, 1995); *Wright v. Salisbury Club, Ltd.*, 479 F. Supp. 378 (E.D. Va. 1979) (applying 42 U.S.C. §§ 1981 and 1982); *Sullivan v. Little Hunting Park, Inc.*, 396 U.S. 229 (1969). See also *U.S. v. Western Resort Properties*, No. 3789456G (N.D. Tex. 1978) (applying Equal Credit Opportunity Act to developer who refused to sell and provide mortgages to black homebuyers).

2. *Actions rising to racial discrimination.* If a community association exercises its right of first refusal to prevent sale of unit to a black couple, has discrimination occurred? See *Wiggins v. Apanas*, No. 79C 2584 (N.D. Ill. May 1981). What about a condominium association or its management company that manages a rental program on behalf of its owners? See generally *Gentry v. Northeast Mgm't Co., Inc.*, 472 F. Supp. 1248 (N.D. Tex. 1979).

3. *Villas West II of Willowridge v. McGlothin*, 841 N.E.2d 584 (Ind. Ct. App. 2006) held that a covenant that prohibited leasing units in a development of "duplex condo-style homes" violated the FFHA because it had a disparate impact on African-Americans, who were disproportionately renters, rather than homeowners, in the area. In addition, the developer's use of the word "restricted" in advertising the development clearly sent a message to that Africa Americans were not welcome.

(1883); *United States v. Morris*, 125 F. 322, 323 (ED Ark. 1903), and, indeed, was enacted before the Fourteenth Amendment was formally proposed, *United States v. Price*, 383 U.S. 787, 804 (1966); *Hurd v. Hodge*, 334 U.S. 24, 32 n. 11 (1948); *Oyama v. California*, 332 U.S. 633, 640 (1948); Civil Rights Cases, supra, 109 U.S., at 22, the 1870 Act was passed pursuant to the Fourteenth, and changes in wording may have reflected the language of the Fourteenth Amendment. See *United States v. Wong Kim Ark*, 169 U.S. 649, 695–696 (1898). The 1866 Act was re-enacted in 1870, and the predecessor of the present § 1981 was to be "enforced according to the provisions" of the 1866 Act. Act of May 31, 1870, § 18, 16 Stat. 144.

12. Respondent McIntyre urges that the judgment in his favor should be affirmed as to him because he was merely a director of Wheaton-Haven and was later defeated in his bid for re-election to its board, and because, in his deposition, he stated that he opposed the Association's exclusionary practices. Neither the District Court nor the Court of Appeals discussed Mr. McIntyre's individual liability, and we find it inappropriate to attempt resolution of this issue on the present record.

4. *Religious discrimination.* The FFHA applies to religious discrimination as well as discrimination on other bases. Can a co-operative board successfully defend a suit claiming religious discrimination in its decision to reject sale of a unit to a single Jewish woman by showing that the members of the board are Jewish and there are other single women in the cooperative? See *Sassower v. Field*, No. 88-5775 (S.D. N.Y. Aug. 12, 1991). Can a condominium association enforce its blanket prohibition against items stored or hung on balconies against display of a Hindu flag and other religious symbols? See *Boodram v. Maryland Farms Condo.*, 16 F. 3d 408 (4th Cir. 1994) cert. den., (unpublished opinion 1994 WL 31025). If the community permits religious displays only during Christmas, but not during religious holidays of non-Christian faiths, does it engage in prohibited discrimination?

B. Board Member Liability and Indemnification

Many people are afraid to serve on community association boards for the simple reason that they are concerned about potential liability. Board service is much safer than popularly believed, particularly in light of indemnification statutes, the business judgment rule and other protections. However, there are risks.

1. Possible Bases for Board Member Liability

Kirtley v. McClelland
Court of Appeals of Indiana
562 N.E.2d 27 (Ind. Ct. App. 1990)

ROBERTSON, J. For the purpose of simplifying the identity of the parties to this appeal, the appellant-defendants will be referred to as the directors or as Kirtley and the appellee-plaintiffs as the Pointe Service Association (PSA). The appellants, William Kirtley, Phyllis Kirtley, Thomas Garrison and Terry Pierson, present or past directors of The Pointe Services Association, Inc., a unit owner's association, appeal from a judgment rendered against them following the bench trial of a shareholders' derivative action. The judgment ordered payment in the sum of approximately $150,000, an accounting and transfer of funds, and ordered payment of attorneys' fees.

We affirm in part, reverse in part, and remand with instructions.

An overview of the basic facts shows that "the Pointe" is a planned residential community built around a golf course and situated on the shore of Lake Monroe. In 1974, Caslon Development Co., the original developer, created the resort community, starting with four independent condominium villages totaling about 250 units. Eventually, plans called for a total of about 1500 residences. To facilitate general community administration, Caslon subjected the development property to certain covenants and restrictions for the benefit of the community as a whole, incorporated PSA, an Indiana not-for-profit corporation, and delegated to PSA responsibility for:

> maintaining and administering the common areas and common facilities, administering and enforcing ... covenants and restrictions, establishing a procedure for assessing its members, and disbursing ... charges and assessments.

Clubhouse at Eagle Pointe Golf Resort (formerly The Pointe), courtesy of Eagle Pointe Golf Resort.

For the most part, PSA acts through its managing agent to perform these duties. It handles, for example, road maintenance, snow removal, general grounds maintenance, accounting services and repairs on the television system, all through contractors. PSA has no employees or equipment other than a television tower and antennae.

Caslon created two classes of membership in PSA as a means of maintaining control over the development process: class A consisted of the owners of units or residential lots while class B referred to the 1500 potential memberships held by Caslon. If all went as planned, Caslon would gradually relinquish control over PSA as well as ultimate financial responsibility [Caslon paid no dues but was to fund deficits in PSA's annual budget], such that PSA, which had high fixed maintenance and security costs, would become self-funding. In any event, by the terms of the Declaration of Covenants, Conditions and Restrictions (Declaration) Callon would be out of PSA by January 1, 1990.

However, by 1982, growth of the Pointe had stagnated. Only 344 units had been sold. Financial considerations caused Caslon's successor, Indun Realty, a subsidiary of Indiana National Corporation, to attempt to sell the development. A buyer for the entire project could not be found; but, the country club, 30 residential units, and the golf course were sold to Resort Management Association (RMA), a limited partnership formed by the directors. As part of the agreement to purchase, RMA became the managing agent of PSA.

Development at the Pointe remained slow. Kirtley became concerned that RMA's investment in the club could be devalued by the plans of potential purchasers of the remaining land and so entered into negotiations with Indun to purchase the undeveloped property at the Pointe. Once the purchase had been consummated, in December, 1982, Kirtley formed a partnership, Pointe Development Company (PDC), and conveyed the property to PDC. Indun assigned the 1500 PSA class B memberships to Kirtley who assigned them to PDC and elected appellants Kirtley, his wife Phyllis Kirtley and brother-in-law Pierson the new directors of PSA. PDC began making changes immediately to encourage the sale of additional units. Among the changes, <u>PDC sold tracts to builders and then diverted part of the purchase price to PSA to fund the deficit</u>.

Over time, discontentment grew among the unit owners who were unable to elect board members, had no say in PSA's decision-making, and were unable to exercise any control over PSA assessments or spending. As a consequence, a group of class A unit owners brought this action against the directors alleging a number of irregularities in the management of the Pointe. One of the points of contention concerns payment to RMA for mowing certain easements and other property shared with PSA. Another involves Kirtley's purchase and sale of television satellite equipment. The issues raised in this appeal are as stated hereafter.

...

III. Whether appellant Kirtley <u>breached a fiduciary duty to PSA by appropriating a corporate opportunity</u> when he upgraded the existing television reception system, provided PSA with satellite based cable television and sold the equipment he had purchased with a covenant not to compete to an independent cable company.

The question arises as a consequence of <u>Kirtley's dual role as developer and director/officer.</u> Kirtley wanted to furnish the development with certain amenities which would enhance the resort image and the desirability of the community overall. Television reception without an unsightly array of antennae was one amenity assured the Pointe residents by Caslon.

Caslon precluded individual unit owners from maintaining outside antennae through the Declaration, which encumbered the entire property making up the Pointe. Caslon then purchased and installed master antennae on developer-owned property, laid cable to the exterior of the units, sold the antennae and tower to PSA on contract at 8% interest, and granted PSA an easement to maintain the system. Hence, PSA owned equipment and provided off air television service to its members.

During the first year of the directors' ownership, it became apparent that the off air set up designed by Caslon was not meeting member expectations. Indun had contacted cable television purveyors to determine whether cable television could be provided members, many of whom were investors, at a rate they were willing to pay. Indun's research indicated that members would agree to a $5.00 per month increase in their assessment for cable television but the lowest proposal called for a $7.50 increase per month. After surveying the members to determine whether two-thirds of them would be willing to pay $5.00 per month for four cable channels, Kirtley took it upon himself to upgrade the system, purchasing top-of-the-line modulators, receivers, converters and satellite dishes.

Instead of selling the system to PSA as Caslon had done, Kirtley operated it himself.[1] Kirtley, through PSA, billed the unit owners at the agreed rate which was commercially reasonable and far below the prevailing market rate. Kirtley therefore had no conflict of interest in the provision of service itself which would render the transaction void or voidable. I.C. 23-7-1.1-61. *See also, Schemmel v. Hill* (1930), 91 Ind.App. 373, 169 N.E. 678.

PSA maintains, however, that Kirtley was obligated at the time he purchased the equipment and began operating the system to obtain the opportunity for PSA as PSA had his-

---

1. Art. II, § 3 of the Declaration reserves in the developer the right, but not the obligation, to convey to PSA such recreational facilities and other amenities as it deems desirable.

torically provided television reception service to its members. A corporate fiduciary may not appropriate to his own use a business opportunity that in equity and fairness belongs to the corporation. *Hartung v. Architects Hartung/Odle/Burke* (1973), 157 Ind.App. 546, 555, 301 N.E.2d 240, 243. *Tower Recreation, Inc. v. Beard* (1967), 141 Ind.App. 649, 652, 231 N.E.2d 154.

Guth v. Loft, Inc. (1939), 23 Del.Ch. 255, 5 A.2d 503 contains the classic statement of a corporate opportunity:

> When a business opportunity comes to a corporate officer or director in his individual capacity rather than in his official capacity, and the opportunity is one which, because of the nature of the enterprise, is not essential to his corporation, and is one in which it has no interest or expectancy, the officer or director is entitled to treat the opportunity as his own, and the corporation has no interest in it, if, of course, the officer or director has not wrongfully embarked the corporation's resources therein.... On the other hand, ... if there is presented to a corporate officer or director a business opportunity which the corporation is financially able to undertake, is, from its nature, in the line of the corporation's business and is of practical advantage to it, is one in which the corporation has an interest or a reasonable expectancy, and, by embracing the opportunity, the self-interest of the officer or director will be brought into conflict with that of his corporation, the law will not permit him to seize the opportunity for himself. And, if, in such circumstances, the interests of the corporation are betrayed, the corporation may elect to claim all the benefits of the transaction for itself, and the law will impress a trust in favor of the corporation upon the property, interests and profits so acquired.

5 A.2d at 510–11.

Briefly summarized, the undisputed evidence of record establishes that Kirtley learned of the need for cable television service in his capacity as director/officer of PSA; that PSA was in the business of providing services to its members, among them television reception; and that PSA was about to obtain cable television for its members when the opportunity to provide it arose. The factual issue seems to center upon whether PSA had the capacity both financially and technically to take advantage of the opportunity. The trial court made numerous findings of fact but ultimately found that PSA had the corporate and financial capacity to provide the service which Kirtley supplied in 1983 and 1984.

[handwritten margin note: Kirtley seized a "corporate opportunity" for himself.]

A complaint alleging a breach of fiduciary duty by converting a corporate opportunity to the fiduciary's benefit places upon the plaintiff the initial burden of establishing that the fiduciary attempted to benefit from a questioned transaction. Once that burden has been met, the law presumes fraud and the burden of proof shifts to the fiduciary to overcome the presumption by showing that his actions were honest and in good faith. *Dotlich*, 475 N.E.2d at 342.

In essence, the trial court found against Kirtley on the issue upon which he had the burden of proof. Hence, he may not question the sufficiency of the evidence to support the findings but may challenge the judgment only as being contrary to law. *Id.* On appellate review, we must accept the trial court's fact-finding, without reweighing the evidence or reassessing the credibility of witnesses, unless the facts and judgment are clearly erroneous. *State Election Bd. v. Bayh* (1988), Ind., 521 N.E.2d 1313, 1315. Indeed, the trial court will not be reversed upon the evidence unless there is a total lack of supporting evidence or the evidence is undisputed and leads only to a contrary conclusion. *Id.*; *Dotlich*, 475 N.E.2d at 453.

Although there is evidence tending to show that Kirtley purchased the satellite cable system believing at the time that PSA was unable to acquire the system itself without his financial assistance and that it would ultimately be in the best interests of the unit owners to keep assessments as low as possible in order to promote sales, the record also shows that the planned development concept undertaken by Kirtley contemplated developer deficit funding regardless of major capital expenditures financed by member assessments and reserves. The Declaration permits increases in annual assessments and special assessments for the purpose of defraying replacement costs of a capital improvement. PSA had 344 assessment paying members at the end of 1983. The evidence showed Kirtley made $10,367 in profit in the six months he operated the system. The equipment and engineering support cost him $13,157. With the increased assessment of $5.00 per unit per month approved by the directors for 1984, the system and costs of operation would have paid for themselves in less than a year. The effect upon unit sales as compared to the third party purveyor method surely would have been negligible. Moreover, it is undisputed and the trial court found that PSA's options simply were not explored or considered. Though Kirtley had no duty to finance the project, Caslon, a subsidiary of Indiana National Corp., was willing to finance the first system at a rate advantageous to the members. Another investor might have emerged had PSA actively sought one. As for technical expertise, Kirtley acquired it by paying for it. PSA could have taken the same approach. After all, it had Kirtley's skills, as a director and through RMA.

Kirtley argues that the trial court's special findings are inadequate to sustain the judgment because the court failed to state specifically the opportunity misappropriated by Kirtley and the resulting breach of fiduciary duty. This argument refers at least in part to PSA's contention that Kirtley misappropriated both a corporate opportunity and a corporate asset, namely, PSA's distribution rights when Kirtley exchanged, on behalf of PSA, the exclusive right to distribute cable television at the Pointe for a service contract with Pegasus on the same day he sold his equipment and a covenant not to compete for $120,000.

Whether a trial court's findings of fact are adequate depends upon whether they are sufficient to disclose a valid basis under the issues for the legal result reached in the judgment and whether they are supported by evidence of probative value. *Ridenour v. Furness* (1987), Ind.App., 504 N.E.2d 336, 339, *affirmed and vacated*, 514 N.E.2d 273; *College Life Insurance Co. v. Austin* (1984), Ind.App., 466 N.E.2d 738, 742. Although conclusions of law are useful in delineating the theories upon which the trial court relied, as a general rule they do not change our scope of review which is to affirm the trial court on any possible basis supported by the factual findings. *Havert v. Caldwell* (1983), Ind., 452 N.E.2d 154, 157.

The trial court's factual findings, all supported by the record, that PSA owned the off air system and cable distribution at the Pointe; that Kirtley purchased his system and began providing service while bids were being accepted and negotiations were being conducted; that Kirtley provided service without a written contract or disclosing to class A members that he was supplying the service to which they had subscribed; that the total cost of installation and amounts due signal providers was significantly less than yearly assessments or the balance of Indun funding after proper credits; and that the PSA directors gave no consideration to obtaining either authorization for a capital assessment to purchase the equipment or financing for the purchases as Caslon had done, disclose a valid basis for concluding that Kirtley appropriated an opportunity belonging to PSA by purchasing and placing in operation satellite receiving equipment. Profits generated from

Holding:

the operation of the system are benefits of the transaction itself which would have accrued to PSA had Kirtley not diverted the opportunity to himself.]

2. Board Member Indemnification

One might find indemnification covered not only in the CCRs or condominium documentation but in the by-laws or articles of incorporation as well. In the final analysis, indemnification is a matter of corporate law, and the statutory authorization is quite important. However, even if indemnification be permitted, there is a further question of whether or not it is adequately funded. What is the relationship between the indemnification requirement and the association's insurance coverage? Always ask whether there is officers and directors liability insurance, and if so, whether it is sufficient to fund the indemnification obligation.

Indemnification is a subject little discussed and more rarely fully understood. However, it is extremely important when problems arise. What can be subject to indemnification? Some actions resulting in liability may not be subject to indemnification for public policy or other reasons. What might these be, and how should an association protect itself in the event claims arise?

Consider the fact that an obligation to indemnify officers and directors may be a small victory if the association has insufficient funds to honor the commitment. How does one fund indemnification? What is the role of insurance and what types of insurance should be utilized? Who should be in a position to adjust claims when covered by insurance? Consider the different interests involved when an insurance defense counsel and an insurance adjuster are in control of a case concerning a challenge to rule making or other "governmental" activities of a community association. The insurance adjuster's primary objective will perhaps differ from the board's objective. An attorney skilled in general insurance defense may not approach the matter in the same way as one whose practice is in community association law. What might be the unintended negative consequences, and how do you deal with them?

Robinson v. La Casa Grande Condo. Ass'n

Appellate Court of Illinois

562 N.E.2d 678 (Ill. Ct. App. 1990)

KNECHT, J. John Robinson, administrator of Kristi Robinson's estate, appeals from an order of the Sangamon County circuit court dismissing count III of his complaint, which was against the individual managers of the board of managers of LaCasa Grande Condominium Association. This case raises issues of first impression involving the Condominium Property Act (Condominium Act) (Ill.Rev.Stat.1985, ch. 30, pars. 301 through 331) and the General Not For Profit Corporation Act of 1986 (Not For Profit Corporation Act) (Ill.Rev.Stat., 1987 Supp., ch. 32, par. 108.70 (eff. Jan. 1, 1987)). We conclude count III did not state a cause of action and affirm.

On March 27, 1987, Kristi Robinson, then 10 years old, drowned in a swimming pool at LaCasa Grande Condominiums in Springfield, Illinois. She and her family lived at LaCasa Grande, where her parents owned a condominium unit.

The plaintiff filed a wrongful death action on May 26, 1989. Count I was against Springfield Marine Bank as trustee of land trust No. 53-0135-0. Count II was against the LaCasa [*wrongful death action*]

Grande Condominium Association. Count III was against the defendants-appellees herein, Sidney Feller, Steven Orr, Rex Livingston, Gene Ferguson, Charles Schmitt, Janice Wolgamot, Angela Williams, and unknown members of the board of managers of LaCasa Grande. The individual named defendants as of March 27, 1987, were members of the board of managers, also known as the board of directors, of the LaCasa Grande Condominium Association. Count IV of Robinson's complaint was against Carol Dossett, a resident of LaCasa Grande.

Count III, at issue here, alleged the defendant managers managed the common elements of LaCasa Grande. They operated and maintained a swimming pool on the premises. The managers purportedly had a duty to maintain the pool in a safe condition and to exercise due care so the decedent could recreate in the pool. The complaint alleged the following acts of negligence, *i.e.*, omissions, by the individual managers: failure to employ lifeguards, failure to provide sufficient lifesaving devices, failure to properly supervise the pool, failure to warn the decedent of the inherent dangers of swimming, failure to keep a proper lookout for the decedent, failure to provide instruction and equipment for association members on the prevention of injury, failure to teach the decedent's parents how to use existing lifesaving equipment, failure to maintain the common areas of the condominium complex in violation of section 18.4(a) of the Condominium Act (Ill.Rev.Stat.1985, ch. 30, par. 318.4(a)), failure to reasonably accommodate the needs of handicapped unit owners (the decedent's parents are blind) (see Ill.Rev.Stat.1985, ch. 30, par. 318.4(q)), failure to anticipate the decedent's parents would use the pool, and failure to provide adequate safeguards for the decedent's safety. Count III also averred the defendants carelessly and negligently caused the decedent's death when they gave her or her parents a key to the pool facility when they knew or should have known injury or death would occur if the decedent used the facilities. Count IV of the complaint, against Dossett, alleged it was Dossett who gave the decedent a key to the pool area. Robinson sought damages in excess of $15,000 on behalf of the estate.

LaCasa Grande filed a motion to dismiss, pursuant to section 2-619 of the Code of Civil Procedure (Code) (Ill.Rev.Stat.1989, ch. 110, par. 2-619) on July 13, 1989, seeking to dismiss count II and the individual defendants-appellees to dismiss count III of the complaint. On the same day, LaCasa Grande also filed a motion to dismiss count II, and the individual defendants-appellees to dismiss count III of the complaint pursuant to section 2-615 of the Code (Ill.Rev.Stat.1989, ch. 110, par. 2-615). The parties briefed and argued the section 2-619 motion. The court deferred a hearing on the section 2-615 motion pending resolution of the section 2-619 motion. The circuit court sent a letter to the attorneys dated October 11, 1989, in which it stated the section 2-615 motion had been allowed. Believing this to be erroneous, the defendants filed a motion to clarify the record and, on November 14, 1989, the court corrected the October 11, 1989, docket entry and allowed the section 2-619 motion as to count III, without stating its reasons for granting the motion and denying the motion as to count II. The court found no just reason to delay enforcement of the order dismissing count III of the complaint with prejudice (the section 2-619 motion), and the plaintiff filed this appeal.

...

The first issue in this case, a narrow one, is whether the Not For Profit Corporation Act protects individual board members from liability, as asserted by defendants in the motion to dismiss and on appeal. Under the Condominium Act, the board of managers, through the association, has the powers and responsibilities of a not-for-profit corporation. (Ill.Rev.Stat.1985, ch. 30, par. 318.3.) The Not For Profit Corporation Act provides:

No director or officer serving <u>without compensation</u>, other than reimbursement for actual expenses, of a corporation organized under this Act and exempt, or qualified for exemption, from taxation pursuant to Section 501(c) of the Internal Revenue Code of 1954 [see 26 U.S.C. § 501(c) (1982 & Supp. IV 1986)], as amended, <u>shall be liable</u>, and <u>no cause of action may be brought</u>, for damages resulting from the <u>exercise of judgment or discretion</u> in connection with the duties or responsibilities of such director or officer <u>unless the act or omission involved willful or wanton conduct</u>...." (Emphasis added.) Ill.Rev.Stat., 1987 Supp., ch. 32, par. 108.70.

[handwritten margin note: Nonstock Corp. Act provides general safe-harbor for directors under certain areas]

To exempt the board of managers from liability under this statute, several prerequisites must be met. First, the directors must serve without compensation. Second, the corporation must be organized under the Not For Profit Corporation Act. Next, the corporation must be exempt from or qualify for exemption from taxation under Federal law. (See 26 U.S.C. § 501(c) (1982 & Supp. IV 1986).) If these requisites are satisfied, then the analysis moves to the final requirement: the conduct of the directors or officers must not have been willful or wanton.

The Not For Profit Corporation Act does not exempt the board of managers of La-Casa Grande from liability, though they evidently serve without compensation. LaCasa Grande <u>was not organized under the Not For Profit Corporation Act</u> in effect at the time (Ill.Rev.Stat.1973, ch. 32, sec. 163a *et seq.*). As shown by the record on appeal, its declaration of condominium states it was organized under the <u>Condominium Act</u> (Ill.Rev.Stat.1973, ch. 30, par. 301 *et seq.*).

LaCasa Grande is not exempt nor does it qualify for exemption from taxation under Federal law (26 U.S.C. § 501(c) (1982 & Supp. IV 1986)). To qualify for tax-exempt status, the common areas at LaCasa Grande would have had to be open to the general public.

[handwritten margin note: But, LaCasa Grande does not fall w/in these parameters.]

Significantly, in 1976 Congress amended the Internal Revenue Code to create a specialized exemption for '<u>homeowners associations</u>' Tax Reform Act of 1976, Pub. Law No. 94-455, 90 Stat. 1520 § 2101. The legislative history of the new section 528 reveals Congress' assessment of the then existing law and particularly the scope of the social welfare exemption provided by section 501(c)(4).

[']Under present law, generally a homeowner association may qualify as an organization exempt from federal income tax (under sec. 501(c)(4) of the Code) only if it meets three requirements. (Rev.Rul. 74-99, 1974-1 C.B. 131). First, the homeowner's association must serve a '<u>community</u>' which bears a reasonably, recognizable relationship to an area ordinarily identified as a governmental subdivision or unit. Second, it must not conduct activities directed to the exterior maintenance of any private residence. Third, common areas or facilities that the homeowner's association owns and maintains must be for the use and enjoyment of the general public.[']

H.R.Rep. No. 94-658, 94th Cong., 1st Sess. at 326–32; S.Rep. No. 94-938, 94th Cong.2d Sess. at 393, U.S.Code Cong. & Admin.News 1976, pp. 2897, 3222–28, 3821. *Flat Top Lake Association, Inc. v. United States* (4th Cir.1989), 868 F.2d 108, 111. See H.R.Rep. No. 658, 94th Cong., 1st Sess. at 326, reprinted in 1976 U.S.Code Cong. & Admin. News (90 Stat.) 2897, 3222, citing Rev.Rul. 74-99, 1974-1 C.B. 131.

Neither the condominium declaration nor the bylaws provide for opening LaCasa Grande's common areas to the public. Therefore, the Not For Profit Corporation Act does not apply to this case and it is unnecessary to discuss whether the allegations of conduct of the members of the board of managers suffice as willful and wanton. The Not For Profit Corporation Act does not exempt the board of managers from liability as they contend.

The second issue plaintiff raises is whether the members of the board of managers of La-Casa Grande, as directors of a corporation, can be held liable for negligent performance of their duties. The defendants argue Illinois case law holding corporate boards of directors are not liable for corporate action, inaction, and malfeasance should be applied to this case. The defendants claim they cannot be sued because the complaint "does not allege that any of the managers did anything outside of their capacity as directors of the corporation." In support of their claim they cite section 108.70 of the Not For Profit Corporation Act (Ill.Rev.Stat., 1987 Supp., ch. 32, par. 108.70(a)). As explained, the statute is inapplicable to this case.

The members of the board of managers cannot be liable for negligent performance of their duties. The Condominium Act specifically makes the members of the board of managers fiduciaries of the unit owners. (Ill.Rev.Stat.1985, ch. 30, par. 318.4.) The law in Illinois is that breach of a fiduciary duty is not a tort. The Illinois Supreme Court has regarded the breach of a fiduciary duty as controlled by the substantive laws of agency, contract and equity. (*Kinzer v. City of Chicago* (1989), 128 Ill.2d 437, 445, 132 Ill.Dec. 410, 414, 539 N.E.2d 1216, 1220.) Thus the members of the board of managers cannot be liable in tort for breaches of their fiduciary duties to the unit owners.

We note in *Wolinsky v. Kadison* (1983), 114 Ill.App.3d 527, 70 Ill.Dec. 277, 449 N.E.2d 151, the plaintiff sought damages from the condominium association, the board of managers, individually and as a board, the companies employed to manage the condominium complex, and an employee of the management company. The plaintiff owned a unit in the condominium and contracted to sell that unit and purchase another unit in the same condominium. The board of managers then notified her it was exercising its right of first refusal and the owner of the second unit terminated his contract to sell to the plaintiff. The plaintiff alleged that in exercising its right of first refusal, the board of managers acted without the affirmative two-thirds vote of the owners, as required by the condominium bylaws, thereby breaching its fiduciary duty. The circuit court granted the defendants' section 2-619 motion to dismiss.

The appellate court stated:

> A fiduciary relationship exists where there is special confidence reposed in one who, in equity and good conscience, is bound to act in good faith with due regard to the interests of the other. (Jones v. Eagle II (1981), 99 Ill.App.3d 64, 72 [54 Ill.Dec. 350, 356] 424 N.E.2d 1253, 1259.) We believe that all condominium association officers and board members become fiduciaries to some degree when they take office. (See P. Rohan and M. Reskin, Condominium Law and Practice sec. 10A.06 (1982); Hyatt & Rhoads, Concepts of Liability in the Development and Administration of Condominium and Home Owners Associations, 12 Wake Forest L.Rev. 915 (1976).) Because the association officers and board members owe a fiduciary or quasi-fiduciary duty to the members of the association, they must act in a manner reasonably related to the exercise of that duty, and the failure to do so will result in liability not only for the association but also for the individuals themselves. (See Hyatt & Rhoads, Concepts of Liability in the Development and Administration of Condominium and Home Owners Associations, 12 Wake Forest L. Rev. 915, 946 (1976).) (Wolinsky, 114 Ill.App.3d at 533–34, 70 Ill.Dec. at 283, 449 N.E.2d at157.)

The case is distinguishable because it was not a negligence action, as is this case. There the counts stated causes based on violation of bylaws, ordinance violation, and willful and wanton disregard for the condominium bylaws. We note, it is not clear the issue before us was raised by the parties in *Wolinsky.*

In 1984, the year following *Wolinsky,* the State legislature amended the Condominium Act, adding the clause within section 18.4 (previously quoted) which sets forth the board of managers' duty of care. Pub. Act 83-833, § 1, eff. July 1, 1984 (1983 Ill.Laws 5424); see Ill.Rev.Stat.1985, ch. 30, par. 318.4.

Also distinguishable is *Schoondyke v. Heil, Heil, Smart & Golee, Inc.* (1980), 89 Ill.App.3d 640, 44 Ill.Dec. 802, 411 N.E.2d 1168. The plaintiff sued the unit owners' association, the condominium association, and Tekton Corporation, not the individual members of the board of managers of the condominium association.

In summary, the Not For Profit Corporation Act does not protect the individual members of LaCasa's board of managers from liability because the statute is inapplicable. Nevertheless, we affirm the circuit court's order dismissing count III of the complaint because it failed to state a cause of action recognized in Illinois. As fiduciaries, the individual members of the board of managers were not and cannot be liable in tort for breach of their fiduciary duties. The circuit court of Sangamon County is affirmed.

Disposition

Affirmed.

Notes & Questions

1. *UCIOA.* UCIOA appears to apply a higher standard of care for developer-appointed directors over the obligations of unit owner elected directors. Specifically, UCIOA provides "in the performance of their duties, officers and members of the executive board appointed by the declarant shall exercise the degree of care and loyalty required of a trustee. Officers and members of the executive board not appointed by the declarant shall exercise the degree of care and loyalty required of an officer or director of a corporation organized under [insert reference to state non-profit corporation law]." UCIOA § 3-103(a). The official comment adds that developer control over the unit owners' property interests necessitates a higher standard. Do you agree with this statement? What reasons may justify a higher standard of care to developer-appointed directors? Or may argue against such a result? Conversely, why would a lower standard of care be necessary for homeowner board members?

2. *Revised Model Business Corporations Act.* In the traditional corporate setting, the standard of care more typically found is the standard of a reasonably prudent person. RMBCA § 35 states:

> A director shall perform his duties as director, including his duties as a member of any committee of the board upon which he may serve, in good faith, in a manner he reasonably believes to be in the best interests of the corporation, and with such care as an ordinarily prudent person in a like position would use under similar circumstances.

As more thoroughly reviewed in Chapter 5, actions of directors are often evaluated in accordance with the business judgment rule. In light of the fiduciary care imposed by several courts on the actions of developer-appointed directors, does the application of the business judgment rule provide any protection to such directors? In other words, is the business judgment rule still relevant in the developer-appointed board context? Explain. See, *e.g., Shinn v. Thrust,* 56 Wash. App. 827, 833, 786 P.2d 285, 289 (1990) (both the "good faith" standard and the "ordinary prudent person" standard applied under the heading of the Business Judgment Rule); *Schwarzmann v. Association of Apart-*

ment Owners, 33 Wash. App. 397, 402, 655 P.2d 1177 (1982) (directors are not liable so long as they demonstrate good faith efforts in the exercise of their duties); *Papalexiou v. Tower West Condominium*, 167 N.J. Super. 516, 520, 401 A.2d 280, 285 (1979) ("Courts will not second guess the actions of directors unless it appears that they are the result of fraud, dishonesty, or incompetency"); see also *Seafirst Corp. v. Jenkins*, 644 F. Supp. 1152, 1159 (W.D. Wash. 1986) (directors held not only to exercise good faith, but also to exercise such care as an ordinarily prudent person would exercise under like circumstances).

3. *Non-Profit statutes.* Among the states, there is general consensus that directors who serve without compensation in an association described in I.R.C. § 501(c) should not be liable to the association or its members for their actions unless their conduct constituted gross negligence or was intended to result in harm to the person asserting the claim. See, *e.g.*, N.Y. Not-For-Profit Corp. Law Section 720-a (1996) and Cal. Corp. Code §§ 5238–39. The rationale frequently asserted for providing such protections in the non-profit area is the need to encourage involvement of volunteers without the fear of becoming liable for their actions on behalf of such entities. Does this same rationale apply to homeowner association boards? Are such protections needed to elicit member involvement in community associations, which are not IRC 501(c) organizations?

4. *Board member indemnification.* As one commentator has remarked, the goal of indemnification is to "seek the middle ground between encouraging fiduciaries to violate their trust, and discouraging them from serving at all." Johnston, *Corporate Indemnification and Liability Insurance for Directors and Officers*, 33 Bus. Law. 1993, 1994 (1978). An uneasiness with the standard of care applied to officers and directors has led to a pervasive use of exculpatory clauses in governing documents which attempt to relieve the officers and directors from all but willful and wanton misconduct. See Robert G. Natelson, Law of Property Owners Associations, § 10.3.3 p.435 (citing 1B P. Rohan and M. Reskin, Condominium Law and Practice, Appendix C-4, at App. 216.39.), Cal. Civil Code § 1365.7; *Kelly v. Astor Investors, Inc.*, 106 Ill. 2d 505, 478 N.E.2d 1346 (1985) (exculpatory clause in the declaration limiting liability of the board to act of willful misconduct does not violate public policy); and, *Pederzani v Guerriere*, No. 930502A, Mass. Superior Ct., August 11, 1995 (recognizing the validity of exculpatory clauses limiting director liability for all but willful misconduct and bad faith). However, in California, such clauses may be held are invalid. (See *Cohen v. Kite Hill Community Ass'n*, 191 Cal. Rptr 209 (Cal. Ct. App. 1983) (blanket protection afforded by an exculpatory clause is unconscionable and unenforceable). However, California law does insulate volunteer officers and directors from tort liability based on ordinary negligence so long as insurance is maintained at certain minimum amounts.

5. *Corporate indemnification.* Indemnification provisions protect the director from personal liability for acts or omissions that have occurred. The extent of board member indemnification in the corporate context turns on the distinction between suits by and in the right of the corporation and suits by third parties. Oesterle, *Limits on a Corporation's Protection of its Directors and Officers from Personal Liability*, 1983 Wis. L. Rev. 513, 540 (1983). Where a suit is brought by a third party, most indemnification statutes provide liberal indemnification for third-party proceedings, including actions by the government and by shareholders. *Id.* at 541. Indemnification can extend to judgments, fines, amounts paid in settlement, and legal expenses if the director "acted in good faith and in a manner he reasonably believed to be in or not opposed to the best interests of the corporation." *Id.* In a criminal context, indemnification may extend where the director had "no reasonable cause to believe his conduct was unlawful." *Id.* Where the suit is brought by or in the name of the corporation, indemnification can extend only for legal expenses

if the case is settled. *Id.* at 542. If the director is found liable, indemnification for legal expenses is only permitted with court approval. *Id.* See also Cal. Corp. Code § 317(b) & (c) (Deering 1996); Del. Code Ann. Tit. 8 § 145(a) & (b) (1996); N.Y. Bus. Corp. Law §§ 722 & 723 (1996); and Revised Model Business Corp. Act § 8.51.

6. *Possible bases for board member liability.* Review *Smith v. Van Gorkam*, 488 A.2d 858 (Del. 1982), discussed in Chapter 5 which explains various bases for potential director liability, and *Stern v. Lucy Webb Hayes*, 381 F. Supp 1003 (D.D.C. 1974), which approaches the question of officer and director liability in the non-profit setting.

7. *Appropriate standards?* Negligent association management can prove to be more costly to individual unit owners than negligent management of a corporation is to its shareholders. Shareholders sell their stock in the market within a shorter time frame than owners can market and sell their unit. Because individual units in newer subdivisions are highly interdependent, association conduct has a substantial influence upon unit value. See Robert G. Natelson, Law of Property Owners Associations, § 10.3.3 p.437. Of course, not just the value of the unit is at stake, as paid assessments may be poorly utilized and wasted. On the flipside of this analysis, negligent association management may be more readily cured by voting in new directors at the next election and hope the "damage" is not beyond repair.

Despite the interrelationship between competent officer and director management and the value of the units themselves, some have argued that the standard of care applied to officers and directors in a non-profit setting should be relaxed. See Oleck, *Non-Profit Corporations, Organizations and Associations* p. 611–12 (1980). Essentially, the rationale for a relaxed standard is premised upon the fact that directors and officers of associations are typically unpaid, part-time volunteers, the reasonable care standard should be relaxed. Should the officers and directors of a community association be held to the same standard as their corporate cousins? Or will such standards result in fewer individuals who will volunteer to run for unpaid director positions?

Should the standard of care run along a sliding scale based on any special knowledge or skill possessed by the individual officer or director? See *Frances T. v. Village Green Owner's Ass'n, supra* (court held that directors are held to the same standard regardless of whether they possessed any special knowledge or experience, or lack thereof).

If you were about to run for a position as director of a community association in a jurisdiction that finds exculpatory clauses unconscionable, how would you protect yourself from potential future liability? How could one draft the community's governing documents to provide appropriate protections?

Do officers and directors who rely on indemnification provisions in the articles or by-laws accept the risk of repeal or modification of those provisions by whoever controls the votes? Are the provisions in effect at the time of the director's initial election irrevocable? Can a director take advantage of subsequent additions granting broader protections? How can a measure of certainty be supplied by careful drafting? See Oesterle, *Limits on a Corporation's Protection of its Directors and Officers from Personal Liability*, 1983 Wis. L. Rev. 513, 519 n.8 (1983) (noting that Loew's Corporation had inserted into its by-law the following indemnification provision: "[T]his section ... shall be deemed to be a contract between the Corporation and each director and officer who serves in such capacity at any time while [it] ... [is] in effect, and any repeal or modification thereof shall not affect any rights or obligations then existing ...").

8. *More on non-profit corporations.* State statutes often limit the liability of persons affiliated with non-profit corporations. The type and scope of protection varies, but most

statutes cover directors, officers, and unpaid board members. See James J. Fishman and Stephen Schwartz, *Nonprofit Organizations*, 199 (1995). See, *e.g.*, Alaska Stat. § 09.17.050(a); and Fla. Stat. Ann. § 617.0285(1). <u>The statutes generally do not protect individuals who engage in intentionally harmful behavior</u>; see, *e.g.*, Ariz. Rev. Stat. Ann. § 10-1017(D), Del. Code. Ann. Tit. 10 § 8133(a); <u>reckless or grossly negligent acts</u>, see Miss. Code Ann. § 9509-1(3)(a), N.J. Stat. Ann. § 2A: 53A-7.1(b); <u>or situations where the individual does not act in good faith,</u> see Minn. Stat. Ann. § 317A.257(1); N.D. Cent. Code §§ 32-03-44 to -45.

Problem

Let's revisit a problem raised in Chapter 5. Tony is a developer-appointed director on the condo board. Three directors are developer appointees, and two are owner elected. The board is considering the question of potential construction defects within several key components of the condominium. Transition of control is approaching, but because the statute of limitations is also nearing its expiration, the board feels that it must address these issues. Tony is concerned about personal liability and wonders whether he should withdraw from deliberations. If he does, at least one other appointee is likely to do so as well. He asks you for advice and a recommendation. You are counsel for the association. How do you respond? Does your response change as counsel for the developer?

Tony next asks about the statute of limitations and what affect it has on his actions and potential exposure. How do you respond? In addition, he asks whether in making his decision he may use knowledge acquired as VP-Construction of Developer. May he? What other issues should Tony consider?

"I get paid to be paranoid." Overheard at pay phone in Denver airport.

C. Members' Exposure to Liability

At the outset of this chapter, we noted that even though an association is held liable, its members, directly or indirectly, are ultimately responsible for satisfying the judgment. The association has limited resources, and such resources as it does possess are owned on behalf of its members. Thus, it is clear that there is some member obligation. The question is what the extent and nature of that obligation is.

The starting spot in this analysis is how the association pays. Obviously, an association which carries public liability insurance may be covered for any civil judgment. However, contractual disputes are generally not going to be covered by insurance, and often even in the presence of insurance, the limits on coverage are too low to satisfy the claims. What happens in the absence of insurance or when the claims exceed the insurance limits?

The second potential source for satisfying a judgment is the association's regular and special assessment income. Obviously, the result will be either an increase in charges against members or a decline in service to permit the diversion of funds to pay the judgment. What if the board does not impose assessments? Can a court order a special assessment to satisfy a judgment?

James F. O'Toole Company, Inc. v.
Los Angeles Kingsbury Court Owners Association

California Court of Appeal
23 Cal.Rptr.3d 894 (Cal. Ct. App. 2005)

VOGEL, J. A plaintiff obtained a judgment against a homeowners association. When the association failed to pay the judgment and refused to levy a special emergency assessment against its members, the plaintiff obtained an order appointing a receiver and compelling the association to levy the emergency assessment. The association appeals, claiming it cannot be ordered to impose an assessment and, inferentially, that the judgment never has to be paid. We reject the association's arguments and affirm the order.

FACTS

A.

After the common areas of the Los Angeles Kingsbury Court, a 46-unit condominium complex in Granada Hills, were damaged in the 1994 Northridge earthquake, the Los Angeles Kingsbury Court Owners Association hired an insurance adjuster, James F. O'Toole Company, Inc., to deal with the Association's insurer. The Association agreed to pay O'Toole 10 percent of the proceeds paid by its insurer but later refused to pay, notwithstanding that the Association received about $1.4 million in insurance proceeds. O'Toole sued the Association for breach of contract and won, and (in March 2002) a judgment was entered directing the Association to pay damages to O'Toole ($140,196.59) plus pre-judgment interest ($59,881.19), with post-judgment interest accruing at the rate of about $80 per day. The Association did not pay the judgment.

B.

In early 2003, O'Toole obtained a writ of execution, recorded an abstract of judgment and, by motion, sought an order directing the Association to assign to it both the regular and special assessments collected by the Association from its members.... The Association, in turn, filed a claim of exemption, asserting that all assessment income was needed for essential services and, therefore, exempt from execution. (Civ.Code, § 1366, subd. (c).)[2]

In May, the trial court agreed with the Association that its claimed expenses were essential, and that all *regular assessments* collected by the Association were exempt from execution. At the same time, the court held that O'Toole's judgment was an "extraordinary expense" within the meaning of subdivision (b) of section 1366, that the Association had "the power to levy an *emergency assessment* to satisfy [the] judgment," that the Association's general duty to maintain its property included a more specific duty to meet its legal obligations, that it was obligated to pay a valid civil money judgment entered against it, and that it was thus required to levy a "*special*" or "*emergency*" *assessment* to raise the money needed to pay the judgment. To that end, the court ordered the Association "to convene a meeting of the individual condominium owners ... to consider and provide for a meaningful emergency assessment so as to satisfy [O'Toole's] judgment."

---

2. Undesignated section references are to the Civil Code, primarily to the Davis-Stirling Common Interest Development Act, section 1350 *et seq*....

C.

The Association held a meeting in May but the members refused to impose an emergency assessment to pay O'Toole's judgment. O'Toole then filed a motion for an order directing the Association to levy a special emergency assessment or, in the alternative, for an order appointing a receiver to levy and administer a special emergency assessment. Over the Association's opposition, the trial court granted O'Toole's motion for the appointment of a receiver to levy and administer a special emergency assessment, then stayed its order to permit the Association to pursue this appeal....

DISCUSSION

Unless otherwise provided in a homeowners association's declaration of common interest development, the association is responsible for the repair and maintenance of the common areas. (§ 1364, subd. (a).) ... [T]he Los Angeles Kingsbury Court Owners Association's Declaration charges the Association with the duty to "maintain, repair, restore, replace and make necessary improvements to the Common Area so that the same are at all times in a first-class condition and good state of repair," and to "pay, out of the general funds of the Association, the costs of any such maintenance and repair...." After the Northridge earthquake, the Association took the first step but not the second, and the question now before us is whether the Association can be compelled to impose an assessment to obtain the money needed to pay for the work that was performed for the benefit of the Association and its members. For the reasons that follow, we answer the question affirmatively.

A.

The relationship between individual homeowners and the managing association of a common interest development is complex (*Lamden v. La Jolla Shores Clubdominium Homeowners Assn.* (1999) 21 Cal.4th 249, 266, 87 Cal.Rptr.2d 237, 980 P.2d 940), and their respective rights depend upon the nature of the particular dispute. Some years ago, in *Duffey v. Superior Court* (1992) 3 Cal.App.4th 425, 428–429, 4 Cal.Rptr.2d 334, the court observed that associations were sometimes treated as landlords (*Frances T. v. Village Green Owners Assn.* (1986) 42 Cal.3d 490, 499–501, 229 Cal.Rptr. 456, 723 P.2d 573 [association could be held liable for rape and robbery of individual owner who was not allowed to install additional lighting at time of crime wave]), sometimes as "minigovernments" (*Laguna Publishing Co. v. Golden Rain Foundation* (1982) 131 Cal.App.3d 816, 844, 182 Cal.Rptr. 813 [gated community could not discriminate among give-away newspapers]), sometimes as businesses (*O'Connor v. Village Green Owners Assn.* (1983) 33 Cal.3d 790, 796, 191 Cal.Rptr. 320, 662 P.2d 427 [condominium project with age restrictions ... was 'business' within the meaning of Unruh Civil Rights Act]), and sometimes as corporations (*Beehan v. Lido Isle Community Assn.* (1977) 70 Cal.App.3d 858, 865–867, 137 Cal.Rptr. 528 [board of directors' good faith refusal to take action against construction of house in arguable contravention of setback restrictions was protected by corporate business judgment rule]).

More recently, the Supreme Court has differentiated between (1) the situation where, for the sake of maximizing the value of the homeowner's investment, each individual owner has an economic interest in the proper management of the development as a whole, and the relationship between the owner and the association is analogous to that of a shareholder to a corporation, and (2) the situation where an individual owner who resides in the development has a personal, "not strictly economic," interest in the appropriate management of the development in a manner that will keep the property secure from risks of physical injury, in which sense the relationship is analogous to that between a tenant and landlord. (*Lamden v. La Jolla Shores Clubdominium Homeowners Assn., supra, ...*)

This case—where the homeowners' interests are strictly economic—is plainly one in which the relationship of the Association to the homeowners is akin to that of a corporation to its shareholders.

B.

We begin by rejecting the Association's contention that it is not required to levy a special emergency assessment to satisfy a civil judgment, and that the trial court had no power to order it to do so. As relevant, section 1366 provides:

(a) Except as provided in this section, the association shall levy regular and special assessments sufficient to perform its obligations under the governing documents and this title. However, annual increases in regular assessments for any fiscal year ... shall not be imposed unless the board has complied with [specified requirements].

(b) Notwithstanding more restrictive limitations placed on the board by the governing documents, the board of directors may not impose a *regular assessment* that is more than 20 percent greater than the regular assessment for the association's preceding fiscal year *or impose special assessments which in the aggregate exceed 5 percent of the budgeted gross expenses of the association for that fiscal year without the approval of owners,* constituting a quorum, casting a majority of the votes at a meeting or election of the association.... *This section does not limit assessment increases necessary for emergency situations.* For purposes of this section, an emergency situation is any one of the following:

(1) An extraordinary expense required by an order of a court.

(2) An extraordinary expense necessary to repair or maintain the common interest development or any part of it for which the association is responsible where a threat to personal safety on the property is discovered.

(3) An extraordinary expense necessary to repair or maintain the common interest development or any part of it for which the association is responsible that could not have been reasonably foreseen by the board in preparing and distributing the pro forma operating budget under Section 1365....

(c) Regular assessments imposed or collected to perform the obligations of an association under the governing documents or this title shall be exempt from execution by a judgment creditor of the association only to the extent necessary for the association to perform essential services, such as paying for utilities and insurance. In determining the appropriateness of an exemption, a court shall ensure that only essential services are protected under this subdivision....

(Emphasis added.)

... O'Toole performed his part of the bargain, and his judgment establishes that he is entitled to be paid for the work he performed for the Association. Although it is true, as the Association contends, that section 1366 does not *expressly obligate* it to impose a special emergency assessment to satisfy O'Toole's civil judgment, the statute most assuredly permits such an assessment in an "emergency situation," including a "situation" where an order of a court is entered in aid of enforcement of a judgment arising out of an extraordinary and unforeseeable expense necessarily incurred to repair the common areas following the Northridge earthquake.... Under the circumstances of this case, section 1366 permits the Association to impose a special emergency assessment to satisfy O'Toole's judgment.

To avoid this result, the Association claims the exemption created by subdivision (c) of section 1366 applies to special emergency assessments and thus prohibits the order made by the trial court. This argument fails for the simple reason that the subdivision (c) exemption applies only to regular assessments, not special or emergency assessments.... Section 1366 provides, "Regular assessments ... collected to perform the obligations of an association ... shall be exempt...."

C.

The Association contends the Legislature's rejection of a proposed amendment to section 1366 shows a legislative intent to prohibit the imposition of an assessment to satisfy a civil judgment. To the contrary, we believe the legislative history shows the opposite intent. [Discussion of legislative history omitted. — Eds.]

...

Quite plainly, the Legislature did exactly what it set out to do — it protected regular assessments to the extent necessary to insure that homeowners were not deprived of essential services, and at the same time protected the rights of judgment creditors (such as O'Toole) by allowing them to execute against an association's *special emergency* assessments and, where available, an association's *excess* (nonexempt) regular assessments. That is precisely what happened in this case, where the trial court *granted* the Association's request for an exemption covering *all* of its regular assessments and limited O'Toole's right of recovery to a fund to be created out of a *special emergency* assessment. [T]he legislative history defeats rather than supports the Association's position.

D.

We summarily reject the Association's remaining contentions.

First, the Association's refusal to impose a special emergency assessment was not a "business decision" of the sort to which the courts must defer under *Lamden v. La Jolla Shores Clubdominium Homeowners Assn., supra,* 21 Cal.4th 249, 87 Cal.Rptr.2d 237, 980 P.2d 940. Generously construed, the Association's refusal to levy a special emergency assessment is a simple refusal to pay a final judgment long since due. While that refusal may in some sense constitute a "business decision," it is not one to which a court must defer by refusing to enforce a valid judgment.

Second, these proceedings do not in any manner violate the homeowners' rights. The imposition of a special emergency assessment will not transform the homeowners into judgment debtors or otherwise make them personally liable for the debts of the Association. This was and will remain an action against the Association, not an action against the homeowners.... [T]he homeowners were not parties to the contract, and the contractor's contractual remedies had to be pursued against the Association, not the homeowners....

O'Toole is doing precisely what he is by law obligated to do. [He] has obtained a judgment against the Association, and is now compelling the Association to look to its members, the homeowners, to create a fund to pay the debt incurred for their common benefit. When the special assessment is levied, the homeowners will be liable to the Association, not to O'Toole, and it will be up to the Association to collect the money that is owed to it....

It follows that the trial court correctly ordered the Association to impose a special emergency assessment and, in light of the Association's refusal to do so, correctly decided to appoint a receiver to carry out the court's order. (Code Civ. Proc., §§ 187, 128, subd. (a)(4); ....

Notes & Questions

1. The provision in § 1366 defining an emergency situation to include an extraordinary expense required by an order of a court and all of subsection (c) were added in 2000. The court, in a portion of the opinion omitted above, described the background for the changes:

> According to the Assembly Committee on Housing and Community Development..., the bill was a response to an extremely unusual and complex problem arising out of the Northridge earthquake. A contractor sued a homeowners association for trade libel and interference with prospective business relations and won a $6.6 million judgment. A receiver was appointed, and he used the association's regular and special assessments to pay the contractor, leaving the association without any money to pay for its essential services. The Committee noted conflicting concerns about (1) the six million California residents who belong to homeowners associations and the effect on our housing market "if consumers become frightened to purchase condominiums and townhouses due to the potential personal risk," and (2) "the potential impact of whether contractors will shy away from conducting repairs if they are left with little remedy in the event a [homeowners association] breaches a contract." (Assem. Com. on Housing and Community Development, Analysis of Assem. Bill No. 1859 (1999–2000 Reg. Sess.) as amended Apr. 26, 2000, p. 5.)

Has the California legislature struck the right balance between protecting residents of common interest communities and protecting creditors of the association?

2. Another possible avenue for creditors is to levy execution on any property owned by the association. Why is this usually not a practical solution to the problem? In condominiums, the association may own no property; in other associations, the common property is usually subject to easements of use in all the community members. If the creditor took title to the common areas in a non-condominium community, could it charge user fees? Could it insist that the association continue to maintain them?

3. Is there anything individual lot or unit owners or their lenders can do to protect themselves from having to pay off, indirectly, liability incurred by the association?

4. In *O'Toole*, the law was clear that the owners were not directly responsible to the associations creditors. Is that always the case? We take up that question next.

1. Individual Liability

Owens v. Dutcher

Court of Appeals of Texas
635 S.W.2d 208 (Tex. Ct. App. 1982)

BROWN, J. This is an appeal by the Plaintiffs from a damage award by the court following a jury trial on a suit for property damages based on negligent tort.

We reverse and render.

Appellants (plaintiffs below) were tenants in a condominium unit in which a fire occurred causing extensive loss to their personal property.

Appellee (defendant below) was the owner of the condominium unit occupied by the appellants as lessees.

The fire began in the wiring which serviced an external light fixture in condominium "common elements" at the condominium known as Eastridge Terrace.

In addition to appellee, the appellants sued Eastridge Terrace Condominium Association, Joe Hill Electric Company, a class of owners of condominiums in Eastridge Terrace, and condominium developer, IHS-8 Ltd., for recovery of their damages. With the exception of appellee, all defendants had obtained a change of venue to Dallas County.

The case was tried before a jury which found that the light fixture in question was defective because of the lack of an insulating box in the exterior wall air space.

The jury further found that Eastridge Condominium Association knew the premises in question were unfit for habitation because of the absence of an insulating box at the light fixture and was negligent in failing to install an insulating box, both of which were found to have been proximate causes of the fire.

The jury found that the Association's negligence alone caused the fire which resulted in damage to the appellants' property in the amount of $69,150.00.

Following the jury verdict the trial court rendered judgment against appellee in the amount of $1,087.04, which represents appellants' damages multiplied by appellee's 1.572% *pro rata* undivided ownership in the common elements of the Eastridge Terrace Condominium.

An agreed statement of facts was filed with this court. The parties stipulated that the sole issue for determination is whether: the *pro rata* judgment rendered by the court is correct; or appellee is liable for the entire damages as appellants contend; or another rule of law should apply.

Appellants contend that the court erred in holding appellee liable only for the proportion of their damages that his undivided ownership in the common elements of the condominium bears to the total damages found by the jury. Appellants base their argument on case law, which provides that members of an association are jointly and severally liable for tortious acts caused by the acts and omissions of the association in the use of property submitted by the members of the association to the control of the association. They cite *Port Terminal Railroad Association v. Leonhardt*, 289 S.W.2d 649 (Tex.Civ.App.— Fort Worth 1956, no writ).

The condominium concept in Texas is the ownership of two estates merged into one, a fee simple ownership or leasehold in the unit occupied and a tenancy in common in the common elements. 11 Hous.L.Rev. 454, *The Condominium and the Corporation—A Proposal for Texas* (1974).

The Texas Condominium Act, V.A.C.S. art. 1301a, is silent on the issue of assessment of damages to a unit owner for injuries sustained by a third person caused by a latent, unknown and nondiscoverable defect in common elements where the condominium association, of which the unit owner is a member, is found to be negligent in maintenance of the common elements.

Therefore, it is left to this court to determine the extent to which individual unit owners may become liable to a third person for tortious conduct arising in the common areas of the condominium project.

Typically, a condominium consists of a single unit or apartment separately owned in a multiple unit structure or structures with common elements. V.A.C.S. art. 1301a sec. 2(d).

General common elements include the foundations, bearing walls and columns, roofs, halls, lobbies, stairways, and entrances and exits or communication ways. V.A.C.S. art. 1301a sec. 2(l)(2).

Individual owners maintain their own apartments, and an association obtains funds for the care of the common areas by charging dues and levying assessments on each apartment owner.

In the absence of a statutory limitation, there appears to be no escape-proof method of insulating the unit owners in a condominium regime from unlimited liability resulting from negligent maintenance and operation of these premises. Consequently, the risk of unlimited tort liability arising from injuries to third persons as a result of unsafe conditions in the common areas or conduct of common servants is great. Powell on Real Property, Part III, Vol. 4B sec. 633.25 (1976).

Many condominium statutes like Texas remain silent on the nature and extent of a unit owner's noncontractual liability. Legal observers therefore conclude that, as co-owners, participants would be jointly and severally liable for tortious conduct in connection with the project. Rohan, Real Estate Transactions-Condominium Law and Practice, Vol. 1 Part 3 sec. 10A.03 Unit Owner Liability (1979).

To avoid this harsh remedy other jurisdictions have enacted legislation which more equitably distributes liability among all members of the association.

The Federal Housing Authority Model Act is intended to guide persons interested in condominium legislation and is regarded by the FHA as the best framework within which to obtain the objectives of condominium ownership. Most statutes in accordance with the FHA Model Act provide that each apartment owner is entitled to an undivided interest in the common areas and facilities in the percentage expressed in the declaration, such percentage to be computed by taking as a basis the value of the apartment in relation to the value of the property. 15A Am.J.2d Condominiums and Co-Operative Apartments, sec. 33 (1976).

Ordinarily, the FHA suggested condominium bylaws contain provisions regarding maintenance, repair, and replacement of common property.

The statutes which follow the FHA Model Act generally provide that the association of apartment owners is responsible for the maintenance and repair of the common elements.

The general rule is that the individual unit owner is liable for torts committed within that portion of his unit over which he has exclusive possession and control and each apartment owner is liable equally with other unit owners for any tort liability growing out of defective construction or maintenance of the common areas and facilities. 15A Am.J.2d Condominiums and Co-Operative Apartments, sec. 43 (1976).

Case law on this issue is sparse and the only case brought to our attention which has attempted to deal with a similar problem involves an action by an owner of a condominium unit for personal injuries he received because of equipment negligently maintained by the condominium association in a common area of the condominium project. *White v. Cox*, 17 Cal.App.3d 824, 826, 95 Cal.Rptr. 259 (1971). There the court stated that control of a condominium is normally vested in a management body over which the individual member has no direct control. It was held in that case that a condominium possessed sufficient aspects of an unincorporated association to make it liable in tort to its members. The majority in that opinion did not consider a unit owner's liability in tort to third persons.

Several provisions in the Texas Condominium Act provide for proportionate contributions by unit owners on a *pro rata* basis of ownership, but none provide directly for assessment of tort liability. They include V.A.C.S. art. 1301a, sec. 7 which states that ownership of common elements is to remain undivided in common among all unit owners; and sec. 19 which states that a condominium co-owner is the beneficiary of whatever insurance may be procured, and that coverage is in percentages or fractions provided in the declaration. Section 20 provides that where reconstruction is impractical, indemnity is figured *pro rata* to co-owners as their interest may appear. Section 21 states that affected co-owners contribute in proportion to the percentage of ownership in the common elements to any uninsured reconstruction cost.

By reciting in detail what we have found relative to the issue before this court, we also reveal clearly what we have found—*i.e.* there is neither case law nor legislation limiting liability in a tort action brought by a third party against a condominium association and its members, each of whom owns his individual unit and all of whom are owners in common of the common elements. Accordingly, we hold that each unit owner, as a tenant in common with all other unit owners in the common elements, is jointly and severally liable for damage claims arising in the common area.

Appellants' point of error is sustained. Judgment reversed and rendered for appellants for $69,150.00, total amount of the damages found by the jury and the amount for which there was prayer, plus legal interest thereon from date of the judgment of the trial court, and all costs.

Reversed and Rendered.

Dutcher v. Owens

Supreme Court of Texas
647 S.W.2d 948 (Tex. 1983)

RAY, J. This is a case of first impression concerning the allocation of liability among condominium co-owners for tort claims arising out of the ownership, use and maintenance of "common elements." The defendant was found to be vicariously liable for the homeowners' association's negligence. The trial court ordered that the plaintiffs recover from the defendant an amount based upon the defendant's proportionate ownership in the condominium project. The court of appeals reversed in part the judgment of the trial court, holding "that each unit owner, as a tenant in common with all other unit owners in the common elements, is jointly and severally liable for damage claims arising in the common elements." 635 S.W.2d 208, 211. We reverse the judgment of the court of appeals and affirm the trial court's judgment.

. . .

By an agreed statement of facts filed with the court of appeals, the parties stipulated that the sole issue for determination on appeal was whether a condominium co-owner is jointly and severally liable or is liable only for a *pro rata* portion of the damages. Tex.R.Civ.P. 377(d).

In enacting the Texas Condominium Act (the Act), Tex.Rev.Civ.Stat.Ann. art. 1301a, the Texas Legislature intended to create "a new method of property ownership."[1] 1963 Tex.Gen.Laws, Ch. 191, §26 at 512. A condominium is an estate in real property consisting of an undivided interest in a portion of a parcel of real property together with a separate fee simple interest in another portion of the same parcel. In essence, condominium ownership is the merger of two estates in land into one: the fee simple ownership of an apartment or unit in a condominium project and a tenancy in common with other co-owners in the common elements. *Scott v. Williams*, 607 S.W.2d 267, 270 (Tex.Civ.App.—

-----

1. Condominium ownership is a tenure unknown at common law. Provisions for a form of condominium ownership can be found in the Roman civil law and the Napoleonic Code. 4B Powell on Real Property (Part III) PP 599, 633.1 *et seq.* (1976).

Texarkana 1980, *writ ref'd n.r.e.*); Tex.Rev.Civ.Stat.Ann. art. 1301a; see also *White v. Cox*, 17 Cal.App.3d 824, 95 Cal.Rptr. 259, 45 A.L.R.3d 1161 (1971); Comment, "The Condominium and the Corporation—A Proposal for Texas," 11 Hous.L.Rev. 454 (1974).

"General common elements" consist of, *inter alia,* the land upon which the building stands, the "foundations, bearing walls and columns, roofs, halls, lobbies, stairways, and entrances and exits or communication ways; ... [a]ll other elements of the building desirable or rationally of common use or necessary to the existence, upkeep and safety of the condominium regime, and any other elements described in the declaration...." Tex.Rev.Civ.Stat.Ann. art. 1301a, §2(l), subsections (1), (2) & (7). An individual apartment cannot be conveyed separately from the undivided interest in the common elements and *vice versa. Id.* §9.

A condominium regime must be established according to the Act. The declaration must be filed with the county clerk, who must record the instrument in the Condominium Records. Once the declarant has complied with the provisions of the Act, each apartment in the project is treated as an interest in real property. *Id.* §§3, 4, & 7. Administration of the regime is established by the Act. *Id.* §§13, 14 & 15.

The condominium association or council is a legislatively created unincorporated association of co-owners having as their common purpose a convenient method of ownership of real property in a statutorily created method of ownership which combines both the concepts of separateness of tenure and commonality of ownership. The California Supreme Court has concluded that "the concept of separateness in the condominium project carries over to any management body or association formed to handle the common affairs of the project, and that both the condominium project and the condominium association must be considered separate legal entities from its unit owners and association members." *White v. Cox*, 95 Cal.Rptr. at 262.

Given the uniqueness of the type of ownership involved in condominiums, the onus of liability for injuries arising from the management of condominium projects should reflect the degree of control exercised by the defendants. We agree with the California court's conclusion that to rule that a condominium co-owner had any effective control over the operation of the common areas would be to sacrifice "reality to theoretical formalism," for in fact a co-owner has no more control over operations than he would have as a stockholder in a corporation which owned and operated the project. *White v. Cox*, 95 Cal.Rptr. at 263. This does not limit the plaintiff's right of action. The efficiency found in a suit directed at the homeowners' association and its board of directors representing the various individual homeowners, as well as any co-owner causally or directly responsible for the injuries sustained, benefits both sides of the docket as well as the judicial system as a whole.

Such a result is not inconsistent with the legislative intent. While the Act creates a new form of real property ownership, it does not address the issue of the allocation of tort liability among co-owners. Nevertheless, we are guided in our decision by the other provisions in the Act which appear in *pari materia*, and which proportionately allocate various financial responsibilities. For example, the Act provides for *pro rata* contributions by co-owners toward expenses of administration and maintenance, insurance, taxes and assessments. *Pro rata* provisions also exist for the application of insurance proceeds. Tex.Rev.Civ.Stat.Ann. art. 1301a, §§15, 18, 19, & 20.

Respondents have cited us to two bills submitted in the legislature in 1981.[2] The bills, which did not pass, included provisions for re-apportionment of liability on a *pro rata* basis.

---

2. House Bills 439 and 2233.

Inasmuch as each bill involved a complete revision of the Act, we cannot draw inferences of the legislature's intent from the failure of the bills to pass. Any such inference would involve little more than conjecture. The legislative history of the Act is so scant that the most that can be said is that the Act is silent as to the matter, and hence the legislative intent is unknown. *Cf. Marmon v. Mustang Aviation, Inc.*, 430 S.W.2d 182, 186 (Tex.1968).

The theories of vicarious and joint and several liability are judicially created vehicles for enforcing remedies for wrongs committed. Justified on public policy grounds, they represent a deliberate allocation of risk. *See Newspapers, Inc. v. Love*, 380 S.W.2d 582, 588–89 (Tex.1964); *Landers v. East Texas Salt Water Disposal Co.*, 151 Tex. 251, 248 S.W.2d 731, 733 (1952); W. Prosser, *Law of Torts*, § 69 at 459 (4th ed. 1971).

Texas follows the rule that statutes in derogation of the common law are not to be strictly construed. Tex.Rev.Civ.Stat.Ann. art. 10, § 8. Nevertheless, it is recognized that if a statute creates a liability unknown to the common law, or deprives a person of a common law right, the statute will be strictly construed in the sense that it will not be extended beyond its plain meaning or applied to cases not clearly within its purview. *Satterfield v. Satterfield*, 448 S.W.2d 456, 459 (Tex.1969); see also 3 C. Sands, *Sutherland Statutory Construction* § 61.02 (4th ed. 1973). Since the Act is silent as to tort liability, we are dealing with rights and liabilities which are not creatures of statute but with the common law, which is our special domain. Hence, the rule we have reached is not a usurpation of the legislative prerogative. To the contrary, it is one reached in the public interest.

We hold, therefore, that because of the limited control afforded a unit owner by the statutory condominium regime, the creation of the regime effects a reallocation of tort liability. The liability of a condominium co-owner is limited to his *pro rata* interest in the regime as a whole, where such liability arises from those areas held in tenancy-in-common. The judgment of the court of appeals is reversed and the judgment of the trial court is affirmed.

Reversed.

———

Ruoff v. Harbor Creek Community Association

California Court of Appeals, Fourth District
13 Cal.Rptr.2d 755 (Cal. Ct. App. 1992)

SONENSHINE, J. Martha Ruoff and Russell Ruoff, individually and as Martha's conservator, challenge summary judgments entered in favor of various defendants in a suit arising out of Martha's slip and fall on a stairway in the common area of the 152-unit Harbor Creek complex. Martha sustained catastrophic injuries. According to appellants, whose statement is uncontradicted by respondents, on August 9, 1988, Martha fell backwards, landing at the bottom of the stairs, her foot wedged in a gap between the side of the building and the edge of the stairs. Comatose and bleeding, she was taken to Mission Hospital and admitted to the intensive care unit (ICU) where she was treated for multiple skull fractures. Due to complications, she underwent partial amputation of her left thumb, index and middle fingers. A month after the accident, a percutaneous endoscopic gastrostomy (insertion of a feeding tube in the stomach) was performed. The following month, a lumbo-peritoneal shunt was inserted in her spine for draining fluids. Martha remained in a coma. A tracheotomy tube inserted at the time of the accident was not removed for two and one-half months. Released from Mission Hospital after 107 days in the ICU, Martha was transferred to the Rehabilitation Institute of Santa Barbara, where she underwent a course of treatment and therapy until, after eight months, the Ruoffs were no longer able to pay for the institutional care. Martha now lives at home, where her 72-year-old husband takes care of her. She is unable to bathe, dress or feed herself. She is incontinent in bladder and bowel. Her diagnosis and prognosis include "probable permanent memory loss, gait disturbance, incontinence and other severe neurological abnormalities." Her only communication is "babble." She will require 24-hours-a-day care for the remainder of her life. Her medical expenses to date exceed $750,000.

The summary judgment argument of the defendants, individual owners of Harbor Creek condominium units, is based on the following undisputed facts: (1) They are tenants-in-common of the common areas of the complex, each owning an undivided 1/152 interest; (2) they have delegated control and management of the common areas to their homeowners association (HOA), which has no ownership interest in the property; (3) the HOA has liability insurance of $1 million; and (4) it is authorized to assess its members for *pro rata* contribution if a judgment exceeds policy limits. The owners argue that for these reasons, (a) Civil Code section 1365.7[2] should be read to immunize them from civil liability, and (b) departure from the common law rule of property owners' liability would serve the greater good and work no substantial detriment to injured third persons.

The Ruoffs contend the immunity of section 1365.7 is expressly limited to volunteer HOA officers or directors and cannot be expanded judicially to include others. The owners, as tenants-in-common in the common area, are subject to the same nondelegable duties to control and manage their property as are other property owners. The trial court agreed with the owners. We agree with the Ruoffs and reverse.

…

II

The summary judgments were granted on the basis that, as a matter of law, the individual condominium owners could not be held liable for injuries sustained in the common area of the Harbor Creek complex. The record establishes that the decision involved no determination of whether the owners had exercised due care; it involved only a determination that no duty existed.[4]

In the usual case, an owner or occupier of real property must exercise ordinary care in managing the property. (§ 1714, subd. (a).) The duty of care is owed to persons who come on the land (see generally, *Rowland v. Christian* (1968) 69 Cal.2d 108, 70 Cal.Rptr. 97, 443 P.2d 561), and ordinarily it is nondelegable. (*Swanberg v. O'Mectin* (1984) 157 Cal.App.3d 325, 331–332, 203 Cal.Rptr. 701.) In the case of a condominium complex, section 1365.7 immunizes a volunteer officer or director of an association managing a common interest residential development from civil tort liability if (1) the injury-producing negligent act or omission was performed within the scope of association duties,

---

2. Civil Code section 1365.7 is part of the Davis-Stirling Common Interest Development Act (Civ.Code, div. 2, pt. 4, ch. 1, § 1350 et seq.). The Act provides conditional immunity from tort damages to "a volunteer officer or director who resides in the common interest development either as a tenant or as an owner of no more than two separate interests in that development." See discussion, post.

All further statutory references are to the Civil Code unless otherwise specified.

4. The court's order granting summary judgment states: "[T]he court finds as a matter of law that the aforementioned defendant homeowners did not breach any duty owed to the plaintiffs herein." The record establishes that no factual evidence regarding the owners' acts or omissions was before the court. The owners relied on the HOA's liability policy, its internal rules, and declarations of individual owners who said they did not exercise control of the common areas.

was in good faith, and was not willful, wanton, or grossly negligent, and (2) the association maintained at least $1 million of applicable general liability insurance if the development exceeds 100 separate interests.[5] (§ 1365.7, subds. (a)(1), (2), (3) and (4)(B).) Subdivision (b) allows the volunteer officer or director to recover actual expenses incurred in executing the duties of the position without losing the statutory immunity. But subdivision (c) excludes from the definition of volunteer any officer or director who, at the time of the negligent act or omission, received compensation as an employee of statutorily-designated persons or entities. Under subdivision (d), the association itself does not enjoy immunity for the negligent acts or omissions of its officers or directors. Finally, subdivision (e) expressly limits the immunity of section 1365.7 to the designated persons: "This section shall only apply to a volunteer officer or director who resides in the common interest development either as a tenant or as an owner of no more than two separate interests in that development." We find this to be a comprehensive and extraordinarily clear immunity statute.

Statutory interpretation presents a question of law. (*Schuhart v. Pinguelo* (1991) 230 Cal.App.3d 1599, 1607, 282 Cal.Rptr. 144.) The owners contend that in section 1365.7, the Legislature intended to immunize them from liability for tortious acts or omissions in the management and control of the commonly-held property. Under established rules of statutory construction, we may not read such an intention into this unambiguous statute. "It is axiomatic that in the interpretation of a statute where the language is clear, its plain meaning should be followed. [Citation.]" (*Lubin v. Wilson* (1991) 232 Cal.App.3d 1422, 1427, 284 Cal.Rptr. 70; *see also Forrest v. Trustees of Cal. State University & Colleges* (1984) 160 Cal.App.3d 357, 362, 206 Cal.Rptr. 595.) Moreover, we must attach significance to every word of a statute. (*See McLarand, Vasquez & Partners, Inc. v. Downey Savings & Loan Assn.* (1991) 231 Cal.App.3d 1450, 1454, 282 Cal.Rptr. 828.) If we were to read the statute as the owners urge, we would need to read out the express limitation of immunity of subdivision (e). We are not permitted or inclined to do that.[6]

We also reject the owners' convoluted argument that by reverse implication, based on a reading of *Davert v. Larson* (1985) 163 Cal.App.3d 407, 209 Cal.Rptr. 445, section 1365.7 endows them with a right to delegate their duties of control and management of the common areas and thus escape liability to which they would otherwise be subjected under established law.

In *Davert,* the Court of Appeal, in a case of first impression, reversed a summary judgment in favor of a defendant property owner who asserted "he owed no duty of care to plaintiffs as a landowner because he took title to his interest in the property subject to a recorded declaration of covenants, conditions and restrictions delegating exclusive control over the subject property to [a property owners' association]." (*Davert v. Larson, supra,* 163 Cal.App.3d at p. 409, 209 Cal.Rptr. 445.) The owner claimed his ownership interest of 1/2500 was too small to provide a basis for liability and he personally exercised

---

5. The Harbor Creek complex contains 152 units and there is no dispute that the number of separate interests exceeds 100.

6. When it enacted section 1365.7, the Legislature was also aware of the Uniform Common Interest Ownership Act of 1982, but did not adopt it. Under section 3-107 of the Uniform Act, an HOA is responsible for maintenance of the common areas of a condominium complex, unless the HOA's declaration provides otherwise. Under section 3-113, individual unit owners are immune from civil liability for injuries occurring in the common areas if the HOA maintains sufficient liability insurance meeting certain standards and naming each condominium owner as an insured party with respect to liability based on his or her ownership of the common areas. Obviously, the Legislature and the authors of the Uniform Act took different paths.

no control over the management of the property. (*Id.* at p. 410, 209 Cal.Rptr. 445.) The appellate court noted with approval the conclusion of "a leading commentator" that "individual owners of common areas in California are liable to third parties for torts arising in common areas. [Citation.]" (*Id.* at p. 411, 209 Cal.Rptr. 445.) In its discussion, the court alluded to the fact that existing California law did "not require insurance to protect third parties in the case of common area torts." (*Id.* at p. 412, 209 Cal.Rptr. 445.) Thus, "relieving individual owners in common of liability would eliminate any motivation on the part of any party to exercise due care in the management and control of commonly owned property and could leave third parties with no remedy at law." (*Ibid.*) The *Davert* court concluded: "[T]enants in common of real property who delegate the control and management of the property to a separate legal entity should not be immunized from liability to third parties for tortious conduct." (*Ibid.*) The owners say *Davert* means that if the duty of control and management is delegated to a separate legal entity and sufficient liability insurance is available for injured parties, then the reason for imposition of liability on the individual owners evaporates. The argument continues: Since section 1365.7 was enacted after publication of *Davert*, and requires HOAs to maintain certain minimum levels of liability insurance, the Legislature must have been reacting to *Davert* and intending to eliminate common law rules regarding property owners' liability.

The argument is crafty, but unavailing. In the first place, when we are urged to find that a statute is intended to silently abrogate an established rule of law, we must heed the Supreme Court's admonition that "it should not 'be presumed that the Legislature in the enactment of statutes intends to overthrow long-established principles of law unless such intention is made clearly to appear either by express declaration or by necessary implication.' [Citation.]" (*Theodor v. Superior Court* (1972) 8 Cal.3d 77, 92, 104 Cal.Rptr. 226, 501 P.2d 234; see also *McLarand, Vasquez & Partners, Inc. v. Downey Savings & Loan Assn.*, *supra*, 231 Cal.3d at p. 1455, 282 Cal.Rptr. 828.) In the second place, the owners' reliance on *Davert* for negative inferences is off the mark. The clear holding of *Davert* is that tenants in common who delegate control and management of the property remain jointly and severally liable for tortious acts or omissions causing injury to third persons. We do not deem the court's observation about the wisdom of retaining landowners' liability where ownership is shared to be judicial advice that a tenant in common can buy his or her way out of liability by purchasing insurance for the property manager.[7]

III

The owners attempt to justify the summary judgment with a number of other policy-type arguments to illustrate why we should rewrite section 1365.7. They assert the HOA's liability insurance of $1 million is sufficient to take care of the needs of the Ruoffs, who would therefore suffer no detriment if liability were not imposed on the individuals. But even if we agreed with the proposition in the abstract — and we do not — the issue of sufficiency of the insurance policy would be a question of fact, inappropriate for determination by summary judgment. (Code of Civ.Procedure, § 437c, subd. (c).)[8]

The owners also contend that because the HOA can make assessments against the association members for *pro-rata* shares of any judgment exceeding the policy limits, immunity for the individuals will not work any hardship on the Ruoffs. But, as the

---

7. We also reject the owners' half-hearted assertion that section 1365.7 violates equal protection under the federal and state constitutions. The matter warrants little discussion....

8. In light of the apparent irremediable nature of Martha's injuries and the continuing accrual of medical expenses which are already approaching the $1 million policy limit, the owners appear to be blowing smoke when they claim the insurance is "sufficient."

Ruoffs astutely observe, "[p]roblems with this approach abound,"[9] and "the power to assess is not the panacea Defendants argue." Indeed, it might prove to be a wholly illusory remedy. The owners assert that under the HOA declaration of covenants, conditions and restrictions, the HOA is incorporated as a nonprofit mutual benefit corporation, therefore the members are entitled to immunity under Corporations Code section 7350, subdivision (a).[10] They argue that because the HOA is a corporation, the Ruoffs must look solely to the corporate assets. The problem with this contention is that the record does not establish the fact of incorporation.[11] Therefore, we express no opinion as to its merits.

The judgments in favor of the owners are reversed and the matter remanded for further proceedings in accordance with this decision. The Ruoffs shall recover their costs on appeal.

Reversed and Remanded.

Retrospective and Observations

The Association's Perspective

David Fuller was hired by the association's insurance company when the Ruoffs sued the developer, the association, and individual homeowners at this project. Ms. Ruoff sustained injuries when she slipped and fell on a stairway in the common area at Harbor Creek. However, Judge Mandel said at the trial that he would not hear the case until the homeowners being sued had been served. Mr. Ruoff turned to Mr. Fuller in court and asked him if he would provide the names and addresses of the homeowners, and Mr. Fuller, of course, said he would not. Mr. Ruoff had to resort to discovery in order to find the individual homeowners' names. It cost Mr. Ruoff $35,000 to $40,000 to serve the individual homeowners, and the case settled for $35,000 regarding individual homeowners.

Mr. Fuller said that the case caused a great deal of consternation in California. The association filed a cross-claim asking the court for summary judgment that tenants-in-common are not responsible for maintaining commonly owned property. The court resorted to common law in California and said that tenants-in-common *are* responsible for maintaining such property.

It is Mr. Fuller's opinion that the California legislature panicked in response to this case. It enacted insurance legislation which requires any project which

---

9. The Ruoffs pose apt questions: "[W]hat happens to the current owners who sell their units before judgment? What happens to a unit owner whose individual insurance company denies coverage for an assessment in contract, but does [sic] over third party injuries occurring in common areas? What about those who sell after judgment, but before the assessment? What happens to a future unit owner whose individual insurance company denies coverage because the 'loss' preceded the commencement of the policy?"

10. Corporations Code section 7350, subdivision (a) relieves members of a nonprofit mutual benefit corporation from personal liability for the debts, liabilities or obligations of the corporation.

11. The only proof of incorporation offered is a copy of article II, section 2.01 of the HOA declaration, stating: "Organization of Association. The Association is or shall be incorporated under the name of HARBOR CREEK COMMUNITY ASSOCIATION, as a corporation not for profit under the Nonprofit Mutual Benefit Corporation Law of the State of California." This is hardly proof. Moreover, the various separate statements of undisputed facts in support of the summary judgment motions do not contain any reference to incorporation and member immunity. Finally, we do not even know if such a defense is at issue in the lawsuit because we have not been provided with a copy of the answers filed by the defendants.

has less than 150 units must carry 1.5 million dollars worth of liability insurance. In addition, all of an association's insurance money must be depleted before a plaintiff can sue individual owners.

Mr. Fuller noted that the case eventually settled with a big settlement figure (he believes it was over seven figures). The settlement was paid by the original developer because California has strict liability regarding construction defects.

The Ruoff's Perspective

After Mr. Mullen was substituted, he hired a title insurance company to copy all of the homeowners' deeds so they could determine who owned units in the project at the time of the accident. They then amended the complaint to add individual homeowners as additional defendants. At that point, the judge was not aware of the involvement of individual homeowners, nor did he know that Mullen's firm had been substituted. At the next status conference, which the judge held every Friday, the judge was overwhelmed when 30 homeowners' defense lawyers appeared at the conference. The judge ordered that the status conference be continued two weeks later and ordered Dennis Mullen to appear personally.

In light of the judge's reaction, Mullen prepared a memorandum of law establishing the homeowners' liability. That memorandum, "The Voluntary Settlement Conference Statement," explained to the judge all rights and remedies for the orderly conduct of the trial. When the continued status conference began, 50 lawyers attended. The judge accused Dennis Mullen of being a charlatan. Mr. Mullen asked the judge if he had read their memorandum of law, and the judge responded that he had not and would not. At the end of that status conference, the judge concluded that he would choose 8 or 9 volunteers to file motions for summary judgment on behalf of the individual homeowners named as defendants and said that he would grant those motions. He precluded any more discovery on the part of the plaintiff, and said that no more defendants would be added to the suit. Of course, he got his volunteers.

Dennis Mullen said his firm did a "Cadillac job" in responding to the motion for summary judgment. He cited the Davis-Stirling Act and felt he had a unique application of that Act. He tried to convince the judge that common law applied, specifically because California chose not to adopt a uniform act and instead adopted the Davis-Stirling Act which applied to this situation. He maintained that under the Davis-Stirling Act, owners in this project owned the common area as tenants-in-common, and therefore they were all liable.

The judge granted summary judgment, and Mullen appealed. Pending appeal, the judge allowed discovery. The appeal took almost four years, and the case was overturned. The judge then allowed time to serve individual homeowners. That time period, five months, was all the time that Mr. Mullen had to prepare for the trial.

Because there was no eyewitness and because Martha Ruoff could not recall anything that happened during her fall and injury, Mullen hired a physicist, a mathematician, a human factor engineer, a safety engineer, and a cost benefit analyst who prepared a computerized re-creation of the fall. That one minute video cost $10,000. At one point in the appeal, Mr. Mullen had spent $270,000 on costs advanced for experts.

Because of the short timeframe in preparation for trial, the plaintiffs also hired a voluntary settlement judge during the time they were taking depositions. At one of the settlement conferences, Mullen's partner happened to overhear a lawyer say that he had an excess insurance policy. It was discovered that the developer had a $5,000,000 excess policy and that the bank which was the lender in this project but was more involved than merely as a lender had a $15,000,000 excess policy.

Mullen was extremely upset by this news and by what he alleged to be intentional perjurious representation by two prior law firms involved in the case and their clients. He filed a motion for sanctions against those lawyers and their clients. While those motions were under advisement by the court, the case settled for what he remembers as slightly under $4,000,000. The greatest contributor to the settlement was the developer, the second greatest contributor was the bank, the individual homeowners and the homeowners association contributed an equal amount to the settlement, and the contractors and architect contributed a total of $100,000.

On the last day of the settlement conference when things were looking grim, the defendants' lawyers asked Mullen if he would accept the figure of under $4,000,000. Mr. Mullen agreed to settle for that amount and told opposing counsel they had until noon the following day to obtain their clients' approval. The following morning, Mr. Mullen received a call from one participant who told him that he could raise $2,000,000 but could not raise the additional $50,000 which was required of him. Mr. Mullen described that moment as a time when he thought he was going to die of a heart attack. He responded in anger to the participant threatening to take the case to trial unless he heard from him before noon that day offering $2,050,000. At five minutes before noon, the participant called to say he would pay the $50,000 as well.

Once the settlement was resolved, Mr. Mullen requested that the probate court appoint separate lawyers for Martha Ruoff and her husband in order to divide the settlement between them. Mr. Ruoff had filed a loss of consortium claim. The probate court decided that Martha Ruoff would receive 60% of the Ruoff's portion of the settlement, and Mr. Ruoff would receive 40%.

Martha Ruoff is still alive, and she has made significant improvements since the accident. Stairwells throughout the entire complex have not been fixed. Mr. Mullen said there are no handrails in the stairwells. They have what he calls a guardrail with no room to put one's hand.

Notes & Question

In a construction defects suit, the builder-declarant cross claimed against the individual unit owners claiming equitable indemnification and seeking damages for the owners' alleged underpayment of assessments. What were the results? See *Lauriedale Assoc. Ltd. v. Wilson*, 9 Cal. Rptr. 2d 774 (Cal. Ct. App. 1992), later in this Chapter.

Restatement (Third) § 6.15 Liability Of Members For Association Torts

The rule of joint and several liability does not apply to tort liability of members arising out of holding the common property as tenants in common. The liability of members is limited to their proportionate share determined by their share of liability for common expenses.

UCIOA § 3-111. Tort & Contract Liability ...

(a) A unit owner is not liable, solely by reason of being a unit owner, for any injury or damage arising out of the condition of use of the common elements....

(b) An action alleging a wrong done by the association, including an action arising out of the condition or use of the common elements, may be maintained only against the association and not against any unit owner....

2. Obligation to Pay for Judgment Challenging Board Actions

Ocean Trail Unit Owners Ass'n, Inc. v. Mead

Supreme Court of Florida
650 So. 2d 4 (Fla. 1994)

WELLS, J. We have for review *Mead v. Ocean Trail Unit Owners Association, Inc.*, 638 So. 2d 963 (Fla. 4th DCA 1993), in which the Fourth District Court of Appeal certified the following question as being of great public importance:

Whether a condominium association can enforce a special assessment imposed to pay judgments, attorney's fees and costs incurred in connection with a lawsuit brought by unit owners against the association in which the association's purchase of real property was invalidated as an unauthorized act and subsequently rescinded.

We have jurisdiction pursuant to article V, section 3(b)(4), Florida Constitution. We answer the certified question "yes."

Having accepted jurisdiction to answer the certified question, we may review the entire record for error. *Lawrence v. Florida E. Coast Ry.*, 346 So. 2d 1012 (Fla.1977). Based on our review, we conclude that the district court erred in reversing the final judgment entered by the circuit court. We therefore quash the decision of the Fourth District and remand to the district court with instructions to affirm the final judgment.

The facts giving rise to this action involve a purchase of property by Ocean Trail Unit Owners Association, Inc. (the Association), which the Fourth District held invalid as beyond the powers of the Association's board of directors. See *Ocean Trail Unit Owners Association, Inc. v. Levy*, 489 So. 2d 103 (Fla. 4th DCA 1986). The board thereafter filed a claim against its insurance carrier and imposed a $500 special assessment upon the unit owners to cover the costs associated with the invalid purchase. Specifically, the funds obtained through the special assessment were used in part to pay the $194,079.37 judgment for attorney fees, which was rendered against the Association in favor of the attorney representing the 150 unit owners who successfully opposed the purchase. The remaining special assessment funds were used to pay judgments rendered against the Association and in favor of unit owners who sued to recover the original $1,500 assessment, which the Association used to make the invalid purchase.

Several months after the special assessment was imposed, the Association settled its claim against its insurance carrier. The Association also obtained $630,000 as a result of a rescission action arising from the invalid purchase. These funds, in addition to the funds obtained from the special assessment, were used to reimburse all unit owners for the original purchase assessment.

Prior to the full reimbursement, however, the respondents brought suit as representatives of the unit owners for a declaratory judgment that the $500 assessment was unauthorized. The respondents also challenged the amount of the insurance settlement and disbursement of the proceeds, claiming that the selective disbursement of the proceeds to only those unit owners who sued the Association for a refund of the purchase assessment constituted a breach of the Association's fiduciary duty.

In evaluating the propriety of the assessment, the district court concluded that assessments used to pay expenses are proper only when the expenses are incurred in carrying out the authorized powers of an association. The court reasoned that a board of directors cannot be unauthorized to do an act and, at the same time, authorized to impose assessments to pay for the consequences of the unauthorized act. *Mead,* 638 So. 2d at 964. Because the judgments were incurred from the litigation attributable to the unauthorized purchase of the property, the district court determined that these expenses were not "properly incurred by the association for the condominium." *Id.* (quoting § 718.103(8), Fla.Stat. (1991)).[1] The district court's decision erroneously ignores that the special assessments were collected in order to pay valid judgments against the Association.

The circuit court, in its final judgment, found that the Association's board of directors reasonably believed that this special assessment was necessary to pay these judgments and protect the Association's common properties and facilities from execution and levy. Accordingly, the trial court concluded, and we agree, that the judgments were a common expense for which the Association had the authority to impose an assessment. Every condominium in Florida is created pursuant to chapter 718, Florida Statutes. § 718.104, Fla.Stat. (1987).[2] A condominium is created by recording a declaration of condominium in the public records of the county where the condominium is to be located. § 718.104(2), Fla.Stat. (1987). A condominium association operates the condominium pursuant to the association's bylaws, which must be included as an exhibit in the recorded declaration. § 718.112(1)(a), Fla.Stat. (1987).

A condominium association has the power to make and collect assessments, and to lease, maintain, repair, and replace the common elements. § 718.111(4), Fla.Stat. (1987). Specifically, the association can make assessments against unit owners to pay for common expenses. § 718.115(2), Fla.Stat. (1987). Common expenses of the association include "the expenses of the operation, maintenance, repair, or replacement of the common elements, costs of carrying out the powers and duties of the association, and any other expense designated as common expense by this chapter, the declaration, the documents creating the condominium, or the bylaws." § 718.115(1), Fla.Stat. (1987).

Condominium associations may also sue or be sued with respect to the exercise or nonexercise of their powers. § 718.111(3), Fla.Stat. (1987). This process necessarily contemplates that judgments may be entered against the association. A judgment against an association renders the property of the association subject to execution and levy.

In the condominium form of ownership, protection of the common elements is vital. Each unit owner owns a proportionate undivided share of the common elements appur-

---

1. Formerly section 718.103(7), Florida Statutes (1987).
2. The 1987 version of the Condominium Act applies in this case because the special assessment was imposed in March 1988.

tenant to the unit. §718.103(10), (24), Fla.Stat. (1987). If assessments cannot be enforced to pay judgments which have been entered against the association and which can be executed against the association property, the condominium could be destroyed, to the detriment of all the owners.

The Association undoubtedly recognized this problem when it included section 6.5 in its declaration of condominium. Section 6.5 provides that any lien upon any portion of the common areas shall be paid by the association as a common expense. The provision is clearly authorized by chapter 718, which provides a condominium association with the powers to manage and operate the condominium property, including the power to maintain the common elements.

The district court's decision, which approves nonpayment of assessments by owners, leaves the Association property vulnerable to levy and execution of the judgments. The court essentially evaluated the judgments against the Association and decided whether an assessment to pay the judgments could be enforced on the basis of its evaluation of the reasons for the judgments. However, it is the existence of the judgments that imperils the Association property. The judgments' existence alone, therefore, authorizes the assessment and necessitates its enforcement.

As set forth in the final judgment entered by the trial court, the reason why the judgments were entered should not determine whether the assessments can be enforced. Rather, a unit owner's duty to pay assessments is conditional solely on whether the unit owner holds title to a condominium unit and whether the assessment conforms with the declaration of condominium and bylaws of the association, which are authorized by chapter 718, Florida Statutes.

The unit owners elect the officers and directors of the association, and those officers and directors have a fiduciary duty to the unit owners. §718.111(1)(a), Fla.Stat. (1987). Accordingly, if the officers or directors act in an unauthorized manner, the unit owners should seek a remedy through elections or, if factually supported, in an action for breach of fiduciary duty. The owners' remedies do not include failing to pay an assessment to protect against a judgment which has been lawfully entered against the association.

Scudder v. Greenbriar C Condominium Association, Inc., 566 So. 2d 359 (Fla. 4th DCA 1990), and *Rothenberg v. Plymouth # 5 Condominium Association*, 511 So. 2d 651 (Fla. 4th DCA), *review denied*, 518 So. 2d 1277 (Fla.1987), on which the unit owners and the Fourth District rely, are clearly distinguishable. The courts in these cases merely determined whether a particular expenditure was proper. The decisions did not involve lawful judgments rendered against the associations for unlawful expenditures and therefore do not compel the decision rendered by the Fourth District in this case.

The trial court's final judgment was also correct with respect to the remaining issues in this case. The insurance settlement and disbursement of proceeds did not require court approval. The settlement was within the discretion of the officers and board of directors acting for the association in managing and operating the condominium property.

It is so Ordered.

KOGAN, J., concurring in part and dissenting in part. I cannot agree with the majority that the Condominium Act sanctions an assessment that would have the effect of forcing unit owners who prevail in an action against the condominium association for unauthorized acts to pay their own judgments. I agree with the court below that a condominium association's board of directors cannot be unauthorized to do an act and at the same time be authorized to impose assessments to pay for the consequences of the unauthorized act. *Mead v. Ocean Trail Unit Owners Association, Inc*, 638 So. 2d 963, 964 (Fla. 4th DCA 1993). The judgments and other expenses incurred by the Association in defending the purchase of the adjoining property are directly attributable to what was determined to be an unauthorized act and, therefore, cannot be considered expenses "properly incurred by the association for the condominium." § 718.103(7), Fla.Stat. (1987). Thus, I cannot agree that expenses so incurred are common expenses that the Association could defray by assessment. I believe the Condominium Act supports this conclusion.

It is clear that the Association is authorized to impose assessments on unit owners for the payment of "common expenses." § 718.103(1), .111(4), .115(2) Fla.Stat. (1987). It is also true that section 718.115(1), Florida Statutes (1987), defines common expenses to include expenses designated as such in the condominium documents and Ocean Trail's condominium documents designate judgments as common expenses. However, it is equally clear that powers granted a condominium association in the condominium documents must be consistent with the Condominium Act. *Towerhouse Condominium, Inc. v. Millman*, 475 So. 2d 674, 676 (Fla.1985); *Rothenberg v. Plymouth No. 5 Condo. Ass'n*, 511 So. 2d 651, 651 (Fla. 4th DCA), *review denied*, 518 So. 2d 1277 (1987); § 718.111(2), Fla.Stat. (1987). As noted by the district court, section 718.103(7), defines "common expenses" as "all expenses and assessments which are *properly incurred by the association for the condominium.*" (Emphasis added). Thus, reading section 718.115(1) *in pari materia* with section 718.103(7), an expense designated as a "common expense" in the condominium documents must be "properly incurred by the Association for the condominium" before the expense can be considered a "common expense" for assessment purposes. I agree with the court below that an expense is not properly incurred if it is incurred in defending an unauthorized act of the Association.

It is undisputed that the purchase of the adjoining property was an unauthorized act. If the Association is allowed to enforce an assessment to pay judgments obtained by the unit owners, plus any costs incurred in defending the unauthorized purchase, the unit owners will effectively be paying for the unauthorized act. Allowing the judgment assessment also would have the effect of forcing the prevailing unit owners to pay their own judgments. I do not read the Condominium Act to sanction such an assessment.

I also must reject the Association's argument that the assessment at issue should be upheld because its board of directors acted in good faith, based on the advice of counsel, when it committed the original unauthorized act of purchasing the adjoining property. Although the proposed good faith standard has appeal, I can find no authority for such a standard in the Condominium Act.

The Association's good faith proposal is particularly unworkable in light of section 718.303(1)(e), Florida Statutes, (1993). Although this provision is not controlling in this case,[3] it seems to militate against application of a good faith standard in this context and lends support to my conclusion that judgments resulting from unauthorized acts of a condominium association should not be considered common expenses. Section 718.303(1)(e) was amended in 1991 to provide that a prevailing unit owner in an action between the unit owner and the condominium association may recover, in addition to a reasonable attorney's fee, amounts necessary to reimburse the owner for assessments levied by the association to fund the expenses of litigation. Ch. 91-103, § 14, Laws of Fla. This provision does not address the situation at hand. Rather, it appears only to apply where the assessment to fund litigation is levied before an adverse judgment has been en-

---

3. The pertinent amendments to section 718.303(1)(e) became effective January 1, 1992. Ch. 91-103, § 28, Laws of Fla.

tered against the Association. Thus, once the action that is the subject of the litigation is found to be unauthorized, the amendment provides a vehicle for the prevailing unit owner to obtain reimbursement for assessments that were levied to fund the litigation. The statute makes no provision for retention of an assessment that was imposed to defray litigation expenses where the litigation arose as the result of a good faith act on the part of the directors. Based on my reading of the Condominium Act, where, as here, unit owners challenge an act of an association as unauthorized, the association may levy an assessment to fund the litigation, as long as there has not been a determination that the challenged act is unauthorized. Until such determination, expenses incurred defending the challenged act are "properly incurred by the association for the condominium." § 718.103(8), Fla.Stat. (1993). However, once the underlying action is held unauthorized, any litigation expenses incurred as a direct result of the unauthorized act are no longer properly incurred common expenses that can be defrayed by assessment. Thus, under the current statutory scheme, if an assessment to fund litigation was levied during the litigation, a prevailing unit owner is entitled to reimbursement of the assessments. 718.303(1)(e). After the challenged act is found to be unauthorized, the Association is without authority to enforce assessments to pay litigation expenses that were incurred in defending the unauthorized act.

I recognize that the current statutory scheme does not control this case. However, I believe my construction of the current scheme lends support to my conclusion that under the 1987 version of the Act, the Association was without authority to enforce the judgment assessment at issue here. There is no reason to believe that the amendment to section 718.303(1)(e) was intended to provide for the reimbursement of an otherwise proper assessment. Rather, it is more likely that this amendment simply was intended to provide an efficient way for a prevailing unit owner to recover assessments that became improper once it was determined that the assessments were incurred in defending or pursuing an unauthorized act.

Accordingly, I would answer the certified question in the negative and approve that portion of the decision under review finding the special assessment improper. However, I agree with the majority that that portion of the decision below disapproving the insurance settlement and disbursement of those proceeds must be quashed because those matters were within the discretion of the Association's officers and board of directors and did not require court approval.

Notes & Questions

1. *Commentary.* Absent an express statutory provision, most commentators have assumed that unit owners would be held jointly and severally liable for association wrongs. See Donald L. Schriefer, *Judicial Action and Condominium Unit Owner Liability: Public Interest Considerations*, 1986 U. Ill. L. Rev. 255 (citing 4B R. POWELL, REAL PROPERTY § 633.25 (2)); 1 P. ROHAN & M. RESKIN, CONDOMINIUM LAW AND PRACTICE, § 10A.03 (1982); John T. Even, *The Administration of Insurance for Condominiums*, 1970 U. Ill. L. Rev. 204, 216; William K. Kerr, *Condominium—Statutory Implementation*, 38 St. John's L. Rev. 1, 17 (1963); Lawrence, *Tort liability of a Condominium Unit Owner*, 2 Real Est. L. J. 789, 797–98 (1974); Patrick J. Rohan, *Perfecting the Condominium as a Housing Tool: Innovations in Tort Liability and Insurance*, 32 Law & Contemp. Probs. 305, 308 (1967). Even where an incorporated association is formed to manage the community, that entity may be treated as an agent of the individual unit owners with each owner as a principal. As a result, the unit owners would be held jointly and severally li-

able in contract and tort for judgments relating to management of the common property. Condominiums and Cooperatives § 43 15 Am. Jur. 2d. Recent dialogue on the subject includes recommendations for judicially created limits on unit owner liability. See Note: *Condominium Unit Owner Tort Liability: Owens v. Dutcher*, 35 Baylor L. Rev. 189 (1983).

2. *UCIOA.* UCIOA requires actions to be brought against the association and not the individual unit owners for wrongful actions of the association. UCIOA § 3-111. See Donald J. Schriefer, *Judicial Action and Condominium Unit Owner Liability: Public Interest Considerations,* 1986 U. Ill. L. Rev. 255, 256 (association wrongs include actions in connection with the general management and maintenance of the complex). When an association is found liable in such matters, liability insurance generally provides the first line of protection for unit owners. Under UCIOA Section 3-113, the association is required to maintain insurance on both individual units and common elements at a rate no less than 80% of the actual cash value of the insured property. Should the insurance fail to cover the judgment, a lien can attach only against individual units, subject to release where the individual unit owner pays his or her proportionate share of the total liability up to the value of the unit. The unit owners' liability is ultimately limited to the value of their units plus their *pro rata* share of any insurance premiums and general maintenance costs already incurred. Only where the judgment exceeds the value of the total insurance plus the equity of the unit owners will the plaintiff not fully be compensated. See, Schriefer, *supra,* at 259. Note that this provision does not, however, protect the unit owner from his own acts or omissions or liability stemming from occurrences within the privately owned unit.

3. *Tenancy in common.* In *Davert v. Larsen*, 209 Cal. Rptr. 445 (Cal. Ct. App.1985), a unit owner with a 1/2500 interest in the common property was held liable in an negligence action brought by an individual whose car struck a horse which had escaped from the property. Tenants in common cannot escape liability by transferring control of the property to a separate legal entity. *Davert's* adherence to common law, however, may have stemmed from the absence of a required insurance minimum to protect third parties under the law of California at the time. Like UCIOA, the present California Civil Code, Section 1365.9 (1997), limits the liability of unit owners if a certain minimum amount of liability insurance covers the common areas. See also 39 A.L.R. 4th 98 (1985); 15A Am. Jur. 2d, *Condominiums and Cooperative Apartments,* § 43 (1996 Cumm. Supp. p.354.)

4. *Statutory Schemes.* Like UCIOA, Georgia law requires plaintiffs to sue the association rather than the individual unit owners for association wrongs. The judgment then constitutes a lien against the common property. The association, in turn, can then place a lien on individual units if unit owners fail to pay the necessary assessments to cover their share of the liability O.C.G.A. § 44-3-106, 107. Georgia also requires a fixed amount of liability insurance. O.C.G.A. § 44-3-106, 107. Accordingly, courts need not assess the reasonableness of the insurance actually procured. Also, because the primary lien attaches to the association property, judgment lien creditors need not deal with multiple unit owners to enforce their liens as is the case under the UCIOA. O.C.G.A. § 44-3-106, 107; see also Miss. Code Ann. §§ 89-9-1 to -37 (1996) and N.J. Stat. Ann. §§ 46:8B-16 (West 1996) (providing indirect liability of unit owners through association assessments for common expenses).

Alabama caps unit owner liability at the owner's percentage interest in the common areas, and provides that in no event may an owner's liability be greater than the value of the unit. Alabama does not require insurance coverage. Ala. Code § 35-8-12 (1996). Although these statutes have different requirements, generally, they limit liability to the value of the privately owned unit and will prevent a judgment lien creditor from pursuing other assets of the unit owners. D. Schriefer, *Judicial Action and Condominium Unit Owner Liability: Public Interest Considerations,* 1986 U. Ill. L. Rev. 255, 262.

Note however that at least five states allocate liability according to the condominium unit owners' proportionate interest in the common area while providing no ultimate cap on liability. These states include Alaska, Colorado, Connecticut, Idaho, and Kentucky. *Id.* These states also do not require the association to maintain any insurance, and the judgment lien creditor can pursue other assets of individual unit owners. *Id.* Still other states provide no statutory guidance for unit owner liability. *Id.*

Statutory treatment of unit owner liability reveals three main trends: (1) capped apportionment with mandatory liability insurance; (2) capped apportionment without insurance; (3) straight apportionment of liability. If you were a unit owner, which would you prefer? Which scheme has the least appeal for plaintiffs?

5. *Member liability for association debts.* Typically, members of non-profit corporations are not personally liable for the liabilities of the corporation. See N.J. Stat. Ann. § 15A:5-25 (West 1996) ("members of a non-profit corporation shall not be personally liable for the debts, liabilities or obligations of the corporation"). However, association members may be individually liable for any unpaid assessments that they may lawfully owe.

Does incorporation really shield individual unit owners from liability? Unit owners remain personally liable to the association for assessments validly imposed. A judicial lien against association property will likely require assessments to prevent the association's management and maintenance from being impaired. Such an assessment would constitute a common expense. While the corporate shield may be "stripp[ed] away" through indirect assessments of judgments, would the unit owners nevertheless be protected by the various statutory schemes? Compare Robert G. Natelson, Law of Property Owners Associations, § 8.4.2 (1989), and Donald. L.Schriefer, *Judicial Action and Condominium Unit Owner Liability: Public Interest Considerations,* 1986 U. Ill. L. Rev. at 255, 262–265.

6. *Unincorporated associations.* If a community association is unincorporated, contractual liability of the members may exist under the general rule that members of unincorporated associations are principals on all duly executed contracts of the association. 15A Am. Jur. 2d, *Condominiums and Cooperatives* § 43. A degree of protection, however, may arise where courts regard the unincorporated association as a separate legal entity. See *White v. Cox,* printed *supra.*

7. *The cost of litigation: a prevailing homeowner's Pyrrhic victory?* In *Ocean Trail Unit Owner's Ass'n v. Mead,* unit owners were forced to pay the costs of the association's litigation even though they prevailed. Since *Ocean Trail,* the Florida statute has been amended. Section 718.303(1) now provides that a unit owner who prevails in a suit against his or her association is entitled to reimbursement for assessments levied to fund the association's litigation expenses. While this amendment may treat individual, victorious unit owners more favorably than those in *Ocean Trail,* what happens if a significant number of unit owners are in the prevailing party to the litigation? Should the assessment burden be shouldered only by those unit owners who did not join the proceedings? How can revised Section 718.303(1) be applied given the language of Section 718.116(9)(a) of the Florida code, which requires all unit owners to be excused from paying their share of assessments or none at all? See Mark F. Grant, Howard D. Cohen, and Manual R. Valcarcel, *Ocean Trail Unit Owners Ass'n, Inc. v. Mead: Democracy or Tyranny—The Supreme Court of Florida Properly Finds in Favor of the Condominium Board,* 20 Nova L. Rev. 513, 527 (1995).

Problems

1. Revisit the board meeting of Seven Oaks Condominium Association, Inc., at the end of Chapter 8. Based upon what you have studied in this Chapter, what new issues and legal principles do you see? How does the material in this Chapter change your overall evaluation of the meeting and of the legal issues you identified?

2. You have succeeded in your fondest employment dream and hold a prestigious clerkship for a well-respected judge. At your regular morning meeting with the judge today, she asked you whether the court could order a special assessment against all of the owners in the community association defendant in the wrongful death case currently pending in her court. She was concerned that the association's assets would be insufficient to satisfy a judgment, and there appeared to be inadequate insurance as well. How do you advise her?

D. Representative Capacity of Association

In almost every community association case, a threshold issue is whether the association can bring the action on behalf of its members or whether one or more members must, on their own, prosecute the case. Why do you think this might be such a critical issue? What might the bases be to permit the community association to bring an action?

As you learned in Chapter 3, standing involves both a question of the power to bring an action (namely the power to sue and be sued) as well as the question of the right to assert the claim. As corporations, community associations clearly have the right to sue, and this same right is extended in most if not all states to unincorporated associations. Thus the first question can be readily answered. What about the second?

For several reasons, a developer defendant will likely raise the defense that the community association may not prosecute a construction defect case. First, you should understand the objective. If the association brings the case, it has the assessment stream to fund the litigation, it has the association structure as a separate entity as a shield for the individual members, and it has the administrative stability of its governance structure to make the difficult process of case management more tractable. If, conversely, the association does not bring the case, some homeowner or homeowners must pay the costs and carry the administrative load while affected by the psychological pressure of litigation cost and risk (including the potential for counterclaims in the personal capacity). Obviously, this makes the plaintiff's position more difficult, and it is a standard defensive strategy to challenge the association's right to assert a claim against the developer or other party.

Upon what basis may an association have the right to represent homeowners on litigation matters? When might it not? Why might the standing issue be resolved differently in the case of a condominium association versus a homeowners association in litigation over common area defects? If the community association acting through its board of directors and in accordance with the will of the majority of the members decides to prosecute or to settle a case, what about the interests of those who would do otherwise? Who should set policy and how? How do you address cases which concern the individually owned property or limited common elements? An interesting final thought deals with the size of the association and whether size does or should have any bearing on the ability to represent the owners in litigation. When and under what circumstances might association size matter?

Del Mar Beach Club Owners Ass'n, Inc. v.
Imperial Contracting Co., Inc.

Court of Appeal of California
176 Cal. Rptr. 886 (Cal. Ct. App. 1981)

WEINER, J. Plaintiff, Del Mar Beach Club Owners Association, Inc. (Association) appeals judgments of dismissal in favor of all defendants.

The principal questions are whether the Association, created to acquire and hold title to property included in a planned development pursuant to Business and Professions Code section 11003 has standing to maintain this action, and if so, whether it can state a cause of action for strict liability against defendants as "manufacturers" of retail housing.

As we will explain, we conclude the Association has standing and has stated a cause of action for strict liability against the developer-builder of the project. We also decide the Association cannot state a cause of action for strict liability against the architects and engineers. We dispose of the judgments accordingly.

GENERAL AND PROCEDURAL BACKGROUND

Before discussing the procedural history, it may be helpful to first identify the participants and to describe the commercial setting giving rise to this litigation.

Association is the managing entity and owner of land and buildings of the Del Mar Beach Club, a planned development (see Bus. & Prof. Code, § 11003), consisting of approximately 192 units located on a scenic bluff overlooking the ocean at Solana Beach, California. The Beach Club was developed and built from about August 1970 through the early part of 1973, pursuant to the terms of Del Mar Venture (Venture), a joint venture agreement between Imperial Contracting Co., Inc. (Imperial), a licensed general contractor, and Rebma California Nine, Inc. (Rebma), a real estate investment company. Imperial was the general contractor for the project; Rebma provided the financial backing. In addition to the living units, the development consists of a clubhouse, swimming pool, parking structure and tennis courts. During the relevant period of planning and construction, Thomas M. Kelly was the president, director, and principal shareholder of Imperial. Tragically, he and his wife were killed in an airplane crash on February 16, 1979. Gary Adcock, a licensed real estate broker, was an officer, director, and shareholder of Imperial and director of the Association until August 1973. William S. Krooskos and Associates (Krooskos), Arevalo and Safino of San Diego, Inc. (Arevalo and Safino), and Wolfe-Woods and Associates, Inc. (Wolfe-Woods), were respectively the soil engineers, structural engineers and architects on the project.

The Beach Club was built in three phases. In November 1972, after completion of the first two stages, erosion problems began to develop on the sea front bluff, a common area, along the western edge of the project. The Association says that actual disbursements for design and construction to prevent further erosion exceed $1.1 million with total damages to exceed $1.6 million. The Association also claims defects in the third phase of the project, Del Mar Beach Club East, pertaining to the grading, paving and installation of decking, parking structures and tennis courts, have caused damages in excess of $178,000.

When negotiations to amicably resolve the problems proved fruitless, the Association sued Imperial, Rebma and Del Mar Venture. This original complaint, filed on July 8, 1975, alleged three causes of action for negligence, breach of contract and declaratory relief. The procedural metamorphosis of this complaint into a fourth amended complaint filed January 31, 1979, is not particularly relevant. That complaint, the pleading before us, contains the same causes of action as the original complaint plus a cause of action sounding in strict liability regarding the bluff-related defects and negligence and strict liability regarding the additional defects within the third phase of the project. Arevelo and Safino, Wolfe-Woods and Krooskos are also named as defendants and theories of alter ego are now alleged against Kelly and Adcock.

Demurrers and motions to strike by Imperial, Venture, Kelly and Adcock were sustained without leave to amend on the grounds the Association lacked standing to sue and could not state a cause of action on strict liability. The remaining defendants successfully moved for judgments on the pleadings. This appeal followed.

STANDING

Code of Civil Procedure section 367 requires that "[every] action must be prosecuted in the name of the real party in interest, except as provided in Sections 369 and 374 of this code." Generally, "the person possessing the right sued upon by reason of the substantive law is the real party in interest." (*Powers v. Ashton* (1975) 45 Cal.App.3d 783, 787 [119 Cal.Rptr. 729]; 3 Witkin, Cal. Procedure (2d ed. 1971) Pleading, § 93, pp. 1768–1770.) In order to state a cause of action for injury to real property, plaintiff's ownership, lawful possession, or right to possession, of the property must be alleged. (*Friendly Village Community Assn. Inc. v. Silva & Hill Constr. Co.* (1973) 31 Cal.App.3d 220, 224 [107 Cal.Rptr. 123, 69 A.L.R.3d 1142]; 3 Witkin, Cal. Procedure (2d ed. 1971) Pleading, §§ 499, 500, p. 2159.)

At oral argument defendants admitted the major problem here was not with the theoretical aspect of plaintiff's standing, but whether standing was properly alleged. Defendants argued that a trial court does not abuse its discretion in sustaining a demurrer without leave to amend where a plaintiff files five different pleadings over a four-year period, each of which is defective.

Defendants correctly acknowledge plaintiff's theoretical status. Unlike the typical planned development under Business and Professions Code section 11003, the Association here acquired title to not only the customary "common areas," but pursuant to the declaration of restrictions recorded May 16, 1971, it also acquired title to the real property and structures. In other words, the individual owners only purchased the "air space" units within the apartment buildings and not the buildings and the land underlying them. Clearly, under such circumstances, the Association as owner has standing.[1]

In addition to the Association's standing as owner, we also conclude the Association may maintain this action in a representative capacity on behalf of its members.

Article VI, sections 6.2 and 6.2.13 of the incorporated declarations of restrictions provides:

> 6.2 The Association has and shall have the following rights and duties:
>
> ...
>
> 6.2.13 To prosecute or defend, under the name of the Association, any action affecting or relating to the Common Areas or the personal property owned by the

---

1. In light of our disposition, we do not address the question of whether Code of Civil Procedure section 374, which was amended effective January 1, 1980, to expressly include associations organized under Business and Professions Code section 11003, may be applied retroactively. (*See Raven's Cove Townhomes, Inc. v. Knuppe Development Co.* (1981) 114 Cal.App.3d 783, 791–793 [171 Cal.Rptr. 334].)

Association, or any action which all of the Owners have an interest in the subject of the action or in whom any right to relief in respect to or arising out of the same transaction or series of transactions is alleged to exist. (Emphasis supplied.)

Code of Civil Procedure section 382 provides in part that "when the question is one of a common or general interest, of many persons, or when the parties are numerous, and it is impracticable to bring them all before the court, one or more may sue ... for the benefit of all." The section is based upon the equitable doctrine of virtual representation which. "'rests upon considerations of necessity and paramount convenience, and was adopted to prevent a failure of justice.'" [Citations.] (*Daar v. Yellow Cab Co.* (1967) 67 Cal.2d 695, 703–704 [63 Cal.Rptr. 724, 433 P.2d 732].)

Courts now eschew a rigid or formal application of the statute particularly where the subject involves a matter of public interest. *(See Residents of Beverly Glen, Inc. v. City of Los Angeles* (1973) 34 Cal.App.3d 117, 122 [109 Cal.Rptr. 724].) There is no particular policy interest to be served, however, by requiring a different interpretation of the statute when the public nature of the issues may be less significant than the financial interests of the parties. Here, where the Association's obligations under the declaration of restrictions are well defined and where it has sustained actual damages as owner, there is no question but that it has, and does intend, to fairly and adequately represent the interests of the individual unit owners, members of the Association. (*See Salton City, etc. Owners Assn. v. M. Penn Phillips Co.* (1977) 75 Cal.App.3d 184, 190 [141 Cal.Rptr. 895].) Because damage to the common areas, such as walkways and stairs, affect all the unit owners, it is not only logical that the common questions of law and fact be resolved in one proceeding, but that it is judicially economical and cost beneficial to do so. In light of the provisions of the declarations of restrictions and the considerations, equitable and practical, underlying the doctrine of permitting representative actions, we hold the Association may maintain this suit in a representative capacity on behalf of its members. (*See Raven's Cove Townhomes, Inc. v. Knuppe Development Co., supra,* 114 Cal.App.3d at pp. 793–796.)

Siller v. Hartz Mountain Assoc., Inc.

Supreme Court of New Jersey
461 A.2d 568 (N.J. 1983)

SCHREIBER, J. We are called upon in this case to consider certain aspects of the Condominium Act, N.J.S.A. 46:8B-1 through -38, in particular those concerning the relationship of the owner of a unit to the associations representing all unit owners with respect to claims against the builder of the condominium. Plaintiffs, owners and inhabitants of housing units in the condominium community "Harmon Cove" in Secaucus, New Jersey, sued the developer, Hartz Mountain Associates (Developer), and the unit owner associations, Harmon Cove I Condominium Association, Inc. (Association), and Harmon Cove Recreation Association, Inc. (Recreation Association) (collectively the Associations). The suit related to alleged defects in and about the units and common areas and facilities and to a settlement that the two associations were prepared to effectuate on behalf of all unit owners, including plaintiffs, with the Developer.

The plaintiffs, as individual unit owners and on behalf of others similarly situated, had instituted the suit by filing a verified complaint and an order to show cause, in which they sought temporary restraints to prevent consummation of the settlement between the Developer and the Associations. The trial court denied any temporary restraints, signed an order directing the parties to file briefs "as to the standing of plaintiffs to bring this action" and set a date for a hearing on the standing issue. In addition to the briefs, the plaintiffs submitted an affidavit of one unit owner with copies of various documents including the master deed. Defendant Hartz Mountain also submitted a certificate of the director of its residential department with certain attachments and the defendant Association submitted a certified statement of its president with certain attachments.[1] The parties and the trial court considered the matter as if defendants had filed a motion for summary judgment on the ground that plaintiffs lacked standing to institute and maintain the action.

The trial court dismissed the complaint against the Developer and permitted the defendants to consummate the settlement at their own risk. It sustained part of one count of plaintiff's complaint against the Associations. 184 N.J. Super. 450 (Ch.Div.1981). Plaintiffs appealed and the Appellate Division affirmed. 184 N.J. Super. 442 (1982). We granted plaintiffs' petition for certification. 91 N.J. 264 (1982).

The complaint contained five counts. The first, second, third and fifth counts were directed solely against the Developer. Generally they asserted that the Developer had planned and built the condominium known as Harmon Cove I in Secaucus and had sold units to the five plaintiffs. They alleged that the condominiums and the common elements had numerous defects and deficiencies, all attributable to the Developer. The complaint specified improper insulation of the individual units; inadequate caulking of windows and doors; improper heating system; inadequate driveways and sound insulation; defects in the marina dock area, swimming pool, and boardwalk; and soil settlement problems throughout the entire development. It is important to note that, though most complaints in these counts pertained to the common elements and areas, some related to the individual units. The trial court dismissed these four counts (first, second, third and fifth) with prejudice.

The fourth count, directed solely against the Associations, alleged that settlement negotiations between the Association, the Recreation Association[2] and the Developer with respect to claims arising from the design and building of the "condominiums and the common elements" were near completion. The trial court sustained that part of the fourth count[3] that challenged the actions taken by both Associations on procedural and substantive grounds and permitted the plaintiffs to amend the complaint to express this clearly. This count, as subsequently amended by plaintiffs, charged that the proposed settlement was unreasonable, unlawful, and inadequate, that the Associations had breached their fiduciary duties and responsibilities to plaintiffs, and that the Developer, which at one time properly controlled the Associations, had continued unlawfully to exercise control and influence over the Associations. Moreover, the plaintiffs asserted that the Associations and the Developer were settling claims pertaining to the individual units as well as the common elements. ...

II

All parties agree that the clear import, express and implied, of the statutory scheme is that the association may sue third parties for damages to the common elements, collect

---

1. The trial court had not examined the defendants' certificates at the time of oral argument because they were submitted shortly before the hearing. It undoubtedly considered them before filing its written opinion.

2. The Association, composed of all unit owners, managed the condominium property. The Recreation Association, also composed of all unit owners, managed the common recreation facilities.

3. The original fourth count also charged that the Associations had no authority to settle the claims against the Developer.

the funds when successful, and apply the proceeds for repair of the property. The statutory provisions empowering the association to sue, imposing the duty on it to repair, and authorizing it to charge and collect "common expenses,"[7] coupled with the prohibition against a unit owner performing any such work on common elements, are compelling indicia that the association may institute legal action on behalf of the unit owners for damages to common elements caused by third persons.

In the absence of any statutory plan, we have acknowledged the standing of an association of tenants in an apartment building to sue their landlord. *Crescent Pk. Tenants Assoc. v. Realty Eq. Corp. of N.Y.*, 58 N.J. 98 (1971). The plaintiff tenant association in *Crescent Park* was a nonprofit organization composed of tenants of a high-rise luxury apartment building. It charged the landlord with responsibility for defects in various parts of the common elements, such as the air conditioning system, elevators, laundry rooms and swimming pool. The complaint was dismissed on the ground that the plaintiff had no standing. Justice Jacobs, writing on behalf of this Court, reversed. He observed that the individual tenants could have brought such a suit and that by acting together their bargaining power was enhanced. *Id.* at 108. He noted that the complaint was

> confined strictly to matters of common interest and [did] not include any individual grievance which might perhaps be dealt with more appropriately in a proceeding between the individual tenant and the landlord. So far as common grievances are concerned they may readily and indeed more appropriately be dealt with in a proceeding between the Association, on the one hand, and the landlord, on the other, thus incidentally avoiding the procedural burdens accompanying multiple party litigation. [*Id.* at 109]

Justice Jacobs concluded that "it [was] difficult to conceive of any policy consideration or any consideration of justice which would fairly preclude the Association from maintaining, on behalf of its member tenants, the present proceeding between itself as plaintiff and the landlord and its parent company as defendants." *Id. See, e.g., Piscataway Apt. Assoc. v. Tp. of Piscataway*, 66 N.J. 106 (1974) (nonprofit association of apartment house owners maintained action).

We find nothing in the legislative scheme governing condominiums to indicate policy considerations different from those expressed in *Crescent Park*. Avoidance of a multiplicity of suits, economic savings incident to one trial, elimination of contradictory adjudications, expedition in resolution of controversies, accomplishment of repairs, and the positive effect on judicial administration are supportive policy reasons.[8] Moreover,

---

7. Common expenses are defined as "expenses for which the unit owners are proportionately liable, including but not limited to:
   (i) all expenses of administration, maintenance, repair and replacement of the common elements;
   (ii) expenses agreed upon as common by all unit owners; and
   (iii) expenses declared common by provisions of this act or by the master deed or by the bylaws." [N.J.S.A. 46:8B-3(e)]
It has been held that an association by virtue of its assessment power may include the litigation costs as a common expense. *See Margate Village Condominium Ass'n, Inc. v. Wilfred, Inc.*, 350 So. 2d 16, 17 (Fla.App.1977) (upholding association's right to assess all owners, including developer, for litigation expenses, including those of an action against developer).

8. The plaintiffs, though not addressing the issue squarely, have implicitly indicated that the Legislature would have no authority to determine whether associations would have a right to sue because this is "procedural" and exclusively within the jurisdiction of the Supreme Court. *Winberry v. Salisbury*, 5 N.J. 240, 255 (1950). It is not necessary for us to address that question since we are in full agreement with the policy expressed.

the financial burden on an individual owner may be so great and so disproportionate to his potential recovery that he could not or would not proceed with litigation. Other jurisdictions have also interpreted their statutes governing condominiums to authorize unit owner associations to sue with respect to claims pertaining to common elements.[9] *1000 Grandview Ass'n v. Mt. Washington Associates*, 290 Pa.Super. 365, 434 A.2d 796 (Pa.Super.1981); *Governors Grove Condominium Ass'n, Inc. v. Hill Development Corp.*, 35 Conn. Sup. 199, 404 A.2d 131, 134 (Conn.Super.Ct.1979); *see also Avila South Condominium Ass'n v. Kappa Corp.*, 347 So. 2d 599, 607–09 (Fla.Sup.Ct.1979), in which the Florida Supreme Court held that the legislature did not have authority to empower the association to sue, but accomplished the same effect by promulgating a court rule. *Contra, Deal v. 999 Lakeshore Ass'n*, 579 P.2d 775, 777–78 (Nev.1978) (dictum); *Friendly Village Community Ass'n, Inc. v. Silva & Hill Constr. Co.*, 31 Cal.App.3d 220, 225, 107 Cal.Rptr. 123, 126, 69 A.L.R.3d 1142, 1146 (1973). *See generally* Annot., "Standing to Bring act relating to real property of condominiums," 72 A.L.R.3d 314 (1976); Annot., "Proper party plaintiff in action for injury to common areas of condominium development," 69 A.L.R.3d 1148 (1976); Note, "Condominium Class Actions," 48 St.Johns L.Rev. 1168, 1180–81 (1974).

III

If, as we have held, the association may sue to protect the rights and interests of the unit owners in the common elements, does it have the exclusive right to maintain those actions? Obviously the unit owner has an interest in claims against the developer arising out of damages to or defects in the common elements. However, the association has been charged with and delegated the primary responsibility to protect those interests. "The association ... shall be responsible for the ... maintenance, repair, replacement, cleaning, and sanitation of the common elements." N.J.S.A. 46:8B-14. So long as it carries out those functions and duties, the unit owners may not pursue individual claims for damages to or defects in the common elements predicated upon their tenant in common interest. The Condominium Act contemplates as much. The association, not the individual unit owner, may maintain and repair the common elements. "No unit owner shall contract for or perform any maintenance, repair, replacement, removal, alteration or modification of the common elements or any additions thereto, except through the association and its officers." N.J.S.A. 46:8B-18. Indeed the statute authorizes the association to assess the membership to raise those funds designated as "common expenses." N.J.S.A. 46:8B-3(e). "A unit owner [is], by acceptance of title ... conclusively presumed to have agreed to pay his proportionate share of common expenses." N.J.S.A. 46:8B-17.

It would be impractical indeed to sanction lawsuits by individual unit owners in which their damages would represent but a fraction of the whole. If the individual owner were permitted to prosecute claims regarding common elements, any recovery equitably would have to be transmitted to the association to pay for repairs and replacements. A sensible reading of the statute leads to the conclusion that such causes of action belong exclusively to the association, which, unlike the individual unit owner, may apply the funds recovered on behalf of all the owners of the common elements. See Wayne S. Hyatt, Condominium and Homeowner Association Practice: Community Association Law 105 (1981), suggesting that only association be permitted to maintain action.

---

9. Many condominium statutes were modeled after the Federal Housing Administration's Model Statute for the Creation of Apartment Ownership, which acknowledges the right of the association to sue on behalf of the unit owner. See § 7 of FHA Model Statute reprinted in Rohan and Reskin, *1A Condominium Law & Practice*, Appendix B-3.

This is not to say that a unit owner may not act on a common element claim upon the association's failure to do so. In that event the unit owner's claim should be considered derivative in nature and the association must be named as a party. Rule 4:32-5 would be applicable. That Rule governs actions "brought to enforce a secondary right on the part of one or more shareholders in an association, incorporated or unincorporated, because the association refuses to enforce rights which may properly be asserted by it."

The unit owner may also sue the developer on behalf of the association irrespective of its governing board's willingness to sue during the period of time that the association remains under the control of the developer. The inherent conflict of interest is such that the association would not be in a position to resolve conflicts with the developer in the absence of the approval of the unit owners, other than the developer.[10] *See Berman v. Gurwicz*, 189 N.J. Super. 89 (Ch.Div.1981), aff'd o.b., 189 N.J. Super. 49 (App.Div.1983), certif. denied, 94 N.J. 549 (1983). In this situation the procedure of R. 4:32-5 would also appear to be appropriate.

The unit owner, of course, does have primary rights to safeguard his interests in the unit he owns. N.J.S.A. 48:8B-4.[11] The physical extent of that property depends upon what has been included in the common elements. This may be ascertained by examination of the statutory definition and the master deed. Moreover, defective conditions in the common elements may also result in injury to the unit owner and damages to his personal property and the unit. For example, a faulty roof may result in personal property damage in the unit. The unit owner's right to maintain an action for compensation for that loss against the wrongdoer is not extinguished or abridged by the association's exclusive right to seek compensation for damage to the common element.

Further, the association's primary right to sue does not diminish any claim that the unit owner may have against the association. The association's board of directors, trustees or other governing body have a fiduciary relationship to the unit owners, comparable to the obligation that a board of directors of a corporation owes to its stockholders. Acts of the governing body should be properly authorized. Fraud, self-dealing or unconscionable conduct at the very least should be subject to exposure and relief. *See, e.g., Papalexiou v. Tower West Condominium*, 167 N.J. Super. 516, 527 (Ch.Div.1979); *Ryan v. Baptiste*, 565 S.W.2d 196, 198 (Mo.Ct.App.1976); *Hidden Harbour Estates, Inc. v. Norman*, 309 So. 2d 180, 182 (Fla.D.Ct.App.1975).

IV

Our attention must next be directed to the application of the stated principles to the facts of this case. Beginning with the election of November 10, 1977, Hartz Mountain selected only one of nine of the Association's board of directors. Further, the Developer had no directors on the board of the Recreation Association after October 19, 1978. In January 1978 the Association's board of directors designated a Legal Action Committee chaired by Sidney Siller, a plaintiff in this case, to investigate claims against the Developer relating to (a) construction and design and (b) misrepresentation or fraud. This Committee

---

10. A similar concern about overreaching by the developer led the Legislature to establish a rebuttable presumption of unconscionability of leases not executed by representatives of condominium unit owners other than the developer. N.J.S.A. 46:8B-32(a). Rebuttable presumptions of unconscionability also apply to numerous provisions that may be found in "leases involving condominium property, including … recreational or other common facilities or areas." N.J.S.A. 46:8B-32.

11. This is expressly recognized in the instant case in the Association's by-laws. Art. 6, §3, p. 75.

reported to the Board of Directors in June 1978 that major deficiencies attributable to the Developer involved heat, air conditioning and insulation; noise, leaks and erosion; and inadequate parking, clubhouse, swimming and marina facilities. There were also questions concerning shrubbery and foliage. The Committee recommended engaging an attorney, who later became plaintiffs' attorney in this action, to institute the necessary litigation. The board of directors adopted this recommendation, but shortly thereafter the board rescinded the action engaging that attorney and instead utilized the Association's general counsel in its negotiations with the Developer.

A settlement was negotiated providing for the Developer to pay $400,000 to the Association and Recreation Association and for the Developer to receive a general release except for "repair and replacement" of underground utility breaks on that part of the common elements known as Sea Isle for a period of three years. Insofar as the claims and general release are confined to the common areas and facilities, we agree with the trial court and the Appellate Division that the Association had exclusive standing to maintain the action. We also agree with the trial court and the Appellate Division that plaintiffs are entitled to proceed under the fourth count of the complaint against the Association and Recreation Association because of allegedly wrongful actions taken by their respective boards of directors.

Plaintiffs as unit owners may also continue with their individual causes of actions based upon damages to their individual units. Their complaint referred to such damages. The common elements as defined in the statute, N.J.S.A. 46:8B-3(d), and in the master deed, do not include certain items peculiar to the individual units, such as doors and windows that open from a unit. The Associations cannot preclude plaintiffs from pursuing these claims. Each plaintiff should be prepared at the pretrial conference to itemize these individual unit owner claims. We do not pass upon the propriety of the class action, an issue which is not before us.

Affirmed in part, Reversed in part and Remanded.

———————

Lauriedale Assoc., Ltd. v. Wilson
Court of Appeal of California
9 Cal. Rptr. 2d 774 (Cal. Ct. App. 1992)

PETERSON, J. The primary issue in this case is straightforward. May the developers of a condominium complex, who have been sued for construction defects by a homeowners association, cross-complain against individual unit owners for equitable indemnity? Under the facts of this case, we conclude the answer is "no."

I. FACTUAL AND PROCEDURAL BACKGROUND

This is an appeal from a judgment entered after a demurrer was sustained without leave to amend. We, thus, recite the facts as set forth in the pleadings.

The Lauriedale Homeowners Association (Association) is a California nonprofit corporation which was created to operate and manage the Lauriedale Condominiums, a 328-unit complex located in San Mateo. On a date which is not disclosed in the record, the Association filed a complaint against various persons and entities who had been involved in the development of the Lauriedale Condominiums.[1] Throughout this opinion, we will

———————

1. The Association alleged it had standing to bring the suit under the authority of Code of Civil Procedure section 374. That section states that an association which has been established to manage

refer to these persons and entities collectively as appellants. Essentially, the complaint alleged that appellants were responsible for defects in the commonly owned areas of the complex—such as roofs, walkways, and decks—under legal theories such as breach of contract, negligence, and misrepresentation. In addition, the complaint alleged that certain appellants, who previously had served as members of the Association's board of directors while the developer was in control of the complex, had failed to adequately assess or collect fees from the various unit owners. As a result, the Association alleged it lacked the funds necessary to make repairs at the complex. Both parties agree that these latter allegations attempt to assert a cause of action for breach of fiduciary duty premised upon *Raven's Cove Townhomes, Inc. v. Knuppe Development Co.* (1981) 114 Cal.App.3d 783 [171 Cal.Rptr. 334], a prior decision from this court.

After being served with the complaint, appellants filed an answer and a cross-complaint. The cross-complaint generates the present appeal. In addition to naming various contractors and subcontractors who allegedly were responsible for damage at the complex, appellants named as cross-defendants over 700 persons who were then, or who in the past had been, owners of units in the Lauriedale Condominiums. We are concerned here only with the allegations of the cross-complaint against these unit owners; we note, however, that appellants also sought relief, equivalent to that sought in their cross-complaint, by affirmative defenses pled in their answer.

Although set forth in three causes of action, the allegations of the cross-complaint against the unit owners were based on only two legal theories. First, appellants denied that the common areas of the complex were damaged; but they alleged that, if such damage were proven, it was caused in whole or in part by individual unit owners who had misused the property. Thus, appellants sought total or partial indemnity from the unit owners under an equitable indemnity theory. Second, appellants denied that those persons who had previously served on the Association's board, while the developer was in control of the complex, had failed to collect adequate fees and assessments; but contended that, if such allegations were true, the unit owners, *inter alia*, would have underpaid the appropriate fees and assessments. Thus, appellants finally contended that, if they were held responsible for such underassessed amounts, they were entitled to indemnity therefor from the individual unit owners, to prevent the latter's unjust enrichment.

The causes of action asserted against the unit owners as a whole were challenged by demurrer of one of the unit owners, respondent Scott Wilson. Wilson essentially contended that the cause of action for equitable indemnity should be dismissed, because it violated public policy and created an unnecessary conflict between himself and the Association. He challenged, for failure to state a cause of action, appellants' contention of entitlement to indemnity to preclude the unit owners' unjust enrichment. The trial court agreed and wholly sustained Wilson's demurrer without leave to amend. After a judgment in favor of Wilson was entered, appellants filed the present appeal.

II. DISCUSSION

Appellants challenge the trial court's ruling sustaining Wilson's demurrer. They maintain they properly asserted causes of action for equitable indemnity and "Unjust Enrichment."

A. Equitable Indemnity

The legal principles governing equitable indemnity are well settled. "The purpose of [the doctrine] is to avoid the unfairness, under joint and several liability theory, of hold-

---

a common interest development has standing to institute litigation for damage to the common areas of the development.

ing one defendant liable for the plaintiff's entire loss while allowing another responsible defendant to escape 'scot free.'" (*GEM Developers v. Hallcraft Homes of San Diego, Inc.* (1989) 213 Cal.App.3d 419, 426 [261 Cal.Rptr. 626].) As a general rule, a defendant "has a right to bring in other tortfeasors who are allegedly responsible for plaintiff's action through a cross-complaint ... for equitable indemnification." (at p. 428.)

However, because indemnification between joint tortfeasors is an equitable rule created to correct potential injustice, the doctrine is not available where it would operate against public policy. Thus, in *Holland v. Thacher* (1988) 199 Cal.App.3d 924, 929–935 [245 Cal.Rptr. 247], this court held that public policy concerns precluded an attorney sued for malpractice from cross-complaining for indemnity against a successor attorney who was retained to extricate the client from the problems created by the first attorney. In *Munoz v. Davis* (1983) 141 Cal.App.3d 420, 427 [190 Cal.Rptr. 400], the court refused to permit an attorney, sued for malpractice for allowing a statute of limitation to expire, to cross-complain against a driver who caused the plaintiff's injuries. The *Munoz* court noted there was "no equitable basis for shifting malpractice liability from the negligent lawyer to the tortfeasor whose actions caused the client's original injuries." (*Ibid.*)

Even more pertinent to the present case is *Jaffe v. Huxley Architecture* (1988) 200 Cal.App.3d 1188 [246 Cal.Rptr. 432]. In *Jaffe*, the issue presented was whether the developers of a condominium complex, who had been sued by a homeowners association for construction defects, could cross-complain for equitable indemnity against individual members of the association's board of directors for acts and omissions which allegedly contributed to the original defects. The *Jaffe* court rejected the cross-complaint for two interrelated reasons. First, noting that the acts of the directors were, in legal effect, the acts of the association itself, the court concluded relief equivalent to that sought in the cross-complaint would be available to the developer through the various affirmative defenses it had asserted. Thus, fairness did not require that the developer be allowed to maintain a cross-complaint. Second, the court observed that a special relationship existed between the homeowners association and its directors, which for public policy reasons, should be preserved. Since the cross-complaint would effectively pit the board members against the association and jeopardize that relationship, the court concluded it would be unwise to allow the cross-complaint to proceed. (*Id.* at pp. 1192–1193.)

The factors which persuaded the *Jaffe* court to reject a cross-complaint for equitable indemnity lead to a similar conclusion in this case. Here, as in *Jaffe*, the cross-complaint against Wilson is unnecessary because equivalent relief is available through affirmative defenses appellants have asserted. In response to the allegation that they were responsible for defects at the complex, appellants alleged by affirmative defense that any damage was caused by individual unit owners who misused the property. The Association has conceded that the legal effect of this affirmative defense is to hold it responsible for damage caused by present and past unit owners. Thus, to the extent appellants can prove their affirmative defense, the Association's recovery will be diminished under principles of comparative negligence. (*See, generally, American Motorcycle Assn. v. Superior Court* (1978) 20 Cal.3d 578, 598 [146 Cal.Rptr. 182 [578 P.2d 899].)

Second, allowing a cross-complaint for equitable indemnity in a case such as this could jeopardize the special relationship between the Association and its members, one characterized as fiduciary in nature. (*Cohen v. Kite Hill Community Assn.* (1983) 142 Cal.App.3d 642, 650–651 [191 Cal.Rptr. 209].) In carrying out their fiduciary duties, the directors of the Association may well have believed they had an obligation to pursue the present suit to protect the interests of the individual unit owners. If such a suit could result in personal liability on the part of the individual unit owners, the decision to bring suit would be much more difficult because the directors understandably would be hesitant to entangle unit owners in litigation. Since board members are also usually unit owners, the decision to initiate litigation, and thus subject oneself to personal liability, would be doubly difficult.

Furthermore, public policy considerations weigh heavily against allowing a cross-complaint such as this from going forward. The high cost of living in California, and particularly in the Bay Area, is well recognized. For many segments of society, condominiums represent one of the last alternatives of affordable home ownership. The prospect of personal liability in a case such as this would place a severe burden on this important housing resource. We decline to permit such a burden where, as here, equivalent relief for the developer via its affirmative defenses was available and sought.

Appellants reject this analysis on several grounds. First, they maintain that the *Jaffe* holding does not apply in this case because they could not obtain equivalent relief through affirmative defenses. In essence, appellants argue that they will be unable to use the negligence of present or past unit owners as a defense to a suit brought by the Association. However, since the Association has properly conceded, as it must, that it is responsible for that portion of the damages caused by present and past unit owners proven in support of the allegations of appellants' affirmative defenses, these arguments are moot.

Next, appellants argue their cross-complaint would not interfere with the relationship between the Association and its members because homeowners associations frequently bring suit against individual members. For example, if a unit owner damages the common areas of a complex, an association often has not only the right, but the obligation, under the applicable governing documents, to hold the unit owner responsible. However, there is a distinct difference between a suit initiated by a homeowners association against a unit owner, and a suit initiated by a third party against a homeowner through a cross-complaint. In the former case, the motivations of the homeowners association initiating suit are generally clear: to hold the person actually causing the damage responsible therefor. Conversely, a cross-complaint such as that appellants seek to assert here can be motivated by nothing more than "spite and a desire to spread confusion, [and] dissention [*sic*] in the opponent's camp." (*Commercial Standard Title Co. v. Superior Court* (1979) 92 Cal.App.3d 934, 945 [155 Cal.Rptr. 393]; *see also Holland v. Thacher, supra*, 199 Cal.App.3d at p. 930.) On this rationale, a cross-complaint for equitable indemnity, such as the one we consider, is rejected when it is clearly and potentially disruptive of the fiduciary relationship between a plaintiff and a cross-defendant. Though the cross-complaint we consider is urged to contain a facade of legitimacy, it realistically constitutes thinly disguised retaliatory litigation, the principal purpose of which is to pursue an adversarial scorched earth posture designed to cripple that relationship and thereby discourage legitimate litigation by the representative homeowners association.

. . .

B. "Unjust Enrichment"

Appellants' alternate cause of action against Wilson is premised upon allegations contained in the Association's complaint. Essentially, appellants denied that those persons who had formerly acted as members of the Association's board had breached their fiduciary duties by failing to collect adequate fees and assessments from the individual unit owners; but if this had occurred, one result would be that individual unit owners would have underpaid the fees and assessments which were appropriate. Thus, appellants alleged that, should they be held responsible for the amount underassessed, they were entitled to indemnity from the individual unit owners so that the unit owners would not be "Unjust[ly] Enrich[ed]."

Initially we note that appellants have mischaracterized the legal theory underlying their cause of action. The phrase "Unjust Enrichment" does not describe a theory of recovery, but an effect: the result of a failure to make restitution under circumstances where it is equitable to do so. (*Dinosaur Development, Inc. v. White* (1989) 216 Cal.App.3d 1310, 1315 [265 Cal.Rptr. 525].) What appellants actually seek is restitution: a term which modernly has been extended to include not only the restoration or giving back of something to its rightful owner, but indemnification such as appellants seek in this case. (*Ibid.*)

Thus clarified, the issue in this case is whether a party which has breached its fiduciary duties may bring an action for restitution against the persons harmed by that breach. We conclude the answer is "no."

It is well settled that restitution will be denied where application of the doctrine would involve a violation or frustration of the law or opposition to public policy. (*Dinosaur Development, Inc. v. White, supra*, 216 Cal.App.3d at p. 1315; *see also Lucky Auto Supply v. Turner* (1966) 244 Cal.App.2d 872, 885 [53 Cal.Rptr. 628].) Indeed, section 140 of the Restatement of Restitution expressly states that a person may be prevented from obtaining restitution for a benefit because of his wrongful conduct in connection with the transaction on which his claim is based. Allowing the director of a homeowners association, who had breached his fiduciary duties by failing to collect adequate assessments, to maintain an action for restitution against the very persons harmed by his breach would be patently inequitable. The demurrer to this cause of action was properly sustained.[2]

III. DISPOSITION

The judgment in favor of Wilson is Affirmed.

Notes & Questions

1. *Association standing and the uniform acts.* UCIOA Section 3-102(a)(4) provides community associations standing to "institute, defend, or intervene in litigation or administrative proceedings in its own name or on behalf of itself or two or more unit owners on matters affecting the common interest community." Absent such statutory authority (or similar language to the same effect), some courts have denied standing to associations lacking an ownership interest in the affected property. See, *e.g., Deal v. 999 Lakeshore Ass'n*, 547 P. 2d 775 (Nev. 1978) (condominium association has no standing to sue as a real party in interest in its own capacity; only unit owners have standing to sue for design defects in the common elements since they must bear the cost of any repairs).

2. *Tax assessments and "common interest."* The court in *In Re Objections & Defenses to Real Property Taxes*, 410 N.W.2d 321 (Minn. 1987), held that a condominium association had standing to bring an action challenging tax assessments of all units which comprised the condominium because the Minnesota condominium statute provided standing to an association when it asserts a claim on behalf of two or more unit owners. Moreover, the court looked to the tax statute which authorized actions to determine the validity of a tax on real property by any person having an estate, right, title, or interest in or lien upon such property. Since the association had a statutorily created lien on every unit for payment of future assessments, the court concluded that the association had the authority to challenge the tax assessments as a lienor. In contrast, the court in *Bonavista Condominium Ass'n v. Bystrom*, 520 So. 2d 84 (Fla. Dist. Ct. App. 1988), denied a condominium asso-

---

2. Having reached this conclusion, we need not consider whether appellants' "Unjust Enrichment" cause of action is barred by the provisions of the Corporations Code.

ciation standing to challenge *ad valorem* assessments on individual units and held that unit owner dissatisfaction with their taxes was not a "common interest" which is a necessary element under the state's statutes regarding association standing.

3. *Exclusive standing?* While the *Siller* case grants the condominium association exclusive standing to bring actions affecting the community's common areas, *Tassan v. United Dev. Co.*, 410 N.E.2d 902 (Ill. App. Ct. 1980), questions the propriety of association standing on construction defect litigation absent explicit statutory language. *Tassan* denied exclusive association standing for the alleged common area defects. Instead, the court in *Tassan* permitted unit owners to sue the developer using the class action device. Also, in *Deal v. 999 Lakeshore Ass'n*, 579 P.2d 775 (Nev. 1978), the court denied a condominium association standing to bring a claim on behalf of the owners absent express statutory authority, or a direct ownership interest by the condominium association in a unit of the development. Finally, in *Carlandia Corp. v. Rogers & Ford*, 626 So. 2d 1350 (Fla. 1993), the Florida Supreme Court declined to follow *Siller's* exclusive standing rationale. The *Carlandia* court allowed unit owners to sue individually for defects in the common elements.

What are some of the practical difficulties implicated by each approach to the association standing question? What is the likelihood of unit owners litigating individually for damages to their units? To the common areas? What factors may inhibit initiation of such litigation? If the association does not have standing to sue in your jurisdiction to bring certain types of litigation against the developer or other third parties, what alternatives may be available to the unit owners to pursue a collective claim?

4. *Necessity of joinder.* Where a state statute expressly provides for community association standing to sue as the real party in interest, joinder of the unit owners is not typically needed. See, *e.g.*, *Orange Grove Terrace Owner's Ass'n v. Bryant Properties, Inc.*, 222 Cal. Rptr. 523 (Cal. Ct. App. 1986), where the court refused to distinguish between the community association and the unit owners since the association was a real party in interest on behalf of everyone. When might joinder of unit owners be required?

5. *Standing and federal antitrust laws.* In the past, developers sometimes required unit owners to accept and ratify an obligation to make rental payments for use of developer-owned recreational facilities. In *Buckley Towers Condo., Inc. v. Buchwald*, 533 F.2d 934 (5th Cir. 1976), the community association attempted to invalidate such an arrangement as a violation of the Sherman Act (15 USCS §§ 1, 2). The court, however, denied the association standing since the association failed to show that the alleged violations caused an injury to its "business or property." The court found that the condominium association acted merely as a conduit in collecting assessments from the unit owners and paying rent to the developer, and, therefore, neither its business nor its property was injured. Do you agree with the court's analysis in *Buckley Towers*? How would you define the scope of "business or property?" See *Burleigh House Condo., Inc. v. Buchwald*, 546 F.2d 57 (5th Cir. 1977) (denying association standing in action against the developer for violations of the Sherman Act); *Chatham Condominium Ass'n v. Century Village, Inc.*, 597 F.2d 1002 (5th Cir. 1979) (denying condominium standing in its action for an alleged tying arrangement in violation of the Sherman Act and § 3 of the Clayton Act).

6. *Settlements and binding effect on unit owners.* In *Frantz v. CBI Fairmac Corp.*, 331 S.E.2d 390 (Va. 1985), individual unit owners were bound by a settlement agreement reached between the condominium association and the developer which granted the association an easement in exchange for releasing the developer from all pending claims. Here, the condominium statute conferred the power to the association to grant and ac-

cept easements and empowered the association to maintain actions for damages or injunctive relief. The court in *Frantz* concluded that since the association had the authority to bring an action on behalf of the unit owners, it necessarily had the power to settle such claims. Do you agree? What policy rationales support this conclusion?

7. *Standing by common law.* Sometimes, an association will achieve standing upon a showing of a direct and substantial injury and a clear stake in the outcome. See, *e.g., Doyle v. A&P Realty Corp.*, 414 A.2d 204 (Conn. Super. Ct. 1980) (granting association standing to sue for alleged construction defects since the association had the duty to maintain the property and would be damaged by way of increased maintenance costs resulting from said defects). In other instances, the association will be granted standing on the basis of its representative character. In *1000 Grandview Ass'n v. Mt. Washington Assoc.*, 434 A.2d 796 (Pa. Super. Ct.1981), the court, citing the Supreme Court decision in *Warth v. Seldin*, 422 U.S. 490, (1975), found that an association may have representational standing to assert the rights of its members, so long as it alleges an immediate, direct, and substantial injury to any one of them.

8. *Capacity to sue versus real party in interest.* In *Equitable Life Assur. Soc. v. Tinsley Mill Village*, 294 S.E.2d 495 (Ga. 1982), the Georgia Supreme court distinguished between the association's capacity to sue as provided by statute and the necessity of being the real party in interest for certain actions. The court found that only the persons who own, lease, or have a legal interest in the affected property were the real parties in interest. Here, the court found that only real parties in interest could maintain an action for damages and an injunction in a nuisance action concerning upstream development activities. What factors would support the community association as being a real party in interest? Does it make a difference if the association is a condominium?

9. *Standing and zoning board decisions.* Just as standing is required to bring a civil action, it is also required to seek judicial review of zoning board decisions.

In *Douglaston Civic Ass'n. v. Galvin*, 364 N.Y.S.2d 830 (N.Y. 1974), a property owner's association had standing to assert the rights of its members where their units may be affected by rezoning, variance, exception, or other determinations of the zoning board. The court emphasized that the relationship between zoning board decisions and public health and welfare justified the association's standing in the matter. The court also examined practical factors which favored an association's representative capacity, including: its capacity to assume an adversary position; the size and composition of the community it seeks to protect; the potential adverse effect of the zoning decision to the entire group; and the availability of full participating membership by the property owners in the affected neighborhood. In *Tuxedo Conservation & Taxpayers Ass'n. v. Town Board of Tuxedo*, 408 N.Y.S.2d 668, *aff'd* 418 N.Y.S.2d 638 (N.Y. App. Div. 1979), a property owner's association was granted standing to challenge a special permit for a 3,900-unit development under the same criteria set forth in *Douglaston*. The *Tuxedo* court also held that there was no need to prove actual harm as a prerequisite to challenge the zoning decision. It was sufficient that the challenged permit might adversely affect the members of the association.

In contrast, the court in *Chabau v. Dade County*, 385 So. 2d 129 (Fla. Dist. Ct. App. 1980), declined to follow *Douglaston* and *Tuxedo*, and it held that a community association must suffer some injury itself in order to maintain standing in a suit challenging zoning board decisions. Other jurisdictions may limit the standing of community associations to only instances where the association actually owns real property which is adversely affected by the zoning board decision. See, *e.g.*, 8 A.L.R. 4th 1087; *Lindenwood Improv. Ass'n v. Lawrence*, 278 S.W.2d 30 (Mo. Ct. App. 1995) (plaintiff association is not an "aggrieved person" within the meaning of the local statute).

Chapter 11

Declarant Control of Association and Transition

The subject of this Chapter is extremely important in the life of any community association and in the evolution of its governance; however, it is so often misunderstood that it goes even by the wrong name. That name, "turnover," exemplifies the extent and nature of the misunderstanding.

Transition refers to the transfer of control from declarant to the home or unit owners. For it to be successful, transition must be a process and not an event. However, in the common parlance of those living in and operating common interest communities, too often the focus is on the actual point at which control is turned over with the resulting misperception being that all activities begin and end at that particular point. That misunderstanding gives rise to many problems.

This Chapter looks at the issue of declarant control as well as the actual passage of that control. These topics are presented together because they are inextricably linked. The extent and methods of control and the way that control is exercised and ended all come together to provide the basis for a significant area of potential declarant liability.

Control is manifested in a variety of ways. In the early years of common interest community development, developers often asserted in their documents, marketing materials, and management practices that the "association doesn't exist" until all or substantially all of the units were sold. In the mean time, so the story went, "the declarant is the association." Obviously, such assertions not only are totally incorrect, but they cause a wide variety of potential problems and liabilities, and not just for the declarant.

In other situations, the documents clearly state that the declarant is in a position of dominance over the association but that the association exists from the outset. Frequently, however, the documents are silent as to the way transition should be effected or how that control is passed. This presents a different set of problems. In some cases, the owners do not desire to take over control, while in others they are extremely anxious to do so.

Regrettably, many documents do not provide for an orderly or phased transition which provides participation in stages, raising the understanding and technical confidence of the owners as they move from being merely owner-members to members in control. Consider the provisions in UCIOA and various state statutes which call for a phased transition.

Obviously, the declarant wants control because of basic business needs. These include flexibility to adjust to changing circumstances and markets, and enforcement of developmental standards and guidelines to ensure the product quality throughout the development's life. The "needs" also include assurance that the budget remain at a level necessary to fund operations of the project at the expected level; this is important not only to the developer for purposes of long-term marketing but also to initial buyers who bought in reliance upon marketing representations.

Basically, the developer needs and desires a sufficient level of control over the association to ensure that its rights to develop in accordance with the basic development plan will be protected. Regrettably, often declarants want control because they have a lack of trust in the owners or because they simply do not understand the positive attributes of sharing or transferring control. In each case you examine, consider why control was needed and whether or not the positive situations could be enhanced by careful drafting and practice.

A. Declarant Control of Board

1. Declarant Obligations and Responsibilities

Restatement (Third) § 6.20 Developer's Duties To The Community

Until the developer relinquishes control of the association to the members, the developer owes the following duties to the association and its members:

(1) to use reasonable care and prudence in managing and maintaining the common property;

(2) to establish a sound fiscal basis for the association by imposing and collecting assessments and establishing reserves for the maintenance and replacement of common property;

(3) to disclose the amount by which the developer is providing or subsidizing services that the association is or will be obligated to provide;

(4) to maintain records and to account for the financial affairs of the association from its inception;

(5) to comply with and enforce the terms of the governing documents, including design controls, land-use restrictions, and the payment of assessments;

(6) to disclose all material facts and circumstances affecting the condition of the property that the association is responsible for maintaining; and

(7) to disclose all material facts and circumstances affecting the financial condition of the association, including the interest of the developer and the developer's affiliates in any contract, lease, or other agreement entered into by the association.

Pederzani v. Guerriere

Massachusetts Superior Court
Civil Action No. 930502A, Mass. Superior Ct.
Aug. 11, 1995

I. INTRODUCTION

The elected unit-owner trustees of a residential condominium have brought suit against the former trustees appointed by the developer. The plaintiffs primarily allege breaches

Units at Summer Hill Condominium, courtesy of Trustees of Summer Hill Condominium.

of fiduciary duty by the former trustees. Applying the business' judgment rule, only the most egregious of these breach of fiduciary duty claims can survive summary judgment. The summary judgment principles to be applied are stated in *Kourouvacilis v. General Motors Corp.*, 410 Mass. 706 (1991).[1]

II. ALLEGATIONS OF BREACH OF FIDUCIARY DUTY AND BAD
FAITH BY TRUSTEES OF THE CONDOMINIUM TRUST (COUNT I)

A. The Business Judgment Rule

Trustees of a condominium trust owe a fiduciary duty to the unit owners collectively. This is a duty of loyalty and good faith. Although our appellate cases have not yet explicitly addressed the issue, I am convinced that the business judgment rule adopted by the Court of Appeals of New York is the appropriate standard to be applied to claims against trustees of a condominium trust. *Levandusky v. One Fifth Avenue*, 75 N.Y. 2d 530, 537–539 (1990); *Macrides v. Mannix*, Plymouth Superior C.A. 89-01618A; 89-0592, Findings, Rulings and Order (R.L. Steadman, C.J.; March 18, 1991) (applying *Levandusky* business judgment rule). Under this standard, trustees are not liable for actions "taken in good faith and in the exercise of honest judgment in the lawful and legitimate furtherance" of the interests of the unit owners. 75 N.Y. 2d at 538.

The most basic meaning of the term fiduciary duty is a duty to act with good faith towards the interests of the unit owners. So long as the trustees have not breached this fiduciary duty, "the exercise of [their powers] for the common and general interests of the ...

---

1. The claims of the plaintiffs as the trustees of the Condominium Trust are limited to damages to individual units. Their claims cannot include damages to individual units. See *Cigal v. Leader Development Corp.*, 408 Mass. 212, 215–216 (1990). The amended complaint does not appear to allege claims for damage to individual units, but if it did such damages would not properly be part of this case.

[unit owners] may not be questioned, although the results show that what they did was unwise or inexpedient." *Id.*

The board of trustees "owes its duty of loyalty to the ... [unit owners] — that is, it must act for the benefit of the residents collectively." *Id.* So long as the board acts "for the purposes of the ... [association of unit owners] within the scope of its authority and in good faith, courts will not substitute their judgment for the board's." *Id.* Unless a plaintiff challenging the trustees' action "is able to demonstrate a breach of this duty, judicial review is not available." *Id.*

Negligence or a failure to use reasonable care in a trustee's management decision does not amount to a cause of action against a condominium trustee. The court will not inquire into the reasonableness of a trustee's decision. *Levandusky,* 75 N.Y. 2d at 538. A bad result does not make a cause of action for the unit owners, even if an unreasonable business decision produced that bad result.

B. Application to the Present Claims

This standard of review is consistent with the provision in the Declaration of Trust in this case providing for limited liability of trustees. Under Article 3, 14, of the Declaration of Trust, trustees "shall not be liable to the Unit Owners for any mistake of judgment, negligence, or otherwise, except for their own individual willful misconduct or bad faith." A similar condominium trust agreement provision was applied by the Appeals Court in *Lilley v. Rich,* 27 Mass. App. Ct. 1212 (1989). The court in *Lilley* held that the judge's findings showed at most an unduly casual attitude by certain of the nonprofessional trustees towards their obligation to the unit owners. The evidence in *Lilley* did not warrant the conclusion that "the [t]rustees display[ed] a willful neglect of their duties amounting to reckless indifference."

In applying the *Levandusky* business judgment rule and the limited liability clause to this case, the court must recognize that the defendants are the developer trustees who controlled the trust prior to the election of new trustees by the unit owners. This does not change the standard of review, but the defendants' positions as developer trustees at least hypothetically permitted a greater potential for conflicting interests.

The court has carefully reviewed the summary judgment materials including the affidavits, deposition excerpts and answers to interrogatories. Applying the *Levandusky* standard to the claims against the condominium trustees in Count I, I conclude that the plaintiffs' materials are sufficient to raise a genuine, material fact issue of breach of fiduciary duty based on the totality of three claims: (1) alleged failure to correct substantial defects in grading, water drainage and retaining walls and to prevent substantial water damage to the buildings; (2) alleged failure to correct substantial problems in the sewage facility; and (3) alleged failure to collect common charge assessments from the developer. The Molleur, Murphy and Nordin affidavits, the Nordin letters to a trustee, and the internal memorandum between two trustees help make out genuine fact issues on these three areas.[2]

A gross failure to correct substantial deficiencies in water drainage, retaining walls, the sewage facility, and collections from the developer may be sufficient in some circumstances to show a lack of good faith and a breach of fiduciary duty by developer trustees in control of a condominium trust. Negligence or poor management would not be enough, but a gross dereliction of duty in such important matters might be enough.

_____

2. The materials show sufficient expert qualification and personal knowledge to warrant a denial of the defendants' motion to strike these affidavits with respect to the three fact issues that are genuine and material.

The summary judgment materials are insufficient to support a claim of breach of fiduciary duty based on the remaining management deficiencies identified in the plaintiffs' memorandum. The summary judgment materials show an absence of evidence to support a claim that the contracts with Smith Realty Management, Inc. or the management by that firm amounted to bad faith or a breach of fiduciary duty. The rental program and the allegedly deficient records may not even show negligence, and they surely do not support a claim of bad faith. Claims about lighting, carpeting, and the expenses of the rental program and the on-site maintenance man are classic questions of business judgment that cannot support a claim for breach of fiduciary duty.

C. Limitations and Repose

The defendants have not shown that their statute of limitations defense entitles them to summary judgment on the claims against the defendants as trustees of the Trust are the only persons with authority to bring suit on behalf of the owners collectively. The elected unit-owner trustees did not take control of the Condominium Trust until April 28, 1992. Before that, the Condominium was in the control of the developer trustees. They were not apt to sue themselves. Assuming arguendo that there was a breach of fiduciary duty by the developer trustees, the elected unit-owner trustees had no legal capacity to bring suit until they took over in April, 1992, *Libman v. Zuckerman*, 33 Mass. App. Ct. 341, 345 (1992). The elected unit-owner trustees brought suit on March 19, 1993, and this was less than three years after their cause of action accrued.

The six year statue or repose for claims of negligence in the design or construction of improvements to real property (G.L. c. 260, 2B) does not apply to the claims against the condominium trustees for breach of fiduciary duty claims are based on alleged failures to properly correct and maintain the grading, drainage, retaining walls and sewage facility, and these claims are not based on negligence in the design, planning, construction, or administration of construction of these improvements.

...

V. ORDER

Summary judgment is ordered for the defendants Guerriere, Buscone, and Pyne on all claims against them in Count I of the amended complaint except the claims that allege breaches of fiduciary duty based on the total effect of alleged failures to carry out their fiduciary duty regarding the grading and water drainage, the retaining walls, the sewage facility, and the collection of condominium charges from the developer.

Summary judgment is ordered for the defendants Guerriere, Buscone and Pyne on the claims in Count II of the amended complaint.

Retrospective and Observations

Paul Stein represented the developer trustees in this case, which was still active at time of publication of the first edition of this book, (the case was appealed and was waiting for a court date to be assigned, and we regret that we were unable to obtain an update). Louis Guerriere and two others saw an opportunity in the late 1980s to purchase and finish a condominium development which was "in limbo." None of the three was a professional developer. One was a builder, one had management experience, and the third had been on the fringes of a developing a project. They all lived in the same town and were acquainted with each other.

Because of their inexperience and because the bottom fell out of the real estate market in Massachusetts, the project failed, and it was taken over by the FDIC. The three tried desperately to find a buyer for the project, but the FDIC dragged its feet on every proposal. When the FDIC finally approved a purchase, the potential purchaser was no longer interested.

Of the 240 units planned for the project, only 140 have been built, and fewer have been sold. The owners are frustrated because they did not get what they expected and because assessments continued to rise. Mr. Stein sees the case as a contest between people who got into something way above their heads and the owners who continue to be frustrated because the project remains unfinished, and there is no money to complete it.

Notes & Questions

1. *Assessments.* Determining whether a developer is liable for assessments for incomplete or unbuilt condominium units depends primarily on: (1) the statutory definition of unit owner and (2) the effect given by courts in the jurisdiction to language in the declaration limiting developer liability for assessments. Typically, a unit is created either when the community's declaration is recorded or when a supplemental declaration is subsequently recorded. By definition, therefore, a developer becomes a unit owner for each unsold unit, even if it exists on paper alone. A condominium developer's attempts to limit exposure to assessments in the condominium declaration may not be upheld by the courts. Refer back to our discussion on this topic in Chapter 6. See also *e.g., Hatfield v. La Charmant Home Owner's Ass'n,* 469 N.E.2d 1218, 1222 (Ind. Ct. App. 1984) (attempts to limit the developer's liability for payment of common expenses on incomplete units in the declaration not enforced). Using the declaration to shift the assessment burden to other unit owners has been rejected by some courts even where the statute seemingly permits assessments to be levied in accordance with the declaration. See, *e.g., Palm Bay Towers Corp. v. Brooks,* 466 So. 2d 1071 (Fla. Dist. Ct. App. 1984).

Some state statutes provide the developer with breathing room. In Florida, for instance, a developer is excused from paying any assessments for up to 24 months following the sale of the first unit. See Fl. St. §718.116(9)(a) (West 1996); see also Ind. Code Ann. §32-1-6-22(d) (Michie 1996) (if the declaration provides, developer may be excused from paying assessments for 24 months following the date the declaration is recorded, but declarant/developer must make up any assessment shortfalls).

2. *Reserve funds.* Maintenance of a reserve fund may be required by statute or by the governing documents. See, *e.g.,* Or. Rev. Stat. §94.595 (1996). Where a reserve fund is established, it is typically funded as a part of the annual budget and general assessments. While reserve funds are generally set aside to cover the depreciation and eventual replacement of a community's capital assets and improvements, sometimes the governing documents also provide for an operational expense reserve fund to cover unexpected shortfalls in the community's annual expenses and revenue. *Id.* Subject to constraints in the governing documents, these funds are often invested until needed.

In *Newport West Condo. Ass'n v. Veniar,* 134 350 N.W.2d 818 (Mich. Ct. App. 1984), defendant unit owners raised as a defense in an action to recover unpaid assessments the developer's failure to maintain reserves in accordance with the by-laws. The court held that the owners' obligation to pay assessments is independent of the developer's obligation to fund a reserve account. Rather than withholding assessment payments, the unit owners instead should have brought an action against the association and developer for acting outside the by-laws. 350 N.W.2d at 823. What advantages are there for the developer to fund such reserve accounts? What disadvantages (or threat) do such reserve funds pose to the developer?

3. *Insurance.* Timely obtaining insurance for the new community association is an important consideration for the declarant/developer. In *Munder v. Circle One Condo. Corp.*, 596 So. 2d 425 (Fla. Dist. Ct. App. 1992), the developer corporation was held liable for failing to renew the fire insurance policy on the community association's clubhouse. However, the developer-director was not liable for breach of fiduciary duty because the clubhouse was unused and the association needed the money saved on the premiums for other purposes.

4. *Hire, supervise, and discharge personnel.* Typically, the developer will not be liable for failing to supervise association personnel after it relinquishes control of the association to the association's board of directors. See, *e.g., Conley v. Coral Ridge Properties, Inc.*, 396 So. 2d 1220 (Fla. Dist. Ct. App. 1981) (developer is not liable where intruder bribed association's security guard to gain access to the building and the developer no longer had any responsibility to oversee the security guard). Why might it be unwise for the developer to "share" personnel with the association?

5. *Failure to bring suit.* The statute of limitations for potential claims against the developer may toll during the period of developer control of the association. Logically, such a tolling period would prevent a developer from delaying turnover until expiration of the relevant statute of limitations period for potential claims against the developer. See, *e.g., Charley Toppino & Sons, Inc. v. Seawatch at Marathon Condo. Ass'n, Inc.*, 658 So. 2d 922 (1994); Fla. Stat. Ann. §718.124 (West 1997). In what situations may a developer argue that it would be inequitable to toll the statute of limitations even though the developer was still in control of the association's board of directors?

6. *Adequate corporate records.* Whether a statute or the by-laws require corporate records to be kept in a specific manner, it is, of course, in the developer's interest to maintain accurate records. See, *e.g.,* Del. Code Ann. Tit. 25 §2218 (1996) (requiring detailed records of receipts and expenditures as well as unit owner access to those records during normal business hours); Fla. St. §718.301(4)(c) (1996) (developer must turn over financial records audited by an independent certified public accountant); see also, *Alternative Dev., Inc. v. St. Lucie Club and Apt. Homes Condo. Ass'n, Inc.*, 608 So. 2d 822 (Fla. Dist. Ct. App. 1992).

In *LaFreniere* v. *Fitzgerald* a summary of the developer's payments and receipts as prepared by an accountant in anticipation of trial was held by an appellate court not to satisfy the business records exception to the hearsay rule. 658 S.W.2d 692 (Tex. Ct. Civ. App. 1983). The developer maintained folders full of receipts and canceled checks, drawn on both his personal and corporate accounts. Note that if the Texas Supreme Court had not reversed and held the business records exception applicable, the developer would have been liable to pay assessments even though he had spent a significant sum of money on behalf of the association. *LaFreniere v. Fitzgerald*, 669 S.W.2d 117 (Tex. 1984).

Both the developer and the accounting firm are potentially liable where the association's financial records fail accurately to reflect the association's financial position during declarant control. See, *Cliff House Condo. Council v. Capaldi*, 1991 WL 165302 (Del. Ch.) *aff'd*, 703 A.2d 643 (Del. 1997). In *Cliff House*, the developer misrepresented the association's financial records by understating expenses, inaccurately describing income, and delaying the transfer of financial information to the transition finance committee. What happens when the association's by-laws require an annual audit of the association's accounts but due to poor record keeping, no CPA is willing to certify an audit report? Be aware of the difference between an audit and a certified audit. Is a homeowner entitled to an audit of the association's financial activities? See, *e.g.*, *Clay v. River Landing Corp.*, 601 So. 2d 919 (Ala. 1992) (no entitlement to an audit).

The Real World: A Developer's Perspective

Communication is especially important in a community such as Champion Hills where a large percentage of the homes are second homes and the owners are not full time residents. When the golf course was resodded and reseeded, we implemented a communications vehicle called "upgrade updates." The updates were sent out weekly because we felt it was important for members to be kept up to date on the status of the work. When something important occurs, accelerating the flow of information is critical.

If we had a second chance to develop this project, we would set up an entity to manage the association. We would do a better job of getting the nuts and bolts of the association set up beyond the documentation. The documents were great, but you don't run an association on documents. You run it with a management company, and we waited far too long in setting up budgets and hiring a professional management company.

—Chuck Mitchell

---

2. Declarant's Rights

Restatement (Third) § 6.21 Developer's Power To Waive Provisions Of The Declaration

A developer may not exercise a power to amend or modify the declaration in a way that would materially change the character of the development or the burdens on the existing community members unless the declaration fairly apprises purchasers that the power could be used for the kind of change proposed.

Residential Communities of America v. Escondido Community Ass'n

District Court of Appeal of Florida
603 So. 2d 122 (Fla. Ct. App. 1992)

SHARP J. Residential Communities of America (RCA) appeals from a judgment in its declaratory suit which determined that its uncompleted units in the Escondido Condominium are bound by an amendment to the declaration of condominium, although the amendment was made without RCA's consent or joinder. The trial court held that since RCA was not presently holding any completed condominium units for sale, it was not a "developer," and its joinder was not necessary. We disagree with the trial court's interpretation of the condominium documents and its application of Florida's Condominium Law (Chapter 718). Accordingly, we reverse.

The facts in this case are not in dispute. Beginning in 1979, RCA developed, acted as general contractor, and initially marketed the Escondido Condominium in Seminole County, Florida. The condominium was planned to be developed in three phases. By 1984 RCA had built and sold 203 units, but it still owned two undeveloped parcels in the last phase when it turned over management and control of the condominium to the Escondido Community Association (ECA).

RCA continued to hold the undeveloped parcels. They were improved to the extent that parking lots were completed, and water, sewer, and telephone lines for the planned additional 27 units were installed. But at the time this lawsuit was filed in 1989, RCA no longer held any completed units for sale.[1]

Article XVII of the Declaration of Condominium sets out how the Declaration can be amended. One is by a two-thirds vote of the Board of Directors, and another is by a two-thirds vote of the owners. Both require that the "developer" consent to or "join" any amendment, in order to "affect" its rights. It provides:

ARTICLE XVII. — AMENDMENTS

Except as expressly set forth elsewhere herein, this Declaration of Covenants and Restrictions may be amended by a two-thirds (2/3) vote of the Board of Directors of the ECA or an instrument executed with the same formalities as a deed by Members of the ECA with at least two-thirds (2/3) of the total outstanding votes of the ECA, which Amendment shall thereafter be recorded in the Public Records of Seminole County, Florida, and shall thereupon become a part of this Declaration of Covenants and Restrictions as though the same were first set forth herein. *Notwithstanding the foregoing, an Amendment to this Declaration shall not affect in any manner whatsoever the rights of the Developer unless the Developer joins in said Amendment.* (emphasis supplied).

The condominium was originally marketed by RCA as an adult community. Pursuant to Article IX(J) of the Declarations, children under the age of seventeen were not permitted to reside in the units for a time longer than sixty days. The condominium population of Escondido was and has remained essentially as it began, as a residential community for senior citizens.

However, the Fair Housing Amendments Act of 1988[2] cast some doubt about the continued enforceability of the condominium's restriction against children. In order for such a restriction to be enforceable, the federal law requires that at least eighty percent of the units have an occupant over the age of fifty-five years.

The Escondido condominium then met the federal age and occupancy requirements, but there was concern by the managers and directors that it might not always be able to qualify. To try to insure that it would, the required two-thirds of the Board of Directors adopted an amendment (the Fifth Amendment) to the Declaration which prohibits the sale or lease of any unit to a person unless an occupant of the unit is fifty-five years of age or older. However, ECA did not notify RCA nor seek its joinder in the amendment.

ECA took the position that RCA's joinder was not required because RCA no longer qualified as a "developer" of the Escondido Condominium since it held no units for sale

---

1. After this lawsuit was filed, RCA sold the two undeveloped parcels to N.J.B. Investments, but has continued the suit for the benefit of its successor in interest.

2. Public Law 100-430, Sept. 13, 1988.

or lease in the ordinary course of business. ECA relied on section 718.303(3), Florida Statutes (1979), which provides:

> If a developer holds units for sale in the ordinary course of business, none of the following actions may be taken without approval in writing by the developer:
>
> (a) Assessment of the developer as a unit owner for capital improvements.
>
> (b) Any action by the association that would be detrimental to the sales of units by the developer. However an increase in assessments for common expenses without discrimination against the developer shall not be deemed detrimental to the sales of the units.

RCA argued that the Fifth Amendment adversely affected its ability to market the planned-for, but-as-yet undeveloped parcels, and that at least those parcels should not be affected by the amendment unless RCA consented to it, and "joined" in the amendment process. RCA pointed out that it qualifies as a "developer" under the definition section of Florida's Condominium Laws. Section 718.103(12), Florida Statutes (1979) which defines developer as:

> *[A] person who creates a condominium or offers condominium parcels for sale or lease* in the ordinary course of business, but does not include an owner or lessee of a unit who has acquired his unit for his own occupancy. (emphasis added)

And RCA noted it is specifically designated as the "Developer" pursuant to Article I(j) of the Escondido Condominium Declaration.[3]

It seems to us that RCA has the better argument. The language used in section 718.301(3) and section 718.103(12) do not settle the issue involved in this case. Section 718.103(3) grants a developer specific protections against adverse actions by an association and later amendments to the declaration. They are similar to Article XVII of the Escondido Declaration, but not identical, since arguably they apply only if a developer is currently holding "units for sale in the ordinary course of business." But, in no manner can we read into section 718.301(3) a prohibition against affording greater protections to a developer in applicable condominium documents.

Similarly, the definition of a developer in section 718.103(12) encompasses RCA. RCA, without dispute, created the condominium in this case even though it now holds no completed unit for sale. But by itself, this section gives RCA no more rights than section 718.301(3) or some other statute might provide.

Article XVII is determinative. It requires RCA's (or its successor-in-interest's) joinder or consent to any amendment to the Escondido Condominium Declaration, if such amendment will be binding on RCA's remaining property interests in the condominium. The article is not limited to RCA remaining actively engaged in selling completed units. Under the language of this article, RCA should be protected regardless of its or the real estate market's activity so long as it owns property in the condominium it acquired as the developer. Since RCA held the ownership interest of the two undeveloped parcels of the Escondido Condominium at the time the amendment was passed and recorded, and since it did not join or consent thereto, the undeveloped parcels are not bound by that amendment.

Accordingly, we reverse the judgment rendered below and remand for further proceedings consistent with this opinion.

Reversed and Remanded.

---

3. Article I(j) of the Declaration defines "Developer" as "Residential Communities of America and any assignee of its rights hereunder."

Notes & Questions

1. *Reservations.* In drafting the association documents, the development team wants to protect the developer's rights during construction and sale and to allow for flexibility in the development plan from concept to reality. The power to reserve such rights is not without limit. See, *e.g., Flamingo Ranch Estates, Inc. v. Sunshine Ranches Homeowners, Inc.*, 303 So. 2d 665, 666 (Fla. Dist. Ct. App. 1974) (developer's reservation unilaterally to amend governing documents "is a valid clause so long as it is exercised in a reasonable manner as not to destroy the general scheme or plan of development"). See also UCIOA §§ 2-105 and 2-110 describing how to draft and exercise development and declaration rights.

a. Annexation. A developer may reserve rights to annex additional land to the association in the declaration. In doing so, it is important to define the additional land that may be subject to annexation, provide the developer with the unilateral right to amend the documents outside the general amendment provisions, and emphasize that any decision to annex additional land is at the developer's option.

Such a right to annex may be limited to the original developer and successors in interest. Others may not be entitled to exercise the right to annex merely because they have acquired title to a portion of the development. See *Fairways of Country Lakes Townhouse Ass'n v. Shenandoah Dev. Corp.*, 447 N.E.2d 1367 (Ill. App. Ct. 1983) (reservation in declaration is personal to the developer and cannot be exercised by subsequent purchasers; no rights ran with title to a portion of the tract sold to another developer). What happens when a developer intends formally to annex newly built units but forgets to record the necessary supplemental declaration? See *In re: Lots 32–42, Colonial Village Townhouses Subdivision, Colonial Village Owners Ass'n, Inc.*, No. 3 AN-90-10566 CIV (Alaska Ct. App., 1991) (holding that annexation was accomplished by the acts of the owners paying annual assessments and accepting association services).

b. Consent requirements. It is not uncommon for developers to place language throughout the declaration requiring the developer's consent to amend certain provisions of the declaration. For example, the amendment provision within the declaration might state: "No amendment may remove, revoke, or modify any right or privilege of Declarant without the written consent of Declarant or the assignee of such right or privilege." See WAYNE S. HYATT, CONDOMINIUMS AND HOMEOWNER ASSOCIATIONS, § 7.93 (1985).

2. *Public policy limits.* In *Callahan v. Ganneston Park Dev. Corp.*, 245 A.2d 274 (Me. 1968), developer sold lots by reference to a recorded plan laying out the future location of roadways. When developer recorded the declaration, he reserved the right to "alter in any way" the provisions contained in the recorded plans. When developer sought to "alter" the plan by removing a cul de sac and forming three additional building lots, plaintiff lot owner sued. The court held that the definition of "alter" did not include the complete removal of any part of the plan, and the developer was estopped from removing the cul de sac because of plaintiff's reliance on the developer's representations. Alternatively, the court stated that the developer was also prohibited from removing the cul de sac based on public policy considerations. The court found that once a roadway had been established in a plan and lots had been sold, only a municipality's officials could remove those streets after a condemnation hearing. *Id.* at 279. ("[I]t is not in the public interest to permit land developers to hold out the hope and expectation of the availability of streets to serve lots being purchased and at the same time retain the power at their whim to subsequently destroy that availability.") How might the developer in the above case better provide for the right he sought to acquire?

3. *Waiver and estoppel.* A developer also may waive its rights under the declaration by failing to act on them or by acquiescing to conduct inconsistent with those rights. See *Englewood Golf, Inc. v. Englewood Golf Condo. Villas Ass'n., Inc.*, 547 So. 2d 1050 (Fla. Dist. Ct. App. 1989).

3. Declarant Bound by Declaration/Governing Documents

Stuewe v. Lauletta

Appellate Court of Illinois
418 N.E.2d 138 (Ill. App. Ct. 1981)

WILSON J. Following a bench trial on count III of the complaint, which alleged that a lease/easement of a portion of the common elements for a single parking space was improper, judgment was entered in favor of defendants (Lauletta) and this count was subsequently dismissed. On appeal, plaintiffs contend that the trial court erred in finding for defendants and dismissing the complaint as the attempted amendment of the condominium declaration was improper and defendants had actual and constructive notice of the fact that the disputed area was part of the common elements. We reverse and remand. The facts are as follows:

In October 1972, defendants entered into a real estate contract to purchase a condominium unit as Les Chateau condominium from the developer, Bern Builders, Inc. Defendants contracted for two parking spaces and were told that these spaces were inside the garage. It was later determined that two spaces were not available inside the garage and so a parking space was designated by the developer outside of the garage. This was a new parking space which had not previously been identified on the survey of the property.

The developer's president, Mr. William Tedtman, and defendants (Lauletta) executed a 99-year lease at closing with a covenant to record an easement.

Defendants moved into their unit in December 1972. At that time only four other units were occupied and owned by others. The shrubbery was removed from the area designated as defendants' parking space in February or March 1973, and they began using the space at that time.

The association took over management of the building from Bern Builders on November 1, 1973. They offered defendants the use of a parking space at the rear of the building for their second car, which was refused.

Defendants testified that they signed a contract and received a copy of a survey in 1972. They were told that they had two parking spaces, both of which were inside the building. At closing, however, the developer realized that they could not have two spaces inside the building and so designated space 3A located at the front of the building. Bern Builders indicated to them that they would amend the condominium declaration to provide for the new parking space so designated; however, to their knowledge, this was not done.

The trial court found in favor of defendants, indicating that the developer made leases and operated the condominium prior to the time the association actually came into being. The court also indicated that it would be inequitable in light of all the circumstances to deprive defendants of the space they contracted for and that the association should have been put on notice that these parties had been given the parking space in dispute.

OPINION

Plaintiffs contend that defendants attempted to purchase or lease from the developer a parking space which the developer did not own and to which it had no right to control and that the attempted amendment of the Declaration to provide for the parking space in question was ineffective and as such, the disputed parking area remains part of the common elements of the Les Chateau condominium. We agree.

The Declaration of Condominium (Declaration) governed the sale of the Les Chateau condominiums and was recorded in February 1972. It designated the common elements as being all portions of the property except the units. It also included a survey, which designated certain areas of the common elements as parking spaces; however, the disputed parking area was not included as such in the survey, and thus would have been considered part of the other common elements. Defendants' argument that the percentage of ownership in the common elements has not been effected and that the amendment merely redesignates a use for a portion of the common elements as a parking space, is unpersuasive since the Declaration specifically indicates that each unit ownership has a perpetual and exclusive easement of a parking space. As such, for all practical purposes, no other tenant can use another's assigned parking space and that particular parking space passes along with the unit if there is any change in unit ownership. In effect, then, the common elements as to all other tenants have thereby been diminished.

Article III of the Declaration states the applicable rules affecting the common elements. Relevant portions of this Article state that:

> Each owner shall own an undivided interest in the common elements as a tenant in common with all the other owners of the property ...

> The extent or amount of such ownership (in the common elements) shall be expressed by a percentage amount, and, once determined, shall remain constant, and may not be changed without unanimous approval of all owners. Art. III, par. 2.

In order to amend article III, article XIII, paragraph 7 provides that:

> The provisions of Article III ... may be changed, modified or rescinded by an instrument in writing setting forth such change, modification or rescission, signed and acknowledged by the Board, all of the owners and all mortgagees having bona fide liens of record against unit ownerships.

Thus, the specific language of the Declaration requires approval of all owners before the common elements could be diminished, and approval of all owners before any provision of article III could be amended which, in either case, the developer did not have.

However, assuming that the area in question fell under the provisions of article I (Parking Area) and article IV, paragraph 3(d), which designates other portions of the common elements as parking spaces, as defendants advocate, then any amendment to these articles would be subject to the following provision of article XIII:

> Other provisions of this Declaration may be changed, modified or rescinded by an instrument in writing setting forth such changes, modification, or rescission, signed and acknowledged by the Board, the owners having at least 3/4ths of the total vote and containing an affidavit by an officer of the Board certifying that a copy of the change, modification or rescission has been mailed by certified mail to all mortgagees having bona fide liens of record against any unit ownership, not less than ten (10) days prior to the date of such affidavit. The change, modification or rescission shall be effective upon recordation of such instrument in the

Office of the Recorder of Deeds of Cook County, Illinois; provided, however, that no provision in this Declaration may be changed, modified or rescinded so as to conflict with the provisions of the Condominium Property Act.

It is undisputed that in December 1972, Bern Builders controlled 15 of the total 19 units (only four other units were occupied and owned by others) and thus along with defendants comprised three-fourths of the ownership of the condominium complex, which was the necessary voting percentage to effect an amendment to these articles. However, the developer would still be bound by this provision setting forth the procedure to follow and requiring notice to the owners. There is no evidence in the record that this procedure was followed, and thus the attempted amendment would still be ineffective.

Moreover, defendant's argument that the rules of equity demand that they be allowed to use the disputed parking area is inapplicable under the circumstances of this case. It is axiomatic that equity follows the law (*Evergreen Savings & Loan Association v. Barnard* (1978), 65 Ill. App. 3d 492, 382 N.E.2d 467; *In re Estate of Wallace* (1932), 266 Ill. App. 500) and cannot be invoked to destroy or supplant a legal right. It therefore follows that where the Declaration establishes the rights inherent in unit ownership and provides for the procedures in order to effect an amendment to it, equity cannot aid in effecting what ought to have been done, in contravention of the Declaration, particularly when other unit owners' rights are involved. Whether the Declaration was properly amended to provide for the disputed parking space is not an equity question but a question of law controlled by the provisions of the Declaration.

Bern Builders, even acting as the board of managers or trustee under article XIII, paragraph 1, could not validly execute a lease to defendants until it was supplemented by a recorded easement as first, the area in question had not been specifically designated in the Declaration with the survey attached, as a parking space, and secondly, there was no proper amendment including recordation to include this area as a parking space to be subject to any lease/easement. Defendants and the developer are both bound by the provisions of the Declaration and could not circumvent its requirements in order to effect an amendment.

For the foregoing reasons, the order appealed from which found in favor of defendants on count III and dismissed the complaint is reversed and this cause is remanded to the trial court with directions that dismissal of the complaint be vacated and judgment be entered in favor of plaintiffs as to count III.

Reversed and Remanded with directions.

Notes & Questions

1. *Unilateral amendments.* While courts have permitted developers unilaterally to amend the covenants after units have been sold, typically the developer must exercise good faith, act reasonably, and adhere to the general development plan if such amendments are to be valid. R. Natelson, § 5.5.2, at 199; *Lakemoor Community Club, Inc. v. Swanson*, 24 Wash. App. 10, 600 P.2d 1022 (1979); *Flamingo Ranch Estates, Inc. v. Sunshine Ranches Homeowners, Inc.*, 303 So. 2d 665 (Fla. Dist. Ct. App. 1974). See also *Johnson v. Three Bays Properties #2, Inc.*, 159 So. 2d 924, 926 (Fla. Dist. Ct. App. 1964) (declarant may amend the restrictive covenants so long as owners are protected against "unreasonable diminution of the building requirements").

2. *Complying with changing mortgage requirements or changing laws.* Reserving the right unilaterally to amend the declaration permits developers to respond to lenders' changing requirements. Agencies that insure, guarantee, or purchase loans have special require-

ments which must be included or reflected in the declaration in order for new loans to be granted on home sales in the community. Oregon statutes specifically permit the developer unilaterally to amend the governing documents to comply with lender requirements until turnover. Or. Rev. Stat. § 94.585 (1996). Singularly, declarants will often reserve the right unilaterally to amend the declarations in order to comply with changing legal requirements of state or federal law.

The Real World: A Developer's Insight

One lesson learned from experiences on previous projects is to get homeowners involved early. On the initial projects on which I worked, the associations had only a minimum amount of control and responsibility, while the developer had maximum control over association operations, both during the developer control period and by extending the length of the developer control period. In those early projects, developer rights took priority. My attitude as a developer has changed over the years. Now I believe that trust must develop between the developer and the owners. The developer must pass the "fairness test."

Communication is also important. Homeowners at Celebration receive a monthly letter to keep them informed about community news, and a resident advisory panel was established. Additionally, the community has a computer network. Disney learned from a poll that 70% of people work on computers. Every home in Celebration is wired for computer technology, and Disney has set up chat rooms where owners can express their ideas about the community. There is an icon on the Celebration network on which one can click to see all aspects of the town.

—Donald E. Killoren

Nothing chastens a planner more than the knowledge that he will have to carry out the plan.

— General James Garvin

B. Transition of Control

Chaos is the law of nature; order is the dream of men.

—Henry Adams

Restatement (Third) § 6.19 Developer's Duty To Create An Association And Turn Over Control

(1) The developer of a common-interest-community project has a duty to create an association to manage the common property and enforce the servitudes unless exempted by statute.

(2) After the time reasonably necessary to protect its interests in completing and marketing the project, the developer has a duty to transfer the common property to the association, or the members, and to turn over control of the association to the members other than the developer.

Developer Transition: How Community Associations Assume Independence from Developer Control
Adapted from A Guide for Association Practitioners
Amanda G. Hyatt (Community Associations Institute 2004) by permission

Method of Transfer

An association's success often depends on how governance is transferred from developer to owners. Ideally, owners should gradually become involved in the association's operations and decisions. However, owners and developers often are reluctant to undertake the transition process. The developer may fear that owners will interfere with building and marketing, thus threatening profitability. Owners may be reluctant to accept responsibility for the association for fear of assuming a financial or legal burden. By understanding the process and the benefits of a successful transition, each party will be more comfortable working with the other.

One way to understand transition is to understand what it is not. For instance, transition is not the act of transfer or acceptance of the common elements or common property.

In condominium developments, for instance, the common property is subject to the condominium regime when the condominium is created, so the property is already "turned over" to the unit owners when they purchase their units. In homeowner associations, the common property frequently is deeded to the association prior to the sale of the first units or during early stages of a multiphase development.

Transition also is not the turnover of the common elements to owners who then have no further recourse for construction defects in the common elements. Furthermore, transfer of control from the developer to the owners does not necessarily ensure that developer construction warranties have been met.

Transition is a process—a series of events—that transfers control of the association from the developer to the individual unit owners. In a well-planned and implemented transition program, actual turnover is a mere formality that marks one event during an extended process when the developer relinquishes control of the association.

Working Together

Experience shows that a well-planned transition, which combines thorough owner-education with the gradual transfer of control, will result in a well-run association. By working together during the transition period, the developer and the unit owners can understand the concerns of each party and protect their interests.

Both parties benefit from a successful transition and early owner involvement. The developer benefits by gaining a good reputation. And owners learn about every facet of association operations. This knowledge enables them to manage the association effectively, matching community needs with the association's financial capabilities. The result is a successful community association, a credit to the developer and a sound investment for the unit owners.

It is important to realize that the level of owner involvement varies depending on the association's character. For example, an owner-occupied residential development can expect a much higher level of participation than a second-home resort development. Also, the complexity of association operations and the size of the common elements can affect involvement. A development that features a large recreational package and exterior building maintenance will involve more owners than one with limited common areas.

Successful transition requires advance planning. Preparation for transition begins with the initial planning of the project and carries through until unit owners are in complete control of the association. It involves all phases of the development process. Though the process may be time consuming, eventually it will return dividends to all involved.

Ideal Transition Scenario

Ideally, the development of a community association begins when the developer meets with those involved in planning the development—attorneys, architects, lenders, accountants, and marketing and management consultants. These professionals should discuss:

- Details of the physical development
- Financing and marketing plan for the project
- The association's structure
- Programs to facilitate involvement and education
- A timetable for the shift of association control to the unit owners

After the planning is completed and the physical development is underway, the developer's attorney drafts the legal documents. While it is necessary for an attorney to draft the documents from a legal point of view, a management practitioner should review them from an operational point of view. The development team also should draft a comprehensive maintenance manual to provide a reliable guide for the association—regardless of who controls the board.

Education of new owners begins with materials and explanations provided during the sales process and with a new owner orientation program given shortly after conveyance. This material should include:

- Explanations of the community association concept.
- Particular aspects of the documents and rules and regulations.
- A description of the association's operation and management.
- The stages of transition from developer to owner control.

The developer identifies activities in which the owners can become immediately involved and solicits participation in these activities. As owners increase in number, the developer or its representative should hold periodic meetings to discuss development progress and association operations. The meetings also should solicit owner input.

The developer should encourage owners to participate in the maintenance, insurance, orientation, communications, architectural review, and finance committees. Their recommendations should have increasing weight in the board's deliberations. When the number of units sold reaches a pre-designated percentage, owners should begin having a more formal involvement in the association's governance. At this stage, the owners elect representatives to serve on an interim committee, an advisory board, or the board of directors, with the percentage and form of representation depending on state statute, association documents, and/or the developer's stated transition plan. These owner representatives would then have the opportunity to present unit owners' views to the developer-controlled board. As additional sale levels are achieved, unit owners are generally entitled to additional representation until, eventually, they hold a majority of the seats on the board. At this point, the owners have complete control of association decisions, unless the developer has retained a veto over certain board decisions until the development is largely complete. In this case, owners gain complete control when the developer's veto right expires.

In the ideal scenario, turnover is a formality. The developer helps phase-in owner responsibility and owners are already in charge of key committee functions when the developer leaves the community. Association operations do not skip a beat. Any disputes between the association and the developer over items such as common-area deficiencies still need to be addressed, but board members can represent owners' interests from the experience they gained during transition. Furthermore, many problems regarding assessment collection, contract awards, and maintenance quality are identified and handled earlier in the transition process.

Although the ideal scenario seems straightforward, the developer must undertake a carefully conceived, multifaceted plan to achieve it.

Legal Framework

The legal framework for transition is one of the most important parts of the transition process. If properly conceived and structured at the outset, this framework can speed the process along to a successful conclusion for both the developer and the homeowners. It also can help limit misunderstanding and court action between the parties. The legal framework for transition, especially for condominiums, typically is set forth in broad terms in state statutes. The statutes set minimum standards for the process. The developer must understand the nature and form of such requirements to provide appropriate language for the association's legal documents.

Developing Leadership and Involvement

The developer's efforts to transfer control will accomplish little if new owners do not become involved. Unfortunately, developers and associations often are faced with owner apathy. Many owners are only interested in paying their assessments on time, obeying rules and regulations, and signing voting proxies—and those actions are important. But running the association requires more. Though owner apathy is a difficult problem faced by many associations, the board can minimize its effects during the development and sell-out phases.

After a new owner has purchased a home in the community and gone through the basic orientation program, the association should attempt to accomplish two goals:

1. Identify the skills and interests of each owner. This can be done through an interview or questionnaire.

2. Introduce owners to each other so they can begin to develop their identity in the community.

Thus, one of the first functions of committee activity is to facilitate these introductions. Whatever the name of the committee—social, hospitality, communication, orientation, or other—its purpose is to provide activities and methods for owners to become acquainted with each other and the association.

Generating Volunteers

Whatever form the committee mentioned above takes, there are key areas for action:

Welcome packet. The developer or the committee should develop a welcome packet containing basic association information, *e.g.*, legal documents, rules, contact list for warranty work, answers to basic questions about the association, emergency numbers, a directory of owners, back issues of any newsletter, and an information form to assist new owners in identifying areas of interest to them.

New owner visit. A personal visit or phone call from a committee member along with a copy of the welcome packet provides an opportunity for new owners to ask questions.

Recognition. Peer recognition is one of the best ways to stimulate leadership. The developer can recognize work done by committees and their members. Bulletin boards—electronic or otherwise—and newsletters are good vehicles for recognizing active volunteers.

Meaningful involvement. The sense of being involved in association life in a meaningful way, that the effort an owner has invested in an activity is productive, and that an owner's involvement in decision making has a recognized effect all result in a positive experience for an owner and continued efforts to contribute.

Association visits. Providing opportunities for owners/leaders to visit other associations and to talk to their board or committee members about experiences broadens the range of options available to them. Exposure to local and national organizations that provide educational materials and programs for association members helps make owners more confident about what they are learning.

Reality checks. Early involvement on a realistic level helps to ensure that, as additional complexity and responsibility develop, owners mature in their capacity to respond.

Working Without a Transition Program

Although the educational programs and committee structure established in the development plan usually help motivate owners to participate in association activities, some developers do not prepare the association for transition. This may occur if the developer is bankrupt or if a lender takes back the property. Concerned owners should ask the developer: "What can we do to become involved in the association and to gain some measure of control over the situation?"

Expressing concern to the developer may be all that is needed, and the owners and developer can then work out a mutually agreeable program. It may be, however, that the developer may not understand or accept the value of early owner involvement and will not respond to owner initiatives.

An unresponsive developer is no excuse for owner inaction. Increasingly, the problem of unresponsive developers, or developers who are insensitive to owner involvement, is diminishing. When owners encounter such situations, they must be ready to assume responsibility to protect their investment.

Goddard v. Fairways Dev. Gen. Partnership

Court of Appeals of South Carolina
426 S.E.2d 828 (S.C. Ct. App. 1992)

CURETON J. At trial, the master-in-equity refused to dissolve or reform a planned unit development (PUD) and denied the plaintiffs other relief. We affirm in part, reverse in part, and remand.

Respondent, Fairways Development General Partnership (Developer), began developing the PUD in the early 1980's. The original design envisioned the building of approximately 90 villas. To date, only five villas have been built; the last one was completed in 1982.

The PUD is governed by a "Declaration of Covenants, Conditions and Restrictions" (Declarations) which grant superior voting rights to the developer until virtual completion of the PUD.[1] It creates "Fairway Villas Homeowners Association" (Association), with mandatory membership for all villa owners. The Declarations require the Association to own the common areas and to be responsible for maintaining these areas. The Association is funded by assessments against each villa. The Declarations provide for amendment by 90% of the villa owners and dissolution with the consent of 100% of the villa owners.

In June 1982, after filing the Declarations, the developer executed a deed conveying the common areas, with the exception of the common areas surrounding appellant Goddard's house, to the then nonexistent Association.[2] The deed was delivered to the Developer's attorney but was not filed. The Developer incorporated the Association in April 1984.

In February 1987, after all five villas were sold, the Association held its first meeting. The Developer filed the deed conveying the common areas to the Association on the same date as this first meeting.

The Association held its second and last meeting in March 1987. At this meeting, the Association elected Ullman, who was dismissed as a party to this action by the master, as president, and the developer notified the villa owners that the Association would thereafter be responsible for maintenance of the common areas. Until this time, the Developer had maintained the common areas at its expense.

The present controversy developed subsequent to the last meeting of the Association. The heart of the disagreement is the "viability" of the PUD. Because there are only six lot owners in the PUD that are required to pay assessments under the Declarations, they are the only sources of funds to maintain the common areas.[3] Present assessments are inadequate to maintain the common areas. Appellants have sought relief by proposing alternatively:

(1) the Developer pay assessments in proportion to its voting power in the Association, or

(2) dissolution of the PUD, transfer of the common areas to the villa owners in fee simple, and conversion of the PUD into a standard subdivision.

These efforts failed. The Developer has refused to pay assessments in proportion to its voting power; it has agreed to pay assessments only on the one lot it owns. Appellants cannot force a dissolution of the PUD because to do so requires a one hundred per cent vote of the lot owners. The Developer and Ullman have refused to consent to a dissolution. However, during oral argument before this court, the Developer's attorney announced it did not object to dissolving the PUD but would not do so over the objection of Ullman.

Assessments for common area expenses are made against lots, not parcels of land. Accordingly, unless and until the Developer subdivides parcels into lots, the undeveloped land in the PUD is not subject to assessment. Because of the Developer's superior voting

---

1. Article III of the Declarations creates two classes of voting rights in the Association. Class "A" is all "Owners" except the Developer; they have one vote for each "Lot" owned. Class "B" is the Developer; it has 50 votes for each "Lot" owned, and a total of 1500 votes for the existing "Parcels." As each "Parcel" is subdivided, the Developer receives 50 votes for each resulting "Lot." This class system continues until the number of Class A votes equals the number of Class B votes.

2. Pursuant to the Declarations, the common areas consist of all roads and all other areas in the PUD with the exception of the actual land located under the villa structures. The common areas surrounding Goddard's villa have never been deeded to the Association. However, the Developer has indicated he is willing to convey these areas to the Association.

3. While the Developer owns several undivided parcels of land in the planned PUD, he owns only one lot.

power, it may unilaterally control assessments. With the exception of electing Ullman as the Association's president, there is no evidence the Developer has exercised this unilateral power.

The appellants claim the master committed reversible error in (1) holding that maintenance of the common areas is the responsibility of the Association because those areas are owned by the Developer, (2) not granting a dissolution of the PUD, (3) not finding a breach of fiduciary duty by respondents and awarding damages,....

Appellants assert the master was incorrect in holding them responsible for assessments for maintenance of the common areas because these areas are owned by the Developer. They argue that because the deed to the common areas was executed before the Association became a legal entity, and the deed was never legally delivered, the conveyance to the Association is invalid. The master's order does not discuss either of these grounds. Moreover, the appellants' Rule 59(e) motion[4] and the order denying the motion do not mention these grounds. Issues on which the trial judge never ruled and which were not raised in post-trial motion are not properly before this court. *SSI Medical Services, Inc. v. Cox*, 301 S.C. 493, 494, 392 S.E.2d 789, 793 (1990).

Appellants also challenge the failure of the master to dissolve the PUD and place ownership of the common areas in the villa owners. Contrary to the holding of the master in dismissing Ullman as a party defendant, she is an indispensable party because changing the form of ownership of the common areas affects her property interests.[5] *Stewart v. State Crop Pest Commission*, S.C., 414 S.E.2d 121, 125 (1992) (a party is indispensable if an action will not afford complete relief among those already parties, will impair or impede an absent party's ability to protect his interest, or will leave parties already in the suit subject to substantial risk of incurring multiple or inconsistent obligations because the absent party was not joined). Ullman's counsel indicated at trial that she was opposed to a dissolution of the PUD. Because Ullman is an indispensable party and is opposed to a dissolution of the PUD, the master could not have dissolved the PUD in her absence. We find no error.

Appellants next contend the master erred in not finding that the Developer and its president owed a fiduciary duty to appellants because of their superior voting strength as compared to appellants. The appellants state:

> [they had] a fiduciary duty to manage and maintain the common property of the development. As such, Respondents should have maintained Fairway Lane in a reasonable condition until such time as there were sufficient reserves in the Association's accounts from assessments to accomplish such repairs. In failing to exercise proper supervisory and managerial responsibilities in the maintenance and upkeep of Fairway Lane, the common grounds and villa exteriors and in failing to establish a fund for such maintenance, Respondents breached their fiduciary duty to Appellants and should be held liable to Appellants for the cost of repairing Fairway Lane.

The appellants make two arguments. First, they argue that because of the Developer's and its president's superior voting strength, the respondents had a fiduciary obligation to assess the villa owners at a level necessary to maintain sufficient reserves to adequately

---

4. We note from the record that the appellants' counsel mentioned the invalidity of the deed during the motion hearing. However, the motion does not assert this ground as a basis for relief.

5. Appellants did not object to Ullman being dismissed as a party defendant because, as stated by the master, "there were no allegations against her."

maintain the common areas. Citing *Raven's Cove Townhomes, Inc. v. Knuppe Development Co.,* 114 Cal. App. 3d 783, 171 Cal. Rptr. 334, 343 (Ct. App. 1981), they also argue that because of their fiduciary relation to the appellants, these respondents had an obligation to expend their own funds to maintain the common areas until sufficient reserves were generated to maintain the areas through assessments.

Assuming a fiduciary relationship exists between the appellants and respondents because of their superior voting power, it is clear that the respondents have refrained from exercising their superior voting strength to effectuate higher assessments in deference to the wishes of the appellants to keep the assessments low. In a dispute between the directors of a homeowners association and aggrieved homeowners, the conduct of the directors should be judged by the "business judgment rule" and absent a showing of bad faith, dishonesty, or incompetence, the judgment of the directors will not be set aside by judicial action. 4 S.C. Juris. *Condominiums* § 42 (1991); *see also Dockside Ass'n, Inc. v. Detyens,* 291 S.C. 214, 352 S.E.2d 714 (Ct. App. 1987), *aff'd,* 294 S.C. 86, 362 S.E.2d 874 (1987). We cannot say that under the circumstances of this case the respondents violated a fiduciary duty to the appellants by not voting for higher assessments.

The appellants also argue that the Developer had a responsibility to insure that the common areas were in good repair at the time they were conveyed to the Association and that the Association had sufficient funds to maintain the common areas. We find that this argument has merit. As we view the facts in this case, the Association was not effectively organized until 1987, when the deed to the common areas was recorded. This appears to have been the intention of the Developer also.

The question of whether the Developer stood in a fiduciary relationship to the villa owners prior to the time the Association was effectively organized and the common elements were conveyed to it was not specifically discussed or ruled upon by the master.[6] "A confidential or fiduciary relationship exists when one reposes a special confidence in another, so that the latter, in equity and good conscience, is bound to act in good faith and with due regard to the interests of the one imposing the confidence." *Island Car Wash, Inc. v. Norris,* 292 S.C. 595, 599, 358 S.E.2d 150, 152 (Ct. App. 1987). Courts of equity have been careful to define fiduciary relationships so as not to exclude new cases that may give rise to the relationship. *Id.*

In the case of *Duncan v. Brookview House, Inc.,* 262 S.C. 449, 205 S.E.2d 707 (1974), our Supreme Court held that the promoters of a corporation are fiduciaries to each other and to the corporation they are creating. *Id.* at 456, 205 S.E.2d at 710. Here, we think there is a corollary between the promoters of a corporation and the developers of a PUD. Both are entrusted by interested investors to bring about a viable organization to serve a specific function. Both should be expected to use good judgment and act in utmost good faith to complete the formation of their organizations. *See* Julia J. Young, Comment, *Areas of Dispute in Condominium Law,* 12 Wake Forest L. Rev. 979, 984 (1976) (comment to Wayne S. Hyatt & James B. Rhoads, *Concepts of Liability in the Development and Administration of Condominium and Home Owners Associations,* 12 Wake Forest L. Rev. 915 (1976)).

While the evidence shows the Developer provided some maintenance of the common areas at its own expense until it belatedly organized the Association, there is evidence that the common areas were substandard at the time the Developer turned them over to the Association. There is also some evidence the Developer seized the opportunity in 1987 to "unload" the common areas on the Association without a plan to establish a reserve or a

---

6. The failure of the master to rule on this issue was raised in the appellants' post-trial motion.

plan to fund the Association until such time as assessments were adequate to cover maintenance expenses. It seems unfair to the villa owners for the Developer to burden them with substandard or deteriorated common areas that required an immediate expenditure of funds to bring them up to standard without a plan or a reserve fund to cover the expenditures. *See Orange Grove Terrace Owners Ass'n v. Bryant Properties, Inc.*, 176 Cal. App. 3d 1217, 222 Cal. Rptr. 523 (Ct. App. 1986); *see also Richard Gill Co. v. Jackson's Landing Owners' Ass'n*, 758 S.W.2d 921 (Tex. App. 1988) (fiduciary relationship established between condominium developer and condominium association because developer assumed responsibility for managing condominium until owners' association could be formed).

We hold that the trial court must consider this issue as a prerequisite to determining the liability of the Developer. Accordingly, the issue is remanded to the trial court for consideration. The trial court is authorized to consider additional evidence. On remand, the trial court should be certain that any liability imposed upon the Developer is limited to the costs that would have been required in 1987 to bring the common areas up to standard. The court should take into account the fact the villa owners apparently agreed at one point to be responsible for the exterior maintenance of their villas.

. . .

We have reviewed the other arguments made by the appellants for reversal of the master's order and find them to be manifestly without merit. They are summarily dismissed pursuant to S.C. Code Ann. § 14-8-250 (Supp. 1991) and Rule 220(b)(2), SCACR.

Affirmed in part, Reversed in part, and Remanded.

Notes & Questions

1. *Control and voting strength.* Developer control of the association may be phased out according to the percentage of units sold by the developer, at a set date provided for in the declaration, or by some other method provided by statute. See, *e.g.,* UCIOA § 3-103(d)-(e); N.J. Stat. Ann. § 46:8B-12.1a. (West 1997); Idaho Code § 55-1505 (1997). Where a statute fails to limit the period of developer control, courts typically permit the period to be defined in the declaration tempered only by public policy limits. See *Barclay v. Deveau*, 11 Mass. App. 236, *rev'd* 384 Mass. 676 (1981) (the declaration provided that the developer would appoint the majority of the board until it owned less than 12 units); *Investors Ltd. Sun Valley v. Sun Mountain Condo., Phase I, Inc. Homeowners Ass'n*, 106 Idaho 855, 683 P.2d 891 (1984) (recognizing the legitimacy of developer control for a certain time period after creation of the condominium). If it could so vote, what are the implications for the obligation to pay?

In *Hill v. Cole*, 591 A.2d 1036 (N.J. Sup. Ct. 1991), the developer ran for election to the board of directors even though more than 75% of the units had been sold. The court held that the purpose of the implicated state statute is to shift control from the developer to unit owners upon sale of 75% of the units. *Id.* at 1039. Under the New Jersey statute, N.J.S.A. 46:8B-12.1a, the developer is entitled to appoint one member to the board after 75% of the units are sold if the developer still holds units for sale in the ordinary course of business. The developer is not also entitled to cast votes in the election. *Hill* at 1039. Does this make good policy or sound governance? What advantages are there for a developer to turn over control of the association's board prior to sell-out? What potential risks exist for the developer if homeowners gain control of the board prior to sell-out? What factors should you consider when drafting the developer turnover provisions for a community association?

2. *Accounting.* The developer's responsibility to turn over the association's financial records also may be prescribed by statute. See *The Colonies Condo. Ass'n, Inc. v. Clairview*

Holdings, Inc., 419 So. 2d 725 (Fla. Dist. Ct. App. 1982) (developer need not produce financial documents for the year following turnover to the association); but see *Id.* at 727 (Sharp, dissent) ("records relating to transactions after the transfer could well lead to discovery of misappropriations of assets wrongfully retained or disposed of by the fiduciary").

3. *Dangerous conditions.* Upon transition of unit owner control, the developer typically will not be liable for injuries caused by the dangerous conditions on the common property that arise thereafter. See, *e.g., First Financial Dev. Corp. v. Hughston*, 797 S.W.2d 286, 290 (Tex. Ct. App. 1990) (adopting the Restatement (Second) of Torts interpretation of vendor liability; unless the developer failed to disclose or actively concealed the dangerous condition, the developer will not be liable).

The Real World: A Developer's Insight

On my first project, I discovered that transition was difficult since there had not been any education of the homeowners on how to run the association. Education should have started earlier.

—*J.J. McCament*

C. Liability Arising from Declarant Control of the Community Association

UCIOA provides that declarant appointees on the board of directors of a common interest community are held to the standards of a fiduciary while the homeowner-elected directors must observe a standard of ordinary and reasonable care. Laying aside for the moment the issue of whether or not such a distinction is valid as a matter of corporate and fiduciary law, does it make sense within the context of the common interest community itself? Is it fair and appropriate, and does it reflect the expectations of the parties?

In this section, you examine issues of liability arising from the declarant's ability to exercise dominion over the association's actions. This is most commonly seen in its ability to appoint the board of directors. Does the fiduciary analogy really fit? Is another treatment more appropriate which might result in the same outcome but be premised on a stronger legal foundation? In reality, the developer is the seller of a product, and the homeowner is the purchaser. As such, there clearly is an "adversarial" relationship to a limited extent. Does that adversarial relationship undercut the argument that the seller should be a fiduciary to the buyer? But do consider the role and liability of a corporate promoter. Consider the arguments and policy issues.

Raven's Cove Townhomes, Inc. v. Knuppe Dev. Co., Inc.
Court of Appeals of California
171 Cal. Rptr. 334 (Cal. Ct. App. 1981)

TAYLOR, J. This is an appeal by Raven's Cove Townhomes, Inc., a homeowners' association (Association), from a judgment of nonsuit in its action against Knuppe Development

Company, Inc., the project developer (Developer) for strict liability and breach of warranty as to defects in common area landscaping, as well as in the exterior walls of individual units, and against the Developer and the Developer's employees as former directors in control of the Association, for breach of fiduciary duty by failing to properly determine operating costs and fund a maintenance reserve account. The major questions presented are: 1) the Association's standing to sue as representing a common interest subdivision (as defined by Bus. & Prof. Code, §11000.1) pursuant to Code of Civil Procedure section 374, or in a representative capacity, pursuant to Code of Civil Procedure section 382; 2) the strict liability of the Developer and appropriate measure of damages pursuant to *Kriegler v. Eichler Homes, Inc.* (1969) 269 Cal.App.2d 224 [74 Cal.Rptr. 749]; 3) the fiduciary liability of the Developer and its employees as former directors in control of the Association; and 4) attorney fees. For the reasons set forth below, we have concluded that the judgment must be reversed.

Viewing the record in favor of the Association, as we must on appeal from the nonsuit pursuant to Code of Civil Procedure section 581c (*cf. Smith v. Roach* (1975) 53 Cal.App.3d 893, 897–898 [126 Cal.Rptr. 29]), the following pertinent facts appear.

The Association is a nonprofit corporation whose members are the owners of 65 townhomes in the Raven's Cove development in Alameda, California. In November 1972, defendants, James and Barbara Knuppe, the sole owners of the Knuppe Development Company, Inc.,[1] conveyed the common areas and facilities in fee simple to the Association. The Developer had been in the residential home building business for over 18 years and had built about 3,000 units, including several townhome developments, before Raven's Cove. The Developer acquired the undeveloped Raven's Cove site in April 1972. The site had been the place of fill activity for many years. The Developer added more fill in the fall of 1972. The overlying compoted fill is not generally characteristic of the native sandy soil.

The Association was incorporated by the Developer in 1972. In August 1973, the Developer recorded its grant deed of the common areas to the Association. By October 1973, construction had been substantially completed and sales commenced. Until May of 1974, when it was turned over to the homeowners, the Association was under the control of the Knuppes, who could not recall any functions that they performed, other than the signing of the Association's by-laws as officers.

The Association holds title to the common areas, including nearly two acres of lawns and shrubbery and landscaped areas. The Association also is responsible for maintenance and repair of the roofs and siding of the individual units, the common areas, and has the responsibility of assessing and collecting dues from the homeowners to establish: 1) an operating fund to pay current costs of upkeep, payment of water bills, and the cost of landscape maintenance personnel; 2) a replacement reserve fund for major costs, such as painting exterior surfaces of the individual units, replacement of roofs and major private street repairs. Replacement reserves have to be accumulated because the Association: 1) cannot assess its members a sufficient amount in a short period of time to pay for the work and materials required for major repairs and improvements; 2) cannot borrow funds for this purpose as the result of the nature of its assets. No reserve or operating funds were ever established or turned over to the Association.

There were serious defects in the landscaping and siding of Raven's Cove in 1974. As to the landscaping, expert testimony established that the problems with the soil, drainage

---

1. The other named defendants, T. A. McKee and J. W. Howard, were employees of Knuppe. Defendant, United Pacific Insurance was the surety on the bonds for the completion of the common areas of Raven's Cove, and is no longer a party.

and irrigation systems of the common areas which resulted in yellow lawns, dead olive trees and unhealthy plants, were the result of the Developer's failure to properly prepare the soil. The soil conditions were not appropriate for the desired landscaping; the soil contained a lot of clay, base rock and in most areas was not more than three or four inches deep before hitting hard pan or base rock. In some areas, there was no soil. The Associations' expert, a landscape architect, testified that the soil type was not proper for the growth of plant materials, as the roots of plants could not penetrate the soil. In addition, the progressive land fill resulted in problems of compaction. The differences in soil textures created layering and improper subsurface drainage for the plants. He opined that although 12 inches was the reasonably satisfactory depth for lawn planting material, the problem could be solved by removing the present shallow top soil layer over the hardpan and replacing it with an 8-inch depth of planting material.

Further, the drainage and irrigation system installed at Raven's Cove varied from the plans and specifications of the Developer's landscape architect. The wrong sprinkler heads were installed so that there was inadequate watering in some areas and too much irrigation in others. In a number of areas, the sprinklers watered the buildings, sidewalks and streets. The irrigation system delivered the same quantity of water to shady, sunny and windswept areas, and to all kinds of plants without adjustment for the differing requirements of trees, lawns and shrubbery. The Association's experts estimated that the costs of correcting the landscaping defects would range from about $219,000 to $240,000; this estimate included redesigning the irrigation system, replacing the olive trees and correcting the lawns.

As to the siding, a painting contractor reaffirmed the testimony of homeowners and property managers as to the conditions of the siding and trim of the individual units. The unpainted siding was decomposing from water and rusting, blacking and mildew, which in some areas was caused or exacerbated by improper sprinkler placement. Apart from mildew, an unpainted wood surface will eventually break down. The use of ungalvanized nails in the trim caused deterioration in the paint and premature chalking in 1974, shortly after the turnover of the Association, as well as seeping rust from the nails. Galvanized nails are customarily used on all exterior surfaces in well constructed projects. He estimated that it would cost between $8,000 and $9,000 to paint the siding, and $17,640 (at $256 for each of the 65 units) to repaint the trim on the individual units.

The instant action was commenced by the Association in 1976. The amended complaint alleged eight causes of action for declaratory relief, strict liability and for breach of warranty as to the landscaping of the common areas and the defects in the individual units, and breach of fiduciary duties by the initial Association directors for failing to establish an adequate reserve fund.

In granting the Developer's motion for nonsuit, the trial court specified three grounds: as to the causes of action involving the individual units on the ground that the Association lacked standing; involving the common areas on the ground that there had been no proof of out-of-pocket loss; and against the individual directors on grounds of no breach of fiduciary or other duties.

The first major contention on appeal pertains to the standing of the Association to sue for the landscaping defects in the common areas and the defects in the exteriors of the individual units....

. . .

... We hold, therefore, that the trial court properly concluded that the Association did not have standing as to the cause of action for damage to the individual units pursuant to Code of Civil Procedure section 374 prior to the 1979 amendment.

The next question is whether the Association has standing to sue in a representative capacity pursuant to Code of Civil Procedure section 382, which provides, so far as pertinent: "… when the question is one of a common or general interest, of many persons, or when the parties are numerous, and it is impracticable to bring them all before the court, *one or more may sue or defend for the benefit of all.*" (Italics added.)

The Developer grudgingly concedes that the Association has the proper capacity to sue and would be a proper class representative, but argues that it has not satisfied the requirements for standing to maintain a class action.[8] We do not consider apposite the Developer's authorities related to class actions. However, we need not deal with the question of whether the Association's cause of action for the defects in the individual units qualifies as a class action. Pursuant to Code of Civil Procedure section 382 the Association has the requisite standing in a representative capacity. The leading authority is *Residents of Beverly Glen, Inc. v. City of Los Angeles* (1973) 34 Cal.App.3d 117 [109 Cal.Rptr. 724]….

…

We conclude that the Association has standing to sue in a representative capacity for the damage to the individual units pursuant to Code of Civil Procedure section 382.

…

We turn next to the Association's second cause of action for breach of fiduciary duty as a result of the failure of the Association's initial board of directors to fund an adequate reserve account for contingencies.

The record indicates that the Developer paid the ordinary costs of maintenance until the Association was turned over to the homeowners after the last unit was sold in May of 1974. The uncontroverted evidence established that the Developer and its employees (who were the incorporating directors and initial officers) totally controlled the Association until May 1974. It is uncontroverted that until the turnover, all directors[10] of the Association were either the owners or employees of the Developer. As a result of its prior experience, the Developer had learned that it was unwise to turn an Association over to "inexperienced homebuyers" and "expect them to run a business." Accordingly, the Developer recommended a professional manager who was employed on the night that the homeowners first were elected to the board of the Association. Six months later, the homeowners' board independently selected and employed a new manager. The new manager had to sue to obtain the Association's financial records from the former manager.

As indicated above, in 1974, no reserve or operating funds had been created; thus, none were [sic] turned over to the Association. As a result, the homeowners had to vote a dues increase for operating costs only. Thus, no funds were available to be set aside for reserves, although in one instance $35 had been set aside in escrow for this purpose. Generally, maintenance reserves are set aside for the purpose of roof replacement, painting and long-term maintenance, and the reserve fund is ordinarily commenced with the conveyance of the common area. At Raven's Cove, the conveyance of the common area occurred in 1973 simultaneously with the sale of the first unit.

---

8. "Standing" refers to the requisite interest to support an action or the right to relief and is distinct from "capacity" (*Friendly Village, supra*, 31 Cal.App.3d, at p. 224).

10. The owner of the Developer could not recall who had served as the president of the Association in this initial period. The record indicates that the owner and his wife were two of the five incorporating directors; she executed the by-laws as secretary for the Association.

The Developer here knew that the bay front exposure of Raven's Cove created particular maintenance problems as to the paint and exterior trim which were the result of severe wind and salt spray exposure of the site. A replacement reserve is a portion of the overall operating budget; in preparing it, the components of the operating budget are used to consider "all those things that will wear out, fall apart, need to be replaced or repaired substantially." Each purchaser at Raven's Cove received copies of the Association's articles and the 1972 estimated operating budget, which set forth a contingency fund comprised of $28–$30 per unit per month. The Association's expert testified that $10 per unit would have been a more reasonable initial replacement reserve budget; by the time of trial, the assessment should have been $15 a month per unit.

The record indicates that pursuant to the declaration of covenants, conditions and restrictions signed by the Developer and each homeowner at the time of purchase, monthly assessments were to start with the conveyance of the common areas to the Association. Necessarily, at the time of purchase, Raven's Cove homeowners bought as yet uncompleted landscaped units. We note that the problems that developed at Raven's Cove have been pervasive as to the common areas of townhouse developments (12 Wake Forest L.Rev., *supra*, p. 957).

The parties have not cited, and our research has not disclosed, any specific authority in this state. Nevertheless, it is well settled that directors of nonprofit corporations are fiduciaries. The statutory provisions here applicable are former Corporations Code section 9002[11] which provided that the provisions of the general corporations law were applicable to nonprofit corporations. The pertinent provision was former general Corporations Code section 820, which required directors and officers to "exercise their powers in good faith, and with a view to the interests of the corporation."

Of particular significance is the conflict of interest presented where, as here, the owner of the Developer and his wife and major coowner, are also directors of the Association in its infancy, along with the Developer's employees. We note that the duty of undivided loyalty (see Scott, *The Fiduciary Principle* (1949) 37 Cal. L.Rev. 539) applies when the board of directors of the Association considers maintenance and repair contracts, the operating budget, creation of reserve and operating accounts, etc. Thus, a developer and his agents and employees who also serve as directors of an association, like the instant one, may not make decisions for the Association that benefit their own interests at the expense of the association and its members (*cf. Northridge Coop. Sec. No. 1 v. 32nd Ave. C. Corp.* (1957) 2 N.Y.2d 514 [161 N.Y.S.2d 404, 141 N.E.2d 802]; *Shore Terrace Cooperative, Inc. v. Roche* (1966) 25 App.Div.2d 666 [268 N.Y.S.2d 278]; *Ireland v. Wynkoop* (Colo.App. 1975) 539 P.2d 1349, 1357). In most jurisdictions, the developer is a fiduciary acting on behalf of unknown persons who will purchase and become members of the association (Note, *Florida Condominiums—Developer Abuses and Securities Law Implications* (1973) 25 U. Fla. L.Rev. 350, 355).

We also find persuasive the following comment on the specific problem here presented. "[Individuals] on the board are held to a high standard of conduct, the breach of which may subject each or all of them to individual liability.... Where a developer or sponsor totally dominates the association, or where the methods of control by the membership are weak or nonexistent, 'closer judicial scrutiny may be felt appropriate,' and the principles of fiduciary duty established with business corporations 'may exist for holding those exercising actual control over the group's affairs to a duty not to use their power in such

---

11. Former Corporations Code section 9002 was repealed and superseded by Statutes of 1978, chapters 567 and 1305, which enacted a new Nonprofit Corporation Law beginning with section 5000, operative January 1, 1980. The pertinent provision of the new law is section 5231, which sets forth the good faith duties of directors in greater detail than the prior law.

a way as to harm unnecessarily a substantial interest of a dominated faction.'" (12 Wake Forest L.Rev. 915, 923.) We are indebted for our approach to these problems to the thoughtful and insightful discussion of the specific issues in the Wake Forest Law Review cited above, which aptly continues at page 976: "The subject of fiscal responsibilities, *e.g.*, 'lowballing' failure to pay assessments on unsold units, the failure to enforce the obligation to pay, is one of the areas of great developer exposure." The article also points to the necessity for good management—with adequate books, records and minutes (see also Annot., *Self-Dealing by Developers of Condominium Project As Affecting Contracts of Leases With Condominium Association* (1976) 73 A.L.R.3d 613).

We also find helpful the reasoning of *Stern v. Lucy Webb Hayes Nat. Train. Sch. for Deacon. & M.* (D.D.C. 1974) 381 F.Supp. 1003, at page 1014, in which the less stringent corporate rules were applied to the directors of a charitable corporation to require due diligence in the supervision of the actions of officers, employees and outside experts over whom they had responsibility under a standard of honesty, good faith and a reasonable amount of diligence and care.

We think that here, the failure of the initial Association directors to exercise supervision which permits mismanagement or nonmanagement is an independent ground for the breach of fiduciary duty by the Developer during the initial period of the Association, when the Developer and its employees controlled the Association.

Here, the initial directors and officers of the Association had a fiduciary relationship to the homeowner members analogous to that of a corporate promoter to the shareholders. These duties take on a greater magnitude in view of the mandatory association membership required of the homeowner. We conclude that since the Association's original directors (comprised of the owners of the Developer and the Developer's employees) admittedly failed to exercise their supervisory and managerial responsibilities to assess each unit for an adequate reserve fund and acted with a conflict of interest, they abdicated their obligation as initial directors of the Association to establish such a fund for the purposes of maintenance and repair. Thus, the individual initial directors are liable to the Association for breach of basic fiduciary duties of acting in good faith and exercising basic duties of good management.

As the Developer concedes that if the Association has standing and adduced sufficient evidence, the applicable theory is strict liability, as first delineated by our seminal decision in *Kriegler v. Eichler Homes, Inc., supra*, 269 Cal.App.2d, at pages 227–228, we turn to the question of the appropriate measure of damages in this case. This question also appears to be one not previously faced by an appellate court in this state in a published opinion.

The record indicates that the trial court, believing that the only proper measure of damages was the "out of pocket" rule (Civ. Code, § 3343), refused an instruction allowing damages equal to the cost of repairs. The record also indicates that the court's ruling was based on its misapprehension that the Association had failed to prove fraud, which is the prerequisite for damages pursuant to Civil Code section 3343.[12]

Here, the applicable statute is Civil Code section 3333, set forth below,[13] which sets forth the measure of damages for actions in tort. In *Avner v. Longridge Estates* (1969) 272

---

12. For the same reason, *Gagne v. Bertron* (1954) 43 Cal.2d 481 [275 P.2d 15], cited by the Developer, is inapposite. *Gagne* held that the out-of-pocket rule applies to determine damages to plaintiffs who had purchased lots in reliance on defendant's representation as to the amount of fill thereon. Here, of course, the Association does not rely primarily on a fraud theory but on strict liability.

13. Civil Code section 3333: "For the breach of an obligation not arising from contract, the measure of damages, except where otherwise expressly provided by this Code, is the amount which will

Cal.App.2d 607 [77 Cal.Rptr. 633], the developer of a lot was held strictly liable for damages suffered by the owner when the rear slope of the plaintiffs' lot failed as a result of uncompacted fill and inadequate drainage. The court, relying on *Kriegler, supra,* 269 Cal.App.2d 224, indicated that the cost of repair pursuant to Civil Code section 3333 was the proper measure of damages. The purpose of tort damages is to make the injured plaintiff whole (4 Witkin, Summary of Cal. Law (8th ed. 1974) Torts, § 842, p. 3137). While, as Witkin also points out, the normal measure of damages for injuries to real property is the difference between the market value of the land before and after the injury, "[another] permissible measure is the reasonable cost of repair or restoration of the property to its original condition, together with the value of the lost use during the period of injury" (Witkin, *supra,* Torts, § 919, p. 3204). This is the correct and practical approach here. Contrary to the Developer's contention, nothing in *Kriegler, supra,* or *Sabella v. Wisler* (1963) 59 Cal.2d 21 [27 Cal.Rptr. 689, 377 P.2d 889], suggests that diminution in value is the only measure. We note that *Sabella* followed *Stewart v. Cox* (1961) 55 Cal.2d 857 [13 Cal.Rptr. 521, 362 P.2d 345], in which a builder was held liable for damages measured by the cost of repairing the damage proximately caused by his negligence. Other commentators agree that regardless of the theory of liability relied upon by a plaintiff, if judgment is rendered against the contractor for construction defects, the proper measure of damages is the cost of repair to the plaintiff's property (Miller & Starr, *Current Law of Cal. Real Estate,* § 9:20, p. 475; see also 8 Pacific L.J. 211 (1977).

. . .

We hold, therefore, that the proper measure of damages here is the cost of remedying the defects in the landscaping and repairing of the homeowners' individual properties, together with the value of the lost use (if any) during the period of injury. Accordingly, we need not discuss the parties' contentions concerning damages based on other theories of liability.

. . .

The judgment of nonsuit is Reversed.

Retrospective and Observations

Raven's Cove's Perspective

Julia Wald represented Raven's Cove Townhomes, Inc., in her first trial as a lawyer. She recalled that Mr. Knuppe came to court wearing very shiny suits that looked as if he had purchased them at a thrift store in order to make it appear that he could not possibly be held responsible for the outcome of this case. The case settled on remand, and Ms. Wald hopes but does not know that it was settled for enough money for the repairs to be made at the project. The attorney who settled the case is dead.

At the trial level, opposing counsel filed a motion for non-suit regarding whether a reserve account had to be established by the developer. To everyone's amazement, the judge ruled that that was a non-issue and also said that developers could build any way they wanted and were not liable for construction defects.

---

compensate for all the detriment proximately caused thereby, whether it could have been anticipated or not."

Knuppe Development Company's Perspective

Joe Joiner, who represented Knuppe Development, noted two interesting things about this case. First, the appeals court, on its own, picked up and emphasized the fiduciary duty issue. Second, on remand, there was no money awarded for damages. During the course of litigation, Mr. Joiner discovered that the association manager had published an article in the association newsletter that the board agreed not to raise assessments because the money it needed would be obtained from the developer through the suit. Mr. Joiner was successful in introducing the newsletter as evidence during the trial on remand and was successful in getting the manager to admit that he wrote the newsletter article.

Notes & Questions

1. *Fiduciary status.* After reading *Raven's Cove Townhomes*, do you agree that a developer in control of a community association has a fiduciary or quasi-fiduciary capacity on behalf of the unit owners? See *B&J Holding Corp. v. Weiss*, 353 So. 2d 141 (Fla. 1977) holding that developer's officers and directors are quasi-fiduciaries; but see ROBERT G. NATELSON, LAW OF PROPERTY OWNERS ASSOCIATIONS, § 10.6.1 (1989) ("where the term fiduciary appears in case opinions, it has been used loosely.... When liability is found, it has almost always been for some violation of the obligations of good faith, or reasonable care—almost never for breach of an obligation truly fiduciary"); *Belvedere Condo. Unit Owner's Ass'n v. R.E. Roark Cos., Inc.*, 617 N.E.2d 1075, 1081 (Ohio 1993) (developers do not owe a fiduciary duty to the association; their relationship, rights, and remedies are defined by the condominium statute).

2. *Self-dealing.* Self-dealing by directors of an association may constitute an actionable wrong unless good faith and fair dealing can be demonstrated. See *Avila South Condo. Ass'n, Inc. v. Kappa Corp.*, 347 So. 2d 599 (Fla. 1977); *Old Port Cove Prop. Owners Ass'n, Inc. v. Ecclestone*, 500 So. 2d 331, 335 (Fla. Dist. Ct. App. 1986) ("Profit motive alone, however, does not constitute a breach of fiduciary duty"); *King Mountain Condo. Ass'n, Inc. v. Gundlach*, 425 So. 2d 569 (Fla. Dist. Ct. App. 1982) (despite statute establishing a rebuttable presumption of unconscionability, unit owners' action to declare recreation lease unconscionable fails); W.E. Shipley, Annotation, *Self-Dealing by Developers of Condominium Project As Affecting Contracts or Leases with Condominium Association*, 73 A.L.R.3d 613 (1976).

Should a developer be permitted to limit his liability for assessments for unbuilt units by drafting language in the declaration shifting the burden to unit owners? Does such a provision really amount to self-dealing? See *Palm Bay Tower Corp. v. Brooks*, 466 So. 2d 1071 (Fla. Dist. Ct. App. 1984); *Point East Mgmt. Corp. v. Point East One Condo. Corp.*, 282 So. 2d 628 (Fla. 1973).

Should a developer avoid signing contracts with entities owned or controlled by the developer or the developer-controlled board altogether? See *King Mountain Condo. Ass'n, Inc. v. Gundlach*, 425 So. 2d 569 (Fla. Dist. Ct. App. 1982) (self-dealing becomes actionable when it results in unjust enrichment not merely enrichment). Should unit owners be able to terminate a contract between a developer entity and the association absent self-dealing? Note that New Jersey terminates management contracts automatically after 90 days from the date the unit owners control a majority of the board of directors. N.J. Stat. Ann. § 46:8B-12.2. Florida permits unit owners to terminate developer entity contracts even if fair and reasonable without any time restriction. See Fla. Stat. Ann. § 718.302 (West 1997). See also 15 U.S.C.A. § 3607 (developer contracts may be terminated by two-thirds vote of the unit owners within two years of transition or 75% unit owner control, whichever occurs first); *181 East 73rd St. Co. v. 181 East 73rd St. Tenants Corp.*, 954 F.2d 45 (2nd Cir. 1992) (no proof of one-sidedness or unconscionability is required to exercise the right to terminate under Condominium and Cooperative Abuse Relief Act of 1980).

3. *Piercing the corporate veil.* Depending on the language of the particular condominium act, it is not always necessary to pierce the corporate veil to hold a developer personally liable for its actions while in control of the association. See, *e.g., Unit Owners Ass'n of Summit Vista Lot 8 Condo. v. Miller*, 677 A.2d 138 (N.H. 1996) (interpreting New Hamphsire's Condominium Act).

4. *Civil penalties.* Developers may be liable to state agencies for civil penalties where the developer fails to abide by the terms of an applicable statute. See, *e.g.,* Fla. Stat. Ann. § 718.501(1)(d)(4) West (1997) (the Florida Division of Land Sales, Condominiums, and Mobile Homes has the authority to impose a civil penalty of not more than $5,000 against a developer for each separate violation of chapter 718 of the Florida Statutes); *RIS Inv. Group v. Dep't of Bus. & Prof'l Regulation*, 695 So. 2d 357 (Fla. Dist. Ct. App. 1997); *First Fed. Sav. & Loan Ass'n of Seminole County v. Dep't of Bus. Regulation*, 472 So. 2d 494 (Fla. Dist. Ct. App. 1985).

5. *The Uniform Act.* According to the *Pederzani* court, the same fiduciary standard applies to board members regardless of whether they are developer-appointed or unit owner elected. The court merely recognizes a "greater potential" for conflicts of interest to arise with developer-appointed board members. *Pederzani v. Guerriere*, No. 930502A (Mass. Superior Ct., August 11, 1995). Do you agree? What are some of the sensitive areas of activity? Contrast this approach with UCIOA § 3-103(a). UCIOA explicitly sets the standard of care for developer-appointed board members at the fiduciary level while suggesting a possible lesser standard for board members elected by the unit owners. Do you agree with this approach? See discussion in Chapter 5 regarding the business judgment rule.

6. *Waiver of declaration terms by declarant.* Should a developer be permitted to waive restrictions contained in the protective covenants, such as a setback restriction, so long as the developer maintains an ownership interest in the development? See *Armstrong v. Roberts*, 325 S.E.2d 769 (Ga. 1985) ("So long as the developer owns an interest in the subdivision being developed his own economic interest will tend to cause him to exercise a right to waive restrictions in a manner which takes into account harm done to other lots in the subdivision").

7. *Transition.* The statutory schemes for transfer of association control from the developer to the unit owners seem simple enough to apply. But what would happen if a developer sells units to limited partnerships whose sole business is the lease of those units? The developer may have transferred control to the association, but the limited partnerships can effectively control the association's elected board by voting in blocs. Are the unit owners who actually occupy their units being disenfranchised? See *Bishop Assoc. L.P. v. Belkin*, 521 So. 2d 158 (Fla. Dist. Ct. App. 1988) (limited partnerships are declared "developers" for purposes of the statute requiring turnover to unit owner control).

8. *Developer as fiduciary when acting as developer.* Does the developer have any special duty to the association? What difference does it make in your answer if you distinguish between the developer as project creator and as the entity appointing members of the association's board? Does the developer have a *duty* to create the entire project? What legal principles support your answer? What if the officers of the development company be-

come aware that the directors of the association have not taken some required action. Does the developer have the power to intercede? A duty to do so? Does it make any difference if a majority of directors are developer appointees? Why?

Problem

Across your desk sits a new client, an eager young couple intent on buying their first home. They have narrowed their choices to two condominium units, one in a new construction townhouse project and one in a highrise conversion. They have come to you for legal advice.

They qualify for a mortgage at either place and are equally well satisfied as to the location and nature of the units. They are interested however, in your advice and suggestions concerning the decision they are about to make. You explain that you will need to review the condominiums' documents before you can give a final opinion, but you nevertheless have some initial considerations for them to evaluate. How do you advise?

The Real World: A Developer's Insight

We created a master association in a resort development at Lake Tahoe. Because the site was remote, we built all the infrastructure, including the water system. Once the property was up and operating, we had a choice: we could operate a jurisdictional water company, we could sell the water system to another private water company in the area, or we could transfer it to the association. We elected to transfer it to the association thinking that in the long term the association had a way of raising necessary capital through assessments. When our relationship with the association deteriorated because of an unrelated suit, they used the water system against us: they tried to cut off service to our future lots, notified the state that there was a water shortage, and warped the structure of the water assessment formula increasing cost to the golf course by 500%.

In the early going when you control the association, you see the association as a colleague, but the association turned out to be an enemy in the worst way. We made the mistake of transferring a service that was absolutely essential to our operation, and it was a critical error. We have since worked it all out; we went to the Nevada Supreme Court and won on all the issues. In retrospect, we made a mistake and learned a lesson. It would have been completely better to put the water system in outside hands.

—*Ron Nahas*

Index